The **Rough Guide** to

Thailand

written and researched by

Paul Gray and Lucy Ridout

with additional contributions by

John Clewley, Ron Emmons, Neil Pettigrew and Fran Sandham

ROUGH GUIDES

NEW YORK • LONDON • DELHI

www.roughguides.com

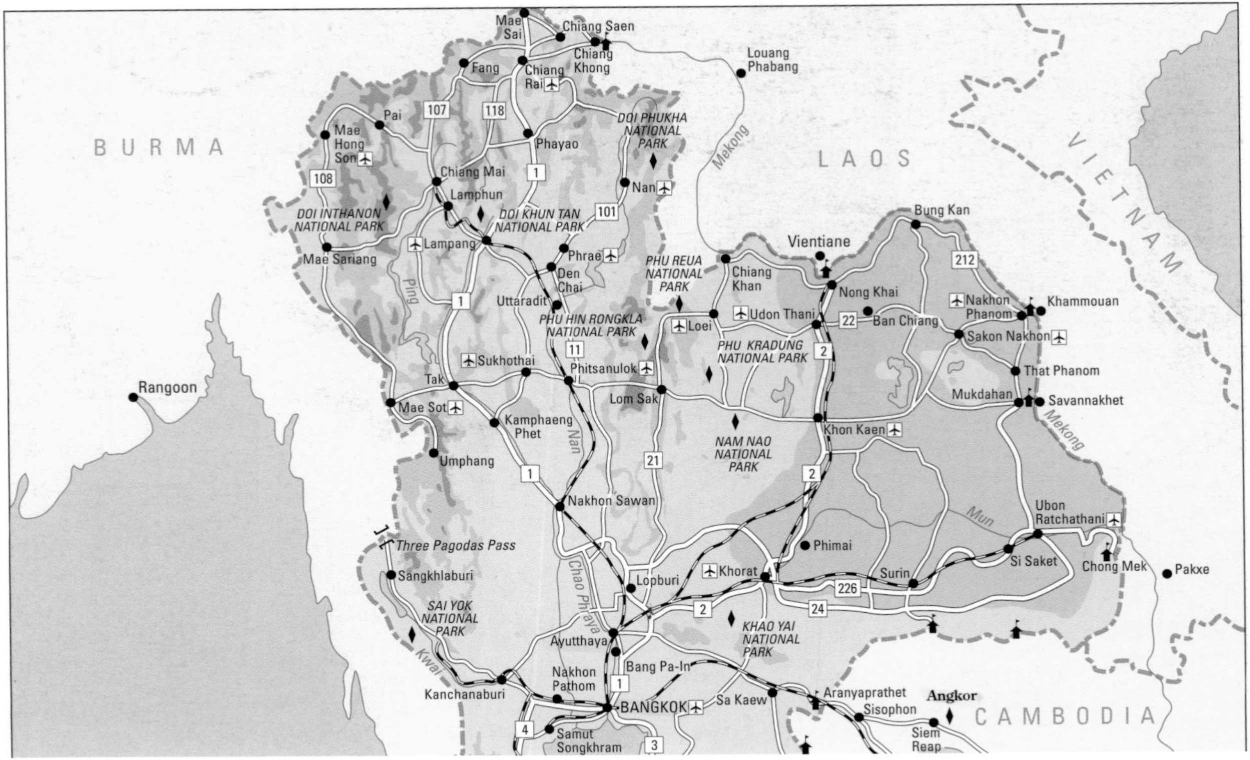

BURMA
LAOS
VIETNAM
CAMBODIA
Rangoon
Mae Sai
Chiang Saen
Chiang Khong
Louang Phabang
Fang
Chiang Rai
Pai
Mae Hong Son
Phayao
DOI PHUKHA NATIONAL PARK
Mekong
Chiang Mai
Lamphun
Nan
DOI INTHANON NATIONAL PARK
DOI KHUN TAN NATIONAL PARK
Lampang
Mae Sariang
Phrae
Den Chai
Ping
Uttaradit
PHU HIN RONGKLA NATIONAL PARK
Sukhothai
Phitsanulok
Tak
Mae Sot
Kamphaeng Phet
Umphang
Nan
Nakhon Sawan
Three Pagodas Pass
Sangkhlaburi
SAI YOK NATIONAL PARK
Kwai
Kanchanaburi
Chao Phraya
Lopburi
Ayutthaya
Bang Pa-In
Nakhon Pathom
BANGKOK
Samut Songkhram
Sa Kaew
Aranyaprathet
Sisophon
Angkor
Siem Reap
Vientiane
Chiang Khan
PHU REUA NATIONAL PARK
Nong Khai
Udon Thani
Loei
Ban Chiang
PHU KRADUNG NATIONAL PARK
Lom Sak
NAM NAO NATIONAL PARK
Khon Kaen
Bung Kan
Nakhon Phanom
Khammouan
Sakon Nakhon
That Phanom
Mukdahan
Savannakhet
Mun
Ubon Ratchathani
Phimai
Khorat
Surin
Si Saket
Chong Mek
Pakxe
KHAO YAI NATIONAL PARK
1
2
3
4
11
21
22
24
101
107
108
118
212
226

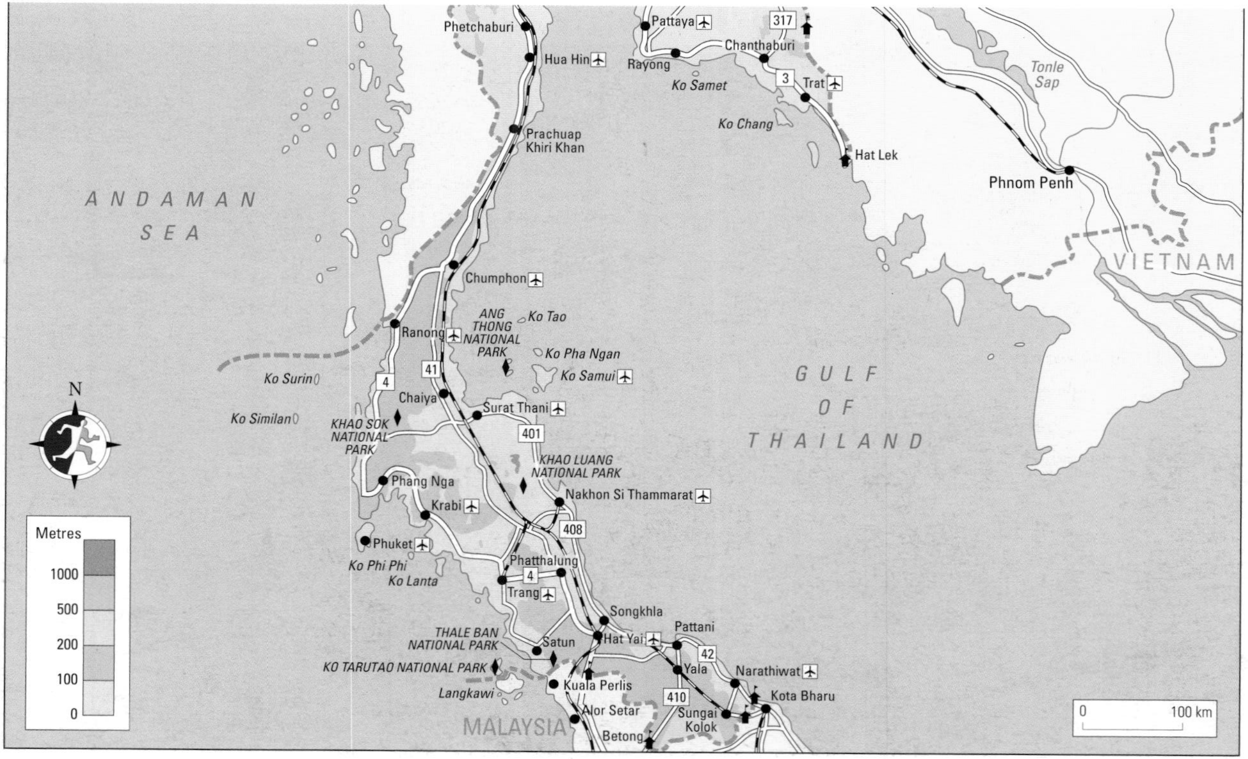

ANDAMAN SEA
GULF OF THAILAND
VIETNAM
MALAYSIA
Phetchaburi
Hua Hin
Prachuap Khiri Khan
Pattaya
Rayong
Chanthaburi
Ko Samet
Trat
Ko Chang
Hat Lek
Tonle Sap
Phnom Penh
Chumphon
Ranong
Ko Tao
ANG THONG NATIONAL PARK
Ko Pha Ngan
Ko Samui
Ko Surin
Ko Similan
Chaiya
Surat Thani
KHAO SOK NATIONAL PARK
KHAO LUANG NATIONAL PARK
Nakhon Si Thammarat
Phang Nga
Krabi
Phuket
Ko Phi Phi
Ko Lanta
Phatthalung
Trang
Songkhla
Hat Yai
Pattani
Satun
THALE BAN NATIONAL PARK
KO TARUTAO NATIONAL PARK
Langkawi
Kuala Perlis
Alor Setar
Yala
Narathiwat
Kota Bharu
Sungai Kolok
Betong
317
3
41
4
401
408
42
410
N
Metres
1000
500
200
100
0
0
100 km

Introduction to

Thailand

With nearly eleven million foreigners flying into the country each year, Thailand has become Asia's primary holiday destination. Yet despite this vast influx of tourists and their cash, Thailand's cultural integrity remains largely undamaged – a country that adroitly avoided colonization has been able to absorb Western influences without wholly succumbing to them. Though the high-rises and neon lights occupy the foreground of the tourist picture, the typical Thai community is still the traditional farming village. Almost fifty percent of Thais earn their living from the land, based around the staple, rice, which forms the foundation of the country's unique and famously sophisticated cuisine.

Tourism has been just one factor in the country's development which, once the deep-seated regional uncertainties surrounding the Vietnam War had faded, was free to proceed at an almost death-defying pace. Indeed Thailand enjoyed the fastest-expanding economy in the world, at an average of nine percent growth a year, until it overstretched itself in 1997, sparking a regional financial crisis – but already, with remarkable resilience, the economy is growing rapidly again. Politics in Thailand, however, has not been able to keep pace. Coups d'état, which used to be the commonest method of changing government, seem to be a thing of the past, but despite a recently revised constitution and robust criticism from students, grass-roots activists and parts of the press, the malnourished democratic system is characterized by corruption and cronyism.

Through all the changes of the last half-century, the much-revered constitutional monarch, King Bhumibol, who sits at the pinnacle of an elaborate hierarchical system of deference covering the whole of Thai society, has lent a large measure of stability. Furthermore, some ninety percent of the population are still practising Theravada Buddhists, a unifying faith that colours all aspects of daily life – from the tiered temple rooftops that dominate every skyline, to the omnipresent saffron-robed monks and the packed calendar of festivals; it is still the norm for a Thai man to spend three months as a monk at some period during his life.

Fact file

- Known as Siam until 1939, Thailand lies wholly within the tropics, covering 511,770 square kilometres and divided into 76 provinces or *changwat*. The population of 63 million is made up of ethnic Thais (75 percent) and Chinese (14 percent), with the rest comprising mainly immigrants from neighbouring countries as well as hill-tribespeople; the national language is *phasaa Thai.* Buddhism is the national religion, with some 90 percent followers, and Islam the largest of the minority religions at around 5 percent. Average life expectancy is 71 years.
- Since 1932 the country has been a constitutional monarchy; King Bhumibol, also known as Rama IX (being the ninth ruler of the Chakri dynasty), has been on the throne since 1946. The elected National Assembly (Rathasapha) has five hundred MPs in the House of Representatives (Sapha Phuthaen Ratsadon), led by a prime minister, and two hundred members of the Senate (Wuthisapha).
- Tourism is the country's main industry, and its biggest exports are computers and components, vehicles and vehicle parts, textiles and rubber.

Where to go

The clash of tradition and modernity is most intense in **Bangkok**, the first stop on almost any itinerary. Within its historic core you'll find resplendent temples, canalside markets and the opulent indulgence of the eighteenth-century **Grand Palace**, while in downtown Bangkok lies the hub of the country's sex industry, the infamous strip known as **Patpong**. After touchdown in Bangkok, much of the package-holiday traffic flows east to **Pattaya**, the country's first and most popular beach resort, but for

The southern reaches of Isaan hold some of Thailand's best-kept secrets.

unpolluted beaches and clear seas you're much better off venturing just a little further afield, to the islands of **Ko Samet** and **Ko Chang**, with their superb sand and idyllic beachfront bungalows.

Fewer tourists strike north from the east coast into **Isaan**, the poorest and in some ways the most traditionally Thai region. Here, a trip through the gently modulating landscapes of the **Mekong River** valley, which defines Thailand's northeastern extremities, takes in archetypal agricultural villages and a fascinating array of religious

Spirit houses

Although the vast majority of Thais are Buddhist, nearly everyone also believes that the physical world is inhabited by spirits. These spirits

can cause trouble if not given enough care and attention, and are apt to wreak havoc when made homeless. Therefore, whenever a new building is constructed – be it a traditional village house or a multi-storey office block – the owners will also construct a home for the spirits who previously occupied that land. Crucially, these spirit houses must be given the best spot on the site – which in Bangkok often means on the roof – and must also reflect the status of the building in question, so their architecture can range from the simplest wooden structure to an elaborate scale model of a particularly ornate temple. Daily offerings of flowers, incense and candles are set inside the spirit house, and sometimes morsels of food. For an introduction to animist and Buddhist practices in Thailand, see p.811.

▲ Wat Arun and the Chao Phraya River, Bangkok

sites, while the southern reaches of Isaan hold some of Thailand's best-kept secrets – the magnificent stone temple complexes of **Phimai**, **Phanom Rung** and **Khao Phra Viharn**, all built by the Khmers of Cambodia almost ten centuries ago. Closer to the capital, in the southwestern corner of Isaan, **Khao Yai National Park** encapsulates the phenomenal diversity of Thailand's flora and fauna, which here range from wild orchids to strangling figs, elephants to hornbills, tigers to macaques.

At the heart of the northern uplands, **Chiang Mai** is both an attractive historic city and a vibrant cultural centre, with a strong tradition of arts and crafts. It does a burgeoning line in self-improvement courses – from

The gecko

Whether you're staying on a beach or in a town, chances are you'll be sharing your room with a few geckos. These pale green tropical lizards, which are completely harmless to humans and usually measure a cute four to ten centimetres in length, mostly appear at night, high up on walls and ceilings, where they feed on insects. Because the undersides of their flat toes are covered with hundreds of microscopic hairs that catch at even the tiniest of irregularities, geckos are able to scale almost any surface, including glass, which is why you usually see them in strange, gravity-defying positions. The largest and most vociferous gecko is known as the *tokay* in Thai, named after the disconcertingly loud sound it makes. Tokays can grow to an alarming 35cm, but are welcomed by most householders, as they devour insects and mice; Thais also consider it auspicious if a baby is born within earshot of a crowing tokay. There's more about Thailand's fauna and flora on p.816.

ascetic meditation to the more earthly pleasures of Thai cookery classes – while the overriding enticement of the surrounding region is the prospect of **trekking** through villages inhabited by a richly mixed population of tribal peoples. Courses and outdoor activities, as well as spas and massages, can be enjoyed at **Pai**, a surprisingly cosmopolitan hill station for backpackers, four hours northwest of Chiang Mai.

With Chiang Mai and the north so firmly planted on the independent tourist trail, the ancient cities of the intervening **central plains** tend to get short shrift. Yet there is rewarding trekking from the Burmese-border towns of **Mae Sot** and **Umphang**, and the elegant ruins of former capitals **Ayutthaya** and **Sukhothai** embody a glorious artistic heritage, displaying Thailand's distinctive ability to absorb influences from quite different cultures. **Kanchanaburi**, stunningly located on the **River Kwai** in the western reaches of the central plains, tells of a much darker episode in Thailand's past, for it was along the course of this river that the Japanese army built the Thailand–Burma Railway during World War II, at the cost of thousands of POW lives.

Sand and sea are what most Thailand holidays are about, and the pick of the coasts are in southern Thailand.

Sand and sea are what most Thailand holidays are about, though, and the pick of the coasts are in southern Thailand, where the Samui archipelago off the **Gulf coast** is one of the highlights. **Ko Samui** itself has the most sweeping white-sand beaches, and the greatest variety of accommodation and

Thai boxing

Such is the national obsession with *muay Thai*, or Thai boxing, that when Wijan Ponlid returned home from the Sydney 2000 Olympics with the country's only gold medal (for international flyweight boxing), he was paraded through town at the head of a procession of 49 elephants, given a new house and over 20 million baht, and offered a promotion at work (he's a policeman). As with soccer and baseball stars in the west, *muay Thai* champions are rarely out of the news even during quieter periods in the sporting calendar, and the national appetite is fed by live TV coverage of major bouts every Sunday afternoon on Channel 7. Though there are boxing venues all around the country, the very best fights are staged at Bangkok's two biggest stadiums, Rajdamnoen and Lumphini, which are well worth attending as a cultural experience even if you have no interest in the sport itself; see p.186 for times and ticket prices and p.67 for more on the rules and rituals of *muay Thai*.

Hill-tribe trekking

Trekking in northern Thailand isn't just about walking through beautiful, rainforested mountain scenery, it also brings you into contact with the hill tribes or *chao khao*, fascinating ethnic minorities who are just clinging on to their traditional ways of life. Sometimes termed Fourth World people, in that they are migrants who continue to migrate without regard for national boundaries, the hill tribes have developed sophisticated customs, laws and beliefs to harmonize relationships between individuals and their environment. Despite the disturbance caused by trekking, most *chao khao* are genuinely hospitable to foreigners, but it's important that you go with a knowledgeable guide who has the interests of the local people at heart – and that you act as a sensitive guest in the face of their hospitality. For more on the hill tribes, see p.836; for trekking practicalities, see p.315.

facilities to go with them. **Ko Pha Ngan** next door is still pure backpacker territory, where you have a stark choice between desolate coves and **Hat Rin**, Thailand's rave capital. The remotest island, rocky **Ko Tao**, is acquiring increasing sophistication as Southeast Asia's largest dive-training centre.

Across on the other side of the peninsula, the **Andaman coast** boasts even more exhilarating scenery and the finest coral reefs in the country, in particular around the spectacular **Ko Similan** island chain, which ranks as one of the best dive sites in the world. The largest Andaman coast island, **Phuket**, is one of Thailand's top tourist destinations and is graced with a dozen fine beaches; many of these have been over-developed with expensive high-rises and throbbing nightlife, but quieter corners can still be found. **Ko Phi Phi** has also suffered under unregulated construction, but its coral-rich sea remains an untainted azure, and the sheer limestone cliffs that characterize the coastline here – and elsewhere around the harbour town and beaches of nearby **Krabi** – are breathtakingly beautiful. The island of **Ko Lanta** has a more understated charm and is a popular destination for both families and backpackers. Inland attractions generally pale in comparison to the coastal splendours, but the rainforests of **Khao Sok National Park** are a notable exception.

Further down the Thai peninsula, in the provinces of the **deep south**, the teeming sea life and unfrequented sands of the **Trang islands** and the **Ko Tarutao National Marine Park** are the main draws.

When to go

The **climate** of most of Thailand is governed by three seasons: rainy (roughly June–Oct), caused by the southwest monsoon dumping moisture gathered from the Andaman Sea and the Gulf of Thailand; cool (Nov–Feb); and hot (March–May). The **rainy season** is the least predictable of the three, varying in length and intensity from year to year, but usually it gathers force between June and August,

▶ Thanon Khao San, Bangkok

Rat or raja?

There's no standard system of transliterating Thai script into Roman, so you're sure to find that the Thai words in this book don't always match the versions you'll see elsewhere. Maps and street signs are the biggest sources of confusion, so we've generally gone for the transliteration that's most common on the spot. However, sometimes you'll need to do a bit of lateral thinking, bearing in mind that a classic variant for the town of Ayutthaya is Ayudhia, while among street names, Thanon Rajavithi could come out as Thanon Ratwithi – and it's not unheard of to find one spelling posted at one end of a road, with another at the opposite end. See pp.853–859 for an introduction to the Thai language.

coming to a peak in September and October, when unpaved roads are reduced to mud troughs and whole districts of Bangkok are flooded. The **cool season** is the pleasantest time to visit, although temperatures can still reach a broiling 30°C in the middle of the day. In the **hot season**, when temperatures often rise to 35°C in Bangkok, the best thing to do is to hit the beach.

Within this scheme, slight variations are found from region to region. The less humid **north** experiences the greatest range of temperatures: at night in the cool season the thermometer occasionally approaches zero on the higher slopes, and this region is often hotter than the central plains between March and May. It's the **northeast** that gets the very worst of the hot season, with clouds of dust gathering above the parched fields, and

▲ Prachuap Khiri Khan

humid air too. In **southern Thailand**, temperatures are more consistent throughout the year, with less variation the closer you get to the equator. The rainy season hits the **Andaman coast** of the southern peninsula harder than anywhere else in the country – heavy rainfall usually starts in May and persists until October.

One area of the country, the **Gulf coast** of the southern peninsula, lies outside this general pattern – with the sea immediately to the east, this coast and its offshore islands feel the effects of the northeast monsoon, which brings rain between October and January, especially in November. This area suffers less than the Andaman coast from the southwest monsoon, getting a comparatively small amount of rain between May and September.

Overall, the **cool season** is generally the **best time** to come to Thailand: as well as having more manageable temperatures and less rain, it offers waterfalls in full spate and the best of the upland flowers in bloom. `Bear in mind, however, that it's also the busiest season, so forward planning is essential.

Thailand's Climate

Average daily temperatures (°C) and monthly rainfall (mm)

	Jan	Feb	Mar	Apr	May	June	July	Aug	Sept	Oct	Nov	Dec
Bangkok												
Max temp (°C)	26	28	29	30	30	29	29	28	28	28	27	26
Rainfall (mm)	11	28	31	72	190	152	158	187	320	231	57	9
Chiang Mai												
Max temp (°C)	21	23	26	29	29	28	27	27	27	26	24	22
Rainfall (mm)	8	6	15	45	153	136	167	227	251	132	44	15
Pattaya												
Max temp (°C)	26	28	29	30	30	29	29	28	28	28	27	26
Rainfall (mm)	12	23	41	79	165	120	166	166	302	229	66	10
Ko Samui												
Max temp (°C)	26	26	28	29	29	28	28	28	28	27	26	25
Rainfall (mm)	38	8	12	63	186	113	143	123	209	260	302	98
Phuket												
Max temp (°C)	27	28	28	29	28	28	28	28	27	27	27	27
Rainfall (mm)	35	31	39	163	348	213	263	263	419	305	207	52

39

things not to miss

It's not possible to see everything that Thailand has to offer in one trip – and we don't suggest you try. What follows is a selective taste of the country's highlights: beautiful beaches, outstanding national parks, magnificent temples, and even good things to eat and drink – arranged in five colour-coded categories to help you find the very best things to see, do and experience. All entries have a page reference to take you straight into the Guide, where you can find out more.

01 Nan Page **366** • Few travellers make the trip out to Nan, but it's a likeable town set in rich mountain scenery, with a strong handicraft tradition and some intriguing Lao-influenced temples, including the beautiful murals at Wat Phumin.

02 Sea-canoeing in the Krabi region Page **706** • Paddling your own canoe is a great way to explore the lagoons, caves and hidden beaches of Krabi's extraordinary coast.

03 Diving and snorkelling off Ko Similan Page **664** • The underwater scenery at this remote chain of national park islands is among the finest in the world.

04 Loy Krathong Page **284** • At this nationwide festival held in honour of the water spirits, Thais everywhere float miniature baskets filled with flowers and lighted candles on canals, rivers, ponds and seashores.

05 Khao Yai National Park Page **478** • Great hornbills are a highlight of Thailand's most popular national park, which also offers guided treks and night safaris.

06 Full moon party at Hat Rin, Ko Pha Ngan Page **611** • *Apocalypse Now* without the war . . .

07 Khmer ruins Page **495** • When the ancient Khmers controlled northeast Thailand in the ninth century, they built a chain of magnificent Angkor Wat-style temple complexes, including this one at Phanom Rung.

08 Silk Page **503** • Sericulture is an important village industry in the northeast, whose weavers produce the country's most exquisite designs, though high-quality silk is sold all over Thailand.

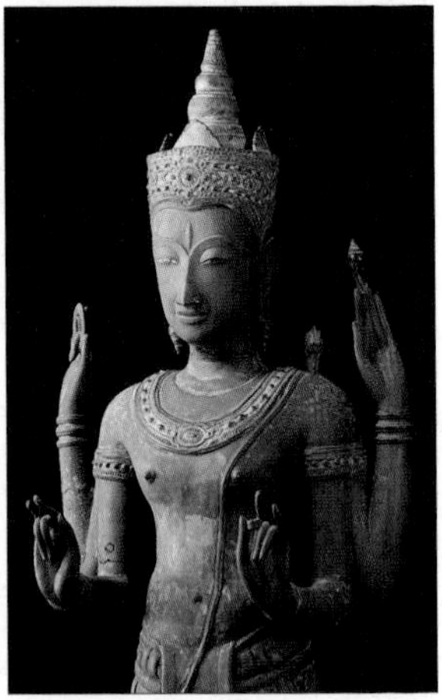

09 The National Museum, Bangkok Page **133** • A colossal hoard of Thailand's artistic treasures.

10 Ko Chang archipelago Page **468** • Enjoy the glorious beaches of Thailand's second-largest island, or escape to a more peaceful corner of the archipelago.

11 Ko Tao Page **620** • Take a dive course, or just explore this remote island's contours by boat or on foot.

12 Traditional massage Page **68** • Combining elements of acupressure and yoga, a pleasantly brutal way to help shed jet lag, or simply to end the day.

13 Umphang treks Page **304** • The best way to reach mighty Tee Lor Su Falls from Umphang is by rafting and hiking your way through the jungle.

14 The Grand Palace, Bangkok Page **122** • No visitor should miss this huge complex, which encompasses the country's holiest and most beautiful temple, Wat Phra Kaeo, and its most important image, the Emerald Buddha.

15 Jim Thompson's House, Bangkok Page **156** • The house of the legendary American adventurer, entrepreneur and art collector is a small, personal museum of Thai crafts and architecture.

16 Ko Samet Page **438** • Petite and pretty, Ko Samet is justifiably popular for its gorgeous white-sand beaches and its proximity to Bangkok.

17 Phetchaburi Page **561** • Many of the temples in this charming, historic town date back three hundred years and are still in use today.

18 Wat Phu Tok Page **548** • A uniquely atmospheric meditation temple on a steep, wooded outcrop – clamber around for the spectacular views, if nothing else.

19 Ko Lanta Page **726** • Sundowners and fresh fish barbecues are a daily feature of life on long, lazy Ko Lanta.

20 Amulet market, Bangkok Page **140** • Nearly everyone wears a sacred talisman – often a miniature Buddha image – to ward off misfortune, and the huge amulet market at Wat Rajnadda is a great place for browsing.

21 **Wat Pho, Bangkok** Page **130** • A lively and lavish temple, encompassing the awesome Reclining Buddha and a great massage school.

22 **Songkhla** Page **768** • A great all-round base, with miles of sandy beach, some fine restaurants and fascinating sights, including the best museum in the south.

23 **Riding the Death Railway, River Kwai** Page **237** • Thailand's most scenic train journey is also its most historic, using the track constructed by World War II POWs, whose story is movingly told in the nearby Hellfire Pass Museum.

24 **The Mae Hong Son loop** Page **372** • A spectacular 600km trip, winding over steep forested mountains and through tightly hemmed farming valleys.

25 Vegetarian festival, Phuket Page **675** • During Taoist Lent, fasting Chinese devotees test their spiritual resolve with acts of gruesome self-mortification.

26 Khao Sok National Park Page **654** • Tree-houses, mist-clad outcrops and whooping gibbons make Khao Sok a memorable place to spend the night.

27 Folklore Museum, Phitsanulok Page **273** • One of Thailand's best ethnology museums, complete with a reconstructed village home and a fascinating array of traditional rural crafts.

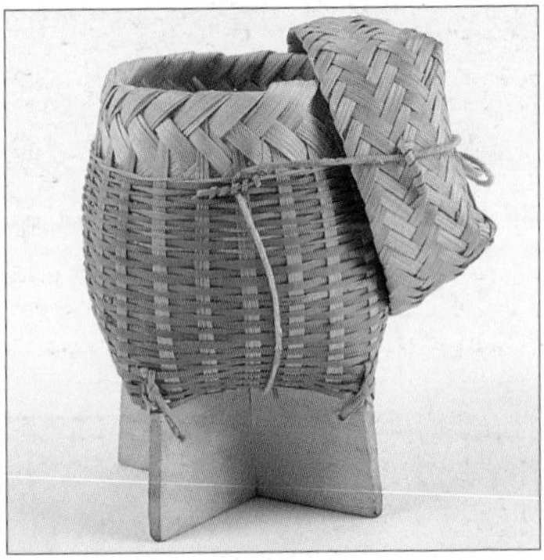

28 Ko Tarutao National Marine Park Page **758** • Spectacular and relatively peaceful islands, sheltering a surprising variety of landscapes and fauna.

29 Night markets Page 48 • After-dark gatherings of dramatically lit pushcart kitchens, which are usually the best-value and most entertaining places to eat in any Thai town.

30 Thai cookery classes in Chiang Mai Page 330 • Of the many courses now on offer in the town, these are the most instantly gratifying, including first-class meals and colourful market visits.

31 Ayutthaya Page 252 • An hour to the north, this former capital provides a sharp contrast to Bangkok, an atmospheric graveyard for temples flanked by good museums and some appealing guest houses.

32 The Mekong River Page 535 • Forming 750km of the border between Thailand and Laos, the mighty Mekong provides an endlessly fascinating scenic backdrop to travels in the northeast.

33 Wat Phra That Doi Suthep, Chiang Mai

Page **348** • One of the most harmonious ensembles of temple architecture in the country, with mountaintop views over half of northern Thailand thrown in.

34 Tom yam kung

Page **50** • Delicious hot and sour soup with prawns and lemon grass, that typifies the strong, fresh flavours of Thai cuisine.

35 Rock-climbing on Laem Phra Nang

Page **709** • Even novice climbers can scale the cliffs here for unbeatable views of the stunning Andaman coastline.

36 Chatuchak Weekend Market, Bangkok

Page **166** • Thailand's top shopping experience features over eight thousand stalls selling everything from windchimes to cooking pots and hill-tribe jewellery to jeans.

37 Sukhothai Page **275** • Stay in one of the many welcoming guest houses in New Sukhothai and hire a bicycle to explore the elegant ruins of the nearby old city, Thailand's thirteenth-century capital.

38 Songkhran Page **63** • Thai New Year is the excuse for a national waterfight – don't plan on getting much done in mid-April, just join in.

39 Axe pillows Page **518** • Much more comfortable than they look, traditional axe pillows are sold everywhere in Thailand, including very cheaply in the village of Ban Sri Than.

Contents

Using this Rough Guide

We've tried to make this Rough Guide a good read and easy to use. The book is divided into five main sections, and you should be able to find whatever you want in one of them.

Colour section

The front colour section offers a quick tour of Thailand. The **introduction** aims to give you a feel for the place, with suggestions on where to go. We also tell you what the weather is like and include a basic country fact file. Next, our authors round up their favourite aspects of Thailand in the **things not to miss** section – whether it's great sights, amazing festivals or a fabulous beach. Right after this comes a full **contents** list.

Basics

The Basics section covers all the **pre-departure** nitty-gritty to help you plan your trip. This is where to find out which airlines fly to your destination, what paperwork you'll need, what to do about money and insurance, about Internet access, food, security, public transport, car rental – in fact just about every piece of **general practical information** you might need.

Guide

This is the heart of the Rough Guide, divided into user-friendly chapters, each of which covers a specific region. Every chapter starts with a list of **highlights** and an **introduction** that helps you to decide where to go, depending on your time and budget. Likewise, introductions to the various towns and smaller regions within each chapter should help you plan your itinerary. We start most town accounts with information on arrival and accommodation, followed by a tour of the sights, and finally reviews of places to eat and drink, and details of nightlife. Longer accounts also have a directory of practical listings. Each chapter concludes with **public transport** details for that region.

Contexts

Read Contexts to get a deeper understanding of what makes Thailand tick. We include a brief history, articles about **Buddhism**, **the arts**, **hill tribes**, **wildlife** and **music**, and a detailed further reading section that reviews dozens of **books** relating to the country.

Language

The **language** section gives useful guidance for speaking Thai and pulls together all the vocabulary you might need on your trip, including a comprehensive menu reader. Here you'll also find a glossary of words and terms peculiar to the country.

Index + small print

Apart from a **full index**, which includes maps as well as places, this section covers publishing information, credits and acknowledgements, and also has our contact details in case you want to send in updates and corrections to the book – or suggestions as to how we might improve it.

Chapter list and map

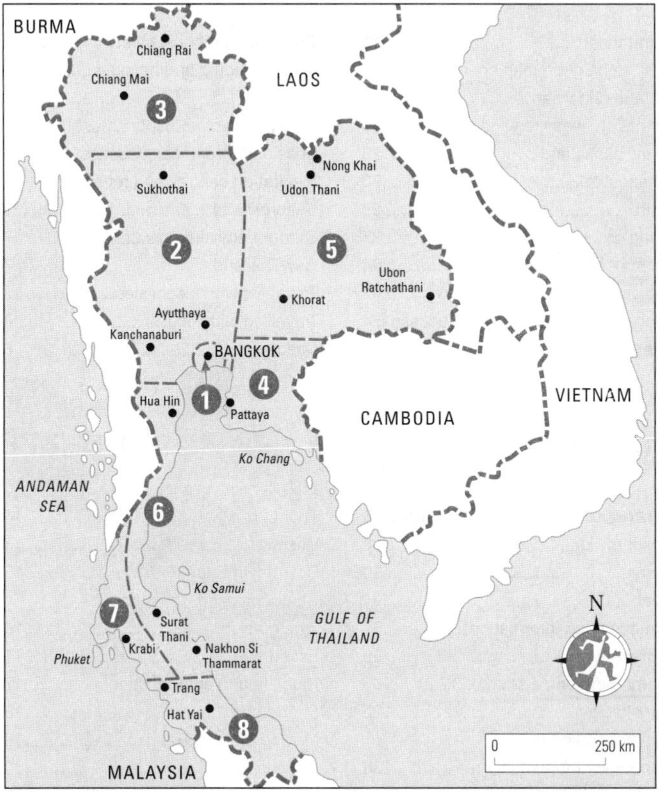

Contents

Colour section i–xxiv

Basics 9–84

The Guide 85–778

Contexts 779–852

Language 853–864

Index + small print 881–896

Basics

Basics

Getting there

Thailand currently has six international airports, in Bangkok, Chiang Mai, Hat Yai, Krabi, Phuket and Ko Samui, but the vast majority of travellers fly into Bangkok. At the time of writing, all international flights into Bangkok use Don Muang, but when the capital's new Suvarnabhumi Airport is completed, possibly in late 2005, all international flights will land there instead; see p.94 for more information about both airports.

Airfares to Thailand always depend on the **season**, with the highest being around mid-November to mid-February, when the weather is best (with premium rates charged for flights between mid-Dec and New Year), and in July and August to coincide with school holidays. You will need to book several months in advance to get reasonably priced tickets during these peak periods. Check the airline's exact seasonal dates through an agent, as you could make major savings by shifting your departure date by as little as one day. Note that however cheap your ticket, you'll still have to pay an **airport departure tax** of B500 in cash when leaving Thailand on an international flight.

You can often cut costs by going through a **specialist flight agent** – either a consolidator, who buys up blocks of tickets from the airlines and sells them at a discount, or a **discount agent**, who in addition to dealing with discounted flights may also offer special student and youth fares as well as travel insurance and tours. Many airlines and discount travel **websites** offer you the opportunity to book your tickets, hotels and holiday packages online, cutting out the costs of agents, but beware of non-refundable, non-changeable deals. Almost all airlines have their own websites, offering flight tickets that can sometimes be just as cheap, and are often more flexible.

Package deals come in two varieties: those offering a return flight and five days or more of accommodation, and specialist tours that organize daytime activities and escorted excursions – sometimes in addition to flights, sometimes not. Flight and accommodation deals can work out good value if you're planning to base yourself in just one or two places. Specialist tour packages, on the other hand, are pretty expensive compared to what you'd pay if you organized everything independently, but may feature activities and itineraries that would take some time to set up yourself. Thailand-wide **tour operators based in Bangkok** are given on p.196, and local operators in other parts of the country are listed throughout the Guide.

If Thailand is only one stop on a longer journey, you might want to consider buying a **round-the-world** (RTW) ticket. Some travel agents can sell you an "off-the-shelf" RTW ticket that will have you touching down in about half a dozen cities (Bangkok is on many itineraries); others will have to assemble one for you, which can be tailored to your needs but is likely to be more expensive.

From the UK and Ireland

The fastest and most comfortable way of reaching Thailand **from the UK** is to fly nonstop from London to Bangkok with Qantas, British Airways, Thai Airways or Eva Airways – a journey time of about eleven and a half hours. These four airlines usually keep their prices fairly competitive, at around £510/710 plus tax in low season/high season. Fares on indirect scheduled flights to Bangkok – with a change of plane en route – are always cheaper than nonstop flights and generally cost between £340/410 and £440/530, though these journeys can take anything from two to twelve hours longer.

The cheapest way of getting straight **to Phuket** and most other **regional Thai airports** is usually to buy a flight to Bangkok and then a domestic add-on with Thai

Airways; their Bangkok–Phuket return costs £75 plus tax. Another option for Phuket would be to fly there with Malaysia Airlines, via Kuala Lumpur, or Singapore Airlines, via Singapore, avoiding Bangkok altogether. You can also go via Singapore for direct connections to Chiang Mai (with Bangkok Airways or Silk Air), Ko Samui (with Bangkok Airways) and Krabi (with Silk Air).

There are no nonstop flights from any regional airports in Britain or from any **Irish airports**, and rather than routing via London, you may find it convenient to fly to another European hub such as Amsterdam (with KLM), Frankfurt (with Lufthansa) or Paris (with Air France), and take a connecting flight from there; flights via Paris with Air France, for example, start at around €710. Agents in Ireland such as Joe Walsh and Twohigs can also offer a wide range of packages to Thailand, or you might consider contacting one of the specialist tour operators in Britain.

Airlines in the UK and Ireland

Air France Republic of Ireland ⓣ01/605 0383, ⓦwww.airfrance.com.
Bangkok Airways UK ⓣ01293/596 626, ⓦwww.bangkokair.com.
British Airways UK ⓣ0870/850 9850, Republic of Ireland ⓣ1800/626 747, ⓦwww.ba.com.
Emirates UK ⓣ0870/243 2222, ⓦwww.emirates.com.
EVA Airways UK ⓣ020/7380 8300, Republic of Ireland ⓣ01/201 3913, ⓦwww.evaair.com.
Finnair UK ⓣ0870/241 4411, Republic of Ireland ⓣ01/844 6565, ⓦwww.finnair.com.
KLM UK ⓣ0870/507 4074, Republic of Ireland ⓣ01/663 6900, ⓦwww.klm.com.
Lufthansa UK ⓣ0845/773 7747, Republic of Ireland ⓣ01/844 5544, ⓦwww.lufthansa.com.
Malaysia Airlines UK ⓣ0870/607 9090, Republic of Ireland ⓣ01/676 2131, ⓦwww.malaysia-airlines.com.
Qantas UK ⓣ0845/774 7767, Republic of Ireland ⓣ01/407 3278, ⓦwww.qantas.co.uk.
Qatar Airways UK ⓣ020/7896 3636, ⓦwww.qatarairways.com.
Royal Jordanian UK ⓣ020/7878 6300, Republic of Ireland ⓣ061/474 995, ⓦwww.rja.com.jo.
Silk Air ⓦwww.silkair.com.
Singapore Airlines UK ⓣ0870/608 8886, Republic of Ireland ⓣ01/671 0722, ⓦwww.singaporeair.com.
Thai Airways UK ⓣ0870/606 0911, ⓦwww.thaiair.com.
Turkish Airlines UK ⓣ020/7766 9300, ⓦwww.thy.com.

Flight agents in the UK and Ireland

Bridge the World UK ⓣ0870/443 2399, ⓦwww.bridgetheworld.com. A wide choice of cut-price flights with good deals aimed at the backpacker market – particularly good for RTW tickets.
cheapflights.co.uk Choose your destination and date to view dozens of airfares, then follow the links or contact details.
ebookers UK ⓣ0870/010 7000, ⓦwww.ebookers.com, Republic of Ireland ⓣ01/241/5689, ⓦwww.ebookers.ie. Low fares on an extensive range of scheduled flights.
expedia ⓦwww.expedia.co.uk. Discount airfares, all-airline search engine and daily deals.
Flightcentre UK ⓣ0870/890 8099, ⓦwww.flightcentre.co.uk. Rock-bottom fares worldwide.
gohop Republic of Ireland ⓣ01/241 2389, ⓦwww.gohop.ie. Irish-owned agent, offering flights, packages, hotels and car rental.
International Association of Air Travel Couriers UK ⓣ0800/0746 481 or 01291/625 656, ⓦwww.aircourier.co.uk. Agent for lots of courier companies.
Joe Walsh Tours Republic of Ireland; Dublin ⓣ01/872 2555, 241 0888 or 241 0846, Cork ⓣ021/277959, ⓦwww.joewalshtours.ie. Well-established discount flight agent and tour operator.
North South Travel UK ⓣ01245/608 291, ⓦwww.northsouthtravel.co.uk. Competitive travel agency offering discounted fares worldwide; profits are used to support projects in the developing world, especially the promotion of sustainable tourism.
opodo.co.uk Popular source of low airfares. Owned by, and run in conjunction with, nine major European airlines.
priceline.co.uk Name-your-own-price website that has deals at around forty percent off standard fares.
Rosetta Travel UK ⓣ028/9064 4996, ⓦwww.rosettatravel.com. Flight and holiday agent, specializing in deals direct from Belfast.
STA Travel UK ⓣ0870/160 0599, ⓦwww.statravel.co.uk. Worldwide specialists in low-cost flights and tours for students and under-26s, though other customers welcome.
Top Deck UK ⓣ020/7244 8000, ⓦwww.topdecktravel.co.uk. Long-established agent dealing in discount flights and tours.

Trailfinders UK ⓣ020/7938 3939, ⓦwww.trailfinders.com, Republic of Ireland ⓣ01/677 7888, ⓦwww.trailfinders.ie. One of the best-informed and most efficient agents for independent travellers.
Travel Bag UK ⓣ0870/890 1456, ⓦwww.travelbag.co.uk. Discount flights to the Far East.
Twohigs Republic of Ireland ⓣ01/677 2666 or 648 0800, ⓦwww.twohigs.com. Specialist long-haul operation, offering low-cost airfares and packages to Thailand.
USIT Dublin ⓣ01/602 1600, Belfast ⓣ028/9032 4073, plus branches in Cork, Derry, Galway, Limerick, Maynooth and Waterford, ⓦwww.usit.ie. Ireland's main outlet for discounted, youth and student fares.

UK Tour operators

Dive Worldwide ⓣ01794/389372, ⓦwww.diveworldwide.com. Live-aboard diving holidays to the Similan and Surin islands, the Mergui archipelago and other Andaman Sea dive highlights. From £1770 for ten nights including flights.
Exodus ⓣ020/8675 5550, ⓦwww.exodus.co.uk. Small-group adventure tours to Thailand such as two weeks' cycling around southern Thailand, with rides to less mainstream spots as well as Trang, Krabi, Phuket and Khao Sok; the price starts at £920 and includes flights but not cycle hire.
Explore Worldwide UK ⓣ01252/760 000, ⓦwww.explore.co.uk. Unusual adventure-tours and small-group exploratory holidays; from £799 for thirteen days including flights. Also offers tailored family holidays.
Footprint Adventures ⓣ01225/8469141, ⓦwww.footprint-adventures.com. Tours catering to walkers as well as wildlife and bird enthusiasts, such as a fifteen-day bird-watching trip to four different national parks (£1260 excluding flights).
Gecko Travel ⓣ023/9225 8859, ⓦwww.geckotravel.com. Southeast Asia specialist operating small-group adventure holidays with off-the-beaten-track itineraries; their 21-day tour of Thailand's northern mountains and southern beaches includes treks, rafting and a cookery course and costs from £1575 including flights. Also offers family-oriented tours and shorter trips out of Bangkok.
Imaginative Traveller ⓣ01473/667337, ⓦwww.imaginative-traveller.com. Small-group adventure tours such as the fifteen-day Wilderness Adventure, which takes in Bangkok, Chiang Mai, a hill-tribe trek, Khao Sok National Park and Krabi, and costs £495 excluding flights.
Intrepid Travel ⓣ020/8960 6333, ⓦwww.intrepidtravel.com. Very well-regarded small-group adventure tour operator that uses local transport and travellers'-style accommodation. Plenty of options, ranging from eight days' trekking and rafting in the north for £230 (excluding flight) to a 29-day tour of northern hills, western rivers and southern beaches for £750.
Kuoni ⓣ01306/747 002, ⓦwww.kuoni.co.uk. Specializes in two-centre holidays, including flights and accommodation, with good family offers. Eight nights in Bangkok and Pattaya from £640. Bookings through most travel agents.
Symbiosis ⓣ0845/123 2844, ⓦwww.symbiosis-travel.com. High-quality tailor-made adventure and special-interest packages, including diving, with a commitment to environmentally sensitive and fair-trade tourism; prices start from around £80 a day, including flights and accommodation.
Travelmood ⓣ0870/444 9911, ⓦwww.flynow.com. Very good flight plus accommodation deals to large and small beach destinations, eg Phuket ten nights from £730, Ko Samet seven nights from £615, and Cha-am eight nights for £500.

From the US and Canada

There are no nonstop flights from North America to Thailand, but plenty of airlines run daily flights to Bangkok from major East and West Coast cities with only one stop en route. Although layover times can vary, the actual flying time is approximately eighteen hours from LA via Asia, around an hour longer from New York via Europe. From Canada, you can expect to spend something like sixteen hours in the air flying from Vancouver (via Tokyo) or at least twenty hours from Montréal (via Europe).

There doesn't seem to be much logic behind the pricing of **fares** from the US to Thailand, although it's generally easier to find a reasonable fare on flights via Asia than via Europe, even if you're departing from the East Coast. The following quoted prices are based on only one stop en route; cheaper rates are often available if you're prepared to make two or three stops and take more time. From the **east coast**, Delta's flights from New York via Seoul are particularly good value at the moment at US$830/940 low/high season; otherwise, expect to pay from US$950/1050 via Asia, and anything from US$1300 via Europe. Among the best current deals from the **west coast** is with China Airlines from LA for US$610/740, while Thai Airways' direct, one-stop flight from the same airport represents decent value at around US$1000; otherwise, you're looking at paying from US$910/1000.

Air Canada has the most convenient service to Bangkok from the largest number of **Canadian cities**. From Vancouver, expect to pay around Can$2000 in low season (Can$300 more in high season), from Toronto, Can$2300 (Can$300 more in high season).

A typical off-the-shelf **round-the-world (RTW) ticket**, starting and ending in New York with stops in London, Mumbai (Bombay), Delhi, Bangkok, Singapore and Hong Kong, costs around US$1500. An alternative would be a **Circle Pacific** deal, which allows you to make a certain number of stopovers en route between the West Coast of the US or Canada and Asia; an itinerary starting out and ending in Los Angeles, for example, taking in Hong Kong, Bangkok, Bali, Perth (overland to Sydney) and Auckland costs from around US$1800.

Airlines in the US and Canada

Air Canada ⓣ1-888/247-2262, ⓦwww.aircanada.com. Flights to Bangkok from most major Canadian cities via Osaka, Hong Kong or London.

Cathay Pacific ⓣ1-800/233-2742, ⓦwww.cathaypacific.com. To Bangkok via Hong Kong from West Coast cities and New York.

China Airlines ⓣ917/368-2000, ⓦwww.china-airlines.com. Cheap flights from LA to Bangkok via Taipei.

Delta ⓣ1-800/241-4141, ⓦwww.delta.com. Cheap flights via Seoul from New York.

JAL Japan Air Lines ⓣ1-800/525-3663, ⓦwww.japanair.com. Flies to Bangkok via Tokyo or Osaka from Chicago, Dallas, Los Angeles, New York, San Francisco and Vancouver.

Lufthansa US ⓣ1-800/645-3880, Canada ⓣ1-800/563-5954, ⓦwww.lufthansa.com. From New York, Chicago, LA, Toronto, Vancouver and other major cities via Frankfurt.

Thai Airways US ⓣ1-800/426-5204, Canada ⓣ1-800/668-8103, ⓦwww.thaiair.com. One-stop flights to Bangkok from most major US and Canadian cities via Osaka, Tokyo, London or Frankfurt (including direct flights from LA with a one-hour stop in Tokyo).

United Airlines ⓣ1-800/538-2929, ⓦwww.united.com. Flights to Bangkok from most major US cities, via Tokyo.

Flight agents in the US and Canada

Air Brokers International ⓣ1-800/883-3273, ⓦwww.airbrokers.com. Consolidator and specialist in round-the-world and Circle Pacific tickets.

Airtech ⓣ212/219-7000, ⓦwww.airtech.com. Standby seat broker; also deals in consolidator fares.

ⓦwww.cheapflights.com (in US), **ⓦwww.cheapflights.ca** (in Canada). Online flight deals, plus links to other travel sites.

ⓦwww.cheaptickets.com Discount flight specialists (US only). Also at ⓣ1-888/922-8849.

Educational Travel Center ⓣ1-800/747-5551 or 608/256-5551, ⓦwww.edtrav.com. Low-cost fares, student/youth discount offers, car rental and tours.

ⓦwww.expedia.com (in US), **ⓦwww.expedia.ca** (in Canada). Discount airfares, all-airline search engine and daily deals.

Flightcentre US ⓣ1-866/WORLD-51, ⓦwww.flightcentre.us, Canada ⓣ1-888/WORLD-55, ⓦwww.flightcentre.ca. Rock-bottom fares worldwide.

ⓦwww.gaytravel.com US gay travel agent, offering accommodation, cruises, tours and more. Also at ⓣ1-800/GAY-TRAVEL.

ⓦwww.hotwire.com Bookings from the US only. Last-minute savings of up to forty percent on regular published fares.

International Association of Air Travel Couriers ⓣ308/632-3273, ⓦwww.courier.org. Courier flight broker. One year's membership costs US$45 in the US or Canada (US$50 elsewhere).

ⓦwww.priceline.com Name-your-own-price website that has deals at around forty percent off standard fares.

ⓦwww.skyauction.com Bookings from the US only. Auctions tickets and travel packages to destinations worldwide.

SkyLink US ⓣ1-800/AIR-ONLY or 212/573-8980, Canada ⓣ1-800/SKY LINK, **ⓦwww.skylinkus.com** Consolidator.

STA Travel US ⓣ1-800/329-9537, Canada ⓣ1-888/427-5639, ⓦwww.statravel.com. Worldwide specialists in independent travel; also student IDs, travel insurance, car rental, rail passes and more.

Travel Avenue ⓣ1-800/333-3335, ⓦwww.travelavenue.com. Full-service travel agent that offers discounts in the form of rebates.

Travel Cuts US ⓣ1-800/592-CUTS, Canada ⓣ1-888/246-9762, ⓦwww.travelcuts.com. Popular, long-established student-travel organization, with worldwide offers.

ⓦ**www.travelocity.com** (in US), ⓦ**www.travelocity.ca** (in Canada). Destination guides, hot fares and great deals for car rental, accommodation and lodging.

Worldtek Travel ⓣ1-800/243-1723, ⓦwww.worldtek.com. Discount travel agency for worldwide travel.

Tour operators in the US and Canada

All prices quoted below exclude international flights, unless stated otherwise.

Abercrombie & Kent ⓣ1-800/323-7308 or 630/954-2944, ⓦwww.abercrombiekent.com. Classy operator with a strong reputation. Thai programmes include eleven-day "Highlights of Thailand" tour (from $2595), taking in Bangkok, Sukhothai, Lampang, Mae Hong Son and Chiang Mai.

Absolute Asia ⓣ1-800/736-8187, ⓦwww.absoluteasia.com. Luxury private tours – which can be customized – ranging from specialist interests such as archeology and Thai cuisine, to a twelve-day "Discover Thailand" trip taking in Bangkok, Chiang Mai, Chiang Rai and Phuket (US$3000).

Adventure Center ⓣ1-800/228-8747 or 510/654-1879, ⓦwww.adventurecenter.com. Hiking and "soft adventure" specialist agent, offering over twenty packages to Thailand with companies such as Gecko, Explore and the Imaginative Traveller. An example is an Explore eleven-day "Hill-tribe Trek" trip in northern Thailand costing from US$720.

Asian Pacific Adventures ⓣ1-800/825-1680 or 818/886-5190, ⓦwww.asianpacificadventures.com. Individualized, small-group tours and tailor-mades, including activities such as sea-canoeing, cruises, mountain-biking, trekking and Thai cooking. The eight-day "Thailand Epic", for example, encompassing Bangkok, Phimai, Ban Chiang, Sukhothai, Chiang Mai and Chiang Rai, costs from US$1300.

Backroads ⓣ1-800/GO-ACTIVE or 510/527-1555, ⓦwww.backroads.com. Cycling, hiking and multi-sport tours, with the emphasis on going at your own pace. Also family-friendly options and singles' trips. Seven days' biking, walking, kayaking and snorkelling on Ko Chang and Ko Samet costs US$2798.

Geographic Expeditions ⓣ1-800/777-8183 or 415/922-0448, ⓦwww.geoex.com. High-end adventure travel and cultural tours, as well as private journeys. "Textiles of Laos and northern Thailand" (21 days) costs from US$5225, including international flights.

Journeys International ⓣ1-800/255-8735 or 734/665-4407, ⓦwww.journeys-intl.com. Prestigious, award-winning operator focusing on eco-tourism and small-group trips. Their eight-day "Secrets of Siam" (US$1495) puts the emphasis on appreciating local culture in northern Thailand, with optional extras such as bird-watching and classes in cooking and massage.

Maupintour ⓣ1-800/255-4266, ⓦwww.maupintour.com. Luxury tours, including "Thailand's Festival of Light", nine days in Bangkok and Hua Hin to take in Loy Krathong (see p.64). From US$2159 (US$3119 including international flights from LA).

Real Traveller ⓣ1-866/REAL-TVL, ⓦwww.realtraveller.com. Canadian agent for a multitude of adventure companies all over the world, taking small groups on specialist programmes that include walking, biking, adventure and cultural trips.

REI Adventures ⓣ1-800/622-2236, ⓦwww.rei.com. Adventure and multi-sport tours. Fifteen days in Thailand trekking, bamboo-rafting and sea-kayaking costs from US$2095.

From Australia and New Zealand

There's no shortage of **scheduled flights** to Bangkok from Australia and New Zealand, with direct services from major Australian cities with Thai Airways, Qantas and British Airways (around nine hours from Sydney and Perth), and plenty of indirect flights via Asian hubs with airlines such as Singapore, Malaysia, Garuda and Royal Brunei, which take at least eleven and a half hours.

There are no nonstop flights from New Zealand, but Thai Airways runs fourteen-hour flights from Auckland to Bangkok with only a short stop in either Sydney or Brisbane, and other major Asian airlines offer indirect flights via their hubs. Both Malaysia Airlines and Singapore Airlines fly direct **to Phuket** from their respective regional hubs, saving you the effort of a Bangkok connection; you can also go via Singapore for direct onward flights to **Chiang Mai** (with Silk Air or Bangkok Airways), **Ko Samui** (with Bangkok Airways) and **Krabi** (with Silk Air).

From Australia, the three airlines that run direct flights to Bangkok keep prices fairly competitive at around Aus$1250/1550 in low/high season from Sydney and most major eastern Australian cities; special promotions are quite common, however, so you could be looking at low-season flights for as little as Aus$900. Indirect flights with Asian airlines start at around Aus$1030/1500. Fares from Perth and Darwin are up to Aus$100/200 cheaper.

From **New Zealand**, direct flights from Auckland to Bangkok on Thai Airways cost from NZ$950/1700 in low/high season, with indirect flights to Bangkok or Phuket on Malaysia Airlines via KL, or on Singapore Airlines via Singapore, priced from NZ$1650/2000. From Christchurch and Wellington you'll pay NZ$150–300 more than from Auckland.

Airlines in Australia and New Zealand

Air New Zealand Australia ⓣ13 24 76, ⓦwww.airnz.com.au, New Zealand ⓣ0800/737 000, ⓦwww.airnz.co.nz.
Bangkok Airways ⓦwww.bangkokair.com.
British Airways Australia ⓣ1300/767 177, New Zealand ⓣ0800/274 847 or 09/356 8690, ⓦwww.britishairways.com.
Garuda Indonesia Australia ⓣ1300/365 330 or 02/9334 9944, New Zealand ⓣ09/366 1862, ⓦwww.garuda-indonesia.com.
Malaysia Airlines Australia ⓣ13 26 27, New Zealand ⓣ0800/777 747, ⓦwww.malaysia-airlines.com.
Qantas Australia ⓣ13 13 13, New Zealand ⓣ0800/808 767 or 09/357 8900, ⓦwww.qantas.com.
Royal Brunei Australia ⓣ07/3017 5000 or 08/8941 0966, New Zealand ⓣ09/977 2240, ⓦwww.bruneiair.com.
Singapore Airlines Australia ⓣ13 10 11, New Zealand ⓣ0800/808 909, ⓦwww.singaporeair.com.
Thai Airways Australia ⓣ1300/651 960, New Zealand ⓣ09/377 3886, ⓦwww.thaiair.com.

Flight agents in Australia and New Zealand

Anywhere Travel Australia ⓣ02/9663 0411, ⓦwww.anywheretravel.com.au. Discounted flights, accommodation packages and tours.
Cheapflights.com Australia ⓦwww.cheapflights.com.au. Flight deals, travel agents, plus links to other travel sites.
Destinations New Zealand ⓣ09/373 4033. Discount fares plus a good selection of tours and holiday packages.
Flight Centre Australia ⓣ13 31 33, ⓦwww.flightcentre.com.au, New Zealand ⓣ0800/243 544, ⓦwww.flightcentre.co.nz. Guarantee to offer the lowest air fares; also sell a wide range of package holidays and adventure tours.
Holiday Shoppe New Zealand ⓣ0800/808 480, ⓦwww.holidayshoppe.co.nz. Great deals on flights, hotels and holidays.
lastminute.com Australia ⓦwww.lastminute.com.au, New Zealand ⓦwww.lastminute.co.nz. Late deals on flights and holidays.
Northern Gateway Australia ⓣ08/8941 1394, ⓔoztravel@norgate.com.au. Specializes in low-cost flights to Asia from Darwin.
OTC Australia ⓣ1300/855 118, ⓦwww.otctravel.com.au. Deals on flights, hotels and holidays.
Plan It Holidays Australia ⓣ03/9245 0747, ⓦwww.planit.com.au. Discounted airfares and accommodation packages.
STA Travel Australia ⓣ1300/733 035, New Zealand ⓣ0508/782 872, ⓦwww.statravel.com. Fare discounts for students and under-26s, as well as visas and travel insurance.
Student Flights Australia ⓣ1800/069 063, ⓦwww.studentflights.com.au. Specialize in cheap flights and other discounts for students. Part of Flight Centre.
Student Uni Travel Australia ⓣ02/9232 8444, ⓦwww.sut.com.au, New Zealand ⓣ09/379 4224, ⓦwww.sut.co.nz. Student/youth discounts and standard discounted fares.
Trailfinders Australia ⓣ02/9247 7666, ⓦwww.trailfinders.com.au. One of the best-informed and most efficient agents for independent travellers.
travel.com.au and **travel.co.nz** Australia ⓣ1300/130 482 or ⓣ02/9249 5444, ⓦwww.travel.com.au, New Zealand ⓣ0800/468 332, ⓦwww.travel.co.nz. Comprehensive online travel company, with discounted fares.
travelshop.com.au Australia ⓣ1800/108 108, ⓦwww.travelshop.com.au. Discounted flights, packages, insurance and online bookings.

Tour operators in Australia and New Zealand

Allways PADI Travel Australia ⓣ1800/259 297, ⓦwww.allwaysdive.com.au. All-inclusive dive packages to prime Thai dive sites.
Explore Worldwide ⓦwww.exploreworldwide.com. Adventure tours, including a fifteen-day Offbeat Thailand to north and west Thailand (Aus$1590 excluding flights), featuring

hill-tribe treks near Nan and rafting and trekking in Umphang. Book through Adventure World: Australia ⓣ02/8913 0755, ⓦwww.adventureworld.com.au, New Zealand ⓣ09/524 5118, ⓦwww.adventureworld. co.nz, or most other travel agents.

Geckos ⓦwww.geckosadventures.com. Small-group adventure tours using local transport and travellers' accommodation. Their fifteen-day Thailand at a Glance (Aus$1170 excluding flights) features the northern hills, hill tribes and cities of Chiang Mai, Chiang Rai and Chiang Dao; the River Kwai; Khao Sok National Park; a Phang Nga boat trip; and Krabi beaches. Sold through Peregrine (see below) and most travel agents.

Imaginative Traveller ⓣ1300/135088, ⓦwww.thinkadventure.com.au. Small-group adventure tours such as the fifteen-day Wilderness Adventure, which takes in Bangkok, Chiang Mai, a hill-tribe trek, Khao Sok National Park and Krabi, and costs Aus$1465 excluding flights. Also does family adventure tours.

Intrepid Travel Australia ⓣ1300/360 667 or 03/9473 2626, ⓦwww.intrepidtravel.com. Very well-regarded small-group adventure tour operator that uses local transport and travellers'-style accommodation. Plenty of options, ranging from eight days' trekking and rafting in the north for Aus$570 (excluding flight) to a 29-day tour of northern hills, western rivers and southern beaches for Aus$1990.

New Horizons Holidays Australia ⓣ08/9268 3777. Largest Southeast Asian wholesaler in Perth, offering an extensive range of trips to Thailand.

Peregrine Adventures Australia ⓣ03/9663 8611, ⓦwww.peregrine.net.au. In New Zealand, contact **Adventure Travel Company** ⓣ09/379 9755. Small-group adventure/cultural trips throughout Thailand; their eight-day Northern Trek and Cycle from Chiang Mai (Aus$990) visits the villages and towns around Chiang Dao, the Kok River, the Golden Triangle region and the city of Chiang Rai. Also act as agents for Geckos above.

Pro Dive Travel Australia ⓣ1800/820 820 or 02/9281 5066, ⓦwww.prodive.com.au. Tailored dive packages to Thailand's top underwater destinations.

Thai Binh Travel ⓣ02/9724 2304, ⓔthaibinh@telstra.com. Specialists in accommodation and tours throughout Thailand.

Thailand Travel ⓣ08/8272 2166. Specialists for tours and flights to Thailand.

Travel via neighbouring countries

Sharing land borders with Burma, Laos, Cambodia and Malaysia, Thailand works well as part of many overland itineraries, both across Asia and between Europe and Australia. In addition, Bangkok is one of the major regional flight hubs for Southeast Asia.

The main restrictions on overland routes in and out of Thailand are determined by **visas**, and by where the permitted land crossings lie. At any of the land borders described below, most passport holders should be able to get an on-the-spot thirty-day entry stamp into Thailand, which can be extended for ten days at Thai provincial immigration offices for a swingeing B1900. It's easy enough, however, to hop across one of the land borders and return on the same day with another, free thirty-day stamp, or you might want to apply for a sixty-day tourist visa instead, obtainable in advance from Thai embassies; full details on visa requirements are given on p.21.

You may need to buy visas for your next port of call when in Thailand, and details of visa requirements for travel to Thailand's immediate neighbours are outlined below. Visa requirements can change so it's worth checking in advance before you travel. All

Asian embassies are located in Bangkok (see p.203 for contact details), but several countries also have visa-issuing consulates outside the capital, where waiting times can be shorter: China and India run consulates in Chiang Mai (see p.346), and Laos and Vietnam have consulates in Khon Kaen (see p.525). Many Khao San tour agents offer to get your visa for you, but beware: some are reportedly **faking the stamps**, which could get you in pretty serious trouble, so it's safer to go to the embassy yourself.

The right paperwork is also crucial if you're planning to **drive your own car or motorbike into Thailand**. For advice on this, consult The Golden Triangle Rider website (Ⓦwww.gt-rider.com/crossing borders.html), which has up-to-date, first-hand accounts of border crossings with a vehicle between many Southeast Asian countries, including lots about Thailand.

Bangkok has become an important centre for **flights** to many parts of Asia, in particular as a transit point for routes between Europe and Vietnam, Laos and Cambodia; indeed on many flights from Europe to Indochina you have no choice but to be routed via Bangkok. In addition it is now also possible to fly into Chiang Mai, Hat Yai, Krabi and Phuket from some Asian cities. If you're doing a longer trip around Southeast Asia, you may want to consider buying a Circle ASEAN ticket, sold by the national airlines of Thailand, Burma, Brunei, Indonesia, Laos, Malaysia, the Philippines, Singapore and Vietnam. The pass entitles you to buy three to six flights between and within these countries for around £300–360/US$500–600; these passes must be bought outside the countries concerned and in conjunction with an international flight on one of the participating airlines.

Burma

At the time of writing, there is no overland access from **Burma** into Thailand and access in the opposite direction is restricted: Western tourists are only allowed to make limited-distance day-trips into Burma at Three Pagodas Pass near Kanchanaburi (see p.249), at Myawaddy near Mae Sot (see p.301), at Mae Sai (where longer trips to Kentung and Mongla are also possible, see p.409), and at Kaw Thaung (Victoria Point) near Ranong (see p.646). In some of these places you may be required officially to exit Thailand, enter Burma on a temporary visa (for a fee of US$5–10), and then re-enter Thailand on a new thirty-day tourist visa; see relevant accounts in the Guide for details.

In addition to numerous flights to Bangkok from Burma, there are regular flights to Chiang Mai from Yangon with Air Mandalay (Ⓦwww.air-mandalay.com) and Thai Airways (Ⓦwww.thaiair.com), and from Mandalay with Air Mandalay. Tourists who intend to enter Burma by air can buy four-week tourist visas at the Burmese embassy in Bangkok (see p.203) for B800; apply to the embassy and you may be able to collect the same day, or definitely the following day.

Cambodia

At the time of writing, six overland crossings on the **Thai-Cambodia border** are open to non-Thais, but check with the Cambodian Embassy in Bangkok as well as with other travellers first, as regulations are changeable. See the relevant town accounts for specific details on all the border crossings, and for travellers' up-to-the-minute experiences of the same, check out Ⓦwww.talesofasia.com/ cambodia-overland.

Most travellers use either the crossing at Poipet, which has transport connections to Sisophon, Siem Reap and Phnom Penh and lies just across the border from the Thai town of Aranyaprathet (see p.451), with its transport to Chanthaburi and Bangkok; or they follow the route from Sihanoukville in Cambodia via Koh Kong and Hat Lek to Trat (see p.455), which is near Ko Chang on Thailand's east coast – the Trat route is the fastest option if you're travelling nonstop from Bangkok to Cambodia. The more recently opened border crossings in northeast Thailand include the Chong Chom–O'Smach border pass, near Kap Choeng in Thailand's Surin province (see p.501), and the Sa Ngam–Choam border in Si Saket province (see p.507) – from both these borders there's transport to Anlong Veng and Siem Reap. There are also two crossings in Chanthaburi province (see p.451), with transport to and from Pailin in Cambodia.

The speedier alternative to the above overland routes is to make use of the Bangkok Airways **flights** that connect both Bangkok and Phuket with Phnom Penh and Siem Reap (ⓦwww.bangkokair.com).

Visas for Cambodia are issued to travellers on arrival at Phnom Penh and Siem Reap airports, and at the Aranyaprathet–Poipet, Hat Lek–Koh Kong and Chong Chom–O'Smach land borders; you need US$20 and two photos for this. You may also want to bring a (real or self-made) International Quarantine Booklet showing dates of your vaccinations, as border guards at overland crossings have been known to (illegally) charge foreigners without vaccination cards a US$5 penalty fee. If you do need to buy an advance thirty-day visa, you can do so from the Cambodian Embassy in Bangkok (see p.203; B1000; apply before noon and you can collect your visa the following day after 5pm).

Laos and Vietnam

There are currently five points along the **Lao border** where it's permissible for tourists to cross into Thailand: Houayxai (for Chiang Khong; see p.415); Vientiane (for Nong Khai; see p.543); Thakhek (for Nakhon Phanom; see p.549); Savannakhet (for Mukdahan; see p.552); and Pakxe (for Chong Mek; see p.517). Provided you have the right visa, all these borders can be used as exits into Laos; see relevant town account for specific details. As well as the numerous routes to and from Bangkok, Lao Airlines (ⓦwww.laoairlines.com) operates handy **flights** between Vientiane, Louang Phabang and Chiang Mai, Thai Airways (ⓦwww.thaiair.com) flies between Louang Phabang and Chiang Mai, and Bangkok Airways (ⓦwww.bangkokair.com) runs outbound flights from Bangkok and Sukhothai to Louang Phabang, with the incoming route landing in Bangkok only (there are no immigration facilities in Sukhothai).

Visas are required for all non-Thai visitors to Laos. A fifteen-day **visa on arrival** can be bought for US$30 (cash only, plus two photos) at Vientiane Airport, Louang Phabang Airport, and all the above-listed land borders. However, these visas cost twice as much and are valid for half the period of **visas bought in advance** from either the Lao Embassy in Bangkok (see p.203) or the Lao Consulate in Khon Kaen (see p.525), both of whom issue thirty-day visas for around B1100, depending on nationality. For this, you need two passport photos, and processing takes three days – or less than 24 hours if you pay an extra B300.

If you have the right Lao visa and Vietnamese exit stamp, you can travel from **Vietnam** to Thailand via Savannakhet in a matter of hours; you'll need to use Vietnam's Lao Bao border crossing, west of Dong Ha, where you can catch a bus to Savannakhet and then a ferry across the Mekong to Mukdahan All travellers into Vietnam need to buy a visa in advance. Thirty-day visas can take up to five working days to process at the embassy in Bangkok (see p.203) and cost about B1800, depending on your nationality; the same visas are issued in 24 hours at the Vietnamese consulate in Khon Kaen (see p.525).

The Eastern and Oriental Express

It's possible to travel between Singapore and Bangkok in extreme style by taking the **Eastern and Oriental Express** train – a Southeast Asian version of the Orient Express – which transports its passengers in great comfort and luxury. The journey, via Kuala Lumpur, takes around 41 hours, departs approximately once a week from either terminus and costs from £990/US$1600/Aus$2620 per person all inclusive. For details, go to ⓦwww.orient-express.com or call ⓣ0845/077 2222 (UK), ⓣ1-866/674-3689 (US), or ⓣ1800/000 395 (Aus). (Once or twice a month, E&O also runs a Bangkok–Chiang Mai overnight trip, costing from £580/US$940/Aus$1600/person, and a two-night version, with additional stops in Ayutthaya and Kanchanaburi from £780/US$1250/Aus$2100.)

Malaysia and Singapore

Travelling between Thailand and **Malaysia and Singapore** is straightforward and a very commonly used route. Most Western tourists can spend thirty days in Malaysia and fourteen days in Singapore without having bought a visa beforehand, and transport linking the three countries is excellent. This makes it an ideal route for tourists and expats needing to renew their Thai visas; there are Thai embassies or consulates in Kuala Lumpur, Penang, Kota Bharu and Singapore (see p.22).

It's possible to take a **train** all the way from Singapore to Bangkok via Malaysia, a journey of just under 2000km. The journey involves several changes, but the overall trip can be done in around 48 hours and for as little as £33/US$50. Taking the train from Singapore or Johor Bahru in southern Malaysia, you can opt for the west coast route, with connections in Kuala Lumpur and Butterworth, or the east coast route, which goes via Kota Bharu, but involves a short taxi ride across the border to Sungai Kolok; the two lines rejoin at the southern Thai town of Hat Yai. Travelling from KL to Hat Yai takes about fifteen hours and costs about £8/US$12 for a second-class sleeper. For a comprehensive guide to this route, and advice on how to save money on your tickets, see ⓦwww.seat61.com/Malaysia.htm; for the current timetable and ticket prices, visit the Malaysian Railways website (ⓦwww.ktmb.com.my). Travelling in the reverse direction, you'll probably get better connections by changing onto a bus or share-taxi at Hat Yai (see p.767), and at Sungai Kolok (p.776) you'll have to get a bus or taxi anyway; details of border formalities are given in the relevant accounts.

Plenty of **buses** also cross the Thai-Malaysian border every day. Hat Yai is the major transport hub for international bus connections, and there are regular buses here from Singapore (around £12/US$18; 18hr) and Kuala Lumpur (£9/US$13; 12hr), and buses and share-taxis from Penang (£9/US$13; 6hr). You'll also find long-distance buses and minibuses to Bangkok, Krabi, Phuket and Surat Thani from Kuala Lumpur, Penang and Singapore, as well as in the reverse direction. If you're coming from Alor Setar, the nearest big town to the border on Malaysia's west coast, you'll have to get a bus to the border at Bukit Kayu Hitam, then take a share-taxi from the Thai side up to Hat Yai.

If you're working your way slowly up the west coast of the peninsula, it's best to cross the border on one of the frequent **boats** that connect Kuala Perlis and Langkawi with Satun in south Thailand; see p.757 for details.

In addition to the numerous daily **flights** on any number of international airlines from Malaysia and Singapore to Bangkok, Bangkok Airways operates daily flights between Singapore and Ko Samui (ⓦwww.bangkokair.com), while Phuket is served by flights from Kuala Lumpur (ⓦwww.malaysia-airlines.com) and Singapore (ⓦwww.silkair.com). There are also regular flights from Singapore to Hat Yai (Singapore Airlines) and Chiang Mai (Silk Air).

Red tape and visas

There are three main entry categories for visitors to Thailand; for all of them your passport must be valid for at least six months from the date of entry. As visa requirements are often subject to change, you should always check before departure with a Thai embassy or consulate, a reliable travel agent, or on the Thai Ministry of Foreign Affairs' website at ⓦwww.mfa.go.th/web/12.php. This webpage gives the official lowdown on every type of visa available (including a new one-year "O–A visa" for over-50s); for further, unofficial details on related matters, such as the perils of overstaying your visa, go to ⓦwww.thaivisa.com.

Most Western passport holders (that includes citizens of the UK, Ireland, the US, Canada, Australia and New Zealand) are allowed to enter the country for **stays of up to thirty days** without having to apply for a visa (officially termed the "tourist visa exemption"); the period of stay will be stamped into your passport by immigration officials upon entry. You're supposed to be able to somehow show proof of means of living while in the country (B10,000/person, B20,000/family), and in theory you may be put back on the next plane without it or sent back to get a sixty-day tourist visa from the nearest Thai embassy, but it's unheard of. It's easy to get a new thirty-day stay by hopping across the border into a neighbouring country, especially Malaysia, or by taking a day-trip into Burma at Kaw Thaung (see p.646), Mae Sot (see p.301) or Thakhilek (see p.409).

If you're fairly certain you may want to stay longer than thirty days, then from the outset you should apply for a **sixty-day tourist visa** from a Thai embassy or consulate, accompanying your application – which generally takes several days to process – with your passport and two photos. The sixty-day visa currently costs B1000 or equivalent (though it's a rip-off £25 in the UK); multiple-entry versions are available, costing B1000 per entry (each giving you another sixty-day stay), which may be handy if you're going to be leaving and re-entering Thailand. Tourist visas are valid for three months, ie you must enter Thailand within three months of the visa being issued by the Thai embassy or consulate. Visa application forms can be downloaded from ⓦwww.thaiinuk.com/visaapplicationform.internet.pdf.

Thai embassies also consider applications for **ninety-day non-immigrant visas** (B2000 or equivalent single entry, valid for three months from date of issue; B5000 multiple entry, valid for one year) as long as you can offer a good reason for your visit, such as study or business (there are different categories of non-immigrant visa for which different levels of proof are needed). As it's quite a hassle to organize a ninety-day visa from outside the country (and generally not feasible for most tourists), it's generally easier, though more expensive, to apply for a thirty-day extension to your sixty-day visa once inside Thai borders.

It's not a good idea to **overstay** your visa limits. Once you're at the airport or the border, it's generally straightforward enough to pay a fine (one-day overstay free, two days B400, thereafter B200/day) before you leave Thailand. However, if you're in the country with an expired visa and you get involved with police or immigration officials for any reason whatsoever, they are obliged to take you to court, possibly imprison you, and deport you.

Extensions and re-entry permits

Thirty-day stays can be **extended** in Thailand for a further ten days, sixty-day tourist visas for a further thirty days, at the discretion of officials; extensions cost B1900 and are issued over the counter at immigration offices (*kaan khao muang*) in nearly every provincial capital – most offices ask for one or two photos as well, plus two photocopies of the main pages of your passport including your Thai arrival card, arrival stamp and visa. Many Khao San tour agents offer to get your visa extension for you, but beware: some are reportedly faking the stamps, which could get you into serious trouble. Immigration offices also issue **re-entry permits** (B1000 single re-entry, B3800 multiple) if for some reason you want to leave the country and come back again while maintaining the validity of your existing visa.

Staying on

Unless you have work or study fixed up before you arrive, staying on in Thailand is a precarious affair. Plenty of people do – teaching English, working in resort bars and guest houses or as dive instructors – but it involves frequent and expensive visa runs to neighbouring countries, and often entails hassle from the local police. All non-residents who acquire income while in Thailand should get a tax clearance certificate from the Revenue Department, which has offices in every provincial capital and on Thanon Phaholyothin in Bangkok (ⓣ02 617 3009). For more on job possibilities in Thailand see p.84.

Thai embassies and consulates abroad

For a full listing of Thai diplomatic missions abroad, check out the Thai Ministry of Foreign Affairs' website at ⓦwww.mfa.go.th/embassy/default.htm

Australia 111 Empire Circuit, Yarralumla, Canberra ACT 2600 ⓣ02/6273 1149; plus consulate at 131 Macquarrie St, Sydney, NSW 2000 ⓣ02/9241 2542, ⓦhttp://thaisydney.idx.com.au.

Burma 73 Manawhari Street, Dagon Township, Rangoon ⓣ01/224647.

Cambodia No.1 V. Samdech Chakrey Nhiek Tioulong, Sangkat Tonle Bassac, Khan Chamcar Mon, Phnom Penh ⓣ023/726306–8.

Canada 180 Island Park Drive, Ottawa, Ontario K1Y 0A2 ⓣ613/722 4444, ⓦwww.magma.ca/~thaiott; plus consulate at 1040 Burrard St, Vancouver, BC, V6Z 2R9 ⓣ604/687 1143.

Ireland Honorary consulate at 18/18 Harcourt St, Dublin 2 ⓣ01/475 3928, or contact the embassy in London.

Laos Route Phonekheng, Vientiane, PO Box 128 ⓣ021/217157–8; plus consulate at Khanthabouly District, Savannakhet Province, PO Box 513 ⓣ041/212373.

Malaysia 206 Jalan Ampang, 50450 Kuala Lumpur ⓣ03/2148 8222; plus consulates at 4426 Jalan Pengkalan Chepa, 15400 Kota Bharu ⓣ09/748 2545; and 1 Jalan Tunku Abdul Rahman, 10350 Penang ⓣ04/226 9484.

New Zealand 2 Cook St, PO Box 17226, Karori, Wellington 6005 ⓣ04/476 8618/9, ⓦwww.thaiembassynz.org.nz.

Singapore 370 Orchard Road, Singapore 238870 ⓣ6737 2158 or 6835 4991, ⓦwww.thaiembsingapore.org.

UK 29–30 Queens Gate, London SW7 5JB ⓣ09003/405456 or 020/7589 2944 (visa applications by post not accepted); plus honorary consulates, which will process postal applications, at Exchange Buildings, Stephenson Place, Birmingham B2 4NN ⓣ0121/643 9481; 9 Mount Stuart Square, Cardiff CF10 5EE ⓣ0292/046577; 4 Woodside Place, Charing Cross, Glasgow ⓣ0141/353 5090; James Bell House, Connaught Rd, Kingwood, Hull HU7 3AQ ⓣ01482/329925; and 35 Lord St, Liverpool L2 9SQ ⓣ0151/255 0504.

US 1024 Wisconsin Ave, NW, Suite 401, Washington, DC 20007 ⓣ202/944-3600, ⓦwww.thaiembdc.org; plus consulates at 700 North Rush St, Chicago, IL 60611 ⓣ312/644-3129; 351 East 52nd St, New York, NY 10022 ⓣ212/754-1770; and 611 North Larchmont Blvd, 2nd Floor, Los Angeles, CA 90004 ⓣ323/962-574, ⓦwww.thai-la.net

Vietnam 63–65 Hoang Dieu St, Hanoi ⓣ04/823-5092; plus consulate at 77 Tran Quoc Thao St, District 3, Ho Chi Minh City ⓣ08/932-7637.

Customs regulations

The duty-free allowance on entry to Thailand is 200 cigarettes (or 250g of tobacco) and a litre of spirits or wine. To export **antiques or religious artefacts** – especially Buddha images – from Thailand, you need to have a licence granted by the Fine Arts Department, which can be obtained through the Office of Archeology and National Museums, 81/1 Thanon Si Ayutthaya (near the National Library), Bangkok (ⓣ02 628 5032), or through the national museums in Chiang Mai (see p.333), Phuket (see p.694) and Songkhla (see p.771). Applications take at least two days in Bangkok, generally more in the provinces, and need to be accompanied by the object itself, two postcard-sized photos of it, taken face-on, and photocopies of the applicant's passport. Some antiques shops will organize this for you.

Information, websites and maps

The efficient Tourism Authority of Thailand (TAT) maintains offices in several cities abroad, where you can pick up a few glossy brochures and get fairly detailed answers to specific pre-trip questions. More comprehensive local information is given at TAT headquarters in Bangkok and its 23 regional branches (all open daily 8.30am–4.30pm), which provide an array of printed information on everything from how to avoid being ripped off to where to learn to dive. In addition, all TAT offices should have up-to-date information on local festival dates and regional transport schedules, but none of them offers accommodation booking and service can be variable. You can contact the TAT Call Centre from anywhere in the country on ⓣ1672 daily from 8am to 8pm. In Bangkok, TAT plays second fiddle to the Bangkok Tourist Bureau, details of which can be found on p.98. In some smaller towns that don't qualify for a local TAT office, the information gap is filled by a municipal tourist assistance office, and at some of these you may find it hard to locate a fluent English speaker.

Independent **tour operators** and information desks crop up in tourist spots all over the country, but be on the lookout for self-interested advice, given by staff desperate for commission. As with TAT offices, independent operators won't book accommodation – unless of course they happen to have business links with specific guest houses or hotels. For offbeat, enthusiastic first-hand advice, you can't do better than guest house **noticeboards** and **comment books** – the best of these boast a whole range of travellers' tips, from anecdotal accounts of cross-country bike trips to recommendations as to where to get the perfect suit made.

You'll find plenty of information about Thailand on the **Internet** as well; a selection of the best websites is given on pp.25–26.

TAT offices abroad

TAT's website is at ⓦwww.tourismthailand.org

Australia Level 2, 75 Pitt St, Sydney, NSW 2000 ⓣ02/9247 7549, ⓦwww.thailand.net.au.

Canada 1393 Royal York Rd, Etobicoke, Toronto, Ontario M9A 4Y9 ⓣ416/614-2625 or 1-800-THAILAND.

New Zealand Level 2, 10 Northcroft St, Takapuna, Auckland ⓣ09/489 1363.

UK and Ireland 3rd Floor, Brook House, 98–99 Jermyn St, London SW1Y 6EE ⓣ020/7925 2511,

recorded information on ⓣ0870/900 2007, ⓦwww.thaismile.co.uk.
US ⓦ1-800-THAILAND; 61 Broadway, Suite 2810, New York, NY 10006 ⓣ212/432-0433, ⓔinfo@tatny.com; 611 North Larchmont Blvd, 1st Floor, Los Angeles, CA 90004 ⓣ323/461-9814, ⓔtatla@ix.netcom.com.

Maps

One thing neither TAT nor tour operators provide is a decent **map**. For most major destinations, the maps in this book should be all you need, though you may want to supplement them with larger-scale versions of Bangkok and the whole country. Bangkok bookshops are the best source of these maps; where appropriate, detailed local maps and their stockists are recommended in the relevant chapters of the Guide. If you want to buy a map before you get there (for outlets at home, see below), Rough Guides' 1:1,200,000 map of Thailand is a good option – and it won't tear because it's printed on special rip-proof paper. Reasonable alternatives include the 1:1,500,000 maps produced by Nelles and Bartholomew.

For drivers, the large-format atlas, *Thailand Highway Map,* is especially good, and is updated annually; it's available at most bookstores in Thailand where English-language material is sold. If you can't get hold of it, you could go for the relevant 1:300,000 maps of each province published by PN Map Centre and sold at better bookshops in Bangkok and all over the country; some of the detail on these maps is only in Thai, but they should have enough English to be useful. Better than both the above are the excellent World Class Drives map-booklets, which are handed out free to customers of Budget car rental: detailed and almost unfailingly accurate, these are designed for tourists, but only cover certain parts of the country.

Trekking maps are hard to come by, except in the most popular national parks where you can usually pick up a free handout showing the main trails.

Travel bookshops and map outlets

The following are specialist map and/or travel bookshops. We're not listing big general bookstores here, although they – and the big Internet retailers such as Amazon (ⓦwww.amazon.com, ⓦwww.amazon.ca and ⓦwww.amazon.co.uk) – will probably stock at least some of the same titles. Stanfords, in the UK, rates as one of the best travel bookshops in the world, boasting a global catalogue, expert knowledge and worldwide mail order. In the US, the website of map wholesalers Map Link (ⓦwww.maplink.com) carries a useful list of specialist map and travel bookstores in every US state: click on Retail Partners.

UK and Ireland

Blackwell's Map Centre 50 Broad St, Oxford ⓣ01865/793550, ⓦmaps.blackwell.co.uk. Branches in Bristol, Cambridge, Cardiff, Leeds, Liverpool, Newcastle, Reading and Sheffield.
Daunt Books 83 Marylebone High St, London W1 ⓣ020/7224 2295; 193 Haverstock Hill, London NW3 ⓣ020/7794 4006.
The Map Shop 30a Belvoir St, Leicester ⓣ0116/247 1400, ⓦwww.mapshopleicester.co.uk.
National Map Centre 22–24 Caxton St, London SW1 ⓣ020/7222 2466, ⓦwww.mapsnmc.co.uk.
National Map Centre Ireland 34 Aungier St, Dublin ⓣ01/476 0471, ⓦwww.mapcentre.ie.
Stanfords 12–14 Long Acre, London WC2 ⓣ020/7836 1321, ⓦwww.stanfords.co.uk. Also at 39 Spring Gdns, Manchester ⓣ0161/831 0250, and 29 Corn St, Bristol ⓣ0117/929 9966.
The Travel Bookshop, 13–15 Blenheim Crescent, London W11 ⓣ020/7229 5260, ⓦwww.thetravelbookshop.co.uk.
Traveller 55 Grey St, Newcastle-upon-Tyne ⓣ0191/261 5622, ⓦwww.newtraveller.com.

US

Book Passage 51 Tamal Vista Blvd, Corte Madera, CA 94925 and in the San Francisco Ferry Building ⓣ1-800/999-7909 or 415/927-0960, ⓦwww.bookpassage.com.
Distant Lands 56 S Raymond Ave, Pasadena, CA 91105 ⓣ1-800/310-3220, ⓦwww.distantlands.com.
Globe Corner Bookstore 28 Church St, Cambridge, MA 02138 ⓣ1-800/358-6013, ⓦwww.globecorner.com.
Longitude Books 115 W 30th St #1206, New York, NY 10001 ⓣ1-800/342-2164, ⓦwww.longitudebooks.com.
Map Link ⓦwww.maplink.com.
110 North Latitude ⓣ336/369-4171, ⓦwww.110nlatitude.com.

Canada

Map Town 400 5 Ave SW #100, Calgary, AB, T2P 0L6 ⓣ1-877/921-6277 or 403/266-2241, ⓦwww.maptown.com.
Open Air Books and Maps 25 Toronto St, Toronto, Ontario, M5R 2C1 ⓣ1-800/360-9185 or 416/363-0719.
Travel Bug Bookstore 3065 W Broadway, Vancouver, BC, V6K 2G9 ⓣ604/737-1122, ⓦwww.travelbugbooks.ca.
Wanderlust 1929 West 4th Ave, Vancouver, BC, V6J 1M7 ⓣ604/739-2182, ⓔwanderlust@telus.ne.
World of Maps 1235 Wellington St, Ottawa, Ontario K1Y 3A3 ⓣ1-800/214-8524 or 613/724-6776, ⓦwww.worldofmaps.com.

Australia

Mapland 372 Little Bourke St, Melbourne ⓣ03/9670 4383, ⓦwww.mapland.com.au.
Map Shop 6 Peel St, Adelaide ⓣ08/8231 2033, ⓦwww.mapshop.net.au.
Map World 371 Pitt St, Sydney ⓣ02/9261 3601, ⓦwww.mapworld.net.au. Also at 900 Hay St, Perth ⓣ08/9322 5733, Jolimont Centre, Canberra ⓣ02/6230 4097 and 1981 Logan Rd, Brisbane ⓣ07/3349 6633.
Travel Bookshop Shop 3, 175 Liverpool St, Sydney ⓣ02/9261 8200.
Worldwide Maps and Guides 187 George St, Brisbane ⓣ07/3221 4330.

New Zealand

Map Centre ⓦwww.mapcentre.co.nz.
Map World 173 Gloucester St, Christchurch ⓣ0800/627 967, ⓦwww.mapworld.co.nz.
Specialty Maps 46 Albert St, Auckland ⓣ09/307 2217, ⓦwww.wisesmap.co.nz.

Thailand online

Only general tourist-oriented websites are listed below. For online accommodation-booking services see p.46, for government travel advisory websites see p.59, for diving websites see p.74, and for websites for gay travellers see p.78.

Ajarn.com ⓦwww.ajarn.com. Great source of info on everything to do with teaching in Thailand, and also has a forum where expats exchange tips on restaurants, entertainment and places to go.
Bangkok Post ⓦwww.bangkokpost.net. Free access to the day's main stories from Thailand's leading English-language daily newspaper, plus travel stories.
Khao San Road ⓦwww.khaosanroad.com. Backpacker-oriented site that's mainly concerned with spreading the word about the Khao San mecca. Also features detailed advice on visiting foreign prisoners in Bangkok, and maps of some Thai rock-climbing sites. Hosts several discussion boards as well.
Lonely Planet Thorn Tree ⓦthorntree.lonelyplanet.com. Worldwide site that includes a very popular, if sometimes rather overheated, Thailand travellers' forum. Also runs forums on other travel-related issues, such as travelling with kids, diving, and gay and lesbian travel.
René Hasekamp's Homepage ⓦwww.hasekamp.net/thaiindex.htm. Created by a Dutch man who is married to a Thai woman, this site lists practical tips for travellers to Thailand, plus information on selected sights and a handy list of FAQs.
Rough Guides ⓦwww.roughguides.com. Interactive site for independent travellers, with forums, bulletin boards, travel tips and features, plus online travel guides.
Siam Net ⓦwww.siam.net/guide. Decent jumping-off point, with general background on Thailand and its main tourist centres, plus an extensive hotel booking service and useful information on visas, etc.
TAT News Rooms ⓦwww.tatnews.org/emagazine. Very interesting archive of articles written by expat journos about a range of Thailand-related subjects from fashion to bird-watching, and often from an unusual angle.
Thai Fiction ⓦwww.thaifiction.com. Marcel Barang, the professional translator of Thai literature who founded the Thai Modern Classics series, posts juicy English extracts from around thirty modern Thai novels and short stories.
Thai Focus ⓦwww.thaifocus.com. The wide-ranging website of a Chiang Mai travel agency, offering a country-wide hotel-booking service, domestic and international air tickets, train tickets, car rental, plus a basic introduction to Thailand's main destinations.
Thailand Travel Forum ⓦwww.travelforum.org/thailand/. Thailand-specific forum that gets plenty of traffic and is a good source of travellers' info. Also provides an accommodation-booking service.
Thaiways Magazine ⓦwww.thaiwaysmagazine.com. The online version of the fortnightly freebie tourist booklet reproduces its lead features on the website, maintains a useful calendar of upcoming events and covers the highlights of the main tourist centres.

Tourism Authority of Thailand (TAT)
Ⓦwww.tourismthailand.org. The official TAT site has general background on the country, plus links to accommodation, weather reports and other standard stuff.
Tourism Authority of Thailand, London
Ⓦwww.thaismile.co.uk. The official website for the London TAT office features a searchable database of affiliated travel agents and tour operators, covers Thailand's highlights and travellers' FAQs and also has an innovative section on Thai culture in the UK, including listings of Thai restaurants across the UK.
2Bangkok.com
Ⓦwww.2bangkok.com/2bangkok/index.shtml. Of most interest to tourists for its very detailed information on gem scams and how to avoid them, and for its accommodation-booking service, but also worth a browse for its unique coverage of some of Thailand's biggest, and most controversial, infrastructure projects, from the expansion of Bangkok's Skytrain network to the digging of a canal across the Isthmus of Kra.
Welcome to Chiang Mai and Chiang Rai
Ⓦwelcome-to.chiangmai-chiangrai.com. The website of the Chiang Mai listings magazine covers some of the obvious northern Thailand highlights, including hill tribes and handicrafts, offers reviews of sights and hotels, and also features a roundup of spas in north Thailand, as well as regularly updated news of forthcoming local events.

Money, banks and costs

Thailand's unit of currency is the baht (abbreviated to "B"), which is divided into 100 satang. Notes come in B10 (though these are becoming rarer nowadays), B20, B50, B100, B500 and B1000 denominations, inscribed with Arabic as well as Thai numerals, and increasing in size according to value. The coinage is more confusing, because new shapes and sizes circulate alongside older ones, which sometimes have only Thai numerals. The tiny brass-coloured 25- and 50-satang pieces are rarely used now, as most prices are rounded off to the nearest baht. There are three different silver one-baht coins, all legal tender; the smallest of these is the newest version, and the one accepted by public call-boxes. Silver five-baht pieces are slightly bigger and have a copper rim; ten-baht coins have a small brass centre encircled by a silver ring.

At the time of writing, **exchange rates** were averaging B42 to US$1 and B66 to £1; note that Thailand has no black market in foreign currency. Because of severe currency fluctuations in the late 1990s, some tourist-oriented businesses now quote their prices in dollars, particularly luxury hotels and dive centres.

Banking hours are Monday to Friday from 8.30am to 3.30 or 4.30pm, but exchange kiosks in the main tourist centres are always open till at least 5pm, sometimes 10pm, and upmarket hotels change money 24 hours a day. The Don Muang Airport exchange counters also operate 24 hours (and exchange kiosks at overseas airports with flights to Thailand usually keep Thai currency), so there's little point arranging to buy baht before you leave home, especially as it takes seven working days to order from most banks outside Thailand.

Costs

In a country where the daily minimum wage is B170 or under, it's hardly surprising that Western tourists find Thailand an extremely cheap place to travel. At the bottom of the scale, you could manage on a **daily budget** of about B400 (£7/US$10) if you're willing to opt for basic accommodation, stay away from the more expensive resorts like Phuket, Ko Samui and Ko Phi Phi, and eat, drink and travel as the locals do. On this budget, you'll be spending B80–150 for a dorm bed or single room (less if you share the cost of a double room), around B150–200 on three meals (eating mainly at night markets and simple noodle shops, and eschewing beer), and the rest on travel (sticking mainly to non-air-con buses and third-class trains) and incidentals. With extras like air-conditioning in rooms (from B300–800 a double in guest houses and simple hotels) and on long-distance buses and trains, taking tuk-tuks (see p.39) rather than buses or shared songthaews for cross-town journeys, and a meal and a couple of beers in a more touristy restaurant (B100–150/person), a day's outlay would look more like B600–800 (£10–13/US$15–20). Staying in comfortable, upmarket hotels and eating in the more exclusive restaurants, you should be able to live in great comfort for around B2000 a day (£35/US$50).

Travellers soon get so used to the low cost of living in Thailand that they start **bargaining** at every available opportunity, much as Thai people do. Although it's expected practice for a lot of commercial transactions, particularly at markets and when hiring tuk-tuks and taxis, bargaining is a delicate art that requires humour, tact and patience. If your price is way out of line, the vendor's vehement refusal should be enough to make you increase your offer: never forget that the few pennies or cents you're making such a fuss over will go a lot further in a Thai person's hands than in your own.

On the other hand, making a tidy sum off foreigners is sometimes official practice: at government-run museums and historical parks, for example, foreigners often pay a B30–40 admission charge while Thais get in for B10. The most controversial **two-tier pricing** system is the innovation at most national parks, where foreigners now have to pay B200 entry while Thais pay just B20. A number of privately owned tourist attractions follow a similar two-tier system, posting an inflated price in English for foreigners and a lower price in Thai for locals.

Traveller's cheques, debit and credit cards

The safest way to carry your money is in **traveller's cheques** (a fee of one or two percent is usually levied when you buy them, though this fee may be waived if you buy the cheques through a bank where you have an account). Sterling and dollar cheques are accepted by banks, exchange booths and upmarket hotels in every sizeable Thai town, and most places also deal in a variety of other currencies; everyone offers better rates for cheques than for straight cash. Generally, a total of B23 in commission and duty is charged per cheque – though kiosks and hotels in isolated places may charge extra – so you'll save money if you deal in larger cheque denominations. All issuers give you a list of numbers to call in the case of **lost or stolen cheques** and will pay refunds if you can produce the purchase agreement and a note of your cheque numbers (which you should keep safe and separate from the cheques themselves). Instructions in cases of loss or theft vary from issuer to issuer, but you'll usually have to notify the police first and then call the issuing company collect to arrange replacements, usually within 24 hours, either by courier or at a local agent.

American Express, Visa and MasterCard/Cirrus **credit and debit cards** are accepted at top hotels as well as in some posh restaurants, department stores, tourist shops and travel agents, but surcharging of up to five percent is rife, and theft and forgery are major industries – always demand the carbon copies, and never leave cards in baggage storage. If you have a personal identification number (PIN) for your debit or credit card, you can also withdraw cash from hundreds of 24-hour **ATMs** ("automatic teller machines" or cash dispensers) around the country. Almost every town now has at least one bank with an ATM that accepts Visa cards and MasterCard/Cirrus cards, and there are a growing number of stand-alone ATMs in places like 7–11, the 24-hour supermarket. For an up-to-the-minute list of ATM locations in Thailand, check the relevant websites (Ⓦwww.mastercard.com and Ⓦwww.visa.com). If in any doubt you could call the issuing bank or credit company to find out whether your particular card works in Thailand and, if so, which Thai bank's ATMs accept it. There's usually a handling fee of 1.5 percent on every withdrawal, little different from the total amount of fees and commissions payable on traveller's cheques, but it's wise not to rely on plastic alone, which is more tempting to thieves and less easy to replace than the trusty traveller's cheque.

Wiring money

Wiring money through a specialist agent is a fast but expensive way to send and receive money abroad. The funds should be available for collection, usually in local currency, from the company's local agent within twenty minutes of being sent via Western Union or Moneygram; both charge on a sliding scale, so sending larger amounts of cash is better value.

It's also possible to have money wired directly from a bank in your home country to a bank in Thailand, although this is somewhat less reliable because it involves two separate institutions. Your home bank will need the address of the branch bank where you want to pick up the money and the address and telex number of the Bangkok head office, which will act as the clearing house; money wired this way normally takes two working days to arrive, and costs around £25/US$40 per transaction.

Money-wiring companies

Travelers Express/MoneyGram US ⓣ1-800/ MoneyGram or 1-800/666-3947, Canada ⓣ1-800/933-3278, Australia ⓣ1800/666 3947, UK ⓣ0800/8971 8971, Ireland and New Zealand ⓣ0800/666 3947. ⓦwww.moneygram.com gives locations of agents in Thailand, including branches of the Siam Commercial and Thai Military banks.

Western Union US and Canada ⓣ1-800/CALL- CASH, Australia ⓣ1800/501 500, New Zealand ⓣ0800/005 253, UK ⓣ0800/833 833, Ireland ⓣ066/947 5603. ⓦwww.westernunion.com gives locations of agents in Thailand, including branches of Bank of Ayudhya, Bank of Asia, Siam City Bank, Central, Robinson, Big C and Zen stores, and post offices; customers in the US and Canada can send money online.

Insurance

If you're unlucky enough to require hospital treatment in Thailand, you'll have to foot the bill – this alone is reason enough to make sure you have adequate travel cover before you leave. Before paying for a new policy, however, it's worth checking whether you are already covered: some all-risks home insurance policies may cover your possessions when overseas, and many private medical schemes include cover when abroad. In Canada, provincial health plans usually provide partial cover for medical mishaps overseas, while holders of official student/teacher/youth cards in Canada and the US are entitled to meagre accident coverage and hospital in-patient benefits. North American students will often find that their student health coverage extends during the vacations and for one term beyond the date of last enrolment.

After exhausting the possibilities above, you might want to contact a specialist **travel insurance** company, or consider the travel insurance deal we offer (see box). A typical travel insurance policy usually provides cover for the loss of baggage, tickets and –

Rough Guides travel insurance

Rough Guides offers its own low-cost **travel insurance**, especially customized for our statistically low-risk readers by a leading British broker, provided by the American International Group (AIG) and registered with the British regulatory body, GISC (General Insurance Standards Council).

There are five main Rough Guides insurance plans: **No Frills**, for the bare minimum for secure travel; **Essential**, which provides decent all-round cover; **Premier**, for comprehensive cover with a wide range of benefits; **Extended Stay**, for cover lasting four months to a year; and **Annual Multi-Trip**, a cost-effective way of getting Premier cover if you travel more than once a year. Premier, Annual Multi-Trip and Extended Stay policies can be supplemented by a "**Hazardous Pursuits Extension**" if you plan to indulge in sports considered dangerous, such as scuba-diving or trekking.

For a **policy quote**, call the Rough Guide Insurance Line: toll-free in the UK ⓣ0800/015 09 06 or +44 1392 314 665 from elsewhere in the world. Alternatively, get an online quote or buy online at ⓦwww.roughguides.com/insurance.

up to a certain limit – cash or cheques, as well as cancellation or curtailment of your journey. Most of them exclude so-called **dangerous sports** unless an extra premium is paid: in Thailand this can mean such things as scuba-diving, whitewater-rafting and trekking. Many policies can be chopped and changed to exclude coverage you don't need – for example, sickness and accident benefits can often be excluded or included at will. If you do take medical coverage, ascertain whether benefits will be paid as treatment proceeds or only after return home, and whether there is a 24-hour medical emergency number. When securing baggage cover, make sure that the per-article limit – typically under £500 – will cover your most valuable possession. If you need to make a **claim**, you should keep receipts for medicines and medical treatment, and in the event you have anything stolen, you must obtain an official statement from the police.

Health

Although Thailand's climate, wildlife and cuisine present Western travellers with fewer health worries than in many Asian destinations, it's as well to know in advance what the risks might be, and what preventive or curative measures you should take.

For a start, there's no need to bring huge supplies of non-prescription medicines with you, as Thai **pharmacies** (*raan khai yaa*; typically open daily 8.30am–8pm) are well stocked with local and international branded medicaments, and of course they are generally much less expensive than at home. Nearly all pharmacies are run by trained English-speaking pharmacists, who are usually the best people to talk to if your symptoms aren't acute enough to warrant seeing a doctor.

Hospital (*rong phayaabahn*) cleanliness and efficiency vary, but generally hygiene and healthcare standards are good and the ratio of medical staff to patients is considerably higher than in most parts of the West. As with head pharmacists, doctors speak

English. All provincial capitals have at least one hospital: if you need to get to one, ask at your accommodation for advice on, and possibly transport to, the nearest or most suitable. In the event of a major health crisis, get someone to contact your embassy (see p.203) and insurance company – it may be best to get yourself flown to Bangkok or even home.

Inoculations

There are no compulsory **inoculation requirements** for people travelling to Thailand from the West, but you should consult a doctor or other health professional for the latest information on recommended immunizations. You'll need to ensure your polio and tetanus boosters are up to date (they last ten years); most doctors also strongly advise vaccinations against typhoid and hepatitis A, and in some cases they might also recommend protecting yourself against Japanese B encephalitis, rabies, hepatitis B, tuberculosis and diphtheria. If you do decide to have several injections, plan your course at least four weeks in advance. There is currently no vaccine against malaria; for information on prophylaxis, see below.

If you forget to have all your inoculations before leaving home, or don't leave yourself sufficient time, you can get them in Bangkok at, for example, the Thai Red Cross Society's Queen Saovabha Institute (see p.203 for details), which also advises on malaria prophylaxis.

A traveller's first-aid kit

Among items you might want to carry with you – especially if you're planning to go trekking – are:

- ❒ Antiseptic.
- ❒ Antihistamine cream.
- ❒ Plasters/band-aids.
- ❒ Lints and sealed bandages.
- ❒ Insect repellent, sunscreen and calamine lotion or similar, to soothe sunburn or insect bites.
- ❒ Imodium, Lomotil or Arret for emergency diarrhoea relief.
- ❒ Paracetamol/aspirin.
- ❒ Multivitamin and mineral tablets.
- ❒ Rehydration sachets.
- ❒ Hypodermic needles and sterilized skin wipes.

Medical resources for travellers

For a comprehensive, and sobering, account of the health problems which travellers can encounter worldwide, pick up a copy of the *Rough Guide to Travel Health* by Dr Nick Jones.

Websites

Ⓦ www.health.yahoo.com Information on specific diseases and conditions, drugs and herbal remedies, as well as advice from health experts.
Ⓦ www.fitfortravel.scot.nhs.uk Scottish NHS website, recommended by health practitioners across the UK, carrying information about travel-related diseases and how to avoid them.
Ⓦ www.istm.org The website of the International Society for Travel Medicine, with a full list of clinics specializing in international travel health. Publishes outbreak warnings, suggested inoculations, precautions and other background information for travellers.
Ⓦ www.tripprep.com Travel Health Online provides an online-only comprehensive database of necessary vaccinations for most countries, as well as destination and medical service provider information.

In the UK and Ireland

British Airways Travel Clinics 156 Regent St, London W1 (Mon–Fri 9.30am–6pm, Sat 10am–5pm, no appointment necessary; Ⓣ0845/600 2236); 101 Cheapside, London EC2 (Mon–Fri 9am–4.45pm, appointment required; Ⓣ0845/600 2236); Ⓦwww.britishairways.com/travel/healthclinintro. Vaccinations, tailored advice from an online database and a complete range of travel healthcare products.
Hospital for Tropical Diseases Travel Clinic 2nd floor, Mortimer Market Centre, off Capper St, London WC1E 6AU (Mon–Fri 9am–5pm, by appointment only; Ⓣ020/7388 9600). A consultation costs £15, which is waived if you have your injections here). A recorded Health Line (Ⓣ0906/133 7733; 50p/min) gives hints on hygiene and illness prevention as well as listing appropriate immunizations.
Liverpool School of Tropical Medicine Pembroke Place, Liverpool L3 5QA Ⓣ0151/708 9393, Ⓦwww.liv.ac.uk/lstm/lstm.html. Walk-in clinic Mon–Fri 1–4pm.

MASTA (Medical Advisory Service for Travellers Abroad) Forty regional clinics in the UK (call ⓣ0870/6062782 or go to ⓦwww.masta.org for the nearest). Also operates a pre-recorded 24-hour Travellers Health Line (ⓣ0906/822 4100, 60p/min), giving written information tailored to your journey by return of post.
Nomad Pharmacy surgeries 40 Bernard St, London WC1N 1LE, and 3–4 Wellington Terrace, Turnpike Lane, London N8 0PX (Mon–Fri 9.30am–6pm, ⓣ020/7833 4114 to book vaccination appointment; ⓦwww.nomadtravel.co.uk). They give advice free if you go in person, or their helpline is ⓣ0906/863 3414 (60p/min). They can give information tailored to your travel needs.
Travel Health Centre Department of International Health and Tropical Medicine, Royal College of Surgeons in Ireland, Mercers Medical Centre, Stephen's St Lower, Dublin 2 ⓣ01/402 2337. Inoculations, expert pre- and post-trip consultations, and a range of travel healthcare products.
Travel Medicine Services PO Box 254, 16 College St, Belfast BT1 6BT ⓣ028/9031 5220. Offers medical advice and services before a trip and help afterwards in the event of a tropical disease.
Tropical Medical Bureau Grafton Buildings, 34 Grafton St, Dublin 2 ⓣ1850/487 674, ⓦwww.tmb.ie. Clinic specializing in travel medicine.

In the US and Canada

Canadian Society for International Health 1 Nicholas St, Suite 1105, Ottawa, ON K1N 7B7 ⓣ613/241-5785, ⓦwww.csih.org. Distributes a free pamphlet *Health Information for Canadian Travellers*, containing an extensive list of travel health centres in Canada.
Centers for Disease Control 1600 Clifton Rd NE, Atlanta, GA 30333 ⓣ1-800/311-3435 or 404/639-3534, ⓦwww.cdc.gov. Publishes outbreak warnings, suggested inoculations, precautions and other background information for travellers. Useful website plus International Travelers' Hotline on ⓣ1-877/FYI-TRIP.
International Association for Medical Assistance to Travelers (IAMAT) 417 Center St, Lewiston, NY 14092 ⓣ716/754-4883, ⓦwww.iamat.org, and 1287 St. Clair Avenue West, Suite #1, Toronto, Ontario M6E 1B8 ⓣ416/652-0137. A non-profit organization supported by donations, IAMAT can provide a list of English-speaking doctors in Thailand, climate charts and leaflets on various diseases and inoculations.
International SOS Assistance Eight Neshaminy Interplex Suite 207, Trevose, PA 19053-6956 ⓣ1-800/523-8930, ⓦwww.intsos.com. Members receive pre-trip medical referral info, as well as overseas emergency services designed to complement travel insurance coverage.
MEDJET Assistance ⓣ1-800/963-3538 or 205/595-6658, ⓦwww.medjetassistance.com. Annual membership program for travellers (US$195 for individuals, US$295 for families) that, in the event of illness or injury, will fly members home or to the hospital of their choice in a medically equipped and staffed jet.
Travel Medicine ⓣ1-800/872-8633, ⓦwww.travmed.com. Sells first-aid kits, mosquito netting, water filters, reference books and other health-related travel products.

In Australia and New Zealand

Travellers' Medical and Vaccination Centres ⓦwww.tmvc.com.au. 27–29 Gilbert Place, Adelaide, SA 5000 ⓣ08/8212 7522; 1/170 Queen St, Auckland ⓣ09/373 3531; 5/247 Adelaide St, Brisbane, Queensland 4000 ⓣ07/3221 9066; 5/8–10 Hobart Place, Canberra, ACT 2600 ⓣ02/6257 7156; 270 Sandy Bay Rd, Sandy Bay, Hobart, Tasmania 7005 ⓣ03/6223 7577; 2/393 Little Bourke St, Melbourne, Victoria 3000 ⓣ03/9602 5788; Level 7, Dymocks Bldg, 428 George St, Sydney, NSW 2000 ⓣ02/9221 7133; Shop 15, Grand Arcade, 14–16 Willis St, Wellington, NZ ⓣ04/473 0991. Travel medicine and vaccination services.

Mosquito-borne diseases

It isn't only malaria that is spread by **mosquitoes** in Thailand; to a lesser extent, there are risks of contracting diseases such as Japanese B encephalitis and dengue fever, especially if you visit during the rainy season.

The main message, therefore, is to **avoid being bitten** by mosquitoes. You should smother yourself and your clothes in **mosquito repellent** containing the chemical compound DEET, reapplying regularly (shops, guest houses and department stores all over Thailand stock it, but if you want the highest-strength repellent, or convenient roll-ons or sprays, do your shopping before you leave home).

DEET is strong stuff, and if you have sensitive skin, a natural alternative is citronella (called Mosi-guard in the UK), made from a blend of eucalyptus oils.

At night you should either sleep under a **mosquito net** sprayed with DEET or in a bedroom with **mosquito screens** across the windows (or in an enclosed air-con room). Accommodation in tourist spots nearly always provides screens or a net (check both for holes), but if you're planning to go way off the beaten track or want the security of having your own mosquito net just in case, wait until you get to Bangkok to buy one, where department stores sell them for much less than you'd pay in the West.

Plug-in insecticide vaporizers, knock-down insect sprays and mosquito coils – also widely available in Thailand – help keep the insects at bay; electronic "buzzers" are useless.

Prophylaxis advice can change from year to year, so it's worth getting the most up-to-date information from your travel health adviser.

Malaria

Thailand is **malarial**, with the disease being carried by mosquitoes that bite from dusk to dawn, but the risks involved vary across the country. There is a significant risk of malaria, mainly in rural and forested areas, in a narrow strip along the **borders with Cambodia and Laos** and along the **Burmese border** as far south as Bangkok.

The only anti-malarial drugs that are likely to be effective in these areas are **Doxycycline** and **Malarone**, whose use should be discussed with your travel health adviser. Either needs to be started a couple of days before entering the malarial zone. You need to keep taking Doxycycline, which can be bought cheaply in Thailand if you don't manage to get it before leaving home, for four weeks after exiting the malarial zone.

The newer Malarone (not currently available in Thailand) is more expensive, but has fewer common side-effects and only needs to be taken for a week after leaving the high-risk area. Elsewhere in the country the risk of malaria is considered to be so low that anti-malarial tablets are not advised.

The **signs of malaria** are often similar to flu, but are very variable. The incubation period for malignant malaria, which can be fatal, is usually 7–28 days, but it can take up to a year for symptoms of the benign form to occur. The most important symptom is a raised temperature of at least 38°C beginning a week or more after the first potential exposure to malaria: if you suspect anything go to a hospital or clinic immediately.

Dengue fever

Like malaria, **dengue fever**, a debilitating and occasionally fatal viral disease, is on the increase throughout tropical Asia, and is endemic to many areas of Thailand. Unlike malaria, though, dengue fever is spread by a mosquito (the *Aedes aegypti*) that bites during daylight hours – usually in early morning or late afternoon, particularly during and just after the rainy season – so you should use mosquito repellent during the day; Ko Pha Ngan seems to suffer a higher than usual incidence of dengue fever. Symptoms include fever, headaches, fierce joint and muscle pain ("breakbone fever" is another name for dengue), and possibly a rash, and usually develop between five and eight days after being bitten.

There is no vaccine against dengue fever; the only treatment is lots of rest, liquids and paracetamol (or any other acetaminophen painkiller, not aspirin), though more serious cases may require hospitalization.

Japanese B encephalitis

If you are travelling in rural areas during the rainy season, especially if it's for long periods or on repeated visits, or in areas known to be infected, you may be at risk of contracting **Japanese B encephalitis**, a viral inflammation of the brain spread by the *Culex* mosquito, which breeds in rice fields.

A vaccine is available, and although the risk of travellers catching the disease is low, you should at least consult your health adviser.

Other health problems

Wearing protective clothing is a good idea when **swimming** or **snorkelling**: a T-shirt will stop you from getting sunburnt in the water, while long trousers can guard against coral grazes. Should you scrape your skin on coral, wash the wound thoroughly with boiled water, apply antiseptic and keep protected until healed. Thailand's seas are home to a few dangerous creatures that you should look out for, notably **jellyfish**, which tend to be washed towards the beach by rough seas during the monsoon season. All manner of stinging and non-stinging jellyfish can be found in Thailand – as a general rule, those with the longest tentacles tend to have the worst stings – but reports of serious incidents are rare; before swimming at this time of the year, ask around at your resort or at a local dive shop to see if there have been any sightings of poisonous varieties. You also need to be wary of poisonous sea snakes, sea urchins and a couple of less conspicuous species – stingrays, which often lie buried in the sand, and stonefish, whose potentially lethal venomous spikes are easily stepped on because the fish look like stones and lie motionless on the sea bed.

If **stung or bitten** you should always seek medical advice as soon as possible, but there are a few ways of alleviating the pain or administering your own first aid in the meantime. If you're stung by a jellyfish, wash the affected area with salt water (not fresh water) and, if possible, with vinegar (failing that, ammonia, citrus fruit juice or even urine may do the trick), and try to remove the fragments of tentacles from the skin with a gloved hand, forceps or thick cloth. The best way to minimize the risk of stepping on the toxic spines of sea urchins, stingrays and stonefish is to wear thick-soled shoes, though these cannot provide total protection; sea urchin spikes should be removed after softening the skin with ointment, though some people recommend applying urine to help dissolve the spines; for stingray and stonefish stings, alleviate the pain by immersing the wound in hot water while awaiting help. In the case of a **poisonous snake bite**, don't try sucking out the poison or applying a tourniquet: wrap up and immobilize the bitten limb and try to stay still and calm until medical help arrives (all provincial hospitals in Thailand carry supplies of antivenins).

Rabies

Rabies is widespread in Thailand, mainly carried by dogs (between four and seven percent of stray dogs in Bangkok are reported to be rabid), but also cats and monkeys, and is transmitted by bites, scratches or even licks. Dogs are everywhere in Thailand and even if kept as pets they're never very well cared for; hopefully their mangy appearance will discourage the urge to pat them, as you should steer well clear of them. Rabies is invariably fatal if the patient waits until symptoms begin, though modern vaccines and treatments are very effective and deaths are rare. The important thing is, if you are bitten, licked or scratched by an animal, to vigorously clean with soap and disinfect the wound, preferably with something containing iodine, and to seek medical advice regarding treatment right away.

Worms and flukes

Worms can be picked up through the soles of your feet, so avoid going barefoot; worms can also be ingested by eating undercooked meat, and liver **flukes** by eating raw or undercooked freshwater fish. Worms which cause schistosomiasis (bilharziasis) by attaching themselves to your bladder or intestines can be found in some freshwater rivers and lakes. The risk of contracting this disease is low, but you should certainly avoid swimming in the southern reaches of the Mekong River and the lakes of northeastern Thailand.

Digestive problems

By far the most common travellers' complaint in Thailand, **digestive troubles** are often caused by contaminated food and water, or sometimes just by an overdose of unfamiliar foodstuffs. Break your system in gently by avoiding excessively spicy curries and too much raw fruit in the first few days, and then use your common sense about

Carrying essential medications

Make sure that you take sufficient supplies of any essential **medications** and carry the complete supply with you whenever you travel (including on public transport), in case of loss or theft (or possibly carry more than you need and split it between your baggage). You should also carry a prescription that includes the generic name in case of emergency. If travelling for a long time, it may be worth arranging for your doctor or hospital to courier extra supplies to a specific address in Thailand, such as a reputable hotel. It's also a good idea to carry a doctor's letter about your drugs prescriptions with you at all times – particularly when passing through customs at Bangkok airport – as this will ensure you don't get hauled up for narcotics transgressions.

If your medication has to be kept cool, buy a **thermal insulation bag** and a couple of freezer blocks before you leave home. That way you can refreeze one of the two blocks every day, while the other is in use; staff in most hotels, guest houses, restaurants and even some bars should be happy to let you use their freezer compartment for a few hours. If you use **needles and syringes**, you should also take a small sharps bin with you, as garbage disposal in Thailand is haphazard and your used syringes might harm someone.

choosing where and what to eat: if you stick to the most crowded restaurants and noodle stalls you should be perfectly safe (for more on food hygiene, see p.47). You need to be more rigorous about **drinking water**, though: stick to bottled water (even when brushing your teeth), which is sold everywhere, or else opt for boiled water or tea.

Stomach trouble usually manifests itself as simple **diarrhoea**, which should clear up without medical treatment within three to seven days and is best combated by drinking lots of fluids. If this doesn't work, you're in danger of getting **dehydrated** and should take some kind of rehydration solution, either a commercial sachet of ORS (oral rehydration solution), sold in all Thai pharmacies, or a do-it-yourself version, which can be made by adding a handful of sugar and a pinch of salt to every litre of boiled or bottled water (soft drinks are *not* a viable alternative). If you can eat, avoid fatty foods. Anti-diarrhoeal agents such as Imodium are useful for blocking you up on long bus journeys, but only attack the symptoms and may prolong infections; an antibiotic such as ciprofloxacin, however, can often reduce a typical attack of self-limiting traveller's diarrhoea to one day. If the diarrhoea persists for a week or more, or if you have blood or mucus in your stools, or an accompanying fever, go to a doctor or hospital.

Heat problems

Aside from the obvious considerations about restricting your exposure to the searing midday sun (using high protection-factor sun creams and protecting your eyes with good sunglasses that screen out UV light and your head with a hat), you should avoid **dehydration** by drinking plenty of (bottled) water and occasionally adding a pinch of salt to fruit shakes. To prevent and alleviate heat rashes, prickly heat and fungal infections, it's a good idea to use a mild antiseptic soap and to dust yourself with prickly heat talcum powder, both of which are sold cheaply in all Thai stores.

HIV and AIDS

AIDS is spreading fast in Thailand, primarily because of the widespread sex trade (see p.165), with an alarming 44 percent of prostitutes in Chiang Mai testing **HIV** positive. Condoms (*meechai*) are sold in pharmacies, department stores, hairdressers, and even on street markets. Should you need to have treatment involving an injection at a hospital, try to check that the needle has been sterilized first; this is not always practicable, however, so you might consider carrying your own syringes. Due to rigorous screening methods, the country's medical blood supply is now considered safe from HIV/AIDS infection.

Getting around

Travel in Thailand is both inexpensive and efficient, if not always speedy. Unless you travel by plane, long-distance journeys in Thailand can be arduous, especially if a shoestring budget restricts you to hard seats and no air-conditioning. Still, the wide range of transport options makes travelling around this country easier than elsewhere in Southeast Asia. Buses are fast and frequent, and can be quite luxurious; trains are slower but safer and offer more chance of sleeping during overnight trips; moreover, if travelling by day you're likely to follow a more scenic route by rail than by road. Inter-town songthaews, share-taxis and air-con minibuses are handy, and ferries provide easy access to all major islands. Local transport comes in all sorts of permutations, both public and chartered, with relatively little separating them in terms of cost.

For an idea of the frequency and duration of bus, train, air and ferry services, check the **travel details** at the end of each chapter.

Inter-town buses

Buses, overall the most convenient way of getting around the country, come in two main categories: **ordinary** (*rot thammadaa*; orange-coloured) and **air-con** (*rot air* or *rot thua*; usually blue). Ordinary and most air-con buses are run by Baw Khaw Saw, the government transport company, while privately owned air-con buses also ply the most popular long-distance routes. Be warned that long-distance overnight buses, particularly the air-con buses, seem to be involved in more than their fair share of accidents; because of this, some travellers prefer to do the overnight journeys by train and then make a shorter bus connection to their destination.

Ordinary buses

Ordinary **buses** are incredibly inexpensive and cover most short-range routes between main towns (up to 150km), running very frequently during daylight hours. Each bus is staffed by a team of two or three – the driver, the fare collector and the optional "stop" and "go" yeller – who often personalize the vehicle with stereo systems, stickers, jasmine garlands and the requisite Buddha image or amulet. With an entertaining team and eye-catching scenery, journeys can be fun, but there are drawbacks. For a start, the teams work on a commission basis, so they pack as many people in as possible and might hang around for thirty minutes after they're due to leave in the hope of cramming in a few extra. They also stop so often that their average speed of 60kph can only be achieved by hurtling along at breakneck speeds between pick-ups, often propelled by amphetamine-induced craziness. To flag down an ordinary bus from the roadside you should wait at the nearest **bus shelter**, or *sala*, usually located at intervals along the main long-distance bus route through town or on the fringes of any decent-sized settlement, for example on the main highway that skirts the edge of town. Where there is only a bus shelter on the "wrong" side of the road, you can be sure that buses travelling in both directions will stop there for any waiting passengers. If you're in the middle of nowhere with no *sala* in sight, any ordinary bus should stop for you if you flag it down.

Air-con buses

Air-con **buses** stop a lot less often (if at all) and cover the distances faster and more comfortably: passengers are allotted specific seats, and on long journeys get blankets, snacks and nonstop videos. On some routes, you also have the option of taking the **VIP** (or even "super VIP") air-con bus services, which have fewer seats (generally 24–32 instead of 44) and more leg room for reclining. On the down side, air-con buses usually cost up to twice as much as the ordinary buses (two or three times as much for VIP buses), depart less frequently and don't cover nearly as many routes; make sure you have some warm clothes, as temperatures can get chilly, even with the blanket. Not all air-con buses have toilets, so it's always worth using bus station facilities before you board.

On a lot of long-distance routes **private air-con buses** are indistinguishable from government ones and operate out of the same Baw Khaw Saw bus terminals. The major private companies, such as Nakorn Chai and Win Tour, offer comparable facilities and standards of service, at roughly similar fares, though naturally with more scope for price variation. The opposite is unfortunately true of a number of the smaller private companies, several of which have a poor reputation for service and comfort, but attract farang customers with bargain fares and convenient timetables. The long-distance tour buses that run **from Thanon Khao San** in Banglamphu to Chiang Mai and Surat Thani are a case in point; travellers on these routes frequently complain about shabby furnishings, ineffective air-conditioning, unhelpful (even aggressive) drivers and a frightening lack of safety awareness – and there are frequent reports of theft from luggage on these routes, too. If you're planning to travel either of these routes, you are strongly recommended to travel with the government or private bus companies from the main bus terminals (who have a reputation with their regular Thai customers to maintain) or to go by train instead – the extra comfort and peace of mind are well worth the extra baht.

Tickets and timetables

Tickets for all buses can be bought from the departure terminals, but for ordinary buses it's normal to buy them on board. Air-con buses may operate from a separate station, and tickets for the more popular routes should be booked a day in advance. As a rough indication of **fares**, a trip from Bangkok to Chiang Mai costs B625 for VIP, B403 for first-class air-con, B314 for second-class air-con and B200–215 by ordinary bus.

Long-distance buses often depart in clusters around the same time (early morning or late at night for example), leaving a gap of five or more hours during the day with no services at all. Local TAT offices often keep up-to-date bus **timetables** in English. Or go to the bus terminal the day before you want to leave and check with staff there. That said, if you turn up at a bus terminal in the morning for a medium-length journey (150–300km), you're almost always guaranteed to be on your way within two hours.

Songthaews, share-taxis and air-conditioned minibuses

In rural areas, the bus network is supplemented – or even substantially replaced – by **songthaews** (literally "two rows"), which are open-ended vans (or occasionally cattle-trucks) onto which the drivers squash as many passengers as possible on two facing benches, leaving latecomers to swing off the running board at the back. As well as their essential role within towns (see "Local Transport" on p.39), songthaews ply set routes from larger towns out to their surrounding suburbs and villages, and, where there's no call for a regular bus service, between small towns: some have destinations written on in Thai, but few are numbered. In most towns you'll find the songthaew "terminal" near the market; to pick one up between destinations just flag it down. To indicate to the driver that you want to get out, the normal practice is to rap hard with a coin on the metal railings as you approach the spot (or press the bell if there is one).

In the deep south (see p.743) they do things with a little more style – **share-taxis**, often clapped-out old limos, connect all the major towns, though they are inexorably being replaced by more comfortable **air-conditioned minibuses**. Similar private air-con minibuses are now cropping up on one or two popular routes elsewhere in the country (eg Ayutthaya–Bangkok, Chiang Mai–Pai– Mae Hong Son), while government-run versions are the norm on certain routes in the Central Plains, most usefully on the Kanchanaburi–Sangkhlaburi and Tak–Mae Sot runs. Air-con minibuses generally depart frequently and cover the distance faster than the ordinary bus service, but can be uncomfortably cramped when full and are not ideal for travellers with huge rucksacks.

In many cases, long-distance songthaews and air-con minibuses will drop you at an exact address (for example a particular guest house) if you warn them far enough in advance – it's generally an expected part of the service. As a rule, the **cost** of inter-town songthaews is comparable to that of air-con buses, that of air-con minibuses perhaps a shade more.

Trains

Managed by the State Railway of Thailand (SRT), the **rail** network consists of four main lines and a few branch lines. The **Northern Line** connects Bangkok with Chiang Mai via Ayutthaya, Lopburi, Phitsanulok and Lampang. The **Northeastern Line** splits into two just beyond Ayutthaya, the lower branch running eastwards to Ubon Ratchathani via Khorat and Surin, the more northerly branch linking the capital with Nong Khai via Khon Kaen and Udon Thani. The **Eastern Line** also has two branches, one of which runs from Bangkok to Aranyaprathet on the Cambodian border, the other of which connects Bangkok with Si Racha and Pattaya. The **Southern Line** extends via Hua Hin, Chumphon and Surat Thani, with spurs off to Trang and Nakhon Si Thammarat, to Hat Yai, where it branches: one line continues down the west coast of Malaysia, via Butterworth, where you change trains for Kuala Lumpur and Singapore; the other heads down the eastern side of the peninsula to Sungai Kolok on the Thailand– Malaysia border (20km from Pasir Mas on Malaysia's interior railway). At Nakhon Pathom a branch of this line veers off to Nam Tok via Kanchanaburi – this is all that's left of the Death Railway, of *Bridge over the River Kwai* notoriety (see p.229).

Fares depend on the class of seat, whether or not you want air-conditioning, and on the speed of the train; those quoted here exclude the "speed" supplements, which are discussed below. Hard, wooden, third-class seats cost about the same as an ordinary bus (Bangkok–Chiang Mai B161), and are fine for about three hours, after which numbness sets in. For longer journeys you'd be wise to opt for the padded and often reclining seats in second class (Bangkok–Chiang Mai B321, or B491 with air-conditioning). On long-distance trains, you also usually have the option of second-class berths (for an extra B180–270 or so), with day seats that convert into comfortable curtained-off bunks in the evening; lower bunks, which are more expensive than upper, have a few cubic centimetres more of space, a little more shade from the lights in the carriage, and a window. Travelling first class (Bangkok–Chiang Mai B1233) means a two-person air-con sleeping compartment, complete with washbasin. Note that you must buy a ticket **before boarding a train**, otherwise you're liable for a fine of B100 on an ordinary train or B250 on a rapid or express train.

There are several different **types of train**: slowest of all is the third-class-only Ordinary service, which is generally (but not always) available only on short and medium-length journeys and has no speed supplement. Next comes the misleadingly named Rapid train (B60 supplement), a trip on which from Bangkok to Chiang Mai, for example, takes over fourteen hours; the Express (B80 supplement) which does the same route in just under fourteen hours; the Special Express (B120 supplement) takes around an hour less to cover the ground; and fastest of all is the Special Express Diesel Railcar (also B120 supplement), which does the journey in eleven to twelve hours. Note that nearly all long-distance trains have **dining cars**, and rail staff will also bring meals to your seat.

Train information

For all train information, phone the 24-hour SRT Hotline on ⓣ1690, or call the main Hualamphong Station office on ⓣ02 225 0300. The SRT **website** (ⓦwww.railway.co.th) gives a breakdown of ticket prices, but currently doesn't carry any timetables.

Booking at least one day in advance is strongly recommended for second- and first-class seats on all lengthy journeys, and sleepers should be booked as far in advance as possible. It should be possible to make bookings at the station in any major town, or by fax to Hualamphong Station in Bangkok on Ⓕ02 226 6068; for further details on how to book trains out of Bangkok, see p.196.

The SRT publishes clear and fairly accurate free **timetables** in English, detailing types of trains and classes available on each route, as well as fares and supplementary charges; the best place to get hold of them is over the counter at Bangkok's Hualamphong Station or, if you're lucky, the TAT office in Bangkok. The information desk at Hualamphong also stocks more detailed local timetables covering, for example, the Bangkok–Ayutthaya route via Don Muang Airport.

The SRT also sells twenty-day **rail passes** (available only in Thailand), covering unlimited train journeys in second- (or third-) class seats for B1500, or B3000 with all supplements thrown in (including air-conditioning, but excluding sleeping berths). However, unless you're on a whistle-stop tour of all four corners of the country, the rail network is not really extensive enough to make them pay.

Ferries

Regular **ferries** connect all major islands with the mainland, and for the vast majority of crossings you simply buy your ticket on board. In tourist areas competition ensures that prices are kept low, and fares tend to vary with the speed of the crossing, if anything: thus Chumphon–Ko Tao costs between B200 (6hr) and B400 (2hr 30min). On the east coast and the Andaman coast boats generally operate a reduced service during the monsoon season (May–Oct), when the more remote spots become inaccessible. Ferries in the Samui archipelago are fairly constant year-round. Details on island connections are given in the relevant chapters.

Flights

The domestic arm of **Thai Airways** (Ⓦwww.thaiair.com) still has the lion's share of the internal flight network, which extends to all extremities of the country, around two dozen airports. However, with deregulation, several smaller airlines have now broken into the volatile market, and there are even one or two cheap, no-frills companies, with more apparently on their way, including a no-frills branch of Thai Airways, and **Air Asia** (Ⓦwww.airasia.com). **Bangkok Airways** (Ⓦwww.bangkokair.com) is still Thai Airways' main competitor at home, covering useful routes such as Bangkok–Ko Samui, Bangkok–Trat, Bangkok–Krabi and Bangkok–Phuket, Trat–Ko Samui, Krabi–Ko Samui, Pattaya–Ko Samui–Phuket and a Bangkok–Sukhothai–Chiang Mai triangle. Among the newcomers on the scene, **Air Andaman** (Ⓦwww.airandaman.com) currently flies from Bangkok to Buriram, Chumphon, Khorat, Loei, Mae Sot, Nan, Narathiwat, Phrae and Surin; **PB Air** (Ⓦwww.pbair.com) to Krabi, Lampang, Nakhon Phanom, Nakhon Si Thammarat, Phetchabun, Roi-Et and Sakon Nakhon; and **Phuket Airlines** (Ⓦwww.phuketairlines.com) to Krabi, Phuket and Ranong, plus Chiang Mai–Chiang Rai. Note that these routings change surprisingly frequently and that at the very minor airports, schedules are erratic and flights are sometimes cancelled, so always check ahead.

In some instances a flight can save you days of travelling: the flight from Chiang Mai to Phuket, for example, takes two hours, as against a couple of days by meandering train and/or bus. To give an idea of **fares**, on the Bangkok–Chiang Mai route Thai and Bangkok Airways charge B2170 one-way, while 1-2-Go (Ⓦwww.onetwo-go.com), the no-frills arm of Orient Thai Airlines, has recently been advertising at B999.

Flights can get booked a long way ahead, so get in early if possible – online reservation is possible on the Thai Airways' and Bangkok Airways' websites. Most towns served by an airport have at least one downtown Thai Airways booking office, while the main Bangkok offices of domestic airlines are detailed on p.202; flight durations and frequencies are listed at the end of each chapter.

If you're planning to use the internal network a lot, you can save money by buying an **airpass**. Of the two available, Bangkok Airways' Discovery Airpass is the easier to use: you buy between three and six flight

80 to Siem Reap

coupons for US$50 each, confirming the first flight before departure, though the others can be left open; once a sector is booked, the date of travel can be changed free of charge, while there's a fee of US$20 for a change of route. Thai Airways' Discover Thailand Airpass is available only outside Thailand from the airlines' offices and travel agents. The pass covers three one-way flights for US$179; you fix the routes when you buy the pass, but dates of travel can be changed in Thailand. Up to five additional flights can be added for US$59 each.

Local transport

Most sizeable towns have some kind of **local transport system**, comprising a network of buses, songthaews or even longtail boats, with set fares and routes but not rigid timetabling; in most cases vehicles leave when they're full – generally at ten- or twenty-minute intervals during the busiest time of day (from about 6am until noon) – and then at least once an hour until 5 or 6pm.

Buses and songthaews

Larger cities like Bangkok, Khorat, Ubon Ratchathani and Phitsanulok have a **local bus** network which usually extends to the suburbs and operates from dawn till dusk (through the night in Bangkok). Most vehicles display route numbers in Arabic numerals, and you pay the conductor B3–10 depending on your destination (on some routes you can choose to take air-con buses, for which you pay a few baht extra).

Within medium-sized and large towns, the main transport role is often played by **songthaews**. The size and shape of vehicle used varies from town to town – and in some places they're known as "tuk-tuks" from the noise they make, not to be confused with the smaller tuk-tuks, described below, that operate as private taxis – but all have the tell-tale two facing benches in the back. In some towns, especially in the northeast, songthaews follow fixed routes; in others they act as communal taxis, picking up a number of people who are going in roughly the same direction and taking each of them right to their destination. To hail a songthaew just flag it down, and to indicate that you want to get out, either rap hard with a coin on the metal railings, or ring the bell if there is one. Fares within towns range between B5 and B20, depending on distance.

Longtail boats

Wherever there's a decent public waterway, there'll be a **longtail boat** ready to ferry you along it. Another great Thai trademark, these elegant, streamlined boats are powered by deafening diesel engines – sometimes custom-built, more often adapted from cars or trucks – which drive a propeller mounted on a long shaft that is swivelled for steering. Longtails carry between ten and twenty passengers: in Bangkok and Krabi the majority follow fixed routes, but elsewhere they're for hire at about B100 an hour per boat, more in tourist spots.

Taxi services

Taxis also comes in many guises, and in bigger towns you can often choose between taking a tuk-tuk, a samlor and a motorbike taxi. The one thing common to all modes of chartered transport, bar Bangkok's metered taxis (see p.105), is that you must establish the **fare** beforehand: although drivers nearly always pitch their first offers too high, they do calculate with traffic and time of day in mind, as well as according to distance – if successive drivers scoff at your price, you know you've got it wrong.

Tuk-tuks

Named after the noise of its excruciatingly unsilenced engine, the three-wheeled, open-sided **tuk-tuk** is the classic Thai vehicle. Painted in primary colours, tuk-tuks blast their way round towns and cities on two-stroke engines, zipping around faster than any car and taking corners on two wheels. They aren't as dangerous as they look though, and can be an exhilarating way to get around, as long as you're not too fussy about exhaust fumes. They're also inexpensive: fares start at around B20 (B30 in Bangkok) regardless of the number

△ Tuk-tuk

of passengers – three is the safe maximum, though six is not uncommon. See p.105 for advice on how to avoid being ripped off by Bangkok tuk-tuk drivers.

Samlors

Tuk-tuks are also sometimes known as samlors (literally "three wheels"), but the original **samlors** are tricycle rickshaws propelled by pedal power alone. Slower and a great deal more stately than tuk-tuks, samlors still operate in many towns around the country, though not in Bangkok. Forget any qualms you may have about being pedalled around by another human being: samlor drivers' livelihoods depend on having a constant supply of passengers, so your most ethical option is to hop on and not scrimp on the fare. In any case, scrimping is not an option in some towns such as Chiang Rai, where drivers price themselves way over the odds as a novelty act for tourists, but they usually charge locals a minimum fee of around B10 and add B10 per kilometre, possibly more for a heavy load.

A further permutation are the motorized samlors, where the driver relies on a motorbike rather than a bicycle to propel passengers to their destination. They look much the same as cycle samlors, often sound as noisy as tuk-tuks and cost something between the two.

Motorbike taxis

Even faster and more precarious than tuk-tuks, **motorbike taxis** feature both in towns and in out-of-the-way places. In towns – where the drivers are identified by coloured, numbered vests – they have the advantage of being able to dodge traffic jams, but are obviously only really suitable for the single traveller, and motorbike taxis aren't the easiest mode of transport if you're carrying luggage. In remote spots, on the other hand, they're often the only alternative to hitching or walking, and are especially useful for getting between bus stops on main roads and to national parks or ancient ruins.

Within towns motorbike-taxi fares can start at B10 or less for short journeys, but for trips to the outskirts the cost rises steeply – about B100–150 for a twenty-kilometre round trip.

Vehicle rental

Despite first impressions, the high accident rate and the obvious mayhem that characterizes Bangkok's roads, **driving** yourself around Thailand can be fairly straightforward and unstressful. Many roads, particularly in the northeast and the south, are remarkably uncongested. Major routes are clearly signed in English, though this only applies to some minor roads; unfortunately there is no perfect English-language map to compensate (see p.24).

Outside the capital, its immediate environs and the eastern seaboard, local drivers are generally considerate and unaggressive; they very rarely use their horns for example, and will often indicate and even swerve away when it's safe for you to overtake. The most inconsiderate and dangerous road-users in Thailand are bus drivers and lorry drivers, many of whom drive ludicrously fast, hog the road, race round bends on the wrong side of the road and use their horns remorselessly; worse still, many of them are tanked up on amphetamines, which makes them quite literally fearless.

Bus and lorry drivers are at their worst after dark (many of them only drive then), so you are strongly advised **never to drive at night** – a further hazard being the inevitable stream of unlit bicycles and mopeds in and around built-up areas, as well as poorly signed roadworks, which are often not made safe or blocked off from unsuspecting traffic.

As for local **rules of the road**, Thais drive on the left, and the speed limit is 60km/h within built-up areas and 90km/h outside them. More unusually, a major road doesn't necessarily have right of way over a minor, but the bigger vehicle *always* has right of way. An oncoming vehicle flashing its lights means it's coming through no matter what; a right indicator signal from the car in front usually means it's not safe for you to overtake, while a left indicator signal usually means that it is safe to do so.

Theoretically, foreigners need an international **driver's licence** to hire any kind of vehicle, but most companies accept national licences, and the smaller operations (especially bicycle rentals) have been known not to ask for any kind of proof whatsoever.

Petrol (*nam man*, which can also mean oil) costs around B15–20 a litre. The big fuel stations are the least costly places to fill up (*hai taem*), and many of these also have toilets and simple restaurants, though some of the more decrepit-looking fuel stations on the main highways only sell diesel. Most small villages have easy-to-spot roadside huts where the fuel is pumped out of a large barrel.

Cars

If you decide to rent a car, go to a reputable dealer, such as Avis, Budget, Hertz or SMT (see below) or a rental company recommended by TAT, and make sure you get insurance from them. There are international car-rental places at many airports, including Bangkok's Don Muang, which is not a bad place to kick off, as you're on the edge of the city and within fairly easy (signed) reach of the major regional highways.

Car-rental places in provincial capitals and resorts are listed in the relevant accounts. Prices for a small car start at about B1200 per day, depending on the vehicle's condition, which is generally not bad. In most parts of the country, you can count on covering about 70km per hour if travelling long distances on major highways. If appropriate, consider the option of hiring a driver along with the car, which you can sometimes do for no extra charge on day rentals.

Jeeps are a lot more popular with farangs, especially on beach resorts and islands like Pattaya, Phuket and Ko Samui, but they're notoriously dangerous; a huge number of tourists manage to roll their jeeps on steep hillsides and sharp bends. Jeep rental usually works out somewhere between B900 and B1500 per day. The pick-up trucks that some companies offer are cheaper again than jeeps to rent, but even greedier for fuel.

International companies will accept your credit-card details as surety, but smaller agents will often ask for a deposit of at least B2000 and/or will want to hold on to your passport.

Car rental agencies

Avis Ⓦwww.avis.com; UK ⓣ0870/606 0100, Irish Republic ⓣ021/428 1111, US ⓣ1-800/230-4898, Canada ⓣ1-800 272 5871, Australia ⓣ13 63 33 or 02/9353 9000, New Zealand ⓣ0800/655 111 or 09/526 2847.
Budget Ⓦwww.budget.com; UK ⓣ01442/276 266, Irish Republic ⓣ09/0662 7711, US ⓣ1-800/527-0700, Canada ⓣ1-800/472 3325, Australia ⓣ1300/362 848, New Zealand ⓣ0800/652227 or 09/976 2222.
Hertz Ⓦwww.hertz.com; UK ⓣ0870/844 8844, Irish Republic ⓣ01/676 7476, US ⓣ1-800/654-3131, Canada ⓣ1-800/263 0600, Australia ⓣ13 30 39 or 03/9698 2555, New Zealand ⓣ0800/654 321.
National Car Rental (SMT in Thailand) Ⓦwww.nationalcar.com; UK ⓣ0870/536 5365, North America ⓣ1-800/962-7070, Australia ⓣ13 10 45, New Zealand ⓣ0800/800 115 or 03/366-5574.

Motorbikes

One of the best ways of exploring the countryside is to rent a motorbike, an especially popular option in the north of the country. Two-seater 80cc bikes with automatic gears are best if you've never ridden a motorbike before, but aren't really suited for long slogs. If you're going to hit the dirt roads you'll certainly need something more powerful, like a 125cc trail bike. These have the edge in gear choice and are the best bikes for steep slopes, though an inexperienced rider may find these machines a handful; the less widely available 125cc road bikes are easier to control and much cheaper on petrol.

Rental prices for the day usually work out at somewhere between B100 (for a fairly beat-up 80cc) and B350 (for a good trail bike), though you can bargain for a discount on a long rental. As with cars, the renters will often ask for a deposit and your passport or credit-card details, though you're unlikely to have to prove that you've ridden a bike before. Insurance is not often available, so it's a good idea to make sure your travel insurance covers you for possible mishaps.

Before signing anything, check the bike thoroughly – test the brakes, look for oil leaks, check the treads and the odometer, and make sure the chain isn't stretched too tight (a tight chain is more likely to break) – and preferably take it for a test run. As you will have to pay an inflated price for any damage when you get back, make a note on the contract of any defects such as broken mirrors, indicators and so on. Make sure you know what kind of petrol the bike takes as well.

As far as **equipment** goes, a helmet is essential – most rental places provide poorly made ones, but they're better than nothing. Helmets are obligatory on all motorbike journeys, and the law is often rigidly enforced with on-the-spot fines in major tourist resorts. You'll need sunglasses if your helmet doesn't have a visor. As well as being more culturally appropriate, long trousers, a long-sleeved top and decent shoes will provide a second skin if you go over, which most people do at some stage. Pillions should wear long trousers to avoid getting nasty burns from the exhaust. For the sake of stability, leave most of your luggage in baggage storage and pack as small a bag as possible, strapping it tightly to the bike with bungy cords – these are usually provided. Once on the road, oil the chain at least every other day, keep the radiator topped up and fill up with oil every 300km or so.

For expert **advice** on motorbike travel in Thailand, check out David Unkovich's website (Ⓦwww.gt-rider.com), which covers everything from how to ship a bike to Thailand to which are the best off-road touring routes in the country.

Bicycles

The safest and most pleasant way of conveying yourself around many towns and rural areas is by **bicycle**, except of course in Bangkok. You won't find bike rentals everywhere, but a lot of guest houses keep a few, and in certain bike-friendly tourist spots, like Kanchanaburi, Chiang Mai, Nong Khai and Sukhothai, you'll find larger-scale rental places, who should charge around B30–50 a day. A few rental outlets in the north also offer mountain bikes, starting from around B50.

Hitching

Public transport being so inexpensive, you should only have to resort to **hitching** in the most remote areas, in which case you'll probably get a lift to the nearest bus or songthaew stop quite quickly. On routes served by buses and trains, hitching is not standard practice, but in other places locals do rely on regular passers-by (such as national park officials), and as a farang you can make use of this "service" too. As with hitching anywhere in the world, think twice about hitching solo or at night, especially if you're female. Like bus drivers, truck drivers are notorious users of amphetamines, so you may want to wait for a safer offer.

Accommodation

Cheap accommodation can be found all over Thailand: for the simplest double room prices start at around B100 in the outlying regions, B150 in Bangkok, and B250 in some of the pricier resorts. Tourist centres invariably offer a huge range of more upmarket choices, and you'll have little problem finding luxury hotels in these places. In most resort areas rates fluctuate according to demand, plummeting during the off-season and, in some places, rising at weekends throughout the year.

Whatever the establishment, staff expect you to look at the room before taking it; in the budget ones especially, try out the door-lock, check for cockroaches and mosquitoes and make sure it's equipped with a decent mosquito net or screens. En-suite showers and flush toilets are common, but at the cheaper places you may well be showering with a bowl dipped into a large water jar, and using squat toilets.

Guest houses and hostels

Any place calling itself a **guest house** – which could be anything from a bamboo hut to a multi-storey concrete block – is almost certain to provide inexpensive, basic accommodation specifically aimed at Western travellers and priced at around B100–250 for a sparse double room with a fan and (sometimes shared) bathroom. You'll find them in all major tourist centres (in their dozens in Bangkok and Chiang Mai), and even in the most unlikely back-country spots: on the beaches, **bungalows** operate in much the same way.

In some main towns, guest houses are concentrated in cheek-by-jowl farang ghettoes, but even if you baulk at the world travellers' scene that characterizes these places, guest houses make great places to stay, with attached cafeterias, clued-up English-speaking staff and informative noticeboards. Many also offer extra **facilities** such as Internet access, safes for valuables, luggage storage, travel and tour operator desks, and their own poste restante. Staying at one of these out in the sticks means you'll often get involved in local life a lot more than if you were encased in a hotel.

At the vast majority of guest houses **check-out time** is noon, which means that during high season you should arrive to check in at about 11.30am to ensure you get a room:

Accommodation prices

Throughout this Guide, guest houses, hotels and bungalows have been categorized according to the **price codes** given below. These categories represent the minimum you can expect to pay in the high season (roughly July, Aug and Nov–Feb) for a **double room**. If travelling on your own, expect to pay anything between sixty and one hundred percent of the rates quoted for a double room. Wherever a **price range** is indicated, this means that the establishment offers rooms with varying facilities – as explained in the write-up. Where an establishment also offers dormitory beds, the price per bed is given in the text, instead of being indicated by a price code.

Remember that the top-whack hotels will add seven percent tax and a ten percent service charge to your bill – the price codes below are based on net rates after taxes have been added.

1 under B150	4 B400–600	7 B1300–1800
2 B150–250	5 B600–900	8 B1800–3000
3 B250–400	6 B900–1300	9 B3000+

few places draw up a "waiting list" and they rarely take advance bookings unless they know you already and you've paid a deposit.

The **upmarket guest house** is almost a contradiction in terms, but there are quite a few such places, charging between B250 and B800 for facilities that may include air-conditioning, bathroom, TV and use of a swimming pool. Beware of pricey guest houses or bungalows in mega-resorts like Pattaya, Phuket and Ko Phi Phi, however, which often turn out to be low-quality fan-cooled establishments making a killing out of unsuspecting holidaymakers.

With just twenty officially registered **youth hostels** in the whole country, it's not worth becoming a YHA member just for your trip to Thailand, especially as card-holders get only a small discount anyway. In general, youth-hostel prices work out the same as guest-house rates and rooms are open to all ages, whether or not you're a member. Online reservations can be made via the Thai Youth Hostels Association website (Ⓦwww.tyha.org).

Budget hotels

Few Thais use guest houses, opting instead for **budget hotels**, which offer rooms costing up to B600. Beds in these places are large enough for a couple, and it's quite acceptable for two people to ask and pay for a single room (*hawng thiang diaw*). Usually run by Chinese-Thais, these three- or four-storey places are found in every sizeable town, often near the bus station. Though the rooms are generally clean and en suite, the hotels tend to be grim and unfriendly, staffed by brusque non-English-speakers, and usually lacking in any communal seating or eating area. A number of budget hotels also double as brothels, though as a farang you're unlikely to be offered this sideline, and you might not even notice the goings-on.

Advance bookings are accepted over the phone, but this is rarely necessary, as such hotels rarely fill up. The only time you may have difficulty finding a budget hotel room is during Chinese New Year (a moveable three-day period in late January or February), when many Chinese-run hotels close and others get booked up fast.

Moderate hotels

Moderate hotels – priced between B600 and B1300 – can sometimes work out to be good value, offering many of the trimmings of a top-end hotel (TV, fridge, air-con, pool), but none of the prestige. They're often the kind of places that once stood at the top of the range, but were downgraded when the multi-national luxury muscled in and hogged the poshest clientele. They still make especially welcome alternatives to the budget hotels in provincial capitals, but, like upmarket guest houses, can turn out to be vastly overpriced in the resorts.

As with the budget hotels, you're unlikely to have trouble finding a room on spec in one of these places, though advance bookings are accepted by phone. Booking online through one of the accommodation finders listed on p.46 can sometimes save you quite a lot of money. Bed size varies a lot more than in the Chinese-run places, though, with some making the strict Western distinction between singles and doubles.

Upmarket hotels

Many of Thailand's **upmarket hotels** belong to international chains like Holiday Inn, Marriott and Sheraton, and home-grown chains such as Amari and Dusit, maintaining top-quality standards in Bangkok and major resorts at prices of B2500 (£40/US$60) and upward for a double – far less than you'd pay for equivalent accommodation in the West. Thailand also boasts an increasing number of exceptionally stylish **super-deluxe hotels**, many of them designed as intimate, small-scale boutique hotels, with chic minimalist decor and excellent facilities that often include a spa (see p.68 for more on spas). A night in one of these places will rarely cost you less than £100/US$150 – and may set you back more than twice as much; see accommodation listings for Bangkok, Chiang Mai, Hua Hin, Ko Samui and Phuket for some suggestions.

Many luxury hotels now quote rates in US dollars, though you can always pay in baht. It's a good idea to reserve ahead in Chiang Mai, Phuket, Ko Samui, Ko Phi Phi or Pattaya during peak season. And consider checking online accommodation-booking services (listed on p.46) as many of these offer big discounts on top hotels.

Booking a hotel online

The following online hotel-booking services offer rates discounted by up to sixty percent on the published prices of selected mid-range and upmarket accommodation. Discounted rates for a double room generally start at US$30, but it is occasionally possible to find rooms for US$20.

Hotels across Thailand

Asia Hotels
Ⓦwww.asia-hotels.com
Asia Ways
Ⓦwww.asiaways.com
Hotel Links
Ⓦwww.wereldreis.net/links/hotelsth.html
Hotel Thailand
Ⓦhotelthailand.com
Sawadee
Ⓦwww.sawadee.com
Thai Focus
Ⓦwww.thaifocus.com
Thailand Hotels Association
Ⓦwww.thaihotels.org
Thailand Hotels and Resorts
Ⓦwww.hotels.siam.net

Regional hotels

Chiang Mai
Ⓦwelcome-to.chiangmai-chiangrai.com
Ko Lanta
Ⓦwww.kolanta.net
Krabi
Ⓦkrabihotels.com
Phuket
Ⓦwww.phuket.com/hotels/index.html
Trang
Ⓦwww.trangonline.com

National parks and camping

Unattractive accommodation is one of the big disappointments of Thailand's **national parks**. Generally built to a standard two-roomed format, these dismal concrete bungalows feature in about half the country's parks, and cost an average B500 for four or more beds plus a basic bathroom. Because most of their custom comes from Thai families and student groups, park officials are sometimes loath to discount these huts for lone travellers, though a few parks do offer dorm-style accommodation at B100 a bed. In most parks, advance booking is unnecessary except at weekends and national holidays.

If you do want to pre-book, the easiest option is to do it online at Ⓦwww.thaiforest-booking.com/nationalpark-eng.htm. The alternatives are to pay on the spot in Bangkok at the Forestry Department offices near Kasetsart University on Thanon Phaholyothin, about 4km north of the Mo Chit Skytrain terminus (Mon–Fri 8.30am–4.30pm, Ⓣ02 579 5734 or 02 579 7223); or to book on the phone (not much English spoken), then send a baht money order and wait for confirmation or to pay through a bank and take the receipt with you when checking in. A few national parks accept phone bookings themselves and these are highlighted in the Guide. If you turn up without booking, check in at the park headquarters, which is usually adjacent to the visitor centre.

In a few parks, private operators have set up low-cost guest houses on the outskirts, and these make much more attractive and economical places to stay.

Camping

You can usually **camp** in a national park for a minimal fee of B30, and some national parks also rent out two-berth tents at anything from B60 to B200; a few, like Khao Yai, even rent out sleeping mats and bags, as well as stoves and pillows. Unless you're planning an extensive tour of national parks, though, there's little point in lugging a tent around Thailand: accommodation everywhere else is too inexpensive to make camping a necessity, and anyway there are no campgrounds inside town perimeters.

Camping is allowed on nearly all **islands and beaches**, many of which are national parks in their own right. Few travellers bother to bring tents for beaches either, though, opting for inexpensive bungalow accommodation or simply sleeping out under the stars.

Food and drink

Thai food is now very popular in most Western countries, with a reputation for using fresh ingredients to quickly create dishes that are fiery but fragrant and subtly flavoured. Lemon grass, basil, coriander, galangal, chilli, garlic, lime juice, coconut milk and fermented fish sauce are some of the vital ingredients that give the cuisine its distinctive taste.

Bangkok and Chiang Mai are the country's big culinary centres, boasting the cream of gourmet Thai restaurants and the best international cuisines. The rest of the country is by no means a gastronomic wasteland, however, and you can eat well and cheaply even in the smallest provincial towns, many of which offer the additional attraction of regional specialities. In fact you could eat more than adequately without ever entering a restaurant, as itinerant food vendors hawking hot and cold snacks materialize in even the most remote spots, as well as on trains and buses, and night markets often serve customers from dusk until dawn.

Hygiene is a consideration when eating anywhere in Thailand, but being too cautious means you'll end up spending a lot of money and missing out on some real local treats. Wean your stomach gently by avoiding excessive amounts of chillies and too much fresh fruit in the first few days, and always drink either bottled or boiled water.

You can be pretty sure that any noodle stall or curry shop that's permanently packed with customers is a safe bet. Furthermore, because most Thai dishes can be cooked in under five minutes, you'll rarely have to contend with stuff that's been left to smoulder and stew. Foods that are generally considered high in risk include salads, raw or undercooked meat or fish, ice and ice cream. If you're really concerned about health standards you could stick to restaurants and food stalls displaying a **"Clean Food Good Taste"** sign, part of a food sanitation project set up by the Ministry of Public Health, TAT and the Ministry of Interior. The criteria for awarding the logo seem to have some rigour: less than half of applicants pass muster, and thirty percent of awardees are randomly chosen and reassessed each year.

Where to eat

Despite their obvious attractions, a lot of tourists eschew the huge range of Thai places to eat and opt instead for the much "safer" restaurants in **guest houses** and **hotels**. Almost all tourist accommodation has a kitchen, and while some are excellent, the vast majority serve up bland imitations of Western fare alongside equally pale versions of common Thai dishes. Having said that, it can be a relief to get your teeth into a processed-cheese sandwich after five days' trekking in the jungle, and guest houses do serve comfortingly familiar Western breakfasts.

Restaurant prices

Broad **price categories** are appended to restaurant listings throughout this guide: "Inexpensive" means you can get a main course for under B60, "Moderate" means B60–130, and "Expensive" means over B130.

Throughout the country most **inexpensive** Thai restaurants and cafés specialize in one general food type or preparation method – a "noodle shop", for example, will do fried noodles and/or noodle soups, plus maybe a basic fried rice, but they won't have curries or meat or fish dishes. Similarly, a restaurant displaying whole roast chickens and ducks in its window will offer these sliced, usually with chillies and sauces and served over rice, but their menu probably won't extend to noodles or fish, while in "curry shops" your options are limited to the vats of curries stewing away in the hot cabinet.

To get a wider array of low-cost food, it's sometimes best to head for the local **night market** (*talat yen*), a term for the gatherings of open-air night-time kitchens found in every town. Often operating from 6pm to 6am, they are typically to be found on permanent patches close to the fruit and vegetable market or the bus station, and as often as not they're the best and most entertaining places to eat, not to mention the least expensive – after a lip-smacking feast of two savoury dishes, a fruit drink and a dessert you'll come away no more than B80 poorer.

A typical night market has some thirty-odd "specialist" pushcart kitchens (*rot khen*) jumbled together, each fronted by several sets of tables and stools. Noodle and fried-rice vendors always feature prominently, as do sweets stalls, heaped high with sticky rice cakes wrapped in banana leaves or thick with bags of tiny sweetcorn pancakes hot from the griddle – and no night market is complete without its fruit-drink stall, offering banana shakes and freshly squeezed orange, lemon and tomato juices. In the best setups you'll find a lot more besides: curries; barbecued sweetcorn; satay sticks of pork and chicken; deep-fried insects; fresh pineapple, watermelon and mango; and – if the town's by a river or near the sea – heaps of fresh fish. Having decided what you want, you order from the cook or the cook's dogsbody and sit down at the nearest table; there is no territorialism about night markets, so it's normal to eat several dishes from separate stalls and rely on the nearest cook to sort out the bill.

Some large markets, particularly in Chiang Mai and Bangkok, have separate **food court** areas where you buy coupons first and select food and drink to their value at the stalls of your choice. This is also the modus operandi in the food courts found on the top floor of department stores and shopping centres across the country.

For a more relaxing ambience, Bangkok and the larger towns have a range of **upmarket restaurants**, some specializing in **"royal" Thai cuisine**, which differs from standard fare mainly in the quality of the ingredients and the way the food is presented. Great care is taken over how individual dishes look: they are served in small portions and decorated with carved fruit and vegetables in a way that used to be the prerogative of royal cooks, but has now filtered down to the common folk. The cost of such delights is not prohibitive, either – a meal in one of these places is unlikely to cost more than B500 per person.

How to eat

Thai food is eaten with a fork (left hand) and a spoon (right hand); there is no need for a knife as food is served in bite-sized chunks, which are forked onto the spoon and fed into the mouth. Steamed **rice** (*khao*) is served with most meals, and indeed the most commonly heard phrase for "to eat" is *kin khao* (literally, "eat rice"); chopsticks are provided only for noodle dishes, and northeastern sticky-rice dishes are always eaten with the fingers of the right hand. Never eat with the fingers of your left hand, which is used for washing after going to the toilet.

So that complementary taste combinations can be enjoyed, the dishes in a Thai meal are served all at once, even the soup, and shared communally. The more people, the more taste and texture sensations; if there are only two of you, it's normal to order three dishes, plus your own individual plates of steamed rice, while three diners would order four dishes, and so on. Only put a serving of one dish on your rice plate each time, and then only one or two spoonfuls.

What to eat

The repertoire of noodles, stir-fries, curries and rice dishes described below is pretty much standard throughout Thailand. When you get out into the provinces, you'll have the chance to sample a few **specialities** as well, which have evolved either from the cuisines of neighbouring countries or from the crops best suited to that area. For a detailed Thai **food and drink glossary**, turn to p.859. Bland food is anathema to Thais, and restaurant tables everywhere come decked out with a **condiment set** featuring the four basic flavours: chopped chillies in watery fish sauce; chopped chillies in vinegar; sugar; and ground red pepper – and often extra bowls of ground peanuts and a bottle of chilli ketchup as well.

Noodle and rice dishes

Thais eat **noodles** (*kway tiaw* or *ba mii*) when Westerners would dig into a sandwich – for lunch, as a late-night snack or just to pass the time – and at B20–30 (around B60 in a posh restaurant) they're the cheapest hot meal you'll find anywhere, whether bought from an itinerant street vendor or ordered in an air-con restaurant. They come in assorted varieties (wide and flat, thin and transparent; made with eggs, soy-bean flour or rice flour) and get boiled up as soups (*kway tiaw nam*), doused in sauces (*kway tiaw rat na*) or stir-fried (*kway tiaw haeng* or *kway tiaw pat*). All three versions include a smattering of vegetables, eggs and meat, but the usual practice is to order the dish with extra chicken, beef, pork or shrimps. Most popular of noodle dishes is *kway tiaw phat thai* (usually abbreviated to *phat thai*), a delicious combination of fried noodles, beansprouts, egg, tofu and spring onions, sprinkled with ground peanuts and the juice of half a lime, and often spiked with tiny dried shrimps.

Fried rice (*khao pat*) is the other faithful standby, much the same price as noodles, and guaranteed to feature on menus right across the country. Curries that come served on a bed of steamed rice are more like stews, prepared long in advance and eaten more as a light meal than a main one; they are usually called *khao na* plus the meat of the chosen dish – thus *khao na pet* is duck curry served over rice.

Curries, stir-fries, fish, soups and salads

Thai **curries** (*kaeng*) are based on coconut milk – which gives them a slightly sweet taste and a soup-like consistency – and get their fire from chilli peppers (*phrik*). The best curries are characterized by their curry pastes, a subtle blend of freshly ground herbs, spices, garlic, shallots and chilli, the most well known being the red or green curry pastes. It's often possible to request one that's "not too hot" (*mai phet*); if you do bite into a chilli, the way to combat the searing heat is to take a mouthful of plain rice – swigging water just exacerbates the sensation. Alternatively, pick the whole chillies out: contrary to what your eyes might think, the green ones are hotter than the red, and the smaller ones are hotter than the large; thus the tiny green "mouse shit" chillies are small but deadly.

Stir-fries tend to be a lot milder, often flavoured with ginger and whole cloves of garlic and featuring a pleasing combination of soft meat and crunchy vegetables or nuts. Chicken with cashew nuts (*kai pat met mamuang*) is a favourite of a lot of farang-oriented places, as is sweet and sour chicken, pork or fish (*kai/muu/plaa priaw waan*). *Pat phak bung* – slightly bitter morning-glory leaves fried with garlic in a black-bean sauce – makes a good vegetable side dish with any of these.

All seaside and most riverside restaurants rightly make a big deal out of locally caught **fish** and **seafood**. If you order fish it will often be served whole, either steamed or grilled with ginger or chillies. Mussels sometimes get stuffed into a batter and shrimps turn up in everything from soups to fried noodles.

You can't make a meal out of a Thai **soup**, but it is an essential component in any shared meal, eaten simultaneously with other dishes, not as a starter. Watery and broth-like, soups are often flavoured with the distinctive tang of lemon grass and kaffir lime leaves, and galangal, and garnished with fresh coriander, and can be extremely hot if the cook adds liberal handfuls of chillies to the pot. Two favourites are *tom kha kai*, a creamy coconut chicken soup; and

Fruits of Thailand

One of the most refreshing snacks in Thailand is fruit (*phõnlamái*), and you'll find it offered everywhere – neatly sliced in glass boxes on hawker carts, blended into delicious shakes at night market stalls and served as a dessert in restaurants. The fruits described below can be found in all parts of Thailand, though some are seasonal. The country's more familiar fruits are not listed here, but include forty varieties of banana (*klûay*), dozens of different mangoes (*mámûang*), three types of pineapple (*sàppàròt*), coconuts (*mapráo*), oranges (*sôm*), lemons (*mánao*) and watermelons (*taeng moh*). To avoid stomach trouble, peel all fruit before eating it, and use common sense if you're tempted to buy it pre-peeled on the street, avoiding anything that looks fly-blown or seems to have been sitting in the sun for hours.

Custard apple (soursop; *nóinà*; July–Sept). Inside the knobbly, muddy green skin you'll find creamy, almond-coloured blancmange-like flesh, having a strong flavour of strawberries and pears, with a hint of cinnamon, and many seeds.

Durian (*thúrian*; April–June). Thailand's most prized, and expensive, fruit (see p.168) has a greeny-yellow, spiky exterior and grows to the size of a football. Inside, it divides into segments of thick, yellow-white flesh which gives off a disgustingly strong stink that's been compared to a mixture of mature cheese and caramel. Not surprisingly, many airlines and hotels ban the eating of this smelly delicacy on their premises. Most Thais consider it the king of fruits, while most foreigners find it utterly foul in both taste and smell.

Guava (*fàràng*; year-round). The apple of the tropics has green textured skin and sweet, crisp flesh that can be pink or white and is studded with tiny edible seeds. Has five times the vitamin C content of an orange and is sometimes eaten cut into strips and sprinkled with sugar and chilli.

Jackfruit (*khan˜un*; year-round). This large, pear-shaped fruit can weigh up to twenty kilograms and has a thick, bobbly, greeny-yellow shell protecting sweet yellow flesh. Green, unripe jackfruit is sometimes cooked as a vegetable in curries.

tom yam kung, a prawn soup without coconut milk (the addition of lime juice gives it its distinctive sour flavour).

Another popular part of any proper Thai meal is a spicy, sour **salad** (*yam*), which is often served warm. *Yam* can be made in many permutations – with noodles, meat, seafood or vegetables, for example – but at the heart of every variety is a liberal squirt of fresh lime juice and a fiery sprinkling of chopped chillies, a combination that can take some getting used to. The most prevalent variation on this theme is the national dish of the northeast, a spicy green-papaya salad called *som tam*, described under "Regional Dishes" below.

Desserts

Desserts (*khanom*) don't really figure on most restaurant menus, but a few places offer bowls of *luk taan cheum*, a jellied concoction of lotus or palm seeds floating in a syrup scented with jasmine or other aromatic flowers. Coconut milk is a feature of most other desserts, notably delicious coconut ice cream, and a royal Thai cuisine special of coconut custard (*sangkhayaa*) cooked inside a small pumpkin, whose flesh you can also eat. **Cakes** are sold on the street and tend to be heavy, sticky affairs made from glutinous rice and coconut cream pressed into squares and wrapped in banana leaves.

Regional dishes

Many of the specialities of the **north** originated over the border in Burma; one such is *khao soi*, in which both boiled and crispy egg noodles are served with beef, chicken or pork in a curried coconut soup. Also popular around Chiang Mai are thick spicy sausages (*nem*) made from minced pork, rice and garlic left to cure for a few days and then sometimes eaten raw with spicy

Lychee (*línjii*; April–May). Under rough, reddish-brown skin, the lychee has sweet, richly flavoured white flesh, rose-scented and with plenty of vitamin C, round a brown, egg-shaped pit.
Longan (*lamyai*; July–Oct). A close relative of the lychee, with succulent white flesh covered in thin, brittle skin.
Mangosteen (*mangkùt*; April–Sept). The size of a small apple, with smooth, purple skin and a fleshy inside that divides into succulent white segments that are sweet though slightly acidic.
Papaya (paw-paw; *málákaw*; year-round). Looks like an elongated watermelon, with smooth green skin and yellowy-orange flesh that's a rich source of vitamins A and C. It's a favourite in fruit salads and shakes, and sometimes appears in its green, unripe form in salads, notably *som tam*.
Pomelo (*sôm oh*; Oct–Dec). The largest of all the citrus fruits, it looks rather like a grapefruit, though it is slightly drier and has less flavour.
Rambutan (*ngáw*; May–Sept). The bright red rambutan's soft, spiny exterior has given it its name – *rambut* means "hair" in Malay. Usually about the size of a golf ball, it has a white, opaque flesh of delicate flavour, similar to a lychee.
Rose apple (*chomphûu*; year-round). Linked in myth with the golden fruit of immortality, the rose apple is small and egg-shaped, with white, rose-scented flesh.
Sapodilla (sapota; *lámút*; Sept–Dec). These small, brown, rough-skinned ovals look a bit like kiwi fruit and conceal a grainy, yellowish pulp that tastes almost honey-sweet.
Tamarind (*mákhăam*; Dec–Jan). A Thai favourite and a pricey delicacy – carrying the seeds is said to make you safe from wounding by knives or bullets. Comes in rough, brown pods containing up to ten seeds, each surrounded by a sticky, dry pulp which has a sour, lemony taste.

salad. Somewhat more palatable is the local curry *kaeng hang lay*, made from pork, ginger, garlic and tamarind, and a delicious spicy dipping sauce, *nam phrik ong*, made with minced pork.

The crop most suited to the infertile lands of **Isaan** is **sticky rice** (*khao niaw*), which replaces the standard grain as the staple diet for northeasterners. Served in its own special rattan "sticky rice basket" (the Isaan equivalent of the Tupperware lunchbox), it's usually eaten with the fingers, rolled up into small balls and dipped once (double-dipping looks crass to Thai people) into chilli sauces and eaten with side dishes such as the local dish *som tam*, a spicy green-papaya salad with garlic, raw chillies, green beans, tomatoes, peanuts and dried shrimps (or fresh crab).

Although you'll find basted barbecued chicken on a stick (*kai yaang*) all over Thailand, it originated in Isaan and is especially tasty in its home region. As with Chiang Mai, Isaan produces its own sausages, called *sai krog isaan*, made from spiced and diced raw pork. Raw minced pork is also the basis of another popular Isaan and northern dish, *larb*, when it is subtly flavoured with mint and served with vegetables.

Aside from putting a greater emphasis on seafood, **southern** Thai cuisine displays a marked Malaysian and Muslim aspect as you near the border. Satays feature more down here, but the two mainstays are the thick, rich and fairly mild Muslim beef curry (*kaeng matsaman*), and the chicken curry served over lightly spiced saffron rice, known as *kaeng karii kai*. You'll find plenty of *roti*s in the south, too – pancakes rolled with sickly sweet condensed milk and sugar and sold hot from pushcart griddles.

Vegetarian food

Although very few Thais are **vegetarian** (*mangsawirat*), it's usually possible to persuade cooks to rustle up a vegetable-only fried rice or noodle dish, though in more out-of-the-way places that's often your only option unless you eat fish – so you'll need to supplement your diet with the nuts, barbecued sweetcorn, fruit and other non-meaty goodies sold by food stalls. In tourist spots, vegetarians can happily splurge on specially concocted Thai and Western veggie dishes, and some restaurants will come up with a completely separate menu if requested. If you're **vegan** (*jeh*) you'll need to stress when you order that you don't want egg, as they get used a lot; cheese and other dairy produce, however, don't feature at all in Thai cuisine. Many towns will have one or more **vegan restaurants** (*raan ahaan jeh*), which are usually run by members of a temple or Buddhist sect and operate from unadorned premises off the main streets; because strict Buddhists prefer not to eat late in the day, most of the restaurants open early, at around 6 or 7am and close by 2pm. Very few of these places have an English-language sign, but they all display the Thai character for vegan, a "*jeh*" (a little like the letter "q" with an elongated arching tail that curves over its head to the left), in yellow on a red background. Nor is there ever a menu: customers simply choose from the trays of veggie stir-fries and curries, nearly all of them made with soya products, that are laid out canteen-style. Most places charge B20–30 for a couple of helpings served over a plate of brown rice.

Drinks

Thais don't drink water straight from the tap, and nor should you; plastic bottles of drinking **water** (*nam plao*) are sold countrywide, even in the smallest villages, for around B5–10. Cheap restaurants and hotels generally serve free jugs of boiled water, which should be fine to drink, though they are not as foolproof as the bottles.

Night markets, guest houses and restaurants do a good line in freshly squeezed **fruit juices** such as lemon (*nam manao*) and orange (*nam som*), which often come with salt and sugar already added, particularly upcountry. The same places will usually do **fruit shakes** as well, blending bananas (*nam kluay*), papayas (*nam malakaw*), pineapples (*nam sapparot*) and others with liquid sugar or condensed milk (or yoghurt, to make lassi). Fresh **coconut water** (*nam maprao*) is another great thirst-quencher – you buy the whole fruit dehusked, decapitated and chilled; Thais are also very partial to freshly squeezed **sugar-cane juice** (*nam awy*), which is sickeningly sweet.

Bottled and canned brand-name **soft drinks** are sold all over the place, with a particularly wide range in the ubiquitous 7–11 chain stores. Soft-drink bottles are returnable, so some shops and drink stalls have an amazing system of pouring the contents into a small plastic bag (fastened with an elastic band and with a straw inserted) rather than charging you the extra for taking away the bottle. The larger restaurants keep their soft drinks refrigerated, but smaller cafés and shops add **ice** (*nam khaeng*) to glasses and bags. Most ice is produced commercially under hygienic conditions, but it might become less pure in transit so be wary – and don't take ice if you have diarrhoea. For those travelling with children, or just partial themselves to **dairy products**, UHT-preserved milk and chilled yoghurt drinks are widely available (especially 7–11 stores), as are a variety of soya drinks.

Weak Chinese **tea** (*nam chaa*) makes a refreshing alternative to water and often gets served in Chinese restaurants and roadside cafés. Posher restaurants keep stronger Chinese and Western-style teas (*chaa*) and **coffee** (*kaafae*), which is nowadays mostly the ubiquitous instant Nescafé. This is usually the coffee offered to farangs, even if freshly ground Thai-grown coffee – notably several kinds of hill-tribe coffee from the mountains of the north – is available. If you would like to try traditional Thai coffee, most commonly found at Chinese-style cafés in the south of the country or at outdoor markets, and prepared through filtering the grounds through a cloth, ask for *kaafae thung* (literally, "bag coffee"), normally served very bitter with sugar as well as sweetened condensed milk alongside a glass of black tea to wash it down with. Fresh Western-style coffee (*kaafae sot*), whether filtered, espresso or percolated, is mostly limited to farang-oriented places, international-style coffee bars and big hotels, in Bangkok, Chiang Mai and beach areas. Tea and coffee are normally served black, perhaps with a sachet of coffee whitener on the side.

Alcoholic drinks

Beer (*bia*) is one of the few consumer items in Thailand that's not a bargain due to the heavy taxes levied on the beverage – at around B60 for a 330ml bottle it works out roughly the same as what you'd pay in the West (larger, 660ml bottles, when available, are always slightly better value). The most famous beer is the slightly acrid locally brewed Singha, but Kloster, which is also brewed by Boon Rawd and costs about B5–10 more than Singha, is easier on the tongue. Some places also stock a lighter version of Singha called Singha Gold, as well as two stronger, cheaper beers by the same brewery, Beer Thai and the slightly maltier Leo. Carlsberg and Heineken are now brewed and widely found in Thailand, and in the most touristy areas you'll find imported bottles from all over the world, even Corona. Carlsberg also produces locally the ubiquitous Chang, usually the cheapest beer available, with a head-banging seven percent alcohol content.

Wine attracts even higher taxation than beer. It's now found on plenty of upmarket and tourist-oriented restaurant menus, but expect to be disappointed both by the quality and by the price. Thai wine is now produced at several vineyards, notably at Château de Loei near Phu Reua National Park in the northeast, which produces quite tasty reds, whites, a rosé, a dessert wine and brandy (see p.534).

At about B60 for a hip-flask-sized 375ml bottle, the local **whisky** is a lot better value, and Thais think nothing of consuming a bottle a night. The most palatable and widely available of these is Mekong, which is very pleasant once you've stopped expecting it to taste like Scotch; distilled from rice, Mekong is 35 percent proof, deep gold in colour and tastes slightly sweet. If that's not to your taste, a pricier Thai **rum** is also available, Sang Thip, made from sugar cane, and even stronger than the whisky at forty percent proof. Check the menu carefully when ordering a bottle of Mekong from a bar in a tourist area, as they often ask up to five times more than you'd pay in a guest house or shop.

You can **buy** beer and whisky in food stores, guest houses and most restaurants at any time of the day; **bars** aren't really an indigenous feature as Thais rarely drink out without eating, but you'll find a fair number of Western-style drinking holes in Bangkok and larger centres elsewhere in the country, ranging from ultra-hip haunts in the capital to basic, open-to-the-elements **"bar-beers"**.

Telephones, mail and Internet access

Thailand has a reasonably fast and efficient communications network: international mail services are relatively speedy, phoning overseas is possible even from some small islands and Internet access is available in just about every town.

Mail

Mail takes around seven days to get between Bangkok and Europe or North America, a little longer from the more isolated areas. Almost all **main post offices** across the country operate a **poste restante** service and will hold letters for one to three months. Mail should be addressed: Name (family name underlined or capitalized), Poste Restante, GPO, Town or City, Thailand. It will be filed by surname, though it's always wise to check under your first initial as well. The smaller post offices pay scant attention to who takes what, but in the busier GPOs you need to show your passport, pay B1 per item received, and sign for them. Most GPO poste restantes follow regular **post office hours** (Mon–Fri 8.30am–4.30pm, Sat 9am–noon; some close Mon–Fri noon–1pm and may stay open until 6pm) – exceptions are explained in the Guide.

Post offices are the best places to buy **stamps**, though hotels and guest houses often sell them too, charging an extra B1 per stamp. An airmail letter of under 10g costs B17 to send to Europe or Australia and B19 to North America; standard-sized postcards cost B12, and aerogrammes B15, regardless of where they're going. All **parcels** must be officially boxed and sealed (for a small fee) at special counters within main post offices or in a private outlet just outside – you can't just turn up with a package and buy stamps for it. In tourist centres (especially at Bangkok's GPO) be prepared to queue, first for the packaging, then for the weighing and then again for the buying of stamps. The surface rate for a parcel of up to 5kg is B1650 to the UK, B1110 to the US and B1090 for Australia, and the package should reach its destination in three months; airmail for up to 5kg costs B2420 to the UK, B2950 to the US and B2150 to Australia and takes about ten days.

Phones and faxes

By and large the Thai phone system works well. Coin **payphones** are straightforward enough and generally come in two varieties: red or pale blue for local calls, blue or stainless steel for local or long-distance **calls within Thailand**. Red and pale blue phones take the small B1 coins and will give you about three minutes per B1, while blue and stainless steel ones gobble up B1, B5 and B10 coins (inter-provincial rates vary between B3 and B12/minute/distance, and work out to be surprisingly pricey). You may well be better off buying a **TOT phonecard** for domestic calls; this comes with a PIN number and is available in a range of denominations from B25 to B240 from hotels and a wide variety of shops: it can be used in designated orange cardphones or in stainless steel payphones. In some provincial towns, enterprising mobile-phone owners hang out on the main streets, often with a simple fold-out table and makeshift cardboard sign, offering cheap long-distance, and sometimes international, calls.

When dialling any number in Thailand, you must now always preface it with what used to be the area code, even when dialling from the same area; in the Guide we've separated off this code, for easy recognition (you'll still come across plenty of business cards and brochures which give only the old local number, to which you'll need to add the area code). Anything that's prefaced with a ⓣ01 is a mobile (cell) phone or satellite phone number (some guest houses on islands like Ko Chang have satellite phones) and will often cost more to call; to add to the confusion, ⓣ06, ⓣ07 and ⓣ09 are also mobile phone codes. Where we've given several line numbers – eg ⓣ02 431 1802–9 – you can substitute the last digit with any number between 3 and 9. [illegible] ies within Thailand, ca[illegible] cal idiosyncrasy: Thai [illegible] ple by their first, not the [illegible]

An increasing nu[illegible] ke their **mobile phon**[illegible] rs from the US may we[illegible] or tri-band phone, [illegible] d 1800Hz, the systems most commonly found in other parts of the world, are both available in Thailand; for a full list of network types and providers in Thailand, go to Ⓦwww.teletechnics.com/reference/telecom/cellular.html. Not all foreign networks have links with Thai networks, so check with your phone provider before you travel whether roaming is available. It's also worth checking how much coverage there is for your network within Thailand, and asking in advance for a summary of rates for incoming as well as outgoing calls while you're there; some networks offer flat-rate deals on international usage, which can save you a lot of money. For further information about using your phone abroad, check out Ⓦwww.telecomsadvice.org.uk/features/using_your_mobile_abroad.htm.

If you want to use your mobile a lot in Thailand, it may well be worth getting hold of a rechargeable **Thai SIM card** with a local phone number. An AIS 1-2-Call card (Ⓦwww.ais900.com or www.one-2-call. com) will give you the widest coverage in Thailand, and top-up cards are available at 7–11 stores across the country. Their call rates aren't the cheapest, however, at B4–8 per minute within Thailand; international rates are around B30 per minute, while texts cost B3 domestic, B9 international. Your own network operator may be able to give you useful advice about exchanging SIM cards before you leave home, but the best place in Thailand to buy a card and have any necessary technical adjustments made is the Mah Boon Krong Centre in Bangkok (see p.188); an AIS 1-2-Call SIM card, for example, will cost you around B650, including your first B300 worth of calls.

Most major post offices offer a domestic and international **fax** service – currently around B75 per page to Australia, North America or the UK. Private phone centres will also send faxes for you, as will most guest houses, for which you can expect to pay up to fifty percent more than government rates.

International calls

For international direct-dial (IDD) phone calls, there are three time periods with different **rates**. The most expensive, or **standard**, time to call is from 7am to 9pm (20 percent discount on Sundays); the **economy** period runs from 9pm to midnight and 5am to 7am; the **reduced** rate applies between midnight and 5am. The per-minute rate for a direct-dial call to Europe is B30 standard, B24 economy and B24 reduced; for North America and Australia it's B22/18/18; at the time of writing, however, plans to cut these international rates by between twenty and seventy percent were announced.

You can use these government rates by buying a **Thaicard**, the international phonecard issued by CAT (Communications Authority of Thailand). Found in B50–3000 denominations at post offices and many shops, Thaicards can be used in designated purple cardphones and at government telephone centres, which are usually located within or adjacent to the town's main post office. On the same phones, you can also use CAT's Internet-based **Phone Net** cards, which come in denominations of B300, B500 and B1000 from the same outlets and

International dialling codes

If you're dialling from abroad, the international code for Thailand is Ⓣ66, after which you leave off the initial zero of the Thai number.

Calling out of Thailand, for Laos dial Ⓣ007856 then the subscriber number, for Malaysia Ⓣ09 then the subscriber number; for anywhere else, dial Ⓣ001 and then the relevant country code:

Australia	**61**
Canada	**1**
Ireland	**353**
New Zealand	**64**
UK	**44**
US	**1**

For **international directory enquiries** and operator services, call Ⓣ100.

give access to far cheaper tariffs: B14 per minute to the US and Australia, for instance, B20 to the UK. (It's unclear at the moment what effect the slashing of the main IDD rates will have on these rates.)

There's also a private international cardphone system called **Lenso**, which operates in Bangkok and the biggest resorts. Lenso's phones are yellow and have been installed all over the place. To use them, you either need a special Lenso phonecard (available from shops near the phones in B300 and B500 denominations), or you can use a credit card. Rates are ten percent higher than government IDD rates.

Private international call offices (where your call is timed and you pay at the end) in tourist areas such as Bangkok's Thanon Khao San tend to be slightly more expensive again, while services offered by the posher hotels are the most expensive way of calling. Cheapest of all is to call via the Internet, and you'll find that many Internet cafés in touristed areas deeply undercut government phone rates.

Collect or **reverse-charge** calls can be made free of charge at government phone centres, or from many guest houses and private phone offices, usually for a fee of B100. From the government phone centres, as well as from some payphones and fixed telephones, you can make Home Country Direct calls to your own international operator, who will arrange for you to make a credit-card or reverse-charge call.

Internet access

Internet access is very widespread and very cheap in Thailand. You'll find traveller-oriented **Internet cafés** in every touristed town and resort in the country – there are at least twenty in the Banglamphu district of Bangkok, for example – and even remote islands like Ko Mak and Ko Phayam provide Internet access via satellite phones. Competition keeps prices low: upcountry you could expect to pay as little as B20 per hour, while rates in tourist centres average B1 per minute. Upmarket hotels are the exception, often charging as much as B100 per half-hour or B3–5 per minute. Nearly every mid-sized town in Thailand also offers a public Internet service, called **Catnet**, at the government telephone office (usually located inside or adjacent to the main post office). To use the service, you need to buy a B100 card with a Catnet PIN (available at all phone offices), which gives you three hours of Internet time at any of these public terminals.

Before leaving home you should check whether your existing **email account** offers a web-based service that enables you to pick up your email from any Internet terminal in the world. This is becoming increasingly common and is very useful and straightforward, though it can sometimes be a bit slow. If this does not apply to you, it's well worth setting yourself up with a free email account for the duration of the trip, either before you leave home or in an Internet café in Thailand. Several companies offer this free email service, but by far the most popular are those run by Hotmail (Ⓦwww.hotmail.com) and Yahoo (Ⓦwww.yahoo.com).

If you plan to email from your **laptop** in Thailand, be advised that very few budget guest houses and cheap hotels have telephone sockets in the room, and that many upmarket hotels charge astronomical rates for international calls. One potentially useful way round the cost issue is to become a temporary subscriber to the Thai ISP Loxinfo (Ⓦwww.loxinfo.co.th), which has local dial-up numbers in every province in Thailand. Their Webnet deal is aimed at international businesspeople and tourists and can be bought online; it allows you 12 hours of Internet access for B160, 30 hours for B380 or 63 hours for B750. The usual phone plug in Thailand is the American standard RJ11 phone jack. See Steve Kropla's Help for World Travellers website (Ⓣwww.kropla.com) for detailed advice on how to set up your modem before you go, and how to hardwire phone plugs where necessary.

The media

To keep you abreast of world affairs, there are several English-language newspapers in Thailand, though a mild form of censorship affects the predominantly state-controlled media, even muting the English-language branches on occasion.

Newspapers and magazines

Of the hundreds of **Thai-language newspapers and magazines** published every week, the sensationalist tabloid *Thai Rath* attracts the widest readership, and the independent *Siam Rath*, founded by M.R. Kukrit Pramoj (see p.165), and the broadly similar *Matichon,* are the most intellectual.

Alongside these, two daily **English-language papers** – the *Bangkok Post* and the *Nation* – are capable of adopting a fairly critical attitude to governmental goings-on and cover major domestic and international stories as well as tourist-related issues. Of the two, the *Bangkok Post* tends to focus more on international stories, while the *Nation* has the most in-depth coverage of Thai and Southeast Asian issues. Both detail English-language cinema programmes, TV schedules and expat social events, and are sold at most newsstands in the capital as well as in major provincial towns and tourist resorts; the more isolated places receive their few copies at least one day late. *Bangkok Metro*, the capital's monthly English-language listings **magazine**, as well as reviews and previews of events in the city, carries lively articles on cultural and contemporary life in Thailand.

The more traveller-oriented monthly magazine *Farang* reviews the bars, clubs, restaurants and guest houses of Thailand's most popular half-dozen tourist destinations and also prints some interesting features on contemporary culture; it is sold most widely in Bangkok but is also available in some major tourist centres.

You can also pick up **foreign publications** such as *Newsweek*, *Time* and the *International Herald Tribune* in Bangkok, Chiang Mai, and the major resorts; expensive hotels sometimes carry air-freighted copies of foreign national newspapers for at least B50 a copy. The weekly current affairs magazine *Far Eastern Economic Review* is also worth looking out for; available in major bookshops and at newsstands in tourist centres, it generally offers a very readable selection of articles on Thailand and the rest of Asia.

Television

Channel 9 is Thailand's major **TV station**, transmitting news, documentaries, quiz shows and predominantly imported cartoons and dramas to all parts of the country. Four other networks broadcast to Bangkok – the privately run Channel 3 and the government-controlled channels 5, 7 and 11 – but not all are received in every province. The new ITV is the only other privately operated channel, but as it's majority-owned by the current prime minister's family, it tends not to veer away from the government politically. **Cable** networks – available in many mid-range and most upmarket hotel rooms – carry channels from all around the world, including CNN from North America, BBC World from the UK, IBC from Australia and the HBO English-language movie channel. Both the *Bangkok Post* and the *Nation* print the daily TV and cable **schedule**, the former offering the better coverage.

Radio

With a shortwave **radio** – or by going online – you can pick up the BBC World Service (Ⓦwww.bbc.co.uk/worldservice), Radio Australia (Ⓦwww.abc.net.au/ra), Voice of America (Ⓦwww.voa.gov), Radio Canada (Ⓦwww.rcinet.ca) and other international stations right across Thailand. Times and wavelengths can change regularly, so get hold of a recent schedule just before you travel or consult the websites for frequency and programme guides. For current, brief listings of major English-language radio stations while you're in Thailand, consult the *Bangkok Post*.

Bangkok is served by a handful of English-language **FM stations**. Radio Thailand broadcasts news in English on 97 MHz several times a day: 7–8am, 12.30–1pm, 7–7.30pm and 8–8.30pm. Apart from a few specialist shows, FMX 95.5 pumps out nonstop upbeat chart hits from 5am to 2am; there are few pauses for chat, except for local and international headlines on the half hour. Proud to dub itself "Bangkok's premier easy-listening station", Smooth 105 FM rarely veers from the middle of the road; international news breaks in on the hour.

At the opposite end of the taste spectrum, Chulalongkorn University Radio (101.5FM) plays classical music from 9.30pm to midnight every night.

Crime and personal safety

As long as you keep your wits about you, you shouldn't encounter much trouble in Thailand. Theft and pickpocketing are two of the main problems – not surprising considering that a huge percentage of the local population scrape by on under US$5 per day – but the most common cause for concern is the number of con-artists who dupe gullible tourists into parting with their cash.

To **prevent theft**, most travellers prefer to carry their valuables with them at all times, either in a moneybelt, neck pouch or inside pocket, but it's sometimes possible to leave your valuables in a hotel or guest-house locker – the safest lockers are those that require your own padlock, as there are occasional reports of valuables being stolen by hotel staff. Padlock your luggage when leaving it in hotel or guest-house rooms, as well as when consigning it to storage or taking it on public transport. Padlocks also come in handy as extra security on your room, particularly on the doors of beachfront bamboo huts.

Theft from some long-distance, **overnight buses** is also a problem, with the majority of reported incidents taking place on the temptingly cheap buses run by private companies direct from Bangkok's Thanon Khao San (as opposed to those that depart from the government bus stations) to destinations such as Chiang Mai and southern beach resorts. The best solution is to go direct from the bus stations.

On any bus, private or government, and on any train journey, never keep anything of value in luggage that is stored out of your sight and be wary of accepting food and drink from fellow passengers as it may be drugged. This might sound paranoid, but there have been enough drug-muggings for TAT to publish a specific warning about the problem.

Violent crime against tourists is not common, but it does occur, and there have been several serious attacks on women travellers in the last few years. However, bearing in mind that over five million foreign tourists visit Thailand every year, the statistical likelihood of becoming a victim is extremely small.

Obvious precautions for travellers of either sex include locking accessible windows and doors at night – preferably with your own padlock (doors in many of the simpler guest houses and beach bungalows are designed for this) – and not travelling alone at night in a taxi or tuk-tuk. Nor should you risk jumping into an unlicensed taxi at Don Muang Airport at any time of day: there have been some very violent robberies in these, so take the well-marked licensed, metered taxis instead, or the airport bus (see p.94).

If you're going hiking on your own for a day, it's a good idea to inform guest-house or hotel staff of where you're planning to go, so they have some idea of where to look for you if necessary.

Unfortunately, it is also necessary for female tourists to think twice about spending time alone with a **monk**, as not all men of the cloth uphold the Buddhist precepts and there have been rapes and murders committed by men wearing the saffron robes of the monkhood (see p.813 for more about the changing Thai attitudes towards the monkhood).

Though unpalatable and distressing, Thailand's high-profile sex industry is relatively unthreatening for Western women, with its energy focused exclusively on farang men; it's also quite easily avoided, being contained within certain pockets of the capital and a couple of beach resorts.

As for **harassment** from men, it's hard to generalize, but most Western women find it less of a problem in Thailand than they do back home. Outside the main tourist spots, you're more likely to be of interest as a foreigner rather than a woman and, if travelling alone, as an object of concern rather than of sexual aggression.

Tourists can get **fined** for overstaying their visa (see p.21), not wearing a motorcycle helmet and violating other traffic laws (see p.43), not having a train ticket (see p.37) and for spitting, littering and discarding cigarette stubs in public areas (up to B2000).

Among hazards to watch out for in the natural world, **riptides** claim a number of tourist lives every year, particularly off Phuket, Ko Chang (Trat) and Ko Samui during stormy periods of the monsoon season, so always pay attention to warning signs and red flags, and always ask locally if unsure.

Jellyfish can be a problem on any coast, especially just after a storm (see p.33 for further advice).

It's advisable to travel with a guide in certain **border areas** or, if you're on a motorbike, to take advice before setting off. As these regions are generally covered in dense unmapped jungle, you shouldn't find yourself alone in the vicinity anyway, but the main stretches to watch are the Burmese border north of Three Pagodas Pass, between Mae Sot and Mae Sariang, around Mae Sai, and between Umphang and Sangkhlaburi – where villages, hideaways and refugee camps occasionally get shelled either by the Burmese military or by rebel Karen or Mon forces – and the border between Cambodia and southern Isaan, which is littered with unexploded mines. There have been violent incidents and bomb attacks, especially in early 2004, in Yala, Pattani and Narathiwat provinces in the deep south, which have been carried out by Muslim separatists/bandits mostly against government institutions and have not been aimed at Westerners (see also p.746). For up-to-the-minute advice on current political troublespots, consult your government's travel advisory.

Scams

Despite the best efforts of guidebook writers, TAT and the Thai tourist police, countless travellers to Thailand get scammed every year. Nearly all **scams** are easily avoided if you are on your guard against anyone

Governmental travel advisories

Australian Department of Foreign Affairs ⓦwww.dfat.gov.au
British Foreign & Commonwealth Office ⓦwww.fco.gov.uk
Canadian Department of Foreign Affairs ⓦwww.dfait-maeci.gc.ca
Irish Department of Foreign Affairs ⓦwww.irlgov.ie/iveagh
New Zealand Ministry of Foreign Affairs ⓦwww.mft.govt.nz
US State Department ⓦtravel.state.gov

who makes an unnatural effort to befriend you. We have outlined the main scams in the relevant sections of the Guide, but con-artists are nothing if not creative, so if in doubt walk away at the earliest opportunity. The worst areas for scammers are the busy tourist centres, including many parts of Bangkok and the main beach resorts.

Many **tuk-tuk drivers** earn most of their living through securing commissions from tourist-oriented shops and this is especially true in Bangkok, where they will do their damnedest to get you to go to a gem shop (see below). The most common tactic is for drivers to pretend that the Grand Palace or other major sight you intended to visit is **closed for the day** (they usually invent a plausible reason, such as a festival or royal occasion; see p.122 for more), and to then offer to take you on a round-city tour instead, perhaps even for free. The tour will invariably include a visit to a gem shop. The easiest way to avoid all this is to take a metered taxi; if you're fixed on taking a tuk-tuk, ignore any tuk-tuk that is parked up or loitering and be firm about where you want to go.

Self-styled **tourist guides**, **touts** and anyone else who might introduce themselves as **students** or **businessmen** and offer to take you somewhere of interest, or invite you to meet their family, are often the first piece of bait in a well-honed chain of con-artists. If you bite, chances are you'll end up either at a gem shop or in a gambling den, or, at best, at a tour operator or hotel that you had not planned to patronise. This is not to say that you should never accept an invitation from a local person, but be extremely wary of doing so following a street encounter in Bangkok or the resorts and note that tourist guides' ID cards are easily faked.

For many of these characters the goal is to get you inside a dodgy **gem shop**, nearly all of which are located in Bangkok. There is a full run-down of advice on how to avoid falling for the notorious low-grade gems scam on p.194, but the bottom line is that if you are not experienced at buying and trading in valuable gems you will definitely be ripped off, possibly even to the tune of several thousand pounds.

Check the 2Bangkok website's account of a typical gem scam (Ⓦwww.2bangkok.com/2bangkok/Scams/Sapphire.shtml) before you shell out any cash at all.

A less common but potentially more frightening scam involves a similar cast of warm-up artists leading tourists into a **gambling** game. The scammers invite their victim home on an innocent-sounding pretext, get out a pack of cards, and then set about fleecing the incomer in any number of subtle ways. Often this can be especially scary as the venue is likely to be far from hotels or recognizable landmarks. And you're unlikely to get any sympathy from police as gambling is **illegal** in Thailand.

Drugs

Drug-smuggling carries a maximum penalty of death in Thailand and **dealing** will get you anything from four years to life in a Thai prison; penalties depend on the drug and the amount involved. Travellers caught with even the smallest amount of drugs at airports and international borders are prosecuted for trafficking, and no one charged with trafficking offences gets bail. Heroin, amphetamines, LSD and ecstasy are classed as Category 1 drugs and carry the most severe penalties: even **possession** of Category 1 drugs for personal use can result in a life sentence. Away from international borders, most foreigners arrested in possession of small amounts of cannabis are released on bail, then fined and deported, but the law is complex and custodial sentences are possible.

Despite occasional royal pardons, don't expect special treatment as a farang: you only need to read one of the first-hand accounts by foreign former prisoners (reviewed in "Books" on p.847) to get the picture, but if that doesn't put you off you could always visit an inmate in a Bangkok jail – details on how to do this are given on p.204. The **police** actively look for tourists doing drugs, reportedly searching people regularly and randomly on Thanon Khao San, for example. They have the power to order a urine test if they have reasonable grounds for suspicion, and even a positive result for marijuana consumption could lead to a year's imprisonment. Be wary also of being shopped by a farang or local dealer keen to earn a financial reward for a successful bust (Chiang Mai samlor drivers are notorious, and there are setups at the Ko Pha Ngan full moon parties, for example), or having substances slipped into your luggage (simple enough to perpetrate unless all fastenings are secured with padlocks).

If you are arrested, ask for your embassy to be contacted immediately, which is your right under Thai law (see p.203 for phone numbers), and embassy staff will talk you through procedures. The British charity Prisoners Abroad (Ⓦwww.prisonersabroad.org.uk) carries a detailed Survival Guide on its website, which outlines what to expect if arrested in Thailand, from the point of apprehension through trial and conviction to life in a Thai jail; if contacted, the charity may also be able to offer direct support to any British citizen facing imprisonment in a Thai jail.

Reporting a crime or emergency

In emergencies, contact the English-speaking **tourist police**, who maintain a 24-hour toll-free nationwide line (Ⓣ1155) and have offices within or adjacent to many regional TAT offices – getting in touch with the tourist police first is invariably more efficient than directly contacting the local police, ambulance or fire service. Their job is to offer advice and tell you what to do next, but they do not file crime reports, which must be done at the nearest police station. TAT has a special department for mediating between tourists, police and accused persons (particularly shopkeepers and tour agents), called the Tourist Assistance Center (TAC); it's based in the TAT office on Thanon Rajdamnoen Nok, Bangkok (daily 8.30am– 4.30pm; Ⓣ02 281 5051).

Opening hours and holidays

Most shops open at least Monday to Saturday from about 8am to 8pm, while department stores operate daily from around 10am to 9pm. Private office hours are generally Monday to Friday 8am to 5pm and Saturday 8am to noon, though in tourist areas these hours are longer, with weekends worked like any other day. Government offices work Monday to Friday 8.30am to noon and 1 to 4.30pm, and national museums tend to stick to these hours too, but some close on Mondays and Tuesdays rather than at weekends.

Most tourists only register **national holidays** because trains and buses suddenly get extraordinarily crowded: although banks and government offices shut on these days, most shops and tourist-oriented businesses carry on regardless, and TAT branches continue to dispense information.

The only time an inconvenient number of shops, restaurants and hotels do close is during Chinese New Year, which, though not marked as an official national holiday, brings many businesses to a standstill for several days in late January or February. You'll notice it particularly in the south, where most service industries are Chinese-managed.

A brief note on **dates**. Thais use both the Western Gregorian calendar and a Buddhist calendar – the Buddha is said to have died (or entered Nirvana) in the year 543 BC, so Thai dates start from that point: thus 2005 AD becomes 2548 BE (Buddhist Era).

National holidays

January 1 Western New Year's Day
February **(day of full moon)** Maha Puja: Commemorates the Buddha preaching to a spontaneously assembled crowd of 1250.
April 6 Chakri Day: The founding of the Chakri dynasty.
April **(usually 13–15)** Songkhran:Thai New Year.
May 5 Coronation Day
May **(early in the month)** Royal Ploughing Ceremony: Marks start of rice-planting season.
May **(day of full moon)** Visakha Puja: The holiest of all Buddhist holidays, which celebrates the birth, enlightenment and death of the Buddha.
July **(day of full moon)** Asanha Puja: Commemorates the Buddha's first sermon.
July **(the day after Asanha Puja)** Khao Pansa: The start of the annual three-month Buddhist rains retreat, when new monks are ordained.
August 12 Queen's birthday
October 23 Chulalongkorn Day: The anniversary of Rama V's death.
December 5 King's birthday
December 10 Constitution Day
December 31 Western New Year's Eve

Festivals

Hardly a week goes by without some kind of local or national festival being celebrated somewhere in Thailand. All the festivals listed below are spectacular or engaging enough to be worth altering your itinerary for, but bear in mind that for some of the more publicized celebrations (notably those in the northeast) you'll need to book transport and accommodation a week or more in advance.

Nearly all Thai festivals have some kind of **religious** aspect. The most theatrical are generally Brahmanic (Hindu) in origin, honouring elemental spirits with ancient rites and ceremonial costumed parades. Buddhist celebrations usually revolve round the local temple, and while merit-making is a significant feature, a light-hearted atmosphere prevails, as the Wat grounds are swamped with food and trinket vendors and makeshift stages are set up to show *likay* folk theatre, singing stars and beauty contests; there may even be funfair rides as well.

Many of the **secular festivals** (like the elephant roundups and the Bridge over the River Kwai spectacle) are outdoor local culture shows, geared specifically towards Thai and farang tourists and thus slightly artificial, though no less enjoyable for that. Others are thinly veiled trade fairs held in provincial capitals to show off the local speciality, which nevertheless assume all the trappings of a temple fair and so are usually worth a look.

Few of the **dates** for religious festivals are fixed, so check with TAT for specifics or consult ⓦwww.thailandgrandfestival.com. The names of the most touristy celebrations are given here in English; the more low-key festivals are more usually known by their Thai name (*ngan* means "festival").

A festival calendar

January–March

Bangkok International Film Festival (usually takes place over ten days in Jan). An annual chance to preview new and unusual Thai films alongside features and documentaries from around the world. Check ⓦwww.bangkokfilm.org for details.

Nakhon Sawan (Chinese New Year) (three days anytime between mid-Jan and late Feb). The new Chinese year is welcomed in with exuberant parades of dragons and lion dancers, Chinese opera performances, an international lion dance competition and a fireworks display. Also celebrated in Chinatowns across the country, especially in Bangkok and Phuket.

Chiang Mai *Flower Festival* (usually first weekend in Feb). Enormous floral sculptures are paraded through the streets.

Nationwide *Maha Puja* (particularly Wat Benjamabophit in Bangkok and Wat Phra That Doi Suthep in Chiang Mai; Feb full-moon day). A day of merit-making marks the occasion when 1250 disciples gathered spontaneously to hear the Buddha preach, and culminates with a candlelit procession round the local temple's bot.

Ngan Phra Buddha Chinnarat Phitsanulok *Ngan Phra Buddha Chinnarat* (mid-Feb). Thailand's second most important Buddha image is honoured with music, dance and *likay* performances.

Phetchaburi *Phra Nakhon Khiri fair* (mid-Feb). *Son-et-lumière* at Khao Wang palace.

Lopburi *King Narai Reign Fair* (Feb). Costumed processions and a *son-et-lumière* show at Narai's palace.

That Phanom *Ngan Phra That Phanom* (Feb). Thousands come to pay homage at the holiest shrine in Isaan, which houses relics of the Buddha.

Pattani *Ngan Lim Ko Niaw* (middle of third lunar month – Feb or March). Local goddess inspires devotees to walk through fire and perform other endurance tests in public.

Nationwide *Kite fights and flying contests* (particularly Sanam Luang, Bangkok; late Feb to mid-April).

Nakhon Si Thammarat *Hae Pha Khun That* (particularly for Maha Puja in Feb and Visakha Puja in May). Southerners gather to pay homage to the Buddha relics at Wat Mahathat, including a procession of long saffron cloth around the chedi.

Yala *ASEAN Barred Ground Dove festival* (first weekend March). International dove-cooing contests.

Phra Phutthabat, near Lopburi *Ngan Phra Phutthabat* (early Feb and early March). Pilgrimages to the Holy Footprint attract food and handicraft vendors and travelling players.

April and May

Mae Hong Son and Chiang Mai *Poy Sang Long* (early April). Young Thai Yai boys precede their ordination into monkhood by parading the streets in floral headdresses and festive garb. See p.385 for more.

Nationwide *Songkhran* (particularly Chiang Mai, Prasat Hin Khao Phanom Rung and Bangkok's Thanon Khao San; usually April 13–15). The most exuberant of the national festivals welcomes the Thai New Year with massive waterfights, sandcastle building in temple compounds and the inevitable parades and "Miss Songkhran" beauty contests.

Prasat Hin Khao Phanom Rung *Ngan Phanom Rung* (usually April). Daytime processions up to the eleventh-century Khmer ruins, followed by a *son-et-lumière*.

Nationwide *Visakha Puja* (particularly Bangkok's Wat Benjamabophit; May full-moon day). The holiest day of the Buddhist year, commemorating the birth, enlightenment and death of the Buddha all in one go; the most public and photogenic part is the candlelit evening procession around the wat.

Sanam Luang, Bangkok *Raek Na* (early May). The royal ploughing ceremony to mark the beginning of the rice-planting season; ceremonially clad Brahmin leaders parade sacred oxen and the royal plough, and interpret omens to forecast the year's rice yield.

Yasothon *Rocket Festival* (*Bun Bang Fai*) (weekend in mid-May). Beautifully crafted painted wooden rockets are paraded and fired to ensure plentiful rains; celebrated all over Isaan, but especially lively in Yasothon.

June–September

Hua Hin *Jazz Festival* (a weekend in late June). Well-known musicians from Thailand and abroad play for free at various special outdoor venues throughout the beach resort.

Dan Sai, near Loei *Phi Ta Khon* (end June or beginning July). Masked re-enactment of the Buddha's penultimate incarnation.

Ubon Ratchathani *Candle Festival* (*Asanha Puja*) (July, three days around the full moon). Ubon citizens celebrate the nationwide festival to mark the Buddha's first sermon and the subsequent beginning of the annual Buddhist retreat period (Khao Pansa) with parades of enormous wax sculptures.

Hua Hin *Elephant Polo Tournament* (five days in late September). Teams from around the world compete on elephant-back in this variation on the traditional game. Also features an elephant parade and various other elephant-related events, all of them free.

Nakhon Si Thammarat *Tamboon Deuan Sip* (Sept or Oct). Merit-making ceremonies to honour dead relatives accompanied by a ten-day fair on the town field.

October–December

Phuket and Trang *Vegetarian Festival* (*Ngan Kin Jeh*) (Oct or Nov). Chinese devotees become vegetarian for a nine-day period and then parade through town performing acts of self-mortification such as pushing skewers through their cheeks. Celebrated in Bangkok's Chinatown with most food vendors and restaurants turning vegetarian for about a fortnight .

Nationwide *Tak Bat Devo* **and** *Awk Pansa* **(especially Ubon Ratchathani and Nakhon Phanom; Oct full-moon day).** Offerings to monks and general merrymaking to celebrate the Buddha's descent to earth from Tavatimsa heaven and the end of the Khao Pansa retreat. Celebrated in Ubon with a procession of illuminated boats along the river and lots of firecrackers, and in Nakhon Phanom with a boat procession and Thailand–Laos dragon-boat races along the Mekong.

Surat Thani *Chak Phra* (mid-Oct). The town's chief Buddha images are paraded on floats down the streets and on barges along the river.

Nan and Phimai *Boat Races* (mid-Oct to mid-Nov). Longboat races and barge parades along town rivers.

Nationwide *Thawt Kathin* (mid-Oct to mid-Nov). The annual ceremonial giving of new robes by the laity to the monkhood at the end of the rains retreat.

Nationwide *Loy Krathong* **(particularly Sukhothai and Chiang Mai; full moon in late Oct or early Nov).** Baskets (*krathong*) of flowers and lighted candles are floated on any available body of water (such as ponds, rivers, lakes, canals and seashores) to honour water spirits and celebrate the end of the rainy season. Nearly every town puts on a big show, with bazaars, public entertainments, fireworks, and in Chiang Mai, the release of balloons; in Sukhothai it is the climax of a nine-day *son-et-lumière* festival.

Wat Saket, Bangkok *Ngan Wat Saket* **(first week of Nov).** Probably Thailand's biggest temple fair, held around the Golden Mount, with all the usual festival trappings.

Surin *Elephant Roundup* **(third weekend of Nov).** Two hundred elephants play team games, perform complex tasks and parade in battle dress.

Kanchanaburi *River Kwai Bridge Festival* **(ten nights from the last week of Nov into the first week of Dec).** Spectacular *son et lumière* at the infamous bridge.

Khon Kaen *Silk Festival* (Nov 29–Dec 10). Weavers from around the province come to town to sell their lengths of silk.

Ayutthaya *World Heritage Site Festival* **(mid-Dec).** Week-long celebration, including a nightly historical *son-et-lumière* romp, to commemorate the town's UNESCO designation.

Entertainment and sport

Most travellers confine their experience of Thai traditional culture to a one-off attendance at a Bangkok tourist show, but these extravaganzas are often less rewarding than authentic folk theatre, music (see p.827) and sports performances. Traditional sport fits neatly into the same category as the more usual theatrical classifications, not only because it can be graceful, even dance-like, to watch, but because, in the case of Thai boxing, Thai classical music plays an important role in the proceedings. Bangkok has a few authentic fixed venues for dance and a couple for Thai boxing; otherwise it's a question of keeping your eyes open in upcountry areas for signs that a travelling troupe may soon turn up. This is most likely at festivals and fairs, which sometimes also feature some of the more traditional pastimes such as (illegal) gambling on the outcome of cock fights and fighting fish contests.

Drama and dance

Drama pretty much equals **dance** in Thai theatre, and many of the traditional dance-dramas are based on the Hindu epic the *Ramayana* (in Thai, *Ramakien*), a classic adventure tale of good versus evil which is taught in all the schools. Not understanding the plots can be a major disadvantage, so try reading an abridged version beforehand (see "Books" p.849) and check out the wonderfully imaginative murals at Wat Phra Kaeo in Bangkok, after which you'll certainly be able to sort the goodies from the baddies, if little else. There are three broad categories of traditional Thai dance-drama – *khon, lakhon* and *likay* – described below in descending order of refinement.

Khon

The most spectacular form of traditional Thai theatre is **khon**, a stylized drama performed in masks and elaborate costumes by a troupe of highly trained classical dancers. There's little room for individual interpretation in these dances, as all the movements follow a strict choreography that's been passed down through generations: each graceful, angular gesture depicts a precise event, action or emotion which will be familiar to educated *khon* audiences. The dancers don't speak, and the story is chanted and sung by a chorus who stand at the side of the stage, accompanied by a classical *phipat* orchestra.

A typical *khon* performance features several of the best-known **Ramayana** episodes, in which the main characters are recognized by their masks, headdresses and heavily brocaded costumes. Gods and humans don't wear masks, but it's generally easy enough to distinguish the hero Rama and heroine Sita from the action; they always wear tall gilded headdresses and often appear in a threesome with Rama's brother Lakshaman. Monkey **masks** are always open-mouthed, almost laughing, and come in several colours: monkey army chief Hanuman always wears white, and his two right-hand men – Nilanol, the god of fire, and Nilapat, the god of death – wear red and black respectively. In contrast, the demons have grim mouths, clamped shut or snarling out of usually green faces; Totsagan, king of the demons, wears a green face in battle and a gold one during peace, but always sports a two-tier headdress carved with two rows of faces.

Khon is performed regularly at Bangkok's National Theatre and nightly at various cultural **shows** staged by tourist restaurants in Bangkok, Phuket and Pattaya. Even if you don't see a show, you're bound to come across copies of the masks worn by the main *khon* characters, which are sold as souvenirs all over the country and constitute an art form in their own right.

Lakhon

Serious and refined, **lakhon** is derived from *khon* but is used to dramatize a greater range of stories, including Buddhist *Jataka* tales, local folk dramas and of course the *Ramayana*. The form you're most likely to come across is *lakhon chatri*, which is performed at shrines like Bangkok's Erawan and *lak muang* as entertainment for the spirits and a token of gratitude from worshippers. Usually female, the *lakhon chatri* dancers perform as a group rather than as individual characters, executing sequences which, like *khon* movements, all have minute and particular symbolism. They wear similarly decorative costumes but no masks, and dance to the music of a *phipat* orchestra.

Unfortunately, as resident shrine troupes tend to repeat the same dances a dozen times a day, it's rarely the sublime display it's cracked up to be. Occasionally the National Theatre features the more elegantly executed *lakhon nai*, a dance form that used to be performed at the Thai court and often retells the *Ramayana*.

Likay

Likay is a much more popular derivative of *khon* – more light-hearted with lots of comic interludes, bawdy jokes and over-the-top acting and singing. Some *likay* troupes perform *Ramayana* excerpts, but a lot of them adapt pot-boiler romances or write their own. Depending on the show, costumes are either traditional as in *khon* and *lakhon*, modern and Western as in films, or a mixture of both. *Likay* troupes travel around the country doing shows on makeshift outdoor stages wherever they think they'll get an audience; temples sometimes hire them out for fairs and there's usually a *likay* stage of some kind at a festival.

Performances are often free and generally last for about five hours, with the audience strolling in and out of the show, cheering and joking with the cast throughout. Televised *likay* dramas get huge audiences and always follow romantic plot-lines.

Nang

Nang, or shadow plays, are said to have been the earliest dramas performed in Thailand, but now are rarely seen except in the far south, where the Malaysian influence ensures an appreciative audience for *nang thalung*. Crafted from buffalo hide, the two-dimensional *nang thalung* puppets play out scenes from popular dramas against a back-lit screen, while the storyline is told through songs, chants and musical interludes. An even rarer *nang* form is the *nang yai*, which uses enormous cut-outs of whole scenes rather than just individual characters, so the play becomes something like an animated film. For more on shadow puppets and puppetry, see p.631.

Film and video

All sizeable towns have a **cinema** or two (Bangkok has over forty; see p.186) and tickets generally start at around B60. In some rural areas, villagers still have to make do with the travelling cinema, or *nang klarng plaeng*, which sets up a mobile screen in Wat compounds or other public spaces, and often entertains the whole village in one sitting (see p.843 for more on these). However makeshift the cinema, the **king's anthem** is always played before every screening, during which the audience is expected to stand up.

Fast-paced Chinese blockbusters have long dominated the programmes at Thai cinemas, serving up a low-grade cocktail of sex, spooks, violence and comedy. Not understanding the dialogue is rarely a drawback, as the storylines tend to be simple and the visuals more entertaining than the words. In the cities, Western **films** are also pretty big, and new releases often get subtitled rather than dubbed. In recent years, however, Thailand's own film industry has been enjoying a bit of a boom, and in the larger cities and resorts you may be lucky enough to come across one of the bigger Thai hits showing with English subtitles. See "Contexts" on p.842 for an introduction to Thai cinema.

Thai boxing

Thai boxing (*muay Thai*) enjoys a following similar to soccer or baseball in the West: every province has a stadium and whenever the sport is shown on TV you can be sure that large noisy crowds will gather round the sets in streetside restaurants and noodle shops. The best place to see Thai boxing is at one of Bangkok's two main stadia, which between them hold bouts every night of the week and on some afternoons as well (see p.187).

There's a strong spiritual and **ritualistic** dimension to *muay Thai*, adding grace to an otherwise brutal sport. Each boxer enters the ring to the wailing music of a three-piece *phipat* orchestra, often flamboyantly attired in a lurid silk robe over the statutory red or blue boxer shorts. The fighter then bows, first in the direction of his birthplace and then to the north, south, east and west, honouring both his teachers and the spirit of the ring. Next he performs a slow dance, claiming the audience's attention and demonstrating his prowess as a performer.

Any part of the body except the head may be used as an **offensive weapon** in *muay Thai*, and all parts except the groin are fair targets. Kicks to the head are the blows which cause most knockouts. As the action hots up, so the orchestra speeds up its tempo and the betting in the audience becomes more frenetic. It can be a gruesome business, but it was far bloodier before modern boxing gloves were made compulsory in the 1930s – combatants used to wrap their fists with hemp impregnated with a face-lacerating dosage of ground glass.

For further **information** about Thai boxing, visit ⓦwww.tat.or.th/do/muay.htm. A number of *muay Thai* gyms and camps offer training **courses** for foreigners, including the Muay Thai Institute in Pathum Thani, Bangkok (ⓣ02 992 0096, ⓕ02 992 0095); Fairtex Muay Thai in Samut Prakan, near Bangkok (ⓣ02 757 5148, ⓦwww.fairtexbkk.com); Lanna Muay Thai in Chiang Mai (ⓣ053 892102, ⓦwww.lannamuaythai.com); and the Muay Thai Martial Arts Academy (MTMAA) in Surat Thani (ⓣ077 282816, ⓦwww.muaythaitraining.com). You can also do one-off training sessions at a couple of gyms in central Bangkok; see p.187 for details.

Takraw

You're very unlikely to stumble unexpectedly on an outdoor bout of *muay Thai*, but you're sure to come across some form of **takraw** game at some point, whether in a public park, a wat compound or just in a backstreet alley. Played with a very light rattan ball (or one made of plastic to look like rattan), the basic aim of the game is to keep the ball off the ground. To do this you can use any part of your body except your hands, so a well-played *takraw* game looks extremely balletic, with players leaping and arching to get a good strike.

There are at least five versions of **competitive takraw**, based on the same principles. The one featured in the Southeast Asian Games and most frequently in school tournaments is played over a volleyball net and involves two teams of three; the other most popular competitive version has a team ranged round a basketball net trying to score as many goals as possible within a limited time period before the next team replaces them and tries to outscore them.

Other *takraw* games introduce more complex rules (like kicking the ball backwards with your heels through a ring made with your arms behind your back) and many assign points according to the skill displayed by individual players rather than per goal or dropped ball. Outside of school playing fields, proper *takraw* tournaments are rare, though they do sometimes feature as entertainment at Buddhist funerals.

Spas and traditional massage

The last few years have seen an explosion in the number of spas being opened around Thailand – mainly in the grounds of the poshest hotels, but also as small, affordable walk-in centres in towns. With their focus on indulgent self-pampering, spas are usually associated with high-spending tourists, but the treatments on offer at Thailand's five-star hotels are often little different from those used by traditional medical practitioners, who have long held that massage and herbs are the best way to restore physical and mental well-being.

Thai massage is based on the principle that many physical and emotional problems are caused by the blocking of vital energy channels within the body. The masseur uses his or her feet, heels, knees and elbows, as well as hands, to exert a gentle pressure on these channels, supplementing this acupressure-style technique by pulling and pushing the limbs into yogic stretches. This distinguishes Thai massage from most other massage styles, which are more concerned with tissue manipulation. One is supposed to emerge from a Thai massage feeling both relaxed and energized, and it is said that regular massages produce long-term benefits in muscles as well as stimulating the circulation and aiding natural detoxification. Thais will visit a masseur for many conditions, including fevers, colds and muscle strain, but bodies that are not sick are also considered to benefit from the restorative powers of a massage, and nearly every hotel and guest house will be able to put you in touch with a masseur. On the more popular beaches, it can be hard to walk a few hundred metres without being offered a massage – something Thai tourists are just as enthusiastic about as foreigners. Thai masseurs do not use oils or lotions and the client is treated on a mat or mattress; you'll often be given a pair of loose-fitting trousers and perhaps a loose top to change into. A session should ideally last two hours and will cost from around B200–300.

The **science** behind Thai massage has its roots in Indian Ayurvedic medicine, which classifies each component of the body according to one of the four elements (earth, water, fire and air), and holds that balancing these elements within the body is crucial to good health. Many of the stretches and manipulations fundamental to Thai massage are thought to have derived from yogic practices introduced to Thailand from India by Buddhist missionaries in about the second century BC; Chinese acupuncture and reflexology have also had a strong influence. In the nineteenth century, King Rama III ordered a series of murals illustrating the principles of Thai massage to be painted around the courtyard of Bangkok's Wat Pho, and they are still in place today, along with statues of ascetics depicted in typical massage poses. **Wat Pho** has been the leading school of Thai massage for hundreds of years, and it is possible to take courses there as well as to receive a massage; see p.130 for details. Masseurs who trained at Wat Pho are considered to be the best in the country and masseurs all across Thailand advertise this as a credential, whether or not it is true. Many Thais consider blind masseurs to be especially sensitive practitioners. While Wat Pho is the most famous place to take a **course** in Thai massage, many foreigners interested in learning this ancient science head for Chiang Mai, which offers the biggest concentration of massage schools, though you will find others all over Thailand, including in Bangkok and at southern beach resorts.

All **spas** in Thailand feature traditional Thai massage and herbal therapies in their programmes, but most also offer dozens of other international treatments, including facials, aromatherapy, Swedish massage and various body wraps. Spa centres in upmarket hotels and resorts are usually open to non-guests but generally need to be booked in advance; day spas that are not attached to hotels are found in some of the bigger cities and resorts, including Bangkok, Chiang Mai, Ko Samui and Phuket, and some of these may not require reservations. Thailand's most famous deluxe spas include the very exclusive Chiva Som holistic therapy centre in Hua Hin (see p.570); the Oriental Spa, run by the renowned five-star *Oriental Hotel* in Bangkok (see p.118); the Banyan Tree Spa at the hotel of the same name in Phuket (see p.680); the Lanna Spa at *The Regent* hotel in Chiang Mai (see p.353); and the Six Senses Spa at the *Evason* in Pak Nam Pran (see p.574).

Meditation centres and retreats

Of the hundreds of meditation temples in Thailand, a few cater specifically for foreigners by holding meditation sessions and retreats in English; novices and practised meditators alike are generally welcome. The meditation taught is mostly Vipassana, or "insight", which emphasizes the minute observation of internal sensations; the other main technique you'll come across is Samatha, which aims to calm the mind and develop concentration (these two techniques are not entirely separate, since you cannot have insight without some degree of concentration). To join a one-off class in Bangkok, call to check times and then just turn up; for overnight and longer visits to wats in more remote areas, you usually have to contact the monastery in advance, either directly or via the WFB (see below).

Longer **retreats** are for the serious-minded only. All the temples listed on p.70 welcome both male and female English-speakers, but strict segregation of the sexes is enforced and many places observe a vow of silence. Reading and writing are also discouraged, and you'll generally not be allowed to leave the retreat complex unless absolutely necessary, so try to bring whatever you'll need in with you. Some retreats require you to wear modest, white clothing – check ahead whether there is a shop at the retreat complex or whether you are expected to bring this with you.

An average day at any one of these monasteries starts with a wake-up call at 4am and includes several hours of group meditation and chanting, as well as time put aside for chores and personal reflection. However long their stay, visitors are usually expected to keep the eight Buddhist precepts, the most restrictive of these being the abstention from food after midday and from alcohol, tobacco, drugs and sex at all times. Most wats ask for a minimal daily donation (around B150) to cover the costs of the simple accommodation and food.

Further details about many of the temples listed below – including how to get there – are given in the relevant sections in the Guide. Though a little out of date, *A Guide to Buddhist Monasteries and Meditation Centres in Thailand* contains plenty of useful general and specific information; originally published by the World Fellowship of Buddhists, it's now accessible online at Ⓦwww.dharmanet.org/thai_94.html.

Meditation centres and retreat temples

For information on **Wat Khao Tham** on Ko Pha Ngan, see p.611; **Wat Mahathat** in Bangkok, p.133; **Wat Phra That Si Chom Thong** near Chiang Mai, p.374; **Wat Ram Poeng** in Chiang Mai, see p.331; and **Wat Suan Mokkh** in Chaiya, p.585.

House of Dhamma Insight Meditation Centre 26 Soi Lardprao 15, Bangkok Ⓣ02 511 0439, Ⓦwww.angelfire.com/al/dhamma/home.html. Vipassana meditation courses in English on the first, second and third Sunday of the month, and weekend and week-long retreats organized. Courses in reiki and other subjects available.

Thailand Vipassana Centre Ⓦwww.dhamma.org. Dhamma Kamala, 200 Ban Nernpasuk, Prachinburi; and at Dhamma Abha, 138 Ban Huayplu, Phitsanulok. Frequent ten-day residential courses in a Burmese Vipassana tradition. Foreign students must pre-register by email (application form available on the website) with Khun Thaveephol or Khun Varattada on Ⓔbehappy@loxinfo.co.th.

Wat Pa Nanachat Ban Bung Wai, Amphoe Warinchamrab, Ubon Ratchathani 34310. A group of foreign monks have established this forest monastery, 17km west of Ubon Ratchathani, specifically for farangs who want to immerse themselves in Anapanasati meditation (mindfulness with breathing, a form of Samatha). Short- and long-term visitors are welcome, but the atmosphere is serious and intense and not for curious sightseers, and accommodation for students is limited, so you should write to the monastery before visiting.

World Fellowship of Buddhists (WFB) 616 Benjasiri Park, Soi Medhinivet off Soi 24, Thanon Sukhumvit, Bangkok Ⓣ02 661 1284–90, Ⓦwww.wfb-hq.org. The main information centre for advice on English-speaking retreats in Thailand. Holds a Buddhist discussion group and meditation session in English on the first Sunday of every month, with dharma lectures and discussions on the second Sunday.

Cultural hints

Tourist literature has so successfully marketed Thailand as the "Land of Smiles" that a lot of farangs arrive in the country expecting to be forgiven any outrageous behaviour. This is just not the case: there are some things so universally sacred in Thailand that even a hint of disrespect will cause deep offence. TAT publishes a special leaflet on the subject, entitled *Dos and Don'ts in Thailand*, which is also reproduced on their website at Ⓦwww.tat.or.th – it's well worth reading before you travel.

The monarchy

The worst thing you can possibly do is to bad-mouth the **royal family**. The monarchy might be a constitutional one, but almost every household displays a picture of King Bhumibol and Queen Sirikit in a prominent position, and respectful crowds mass whenever either of them makes a public appearance. The second of their four children, Crown Prince Vajiralongkorn, is the heir to the throne; his younger sister, Princess Royal Maha Chakri Sirindhorn, is often on TV and in the English newspapers as she is involved in many charitable projects. When addressing or speaking about royalty, Thais use a special language full of deference, called *rajasap* (literally "royal language").

Aside from keeping any anti-monarchy sentiments to yourself, you should be prepared to stand when the **king's anthem** is played at the beginning of every cinema programme, and to stop in your tracks if the town you're in plays the **national anthem** over its public address system – many small towns do this twice a day at 8am and again at 6pm, as do some train stations. A less obvious point: as the king's head features on all Thai currency, you should never step on a coin or banknote, which is tantamount to kicking the king in the face.

Religion

Almost equally insensitive would be to disregard certain **religious precepts**. Buddhism plays an essential part in the lives of most Thais, and Buddhist monuments should be treated with respect – which basically means wearing long trousers or knee-length skirts, covering your arms and removing your shoes whenever you visit one.

All **Buddha images** are sacred, however small, however tacky, however ruined, and should never be used as a backdrop for a portrait photo, clambered over, placed in a position of inferiority or treated in any manner that could be construed as disrespectful. In an attempt to prevent foreigners from committing any kind of transgression the government requires a special licence for all Buddha statues exported from the country.

Monks come only just beneath the monarchy in the social hierarchy, and they too are addressed and discussed in a special language. If there's a monk around, he'll always get a seat on the bus, usually right at the back. Theoretically, monks are forbidden to have any close contact with women, which means, as a female, you mustn't sit or stand next to a monk, or even brush against his robes; if it's essential to pass him something, put the object down so that he can then pick it up – never hand it over directly. Nuns, however, get treated like ordinary women.

See Contexts p.811 for more on religious practices in Thailand.

The body

The Western liberalism embraced by the Thai sex industry is very unrepresentative of the majority Thai attitude to the body. **Clothing** – or the lack of it – is what bothers Thais most about tourist behaviour. As mentioned above, you need to dress modestly when entering temples, but the same also applies to other important buildings and all public places. Stuffy and sweaty as it sounds, you should keep short shorts and vests for the real tourist resorts, and be especially diligent about covering up and, for women, wearing bras in rural areas. Baring your flesh on beaches is very much a Western practice: when Thais go swimming they often do so fully clothed, and they find topless and nude bathing extremely unpalatable. It's not illegal, but it won't win you many friends.

According to ancient Hindu belief, the **head** is the most sacred part of the body and the **feet** are the most unclean. This belief, imported into Thailand, means that it's very rude to touch another person's head or to point your feet either at a human being or at a sacred image – when sitting on a temple floor, for example, you should tuck your legs beneath you rather than stretch them out towards the Buddha. These hierarchies also forbid people from wearing shoes (which are even more unclean than feet) inside temples and most private homes, and – by extension – Thais take offence when they see someone sitting on the "head", or prow, of a boat. Putting your feet up on a table, a chair or a pillow is also considered very uncouth, and Thais will always take their shoes off if they need to stand on a train or bus seat to get to the luggage rack, for example. On a more practical note, the **left hand** is used for washing after defecating, so Thais never use it to put food in their mouth, pass things or shake hands – as a farang though, you'll be assumed to have different customs, so left-handers shouldn't worry unduly.

Social conventions

In fact, Thais very rarely shake hands anyway, using the **wai** to greet and say goodbye and to acknowledge respect, gratitude or apology. A prayer-like gesture made with raised hands, the *wai* changes according to the relative status of the two people involved: Thais can instantaneously assess which *wai* to use when, but as a farang your safest bet is to go for the "stranger's" *wai*, which requires that your hands be raised close to your chest and your fingertips placed just below your chin. If someone makes a *wai* at you, you should generally *wai* back, but it's safer not to initiate.

Public displays of **physical affection** in Thailand are more common between friends of the same sex than between lovers, whether hetero- or homosexual. Holding hands and hugging is as common among male friends as with females, so if you're given fairly intimate caresses by a Thai acquaintance of the same sex, don't assume you're being propositioned.

Finally, there are three specifically Thai **concepts** you're bound to come across, which may help you comprehend a sometimes *laissez-faire* attitude to delayed buses and other inconveniences. The first, **jai yen**, translates literally as "cool heart" and is something everyone tries to maintain – most Thais hate raised voices, visible irritation and confrontations of any kind. Related to this is the oft-quoted response to a difficulty, **mai pen rai** – "never mind", "no problem" or "it can't be helped" – the verbal equivalent of an open-handed shoulder shrug, which has its basis in the Buddhist notion of karma (see "Religion", p.814). And then there's **sanuk**, the wide-reaching philosophy of "fun", which, crass as it sounds, Thais do their best to inject into any situation, even work. Hence the crowds of inebriated Thais who congregate at waterfalls and other beauty spots on public holidays, the inability to do almost anything without high-volume musical accompaniment, and the national water-fight which takes place every April on streets right across Thailand.

Thai names

Although all Thais have a first **name** and a family name, everyone is addressed by their first name – even when meeting strangers – prefixed by the title **"Khun"** (Mr/Ms); no one is ever addressed as Khun Surname, and even the phone book lists people by their given name. In Thailand you will often be addressed in an Anglicized version of this convention, as Mr Paul or Miss Lucy for example. Bear in mind though, that when a man is introduced to you as Khun Pirom, his wife will definitely not be Khun Pirom as well, as that would be like calling them Mr and Mrs Paul (or whatever). Among friends and relatives, **Phii** ("older brother/sister") is used instead of Khun when addressing older familiars (though as a tourist you're on surer ground with Khun), and **Nong** is used for younger ones.

Many Thai **first names** come from ancient Sanskrit and have an auspicious meaning; for example, Boon means good deeds, Porn means blessings, Siri means glory and Thawee means to increase. However, Thais of all ages are commonly known by the **nickname** given them soon after birth rather than by their official first name. This tradition arises out of a deep-rooted superstition that once a child has been officially named the spirits will begin to take an unhealthy interest in them, so a nickname is used instead to confuse the spirits. Common nicknames – which often bear no resemblance to the adult's personality or physique – include Yai (Big), Oun (Fat) and Muu (Pig); Lek or Noi (Little), Nok (Bird), Noo (Mouse) and Kung (Shrimp); Neung (Number One/Eldest), Sawng (Number Two), Saam (Number Three); and English nicknames like Apple and Joy.

Family names were only introduced in 1913 (by Rama VI, who invented many of the aristocracy's surnames himself), and are used only in very formal situations, always in conjunction with the first name. It's quite usual for good friends never to know each other's surname. Ethnic Thais generally have short surnames like Somboon or Srisai, while the long, convoluted family names – such as Sonthanasumpun – usually indicate Chinese origin, not because they are phonetically Chinese but because many Chinese immigrants have chosen to adopt new Thai surnames and Thai law states that every newly created surname must be unique. Thus anyone who wants to change their surname must submit a shortlist of five unique Thai names – each to a maximum length of ten Thai characters – to be checked against a database of existing names. As more and more names are taken, Chinese family names get increasingly unwieldy, and more easily distinguishable from the pithy old Thai names.

snorkelling **equipment** goes, the most important thing is that you buy or rent a mask that fits. To check the fit, hold the mask against your face, then breathe in and remove your hands – if it falls off, it'll leak water. If you're buying equipment, you should be able to kit yourself out with a mask, snorkel and fins for about B1000, available from most dive centres. Few places rent fins, but a mask and snorkel set usually costs about B50 a day to rent, and if you're going on a snorkelling day-trip they are often included in the price. When renting equipment you'll nearly always be required to pay a deposit.

National parks

Over the last half century more than one hundred areas across Thailand have been singled out for conservation as **national parks**, with the dual aim of protecting the country's natural resources and creating educational and recreational facilities for the public; these parks generally make the best places to observe wildlife. One of the best for seeing larger animals is **Khao Yai** (see p.478), the most popular national park, about three hours northeast of Bangkok. If you join a night safari here, you could be rewarded with sightings of elephants, deer, civets, even tigers, whilst during the day you'll come across gibbons and hornbills at the very least. Bird-watchers consider the national park mountains of **Doi Suthep** (see p.347) and **Doi Inthanon** (see p.373) – both close to Chiang Mai – primary observation spots, and the coastal flats at **Khao Sam Roi Yot** (see p.575) and the sanctuaries of **Thale Noi** (see p.747) and **Khu Khut** (see p.774) in the south are also good spots. Many of southern Thailand's protected reserves are marine parks, including the archipelago of **Ko Similan** (see p.664), **Ko Surin** (see p.652), **Ang Thong** (see p.593) and **Ko Tarutao** (see p.758).

All the national parks are administered by the **Royal Forestry Department** at 61 Thanon Phaholyothin, Chatuchak District, Bangkok 10900 (Ⓣ02 579 5734 or 02 579 7223, Ⓦwww.forest.go.th/default_e.asp and www.thaiforestbooking.com/national-park-eng. htm), about forty minutes' bus ride north of Democracy Monument. To book national park bungalows in advance (advisable for weekends and public holidays) you need to pay up front; see "Accommodation" on p.46 for details.

For all their environmental benefits, national parks are a huge source of **controversy** in Thailand, with vested interests such as fishermen, farmers, loggers, poachers and the tourist industry pitted against environmentalists and certain sections of the government. The Royal Forestry Department has itself come in for voluble criticism over the last few years, particularly over the filming of *The Beach* on the national park island of Ko Phi Phi Leh, and in 2000 when – without warning – it raised the **foreigners' entrance fee** levied at most national parks from B20 to B200 (B100 for children). See "Flora, Fauna and Environmental Issues" on p.816 for a fuller account of these issues and for a more detailed introduction to Thailand's wildlife.

Most parks have limited public facilities, very few signposted walking trails and a paucity of usable maps. Nor are many of the parks well served by public transport – some can take a day to reach from the nearest large town, via a route that entails several bus and songthaew changes and a final lengthy walk. This factor, combined with the expense and poor quality of most national park accommodation, means that if you're planning to do a serious tour of the parks you should consider **bringing a tent** (all parks allow this; see p.46 for details) and be prepared to rent your own transport.

Rock-climbing

The limestone karsts that pepper south Thailand's Andaman coast make ideal playgrounds for **rock-climbers**, and the sport has really taken off here in the last decade. Most climbing is centred round **East Railay** and **Ton Sai** beaches on Laem Phra Nang in Krabi province (see p.709), where there are dozens of routes within easy walking distance of tourist bungalows, restaurants and beaches. Several climbing schools have already established centres here, providing instruction, guides and all the necessary equipment. Half-day introductory courses at East Railay and Ton Sai cost B800, a full day's guided climbing is B1500 and a three-day course B5000. Equipment rental is charged at about B1000 per day for two people. Ko Phi Phi (see p.721) also offers a few interesting routes and a couple of climbing schools. There are also less developed climbing areas near Chiang Mai (see p.322) and Ko Tao (see p.627), as well as in Lopburi and Phetchaburi. For further details about climbing courses, visit the rock-climbing schools' websites listed on p.709. For an introduction to climbing in Thailand, plus advice on where to climb and what equipment to bring, as well as reviews of climb shops and a climbers' forum, see Ⓦwww.simonfoley.com/climbing.

Sea-kayaking and whitewater-rafting

Sea-kayaking is also centred around Thailand's Andaman coast, whose limestone outcrops, sea caves, hongs (hidden lagoons), mangrove swamps and picturesque shorelines all make for rewarding paddling. See p.706 for an introduction to the kayaking highlights of the Krabi area on the Andaman coast.

The longest-established **sea-kayaking operator** in Thailand is trailblazing John Gray SeaCanoe (Ⓦwww.seacanoe.com), which always seems to get good reviews. They run day-trips out of Phuket (see p.679), Phang Nga and Ao Nang, which cost B1400–3500 per person (children aged 4–12 half-price), and also offer three- to six-day kayaking expeditions. In typical Thai style, John Gray SeaCanoe's success has spawned a lot of copycat operations, most of which are based in Krabi (see p.706), Ao Nang (see p.713) and Phuket (see p.679), averaging B2700 for a full day or about B900 for half a day. Some of these operators also rent out kayaks from about B100 per hour, as does one outfit on Ko Phi Phi. Phuket-based Paddle Asia (Ⓦwww.paddleasia.com) also offer week-long sea-kayaking trips around the Trang islands and the Tarutao National Marine Park islands at US$100–150 per person per day. There are a handful of kayaking operators over on Ko Samui, listed on p.594, who organize trips around the picturesque islands of the Ang Thong National Marine Park.

You can go **river-kayaking** and **whitewater-rafting** on several rivers in north, west and south Thailand. Some stretches of these rivers can run quite fast, particularly during the rainy season from July to November, but there are plenty of options for novices, too. The best time is from October through February; during the hot season (Mar–June), many rivers run too low. The most popular whitewater-rafting rivers include the Umphang and Mae Khlong rivers near Umphang (see p.304) and the Pai River near Pai (see p.391). Gentler rafting excursions take place on the River Kwai and its tributaries near Kanchanaburi (see p.235), and on the Sok River in Khao Sok National Park (see p.659). Southwest of Chiang Mai, rafts can be rented from the adjacent national park headquarters for trips in Ob Luang Gorge (see p.377).

Gay Thailand

Buddhist tolerance and a national abhorrence of confrontation and victimization combine to make Thai society relatively tolerant of homosexuality, if not exactly positive about same-sex relationships. Most Thais are extremely private and discreet about being gay, generally pursuing a "don't ask, don't tell" understanding with their family. However, most Thais are horrified by the idea of gay-bashing and generally regard it as unthinkable to spurn a child or relative for being gay.

Hardly any public figures are out, yet the predilections of several respected social, political and entertainment figures are widely known and accepted. **Transvestites** (known as *katoey* or ladyboys) and **transsexuals** are also a lot more visible in Thailand than in the West. You'll find cross-dressers doing ordinary jobs, even in small upcountry towns, and there are a number of transvestites and transsexuals in the public eye too – including national volleyball stars and champion *muay Thai* boxers. The government tourist office vigorously promotes the transvestite cabarets in Pattaya and Phuket, all of which are advertised as family entertainment. *Katoey* also regularly appear as characters in soap operas, TV comedies and films, where they are depicted as harmless figures of fun. Richard Totman's *The Third Sex* offers an interesting insight into Thai *katoey*, their experiences in society and public attitudes towards them; see "Books" on p.847 for a review.

There is no mention of homosexuality at all in Thai law, which means that the age of consent for gay sex is sixteen, the same as for heterosexuals. However, this also means that gay rights are not protected under Thai law.

The scene

Thailand's gay scene is mainly focused on mainstream **venues** like karaoke bars, restaurants, massage parlours, gyms, saunas and escort agencies. For the sake of discretion, gay venues are usually intermingled with equivalent straight venues. As in the straight scene, venues reflect class and status differences. Expensive international-style places are very popular in Bangkok, attracting upper- and middle-class gays, many of whom have travelled or been educated abroad and developed Western tastes. These places also attract a contingent of Thais seeking foreign sugar daddies. The biggest concentrations of farang-friendly gay bars and clubs are found in Bangkok, Chiang Mai, Phuket and Pattaya, and are listed in the Guide; the gay communities of Bangkok, Phuket and Pattaya all host flamboyant annual **Gay Pride festivals** (check upcoming dates on the websites listed below).

Thailand's gay scene is heavily male, and there are hardly any **lesbian**-only venues, though Bangkok has a few mixed gay bars. Thai lesbians generally eschew the word lesbian, which in Thailand is associated with male fantasies, instead referring to themselves as either *tom* (for tomboy) or *dee* (for lady). Where possible, we've listed lesbian meeting-places, but unless otherwise specified, gay means male throughout this Guide.

Although excessively physical displays of affection are frowned upon for both heterosexuals and homosexuals, Western gay couples should get no hassle about being seen together in public – it's much more acceptable, and common, in fact, for friends of the same sex (gay or not) to walk hand-in-hand, than for heterosexual couples to do so.

The farang-oriented gay **sex industry** is a tiny but highly visible part of Thailand's gay scene. With its tawdry floor shows and host services, it bears a dispiriting resemblance to the straight sex trade, and is similarly most active in Bangkok, Pattaya, Patong (on Phuket) and Chiang Mai. Like their female counterparts in the heterosexual fleshpots, many of the boys working in the gay sex bars that dominate these districts are underage (anyone caught having sex with a prostitute below the age of 18 faces imprisonment). A significant number of gay prostitutes are gay by economic necessity rather than by inclination. As with the straight sex scene, we do not list the commercial gay sex bars in the Guide.

Information and contacts for gay travellers

Anjaree PO Box 322, Rajdamnoen PO, Bangkok 10200 Ⓔ anjaree@loxinfo.com. General information on the lesbian community in Thailand.
Dragon Castle's Gay Asia Ⓦ dragoncastle.net. Carries informed advice on getting involved in the gay scene, plus some venue listings.
Dreaded Ned's Ⓦ www.dreadedned.com. Information on almost every gay venue in the country, plus plenty of links.
Gay Phuket Ⓦ www.gayphuket.com. Phuket's Patong Beach is Thailand's biggest gay centre after Bangkok, and the website list dozens of gay bars and clubs, as well as gay-friendly hotels. Also sponsors the annual Gay Festival every Jan/Feb.
Thai Guys Ⓦ www.thaiguys.org. Online version of the magazine, mostly comprising contributors' stories about gay life in Thailand.
Utopia Ⓦ www.utopia-asia.com. Asia's best gay and lesbian website lists clubs, events and accommodation for gays and lesbians and has useful links to other sites in Asia and the rest of the world. Its offshoot, Utopia Tours, is a gay-oriented travel agency for trips within Thailand and the rest of Asia; it also offers a gay tour-guide service, called Thai Friends, through which English-speaking Thai gay men volunteer to show tourists the sights of Bangkok. It's a strictly non-sexual arrangement and can be organized through their website or at their desk inside the Tarntawan Palace Hotel, 119/5–10 Thanon Suriwong (Ⓣ 02 238 3227, Ⓦ www.utopia-tours.com).

Travellers with disabilities

Thailand makes few provisions for its disabled citizens and this obviously affects travellers with disabilities, but these drawbacks are often balanced out by the affordability of small luxuries such as taxis, comfortable hotels and personal tour guides, all of which can help smooth the way considerably. Most travellers with disabilities find Thais only too happy to offer assistance where they can, but hiring a local tour guide to accompany you on a day's sightseeing is particularly recommended – for example, with the help of a Thai speaker you will find it much easier to arrange access to temples, museums and other places that may at first not seem wheelchair-friendly. Government tour guides can be arranged through any TAT office.

Wheelchair-users will have a hard time negotiating the uneven pavements, which are high to allow for flooding and invariably lack dropped kerbs, and will find it difficult to board buses and trains; however, in Bangkok, some Skytrain stations and all subway stations have lifts. Crossing the road can be a trial, particularly in Bangkok and other big cities, where it's usually a question of climbing steps up to a bridge rather than taking a ramped underpass.

One way to cut down the hassle is to go with a **tour** that guarantees adapted facilities and accessible transport and/or escorts to otherwise inaccessible sights. In the UK, Kuoni (see p.13) tailors package deals to specific needs. You might also want to contact the Bangkok based Help and Care Travel Company (ⓣ02 720 5395, ⓦwww.wheelchairtours.com), which designs accessible holidays in Thailand for slow walkers and wheelchair-users, can provide transport and escort services, and on its website carries a (short) list of wheelchair-accessible hotels in the main tourist centres. In Chiang Mai, *Baan Khun Daeng* (ⓣ053 242874, ⓦmembers.chello.nl/danblokker/e_home.html) is a wheelchair-accessible guest house run by a wheelchair-user who can also arrange accessible tours around north Thailand.

The more expensive international **airlines** tend to be the better equipped: British Airways, Thai Airways and Qantas all carry aisle wheelchairs and have at least one toilet adapted for disabled passengers, but need to be notified in advance. The All Go Here website (ⓦwww.allgohere.com) reviews the accessibility and services of many major international airlines. Staff at Bangkok airport are generally helpful and, if asked, should be able to whisk you past immigration queues; they will also provide wheelchairs if necessary.

Contacts for travellers with disabilities

For general **information** on travelling abroad with a disability, get in touch with the organizations listed below, browse the exhaustive links at ⓦwww.independentliving.org/links/links-travel-and-leisure.html or post a query on the forum for travellers with disabilities at ⓦthorntree.lonelyplanet.com.

UK and Ireland

Access Travel ⓣ01942/888844, ⓦwww.access-travel.co.uk. Tour operator who can arrange flights, transfers and accommodation for travellers with disabilities.

Holiday Care Service ⓣ0845/124 9971 or 0208/760 0072, ⓦwww.holidaycare.org.uk. Free lists of accessible accommodation abroad.

Irish Wheelchair Association ⓣ01/818 6400, ⓦwww.iwa.ie. Useful information about travelling abroad with a wheelchair.

RADAR (Royal Association for Disability and Rehabilitation) ⓣ020/7250 3222, minicom ⓣ020/7250 4119, ⓦwww.radar.org.uk. Offers advice on holidays and travel abroad.

Tripscope ⓣ08457/585 641, ⓦwww.tripscope.org.uk. This registered charity provides a national telephone information service offering free advice on international transport for those with a mobility problem.

US and Canada

Access-Able ⓦwww.access-able.com. An online resource for travellers with disabilities.

Directions Unlimited ⓣ1-800/533-5343 or 914/241-1700. Tour operator specializing in custom tours for people with disabilities.

Mobility International US ⓣ541/343-1284, ⓦwww.miusa.org. Information and referral services, access guides and tours.

Society for the Advancement of Travelers with Handicaps (SATH) ⓣ212/447-7284, ⓦwww.sath.org. Non-profit educational organization that has actively represented travellers with disabilities since 1976.

Wheels Up! ⓣ1-888/389-4335, ⓦwww.wheelsup.com. Provides discounted airfares, tour and cruise prices; also publishes a free monthly newsletter and has a comprehensive website.

Australia and New Zealand

ACROD (Australian Council for Rehabilitation of the Disabled) ⓣ02/6282 4333 (also TTY ⓦwww.acrod.org.au). Provides lists of travel agencies and tour operators for people with disabilities.

Disabled Persons Assembly New Zealand ⓣ4/801-9100 (also TTY ⓦwww.dpa.org.nz). Resource centre with lists of travel agencies and tour operators for people with disabilities.

Travelling with kids

Thais are very tolerant of children, so you can take them almost anywhere without restriction. The only drawback might be the constant attention lavished on your kids by complete strangers, which can get tiring for adults and children alike.

Activities for kids

There's plenty in Thailand to appeal to children – especially the **beach**, the swimming pools and the water-based activities in the more developed resorts. Many **dive centres** will teach the PADI children's scuba courses on request: their Bubblemaker programme is open to 8-year-olds and the Junior Open Water is designed for anyone over ten. An increasing number of upmarket hotels in the big **resorts** arrange special activities for kids: the *Laguna Resort* hotels complex on Ao Bang Tao, Phuket (see p.679) is particularly recommended for its family-friendly accommodation and kids' activities camp, as are the *Novotel Phuket Resort*, and the *Holiday Inn*, both on Patong Beach, Phuket (p.684). The activity-centred Club Med chain of hotels (Ⓦwww.clubmed.com) also has a resort on Phuket, on Ao Kata Yai (see p.689). In Pattaya, the *Hard Rock Hotel* (see p.431) offers popular kids' facilities, including the Lil' Rock Kids' Club and a huge freeform swimming pool. Some of these hotels will also provide a **babysitting** service.

Older children will relish the cheap supply of electronic games and brand-name clothing on sale in the main tourist centres, and might enjoy taking up the countless offers from beach masseuses to "plait your hair" and "have manicure".

Despite its lack of obvious child-centred activities, many parents find that the moderately developed island of Ko Lanta (see p.726) makes a good destination for kids of all ages, with reasonably priced accommodation, fairly uncrowded sandy beaches and safe seas. However, as with almost any non-mainstream destination in Thailand, the nearest top-class health centre is several hours' away from Ko Lanta, in Phuket. On Ko Lanta and many other beaches, open-air shorefront restaurants are the norm, so adults can eat in relative peace while kids play within view.

Active children also enjoy the **national parks** and their inevitable waterfalls, plus the opportunities to go **rafting** – available in both sedate and whitewater versions – and **elephant-riding**. Kanchanaburi (see p.235) is a rewarding centre for all these outdoor pursuits, with the added attraction that many of the town's guest houses are set round decent-sized lawns. Chiang Mai (see p.318) can also offer these activities, as well as elephant-logging shows, an attractive, modern zoo, watching umbrella-makers and other craftspeople at work, and a trip to the Mae Sa valley, which is lined with many family-oriented attractions, such as the botanical gardens and **butterfly farms**. Bangkok has several child-friendly **theme parks** and activity centres, listed on p.184.

Practicalities

Many of the expensive **hotels** listed in this Guide offer special deals for families, usually allowing one or two under-twelves to share their parents' room for free, as long as no extra bedding is required. It's often possible to cram two adults and two children into the double rooms in inexpensive and mid-range hotels (as opposed to guest houses), as beds in these places are usually big enough for two (see p.45). An increasing number of guest houses now offer three-person rooms, and some even provide special family accommodation: see accommodation listings throughout the Guide for details.

Few museums or transport companies offer student reductions, but in some cases children get **discounts**; these vary a lot, one of the more bizarre provisos being the State Railway's regulation that a child aged three to twelve qualifies for half-fare only if under

150cm tall; in some stations you'll see a measuring scale painted onto the ticket-hall wall. On most domestic flights, under-twos pay ten percent of the full fare, and under-twelves pay fifty percent.

Although most Thai babies don't wear them, **disposable nappies** (diapers) are sold in Thailand at convenience stores, pharmacies and supermarkets in big resorts and sizeable towns; for longer, more out-of-the-way journeys and stays on lonely islands and beaches, consider bringing some washable ones as back-up. A **changing mat** is another necessity as there are few public toilets in Thailand, let alone ones with baby facilities (though posh hotels are always a useful option). If your baby is on powdered milk, it might be an idea to bring some of that; you can certainly get it in Thailand but it may not taste the same as at home. Dried **baby food**, too, could be worth taking, though you can get international-brand baby food in big towns and resorts, and some parents find restaurant-cooked rice and bananas go down just as well.

For touring, child-carrier backpacks are ideal. Opinions are divided on whether or not it's worth bringing a **buggy** or three-wheeled **stroller**. Where they exist, Thailand's pavements are bumpy at best, and there's an almost total absence of ramps; sand is especially difficult for buggies, though less so for three-wheelers. Buggies and strollers do, however, come in handy for feeding and even bedding small children, as highchairs and cots are only provided in the most upmarket hotels. You can buy buggies cheaply in most moderate-sized Thai towns, but if you bring your own and then wish you hadn't, most hotels and guest houses will keep it for you until you leave. Taxis and car-rental companies never provide baby seats.

Children's **clothes** are also very cheap in Thailand, and have the advantage of being designed for the climate. If you haven't already got beach shoes or sports sandals for your child to swim in (essential protection against coral, sea urchins and the like), you can buy these in the big cities and in every resort. Even if you've forgotten a crucial piece of children's equipment, you'll probably find it in Bangkok, where department stores have everything from bottles and dummies, and there's even a branch of Mothercare, as well as a special kids' department store selling English-language kids' books and games.

Even more than their parents, children need protecting from the sun, unsafe drinking water, heat and unfamiliar **food**. All that chilli in particular may be a problem, even with older kids; consider packing a jar of Marmite or equivalent child's favourite, so that you can always rely on toast if the local food doesn't go down so well. As with adults, you should be careful about unwashed fruit and salads and about dishes that have been left uncovered for a long time (see p.50). As diarrhoea could be dangerous for a child, rehydration solutions (see under "Health", p.34) are vital if your child goes down with it. Other significant **hazards** include thundering traffic; huge waves, strong currents and jellyfish; and the **sun** – not least because many beaches offer only limited shade, if at all. Sunhats, sunblock and waterproof suntan lotions are essential, and can be bought in the major resorts. You should also make sure, if possible, that your child is aware of the dangers of rabies; keep children away from animals, especially dogs and monkeys, and ask your medical advisor about rabies jabs.

Information and advice

The **website** of the Bangkok-based expat parents' group Bambi (Ⓦwww.bambi-bangkok.org) has useful tips on parents' common concerns, as well as ideas for child-friendly activities in Thailand. The Kids To Go forum at Ⓦthorntree.lonelyplanet. com gets quite a lot of postings from parents who've already taken their kids to Thailand and is a good source of advice and recommendations; for other travel websites see p.25. The logistics of travelling with kids in Asia are addressed in the **book** *Your Child's Health Abroad* by Dr Jane Wilson-Howarth and Dr Matthew Ellis (Bradt Publications). For specific advice about kids' health issues, either contact your doctor, or consult one of the travellers' medical services listed on p.30 or, in the UK, the Nomad Medical Centre (Ⓣ020/8889 7014, Ⓦwww.nomadtravel.co.uk) produces an information sheet on keeping kids healthy when abroad.

Directory

Addresses Thai addresses can be immensely confusing, mainly because property is often numbered twice, first to show which real estate lot it stands in, and then to distinguish where it is on that lot. Thus 154/7–10 Thanon Rajdamnoen means the building is on lot 154 and occupies numbers 7–10. There's an additional idiosyncrasy in the way Thai roads are sometimes named: in large cities a minor road running off a major road is often numbered as a soi ("lane" or "alley", though it may be a sizeable thoroughfare), rather than given its own street name. Thanon Sukhumvit for example – Bangkok's longest – has minor roads numbered Soi 1 to Soi 103, with odd numbers on one side of the road and even on the other; so a Thanon Sukhumvit address could read something

Giving something back

Reassured by the plethora of well-stocked shopping plazas, efficient services and apparent abundance in the ricefields, it is easy to forget that life is extremely hard for many people in Thailand. Countless **charities** work with Thailand's many poor and disadvantaged communities: listed below are a few that would welcome help in some way from visitors. The website of the *Bangkok Post* also carries an extensive list of charitable foundations and projects in Thailand at ⓦwww.bangkokpost.com/outlookwecare. For links to organizations in Thailand that welcome non-specialist **volunteers** for one- or two-week projects, see ⓦbolt.icestorm.com/lyric/asia.html.

Baan Unrak, Home of Joy Sangkhlaburi, ⓣ034 595428, ⓦwww.geocities.com/baanunrak, ⓔbaanunrak@hotmail.com. Based near Kanchanaburi, this project houses and educates destitute orphans, most of whom are ethnic minority refugees from Burma. It was founded by a woman working with the international Neo Humanist Foundation of Ananda Marga and now has two homes in the Sangkhlaburi area, where it cares for over 60 children, as well as a weaving centre and community outreach and education programmes. The easiest way to support Baan Unrak is to drop by their *Bakery* café in Sangkhlaburi (see p.249), where you can have lunch, buy their woven cotton clothes, bags and sarongs, and find out how to visit the school. Donations of books, clothes and money may also be welcome.

Chiang Mai Disabled Centre Thanon Ratchaphakinai, Chiang Mai ⓦdisabled.infothai.com. Centrally placed, disabled-managed outlet for a foundation that provides, among other things, a training, resource and social centre for disabled people. Skilled long-term volunteers, donations and wheelchair sponsorships are sought, or just take your custom there for such services as Internet access, laundry and massage.

Human Development Foundation 100/11 Kae Ha Klong Toey 4, Thanon Damrongrathhaphipat, Klong Toey, Bangkok ⓣ02 671 5313, ⓦwww.mercycentre.org. Since 1972, this organization – founded by locally famous Catholic priest Father Joe – has been providing education and support for Bangkok's street kids and slum-dwellers as well as caring for those with HIV-AIDS. It now runs more than thirty kindergartens in Bangkok's slums and is staffed almost entirely by people who grew up in the slums themselves. Contact the centre for information about donations and volunteering, or visit it to purchase cards and gifts. Father Joe like 27/9–11 Soi 15, Thanon Sukhumvit, which would mean the property occupies numbers 9–11 on lot 27 on minor road number 15 running off Thanon Sukhumvit.

Contact lens solutions Opticians in all reasonable-sized towns sell international brand-name contact lens cleaning and disinfection solutions.

Contraceptives Condoms (*meechai*) are sold in all pharmacies and in many hairdressers and village shops as well. Birth-control pills can be bought in Bangkok (see p.203) and at some pharmacies in major towns and resorts; supplies of any other contraceptives should be brought from home.

Cookery classes You can take short courses in authentic Thai cookery at schools in Bangkok, Chiang Mai, Hua Hin, Kanchanaburi, Ko Samui, Pai, Phuket and Sukhothai; see relevant accounts for details.

Electricity Supplied at 220 volts AC and available at all but the most remote villages and basic beach huts. If you're packing a hair-dryer, laptop or other appliance, you'll need to take a set of travel-plug adapters with you as several plug types are commonly in use, most usually with two round pins, but also with two flat-blade pins, and sometimes with both options. Check out the Help for World Travellers website

Maier's book, *The Slaughterhouse: Stories from Bangkok's Klong Toey Slum*, is an eye-opening insight into this side of Thai life that tourists rarely encounter; it's available from most Bangkok bookshops and profits go to the Foundation (see p.847 for a review).

Mae Tao Clinic Mae Sot, ⓦwww.burmachildren.org. Every year, thousands of refugees from Burma's pernicious military regime flee across Thailand's western borders in search of sanctuary. Many are housed in refugee camps, where they at least have access to food and medical care, but thousands more fall outside the remit of the refugee camps and end up at the Mae Tao Clinic. The clinic, which provides free medical care for around 30,000 Burmese refugees a year, was founded in 1989 by a Karen refugee, Dr Cynthia, now internationally renowned for her work. Several guest houses and restaurants in Mae Sot accept donations of clothes, medical supplies and money for the Mae Tao clinic, and the town is also home to a number of other organizations concerned with the welfare of the refugee communities. See p.298 for details.

The Mirror Art Group 106 Moo 1, Ban Huay Khom, Tambon Mae Yao, Chiang Rai ⓣ053 737412, ⓦwww.mirrorartgroup.org. NGO working with the hill tribes in the Mae Yao sub-district of Chiang Rai province to help combat such issues as drug abuse, erosion of culture and trafficking of women and children. Long-term volunteers with IT, English and teaching skills are sought, as well as donations such as old books, clothes or even scholarships for schools.

The Students' Education Trust (SET) ⓦwww.thaistudentcharity.org. High-school and further education in Thailand is a luxury that the poorest kids cannot afford – not only is there a lack of funds for fees, books, uniforms and even bus fares, but they often need to work to help support the family. Many are sent to live in temples to ease the burden on their relatives. The SET was founded by British-born Phra Peter Pannapadipo to help these kids pursue their education and escape from the poverty trap. He lived as a Thai monk for ten years and tells the heart-breaking stories of some of the boys at his temple in his book, *Little Angels: The real-life stories of twelve Thai novice monks* (see p.847 for a review). SET welcomes donations and sponsorship; see their website for details.

We-Train International House Bangkok ⓣ02 967 8550–4, ⓦwww.we-train.co.th. Run by the Association for the Promotion of the Status of Women (APSW), this is a hotel close to Bangkok airport whose profits go towards helping APSW support, house and train disadvantaged women and children. See p.95 for details.

(Ⓦ www.kropla.com) which has a very helpful list, complete with pictures, of the different sockets, voltage and phone plugs used in Thailand.

Employment The most common source of employment in Thailand is English teaching, and Bangkok and Chiang Mai are the best places to look. The website Ⓦ www.ajarn.com is a great source of advice on everything to do with teaching in Thailand, and it also carries job adverts. In addition, keep an eye on guest-house noticeboards in the two cities as teachers often advertise for replacements here. The *Bangkok Post* and *Bangkok Metro* listings magazine also sometimes carry teachers-wanted ads. If you're a qualified dive instructor, you might be able to get seasonal work at one of the major resorts – in Phuket, Khao Lak and Ao Nang and on Ko Phi Phi, Ko Lanta, Ko Samui and Ko Tao, for example. Guest-house noticeboards occasionally carry adverts for more unusual jobs, such as playing extras in Thai movies.

Film The price of film in Thailand is comparable to that in the West. Slide film is hard to get outside the main tourist centres, but videotape is more widely available. Developing film is a lot less expensive than in the West and is done in a couple of hours in the main tourist areas, to about the same quality.

Laundry services Guest houses and hotels all over the country run low-cost, same-day laundry services. In some places you pay per item, in others you're charged by the kilo; ironing is often included in the price.

Left luggage Most major train stations have left-luggage facilities, where bags can be stored for up to twenty days; at bus stations you can usually persuade someone official to look after your stuff for a few hours. Many guest houses and hotels also offer an inexpensive and reliable service.

Tampons Few Thai women use tampons, which are not widely available, except from branches of Boots in Bangkok and the resorts, and from a few tourist-oriented mini-markets in the biggest resorts.

Thai language classes Even more than in Chiang Mai (see p.331), there's plenty of choice in Bangkok, including private and group lessons for both tourists and expats. Try AUA (American University Alumni (Ⓦ www.auathai.com), Jentana and Associates (Ⓔ jentana@loxinfo.co.th), or Nisa Thai Language School (Ⓦ nisathai@ cscoms.com). For more information and directories of language schools, see Ⓦ www.learningthai.com and www.thailandguidebook.com.

Time differences Bangkok is seven hours ahead of GMT, twelve hours ahead of US Eastern Standard Time and three hours behind Australian Eastern Standard Time.

Tipping Some upmarket hotels and restaurants will add an automatic ten-percent service charge to your bill. It is usual to tip hotel bellboys and porters B10–20, and to round up taxi fares to the nearest B10.

Women's groups For an extensive list of women's organizations in Thailand, see Ⓦ www.euronet.nl/~fullmoon/womlist/countries/thailand.html.

Guide

Guide

1

Bangkok

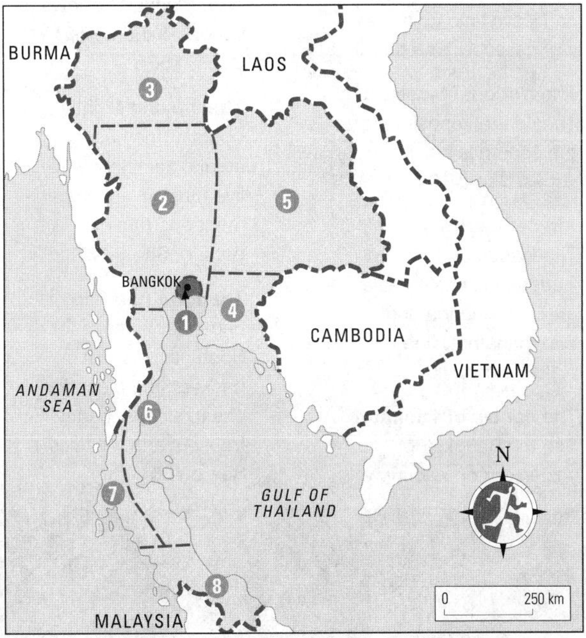
BURMA
LAOS
3
2
5
BANGKOK
4
1
CAMBODIA
VIETNAM
ANDAMAN SEA
6
7
GULF OF THAILAND
8
MALAYSIA
N
0
250 km

CHAPTER 1

Highlights

* **The Grand Palace** The country's least missable sight, incorporating its holiest and most dazzling temple, Wat Phra Kaeo. See p.122
* **Wat Pho** Admire the Reclining Buddha and the lavish architecture, and leave time for a relaxing massage. See p.130
* **The National Museum** The central repository of the country's artistic riches. See p.134
* **Amulet markets** Thousands of tiny Buddha images on sale at Wat Rajnadda and Wat Mahathat. See p.132 and p.140
* **The canals of Thonburi** See the Bangkok of yesteryear on a touristy but memorable longtail boat ride. See p.150
* **Jim Thompson's House** An elegant Thai design classic. See p.159
* **Chatuchak Weekend Market** Eight thousand stalls selling everything from triangular pillows to second-hand Levis. See p.166
* **Thai boxing** Nightly bouts at the national stadia, complete with live musical accompaniment and frenetic betting. See p.187
* **Thanon Khao San** Legendary mecca for Southeast Asia backpackers; the place for cheap sleeps, baggy trousers and tall tales. See p.106

△ Wat Pho

1

Bangkok

The headlong pace and flawed modernity of Bangkok match few people's visions of the capital of exotic Siam. Spiked with scores of high-rise buildings of concrete and glass, it's a vast flatness that holds a population of at least nine million, and feels even bigger. But under the shadow of the skyscrapers you'll find a heady mix of chaos and refinement, of frenetic markets and hushed golden temples, of dispiriting, zombie-like sex shows and early-morning almsgiving ceremonies. One way or another, the place will probably get under your skin – and if you don't enjoy the challenge of slogging through jams of buses and tuk-tuks, which fill the air with a chainsaw drone and clouds of pollution, you can spend a couple of days on the most impressive temples and museums, have a quick shopping spree and then strike out for the provinces.

Most budget travellers head for the **Banglamphu** district, where if you're not careful you could end up watching videos all day long and selling your shoes when you run out of money. The district is far from having a monopoly on Bangkok accommodation, but it does have the advantage of being just a short walk from the major sights in the **Ratanakosin** area: the dazzling ostentation of **Wat Phra Kaeo**, lively and grandiose **Wat Pho** and the **National Museum**'s hoard of exquisite works of art. Once those cultural essentials have been seen, you can choose from a whole bevy of lesser sights, including **Wat Benjamabophit** (the "Marble Temple"), especially at festival time, and **Jim Thompson's House**, a small, personal museum of Thai design.

For livelier scenes, explore the dark alleys of **Chinatown**'s bazaars or head for the water: the great **Chao Phraya River**, which breaks up and adds zest to the city's landscape, is the backbone of a network of **canals and floating markets** that remains fundamentally intact in the west-bank Thonburi district. Inevitably the waterways have earned Bangkok the title of "Venice of the East", a tag that seems all too apt when you're wading through flooded streets in the rainy season; indeed, the city is year by year subsiding into the marshy ground, literally sinking under the weight of its burgeoning concrete towers.

Shopping on dry land varies from touristic outlets selling silks, handicrafts and counterfeit watches, through international fashion emporia and home-grown, street-wise boutiques, to completely and sometimes undesirably authentic marketplaces – notably Chatuchak, where caged animals cringe among the pots and pans. Similarly, the city offers the country's most varied **entertainment**, ranging from traditional dancing and the orchestrated bedlam of Thai boxing, through hip bars and clubs playing the latest imported sounds, to the farang-only sex bars of the notorious Patpong district, a tinseltown Babylon that's the tip of a dangerous iceberg. Even if the above doesn't appeal, you'll almost certainly pass through Bangkok once, if not several times – not only is it

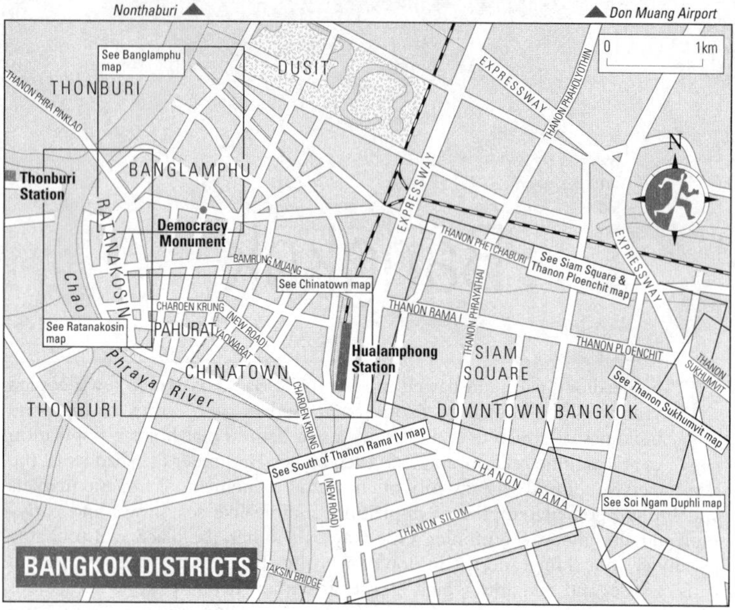

Thailand's main port of entry, it's also the obvious place to sort out **onward travel**, with some of the world's best deals on international air tickets, as well as a convenient menu of embassies for visas to neighbouring countries.

A little history

Bangkok is a relatively young capital, established in 1782 after the Burmese sacked Ayutthaya, the former capital. A temporary base was set up on the western bank of the Chao Phraya River, in what is now **Thonburi**, before work started on the more defensible east bank, where the French had built a grand, but short-lived fort in the 1660s. The first king of the new dynasty, Rama I, built his palace at **Ratanakosin**, within a defensive ring of two (later expanded to three) canals, and this remains the city's spiritual heart.

Initially, the city was largely **amphibious**: only the temples and royal palaces were built on dry land, while ordinary residences floated on thick bamboo rafts on the river and canals; even shops and warehouses were moored to the river bank. A major shift in emphasis came in the second half of the nineteenth century, first under Rama IV (1851–68), who as part of his effort to restyle the capital along European lines built Bangkok's first roads, and then under Rama V (1868–1910), who constructed a new residential palace in Dusit, north of Ratanakosin, and laid out that area's grand boulevards.

Since World War II, and especially from the mid-1960s onwards, Bangkok has seen an explosion of **modernization**, which has blown away earlier attempts at orderly planning and left the city without an obvious centre. Most of the canals have been filled in, to be replaced by endless rows of cheap and functional concrete shophouses, sprawling over a built-up area of 330 square kilometres. The benefits of the **economic boom** of the 1980s and early 1990s were concentrated in Bangkok, as well as the calamitous effects of the late

City of angels

When Rama I was crowned in 1782, he gave his new capital a grand 43-syllable name to match his ambitious plans for the building of the city. Since then, 21 more syllables have been added. Krungthepmahanakhornbowornrattanakosinmahintarayutthayamahadilokpopnopparatratchathaniburiromudomratchaniwetmahasathanamornpimanavatarnsathitsakkathattiyavisnukarprasit is certified by the Guinness Book of Records as the longest place name in the world, roughly translating as "Great city of angels, the supreme repository of divine jewels, the great land unconquerable, the grand and prominent realm, the royal and delightful capital city full of nine noble gems, the highest royal dwelling and grand palace, the divine shelter and living place of the reincarnated spirits". Fortunately, all Thais refer to the city simply as Krung Thep, though plenty can recite the full name at the drop of a hat. Bangkok – "Village of the Plum Olive" – was the name of the original village on the Thonburi side; with remarkable persistence, it has remained in use by foreigners since the time of the French garrison.

1990s **economic crisis**, both of which attracted migration from all over Thailand and made the capital ever more dominant: the population, over half of which is under 30 years of age, is now forty times that of the second city, Chiang Mai. Bangkokians now own four-fifths of the nation's automobiles, and there's precious little chance to escape from the pollution in green space: the city has only 0.4 square metres of public parkland per inhabitant, the lowest figure in the world, compared, for example, to London's 30.4 square metres per person.

Arrival and accommodation

Finding a place to stay in Bangkok is usually no problem: the city has a huge range of **accommodation**, from the murkiest backstreet bunk to the plushest five-star riverside suite, and you don't have to spend a lot to get a comfortable place. Getting to your guest house or hotel, however, is unlikely to put you in a good mood, for there can be few cities in the world where **transport** is such a headache. Bumper-to-bumper vehicles create fumes so bad that some days the city's carbon monoxide emissions come close to the international danger level, and it's not unusual for residents to spend three hours getting to work – and these are people who know where they're going. However, the recent opening of the elevated train network called the Bangkok Transit System, or BTS Skytrain, has radically improved public transport in a few parts of the city, notably the Siam Square, Silom and Sukhumvit areas, and it's hoped that the new subway system will have a similar effect on the areas it runs to. Unfortunately for tourists, the Skytrain and subway systems do not stretch as far as Ratanakosin or Banglamphu, where boats still provide the fastest means of hopping from one sight to another.

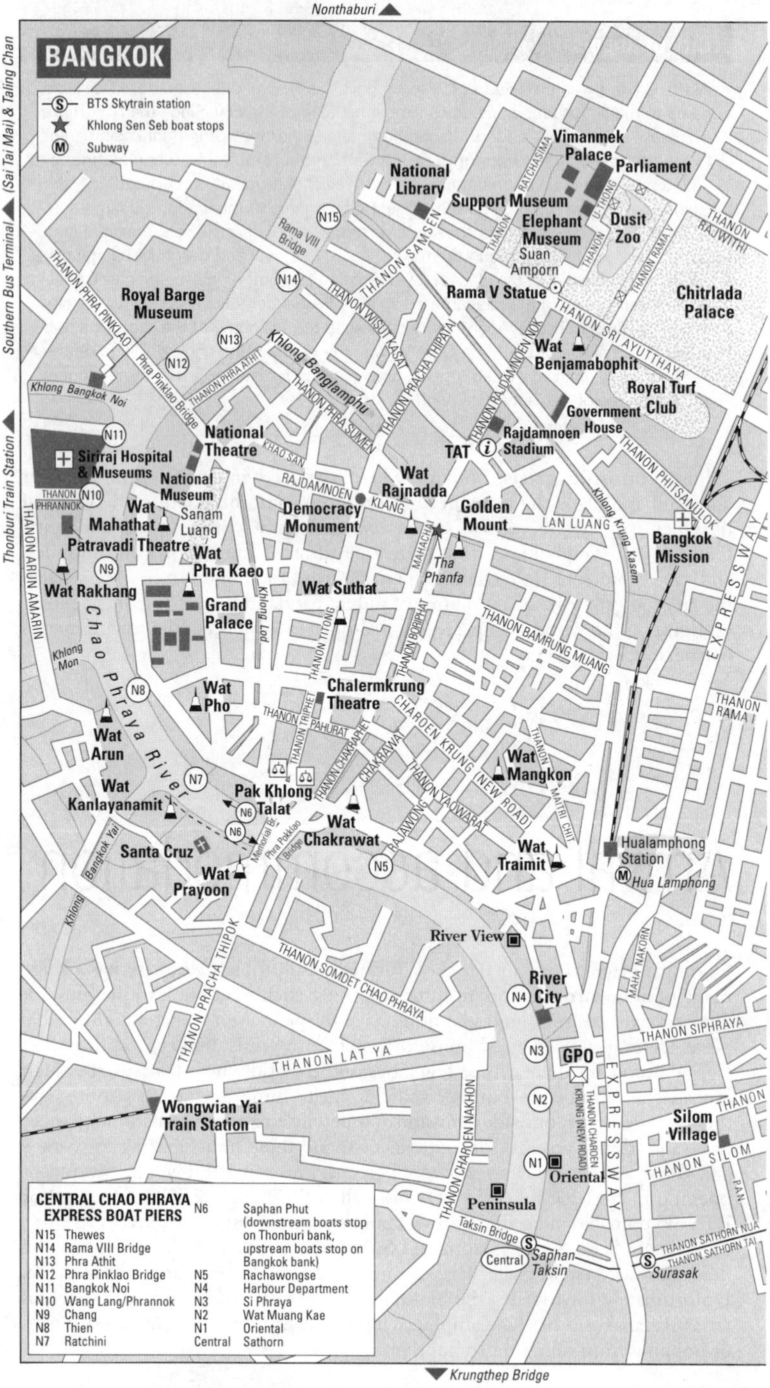
BANGKOK
BTS Skytrain station
Khlong Sen Seb boat stops
Subway
Nonthaburi
Southern Bus Terminal (Sai Tai Mai) & Taling Chan
Thonburi Train Station
Krungthep Bridge
Vimanmek Palace
Parliament
National Library
Support Museum
Elephant Museum
Dusit Zoo
Suan Amporn
Rama V Statue
Chitrlada Palace
Wat Benjamabophit
Royal Turf Club
Government House
Rajdamnoen Stadium
TAT
Royal Barge Museum
Khlong Bangkok Noi
Khlong Banglamphu
National Theatre
Siriraj Hospital & Museums
National Museum
Wat Mahathat
Sanam Luang
Patravadi Theatre
Wat Phra Kaeo
Wat Rakhang
Grand Palace
Democracy Monument
Wat Rajnadda
Golden Mount
Tha Phanfa
Bangkok Mission
Wat Suthat
Wat Pho
Chalermkrung Theatre
Wat Arun
Chao Phraya River
Wat Kanlayanamit
Pak Khlong Talat
Wat Chakrawat
Wat Mangkon
Wat Traimit
Hualamphong Station
Hua Lamphong
Santa Cruz
Wat Prayoon
River View
River City
GPO
Wongwian Yai Train Station
Silom Village
Oriental
Peninsula
Saphan Taksin
Surasak
Central
Taksin Bridge
Rama VIII Bridge
Phra Pinklao Bridge
Memorial Br.
Phra Pokklao Bridge
Khlong Mon
Khlong Lod
Khlong Krung Kasem
Bangkok Yai
THANON SAMSEN
THANON RATCHASIMA
THANON U-THONG
THANON RAMA V
THANON RAJWITHI
THANON SRI AYUTTHAYA
THANON PHITSANULOK
THANON PHRA PINKLAO
THANON PHRA ATHIT
THANON PHRA SUMEN
THANON WISUT KASAT
THANON PRACHA THIPATAI
THANON RAJDAMNOEN NOK
KHAO SAN
RAJDAMNOEN KLANG
MAHACHAI
LAN LUANG
THANON PHRANNOK
THANON ARUN AMARIN
THANON BAMRUNG MUANG
THANON BORIPHAT
THANON TITONG
THANON TRIPHET
THANON PAHURAT
THANON CHAKRAPHET
CHAKRAWAT
CHAROEN KRUNG (NEW ROAD)
THANON YAOWARAT
RAJAWONG
THANON MAITRI CHIT
THANON RAMA I
EXPRESSWAY
THANON PRACHA THIPOK
THANON SOMDET CHAO PHRAYA
THANON LAT YA
THANON CHAROEN NAKHON
MAHA NAKORN
THANON SIPHRAYA
THANON CHAROEN KRUNG (NEW ROAD)
THANON SILOM
PAN
THANON SATHORN NUA
THANON SATHORN TAI
CENTRAL CHAO PHRAYA EXPRESS BOAT PIERS
N15 Thewes
N14 Rama VIII Bridge
N13 Phra Athit
N12 Phra Pinklao Bridge
N11 Bangkok Noi
N10 Wang Lang/Phrannok
N9 Chang
N8 Thien
N7 Ratchini
N6 Saphan Phut (downstream boats stop on Thonburi bank, upstream boats stop on Bangkok bank)
N5 Rachawongse
N4 Harbour Department
N3 Si Phraya
N2 Wat Muang Kae
N1 Oriental
Central Sathorn

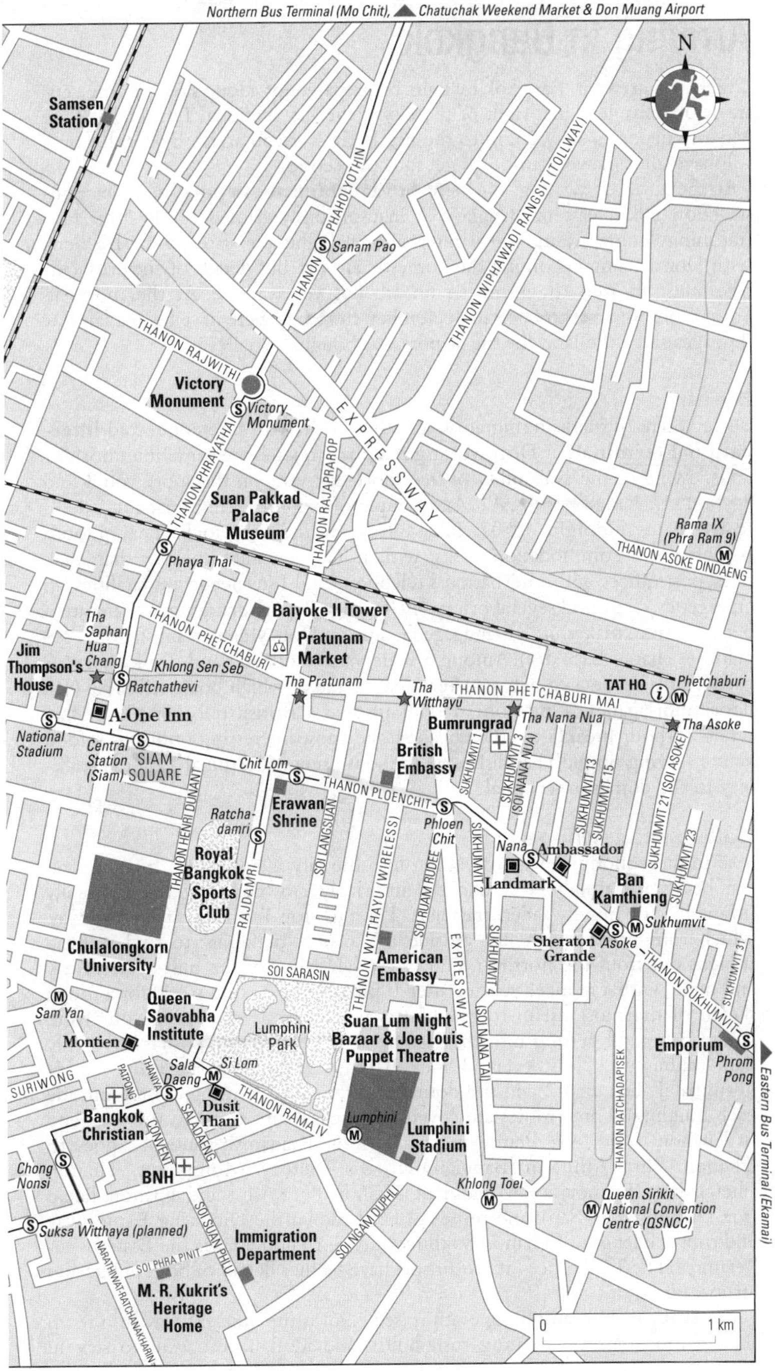

Northern Bus Terminal (Mo Chit), Chatuchak Weekend Market & Don Muang Airport
N
Samsen Station
Sanam Pao
THANON PHAHOLYOTHIN
THANON WIPHAWADI RANGSIT (TOLLWAY)
THANON RAJWITHI
Victory Monument
Victory Monument
EXPRESSWAY
THANON PHRAYATHAI
THANON RAJAPRAROP
Suan Pakkad Palace Museum
Phaya Thai
Rama IX (Phra Ram 9)
THANON ASOKE DINDAENG
Baiyoke II Tower
THANON PHETCHABURI
Tha Saphan Hua Chang
Pratunam Market
Jim Thompson's House
Khlong Sen Seb
Ratchathevi
Tha Pratunam
Tha Witthayu
THANON PHETCHABURI MAI
TAT HQ
Phetchaburi
A-One Inn
National Stadium
Bumrungrad
Tha Nana Nua
Tha Asoke
Central Station (Siam)
SIAM SQUARE
Chit Lom
British Embassy
SUKHUMVIT 1
SUKHUMVIT 3 (SOI NANA NUA)
SUKHUMVIT 13
SUKHUMVIT 15
SUKHUMVIT 21 (SOI ASOKE)
THANON PLOENCHIT
THANON HENRI DUNANT
Erawan Shrine
Ratchadamri
SOI LANGSUAN
THANON WITTHAYU (WIRELESS)
Phloen Chit
SUKHUMVIT 2
Nana
Ambassador
SUKHUMVIT 23
Royal Bangkok Sports Club
RAJDAMRI
SOI RUAM RUDEE
Landmark
Ban Kamthieng
Sukhumvit
Sheraton Grande
Asoke
SUKHUMVIT 4 (SOI NANA TAI)
Chulalongkorn University
SOI SARASIN
American Embassy
EXPRESSWAY
THANON SUKHUMVIT
SUKHUMVIT 31
Sam Yan
Queen Saovabha Institute
Lumphini Park
Suan Lum Night Bazaar & Joe Louis Puppet Theatre
Emporium
Phrom Pong
Montien
THANON RATCHADAPISEK
SURIWONG
PATPONG
THANIYA
Sala Daeng
Si Lom
THANON RAMA IV
Dusit Thani
SALADAENG
Bangkok Christian
CONVENT
Lumphini
Lumphini Stadium
Eastern Bus Terminal (Ekamai)
Chong Nonsi
BNH
Khlong Toei
Queen Sirikit National Convention Centre (QSNCC)
Suksa Witthaya (planned)
SOI SUAN PHLU
Immigration Department
SOI NGAM DUPHLI
SOI PHRA PINIT
NARATHIWAT-RATCHANAKHARIN
M. R. Kukrit's Heritage Home
0
1 km

Arriving in Bangkok

Unless you arrive in Bangkok by train, be prepared for a long slog into the centre. Most travellers' first sight of the city is the International Terminal at Don Muang Airport, a slow 25km to the north. Even if you arrive by coach, you'll still have a lot of work to do to get into the centre.

At the time of writing, the new **Suvarnabhumi Airport** is under construction 30km east of Bangkok at inauspiciously named Nong Ngu Hao (meaning "cobra swamp"). All international flights are slated to arrive here, with Don Muang becoming the domestic airport, but details of airport facilities, transport into town and so on are not yet available. At the moment, Suvarnabhumi is set to open in September 2005, but there have been a fair few slippages since the land for the airport was bought – in 1973.

By air

Once you're through immigration at either of the two interconnected **international terminals** at **Don Muang Airport** (queues are sometimes horrendous, owing to the availability of free short-stay visas on the spot), you'll find 24-hour exchange booths, ATMs, a couple of helpful TAT information desks (daily 9am–midnight; ⓣ02 523 8973), round-the-clock Thai Hotels Association accommodation desks, with prices generally cheaper than rack rates, post offices with international telephone and Internet access facilities, an emergency clinic and several pricey left-luggage depots, charging B90 per item per day (more makeshift left-luggage facilities at Don Muang train station – see below – charge B15/day). Among a wide variety of food and drink outlets – particularly in the area between Terminals 1 and 2, which boasts Chinese (4th floor) and Japanese (2nd floor) restaurants and a British pub (4th floor) that offers 24-hour breakfast – the cheapest and most interesting option is a food centre serving simple Thai dishes on the south side of Terminal 2 on the walkway to the domestic terminal.

Getting into town

The most economical way of getting into the city is by **public bus**, but this can be excruciatingly slow and the invariably crowded vehicles are totally unsuitable for heavily laden travellers. The bus stop is on the main highway, which runs north–south just outside the airport buildings: to find it, head straight out from the northern end of arrivals. Most of the buses run all day and night, with a reduced service after 10pm; see the box on p.100 for a rough sketch of the most useful routes. Unless you're already counting your baht, you're better off getting into the city by air-conditioned **airport bus** (daily 5am–midnight; at least every 30min; B100); the buses depart from outside Terminal 1, Terminal 2 and the domestic terminal (clearly signposted outside each building). Three routes are covered: route A1 runs along to the west end of Thanon Silom, via Pratunam and Thanon Rajdamri; route A2 goes to Thanon Phra Athit in Banglamphu, via Victory Monument, Thanon Phetchaburi, Democracy Monument, Thanon Phra Athit and Thanon Tanao (for Thanon Khao San); and route A3 heads down the Dindaeng Expressway and runs the length of Thanon Sukhumvit to Soi Thonglor via the Eastern Bus Terminal. The TAT offices at the airport have further details of both public and airport buses.

The **train** to Hualamphong Station (see p.96) is the quickest way into town during morning and evening rush hours, and ideal if you want to stay in

Chinatown or change onto the subway system (either at Hualamphong or at Bang Sue Station), but services are irregular. To reach the station at Don Muang Airport follow the signs from arrivals in Terminal 1 (if in doubt head towards the big *Amari Airport Hotel*, across the main highway, carry on through the hotel foyer and the station is in front of you). More than thirty trains a day make the fifty-minute trip to Hualamphong, with fares starting from B5 in third class (though rapid and express trains command surcharges of up to B80), with services most frequent around the early morning – at other times of the day you might have to wait over an hour.

Taxis to the centre are comfortable, air-conditioned and not too extravagantly priced, although the driving can be hairy. Turn down any tout who may offer a cheap ride in an unlicensed and unmetered vehicle, as newly arrived travellers are seen as easy prey for robbery, and the cabs are untraceable. Licensed and metered public taxis are operated from clearly signposted counters, operated by the Airports Authority of Thailand, outside Arrivals. Even including the B50 airport pick-up fee and B70 tolls for the overhead expressways, a journey to Thanon Silom downtown, for example, should set you back around B300, depending on the traffic.

Airport accommodation

With time to kill and money to spare before your onward journey, you might want to rest, clean up and maybe have a swim at the *Amari Airport Hotel* (Ⓣ02 566 1020–1, Ⓦwww.amari.com; ❾; 50 percent discount for Thai Airways international passengers), just across the road from the international terminal, which rents out very upmarket **bedrooms** at special **daytime rates** between 8am and 6pm (from US$25 for 3hr). Passengers in transit can make use of the day rooms in the airport's transit area for up to four hours (US$35). To **stay near the airport**, more economical choices are the huge *Asia Airport Hotel* (Ⓣ02 992 6999, Ⓦwww.asiahotel.co.th; ❽) and the *Comfort Inn* (Ⓣ02 552 8921–9, Ⓔpinap@loxinfo.co.th; ❼), both of which have swimming pools and offer free transport to and from the airport. Cheaper still is the *We-Train International House*, about 3km west of the airport (Ⓣ02 967 8550–4, Ⓦwww.we-train.co.th; ❸–❹), run by the Association for the Promotion of the Status of Women, where proceeds go to help disadvantaged women and children. In a peaceful lakeside setting, there are dorms (from B100), comfortable fan- or air-conditioned rooms, Internet access, a gym and a swimming pool. To get there, take a taxi from the airport, or a taxi or motorbike from Don Muang train station (saving the B50 airport pick-up fee); if in doubt, phone the guest house who will book a taxi to come and pick you up.

Getting to the rest of the country

To catch a connecting **internal flight**, head to the **domestic terminal** at Don Muang, 500m away from Terminal 2, connected by an air-conditioned covered walkway and by a free shuttle bus (daily 5am–11pm; every 20min). Facilities here include exchange booths, ATMs, a Thai Hotels Association accommodation desk, with prices generally cheaper than rack rates, a post office with international telephones and Internet access, and left luggage (B70/item/day); metered taxi counters can be found outside arrivals on the ground floor, while the airport bus (see opposite) stops outside the northern end of arrivals.

You can spare yourself the trip into Bangkok if you're planning to head straight to the **north or northeast** by train or bus: all trains to these parts of the country stop at Don Muang train station, while the Northern Bus Terminal

(Mo Chit) is a short taxi-ride away. Thai Airways also runs an air-conditioned bus from the airport direct to **Pattaya** three times a day for B200 per person (9am, noon & 7pm; 2hr 30min).

By train

Travelling to Bangkok by **train** from Malaysia and most parts of Thailand, you arrive at **Hualamphong Station**, which is centrally located, at the southern end of the subway line. The most useful of the numerous city buses serving Hualamphong are #53 (non-air-con), which stops on the east side (left-hand exit) of the station and runs to the budget accommodation in Banglamphu; and the #25 (ordinary and air-con), which runs east to Siam Square (for Skytrain connections) and along Thanon Sukhumvit to the Eastern Bus Terminal, or west through Chinatown to Tha Chang (for the Grand Palace). See box on p.100 for bus-route details. Station **facilities** include a post office, an exchange booth, an ATM (just inside the main exit), an Internet centre and a **left-luggage** office (daily 4am–10.30pm), which charges B10–30 per day, depending on the size of the bag (almost any rucksack counts as large). A more economical place to store baggage is at the *TT2 Guest House* (see p.113), about fifteen minutes' walk from the station, which provides the same service for only B10 per item per day, whatever the size.

One service the station does not provide is itinerant tourist assistance staff – anyone who comes up to you in or around the station concourse and offers help/information/transport or ticket-booking services is almost certainly a **con-artist**, however many official-looking ID tags are hanging round their neck. This is a well-established scam to fleece new arrivals and should be avoided at all costs (see p.59 for more details). For train-related questions, contact the 24-hour "Information" counter close by the departures board (there's more information on buying onward rail tickets on p.197). The station area is also fertile ground for **dishonest tuk-tuk drivers**, so you'll need to be extra suspicious to avoid them – take a metered taxi or a bus instead.

Trains from Kanchanaburi pull in at the small and not very busy **Thonburi Station**, which is an 850-metre walk west of the N11 (Bangkok Noi) express-boat stop, just across the Chao Phraya River from Banglamphu and Ratanakosin.

By bus

Buses come to a halt at a number of far-flung spots. All services from the north and northeast terminate at the **Northern Bus Terminal** (**Mo Chit**) on Thanon Kamphaeng Phet 2; some east-coast buses also use Mo Chit (rather than the Eastern Terminal), including several daily services from Pattaya, and a few daily buses from Rayong (for Ko Samet), Chanthaburi and Trat (for Ko Chang and the Cambodian border). The quickest way to get into the city centre from Mo Chit is to hop onto the Skytrain (see p.104) at the Mo Chit Station (or the subway at the adjacent Chatuchak Park Station – see p.99), fifteen minutes' walk from the bus terminal on Thanon Phaholyothin, and then change onto a city bus if necessary. Otherwise, it's a long bus, tuk-tuk or taxi ride into town: city buses from the Mo Chit area include air-conditioned #502/#2 to Thanon Silom; regular and air-conditioned #3, and air-conditioned #509/#9 and #512/#12 to Banglamphu; and both regular and air-conditioned #29 to Hualamphong train station; for details of these routes see the box on pp.100–101.

Most buses from the east coast use the **Eastern Bus Terminal** (**Ekamai**) between sois 40 and 42 on Thanon Sukhumvit. This bus station is right beside the Ekamai Skytrain stop (see p.104), and is also served by lots of city buses, including air-conditioned #511/#11 to Banglamphu and the Southern Bus Terminal (see box on pp.100–101 for details), or you can take a taxi down Soi 63 to Tha Ekamai, a pier on Khlong Sen Seb, to pick up the canal boat service to the Golden Mount near Banglamphu (see p.103). There's a left-luggage booth at the bus terminal (daily 7am–8pm; B30/day).

Bus services from Malaysia and the south, as well as from Kanchanaburi, use the **Southern Bus Terminal** (**Sai Tai Mai**) at the junction of Thanon Borom Ratchonni and the Nakhon Chaisri Highway, west of the Chao Phraya River in Thonburi. Drivers on these services always make a stop to drop passengers on the east side of Thanon Borom Ratchonni, in front of a Toyota dealer, before doing a time-consuming U-turn for the terminus on the west side of the road; if you're heading across the river to Banglamphu or downtown Bangkok you should get off here, along with the majority of the other passengers. Numerous **city buses** cross the river from this bus stop, including air-con #507/#7 to Banglamphu, Hualamphong Station and Thanon Rama IV, air-con #511/#11 to Banglamphu and Thanon Sukhumvit, and non-air-con #159 to the Northern Bus Terminal (see box on pp.100–101 for routes). This is also a better place to grab a **taxi** into town, as rides are faster and cheaper when started from here.

Orientation and information

Bangkok can be a tricky place to get your bearings as it's huge and ridiculously congested, with largely featureless modern buildings and no obvious centre. The boldest line on the map is the **Chao Phraya River**, which divides the city into Bangkok proper on the east bank, and **Thonburi**, part of Greater Bangkok, on the west.

The historical core of Bangkok proper, site of the original royal palace, is **Ratanakosin**, which nestles into a bend in the river. Three concentric canals radiate eastwards around Ratanakosin: the southern part of the area between the canals is the old-style trading enclave of **Chinatown** and Indian **Pahurat**, linked to the old palace by Thanon Charoen Krung (aka New Road); the northern part is characterized by old temples and the **Democracy Monument**, west of which is the backpackers' ghetto of **Banglamphu**. Beyond the canals to the north, **Dusit** is the site of many government buildings and the nineteenth-century palace, which is linked to Ratanakosin by the three stately avenues, Thanon Rajdamnoen Nok, Thanon Rajdamnoen Klang and Thanon Rajdamnoen Nai.

"New" Bangkok begins to the east of the canals and beyond the main rail line and Hualamphong Station, and stretches as far as the eye can see to the east and north. The main business district and most of the embassies are south of **Thanon Rama IV**, with the port of Khlong Toey at the southern edge. The diverse area north of Thanon Rama IV includes the sprawling campus of Chulalongkorn University, huge shopping centres around **Siam Square** and a variety of other businesses. A couple of blocks northeast of Siam Square stands the tallest building in Bangkok, the 84-storeyed **Baiyoke II Tower** whose golden spire makes a good point of reference. To the east lies the swish residential quarter off **Thanon Sukhumvit**.

Information and maps

The Bangkok Tourist Bureau (BTB) provides a decent information service from its headquarters, the **Bangkok Information Centre**, located next to Phra Pinklao Bridge at 17/1 Thanon Phra Athit in Banglamphu (daily 9am–7pm; ⓣ02 225 7612–4, ⓦbangkoktourist.bma.go.th/english/index.php), and from its twenty or so strategically placed information booths around the capital, which all provide reasonable free city maps, and also run a variety of interesting city tours by boat, bus and bicycle (see below). Among the most usefully located BTB booths are those at the Erawan Shrine, at River City, in front of Mah Boon Krong Shopping Centre, in front of Robinson Department Store on Thanon Silom, and in front of Banglamphu's Wat Chana Songkhram.

The BTB is the most useful resource for information on the capital, but for destinations further afield you need to visit the **Tourism Authority of Thailand (TAT)** which maintains a Tourist Service Centre within walking distance of Banglamphu, at 4 Rajdamnoen Nok (daily 8.30am–4.30pm; ⓣ02 282 9773, 24-hr freephone tourist assistance ⓣ1672, ⓦwww.tat.or.th), a twenty-minute stroll from Thanon Khao San, or a short ride in air-conditioned bus #503/#3. TAT also has a couple of booths in the airport arrivals concourse, but its headquarters is rather inconveniently located out at 1600 Thanon Phetchaburi Mai, near the junction with Sukhumvit Soi 21 (daily 8.30am–4.30pm; ⓣ02 250 5500): easiest access is by subway to Phetchaburi or by Khlong Sen Seb canal boat to Tha Asoke. Other useful sources of information, especially about what to avoid, are the travellers' **noticeboards** in many of the Banglamphu guest houses, and the websites and Internet forums listed in Basics on p.25.

Tours of the city

If you can't face negotiating the public transport network, any taxi or tuk-tuk driver can be hired for the day to take you around the major or minor sights (B700–800), and every travel agent in the city can arrange this for you as well. Alternatively, the Bangkok Tourist Bureau (BTB) runs several quite unusual tours of the capital, including a night-time bicycle tour of Ratanakosin (every Sat 7–9.30pm; B390 including bicycle), weekend walking tours according to demand (B100), and a highly recommended 35-kilometre bike ride along the canal towpaths of Thonburi (see box on p.150). Of more limited interest is the BTB's tourist "tram" (more like an open-topped single-decker bus) which covers a forty-minute circuit from the Grand Palace down to Wat Pho, up to Banglamphu, and back to the palace, roughly every half an hour (daily 9.30am–5pm; B30).

A very popular, long-running bicycle tour, the **ABC Amazing Bangkok Cyclist Tour**, begins from Thanon Sukhumvit and takes you across the river to the surprisingly rural khlong- and riverside communities of Bang Krajao; these thirty-kilometre-long tours operate every afternoon year-round but need to be reserved in advance through Real Asia (ⓣ02 712 9301, ⓦwww.realasia.net; B1000 including bicycle). **Real Asia** also leads an interesting-sounding outing to the historic fishing port of Samut Sakhon (from B1750), and does boat trips through the Thonburi canals. **Tamarind Tours** runs imaginative and well-regarded (if pricey) tours of the city, including specialized options such as Bangkok X-Files and Bangkok After Dark (ⓣ02 238 3227, ⓦwww.tamarindtours.com; from US$50).

For details of Thonburi canal tours, see p.150; for Chao Phraya Express tourist boats, see p.102; and for dinner cruises along the Chao Phraya River, see p.172.

To get the most out of the city, it's worth getting hold of *Metro*, a monthly expats-oriented **listings magazine** available in bookstores, hotel shops and 7–11 stores. For B100, you get useful sections on restaurants, cinemas, nightlife and gay life. The less widely distributed *Farang* magazine (monthly; B100; mainly sold in Banglamphu) is more hip and straight-talking; it's aimed at backpackers and includes brief roundups of guest houses, bars, clubs, restaurants and sights in Bangkok and the rest of the country, as well as in Laos and Cambodia. The two English-language dailies, the *Nation* and the *Bangkok Post*, also give limited information about what's on across the city.

To get around Bangkok without spending much money, you'll need to buy a **bus map**. Of the several available at bookshops, hotels and some guest houses, the most useful is Bangkok Guide's *Bus Routes & Map*, which not only maps all major air-conditioned and non-air-conditioned bus routes but also carries detailed written itineraries of some two hundred bus routes. The long-running bright blue and yellow bus map published by Tour 'n' Guide also maps bus routes and dozens of smaller sois, but its street locations are not always reliable, and it can be hard to decipher exact bus routings. The bus routes on *Litehart's Groovy Map and Guide* are clearly colour-coded but only selected ones are given. The most accurate map for locating small streets and places of interest in the city is GeoCenter's *Bangkok 1:15,000*, best bought before you leave home, though it's also available in some Bangkok bookshops. Serious shoppers will want to buy a copy of the idiosyncratic *Nancy Chandler's Map of Bangkok*, which has lots of annotated recommendations on shops, markets and interesting neighbourhoods across the city and is reliably accurate; it's available in most tourist areas and from Ⓦwww.nancychandler.net.

City transport

The main form of transport in the city is **buses**, and once you've mastered the labyrinthine complexity of the route maps you'll be able to get to any part of the city, albeit slowly. Catching the various kinds of **taxi** can make a serious dent in your budget, and you'll still get held up by the daytime traffic jams. **Boats** are obviously more limited in their range, but they're regular and as cheap as buses, and you'll save a lot of time by using them whenever possible – a journey between Banglamphu and the GPO, for instance, will take around thirty minutes by water, half what it would take on land. The **Skytrain** and **subway** each have a similarly limited range but are also worth using whenever suitable for all or part of your journey; their networks roughly coincide with each other at the east end of Thanon Silom, at the corner of Soi Asoke and Thanon Sukhumvit, and on Thanon Phaholyothin by Chatuchak Park (Mo Chit), while the Skytrain joins up with the Chao Phraya River express boats at the vital hub of Sathorn/Saphan Taksin (Taksin Bridge) and the subway intersects the mainline railway at Hualamphong and Bang Sue stations. **Walking** might often be quicker than travelling by road, but the heat can be unbearable, distances are always further than they look on the map, and the engine fumes are stifling.

Useful bus routes

For more details on Banglamphu bus stops and routes, see p.110.

#3 (ordinary and air-con, 24hr): Northern Bus Terminal–Chatuchak Weekend Market–Thanon Phaholyothin–Thanon Samsen–Thanon Phra Athit (for Banglamphu guest houses)–Thanon Sanam Chai–Thanon Triphet–Memorial Bridge (for Pak Khlong Talat)–Taksin Monument–Wat Suwan.
#16 (ordinary and air-con): Thanon Srinarong–Thanon Samsen–Thewes (for guest houses)–Thanon Phitsanulok–Thanon Phrayathai–Siam Square–Thanon Suriwong–GPO–Tha Si Phraya.
#25 (ordinary and air-con, 24hr): Eastern Bus Terminal–Thanon Sukhumvit–Siam Square–Hualamphong Station–Thanon Yaowarat (for Chinatown)–Pahurat–Wat Pho–Tha Chang (for the Grand Palace).
#29 (ordinary and air-con, 24hr): Airport–Chatuchak Weekend Market–Victory Monument–Siam Square–Thanon Phrayathai–Thanon Rama 1V–Hualamphong Station.
#38 (ordinary): Chatuchak Weekend Market–Victory Monument–Thanon Phrayathai–Thanon Phetchaburi–Soi Asoke–Thanon Sukhumvit–Eastern Bus Terminal.
#39 (ordinary and air-con): Chatuchak Weekend Market–Victory Monument–Thanon Sri Ayutthaya–Thanon Lan Luang–Democracy Monument–Rajdamnoen Klang (for Thanon Khao San guest houses)–Sanam Luang.
#53 circular (also anti-clockwise; ordinary): Thewes–Thanon Krung Kasem–Hualamphong Station–Thanon Yaowarat–Pahurat–Pak Khlong Talat–Thanon Maharat (for Wat Pho, the Grand Palace and Wat Mahathat)–Sanam Luang (for National Museum)–Thanon Phra Athit and Thanon Samsen (for Banglamphu guest houses)–Thewes.
#56 circular (also clockwise; ordinary): Thanon Phra Sumen–Wat Bowoniwes–Thanon Pracha Thipatai–Thanon Ratchasima (for Vimanmek Palace)–Thanon Rajwithi–Krung Thon Bridge–Thonburi–Memorial Bridge–Thanon Chakraphet (for Chinatown)–Thanon Mahachai–Democracy Monument–Thanon Tanao (for Khao San guest houses)–Thanon Phra Sumen.
#59 (ordinary and air-con, 24hr): Airport–Chatuchak Weekend Market–Victory Monument–Thanon Phrayathai–Thanon Phetchaburi–Phanfa (for Khlong Sen Seb and Golden Mount)–Democracy Monument (for Banglamphu guest houses)–Grand Palace–Sanam Luang.
#124 (ordinary): Southern Bus Terminal–Phra Pinklao Bridge–Sanam Luang (for Banglamphu guest houses)–Wat Pho.

Buses

Bangkok is served by over four hundred bus routes, reputedly the world's largest bus network, on which operate three main types of bus service. **Ordinary** (non-air-con) buses come in a variety of colours and sizes, on which fares range from B3.50 to B5.50; most routes operate from about 4am to 10pm, but some maintain a 24-hour service, as noted in the box above. **Air-conditioned** buses are either blue, orange or white (some of these are articulated) and charge between B8 and B24 according to distance travelled; most stop at around 8–8.30pm, but a few of the more popular routes run late-night services. As buses can only go as fast as the car in front, which at the moment is averaging 4 kilometres per hour, you'll probably be spending a long time on each journey, so you'd be well advised to pay the extra for cool air – and the air-conditioned buses are usually less crowded, too. Note that an attempt to clarify the numbering of the main air-con buses by

#159 (ordinary): Southern Bus Terminal – Phra Pinklao Bridge–Democracy Monument–Hualamphong Station–MBK Shopping Centre–Thanon Ratchaprarop–Victory Monument–Chatuchak Weekend Market–Northern Bus Terminal.
#502 or #2 (air-con): Loetsin Hospital–Thanon Silom–Thanon Rama IV–MBK Shopping Centre (for Siam Square)–Thanon Phrayathai–Victory Monument–Chatuchak Weekend Market–Lard Phrao–Suwinthawong.
#503 or #3 (air-con): Southern Bus Terminal–Thanon Phra Pinklao–Phra Pinklao Bridge (for Banglamphu guest houses)–Democracy Monument–Rajdamnoen Nok (for TAT and boxing stadium)–Wat Benjamabophit–Thanon Sri Ayutthaya (for Thewes guest houses)–Victory Monument–Chatuchak Weekend Market–Rangsit.
#504 or #4 (air-con): Airport–Thanon Rajaprarop–Thanon Rajdamri–Thanon Silom–Thanon Charoen Krung–Krungthep Bridge–Thonburi.
#507 or #7 (air-con): Southern Bus Terminal–Thanon Phra Pinklao–Phra Pinklao Bridge (for Banglamphu guest houses)–Sanam Luang–Thanon Charoen Krung (New Road)–Thanon Chakraphet–Thanon Yaowarat (for Chinatown and Wat Traimit)–Hualamphong Station–Thanon Rama IV (for Soi Ngam Duphli guest houses)–Bang Na Intersection–Pak Nam (for Ancient City buses).
#508 or #8 (air-con): Wat Pho–Grand Palace–Thanon Charoen Krung–Thanon Krung Kasem–Siam Square–Thanon Ploenchit–Thanon Sukhumvit–Eastern Bus Terminal–Pak Nam (for Ancient City buses).
#509 or #9 (air-con): Nonthaburi Pier–Chatuchak Weekend Market–Victory Monument–Thanon Rajwithi–Thanon Sawankhalok–Thanon Phitsanulok–Thanon Rajdamnoen Nok–Democracy Monument–Rajdamnoen Klang (for Banglamphu guest houses)–Phra Pinklao Bridge–Thonburi.
#510 or #10 (air-con): Airport–Chatuchak Weekend Market–Victory Monument–Dusit Zoo–Thanon Rajwithi–Krung Thon Bridge (for Thewes guest houses)–Thonburi.
#511 or #11 (air-con): Southern Bus Terminal–Phra Pinklao Bridge–Rajdamnoen Klang–Wat Bowoniwes (for Banglamphu guest houses)–Democracy Monument–Thanon Lan Luang–Thanon Phetchaburi–Thanon Sukhumvit–Eastern Bus Terminal–Pak Nam (for Ancient City buses).
#512 or #12 (air-con): Northern Bus Terminal–Chatuchak Weekend Market–Thanon Phetchaburi–Thanon Lan Luang–Democracy Monument (for Banglamphu guest houses)–Sanam Luang–Tha Chang (for Grand Palace)–Pak Khlong Talat.
#513 or #13 (air-con): Airport–Chatuchak Weekend Market–Victory Monument–Thanon Phraya Thai–Thanon Sri Ayutthaya–Thanon Rajaprarop–Thanon Sukhumvit–Eastern Bus Terminal–Sukhumvit Soi 62.

adding a "5" on the front has so far not been fully enforced – you're likely to find, for example, both air-con #11 and air-con #511 plying the same route between the Southern Bus Terminal and Thanon Sukhumvit. It's also possible during the day to travel certain routes on pink, air-conditioned private **microbuses**, which were designed with the commuter in mind and offer the certainty of a seat (no standing allowed). The fare is generally a flat B20 (exact money only), which is dropped into a box beside the driver's seat, though on some routes short journeys are charged at B10, as advertised on a placard in the bus's front window.

Some of the most useful city-bus routes are described in the box above; for a comprehensive roundup of bus routes in the capital, buy a copy of Bangkok Guide's *Bus Routes & Map* (see p.99), or log onto the Bangkok Mass Transit Authority website (Ⓦwww.bmta.co.th), which gives details of all city-bus routes, bar microbuses and airport buses.

Boats

Bangkok was built as an amphibious city around a network of canals – or **khlongs** – and the first streets were constructed only in the second half of the nineteenth century. Many canals remain on the Thonburi side of the river, but most of those on the Bangkok side have been turned into roads. The Chao Phraya River itself is still a major transport route for residents and non-residents alike, forming more of a link than a barrier between the two halves of the city.

Express boats

The Chao Phraya Express Boat Company operates the vital **express-boat** (*reua duan*) service, using large water buses to plough up and down the river, between clearly signed piers (*tha*), which appear on all Bangkok maps. Tha Sathorn, which gives access to the Skytrain network at Saphan Taksin Station, has recently been designated "Central Pier", with piers to the south of here numbered S1, S2, etc, those to the north N1, N2 and so on – the important stops in the centre of the city are outlined in the box opposite and marked on our city map (see pp.92–3). Its basic route, one hour thirty minutes in total, runs between Wat Rajsingkorn, just upriver of Krung Thep Bridge, in the south, and Nonthaburi in the north. These "**standard**" boats set off every fifteen minutes or so between around 6am and 7.15pm (6.30pm on Sat & Sun), the last boat in each direction flying a dark-blue flag. Boats do not necessarily stop at every landing – they only pull in if people want to get on or off, and when they do stop, it's not for long – when you want to get off, be ready at the back of the boat in good time for your pier. During busy periods, certain "**special express**" boats operate limited-stop services on set routes, flying either a **yellow flag** (Nonthaburi to Rajburana, far downriver beyond Krung Thep Bridge, in about 50min; Mon–Fri roughly 6–9am & 4–7pm) or an **orange flag** (Nonthaburi to Wat Rajsingkorn in 1hr; Mon–Fri roughly 6–9am & 2–7pm, Sat 7–9am & 4–6pm).

Tickets can be bought on board, and cost B6–10 on standard boats according to distance travelled, B10 flat rate on orange-flag boats and B15 on yellow-flag boats. Don't discard your ticket until you're off the boat, as the staff at some piers impose a B1 fine on anyone disembarking without one.

The Chao Phraya Express Boat Company now also runs **tourist boats**, distinguished by their light-blue flags, between Sathorn (departs every 30min 9.30am–3pm on the hour and half-hour) and Banglamphu (departs every 30min 10am–3.30pm on the hour and half-hour). In between (in both directions), these boats call in at Oriental, Si Phraya, Rachawongse, the Princess Mother Memorial Park in Thonburi, Thien, Maharaj (near Wat Mahathat and the Grand Palace, with free connecting boats across to the Royal Barge Museum) and Wang Lang. On-board guides provide running commentaries, and a one-day ticket for unlimited trips, which also allows you to use other express boats within the same route between 9am and 7.30pm, costs B75.

Cross-river ferries

Smaller than express boats are the slow **cross-river ferries** (*reua kham fak*), which shuttle back and forth between the same two points. Found at or beside every express stop and plenty of other piers in between, they are especially useful for exploring Thonburi and for connections to Chao Phraya special express-boat stops during rush hours. Fares are B2, which you usually pay at the entrance to the pier.

Central stops for the Chao Phraya express boats

N15	Thewes (all standard and special express boats) – for Thewes guest houses.
N14	Rama VIII Bridge (standard and orange flag) – for Samsen Soi 5.
N13	Phra Athit (standard) – for Thanon Phra Athit, Thanon Khao San and Banglamphu guest houses.
N12	Phra Pinklao Bridge (all standard and special express boats) – for Royal Barge Museum and Thonburi shops.
N11	Bangkok Noi (or Thonburi Railway Station; standard) – for trains to Kanchanaburi.
N10	Wang Lang for boats going downstream, adjacent Prannok for upstream boats (all standard and special express boats) – for Siriraj Hospital and hospital museums.
N9	Chang (standard and orange flag) – for the Grand Palace.
N8	Thien (standard) – for Wat Pho, and the cross-river ferry to Wat Arun.
N7	Ratchini (aka Rajinee; standard).
N6	Saphan Phut (Memorial Bridge; standard and orange flag) – for Pahurat, Pak Khlong Talat and Wat Prayoon. Due to increasing congestion on the river, boats going downstream now stop on the Thonburi bank, upstream boats on the Bangkok side; frequent cross-river ferries connect the two sides.
N5	Rachawongse (aka Rajawong; all standard and special express boats) – for Chinatown.
N4	Harbour Department (standard).
N3	Si Phraya (all standard and special express boats) – walk north past the *Sheraton Royal Orchid Hotel* for River City shopping complex.
N2	Wat Muang Kae (standard) – for GPO.
N1	Oriental (standard and orange flag) – for Thanon Silom.
Central	Sathorn (all standard and special express boats) – for the Skytrain (Saphan Taksin Station) and Thanon Sathorn.

Piers are marked on the map on pp.92–93.

Longtail boats

Longtail boats (*reua hang yao*) ply the khlongs of Thonburi like buses, stopping at designated shelters (fares are in line with those of express boats), and are available for individual rental here and on the river (see box on p.150). On the Bangkok side, **Khlong Sen Seb** is well served by longtails, which run at least every fifteen minutes during daylight hours from the Phanfa pier at the Golden Mount (handy for Banglamphu, Ratanakosin and Chinatown), and head way out east to Wat Sribunruang, with useful stops at Thanon Phrayathai, aka Saphan Hua Chang (for Jim Thompson's House and Ratchathevi Skytrain stop); Pratunam (for the Erawan Shrine); Thanon Witthayu (Wireless Road); and Soi Nana Nua (Soi 3), Soi Asoke (Soi 21, for TAT headquarters and Phetchaburi subway stop), Soi Thonglo (Soi 55) and Soi Ekamai (Soi 63), all off Thanon Sukhumvit. This is your quickest and most interesting way of getting between the west and east parts of town, if you can stand the stench of the canal. You may have trouble actually locating the piers as none are signed in English and they all look very unassuming and rickety; see the map on pp.92–93 for locations and keep your eyes peeled for a plain wooden jetty – most jetties serve boats running in both directions. Once on the boat, state your destination to the conductor when he collects your fare, which will be between B7 and B15. Due to the construction of some low bridges, all passengers change onto a different boat at Tha Pratunam and then again at the stop way out east on Sukhumvit Soi 71 – just follow the crowd.

The Skytrain and the subway

Although its network is limited, the **BTS Skytrain**, or *rot fai faa* (Ⓦwww.bts.co.th), provides a much faster alternative to the bus, is clean, efficient and vigorously air-conditioned, and – because fares are comparatively high for Bangkokians – is rarely crowded. There are only two Skytrain lines, both running every few minutes from 6am to midnight, with **fares** of B10–40 per trip depending on distance travelled. You'd really have to be motoring to justify buying a day **pass** at B100, but the B280 "three-day" pass is more likely to appeal – especially as it's not a strictly 72-hour pass but is valid until midnight on the final day, so by buying yours early in the morning, you can effectively turn it into a four-day pass. Other passes available include ten-trip, fifteen-trip and thirty-trip cards for B250, B300 and B540 respectively, valid for thirty days.

The **Sukhumvit Line** runs from Mo Chit (stop #N8) in the northern part of the city (near Chatuchak Market and the Northern Bus Terminal) south via Victory Monument (N3) to the interchange, **Central Station**, at Siam Square, and then east along Thanon Ploenchit and Thanon Sukhumvit, via the Eastern Bus Terminal (Ekamai; E7), to On Nut (Soi 77, Thanon Sukhumvit; E9); the whole journey to the eastern end of town from Mo Chit takes around thirty minutes.

The **Silom Line** runs from the National Stadium (W1), just west of Siam Square, through Central Station, and then south along Thanon Rajdamri, Thanon Silom and Thanon Sathorn, via Sala Daeng near Patpong (S2), to Saphan Taksin (Sathorn Bridge; S6), to link up with the full gamut of express boats on the Chao Phraya River. Free feeder buses for Skytrain passholders, currently covering six circular routes, mostly along Thanon Sukhumvit, are geared more for commuters than visitors, but pick up a copy of the ubiquitous free BTS **map** if you want more information.

The Skytrain network is just the first phase of a planned city transport programme that will be greatly enhanced by an underground rail system, the **subway** (or metro; in Thai, *rot fai faa mahanakhon*). At the time of writing, only one line was imminent, the Blue Line, due to become operational in 2004 (a partial opening from Bang Sue to Huai Khwang, followed by the whole line a few months later). With fares comparable to those on the Skytrain, the subway will run a frequent service (up to every 2min in rush hour) from Hualamphong train station, first heading east along Thanon Rama IV, with useful stops at Sam Yan (for Si Phraya and Phrayathai roads), Silom (near the Sala Daeng Skytrain station) and Lumphini (Thanon Sathorn/southeast corner of Lumphini Park). The line then turns north up Soi Asoke/Thanon Ratchadapisek via the Queen Sirikit National Convention Centre, Sukhumvit Station (near Asoke Skytrain station), Phetchaburi (handy for Khlong Sen Seb boats) and the Thailand Cultural Centre, before looping around via Chatuchak Park (near Mo Chit Skytrain station) and Kampaeng Phet (best stop for the weekend market) to terminate at Bang Sue railway station in the north of the city.

Taxis

Bangkok **taxis** come in three forms, and are so plentiful that you rarely have to wait more than a couple of minutes before spotting an empty one of any description. Neither tuk-tuks nor motorbike taxis have meters, so you should agree on a price before setting off, and expect to do a fair amount of haggling.

For nearly all journeys, the best and most comfortable option is to flag down one of Bangkok's metered, air-conditioned **taxi cabs**; look out for the "TAXI METER" sign on the roof, and a red light in the windscreen in front of the passenger seat, which means the cab is available for hire. Fares start at B35, and are displayed on a clearly visible meter that the driver should reset at the start of each trip, and increase in stages on a combined distance/time formula; as an example, a journey from Banglamphu to Silom will cost around B80–90 at a quiet time of day. Try to have change with you as cabs tend not to carry a lot of money; tipping of up to ten percent is common, though occasionally a cabbie will round down the fare on the meter. If a driver tries to quote a flat fare rather than using the meter, let him go, and avoid the now-rare unmetered cabs (denoted by a "TAXI" sign on the roof).

Somewhat less stable though typically Thai, **tuk-tuks** have little to recommend them. These noisy, three-wheeled, open-sided buggies, which can carry three medium-sized passengers comfortably, fully expose you to the worst of Bangkok's pollution and weather, but they're a lot nippier than taxi cabs, and the drivers have no qualms about taking semi-legal measures to avoid gridlocks. Locals might use tuk-tuks for short journeys – though you'll have to bargain hard to get a fare lower than the taxi-cab flagfall of B35 – while a longer trip from Banglamphu to Silom, for example, will set you back around B100. Be aware, also, that tuk-tuk drivers tend to speak less English than taxi drivers – and there have been cases of robberies and attacks on women passengers late at night. During the day it's quite common for tuk-tuk drivers to try and **con** their passengers into visiting a jewellery or expensive souvenir shop with them, for which they get a hefty commission; the usual tactic involves falsely informing tourists that the Grand Palace, or whatever their destination might be, is closed (see p.122), and offering instead a ridiculously cheap, even free, city tour.

Motorbike taxis generally congregate at the entrances to long sois – pick the riders out by their numbered, coloured vests – and charge B5–15 for short trips down into the side streets. If you're short on time and have nerves of steel, it's also possible to charter them for hairy journeys out on the main roads (a short trip, say from Patpong to Lumphini Stadium, should cost around B40). Crash helmets are compulsory on all main roads in the capital (traffic police fine non-wearers on the spot), though they're rarely worn on trips down the sois and the local press has reported complaints from people who've caught head-lice this way (they suggest wearing a headscarf under the helmet).

Accommodation

If your time in Bangkok is limited, you should think especially carefully about what you want to do in the city before deciding which part of town to stay in. Traffic jams are so appalling here that you may not want to explore too far from your hotel, and accommodation in some parts of the city is significantly more expensive than others.

For double rooms under B400, your widest choice lies with the **guest houses** of Banglamphu and the smaller, dingier travellers' ghetto that has grown up around Soi Ngam Duphli, off the south side of Thanon Rama IV. The most inexpensive rooms here are no-frills crash-pads: small and often windowless, with thin walls and shared bathrooms. Unless you pay cash in advance, bookings are rarely accepted by guest houses, but it's often worth phoning to establish whether a place is full already. During peak season (Nov–Feb) you may have difficulty getting a room after noon.

Banglamphu is also starting to cater for the slightly better-off tourist and you'll find some good mid-priced options along Thanon Khao San. But the majority of the city's **moderate and expensive** rooms are concentrated downtown around Siam Square and Thanon Ploenchit and in the area between Thanon Rama IV and Thanon Charoen Krung (New Road), along Thanon Sukhumvit, and to a lesser extent in Chinatown. Air-conditioned rooms with hot-water bathrooms can be had for as little as B500 in these areas, but for that you're looking at a rather basic cubicle; you'll probably have to pay more like B800 for smart furnishings and a swimming pool. The cream of Bangkok's **deluxe** tourist accommodation, with rates starting from B3000, is scenically sited along the banks of the Chao Phraya River, though there are a few top-notch hotels in the downtown area too, which is also where you'll find the best business hotels. Details of accommodation **near Don Muang Airport** are given on p.95.

For **long-stay accommodation**, the most economical option is usually a room with a bathroom in an apartment building, which is likely to set you back at least B5000 a month. The *Bangkok Post* carries rental ads in its Thursday property section, as does the monthly listings magazine *Metro*; vacancies are also sometimes advertised on the noticeboards in the AUA Language Centre on Thanon Rajdamri. Many foreigners end up living in apartments off Thanon Sukhumvit, around Victory Monument and Pratunam, or on Soi Boonprarop, off Thanon Rajaprarop just north of Pratunam. Visit the Teaching in Thailand website, Ⓦ www.ajarn.com, for useful advice on how to find a place to live in Bangkok.

Banglamphu

Nearly all backpackers head straight for **Banglamphu**, Bangkok's long-established travellers' ghetto, location of the cheapest accommodation and some of the best nightlife in the city, and arguably the most enjoyable area to base yourself in the city. It's within easy reach of the Grand Palace and other major sights in Ratanakosin, and has enough bars, restaurants and shops to keep any visitor happy for a week or more, though some people find this insularity tiresome after just a few hours.

At the heart of Banglamphu is the legendary **Thanon Khao San**, almost a caricature of a travellers' centre, crammed with Internet cafés, dodgy travel agents and restaurants serving yoghurt shakes and muesli, the sidewalks lined with stalls flogging cheap backpackers' fashions, racks of bootleg music and video CDs, tattooists and hair-braiders. It's a lively, high-energy base: great for shopping and making travel arrangements (though beware the innumerable Khao San scams, as outlined in Basics, p.59) and a good place to meet other travellers. It's especially fun at night when young Thais from all over the city gather here to browse the countless clothes stalls, mingle with the crowds of foreigners and squash into the bars and clubs that have made Khao San *the* place to party.

The increasingly sophisticated nightlife scene has enticed more moneyed travellers into Banglamphu and a growing number of Khao San **guest houses** are reinventing themselves as good-value mini-hotels boasting chic decor, swimming pools, and even views from the windows – a remarkable facelift for the cardboard cells of old. The cheap sleeps are still there though – in the darker corners of Khao San itself, as well as on the smaller, quieter roads off and around it, in particular on **Soi Chana Songkhram**, which encircles the wat of the same name; along **Phra Athit**, which runs parallel to the Chao Phraya River and is packed with trendy Thai café-bars and restaurants (and also has a useful express-boat stop); and in the residential alleyways that parallel Thanon Khao San to the south: **Trok Mayom** and **Damnoen Klang Neua**. About ten minutes' walk north from Thanon Khao San, the handful of guest houses scattered amongst the neighbourhood shophouses of the **Thanon Samsen sois** offer a more authentically Thai atmosphere. A further fifteen minutes' walk in the same direction will take you to **Thanon Sri Ayutthaya**, behind the National Library in **Thewes** (a seven-minute walk from the express-boat stop), the calmest area in Banglamphu, where rooms are larger and guest houses smaller. We've listed only the cream of what's on offer in each small enclave of Banglamphu: if your first choice is full there'll almost certainly be a vacancy somewhere just along the soi, if not right next door. **Theft** is a problem in Banglamphu, particularly at the cheaper guest houses, so don't leave anything valuable in your room and heed the guest houses' notices about padlocks and safety lockers.

Banglamphu is served by plenty of **public transport**. All the guest houses listed lie only a few minutes' walk from Chao Phraya **express boat** stops N13 (Phra Athit, sometimes known as Banglamphu), N14 (Rama VIII Bridge) and N15 (Thewes), as detailed in the box on p.103. Note that if you're using the boat service in the evening to head downtown via the Central BTS train station at Saphan Taksin, the last boat leaves N13 at about 7pm. If you're simply crossing the river, there's no need to wait for the Chao Phraya Express as a **cross-river shuttle boat** runs continually during daylight hours between a second Phra Athit pier (about 150m south of the N13 pier) and Tha Phra Pinklao on the Thonburi bank. Banglamphu is also served by **public longtail boats** along Khlong Sen Seb (see p.103). For details of the most useful **buses** in and out of Banglamphu and where to catch them, see the box on p.110. **Airport bus** A2 has several stops in Banglamphu (see p.94), though for the cheapest route from Don Muang to Banglamphu, take ordinary bus #29 from the road 100m right of International Terminal 1 as far as Mo Chit Skytrain station and change onto ordinary bus #3, which will take you to Thanon Phra Athit in Banglamphu: the trip will probably take about 90 minutes but costs just B7. The same route works in reverse, and leaves from Bus Stop 3 on Thanon Phra Athit (see map pp.108–109).

Traveller-oriented facilities in Banglamphu are second to none. The **Bangkok Information Centre** is on Thanon Phra Athit (see p.98), and there's a 24-hour **tourist information and assistance booth** in front of the police station on the west corner of Thanon Khao San. The closest **poste restante** service to Khao San is at Ratchadamnoen Post Office on the eastern stretch of Soi Damnoen Klang Neua, but the one at Banglamphubon Post Office near Wat Bowoniwes is also handy (for full details see p.204). Almost every alternate building on Thanon Khao San and on the west arm of Soi Ram Bhuttri offers **Internet access**, as do many of the guest houses; intense competition keeps the rates very low. There are also Catnet Internet terminals (see Basics, p.56) at the Ratchadamnoen Post Office. As well as numerous money **exchange** places on Thanon Khao San, there are two branches of national banks (with ATMs), an outlet for Boots the Chemist and a couple of self-service laundries.

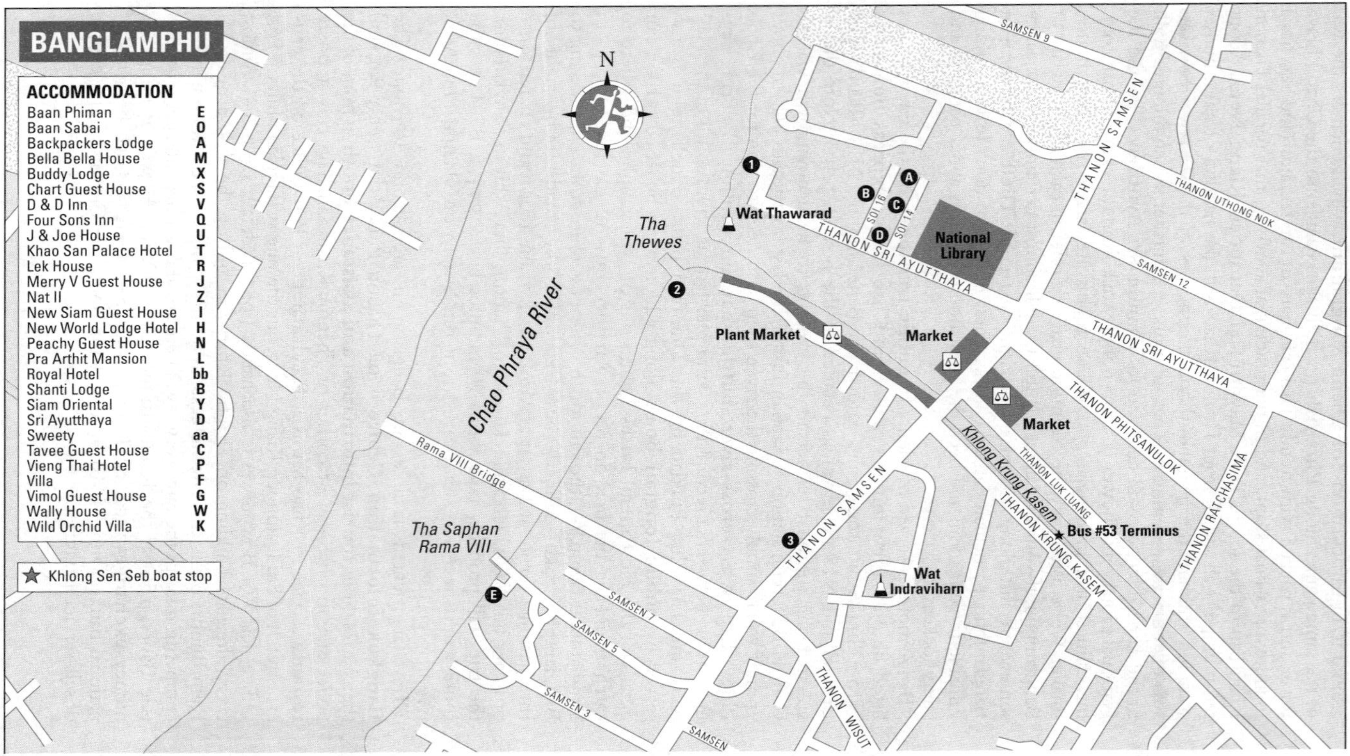
BANGLAMPHU
ACCOMMODATION
Baan Phiman E
Baan Sabai O
Backpackers Lodge A
Bella Bella House M
Buddy Lodge X
Chart Guest House S
D & D Inn V
Four Sons Inn Q
J & Joe House U
Khao San Palace Hotel T
Lek House R
Merry V Guest House J
Nat II Z
New Siam Guest House I
New World Lodge Hotel H
Peachy Guest House N
Pra Arthit Mansion L
Royal Hotel bb
Shanti Lodge B
Siam Oriental Y
Sri Ayutthaya D
Sweety aa
Tavee Guest House C
Vieng Thai Hotel P
Villa F
Vimol Guest House G
Wally House W
Wild Orchid Villa K
Khlong Sen Seb boat stop
N
Chao Phraya River
Tha Thewes
Tha Saphan Rama VIII
Rama VIII Bridge
Wat Thawarad
National Library
Plant Market
Market
Market
Wat Indraviharn
Bus #53 Terminus
Khlong Krung Kasem
THANON SAMSEN
THANON SRI AYUTTHAYA
THANON PHITSANULOK
THANON RATCHASIMA
THANON UTHONG NOK
THANON LUK LUANG
THANON KRUNG KASEM
THANON WISUT
SAMSEN 9
SAMSEN 12
SAMSEN 7
SAMSEN 5
SAMSEN 3
SAMSEN
SOI 16
SOI 14

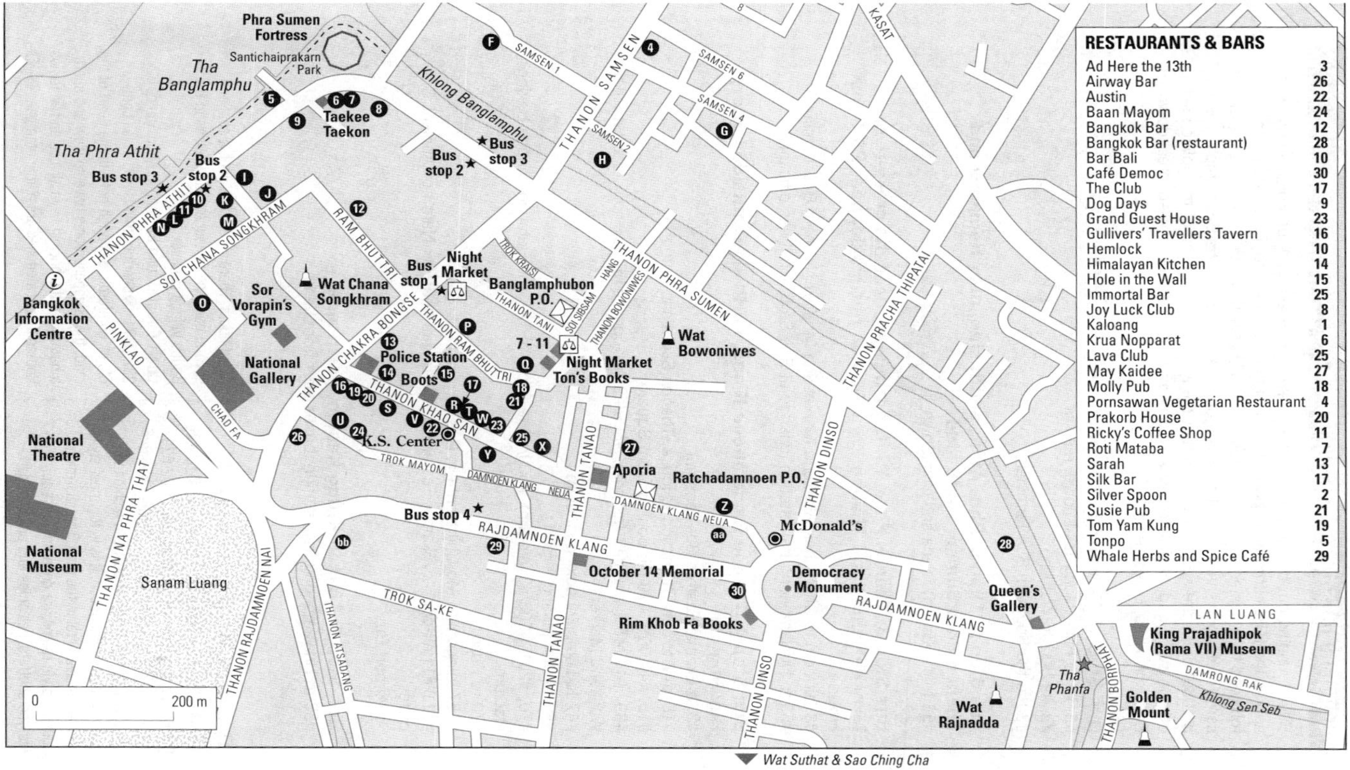
RESTAURANTS & BARS
Ad Here the 13th 3
Airway Bar 26
Austin 22
Baan Mayom 24
Bangkok Bar 12
Bangkok Bar (restaurant) 28
Bar Bali 10
Café Democ 30
The Club 17
Dog Days 9
Grand Guest House 23
Gullivers' Travellers Tavern 16
Hemlock 10
Himalayan Kitchen 14
Hole in the Wall 15
Immortal Bar 25
Joy Luck Club 8
Kaloang 1
Krua Nopparat 6
Lava Club 25
May Kaidee 27
Molly Pub 18
Pornsawan Vegetarian Restaurant 4
Prakorb House 20
Ricky's Coffee Shop 11
Roti Mataba 7
Sarah 13
Silk Bar 17
Silver Spoon 2
Susie Pub 21
Tom Yam Kung 19
Tonpo 5
Whale Herbs and Spice Café 29
Phra Sumen Fortress
Santichaiprakarn Park
Tha Banglamphu
Khlong Banglamphu
Taekee Taekon
Tha Phra Athit
Bus stop 3
Bus stop 2
Bus stop 1
Bus stop 4
THANON PHRA ATHIT
SOI CHANA SONGKHRAM
RAM BHUTTRI
Wat Chana Songkhram
Sor Vorapin's Gym
National Gallery
Bangkok Information Centre
PINKLAO
CHAD FA
National Theatre
National Museum
THANON NA PHRA THAT
Sanam Luang
THANON RAJDAMNOEN NAI
THANON CHAKRA BONGSE
Night Market
Banglamphubon P.O.
TROK KRAIS
THANON TANI
SOI SIBSAM
HANG
THANON BOWONIWES
THANON RAM BHUTTRI
Police Station
Boots
7 - 11
Night Market
Ton's Books
THANON KHAO SAN
K.S. Center
TROK MAYOM
DAMNOEN KLANG NEUA
THANON TANAO
Aporia
Ratchadamnoen P.O.
DAMNOEN KLANG NEUA
McDonald's
RAJDAMNOEN KLANG
October 14 Memorial
Democracy Monument
Rim Khob Fa Books
TROK SA-KE
THANON ATSADANG
THANON TANAO
THANON DINSO
THANON DINSO
Wat Bowoniwes
THANON PHRA SUMEN
THANON SAMSEN
SAMSEN 1
SAMSEN 2
SAMSEN 4
SAMSEN 6
KASAT
THANON PRACHA THIPATAI
Queen's Gallery
LAN LUANG
King Prajadhipok (Rama VII) Museum
DAMRONG RAK
Khlong Sen Seb
THANON BORIPHAT
Tha Phanfa
Golden Mount
Wat Rajnadda
0 200 m
Wat Suthat & Sao Ching Cha

Banglamphu's bus stops and routes

Buses running out of Banglamphu have several different pick-up points in the area, and as the BTB information booth has assigned numbers to these bus stops we've followed their system to make things simpler. Where there are two bus stops on the same route they share a number. Bus stops are marked on the Banglamphu map on p.108. For on-the-spot advice, contact the BTB booth in front of the police station off the west end of Thanon Khao San, and for a more detailed breakdown of Bangkok's bus routes see p.100.

Bus Stop 1: Thanon Chakrabongse, in front of the 7-11
#6, #9 to Pak Khlong Talat flower market
#6, #9, #32 to Wat Pho
#30 to the Southern Bus Terminal

Bus Stop 2: Thanon Phra Athit, south side, near Hemlock; and Thanon Phra Sumen, south side
#53 to the Grand Palace and Chinatown

Bus Stop 3: Thanon Phra Athit, north side, near the cross-river ferry entrance; and Thanon Phra Sumen, north side, near PS Guest House
#3 (air-con) to Chatuchak Weekend Market and Mo Chit Northern Bus Terminal
#53 to Hualamphong train station (change at Bus Stop 5, but same ticket)

Bus Stop 4: Thanon Rajdamnoen Klang, north side, outside Lottery Building
#2 to Ekamai Eastern Bus Terminal
#15, #47 to Jim Thompson's House, Thanon Silom and Patpong
#15, #47, #79, #79 (air-con) to Siam Square
#39, #44, #59, #503/#3 (air-con), #509/#9 (air-con), #157 (air-con) to Chatuchak Weekend Market
#47 to Lumphini boxing stadium
#59 to Don Muang Airport
#70, #201, #503/#3 (air-con), #509/#9 (air-con) to TAT and Ratchadamnoen boxing stadium
#70 to Dusit
#157 (air-con) to Mo Chit Northern Bus Terminal
#511/#11(air-con) to Ekamai Eastern Bus Terminal and Pak Nam (for Ancient City buses)
A2 Airport Bus

Bus Stop 5: Thanon Krung Kasem, north side
#53 to Hualamphong train station (buses start from here)

Thanon Khao San and Soi Damnoen Klang Neua

Buddy Lodge 265 Thanon Khao San ⓣ 02 629 4477, ⓦ www.buddylodge.com. Setting the standard for the new breed of chic and fashionable Khao San accommodation, this is the most stylish and expensive hotel in the area. The charming, colonial-style rooms are done out in cream, with louvred shutters, balconies and polished dark-wood floors. There's a rooftop pool, a spa, and several bars and restaurants downstairs in the Buddy Village complex. ❽

Chart Guest House 62 Thanon Khao San ⓣ 02 282 0171, ⓔ chartguesthouse@hotmail.com. Clean, comfortable enough hotel in the heart of the road; the cheapest rooms have no view and share a bathroom; the priciest have air-con and windows. Rooms in all categories are a little cramped. ❸–❹

D & D Inn 68–70 Thanon Khao San ⓣ02 629 5252, ⓦwww.ddinn.com. The delightful rooftop pool, with expansive views, is the clincher at this good-value hotel located in the midst of the throng. The rooms are comfortably furnished and perfectly fine, if not immaculate, but avoid the cheapest windowless ones and choose instead between views over the city or Khao San. All rooms are en suite and air-conditioned. ❹–❺
Four Sons Inn 327 Thanon Ram Bhuttri ⓣ02 629 5812, ⓦwww.foursonsinn.com. Good, clean mid-range little hotel just 50m from Khao San. Rooms are well designed and all have air-con and TV, but the cheapest don't have windows. ❹–❺
J & Joe House 1 Trok Mayom ⓣ02 281 2949. Simple, inexpensive rooms, all with shared bathrooms, in a traditional wooden house located among real Thai homes (very unusual for Banglamphu) in a narrow alley off Khao San. ❷
Khao San Palace Hotel 139 Thanon Khao San ⓣ02 282 0578. Clean and well-appointed hotel with a rooftop pool. All rooms have bathrooms and windows and some also have air-con and TV. The best rooms are in the new wing – they're nicely tiled and some have rooftop views. ❸–❺
Lek House 125 Thanon Khao San ⓣ02 281 8441. Classic old-style Khao San guest house, with small, basic rooms and shared facilities, but less shabby than many others in the same price bracket and a lot friendlier than most. Could get noisy at night as it's right next to the popular *Silk Bar*. ❷
Nat II 91–95 Soi Damnoen Klang Neua (aka Soi Post Office) ⓣ02 282 0211. Shabby but cheap rooms, some with windows and some en suite, in a fairly quiet location, though you may be woken by the 5am prayer calls at the local mosque. There are only a couple of other guest houses on this road, so it has a friendly, neighbourhood feel to it, even though Khao San is less than 200m away. ❷
Royal (Ratanakosin) Hotel 2 Thanon Rajdamnoen Klang ⓣ02 222 9111, ⓦwww.ratanakosinhotel.com. Determinedly old-fashioned hotel that's used mainly by older Thai tourists and for conferences. Air-con rooms in the new wing are smart if unexciting and there's a pool and a restaurant, but the chief attraction is the location, just a 5-min stroll from Sanam Luang (or a further 10min to the Grand Palace) – though getting to Thanon Khao San entails a life-endangering leap across two very busy main roads. ❼
Siam Oriental 190 Thanon Khao San ⓣ02 629 0312, ⓕ02 629 0310. Small hotel right in the middle of Thanon Khao San, offering spartan but clean rooms, all with attached bathrooms and some with windows. Some rooms have air-con and a few also have balconies. ❸–❺
Sweety Soi Damnoen Klang Neua ⓣ02 280 2191, ⓔsweetygh@hotmail.com. Popular place that's one of the least expensive in Banglamphu; it's nicely located away from the fray but convenient for Khao San. Rooms are very small and a bit grotty, but many have windows, and beds come with thick mattresses; some have private bathrooms and some also have air-con. ❷–❹
Vieng Thai Hotel 42 Thanon Ram Bhuttri ⓣ02 280 5392, ⓦwww.viengtai.co.th. The second best of the options in Banglamphu's upper price bracket, with a good location on a fairly quiet road that's just a few metres from the shops and restaurants of Thanon Khao San. Rooms are a decent size if not especially stylish, they all have air-con and TV, and there's a big pool. ❼
Wally House 189/1–2 Thanon Khao San ⓣ02 282 7067. Small guest house behind the restaurant of the same name, where the simplest rooms – just a bed and four tiled walls – are among the cheapest in the area, or you can pay a bit extra for a bathroom and fan. ❷–❸

Soi Chana Songkhram and Phra Athit

Baan Sabai 12 Soi Rongmai, between Soi Chana Songkhram and Thanon Chao Fa ⓣ02 629 1599, ⓔbaansabai@hotmail.com. Built round a courtyard, this large, hotel-style guest house has a range of bright, fresh and decent-sized en-suite rooms, some of them air-con, though the cheapest have no windows. ❸–❹
Bella Bella House 74 Soi Chana Songkhram ⓣ02 629 3090. Delightful guest house where all the pale-pink rooms are immaculate and some boast lovely views over Wat Chana Songkhram. The cheapest share bathrooms, and the most expensive have air-con. Good value for the standard so fills up fast. ❷–❹
Merry V 35 Soi Chana Songkhram ⓣ02 282 9267. Large, efficiently run guest house offering some of the cheapest accommodation in Banglamphu. Rooms are basic and small, they all share bathrooms and it's pot luck whether you get a window or not. Good noticeboard in the downstairs restaurant. ❷
New Siam Guest House 21 Soi Chana Songkhram ⓣ02 282 4554, ⓦwww.newsiam.net. Well-organized, hotel-style guest house offering decent if rather faded rooms, all with fans and windows, and plenty of clothes hooks. The cheapest rooms share bathrooms, the priciest have air-con. Guests can use the pool at nearby *New Siam 2* for B60. ❸–❹

Peachy Guest House 10 Thanon Phra Athit ⓣ02 281 6471. Popular, cheap place set round a small courtyard, with clean, spartan rooms, most with shared bathrooms but some with air-con. ❷–❸

Pra Arthit Mansion 22 Thanon Phra Athit ⓣ02 280 0744, ⓔpraarthit@bkk.anet.net.th. Low-key, mid-range place where the good, comfortable rooms all come with air-con and TV. The fifth-floor rooms have the best views of Banglamphu's rooftops. No restaurant, lobby or other hotel facilities, but staff are friendly and the location is quiet and convenient. ❺

Wild Orchid Villa 8 Soi Chana Songkhram ⓣ02 629 4378, ⓔwild_orchid_villa@hotmail.com. Painted in an appropriately wild colour scheme of lemon, aqua and blackberry, this hotel features some cosily furnished air-con rooms at the top of its price range (though their bathrooms are inconveniently accessed via the balcony), and some much less interesting windowless options, with shared bathrooms, at the bottom end. Has a very pleasant seating area out front. ❸–❺

Samsen sois and Thewes

Baan Phiman 123 Samsen Soi 5 ⓣ02 282 5594, ⓔbaanphiman@hotmail.com. Bangkok's most unusual guest house is located just atop the muddy bank of the (occasionally pongy) Chao Phraya River in a little garden full of flotsam sculptures. Comprising a few rattan huts plus some more conventional rooms, the atmosphere here is exceptionally friendly and you're in the heart of a traditional riverside neighbourhood. To get there, take a left at the far, river, end of Soi 5, then first right, and follow the signs; it's just a 2-min walk from the Rama VIII Bridge Chao Phraya express ferry stop. ❷–❸

Backpackers Lodge Soi 14, 85 Thanon Sri Ayutthaya ⓣ02 282 3231. Quiet, family-run place in the peaceful Thewes quarter of north Banglamphu. Just a handful of simple rooms, all with shared bathroom, and a communal area downstairs. ❸

New World Lodge Hotel Samsen Soi 2 ⓣ02 281 5596, ⓦwww.newworldlodge.com. Friendly, Muslim hotel offering large, unadorned but en-suite rooms with TV, and either fan or air-con. All rooms have balconies, some have khlong views, and there's also a pleasant khlongside seating area. The cheapest rooms in the less appealing guest-house wing are shabby and share bathrooms. ❷–❻

Shanti Lodge Soi 16, 37 Thanon Sri Ayutthaya ⓣ02 281 2497. Quiet place with a variety of small but fairly characterful rooms – some have rattan walls, others are decorated with Indian motifs. The cheapest share bathrooms, the most expensive have air-con. The predominantly vegetarian restaurant downstairs is to be recommended. ❸–❺

Sri Ayutthaya Soi 14, 23/11 Thanon Sri Ayutthaya ⓣ02 282 5942. The most attractive guest house in Thewes, where the good-sized rooms are elegantly done out with beautiful wood-panelled walls and polished wood floors. All rooms have fans, and some are also en suite. ❸

Tavee Guest House Soi 14, 83 Thanon Sri Ayutthaya ⓣ02 282 5983. Decent-sized rooms; quiet and friendly and one of the cheaper places in the Thewes quarter. Offers rooms with shared bathroom plus some en-suite ones with air-con. ❸–❹

Villa 230 Samsen Soi 1 ⓣ02 281 7009. One of Banglamphu's more therapeutic guest houses, in a lovely old Thai home and garden with just ten large rooms, each idiosyncratically furnished in simple, semi-traditional style; bathrooms are shared and rooms are priced according to their size. Fills up quickly in high season. ❸–❹

Vimol Guest House 358 Samsen Soi 4 ⓣ02 281 4615. Old-style, family-run guest house in a quiet but interesting neighbourhood that has just a smattering of other tourist places. The simple, cramped rooms are basic and have shared bathrooms but are possibly the cheapest in Banglamphu. ❶

Chinatown and Hualamphong Station area

Not far from the Ratanakosin sights, **Chinatown (Sampeng)** is one of the most frenetic and quintessentially Asian parts of Bangkok. Staying here, or in one of the sois around the conveniently close **Hualamphong Station**, can be noisy, but there's always plenty to look at, and some people choose to base themselves in this area in order to get away from the travellers' scene in Banglamphu. All listed accommodation is marked on the map on p.143.

Hualamphong is on the **subway** system, and Chinatown is served by a number of useful **bus** routes, including west-bound air-conditioned #507/#7 and ordinary buses #25, #40 and #53, which all go to Ratanakosin (for Wat Pho and the Grand Palace); the east-bound #16, #25 and #40 buses all go to Siam Square, where you change onto the Skytrain. For more details, see box on pp.100–101.

Baan Hualamphong Trok Chalongkrung ⓣ02 637 8095, ⓔsriyot@yahoo.de. Custom-built wooden guest house that's attractively designed, has a stylish modern decor and is fitted with contemporary bathrooms and furnishings. Big, bright, double rooms and five-person dorms at B200 per bed; all rooms share facilities. Serves German breakfasts and provides a left-luggage service. ❹

Bangkok Center 328 Thanon Rama IV ⓣ02 238 4848, ⓦwww.bangkokcentrehotel.com. Handily placed upper-mid-range option with efficient service right by the subway station and just across the road from the train station. Rooms are smartly furnished, and all have air-con and TV; there's a pool, restaurant and Internet access on the premises. ❻

FF Guest House 338/10 Trok La-O, off Thanon Rama IV ⓣ02 233 4168. Budget accommodation at the end of an alley just a 5-min walk from the station, offering ten basic rooms with shared facilities. ❷

Grand China Princess 215 Thanon Yaowarat ⓣ02 224 9977, ⓦwww.grandchina.com. The poshest hotel in Chinatown boasts very luxurious accommodation in its medium-rise tower close to the heart of the bustle, with stunning views over all the city landmarks, a rooftop swimming pool, revolving panoramic restaurant and several other food outlets. Well worth the money. ❽

New Empire Hotel 572 Thanon Yaowarat ⓣ02 234 6990, ⓦwww.newempirehotel.com. Medium-sized hotel right in the thick of the Chinatown bustle, offering exceptionally good-value superior rooms with air-con, TV and panoramic views towards the river. The standard rooms have the same facilities and are fine but rather faded. ❹–❺

River View Guest House 768 Soi Panurangsri, Thanon Songvad ⓣ02 235 8501, ⓕ02 237 5428. Large but uninteresting rooms, with fans at the lower end of the range, air-con, and TVs at the top. Great views over the bend in the river, especially from the top-floor restaurant. To find it, head north for 400m from River City shopping centre (on the express-boat line) along Soi Wanit 2, before following signs to the guest house to the left. ❹–❺

TT2 Guest House 516 Soi Sawang, off Thanon Maha Nakorn ⓣ02 236 2946, ⓔttguesthouse@hotmail.com. The most traveller-friendly budget place in the station area, this guest house is clean, friendly and well run, keeps good bulletin boards, has Internet access and a small library and stores left luggage at B10 a day. All rooms share bathrooms. During high season, there are B100 beds in a three-person dorm. Roughly a 15min walk from either the station or the N3 Si Phraya express-boat stop; to get here from the station, cross Thanon Rama IV, then walk left for 250m, cross Thanon Maha Nakorn and walk down it (following signs for *TT2*) as far as a seafood restaurant (opposite the lane signed as Trok Fraser and Neave), where you turn left and then first right. ❸

Downtown: around Siam Square and Thanon Ploenchit

Siam Square – not really a square, but a grid of shops and restaurants between Thanon Phrayathai and Thanon Henri Dunant – and nearby **Thanon Ploenchit** are as central as Bangkok gets, at the heart of the Skytrain system and with all kinds of shopping on hand. There's no budget accommodation here, but a few scaled-up guest houses have sprung up alongside the expensive hotels. Concentrated in their own "ghetto" on **Soi Kasemsan 1**, which runs north off Thanon Rama I just west of Thanon Phrayathai and is the next soi along from Jim Thompson's House (see p.156), these offer an informal guest-house atmosphere, with hotel comforts – air-conditioning and en-suite hot-water bathrooms – at moderate prices. Several luxury hotels have set up on **Thanon Witthayu**, aka **Wireless Road**, home of the American and British embassies (among others). Accommodation here is marked on the map on p.157.

Moderate

A-One Inn 25/13 Soi Kasemsan 1, Thanon Rama I ⓣ02 215 3029, ⓦwww.aoneinn.com. The original upscale guest house, and still justifiably popular, with helpful staff, Internet access and a reliable left-luggage room. Bedrooms all have satellite TV and come in a variety of sizes, including family rooms (but no singles). ❹

The Bed & Breakfast 36/42 Soi Kasemsan 1, Thanon Rama I ⓣ02 215 3004, ⓕ02 215 2493. Bright, clean, family-run and friendly, though the rooms – carpeted and with en-suite telephones – are a bit cramped. As the name suggests, a simple breakfast is included. ❹

Jim's Lodge 125/7 Soi Ruam Rudee, Thanon Ploenchit ⓣ02 255 3100, ⓔanant@asiaaccess.net.th. In a relatively peaceful residential area, convenient for the British and American embassies; offers international standards, including satellite TV and mini-bars, on a smaller scale and at bargain prices; no swimming pool, but there is a roof garden with outdoor Jacuzzi. ❼

Patumwan House 22 Soi Kasemsan 1, Thanon Rama I ⓣ02 612 3580–99, ⓔpatumwan_house@hotmail.com. At the far end of the soi, with very large, though rather bare rooms with TV and wardrobes; facilities include a very small fitness room, table-tennis, a café and Internet access. At the lower end of its price code; discounted weekly and monthly rates. ❻

Reno Hotel 40 Soi Kasemsan 1 Thanon Rama I ⓣ02 215 0026, ⓕ02 215 3430. Friendly hotel, boasting large, en-suite rooms with air-con and TV, a small swimming pool and an attractive bar-restaurant where breakfast is served (included in the price). Internet access and free left-luggage facility. ❺

Siam Orchid Inn 109 Soi Rajdamri, Thanon Rajdamri ⓣ02 251 4417, ⓔsiam_orchidinn@hotmail.com. Very handily placed behind the Narayana Phand souvenir centre, this is a friendly, cosy place with an ornately decorated lobby, a coffee shop, and air-con, hot water, cable TV, mini-bars and phones in the comfortable bedrooms. The room rate includes breakfast. ❻

VIP Guest House 1025/5–9 Thanon Ploenchit ⓣ02 252 9535–8, ⓦwww.goldenhouses.net. Very clean, self-styled "boutique" hotel in a peerless location. In the attractive, parquet-floored rooms (all with air-con and hot water), large beds leave just enough space for a couple of armchairs and a dressing table, as well as cable TV, mini-bar and tea- and coffee-making facilities. ❻

Wendy House 36/2 Soi Kasemsan 1, Thanon Rama I ⓣ02 214 1149–50, ⓔwendyweb@cscoms.com. Most functional of this soi's upmarket guest houses, and no frills in the service either, but clean and comfortable enough, with fridge and TV in some rooms. Discounted weekly and monthly rates. ❹

White Lodge 36/8 Soi Kasemsan 1, Thanon Rama I ⓣ02 216 8867 or 215 3041, ⓕ02 216 8228. Cheapest guest house on the soi, with well-maintained, shining white cubicles, a welcoming atmosphere, and very good breakfasts at *Sorn's* next door. ❹

Expensive

Conrad All Seasons Place, 87 Thanon Witthayu ⓣ02 690 9999, ⓦwww.conradhotels.com. One of Bangkok's newest luxury hotels, which places a high premium on design, aiming to add a cutting edge to traditional Thai style. Bathroom fittings include free-standing baths, glass walls and huge shower heads, and there's an enticing pool, spa, gym and two floodlit tennis courts. Eating options include the modern Chinese *Liu*, a branch of Beijing's hottest restaurant. ❾

Four Seasons 155 Thanon Rajdamri ⓣ02 250 1000, ⓦwww.fourseasons.com. The stately home of Bangkok's top hotels, formerly the Regent, where afternoon tea is still served in the monumental lobby. Choose between large, well-endowed rooms and resort-style "cabanas", with private patios, in the landscaped gardens. ❾

Nai Lert Park Hotel 2 Thanon Witthayu ⓣ02 253 0123, ⓦwww.swissotel.com. The main distinguishing feature of the former Hilton hotel is its acres of beautiful gardens, overlooked by many of the spacious, balconied bedrooms; set into the grounds are a landscaped swimming pool, jogging track, tennis courts and popular spa and health club. Good deli-café and French and Japanese restaurants. ❾

Holiday Mansion Hotel 53 Thanon Witthayu ⓣ02 255 0099, ⓔhmtel@ksc.th.com. Handily placed opposite the British Embassy, this hotel's main selling point is its large, attractive swimming pool. The bright and spacious bedrooms are nothing to write home about, but come with cable TV, air-con and hot water. Rates, which are often heavily discounted, include breakfast. ❽

Hotel Plaza Athénée Thanon Witthayu ⓣ02 650 8800, ⓦwww.hotel-plaza-athenee.com. Recently opened branch of the well-known New York luxury hotel, offering high standards of service and design and an air of efficient opulence. The spa and health club include a squash court and a large, landscaped swimming pool with fine views of the city. ❾

Pathumwan Princess Hotel 444 Thanon Phrayathai ⓣ 02 216 3700, ⓦ www.pprincess.com. At the southern end of the Mah Boon Krong (MBK) Shopping Centre, affordable luxury (with heavy discounting common) that's popular with families and businessmen. Facilities run to Korean and Japanese restaurants, a large, saltwater swimming pool, a health spa and a huge fitness club (including saunas, jogging track and squash and tennis courts). ❾

Siam City Hotel 477 Thanon Sri Ayutthaya ⓣ 02 247 0123, ⓦ www.siamhotels.com. Elegant, welcoming luxury hotel on the northern side of downtown (next to Phaya Thai Skytrain station and opposite Suan Pakkad), with rates towards the lower end of this price code. Rooms are tastefully done out in dark wood and subdued colours, and there's a health club, swimming pool, business centre and a comprehensive array of restaurants: Thai, Chinese, Japanese, Italian, international and a bakery. ❾

Downtown: south of Thanon Rama IV

South of Thanon Rama IV, the left bank of the river contains a full cross-section of places to stay. Tucked away at the eastern edge of this area is **Soi Ngam Duphli**, a ghetto of budget guest houses which is handy for Lumphini subway station, but is often choked with traffic escaping the jams on Thanon Rama IV – the neighbourhood is generally on the slide, although the best guest houses, tucked away on quiet **Soi Saphan Khu**, can just about compare with Banglamphu's finest.

Some medium-range places are scattered between Thanon Rama IV and the river, ranging from the notorious (the *Malaysia*) to the sedate (the *Bangkok Christian Guest House*). The area also lays claim to the capital's biggest selection of top hotels, which are among the most opulent in the world. Traversed by the Skytrain, this area is especially good for eating and nightlife. Staying by the river itself off **Thanon Charoen Krung**, aka **New Road**, has the added advantage of easy access to express boats, which will ferry you upstream to view the treasures of Ratanakosin.

Inexpensive

ETC Guest House 5/3 Soi Ngam Duphli ⓣ 02 287 1477–8, ⓔ etc@mozart.inet.co.th. Above a branch of the recommended travel agent of the same name, and very handy for Thanon Rama IV, though consequently noisy. Friendly, helpful and very clean, catering mainly to Japanese travellers. Rooms can be dingy, and come with fan or air-con, as well as shared or en-suite hot-water bathrooms; breakfast is included with the more expensive rooms. ❶–❸

Freddy's 2 27/40 Soi Sri Bamphen ⓣ 02 286 7826, ⓔ freddyguesthouse2@hotmail.com. Popular, clean, well-organized guest house with a variety of rooms with shared bathrooms and plenty of comfortable common areas, including a small café and beer garden at the rear. Rather noisy. ❷

Lee 3 Guest House 13 Soi Saphan Khu ⓣ 02 679 7045. In an old wooden house, the best of the Lee family of guest houses spread around this and adjoining sois. Decent and quiet, with reasonably sized rooms. ❶

Madam Guest House 11 Soi Saphan Khu ⓣ 02 286 9289, ⓕ 02 213 2087. Cleanish, often cramped, but characterful bedrooms, some with their own bathrooms, in a warren-like, balconied wooden house. Friendly. ❶–❷

Sala Thai Daily Mansion 15 Soi Saphan Khu ⓣ 02 287 1436. The pick of the area. A clean and efficiently run place at the end of this quiet, shaded alley, with bright, modern rooms (priced according to size) with wall fans, sharing hot-water bathrooms; a roof terrace makes it all the more pleasant. ❸–❹

Moderate

Bangkok Christian Guest House 123 Soi 2, Saladaeng, off the eastern end of Thanon Silom ⓣ 02 233 2206, ⓦ www.bcgh.org. Well-run, orderly missionary house in a shiny, modern building, where plain but immaculately kept rooms come with air-con and hot-water bathrooms. Breakfast included. ❼

Charlie House 1034/36–37 Soi Saphan Khu ⓣ 02 679 8330–1, ⓦ www.charliehousethailand.com. Good mid-range alternative to the crash-pads of Soi Ngam Duphli: bright, clean lobby restaurant, serving good, reasonably priced food, and small, carpeted bedrooms with hot-water bathrooms, air-con and TV, close to Thanon Rama IV. Cheap Internet access. No smoking. ❹

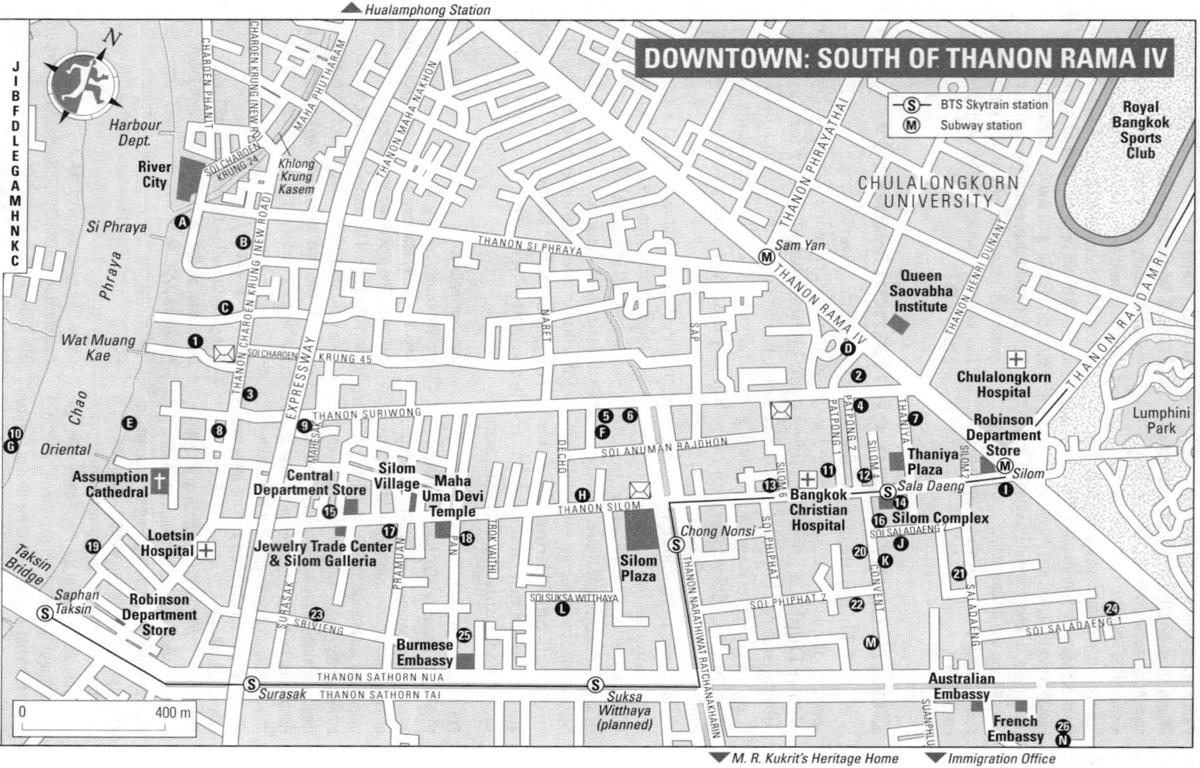

ACCOMMODATION

Bangkok Christian Guest House	J
Dusit Thani	I
Intown Residence	B
La Résidence	F
Montien	D
Niagara	L
Oriental	E
Peninsula Bangkok	G
Royal Orchid Sheraton	A
Ryn's Café & Bed	M
Sofitel Silom	H
Sukhothai	N
Swiss Lodge	K
Woodlands Inn	C

RESTAURANTS & BARS

All Gaengs	5
Angelini's at Shangri-La	19
Anna's Café	21
Aoi	13
Ban Chiang	23
Barbican	7
Bussaracum	25
Celadon	26
Chai Karr	15
Charuvan	12
Deen	17
Dick's Café	2
Eat Me	22
Harmonique	1
Himali Cha-Cha	3
Indian Hut	9
Irish Xchange	16
Jim Thompson's Farmers' Market and Café	24
Khrua Aroy Aroy	18
La Boulange	20
Le Bouchon	4
Lucifer	11
Mei Jiang	10
Somboon Seafood	6
Talat Nam	14
Tongue Thai	8

Intown Residence 1086/6 Thanon Charoen Krung ⓣ02 639 0960–2, ⓔintownbkk@hotmail.com. Clean, welcoming, rather old-fashioned hotel sandwiched between shops on the noisy main road (ask for a room away from the street). Slightly chintzy but comfortable rooms, at the lower end of their price code, come with air-con, hot-water bathrooms, mini-bars, satellite TVs and phones. ❺

La Residence 173/8–9 Thanon Suriwong ⓣ02 266 5400–1, ⓦwww.laresidencebangkok.com. Above *All Gaengs* restaurant, a small, intimate boutique hotel where the tasteful, individually decorated rooms stretch to TVs and mini-bars. Continental breakfast included; decent rates for single rooms. ❼

Malaysia Hotel 54 Soi Ngam Duphli ⓣ02 679 7127–36, ⓕ02 287 1457, ⓔmalaysia@ksc15.th.com. Once a travellers' legend famous for its compendious noticeboard, now better known for its seedy 24hr coffeeshop and massage parlour. The accommodation itself is reasonable value though: the rooms are large and have air-con, and hot-water bathrooms; some have fridge, TV and video. There's a swimming pool (B50/day for non-guests) and Internet access. ❺

Niagara 26 Soi Suksa Witthaya, off the south side of Thanon Silom ⓣ02 233 5783, ⓕ02 233 6563. No facilities other than a coffeeshop, but the clean bedrooms, with air-con, hot-water bathrooms, satellite TV, telephones and rates at the lower end of this price code, are a snip. ❺

Ryn's Café and Bed 44/16 Thanon Convent ⓣ02 632 1327, ⓦwww.cafeandbed.com. Upmarket guest house in a surprisingly central location just off Sathorn and a short walk from the east end of Silom. Above a European and Thai café, there are just seven diverse bedrooms, all air-conditioned: some are en suite, some share bathrooms, and some have bunk-beds, including small dorm rooms (B250/person). Internet access. ❹–❻

Woodlands Inn 1158/5–7 Soi 32, Thanon Charoen Krung ⓣ02 235 3894 or 6640–1, ⓦwww.woodlandsinn.org. Simple but well-run hotel next to the GPO, under South Indian management and popular with travellers from the subcontinent. All rooms have air-con, fridge, cable TV and hot-water bathrooms, and there's a good-value South Indian restaurant on the ground floor. ❹

Expensive

Dusit Thani Hotel 946 Thanon Rama IV, on the corner of Thanon Silom ⓣ02 236 9999, ⓦwww.dusit.com. Centrally placed top-class hotel, famous for its restaurants, including the *Tiara*, which has some spectacular top-floor views. ❾

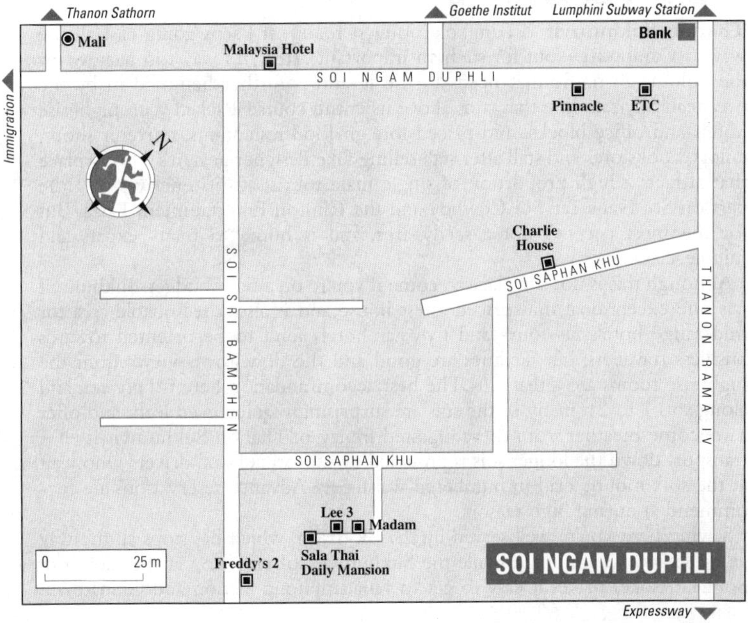

Montien Hotel 54 Thanon Surawongse, on the corner of Rama IV ⓣ 02 233 7060, ⓦ www.montien.com. Grand, airy and solicitous luxury hotel, with a strongly Thai character, very handily placed for business and nightlife. ⑨

Oriental Hotel 48 Oriental Avenue, off Thanon Charoen Krung ⓣ 02 659 9000, ⓦ www.mandarinoriental.com. One of the world's best, this effortlessly stylish riverside hotel boasts immaculate standards of service. ⑨

Peninsula Bangkok 333 Thanon Charoennakorn, Klongsan ⓣ 02 861 2888, ⓦ www.peninsula.com. Superb top-class hotel which self-consciously aims to rival the *Oriental* across the river. Service is flawless, the decor stylishly blends traditional and modern Asian design, and every room has a panoramic view of the Chao Phraya. Although it's on the Thonburi side of the river, the hotel operates a shuttle boat across to a pier and reception area by the *Shangri-La Hotel* off Thanon Charoen Krung. ⑨

Pinnacle 17 Soi Ngam Duphli ⓣ 02 287 0111–31, ⓦ www.pinnaclehotels.com. Bland but reliable international-standard place, with rooftop Jacuzzi and fitness centre; rates, which are usually heavily discounted, include breakfast. ⑧

Royal Orchid Sheraton 2 Captain Bush Lane, Thanon Charoen Krung ⓣ 02 266 0123, ⓦ www.royalorchidsheraton.com. Luxury hotel by the Chao Phraya and River City shopping centre, with expansive river views from all the rooms. Facilities include a spa and two fine swimming pools, one by the fitness centre, the other in the garden near a floodlit tennis court. ⑨

Sofitel Silom 188 Thanon Silom ⓣ 02 238 1991, ⓦ www.sofitel.com. Towards the quieter end of Thanon Silom, a clever renovation combines contemporary Asian artworks and furnishings with understated French elegance. A wine bar and Mediterranean, Japanese and rooftop Chinese restaurants, as well as a spa, fitness club and small pool, complete the picture. ⑨

Sukhothai 13/3 Thanon Sathorn Tai ⓣ 02 287 0222, ⓦ www.sukhothai.com. The most elegant of Bangkok's top hotels, its decor inspired by the walled city of Sukhothai: low-rise accommodation coolly furnished in silks, teak and granite, around six acres of gardens and lotus ponds. Excellent Italian and Thai restaurants. ⑨

Swiss Lodge 3 Thanon Convent ⓣ 02 233 5345, ⓦ www.swisslodge.com. Swish, friendly, good-value, boutique hotel, with high standards of service, just off Thanon Silom and ideally placed for business and nightlife. *Café Swiss* serves fondue, raclette and all your other Swiss favourites, while the tiny terrace swimming pool confirms the national stereotypes of neatness and clever design. ⑨

Thanon Sukhumvit

Thanon Sukhumvit is Bangkok's longest road – it keeps going east all the way to Cambodia – but for such an important artery it's way too narrow for the volume of traffic that needs to use it, and is further hemmed in by the overhead Skytrain line that runs above its entire course. Packed with high-rise hotels and office blocks, mid-priced foreign-food restaurants, souvenir shops, tailors, bookstores and stall after stall selling fake designer gear, it's a lively place that attracts a high proportion of single male tourists to its enclaves of girlie bars on Soi Nana Tai, Soi Cowboy and the Clinton Entertainment Plaza. But for the most part it's not a seedy area, and is home to many expats and middle-class Thais.

Although this is not the place to come if you're on a tight budget, Sukhumvit has one exceptional mid-priced guest house and is also a reasonable area for mid-range hotels; its four- and five-star hotels tend to be oriented towards business travellers, but facilities are good and the downtown views from the high-rise rooms are a real plus. The best accommodation here is between and along sois 1 to 21; many of the sois are surprisingly quiet, even leafy, and offer a welcome breather from the congested frenzy of Thanon Sukhumvit itself – transport down the longer sois is provided by motorbike-taxi drivers who wait at the soi's mouth, clad in numbered waistcoats. Advance reservations are recommended during high season.

Staying here, you're well served by the **Skytrain**, which has stops all the way along Thanon Sukhumvit, while the Sukhumvit **subway** stop at the mouth of Soi 21 (Asoke) makes it easy to get to Hualamphong Station and Chinatown.

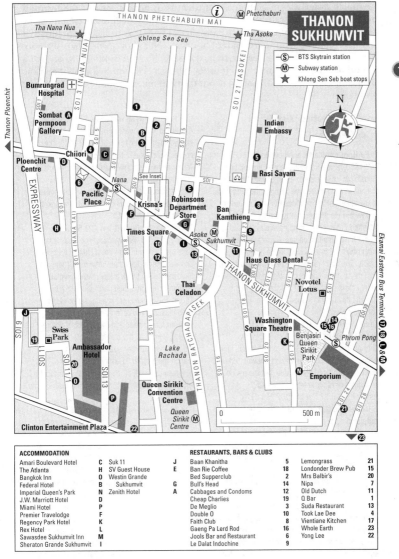

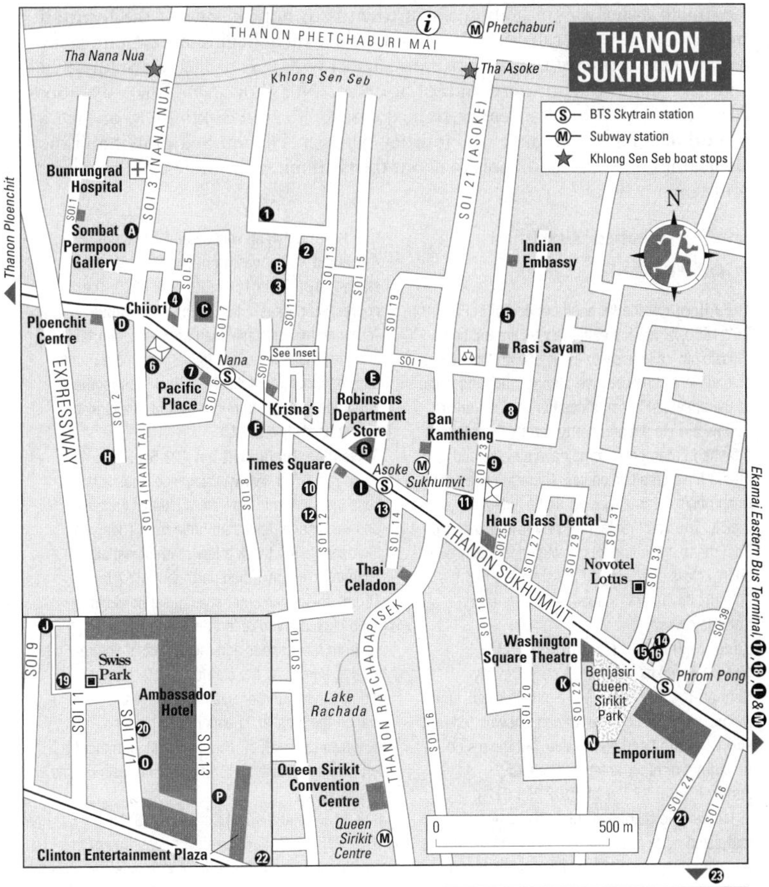

ACCOMMODATION			
Amari Boulevard Hotel	C	Suk 11	J
The Atlanta	H	SV Guest House	E
Bangkok Inn	O	Westin Grande Sukhumvit	G
Federal Hotel	B	Zenith Hotel	A
Imperial Queen's Park	N		
J.W. Marriott Hotel	D		
Miami Hotel	P		
Premier Travelodge	F		
Regency Park Hotel	K		
Rex Hotel	L		
Sawasdee Sukhumvit Inn	M		
Sheraton Grande Sukhumvit	I		

RESTAURANTS, BARS & CLUBS			
Baan Khanitha	5	Lemongrass	21
Ban Rie Coffee	18	Londonder Brew Pub	15
Bed Supperclub	2	Mrs Balbir's	20
Bull's Head	14	Nipa	7
Cabbages and Condoms	12	Old Dutch	11
Cheap Charlies	19	Q Bar	1
De Meglio	3	Suda Restaurant	13
Double O	10	Took Lae Dee	4
Faith Club	8	Vientiane Kitchen	17
Gaeng Pa Lerd Rod	16	Whole Earth	23
Jools Bar and Restaurant	6	Yong Lee	22
Le Dalat Indochine	9		

On the downside, you're a long way from the main Ratanakosin sights, and the volume of traffic on Sukhumvit means that travelling by **bus** across town can take an age – if possible, try to travel to and from Thanon Sukhumvit outside rush hour (7–9am & 3–7pm); it's almost as bad in a taxi, which will often take at least an hour to get to Ratanakosin. Useful buses for getting to Ratanakosin include #508/#8 (air-con) and #25 (ordinary); full details of bus routes are given on pp.100–101. Airport bus A3 makes stops all the way along Thanon Sukhumvit (see p.94).

A much faster way of getting across town is to hop on one of the **longtail boats** that ply the canals: Khlong Sen Seb, which begins near Democracy Monument in the west of the city, runs parallel with part ofThanon Sukhumvit and has stops at the northern ends of Soi Nana Nua (Soi 3) and Soi Asoke (Soi 21), from where you can either walk down to Thanon Sukhumvit, or take a motorbike taxi. This reduces the journey between Thanon Sukhumvit and the Banglamphu/Ratanakosin area to about thirty minutes; for more details on boat routes, see p.103.

Inexpensive and moderate

The Atlanta At the far southern end of Soi 2 ⓣ02 252 1650, ⓦwww.theatlantahotel.bizland.com. Classic old-style five-storey hotel with lots of colonial-era character, welcoming staff, and some of the cheapest accommodation on Sukhumvit. Rooms are simple and pretty scruffy, but all have attached bathrooms; some have air-con, and others have small balconies. There are two swimming pools, Internet access and a left-luggage facility. The hotel restaurant serves an extensive Thai menu, including lots of vegetarian dishes, and shows classic movies set in Asia every night; a Thai dance show is staged for guests every Saturday. ❹

Bangkok Inn Soi 11/1 ⓣ02 254 4834, ⓦwww.bangkok-inn.com. A cosy, friendly, German-run place with just eighteen clean, smart rooms, all of which have air-con, shower, fridge and TV. Central and good value, but there's no restaurant or other hotel facilities. ❻

Federal Hotel 27 Soi 11 ⓣ02 253 0175, ⓔfederalhotel@hotmail.com. Efficiently run, mid-sized hotel at the far end of Soi 11 so there's a feeling of space and a relatively uncluttered skyline; many rooms look out on the appealing poolside seating area, though the cheapest have no window. All rooms have air-con and TV; the upstairs ones are in better condition and worth paying a little extra for. ❺–❻

Miami Hotel Soi 13 ⓣ02 253 5611, ⓔmiami hotel@thaimail.com. Very popular, long-established budget hotel built around a swimming pool. The cheapest rooms, which are pretty grim windowless boxes, have shared bathrooms, the priciest come with bathroom, air-con and windows. Close to the girlie bars of the Clinton Entertainment Plaza and seems to share quite a few customers. ❸–❺

Premier Travelodge Soi 8 ⓣ02 251 3031, ⓔpremierlodge@yahoo.com. Well-equipped, centrally located small hotel offering good-value, unadorned rooms with shower, bathtub, air-con and TV. ❺

Rex Hotel Between sois 32 and 34 (opposite Soi 49), about 300m west from Thong Lo Skytrain station ⓣ02 259 0106, ⓕ02 258 6635. The nearest upmarket option to the Eastern Bus Terminal, this old-fashioned hotel is comfortable and well maintained and has a pool and a restaurant to complement its sizeable air-con rooms, but is too isolated from the best of Sukhumvit for a longer stay. ❺–❻

Sawasdee Sukhumvit Inn 123 Soi 57 ⓣ02 714 0703, ⓦwww.sawasdee-hotels.com. Less than a 15min walk from Ekamai Eastern Bus Terminal or less than 5min from Thong Lo Skytrain station (walk a few metres east along Thanon Sukhumvit then north up Soi 57 for 150m), this small hotel-style guest house is a good choice if you're in transit, though quite far from most shops and restaurants if you're staying longer. All the comfortably furnished rooms have bathrooms, air-con and cable TV, though the smaller, cheaper ones have no windows to speak of. There's a restaurant and a left-luggage facility (B10/day). Phone reservations advisable. ❹

Suk 11 Behind the 7–11 store at 1/3 Soi 11 ⓣ02 253 5927, ⓦwww.suk11.com. One of the most unusual and characterful little hotels in Bangkok, this is also the most backpacker-orientated guest house in the area. The interior of the apparently ordinary apartment-style building has been transformed to resemble a village of traditional wooden houses, accessed by a dimly lit plankway that winds past a variety of guest rooms and a breezy outdoor terrace. The rooms themselves are simple but very clean, they're all air-conditioned and some are en suite. In high season, B250 beds in five-person air-con dorms are also available. It's friendly and well run, keeps informative noticeboards, stores left luggage (B20/day), and accepts advance reservations via the website. ❹–❺

SV Guest House Soi 19 ⓣ02 253 1747, ⓕ02 255 7174. Some of the least expensive beds in the area; the rooms, some of which have air-con, are clean and well maintained, but all share bathrooms. ❸–❹

Expensive

Amari Boulevard Hotel Soi 5 ⓣ02 255 2930, ⓦwww.amari.com. Medium-sized, unpretentious and friendly upmarket tourist hotel. Rooms are comfortably furnished and all enjoy fine views of the Bangkok skyline from their balcony or terrace. There's an attractive rooftop swimming pool and garden terrace which becomes the Thai-food restaurant *Season* in the evenings. ⑨

Imperial Queen's Park Soi 22 ⓣ02 261 9000, ⓦwww.imperialhotels.com. Enormous and very swish high-rise hotel, whose large, comfortable rooms are nicely decorated with Thai-style furnishings and enjoy views out over the park. Facilities include seven restaurants, two rooftop swimming pools, a spa and an air-conditioned squash court. ⑨

J.W. Marriott Hotel Soi 2 ⓣ02 656 7700, ⓦwww.marriotthotels.com. Deluxe hotel, offering comfortable rooms geared towards business travellers, three restaurants (including one that serves exceptionally good all-day buffets), a swimming pool, spa and fitness centre. ⑨

Regency Park Hotel 12/3 Soi 22 ⓣ02 259 7420, ⓦwww.accorhotels.com. Personable little hotel built around a plant-filled central atrium. The rooms are large and comfortable if not especially stylish, and have air-con, TVs and bathtubs, and there's a rooftop swimming pool. The location is not ideal, about 500m from the Emporium Skytrain station and nearby shopping plaza, and the soi is home to several bar-beer complexes. ⑧

Sheraton Grande Sukhumvit Between sois 12 and 14 ⓣ02 653 0333, ⓦwww.luxurycollection.com. Deluxe accommodation in stylishly understated rooms, all of which offer fine views of the cityscape (the honeymoon suites have their own rooftop plungepools). Facilities include a gorgeous free-form swimming pool and tropical garden on the ninth floor, a spa with a range of treatment plans, the trendy *Basil* Thai restaurant and the *Living Room* bar, which is famous for its jazz singers. Those aged 17 and under stay for free if sharing adults' room. ⑨

Westin Grande Sukhumvit Above Robinson's Department Store, between sois 17 and 19 ⓣ02 651 1000, ⓦwww.westin.com/bangkok. Conveniently located four-star hotel that's aimed at the fashion-conscious business traveller but would suit holidaymakers too. The decor is modish but cheerful, with groovy pale-wood desks, flat-screen TVs and Westin's trademark super-deluxe "heavenly" mattresses. Facilities include several restaurants, a swimming pool, gym and spa, a kids' club and a business centre. Good value for its class. ⑨

Zenith Hotel 29 Soi 3 ⓣ02 655 4999, ⓦwww.zenith-hotel.com. Central and extremely smart but nevertheless affordable upmarket option, where the high-rise rooms are large and sleek (all have air-con and TV) and there's a rooftop swimming pool. Discounts sometimes available. ⑨

The City

Bangkok is sprawling, chaotic and exhausting: to do it justice and to keep your sanity, you need time, boundless patience and a bus map. The place to start is **Ratanakosin**, the royal island on the east bank of the Chao Phraya, where the city's most important and extravagant sights are to be found. On the edges of this enclave, the area around the landmark **Democracy Monument** includes some interesting and quirky religious architecture, a contrast with the attractions of neighbouring **Chinatown**, whose markets pulsate with the much more aggressive business of making money. Quieter and more European in ambience are the stately buildings of the new royal district of **Dusit**, 2km northeast of Democracy Monument. Very little of old Bangkok remains, but the back canals of **Thonburi**, across the river from Ratanakosin and Chinatown, retain a traditional feel quite at odds with the modern high-rise jungle of **downtown Bangkok**, which has evolved across on the eastern perimeter of the city and can take an hour to reach by bus from Ratanakosin. It's here that you'll find the best shops, bars, restaurants and nightlife, as well as a couple of worthwhile sights. Greater Bangkok now covers an area some 30km in diameter; though unsightly urban development predominates, an expedition to **the outskirts** is made worthwhile by several museums and the city's largest market, **Chatuchak**.

Ratanakosin

When Rama I developed **Ratanakosin** as his new capital in 1782, after the sacking of Ayutthaya and a temporary stay across the river in Thonburi, he paid tribute to its precursor by imitating Ayutthaya's layout and architecture – he even shipped the building materials downstream from the ruins of the old city. Like Ayutthaya, the new capital was sited for protection beside a river and turned into an artificial island by the construction of defensive canals, with a central **Grand Palace** and adjoining royal temple, **Wat Phra Kaeo**, fronted by an open cremation field, **Sanam Luang**; the Wang Na (Palace of the Second King), now doing service as the **National Museum**, was also built at this time. **Wat Pho**, which predates the capital's founding, was further embellished by Rama I's successors, who have consolidated Ratanakosin's pre-eminence by building several grand European-style palaces (now housing government institutions); Wat Mahathat, the most important centre of Buddhist learning in southeast Asia; the National Theatre; and Thammasat University.

Bangkok has expanded eastwards away from the river, leaving the Grand Palace a good 5km from the city's commercial heart, and the royal family have long since moved their residence to Dusit, but Ratanakosin remains the ceremonial centre of the whole kingdom – so much so that it feels as if it might sink into the boggy ground under the weight of its own mighty edifices. The heavy, stately feel is lightened by noisy **markets** along the riverside strip and by **Sanam Luang**, still used for cremations and royal ceremonies, but also functioning as a popular open park and the hub of the modern city's bus system. Despite containing several of the country's main sights, the area is busy enough in its own right not to have become a swarming tourist zone, and strikes a neat balance between liveliness and grandeur.

Ratanakosin is within easy walking distance of Banglamphu, but is best approached from the river, via the express-boat piers of Tha Chang (for the Grand Palace) or Tha Thien (for Wat Pho). A **word of warning**: when you're heading for the Grand Palace or Wat Pho, you may well be approached by someone pretending to be a student or an official, who will tell you that the sight is closed when it's not, because they want to lead you on a shopping trip. Although the opening hours of the Grand Palace in particular are sometimes erratic because of state occasions or national holidays, it's far better to put in a bit of extra legwork and check it out for yourself.

Wat Phra Kaeo and the Grand Palace

Hanging together in a precarious harmony of strangely beautiful colours and shapes, **Wat Phra Kaeo** (Ⓦ www.palaces.thai.net) is the apogee of Thai religious art and the holiest Buddhist site in the country, housing the most important image, the **Emerald Buddha**. Built as the private royal temple, Wat Phra Kaeo occupies the northeast corner of the huge **Grand Palace**, whose official opening in 1785 marked the founding of the new capital and the rebirth of the

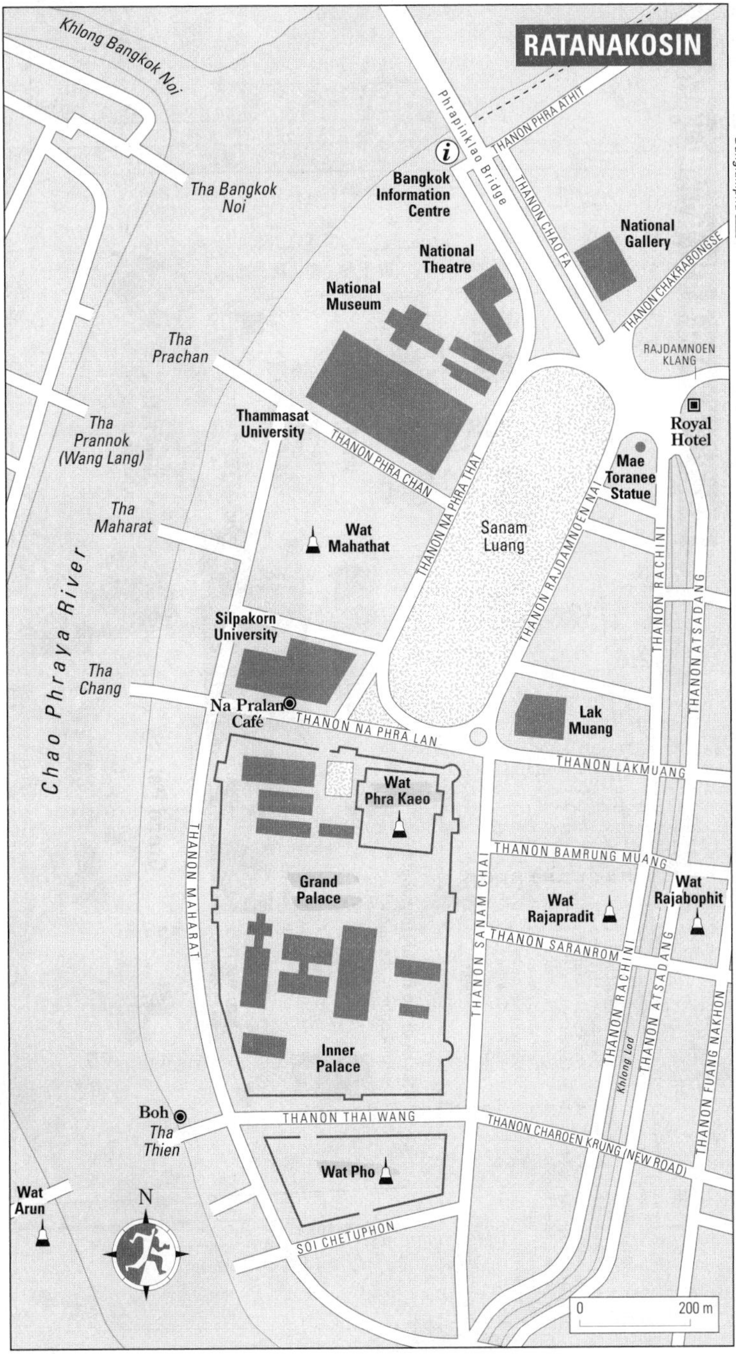
RATANAKOSIN
Khlong Bangkok Noi
Phrapinklao Bridge
THANON PHRA ATHIT
Banglamphu
Bangkok Information Centre
Tha Bangkok Noi
THANON CHAO FA
National Gallery
National Theatre
National Museum
THANON CHAKRABONGSE
RAJDAMNOEN KLANG
Tha Prachan
Royal Hotel
Thammasat University
THANON PHRA CHAN
Tha Prannok (Wang Lang)
Mae Toranee Statue
Tha Maharat
Wat Mahathat
THANON NA PHRA THAT
Sanam Luang
THANON RAJDAMNOEN NAI
THANON RACHINI
THANON ATSADANG
Chao Phraya River
Silpakorn University
Tha Chang
Na Pralan Café
THANON NA PHRA LAN
Lak Muang
THANON LAKMUANG
Wat Phra Kaeo
THANON MAHARAT
THANON BAMRUNG MUANG
Grand Palace
Wat Rajapradit
Wat Rajabophit
THANON SANAM CHAI
THANON SARANROM
THANON FUANG NAKHON
Khlong Lod
Inner Palace
Boh
Tha Thien
THANON THAI WANG
THANON CHAROEN KRUNG (NEW ROAD)
Wat Pho
Wat Arun
N
SOI CHETUPHON
0
200 m

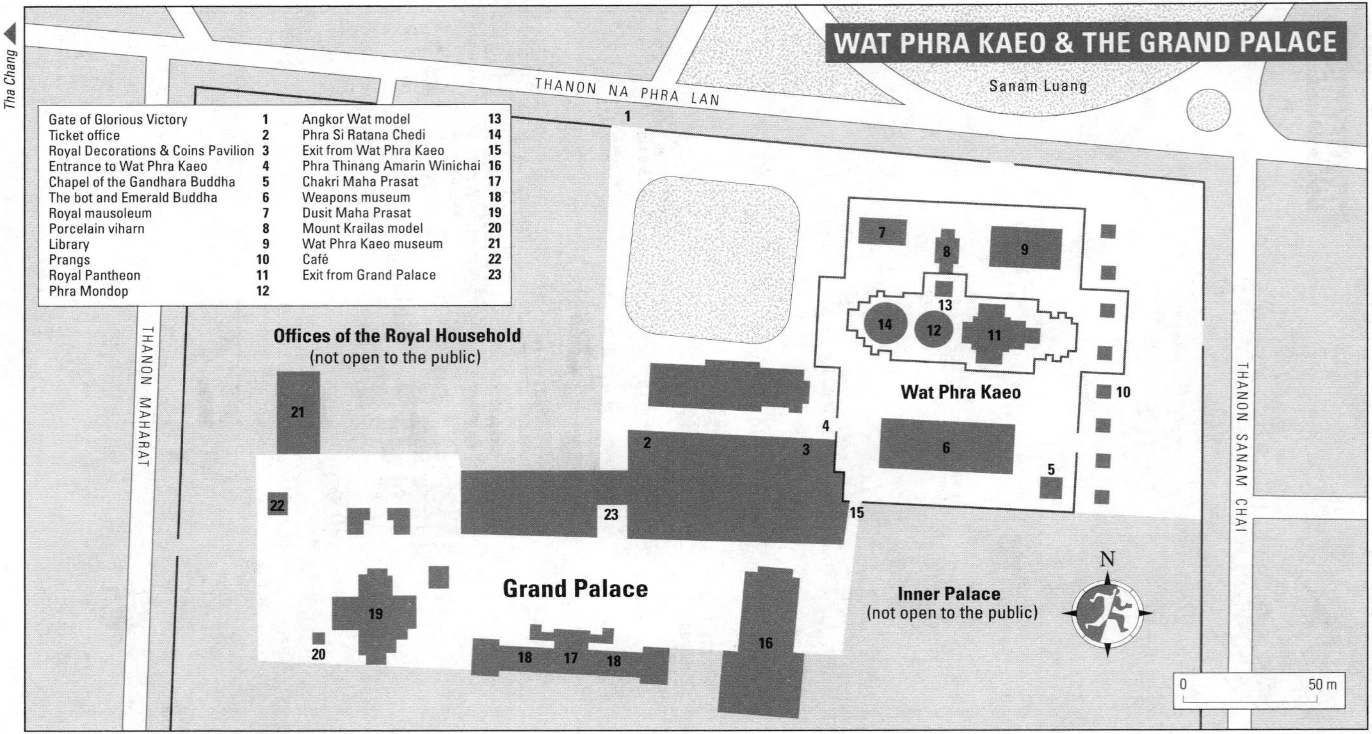
WAT PHRA KAEO & THE GRAND PALACE
Gate of Glorious Victory 1
Ticket office 2
Royal Decorations & Coins Pavilion 3
Entrance to Wat Phra Kaeo 4
Chapel of the Gandhara Buddha 5
The bot and Emerald Buddha 6
Royal mausoleum 7
Porcelain viharn 8
Library 9
Prangs 10
Royal Pantheon 11
Phra Mondop 12
Angkor Wat model 13
Phra Si Ratana Chedi 14
Exit from Wat Phra Kaeo 15
Phra Thinang Amarin Winichai 16
Chakri Maha Prasat 17
Weapons museum 18
Dusit Maha Prasat 19
Mount Krailas model 20
Wat Phra Kaeo museum 21
Café 22
Exit from Grand Palace 23
Tha Chang
THANON NA PHRA LAN
Sanam Luang
THANON MAHARAT
THANON SANAM CHAI
Offices of the Royal Household
(not open to the public)
Wat Phra Kaeo
Grand Palace
Inner Palace
(not open to the public)
N
0
50 m

Thai nation after the Burmese invasion. Successive kings have all left their mark here, and the palace complex now covers 61 acres, though very little apart from the wat is open to tourists.

The only **entrance** to the complex in 2km of crenellated walls is the Gate of Glorious Victory in the middle of the north side, on Thanon Na Phra Lan. This brings you onto a driveway with a tantalizing view of the temple's glittering spires on the left and the dowdy buildings of the Offices of the Royal Household on the right: this is the powerhouse of the kingdom's ceremonial life, providing everything down to chairs and catering, even lending an urn when someone of rank dies. Turn left at the end of the driveway for the ticket office and entrance turnstiles: **admission** to Wat Phra Kaeo and the palace is B200 (daily 8.30am–3.30pm, palace halls and weapons museum closed Sat & Sun; free tours in English at 10am & 1.30pm, plus 10.30am & 2pm most days; 2hr personal audioguide B100, with passport, credit card or B5000 as surety), which includes a free brochure and map, as well as admission (within seven days) to the Vimanmek Palace in the Dusit area (see p.154). As it's Thailand's most sacred site, you have to show respect by **dressing in smart clothes** – no vests, shorts, see-through clothes, sarongs, mini-skirts, fisherman's trousers, slip-on sandals or flip-flops– but if your rucksack won't stretch that far, head for the office to the right just inside the Gate of Glorious Victory, where suitable garments or shoes can be provided (free, socks B15) as long as you leave some identification (passport, driver's licence or credit card) as surety or pay a deposit of B100 per item.

Wat Phra Kaeo

Entering the temple is like stepping onto a lavishly detailed stage set, from the immaculate flagstones right up to the gaudy roofs. Although it receives hundreds of foreign sightseers and at least as many Thai pilgrims every day, the temple, which has no monks in residence, maintains an unnervingly sanitized look, as if it were built only yesterday. Its jigsaw of structures can seem complicated at first, but the basic layout is straightforward: the turnstiles in the west wall open onto the back of the bot, which contains the Emerald Buddha; to the left, the upper terrace runs parallel to the north side of the bot, while the whole temple compound is surrounded by arcaded walls, decorated with extraordinary murals of scenes from the *Ramayana* (see box on p.127).

The approach to the bot

Immediately inside the turnstiles, you're confronted by six-metre tall *yaksha*, gaudy demons from the *Ramayana*, who watch over the Emerald Buddha from every gate of the temple and ward off evil spirits. Less threatening is the toothless old codger, cast in bronze and sitting on a plinth by the back wall of the bot, who represents a Hindu hermit credited with inventing yoga and herbal medicine. In front of him is a large grinding stone where previously herbal practitioners could come to grind their ingredients – with enhanced powers, of course. Skirting around the bot, you'll reach its **main entrance** on the eastern side, in front of which stands a cluster of grey **statues**, which have a strong Chinese feel: next to Kuan Im, the Chinese goddess of mercy, are a sturdy pillar topped by a lotus flower, which Bangkok's Chinese community presented to Rama IV during his 27 years as a monk; and two handsome cows which commemorate Rama I's birth in the Year of the Cow. Worshippers make their offerings to the Emerald Buddha in among the statues, where they can look at the image through the open doors of the bot without messing up its pristine interior with candle wax and joss-stick ash.

Nearby, in the southeastern corner of the temple precinct, look out for the beautiful country scenes painted in gold and blue on the doors of the **Chapel of the Gandhara Buddha**, a building that was crucial to the old royal rain-making ritual. Adorning the roof are thousands of nagas (serpents), symbolizing water; inside the locked chapel, among the paraphernalia used in the ritual, is kept the Gandhara Buddha, a bronze image in the gesture of calling down the rain with its right hand, while cupping the left to catch it. In times of drought the king would order this week-long ceremony to be conducted, during which he was bathed regularly and kept away from the opposite sex while Buddhist monks and Hindu Brahmins chanted continuously.

The bot and the Emerald Buddha

The **bot**, the largest building of the temple, is one of the few original structures left at Wat Phra Kaeo, though it has been augmented so often it looks like the work of a wildly inspired child. Eight *sema* stones mark the boundary of the consecrated area around the bot, each sheltering in a psychedelic fairy castle, joined by a low wall decorated with Chinese porcelain tiles, which depict delicate landscapes. The walls of the bot itself, sparkling with gilt and coloured glass, are supported by 112 golden garudas (birdmen) holding nagas, representing the god Indra saving the world by slaying the serpent-cloud that had swallowed up all the water. The symbolism reflects the king's traditional role as a rain-maker.

Inside the bot, a nine-metre-high pedestal supports the tiny **Emerald Buddha**, a figure whose mystique draws pilgrims from all over Thailand – here especially you must act with respect, sitting with your feet pointing away from the Buddha. The spiritual power of the sixty-centimetre jadeite image derives from its legendary past. Reputed to have been created in Sri Lanka, it was discovered when lightning cracked open an ancient chedi in Chiang Rai in the early fifteenth century. The image was then moved around the north, dispensing miracles wherever it went, before being taken to Laos for two hundred years. As it was believed to bring great fortune to its possessor, the future Rama I snatched it back when he captured Vientiane in 1779, installing it at the heart of his new capital as a talisman for king and country.

The Emerald Buddha has three costumes, one for each season: the crown and ornaments of an Ayutthayan king for the hot season; a gilt monastic robe dotted with blue enamel for the rainy season, when the monks retreat into the temples; and a full-length gold shawl to wrap up in for the cool season. To this day it's the job of the king himself to ceremonially change the Buddha's costumes – though in recent years, due to the present king's age, the Crown Prince has conducted proceedings. (The Buddha was granted a new set of these three costumes in 1997: the old set is now in the Wat Phra Kaeo Museum – see p.129 – while the two costumes of the new set that are not in use are put on display among the blinding glitter of crowns and jewels in the Royal Decorations and Coins Pavilion, which lies between the ticket office and the entrance to Wat Phra Kaeo.) Among the paraphernalia in front of the pedestal is the tiny, black Victory Buddha, which Rama I always carried with him into war for luck.

The upper terrace

The eastern end of the **upper terrace** is taken up with the **Prasat Phra Thep Bidorn**, known as the **Royal Pantheon**, a splendid hash of styles. The pantheon has its roots in the Khmer concept of *devaraja*, or the divinity of kings: inside are bronze and gold statues, precisely life-size, of all the

The Ramayana

The **Ramayana** is generally thought to have originated as an oral epic in India, where it appears in numerous dialects. The most famous version is that of the poet Valmiki, who as a tribute to his king drew together the collection of stories over two thousand years ago. From India, the *Ramayana* spread to all the Hindu-influenced countries of South Asia and was passed down through the Khmers to Thailand, where as the **Ramakien** it has become the national epic, acting as an affirmation of the Thai monarchy and its divine Hindu links. As a source of inspiration for literature, painting, sculpture and dance-drama, it has acquired the authority of holy writ, providing Thais with moral and practical lessons, while its appearance in the form of films and comic strips shows its huge popular appeal. The version current in Thailand was composed by a committee of poets sponsored by Rama I, and runs to three thousand pages.

The central story of the *Ramayana* concerns **Rama** (in Thai, Phra Ram), son of the king of Ayodhya, and his beautiful wife **Sita**, whose hand he wins by lifting and stringing a magic bow. The couple's adventures begin when they are exiled to the forest, along with Rama's good brother, **Lakshaman** (Phra Lak), by the hero's father under the influence of his evil stepmother. Meanwhile, in the city of Lanka (Longka), the demon king **Ravana** (Totsagan) has conceived a passionate desire for Sita and, disguised as a hermit, sets out to kidnap her. By transforming one of his subjects into a beautiful deer, which Rama and Lakshaman go off to hunt, Ravana catches Sita alone and takes her back to Lanka. Rama then wages a long war against the demons of Lanka, into which are woven many battles, spy scenes and diversionary episodes, and eventually kills Ravana and rescues Sita.

The Thai version shows some characteristic differences from the Indian. Hanuman, the loyal monkey king, is given a much more playful role in the *Ramakien*, with the addition of many episodes which display his cunning and talent for mischief, but the major alteration comes at the end of the story, when Phra Ram doubts Sita's faithfulness after rescuing her from Totsagan. In the Indian story, this ends with Sita being swallowed up by the earth so that she doesn't have to suffer Rama's doubts any more; in the *Ramakien* the ending is a happy one, with Phra Ram and Sita living together happily ever after.

kings since Bangkok became the Thai capital. The building is open only on special occasions, such as Chakri Day (April 6), when the dynasty is commemorated.

From here you get the best view of the **royal mausoleum**, the **porcelain viharn** and the **library** to the north (all of which are closed to the public), and, running along the east side of the temple, a row of eight bullet-like **prangs**, each of which has a different nasty ceramic colour. Described as "monstrous vegetables" by Somerset Maugham, they represent, from north to south, the Buddha, Buddhist scripture, the monkhood, the nunhood, the Buddhas who attained enlightenment but did not preach, previous emperors, the Bodhisattva and the future Buddha.

In the middle of the terrace, dressed in deep-green glass mosaics, the **Phra Mondop** was built by Rama I to house the *Tripitaka*, or Buddhist scripture. It's famous for the mother-of-pearl cabinet and solid-silver mats inside, but is never open. Four tiny **memorials** at each corner of the mondop show the symbols of each of the nine Chakri kings, from the ancient crown representing Rama I to the present king's sun symbol, while the bronze statues surrounding the memorials portray each king's lucky white elephants, labelled by name and pedigree. A contribution of Rama IV, on the north side of the mondop, is a **scale model of Angkor Wat**, the prodigious Cambodian temple, which during his reign (1851–68) was under Thai rule. At the western end of the terrace, you can't miss the golden dazzle of the **Phra Si Ratana Chedi**, which Rama IV erected to enshrine a piece of the Buddha's breastbone.

The murals

Extending for over a kilometre in the arcades that run inside the wat walls, the **murals of the Ramayana** depict every blow of this ancient story of the triumph of good over evil, using the vibrant buildings of the temple itself as backdrops, and setting them off against the subdued colours of richly detailed landscapes. Because of the damaging humidity, none of the original work of Rama I's time survives: maintenance is a never-ending process, so you'll always find an artist working on one of the scenes. The story is told in 178 panels, labelled and numbered in Thai only, starting in the middle of the northern side: in the first episode, a hermit, while out ploughing, finds the baby Sita, the heroine, floating in a gold urn on a lotus leaf and brings her to the city. Panel 109 shows the climax of the story, when Rama, the hero, kills the ten-headed demon Totsagan (Ravana), and the ladies of the enemy city weep at the demon's death. Panel 110 depicts his elaborate funeral procession, and in 113 you can see the funeral fair, with acrobats, sword-jugglers and tightrope-walkers. In between, Sita – Rama's wife – has to walk on fire to prove that she has been faithful during her fourteen years of imprisonment by Totsagan. If you haven't the stamina for the long walk round, you could sneak a look at the end of the story, to the left of the first panel, where Rama holds a victory parade and distributes thankyou gifts.

The palace buildings

The exit in the southwest corner of Wat Phra Kaeo brings you to the palace proper, a vast area of buildings and gardens, of which only the northern edge is on show to the public. Though the king now lives in the Chitrlada Palace in Dusit, the Grand Palace is still used for state receptions and official ceremonies, during which there is no public access to any part of the palace; in addition the weapons museum and the interiors of the Phra Thinang Amarin Winichai and the Dusit Maha Prasat are closed at weekends.

Phra Maha Monthien

Coming out of the temple compound, you'll first of all see to your right a beautiful Chinese gate covered in innumerable tiny porcelain tiles. Extending in a straight line behind the gate is the **Phra Maha Monthien**, which was the grand residential complex of earlier kings.

Only the **Phra Thinang Amarin Winichai**, the main audience hall at the front of the complex, is open to the public. The supreme court in the era of the absolute monarchy, it nowadays serves as the venue for the king's birthday speech; dominating the hall is the *busbok*, an open-sided throne with a spired roof, floating on a boat-shaped base. The rear buildings are still used for the most important part of the elaborate coronation ceremony, and each new king is supposed to spend a night there to show solidarity with his forefathers.

Chakri Maha Prasat and the Inner Palace

Next door you can admire the facade of the "farang with a Thai hat", as the **Chakri Maha Prasat** is nicknamed. Rama V, whose portrait you can see over its entrance, employed an English architect to design a purely Neoclassical residence, but other members of the royal family prevailed on the king to add the three Thai spires. This used to be the site of the elephant stables: the large red tethering posts are still there and the bronze elephants were installed as a reminder. The building displays the emblem of the Chakri dynasty on its gable, which has a trident (*ri*) coming out of a *chak*, a discus with a sharpened rim. The only part of the Chakri Maha Prasat open to the public is the **weapons museum**, which occupies two rooms on the ground floor on either side of the grand main entrance, and houses a forgettable display of hooks, pikes, tridents, guns and cannon.

The **Inner Palace**, which used to be the king's harem (closed to the public), lies behind the gate on the left-hand side of the Chakri Maha Prasat. The harem was a town in itself, with shops, law courts and a police force for the huge all-female population: as well as the current queens, the minor wives and their servants, this was home to the daughters and consorts of former kings, and the daughters of the aristocracy who attended the harem's finishing school. Today, the Inner Palace houses a school of cooking, fruit-carving and other domestic sciences for well-bred young Thais.

Dusit Maha Prasat

On the western side of the courtyard, the delicately proportioned **Dusit Maha Prasat**, an audience hall built by Rama I, epitomizes traditional Thai architecture. Outside, the soaring tiers of its red, gold and green roof culminate in a gilded *mongkut*, a spire shaped like the king's crown, which symbolizes the 33 Buddhist levels of perfection. Each tier of the roof bears a typical *chofa*, a slender, stylized bird's-head finial, and several *hang hong* (swans' tails), which represent three-headed nagas. Inside, you can still see the original throne, the **Phra Ratcha Banlang Pradap Muk**, a masterpiece of mother-of-pearl inlaid work. When a senior member of the royal family dies, the hall is used for the lying-in-state: the body, embalmed and seated in a huge sealed urn, is placed in the west transept, waiting up to two years for an auspicious day to be cremated.

To the right and behind the Dusit Maha Prasat rises a strange model mountain, decorated with fabulous animals and topped by a castle and prang. It represents **Mount Krailas**, a version of Mount Meru, the centre of the Hindu universe, and was built as the site of the royal tonsure ceremony. In former times, Thai children had shaved heads, except for a tuft on the crown, which, between the age of five and eight, was cut in a Hindu initiation rite to welcome adolescence. For the royal children, the rite was an elaborate ceremony that sometimes lasted five days, culminating with the king's cutting of the hair knot. The child was then bathed at the model Krailas, in water representing the original river of the universe flowing down the central mountain.

The Wat Phra Kaeo Museum

In the nineteenth-century Royal Mint in front of the Dusit Maha Prasat – next to a small, basic **café** – the **Wat Phra Kaeo Museum** houses a mildly interesting collection of artefacts associated with the Emerald Buddha along with architectural elements rescued from the Grand Palace grounds during restoration in the 1980s. Highlights include the bones of various kings' white elephants, and upstairs, the Emerald Buddha's original costumes and two useful scale models of the Grand Palace, one as it is now, the other as it was when first built. Also on the first floor stands the grey stone slab of the Manangasila Seat, where Ramkhamhaeng, the great thirteenth-century king of Sukhothai, is said to have sat and taught his subjects. It was discovered in 1833 by Rama IV during his monkhood and brought to Bangkok, where Rama VI used it as the throne for his coronation.

Wat Pho

Where Wat Phra Kaeo may seem too perfect and shrink-wrapped for some, **Wat Pho** (daily 8am–6pm; B20; personal guides available, charging B150/200/300 for 1, 2 or 3 visitors; ⓦwww.watpho.com), covering twenty acres to the south of the Grand Palace, is lively and shambolic, a complex arrangement of lavish structures which jostle with classrooms, basketball courts and a turtle pond. Busloads of tourists shuffle in and out of the **north entrance**, stopping only to gawp at the colossal Reclining Buddha, but you can avoid the worst of the crowds by using the **main entrance** on Soi Chetuphon to explore the huge compound, where you're likely to be approached by friendly young monks wanting to practise their English.

Wat Pho is the oldest temple in Bangkok and older than the city itself, having been founded in the seventeenth century under the name Wat Photaram. Foreigners have stuck to the contraction of this old name, even though Rama I, after enlarging the temple, changed the name in 1801 to Wat Phra Chetuphon, which is how it is generally known to Thais. The temple had another major overhaul in 1832, when Rama III built the chapel of the Reclining Buddha, and turned the temple into a public centre of learning by decorating the walls and pillars with inscriptions and diagrams on subjects such as history, literature, animal husbandry and astrology. Dubbed Thailand's first university, the wat is still an important centre for traditional medicine, notably **Thai massage**, which is used against all kinds of illnesses, from backaches to viruses. Thirty-hour training courses are conducted here in English, over a five- to ten-day period, costing B7000, as well as fifteen-hour, three-day foot-massage courses for B3600 (ⓣ02 221 2974 or ⓔwatpottm@netscape.net for more information). Alternatively you can simply turn up and suffer a massage yourself in the ramshackle buildings on the east side of the main compound; allow two hours for the full works (B300/hr; foot reflexology massage B300/45min).

The eastern courtyard

The main entrance on Soi Chetuphon is one of a series of sixteen monumental gates around the main compound, each guarded by stone **giants**, many of them comic Westerners in wide-brimmed hats – ships which exported rice to China would bring these statues back as ballast.

The entrance brings you into the eastern half of the main complex, where a courtyard of structures radiates from the bot in a disorientating symmetry. To get to the bot, the principal congregation and ordination hall, turn right and cut through the two surrounding cloisters, which are lined with hundreds of Buddha images. The elegant **bot** has beautiful teak doors decorated with mother-of-pearl, showing stories from the *Ramayana* in minute detail. Look out also for the stone bas-reliefs around the base of the bot, which narrate a longer version of the *Ramayana* in 152 action-packed panels. The plush interior has a well-proportioned altar on which ten statues of disciples frame a graceful, Ayutthayan Buddha image containing the remains of Rama I, the founder of Bangkok (Rama IV placed them there so that the public could worship him at the same time as the Buddha).

Back outside the entrance to the double cloister, keep your eyes open for a miniature mountain covered in statues of naked men in tall hats who appear to be gesturing rudely: they are *rishis* (hermits), demonstrating various positions of healing massage. Skirting the southwestern corner of the cloisters, you'll come to a pavilion between the eastern and western courtyards, which displays plaques inscribed with the precepts of traditional medicine, as well as

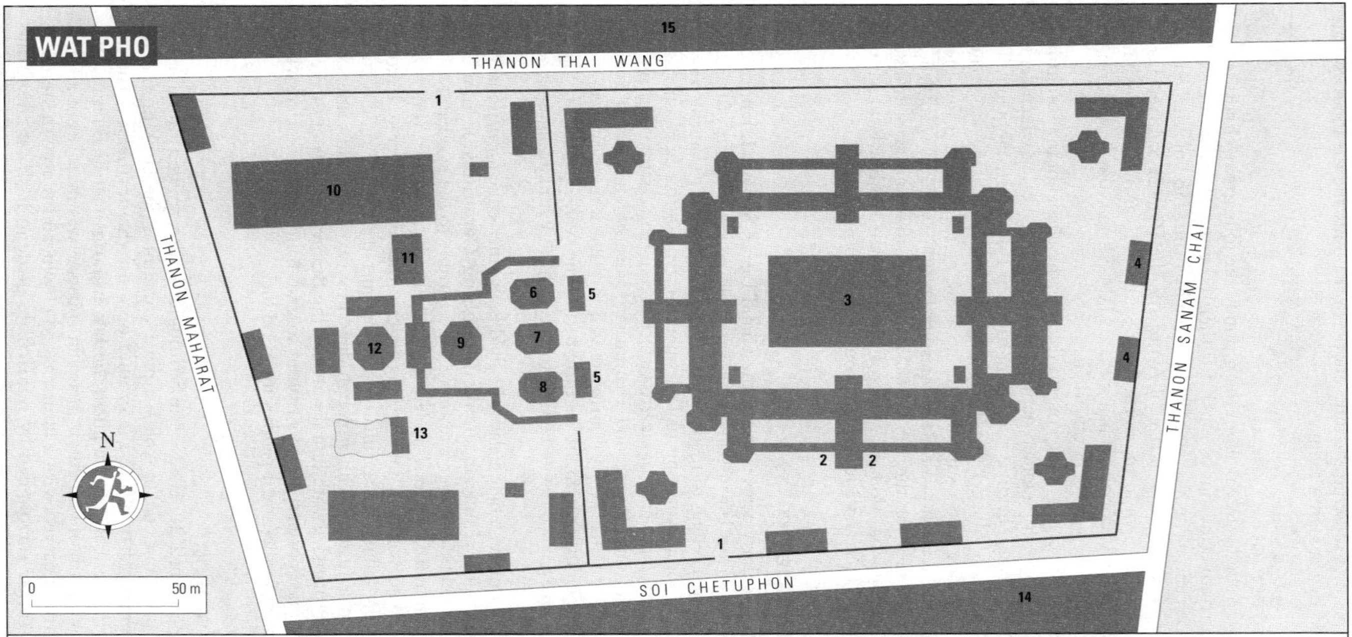

Visitors' entrances	1	Traditional Medicine Pavilions	5	Rama IV Chedi	9	European Pavilion	13
Entrances to Bot	2	Rama II Chedi	6	Chapel of the Reclining Buddha	10	Monks' Quarters	14
Bot	3	Phra Si Sanphet Chedi	7	Chinese Pavilion	11	Grand Palace	15
Massage Pavilions	4	Rama III Chedi	8	Library	12		

anatomical pictures showing the different pressure points and the illnesses that can be cured by massaging them.

The western courtyard

Among the 99 chedis strewn about the grounds, the four **great chedis** in the western courtyard stand out as much for their covering of garish tiles as for their size. The central chedi is the oldest, erected by Rama I to hold the remains of the most sacred Buddha image of Ayutthaya, the Phra Si Sanphet. Later, Rama III built the chedi to the north for the ashes of Rama II and the chedi to the south to hold his own remains; Rama IV built the fourth, with bright blue tiles, though its purpose is uncertain.

In the northwest corner of the courtyard stands the chapel of the **Reclining Buddha**, a 45-metre-long gilded statue of plaster-covered brick which depicts the Buddha entering Nirvana, a common motif in Buddhist iconography. The chapel is only slightly bigger than the statue – you can't get far enough away to take in anything but a surreal close-up view of the beaming five-metre smile. As for the feet, the vast black soles are beautifully inlaid with delicate mother-of-pearl showing the 108 *lakshanas*, or auspicious signs, which distinguish the true Buddha. Along one side of the statue are 108 bowls which will bring you good luck and a long life if you put a coin in each.

Sanam Luang

Sprawling across thirty acres north of the Grand Palace, **Sanam Luang** is one of the last open spaces left in Bangkok, a bare field where residents of the capital gather in the evening to meet, eat and play. The nearby pavements are the marketplace for some exotic spiritual salesmen: on the eastern side sit astrologers and palm-readers, and sellers of bizarre virility potions and contraptions; on the western side and spreading around Thammasat University and Wat Mahathat, scores of small-time hawkers sell **amulets** (see p.140), taking advantage of the spiritually auspicious location. In the early part of the year, especially in March during the Thai Sports and Kite Festival, the sky is filled with kite-fighting contests (see box opposite).

As it's in front of the Grand Palace, the field is also the venue for national ceremonies, such as royal funerals and the **Ploughing Ceremony**, held in May at a time selected by astrologers to bring good fortune to the rice harvest. The elaborate Brahmin ceremony is led by an official from the Ministry of Agriculture, who stands in for the king in case the royal power were to be reduced by any failure in the ritual. At the designated time, the official cuts a series of circular furrows with a plough drawn by two oxen, and scatters rice that has been sprinkled with lustral water by the Brahmin priests of the court. When the ritual is over, spectators rush in to grab handfuls of the rice, which they then plant in their own paddies for good luck.

The lak muang

At 6.54am on April 21, 1782 – the astrologically determined time for the auspicious founding of Bangkok – a pillar containing the city's horoscope was ceremonially driven into the ground opposite the northeast corner of the Grand Palace. This phallic pillar, the **lak muang** – all Thai cities have one, to provide a home for their guardian spirits – was made from a four-metre tree trunk carved with a lotus-shaped crown, and is now sheltered in an elegant shrine surrounded by immaculate gardens. It shares the shrine

Kite-flying

Flying intricate and colourful **kites** is now done mostly for fun in Thailand, but it has its roots in more serious activities. Filled with gunpowder and fitted with long fuses, kites were deployed in the first Thai kingdom at Sukhothai (1240–1438) as machines of war. In the same era, special *ngao* kites, with heads in the shape of bamboo bows, were used in Brahmin rituals: the string of the bow would vibrate in the wind and make a noise to frighten away evil spirits (nowadays noisy kites are still used, though only by farmers, to scare the birds). By the height of the Ayutthayan period (1351–1767) kites had become largely decorative: royal ceremonies were enhanced by fantastically shaped kites, adorned with jingling bells and ornamental lamps.

In the nineteenth century, Rama V, by his enthusiastic lead, popularized kite-flying as a wholesome and fashionable recreation. **Contests** are now held all over the country between February and April, when winds are strong and farmers traditionally have free time after harvesting the rice. These contests fall into two broad categories: those involving manoeuvrable flat kites, often in the shapes of animals; and those in which the beauty of static display kites is judged. The most popular contest of all, which comes under the first category, matches two teams, one flying star-shaped *chulas*, two-metre-high "male" kites, the other flying the smaller, more agile *pakpaos*, diamond-shaped "females". Each team uses its skill and teamwork to ensnare the other's kites and drag them back across a dividing line.

with the taller *lak muang* of Thonburi, which was recently incorporated into Greater Bangkok.

Hundreds of worshippers come every day to pray and offer flowers, particularly childless couples seeking the gift of fertility. In one corner of the gardens you can often see short performances of **classical dancing**, paid for by well-off families when they have a piece of good fortune to celebrate.

Wat Mahathat

On Sanam Luang's western side, with its main entrance on Thanon Maharat, **Wat Mahathat** (daily 9am–5pm; free), founded in the eighteenth century, provides a welcome respite from the surrounding tourist hype, and a chance to engage with the eager monks studying at **Mahachulalongkorn Buddhist University** here. As the nation's centre for the Mahanikai monastic sect, and housing one of the two Buddhist universities in Bangkok, the wat buzzes with purpose. It's this activity, and the chance of interaction and participation, rather than any special architectural features, which make a visit so rewarding. The many university-attending monks at the wat are friendly and keen to practise their English, and are more than likely to approach you: diverting topics might range from the poetry of Dylan Thomas to English football results gleaned from the BBC World Service.

Situated in Section Five of the wat is its **Vipassana Meditation Centre**, where sitting and walking meditation practice is available in English (daily 7–10am, 1–4pm & 6–8pm; ⓣ02 222 6011 or 623 5685 for further information). Participants are welcome to stay in the simple surroundings of the meditation building itself (donation requested), as long as they wear white clothes (available at the centre) and observe the eight main Buddhist precepts, see p.69. Talks in English on meditation and Buddhism are held here every evening (8–10pm), as well as at the International Buddhist Meditation Centre (Room 105 or 209) in the Mahachulalongkorn University building on the second and fourth Saturdays of every month (3–5pm).

The National Museum

Near the northwest corner of Sanam Luang, the **National Museum** (Wed–Sun 9am–4pm; B40 including free leaflet with map; Ⓦwww.thailandmuseum.com) houses a colossal hoard of Thailand's chief artistic riches, ranging from sculptural treasures in the north and south wings, through bizarre decorative objects in the older buildings, to outlandish funeral chariots and the exquisite Buddhaisawan Chapel, as well as occasionally staging worthwhile temporary exhibitions (details on Ⓣ02 224 1333). It's worth making time for the free **guided tours in English** (Wed & Thurs 9.30am): they're generally entertaining and their explication of the choicest exhibits provides a good introduction to Thai religion and culture. By the ticket office are a bookshop and a pleasant, air-conditioned **café**, serving drinks and cakes, while the **restaurant** inside the museum grounds, by the funeral chariots building, dishes up decent, inexpensive Thai food.

The first building you'll come to near the ticket office houses an informative overview of the history of Thailand, including a small archeological gem: a black stone **inscription**, credited to King Ramkhamhaeng of Sukhothai, which became the first capital of the Thai nation (c.1278–99) under his rule. Discovered in 1833 by the future Rama IV, it's the oldest extant inscription using the Thai alphabet. This, combined with the description it records of prosperity and piety in Sukhothai's Golden Age, has made the stone a symbol of Thai nationhood. (The prehistory section, including artefacts from Ban Chiang in the northeast of Thailand, one of the earliest Bronze Age cultures ever discovered, which used to be housed behind here, is scheduled to get a new display in the southern building of the main collection.)

The main collection: southern building

At the back of the compound, two large modern buildings, flanking an old converted palace, house the museum's **main collection**, kicking off on the ground floor of the **southern building**. Look out here for some historic sculptures from the rest of Asia, including one of the earliest representations of the Buddha, from Gandhara in northwest India. Alexander the Great left a garrison at Gandhara, which explains why the image is in the style of Classical Greek sculpture: for example, the *ushnisha*, the supernatural bump on the top of the head, which symbolizes the Buddha's intellectual and spiritual power, is rationalized into a bun of thick, wavy hair.

Upstairs, in the **Dvaravati** room (sixth to eleventh centuries), the pick of the stone and terracotta Buddhas is a small head in smooth, pink clay, whose downcast eyes and faintly smiling full lips typify the serene look of this era. At the far end of the first floor, you can't miss a voluptuous Javanese statue of elephant-headed Ganesh, Hindu god of wisdom and the arts, which, being the symbol of the Fine Arts Department, is always freshly garlanded. As Ganesh is known as the clearer of obstacles, Hindus always worship him before other gods, so by tradition he has grown fat through getting first choice of the offerings – witness his trunk jammed into a bowl of food in this sculpture.

Room S9 next door contains the most famous piece of **Srivijaya** art (seventh to thirteenth centuries), a bronze Bodhisattva Avalokitesvara found at Chaiya (according to Mahayana Buddhism, a *bodhisattva* is a saint who has postponed his passage into Nirvana to help ordinary believers gain enlightenment). With its pouting face and sinuous torso, this image has become the ubiquitous emblem of southern Thailand. The rough chronological order of the collection continues back downstairs with an exhibition of **Khmer** and **Lopburi** sculpture (seventh to fourteenth centuries), most notably some dynamic bronze statuettes and stone lintels. Look out for an elaborate lintel that depicts Vishnu reclining on a dragon in the sea of eternity, dreaming up a new universe after the old one has been annihilated in the Hindu cycle of creation and destruction. Out of his navel comes a lotus, and out of this emerges four-headed Brahma, who will put the dream into practice.

The main collection: northern building

The second half of the survey, in the northern building, begins upstairs with the **Sukhothai** collection (thirteenth to fifteenth centuries), which features some typically elegant and sinuous Buddha images, as well as chunky bronzes of Hindu gods and a wide range of ceramics. The **Lanna** rooms (roughly thirteenth to sixteenth centuries) include a miniature set of golden regalia, among them tiny umbrellas and a cute pair of filigree flip-flops, which would have been enshrined in a chedi. An ungainly but serene Buddha head, carved from grainy, pink sandstone, represents the **Ayutthaya** style of sculpture (fourteenth to eighteenth centuries): the faintest incision of a moustache above the lips betrays the Khmer influences that came to Ayutthaya after its conquest of Angkor. A sumptuous scripture cabinet, showing a cityscape of old Ayutthaya, is a more unusual piece, one of a surviving handful of such carved and painted items of furniture.

Downstairs in the section on **Bangkok** or **Ratanakosin** art (eighteenth century onwards), a stiffly realistic standing bronze brings you full circle. In his zeal for Western naturalism, Rama V had the statue made in the Gandhara style of the earliest Buddha image displayed in the first room of the museum.

The funeral chariots

To the east of the northern building, beyond the café on the left, stands a large garage where the fantastically elaborate **funeral chariots** of the royal family are stored. Pre-eminent among these is the Vejayant Rajarot, built by Rama I in 1785 for carrying the urn at his own funeral. The thirteen-metre-high structure symbolizes heaven on Mount Meru, while the dragons and divinities around the sides – piled in five golden tiers to suggest the flames of the cremation – represent the mythological inhabitants of the mountain's forests. Weighing forty tons and pulled by three hundred men, the teak chariot was used as recently as 1985 for the funeral of Queen Rambhai Bharni, wife of Rama VII.

Wang Na (Palace of the Second King)

The sprawling central building of the compound was originally part of the **Wang Na**, a huge palace stretching across Sanam Luang to Khlong Lod, which housed the "second king", appointed by the reigning monarch as his heir and deputy. When Rama V did away with the office in 1887, he turned the "Palace of the Second King" into a museum, which now contains a fascinating array of Thai *objets d'art*. As you enter (room 5), the display of sumptuous rare gold pieces behind heavy iron bars includes a well-preserved armlet taken from the ruined prang of fifteenth-century Wat Ratburana in Ayutthaya. In adjacent room 6, an intricately carved ivory seat turns out, with gruesome irony, to be a *howdah*, for use on an elephant's back. Among the masks worn by *khon* actors next door (room 7), look out especially for a fierce Hanuman, the white monkey-warrior in the *Ramayana* epic, gleaming with mother-of-pearl.

The huge and varied ceramic collection in room 8 includes some sophisticated pieces from Sukhothai, while the room behind (9) holds a riot of mother-of-pearl items, whose flaming rainbow of colours comes from the shell of the turbo snail from the Gulf of Thailand. It's also worth seeking out the display of richly decorated musical instruments in room 15.

The Buddhaisawan chapel

The second holiest image in Thailand, after the Emerald Buddha, is housed in the **Buddhaisawan Chapel**, the vast hall in front of the eastern entrance to the Wang Na. Inside, the fine proportions of the hall, with its ornate coffered ceiling and lacquered window shutters, are enhanced by painted rows of divinities and converted demons, all turned to face the chubby, glowing **Phra Sihing Buddha**, which according to legend was magically created in Sri Lanka and sent to Sukhothai in the thirteenth century. Like the Emerald Buddha, the image was believed to bring good luck to its owner and was frequently snatched from one northern town to another, until Rama I brought it down from Chiang Mai in 1795 and installed it here in the second king's private chapel. Two other images (in Nakhon Si Thammarat and Chiang Mai) now claim to be the authentic Phra Sihing Buddha, but all three are in fact derived from a lost original – this one is in a fifteenth-century Sukhothai style. It's still much loved by ordinary people and at Thai New Year is carried out onto Sanam Luang, where worshippers sprinkle it with water as a merit-making gesture.

The careful detail and rich, soothing colours of the surrounding 200-year-old **murals** are surprisingly well preserved; the bottom row between the windows narrates the life of the Buddha, beginning in the far right-hand corner with his parents' wedding.

Tamnak Daeng

On the south side of the Buddhaisawan chapel, the sumptuous **Tamnak Daeng** (Red House) stands out, a large, airy Ayutthaya-style house made of rare golden teak, surmounted by a multi-tiered roof decorated with carved foliage and swan's-tail finials. Originally part of the private quarters of Princess Sri Sudarak, elder sister of Rama I, it was moved from the Grand Palace to the old palace in Thonburi for Queen Sri Suriyen, wife of Rama II; when her son became second king to Rama IV, he dismantled the edifice again and shipped it here to the Wang Na compound. Inside, it's furnished in the style of the early Bangkok period, with some of the beautiful objects that once belonged to Sri Suriyen, a huge, ornately carved box bed, and the uncommon luxury of an indoor toilet and bathroom.

The National Gallery and Silpakorn University Gallery

If the National Museum hasn't finished you off, two other lesser galleries nearby might. The **National Gallery**, across from the National Theatre on the north side of Sanam Luang at 4 Thanon Chao Fa (daily 9am–4pm; B30; Ⓣ02 282 2639–40, Ⓦwww.thailandmuseum.com), houses a permanent collection of largely uninspiring and derivative twentieth-century Thai art, but its temporary exhibitions can be pretty good. The fine old wooden building that houses the gallery is also worth more than a cursory glance – it used to be the Royal Mint, and is constructed in typical early-twentieth-century style, around a central courtyard.

The **Silpakorn University Gallery** (Mon–Fri 9am–7pm, Sat 10am–4pm; free; ⓣ02 880 7374–6, ⓦwww.su.ac.th) on Thanon Na Phra Lan, across the road from the entrance to the Grand Palace, also stages regular exhibitions of modern Thai work.

Banglamphu and the Democracy Monument area

Best known as the site of the travellers' mecca, Thanon Khao San (for more on which, see p.106), the **Banglamphu** district (see map on p.108–109) also has a couple of noteworthy temples. But the most interesting sights in this part of the city are found to the south and east of **Democracy Monument**, within walking distance of Khao San guest houses and equally accessible from the Grand Palace. If coming from downtown Bangkok, the fastest way to get to this area is by longtail canal boat along Khlong Sen Seb (see p.103): the Phanfa terminus for this boat service is right next to the Golden Mount compound. For details on bus and express-boat services to Banglamphu, see p.107.

Wat Chana Songkhram

Sandwiched between Thanon Khao San and the Chao Phraya River at the heart of the Banglamphu backpackers' ghetto stands the lusciously renovated eighteenth-century **Wat Chana Songkhram**. As with temple compounds throughout the country, Wat Chana Songkhram is used for all sorts of neighbourhood activities (including car-parking and football games) and is not at all an ivory tower; in this instance, part of the temple yard has been appropriated by stallholders selling second-hand books and travellers' clothes, making the most of the constant stream of tourists who use the wat as a shortcut between the river and Khao San. It's worth slowing down for a closer look though, as the gables of the bot roof are beautifully ornate, embossed with a golden relief ofVishnu astride Garuda enmeshed in an intricate design of red and blue glass mosaics, and the golden finials are shaped like nagas. Peeking over the compound walls onto the guest houses and bars of Soi Ram Bhuttri are a row of *kuti*, or monks' quarters: elegantly simple wooden cabins on stilts with steeply pitched roofs.

Phra Athit

Thanon **Phra Athit**, the Banglamphu road that runs alongside the (mostly obscured) Chao Phraya River, is known for its arty atmosphere and numerous little bar-restaurants that draw crowds of students from nearby Thammasat University. Many of these places open only in the evenings (see p.174), but some serve passing tourists during daylight hours and there's also a little knot of shops selling unusual Thai crafts and art-photocards towards the northern end of the road. This northern stretch of Thanon Phra Athit is dominated by the crenellated whitewashed tower of **Phra Sumen Fortress** (aka Phra Sumeru), a renovated corner of the original eighteenth-century city walls that stands beside the river and its juncture with Khlong Banglamphu. The fortress was the northernmost of fourteen octagonal towers built by Rama I in 1783 to protect the royal island of Ratanakosin and originally contained 38 rooms for storing ammunition. (The only other surviving tower, also renovated, is Phra Mahakan Fortress, next to the

Golden Mount; see p.140.) Nowadays there's nothing to see inside the Phra Sumen tower, but it makes a striking landmark, and the area around it has been made into a pleasant grassy riverside recreation area, **Santichaiprakarn Park**, with English-language signs describing the history of the fortifications. A park sign also highlights one of the last remaining lamphu trees (*duabanga grandiflora*) in the area, which continues to grow in a muddy pool on the edge of the river to the left of the royal *sala*; lamphu trees were once so common in this neighbourhood that they gave the area its name: Banglamphu means "the place with lamphu trees", though they've all but disappeared now.

The fort marks the northernmost limit of a **riverside walkway** that runs down to the Bangkok Information Centre at Phra Pinklao Bridge, passing en route the front entrances of two very grand old buildings from the late nineteenth and early twentieth centuries, both of them beautifully restored and currently occupied by international organizations. They show their most elegant faces to the river, as in those days most visitors would have arrived by boat. On the eastern side of Thanon Phra Athit, there's another fine early-twentieth-century mansion, **Baan Phra Athit**, at #201/1; most of this building is now occupied by a private company, but one wing has been turned into the café-bar *Coffee and More*, with views onto the courtyard.

Wat Indraviharn

Located in the northern reaches of the Banglamphu district on Thanon Wisut Kasat, **Wat Indraviharn** (also known as Wat In) is famous for the enormous standing Buddha that dominates its precincts. Commissioned by Rama IV in the mid-nineteenth century to enshrine a Buddha relic from Sri Lanka, the 32-metre-high image certainly doesn't rate as a work of art: its enormous, overly flattened features give it an ungainly aspect, while the gold mirror-mosaic surface emphasizes its faintly kitsch overtones. But the beautifully pedicured foot-long toenails peep out gracefully from beneath devotees' garlands of fragrant jasmine, and you can get reasonable views of the neighbourhood by climbing the stairways of the tower supporting the statue from behind; when unlocked, the doorways in the upper part of the tower give access to the interior of the hollow image, affording vistas from shoulder level. Elsewhere in the wat's compact grounds you'll find the usual amalgam of architectural and spiritual styles, including a Chinese shrine and statues of Ramas IV and V.

Wat Indraviharn is one of an increasing number of favourite hangouts for **con-artists**, and the popular scam here is to offer tourists a tuk-tuk tour of Bangkok for a bargain B20, which invariably features a hard-sell visit to a jewellery shop – see p.194 for more on the famous Bangkok jewellery scam and p.59 for more on con-artists. Avoid all these hassles by hailing a passing metered taxi instead, or move on by **public transport**: Chao Phraya express boat stops N14 and N15 are within reach, and bus #3 runs from Thanon Samsen to Thanon Phra Athit.

Democracy Monument and October 14 Memorial

About 300m southeast of Thanon Khao San and midway along Rajdamnoen Klang, the avenue that connects the Grand Palace and the new royal district of Dusit, looms the imposing **Democracy Monument** (*Anu Sawari Pracha Tippatai*). Designed in 1939 by Italian sculptor Corrado Feroci (who founded Thailand's first Institute of Fine Arts and is often known by his Thai name, Silpa Bhirasi), it was conceived as a testimony to the ideals that fuelled the 1932 revolution and the changeover to a constitutional monarchy, hence its symbolic positioning between the royal residences. It contains a copy of the constitution and its dimensions are also significant: the four wings tower to a height of 24m, the same as the radius of the monument – allusions to June 24, the date the system was changed – and the 75 cannons around the perimeter refer to the year, 2475 BE (1932 AD).

Rajdamnoen Klang and Democracy Monument have long been the rallying point for political demonstrations, including the fateful student-led protests of October 14, 1973, when half a million people gathered here to demand a new constitution and an end to the autocratic regime of the so-called "Three Tyrants". The October 14 demonstration was savagely repressed: it turned into a bloody riot and culminated in the death of several hundred protesters at the hands of the police and the military. After years of procrastination, the events of this catastrophic day were finally commemorated in 2002 with the erection of the **October 14 Memorial**, a small granite amphitheatre encircling an elegant modern chedi bearing the names of some of the dead. The memorial stands in front of the former headquarters of Colonel Narong Kittikachorn, one of the Three Tyrants, 200m west of Democracy Monument, at the corner of Rajdamnoen Klang and Thanon Tanao.

The Queen's Gallery

It's an easy stroll from the long-running, rather staid, National Gallery (see p.136) to the newest art museum in the area, **The Queen's Gallery** (Thurs–Tues 10am–7pm; B20), a privately funded five-storey space on the corner of Rajdamnoen Klang and Thanon Phra Sumen that stages temporary exhibitions of contemporary Thai art, plus the occasional show by foreign artists. Reading rooms on each floor contain a vast selection of artists' monographs, many of them with English-language texts, and the bookshop beside the gallery entrance sells hard-to-find Thai art books.

King Prajadhipok (Rama VII) Museum

Appropriately located just 400m east of Democracy Monument, within the rather elegant European-style walls of an early-twentieth-century shop, the **King Prajadhipok Museum** (Tues–Sun 9am–4pm; B40) on Thanon Lan Luang charts the life and achievements of **Rama VII**, the king whose ten-year reign embraced Thailand's 1932 transition from rule by absolute monarchy to rule by democratic constitutional monarchy. Though the museum is hardly an unmissable attraction, the section explaining the background to the 1932 revolution is important, and there's also a miniature replica of one of Thailand's earliest cinemas here, the extant Chalermkrung Theatre, which was commissioned by Rama VII in 1933 (see p.185); the king was a keen amateur film-maker and old films from his era are screened at the museum's cinema twice daily, at 10am and 2pm.

Wat Rajnadda, Loh Prasat and the amulet market

Five minutes' walk southeast of Democracy Monument, at the point where Rajdamnoen Klang meets Thanon Mahachai, stands the assortment of religious buildings known collectively as **Wat Rajnadda**. It's immediately recognizable by the dusky-pink, multi-tiered, castle-like structure called **Loh Prasat**, or "Iron Monastery" – a reference to its 37 metal spires, which represent the 37 virtues that lead to enlightenment. The only structure of its kind in Bangkok, Loh Prasat is the dominant and most bizarre of Wat Rajnadda's components. Each tier is pierced by passageways running north–south and east–west (fifteen in each direction at ground level), with small meditation cells at each point of intersection. The Sri Lankan monastery on which it is modelled contained a thousand cells; this one probably has half that number.

In the southeast (Thanon Mahachai) corner of the temple compound, Bangkok's biggest amulet market, the **Wat Rajnadda Buddha Center**, comprises at least a hundred stalls selling tiny Buddha images of all designs, materials and prices. Alongside these miniature charms are statues of Hindu deities, dolls and carved wooden phalluses, also bought to placate or ward off disgruntled spirits, as well as love potions and tapes of sacred music. While the amulet market at Wat Rajnadda is probably the best in Bangkok, you'll find less pricey examples from the streetside vendors who congregate daily along the pavement in front of Wat Mahathat. Prices start as low as B20 and rise into the thousands.

The Golden Mount

The grubby yellow hill crowned with a gleaming gold chedi just across the road from Wat Rajnadda is the grandiosely named Golden Mount, or Phu Khao Tong. It rises within the compound of **Wat Saket**, a dilapidated late-eighteenth-century temple built by Rama I just outside his new city walls to serve as the capital's crematorium. During the following hundred years the temple became the dumping ground for some sixty thousand plague victims – the majority of them too poor to afford funeral pyres, and thus left to the vultures.

Amulets

To gain protection from malevolent spirits and physical misfortune, Thais wear or carry at least one **amulet** at all times. The most popular **images** are copies of sacred statues from famous wats, while others show revered holy men, kings (Rama V is a favourite), healers or a many-armed monk depicted closing his eyes, ears and mouth so as to concentrate better on reaching Nirvana – a human version of the hear-no-evil, see-no-evil, speak-no-evil monkeys. On the reverse side a *yantra* is often inscribed, a combination of letters and figures also designed to ward off evil, sometimes of a very specific nature: protecting your durian orchards from gales, for example, or your tuk-tuk from oncoming traffic. Individually hand-crafted or mass-produced, amulets can be made from bronze, clay, plaster or gold, and some even have sacred ingredients added, such as the ashes of burnt holy texts. But what really determines an amulet's efficacy is its history: where and by whom it was made, who or what it represents and who consecrated it. Monks are often involved in the making of the images and are always called upon to consecrate them – the more charismatic the monk, the more powerful the amulet. In return, the proceeds from the sale of amulets contributes to wat funds.

The **belief in amulets** is thought to have originated in India, where tiny images were sold to pilgrims who visited the four holy sites associated with the Buddha's birth, enlightenment, first sermon and death. But not all amulets are Buddhist-related – there's a whole range of other enchanted objects to wear for protection, including tigers' teeth, rose quartz, tamarind seeds, coloured threads and miniature phalluses. Worn around the waist rather than the neck, the phallus amulets provide protection for the genitals as well as being associated with fertility, and are of Hindu origin.

For some people, amulets are not only a vital form of spiritual protection, but valuable **collectors' items** as well. Amulet-collecting mania is something akin to stamp collecting – there are at least six Thai magazines for collectors, which give histories of certain types, tips on distinguishing between genuine items and fakes, and personal accounts of particularly powerful amulet experiences.

The **Golden Mount** was a late addition to the compound and dates back to the early nineteenth century, when Rama III built a huge chedi on ground that proved too soft to support it. The whole thing collapsed into a hill of rubble, but Buddhist law states that a religious building can never be destroyed, however tumbledown, so fifty years later Rama V topped the debris with a more sensibly sized chedi in which he placed a few Buddhist relics, believed by some to be the Buddha's teeth.

To reach the base of the mount, follow the renovated crenellations of the eighteenth-century Phra Mahakan Fortress and the old city wall, past the small bird and antiques market that operates from one of the recesses. Climbing to the top, you'll pass remnants of the collapsed chedi and plaques commemorating donors to the temple. The **terrace** surrounding the base of the new chedi is a good place for landmark-spotting: immediately to the west are the gleaming roofs of Wat Rajnadda and the salmon-pink Loh Prasat; behind them the spires of the Grand Palace can be seen and, even further beyond, the beautifully proportioned prangs of Wat Arun on the other side of the river.

Wat Saket hosts an enormous annual **temple fair** in the first week of November, when the mount is illuminated with coloured lanterns and the whole compound seethes with funfair rides, food-sellers and travelling performers.

Wat Suthat and Sao Ching Cha

Located about 700m southwest of the Golden Mount, or a similar distance directly south of Democracy Monument along Thanon Dinso, **Wat Suthat** (daily 9am–9pm; B20) is one of Thailand's six most important temples and contains Bangkok's tallest **viharn**, built in the early nineteenth century to house the meditating figure of **Phra Sri Sakyamuni Buddha**. This eight-metre-high statue was brought all the way down from Sukhothai by river, and now sits on a glittering mosaic dais surrounded with surreal **murals** that depict the last twenty-four lives of the Buddha rather than the more usual ten. The galleries that encircle the viharn contain 156 serenely posed Buddha images, making a nice contrast to the **Chinese statues** dotted around the viharn's courtyard and that of the bot in the adjacent compound, most of which were brought over from China during Rama I's reign, as ballast in rice boats: check out the depictions of gormless Western sailors and the pompous Chinese scholars.

The area just in front of Wat Suthat is dominated by the towering, red-painted teak posts of **Sao Ching Cha**, otherwise known as the **Giant Swing**, once the focal point of a Brahmin ceremony to honour Shiva's annual visit to earth. Teams of two or four young men would stand on the outsized seat (now missing) and swing up to a height of 25m, to grab between their teeth a bag of gold suspended on the end of a bamboo pole. The act of swinging probably symbolized the rising and setting of the sun, though legend also has it that Shiva and his consort, Uma were banned from swinging in their heavenly abode because doing so caused cataclysmic floods on earth – prompting Shiva to demand that the practice be continued on earth as a rite to ensure moderate rains and bountiful harvests. Accidents were so common with the terrestrial version that it was outlawed in the 1930s.

The streets leading up to Wat Suthat and Sao Ching Cha are renowned as the best place in the city to buy **religious paraphernalia**, and are well worth a browse even for tourists. Thanon Bamrung Muang in particular is lined with shops selling everything a good Buddhist could need, from household offertory tables to temple umbrellas and six-foot Buddha images. They also sell special alms packs for devotees to donate to monks; a typical pack is contained within a (holy saffron-coloured) plastic bucket (which can be used by the monk for washing his robes, or himself), and comprises such daily necessities as soap, toothpaste, soap powder, toilet roll, candles and incense.

Wat Rajabophit

From Wat Suthat, walk south down Thanon Titong for a few hundred metres before turning right (west) onto Thanon Rajabophit, on which stands **Wat Rajabophit** (see map on p.123), one of the city's prettiest temples and another example of Chinese influence. It was built by Rama V and is characteristic of this progressive king in its unusual design, with the rectangular bot and viharn connected by a circular cloister that encloses a chedi. Every external wall in the compound is covered in the pastel shades of Chinese *bencharong* ceramic tiles, creating a stunning overall effect, while the bot interior looks like a tiny banqueting hall, with gilded Gothic vaults and intricate mother-of-pearl doors.

If you now head west towards the Grand Palace from Wat Rajabophit, you'll pass a gold **statue of a pig** as you cross the canal. The cute porcine monument was erected in tribute to one of Rama V's wives, born in the Chinese Year of the Pig. Alternatively, walking in a southerly direction down Thanon Banmo takes you all the way down to the Chao Phraya River and Memorial Bridge, passing some fine old Chinese shophouses and the exuberant flower and vegetable market, Pak Khlong Talat, en route (see p.147).

Chinatown and Pahurat

When the newly crowned Rama I decided to move his capital across to the east bank of the river in 1782, the Chinese community living on the proposed site of his palace was given no choice but to relocate downriver, to the **Sampeng** area. Two hundred years on, **Chinatown** has grown into the country's largest Chinese district, a sprawl of narrow alleyways, temples and shophouses packed between Charoen Krung (New Road) and the river, separated from Ratanakosin by the Indian area of **Pahurat** – famous for its cloth and dressmakers' trimmings – and bordered to the east by Hualamphong train station. Real estate in this part of the city is said to be amongst the most valuable in the country, and there are over a hundred gold and jewellery shops along Thanon Yaowarat alone. For the tourist, Chinatown is chiefly interesting for its markets, shophouses, open-fronted warehouses and remnants of colonial-style architecture, though it also harbours a few noteworthy temples. The following account covers Chinatown's main attractions and most interesting neighbourhoods, sketching a meandering and quite lengthy route which could easily take a whole day to complete on foot. For the most authentic Chinatown experience it's best to come during the week, as some shops and stalls shut at weekends; on weekdays they begin closing around 5pm.

Easiest access is either by **subway** to Hualamphong Station, or by Chao Phraya **express boat** to Tha Rajavongse (Rajawong) at the southern end of Thanon Rajawong, which runs through the centre of Chinatown. This part of the city is also well served by **buses** from downtown Bangkok, as well as from Banglamphu and Ratanakosin (see boxes on pp.100 and 110); from Banglamphu either take any Hualamphong-bound bus and then walk from the train station, or catch the non-air-conditioned bus #56, which runs along Thanon Tanao at the end of Thanon Khao San and then goes all the way down

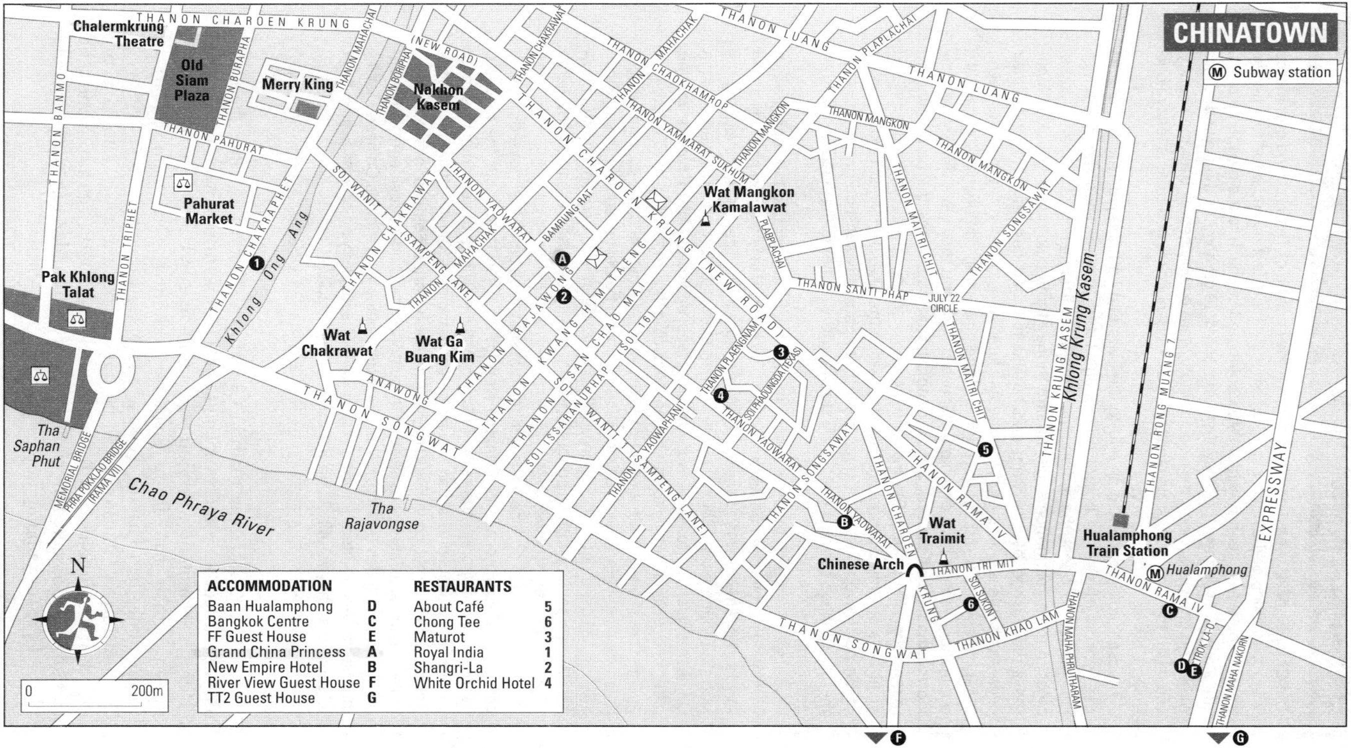
CHINATOWN
M Subway station
ACCOMMODATION
Baan Hualamphong D
Bangkok Centre C
FF Guest House E
Grand China Princess A
New Empire Hotel B
River View Guest House F
TT2 Guest House G
RESTAURANTS
About Café 5
Chong Tee 6
Maturot 3
Royal India 1
Shangri-La 2
White Orchid Hotel 4
Chalermkrung Theatre
Old Siam Plaza
Merry King
Nakhon Kasem
Pahurat Market
Pak Khlong Talat
Wat Chakrawat
Wat Ga Buang Kim
Wat Mangkon Kamalawat
Wat Traimit
Chinese Arch
Hualamphong Train Station
Hualamphong
Khlong Krung Kasem
Khlong Ong Ang
Chao Phraya River
Tha Saphan Phut
Tha Rajavongse
THANON CHAROEN KRUNG
(NEW ROAD)
THANON YAOWARAT
THANON RAMA IV
THANON SONGWAT
THANON LUANG
THANON SONGSAWAT
THANON MAITRI CHIT
THANON SANTI PHAP
JULY 22 CIRCLE
THANON KRUNG KASEM
THANON RONG MUANG 7
THANON TRI MIT
THANON KHAO LAM
THANON MAHA PHRUTHARAM
THANON MAHA NAKORN
TROK LA-O
EXPRESSWAY
THANON PAHURAT
THANON CHAKRAPHET
THANON TRIPHET
THANON BANMO
THANON BURAPHA
THANON MAHACHAI
THANON CHAKRAWAT
THANON MAHACHAK
THANON CHAOKHAMROP
THANON YAMMARAT SUKHUM
THANON MANGKON
THANON PLAPLACHAI
THANON RAJAWONG
THANON ANAWONG
THANON PLAENGNAM
SOI PHADUNGDAO (TEXAS)
SOI WANIT 1 (SAMPENG LANE)
SOI ISSARANUPHAP
THANON YAOWAPHANIT
SOI SUKON 1
BAMRUNG RAT
PLABPLACHAI
SOI KWANG HIM TAENG
CHAO MAI (SOI 16)
MEMORIAL BRIDGE
PHRA POKKLAO BRIDGE (RAMA VIII)
N
0 200m

The Chinese in Thailand

The **Chinese** have been a dominant force in the shaping of Thailand, and **commerce** is the foundation of their success. Chinese merchants first gained a toehold here in the mid-fourteenth century, when they contributed so much to the prosperity of the city-state of Ayutthaya that they were the only foreign community allowed to live within the city walls. Soon their compatriots were established all over the country, and when the capital was eventually moved to Bangkok it was to an already flourishing Chinese trading post.

The Bangkok era marked an end to the wars that had dogged Thailand and as the economy began to boom, both Rama I and Rama II encouraged Chinese immigration to boost the indigenous workforce. Thousands of migrants came, most of them young men eager to earn money that could be sent back to families impoverished by civil wars and persistently bad harvests. They saw their overseas stints as temporary measures, intending to return after a few years, though many never did. By the middle of the nineteenth century half the capital's population were of pure or mixed Chinese blood, and they were quickly becoming the masters of the new import-export trade, particularly the burgeoning tin and rubber industries. By the end of the century, the Chinese dominated Thailand's commercial and urban sector, while the Thais remained in firm control of the political domain, an arrangement that apparently satisfied both parties: as the old Chinese proverb goes, "We don't mind who holds the head of the cow, providing we can milk it".

Up until the beginning of the twentieth century, **intermarriage** between the two communities had been common, because so few Chinese women had emigrated – indeed, there is some Chinese blood in almost every Thai citizen, including the king. But in the early 1900s Chinese women started to arrive in Thailand, making Chinese society increasingly self-sufficient and enclosed. **Anti-Chinese feeling** grew and discriminatory laws ensued, including the restricting of Chinese-language education and the closing of some jobs to Chinese citizens, a movement that increased in fervour as Communism began to be perceived as a threat. Since the late 1970s, strict immigration controls have been enforced, limiting the number of new settlers to one hundred per nationality per year, a particularly harsh imposition on the Chinese.

The Chinese still dominate the commercial sector, as can be witnessed over the annual three-day holiday at **Chinese New Year**, when throughout the kingdom nearly all shops, hotels and restaurants shut down. This is the community's most important festival, but is celebrated much more as a family affair than in the Chinatowns of other countries. The nine-day **Vegetarian Festival** in October is a more public celebration, observed with gusto by the Chinese residents of Phuket and Trang provinces (see p.675); in Bangkok, nearly all the city's Chinese restaurants stop serving meat for the duration of the festival, flying special yellow flags to show that they're upholding the community's tradition.

Mahachai and Chakraphet roads in Chinatown – get off just after the Merry King department store for Sampeng Lane. Coming from downtown Bangkok and/or the Skytrain network, jump on a non-air-conditioned bus #25 or #40, both of which run from Thanon Sukhumvit, via Siam Square to Hualamphong, then Thanon Yaowarat and on to Pahurat.

Orientation in Chinatown can be quite tricky: the alleys (known as trok rather than the more usual soi) are extremely narrow, their turn-offs and other road signs often obscured by the mounds of merchandise that clutter the sidewalks and the surrounding hordes of buyers and sellers.

Wat Traimit and the Golden Buddha

Given the confusing layout of the district, it's worth starting your explorations at the eastern edge of Chinatown, just west of Hualamphong train and subway stations, with the triangle of land occupied by **Wat Traimit** (daily 9am–5pm; B20). Cross the khlong beside the station and walk 200m down (signed) Thanon Tri Mit to enter the temple compound. Outwardly unprepossessing, the temple boasts a quite stunning interior feature: the world's largest solid-gold Buddha is housed here, fitting for a community so closely linked with the gold trade, even if the image has nothing to do with China's spiritual heritage. Over 3m tall and weighing five and a half tons, the **Golden Buddha** gleams as if coated in liquid metal, seated amidst candles and surrounded with offerings of lotus buds and incense. A fine example of the curvaceous grace of Sukhothai art, the beautifully proportioned figure is best appreciated by comparing it with the much cruder Sukhothai Buddha in the next-door bot, to the east.

Cast in the thirteenth century, the image was brought to Bangkok by Rama III, completely encased in stucco – a common ruse to conceal valuable statues from would-be thieves. The disguise was so good that no one guessed what was underneath until 1955 when the image was accidentally knocked in the process of being moved to Wat Traimit, and the stucco cracked to reveal a patch of gold. The discovery launched a country-wide craze for tapping away at plaster Buddhas in search of hidden precious metals, but Wat Traimit's is still the most valuable – it's valued, by weight alone, at over US$10 million. Sections of the stucco casing are now on display alongside the Golden Buddha.

Sampeng Lane, Soi Issaranuphap and Wat Mangkon Kamalawat

Leaving Wat Traimit by the Charoen Krung/Yaowarat exit (at the back of the temple compound), walk northwest along Thanon Yaowarat, and make a left turn onto Thanon Songsawat, to reach **Sampeng Lane** (also signposted as Soi Wanit 1), an area that used to thrive on opium dens, gambling houses and brothels, but now sticks to a more reputable (if tacky) commercial trade. Stretching southeast–northwest for about 1km, Sampeng Lane is a fun place to browse and shop, unfurling itself like a ramshackle department store selling everything from Chinese silk pyjama pants to computer games at bargain-basement rates. Like goods are more or less gathered in sections, so at the eastern end you'll find mostly cheap jewellery and hair accessories, for example, before passing through stalls specializing in ceramics, Chinese lanterns and shoes,followed by clothes (west of Thanon Rajawong), sarongs and haberdashery.

For a rather more sensual experience, take a right about halfway down Sampeng Lane, into **Soi Issaranuphap** (also signed in places as Soi 16). Packed with people from dawn till dusk, this long, dark alleyway, which also traverses Charoen Krung (New Road), is where you come in search of ginseng roots (essential for good health), quivering fish heads, cubes of cockroach-killer chalk and pungent piles of cinnamon sticks. You'll see Chinese grandfathers discussing business in darkened shops, ancient pharmacists concocting bizarre potions to order, alleys branching off in all directions to gaudy Chinese temples and market squares. Soi Issaranuphap finally ends at the Thanon Plaplachai intersection amid a flurry of shops specializing in paper **funeral art**. Believing that the deceased should be well provided for in their afterlife, Chinese people buy miniature paper replicas of necessities to be burned with the body: especially popular are houses, cars, suits of clothing and, of course, money.

If Soi Issaranuphap epitomizes traditional Chinatown commerce, then **Wat Mangkon Kamalawat** (also known as **Wat Leng Nee Yee** or, in English, "Dragon Flower Temple") stands as a superb example of the community's spiritual practices. Best approached via its dramatic multi-tiered gateway 10m up Thanon Charoen Krung (New Road) from the Soi Issaranuphap junction, Wat Mangkon receives a constant stream of devotees, who come to leave offerings at one or more of the small altars inside this important Mahayana Buddhist temple. As with the Theravada Buddhism espoused by the Thais, Mahayana Buddhism (see "Religion: Thai Buddhism" in Contexts) fuses with other ancient religious beliefs, notably Confucianism and Taoism, and the statues and shrines within Wat Mangkon cover the whole spectrum. Passing through the secondary gateway, under the glazed ceramic gables topped with undulating Chinese dragons, you're greeted by a set of four outsize statues of bearded and rather forbidding sages, each clasping a symbolic object: a parasol, a pagoda, a snake's head and a mandolin. Beyond them, a series of Buddha images swathed in saffron netting occupies the next chamber, a lovely open-sided room of gold paintwork, red-lacquered wood, lattice lanterns and pictorial wall panels inlaid with mother-of-pearl. Elsewhere in the compound are little booths selling devotional paraphernalia, a Chinese medicine stall and a fortune-teller.

Wat Ga Buang Kim and Wat Chakrawat

Less than 100m up Thanon Charoen Krung (New Road) from Wat Mangkon, a left turn into Thanon Rajawong, followed by a right turn into Thanon Anawong and a further right turn into the narrow, two-pronged Soi Krai brings you to the typical neighbourhood temple of **Wat Ga Buang Kim**. Here, as at Thai temples upcountry, local residents socialize in the shade of the tiny, enclosed courtyard and the occasional worshipper drops by to pay homage at the altar. This particular wat is remarkable for its exquisitely ornamented "vegetarian hall", a one-room shrine with altar centrepiece framed by intricately carved wooden tableaux – gold-painted miniatures arranged as if in sequence, with recognizable characters reappearing in new positions and in different moods. The hall's outer wall is adorned with small tableaux, too, the area around the doorway at the top of the stairs peopled with finely crafted ceramic figurines drawn from Chinese opera stories. The other building in the wat compound is a stage used for Chinese opera performances.

Back on Anawong, a right turn down Thanon Chakrawat leads to the quite dissimilar **Wat Chakrawat**, home to several long-suffering crocodiles, not to mention monkeys, dogs and chess-playing local residents. **Crocodiles** have lived in the tiny pond behind the bot for about fifty years, ever since one was brought here after being hauled out of the Chao Phraya, where it had been endangering the limbs of bathers. The original crocodile, stuffed, sits in a glass case overlooking the current generation in the pond.

Across the other side of the wat compound is a grotto housing two unusual Buddhist relics. The first is a black silhouette on the wall, decorated with squares of gold leaf and believed to be the Buddha's shadow. Nearby, the statue of a fat monk looks on. The story goes that this monk was so good-looking that he was forever being tempted by the attentions of women; the only way he could deter them was to make himself ugly – which he did by gorging himself into obesity.

Pahurat

The ethnic emphasis changes west of Khlong Ong Ang, where **Pahurat** begins, for here, in the small square south of the intersection of Chakraphet and Pahurat roads, is where the capital's sizeable Indian community congregates. Curiosity-shopping is not as rewarding here as in Chinatown, but if you're interested in buying **fabrics** this is definitely the place; Thanon Pahurat is chock-a-block with cloth merchants specializing in everything from curtain materials, through saree lengths to *lakhon* dance costumes complete with accessories.

Also here, at the Charoen Krung (New Road)/Thanon Triphet intersection, is the **Old Siam Plaza**: its mint-green and cream exterior, resplendent with shutters and balustraded balconies, is redolent of a colonial summer palace, and its airy, three-storey interior is filled with a strange combination of shops selling either upmarket gifts or hi-tech consumer goods. Most rewarding are the half-dozen shops on the ground floor that carry an excellent range of silk from north and northeast Thailand; many of them offer dressmaking services as well. But most of the ground floor is taken up by a permanent food festival and is packed with stalls selling snacks, sweets and sticky desserts. Pahurat is also renowned for its Indian restaurants, and a short stroll along Thanon Chakraphet takes you past a choice selection of curry houses and street vendors.

Pak Khlong Talat

A browse through the 24-hour flower and vegetable market, **Pak Khlong Talat**, is a fine and fitting way to round off a day in Chinatown, though if you're an early riser it's also a great place to come before dawn, when market gardeners from Thonburi boat and truck their freshly picked produce across the Chao Phraya ready for sale to the shopkeepers, restaurateurs and hoteliers. Occupying an ideal position close to the river, the market has been operating from covered halls between the southern ends of Khlong Lod, Thanon Banmo, Thanon Chakraphet and the river bank since the nineteenth century and is the biggest wholesale market in the capital. The flower stalls, selling twenty different varieties of cut orchids and myriad other tropical blooms, spill onto the streets along the riverfront as well and, though prices are lowest in the early morning, you can still get some good bargains here in the afternoon. The riverside end of nearby Thanon Triphet and the area around the base of Memorial Bridge (Saphan Phut) hosts a huge **night bazaar** every evening except Wednesday from about 8pm; it's dominated by cheap and idiosyncratic fashions – and by throngs of teenage fashion victims.

For the most interesting approach to the flower market from the Old Siam Plaza, turn west across Thanon Triphet to reach Thanon Banmo, and then follow this road south down towards the Chao Phraya River. As you near the river, notice the facing rows of traditional Chinese shophouses, still in use today, which retain their characteristic (peeling) pastel-painted facades, shutters and stucco curlicues; there's an entrance into the market on your right. The upstream Chao Phraya **express boat** service stops just a few metres from the market at Tha Saphan Phut, but if you're on the downstream service (coming from Banglamphu) you're obliged to alight on the Thonburi side of the bridge and take a cross-river shuttle to the market. Numerous city **buses** stop in front of the market and pier, including the northbound non-air-conditioned #3 and air-conditioned #512/#12, which both run to Banglamphu (see boxes on pp.100–101).

△ Rama IX Bridge, southern Thonburi

Thonburi

Bangkok really began across the river from Ratanakosin in the town of **Thonburi**. Devoid of grand ruins and isolated from central Bangkok, it's hard to imagine Thonburi as a former capital of Thailand, but so it was for fifteen years, between the fall of Ayutthaya in 1767 and the establishment of Bangkok in 1782. General Phraya Taksin chose to set up his capital here, strategically near the sea and far from the marauding Burmese, but the story of his brief reign is a chronicle of battles that left little time and few resources to devote to the building of a city worthy of its predecessor. When General Chao Phraya displaced the by now demented Taksin to become Rama I, his first decision as founder of the Chakri dynasty was to move the capital to the more defensible site across the river. It wasn't until 1932 that Thonburi was linked to its replacement by the **Memorial Bridge** (aka Phra Buddha Yodfa Bridge), built to commemorate the 150th anniversary of the foundation of the Chakri dynasty and of Bangkok, and dedicated to Rama I, whose bronze statue sits at the Bangkok approach. Thonburi retained its separate identity for another forty years until, in 1971, it officially became part of Bangkok.

While Thonburi may lack the fine monuments of Thailand's other ancient capitals, it nevertheless contains some of the most traditional parts of Bangkok and makes a pleasant and evocative place to explore, either on foot, by boat or even by bicycle (see box on p.150). As well as the imposing riverside structure of **Wat Arun**, Thonburi is home to the **Royal Barge Museum**, the bizarre anatomical exhibits of the **Siriraj Hospital museums**, and the moderately interesting temples of **Wat Rakhang** and **Wat Prayoon.** In addition, life on this side of the river still revolves around the khlongs: vendors of food and household goods paddle their boats along the canals that crisscross the residential areas, and canalside factories use them to transport their wares to the Chao Phraya River artery. Venture onto the Thonburi backroads just three or four kilometres west of the river and you find yourself surrounded by market gardens and rural homes, with no hint of the throbbing metropolis across on the other bank. Modern Thonburi, on the other hand, sprawling to each side of Thanon Phra Pinklao, consists of the prosaic line-up of department stores, cinemas, restaurants and markets found all over urbanized Thailand.

Getting to Thonburi is simply a matter of crossing the river – use one of the numerous bridges (Memorial/Phra Pokklao and Phra Pinklao are the most central), take a cross-river ferry, or hop on the express ferry, which makes stops at Phra Pinklao Bridge and Memorial Bridge, and two stops in between. Thonburi Station, 850m west of the Tha Bangkok Noi ferry stop, is the departure point for trains to Kanchanaburi, but should not to be confused with Thonburi's other even smaller train station, Wongwian Yai (for trains to Samut Sakhon), which is further south. The Southern Bus Terminal is also in Thonburi, at the junction of Thanon Borom Ratchonni and the Nakhon Chaisri Highway, and all public and air-conditioned buses to southern destinations leave from here (see p.199).

Getting around Thonburi is a bit more complicated: the lack of footbridges over canals means that walking between sights often involves using the heavily trafficked Thanon Arun Amarin, so for these stretches it's more comfortable to hop onto a motorbike taxi, though there is a peaceful riverside walkway between Wat Kanlayanamit and Memorial Bridge. The slower, more convoluted alternative would be to leapfrog your way up or down the river by boat, using the numerous cross-river ferries that sail from small piers all the way down the Thonburi bank to link up with the Chao Phraya express-boat stops on the other side.

Exploring Thonburi by boat and bike

The most popular way to explore the sights of Thonburi is by **longtail boat**, taking in Wat Arun and the Royal Barge Museum, then continuing along Thonburi's network of small canals. The easiest option is to take a fixed-price trip from one of the piers on the Bangkok side of the Chao Phraya, and most of these companies also feature visits to Thonburi's two main floating markets, both of which are heavily touristed and rather contrived (Amphawa's Tha Ka floating markets are much more authentic, but also much more of an expedition; see p.220). **Wat Sai floating market** happens daily from Monday to Friday but is very commercialized, and half of it is land-based anyway, while **Taling Chan floating market** is also fairly manufactured but more fun, though it only operates on Saturdays and Sundays. (Taling Chan market is held on Khlong Chakphra in front of Taling Chan District Office, a couple of kilometres west of Thonburi train station, and can also be reached by taking bus #79 from Democracy Monument/Ratchadamnoen Klang to Khet Taling Chan.)

Fixed-priced trips with The Boat Tour Centre (ⓣ02 235 3108) at Tha Si Phraya cost B500 per boat for one whistle-stop hour, B800 for two hours and go either to Wat Sai (for which you need to be at the pier by about 8am; Mon–Fri only), or around the Thonburi canals, taking in Wat Arun and the Royal Barge Museum (can depart any time). The Mitchaopaya Travel Service (ⓣ02 623 5340), operating out of Tha Chang, offers a one-hour trip that takes in the Royal Barge Museum and Wat Arun, as well as Wat Sai (Mon–Fri) or Taling Chan (Sat & Sun), for B600 per boat, or two hours with the addition of a visit to an orchid farm for B1200. Real Asia (ⓣ02 712 9301, ⓦwww.realasia.net) runs guided full-day tours of Bangkok's waterways, taking in Nonthaburi (see p.168) as well as the Thonburi canals (daily depending on bookings; from B1350/person). For details of dinner cruises down the Chao Phraya River, see p.172.

It's also possible to **organize your own boat trip** around Thonburi from other piers, including Tha Orienten (at the *Oriental Hotel*), and Tha Wang Nah, next to the Bangkok Information Centre on Thanon Phra Athit in Banglamphu, but bear the above prices in mind and be prepared for some heavy bargaining.

A less expensive option is to use the **public longtails** that run bus-like services along back canals from central Bangkok-side piers, departing every ten to thirty minutes and charging from B15 to B30 for a round trip. Potentially interesting routes include the Khlong Bangkok Noi service from Tha Chang; the Khlong Mon service from Tha Thien, in front of Wat Pho; the Khlong Bang Waek service from Tha Saphan Phut, at Memorial Bridge; and the Khlong Om service from Tha Nonthaburi. There have however been reports that taxi-boat drivers are making it impossible for tourists to board the public services from Tha Chang and Tha Thien, so the tourist office suggests starting in Nonthaburi instead.

The most peaceful and least touristed way to enjoy the canals of Thonburi is to join the monthly **bicycle tour** organized by the Bangkok Tourist Bureau on Thanon Phra Athit in Banglamphu (ⓣ02 225 7612–4, ⓔbangkoktour@hotmail.com; B650 including bike rental). You need to be reasonably fit to tackle the 35-kilometre route, which is specially designed to follow canal towpaths wherever possible; the tour guides you through exceptionally scenic parts of both Thonburi and Nonthaburi, taking in khlongside settlements, floating markets, market gardens, orchid nurseries and neighbourhood temples. The tour currently takes place from 7am to 4.30pm on the first Sunday of every month, but call ahead to check.

Royal Barge Museum

Since the Ayutthaya era, kings of Thailand have been conveyed along their country's waterways in royal barges. For centuries these slender, exquisitely elegant, black-and-gold wooden vessels were used on all important royal outings, and even up until 1967 the current king used to process down the Chao Phraya River to Wat Arun in a flotilla of royal barges at least once a year, on the occasion of Kathin, the annual donation of robes by the laity to the temple at the end of the rainy season. But the 100-year-old boats are becoming quite frail, so such a procession is now a rare event: the last royal procession was in 1999, to mark the king's 72nd birthday, and is set to be repeated on his sixtieth anniversary in 2006 (a special procession was held in honour of visiting heads of state in 2003, but no members of the royal family participated). A **royal barge procession** along the Chao Phraya is a magnificent event, all the more spectacular because it happens so infrequently. Fifty or more barges fill the width of the river and stretch for almost 1km, drifting slowly to the measured beat of a drum and the hypnotic strains of ancient boating hymns, chanted by over two thousand oarsmen dressed in luscious brocades.

The eight beautifully crafted vessels at the heart of the ceremony are housed in the **Royal Barge Museum** on the north bank of Khlong Bangkok Noi (daily 9am–5pm; B30). Up to 50m long and intricately lacquered and gilded all over, they taper at the prow into imposing mythical figures after a design first used by the kings of Ayutthaya. Rama I had the boats copied and, when those fell into disrepair, Rama VI commissioned the exact reconstructions still in use today. The most important is *Sri Suphanahongse*, which bears the king and queen and is graced by a glittering five-metre-high prow representing the golden swan Hamsa, mount of the Hindu god Brahma. In front of it floats *Anantanagaraj*, fronted by a magnificent seven-headed naga and bearing a Buddha image. The newest addition to the fleet is *Narai Song Suban*, which was commissioned by the current king for his golden jubilee in 1996; it is a copy of the mid-nineteenth-century original and is crowned with a black Vishnu (Narai) astride a garuda figurehead. A display of miniaturized royal barges at the back of the museum recreates the exact formation of a traditional procession.

The museum is a feature of most canal tours but is easily visited on your own. Just take the Chao Phraya **express boat** to Tha Phra Pinklao or, if coming from Banglamphu, take the cheaper, more frequent cross-river ferry from Tha Phra Athit to Tha Phra Pinklao, then walk up the road a hundred metres and take the first left down Soi Wat Dusitaram. If coming by **bus** from the Bangkok side (air-con buses #503/#3, #507/#7, #509/#9, #511/#11 and #32 all cross the river here), get off at the first stop on the Thonburi side, which is right beside the mouth of Soi Wat Dusitaram. Signs from Soi Wat Dusitaram lead you through a jumble of walkways and stilt-houses to the museum, about ten minutes' walk away.

Siriraj Hospital Museums

For some bizarre reason, a surprising number of tourists make a point of visiting the **Anatomical Museum** (Mon–Fri 9am–noon & 1–4pm; free), one of six small collections of medical curiosities housed in Thonburi's enormous Siriraj teaching hospital. The Anatomical Museum was set up to teach students how to dissect the human body, but its most notorious exhibits are the specimens of conjoined twins kept in jars in a couple of old wooden display cabinets. There is also a picture of the most famous conjoined twins in history, the genuinely Siamese twins, Chang and Eng, who were born just outside Bangkok in Samut Songkhram (see p.218). The collection was established in 1927 and looks very dated in comparison to modern museums; there is almost no information in English. Exit right from the back door of the Anatomical Building and take the first left to find the **Museum of History of Thai Medicine** (Mon–Fri

9am–noon & 1–4pm; free), a potentially more stimulating exhibition whose wax tableaux recreate the traditional medical practices of midwives, masseuses, pharmacists and yogis, though these also have no English-language captions.

Easiest **access** to the hospital is by Chao Phraya express boat to Tha Wang Lang/Siriraj (downstream service) or nearby Tha Phrannok (upstream service). From the piers walk a few metres up Thanon Phrannok and enter the hospital via its side entrance. Follow the road through the hospital compound for about 350m, turn left just before the (signed) Museum of History of Thai Medicine, and the Anatomical Museum is the first building on your left.

Wat Rakhang

The charming riverside temple of **Wat Rakhang** (Temple of the Bells) gets its name from the five large bells donated by King Rama I and is notable for the hundreds of smaller chimes that tinkle away under the eaves of the main bot and, more accessibly, in the temple courtyard, where devotees come to strike them and hope for a run of good luck. To be extra certain of having wishes granted, visitors sometimes also buy turtles from the temple stalls outside and release them into the Chao Phraya River below. Behind the bot stands an attractive eighteenth-century wooden *ho trai* (scripture library) that still boasts some original murals on the wooden panels inside, as well as exquisitely renovated gold-leaf paintwork on the window shutters and pillars. A cross-river **ferry** shuttles between Wat Rakhang's pier and the Tha Chang (Grand Palace) express-boat pier, or you can **walk** to Wat Rakhang in five minutes from the Tha Wang Lang/Siriraj and Phrannok express-boat piers: turn south (left) through the Phrannok pierside market and continue until you reach the temple, passing the posh *Supatra River House* restaurant (see p.186) and Patravadi Theatre on the way.

Wat Arun

Almost directly across the river from Wat Pho rises the enormous, five-pranged **Wat Arun** (daily 7am–5pm; B20), the Temple of Dawn, probably Bangkok's most memorable landmark and familiar as the silhouette used in the TAT logo. It looks particularly impressive from the river as you head downstream from the Grand Palace towards the *Oriental Hotel*, but is ornate enough to be well worth stopping off for a closer look. All boat tours include half an hour here, but Wat Arun is also easily visited by yourself, although tour operators will try to persuade you otherwise: just take a B2 cross-river ferry from the pier adjacent to the Chao Phraya express-boat pier at Tha Thien. In January and February, Wat Arun hosts a free *son-et-lumière* show every night at 7, 8 and 9pm: visit Ⓦwww.thailandgrandfestival.com or contact TAT for details.

A wat has occupied this site since the Ayutthaya period, but only in 1768 did it become known as the Temple of Dawn – when General Phraya Taksin reputedly reached his new capital at the break of day. The temple served as his royal chapel and housed the recaptured Emerald Buddha for several years until the image was moved to Wat Phra Kaeo in 1785 (see p.126). Despite losing its special status after the relocation, Wat Arun continued to be revered and was reconstructed and enlarged to its present height of 104m by Rama II and Rama III.

The Wat Arun that you see today is a classic prang structure of Ayutthayan style, built as a representation of Mount Meru, the home of the gods in Khmer mythology. Climbing the two tiers of the square base that supports the **central prang**, you not only enjoy a good view of the river and beyond, but also get a chance to examine the tower's curious decorations. Both this main prang and the four minor ones that encircle it are covered in bits of broken porcelain, arranged to create an amazing array of polychromatic flowers (local people gained much merit by donating their crockery for the purpose). Statues of mythical figures such as *yaksha* demons and half-bird, half-human *kinnari* support the different levels and, on the first terrace, the mondops at each cardinal point contain statues of the Buddha at the most important stages of his life: at birth (north), in meditation (east), preaching his first sermon (south) and entering Nirvana (west). The second platform surrounds the base of the prang proper, whose closed entranceways are guarded by four statues of the Hindu god Indra on his three-headed elephant Erawan. In the niches of the smaller prangs stand statues of Phra Pai, the god of the wind, on horseback.

Santa Cruz and Wat Prayoon

About 700m downstream of Wat Arun, the bot at **Wat Kanlayanamit** stands very tall in order to accommodate its huge Buddha image, but is chiefly of interest because it marks the start of the riverside walkway to Memorial Bridge. En route, you'll pass the distinctive pastel facade and pretty stained-glass windows of **Santa Cruz** (also known as **Wat Kudi Jeen**), a Catholic church that sits at the heart of what used to be Thonburi's Portuguese quarter. The Portuguese came to Thailand both to trade and to proselytize, and by 1856 had established the largest of the European communities in Bangkok: four thousand Portuguese Christians lived in and around Thonburi at this time, about one percent of the total population. The Portuguese ghetto is a thing of the distant past, but plenty of local residents still have Portuguese blood in them and the church and its adjacent school continue to be well attended.

The walkway stops at the base of Memorial Bridge, where you can pick up the downstream service of the Chao Phraya express boats (upstream services leave from across the river). Before leaving Thonburi, however, it's worth stopping off at nearby **Wat Prayoon** for a wander around the temple's **Khao Mor cemetery**, which is located in a separate compound to the southeast side of the wat, just off Thanon Pracha Thipok, three minutes' walk from the bridge. The cemetery's unusual collection of miniature chedis and shrines are set on an artificial hill, which was constructed on a whim of Rama III's, after he'd noticed the pleasing shapes made by dripping candle wax. Wedged in among the grottoes, caverns and ledges of this uneven mass are numerous shrines to departed devotees, forming a phenomenal gallery of different styles, from traditionally Thai chedis, bots or prangs to such obviously foreign designs as the tiny Wild West house complete with cactuses at the front door. Turtles fill the pond surrounding the mound – you can feed them with the bags of banana and papaya sold nearby. At the edge of the pond stands a memorial to the unfortunate few who lost their lives when one of the saluting cannons exploded at the temple's dedication ceremony in 1836.

Dusit

Connected to Ratanakosin via the boulevards of Rajdamnoen Klang and Rajdamnoen Nok, the spacious, leafy area known as **Dusit** has been a royal district since the reign of Rama V, King Chulalongkorn (1860–1910). The first Thai monarch to visit Europe, Rama V returned with radical plans for the modernization of his capital, the fruits of which are most visible in Dusit: notably at **Vimanmek Palace** and **Wat Benjamabophit**, the so-called "Marble Temple". Even now, Rama V still commands a loyal following and his statue, which stands at the Thanon U-Thong-Thanon Sri Ayutthaya crossroads, is presented with offerings every week and is also the focus of celebrations on Chulalongkorn Day (Oct 23). Today, the peaceful Dusit area retains its European feel, and much of the country's decision-making goes on behind the high fences and impressive facades along its tree-lined avenues: the building that houses the National Parliament is here, as is Government House (which is used mainly for official functions), and the king's official residence, Chitrlada Palace, occupies the eastern edge of the area. Across from Chitrlada Palace, **Dusit Zoo** makes a pleasant enough place to take the kids.

From Banglamphu, you can get to Dusit by taking the #70 **bus** from Rajdamnoen Klang (see box on p.110) and getting off outside the zoo and Elephant Museum on Thanon U-Thong; or take the **express boat** to Tha Thewes and then walk. From downtown Bangkok, easiest access is by bus from the Skytrain and subway stops at Victory Monument; there are many services from here, including air-con #510/#10 and #16, both of which run all the way along Thanon Rajwithi.

Vimanmek Palace and the Royal Elephant National Museum

Breezy, elegant **Vimanmek Palace** (daily 9.30am–4pm; compulsory free guided tours every 30min, last tour 3.15pm; B100, or free with a Grand Palace ticket, which remains valid for one month) was built by Rama V as a summer retreat on Ko Si Chang (see p.425), from where it was transported bit by bit in 1901. The ticket price also covers entry to half a dozen other small museums in the palace grounds, including the Support Museum and Elephant Museum described below, and all visitors are treated to free performances of traditional Thai dance daily at 10.30am and 2pm. Note that the same **dress rules** apply here as to the Grand Palace (see p.125). The main **entrance** to the extensive Vimanmek Palace compound is on Thanon Rajwithi, but there are also ticket gates on Thanon Ratchasima, and opposite Dusit Zoo on Thanon U-Thong.

Vimanmek Palace

Built almost entirely of golden teak without a single nail, the coffee-coloured, L-shaped Vimanmek Palace is encircled by delicate latticework verandas that look out onto well-kept lawns, flower gardens and lotus ponds. Not surprisingly, this "Celestial Residence" soon became Rama V's favourite palace, and he and his enormous retinue of officials, concubines and children stayed here for lengthy periods between 1902 and 1906. All of Vimanmek's 81 rooms were out of bounds to male visitors, except for the king's own apartments, in the octagonal tower, which were entered by a separate staircase.

On display inside is Rama V's collection of artefacts from all over the world, including *bencharong* ceramics, European furniture and bejewelled Thai betel-nut sets. Considered progressive in his day, Rama V introduced many new-fangled ideas to Thailand: the country's first indoor bathroom is here, as is the earliest typewriter with Thai characters, and some of the first portrait paintings – portraiture had until then been seen as a way of stealing part of the sitter's soul.

The Support Museum

Elsewhere in the Vimanmek grounds several small throne halls have been converted into tiny museums displaying royal portraits, antique clocks and

The royal white elephants

In Thailand the most revered of all elephants are the so-called **white elephants** – actually tawny brown albinos – which are considered so sacred that they all, whether wild or captive, belong to the king by law. Their special status originates from Buddhist mythology, which tells how the previously barren Queen Maya became pregnant with the future Buddha after dreaming one night that a white elephant had entered her womb. The thirteenth-century King Ramkhamhaeng of Sukhothai adopted the beast as a symbol of the great and the divine, and ever since, a Thai king's greatness is said to be measured by the number of white elephants he owns. The present king, Rama IX, has twelve, the largest royal collection to date.

Before an elephant can be granted official "white elephant" status, it has to pass a stringent assessment of its physical and behavioural **characteristics**. Key qualities include a paleness of seven crucial areas – eyes, nails, palate, hair, outer edges of the ears, tail and testicles – and an all-round genteel demeanour, manifested, for instance, in the way in which it cleans its food before eating, or in a tendency to sleep in a kneeling position. The most recent addition to King Bhumibol's stables was first spotted in Lampang in 1992, but experts from the Royal Household had to spend a year watching its every move before it was finally given the all-clear. Tradition holds that an elaborate ceremony should take place every time a new white elephant is presented to the king: the animal is paraded with great pomp from its place of capture to Dusit, where it's anointed with holy water in front of an audience of the kingdom's most important priests and dignitaries, before being housed in the royal stables. Recently though, the king has decreed that as a cost-cutting measure there should be no more ceremonies for new acquisitions, and only one of the royal white elephants is now kept inside the royal palace; the others live in less luxurious rural accommodation.

The expression "white elephant" probably derives from the legend that the kings used to present certain enemies with one of these exotic creatures. The animal required expensive attention but, being royal, could not be put to work in order to pay for its upkeep. The recipient thus went bust trying to keep it.

other collectors' items. The most interesting of these is the **Support Museum Abhisek Dusit Throne Hall**, which is housed in another very pretty building immediately behind (to the east of) Vimanmek. The Support Museum showcases the exquisite handicrafts produced under Queen Sirikit's charity project, Support, which works to revitalize traditional Thai arts and crafts. Outstanding exhibits include a collection of handbags, baskets and pots woven from the *lipao* fern that grows wild in southern Thailand; jewellery and figurines inlaid with the iridescent wings of beetles; gold and silver nielloware; and lengths of intricately woven silk from the northeast.

Chang Ton Royal Elephant National Museum

Just behind (to the east of) the Support Museum, inside the Thanon U-Thong entrance to the Vimanmek compound, stand two whitewashed buildings that once served as the stables for the king's white elephants. Now that the sacred pachyderms have been relocated, the stables have been turned into the **Royal Elephant National Museum**. Inside you'll find some interesting pieces of elephant paraphernalia, including sacred ropes, mahouts' amulets and magic formulae, as well as photos of the all-important ceremony in which a white elephant is granted royal status (see above).

Dusit Zoo (Khao Din)

Across Thanon U-Thong from the Elephant Museum is the side entrance into **Dusit Zoo**, also known as **Khao Din** (daily 8am–6pm; B30, children B5), which was once part of the Chitrlada Palace gardens, but is now a public park; the main entrance is on Thanon Rajwithi, and there's a third gate on Thanon Rama V, within walking distance of Wat Benjamabophit. All the usual suspects are here in the zoo, including big cats, elephants, orang-utans, chimpanzees and a reptile house, but the enclosures are pretty basic. However, it's a reasonable place for kids to let off steam, with plenty of shade, a full complement of English-language signs, a lake with pedalos and lots of foodstalls.

Wat Benjamabophit

Wat Benjamabophit (aka Wat Bencha; daily 7am–5pm; B20) is the last major temple to have been built in Bangkok. It's an interesting fusion of classical Thai and nineteenth-century European design, with its Carrara marble walls – hence the touristic tag "The Marble Temple" – complemented by the bot's unusual stained-glass windows, Victorian in style but depicting figures from Thai mythology. Inside, a fine replica of the highly revered Phra Buddha Chinnarat image of Phitsanulok (see p.272) presides over the small room containing Rama V's ashes. The courtyard behind the bot houses a gallery of Buddha images from all over Asia, set up by Rama V as an overview of different representations of the Buddha.

Wat Benjamabophit is one of the best temples in Bangkok to see religious **festivals** and rituals. Whereas monks elsewhere tend to go out on the streets every morning in search of alms, at the Marble Temple the ritual is reversed, and merit-makers come to them. Between about 6 and 7.30am, the monks line up on Thanon Nakhon Pathom, their bowls ready to receive donations of curry and rice, lotus buds, incense, even toilet paper and Coca-Cola; the demure row of saffron-robed monks is a sight that's well worth getting up early for. The evening candlelight processions around the bot during the Buddhist festivals of Maha Puja (in Feb) and Visakha Puja (in May) are among the most entrancing in the country.

Wat Benjamabophit is just a two-hundred-metre walk south of the zoo's Thanon Rama V entrance, or about 600m from Vimanmek's U-Thong gate. Coming by bus #70 from Banglamphu, get off at the crossroads in front of the Rama V statue and walk east along Thanon Sri Ayutthaya.

Downtown Bangkok

Extending east from the rail line and south to Thanon Sathorn, **downtown Bangkok** is central to the colossal expanse of Bangkok as a whole, but rather peripheral in a sightseer's perception of the city. This is where you'll find the main financial district, around Thanon Silom, and the chief shopping centres, around Siam Square, in addition to the smart hotels and restaurants, the embassies and airline offices. Scattered widely across the downtown area are just a few attractions for visitors, including the noisy and glittering **Erawan Shrine**, and four attractive museums housed in traditional teak buildings: **Jim Thompson's House**, the **Ban Kamthieng**, the **Suan Pakkad Palace Museum** and **M.R. Kukrit's Heritage Home**. The infamous **Patpong** district hardly shines as a tourist sight, yet, lamentably, its sex bars provide Thailand's single biggest draw for foreign men.

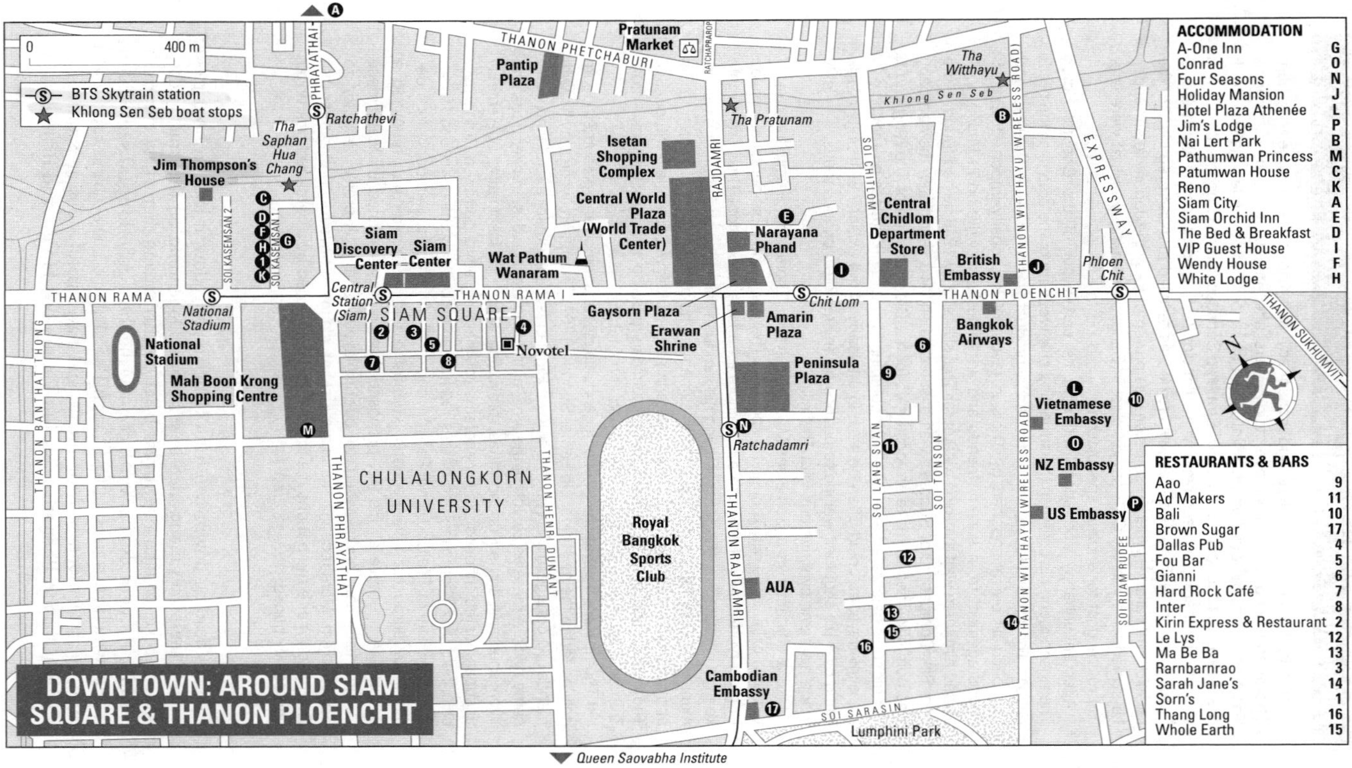
DOWNTOWN: AROUND SIAM SQUARE & THANON PLOENCHIT
0 400 m
BTS Skytrain station
Khlong Sen Seb boat stops
ACCOMMODATION
A-One Inn G
Conrad O
Four Seasons N
Holiday Mansion J
Hotel Plaza Athenée L
Jim's Lodge P
Nai Lert Park B
Pathumwan Princess M
Patumwan House C
Reno K
Siam City A
Siam Orchid Inn E
The Bed & Breakfast D
VIP Guest House I
Wendy House F
White Lodge H
RESTAURANTS & BARS
Aao 9
Ad Makers 11
Bali 10
Brown Sugar 17
Dallas Pub 4
Fou Bar 5
Gianni 6
Hard Rock Café 7
Inter 8
Kirin Express & Restaurant 2
Le Lys 12
Ma Be Ba 13
Rarnbarnrao 3
Sarah Jane's 14
Sorn's 1
Thang Long 16
Whole Earth 15
THANON PHETCHABURI
THANON RAMA I
THANON PLOENCHIT
THANON SUKHUMVIT
EXPRESSWAY
PHRAYATHAI
THANON PHRAYATHAI
THANON HENRI DUNANT
THANON RAJDAMRI
RAJDAMRI
RATCHAPRAROP
THANON WITTHAYU (WIRELESS ROAD)
THANON BANTHAT THONG
SOI KASEMSAN 1
SOI KASEMSAN 2
SOI CHITLOM
SOI LANG SUAN
SOI TONSON
SOI RUAM RUDEE
SOI SARASIN
Khlong Sen Seb
Tha Saphan Hua Chang
Tha Pratunam
Tha Witthayu
Ratchathevi
Central Station (Siam)
National Stadium
Chit Lom
Phloen Chit
Ratchadamri
Jim Thompson's House
Pantip Plaza
Pratunam Market
Isetan Shopping Complex
Central World Plaza (World Trade Center)
Wat Pathum Wanaram
Siam Discovery Center
Siam Center
SIAM SQUARE
Novotel
National Stadium
Mah Boon Krong Shopping Centre
CHULALONGKORN UNIVERSITY
Royal Bangkok Sports Club
Narayana Phand
Gaysorn Plaza
Erawan Shrine
Amarin Plaza
Peninsula Plaza
Central Chidlom Department Store
British Embassy
Bangkok Airways
Vietnamese Embassy
NZ Embassy
US Embassy
AUA
Cambodian Embassy
Lumphini Park
Queen Saovabha Institute

The legend of Jim Thompson

Thai silk-weavers, art-dealers and conspiracy theorists all owe a debt to **Jim Thompson**, who even now, over thirty years after his disappearance, remains Thailand's most famous farang. An architect by trade, Thompson left his New York practice in 1940 to join the Office of Strategic Services (later to become the CIA), a tour of duty that was to see him involved in clandestine operations in North Africa, Europe and, in 1945, the Far East, where he was detailed to a unit preparing for the invasion of Thailand. When the mission was pre-empted by the Japanese surrender, he served for a year as OSS station chief in Bangkok, forming links that were later to provide grist for endless speculation.

After an unhappy and short-lived stint as part-owner of the *Oriental Hotel*, Thompson found his calling in the struggling **silk-weavers** of the area near the present Jim Thompson House, whose traditional product was unknown in the West and had been all but abandoned by Thais in favour of less costly imported textiles. Encouragement from society friends and an enthusiastic write-up in *Vogue* convinced him there was a foreign market for Thai silk, and by 1948 he had founded the Thai Silk Company Ltd. Success was assured when, two years later, the company was commissioned to make the costumes for the Broadway run of *The King and I*. Thompson's celebrated eye for colour combinations and his tireless promotion – in the early days, he could often be seen in the lobby of the *Oriental* with bolts of silk slung over his shoulder, waiting to pounce on any remotely curious tourist – quickly made his name synonymous with Thai silk.

Like a character in a Somerset Maugham novel, Thompson played the role of Western exile to the hilt. Though he spoke no Thai, he made it his personal mission to preserve traditional arts and architecture (at a time when most Thais were more keen to emulate the West), assembling his famous Thai house and stuffing it with all manner of Oriental *objets d'art*. At the same time he held firmly to his farang roots and society connections: no foreign gathering in Bangkok was complete without Jim Thompson, and virtually every Western luminary passing through Bangkok – from Truman Capote to Ethel Merman – dined at his table.

If Thompson's life was the stuff of legend, his disappearance and presumed death only added to the mystique. On Easter Sunday, 1967, Thompson, while staying with friends in a cottage in Malaysia's Cameron Highlands, went out for a stroll and never came back. A massive search of the area, employing local guides, tracker dogs and even shamans, turned up no clues, provoking a rash of fascinating but entirely unsubstantiated theories. The grandfather of them all, advanced by a Dutch psychic, held that Thompson had been lured into an ambush by the disgraced former prime minister of Thailand, Pridi Panyonyong, and spirited off to Cambodia for indeterminate purposes; later versions, supposing that Thompson had remained a covert CIA operative all his life, proposed that he was abducted by Vietnamese Communists and brainwashed to be displayed as a high-profile defector to Communism. More recently, an amateur sleuth claims to have found evidence that Thompson met a more mundane fate, having been killed by a careless truck driver and hastily buried.

If you're heading downtown from Banglamphu, allow at least an hour to get to any of the places mentioned here by **bus**. Depending on the time of day, it may be quicker to take an **express boat** downriver, and then change onto the **Skytrain**. It might also be worth considering the regular **longtails** on Khlong Sen Seb, which runs parallel to Thanon Phetchaburi. They start at the Golden Mount, near Democracy Monument, and have useful stops at Saphan Hua Chang on Thanon Phrayathai (for Jim Thompson's House) and Pratunam (for the Erawan Shrine).

Siam Square to Thanon Sukhumvit

Though Siam Square has just about everything to satisfy the Thai consumer boom – big shopping centres, Western fast-food restaurants, cinemas – don't come looking for an elegant commercial piazza: the "square" is in fact a grid of small streets on the south side of Thanon Rama I, between Thanon Phrayathai and Thanon Henri Dunant, and the name is applied freely to the surrounding area. Further east, you'll find yet more shopping malls around the Erawan Shrine, where Rama I becomes Thanon Ploenchit. Life becomes marginally less frenetic along Ploenchit, which is flanked by several grand old embassies, but picks up again once you pass under the expressway flyover and enter the shopping and entertainment quarter of Thanon Sukhumvit.

Jim Thompson's House

Just off Siam Square at the north end of Soi Kasemsan 2, Thanon Rama I, **Jim Thompson's House** (daily from 9am, viewing on frequent 30–40min guided tours in several languages, last tour 5pm; B100, students & under-25s B50; Ⓦ www.jimthompson.com) is a kind of Ideal Home in elegant Thai style, and a peaceful refuge from downtown chaos. The house was the residence of the legendary American adventurer, entrepreneur, art collector and all-round character whose mysterious disappearance in the jungles of Malaysia in 1967 has made him even more of a legend among Thailand's farang community.

Apart from putting together this beautiful home, Thompson's most concrete contribution was to turn traditional silk-weaving from a dying art into the highly successful international industry it is today. The complex now includes a **shop** (closes 6pm), part of the Jim Thompson Thai Silk Company chain (see p.191), and a **café** (last orders 5pm), which serves a similar menu to *Jim Thompson's Farmer's Market and Café* (see p.177); and a centre for temporary exhibitions on textiles and the arts is planned in a new building. Ignore any conmen at the entrance to the soi looking for mugs to escort on rip-off shopping trips, who'll tell you that the house is closed when it isn't.

The grand, rambling **house** is in fact a combination of six teak houses, some from as far afield as Ayutthaya and most more than two hundred years old. Like all traditional houses, they were built in wall sections hung together without nails on a frame of wooden pillars, which made it easy to dismantle them, pile them onto a barge and float them to their new location. Although he had trained as an architect, Thompson had more difficulty in putting them back together again; in the end, he had to go back to Ayutthaya to hunt down a group of carpenters who still practised the old house-building methods. Thompson added a few unconventional touches of his own, incorporating the elaborately carved front wall of a Chinese pawnshop between the drawing room and the bedroom, and reversing the other walls in the drawing room so that their carvings faced into the room.

The impeccably tasteful **interior** has been left as it was during Thompson's life, even down to the cutlery on the dining table. Complementing the fine artefacts from throughout Southeast Asia is a stunning array of Thai arts and crafts, including one of the best collections of traditional Thai paintings in the world. Thompson picked up plenty of bargains from the Thieves' Quarter (Nakhon Kasem) in Chinatown, before collecting Thai art became fashionable and expensive. Other pieces were liberated from decay and destruction in upcountry temples, while many of the Buddha images were turned over by ploughs, especially around Ayutthaya. Some of the exhibits are very rare, such as a seventeenth-century Ayutthayan teak Buddha, but Thompson also bought pieces of little value and fakes simply for their looks – a shopping strategy that's all the more sensible in the jungle of today's Thai antiques trade.

The Erawan Shrine

For a break from high culture, drop in on the **Erawan Shrine** (*Saan Phra Prom* in Thai), at the corner of Thanon Ploenchit and Thanon Rajdamri. Remarkable as much for its setting as anything else, this shrine to Brahma, the ancient Hindu creation god, and Erawan, his elephant, squeezes in on one of the busiest and noisiest corners of modern Bangkok, in the shadow of the *Grand Hyatt Erawan Hotel* – whose existence is the reason for the shrine. When a string of calamities held up the building of the original hotel in the 1950s, spirit doctors were called in, who instructed the owners to build a new home for the offended local spirits: the hotel was then finished without further mishap.

Be prepared for sensory overload: the main structure shines with lurid glass of all colours and the overcrowded precinct around it is almost buried under scented garlands and incense candles. You might also catch a lacklustre group of traditional dancers performing here to the strains of a small classical orchestra – worshippers hire them to give thanks for a stroke of good fortune. To increase their future chances of such good fortune, visitors buy a bird or two from the flocks incarcerated in cages here; the bird-seller transfers the requested number of captives to a tiny hand-held cage, from which the customer duly liberates the animals, thereby accruing merit. People set on less abstract rewards will invest in a lottery ticket from one of the physically handicapped sellers: they're thought to be the luckiest you can buy.

Ban Kamthieng

Another reconstructed traditional Thai residence, **Ban Kamthieng** (Tues–Sat 9am–5pm; B100) was moved in the 1960s from Chiang Mai to 131 Soi Asoke (Soi 21), off Thanon Sukhumvit, and set up as an ethnological museum by the Siam Society. The delightful complex of polished teak buildings makes a pleasing oasis beneath the towering glass skyscrapers that dominate the rest of Sukhumvit, and is easily reached from the Asoke Skytrain and Sukhumvit subway stops. It differs from Suan Pakkad, Jim Thompson's House and M.R. Kukrit's Heritage Home in being the home of a rural family, and the objects on display give a fair insight into country life for the well-heeled in northern Thailand, though unless you've already visited the north you may find the twenty-first-century metropolitan context unhelpfully anomalous.

The house was built on the banks of the Ping River in the mid-nineteenth century, and the ground-level display of farming tools and fish traps evokes the upcountry practice of fishing in flooded rice paddies to supplement the supply from the rivers. Upstairs, the main display focuses on the ritual life of a typical Lanna household, explaining the role of the spirits, the practice of making offerings, and the belief in talismans, magic shirts and male tattoos. The rectangular lintel above the door is a *hum yon*, carved in floral patterns that represent testicles and designed to ward off evil spirits. Walk along the open veranda to the authentically equipped kitchen to see a video lesson in making spicy frog soup, and to the granary to find an interesting exhibition on the ritual practices associated with rice-farming. Elsewhere in the Siam Society compound you'll find an esoteric bookshop (see p.194) and an antiques outlet.

Northern downtown

The area above Thanon Phetchaburi, which becomes increasingly residential as you move north, is cut through by two major roads lined with monolithic company headquarters: Thanon Phaholyothin, which runs past the Northern Bus Terminal and the weekend market, and Thanon Wiphawadi Rangsit, leading eventually to Don Muang Airport. The start of Thanon Phaholyothin is marked by the stone obelisk of **Victory Monument** (*Anu Sawari Chaisamoraphum*, or just *Anu Sawari*), which can be seen most spectacularly from Skytrains as they snake their way round it. It was erected after the Indo-Chinese War of 1940–41, when Thailand pinched back some territory in Laos and Cambodia while the French government was otherwise occupied in World War II, but nowadays it commemorates all of Thailand's past military glories.

Suan Pakkad Palace Museum

The **Suan Pakkad Palace Museum** (daily 9am–4pm; B100; Ⓦwww.suanpakkad.com), five minutes' walk from Phaya Thai Skytrain station, at 352–4 Thanon Sri Ayutthaya, stands on what was once a cabbage patch but is now one of the finest gardens in Bangkok. Most of this private collection of beautiful Thai objects from all periods is displayed in four groups of traditional wooden houses, which were transported to Bangkok from various parts of the country. You can either take a guided tour in English (free) or explore the loosely arranged collection yourself (a leaflet and bamboo fan are handed out at the ticket office, and some of the exhibits are labelled). The attached **Marsi Gallery**, in the modern Chumbhot-Pantip Center of Arts on the east side of the garden, displays some interesting temporary exhibitions of contemporary art (Ⓣ02 246 1775–6 for details).

The highlight of Suan Pakkad is the renovated **Lacquer Pavilion**, across the reedy pond at the back of the grounds. Set on stilts, the pavilion is actually an amalgam of two eighteenth- or late-seventeenth-century temple buildings, a *ho trai* (library) and a *ho khien* (writing room), one inside the other, which were found between Ayutthaya and Bang Pa-In. The interior walls are beautifully decorated with gilt on black lacquer: the upper panels depict the life of the Buddha while the lower ones show scenes from the *Ramayana*. Look out especially for the grisly details in the tableau on the back wall, showing the earth goddess drowning the evil forces of Mara. Underneath are depicted some European dandies on horseback, probably merchants, whose presence suggests that the work was executed before the fall of Ayutthaya in 1767.

The carefully observed details of daily life and nature are skilful and lively, especially considering the restraints which the **lacquering technique** places on the artist, who has no opportunity for corrections or touching up. The design has to be punched into a piece of paper, which is then laid on the panel of black lacquer (a kind of plant resin); a small bag of chalk dust is pressed on top so that the dust penetrates the minute holes in the paper, leaving a line of dots on the lacquer to mark the pattern; a gummy substance is then applied to any background areas that are to remain black, before the whole surface is covered in microscopically thin squares of gold leaf; thin sheets of blotting paper, sprinkled with water, are then laid over the panel, which when pulled off bring away the gummy substance and the unwanted pieces of gold leaf. This leaves the rest of the gold decoration in high relief against the black background.

Divided between House no. 8 and the Ban Chiang Gallery in the Chumbhot-Pantip Center of Arts is a very good collection of elegant, whorled pottery and bronze jewellery, which the former owner of Suan Pakkad Palace, Princess Chumbhot, excavated from tombs at Ban Chiang, the major Bronze Age settlement in the northeast. Scattered around the rest of the museum are some attractive Thai and Khmer religious sculptures among an eclectic jumble of artefacts, including fine ceramics and some intriguing kiln-wasters, failed pots which have melted together in the kiln to form weird, almost rubbery pieces of sculpture; an extensive collection of colourful papier-mâché *khon* masks; beautiful betel-nut sets (see box on p.523); monks' elegant ceremonial fans; and some rich teak carvings, including a 200-year-old temple door showing episodes from *Sang Thong*, a folk tale about a childless king and queen who discover a handsome son in a conch shell.

Southern downtown

South of Thanon Rama I, commercial development gives way to a dispersed assortment of large institutions, dominated by Thailand's most prestigious centre of higher learning, Chulalongkorn University, and the green expanse of **Lumphini Park**. Thanon Rama IV marks another change of character: downtown proper, centring around the high-rise, American-style boulevard of Thanon Silom, heart of the financial district, extends from here to the river. Alongside the smoked-glass banks and offices, the plush hotels and tourist shops, and opposite Bangkok's Carmelite convent, lies the dark heart of Bangkok nightlife, **Patpong**. Further west along Silom, at the corner of Thanon Pan, lies another incongruous landmark, the Maha Uma Devi Temple (aka Sri Mahamariamman or Wat Khaek), a gaudily coloured, South Indian, Hindu shrine in honour of Uma Devi. Carrying on to the river, the strip west of Charoen Krung (New Road) reveals some of the history of Bangkok's early dealings with foreigners in the fading grandeur of the old trading quarter. Here you'll find the only place in Bangkok where you might be able to eke out an architectural walk, though it's hardly compelling. Incongruous churches and "colonial" buildings (the best of these is the Authors' Wing of the *Oriental Hotel*, where nostalgic afternoon teas are served) are hemmed in by the spice shops and *halal* canteens of the growing Muslim area along Thanon Charoen Krung and the outskirts of Chinatown to the north.

The Queen Saovabha Memorial Institute (Snake Farm)

The **Queen Saovabha Memorial Institute** (*Sathan Saovabha*), often simply known as the **Snake Farm**, at the corner of Thanon Rama IV and Thanon Henri Dunant, is a bit of a circus act, but an entertaining, informative and worthy one at that. Run by the Thai Red Cross, it has a double function: to produce snake-bite serums, and to educate the public on the dangers of Thai snakes. The latter mission involves putting on displays (Mon–Fri 10.30am & 2pm, Sat, Sun & hols 10.30am; B70; ⓣ02 252 0161, ⓦwww.redcross.or.th) that begin with a slick half-hour slide-show illustrating, among other things, how to apply a tourniquet and immobilize a bitten limb. Things warm up with a live, half-hour demonstration of snake-handling and -feeding and venom extraction, which is well presented and safe, and gains a perverse fascination from the knowledge that the strongest venoms of the snakes on show can kill in only three minutes. If you're still not herpetologically sated, a wide range of Thai snakes can be seen live in cages around the grounds, as well as preserved and bottled in a small snake museum.

Lumphini Park

If you're sick of cars and concrete, head for **Lumphini Park** (*Suan Lum*; daily 4.30am–8pm), at the east end of Thanon Silom, where the air is almost fresh and the traffic noise dies down to a low murmur. Named after the town in Nepal where the Buddha was born, the park is arrayed around two lakes, where you can join the locals in feeding the turtles and fish with bread or take out a pedalo or a rowing boat (B40/hr), and is landscaped with a wide variety of local trees and numerous pagodas and pavilions, usually occupied by Chinese-chess players. In the early morning and at dusk, exercise freaks hit the outdoor gym on the southwest side of the park, or en masse do some jogging along the yellow-marked circuit or some balletic t'ai chi, stopping for the twice-daily broadcast of the national anthem. The wide open spaces here are a popular area for gay cruising, and you might be offered dope, though the police patrol regularly – for all that, it's not at all an intimidating place. To recharge your batteries, make for the inexpensive garden restaurant, *Pop*, in the northwest corner, or the pavement foodstalls at the northern edge of the park.

Patpong

Concentrated into a small area between the eastern ends of Thanon Silom and Thanon Suriwong, the neon-lit go-go bars of the **Patpong** district loom like rides in a tawdry sexual Disneyland. In front of each bar, girls cajole passers-by with a lifeless sensuality while insistent touts proffer printed menus detailing the degradations on show. Inside, bikini-clad or topless women gyrate to Western music and play hostess to the (almost exclusively male) spectators; upstairs, live shows feature women who, to use Spalding Gray's phrase in *Swimming to Cambodia*, "do everything with their vaginas except have babies".

Patpong was no more than a sea of mud when the capital was founded on the marshy river bank to the west, but by the 1960s it had grown into a flash district of nightclubs and dance halls for rich Thais, owned by a Chinese millionaire godfather who gave his name to the area. In 1969, an American entrepreneur turned an existing teahouse into a luxurious nightclub to satisfy the tastes of soldiers on R&R trips from Vietnam, and so Patpong's transformation into a Western sex reservation began. At first, the area was rough and violent, but over the years it has wised up to the desires of the affluent farang, and now markets itself as a packaged concept of Oriental decadence. The centre of the skin trade lies along the interconnected sois of **Patpong 1 and 2**, where lines of go-go bars share their patch with respectable restaurants, a 24-hour supermarket and an overabundance of pharmacies. By night, it's a thumping theme park, whose blazing neon promises tend towards self-parody, with names like *Thigh Bar* and *Chicken Divine*. Budget travellers, purposeful safari-suited businessmen and noisy lager louts throng the streets, and even the most demure tourists – of both sexes – turn out to do some shopping at the night market down the middle of Patpong 1, where hawkers sell fake watches, bags and designer T-shirts. By day, a relaxed hangover descends on the place. Bar-girls hang out at foodstalls and cafés in respectable dress, often recognizable by faces that are pinched and strained from the continuous use of antibiotics and heroin in an attempt to ward off venereal disease and boredom. Farang men slump at the bars on Patpong 2, drinking and watching videos, unable to find anything else to do in the whole of Bangkok.

The small dead-end alley to the east of Patpong 2, **Silom 4** (ie Soi 4, Thanon Silom), hosts some of Bangkok's hippest nightlife, its bars, clubs and pavements heaving at weekends with the capital's bright young things. Several gay venues can be found on Silom 4, but the focus of the scene has shifted to **Silom 2**. In between, **Thanon Thaniya**'s hostess bars and restaurants cater to Japanese tourists, while **Silom 6** (Soi Tantawan), to the west of Patpong 1, attracts a curious mix of Korean and hardcore gay visitors.

M.R. Kukrit's Heritage Home

Ten minutes' walk south ofThanon Sathorn, at 19 Soi Phra Pinit (Soi 7,Thanon Narathiwat Ratchanakharin), lies **M.R. Kukrit's Heritage Home** (*Baan Mom Kukrit*; Sat, Sun & public hols 10am–5pm; B50), the beautiful traditional house

Thailand's sex industry

Bangkok owes its reputation as the carnal capital of the world to a highly efficient sex industry adept at peddling fantasies of cheap sex on tap. More than a thousand sex-related businesses operate in the city, but the gaudy neon fleshpots of Patpong give a misleading impression of an activity that is deeply rooted in Thai culture – the overwhelming majority of Thailand's prostitutes of both sexes (estimated at anywhere between 200,000 and 700,000) work with Thai men, not farangs.

Prostitution and polygamy have long been intrinsic to the Thai way of life. Until Rama VI broke with the custom in 1910, Thai kings had always kept a retinue of concubines around them, a select few of whom would be elevated to the status of wife and royal mother, the rest forming a harem of ladies-in-waiting and sexual playthings. The practice was aped by the status-hungry nobility and, from the early nineteenth century, by newly rich merchants keen to have lots of sons and heirs. Though the monarch is now monogamous, many men of all classes still keep mistresses, known as *mia noi* (minor wives), a tradition bolstered by the popular philosophy that an official wife (*mia luang*) should be treated like the temple's main Buddha image – respected and elevated upon the altar – whereas the minor wife is an amulet, to be taken along wherever you go. For those not wealthy enough to take on *mia noi*, prostitution is a far less costly and equally accepted option. Statistics indicate that at least two-fifths of sexually active Thai men are thought to use the services of prostitutes twice a month on average, and it's common practice for a night out with the boys to wind up in a brothel or massage parlour.

The **farang sex industry** is a relatively new development, having had its start during the Vietnam War, when the American military set up seven bases around Thailand. The GIs' appetite for "entertainment" fuelled the creation of instant red-light districts near the bases, attracting women from surrounding rural areas to cash in on the boom; Bangkok joined the fray in 1967, when the US secured the right to ferry soldiers in from Vietnam for R&R breaks. By the mid-1970s, the bases had been evacuated, but the sex infrastructure remained and tourists moved in to fill the vacuum, lured by advertising that diverted most of the traffic to Bangkok and Pattaya. Sex tourism has since grown to become an established part of the Thai economy.

The majority of the women who work in the Patpong bars come from the poorest rural areas of north and northeast Thailand. **Economic refugees** in search of a better life, they're easily drawn into an industry in which they can make in a single night what it takes a month to earn in the rice fields. In some Isaan villages, money sent home by prostitutes in Bangkok far exceeds financial aid given by the government. Women from rural communities have always been expected to contribute an equal share to the family income, and many opt for a couple of lucrative years in the sex bars and brothels as the most effective way of helping to pay off family debts and improve the living conditions of parents stuck in the poverty trap. Reinforcing this social obligation is the pervasive Buddhist notion of karma, which holds that your lot, however unhappy, is the product of past-life misdeeds and can only be improved by making sufficient merit to ensure a better life next time round.

and gardens of one of Thailand's leading figures of the twentieth century. M.R. (*Mom Rajawongse*, a princely title) **Kukrit Pramoj** (1911–95) was a remarkable all-rounder, descended from Rama II on his father's side and, on his mother's side, from the influential ministerial family, the Bunnags. Kukrit graduated in Philosophy, Politics and Economics from Oxford University and went on to become a university lecturer back in Thailand, but his greatest claim to fame is probably as a writer: he founded, owned and penned a daily column for *Siam Rath*, the most influential Thai-language newspaper, and wrote short stories, novels, plays and poetry. He was also a respected performer in classical

While most women enter the racket presumably knowing at least something of what lies ahead, younger girls definitely do not. **Child prostitution** is rife: an estimated ten percent of prostitutes are under 14, some are as young as 9. They are valuable property: in the teahouses of Chinatown, a prepubescent virgin can be rented to her first customer for B6000, as sex with someone so young is believed to have rejuvenating properties. Most child prostitutes have been sold by desperate parents as **bonded slaves** to pimps or agents, and are kept locked up until they have fully repaid the money given to their parents, which may take two or more years.

Despite its ubiquity, prostitution has been **illegal** in Thailand since 1960, but sex-industry bosses easily circumvent the law by registering their establishments as bars, restaurants, barbers, nightclubs or massage parlours, and making payoffs to the police. Sex workers, on the other hand, often endure exploitation and violence from employers, pimps and customers rather than face fines and long rehabilitation sentences in prison-like reform centres. Life is made even more difficult by the fact that abortion is illegal in Thailand. In an attempt to redress some of the iniquities, and protect the youngest prostitutes at least, an amendment to the **anti-prostitution law**, passed in April 1996, attempts to treat sex workers as victims rather than criminals. Besides penalizing parents who sell their children to the flesh trade, the amended law is supposed to punish owners, managers and customers of any place of prostitution with a jail sentence or a heavy fine, but this has been met with some cynicism, owing to the number of influential police and politicians allegedly involved in the sex industry. Under this amendment anyone caught having sex with an under-15 is charged with rape, though this has apparently resulted in an increase in trafficking of young children from neighbouring countries as they are less likely to seek help. In 2003, the Taksin government instigated a public debate on the potential **legalisation of prostitution**, a move which would register all sex workers and make prostitution a legitimate taxable source of income, theoretically curtailing much of the associated extortion and violence. It is a phenomenally lucrative industry, thought to be worth some US$4.3 billion, and critics of the proposal see the government's motive as financial rather than as a way of protecting the sex workers. In addition, sex workers are concerned that once registered they will be stigmatized for the rest of their lives, regardless of how brief a period they may have spent working as prostitutes.

In recent years, the spectre of **AIDS** has put the problems of the sex industry into sharp focus: UN AIDS statistics from 2001 reported that about one in sixty Thais was infected with HIV/AIDS; in the same year there were 55,000 AIDS-related deaths in the country, a disproportionate number of them in the northern provinces. Since 1988, the government has conducted an aggressive, World Health Organization-approved AIDS awareness campaign, a vital component of which has been to send health officials into brothels to administer blood tests and give out condoms. The programme seems to have had some effect, and the number of new HIV infections has declined sharply from 143,000 in 1991 to 29,000 in 2001.

dance-drama (*khon*), and he starred as an Asian prime minister, opposite Marlon Brando, in the Hollywood film, *The Ugly American*. In 1974, during an especially turbulent period for Thailand, life imitated art, when Kukrit was called on to become Thailand's PM at the head of a coalition of seventeen parties. However, just four hundred days into his premiership, the Thai military leadership dismissed him for being too anti-American.

The **residence**, which has been left just as it was when Kukrit was alive, reflects his complex character. In the large, open-sided *sala* (pavilion) for public functions near the entrance is an attractive display of *khon* masks, including a gold one which Kukrit wore when he played the demon king, Totsagan (Ravana). In and around the adjoining Khmer-styled garden, keep your eyes peeled for the the *mai dut*, sculpted miniature trees similar to bonsai, some of which Kukrit worked on for decades. The living quarters beyond are made up of five teak houses on stilts, assembled from various parts of central Thailand and joined by an open veranda. The bedroom, study and various sitting rooms are decked out with beautiful *objets d'art*; look out especially for the carved bed that belonged to Rama II and the very delicate, 200-year-old nielloware (gold inlay) from Nakhon Si Thammarat in the formal reception room. In the small family prayer room, Kukrit Pramoj's ashes are enshrined in the base of a reproduction of the Emerald Buddha.

Chatuchak and the outskirts

The amorphous clutter of Greater Bangkok doesn't harbour many attractions, but there are a handful of places – principally **Chatuchak Weekend Market**, the cultural theme park of **Muang Boran**, the rather more esoteric **Prasart Museum**, the upstream town of **Nonthaburi** and the tranquil artificial island of **Ko Kred** – which make pleasant half-day escapes. Theoretically, you could also see any one of these sights en route to destinations north, east or west, though lumping luggage around makes negotiating city transport even more trying.

Chatuchak Weekend Market (JJ)

With eight thousand open-air stalls to peruse, and wares as diverse as Lao silk, Siamese kittens and designer lamps to choose from, the enormous **Chatuchak Weekend Market**, or **JJ** as it's usually known (Sat & Sun 7am–6pm), is Bangkok's most enjoyable shopping experience. It occupies a huge patch of ground between the Northern Bus Terminal and Mo Chit Skytrain (N8) and subway stations, and is best reached by Skytrain or subway if you're coming from downtown areas, though some people prefer to get off at Saphan Kwai (N7) and then walk through the amulet stalls that line the road up to the southern (handicraft) part of the market. Coming from Banglamphu, you can either get a bus to the nearest Skytrain stop (probably Ratchathewi or Phya Thai) and then take the train, or take the #503/#3 or #509/#9 bus all the way from Rajdamnoen Klang (1hr); see p.110 for details.

Though its primary customers are Bangkok residents in search of inexpensive clothes and home accessories, Chatuchak also has plenty of collector- and tourist-oriented **stalls**. Best buys include antique lacquerware, unusual sarongs, cotton clothing and crafts from the north, jeans, traditional musical instruments, silver jewellery and ceramics, particularly the five-coloured *bencharong*. The market is divided into 26 numbered **sections**, plus a dozen unnumbered ones, each of which is more or less dedicated to a certain range of goods, for example household items, plants, second-hand books or crafts. If you have several hours to spare, it's fun just to browse at whim, but if you're looking for souvenirs, handicrafts or traditional textiles you should start with sections 22, 24, 25 and 26, which are all in a cluster at the southwest (Saphan Kwai) end of the market; the "Dream" section (27) behind the TAT office is also full of interesting artefacts. *Nancy Chandler's Map of Bangkok* has a fabulously detailed and informatively annotated **map** of all the sections in the market, but should be bought before you arrive. Alternatively, drop in at the TAT office, located in the Chatuchak market building on the southwest edge of the market, across the car park, as they dish out smaller but useful free plans of the market.

The market also contains a large, and controversial, **wildlife** section and has long been a popular clearing-house for protected and endangered species such as gibbons, palm cockatoos and Indian pied hornbills, many of them smuggled in from Laos and Cambodia and sold to private animal collectors and foreign zoos, particularly in eastern Europe. The illegal trade goes on beneath the counter, and may be in decline following a spate of crackdowns, but you're bound to come across fighting cocks around the back (demonstrations are almost continuous), miniature flying squirrels being fed milk through pipettes, and iridescent red and blue Siamese fighting fish, kept in individual jars and shielded from each other's aggressive stares by sheets of cardboard.

There's no shortage of **foodstalls** inside the market compound, particularly at the southern end, where you'll find plenty of places serving inexpensive *phat thai* and Isaan snacks. Close by these stalls is a classy little juice bar called *Viva* where you can rest your feet while listening to the manager's jazz tapes. The biggest restaurant here is *Toh Plue*, behind TAT on the edge of the Dream section, which makes a good rendezvous point. For vegetarian sustenance, head for *Chamlong's* (also known as *Asoke*), an open-air, cafeteria-style restaurant just outside the market on Thanon Kamphaeng Phet (across Thanon Kamphaeng Phet 2), set up by Bangkok's former governor as a service to the citizenry (Sat & Sun 8am–noon). You can **change money** (Sat & Sun 7am–7pm) in the market building at the south end of the market, across the car park from the stalls area, and there's an ATM here too.

The Prasart Museum

Located right out on the eastern edge of the city (and still surrounded by fields), the **Prasart Museum** at 9 Soi 4A, Soi Krungthep Kreetha, Thanon Krungthep Kreetha (Tues–Sun 10am–3pm; B1000 for one or two people; call ⓣ02 379 3601 to book the compulsory tour) is an unusual open-air exhibition of traditional Asian buildings, collected and reassembled by wealthy entrepreneur and art-lover Khun Prasart. The museum is rarely visited by independent tourists – partly because of the intentionally limited opening hours and inflated admission price, and partly because it takes at least an hour and a half to get here by bus from Banglamphu or Silom – but it makes a pleasant day out and is worth the effort.

Set in a gorgeously lush tropical garden, the museum comprises about a dozen replicas of **traditional buildings**, including a golden teak palace inspired by the royal residence now housed at the National Museum, a Chinese temple and water garden, a Khmer shrine, a Sukhothai-era teak library set over a lotus pond, and a European-style mansion, fashionable with Bangkok royalty in the late nineteenth century. Some of these structures have been assembled from the ruins of buildings found all over Asia, but there's no attempt at purist authenticity – the aim is to give a flavour of architectural styles, not an exact reproduction. Many of the other buildings, including the Thai wat and the Chinese temple, were constructed from

Durians

The naturalist Alfred Russel Wallace, eulogizing the taste of the **durian**, compared it to "rich butter-like custard highly flavoured with almonds, but intermingled with wafts of flavour that call to mind cream cheese, onion sauce, brown sherry and other incongruities". He neglected to discuss the smell of the fruit's skin, which is so bad – somewhere between detergent and dogshit – that durians are barred from Thai hotels and aeroplanes. The different **varieties** bear strange names which do nothing to make them more appetizing: "frog", "golden pillow", "gibbon" and so on. However, the durian has fervent admirers, perhaps because it's such an acquired taste, and because it's considered a strong aphrodisiac. Aficionadoes discuss the varieties with as much subtlety as if they were vintage champagnes, and they treat the durian as a social fruit, to be shared around, despite a price tag of up to B3000 each.

Durian season is roughly April to June and the most famous durian orchards are around Nonthaburi, where the fruits are said to have an incomparably rich and nutty flavour due to the fine clay soil. If you don't smell them first, you can recognize durians by their sci-fi appearance: the shape and size of a rugby ball, but slightly deflated, they're covered in a thick, pale-green shell which is heavily armoured with short, sharp spikes (*duri* means "thorn" in Malay). By cutting along one of the faint seams with a good knife, you'll reveal a white pith in which are set a handful of yellow blobs with the texture of a wrinkled soufflé: this is what you eat. The taste is best when the smell is at its highest, about three days after the fruit has dropped. Be careful when out walking near the trees: because of its great weight and sharp spikes, a falling durian can lead to serious injury, or even an ignominious death.

scratch, using designs dreamt up by Khun Prasart and his team. Whatever their ancestry, all the buildings are beautifully crafted, with great attention paid to carvings and decorations, and many are filled with antique **artefacts**, including Burmese woodcarvings, prehistoric pottery from Ban Chiang and Lopburi-era statuettes. There are also some unusual pieces of royal memorabilia and an exquisite collection of *bencharong* ceramics. Khun Prasart also owns a ceramics workshop, which produces reproductions of famous designs; they can be bought either at the museum, or at his showroom, the Prasart Collection, on the second floor of the Peninsula Plaza shopping centre on Thanon Rajdamri.

The easiest way to get there is by regular **bus** #93, which you can pick up either on Thanon Si Phraya near River City and the GPO, or anywhere along its route on Phetchaburi and Phetchaburi Mai roads. The #93 terminates on Thanon Krungthep Kreetha, but you should get off a couple of stops before the terminus, at the first stop on Thanon Krungthep Kreetha, as soon as you see the sign for the Prasart Museum (about 1hr 15min by bus from Si Phraya). Follow the sign down Soi Krungthep Kreetha, go past the golf course and, after about a fifteen-minute walk, turn off down Soi 4A.

Nonthaburi

A trip to **NONTHABURI**, the first town beyond the northern boundary of Bangkok, is the easiest excursion you can make from the centre of the city and affords a perfect opportunity to recharge your batteries. Nonthaburi is the last stop upriver for express boats, around one hour fifteen minutes from Central Pier (Sathorn) Sathorn Bridge, under an hour if you catch a "special express".

The ride itself is most of the fun, weaving round huge, crawling sand barges and tiny canoes, and the slow pace of the boat gives you plenty of time to take in the sights on the way. On the north side of Banglamphu, beyond the elegant, new Rama VIII Bridge, you'll pass the royal boat house in front of the National Library on the east bank, where you can glimpse the minor ceremonial boats that escort the grand royal barges. Further out are dazzling Buddhist temples and drably painted mosques, catering for Bangkok's growing Muslim population, as well as a few remaining communities who still live in houses on stilts or houseboats – around Krungthon Bridge, for example, you'll see people living on the huge teak vessels used to carry rice, sand and charcoal.

Disembarking at suburban Nonthaburi, on the east bank of the river, you won't find a great deal to do, in truth. There's a market that's famous for the quality of its fruit, while the attractive, old Provincial Office across the road is covered in rickety wooden latticework. To break up your trip with a slow, scenic drink or lunch, you'll find a floating seafood restaurant, *Rim Fang*, to the right at the end of the prom which, though a bit overpriced, is quiet and breezy.

Set in relaxing grounds about 1km north of Nonthaburi pier on the west bank of the river, elegant **Wat Chalerm Phra Kiat** injects a splash of urban refinement among a grove of breadfruit trees. You can get there from the express-boat pier by taking the ferry straight across the Chao Phraya and then catching a motorbike taxi. The beautifully proportioned temple, which has been lavishly restored, was built by Rama III in memory of his mother, whose family lived in the area. Entering the walls of the temple compound, you feel as if you're coming upon a stately folly in a secret garden, and a strong Chinese influence shows itself in the unusual ribbed roofs and elegantly curved gables, decorated with pastel ceramics. The restorers have done their best work inside: look out especially for the simple, delicate landscapes on the shutters.

Ko Kred

About 7km north of Nonthaburi, the tiny island of **KO KRED** lies in a particularly sharp bend in the Chao Phraya, cut off from the east bank by a waterway created to make the cargo route from Ayutthaya to the Gulf of Thailand just that little bit faster. Although it's slowly being discovered by day-trippers from Bangkok, this artificial island remains something of a time capsule, a little oasis of village life completely at odds with the metropolitan chaos downriver. Roughly ten square kilometres in all, Ko Kred has no roads, just a concrete path that follows its circumference, with a few arterial walkways branching off towards the interior. Villagers, the majority of whom are Mon (see p.246 for more on the Mon people), use a small fleet of motorbike taxis to cross their island, but as a sightseer you're much better off on foot: a round-island walk takes less than an hour and a half.

There are few sights as such on Ko Kred, but its lushness and comparative emptiness make it a perfect place in which to wander. You'll no doubt come across one of the island's potteries and kilns, which churn out the regionally famous earthenware flower-pots and small water-storage jars and employ a large percentage of the village workforce; several shops dotted around the island sell Ko Kred terracotta, including what's styled as the Ancient Mon Pottery Centre near the island's northeast corner, which also displays delicate and venerable museum pieces and Mon-style Buddha shrines. The island's clay is very rich in nutrients and therefore excellent for fruit-growing, and banana trees, coconut palms, pomelo, papaya and durian trees all grow in abundance on Ko Kred, fed by an intricate network of irrigation channels that crisscrosses the interior. In among the orchards, the Mons have built their wooden houses, mostly in traditional style and raised high above the marshy ground on stilts. A handful of attractive riverside wats complete the picture, most notably **Wat Paramaiyikawat** (aka Wat Poramai), at the main pier at the northeast tip of the island. This engagingly ramshackle eighteenth-century temple was restored by Rama V in honour of his grandmother, with a Buddha relic placed in its Mon-style chedi. Among an open-air scattering of Burmese-style alabaster Buddha images, the tall bot shelters some fascinating nineteenth-century murals, depicting scenes from temple life at ground level and the life of the Buddha above, all set in delicate imaginary landscapes.

Practicalities

The best day to go to Ko Kred is **Sunday**, when the Chao Phraya Express Boat Company (Ⓣ02 623 6001–3) and Mitchaopaya Travel Service (Ⓣ02 623 5340) both run **tours** there from central Bangkok (B250). They head upriver from Ratanakosin at 9am (Chao Phraya Express Boat Company from Tha Maharat, Mitchaopaya from Tha Chang), taking in Wat Poramai and the Ancient Mon Pottery Centre, before circling the island via Ban Khanom Thai, where you can buy traditional sweets and watch them being made, and dropping in at Wat Chalerm Phra Kiat in Nonthaburi (see p.169) on the way back. Chao Phraya Express Boat Company arrives back at Tha Maharat at about 3pm, while Mitchaopaya also takes in the Royal Barge Museum (see p.150), returning to Tha Chang at around 4.30pm.

At other times, the main drawback of a day-trip to Ko Kred is the difficulty of **getting there**. Your best option is to take a Chao Phraya express boat to Nonthaburi, then bus #32 to Pakkred pier – or, if you're feeling flush, a chartered longtail boat direct to Ko Kred (about B200–300). From Pakkred, the easiest way of getting across to the island is to hire a longtail boat, although shuttle boats cross at the river's narrowest point to Wat Poramai from Wat Sanam Nua, about a kilometre's walk or a short samlor or motorbike-taxi ride south of the Pakkred pier.

Muang Boran Ancient City

A day-trip out to the **Muang Boran Ancient City** open-air museum (daily 8am–5pm; B100, children B50), 33km southeast of Bangkok, is a great way to enjoy the best of Thailand's architectural heritage in relative peace and without much effort. Occupying a huge park shaped like Thailand itself, the museum comprises more than 115 traditional Thai buildings scattered around pleasantly landscaped grounds and is best toured by rented **bicycle** (B50; B150/tandem; B200/three-seater), though you can also make use of the circulating **tram** (B150 round trip, kids B75), and doing it on foot is just about possible. Many of the buildings are copies of the country's most famous monuments, and are located in the appropriate "region" of the park, with everything from Bangkok's Grand Palace (central region) to the spectacularly sited hilltop Khmer Khao Phra Viharn sanctuary (northeast) represented here. There are also some original structures, including a rare scripture repository (library) rescued from Samut Songkhram (south), as well as some painstaking reconstructions from contemporary documents of long-vanished gems, of which the Ayutthaya-period Sanphet Prasat palace (central) is a particularly fine example. A sizeable team of restorers and skilled craftspeople maintains the buildings and helps keep some of the traditional techniques alive; if you come here during the week you can watch them at work.

To get to Muang Boran from Bangkok, take air-conditioned **bus** #511/#11 from Banglamphu/Thanon Rama I/Thanon Sukhumvit to **Samut Prakan** on the edge of built-up Greater Bangkok, then change onto songthaew #36, which passes the entrance to Muang Boran. If you're starting from Banglamphu it's often faster to do the journey in stages, taking the Chao Phraya ferry down to Tha Sathorn, changing on to the Skytrain as far as Ekamai and then picking up the #511/#11 from there; from Rama 1 you could take the Skytrain as far as Ekamai and then change onto the #511/#11.

A couple of kilometres east of Samut Prakan, the **Crocodile Farm** (daily 7am–6pm; B300, kids B200) figures on tour-group itineraries, but is a depressing place. The thirty thousand reptiles kept here are made to "perform" for their trainers in hourly shows (daily 9, 10 & 11am & 1, 2, 3 & 4pm) and are subsequently turned into handbags, shoes, briefcases and wallets, a selection of which are sold on site. Songthaews run from Samut Prakan. There's also a dinosaur museum at the farm (B60).

Food, entertainment, shopping and moving on

As you'd expect, nowhere in Thailand can compete with Bangkok's diversity when it comes to eating and entertainment, and, although prices are generally higher here than in the provinces, it's still easy to have a good time while on a budget. Bangkok boasts an astonishing fifty thousand **places to eat** – that's almost one for every hundred citizens – ranging from grubby streetside noodle shops to the most elegant of restaurants. Below we run through the best of the city's indigenous eateries, with a few representatives of the capital's numerous ethnic minorities.

Bangkok nightlife has at last outgrown its reputation for catering only to single men and now centres around dozens of fashionable **bars** and sophisticated **clubs**, where hip design and trend-setting DJs draw in capacity crowds of stylish young Thais and partying travellers. Getting back to your lodgings is no problem in the small hours: many bus routes run a (reduced) service throughout the night, and tuk-tuks and taxis are always at hand – though it's probably best for unaccompanied women to avoid using tuk-tuks late at night.

Introductions to more traditional elements of Thai culture are offered by the raucous ambience of the city's **boxing arenas**, its **music and dancing** troupes and its profusion of **shops**, stalls and markets – all of them covered here. This section concludes with an overview of the options for **moving on** from the city – not only to elsewhere in Thailand, but to other countries too, as Bangkok is one of Asia's bargain counters when it comes to buying flights.

Eating

Thai restaurants of all types are found all over the city. The best **gourmet Thai** restaurants operate from the downtown districts around Thanon Sukhumvit and Thanon Silom, proffering wonderful royal, traditional and regional cuisines that definitely merit an occasional splurge. Over in Banglamphu, Thanon Phra Athit has become famous for its dozen or so trendy little restaurant-bars, each with distinctive decor and a contemporary Thai menu that's angled at young Thai diners. At the other end of the scale there are the **night markets** and **street stalls**, so numerous in Bangkok that we can only flag the most promising areas – but wherever you're staying, you'll hardly have to walk a block in any direction before encountering something appealing.

For the non-Thai cuisines, Chinatown naturally rates as the most authentic district for pure **Chinese** food; likewise neighbouring Pahurat, the capital's Indian enclave, is best for unadulterated **Indian** dishes; and good, comparatively cheap **Japanese** restaurants are concentrated on Soi Thaniya, at the east end of Thanon Silom. The place to head for Western, **travellers' food** – from herbal teas and hamburgers to muesli – as well as a hearty range of veggie options, is Thanon Khao San, packed with small, inexpensive tourist restaurants; standards vary, but there are some definite gems among the blander establishments.

Fast food comes in two forms: the mainly Thai version, which stews canteen-style in large tin trays on the upper floor **food courts** of department stores all over the city, and the old Western favourites like *McDonald's* and *Kentucky Fried Chicken* that mainly congregate around Thanon Sukhumvit and Siam Square – an area that also has its share of decent Thai and foreign restaurants. In addition, downtown Bangkok has a good quota of **coffee shops**,

A night on the river

The **Chao Phraya River** looks fabulous at night, when most of the noisy longtails have stopped terrorizing the ferries, and the riverside temples and other grand monuments – including the Grand Palace and Wat Arun – are elegantly illuminated. Joining one of the nightly dinner cruises along the river is a great way to appreciate it all. Call ahead to reserve a table and check departure details – some places offer free transport from hotels, and some cruises may not run during the rainy season (May to October).

Loy Nava ⓣ02 235 3108. Departs Si Phraya pier at 6pm (returning 8pm) and 8pm (returning 10pm). Six-course Thai or seafood meal. B1100.

Maeyanang Run by the *Oriental Hotel* ⓣ02 236 0400. Departs *Oriental* at 7.30pm, returning at 10pm. Thai and international buffet. B1600.

Manohra Run by the *Marriott Royal Garden Riverside Hotel*, south of Taksin Bridge in Thonburi ⓣ02 883 1588, ⓦwww.manohracruises.com. Departs Krungthon Bridge pier at 7.15pm, returning 9pm, with pick-ups at Tha Sathorn and Tha Oriental possible. Thai buffet B1200, or B120 for the boat trip plus the cost of your food.

Pearl of Siam ⓣ02 292 1649. Departs River City at 7.30pm, returning at 9.30pm. Thai and international buffet. B1100.

Shangri-La Horizon ⓣ02 236 7777. Departs *Shangri-La Hotel* pier, north of Taksin Bridge, at 7.30pm, returning at 9.30pm. International buffet. B1400.

Wan Fah ⓣ02 237 0077, ⓦwww.wanfah.com. Departs Si Phraya pier or River City at 7pm, returning at 9pm. Thai or seafood set menu. B850.

including several branches of Black Canyon and Starbucks, the latter expensive but usually graced with armchairs and free newspapers.

The restaurants listed below are graded by three general price categories, based on the cost of a main dish: "Inexpensive" (under B60), "Moderate" (B60–130) and "Expensive" (over B130). In the more expensive places you may have to pay a ten percent service charge and seven percent government tax. Telephone numbers are given for the more popular or out-of-the-way establishments, where booking may be advisable. Most restaurants in Bangkok are open every day for lunch and dinner; we've noted exceptions in the listings below.

Banglamphu and the Democracy Monument area

Banglamphu is a great area for eating. **Khao San** is stacked full of guest-house restaurants serving the whole range of cheap and cheerful travellers' fare; there are also some good Thai places here, as well as veggie, Indian, Israeli and Italian joints. For a complete contrast you need only walk a few hundred metres down to riverside **Thanon Phra Athit**, where the pavement positively heaves with arty little café-restaurants; these are patronized mainly by students from Thammasat University up the road, but most offer English-language menus to any interested tourists. The food in these places is generally modern Thai, nearly always very good and reasonably priced. There are also some recommended trendy Thai places on the Banglamphu **fringes**, plus a few traditional options too. Small knots of hot-food stalls serving very cheap **night-market** fare set up nightly from around 5.30pm in front of 7–11 at the Thanon Tani/Soi Ram Bhuttri intersection; at the Soi Ram Bhuttri/Thanon Chakrabongse intersection; and in the forecourt of the Shell petrol station on Thanon Chakrabongse. For restaurant locations see the map on p.108–109.

Around Khao San

Baan Mayom 15 Trok Mayom. Notable for its huge menu of spicy Thai salads (*yam*) – two dozen at the last count – as well as curries, soups and a recommended version of the ever-popular chicken wrapped in pandanus leaves. Diners sit in the tiny garden courtyard as a DJ spins tunes in the background. Daily 6pm–2am, closed second and third Suns. Moderate.

Himalayan Kitchen 1 Thanon Khao San. Currently serving Banglamphu's best South Asian food, this first-floor restaurant – which gives good bird's-eye views of Khao San action – is decorated with Nepalese *thanka* paintings and dishes out decent Nepalese veg and non-veg thalis. Moderate.

May Kaidee 123–125 Thanon Tanao, though actually on the parallel soi to the west; easiest access is to take first left on Soi Damnoen Klang Neua. Simple, soi-side foodstall plus tables serving the best vegetarian food in Banglamphu. Try the tasty green curry with coconut, the curry-fried tofu with vegetables or the sticky black-rice pudding. May Kaidee herself also runs veggie cookery classes, detailed on p.203. Shuts about 9pm. Inexpensive.

Prakorb House Thanon Khao San. Archetypal travellers' haven, with only a few tables, and an emphasis on wholesome ingredients. Herbal teas, mango shakes, delicious pumpkin curry, and lots more besides. Inexpensive.

Sarah Off Thanon Chakrabongse, between the Shell petrol station and the police station. Israeli restaurant, serving hearty platefuls of falafels, hummus, salads and dips. Inexpensive.

Tom Yam Kung Thanon Khao San. Delicious, occasionally mouth-blastingly authentic Thai food served in a beautiful early-twentieth-century villa that's hidden behind Khao San's modern clutter. The menu includes spicy fried catfish, coconut-palm curry with tofu and shrimps in sugar cane. You can savour it inside the villa's elegant dining rooms or outside under the latticework colonnade. Well-priced cocktails, draught beer and a small wine list. Open 24hr. Moderate to expensive.

Whale Herbs and Spice Café Thanon Rajdamnoen Klang. Though it looks and feels like a fast-food joint, this place serves genuinely healthy set meals, many of them vegetarian, such as brown-rice soup and tofu steak. Also brews several blends of fresh coffee, and sells snacks and bakery items. Moderate.

Phra Athit area

Hemlock 56 Thanon Phra Athit, next door but one from *Pra Arthit Mansion*; the sign is visible from the road but not from the pavement ⓣ02 282 7507. Small, stylish, highly recommended air-con restaurant that's very popular with students and young Thai couples. Offers a long and interesting menu of unusual Thai dishes, including banana-flower salad (*yam hua plii*), coconut and mushroom curry, grand lotus rice and various *larb* and fish dishes. The traditional *miang* starters (shiny green wild tea leaves filled with chopped vegetables, fish and meat) are also very tasty, and there's a good vegetarian selection. Mon–Sat 5pm–midnight; worth reserving a table on Friday and Saturday nights. Moderate.

Joy Luck Club 8 Thanon Phra Sumen. Despite its name, the only things noticeably Chinese about this cute little art-house café-restaurant are the red lanterns hanging outside. Inside are just half a dozen tables – each designed with a glassed-in display of artefacts – modern art on the walls and occasional live music at night. The Thai food is delicious, and there's a big veggie menu too, including various green and *matsaman* curries, plus lots of cocktails. Inexpensive to moderate.

Krua Nopparat 130–132 Thanon Phra Athit. The decor in this unassuming air-con restaurant is noticeably plain compared to all the arty joints on this road, but the Thai food is good, especially the eggplant wing-bean salad and the battered crab. Inexpensive.

Ricky's Coffee Shop 22 Thanon Phra Athit. With its atmospherically dark woodwork, red lanterns and marble-top tables, this contemporary take on a traditional Chinese coffee house is an enjoyable spot to idle over fresh coffee (choose from six blends) and feast on the deli-style offerings – pastrami, imported cheeses – served over baguettes and croissants, not to mention the all-day breakfasts. Mon–Sat 8am–8pm. Moderate.

Roti Mataba 136 Thanon Phra Athit. Famous outlet for the ever-popular fried Indian breads, or rotis, served here in lots of sweet and savoury varieties, including with vegetable and meat curries, and with bananas and condensed milk. Closed Sun. Inexpensive.

Tonpo Thanon Phra Athit, next to Tha Banglamphu express-boat pier. Sizeable seafood menu and a relatively scenic riverside location; good place for a beer and a snack at the end of a long day's sightseeing. Moderate.

Thanon Samsen, Thewes and the fringes

Bangkok Bar 591 Thanon Phra Sumen. Housed in an elegant 150-year-old canalside house, complete with high ceilings, wooden floors and fine fretwork, this place is well worth trying both for its setting and for its good-value upmarket Thai cuisine. There's a gallery upstairs to entertain you while you're waiting for food. Recommendations include seafood with young coconut, fish-head curry and deep-fried pillows of tofu. Daily 6pm–2am. Moderate.

Isaan restaurants Behind the Rajdamnoen Boxing Stadium on Thanon Rajdamnoen Nok. At least five restaurants in a cluster serving northeastern fare to hungry boxing fans: take your pick for hearty plates of *kai yang* and *khao niaw*. Inexpensive.

Kaloang Beside the river at the far western end of Thanon Sri Ayutthaya. Flamboyant service and excellent seafood attracts an almost exclusively Thai clientele to this open-air riverside restaurant.

Yellow-flag heaven for veggies

Every autumn, for nine days during the ninth lunar month (October or November), Thailand's Chinese community goes on a **meat-free** diet in order to mark the onset of the Vegetarian Festival (Ngan Kin Jeh), a sort of Taoist version of Lent. Though the Chinese citizens of Bangkok don't go in for skewering themselves like their compatriots in Trang and Phuket (see p.675), they do celebrate the Vegetarian Festival with gusto: nearly every restaurant and foodstall in Chinatown turns vegetarian for the period, flying small yellow flags to show that they are upholding the tradition. For vegetarian tourists this is a great time to be in town – just look for the yellow flag and you can be sure all dishes will be one hundred percent vegan. Soya substitutes are a popular feature on the vegetarian Chinese menu, so don't be surprised to find pink prawn-shaped objects floating in your noodle soup or unappetizingly realistic slices of fake duck. Many hotel restaurants also get in on the act during the Vegetarian Festival, running special veggie promotions for a week or two.

Dishes well worth shelling out for include the fried rolled shrimps served with a sweet dip, the roast squid cooked in a piquant sauce and the steamed butter fish. Expensive.

Na Pralan Café Almost opposite the Gate of Glorious Victory, Thanon Na Phra Lan. Technically in Ratanakosin (it's marked on the map on p.123) but very close to Banglamphu, this small café, only a couple of doors up the street from the Silpakorn University Art College, is ideally placed for refreshment after your tour of the Grand Palace. Popular with students, it occupies a quaint old air-con shophouse with battered, artsy decor. The menu, well thought out with some unusual twists, offers tasty daily specials – mostly one-dish meals with rice – and a range of Thai desserts, coffees, teas and beers. Mon–Sat 10am–10pm. Inexpensive.

Pornsawan Vegetarian Restaurant 80 Thanon Samsen, between sois 4 and 6. Perfectly decent Thai veggie café that uses soya products instead of meat in its curries and stir-fries. Daily 7am–6.30pm. Inexpensive.

Silver Spoon Beside the Tha Thewes express-boat pier at 2/1 Thanon Krung Kasem. Popular place for seafood – and riverine breezes, with decent Chao Phraya views and a huge menu including baked cottonfish in mango sauce, steamed snakehead fish with chillies, and *tom yam kung*. Moderate.

Chinatown and Pahurat

The places listed below are marked on the map on p.143.

Chong Tee 84 Soi Sukon 1, Thanon Trimit, between Hualamphong Station and Wat Traimit. Delicious and moreishly cheap pork satay and sweet toast.

Maturot Soi Phadungdao (aka Soi Texas), Thanon Yaowarat. In a soi famous for its seafood stalls, the fresh, meaty prawns served up here, accompanied by *phak bung fai daeng* (fried morning glory) and *tom yam kung*, stand out. Evenings only, until late. Inexpensive to moderate.

Royal India Just off Thanon Chakraphet at 392/1. Famously good curries served in the heart of Bangkok's most Indian of neighbourhoods to an almost exclusively South Asian clientele. Moderate.

Shangri-La 306 Thanon Yaowarat (cnr of Thanon Rajawong). Cavernous place serving Chinese classics, including lots of seafood, and lunchtime *dim sum*. Very popular, especially for family outings. Moderate.

White Orchid Hotel 409–421 Thanon Yaowarat. Recommended for its *dim sum*, with bamboo baskets of prawn dumplings, spicy spare ribs, stuffed beancurd and the like, served in three different portion sizes. *Dim sum* 11am–2pm & 5–10pm. All-you-can-eat lunchtime buffets also worth stopping by for. Moderate to expensive.

Downtown: around Siam Square and Thanon Ploenchit

The map on p.157 shows the places listed below.

Aao 45/4–8 Soi Lang Suan, Thanon Ploenchit ⓣ02 254 5699. Bright, almost unnerving retro-Sixties decor is the setting for friendly service and very tasty Thai dishes – notably wing-bean salad and *kaeng phanaeng kai* – most of which are available spiced to order and/or in vegetarian versions. Moderate.

Bali 15/3 Soi Ruam Rudee ⓣ02 250 0711. Top-notch Indonesian food in a cosy nook. Blow out on seven-course *rijstaffel* for B250. Closed Sun. Moderate.

Food Loft Floor 7, Central Chidlom, Thanon Ploenchit. Bangkok's top department store lays on a suitably upmarket food court of all hues – Thai, Vietnamese, Chinese, Japanese, Indian, Italian. Choose your own ingredients and watch them cooked in front of you, eat in the stylish, minimalist seating areas and then ponder whether you have room for a Thai or Western dessert. Moderate.

Gianni 34/1 Soi Tonson, Thanon Ploenchit ⓣ02 252 1619. One of Bangkok's best independent Italian restaurants, successfully blending traditional and modern in both its decor and food. Offerings include a belt- (and bank-) busting tasting menu, innovative pastas, and home-made cantuccini with vinsanto. Expensive.

Inter 432/1–2 Soi 9, Siam Square. Honest, efficient Thai restaurant that's popular with students and shoppers, serving good one-dish meals and more expensive curries in a no-frills, fluorescent-lit canteen atmosphere. Inexpensive.

Kirin Express & Restaurant 226/1 Soi 2, Siam Square ☎02 251 2326–9. Long-standing and highly regarded Chinese restaurant with swanky, modern dining rooms on the first and second floors (moderate–expensive), plus cheap fast food, including stir-fries and all-day *dim sum*, on the ground floor.

Le Lys 75/2 Soi Lang Suan 3 ☎02 652 2401. In a cosy, characterful house off Soi Lang Suan with a petanque court out the back, the French-Thai owners rustle up excellent, authentic Thai food – try the squid in tamarind sauce. Moderate.

Ma Be Ba 93 Soi Lang Suan ☎02 254 9595. Lively, spacious and extravagantly decorated Italian restaurant dishing up a good variety of antipasti, excellent pizzas (in two sizes) and pastas, and traditional main courses strong on seafood. Live music nightly, mostly pop covers, plus jazz early evenings at the weekend. Expensive.

Mah Boon Krong Food Centre Floor 6, MBK shopping centre, corner of Thanon Rama I and Thanon Phrayathai. Increase your knowledge of Thai food here: ingredients, names and pictures of dishes (including plenty of vegetarian ones, and a wide range of desserts) from all over the country are displayed at the various stalls. Inexpensive.

Sarah Jane's Ground Floor, Sindhorn Tower 1, 130–132 Thanon Witthayu ☎02 650 9992–3. Long-standing restaurant, popular with Bangkok's Isaan population, serving excellent, simple north-eastern food. It's in slick but unfussy modern premises that can be slightly tricky to find at night, towards the rear of a modern office block. Moderate.

Sorn's 36/8 Soi Kasemsan 1, Thanon Rama I. In this quiet lane of superior guest houses, a laid-back hangout strewn with plants and vines. Delicious versions of standard Thai dishes – the *tom kha kai* is especially good – as well as Western meals, a huge breakfast menu including reasonably priced set meals, good teas and coffees and a full-service bar. Moderate.

Thang Long 82/5 Soi Lang Suan ☎02 251 3504. Excellent Vietnamese food in this stylish, minimalist and popular restaurant, all stone floors, plants and whitewashed walls. Moderate to expensive.

Whole Earth 93/3 Soi Lang Suan ☎02 252 5574. Long-standing veggie-oriented restaurant, serving interesting and varied Thai and Indian-style food for both vegetarians and omnivores in a relaxing atmosphere. Moderate.

Zen Floor 6, Central World Plaza, corner of Thanon Ploenchit and Thanon Rajdamri ☎02 255 6462; and Floor 4, Siam Center, Thanon Rama I ☎02 658 1183–4 (plus a branch at 1/1 Thanon Convent ☎02 266 7150–1). Good-value Japanese restaurant with wacky modern wooden design and seductive booths. Among a huge range of dishes, the complete meal sets (with pictures to help you choose) are filling and particularly good. Moderate to expensive.

Downtown: south of Thanon Rama IV

The places listed below are marked on the maps on p.116 and p.117.

All Gaengs 173/8–9 Thanon Suriwong. Large menu of tasty curries (*kaeng*, sometimes spelt *gaeng*) served in cool, modern, black-and-white-tiled surrounds. Closed Sat & Sun lunchtimes. Moderate.

Angelini's *Shangri-La Hotel*, 89 Soi Wat Suan Plu, Thanon Charoen Krung (New Rd) ☎02 236 7777. One of the capital's best Italians, pricey but not too extravagant. The setting is lively and relaxed, with open-plan kitchen and big picture windows onto the pool and river. There are some unusual main courses as well as old favourites like ossobucco, or you can invent your own wood-oven-baked pizza. Expensive.

Anna's Café Thanon Saladaeng ☎02 632 0619. In a large, elegant villa between Silom and Sathorn roads, reliable and reasonably priced Thai and Western dishes and desserts, including a very good *som tam*, *kai yang* and sticky rice combo, and tasty fried tofu with chives for veggies. Moderate to expensive.

Aoi 132/10–11 Soi 6, Thanon Silom ☎02 235 2321–2 (plus a branch in Emporium on Thanon Sukhumvit ☎02 664 8590). The best place in town for a Japanese blowout, justifiably popular with the expat community. Excellent authentic food and elegant decor. Good-value lunch sets available and a sushi corner. Expensive.

Ban Chiang 14 Soi Srivieng, off Thanon Surasak, between Thanon Silom and Thanon Sathorn ☎02 236 7045. Fine central and northeastern Thai cuisine in an elegant wooden house. Moderate to expensive.

Bussaracum 139 Sethiwan Building, Thanon Pan ☎02 266 6312–8. Superb royal Thai cuisine, well worth a splurge. Expensive.

Celadon *Sukhothai Hotel*, 13/3 Thanon Sathorn Tai ☎02 287 0222. Consistently rated as one of the best hotel restaurants in Bangkok and a favourite with locals, serving outstanding Thai food in an elegant setting surrounded by lotus ponds. Expensive.

Chai Karr 312/3 Thanon Silom ☎02 233 2549. Opposite *Holiday Inn*. Folksy, traditional-style wooden decor is the welcoming setting for a wide variety of well-prepared Thai and Chinese dishes, followed by liqueur coffees and home-made coconut ice cream. Closed Sun. Moderate.

Charuvan 70–2 Thanon Silom, near the entrance to Soi 4. Cleanish but lackadaisical place, with an air-con room, specializing in tasty duck on rice; the beer's a bargain too. Inexpensive.

Deen 786 Thanon Silom, almost opposite Silom Village. Small, basic, air-con Muslim café (no alcohol), which offers Thai and Chinese standard dishes with a southern Thai twist, as well as spicy Indian-style curries and specialities such as *grupuk* (crispy fish) and *roti kaeng* (Muslim pancakes with curry). Inexpensive to moderate.

Eat Me 1/6 Soi Phiphat 2, Thanon Convent ☎02 238 0931. Highly fashionable art gallery and restaurant in a striking, white-painted modernist building, with changing exhibitions on the walls and a temptingly relaxing balcony. The far-reaching menu is more international – pork tenderloin with thyme, grilled aubergines with mozzarella and pesto – than fusion, though the lemon-grass crème brûlée is not to be missed. Expensive.

Harmonique 22 Soi 34, Thanon Charoen Krung, on the lane between Wat Muang Kae express-boat pier and the GPO ☎02 237 8175. A relaxing, welcoming restaurant that's well worth a trip: tables are scattered throughout several converted houses, decorated with antiques, and a quiet, leafy courtyard, and the Thai food is varied and excellent – among the seafood specialities, try the red shrimp curry, or else plump for one of the good-value three-dish set menus. Moderate.

Himali Cha-Cha 1229/11 Thanon Charoen Krung, south of GPO ☎02 235 1569 (plus a branch at 2 Soi 35, Thanon Sukhumvit ☎02 258 8846). Fine North Indian restaurant, founded by a character who was chef to numerous Indian ambassadors, and now run by his son; good vegetarian selection. Moderate.

Indian Hut 311/2–5 Thanon Suriwong, ☎02 635 7876–7. Bright, white-tablecloth, North Indian restaurant – look out for the *Pizza Hut*-style sign – that's justly popular with local Indians. For carnivores, tandoori's the thing, with an especially good kastoori chicken kebab with saffron and cumin. There's a huge selection of mostly vegetarian pakoras as appetizers, as well as plenty of veggie main courses and breads, and a hard-to-resist house dahl, made with ginger, garlic, onion and tomato. Moderate to expensive.

Jim Thompson's Farmers' Market and Café 120/1 Soi 1, Thanon Saladaeng ☎02 266 9167–8. A civilized haven with tables in the elegantly informal air-con interior or out in the leafy garden. Thai food stretches to daily blackboard specials and some unusual dishes such as deep-fried morning glory with shrimp and spicy sauce. There's pasta, salads and other Western dishes, plus a few stabs at fusion including a delicious linguini *tom yam kung*. The array of Western cakes and Thai desserts is mouthwatering, rounded off by good coffee and a wide choice of teas. Moderate.

Khrua Aroy Aroy 3/1 Thanon Pan. In a fruitful area for cheap food (including a night market across Silom on Soi 20), this simple shophouse restaurant stands out for its choice of tasty, well-prepared dishes from all around the kingdom, notably *khao soi*, *kaeng matsaman* and *khanom jiin*. Roughly Mon–Fri 8am–6pm, Sat & Sun 8am–4pm. Inexpensive.

La Boulange 2–2/1 Thanon Convent. A fine choice for breakfast with great croissants and all sorts of tempting patisserie made on the premises, with good-value set menus. For savoury meals later in the day, choose from a variety of quiches, filled croissants, salads and French meats and cheeses. Daily 6.30am–8.30pm. Inexpensive to moderate.

Le Bouchon 37/17 Patpong 2, near Thanon Suriwong ☎02 234 9109. Cosy, welcoming bar-bistro that's much frequented by the city's French expats, offering French home-cooking, such as lamb shank in a white bean sauce, on a regularly changing menu; booking is strongly recommended. Closed Sun lunchtime. Expensive.

Mali Soi Jusmag, just off Soi Ngam Duphli. Cosy, informal, low-lit restaurant, mostly air-con with a few cramped tables out front. The Thai menu specializes in salads and northeastern food, with plenty of veggie options, while Western options run as far as burgers, potato salad, all-day breakfasts and delicious banana pancakes. Moderate.

Mei Jiang *Peninsula Hotel*, 333 Thanon Charoennakorn, Klongsan ☎02 861 2888. Probably Bangkok's best Chinese restaurant, with beautiful views of the hotel gardens and the river night and day. It's designed like an elegant teak box, without the gaudiness of many Chinese restaurants, and staff are very attentive and graceful. Specialities include duck smoked with tea and excellent lunchtime *dim sum* – a bargain at around B70 a dish. Expensive.

Somboon Seafood Thanon Suriwong, corner of Thanon Narathiwat Ratchanakharin ☎ 02 234 4499. Highly favoured seafood restaurant, known for its crab curry and soy-steamed sea bass, with reassuringly simple decor and an array of marine life lined up in tanks outside awaiting its gastronomic fate. Moderate to expensive.

Talat Nam Thanon Silom opposite Thaniya Plaza, between Soi 1 and Thanon Rama IV. Popular street stall, surrounded by many similar competitors, with twenty or so tables in the adjoining dark alley and all manner of fresh seafood temptingly displayed on ice. Evenings only. Inexpensive to moderate.

Tongue Thai 18–20 Soi 38, Thanon Charoen Krung ☎ 02 630 9918–9. In front of the Oriental Place shopping mall. Very high standards of food and cleanliness, with charming, unpretentious service, in a 100-year-old shophouse elegantly decorated with Thai and Chinese antiques and contemporary art. Veggies are amply catered for with delicious dishes such as tofu in black bean sauce and deep-fried banana-flower and corn cakes, while carnivores should try the fantastic beef curry (*panaeng neua*). Moderate to expensive.

Thanon Sukhumvit

See the map on p.119 for locations of the places listed below. For those restaurants east of sois 39 and 26 that are not shown on the map, we've given directions from the nearest Skytrain station.

Baan Khanitha Soi 23 ☎ 02 258 4128. The big attraction at this long-running favourite haunt of Sukhumvit expats is the setting in a traditional Thai house. The food is upmarket Thai and includes lots of fiery salads (*yam*), and a good range of *tom yam* soups, green curries and seafood curries. Expensive.

Ban Rie Coffee Opposite Ekamai Eastern Bus Station and beside the Ekamai Skytrain station on the corner of Soi 63. Surely the perfect place to await your next east-coast bus, this chic, modern teakwood pavilion welcomes you via a wooden walkway across a narrow fringe of ricefields and works hard to create a soothing ambience inside. It serves a decent selection of hot and iced coffees, as well as Thai desserts, and also offers Internet access and terrace seating. Moderate.

Basil *Sheraton Grande Hotel*, between sois 12 and 14. Mouthwateringly fine traditional Thai food with a modern twist is the order of the day at this trendy, relatively informal restaurant in the super-deluxe five-star Sheraton. Recommendations include the grilled river prawns with chilli, the *matsaman* curry (both served with red and green rice) and the surprisingly delicious durian cheesecake. Vegetarian menu on request. Expensive.

Cabbages and Condoms 6–8 Soi 12. Run by the Population and Community Development Association of Thailand (PDA): diners are treated to authentic Thai food in the Condom Room, and relaxed scoffing of barbecued seafood in the beer garden. Try the *plaa samlii* (fried cottonfish with mango and chilli) or the *kai haw bai toey* (marinated chicken baked in pandanus leaves). All proceeds go to the PDA, and there's an adjacent shop selling all kinds of double-entendre T-shirts, keyrings and of course, condoms. Moderate.

De Meglio Soi 11. Upmarket Italian where the antipastos are unusual Thai-Italian hybrids, and the linguini with clams and the crab cannelloni with fennel salad are recommended. Authentic wood-fired pizzas a speciality. Expensive.

Gaeng Pa Lerd Rod Soi 33/1; no English sign but it's just before the *Bull's Head*. Hugely popular outdoor restaurant whose tables are clustered under trees in a streetside yard and get packed with office workers at lunchtime. Thai curries are the speciality here, with dishes ranging from conventional versions, like catfish and beef curries, to more adventurous offerings like fried cobra with chilli, and curried frog. Inexpensive.

Le Dalat Indochine 14 Soi 23 ☎ 02 661 7967. There's Indochinese romance aplenty at this delightfully atmospheric restaurant, which is housed in an early-twentieth-century villa decked out in homely style with plenty of photos, pot plants at every turn and eclectic curiosities in the male and female toilets. The extensive, Vietnamese menu features favourites such as a *goi ca* salad of aromatic herbs and shredded pork, *chao tom* shrimp sticks and *ga sa gung*, chicken curry with caramelized ginger. Expensive.

Lemongrass Soi 24 ☎ 02 258 8637. Known for its delicious Thai nouvelle cuisine – including a particularly good minced chicken with ginger – and for its pleasant setting in a converted traditional house. A vegetarian menu is available on request. Advance reservations recommended. Moderate to expensive.

Mrs Balbir's 155/8 Soi 11/1. All dishes are cooked to order at this popular North Indian restaurant run by TV cook Mrs Balbir. The menu features both veg and non-veg selections, and specialities include the spicy dry chicken and lamb curries (*masala kerai*). Ask to sit on the cushions in the cosy upstairs gallery where you can browse the pile of magazines while you wait for your meal. Indian and Thai cookery courses are held here every week – see "Listings" on p.202 for details. Closed Mon. Moderate to expensive.

Nipa 3rd Floor, Landmark Plaza, between sois 4 and 6. Tasteful traditional Thai-style place with a classy menu that features an adventurous range of dishes, including spicy fish curry, several *matsaman* and green curries, excellent *som tam* and mouthwatering braised spare ribs. Also offers a sizeable vegetarian selection. Regular cookery classes are held here – see "Listings" on p.202 for details. Moderate to expensive.

Suda Restaurant Soi 14. Unpretentious shop-house restaurant whose formica tables and plastic chairs spill out onto the soi and are mainly patronized by budget-conscious expats and their Thai friends. The friendly proprietor serves a good, long menu of Thai favourites, including deep-fried chicken in banana leaves, battered shrimps, fried tuna with cashews and chilli, and sticky rice with mango. Inexpensive.

Took Lae Dee Inside the Foodland supermarket on Soi 5. The place to come for very cheap breakfasts: hearty American breakfasts eaten at the counter cost B39 before 9am, or B55 after. Inexpensive.

Vientiane Kitchen (Khrua Vientiane) 8 Soi 36, about 50m south off Thanon Sukhumvit. Just a 3min walk west then south from Thong Lo Skytrain station and you're transported into a little piece of Isaan, where the menu's stocked full of northeastern delicacies, a live band sets the mood with its repertoire of heart-felt folk songs, and there's even a troupe of upcountry dancers. The Lao- and Isaan-accented menu includes vegetable curry with ants' eggs, spicy-fried frog, jackfruit curry, and farm chicken with cashews, plus there's a decent range of veggie options such as meat-free *larb* and sweet and sour dishes. With its airy, barn-like interior and a mixed clientele of Thais and expats, it all adds up to a very enjoyable dining experience. Moderate.

Whole Earth A 10min walk down Soi 26, beyond the *Four Wings Hotel*, at no. 71. Vegetarian-oriented restaurant serving meat-free Thai and Indian food plus an equivalent number of dishes for carnivores. The mushroom and tofu *larb* served over baked rice is worth the walk, especially if you can get one of the low tables on the first floor where there's more atmosphere than in the ground-floor restaurant. Moderate.

Yong Lee Corner of Soi 15. One of the few refreshingly basic – and brusque – rice-and-noodle shops on Sukhumvit. Daily 11.30am–8.30pm. Inexpensive.

Nightlife and entertainment

For many of Bangkok's male visitors, nightfall in the city is the signal to hit the sex bars, the neon sumps that disfigure three distinct parts of town: along Thanon Sukhumvit's Soi Cowboy (between sois 21 and 23) and Nana Plaza (Soi 4), and, most notoriously, in the two small sois off the east end of Thanon Silom known as Patpong 1 and 2 (see p.163). Fortunately, Bangkok's **nightlife** has grown up and diversified beyond these sleazy ghettos in the last few years: within spitting distance of the beer bellies flopped onto Patpong's bars, for example, lies Soi 4, Thanon Silom, one of Bangkok's most happening after-dark haunts. Along with Silom 4, the high-concept clubs and bars of Sukhumvit and the lively, teeming venues of Banglamphu pull in the style-conscious cream of Thai youth and are tempting an increasing number of travellers to stuff their party gear into their rucksacks. Though Silom 4 started out as a purely **gay** area, it now offers a range of styles in gay, mixed and straight pubs, DJ bars and clubs, while the city's other main gay area is the more exclusive Silom 2 (towards Thanon Rama IV). As with the straight scene, many gay bars feature go-go dancers and live sex shows. Those listed here do not. Most bars and clubs open nightly until 1 or 2am, with closing time strictly enforced under the current government's Social Order Policy. This has also involved sporadic clampdowns on illegal drugs, including urine testing of bar customers, and more widespread ID checks to curb under-age drinking – you're supposed to be over 21 to drink in bars and clubs, though Thais seem to be more rigorously checked than foreigners.

On the cultural front, the most accessible of the capital's performing arts are **Thai dancing**, particularly when served up in bite-size portions on tourist restaurant stages, and the graceful and humorous **traditional puppet shows** at the Joe Louis Puppet Theatre on Thanon Rama IV. **Thai boxing** is also well worth watching: the live experience at either of Bangkok's two main national stadia far outshines the TV coverage.

Bars and clubs

For convenient drinking and dancing, we've split the most recommended of the city's bars and clubs into three central areas. The travellers' enclave of **Banglamphu** takes on a whole new personality after dark, when its hub – Thanon Khao San – becomes a "walking street", closed to all traffic but open to almost any kind of makeshift stall, selling everything from fried bananas and cheap beer to bargain fashions and idiosyncratic art works. Young Thais crowd the area to browse and snack before piling in to Banglamphu's countless bars and clubs, most of which host a good mix of local and foreign drinkers and ravers. Venues here tend to be low-key, with free entry (though some places ask you to show ID first), reasonably priced drinks and up-to-date sounds, or there's always plenty of kerbside restaurant tables, which make great places to nurse a few beers and watch the parade. Away from Khao San and nearby Soi Ram Bhuttri, Thanon Phra Athit is more of a Thai scene, though again there are always some Western drinkers in the mix. Here, the style-conscious little restaurant-bars have their tables spill over onto the pavement, and the live music is likely to be a lone piano-player or guitarist.

Downtown bars, which tend to attract both foreign and Thai drinkers, are concentrated on adjoining Soi Lang Suan and Soi Sarasin (between Thanon Ploenchit and Lumphini Park), and in studenty Siam Square, as well as around the east end of Thanon Silom. Lang Suan and Sarasin have their fair share of live-music bars, but Western covers are often less than inspiring; the better live-music venues are listed below. On Silom 4, while most of the gay venues have been around for some years now, other bars and clubs have opened and closed with bewildering speed – only *Tapas* seems to have stood the test of time, so far. All the same – once you've passed through the ID check at the entrance – on a short, slow bar-crawl around this wide, traffic-free alley lined with pavement tables, it would be hard not to find somewhere to enjoy yourself. If, among all the choice of nightlife around Silom, you do end up in one of Patpong's sex bars, be prepared to shell out up to B600 for a small beer. Though many Patpong bars trumpet the fact that they have no cover charge, almost every customer gets ripped off in some way, and stories of menacing bouncers are legion. **Thanon Sukhumvit** also has its share of girlie bars and bar-beers (open-sided drinking halls with huge circular bars) packed full of hostesses, but it's also garnering quite a reputation for high-concept "destination bars" (where the decor is as important as the drinks menu), as well as being the home of several long-established British-style pubs.

During the cool season (Nov–Feb), an evening out at one of the seasonal **beer gardens** is a pleasant way of soaking up the urban atmosphere (and the traffic fumes). You'll find them in hotel forecourts or sprawled in front of shopping centres – the huge beer garden that sets up in front of the Central World Plaza (formerly the World Trade Center) on Thanon Rajdamri is extremely popular, and recommended; beer is served in pitchers here and bar snacks are available too.

Banglamphu, Ratanakosin and Hualamphong

Except where indicated, all bars listed below are marked on the map on p.108.

About Café A 5-min walk from Hualamphong Station at 418 Thanon Maitri Chit (see map on p.143). Arty café-bar that's popular with trendy young Thais. There's a gallery space upstairs and exhibits usually spill over into the ground-floor eating and drinking area, where tables and sofas are scattered about in an informal and welcoming fashion. Mon–Sat 7pm–midnight.

Ad Here the 13th 13 Thanon Samsen. Friendly, intimate little jazz bar where half a dozen tables of Thai and expat musos congregate to listen to nightly sets from the in-house blues 'n' jazz quartet (10.30pm onwards). Well-priced beer and plenty of cocktails.

Airway Bar 18 Thanon Chakrabongse, on the rooftop above the *Sawasdee Khaosan Inn*. Struggle up five flights of stairs to the rooftop terrace to be rewarded with a stunning view that takes in the Grand Palace to the south, the Golden Mount and the towering red and blue neon of the *Conrad Hotel* to the east, and Rama VIII Bridge to the north. There's a small bar up here and turntables, which makes this the perfect place for a gentle dance, weather permitting. Daily 9pm–2am.

Austin 164 Thanon Khao San, in the scrum behind *D&D Inn*. Named in honour of the car (hence the neon silhouette), this homely three-floored bar plays loud music and gets crammed with students from nearby Thammasat University, though it doesn't attract much of a Western crowd. The favoured drink is a jug of Sang Som rum over ice, mixed with soda and lemon and served with straws to share with your mates. Also on offer are lots of cocktails and fairly pricey beer.

Bangkok Bar 149 Soi Ram Bhuttri. Not to be confused with the restaurant of the same name on Thanon Phra Sumen, this skinny dance bar is fronted by a different DJ every night and draws capacity crowds of drinkers and clubbers.

Bar Bali 58 Thanon Phra Athit. Typical Phra Athit bar-restaurant, with just a half-dozen tables, a small menu of salads and drinking foods and a decent selection of well-priced cocktails. Good place for a chat, but don't expect much in the way of entertainment.

Boh 230 Tha Thien, Thanon Maharat (see map on p.123). When the Chao Phraya express boats stop running around 6.30pm, this bar takes over the rustic wooden pier with its great sunset views across the river. Beer and Thai whisky with accompanying Thai food and loud Thai pop music – very popular with Silpakorn and Thammasat university students.

Café Democ 78 Thanon Rajdamnoen Klang. Fashionable, dark and dinky bar that overlooks Democracy Monument and is spread over one and a half cosy floors, with extra seating on the semi-circular mezzanine. Lots of cocktails, nightly sessions from up-and-coming Thai DJs, and regular hip-hop evenings. Closed on Mon.

The Club Thanon Khao San. The kitsch, pseudo Italianate interior – designed to evoke a classical courtyard garden, complete with central fountain and statue of a chubby child hugging a fish – is unlikely to appeal to many Western clubbers, but Thais love this place, putting up with the ID checks at the door and making the most of the two bars and resident DJs.

Grand Guest House Middle of Thanon Khao San. Cavernous place lacking in character but popular because it stays open 24hr. Videos are shown non-stop, usually movies in the day and MTV in the early hours.

Gullivers' Travellers Tavern Thanon Khao San. Backpacker-oriented air-con sports pub with two pool tables, sixteen TV screens, masses of sports memorabilia and reasonably priced beer. Daily 11am–2am.

Hole in the Wall Bar Thanon Khao San, down the alleyway beside Boots. Small, dark, low-key drinking-spot at the heart of the backpackers' ghetto. Dim lighting, a pool table, a more varied than average CD selection and competitively priced beer.

Immortal Bar Bayon Building, 209 Thanon Khao San. Loud hip-hop and drum 'n' bass nightly 5pm–2am. Farangs are sometimes asked to show ID (passports) at the door.

Lava Club Bayon Building, 209 Thanon Khao San. Self-consciously sophisticated basement lounge bar done out in "volcanic" red and black with laser displays to enhance the look. DJs play mainly house and rave from 8pm.

Molly Pub Thanon Ram Bhuttri. The attractive, colonial-style facade, complete with pastel-coloured shutters, make a pleasant backdrop for the outdoor tables and low-slung wooden chairs that are perfectly located for people-watching over a Beer Chang or two. Also serves food.

Silk Bar 129–131 Thanon Khao San. The two-tiered outdoor decks are a popular spot for sipping cocktails while watching the nightly Khao San fashion parade; inside there's air-con, a pool table, comfy chairs and a DJ. Daily 6am–2am.

Susie Pub Next to *Marco Polo Guest House* on the soi between Thanon Khao San and Thanon Ram Bhuttri. Big, dark, phenomenally popular pub that's usually standing-room-only after 9pm. Has a pool table, decent music, resident DJs and cheapish beer. Packed with travellers and young Thais. Sometimes asks farangs to show ID (passports) at the door. Daily 11am–2am.

Siam Square, Thanon Ploenchit and northern downtown

The venues listed below are marked on the map on p.157.

Ad Makers 51/51 Soi Langsuan ⓣ02 652 0168. Friendly, spacious bar with Wild West-style wooden decor and good food, attracting a cross-section of Thais and foreigners and featuring nightly folk and rock bands.

Brown Sugar 231/19–20 Soi Sarasin ⓣ02 250 1825–6. Chic, pricey, lively bar, acknowledged as the capital's top jazz venue.

Club 87 *Conrad Hotel*, All Seasons Place, 87 Thanon Witthayu ⓣ02 690 9999. Stylish, upmarket lounge-bar, restaurant and club, reflecting its "World Food Global Grooves" theme in a pricey menu of cutting-edge fusion food and in a fast-changing rota of DJs, playing everything from funky house to Cuban grooves.

Concept CM² *Novotel*, Soi 6, Siam Square ⓣ02 255 6888. More theme park than nightclub, with live bands and various, barely distinct entertainment zones, including karaoke, an Italian restaurant and techno in the Boom Room. Admission (including one drink) B330 Fri & Sat, B220 Sun–Thurs.

Dallas Pub Soi 6, Siam Square ⓣ02 255 3276. Typical dark, noisy "songs for life" hangout – buffalo skulls, Indian heads, American flags – but a lot of fun: singalongs to decent live bands, dancing round the tables, cheap beer and friendly, casual staff.

Fou Bar 264/4–6 Soi 3, Siam Square. Smart, modernist but easy-going hangout for students and 20-somethings, with reasonably priced drinks, TV football, a good choice of accompanying snacks and some interesting Thai/Italian crossovers for main dishes. A little hard to find up some stairs by Siam Square's Centerpoint.

Hard Rock Café Soi 11, Siam Square. Genuine outlet of the famous chain, better for drink than food. Big sounds, brash enthusiasm, bank-breaking prices.

Rarnbarnrao 258/15 Soi 3, Siam Square. Hip, laid-back bar-restaurant hosting monthly art exhibitions, with cool sounds and live pop music every Fri & Sat evening. Hard to find on the first floor by the Lido Cinema.

Saxophone 3/8 Victory Monument (southeast corner), Thanon Phrayathai ⓣ02 246 5472. Lively, spacious venue that hosts nightly jazz, blues, folk and rock bands and attracts a good mix of Thais and farangs; decent food, relaxed drinking atmosphere and, all things considered, reasonable prices.

Southern downtown: south of Thanon Rama IV

See the map on p.116 for locations of the venues listed below.

The Barbican 9/4–5 Soi Thaniya, east end of Thanon Silom ⓣ02 234 3590. Stylishly modern fortress-like decor to match the name: dark woods, metal and undressed stone. With Guinness on tap and the financial pages posted above the urinals, it could almost be a smart City of London pub – until you look out of the windows onto the soi's incongruous Japanese hostess bars. Good food, DJ sessions and happy hours Mon–Fri 5–7pm.

Irish Xchange 1/5 Thanon Convent, off the east end of Thanon Silom ⓣ02 266 7160. Blarney Bangkok-style: a warm, relaxing Irish pub, tastefully done out in dark wood and familiar knick-knacks and packed with expats, especially on Fri night. Guinness and Kilkenny Bitter on tap, expensive food such as Irish stew and beef and Guinness pie, and a rota of house bands.

Lucifer 76/1–3 Patpong 1. Popular dance club in the dark heart of Patpong, largely untouched by the sleaze around it. Done out with mosaics and stalactites like a satanic grotto, with balconies to look down on the dance-floor action. *Radio City*, the interconnected bar downstairs, is only slightly less raucous, with jumping live bands, including famous Elvis and Tom Jones impersonators, and tables out on the sweaty pavement.

Tapas Bar Soi 4, Thanon Silom ⓦwww.tapasroom.com. Vaguely Spanish-oriented bar (but no tapas) with Moorish-style decor, whose outside tables are probably the best spot for checking out the comings and goings on the soi; inside, the main dance floor is upstairs (B200 to go up) and music ranges from house and hip-hop to Latin jazz and funk.

Tawandang German Brewery 462/61 Thanon Rama III ☎02 678 1114–6. A taxi-ride south of Thanon Sathorn down Thanon Narathiwat Ratchanakharin – and best to book a table in advance – this vast all-rounder is well worth the effort. Under a huge dome, up to 1300 revellers can enjoy good food and great micro-brewed beer, but the main attraction is the mercurial cabaret (Mon–Sat from 8.30pm), featuring Fong Naam, led by Bruce Gaston, who blend Thai classical and popular with Western styles of music.

Thanon Sukhumvit

The places listed below are marked on the map on p.119.

Bed Supperclub 26 Soi 11 ☎02 651 3537. Worth visiting just for the futuristic visuals, this seductively curvaceous spacepod bar squats self-consciously in an otherwise quite ordinary soi. Inside, the all-white interior is dimly lit and surprisingly cosy, with the eponymous bed-style couches inviting drinkers to recline around the edges of the upstairs gallery, getting a good view of the downstairs bar and DJ. The restaurant section is starker, lit with glacial ultra-violet, and serving a Pacific Rim fusion menu from 7.30–9pm (reservations essential). Bar opens nightly from 8pm–2am.

The Bull's Head Soi 33/1. A Sukhumvit institution that takes pride in being Bangkok's most authentic British pub, right down to the horse brasses, jukebox and typical pub food. Famous for its Sunday evening "toss the boss" happy hours (5–7pm), when a flip of a coin determines whether or not you have to pay for your round. Daily 11am–1.30am.

Cheap Charlies Soi 11. Idiosyncratic, long-running pavement bar that's famous for its cheap beer and lack of tables and chairs. A few lucky punters get to occupy the bar-stools but otherwise it's standing room only. Daily 3pm–2am.

Faith Club Soi 23. Highly rated little club with a vaguely industrial but intimate feel (lots of raw concrete and plenty of sofas), an upstairs pool table, and a timetable of regular club nights, including weekly reggae, hip-hop, techno and chillout evenings: check *Metro* or *Farang* magazines for current schedules. Has a loyal following but rarely gets packed out. Daily 8pm–2am.

Jools Bar and Restaurant Soi 4. Easy-going British-run pub whose cosy downstairs bar is popular with expat drinkers (photos of regular customers plaster the walls). Traditional British food is served at tables upstairs.

Londoner Brew Pub Mouth of Soi 33. Aside from the pool table, darts board, big-screen sports TV and live music (nightly from about 9pm), it's the specially brewed pints of Londoner's Pride Cream Bitter and London Pilsner 33 that draw in the punters.

dbl 0 (Double 0) Soi 12. This is the city's largest all-in-one nightlife complex, comprising the *Sib Song* live-music pub on the ground floor, the *Dance Club* clubbing experience on the first floor, and the *Sugar* 1970s-style vodka-cocktail bar on the mezzanine level (complete with its own DJ). The dance floor is the big draw, chiefly because of its spectacular hi-tech laser light shows and phenomenal sound system – the best in Bangkok – which pumps out high-decibel house on Fridays and Saturdays and mainstream dance hits through the rest of the week. Entry costs B150 including one drink, except on Fri & Sat after 11pm when it's B250 including one drink. Tues–Sun 9pm–2am.

Old Dutch Soi 23, at the mouth of the Soi Cowboy strip. Cool, dark, peaceful oasis at the edge of Sukhumvit's frenetic sleaze; a reasonable basic menu and a big stock of current US and European newspapers make this an ideal daytime or early evening watering hole.

Q Bar 34 Soi 11. Very dark, very trendy, New York-style bar occupying two floors and a terrace. Famous for its big choice of chilled vodkas, and for its music, *Q Bar* appeals to a mixed crowd of fashionable people, particularly on Friday and Saturday nights when the DJs fill the dance floor and there's a B600 cover charge after 10pm that includes two free drinks. Arrive before 11pm if you want a seat, and don't turn up in shorts, singlets or sandals if you're male. Daily 8pm–2am.

Gay scene

The bars, clubs and bar-restaurants listed here are the most notable of Bangkok's gay nightlife venues; for more general background on gay life in Thailand, contacts and sources of information, most of them concentrated in Bangkok, see p.77. Don't forget **Bangkok Pride** in mid-November, when the capital's gay community struts its stuff in a week of parades, cabarets, fancy-dress shows and sports contests that culminates with a jamboree in Lumphini Park on the Saturday.

Bangkok for kids

The following theme parks and amusement centres are all designed for kids, the main drawback being that many are located a long way from the city centre. Other attractions kids should enjoy include Dusit Zoo (see p.155), the Snake Farm (see p.162), the ice-skating rink inside the Central World Plaza (formerly World Trade Center) on Thanon Rajdamri, and the Joe Louis Puppet Theatre at Suan Lum Night Bazaar (see p.186).

Adventureland Seacon Square, 904 Thanon Sri Nakarin (Mon–Fri 11am–9pm, Sat & Sun 10am–10pm; ⓣ02 721 9444). Shopping-mall amusement park featuring rollercoasters, go-karts, a "stimulator" cinema and a rollerblade rink. Skytrain to On Nut, then regular bus #133 from Sukhumvit Soi 77.

Children's Discovery Museum Opposite Chatuchak Weekend Market on Thanon Kamphaeng Phet 4 (Tues–Fri 9am–5pm, Sat & Sun 10am–6pm; B70, kids B50; ⓣ02 615 7333, ⓦwww.bkkchildrenmuseum.com/english). Interactive and hands-on displays covering science, the environment, human and animal life. Skytrain or subway to Mo Chit or, from Banglamphu, any bus bound for Chatuchak or the Northern Bus Terminal (see p.110).

Dream World Ten minutes' drive north of Don Muang Airport at kilometre-stone 7 Thanon Rangsit-Ongharak (Mon–Fri 10am–5pm, Sat & Sun 10am–7pm; B120, children B95; ⓣ02 533 1152, ⓦwww.dreamworld-th.com). Theme park with different areas such as Fantasy Land, Dream Garden and Adventure Land. Water rides, a hanging coaster and other amusements. Regular buses #39 and #59 from Rajdamnoen Klang in Banglamphu to Rangsit, then songthaew or tuk-tuk to Dream World; or bus, Skytrain or subway to Mo Chit/Chatuchak Park, then air-con bus #523.

The Balcony Soi 4, Thanon Silom. Unpretentious, fun place with a large, popular terrace, cheap drinks, karaoke and decent Thai and Western food.
Dick's Café Duangthawee Plaza, 894/7–8 Soi Pratuchai, Thanon Suriwong. Stylish day-and-night café-restaurant (daily 11am–2am), hung with exhibitions by gay artists, on a traffic-free soi opposite the prominent Wall St Tower, ideal for drinking, eating decent Thai and Western food or just chilling out.
Disco Disco Soi 2, Thanon Silom. Small, well-designed bar-disco with an industrial feel, serving up reasonably priced drinks and good dance music to a fun young crowd.
DJ Station Soi 2, Thanon Silom. Highly fashionable but unpretentious disco, packed at weekends, attracting a mix of Thais and farangs; cabaret show nightly at 11.30pm. B100 including one drink (B200 including two drinks Fri & Sat).
Dog Days 100/2–6 Thanon Phra Athit. Unadorned little bar-restaurant whose cosy atmosphere and mid-priced food and drink is a favourite with lesbians. Tues–Sun 5pm–midnight.
Expresso Soi 2, Thanon Silom. Immaculately designed bar-lounge with cool water features and subtle lighting.
Freeman Dance Arena, 60/18–21 Thanon Silom (in the small, unnamed soi between Soi Thaniya and Soi 2). Busy disco, somewhat more Thai-oriented than *DJ Station*, with slick midnight cabaret shows. B100 including one drink (B200 including two drinks Fri & Sat). Under the same management is *The Mix*, a smart, pre- and post-club bar-restaurant next door.
JJ Park 8/3 Soi 2, Thanon Silom. Classy, Thai-oriented bar-restaurant, for relaxed socializing rather than raving, with nightly singers, comedy shows and good food.
Sphinx 98–104 Soi 4, Thanon Silom. Chic decor, terrace seating and good Thai and Western food attract a sophisticated crowd to this ground-floor bar and restaurant; karaoke and live music upstairs at *Pharoah's*.
Telephone Pub 114/11–13 Soi 4, Thanon Silom. Cruisey, dimly lit, long-standing eating and drinking venue with a terrace on the alley.
Vega Soi 39, Thanon Sukhumvit. Trendy bar-restaurant run by a group of lesbians. The live music, karaoke and dance floor attract a mixed, fashionable crowd. Mon–Sat 11am–1pm.

Leoland Water Park 6th Floor, Central City Bangna at kilometre-stone 3 on Thanon Bangna Trat (Mon–Fri 11am–6pm, Sat & Sun 10am–7pm; B250, kids B150; ⓣ02 361 0888). Huge rooftop waterpark atop a shopping mall on the eastern outskirts of the city. Waterslides, tube rides and sunbeds. Skytrain to On Nut, then regular bus #38, #48, #132 or air-con #38.

MBK Magic Land 8th Floor, Mah Boon Krong Shopping Centre, at the Rama I/Phrayathai intersection (Mon–Fri 10.30am–6.30pm, Sat & Sun 10.30am–8pm). Centrally located amusements centre in downtown Bangkok, with cheap indoor fairground rides. Skytrain to National Stadium.

Safari World On the northeastern outskirts at 99 Thanon Ramindra, Minburi (daily 9am–5pm; B700, children B450; ⓣ02 518 1000, ⓦwww.safariworld.com). Drive-through safari park, complete with monkeys, lions, rhinos, giraffes and zebras, plus a sea-life area with dolphins and sea lions. If you don't have your own car, you can be driven through the park in a Safari World coach. Take air-con bus #60 from Rajdamnoen Klang in Banglamphu or air-con #26 from Victory Monument, then a songthaew to Safari World.

Siam Park On the far eastern edge of town at 101 Thanon Sukhapiban 2 (Mon–Fri 10am–6pm, Sat & Sun 9am–7pm; B400, children B300; ⓣ02 919 7200, ⓦwww.siamparkcity.com). Waterslides, whirlpools and artificial surf, plus rollercoasters, a small zoo and a botanical garden. Air-con bus #60 from Rajdamnoen Klang in Banglamphu or air-con #501/#1 from Hualamphong Station.

Traditional theatre and culture shows

Even in the Thai capital, you'll have your work cut out to see a live display of authentic **traditional dance or theatre**. The main venue is the National Theatre (ⓣ02 224 1342), next to the National Museum on the northwest corner of Sanam Luang, which puts on irregular shows of *lakhon* (classical dance-drama) and *likay* (folk drama), with tickets starting at around B100. However, publicity for performances is next to nil, and little more information in English can be gleaned by contacting the theatre or the tourist information offices. Their most accessible current output seems to be outdoor shows of classical music and dancing at the National Museum (Dec–April Sat & Sun 5.30–7.30pm; B20). It's also worth trying the Thailand Cultural Centre, the country's most prominent performing arts space, located in the northeastern part of the city on Thanon Ratchadapisek and on the subway line (ⓣ02 247 0028, ext 4280, ⓦwww.thaiculturalcenter.com), which hosts free performances every Saturday at 5pm that may feature music, folk dances, *nang thalung* (shadow-puppet plays) or drama such as *likay*.

The Sala Chalermkrung Theatre (ⓣ02 225 8757) at 66 Thanon Charoen Krung (New Road; on the intersection with Thanon Triphet in Pahurat, next to Old Siam Plaza) shows **contemporary Thai drama and comedy** most of the week, but in February and March stages performances of traditional, tourist-friendly dance-dramas every Sunday at 2pm and 7pm (B350–500). The Patravadi Theatre in Thonburi is known for its experimental, contemporary shows, some of them accessible to non-Thai speakers (ⓣ02 412 7287, ⓦwww.patravadi.com; free shuttle boat transport from Tha Maharaj in front of Wat Mahathat), while the more mainstream Thailand Cultural Centre (see above for details) hosts **classical concerts** and visiting international dance and theatre companies.

Many tourist restaurants feature nightly **culture shows** – usually a hotchpotch of Thai dancing and classical music, with a martial-arts demonstration thrown in; it's always worth calling ahead to reserve, especially if you want a vegetarian version of the set menu. Worth checking out are the upmarket, riverside *Supatra River House* in Thonburi (ⓣ02 411 0305), where twice a week diners are entertained by performers from the nearby Patravadi Theatre (Fri & Sat at 8.30pm; B650–850 including food); *Baan Thai* (ⓣ02 258 5403), a traditional teak house on Sukhumvit Soi 32 (performances at 8.30pm; B550); and Silom Village (ⓣ02 234 4581) on Thanon Silom, which stages a nightly fifty-minute indoor show (8.30pm; B550) to accompany a set menu of Thai food, as well as a rather desultory free show at 8pm at its outdoor restaurant. In Banglamphu, most tour agents offer a dinner-show package including transport for around B600 per person.

The **Joe Louis Puppet Theatre** (ⓣ02 252 9683–4, ⓦwww.joelouis-theater.com), at Suan Lum Night Bazaar on Thanon Rama IV, stages entertaining tourist-oriented performances, which, though pricey, are well worth it for both adults and children. The puppets in question are jointed stick-puppets (*hun lakhon lek*), an art form that was developed under Rama IV in the mid-nineteenth century and had all but died out before the owner of the theatre, Sakorn Yangkeowsod (aka Joe Louis), came to its rescue in the 1980s. Each sixty-centimetre-tall puppet is manipulated by three puppeteers, who are accomplished Thai classical dancers in their own right, complementing their charges' elegant and precise gestures with graceful movements in a harmonious ensemble. Hour-long shows (B600, kids B300) are put on daily at the theatre at 7.30pm, with extra Saturday and Sunday shows at 5pm, but you should turn up half an hour in advance for demonstrations of how the puppets and *khon* masks are made. The puppets perform mostly stories from the *Ramakien*, accompanied by commentary in English and traditional music of a high standard.

More glitzy and occasionally ribald entertainment is the order of the day at the capital's two **ladyboy cabaret shows**, where a bevy of luscious transvestites dons glamorous outfits and performs over-the-top song and dance routines: Mambo Cabaret plays at the theatre in Washington Square, between Sukhumvit sois 22 and 24 (ⓣ02 259 5715; nightly 8pm; Nov–Feb also at 10pm; B600–800), and New Calypso Cabaret performs inside the *Asia Hotel*, close by Ratchathevi Skytrain station at 296 Thanon Phayathai (ⓣ02 216 8937; nightly 8.15 & 9.45pm; B800).

Thai dancing is performed for its original ritual purpose, usually several times a day, at the Lak Muang Shrine behind the Grand Palace and the Erawan Shrine on the corner of Thanon Ploenchit. Both shrines have resident troupes of dancers who are hired by worshippers to perform *lakhon chatri*, a sort of *khon* dance-drama, to thank benevolent spirits for answered prayers. The dancers are always dressed up in full gear and accompanied by musicians, but the length and complexity of the dance and the number of dancers depends on the amount of money paid by the supplicant: a price list is posted near the dance area. The musicians at the Erawan Shrine are particularly highly rated, though the almost comic apathy of the dancers there doesn't do them justice.

Cinemas

Central Bangkok has more than forty **cinemas**, many of which show recent American and European releases with their original dialogue and Thai subtitles. Most cinemas screen shows around four times a day: programmes are detailed every day in the *Nation* and *Bangkok Post*, and reviews and some listings appear in the monthly listings magazine, *Metro*. Alternatively go to Ⓦwww.movieseer.com, which allows you to search by movie or by area in Bangkok (or indeed around the country), up to a week ahead; cinema locations are printed on *Nancy Chandler's Map of Bangkok*. Seats cost from around B60 to B140, depending on the plushness of the cinema; whatever cinema you're in, you're expected to stand for the national anthem, which is played before every performance.

There are half a dozen cinemas in and around Siam Square, and nearly every major downtown shopping plaza has two or three screens on its top floor. Western films are also regularly shown at the DK Filmhouse in Thammasat University's Pridi Phanomyong Library: check *Metro* or the other English-language press for details. And if it's been a while since you've caught up on the new releases, check out the dozens of video-showing restaurants along Banglamphu's Thanon Khao San, where recent blockbusters are screened back-to-back every day and night of the year, all for the price of a banana smoothie or a cheese sandwich.

Thai boxing

The violence of the average **Thai boxing** match may be offputting to some, but spending a couple of hours at one of Bangkok's two main stadiums can be immensely entertaining, not least for the enthusiasm of the spectators and the ritualistic aspects of the fights. Bouts, advertised in the English-language newspapers, are held in the capital every night of the week at the **Rajdamnoen Stadium**, next to the TAT office on Rajdamnoen Nok (Ⓣ02 281 4205; Mon, Wed & Thurs 6pm, Sun 5pm), and at **Lumphini Stadium** on Thanon Rama IV (Ⓣ02 252 8765, Ⓦwww.muaythailumpinee.com; Tues & Fri 6.30pm, Sat 5pm & 8.30pm). Tickets go on sale one hour before and, unless the boxers are big stars, start at B220, rising to B1000 for a ringside seat; tickets for the Sunday bouts at Rajdamnoen cost from B50. You might have to queue for a few minutes, but there's no need to get there early unless there's a really important fight on. Sessions usually feature ten bouts, each consisting of five three-minute rounds (with two-minute rests in between each round), so if you're not a big fan it may be worth turning up an hour late, as the better fights tend to happen later in the billing. It's more fun if you buy one of the less expensive standing tickets, enabling you to witness the wild gesticulations of the betting aficionadoes at close range. For more on Thai boxing and on training camps outside the city, see p.67.

To engage in a little *muay Thai* yourself, visit Sor Vorapin's Gym at 13 Trok Kasap off Thanon Chakrabongse in Banglamphu, which holds *muay Thai* **classes** twice daily (B500; Ⓣ02 282 3551, Ⓦthaiboxings.genesis.mweb.co.th). Jitti's Gym on Soi Amon off Sukhumvit Soi 49 also offers well-regarded training sessions for foreigners (Ⓣ02 2392 5890, Ⓦwww.thailandroad.com/jittigym). For more in-depth training and further information about Thai boxing, contact the Muay Thai Institute at 336/932 Prachathipat, Thanyaburi, Pathum Thani, Bangkok 12130 (Ⓣ02 992 0096, Ⓦwww.tat.or.th/do/learn.htm), which runs training courses for foreigners (US$160 for 40hr), including practical instruction, as well as history and theory.

Shopping

Bangkok has a good reputation for shopping, particularly for silk, gems and fashions, where the range and quality are streets ahead of other Thai cities, and antiques and handicrafts are good buys too. As always, watch out for old, damaged goods being passed off as antiques: if you're concerned about the quality or authenticity of your purchases, stick to TAT-approved shops (contact TAT for a list). Bangkok also has the best English-language bookshops in the country. Department stores and tourist-oriented shops in the city keep late hours, opening daily at 10 or 11am and closing at about 9pm; many small, upmarket boutiques, for example along Thanon Charoen Krung and Thanon Silom, close on Sundays.

Downtown Bangkok is full of smart, multi-storeyed **shopping plazas** like Siam Centre, Emporium and the Peninsula Plaza, which is where you'll find the majority of the city's fashion stores, as well as designer lifestyle goods and bookshops. The plazas tend to be pleasantly air-conditioned and thronging with trendy young Thais, but don't hold much interest for tourists unless you happen to be looking for a new outfit. You're more likely to find useful items in one of the city's numerous **department stores**, most of which are also scattered about the downtown areas. Seven-storey Central Chidlom on Thanon Ploenchit, which boasts handy services like watch-, garment- and shoe-repair booths as well as a huge product selection, is probably the city's best (with other Central branches on Thanon Silom and around town), but Robinson's (on Sukhumvit Soi 19, and at the Silom/Rama IV junction) and Big C (on Thanon Charoen Krung near Thanon Sathorn) are also good. Should you need to buy a crucial piece of **children's gear**, you'll find everything from bottles and slings to English-language kids' books and games in the children's department store Buy Buy Kiddo at the far southern end of Sukhumvit Soi 24 (opposite *Camp Davis* hotel), though all the department stores also have decent children's sections, and there's a branch of Mothercare in Emporium between Sukhumvit sois 22 and 24. The British chain of **pharmacies**, Boots the Chemist, has lots of branches across the city, including on Thanon Khao San, in the Siam Centre opposite Siam Square, in the Times Square complex between Sukhumvit sois 12 and 14, and in Emporium on Sukhumvit; Boots is the easiest place in the city to buy tampons.

The best place to buy anything to do with **mobile phones**, including rechargeable Thai SIM cards with a local phone number (see p.55), is the Mah Boon Krong (MBK) Shopping Centre at the Rama I/Phrayathai intersection; among scores of booths on the third floor here devoted to nothing but mobiles, WAS Shop (Ⓣ02 736 7372) is reliable, with English spoken.

Counterfeit culture

Faking it is big business in Bangkok, a city whose copyright regulations carry about as much weight as its anti-prostitution laws. Forged **designer clothes** and accessories are the biggest sellers; street vendors along Patpong, Silom, Sukhumvit and Khao San roads will flog you a whole range of inexpensive lookalikes, including Burberry shirts, Diesel jeans, Calvin Klein wallets, Prada bags and Hermes scarves.

Along Patpong, after dark, plausible would-be Rolex, Cartier and Tag **watches** from Hong Kong and Taiwan go for B1000 or less if you bargain hard – and are fairly reliable considering the price. If your budget won't stretch to a phoney Rolex Oyster, there's plenty of opportunities for lesser expenditure here and at the stalls concentrated on Thanon Khao San, where pirated **DVDs and music and video CDs** and **software and games CD-ROMs** are sold at a fraction of their normal price. Quality is usually fairly high but the choice is often less than brilliant, with a concentration on mainstream pop and rock albums. Finally, several stallholders along Thanon Khao San even make up passable international **student and press cards** as well as international driver's licences – though travel agencies and other organizations in Bangkok aren't easily fooled.

△ T-shirt stall, Thanon Khao San

Markets

For travellers, spectating, not shopping, is apt to be the main draw of Bangkok's neighbourhood **markets** – notably the bazaars of Chinatown (see p.145) and the blooms and scents of Pak Khlong Talat, the flower and vegetable market just west of Memorial Bridge (see p.147). The massive Chatuchak Weekend Market is an exception, being both a tourist attraction and a marvellous shopping experience (see p.166 for details). If you're planning on some serious market exploration, get hold of *Nancy Chandler's Map of Bangkok*, an enthusiastically annotated creation with special sections on the main areas of interest. With the chief exception of Chatuchak, most markets operate daily from dawn till early afternoon; early morning is often the best time to go to beat the heat and crowds. The Patpong **night market**, which also spills out onto Thanon Silom and Thanon Suriwong, is *the* place to stock up on fake designer goods, from pseudo-Rolex watches to Burberry shirts; the stalls open at about 5pm until late into the evening. A recent arrival on the evening shopping scene is the **Suan Lum Night Bazaar**, opposite Lumphini Park at the corner of Thanon Rama IV and Thanon Witthayu (Wireless Road) (daily 3pm–midnight; Ⓦwww.thainight bazaar.com), a huge development of more than three thousand booths, though nothing like that many were occupied by the time of writing so it's not a patch on Chatuchak. At the centre stands the Joe Louis Puppet Theatre (see p.186) and the attractive clothes, cloth and furnishings of the Mae Fah Luang shop (see p.191), with a hip Doi Tung coffee house attached. Other options for eating and drinking are uninspiring – your best bet is probably the open-air food court and beer garden, with a stage for nightly live music, by Thanon Witthayu.

Handicrafts, textiles and contemporary interior design

Samples of nearly all regionally produced **handicrafts** end up in Bangkok, so the selection is phenomenal. Many of the shopping plazas have at least one classy handicraft outlet, and competition keeps prices in the city at upcountry levels, with the main exception of household objects – particularly wickerware and tin bowls and basins – which get palmed off relatively expensively in Bangkok. Handicraft sellers in Banglamphu tend to tout a limited range compared to the shops downtown, but several places on Thanon Khao San sell reasonably priced triangular "axe" pillows (*mawn khwaan*) in traditional fabrics, which make fantastic souvenirs but are heavy to post home; some places sell unstuffed versions which are simple to mail home, but a pain to fill when you return. This is also a good place to pick up Thai shoulder bags woven to all specifications and designed with travellers' needs in mind. The cheapest outlet for traditional northern and northeastern textiles – including sarongs, axe pillows and farmers' shirts – is **Chatuchak Weekend Market** (see p.166), where you'll also able to nose out some interesting handicrafts.

Noted for its thickness and sheen, **Thai silk** became internationally recognized only about fifty years ago after the efforts of American Jim Thompson (see box on p.158). Much of it comes from the northeast, but you'll find a good range of outlets in the capital. Prices start at about B350 per metre for two-ply silk (suitable for thin shirts and skirts), or B500 for four-ply (for suits).

Bangkok is rapidly establishing a reputation for its **contemporary interior design**, fusing minimalist Western ideals with traditional Thai and other Asian elements. The best places to sample this are the fourth floor of the Siam Discovery Centre on Thanon Rama I and, more notably, the third floor of the Gaysorn Plaza on Thanon Ploenchit, where Cocoon, with its thoroughly modern axe pillows and funky chopsticks, occupies the cutting edge. Look out here also for bronze bowls decorated with Buddha's curls at Lamont, and the more traditional Triphum, which sells affordable, hand-painted reproductions of temple mural paintings and Buddhist manuscripts from Burma.

Banglamphu

Taekee Taekon 118 Thanon Phra Athit. Tasteful assortment of traditional textiles and scarves, plus a good selection of Thai art cards, black-and-white photocards and Nancy Chandler greetings cards.

Downtown: around Siam Square and Thanon Ploenchit

Come Thai 2nd Floor, Amarin Plaza, Thanon Ploenchit. Currently has no English sign, but easily spotted by its carved wooden doorframe. Impressive range of unusual handwoven silk and cotton fabrics, much of it made up into traditional-style clothes such as Chinese mandarin shirts and short fitted jackets.
Earthasia 1045 Thanon Ploenchit (opposite Soi Ruam Rudee). Contemporary basketware, furniture and beautiful lotus-bud lamps in vivid colours.
The Legend 3rd Floor, Amarin Plaza, Thanon Ploenchit, and 3rd Floor, Thaniya Plaza, Thanon Silom. Stocks a small selection of well-made Thai handicrafts, from wood and wickerware to fabrics and ceramics – including quirky items such as a celadon nativity scene – at reasonable prices.
Mae Fah Luang 4th Floor, Siam Discovery Centre, Thanon Rama I, and Suan Lum Night Bazaar, Thanon Rama IV ⓦwww.doitung.org. Part of the late Princess Mother's development project based at Doi Tung, selling very attractive fabrics (mostly cotton and linen) in warm colours, either in bolts or made up into clothes, cushion covers, rugs and so on.
Narayana (or Narai) Phand 127 Thanon Rajdamri (ⓦwww.naraiphand.com). This souvenir centre was set up as a joint venture with the Ministry of Industry to ensure the preservation of traditional crafts and to maintain standards of quality, and makes a reasonable one-stop shop for last-minute presents, though its layout is unappealing. It offers a huge assortment of very reasonably priced goods from all over the country, including silk and cotton, *khon* masks and shadow puppets, musical instruments and kites, *bencharong*, nielloware and celadon, woodcarving and hill-tribe crafts.
Panta 4th Floor, Siam Discovery Centre. Contemporary design store which stands out for its experimental furniture, including way-out-there woven items and everything from cushions to bags covered in dried water-hyacinth stalks.
Treasure Siam 3rd Floor, Siam Centre, Thanon Rama I. A good place to buy that chunky, elegant Thai-style cutlery you may have been eating your dinner with in Bangkok's posher restaurants, with both traditional and contemporary designs.

Downtown: south of Thanon Rama IV

Jim Thompson's Thai Silk Company Main shop at 9 Thanon Suriwong (including a branch of their very good café – see p.177), plus branches in Isetan in the Central World Plaza (formerly World Trade Center), Central Chidlom department store on Thanon Ploenchit, at Emporium on Thanon Sukhumvit, at the Jim Thompson House Museum, and at many hotels around the city, ⓦwww.jimthompson.com. A good place to start looking for traditional Thai fabric, or at least to get an idea of what's out there. Stocks silk and cotton by the yard and ready-made items from dresses to cushion covers, which are well designed and of good quality, but pricey. They also have a home furnishings section and a good tailoring service. A couple of hundred metres along Thanon Suriwong from the main branch, at no. 149/4–6, the Jim Thompson Factory Sales Outlet sells remnant home-furnishing fabrics and accessories at knock-down prices.
Silom Village 286/1 Thanon Silom. A complex of low-rise buildings that attempts to create a relaxing, upcountry atmosphere as a backdrop for its pricey fabrics and Chinese antiques and occasionally unusual souvenirs, such as woven rattan goods and grainy *sa* paper made from mulberry bark.
Tamnan Mingmuang 3rd Floor, Thaniya Plaza, Soi Thaniya, east end of Thanon Silom. Subsidiary of The Legend opposite (see above) which concentrates on basketry from all over the country. Among the unusual items on offer are trays and boxes for tobacco and betel nut made from *yan lipao* (intricately woven fern vines), and bambooware sticky rice containers, baskets and lampshades. The Legend's other subsidiary, the adjacent Eros, sells rather tacky erotic craft items such as naked chess sets.

Thanon Sukhumvit

Chiiori Between sois 3/1 and 5. Produces and sells a stunning selection of traditional five-coloured *bencharong* chinaware, all handmade by a couple of families in the Damnoen Saduak area, plus a fine array of modern celadon crafted in Chiang Mai.

Rasi Sayam A 10min hike down Soi 23, opposite *Le Dalat Vietnamese* restaurant. Very classy handicraft shop, specializing in eclectic and fairly pricey decorative and folk arts such as tiny betel-nut sets woven from *lipao* fern, sticky rice lunch baskets, coconut wood bowls and *mut mee* textiles. Mon–Sat 9am–5.30pm.

Thai Celadon Soi 16 (Thanon Ratchadapisek). Classic celadon stoneware made without commercial dyes or clays and glazed with the archetypal blues and greens that were invented by the Chinese to emulate the colour of precious jade. Mainly dinner sets, vases and lamps, plus some figurines.

Tailored clothes

Inexpensive **tailoring shops** crowd Silom, Sukhumvit and Khao San roads, but the best single area to head for is the short stretch of Thanon Charoen Krung between the GPO and Thanon Silom, close by the Chao Phraya express boat stops at Tha Oriental and Tha Wat Muang Kae, or ten minutes' walk from Saphan Taksin Skytrain station. It's generally best to avoid tailors in tourist areas such as Thanon Khao San, shopping malls and Thanon Sukhumvit's Soi Nana and Soi 11, although if you're lucky it's still possible to come up trumps here: one that stands apart is Banglamphu's well-regarded Chang Torn, located at 95 Thanon Tanao (ⓣ02 282 9390). All the outlets listed below are recommended. See the box below for advice on having clothes tailor-made.

Having clothes tailor-made

Bangkok can be an excellent place to get tailor-made suits, dresses, shirts and trousers at a fraction of the price you'd pay in the West. Tailors here can copy a sample brought from home and will also work from any photographs you can provide; most also carry a good selection of catalogues. The bad news is that many tourist-oriented tailors aren't terribly good, often attempting to get away with poor work and shoddy materials, so lots of visitors end up wasting their time and money. However, with a little effort and thought, both men and women can get some fantastic clothes made to measure.

Choosing a tailor can be tricky, and unless you're particularly knowledgeable about material, shopping around won't necessarily tell you much. However, don't make a decision wholly on prices quoted – picking a tailor simply because they're the cheapest usually leads to poor work, and cheap suits don't last. Special deals offering two suits, two shirts, two ties and a kimono for US$99 should be left well alone. Above all, ignore recommendations by anyone with a vested interest in bringing your custom to a particular shop.

Prices vary widely depending on material and the tailor's skill. As a very rough guide, for labour alone expect to pay B5000–6000 for a two-piece suit, though some tailors will charge rather more. For middling **material**, expect to pay about the same again, or anything up to four times as much for top-class cloth. With the exception of silk, local materials are frequently of poor quality and for suits in particular you're far better off using English or Italian cloth. Most tailors stock both imported and local fabrics, but bringing your own from home can work out significantly cheaper.

Give yourself as much **time** as possible. For suits, insist on two fittings. Most good tailors require around three days for a suit (some require ten days or more), although a few have enough staff to produce good work in a day or two. The more **detail** you can give the tailor the better. As well as deciding on the obvious features such as single- or double-breasted and number of buttons, think about the width of lapels, style of trousers, whether you want the jacket with vents or not, and so forth. Specifying factors like this will make all the difference to whether you're happy with your suit, so it's worth discussing them with the tailor; a good tailor should be able to give good advice. Finally, don't be afraid to be an awkward customer until you're completely happy with the finished product – after all, the whole point of getting clothes tailor-made is to get exactly what you want.

For cheap and reasonable shirt and dress material other than silk go for a browse around **Pahurat** market (see p.147), though the suit materials are mostly poor, and best avoided.

A Song Tailor 8 Trok Chartered Bank, off Thanon Charoen Krung, near the *Oriental Hotel* ⓣ02 630 9708, ⓔasongtailor@yahoo.com. Friendly, helpful and a good first port of call if you're on a budget.

Ah Song Tailor 1203 Thanon Charoen Krung (opposite Soi 36) ⓣ02 233 7574, ⓔah_song_1936@hotmail.com. Meticulous tailor who takes pride in his work. Men's only.

Golden Wool 1340–1342 Thanon Charoen Krung ⓣ02 233 0149, ⓔgoldenwool@hotmail.com; and World Group 1302–1304 Thanon Charoen Krung, ⓣ02 234 1527, ⓔworldgroupbkk@hotmail.com. Part of the same company, they can turn around decent work in a couple of days. One of the tailors here has made suits for the king.

Marco Tailor Soi 7, Siam Square ⓣ02 252 0689 Long-established tailor with a good reputation, though not cheap by Bangkok standards; they require two weeks for a suit. Men's only.

Marzotto Tailor 3 Soi Shangri-la Hotel, Thanon Charoen Krung ⓣ02 233 2880, ⓔtanonchaip@hotmail.com. Friendly business which makes everything from trousers to wedding outfits.

Fashions

Thanon Khao San is lined with stalls selling low-priced **fashions**: the tie-dyed vests, baggy cotton fisherman's trousers and embroidered blouses are all aimed at backpackers, but they're supplemented by cheap contemporary fashions that appeal to urban Thai trendies as well. The stalls of Banglamphu Market, near the post office on Soi Sibsam Hang and along nearby Trok Kraisi, have the best range of inexpensive Thai fashions in this area. For the best and latest trends, however, check out the shops in the Siam Centre and the Siam Discovery Centre, both across from Siam Square, and the high-fashion outlets at the upmarket Emporium on Sukhumvit (it may also be worth scoping Amarin Plaza, where at the time of writing a new "Bangkok Fashion Centre", showcasing the work of Thai clothes designers, was on the cards; and look out for Siam Paragon, a huge new mall due to open in 2005 next to the Siam Centre). Prices at most fashion outlets are generally competitive but not breathtakingly lower than in the West; larger sizes can be hard to find. **Shoes** and **leather goods** are good buys in Bangkok, being generally hand-made from high-quality leather and quite a bargain: check out branches of the stylish, Italian-influenced Ragazze in the Silom Complex, Thanon Silom, at Isetan in the Central World Plaza or the MBK Shopping Centre (both Thanon Rama I), or Amarin Plaza, Thanon Ploenchit.

Emporium Thanon Sukhumvit, between sois 22 and 24. Enormous and rather glamorous shopping plaza, with a good range of fashion outlets, from exclusive designer wear to trendy high-street gear. Brand name outlets include Versace, Prada, DKNY, Chanel and Louis Vuitton.

Mah Boon Krong (MBK) At the Rama I/Phrayathai intersection. Labyrinthine shopping centre which houses hundreds of small, mostly fairly inexpensive outlets, including plenty of high-street fashion shops.

Peninsula Plaza Thanon Rajdamri. Considered the most upmarket shopping plaza in the city, so come here for genuine Versace and the like.

Siam Centre Thanon Rama I, across the road from Siam Square. Particularly good for trendy local labels as well as international high-street chains; Mambo, Greyhound and Soda Pop are typical outlets.

Siam Discovery Centre Thanon Rama I, across the road from Siam Square. Flash designer gear, including plenty of name brands like DKNY and Armani.

Siam Square Worth poking around the alleys here, especially near what's styled as the area's "Centerpoint" between sois 3 and 4. All manner of inexpensive boutiques, some little more than booths, sell colourful street gear to the capital's fashionable students and teenagers.

Books

English-language **bookstores** in Bangkok are always well stocked with everything to do with Thailand, and most carry fiction classics and popular paperbacks as well. The capital's few **second-hand** bookstores are surprisingly poor value, but you might turn up something worthwhile – or earn a few baht by selling your own cast-offs – in the shops and stalls along Thanon Khao San.

Aporia Thanon Tanao, Banglamphu. Run by knowledgeable book-loving staff, this is one of Banglamphu's main outlets for new books and keeps a good stock of titles on Thai and Southeast Asian culture, a decent selection of travelogues, plus some English-language fiction. Also sells second-hand books.

Asia Books Branches on Thanon Sukhumvit between sois 15 and 19, in Landmark Plaza between sois 4 and 6, in Times Square between sois 12 and 14, and in Emporium between sois 22 and 24; in Peninsula Plaza and in the Central World Plaza (formerly World Trade Center) both on Thanon Rajdamri; in Siam Discovery Centre on Thanon Rama I; and in Thaniya Plaza near Patpong off Thanon Silom. English-language bookstore that's especially recommended for its books on Asia – everything from guidebooks to cookery books, novels to art (the Sukhumvit 15–19 branch has the very best Asian selection). Also stocks bestselling novels and coffee-table books.

Bookazine Branches on Thanon Silom in the CP Tower (Patpong) and in the Silom Complex; in Siam Square; in the Amarin Plaza on Thanon Ploenchit; in All Seasons Place on Thanon Witthayu; and at the mouth of Sukhumvit Soi 5. Alongside a decent selection of English-language books about Asia and novels, these shops stock a huge range of foreign newspapers and magazines.

Books Kinokuniya 3rd Floor, Emporium Shopping Centre, between sois 22 and 24 on Thanon Sukhumvit, with a branch in Isetan in the Central World Plaza (formerly World Trade Center). Huge English-language bookstore with a broad range of books ranging from bestsellers to travel literature and from classics to sci-fi; not so hot on books about Asia though.

Rim Khob Fa Bookshop Democracy Monument roundabout, Rajdamnoen Klang, Banglamphu. Useful outlet for the more obscure and esoteric English-language books on Thailand and Southeast Asia, as well as mainstream titles on Thai culture.

Robinson's Department Store at the mouth of Sukhumvit Soi 19. The third-floor book department is worth a mention for its decent range of Thai maps and road atlases, including the full complement of 1:300 000 province maps published by PN Map Centre. Also keeps a small stock of English-language fiction and non-fiction, plus books about Asia.

Shaman Books Two branches on Thanon Khao San, Banglamphu. The best-stocked and most efficient second-hand bookshop in the city, where all books are displayed alphabetically as well as being logged on the computer – which means you can locate your choice in seconds. Lots of books on Asia (travel, fiction, politics and history) as well as a decent range of novels and general interest books. Don't expect bargains though.

Siam Society Bookshop 131 Sukhumvit Soi 21, inside the Ban Kamthieng compound. Extensive collection of esoteric and academic books about Thailand, including many ethnology studies published by White Lotus and by the Siam Society itself. Closed Sun & Mon.

Silpakorn Book Centre Corner of Na Phra Lan and Na Phra That roads. Very handily placed opposite the entrance to the Grand Palace, this smart little bookshop keeps a good selection of English-language titles, especially on Thailand and Southeast Asia.

Ton's Bookseller 327/5 Thanon Ram Bhuttri, Banglamphu. One of Banglamphu's best-stocked outlets for books about Thailand and Southeast Asia; also sells the best Bangkok map, *Bangkok Guide's Bus Routes and Map*, and some English-language fiction.

Jewellery, gems and other rare stones

Bangkok boasts the country's best **gem and jewellery** shops, and some of the finest lapidaries in the world, making this *the* place to buy cut and uncut stones such as rubies, blue sapphires and diamonds. However, countless gem-buying tourists get badly **ripped off**, so be extremely wary. Never buy anything through a tout or from any shop recommended by a government official/student/businessperson/tuk-tuk driver who just happens to engage you in conversation on the street, and note that there are no government jewellery shops despite any information you may be given to the contrary. Always check that the shop is a member of the **Thai Gem and Jewelry Traders Association** by calling the association or visiting their website (Ⓣ02 630 1390–7, Ⓦwww.thaigemjewelry.or.th). To be doubly sure, you may want to seek out shops that also belong to the TGJTA's **Jewel Fest Club** (Ⓦwww.jewelfest.com), which guarantees quality and will offer refunds; see their website for a directory of members. For independent professional advice or precious stones certification, contact the Asian Institute of Gemological Sciences, located on the sixth floor of the Jewelry Trade Center Building, 919/1 Thanon Silom (Ⓣ02 267 4325–7, Ⓦwww.aigsthailand.com), which also runs reputable **courses**, such as a five-day (15hr) introduction to gemstones (B7500) and one day on rubies and sapphires (B1500). A common **scam** is to charge a lot more than what the gem is worth based on its carat weight. Get it tested on the spot, ask for a written guarantee and receipt. Don't even consider **buying gems in bulk** to sell at a supposedly vast profit elsewhere: many a gullible traveller has invested thousands of dollars on a handful of worthless multi-coloured stones, believing the vendor's reassurance that the goods will fetch a hundred times more when resold at home. Gem scams are so common in Bangkok that TAT has published a brochure about it and there are several websites on the subject, including the very informative Ⓦwww.2bangkok.com/2bangkok/Scams/Sapphire.shtml, which describes the typical scam in detail and advises on what to do if you get done. Most victims get no recompense at all, but you have more chance of doing so if you contact the website's recommended authorities while still in Thailand. See p.60 for more on common scams in Thailand.

The most exclusive of the reputable **gem outlets** are scattered along Thanon Silom, but many tourists prefer to buy from hotel shops, like Kim's inside the *Oriental*, where reliability is assured. Other recommended outlets include Johnny's Gems at 199 Thanon Fuang Nakhon, near Wat Rajabophit in Ratanakosin; and Merlin et Delauney at 1 Soi Pradit, off Thanon Suriwong. Thongtavee, Floor 2, River City, an outlet of a famous Burmese **jade** factory in Mae Sai in northern Thailand, sells beautiful jade jewellery, as well as carved Buddha statues, chopsticks and the like. For cheap and cheerful silver earrings, bracelets and necklaces, you can't beat the traveller-orientated jewellery shops along Thanon Khao San in Banglamphu.

Among the more esoteric of Bangkok's outlets is the **Rare Stone Museum** at 1048–1054 Thanon Charoen Krung (Ⓣ02 236 5655, Ⓦwww.rarestonemuseum.com), near Soi 26 and the GPO. Here, for B50–100, you can buy tektites, pieces of glassy rock found in Thai fields and thought to be the 750,000-year-old products of volcanic activity on the moon, as well as fossilized plants and shells, 60- to 200-million-year-old petrified dinosaur droppings (properly known as coprolite) unearthed in Thailand's Isaan region, and some fantastic rock formations. Of these last-mentioned, the best, resembling anything from owls and polar bears to grander scenes such as a dog contemplating the moon, are kept for display in the adjoining museum (daily 10am–5.30pm; B100).

Antiques and paintings

Bangkok is the entrepôt for the finest Thai, Burmese and Cambodian **antiques**, but the market has long been sewn up, so don't expect to happen upon any undiscovered treasure. Even experts admit that they sometimes find it hard to tell real antiques from fakes, so the best policy is just to buy on the grounds of attractiveness. The River City shopping complex, off Thanon Charoen Krung

(New Road), devotes its third and fourth floors to a bewildering array of pricey treasures, as well as holding an auction on the first Saturday of every month (viewing during the preceding week). Worth singling out here are Old Maps and Prints on the fourth floor (Ⓦwww.classicmaps.com), which has some lovely old prints of Thailand and Asia from about B2000 up, as well as rare books and maps; and Ingon on the third floor, which specializes in small Chinese pieces made of jade and other precious stones, such as snuff boxes, jewellery, statuettes and amulets. The other main area for antiques is the section of Charoen Krung that runs between the GPO and the bottom of Thanon Silom, and the stretch of Silom running east from here up to and including the multi-storey Silom Galleria. Here you'll find a good selection of largely reputable individual businesses specializing in woodcarvings, ceramics, bronze statues and stone sculptures culled from all parts of Thailand and neighbouring countries as well. Remember that most antiques require an export permit (see p.23).

Street-corner stalls all over the city sell poor-quality mass-produced traditional Thai **paintings**, but for a huge selection of better-quality Thai art, visit Sombat Permpoon Gallery on Sukhumvit Soi 1, which carries thousands of canvases, framed and unframed, spanning the range from classical Ayutthayan-era-style village scenes to twenty-first-century abstracts. The gallery does have works by famous Thai artists like Thawan Duchanee, but prices for the more affordable works by less well-known painters start at B1500.

Package tours and tour operators

If your time is short and you want to pack as much as you can into your stay, you might consider booking a package tour once you're in Thailand; some recommended tour operators are listed below. A number of tour operators offer inexpensive packages, with deals that range from overnight trips to tailor-made tours of a week or more. All of them include transport and budget accommodation, and many include food as well; prices start at around B1000 for two-day packages. Some of the most popular packages include one or two nights in the Kanchanaburi and Sangkhlaburi area (for trekking, river-rafting and elephant-riding); three to five nights in Umphang (trekking); two or three nights in Chiang Rai, Chiang Mai or Pai (trekking, river-rafting and elephant-riding); and two to four nights in Khao Sok national park (trekking, river-rafting and elephant-riding). There are also a number of specialist activity tours worth investigating, including rock-climbing, kayaking, diving and cycling.

Many of the same tour operators also offer **day-trips** from Bangkok to outlying destinations. These tend to be quite good value as they combine several places that would otherwise take a couple of days to see on your own. The most popular itinerary takes in Damnoen Saduak, Nakhon Pathom and Kanchanaburi.

Bike and Travel 802/756 River Park, Mu 12, Thanon Phaholyothin Ⓣ02 990 0274, Ⓦwww.cyclingthailand.com. Joint and private cycling trips to different parts of Thailand, with mountain bikes and support vehicle provided.

Educational Travel Centre (ETC) *Royal Hotel*, Room 318, 2 Thanon Rajdamnoen Klang, Banglamphu Ⓣ02 224 0043, Ⓦwww.etc.co.th, also at 180 Thanon Khao San, Banglamphu Ⓣ02 282 2958 and 5/3 Soi Ngam Duphli Ⓣ02 286 9424. Highlights include: two- and three-day cruises on a converted traditional rice barge up the Chao Phraya River between Bangkok and Ayutthaya; five-day Khao Sok safaris; six-day treks in the Chiang Mai region.

Intrepid *Vieng Thai Hotel*, 3rd Floor, Thanon Ram Bhuttri, Banglamphu Ⓣ02 629 0127, Ⓦwww.intrepidtravel.com. Very well-regarded adventure tour operator that's

Moving on from Bangkok

Bangkok is the terminus of all major highways and rail lines, and **public transport** between the capital and the provinces is inexpensive and plentiful, if not particularly speedy. Bangkok is also the best place to make arrangements for onward travel from Thailand – the city's travel agents can offer some good flight deals and all the major Asian embassies are here, so getting the appropriate **visas** should be no problem.

Travel within Thailand

Having to change trains or buses in Bangkok might sound a tiresome way to travel the country, but it has its advantages – breaking up what would otherwise be an unbearably long trip, and giving the chance to confirm plane tickets and stock up on supplies not so widely available elsewhere. It also means that you can store unwanted clothes in a guest house or hotel.

By train

Nearly all trains depart from **Hualamphong Station**, exceptions being the twice-daily service to Nakhon Pathom and Kanchanaburi, a couple of the Hua Hin trains, which leave from **Thonburi Station** (sometimes still referred to by

based in Australia (see p.17) and mainly caters for travellers booking from abroad, but will accept bookings at its Bangkok office. Known for choosing unusual routes and characterful travellers'-style accommodation. Their most popular package is the 16-day Northern Thailand tour, which includes a four-day trek.

Lost Horizons Ban Chaophraya Rm 1907, Somded Chaophraya Soi 17, Thonburi ⓣ02 860 3936, ⓦlosthorizonsasia.com. Manages and owns several mid-priced eco-resorts in secluded spots in southern Thailand, and arranges lots of different activity packages, including yoga holidays and turtle-conservation projects, plus cycling, kayaking, trekking etc. Destinations include Khao Sok, the River Kwai, Mae Hong Son and southern beaches.

Nature Trails 49 Soi 64, Thanon Ramkhamhaeng, ⓣ02 735 0644, ⓦwww.naturetrailsthailand.com. Specialist bird-watching tours, from half a day to four days, in Thailand's national parks.

Open World 89/14–15 Soi 54/1, Thanon Phaholyothin ⓣ02 974 3866–7, ⓦwww.openworldthailand.com. Award-winning operator offering a diverse programme of trips, notably bird-watching expeditions, cultural tours and Buddhism and meditation trips.

Tamarind Tours *Tantawan Place Hotel*, 119/5–10 Thanon Suriwong ⓣ02 238 3227, ⓦwww.tamarindtours.com. Imaginative and well-regarded (if pricey) tours to Chiang Mai, Chiang Rai, Sukhothai and southern beaches. Also runs a gay travel service, Utopia Tours, ⓦwww.utopia-tours.com.

Wild Planet and Planet Scuba Across from Thanon Khao San on Thanon Chakrabongse, Banglamphu ⓣ02 629 0977; and Floor 2, Terminal Centre, Sukhumvit Soi 24, ⓣ02 261 4412 ⓦwww.thewildplanet.com. Active adventure packages including trail-biking, trekking, kayaking and mountain-biking, mostly in the hills of northern Thailand, plus scuba-diving in all the major spots.

its former name, **Bangkok Noi Station**), across the river from Banglamphu in Thonburi, about an 850-metre walk west of the express-boat stop; and the hourly service to Samut Sakhon (aka Mahachai), for connections to Samut Songkhram, that leaves from **Wongwian Yai Station**, south of the Thanon Pracha Thipok/Thanon Lat Ya intersection, also in Thonburi. All north- and northeast-bound trains from Hualamphong make a stop at the **Don Muang** Airport station. The 24-hour "Information" booth at Hualamphong Station keeps English-language timetables, or you can try phoning the Train Information Hotline on ⓣ1690; the State Railway of Thailand website (ⓦwww.railway.co.th) carries a fare chart for major destinations. For a guide to destinations and journey times from Bangkok, see "Travel Details" on p.205. For details on city transport to and from Hualamphong, left-luggage facilities at the station, and a warning about con-artists operating at the station, see the section on "Arriving in Bangkok" on p.96.

Tickets for overnight trains and other busy routes should be booked at least a day in advance (or at least a week in advance for travel on national holidays), and are best bought from Hualamphong. During normal office hours you can buy rail tickets from the clearly signed State Railway **advance booking office** at the back of the station concourse (daily 8.30am–4pm); at other times you can buy them from ticket counter #2, which is labelled "foreign tourist priority" (daily 5–8.30am & 4–10pm); counters #1 and #2 deal with ticket refunds and alterations. Train tickets can also be bought through almost any travel agent and through some hotels and guest houses for a booking fee of about B50. In addition to all types of normal rail ticket, the Advance Booking Office sells **joint rail and boat or rail and bus tickets** to Ko Samui, Ko Pha Ngan, Ko Tao, Krabi and Ko Phi Phi. Sample prices include B650 to Surat Thani (second-class air-con sleeper), plus B150 for bus and boat connections to Ko Samui or B200 for bus connections to Krabi.

By bus

Bangkok's three main bus terminals are distributed around the outskirts of town. Leave plenty of time to get to the bus terminals, especially if setting off from Banglamphu, from where you should allow at least an hour and a half (outside rush hour) to get to the Eastern Bus Terminal, and a good hour to get to the Northern or Southern terminals. Seats on the most popular long-distance air-con bus services (such as to Chaing Mai, Krabi, Phuket and Surat Thani) should be **reserved** ahead of time either at the relevant bus station or through hotels and guest houses.

The **Northern Bus Terminal**, or **Sathaanii Mo Chit** (departure info for both air-con and regular services on ⓣ02 936 2852–66), is the departure point for all buses to northern and northeastern towns, including Chiang Mai, Chiang Rai, Nong Khai and Pak Chong (for Khao Yai), and for most destinations in the central plains, including Ayutthaya, Sukhothai and Mae Sot (but excluding Nakhon Pathom and Kanchanaburi, services to which run from the Southern Bus Terminal). Mo Chit also runs a few buses to the east-coast destinations of Pattaya, Chanthaburi and Trat: though there are more regular services to the east coast from the Eastern Bus Terminal, journey times from Mo Chit are usually slightly shorter. The Northern Bus Terminal is on Thanon Kamphaeng Phet 2, near Chatuchak Weekend Market in the far north of the city; Skytrain's Mo Chit station and Kampaeng Phet subway station are within a short motorbike taxi or tuk-tuk ride, or take a city bus direct to the bus terminal: air-con #503/#3, #512/#12 and #157 run from Banglamphu and non-air-con #159 runs from the Southern Bus Terminal; see box on p.100 for bus route details.

The **Eastern Bus Terminal**, or **Sathaanii Ekamai** (air-con services ⓣ02 391 2504; regular services ⓣ02 391 8097), between Sukhumvit sois 40 and 42, serves east-coast destinations such as Pattaya, Ban Phe (for Ko Samet) and Trat (for Ko Chang). The Skytrain stops right by the bus terminal at Ekamai Station, as do city buses #511/#11 (from Banglamphu) and #59 (from the Northern Bus Terminal); see box on p.100 for bus route details. Alternatively you can take the Khlong Sen Seb boat service from the Golden Mount (see p.103) to Tha Ekamai (Sukhumvit Soi 63) and then hop into a taxi down Soi 63 to the bus terminal. There's a **left-luggage** booth at Ekamai (daily 7am–8pm; B30/day), but *Sawasdee Sukhumvit Inn* on Soi 57, less than fifteen minutes' walk from Ekamai or one stop on the Skytrain, offers a much cheaper service to its guests at B10 per day; see p.120 for details. If you find yourself at Ekamai with nothing to do for a few hours, you can sip coffee and check emails at the plush *Ban Rie Coffee* experience across the road (see p.178), or there's the Major Cineplex a few minutes' walk west, between sois 61 and 63.

The **Southern Bus Terminal**, or **Sathaanii Sai Tai Mai** (air-con services ⓣ02 435 1199; regular services ⓣ02 434 5537), is at the junction of Thanon Borom Ratchonni and the Nakhon Chaisri Highway, west of the Chao Phraya River in Thonburi. It handles departures to all points south of the capital, including Hua Hin, Chumphon (for Ko Tao), Surat Thani (for Ko Samui and Ko Pha Ngan), Phuket and Krabi (for Ko Phi Phi and Ko Lanta), as well as departures for destinations west of Bangkok, such as Nakhon Pathom and Kanchanaburi. Regular and air-con buses leave from different sections of the Southern Bus Terminal, and anyone there will be able to point you in the right direction for your bus. To get here, take city bus #507/#7 (air-con) from Banglamphu or Hualamphong Station, air-con #511/#11 from Banglamphu or Thanon Sukhumvit, or non-air-con #159 from the Northern Bus Terminal (see box on p.100 for bus route details).

Budget transport

Many Bangkok tour operators offer **budget transport** to major tourist destinations such as Chiang Mai, Surat Thani, Krabi, Ko Samet and Ko Chang. In many cases this works out as cheap if not cheaper than the equivalent fare on a public air-con bus and, as most of the budget transport deals leave from the Thanon Khao San area in Banglamphu, they're often more convenient. The main drawbacks, however, are the **lack of comfort** and **poor safety**: some travellers end up wishing they'd taken a public air-con bus instead (see below, and Basics p.36 for more info). The best advice is to consult other travellers before booking with budget transport operators, and to keep your valuables with you at all time. **Tour operators** open up and go bust all the time, particularly in the Thanon Khao San area, so ask around for recommendations; never hand over any money until you see the ticket.

For the shorter trips, for example to **Ko Samet** (around B230 excluding boat), **Laem Ngop**, departure point for Ko Chang (B250–300), and **Kanchanaburi** (B100), transport operators always take passengers in minibuses which, if crowded, can be unbearably cramped, and often have insufficient air-conditioning. Drivers usually go as fast as possible, which some travellers find scary. For destinations further afield, such as **Chiang Mai** (11hr) and **Surat Thani** (11hr), travellers are usually taken by larger tour bus; again these tend to be clapped-out old things (despite invariably being advertised as VIP-style) and drivers on these journeys have an even worse safety record. **Security** on these buses is also a serious problem, and because they're run by private companies there is no insurance against loss or theft of baggage: don't keep anything of value in luggage that's stored out of sight, even if it's padlocked. In addition, passengers often find themselves dumped on the outskirts of their destination city, at the mercy of unscrupulous touts. If you are planning a journey to Chiang Mai or Surat Thani, consider taking the train instead – the extra comfort and peace of mind are well worth the extra baht – or at the least, opt for a government bus from the relevant terminal (see above).

If you're heading for an **island** (such as **Ko Samui**, **Ko Tao** or **Ko Chang**), your bus should get you to the ferry port in time to catch the boat, though there have been complaints from travellers that this does not always happen; check whether your bus ticket covers the ferry ride. Sample prices for joint bus and boat tickets include B370 for Ko Samui, B420 for Ko Pha Ngan, B300 for Ko Tao and B470 for Ko Phi Phi.

By air

During high season, **flights** on the most popular domestic routes (to Chiang Mai, Ko Samui, Phuket and Krabi) should be booked as far in advance as possible. Most domestic airlines offer online booking services, and tickets can also be bought at the airport if available; the **domestic departure tax** is included in the price of the ticket. Thai Airways is the main domestic carrier and flies to over twenty major towns and cities; between them, the other main domestic carriers – Bangkok Airways, Air Andaman, PB Air and Phuket Airlines – currently cover another twenty minor routes out of the capital (see Basics p.38 for details), though schedules are often erratic on the least popular routings. All domestic flights leave from Don Muang Airport (see p.94); for advice on how to get to the airport see the box below; for details on hotels within ten minutes' drive of the airport see p.95; and for airline phone numbers and websites see "Listings", p.202.

Getting to Don Muang Airport

The fastest, most expensive way of getting to the airport is by **metered taxi,** which can cost anything from B120 to B350 (plus B70 in expressway tolls), depending on where you are and how bad the traffic is. If you leave the downtown areas before 7am you can get to the airport in half an hour, but at other times you should set off at least an hour before you have to check in. A cheaper and (during rush hour) faster option from downtown areas is to take the **Skytrain** or **subway** to Mo Chit/Chatuchak Park in the north of the city and pick up a taxi for the last few kilometres to the airport from there.

Every guest house and travel agent in Banglamphu, and many hotels elsewhere in the city, can book you onto one of the **private minibuses** to the airport. Those running from Banglamphu depart approximately every hour, day and night, and cost B60–80; though you'll get picked up from your accommodation, you should book yourself onto a minibus that leaves at least an hour and a half before check-in commences as it can take up to 45 minutes to pick up all passengers, after which there's the traffic to contend with.

The **airport bus services** that are so useful when arriving at Don Muang are less reliable on the outward journey, mainly because the traffic often makes it impossible for them to stick to their half-hourly schedules; at B100 it's not a risk worth taking.

As with in-bound **trains**, schedules for trains from Hualamphong to Don Muang are not helpfully spread throughout the day (ask at the station for the timetable), but the service is cheap and fast. A number of **city buses** run from the city to the airport and are detailed in the box on p.100; they are slow and crowded however.

SUVARNABHUMI airport status?

Leaving Thailand

Whether you're moving on within Asia or just trying to get home, Bangkok is one of the best places in the world to buy **low-priced international air tickets**, and there are hundreds of travel agents to buy them from. You'll get the rock-bottom deals from agents who don't belong to the **Association of Thai Travel Agents** (ATTA), but as with their Western counterparts many of these are transient and not altogether trustworthy. Thanon Khao San is a notorious centre for such dodgy operations, some of which have been known to flee with travellers' money overnight: if you buy from a non-ATTA outlet it's a good idea to ring the airline and check your reservation yourself – don't hand over any money until you've done that and been given the ticket. The slightly more expensive ATTA agencies still work out good value by international standards: to check if an agency is affiliated either get hold of the TAT list, ask for proof of membership or contact the ATTA office (Ⓣ02 237 6046–8, Ⓦwww.atta.or.th). Some tried and tested travel agents are given in "Listings", p.205.

All major **airline offices** are in downtown Bangkok. There's no advantage in buying tickets directly from the airlines – their phone numbers are given in "Listings", p.202, so you can confirm reservations or change dates.

The **international departure tax** on all foreigners leaving Thailand by air is B500; buy your voucher near the check-in desks at the airport. For advice on getting to the airport see the box on p.200; for a list of accommodation within ten minutes' drive of the airport, see p.95.

Getting to other Asian countries

Bangkok is the regional hub for **flights to Indochina**, and many long-haul flights from Europe to Indochina involve a change of plane in Bangkok. However, if you plan to travel around Thailand before moving on to Laos, Cambodia, China or Singapore, you may not have to return Bangkok as there are an increasing number of interesting inter-Asia flights from Thailand's **regional airports**, including from Chiang Mai to Vientiane, Rangoon, Jinghong, Xian, KL and Singapore; from Sukhothai to Louang Phabang; from Phuket to Siem Reap, KL and Singapore; from Hat Yai to Malaysia and Singapore; and from Ko Samui to Singapore; for more on all these check the relevant accounts in the guide.

Most travellers who choose to make their way **overland from Thailand** to Laos, Cambodia or Malaysia do so slowly, stopping at various places in Thailand en route, but it is possible to make these overland trips in one fell swoop from Bangkok, though in most cases you'll need to spend a night somewhere on the way. To get **from Bangkok to Laos**, you have to take a train or bus to the border at Chiang Khong (see p.415), Nong Khai (see p.540), Nakhon Phanom (see p.549), Mukdahan (see p.552) or Chong Mek (see p.517). For transport **to Cambodia**, you'll need to begin by either taking a bus from Bangkok to Trat (see p.452); a train or bus from Bangkok to Aranyaprathet (see p.451); or a bus or train to Surin (see p.498). The easiest way of travelling from Bangkok **to Malaysia** is by train to the west coast of the peninsula. There is currently one train a day from Bangkok's Hualamphong Station to Butterworth (for Penang; 21hr), which costs about B1000 in a second-class sleeper. It's also possible to make onward train connections to Kuala Lumpur (for an extra B420) and Singapore (for an extra B900). A more convoluted option would be to take a bus from Bangkok's Southern Bus Terminal down to Hat Yai (14hr) and then change onto a bus or share-taxi to Penang (6hr); see Basics, p.20, for more.

All the **foreign embassies and consulates** in Bangkok are located in the downtown area; see "Listings", opposite, for details. Before heading off to the embassy, ring ahead to check on the opening hours (usually very limited) and documentation required. Entry formalities for Thailand's near neighbours (other than Malaysia) have undergone radical transformations over the past few years, and may well change again; for an overview of visa requirements and travel options for Burma, Cambodia, Laos, Malaysia, Singapore and Vietnam see Basics, pp.18–20. Some travellers prefer to avoid the hassle of trudging out to the relevant embassy by paying one of the Khao San travel agencies to get their visa for them; beware of doing this, however, as some agencies are reportedly **faking the stamps**, which causes serious problems at immigration.

Listings

Airport enquiries General enquiries ⓣ02 535 1111; international departures ⓣ02 535 1386; international arrivals ⓣ02 535 1149; domestic departures ⓣ02 535 1277; domestic arrivals ⓣ02 535 1305.

Airlines, domestic Air Andaman, 3388/56 16th Floor, Sirinrat Bldg, Thanon Rama IV, ⓣ02 229 9555; Bangkok Airways, 1111 Thanon Ploenchit ⓣ02 254 2903; PB Air, UBC 2 Bldg, 591 Sukhumvit Soi 33 ⓣ02 2610220–5; Phuket Airlines, 1168/102 34th Floor Lumpini Tower Bldg, Thanon Rama IV ⓣ02 679 8999; Thai Airways, 485 Thanon Silom ⓣ02 232 8000, and 6 Thanon Lan Luang near Democracy Monument ⓣ02 280 0060, 24-hour reservations ⓣ02 628 2000.

Airlines, international Aeroflot ⓣ02 254 1180–2; Air Canada ⓣ02 670 0400; Air France ⓣ02 635 1186–7; Air India ⓣ02 235 0557–8; Air New Zealand ⓣ02 254 8440; Biman Bangladesh Airlines ⓣ02 233 3640; British Airways ⓣ02 636 1747 or 02 236 2800; Cathay Pacific ⓣ02 263 0616; China Airlines ⓣ02 253 4242–3; Druk Air ⓣ02 535 1960; Egyptair ⓣ02 231 0505–8; Emirates ⓣ02 664 1040; Eva Air ⓣ02 240 0890; Finnair ⓣ02 635 1234; Garuda ⓣ02 679 7371–2; Gulf Air ⓣ02 254 7931–4; Japan Airlines ⓣ02 234 9114–5; KLM ⓣ02 679 1100; Korean Air ⓣ02 635 0465; Lao Aviation ⓣ02 237 6982; Lauda Air ⓣ02 267 0873; Lufthansa ⓣ02 264 2400; Malaysia Airlines ⓣ02 263 0565–71; Olympic Airways ⓣ02 237 6141; Pakistan International (PIA) ⓣ02 234 2961–5; Philippine Airlines ⓣ02 633 5713; Qantas Airways ⓣ02 636 1747; Royal Brunei ⓣ02 637 5151; Singapore Airlines ⓣ02 236 0440; Sri Lankan Airlines ⓣ02 236 4981; Swiss ⓣ02 636 2150; Thai Airways ⓣ02 280 0060, 24-hour reservations ⓣ02 628 2000; United Airlines ⓣ02 253 0558; Vietnam Airlines ⓣ02 655 4137–40.

Car rental Avis ⓦwww.avis.com; head office, 2/12 Thanon Witthayu (Wireless Road) ⓣ02 255 5300–4; also at Don Muang international airport ⓣ02 535 4052; the *Grand Hyatt Erawan Hotel*, 494 Thanon Rajdamri ⓣ02 254 1234; *Le Meridien President Hotel*, 971 Thanon Ploenchit ⓣ02 253 0444; and the *Amari Airport Hotel* ⓣ02 566 1020. Budget ⓦwww.budget.co.th; head office, 19/23 Building A, Royal City Avenue, Thanon Phetchaburi Mai ⓣ02 203 0250; also at Don Muang Airport train station, Thanon Vibhavadi Rangsit ⓣ02 566 5067; and Rama IV Tesco Lotus, 3300 Thanon Rama IV ⓣ02 671 6813. SMT Rent-A-Car (part of National) ⓦwww.smtrentacar.com; central reservations ⓣ02 722 8487; and at *Amari Airport Hotel* ⓣ02 928 1525.

Cookery classes Nearly all the five-star hotels will arrange Thai cookery classes for guests if requested; the most famous are held at the *Oriental Hotel* (ⓣ02 437 6211; US$120/day), which mainly focus on demonstrating culinary techniques (Mon–Thurs each week), with a chance to practise what you have learnt on Fri and Sat. There's a more hands-on approach at the *Nipa Thai* restaurant (ⓣ02 254 0424, ext 4823), which runs one- to five-day cookery courses on demand (B1950/person/day, but cheaper in groups and for longer courses), and regular fruit-carving lessons (daily 2–4pm; B450) at the restaurant on the third floor of the Landmark Plaza, between sois 4 and 6 on Thanon Sukhumvit. In a grand, century-old building at 233 Thanon Sathorn Tai (ⓣ02 673 9353–4, ⓦwww.blueelephant.com), the *Blue Elephant* offers courses that range from B2800 for a half-day to a five-day private course for professional chefs for B68,000. Tour company Real Asia (ⓣ02 712 9301, ⓦwww.realasia.net) organizes afternoon courses for B1250 (minimum six people). TV chef and restaurateur Mrs Balbir holds regular classes (B1200) in Thai cookery (Fri 10am–1pm) and Indian cookery (Tues 10am–1pm & Sat 4–7pm) at her restaurant on Sukhumvit Soi 11/1 (Ⓣ02 651 0498, Ⓦwww.mrsbalbir.com), and Banglamphu's famous veggie cook, May Kaidee, shares her culinary expertise at her restaurant at 123–125 Thanon Tanao (Ⓣ02 629 4839, ext 0 or 1, Ⓦwww.maykaidee.com) for B1000 per day. Set in an orchard in a rural part of Nonthaburi, *Thai House* (Ⓣ02 903 9611 or 997 5161, Ⓦwww.thaihouse.com) runs one- (B3500) to three-day (B16,650) cooking courses, including vegetable- and fruit-carving, and offers accommodation in traditional wooden houses (❼).

Couriers DHL Worldwide has several central Bangkok depots, including on Thanon Silom and Thanon Sukhumvit; call Ⓣ02 658 8000 or visit Ⓦwww.dhl.com.sg for details.

Embassies and consulates Australia, 37 Thanon Sathorn Tai Ⓣ02 287 2680; Burma (Myanmar), 132 Thanon Sathorn Nua Ⓣ02 234 0278; Cambodia, 185 Thanon Rajdamri (enter via Thanon Sarasin) Ⓣ02 254 6630; Canada, 15th floor, Abdulrahim Place, 990 Thanon Rama IV Ⓣ02 636 0560; China, 57 Thanon Rajadapisek Ⓣ02 245 7030–45; Germany, 9 Thanon Sathorn Tai (Ⓣ02 213 2331–6); India, 46 Soi Prasarnmitr, Soi 23, Thanon Sukhumvit Ⓣ02 258 0300; Indonesia, 600–602 Thanon Phetchaburi Ⓣ02 252 3135–40; Ireland, 12th Floor, TISCO Tower, 48/20 Thanon Sathorn Nua Ⓣ02 638 0303; Laos, 520 Ramkhamhaeng Soi 39 Ⓣ02 539 6667–8, ext 1053; Malaysia, 35 Thanon Sathorn Tai Ⓣ02 679 2190–9; Nepal, 189 Sukhumvit Soi 71 Ⓣ02 391 7240; Netherlands, 106 Thanon Witthayu (Wireless Road) Ⓣ02 253 8693; New Zealand, 93 Thanon Witthayu Ⓣ02 254 3856, 253 5363 or 253 0429; Pakistan, 31 Sukhumvit Soi 3 Ⓣ02 253 5325; Philippines, 760 Thanon Sukhumvit, opposite Soi 47 Ⓣ02 259 0139–40; Singapore, 129 Thanon Sathorn Tai Ⓣ02 286 2111; Sri Lanka, 89 Sukhumvit Soi 15 Ⓣ02 251 2788–9; Vietnam, 83/1 Thanon Witthayu Ⓣ02 251 7201–3; UK, 1031 Thanon Witthayu, embassy Ⓣ02 305 8333, consulate Ⓣ02 305 8318; US, 120 Thanon Witthayu Ⓣ02 205 4000.

Emergencies For all emergencies, either call the tourist police (free 24hr phoneline Ⓣ1155), who also maintain a 24-hour booth in the Suan Lum Night Bazaar on Thanon Rama IV, visit the Banglamphu Police Station at the west end of Thanon Khao San, or contact the Tourist Police Headquarters, CMIC Tower, 209/1 Soi 21 (Asoke), Thanon Sukhumvit Ⓣ02 664 0222–6.

Exchange The Don Muang Airport exchange desk and those in the upmarket hotels are open 24 hours; many other exchange desks stay open till 8pm, especially along Khao San, Sukhumvit and Silom. If you have a MasterCard/Cirrus or Visa debit or credit card, you can also withdraw cash from hundreds of ATMs around the city, and at Don Muang Airport, at branches of the Bangkok Bank, the Bank of Ayudhaya, Thai Farmers Bank and Siam Commercial Bank.

Hospitals, clinics and dentists Most expats rate the private Bumrungrad Hospital, 33 Sukhumvit Soi 3 Ⓣ02 667 1000, emergency Ⓣ02 667 2999, as the best and most comfortable in the city, followed by the Bangkok Nursing Home Hospital (BNH), 9 Thanon Convent Ⓣ02 632 0550; the Bangkok General Hospital, 2 Soi Soonvijai 7, Thanon Phetchaburi Mai, Ⓣ02 310 3102; and the Samitivej Sukhumvit Hospital, 133 Sukhumvit Soi 49 Ⓣ02 392 0011. Other recommended private hospitals include Bangkok Mission Hospital, 430 Thanon Phitsanulok, cnr Thanon Lan Luang, just east of Banglamphu Ⓣ02 282 1100, and Bangkok Christian Hospital, 124 Thanon Silom Ⓣ02 233 6981–9. You can get vaccinations and malaria advice, as well as rabies advice and treatment, at the Thai Red Cross Society's Queen Saovabha Memorial Institute (QSMI) and Snake Farm on the corner of Thanon Rama IV and Thanon Henri Dunant (Mon–Fri 8.30am–noon & 1–4.30pm; Ⓣ02 252 0161–4 or 0167, Ⓦwww.redcross.or.th). Among general clinics, the Australian-run Travmin Bangkok Medical Centre, 8th Floor, Alma Link Building, next to the Central Department Store at 25 Soi Chitlom, Thanon Ploenchit (Ⓣ02 655 1024–5; B650/consultation), is recommended. For dental problems, try the Bumrungrad Hospital's dental department on Ⓣ02 667 2300, or the following dental clinics (not 24hr): Dental Hospital 88/88 Sukhumvit Soi 49 Ⓣ02 260 5000–15, Glas Haus Dental Centre, mouth of Sukhumvit Soi 25, Ⓣ02 260 6120–2, Siam Family Dental Clinic 292/6 Siam Square Soi 4 Ⓣ02/255 6664–5.

Immigration office About 1km down Soi Suan Phlu, off Thanon Sathorn Tai (Mon–Fri 8.30am–4.30pm, plus Sat 8.30am–noon for visa extensions only; Ⓣ02 287 3101–10); visa extensions take about an hour. They also send a weekly mobile office to the *Emerald Hotel*, Thanon Ratchadaphisek near the Huay Khwang intersection, in the northeast of the city (Wed 9am–noon; Ⓣ02 693 9333–8). Be very wary of any Khao San tour agents who offer to organize a visa extension for you: some are reportedly faking the relevant stamps and this has caused problems at immigration.

Internet access Banglamphu is packed with places offering Internet access, in particular along Thanon Khao San. Competition keeps prices very low, so this is the best area of the city for all cyber activities. The Ratchadamnoen Post Office on Banglamphu's Soi Damnoen Klang Neua (daily 8am–7pm) also has very cheap public Catnet Internet booths (see p.56). Outside Banglamphu, mid-range and upmarket hotels also offer Internet access, but at vastly inflated prices. Thanon Sukhumvit has a number of makeshift phone/Internet offices, as well as several more formal and more clued-up Internet cafés, including *Login*, Ground Floor, Ploenchit Center, Sukhumvit Soi 2 (daily 10am–7pm), and Time Internet Centre on the second floor of Times Square, between sois 12 and 14 (Mon–Sat 9am–midnight, Sun 10am–midnight); the Soi Nana Post Office between sois 4 and 6 also has some Catnet Internet terminals. In the Silom area, head for Patpong Internet on Patpong 2 (daily noon–10pm). There are Catnet centres in the 24-hour public telephone office adjacent to the GPO on Thanon Charoen Krung (New Road), and at both international terminals of Don Muang Airport, in the check-in areas and in airside departures areas, as well as at the domestic terminal.

Laundry Nearly all guest houses and hotels offer same-day laundry services, or there are several self-service laundries on Thanon Khao San.

Left luggage At Don Muang airport (international and domestic; B90/day); Don Muang train station (B15/day); Ekamai Eastern Bus Terminal (B30/day), Hualamphong train station (B10–30/day), and at most hotels and guest houses (B10–20/day).

Mail The GPO is at 1160 Thanon Charoen Krung (New Road), a few hundred metres left of the exit for Wat Muang Kae express-boat stop. Poste restante can be collected here Mon–Fri 8am–8pm, Sat, Sun & holidays 8am–1pm; letters are kept for three months. The parcel-packing service at the GPO operates Mon–Fri 8am–4.30pm, Sat 9am–noon. If you're staying on or near Thanon Khao San in Banglamphu, it's more convenient to use the poste restante service at one of the two post offices in Banglamphu itself. The one closest to Khao San is Ratchadamnoen Post Office on the eastern stretch of Soi Damnoen Klang Neua (Mon–Fri 8am–5pm, Sat 9am–noon); letters are kept for two months and should be addressed c/o poste restante, Ratchadamnoen PO, Bangkok 10200. Banglamphu's other post office is on Soi Sibsam Hang, just west of Wat Bowoniwes (Mon–Fri 8.30am–5.30pm, Sat 9am–noon); its poste restante address is Banglamphubon PO, Bangkok 10203. You can also send and receive faxes there on Ⓕ 02 281 1579. In the Thanon Sukhumvit vicinity, poste restante can be sent to the Thanon Sukhumvit post office between sois 4 and 6, c/o Nana PO, Thanon Sukhumvit, Bangkok 10112 (daily 8am–7pm).

Massage and spas Traditional Thai massage sessions and courses are held at Wat Pho (see p.130), and at dozens of guest houses in Banglamphu. More luxurious and indulgent spa and massage treatments are available at many posh hotels across the city, including most famously at the *Banyan Tree Hotel* on Thanon Sathorn Tai (Ⓣ 02 679 1054) and the *Oriental* on Thanon Charoen Krung (Ⓣ 02 439 7613), and more affordably at *Buddy Lodge* on Thanon Khao San in Banglamphu (Ⓣ 02 629 4477). For more on spa treatments see Basics p.68.

Pharmacies There are English-speaking staff at most of the capital's pharmacies, including the city-wide branches of Boots the Chemist (most usefully on Thanon Khao San, in the Siam Centre on Thanon Rama I and inside the Emporium on Thanon Sukhumvit).

Prison visits A number of foreigners are serving long sentences in Nonthaburi's Bang Kwang Jail, and they appreciate visits from other foreigners. When visiting, you need to know the name of the prisoner, which block number they're in, and the relevant visiting hours. Embassy staff keep this information, and guest-house noticeboards often have more details as well as accounts from recent prison visitors; similar info is available at Ⓦwww.bangkwang.net and Ⓦwww.khaosanroad.com/bangedup.htm. Prisoners are only allowed one visitor at a time, and visitors must look respectable (no shorts or singlets); all visitors must show their passports at the jail. You can only bring certain gifts with you (such as books, newspapers, fruit, sweets and clothes), as other stuff has to be bought at the prison shop. For directions to Nonthaburi, see p.168; at Nonthaburi pier, take the road ahead, and then turn first left for the prison visitor centre.

Telephones International cardphones are dotted all over the city, so there's now little call for the public telephone offices in or adjacent to post offices, though their booths do at least guarantee some peace and quiet. The largest and most convenient public telephone office is in the compound of the GPO on Thanon Charoen Krung (New Road), which is open 24 hours and also offers a fax and Internet service and a free collect-call service (see above for location details). The post offices at Hualamphong Station, on Thanon Sukhumvit (see above), and in Banglamphu (see above) also have international telephone offices attached, but these close at 7pm. Many fly-by-night entrepreneurs, particularly on Thanon Khao San, advertise very cheap international calls through the Internet: see Basics for details.

Travel agents Diethelm Travel has branches all over Thailand and Indochina and is especially good for travel to Burma, Cambodia, Laos and Vietnam: 12th Floor, Kian Gwan Building II, 140/1 Thanon Witthayu (Wireless Road) ⓣ02 255 9200, ⓦwww.diethelm-travel.com; Educational Travel Centre (ETC) sells air tickets and Thailand tours and has offices inside the *Royal Hotel*, Room 318, 2 Thanon Rajdamnoen Klang, Banglamphu ⓣ02 224 0043, ⓦwww.etc.co.th, at 180 Thanon Khao San, Banglamphu ⓣ02 282 2958, and at 5/3 Soi Ngam Duphli ⓣ02 286 9424; Educational Travel Centre NS Tours sells air tickets and budget transport within Thailand and, has offices inside the *Vieng Thai Hotel*, Thanon Ram Bhuttri, Banglamphu ⓣ02 629 0509, ⓔnstravel@hotmail. com, and at 46/1 Thanon Khao San ⓣ02 282 1900; Olavi Travel, a similar outfit, is based inside the Buddy Village complex on Thanon Khao San ⓣ02 629 4711–4, ⓦwww.olavi.com; Royal Exclusive is good for travel to Burma, Cambodia, Laos and Vietnam, and also sells air and train tickets: 21 Thanon Silom ⓣ02 267 1536, ⓦwww.royal exclusive.com; and the Bangkok branch of the worldwide STA Travel is a reliable outlet for cheap international flights: 14th Floor, Wall Street Tower, 33 Thanon Suriwong ⓣ02 236 0262, ⓦwww.statravel.co.th. For Bangkok tour operators specializing in trips within Thailand see p.196.

Travel details

Trains

Bangkok Hualamphong Station to: Aranyaprathet (2 daily; 5–6hr); Ayutthaya (20 daily; 1hr 30min); Butterworth (Malaysia; 1 daily; 23hr); Chiang Mai (7 daily; 12–14hr); Chumphon (9 daily; 6hr 45min–8hr 20min); Don Muang airport (30 daily; 50min); Hat Yai (5 daily; 14–16hr); Hua Hin (9 daily; 3–4hr); Khon Kaen (5 daily; 7hr 30min–10hr 30min); Khorat (9 daily; 4–5hr); Lampang (7 daily; 10–12hr); Lamphun (6 daily; 12–14hr); Lopburi (15 daily; 2hr 30min–3hr); Nakhon Pathom (14 daily; 1hr 20min); Nakhon Si Thammarat (2 daily; 15–16hr); Nong Khai (4 daily; 11hr 30min–12hr 30min); Pak Chong (for Khao Yai National Park; 6 daily; 2hr 45min–3hr 30min); Pattaya (1 daily; 3hr 45min); Phatthalung (5 daily; 12–15hr); Phitsanulok (9 daily; 5hr 15min–9hr 30min); Si Racha (1 daily; 3hr 15min); Sungai Kolok (2 daily; 20hr); Surat Thani (11 daily; 9–12hr); Surin (10 daily; 7–10hr); Trang (2 daily; 15–16hr); Ubon Ratchathani (6 daily; 10hr 20min–13hr 15min); Udon Thani (5 daily; 9hr–12hr 30min); Yala (4 daily; 15–19hr).

Don Muang Airport to: Ayutthaya (23 daily; 40min); Chiang Mai (7 daily; 10hr 20min–13hr 25min); Khon Kaen (5 daily; 6hr 40min–9hr 40min); Khorat (9 daily; 3hr 10min–4hr 10min); Lampang (7 daily; 10hr); Lamphun (6 daily; 12hr); Lopburi (9 daily; 1hr 25min–2hr 10min); Nong Khai (3 daily; 11–12hr); Pak Chong (for Khao Yai National Park; 6 daily; 2hr–2hr 40min); Phitsanulok (9 daily; 4hr 25min–8hr 40min); Surin (10 daily; 6–9hr); Ubon Ratchathani (6 daily; 9hr 30min–12hr 25min); Udon Thani (5 daily; 9hr).

Thonburi (Bangkok Noi) Station to: Hua Hin (2 daily; 4hr–4hr 30min); Kanchanaburi (2 daily; 2hr 40min); Nakhon Pathom (3 daily; 1hr 10min); Nam Tok (2 daily; 4hr 35min).

Buses

Eastern Bus Terminal to: Ban Phe (for Ko Samet; 12 daily; 3hr 30min); Chanthaburi (every 30min; 5–7hr); Pattaya (every 30min; 2hr 30min); Rayong (every 15min; 2hr 40min); Si Racha (for Ko Si Chang; every 30min; 2–3hr); Trat (for Ko Chang; at least every 90min; 6–8hr).

Northern Bus Terminal to: Aranyaprathet (hourly; 4hr); Ayutthaya (every 15min; 2hr); Chanthaburi (5 daily; 3–4hr); Chiang Khong (10 daily; 13–14hr); Chiang Mai (19 daily; 10–11hr); Chiang Rai (16 daily; 12hr); Khon Kaen (23 daily; 6–7hr); Khorat (every 15min; 3–4hr); Lampang (10 daily; 8hr); Loei (18 daily; 10hr); Lopburi (every 20min; 3hr); Mae Hong Son (2 daily; 18hr); Mae Sai (8 daily; 13hr); Mae Sot (10 daily; 8hr 30min); Mukdahan (13 daily; 11hr); Nakhon Phanom (17 daily; 12hr); Nan (13 daily; 13hr); Nong Khai (17 daily; 10hr); Pak Chong (for Khao Yai National Park; every 15min; 3hr); Pattaya (every 30min;2hr 30min); Phitsanulok (up to 19 daily; 5–6hr); Si Racha (every 30min; 2hr);

Sukhothai (17 daily; 6–7hr); Surin (up to 20 daily; 8–9hr); Tak (13 daily; 7hr); Trat (4 daily; 4hr 30min); Ubon Ratchathani (19 daily; 10–12hr); Udon Thani (every 15min; 9hr).
Southern Bus Terminal to: Chumphon (9 daily; 7hr); Damnoen Saduak (every 20min; 2hr); Hat Yai (21 daily; 12–15hr); Hua Hin (every 25min; 3–3hr 30min); Kanchanaburi (every 15min; 2–3hr); Ko Samui (5 daily; 15hr); Krabi (9 daily; 12–14hr); Nakhon Pathom (every 10min; 40min–1hr 20min); Nakhon Si Thammarat (11 daily; 12hr); Narathiwat (4 daily; 17–19hr); Phang Nga (4 daily; 11hr–12hr 30min); Phatthalung (4 daily; 13hr); Phuket (at least 10 daily; 14–16hr); Ranong (7 daily; 9–10hr); Satun (2 daily; 16hr); Sungai Kolok (3 daily; 18–20hr); Surat Thani (7 daily; 10–11hr); Takua Pa (10 daily; 12–13hr); Trang (8 daily; 12–14hr); Yala (6 daily; 16–19hr).

Flights

Bangkok to: Buriram (daily; 1hr 10min); Chiang Mai (14–17 daily; 1hr); Chiang Rai (5 daily; 1hr 15min); Chumphon (3 weekly; 1hr 10min); Hat Yai (7 daily; 1hr 30min); Khon Kaen (4 daily; 55min); Khorat (6 weekly; 50min); Ko Samui (15 daily; 1hr 20min); Krabi (5–7 daily; 1hr 20min); Lampang (1–2 daily; 1hr); Loei (4 weekly; 1hr 20min); Mae Sot (4 weekly; 1hr 20min); Nakhon Phanom (daily; 1hr 5min); Nakhon Si Thammarat (2–3 daily; 1hr 15min); Nan (1 daily; 1hr 40min); Narathiwat (1–2 daily; 1hr 40min–2hr 20min); Phitsanulok (3 daily; 55min); Phrae (1 daily; 2hr 40min);Phuket (16 daily; 1hr 20min); Ranong (daily; 1hr 10min); Roi Et (6 weekly; 1hr); Sukhothai (1–2 daily; 1hr 10min); Surat Thani (2 daily; 1hr 10min); Surin (4 weekly; 1hr 30min); Trang (1–2 daily; 1hr 30min); Trat (2 daily; 50min); Ubon Ratchathani (3 daily; 1hr 5min); Udon Thani (3 daily; 1hr).

2

The central plains

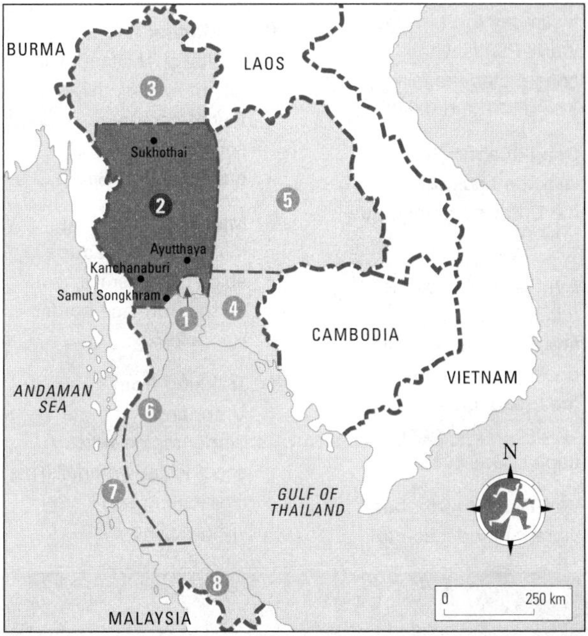

CHAPTER 2

Highlights

* **Kanchanaburi** Stay in a raft house on the River Kwai. See p.223

* **The Death Railway** Chug through the scenic River Kwai valley and then visit the **Hellfire Pass Memorial Museum**, a moving testimony to the World War II POWs who constructed the railway. See p.237 and p.242

* **Sangkhlaburi** Peaceful lakeside backwater near the Burmese border. See p.244

* **Ayutthaya** Atmospheric ruined temples, three fine museums and laid-back guest houses in the broad, grassy spaces of the former capital. See p.252

* **Wat Phra Phutthabat** A vibrant introduction to Thai religion at the Temple of the Buddha's Footprint. See p.267

* **Phitsanulok Folklore Museum** A fascinating look at traditional rural life, complete with reconstructed village homes. See p.273

* **Sukhothai** A former capital of Thailand, with lots of elegant thirteenth-century ruins and several exceptional guest houses. See p.275

* **Mae Sot** An alluring mix of cultures adds spice to this small town on the Burmese border. See p.298

* **Trekking from Umphang** A remote border region with spectacular waterfalls, river-rafting and Karen villages. See p.304

△ Buddha in a bodhi tree, Wat Phra Mahathat, Ayutthaya

2

The central plains

North and west of the capital, the unwieldy urban mass of Greater Bangkok peters out into the vast, well-watered **central plains**, a region that for centuries has grown the bulk of the nation's food and been a tantalizing temptation for neighbouring power-mongers. The most densely populated region of Thailand, with sizeable towns sprinkled among patchworks of paddy, orchards and sugar-cane fields, the plains are fundamental to Thailand's agricultural economy. Its rivers are the key to this area's fecundity, especially the Nan and the Ping, whose waters irrigate the northern plains before merging to form the Chao Phraya, which meanders slowly south through Bangkok and out into the Gulf of Thailand. Further west, the Mae Khlong River sustains the many market gardens and fills the canals that dominate the hinterlands of the estuary at **Samut Songkhram**.

Sited at the confluence of the Kwai Yai and Kwai Noi rivers, the town of **Kanchanaburi** has long attracted visitors to the notorious Bridge over the River Kwai and is now well established as a budget-travellers' hangout, mainly because of its unique raft-house accommodation. Few tourists venture further upriver, except as passengers on the remaining stretch of the **Death Railway** – the most tangible wartime reminder of all – but the remote and tiny hilltop town of **Sangkhlaburi** holds enough understated allure to make the extra kilometres worthwhile.

On the plains north of Bangkok, the historic heartland of the country, the major sites are ruined ancient cities, which cover the spectrum of Thailand's art and architecture. Closest to Bangkok, **Ayutthaya** served as the country's capital for the four hundred years prior to the 1782 foundation of Bangkok, and its ruins evoke an era of courtly sophistication. A short hop north of here, the remnants of **Lopburi** hark back to an earlier time, when the predominantly Hindu Khmers held sway over this region, building a constellation of stone temples across central and northeastern Thailand and introducing a complex grammar of sacred architecture that still dictates aspects of wat design today.

A separate nucleus of sites in the northern neck of the plains centres on **Sukhothai**, birthplace of the Thai kingdom in the thirteenth century. The buildings and sculpture produced during the Sukhothai era are the acme of Thai art, and the restored ruins of the country's first official capital are the best place to appreciate them, though two satellite cities – **Si Satchanalai** and **Kamphaeng Phet** – provide further incentives to linger in the area, and the engaging city of **Phitsanulok** also serves as a good base. West of Sukhothai, on the Burmese border, the town of **Mae Sot** makes a refreshing change from ancient history and is the departure point for the rivers and waterfalls of **Umphang**, a remote border region that's becoming increasingly popular for trekking and rafting.

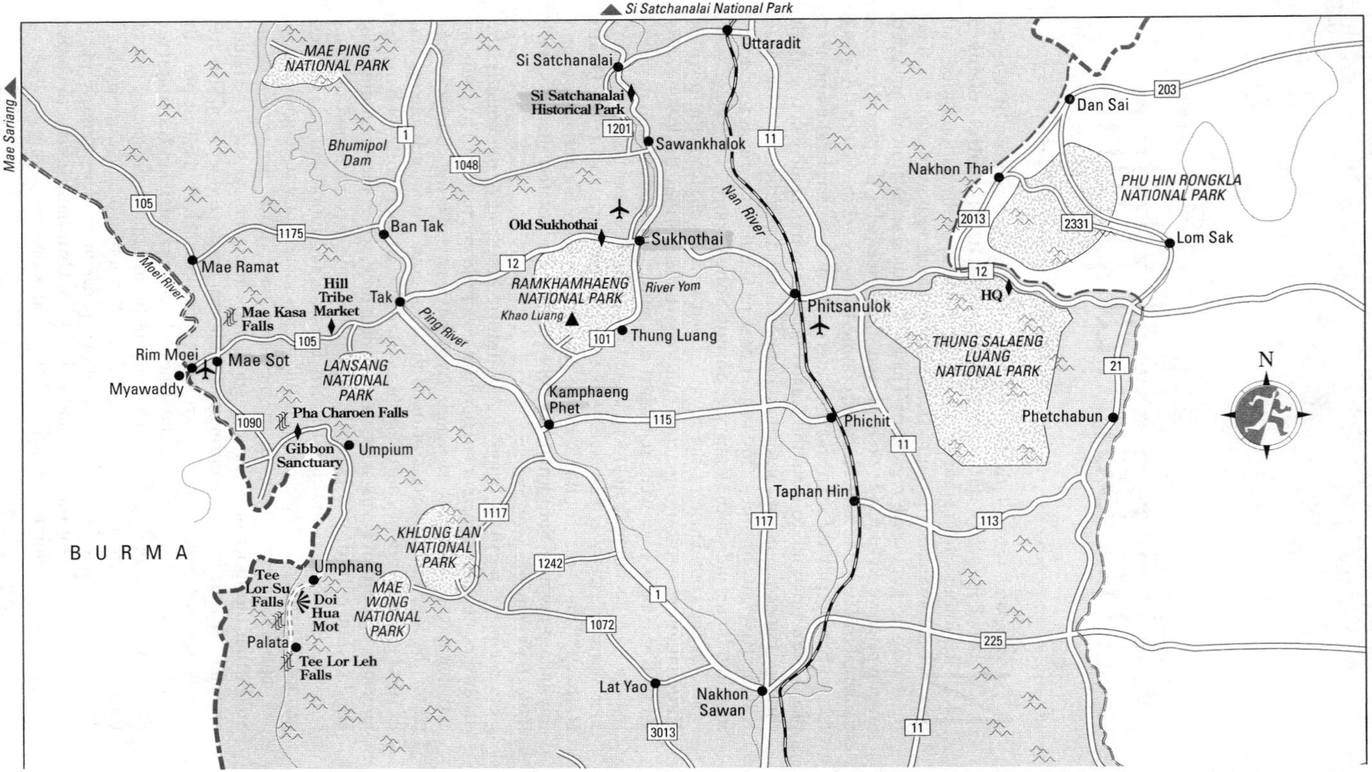
Si Satchanalai National Park
Mae Sariang
MAE PING NATIONAL PARK
Bhumipol Dam
Si Satchanalai
Si Satchanalai Historical Park
Uttaradit
Sawankhalok
Old Sukhothai
Sukhothai
Nan River
Dan Sai
Nakhon Thai
PHU HIN RONGKLA NATIONAL PARK
Lom Sak
Ban Tak
Mae Ramat
Moei River
Hill Tribe Market
Tak
Ping River
RAMKHAMHAENG NATIONAL PARK
River Yom
Khao Luang
Thung Luang
Phitsanulok
HQ
THUNG SALAENG LUANG NATIONAL PARK
Mae Kasa Falls
Rim Moei
Mae Sot
Myawaddy
LANSANG NATIONAL PARK
Kamphaeng Phet
Phichit
Phetchabun
Pha Charoen Falls
Gibbon Sanctuary
Umpium
Taphan Hin
KHLONG LAN NATIONAL PARK
BURMA
Umphang
Tee Lor Su Falls
Doi Hua Mot
MAE WONG NATIONAL PARK
Palata
Tee Lor Leh Falls
Lat Yao
Nakhon Sawan
N
203
105
1175
1
1048
1201
11
12
2013
2331
105
101
21
1090
115
11
1117
117
113
1242
1
1072
225
3013
11

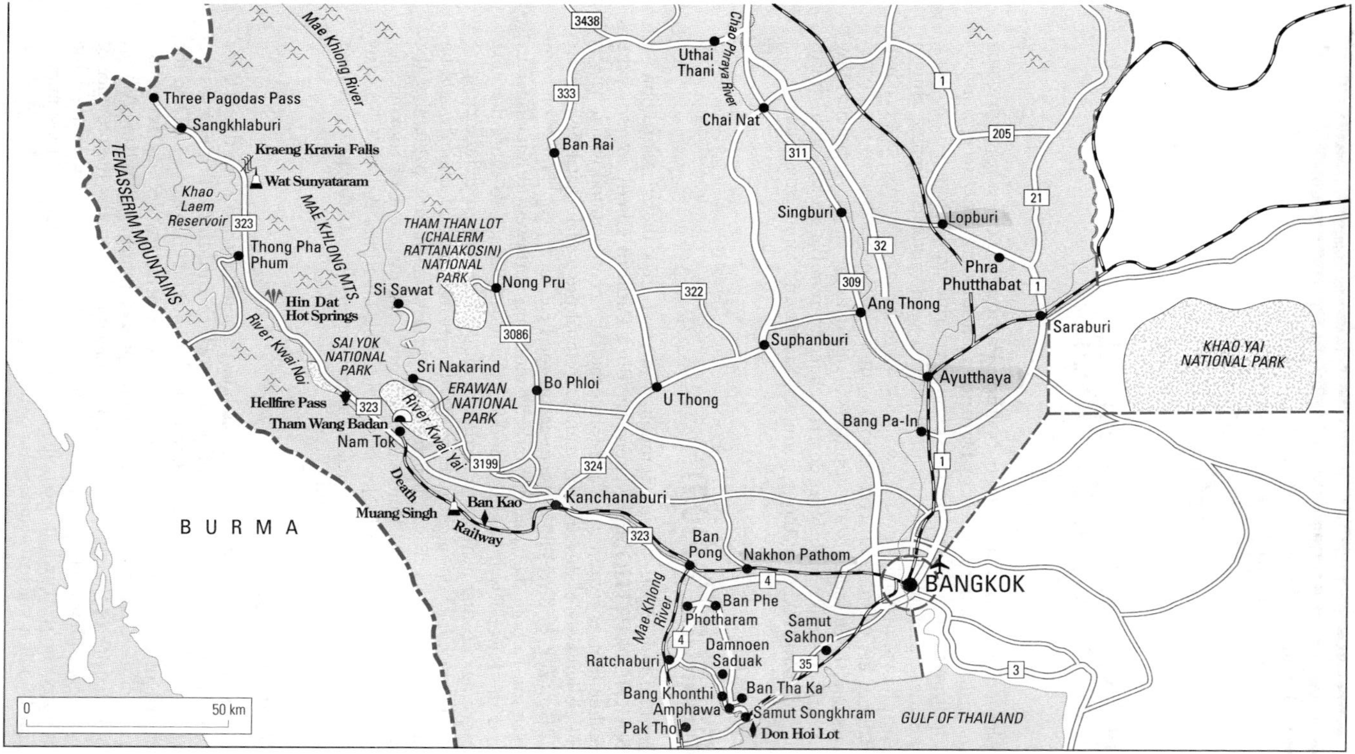
Three Pagodas Pass
Sangkhlaburi
Kraeng Kravia Falls
Wat Sunyataram
TENASSERIM MOUNTAINS
Khao Laem Reservoir
323
Thong Pha Phum
MAE KHLONG MTS.
Mae Khlong River
Hin Dat Hot Springs
River Kwai Noi
SAI YOK NATIONAL PARK
Hellfire Pass
Tham Wang Badan
Nam Tok
Si Sawat
Sri Nakarind
River Kwai Yai
ERAWAN NATIONAL PARK
THAM THAN LOT (CHALERM RATTANAKOSIN) NATIONAL PARK
Nong Pru
3086
Bo Phloi
3199
Death Railway
Muang Singh
Ban Kao
Kanchanaburi
324
U Thong
322
Ban Rai
333
3438
Uthai Thani
Chao Phraya River
Chai Nat
311
Singburi
32
309
Suphanburi
Ang Thong
Lopburi
Phra Phutthabat
205
21
1
Saraburi
KHAO YAI NATIONAL PARK
Ayutthaya
Bang Pa-In
BANGKOK
Ban Pong
Nakhon Pathom
4
Ban Phe
Photharam
Mae Khlong River
Ratchaburi
Damnoen Saduak
Samut Sakhon
35
3
Bang Khonthi
Amphawa
Ban Tha Ka
Samut Songkhram
Pak Tho
Don Hoi Lot
GULF OF THAILAND
BURMA
0
50 km

Chiang Mai makes an obvious next stop after exploring the sights north of Bangkok, chiefly because the Northern Rail Line makes **connections** painless. Or you could branch east into Isaan, by train or bus. It's also possible to fly out of Sukhothai, Mae Sot and Phitsanulok.

West of Bangkok

Although the enormous chedi of **Nakhon Pathom** and the increasingly commercialized floating markets of **Damnoen Saduak** are easily seen in a day-trip from the capital, the much less visited riverine sites of Samut Songkhram province, particularly the floating markets and historic temples around **Amphawa**, make this area a rewarding focus for an overnight stay. Nakhon Pathom has useful **train** connections with both Kanchanaburi to the northwest and Phetchaburi to the southwest, but **buses** are the most practical way of exploring this region: buses depart frequently from Bangkok's Southern Bus Terminal to Nakhon Pathom, Damnoen Saduak and Samut Songkhram.

Nakhon Pathom

Even if you're just passing through, you can't miss the star attraction of **NAKHON PATHOM**: the enormous **Phra Pathom Chedi** dominates the skyline from every direction, and forms the calm centre around which wheels the daily bustle of this otherwise unexceptional provincial capital, 56km west of Bangkok. As there's little else to detain you here, most people move on from Nakhon Pathom the same day, either continuing northwest to Kanchanaburi and the River Kwai, heading south to Damnoen Saduak to catch the next morning's floating markets, or further south still to Hua Hin and the coast.

The one time you might want to stay longer in Nakhon Pathom would be during either of its two annual **festivals**: for a week in early September the town hosts a food and fruits fair, featuring demonstrations of cooking and fruit-carving; then in mid-November the week-long Phra Pathom Chedi fair brings together itinerant musicians, fortune-tellers – and crowds of devotees from all over central Thailand.

The Town

Probably Thailand's oldest town, Nakhon Pathom (derived from the Pali for "First City") is thought to be the point at which **Buddhism** first entered the region now known as Thailand, more than two thousand years ago. Then the capital of a sizeable Mon kingdom, the settlement was deemed important enough to rate a visit from a pair of missionaries dispatched by King Ashoka of India, one of Buddhism's great early evangelists. Even today, the province of Nakhon Pathom retains a high Buddhist profile – aside from housing the country's holiest chedi, it also contains Phuttamonthon, Thailand's most important Buddhist sanctuary and home of its supreme patriarch.

Arriving at Nakhon Pathom's **train station**, a two-hundred-metre walk south across the khlong and through the market will get you to the chedi compound's north gate. Try to avoid being dumped at the **main bus terminal**, which is about 1km east of the town centre: most buses pass the chedi first, dropping passengers either in front of the police station across from the chedi's southern entrance, or beside the khlong, 100m from the northern gate. Staff at the train station will look after luggage for an hour or two, as will ticket collectors at the booth inside the chedi's south gate, a few metres from the bus drop. Finding your way around town is no problem as the chedi is an omnipresent landmark: nearly everything described below is within ten minutes' walk of it.

Phra Pathom Chedi

Phra Pathom Chedi (daily dawn–dusk; B20) has been twice rebuilt since its initial construction, its earliest fragments remaining entombed within the later layers. The origin of the chedi has become indistinguishable from folklore; although the Buddha never actually came to Thailand, legend has it that he rested here after wandering the country, and the original Indian-style (inverted bowl-shaped) chedi, similar to Ashoka's great stupa at Sanchi in India, may have been erected to commemorate this. Local chronicles, however, tell how the chedi was built as an act of atonement by the patricidal Phraya Pan. Abandoned at birth because of a prediction that he would one day murder his father, the Mon king, Pan was found by a village woman and raised to be a champion of the downtrodden. Vowing to rid the Mon of oppressive rule, Pan killed the king, and then, learning that he had fulfilled the tragic prophecy, blamed his adoptive mother and murdered her as well. To expiate his sin, the monks advised him to build a chedi "as high as the wild pigeon flies", and thus the original 39-metre-high stupa was born. Statues of both father and son stand inside the viharns of the present chedi.

Whatever its true beginnings, the first chedi fell into disrepair, only to be rebuilt with a **Khmer** prang during the time the Khmers controlled the region, between the eighth and twelfth centuries. Once again it was abandoned to the jungle until Rama IV rediscovered it during his 27-year monkhood. Mindful of the Buddhist tradition that all monuments are sacred, in 1853 Rama IV set about encasing the old prang in the enormous new 120-metre-high plunger-shaped **chedi** (making it reputedly the tallest stupa in the world), adding four viharns, a circular cloister and a bot as well as a model of the original prang. Rama IV didn't live to see the chedi's completion, but his successors covered it in golden-brown tiles from China and continued to add statues and murals as well as new buildings.

Around the chedi

Approaching the chedi from the main (northern) staircase, you're greeted by the eight-metre-high Sukhothai-style Buddha image known as **Phra Ruang Rojanarit**, installed in front of the north viharn. Each of the viharns – there's one at each of the cardinal points – has an inner and an outer chamber containing tableaux of the life of the Buddha. The figures in the outer chamber of the **north viharn** depict two princesses paying homage to the newly born Prince Siddhartha (the future Buddha), while the inner one shows a monkey and an elephant offering honey and water to the Buddha at the end of a forty-day fast.

Proceeding clockwise around the chedi, as is the custom at all Buddhist monuments, you can weave between the outer promenade and the inner cloister via ornate doors that punctuate the dividing wall; the promenade is dotted with **trees**, many of which have religious significance, such as the bodhi tree (*ficus religiosa*) under which the Buddha was meditating when he achieved enlightenment. Moving on, you come to the **east viharn**, on whose wall is painted a clear cross-section of the chedi construction that shows the encased original. Flanking the staircase that leads up to the **south viharn** are a three-dimensional replica of the original chedi with its Khmer prang (east side) and a model of the venerated chedi at Nakhon Si Thammarat (west side). The west viharn houses two reclining Buddhas: a sturdy, nine-metre-long figure in the outer chamber and a more delicate portrayal in the inner one.

The museums

There are two museums within the chedi compound and, confusingly, they have similar names. The newer, more formal setup, the **Phra Pathom Chedi National Museum** (Wed–Sun 9am–noon & 1–4pm; B30), is clearly sign-posted from the bottom of the chedi's south staircase. It displays a good collection of Dvaravati-era (sixth to eleventh centuries) artefacts excavated near-

A stupa is born

One of the more colourful explanations of the origin of the Buddhist **stupa** (chedi in Thai) comes from a legend describing the death of the Buddha. Anxious about how to spread the Buddha's teachings after his death, one of his disciples asked for a symbol of the Dharma philosophy. Famously lacking in material possessions, the Buddha assembled his worldly goods – a teaching stick, a begging bowl and a length of cloth – and constructed the stupa shape using the folded cloth as the base, the inverted bowl as the central dome and the stick as the spire.

Upon the Buddha's death, disciples from all over Asia laid claim to his **relics**, burying many of them in specially constructed stupa structures. In Thailand, the temples containing such chedis were given the title **Wat Phra Mahathat** (Temple of the Great Relic) and each royal city had one; today you'll find a Wat Phra Mahathat in Ayutthaya, Lopburi, Phetchaburi, Phitsanulok, Sukhothai, Nakhon Si Thammarat and Bangkok, all enjoying a special status, although the presence of a genuine piece of the Buddha in each is open to question.

Stupa design has undergone many changes since the Buddha's makeshift example, and there are chedis in Thailand reflecting the architectural style of every major historical period. The **Sukhothai** chedi (thirteenth to fifteenth centuries), for example, is generally an elegant reworking of the original Sri Lankan model: early ones are bell-shaped (the bell symbolizing the ringing out of the Buddha's teachings), while the later, slimmer versions evoke the contours of a lotus bud. **Ayutthayan** architects (fourteenth to eighteenth centuries) owed more to the Khmers, elongating their chedis and resting them on a higher square platform, stepped and solid. Meanwhile, the independent **Lanna** kingdom (thirteenth to sixteenth centuries) of northern Thailand built some stupas to a squat pyramidal design that harked back to the seventh century, and other more rotund ones that drew on Burmese influences.

Contemporary chedi-builders have tended to combine historical features at will, but most still pay some heed to the traditional **symbolism** of each stupa component. In theory, the base or platform of the chedi structure should be divided into three layers to represent hell, earth and heaven. The dome usually supports the cube-shaped reliquary, known as a *harmika* after the Sanskrit term for the Buddha's seat of meditation. Crowning the structure, the "umbrella" spire is graded into 33 rings, one for each of the 33 Buddhist heavens.

Over the centuries, Thailand's chedis have been used to house the ashes of kings and important monks and, in the last two hundred years or so, as reliquaries and memorials for anyone who can afford to have one erected.

by, including Wheels of Law – an emblem introduced by Theravada Buddhists before naturalistic images were permitted – and Buddha statuary with the U-shaped robe and thick facial features characteristic of Dvaravati sculpture.

For a broader, more contemporary overview, hunt out the other magpie's nest of a collection, the **Phra Pathom Chedi Museum** (Wed–Sun 9am–noon & 1–4pm; free), which is halfway up the steps near the east viharn. More a curiosity shop than a museum, the small room is an Aladdin's cave of Buddhist amulets, seashells, gold and silver needles, Chinese ceramics, Thai musical instruments and ancient statues.

Sanam Chan Palace

A ten-minute walk west of the chedi along Thanon Rajdamnoen takes you through a large park to the moderately interesting **Sanam Chan Palace** complex (Thurs–Sun 9am–4pm; B50), which was built as the country retreat of Rama VI in 1907. Sanam Chan is located across the road from the main campus of Silpakorn University and can also be reached by following signs for the university: from the chedi's southwest corner head west along Thanon Rajvithee, continue past the Whale Hotel for about 1km and then turn right down Thanon Rajamanka Nai – a B20 ride on a motorbike taxi.

The **palace** was designed to blend Western and Eastern styles: its principal structure, the Chaeemongkolosana Hall, evokes a miniature Bavarian castle, complete with turrets and red-tiled roof; the Mareeratcharatabulung Hall is a more oriental-style pavilion, built of teak and painted a deep rose colour inside and out; and the Thubkwan Hall is an unadorned traditional Thai-style house of polished, unpainted teak. Behind the Thubkwan Hall, in among a complementary series of pretty white wooden villas, stands a sizeable **art gallery**, which stages temporary exhibitions of modern works.

Practicalities

The most traveller-friendly of Nakhon Pathom's **accommodation** options is the conveniently located *Mitpaisal Hotel* (Ⓣ034 242422, Ⓔmitpaisal@hotmail.com; ❷–❸). Less than 200m from the chedi's north gateway, it has one entrance just a few metres to the right of the station exit, and another across from the north bank of the khlong (near the stop for buses to Bangkok), at 120/30 Thanon Phaya Pan. Rooms are a good size and are all en suite, and you can choose between fan or air-con. The other passable budget option is the less central and shabbier *Mitrsampant Hotel* (Ⓣ034 242422; ❷), located above a shop opposite the west gate of the chedi compound at the Lang Phra/Rajdamnoen intersection; all rooms here have fan and shower. Thanon Rajvithee, which starts at the southwestern corner of the chedi compound, leads to a couple of comfortable, air-con-only hotels: *Nakorn Inn Hotel* on Soi 3 (Ⓣ034 251152, Ⓕ034 254998; ❹) is the town's best, though the *Whale Hotel* (Ⓣ034 251020, Ⓕ034 253864; ❹), on Soi 19 and signposted from the main road (about ten minutes' walk from the chedi), is pretty similar, and has a disco.

For inexpensive Thai and Chinese food head for any of the **restaurants** along the eastern arm of Thanon Phraya Gong, which runs along the south (chedi) side of the canal; the place with the "Thai Food" sign is used to serving foreigners. Or try one of the garden restaurants along Thanon Rajdamnoen, which runs west from the chedi's west gate. Night-time foodstalls on Thanon Rajvithee are another good bet, and during the day the market in front of the station serves the usual takeaway goodies, including reputedly the tastiest *khao laam* (bamboo cylinders filled with steamed rice and coconut) in Thailand. If you're down at Sanam Chan palace, exit the compound on to Thanon Rajamanka Nai (across from the university campus) to find a string of idiosyncratic, student-oriented restaurants, including the *Home Made Shop*, which does pizzas, pastas, rice and curry dishes, plus cakes and fresh coffee, and several tiny cafés along nearby "Art Street" where you can get coffee and ice cream.

You can **change money** at the exchange booth (open banking hours only) on Thanon Phaya Pan, beside the bridge over the khlong, one block south of the train station; several nearby banks also have ATMs. There's **Internet access** on the road between the khlong and the chedi.

Buses heading for Kanchanaburi, Damnoen Saduak and Phetchaburi collect passengers from stops outside the police station across the road from the chedi's southern gate, and further west along Thanon Rajvithee, near the *Nakorn Inn Hotel*. Buses bound for Bangkok pick up from Thanon Phaya Pan on the north bank of the khlong, across from the *Mitpaisal Hotel*.

Damnoen Saduak floating markets

To get an idea of what shopping in Bangkok used to be like before all the canals were tarmacked over, many people take an early-morning trip to the **floating markets** (*talat khlong*) of **DAMNOEN SADUAK**, 60km south of Nakhon Pathom. Vineyards and orchards here back onto a labyrinth of narrow canals, and every morning between 6 and 11am local market gardeners ply these waterways in paddle boats full of fresh fruit and vegetables, selling their produce to each other and the canalside residents. As most of the vendors dress in the deep-blue jacket and high-topped straw hat traditionally favoured by Thai farmers, it's all richly atmospheric, but the setup feels increasingly manufactured, and some visitors have complained of seeing more tourists than vendors, however early they arrive. For a more authentic version, consider going instead to the floating market near Amphawa, 10km south of Damnoen Saduak (see p.220).

The target for most tourists is the main **Talat Khlong Ton Kem**, 2km west of Damnoen Saduak's tiny town centre at the intersection of Khlong Damnoen Saduak and Khlong Thong Lang. Many of the wooden houses here have been converted into warehouse-style souvenir shops and tourist restaurants, diverting trade away from the khlong vendors and into the hands of large commercial enterprises. But, for the moment at least, a semblance of the traditional water trade continues, and the two bridges between Ton Kem and **Talat Khlong Hia Kui** (a little further south down Khlong Thong Lang) make decent vantage points. Touts invariably congregate at the Ton Kem pier to hassle you into taking a **boat trip** around the khlong network (asking an hourly rate of around B150/person), but there are distinct disadvantages in being propelled between markets at top speed in a noisy motorized boat. For a less hectic and more sensitive look at the markets, explore via the walkways beside the canals.

Practicalities

Damnoen Saduak is 109km from Bangkok, so to reach the market in good time you have to catch one of the earliest **buses** from Bangkok's Southern Bus Terminal (from 6am; 2hr 30min). Or join one of the numerous half- or full-day trips (from B250). In Nakhon Pathom, buses and songthaews pick up passengers outside the police station and outside *Nakorn Inn Hotel* (from 6am; 1hr). From Kanchanaburi, take bus #461 to Ban Phe (every 15min from 5.25am; 1hr 15min), then change to bus #78. To get to Damnoen Saduak from Phetchaburi or any points further south, catch any Bangkok-bound bus and, depending on which route it takes, change either at Samut Songkhram or at the Photharam intersection.

Damnoen Saduak's **bus terminal** is just north of Thanarat Bridge and Khlong Damnoen Saduak, on the main Bangkok/Nakhon Pathom–Samut Songkhram road, Highway 325. Frequent yellow **songthaews** cover the 2km to Ton Kem, but walk if you've got the time: a walkway follows the canal, which you can get to from Thanarat Bridge, or you can cross the bridge and take the road to the right (west), Thanon Sukhaphiban 1, through the orchards. Drivers on the earliest buses from Bangkok sometimes do not terminate at the bus station near Thanarat Bridge but instead cross the bridge and then drop unsuspecting tourists a few hundred metres along Thanon Sukhaphiban 1, into the arms of a local boat operator. If you're happy to join a boat tour straightaway, this is not necessarily a problem, but it can be difficult to extricate yourself; to avoid this, get off with the rest of the Thai passengers at the bus station near the bridge.

The best way to see the markets is to stay overnight in Damnoen Saduak and get up at dawn, well before the buses and coach tours from Bangkok arrive. There's decent budget **accommodation** at the *Little Bird Hotel*, also known as *Noknoi* (Ⓣ032 254382; ❷–❸), whose sign is clearly visible from the main road and Thanarat Bridge. Rooms here are good value: enormous, clean and all with en-suite bathrooms, and there's air-con if you want it. Staff at *Little Bird* can also arrange floating market boat trips.

Samut Songkhram and around

Rarely visited by foreign tourists and yet within easy reach of Bangkok, the tiny estuarine province of **SAMUT SONGKHRAM** is nourished by the Mae Khlong River as it meanders through on the last leg of its route to the Gulf. Fishing is an important industry round here, and big wooden boats are still built in riverside yards near the estuary, within easy reach of the Gulf waters; further inland, fruit is the main source of income, particularly pomelos, lychees, guavas and coconuts. But for visitors it is the network of three hundred canals woven around the river, and the traditional way of life the waterways still support, that is most intriguing. As well as some of the most genuine floating markets in Thailand, there are chances to witness traditional cottage industries such as palm-sugar production and *bencharong* ceramic painting, plus more than a hundred historic temples to admire, a number of them dating back to the reign of Rama II, who was born in the province. The other famous sons of the region are Eng and Chang, the "original" Siamese twins, who grew up in Samut Songkhram and are commemorated with a small museum in the town.

Despite the region's tangible charm, tourism is very much in its infancy here, so hotel options are limited. If you're dependent on public transport, your first stop will be the provincial capital of Samut Songkhram, also commonly known as Mae Khlong, after the river that cuts through it, but there's no reason to linger here as the sights and accommodation are all out of town, mainly in the **Amphawa** district a few kilometres upriver.

If you get the chance, it's well worth venturing out onto the canals after dark to **watch the fireflies** twinkling romantically in their favourite lamphu trees like delicate strings of fairylights; any boatman should know where to find them. The lights are a mating call and can operate day or night, though they're only visible to the human eye after dark and are easiest to spot in the rainy season, and when the moon's not too bright.

Eng and Chang, the Siamese twins

Eng (In) and Chang (Chan), the "original" **Siamese twins**, were born in Samut Songkhram in 1811, when the town was known as Mae Khlong after the estuary on which it sits, and the country was known as Siam. The boys' bodies were joined from breastbone to navel by a short fleshy ligament, but they shared no vital organs and eventually managed to stretch their connecting tissue so that they could stand almost side by side instead of permanently facing each other.

In 1824, the boys were spotted by entrepreneurial Scottish trader Robert Hunter, who returned five years later with an American sea merchant, Captain Abel Coffin, to convince the twins' mother to let them take her sons on a world tour. Hunter and Coffin anticipated a lucrative career as producer-managers of an exotic **freak show**, and were not disappointed. They launched the twins in Boston, advertising them as "the Monster" and charging the public 50 cents to watch the boys demonstrate how they walked and ran. Though shabbily treated and poorly paid, the twins soon developed a more theatrical show, enthralling their audiences with impressive acrobatics and feats of strength, and earning the soubriquet "the eighth wonder of the world". At the age of 21, having split from their exploitative managers, the twins became self-employed, but continued to tour with other companies across the world. Wherever they went, they would always be given a thorough examination by local **medics**, partly to counter accusations of fakery, but also because this was the first time the world and its doctors had been introduced to conjoined twins. Such was the twins' international celebrity that the term "Siamese twins" has been used ever since. Chang and Eng also sought advice from these doctors on surgical separation – an issue they returned to repeatedly right up until their deaths but never acted upon, despite plenty of gruesome suggestions.

By 1840 the twins had become quite wealthy and decided to settle down. They were granted American citizenship, assumed the family name Bunker, and became slave-owning **plantation farmers** in North Carolina. Three years later they married two local sisters, Addie and Sally Yates, and between them went on to father 21 children. The families lived in separate houses and the twins shuttled between the two, keeping to a strict timetable of three days in each household; for an intriguing imagined account of this bizarre state of affairs, read Darin Strauss's novel *Chang and Eng*, reviewed on p.851. Chang and Eng had quite different personalities, and relations between the two couples soured, leading to the division of their assets, with Chang's family getting most of the land, and Eng's most of the slaves. To support their dependants, the twins were obliged to take their show back on the road several times, on occasion working with the infamous showman P.T. Barnum. Their final tour was born out of financial desperation following the 1861–65 Civil War, which had wiped out most of the twins' riches and led to the liberation of all their slaves.

In 1874, Chang succumbed to bronchitis and died; Eng, who might have survived on his own if an operation had been performed immediately, died a few hours later, possibly of shock. They were 62. The twins are buried in White Plains in North Carolina, but there's a **memorial** to them near their birthplace in Samut Songkhram, where a statue and the makeshift little In-Chan Museum (Mon–Fri 8.30am–4.30pm; free) have been erected 4km north of the provincial capital's centre on Thanon Ekachai (Route 3092).

Practicalities

The traditional way of travelling to Samut Songkhram from Bangkok – by **train** – is still the most scenic, albeit rather convoluted. Trains leave from Wongwian Yai station in southern Thonburi (not to be confused with Thonburi train station further north), and take you through a serene and fertile landscape as far as **Samut Sakhon**, also known as **Mahachai** (approximately hourly; 1hr); here you take a ferry across the Tha Chin River (there's no rail bridge) and then wait for the departure of the connecting train from **Ban Laem** on the other bank to Samut Songkhram at the end of the line (4 daily; 1hr). The **bus** ride to Samut Songkhram from Bangkok's Southern Bus terminal (every 20min; 1hr 30min) is faster, but the views are dominated by urban sprawl until the last stretch, when Highway 35 runs through a swathe of **salt farms** whose windmills pump in the sea water via a web of canals, leaving the brine to evaporate into photogenic little pyramids of white crystals.

Once in Samut Songkhram, you have various options for local transport, though the public transport network is limited and doesn't encompass all the sights. **Taxi-boats** and other chartered river transport operate from the Mae Khlong River pier, which is close to the train station and market in the town centre. **Songthaews** to Amphawa and **local buses** to Amphawa and Damnoen Saduak, via Highway 325, leave from the central market, between the train and bus stations. A big part of this area's appeal is that it's best explored by boat, most rewardingly on a **tour** from *Baan Tai Had Resort* (B150–200/person) or one of the home-stays (B300–700/boat), though it's also possible to charter a boat from the town centre pier in Samut Songkhram. Independent exploration is possible if you have your own vehicle, and *Baan Tai Had* rents out bicycles, kayaks and jet skis.

Alternatively, you could join a one-day **cycling tour** from Bangkok: Bike and Travel (Ⓦwww.cyclingthailand.com) runs day-trips to Amphawa from the capital, with minibus transport from Bangkok and bicycle rental included.

Accommodation and eating

English-speaking hotel staff and tour guides are thin on the ground in Samut Songkhram, which is one of several reasons why it's worth splashing out on **accommodation** at the luxurious but good-value *Baan Tai Had Resort* (Ⓣ034 767220, Ⓦwww.hotelthailand.com/samutsongkram/baantaihad, Ⓔbaantaihad@hotmail.com; ❻), located beside the Mae Khlong River in the Amphawa district, about 6km upstream from Samut Songkhram. Taxi-boats from Samut Songkhram's pier to *Baan Tai Had* cost B60 and take about fifteen minutes; if coming by car, it's best to email the hotel for a map. With its stylish, comfortable bungalows set around a Bali-style garden, swimming pool and restaurant, *Baan Tai Had* makes a good base, not least because of its local tour programmes and English-speaking guides. There's also a potentially interesting **home-stay programme** in two nearby villages, Ban Tha Ka (15km north of Samut Songkhram) and Plai Phong Pang (9km west of Samut Songkhram on Route 3093), where many households have joined together to offer accommodation and meals in their traditional homes (B350/person half-board), though you're unlikely to be able to converse with them in English. Home-stays must be booked through the headman (*kamnan*) of each village: for Plai Phong Pang call Ⓣ01 403 7907 or 01 406 4057, and for Ban Tha Ka call Ⓣ034 766190; if you don't speak Thai, Bangkok TAT may be able to help (Ⓣ02 282 9773).

Seafood is the obvious regional speciality and the most famous local dish is *hoi lot pat cha*, a spicy stir-fry that centres round the tubular worm shells –

hoi lot – that are harvested in their sackloads at low tide from a muddy sandbank known as Don Hoi Lot at the mouth of the Mae Khlong estuary. Don Hoi Lot is probably the most famous spot in the province to eat seafood, and a dozen restaurants occupy the area around the nearby pier, many offering views out over the Gulf and its abundant sandbar; the pier is 5km south of Highway 35 and is reached from Samut Songkhram by following the Highway 35 signs for Phetchaburi until directed down a side road. If you're staying at *Baan Tai Had*, make use of the free taxi-boat service from the *Chao Lay* restaurant, a ten-minute boat ride away on the banks of a nearby khlong: the setting is very pleasant and the mid-priced menu has plenty of fresh fish and seafood, usually including locally caught giant prawns (*kung yai*).

Tha Ka Floating Market and the palm-sugar centres

Unlike at the over-touristed markets of nearby Damnoen Saduak, the **floating market at Tha Ka** is still the province of local residents, with market gardeners either paddling up here in their small wooden sampans, or motoring along in their noisy longtails, the boats piled high with whatever's in season, be it pomelos or betel nuts, rambutans or okra, or even hot noodle soup and freshly cooked satay. Their main customers are canalside residents and other traders, so the atmosphere is still pleasingly but not artificially traditional and as yet the market is not a major feature on the coach-tour trail. Thai tourist groups do visit, but mainly if market day happens to fall on a weekend. The Tha Ka market operates only six times a month, on a **timetable** that's dependent on the tides (for boat access) and is therefore dictated by the moon; thus market days are restricted to the second, seventh and twelfth mornings of every fifteen-day lunar cycle, from around 7 to 11am. The market takes place on Khlong Phanla in the village of Ban Tha Ka, a half-hour **boat ride** from *Baan Tai Had Resort*, or ten to forty minutes from the home-stays, and about an hour from Damnoen Saduak; it's usually incorporated into a day-trip (about B200/person). The boat ride to the market is half the fun, but you can also get there by **road**, following Highway 325 out of Samut Songkhram for 10km, then taking a five-kilometre access road to Ban Tha Ka.

Most boat trips to Tha Ka also make a stop at one of the nearby **palm-sugar-making centres**. The sap of the coconut palm is a crucial ingredient in many Thai sweets and the fertile soil of Samut Songkhram province supports many small-scale sugar-palm plantations. There are several palm-sugar cottage industries between Amphawa and Ban Tha Ka, off Highway 325, accessible by car, by Damnoen Saduak-bound bus or by longtail boat.

Amphawa and around

The district town of **AMPHAWA** is smaller and more atmospheric than Samut Songkhram, retaining traditional charm alongside modern development. Its old neighbourhoods hug the banks of the Mae Khlong River and the Khlong Amphawa tributary, the wooden homes and shops facing the water and accessed either by boat or on foot along one of the waterfront walkways. Frequent **songthaews** and local **buses** (both approximately every 30min; 15min) connect Samut Songkhram market with Amphawa market, which sets up beside the khlong, just back from its confluence with the river.

King Rama II Memorial Park and Wat Amphawan

King Rama II was born in Amphawa (his mother's home town) in 1767 and is honoured with a memorial park and temple erected on the site of his probable birthplace, beside the Mae Khlong River on the western edge of Amphawa town, five minutes' walk west of Amphawa market and khlong. It's accessible both by boat and by road, 6km from Samut Songkhram on the Amphawa–Bang Khonthi road.

Rama II, or Phra Buddhalertla Naphalai as he is known in Thai, was a famously cultured king and a respected poet and playwright, and the **museum** (Wed–Sun 9am–4pm; B10) at the heart of the **King Rama II Memorial Park** (daily 9am–6pm) displays lots of rather esoteric Rama II memorabilia, including a big collection of nineteenth-century musical instruments and a gallery of *khon* masks used in traditional theatre. On the edge of the park, **Wat Amphawan** is graced with a statue of the king and decorated with murals that depict scenes from his life, including a behind-the-altar panorama of nineteenth-century Bangkok, with Ratanakosin Island's Grand Palace, Wat Pho and Sanam Luang still recognizable to modern eyes.

Wat Chulamani and Ban Pinsuwan bencharong workshop

The canalside **Wat Chulamani** was until the late 1980s the domain of the locally famous abbot Luang Poh Nuang, a man believed by many to possess special powers, and followers still come to the temple to pay respects to his body, which is preserved in a glass-sided coffin in the main viharn. The breathtakingly detailed decor inside the viharn is testament to the devotion he inspired: the intricate black-and-gold lacquered artwork that covers every surface has taken years and cost millions of baht to complete. Across the temple compound, the bot's modern, pastel-toned murals tell the story of the Buddha's life, beginning inside the door on the right with a scene showing the young Buddha emerging from a tent (his birth) and being able to walk on lilypads straightaway. The death of the Buddha and his entry into nirvana is depicted on the wall behind the altar. Wat Chulamani is located beside Khlong Amphawa, a twenty-minute walk east of Amphawa market, or a five-minute boat-ride. It is also signed off Highway 325, so any bus going to Damnoen Saduak from Samut Songkhram will drop you within reach.

A few hundred metres down the road from Wat Chulamani, and also accessible on foot, by bus and by canal, the Ban Pinsuwan **bencharong workshop** specializes in reproductions of famous antique *bencharong* ceramics, the exquisite five-coloured pottery that used to be the tableware of choice for the Thai aristocracy and is now a prized collector's item. A *bencharong* museum, exhibiting the chronology of styles, is planned.

Kanchanaburi and the River Kwai valleys

Set in a landscape of limestone hills just 120km from Bangkok, the provincial capital of **Kanchanaburi** occupies a strategic and scenic spot at the point where the **River Kwai Noi** merges with the **River Kwai Yai** to become the Mae Khlong. (Though, in truth, Kwai Yai is just the name that's been appropriated for the Mae Khlong as it flows through this region.) The town is most famous for its World War II role as a POW camp and base for construction work on the Thailand–Burma Railway, chiefly because of the notorious Bridge

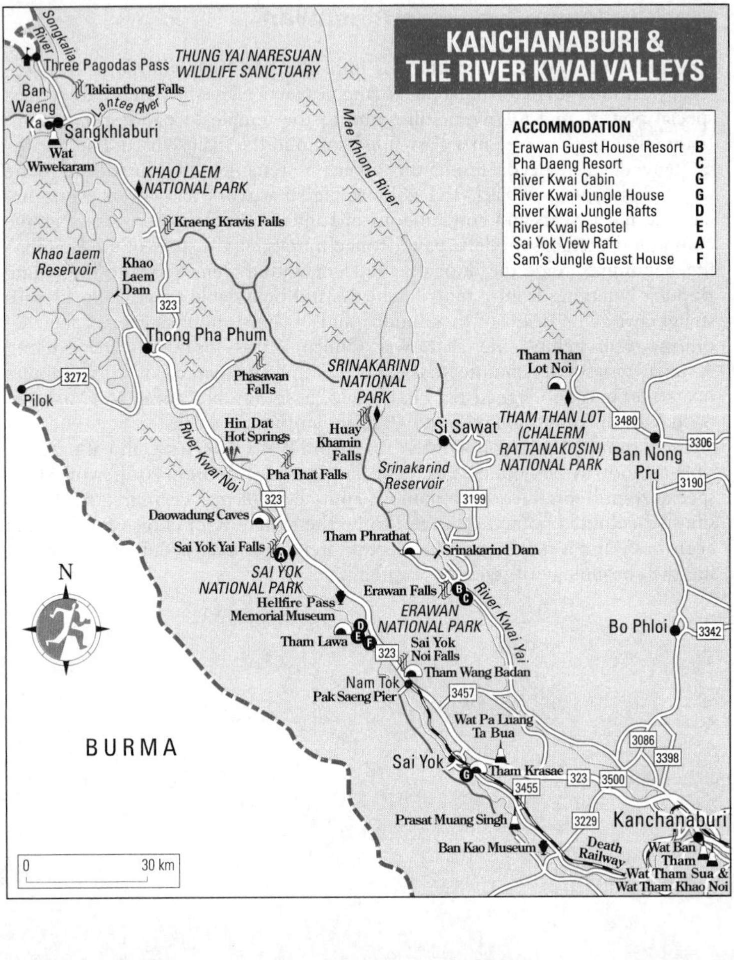

over the River Kwai, which spans the river here. But there are plenty more important wartime sights in and around Kanchanaburi, and the town is also an appealing destination in its own right, with lots of riverside guest houses that make wonderful places to unwind for a few days. The surrounding area offers numerous caves, wats and historical sites to explore, some of them easily reached by bicycle, and organized treks and rafting trips are also a major feature.

Beyond Kanchanaburi, the main area of interest is the Kwai Noi valley as this was the route followed by the **Death Railway**. Riding the train along the remaining section of this line is a popular activity and combines well with a visit to the sobering museum north of the current terminus at the aptly named **Hellfire Pass**. Following the Kwai Noi to its headwaters brings you to the unhyped, ethnically mixed little lakeside town of **Sangkhlaburi**, close by the Burmese border at **Three Pagodas Pass**. Further east, the Kwai Yai valley offers fewer obvious attractions, but is the site of the much-visited **Erawan Falls**, while nearby **Tham Than Lot National Park** appeals to hikers because of its impressive caves.

Kanchanaburi

With its plentiful supply of traveller-oriented accommodation and countless possibilities for easy forays into the surrounding countryside, **KANCHANABURI** makes the perfect getaway from Bangkok, a two-hour bus ride away. The big appeal here is the river: that it's the famous River Kwai is a bonus, but the more immediate attractions are the guest houses whose rooms overlook the waterway, most of them offering fine views of the serrated limestone hills beyond. The heart of this ever-expanding travellers' scene dominates the southern end of Thanon Maenam Kwai (also spelt Kwae) and is within easy reach of the train station, but the real town centre is some distance away, running north from the bus station up Kanchanaburi's main drag, Thanon Saeng Chuto.

Nearly all Kanchanaburi's official attractions relate to World War II and the building of the Thailand–Burma Railway. Day-trippers and tour groups descend in their hundreds on the infamous **Bridge over the River Kwai**, the symbol of Japanese atrocities in the region, though the town's main **war museums** and **cemeteries** are much more moving. Many veterans returning to visit the graves of their wartime comrades are understandably resentful that others have in some cases insensitively exploited the POW experience – the commercial paraphernalia surrounding the Bridge is a case in point. On the other hand, the Thailand–Burma Railway Centre provides shockingly instructive accounts of a period not publicly documented outside this region. The town's main war sights are located along the east bank of the Kwai Yai and Mae Khlong, but it's easy to cross the river – by road, ferry or longtail – and explore some of the more tranquilly located temples along the Kwai Noi and west bank of the Mae Khlong.

The Bridge forms the dramatic centrepiece of the annual *son-et-lumière* **River Kwai Bridge Festival**, held over ten nights from the end of November to commemorate the first Allied bombing of the Bridge on November 28, 1944. The hour-long show uses spectacular effects to sketch the history of the region's wartime role, and the area around the Bridge turns into an enormous funfair. Tourists of all nationalities flock to Kanchanaburi during this time, so book accommodation and transport well in advance, or join one of the many special tours operating out of Bangkok.

Arrival

Trains from Thonburi station in Bangkok or from Nakhon Pathom are the most scenic way to get to Kanchanaburi, but there are only two daily in each direction. The State Railway also runs special day-trips from Bangkok's Hualamphong Station, which include short stops at Nakhon Pathom, the Bridge over the River Kwai and Nam Tok, the terminus of the line (Sat, Sun & holidays only; advance booking is essential, see p.198). Coming from Hua Hin, Chumphon and points further south, take the train to Ban Pong and then change to a Kanchanaburi-bound train (or bus). When moving on to the south, the best option is to take a train or bus to Nakhon Pathom and change to a night train headed for Chumphon, Surat Thani or beyond, but you must book tickets for these sleepers in advance. The main **Kanchanaburi train station** (Ⓣ034 511285) is on Thanon Saeng Chuto, about 2km north of the town centre, but within walking distance of some of the riverside accommodation along Soi Rongheabaow and Thanon Maenam Kwai. However, if you're staying at *Bamboo House* or the *Felix River Kwai*, or are doing a day-trip and want to see the Bridge, get off at the next stop instead, which is **River Kwai Bridge train station**, seven minutes further on and located just in front of the Bridge, on the east bank of the river.

Faster than the train are the various **buses** (air-con only) from Bangkok's Southern Bus Terminal: the #81 is a first-class service (every 15min; 2hr), while the slightly cheaper series of buses numbered #81-1 to #81-36 (every 20min; 2hr) form the second-class service. When leaving Kanchanaburi, the first-class ticket office and departure point is right beside the main road on the edge of the bus station, while the main ticket office for all other services is further back inside the depot. From Lopburi, Ayutthaya (for trains from Chiang Mai), or points further north, you'll have to return to Bangkok or change buses at Suphanburi, about 90km north of Kanchanaburi (#411; every 20min; 2hr). The Suphanburi route is quite workable in reverse if you're heading north to Ayutthaya and/or Chiang Mai. From Phetchaburi and Hua Hin you need to change buses at Ratchaburi for connections to Kanchanaburi (#461; every 15min; 1hr 45min). Arriving at Kanchanaburi **bus station** (Ⓣ034 511182), at the southern edge of the town centre, it's a ten- to twenty-minute walk, B15 motorbike-taxi ride or B40–50 samlor ride along Thanon Lak Muang to the raft houses off Thanon Song Kwai; to get to the Soi Rongheabaow and Thanon Maenam Kwai guest houses, either take a B40–50 samlor or tuk-tuk ride, or hop on the public songthaew service described below.

If you're coming from Bangkok, the fastest transport of all is to take one of the **tourist minibuses** from Thanon Khao San, which travel at breakneck speeds and take just two hours door to door, though they generally only drop passengers at *Jolly Frog*, despite advertising otherwise. The same minivans make the return trip to Thanon Khao San every afternoon and can be booked through most Kanchanaburi guest houses and tour operators. Minivans can also be chartered for transport to **Don Muang Airport** at a cost of B1800 for a minibus that seats up to nine people. Tourist minibuses also run between Kanchanaburi and Ayutthaya, taking two hours.

Town transport and information

The cheapest way of getting between the bus station, Thanon Maenam Kwai guest houses and the Bridge is to take one of the public **songthaews** that run along Thanon Saeng Chuto via the Kanchanaburi War Cemetery (Don Rak)

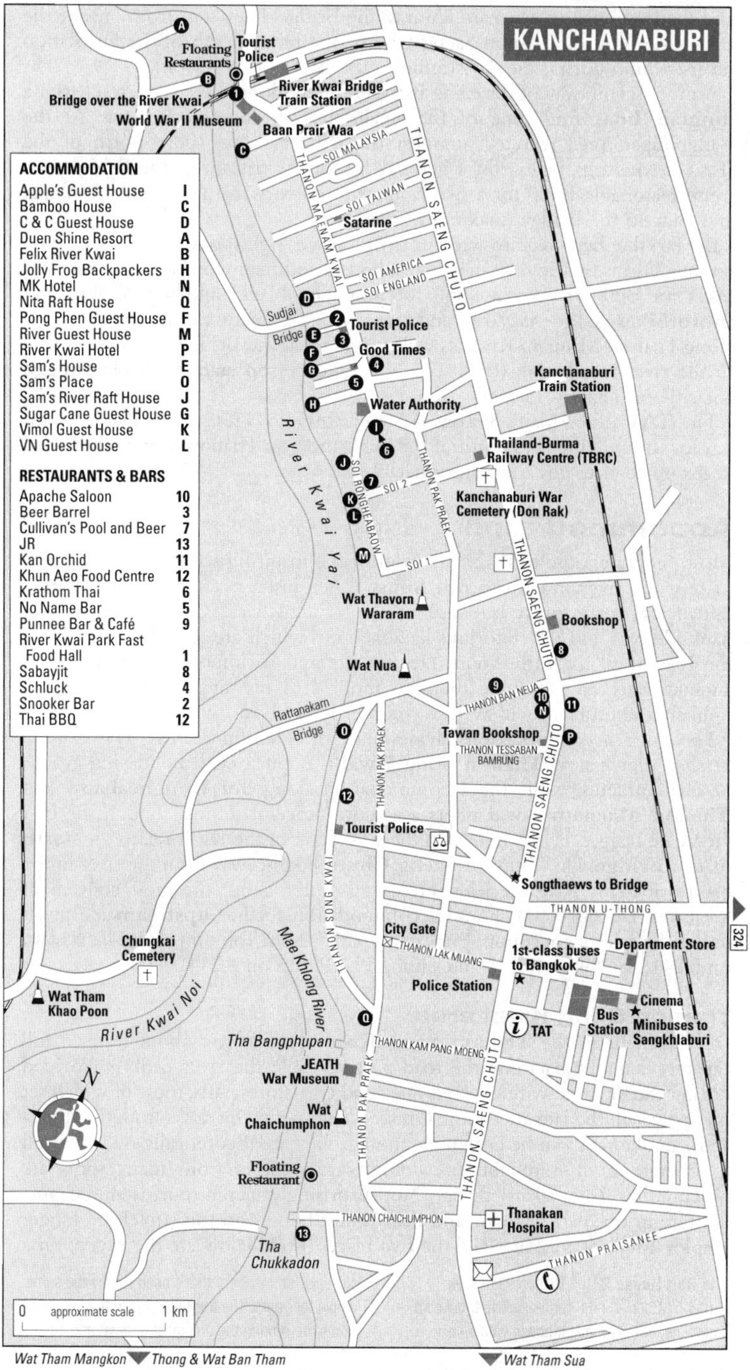
KANCHANABURI
ACCOMMODATION
Apple's Guest House I
Bamboo House C
C & C Guest House D
Duen Shine Resort A
Felix River Kwai B
Jolly Frog Backpackers H
MK Hotel N
Nita Raft House Q
Pong Phen Guest House F
River Guest House M
River Kwai Hotel P
Sam's House E
Sam's Place O
Sam's River Raft House J
Sugar Cane Guest House G
Vimol Guest House K
VN Guest House L
RESTAURANTS & BARS
Apache Saloon 10
Beer Barrel 3
Cullivan's Pool and Beer 7
JR 13
Kan Orchid 11
Khun Aeo Food Centre 12
Krathom Thai 6
No Name Bar 5
Punnee Bar & Café 9
River Kwai Park Fast Food Hall 1
Sabayjit 8
Schluck 4
Snooker Bar 2
Thai BBQ 12
Floating Restaurants
Tourist Police
Bridge over the River Kwai
World War II Museum
River Kwai Bridge Train Station
Baan Prair Waa
SOI MALAYSIA
SOI TAIWAN
Satarine
SOI AMERICA
SOI ENGLAND
THANON MAENAM KWAI
THANON SAENG CHUTO
Sudjai Bridge
Tourist Police
Good Times
Water Authority
Kanchanaburi Train Station
Thailand-Burma Railway Centre (TBRC)
River Kwai Yai
SOI RONGHEABAOW
SOI 2
SOI 1
THANON PAK PRAEK
Kanchanaburi War Cemetery (Don Rak)
Wat Thavorn Wararam
Bookshop
Wat Nua
THANON BAN NEUA
Rattanakarn Bridge
Tawan Bookshop
THANON TESSABAN BAMRUNG
Tourist Police
THANON SONG KWAI
Songthaews to Bridge
THANON U-THONG
324
City Gate
THANON LAK MUANG
1st-class buses to Bangkok
Department Store
Police Station
Cinema
Bus Station
Minibuses to Sangkhlaburi
TAT
Chungkai Cemetery
Wat Tham Khao Poon
River Kwai Noi
Mae Khlong River
Tha Bangphupan
THANON KAM PANG MOENG
JEATH War Museum
Wat Chaichumphon
N
Floating Restaurant
THANON CHAICHUMPHON
Thanakan Hospital
Tha Chukkadon
THANON PRAISANEE
0 approximate scale 1 km
Wat Tham Mangkon Thong & Wat Ban Tham
Wat Tham Sua

and then up Thanon Maenam Kwai to the Bridge. They start from outside the Bata shoe shop on Thanon Saeng Chuto, one block north of the bus station (every 15min during the day; 15min to the Bridge; B5/person).

A more scenic way of travelling between sights along the river is to charter a **longtail boat** from one of the small piers in the tourist areas. At the Bangphupan pier, secreted amongst the trinket shops 100m north of the JEATH Museum, boats cost a hefty B150 for the trip up to the Bridge, or a more reasonable B400 for a two-hour trip out to Khao Poon and Chungkai and back to the Bridge (maximum six people).

By far the best way to see the main town sights, and the surrounding countryside, is by **bicycle**; most guest houses and many tour agencies rent out bikes for B20–30 per day (B50 for mountain bikes), and several also have **motorbikes** (B150–350/day) and jeeps for hire. There are dozens of outlets along Thanon Maenam Kwai, as well as one up at the Bridge. Or you can take to the river in a **kayak** (B500/3hr for a two-person craft), available through Safarine on Thanon Taiwan.

The **TAT** office (daily 8.30am–4.30pm; ⓣ034 511200, ⓔtatkan@tat.or.th) is a few hundred metres south of the bus station on Thanon Saeng Chuto and keeps up-to-date bus and train timetables.

Accommodation

Most people choose to make the most of the inspiring scenery by staying on or near the river, in either a **raft house** (often just a rattan hut balanced on a raft of logs) or a **guest house**. The one big drawback is the noise from the bankside bars and the notorious karaoke rafts, which are towed up and down the river until the early hours. Despite attempts to impose a curfew on the karaoke rafts, and to force them to moor at a distant spot downriver, it's unlikely the problem will ever be completely resolved.

The river accommodation divides into three distinct areas. The noisier, brasher stretch near **Thanon Song Kwai** is popular with holidaying groups of Thai students, while the accommodation along **Soi Rongheabaow** and **Thanon Maenam Kwai** offers a a more peaceful setting, though the best views are bagged by the hotels on the west bank of the Kwai Yai, to the **north of the Bridge**. The **Thanon Saeng Chuto** hotels, away from the river in the centre of town, have the least interesting outlooks but the most convenient locations. Details of raft-house accommodation further **upstream** are given under the relevant accounts: Erawan on p.237, Nam Tok on p.241, Tham Lawa on p.241, Sai Yok on p.243 and Thong Pha Phum on p.244.

Thanon Song Kwai area

Development in the **Thanon Song Kwai** area has just about reached full capacity: karaoke bars line the road proper, while the river bank is crowded during the daytime with covered one- and two-storey rafts, most of which set off upriver in the late afternoon. On weekend nights the noise from the disco- and karaoke rafts can be deafening, though they are theoretically only allowed to operate until midnight. In addition, river views from many spots are obscured by Rattanakarn Bridge. Not surprisingly, farang tourists are becoming rare in this part of town, and many guest houses on this stretch no longer employ English-speaking staff: the two places listed below are the exception.

Nita Raft House 271/1 Thanon Pak Praek ⓣ034 514521, ⓔnita_rafthouse@hotmail.com. A genuine, old-style guest house with a very laid-back atmosphere that's been run by the same couple for years. The fourteen simple floating rooms are among the cheapest in town and all offer some sort of river view; some are en suite. There's also a nice floating lounge for watching DVDs, and sampling the tasty guest-house food. Located away from the main Thanon Song Kwai fray, near the JEATH Museum. ❶–❷

Sam's Place Thanon Song Kwai ⓣ034 513971, ⓦwww.samsguesthouse.com. Comfortable and attractively designed range of en-suite raft houses, all with a partial view of the Mae Khlong River from their own little veranda, though noise levels could be an issue. ❸

Soi Rongheabaow and Thanon Maenam Kwai area

Soi Rongheabaow (or **Rong Heeb Oil**, as it's sometimes spelt) is little more than a narrow village lane with a handful of pleasant raft houses and a couple of small bar-restaurants, where bicycles and dogs constitute the main traffic and householders sell a few groceries from their front rooms. **Thanon Maenam Kwai** is more of a thoroughfare, stretching 2km from Soi Rongheabaow to the Bridge, and is *the* backpackers' hub, full of small bars, restaurants, tour operators and tourist-oriented minimarts, as well as guest houses, though most of these are well off the main road on the river bank.

Apple's Guest House 52 Soi Rongheabaow 3 ⓣ034 512017, ⓦwww.applenoi-kanchanaburi.com. Small, welcoming guest house whose indefatigable owners run imaginative, well-regarded tours and have made their restaurant the town's best. The twenty spotless rooms are set round a lawn away from the river and are all en suite; price depends on size, furnishings and whether you want fan or air-con. ❷–❹

Bamboo House Soi Vietnam, off the Bridge end of Thanon Maenam Kwai ⓣ034 624470, ⓔbamboo-house@thaimail.com. Kanchanaburi's most secluded and peaceful accommodation occupies a lovely stretch of the river not far from the Bridge, though it is a little inconvenient for the shops and restaurants of southern Thanon Maenam Kwai, 2km away. The nicest bungalows are en suite and set round a decent-sized lawn that's good for kids; there are also some simple floating huts with a mattress on the floor and shared bathrooms, and a couple of air-con rooms on dry land. If arriving by train, get off at the River Kwai Bridge station, which is closer than Kanchanaburi station. ❷–❹

C & C Guest House Soi England, 265/2 Thanon Maenam Kwai ⓣ034 624547, ⓔcctrekking@yahoo.com. Riverside compound of basic and very cheap floating huts with shared bathrooms, plus some simple en-suite huts (with the option of air-con) set in the garden. It's a very quiet spot, at the end of a winding soi, and serves guest-house food at its floating restaurant. Call for free transport from the bus or train station. ❶–❸

Jolly Frog Backpackers 28 Soi China, just off the southern end of Thanon Maenam Kwai ⓣ034 514579, ⓦwww.jollyfrog.fsnet.co.uk. Most backpackers' first choice, this large complex features comfortable en-suite bamboo huts (some with air-con) ranged around a riverside garden plus a few cheaper floating rafts with shared facilities. You can swim off the jetty (though be careful of the strong current), and the lawn's nice and large. On the down side, the place can be noisy at night and is a bit impersonal. Call for free transport from the bus or train station. ❷–❸

Pong Phen Guest House 5 Soi Bangladesh (Bangklated), off Thanon Maenam Kwai ⓣ034 512981, ⓔpongphen@hotmail.com. Small, modern raft-house rooms with shared bathrooms but great views from the common veranda.. On land, choose between well-designed fan and air-con rooms, all en suite, set in a row around the lawn area. Also has a pleasant riverside terrace for soaking up the impressive vistas. ❷–❸

River Guest House 42 Soi Rongheabaow ⓣ034 511637. Prettily located set of very simple raft houses, all with private bathrooms, moored 30m from the river bank. ❷

Sam's House Thanon Maenam Kwai ⓣ034 515956, ⓦwww.samsguesthouse.com. The poshest and most popular of the three *Sam's* places in town, this one features a set of attractively positioned, if rather congested, wooden huts floating among a dense tangle of lotuses – all are en suite, furnished to a high standard, and fronted by a small private balcony, and some have air-con. There are some less interesting fan and air-con rooms on the river bank. ❷–❺

Sam's River Raft House 48/1 Soi Rongheabaow ⓣ034 624231, ⓦwww.samsguesthouse.com. This arm of the *Sam's* empire offers thirty comfortably equipped floating rooms, built on pontoons, some with direct access to the riverfront walkway, others with river-bank views, but all of them are en suite and a few have air-con. There are cheaper rooms in the garden across the road. ❷–❸

Sugar Cane Guest House 22 Soi Pakistan, off Thanon Maenam Kwai ⓣ034 624520, ⓔsugarcaneguesthouse@hotmail.com. Peaceful, family-run place with a dozen en-suite terraced and detached huts set round a lawn overlooking the river, plus a block of en-suite floating rooms, some of which enjoy stunning river views and have air-con. ❷–❹

Vimol Guest House Soi Rongheabaow ⓣ & ⓕ034 514831. Offers smart, wood-panelled floating rooms, all en suite and with air-con, plus some A-frame bamboo huts with sleeping quarters in the roof section and bathrooms downstairs, but no views at all. Friendly management and good food. ❶–❺

VN Guest House 44 Soi Rongheabaow ⓣ034 514082, ⓔvnguesthouse@yahoo.com. Very basic, very cheap floating huts (shared facilities), plus some unimaginatively designed concrete huts on the bank, all en suite and some with air-con. Phone for free transport from bus and train stations. ❶–❸

Thanon Saeng Chuto

Thanon Saeng Chuto is the town's main thoroughfare, so staying here gives you easy access to shops and town-centre businesses, but offers no prospect of a river view.

MK Hotel 277/41 Thanon Saeng Chuto ⓣ034 621143. Smartly maintained city-style hotel that lacks character but compensates with genuinely comfortable air-con rooms and reasonable prices. ❸–❹

River Kwai Hotel 284/3–16 Thanon Saeng Chuto ⓣ034 513349, ⓦwww.riverkwai.co.th. The town centre's top hotel is nowhere near the river, but all rooms have air-con, and facilities include a swimming pool, nightclub and Internet access. Good value for its class but not much atmosphere compared to the competition. Thirty percent discounts routinely offered. ❼

North of the Bridge

The hotels on the west bank of the Kwai Yai, to the **north of the Bridge**, are the most luxurious in the area, but, although they make the most of their picturesque locations, these places are beyond walking distance from most of the restaurants and sights.

Duen Shine Resort On the west bank of the Kwai Yai ⓣ034 653345, ⓔduenshine@yahoo.com. Upmarket riverside resort that caters more to Thai tourists than the nearby *Felix*; offers pretty good-value rooms, all with air-con and TV, in raft houses, cottages and a small hotel block. There's a swimming pool in the landscaped tropical garden, and a restaurant. ❼

Felix River Kwai On the west bank of the Kwai Yai ⓣ034 515061, ⓦwww.felixriverkwai.co.th. Occupying a lovely riverside spot within walking distance of the Bridge (or a 2km drive from Thanon Maenam Kwai – a little inconvenient if you don't have transport), this is the most upmarket resort in the area and offers over two hundred large deluxe rooms with air-con, TV and mini-bar, plus two swimming pools and several not very interesting restaurants. Rates depend on whether or not you want a river view, and are discounted during the week; reservations are essential for weekends. ❽

The Town

Strung out along the east bank of the River Kwai and its continuation, south of the Kwai Noi confluence, as the Mae Khlong, Kanchanaburi is a long, narrow ribbon of a town. The **war sights** are sandwiched between the river and the busy main drag, Thanon Saeng Chuto, with the Bridge over the River Kwai marking the northern limit, and the JEATH Museum towards the town's southern edge. If you have the time, it makes sense to start with the fairly central Thailand–Burma Railway Centre, across the road from the train station, which offers a good introduction to the World War II sights.

The Thailand-Burma Railway Centre

The **Thailand–Burma Railway Centre** (daily 9am–5pm; B60) is the best place to start any tour of Kanchanaburi's World War II memorials. Located across

The Death Railway

Shortly after entering World War II in December 1941, Japan, fearing an Allied blockade of the Bay of Bengal, began looking for an alternative supply route to connect its newly acquired territories that stretched from Singapore to the Burma–India border. In spite of the almost impenetrable terrain, the River Kwai basin was chosen as the route for a new **Thailand–Burma Railway**, the aim being to join the existing terminals of Nong Pladuk in Thailand (51km southeast of Kanchanaburi) and Thanbuyazat in Burma – a total distance of 415km.

About 60,000 Allied POWs were shipped up from captured Southeast Asian territories to work on the link, their numbers later augmented by as many as 200,000 conscripted Asian labourers. Work began at both ends in June 1942. Three million cubic metres of rock were shifted and 14km of bridges built with little else but picks and shovels, dynamite and pulleys. By the time the line was completed, fifteen months later, it had more than earned its nickname, the **Death Railway**: an estimated 16,000 POWs and 100,000 Asian labourers died while working on it.

The appalling conditions and Japanese brutality were the consequences of the **samurai code**: Japanese soldiers abhorred the disgrace of imprisonment – to them, ritual suicide was the only honourable option open to a prisoner – and therefore considered that Allied POWs had forfeited any rights as human beings. Food rations were meagre for men forced into backbreaking eighteen-hour shifts, often followed by night-long marches to the next camp. Many suffered from beri-beri, many more died of dysentery-induced starvation, but the biggest killers were cholera and malaria, particularly during the monsoon. It is said that one man died for every sleeper laid on the track.

The two lines finally met at Konkuita, just south of present-day Sangkhlaburi. But as if to underscore its tragic futility, the Thailand–Burma link saw less than two years of active service: after the Japanese surrender on August 15, 1945, the railway came under the jurisdiction of the British who, thinking it would be used to supply Karen separatists in Burma, tore up 4km of track at Three Pagodas Pass, thereby cutting the Thailand to Burma link forever. When the Thais finally gained control of the rest of the railway, they destroyed the track all the way down to Nam Tok, apparently because it was uneconomic. Recently, however, an Australian-Thai group of volunteers and former POWs has salvaged sections of track near the fearsome stretch of line known as Hellfire Pass, clearing a memorial walk at the pass and founding an excellent museum at the site, described on p.242.

There have been a number of books written about the Death Railway, including several by former POWs; the Thailand–Burma Railway Centre's bookshop stocks a selection, as do the town's bookshops, listed on p.234.

the road from the train station, next to the Don Rak Kanchanaburi War Cemetery, it was founded by the local supervisor of the Commonwealth War Graves Commission, Rod Beattie, specifically to provide an informed context for the thousands of people who visit the POW graves every week. He spent years exploring the entire route of the Thailand–Burma Railway and the result is a comprehensive and sophisticated history of the line itself, with plenty of original artefacts, illustrations and scale models, and particularly strong sections on the planning and construction of the railway, and on the subsequent operation, destruction and decommissioning of the line. There is more of a focus on the line itself here than at the more emotive Hellfire Pass Memorial Museum (see p.242), but the human stories are well documented too, notably via some extraordinary original photographs and video footage shot by Japanese engineers, as well as through unique interviews with surviving Asian labourers on the railway.

The shop inside the entrance sells a number of interesting books on the railway and also sells some of the products made by the Women for Weaving project in Sangkhlaburi (see p.246).

The Kanchanaburi War Cemetery (Don Rak)

Thirty-eight Allied POWs died for each kilometre of track laid on the Thailand–Burma Railway, and many of them are buried in Kanchanaburi's two war cemeteries. Of all the region's war sights, the cemeteries are the only places to have remained untouched by commercial enterprise. Opposite the train station on Thanon Saeng Chuto, the **Kanchanaburi War Cemetery** (**Don Rak**; daily 8am–4pm; free), is the bigger of the two (the other cemetery, Chungkai, is described opposite), with 6982 POW graves laid out in straight lines amid immaculately kept lawns and flowering shrubs. It was established after the war, on a plot adjacent to the town's Chinese cemetery, as the final resting place for the remains that had been hurriedly interred at dozens of makeshift POW-camp gravesites all the way up the course of the railway line. Many of the identical stone memorial slabs in Don Rak state simply, "A man who died for his country"; others, inscribed with names, dates and regiments, indicate that the overwhelming majority of the dead were under 25 years old. A commemorative service is held here every year on April 25, Anzac Day.

The Bridge over the River Kwai

For most people, the plain steel arches of the **Bridge over the River Kwai** come as a disappointment: as a war memorial it lacks both the emotive punch of the museums and the perceptible drama of spots further up the line, and as a bridge it looks nothing out of the ordinary – certainly not as awesomely hard to construct as it appears in David Lean's famous 1957 film, *Bridge on the River Kwai* (which was in fact shot in Sri Lanka). But it is the link with the multi-Oscar-winning film, of course, that draws tour buses by the dozen, and makes the Bridge approach seethe with trinket-sellers and touts. For all the commercialization of the place, however, you can't really come to the Kwai and not see it. To get here, take any songthaew heading north up Thanon Saeng Chuto, hire a samlor, or cycle – it's 5km from the bus station. You can charter longtails from the pier beside the Bridge for trips to JEATH or out to sights along the Kwai Yai.

The fording of the Kwai Yai at the point just north of Kanchanaburi known as Tha Makkham was one of the first major obstacles in the construction of the Thailand–Burma Railway. Sections of a steel bridge were brought up from Java and reassembled by POWs using only pulleys and derricks. A temporary **wooden bridge** was built alongside it, taking its first train in February 1943; three months later the steel bridge was finished. Both bridges were severely damaged by Allied bombers (rather than commando-saboteurs as in the film) in 1944 and 1945, but the steel bridge was repaired after the war and is still in use today. In fact the best way to see the Bridge is by taking the train over it: the Kanchanaburi–Nam Tok train crosses it three times a day in each direction, stopping briefly at the River Kwai Bridge station on the east bank of the river.

Some of the original World War II **railway engines** used on this stretch have been spruced up and parked beside the Bridge; nearby, a memorial stone commemorates the Japanese soldiers who died while overseeing the construction work.

World War II Museum and Art Gallery

While at the Bridge, you can't fail to see the advertisements for the nearby **World War II Museum** (daily 8am–6pm; B30), 30m south along Thanon Maenam Kwai. Despite mendacious signs that call this the "World War II Museum and JEATH War Museum", this should not be confused with the real JEATH War Museum (see below), for this is an entirely different, privately owned collection that cynically uses the war to pull in the coach parties. The war section comprises an odd mixture of memorabilia (a rusted bombshell, the carpet used by the local Japanese commander) and reconstructed tableaux featuring emaciated POWs, while the top-floor gallery in the same building displays selected "Miss Thailand" portraits from 1934 onwards. Across the courtyard, a second building seeks to present an overview of Thailand's most venerated institutions with the help of specially commissioned wall-paintings: Buddhism on the ground floor, prime ministers and kings on the middle storeys, and family portraits of the museum's founders – the Chansiris – at the top.

The JEATH War Museum

Founded by the chief abbot of Wat Chaichumpon and housed within the temple grounds in a reconstructed Allied POW hut of thatched palm, the ramshackle and unashamedly low-tech **JEATH War Museum** (daily 8.30am–6pm; B30) was the town's first public repository for the photographs and memories of the POWs who worked on the Death Railway. JEATH is an acronym of six of the countries involved in the railway: Japan, England, Australia, America, Thailand and Holland. The museum has since been surpassed by the slicker and more informative exhibitions at the Thailand–Burma Railway Centre (see p.228) and the Hellfire Pass Memorial Museum (see p.242) and is now of most interest for its small collection of wartime photographs and for its archive of newspaper articles about and letters from former POWs who have revisited the River Kwai. The museum is located beside the Mae Khlong on Thanon Pak Praek, at the southern end of town. It's about 700m from the TAT office, or 5km from the Bridge. From the nearby pier, Tha Banphuphen, you can take a longtail boat ride up to the Bridge and out to sights along the Kwai Noi.

Across the river

Kanchanaburi's other war cemetery, at **Chungkai**, and a handful of moderately interesting temples – including cave temples at **Wat Tham Khao Poon** and **Wat Ban Tham**, the hilltop twins of **Wat Tham Sua** and **Wat Tham Khao Noi**, and a wat featuring a rather bizarre **floating nun** – provide the focus for pleasurable trips west of the town centre, to various locations along the Kwai Noi and the Mae Khlong. All these sights are accessible by bicycle from central Kanchanaburi, and can also be reached by longtail (hired through guest houses or at one of the east-bank piers), or even by kayak (see p.235).

Chungkai Cemetery and Wat Tham Khao Poon

Chungkai Cemetery occupies a peaceful spot on the west bank of the Kwai Noi, at the site of a former POW camp. Some 1750 POWs are buried here; most of the gravestone inscriptions include a name and regimental insignia, but a number remain unnamed – at the upcountry camps, bodies were thrown onto mass funeral pyres, making identification impossible.

One kilometre on from Chungkai Cemetery, at the top of the road's only hill, sits the cave temple **Wat Tham Khao Poon** (daily 8am–6pm; donation).

This labyrinthine Santa's grotto is presided over by a medley of religious icons, the star being a Buddha reclining under a fanfare of flashing lights. The scenery around here is a good reason for continuing along the road for another few kilometres; once over the hill, the prospect widens to take in endless square kilometres of sugar-cane plantation (for which Kanchanaburi has earned the title "sugar capital of Thailand") fringed by dramatically looming limestone crags.

To reach Chungkai Cemetery and Wat Tham Khao Poon, either take the two-minute ferry ride (for pedestrians and bikes) from the pier at the confluence of the two rivers on Thanon Song Kwai, or follow the main road over Rattanakarn Bridge, 1km north of the pier.

Wat Tham Mangkon Thong (Floating Nun Temple)

The impressive scenery across on the east of the River Kwai Noi makes for an equally worthwhile bike trip, but the cave temple on this side – **Wat Tham Mangkon Thong**, otherwise known as the "**Floating Nun Temple**" – is fairly tacky. The attraction here is a Thai nun who, clad in white robes, will get into the temple pond and float there, meditating – if tourists give her enough money to make it worth her while. It's difficult not to be cynical about such a commercial stunt, though Taiwanese visitors are said to be particularly impressed. The floating takes place on a round pond at the foot of the enormous dragon staircase that leads up to the temple embedded in the hillside behind. The temple comprises an unexceptional network of low, bat-infested limestone caves, punctuated at intervals with Buddha statues.

There's no direct access from the west to the east bank of the Kwai Noi, so to get to Wat Tham Mangkon Thong from Chungkai and Wat Tham Khao Poon you have to return to town and start again. Travelling by bicycle or motorbike, take the ferry across the Mae Khlong River at Tha Chukkadon and then follow the road on the other side for about 4km. By car, turn west off Thanon Saeng Chuto (Highway 323) about 3km south of TAT onto Route 3429, which bridges the river and takes you north then west to the temple. Alternatively, take **bus** #8191 (every 30min; 20min) from Kanchanaburi bus station; the last return bus passes the temple at about 4.15pm.

Wat Ban Tham

Because of the limestone landscape, caves are all too common around Kanchanaburi and many of them have been sanctified as shrines. **Wat Ban Tham** is yet another example, but it's quite intriguing and is worth the twelve-kilometre trip from the town centre. Travelling south down the Mae Khlong to get to the temple is especially pleasant by longtail or kayak, but can also be fun by road: cross the river at Thanon Mae Khlong, then turn left for the six-kilometre ride along a partially unmade road or, if combining with Wat Tham Mangkon, see directions above and then head south.

Wat Ban Tham was founded around 600 years ago but its fame rests on the seventeenth-century love story that was supposedly played out in a cave on this site. A young woman called Nang Bua Klee was forced to choose between duty to her criminal father and love for the local hero by whom she had fallen pregnant; her father eventually persuaded Bua Klee to poison her sweetheart's food, but the soldier learned of the plot and killed both his wife and their unborn son, whose souls are now said to be trapped in the cave at Wat Ban Tham. The cave is approached via an ostentatious Chinese-style dragon's mouth staircase, whose upper levels relate the legend in a gallery of brightly painted modern murals on the right-hand walls. Inside the cave, a woman-shaped stone has been painted in the image of the dead mother and is a popular object of worship for women trying to conceive: hopeful devotees bring pretty dresses and shoes for the image, which are hung in wardrobes to the side of the shrine when not in use, as well as toys for her son.

Wat Tham Sua and Wat Tham Khao Noi

If you're in the mood for more temples, continue south along the Mae Khlong for another 5km to reach the modern hilltop wats of Tham Sua and Tham Khao Noi, which both afford expansive views over the river valley and out to the mountains beyond. Coming by car, the quickest route is to head south out of town along Highway 323 and cross the river via the signed Mae Khlong Dam. Otherwise, take any non-air-con Bangkok- or Nakhon Pathom-bound bus as far as Tha Muang, 12km south along Highway 323, then change to a motorbike taxi to the temples (about B40).

Designed by a Thai architect, **Wat Tham Sua** was conceived in typical grandiose style around a massive chedi covered with tiles similar to those used at Nakhon Pathom. Inside, a placid seated Buddha takes centre stage, his huge palms raised to show the Wheels of Law inscribed like stigmata across them; a conveyor belt transports devotees' offerings into the enormous alms bowl set into his lap. The neighbouring Chinese-designed **Wat Tham Khao Noi** is a fabulously gaudy, seven-tiered Chinese pagoda within which a laughing Buddha competes for attention with a host of gesturing and grimacing statues and painted characters.

Eating and drinking

All of Kanchanaburi's guest houses and raft houses have **restaurants**, in addition to which there are two main clusters of floating restaurants, around Tha Chukkadon, and beside the Bridge, which serve authentic if rather pricey seafood as well as enjoying great river views. A cheaper place to enjoy genuine local food is at the ever-reliable **night market**, which sets up alongside Thanon Saeng Chuto on the edge of the bus station. There are also a few foodstalls at the thrice-weekly **night bazaar** (aka JJ in homage to Bangkok's Chatuchak Market), which operates in front of the train station every Monday, Thursday and Saturday evening from 6 to 10pm, but the focus here is mainly on cheap fashions, CDs and sarongs – it's not at all tourist-oriented.

Restaurants

JR South of Tha Chukkadon. Floating restaurant that affords especially pretty views across the Mae Khlong and serves good-value, set meals of typical Thai-Chinese dishes, as well as à la carte standards. Moderate.

Kan Orchid Next to the *River Kwai Hotel* on Thanon Saeng Chuto. Air-con restaurant with a scrumptious, menu of farang-friendly Thai dishes, including recommended steamed river fish with plum sauce. Run by the same family as *Krathom Thai*. Moderate.

Khun Aeo Food Centre and **Thai BBQ** Thanon Song Kwai. These two large, adjacent canteens cater mainly to the crowds of Thai students who party at the rafts moored along this stretch of the road. The *Food Centre* dishes out plates of Thai fast food, while the almost as cheap *Thai BBQ* place next door lets you grill your choice of meat cuts at the hot-table in front of you. Inexpensive.

Krathom Thai At *Apple's Guest House*, 52 Soi Rongheabaow 3. Exceptionally delicious food, prepared by guest-house owner Apple to traditional Thai recipes. The extensive menu includes coconut- and cashew-laced *matsaman* curries – both meat and vegetarian varieties – as well as outstanding yellow curries and multi-course set dinners. Because every dish is prepared to order, service can be slow. Moderate.

Nita Raft House Thanon Pak Praek. Home-style cooking is the thing at the kitchen attached to this raft house (see p.226), especially the famous "no name" deep-fried vegetable and chicken fritters. Seating is home-style too, on floor cushions, and there are usually DVD screenings in the evenings. Inexpensive.

River Kwai Park Fast Food Hall 50m south of the Bridge on Thanon Maenam Kwai. The cheapest place to eat in the vicinity of the Bridge, this is a collection of curry and noodle stalls where you buy coupons for meals that cost just B25 or B30. Only a few of the stalls have English menus, but it's easy enough to point at what you'd like. Inexpensive.

Sabayjit Just north of the *River Kwai Hotel*, at 284/54 Thanon Saeng Chuto. Cheap, unpretentious place with a large and tasty menu of sweet-and-sour soups, curries, spicy salads, *wontons* and juices.

Schluck Thanon Maenam Kwai. Misleadingly uninviting from the exterior, this dark, fairly cosy air-con restaurant entices a regular crowd of expats with its menu of pizzas, salads and steaks, plus its decent selection of authentically spicy fish and *yam* dishes. Also has a few tables outside. Evenings only. Moderate–expensive.

Snooker Bar Thanon Maenam Kwai. Standard travellers' fare plus back-to-back video shows nightly. Inexpensive.

Vimol Cruise Departs from *Vimol Guest House* on Soi Rongheabaow ☎034 517131. A Thai buffet inner is served aboard the *Vimol's* boat as it cruises slowly up to the Bridge and back down to the Kwai Noi and Mae Khlong. The cruise departs at 7pm (phone or ask at the guest house to check), lasts three hours and features the obligatory karaoke; it's B450 including dinner or B200 without food.

Bars

Apache Saloon Across from the *River Kwai Hotel* on Thanon Saeng Chuto. Done up inside and out to look like a Wild West bar, this is the place to come for live music (mostly soft rock), mid-priced beer and whisky, and a short menu of snacks.

Beer Barrel Thanon Maenam Kwai. Rustic-styled outdoor beer garden where the decking is made from Death Railway sleepers and you sit at rough-hewn wooden tables amid a jungle of low-lit trees and vines. The star feature here is the ice-cold draught beer, but there's also a short menu of bar meals including *som tam*, *kai pat bai kaphrao* (chicken with basil) and *khao pat kung*.

Cullivan's Pool and Beer Opposite *Vimol Guest House* on Soi Rongheabaow. Cosy little two-storey bar with a pool table on a quiet stretch of road. Open 5pm–2am.

No Name Bar Thanon Maenam Kwai. Popular farang-run travellers' hangout that invites punters to "get shit-faced on a shoestring". Key attractions are the satellite TV screenings of major sporting events, the pool table and the well-priced beer. Also serves British food, including roast beef and Yorkshire pudding. Open evenings till the early hours.

Listings

Books For the town's best selection of books about Thailand and English-language novels head for Tawan bookshop and stationery store on Thanon Saeng Chuto; further north up the same road, the bookstore across from Thanon Ban Neua also carries a couple of racks of English-language books. The shop at the Thailand–Burma Railway Centre is the best outlet for books about the Death Railway. *Punnee Bar* on Thanon Ban Neua buys and sells second-hand titles.

Cinema At the back of the bus station.

Cookery classes At *Apple's Guest House*, 52 Soi Rongheabaow 3: shop at the morning market and learn how to cook the seven basic Thai dishes. Minimum three participants; book the day before (10am–4pm; B700). Also at *C&C Guest House*, Soi England.

Emergencies For all emergencies, call the tourist police on the free, 24hr phone line ☎1155, or contact them at one of their booths in town: right beside the Bridge ☎034 512795; near *Beer Barrel* on Thanon Maenam Kwai; and on Thanon Song Kwai.

Exchange There are several banks with money-changing facilities and ATMs on the stretch of Thanon Saeng Chuto immediately to the north of the Thanon U Thong junction. Outside banking hours contact either *Apple's Guest House* on Thanon Maenam Kwai, or *Punnee Bar* on Thanon Ban Neua.

Hospitals The private Thanakan Hospital is at 20/20 Thanon Saeng Chuto, at the southern end of town, near the junction with Thanon Chukkadon ☎034 622366; the government-run Phahon Phonphayulasena Hospital is further south at 572/1 Thanon Saeng Chuto, near the junction with Thanon Mae Khlong ☎034 622999.

Immigration office At 100/22 Thanon Mae Khlong ☎034 513325.

Day-trips, trekking, rafting and kayaking

All the places listed below advertise **treks** around the Kanchanaburi and Sangkhlaburi areas, though few itineraries actually feature any trekking: most concentrate on waterfalls, elephant rides and river-rafting instead. Prices listed are per person in a group of four people minimum; smaller groups usually have to pay proportionally more. Rates do fluctuate a little according to season, demand and competition. All the tour operators listed below also do tailor-made guided tours to the war sights (often by boat or raft) and to Damnoen Saduak floating markets, and most will also provide a cheap transport service – car plus driver but no guide – for the more accessible sights.

A.S. Mixed Travel 52 Soi Rongheabaow 3 ⓣ034 512017, ⓦwww.applenoi-kanchanaburi.com. Small and friendly operation that runs out of *Apple's Guest House*, is led by enthusiastic and well-informed guides, and gets lots of positive feedback. Their specialities include various cycling expeditions (from B950), and serious two- and three-day treks that feature (optional) 6–8 hours' walking per day, a night in a remote Karen village where A.S. Mixed supports a weaving and education project, plus rafting, elephant-riding, Tham Than Lot National Park and Erawan Falls (B1450–3000), They also run overnight trips to Sangkhlaburi and Three Pagodas Pass, and standard one-day trips featuring various combinations of Erawan Falls, elephant-riding, rafting and the Death Railway (B400–950).

Good Times Travel 63/1 Thanon Maenam Kwai ⓣ034 624441, ⓔgood_times_travel@hotmail.com. Energetically run, competitively priced day- and half-day trips (B120–850) that get good reviews. Especially popular for its late-afternoon programme where tourists get to soap and shower elephants (and themselves) in the river and then have a barbecue dinner. Also offer infinite permutations of rafting, elephant-riding, Erawan Falls, Hellfire Pass and the Death Railway, plus an overnight trip to Sangkhlaburi.

Punnee Bar and Café Thanon Ban Neua ⓣ034 513503. Expat resident Danny will take people pretty much anywhere in the locality for around B600 per person per day, but he is especially knowledgeable about Hellfire Pass and the other World War II sights. He can also arrange elephant-riding and rafting trips.

Safarine 4 Soi Taiwan, off Thanon Maenam Kwai ⓣ & ⓕ034 624140, ⓦwww.safarine.com. Canoeing and kayaking specialist offering a programme of packaged and tailor-made canoeing trips, including equipment, lunch, connecting transport and optional guide. Kayak trips from one hour to a full day in the Kanchanaburi area (B300–900), or a day's kayaking including a visit to Hellfire Pass, and either elephant-riding (B1400) or a trip on the Death Railway (B850).

Internet access Available at almost every guest house on Thanon Maenam Kwai, as well as at several dedicated Internet centres on Thanon Maenam Kwai, and a few more just south of the *River Kwai Hotel* on Thanon Saeng Chuto. Catnet terminals at the CAT telephone office in the south of town on Soi Praisanee/ Soi 38 off Thanon Saeng Chuto (daily 8.30am–8pm).

Mail The GPO is 1km south of the TAT office on Thanon Saeng Chuto, but there's a more central post office on Thanon Lak Muang, one block west of Thanon Song Kwai.

Pharmacies Several dispensaries in the fresh-market area south of Wat Thavorn.

Telephones The CAT international telephone office (daily 8.30am–8pm) is on a side road near the GPO, about 1.2km south of the TAT office, on Soi Praisanee/ Soi 38, off Thanon Saeng Chuto. There are several private telephone offices at guest houses and on Thanon Maenam Kwai.

Around Kanchanaburi

After the war sights and a ride on the Death Railway, the most popular attraction around Kanchanaburi is the seven-tiered **Erawan Falls**, sometimes combined with a trek to the caves of **Tham Than Lot National Park**. With your own transport you could also add in a visit to Hellfire Pass.

Erawan and Srinakarind national parks

Chances are that when you see a poster of a waterfall in Thailand, you'll be looking at a picture of the falls in **Erawan National Park** (daily 8am–4pm; B200), 65km northwest of Kanchanaburi. The seven-tiered waterfall, topped by a triple cascade, is etched into the national imagination not just for its beauty, but also for its alleged resemblance to a three-headed elephant – this elephant (*erawan* in Thai) is the former national symbol and the usual mount of the Hindu god Indra. It makes a lovely setting for a picnic, especially just after the rainy season, and on Sundays and holidays Thais flock here to eat, drink and take family photographs against the falls; weekdays are generally a more peaceful time to come.

Although the park covers an area of 550 square kilometres, the main **trail** is the one that leads you up the course of the rivulet, past each of its seven tiers. Each of these levels comprises a waterfall feeding a pool of invitingly clear water partly shaded by bamboos, rattans and lianas. It's a fairly easy climb up to the fifth stage, but the route onto the sixth and seventh levels gets very steep and slippery and involves negotiating a few dilapidated bridges and ladders: be sure to wear strong shoes, not flip-flops, and avoid doing levels six and seven alone if you can. The best pools for swimming are level two (which gets the most crowded) and level seven (which is a hard slog but rarely busy, and also boasts stunning views over the jungle).

If you follow the main road along its westerly branch from Srinakarind market for another 10km you'll reach Wat Phrathat, from where it's a five-hundred-metre walk to **Tham Phrathat** (last entry at 3pm); a chartered songthaew from the market to the wat costs about B300: buses don't come this far. The stalactite cave has several large chambers, but is of interest to geologists for the fault lines that run under the Kwai Noi and are clearly visible in the disjointed strata.

A few kilometres north of the turn-off to Erawan, the landscape is dominated by the scenic **Srinakarind Reservoir**, which is fed by the dammed waters of the Mae Khlong and the Kha Khaeng and gives rise to the Kwai Yai. It's a popular recreation spot and site of several resorts, all of which lie within the **Srinakarind National Park** (sometimes spelt Sri Nakarin or Si Nakharin). From the dam you can hire boats (about B1500) to make the two-hour journey northwest across the reservoir to **Huay Khamin Falls**, which are said to be the most powerful in the district, and reputedly get the name "Turmeric Streak" from the ochre-coloured limestone rockface. However, it's quicker and less hassle to join one of the tours from Kanchanaburi.

Practicalities

Buses to Erawan (#8170; 2hr) leave Kanchanaburi every fifty minutes between 8am and 5.20pm and stop at **Srinakarind** market, from where it's a one-kilometre walk to the National Park headquarters and trailhead; if you miss the 4pm bus back, you'll probably be there for the night. Erawan features on many tours, and most Kanchanaburi guest houses will also arrange

songthaew transport to and from the falls for about B80 per person, giving you around five hours in the park. If you have your own transport, simply follow signs from Kanchanaburi for Route 3199 and the falls.

It's possible to stay in the Erawan National Park **bungalows** (B250–1000 for two to fifteen people), though these are often full and should ideally be reserved in advance by contacting the Royal Forestry Department in Bangkok (ⓣ02 579 5734 or 02 579 7223); you can also pitch your own tent for a nominal fee. Several **foodstalls**, restaurants and shops near the trailhead open daily until about 8pm. There's more upmarket **accommodation** just outside the park boundaries, at *Erawan Guest House Resort* (ⓣ01 907 8210; ❷–❻) and, further out, near kilometre-stone 46, *Pha Daeng Resort* (ⓣ034 513909; ❹–❽).

Tham Than Lot (Chalerm Rattanakosin) National Park

Ninety-seven kilometres north of Kanchanaburi, off Route 3086, tiny little **Tham Than Lot National Park** (also known as **Chalerm Rattanakosin National Park**) covers just 59 square kilometres but boasts two very nice caves, a decent waterfall and an enjoyable hiking trail that links them; wear comfortable shoes and bring a torch.

It is possible but time consuming to get to the park without your own transport and would be rather rushed as a day-trip. Take regular **bus** #325 from Kanchanaburi and get off at **BAN NONG PRU** (every 20min; 2–3hr), then change onto a motorbike taxi (B100) for the 22-kilometre ride to the park entrance (B200 admission) and visitors' centre. There are five **national park bungalows** (B500–1000 for four to twelve people; ⓣ02 579 5734 or 02 579 7223) near the visitors' centre, which should be booked in advance for weekends. Alternatively, rent your own motorbike from Kanchanaburi, or take a tour (see p.235).

From the visitors' centre, follow the signed trail for about ten minutes to reach the first cave, **Tham Than Lot Noi**, which is 400m deep and illuminated if there are enough people (for example at weekends). A very picturesque 2.5-kilometre, two-hour trail runs on from the other side of Tham Than Lot Noi, along a stream and through a ravine to the first of three **waterfalls**, about an hour and a half's easy walk away and passing towering dipterocarps, fine jungle views and plenty of butterflies en route. The path gets more difficult after the first waterfall, and dangerously slippery in the wet season, running via another couple of waterfalls before coming to the larger of the park's two caves, the impressively deep sink-hole **Tham Than Lot Yai**, site of a small Buddhist shrine. Another ten minutes along the trail brings you to a small forest temple, from where you'll need to retrace your steps to return to the visitors' centre.

The Death Railway: to Nam Tok and Hellfire Pass

The two-hour journey along the notorious Thailand–Burma **Death Railway** from Kanchanaburi to **Nam Tok** is one of Thailand's most scenic, and most popular. Though the views are lovely, it is the history that makes the ride so special, so it's worth visiting the Thailand–Burma Railway Centre in town (see p.228) before making the trip, as this provides a context for the enormous loss of human life and the extraordinary feat of engineering behind the line's construction (see the box on p.229). Alternatively, take the bus straight up to the **Hellfire Pass Memorial Museum**, just north of the line's current Nam Tok terminus, which provides an equally illuminating introduction to the railway's history, then return to Kanchanaburi by train. The peaceful stretch of the River Kwai Noi between Nam Tok and Hellfire Pass is now the site of a few low-key riverside hotels, in particular around **Tham Lawa**.

The obvious way to travel through this area is by train, though the #8203 **bus** service from Kanchanaburi to Nam Tok (every 30min; 1hr 30min) and beyond is faster and more frequent. If you are planning to use the train as transport to sights, be aware that they often run very late. With your own transport, you have the chance to visit some of the less mainstream sights between Kanchanaburi and Nam Tok, notably the region's Stone Age artefacts at the **Ban Kao Museum**, and the nearby ruins of a twelfth-century Khmer temple sanctuary at **Muang Singh**.

Riding the Death Railway

Three **trains** run daily along the Death Railway in both directions, which means it's possible to make day-trips from Kanchanaburi to Muang Singh and Nam Tok if you get the timing right, though most tourists simply enjoy the ride as an attraction itself. At the time of writing, the train is scheduled to leave Kanchanaburi at 6.07am, 10.50am and 4.30pm and to return from Nam Tok at 5.25am, 1pm and 3.15pm; Kanchanaburi TAT keeps up-to-date **timetables**. If you're up at the Bridge, you can join the train five minutes later. As it's such a popular trip, the State Railway adds a couple of "**Special Cars**" for tourists on the 10.50am Kanchanaburi–Nam Tok train, for which they charge B150 instead of the usual B17; the seats are exactly the same as those in the cheap carriages, but you get a reserved place and several soft drinks and snacks. Whatever ticket you opt for, sit on the left-hand side of the train for the best views, or the right-hand side for shade.

Leaving Kanchanaburi via the Bridge over the River Kwai, the train chugs through the Kwai Noi valley, stopping frequently at country stations decked with frangipani and jasmine. The first stop of note is Tha Kilen (1hr 15min), where you should alight for Prasat Muang Singh (see opposite), and about twenty minutes later the most hair-raising section of track begins. At **Wang Sing**, also known as Arrow Hill, the train squeezes through thirty-metre-deep solid rock cuttings, dug at the cost of numerous POW lives; 6km further, it slows to a crawl at the approach to the **Wang Po viaduct**, where a 300-metre-long trestle bridge clings to the cliff face as it curves with the Kwai Noi – almost every man who worked on this part of the railway died. The station at the northern end of the trestle bridge is called **Tham Krasae**, after the cave that's hollowed out of the rockface beside the bridge; you can see the cave's resident Buddha image from the train. A couple of raft-house operations have capitalized on the drama of the stretch of river alongside Wang Po. On the viaduct side, *River Kwai Cabin* (ⓣ01 944 0898, ⓕ02 967 8184; ❻–❽) offers upmarket bungalow accommodation; on the other bank, *River Kwai Jungle House* (ⓣ034 561052, ⓕ034 636713; ❽) has well-positioned raft houses. At both places meals are included in the nightly package rates quoted here and accommodation should be booked in advance. North of Tham Krasae, the train pulls in at **Wang Po Station** before continuing alongside a particularly lovely stretch of the Kwai Noi, its banks thick with jungle and not a raft house in sight, the whole vista framed by distant tree-clad peaks. Thirty minutes later, the train reaches Nam Tok, a small town that thrives chiefly on its position at the end of the line.

To Nam Tok by road

For most people, the main reason for heading out of Kanchanaburi towards Nam Tok is to take the train along the infamous Death Railway, but there are several sights along the way that can only be visited by road, either with your own transport or as part of a tour (perhaps combined with a one-way trip on the train). Chief among these are the prehistoric relics at **Ban Kao Museum** and the Khmer ruins of nearby **Prasat Muang Singh**.

Ban Kao Museum

The **Ban Kao Museum** (Wed–Sun 8.30am–4.30pm; B30) is devoted to relics from an advanced prehistoric civilization (8000 to 1000 BC) that once settled on the banks of the Kwai Noi. Items on display include unique, curiously designed pots dated to around 1770 BC that were found buried at the head and feet of fifty skeletons; polished stone tools from around 8000 BC; and inscribed bronze pots and bangles transferred from a nearby bronze-culture site, which have been placed at around 1000 BC – somewhat later than the bronze artefacts from Ban Chiang in the northeast (see p.526). The hollowed-out tree trunks in front of the museum are also unusual: they may have been used as boats or as coffins – or possibly as a metaphorical combination of the two.

The museum is 35km west of Kanchanaburi and 8km from Prasat Muang Singh. Follow Highway 323 north out of Kanchanaburi until you get to the junction with minor road 3229, then follow this road southwest for about 16km before veering on to minor road 3445 for the last couple of kilometres. There's no public transport.

Prasat Muang Singh

Eight hundred years ago, the Khmer empire extended west as far as Muang Singh (City of Lions), an outpost strategically sited on the banks of the River Kwai Noi, 43km west of present-day Kanchanaburi. Thought to have been built at the end of the twelfth century, the temple complex of **Prasat Muang Singh** (daily 9am–5pm; B40) follows Khmer religious and architectural precepts (see p.492), but its origins are obscure – the City of Lions gets no mention in any of the recognized chronicles until the nineteenth century.

Prasat Muang Singh covers one-third of a square kilometre, bordered by moats and ramparts that probably had cosmological as well as defensive significance, but unless you fancy a long stroll, you'd be wise to stick to the enclosed **shrine complex** at its heart. Restoration work on this part has been sensitively carried out to give an idea of the crude grandeur of the original structure, which was constructed entirely from blocks of rough russet laterite.

As with all Khmer prasats, the pivotal feature of Muang Singh is the main prang, as always surrounded by a series of walls and a covered gallery, with gateways marking the cardinal points. The prang faces east, towards Angkor, and is guarded by a fine sandstone statue of **Avalokitesvara**, one of the five great bodhisattvas of Mahayana Buddhism, would-be Buddhas who have postponed their entrance into Nirvana to help others attain enlightenment. He's depicted here in characteristic style, his eight arms and torso covered with tiny Buddha reliefs and his hair tied in a top-knot. In Mahayanist mythology, Avalokitesvara represents mercy, while the other statue found in the prasat, the female figure of **Prajnaparamita**, symbolizes wisdom – when wisdom and mercy join forces, enlightenment ensues. Just visible on the inside of the north wall surrounding the prang is the only intact example of the stucco carving that once ornamented every facade. Other fragments and sculptures found at this and nearby sites are displayed beside the north gate; especially tantalizing is the single segment of what must have been a gigantic face hewn from several massive blocks of stone.

Muang Singh is 8km northwest of Ban Kao Museum, on minor road 3445. Easiest **access** from Kanchanaburi is by road: either follow directions as for Ban Kao Museum, above, or continue along Highway 323 as far as kilometrestone 15 to take Route 3445 southwest to Muang Singh. You can also get to Muang Singh by taking the Death Railway train: get off at Tha Kilen (1hr 15min from Kanchanaburi), walk straight out of the station for 500m, turn right at the crossroads and continue for another 1km to reach the ruins.

Wat Pa Luang Ta Bua Yannasampanno: the Tiger Sanctuary Temple

Kanchanaburi's oddest and most controversial attraction is the chance to stroke a tiger at the so-called "Tiger Sanctuary Temple", **Wat Pa Luang Ta Bua Yannasampanno** (afternoons only; B100 donation; do not wear red clothes, which antagonize the tigers). Many tourists are seduced by the idea and join one of the numerous tours to the temple, but a lot of people return discouraged by the experience, not least because the animals are housed in small bare cages and only let out to be paraded in front of visitors in the afternoons.

Temples are traditionally regarded as sanctuaries for unwanted and illegally captured animals and Wat Pa Luang Ta Bua has been taking in tigers since 1999, when a distressed young tiger cub was brought to them, probably orphaned by poachers keen to tap into the lucrative trade in tiger body parts. The temple has attracted a lot of media interest and has been accused of exploiting the animals as a money-making tourist attraction; there was more negative publicity after one of the tigers mauled a Thai tourist. The temple is 37km from town and signed off Highway 323 at kilometre-stone 21, a few kilometres beyond the Route 3445 turn-off to Muang Singh.

Nam Tok and around

There's not much to **NAM TOK**, the terminus of the Death Railway line. The **train station** is at the top of the town, 900m north of Highway 323, and a further 2km from the Kwai Noi; buses usually stop near the T-junction of the highway and the station road.

On rainy-season weekends, Thais flock to Nam Tok's roadside **Sai Yok Noi Falls**, but if you're filling time between trains, you'd be better off stretching your legs on the short trek to the nearby Wang Badan cave or taking a boat trip from Pak Saeng pier to Tham Lawa or Sai Yok Yai Falls (see p.243). Impressive stalactites, fathomless chambers and unerving heat make **Tham Wang Badan** (daily 8.30am–4.30pm) one of the more interesting underground experiences in the region and it's easily reached by a trail that begins from Highway 323 about 1500m northwest of the train station. From the station, walk up the station approach road, cross the tracks, turn left at the roundabout, then first right through the small town, passing a water tower on your left; you'll reach the T-junction with Highway 323 after 900m. The **trail** to the cave is signposted 600m northwest (right) up Highway 323, from the right-hand (east) side of the road. About 1km into the trail, you arrive at the park warden's office where you can rent feeble torches; it's better to bring your own or to pay the warden at least B50 to accompany you and turn on the cave lights, which is well worth the money. From the office it's 2km of easy walking to the cave.

Longtail **boats** can be rented from the restaurant beside **Pak Saeng pier** for the forty-minute boat ride upstream to Tham Lawa and its nearby riverside accommodation, described below. To reach the pier from the Highway 323 T-junction, cross the road, turn left (southeast) towards Kanchanaburi, then take the first road on your right. The return journey to the cave takes roughly two hours, including half an hour there, and costs about B700 for the eight-seater boat. Add on at least four more hours and another B800 if you want to continue on to Sai Yok Yai Falls.

The best-value **accommodation** in Nam Tok is at the *Sai Yok Noi Bungalows* (Ⓣ034 591075; ❸–❹); to get there from the train station, turn northwest at the T-junction (towards Sangkhlaburi), walk about ten minutes and then turn right at the hotel sign by the fuel station. Or you can sleep in a floating room, comfortably kitted out with attached bathroom and veranda, beside Pak Saeng pier, at *Kitti Raft* (Ⓣ034 634168; ❹).

Tham Lawa and around

About 10km north of Nam Tok, a side road turns off Highway 323 at kilometre-stone 54 and runs down to the river, giving access to a beautiful stretch of the Kwai Noi, the *Resotel* pier, and several pleasant places to stay. Any Kanchanaburi–Thong Pha Phum bus will drop you at the turn-off. The most famous attraction around here is **Tham Lawa**, the largest stalactite cave in the area and home to three species of bat; it's a ten-minute longtail ride upriver from the pier. The river is about 50m wide at this point, embraced by sheer limestone cliffs that are artistically pitted, dramatically streaked in red and white, and grown thick with lianas and bamboos tumbling down to the water's edge – be careful when swimming as the current is very strong (hotels should have lifejackets available). There's no development along the banks apart from a few raft houses and shore-bound little resorts, so staying here means there is no easy access to restaurants, shops and local sights, although all the resorts offer transport to nearby attractions, or you can charter your own **boat** (for up to 8 people, prices quoted are for return trips) from the *Resotel* pier to Tham Lawa cave (10min; B500), Hellfire Pass (B700 to the nearest pier, then a 4km walk), and Sai Yok Yai Falls (1hr 30min; B1200). You might also want to visit the **Mon Village** behind the *River Kwai Jungle Rafts* resort, where you're encouraged to browse the sarongs and other artefacts made and sold by the villagers, take an elephant-ride (B800/hour), and visit the school. The Mon villagers fled here from Burma in the late 1950s but have still not been granted Thai ID papers, which means the children can't study at Thai secondary schools and adults have difficulty finding work. This village has close links with *Jungle Rafts* and many of its residents work at the hotel. For more on the Mon people, see p.246.

Occupying a large swathe of steep and densely grown river bank about 1km off the highway at kilometre-stone 54, *Sam's Jungle Guest House* (Ⓣ01 948 3448, Ⓦwww.samsguesthouse.com; ❶–❹) offers a range of well-priced **accommodation** in a strange and rather unstylish assortment of buildings that nonetheless enjoy an exceptional tranquil setting. The cheapest rooms share facilities, the better ones have bathrooms, balconies and air-con, and there's a swimming pool. The nearby *Resotel* pier is the departure point for the two other places to stay around here, both of them owned by the River Kwai Floatel company (Ⓣ02 642 6361, Ⓦwww.riverkwaifloatel.com). Located on the west bank of the river, a few metres downstream from Tham Lawa, *River Kwai Resotel* is the more upmarket of the two, comprising some charming thatched riverside huts and a swimming pool. A short distance upstream, the more rustic but very popular *River Kwai Jungle Rafts* offers simple but tasteful floating rooms, complete with hammocks, a swimming area, canoe rental (B350/hour) and a bar. Rooms have no electricity so there are no fans or air-con and only oil-lamps at night. Everyone at these two resorts is on a full-board basis at B1300–1650 per person per day, which includes boat transfers.

Hellfire Pass

Although the rail line north of Nam Tok was ripped up soon after the end of World War II, it casts its dreadful shadow all the way up the Kwai Noi valley into Burma. The remnants of track are most visible at **Hellfire Pass**, and many of the villages in the area are former POW sites – locals frequently stumble across burial sites, now reclaimed by the encroaching jungle. To keep the Death Railway level through the uneven course of the Kwai valley, the POWs had to build a series of embankments and trestle bridges and, at dishearteningly frequent intervals, gouge deep cuttings through solid rock. The most concentrated digging was at **Konyu**, 18km beyond Nam Tok, where seven separate cuttings were made over a 3.5-kilometre stretch. The longest and most brutal of these was Hellfire Pass, which got its name from the hellish-looking lights and shadows of the fires the POWs used when working at night. The job took three months of round-the-clock labour with the most primitive tools.

Hellfire Pass has now been turned into a memorial walk in honour of the POWs who worked and died on it, and their story is documented at the beautifully designed **Hellfire Pass Memorial Museum** (daily 9am–4pm; donation) which stands at the trailhead. This is the best and most informative of all the World War II museums in the Kanchanaburi region, using war-time relics, and POW memorabilia, photos and first-hand accounts to tell the sobering history of the construction of this stretch of the Thailand–Burma Railway. Founded by an Australian-Thai volunteer group, the museum now serves as a sort of pilgrimage site for the families and friends of Australian POWs.

The same Australian-Thai group has also cleared a four-kilometre, ninety-minute circular **memorial walk**, which begins at the museum and follows the old rail route through the eighteen-metre-deep cutting and on to Hin Tok creek along a course relaid with some of the original narrow-gauge track. The creek was originally forded by a trestle bridge so unstable that it was nicknamed the Pack of Cards Bridge, but this has long since crumbled away. The trail doubles back on itself, passing through bamboo forest and a viewpoint that gives some idea of the phenomenal depth of rock the POWs had to dig through.

Most Kanchanaburi tour operators offer **day-trips** featuring Hellfire Pass. It's also quite easy to get to Hellfire Pass on your own, and to combine it with your own trip on the Death Railway: from Kanchanaburi or Nam Tok, take any **bus** bound for Thong Pha Phum or Sangkhlaburi and ask to be dropped off at Hellfire Pass, which is signposted on the west side of Highway 323 just after kilometre-stone 64; it's about a 75-minute journey from Kanchanaburi or 20 minutes from Nam Tok. The last return bus to Kanchanaburi passes Hellfire Pass at about 4.45pm; if you're continuing to Sangkhlaburi, the last onward bus comes past at about 1.15pm.

North to Thong Pha Phum

Expanses of impenetrable mountain wilderness characterize the Kwai Noi valley to the north of Hellfire Pass, a landscape typified by the dense monsoon forests of **Sai Yok National Park**, which stretches all the way to the Burmese border. The first significant town beyond Sai Yok is **Thong Pha Phum** (147km from Kanchanaburi), which sits at the southern edge of the massive **Khao Laem Reservoir** and features some pleasant waterside accommodation.

Sai Yok National Park, Pha That Falls and Hin Dat hot springs

Signed off the highway between kilometre-stones 80 and 81, 104km north of Kanchanaburi, **Sai Yok National Park** (B200 entry) is best known for its much-photographed though unexceptional **Sai Yok Yai Falls** and for the stalactite-filled Daowadung Caves. It is also home to the smallest-known mammal in the world, the elusive hog-nosed or bumblebee bat, which weighs just 1.75g and has a wingspan of 1.6cm. The park makes a refreshing enough stopover between Nam Tok and Sangkhlaburi, particularly if you have your own transport, and you can stay in the national park **bungalows** (B500–1500 for four to twelve people) or the more inviting *Sai Yok View Raft* (Ⓣ034 514194; ❹) raft houses near the waterfall; get there early to secure a room. The raft house serves food and there are plenty of hot-food stalls near the visitor centre. Any of the Kanchanaburi–Thong Pha Phum **buses** will stop at the road entrance to Sai Yok, from where it's a three-kilometre walk to the **visitor centre**, trailheads and river. The last buses in both directions pass the park at about 4.30pm. Motorbike taxis sometimes hang around the road entrance, but a more scenic approach would be by longtail from Nam Tok (see p.241). All the trails start from near the visitor centre, and are clearly signposted from there as well as being marked on the map available from the centre.

North of Sai Yok National Park, signs off Highway 323 direct you to the two long, gently sloping cascades of **Pha That Falls** (12km east of the highway's kilometre-stone 103), accessible only with your own transport or on a tour; and to **Hin Dat** (Hindad) **hot springs** (1km east off the highway's kilometre-stone 105; B5 entry), where you can immerse yourself in big pool of soothingly warm water, and make use of the nearby showers and foodstalls. Any Thong Pha Phum bus will drop you at the access track, and the restaurant near the springs has a couple of basic rooms for rent (❸), though there's not much to detain you here.

Thong Pha Phum and the lakeside hotels

From Sai Yok National Park, Highway 323 continues northwest, following the course of the Kwai Noi. Forty-seven kilometres on, the road skirts **THONG PHA PHUM**, a mid-sized market town with bus connections to Sangkhlaburi and Kanchanaburi, plenty of small food shops, and the bungalow-hotel *Som Chainuk* (Ⓣ034 599067; ❶–❹), which offers basic fan rooms and better air-con versions on the main street, within easy walking distance of the bus drop.

With your own transport, a much better alternative to staying overnight in town is to drive 12km west of Thong Pha Phum market to the southeastern fringes of nearby **Khao Laem Reservoir**. Also known as the Kreung Kra Wia Reservoir, this vast body of water stretches all the way to Sangkhlaburi 73km to the north and, when created in the early 1980s, flooded every village in the vicinity. The former villagers have been rehoused along the reservoir's banks, and hotels have sprung up here too, making the most of the refreshing, almost Scandinavian, landscape of forested hills and clear, still water that's perfect for swimming. Here you'll find a string of appealing **raft-house hotels** including *Phae VIP* (☎034 599001), which has both simple, family-sized raft houses (B2000 for up to ten people) as well as more comfortable air-conditioned doubles (❺); and 1500m east, the more upmarket *Lake Valley* (☎02 433 6688; ❽). Even if you've no intention of staying, the moderately priced lakeside **restaurant** at *VIP* makes a soothing place for an hour's break on the way to or from Sangkhlaburi. To reach the hotels, follow signs from Thong Pha Phum for the Khao Laem Dam, but instead of turning right for the dam continue along the left-hand branch of the road for another 7km.

Sangkhlaburi and Three Pagodas Pass

Beyond Thong Pha Phum the views get increasingly spectacular as Highway 323 climbs through the remaining swathes of montane rainforest, occasionally hugging Khao Laem's eastern shore, until 73km later it comes to an end at the small town of **Sangkhlaburi**, just across the lake from the Mon village of Ban Waeng Ka and a mere 18km short of the Burmese border at **Three Pagodas Pass**. Note that even if you have a visa you won't be allowed to travel any more than 1km into Burma at the pass.

Sangkhlaburi is easily reached by bus from Kanchanaburi, and runs transport to Three Pagodas Pass. Travelling to Sangkhlaburi under your own steam can be tiring as the **road** is full of twists after Thong Pha Phum; the last 25km are particularly nerve-wracking for bikers because of the gravel spots in the many bends. Nonetheless, the scenery is fabulous, particularly at the **viewpoint** just north of kilometre-stone 35 (about 40km south of Sangkhlaburi), where there's a lakeside lay-by that's just perfect for taking photos. You may also be tempted to stop at the roadside **Kraeng Kravia Falls**, 1km south of the view-point at kilometre-stone 34, beside the army checkpoint. Though not very high, the three-tiered cascade does get quite powerful in and just after the rainy season, and makes a pleasant spot for picnicking on barbecued chicken sold at the nearby stall.

Sangkhlaburi and around

In the early 1980s, the old town of **SANGKHLABURI** (often called Sangkhla for short) was lost under the rising waters of the newly created Khao Laem Reservoir and its residents were relocated to the northeastern tip of the lake, beside the Songkalia River. Modern-day Sangkhla now overlooks the remnants of its former incarnation, an eerily beautiful scene of semi-submerged trees and raft houses. It's a tiny town with no unmissable attractions, but the atmosphere is pleasantly low-key and the best of the tourist accommodation occupies scenic spots along the lake-shore; there is cultural interest in the villages, markets and temples of the area's Mon, Karen and Thai population, as well as natural beauty in various waterfalls, whitewater rivers, and the remote Thung Yai Naresuan Wildlife Sanctuary. Though it sees relatively few farang tourists, Sangkhla is getting increasingly popular among weekending Thais, so come during the week for a bit of peace and better deals on accommodation.

Aside from crossing the famous wooden bridge over the lake to the Mon village of Ban Waeng Ka (see below), the other main pastime in town is

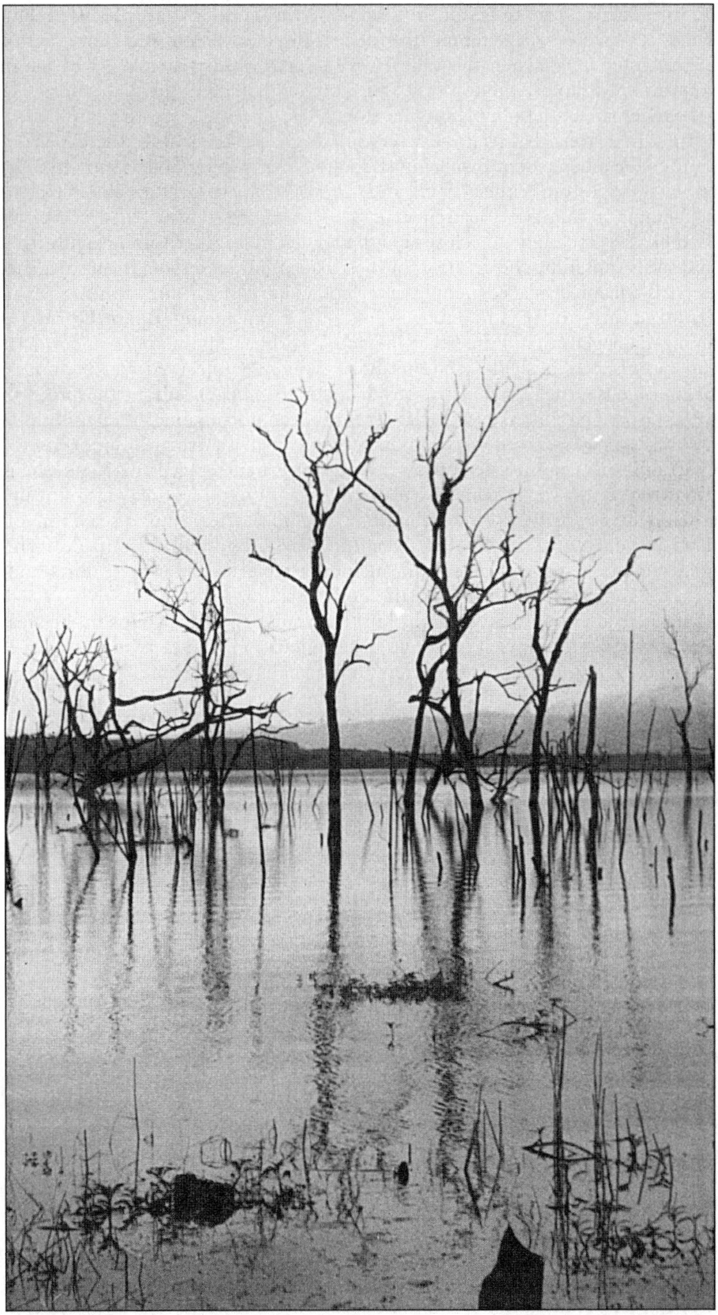

△ Early morning, Sangkhlaburi

boating across the reservoir in search of the **sunken temple** Wat Sam Phrasop, a former village temple that once stood on a hill but was almost completely submerged when the valley was flooded. When water levels are high you can only glimpse the top of its spire, but by the end of the dry season you get to see part of the temple's upper storey as well; it's close to the confluence of the three rivers that feed the reservoir. *P Guest House* rents out two-person **canoes** for independent exploring (B25/hour), or you can join a sunset longtail-boat trip from either *P Guest House* or *Burmese Inn* (B350–500/boat depending on number of passengers).

Sangkhla's location so close to the Burmese border, along with the upheavals caused by the creation of the Khao Laem Reservoir, mean that the town is full of displaced people, many of whom are in dire straits. Several organizations work with refugees in the area, including **Baan Unrak**, a farang-managed programme that has run an orphans' home here since 1991 and has also established a school and a weaving project. At Baan Unrak's *Bakery café* (see p.249) you can buy handicrafts, find out about the project, make donations and take yoga classes; for more information on Baan Unrak, see Basics p.82. Another community project that's worth supporting is **Women for Weaving**, set up by a group of Karen refugees in 1989. Their shop is located about 450m down the hill from the post office, or 150m up the hill from the turn-off to *Burmese Inn*, and carries a huge selection of hand-woven items, much of it in *mut mee* design and all of it made from good-quality Chiang Mai cotton, including tablecloths, sarongs, shirts and bags; for more on the Karen, see the box on p.296.

The two guest houses in Sangkhlaburi both run **organized trips** in the area for their guests. As well as their accommodation and activities package described below, *P Guest House* offers an overnight camp at an elephant village near the Lantee (Runtee) River, about 40km southeast of Sangkhla (B1300). *Burmese Inn* does one-day rafting excursions on the Songkalia River (B400); two- and three-day treks in the Thung Yai Naresuan Wildlife Sanctuary, around the Karen village of Ban Sane Pong (B1300–1700); and two-day cooking classes (B500). They also keep a book of useful information on motorbike routes in the area, including to Takianthong waterfall and Sawan Badan cave, both accessed via the road to Three Pagodas Pass.

The wooden bridge, Ban Waeng Ka and Wat Wang Wiwekaram

The Mon village of **BAN WAENG KA**, across the reservoir from Sangkhlaburi, grew up in the late 1940s after the outbreak of civil war in Burma, when the emergence of an intolerant nationalist regime prompted the country's ethnic minorities – including vast numbers of Karen (see box on p.296) and Mon – to flee across the border. The **Mon** people's homeland, Mon State, lies just west of the Tenasserim Mountains, so thousands of Mon ended up in Sangkhlaburi. Illegal immigrants in Thailand, their presence was permitted but not officially recognized, so that thirty years later, when the dam was constructed and the valley villages flooded, the Mon refugees were entitled to neither compensation nor new agricultural land. Despite this, an influential local Mon abbot, Pa Uttama, managed to secure the right to relocate five hundred submerged households to the northern shore of the reservoir, a settlement that has mushroomed into the one-thousand-household village of Ban Waeng Ka. Although most of the Mon villagers now have official Sangkhlaburi residency, they still have limited rights and must apply for expensive seven-day permits if they wish to travel out of the district, a system that lends itself to corruption.

Getting to the village is simply a matter of crossing the narrow northern neck of the lake, near the influx of the Songkalia River. Pedestrians can use the spider's web of a **wooden bridge** that is Sangkhla's unofficial town symbol: at almost 400m it is said to be the longest hand-built wooden bridge in the world and can be reached either by following signs from near the post office to *Samprasop Resort*, which overlooks the structure, or by using the new connecting footbridge near the *Burmese Inn*. If you're on a motorbike or in a car, you'll have to use the concrete roadbridge several hundred metres further north. Once across the wooden bridge, turn left to get into the village – a sprawling collection of traditional wooden houses lining a network of steep tracks, with a small but lively dry-goods market at its heart. You might want to hail a B10 motorbike taxi to get to Wat Wang Wiwekaram, which is about 2km from the bridgehead. Alternatively, *P Guest House* offers a two-hour tuk-tuk tour of Ban Waeng Ka and the wat for B250 for two people.

Wat Wang Wiwekaram (or Wat Luang Pho Uttama), Ban Waeng Ka's most dramatic sight, stands at the western edge of the village, its massive, golden **chedi** clearly visible from Sangkhlaburi. Built in a fusion of Thai, Indian and Burmese styles, the imposing square-sided stupa is modelled on the centrepiece of India's Bodh Gaya, the sacred site of the Buddha's enlightenment, and contains a much-prized Buddha relic (said to be a piece of his skeleton) brought to Ban Waeng Ka from Sri Lanka. The wat is hugely popular with Buddhist pilgrims from all over Thailand, and is also a focal point for the Mon community on both sides of the Thai–Burma border; at Mon New Year in April, the wat is packed with men sent by their Mon families to pay their respects. Mon, Karen, Burmese and Thai devotees donate enormous sums of money to the temple coffers in honour of the nonagenarian **Pa Uttama**, now the wat's abbot, who has been revered as a unifying force and champion of Mon culture ever since he crossed the border into Thailand in 1955. His photograph is displayed in the temple compound, and the opulence of the wat buildings is testimony to his status. There's a good **tourist market** in the covered cloisters at the chedi compound, with plenty of reasonably priced Burmese woodcarvings, checked *longyis* and jewellery. The wat is spread over two compounds, with the gleaming new bot, **viharn** and monks' quarters about 1km away from the chedi, at the end of the right-hand fork in the road. The interior of the viharn is decorated with murals showing tableaux from the five hundred lives of the Buddha, designed to be viewed in anticlockwise order.

Practicalities

Sangkhlaburi is connected to Kanchanaburi by three different **bus services**. The fastest option is the air-conditioned **minibus** service (daily at 7.30am, 11.30am & 4.30pm; 3hr; reserve seats a few hours in advance), which departs from the office in the far southeast corner of Kanchanaburi bus station. The minibuses make no pick-ups en route and terminate on the northern edge of Sangkhla, across the road from a motorbike taxi stand and around the corner from the *Pornpailin Hotel*. The return minibuses (8 daily between 6.30am and 3.30pm; 3hr; reserve ahead) depart from the same spot: find the adjacent ticket office (unsigned in English) next to a small restaurant in a row of shops diagonally across from the Fuji shop and police box. Three **air-con** and four **non-air-con** buses (all #8203) cover the same route in both directions, terminating at the bus station on the western edge of Sangkhla. The air-con service makes a few stops en route, including at Thong Pha Phum, and takes four hours; the last departure from Kanchanaburi is at 3.30pm and from Sangkhla at 2.30pm. The non-air-con service will pick up passengers from anywhere along Highway 323 and takes up to six hours to make the whole Kanchanaburi–Sangkhla trip; the last departure from Kanchanaburi is at midday and from Sangkhlaburi at 1.15pm.

Sangkhlaburi is small enough to walk round in an hour, and there are plenty of **motorbike taxis** for rent, too; rates start at about B15 from the bus station to the guest houses and rise to around B50 for a ride from the guest houses to Wat Wang Wiwekaram across the water. *P Guest House* rents **motorbikes** (B200/day) and Armin at *Burmese Inn* can organize the hiring of a pick-up **truck** and driver for around B750 a day or a four-wheel-drive plus driver for B2000.

The reservoir marks the western limit of Sangkhla. The town's westernmost (signless) road is the most useful thoroughfare, with the bus station at its northern end, *P Guest House* 1.3km down the hill towards the southern end, and the post-office, *Burmese Inn* and *Bakery* in between. The market is the focus of the tiny grid of streets that runs east of the bus station and post office. The post office, 100m down the hill from the bus station, has one Catnet **Internet** terminal. Traveller's cheques and dollars can be changed at the **bank**, on the edge of the market in the town centre, though there is as yet no ATM. If you're heading up to Three Pagodas Pass and want to **cross the border** into the Burmese side of the market (see p.249), you'll need to take US$10 (there's no exchange at the border) and a border permit, which is only available from the immigration office in Sangkhlaburi, not at Three Pagodas itself. Sangkhla's **immigration** office (daily 6am–6pm) is 150m east of the post office; to get the permit you will need to surrender your passport and hand over two photographs and a photocopy of the details page of your passport and your departure card (you can get photos and photocopies at the Fuji shop two blocks north of the immigration office).

Accommodation

Not many independent foreign travellers make it to Sangkhlaburi, but those who do all seem to head for one of the town's two inexpensive **guest houses**: both are run by informative managers, and both offer day-trips. The two guest houses are also used by backpacking tour groups, so it might be worth phoning ahead to reserve a room; you will definitely need to book for weekends and national holidays. Both guest houses are well signed from the bus station.

Burmese Inn 700m down the hill from the bus station, then right down Soi 1, or 150m west from the minivan terminus to the bus station, then down the hill ⓣ06 168 1801, ⓦwww.sangkhlaburi.com. This traveller-oriented Thai-Austrian-managed guest house overlooks the northeastern spur of the lake just behind the new bridge, offering easy access to the Mon village, but slightly truncated lake views. Most of the bungalows look right over the water and nearly all are en suite; the more expensive are attractively furnished and some have air-con and TV. ❶–❺

Forget Me Not On the reservoir, between *Burmese Inn* and *P Guest House*, about 1km down the hill from the bus station ⓣ034 595014. A Thai-oriented resort that occupies a lovely waterside location and has decent rooms with fan or air-con. ❹–❺

P Guest House About 1.3km down the hill from the bus station, or 150m west from the minivan drop to the bus station, then down the hill ⓣ034 595061, ⓦwww.pguesthouse.com. Efficiently run, Mon-owned place that sits prettily on the banks of the reservoir and offers comfortable travellers' accommodation in stone huts with shared bathrooms, and en-suite rooms with air-con. However, as priority is given to guests booking *P*s special B850 packages, which include one night's fan accommodation plus a day of activities like rafting, elephant-riding and a trip on the lake, you may find it hard to stay here on a room-only basis. ❷–❺

Pornpailin Hotel On the east edge of town, one block south of the minivan drop or one block north of the hospital ⓣ034 595039, ⓣ034 595026. Standard, fairly cheap hotel that's nowhere near the lake but offers large, clean, en-suite rooms with fan or air-con. ❷–❸

Pornpailin Riverside About 2km down the hill from the bus station ⓣ034 595039, ⓕ034 595026. Attractive sister outfit to the *Pornpailin Hotel* (ask there for transport) whose fan and air-con bungalows are scenically located on the lake-shore, a few hundred metres beyond *P*. ❻–❼

Eating

The cheapest places to **eat** are at and around the market in the town centre, and at the night market that sets up in the marketplace every evening. *P*'s large but cosy restaurant offers fine lake views and serves good Thai, Burmese and European food. The welcoming *Bakery* (open daytime only), 900m south down the hill from the post office, mid-way between the turn-offs for *Burmese Inn* and *P Guest House*, makes a nice chilled-out spot to sample brown-bread sandwiches, veggie pizzas and banana cake and is staffed by volunteers from the nearby Baan Unrak orphans' home.

Three Pagodas Pass (Ban Chedi Sam Ong)

Four kilometres before Sangkhlaburi, a road branches off Highway 323 to **Three Pagodas Pass** (signed as **Jadee Sam Ong**), winding its way through cloud-capped, forested hills and passing a few Karen and Mon settlements before reaching the border terminus 18km further on. Songthaews for the pass leave Sangkhlaburi bus station every forty minutes from 6am until about 5pm and take forty minutes; the last songthaew back to Sangkhla leaves at 6pm.

All **border trade** for hundreds of kilometres north and south has to come through Three Pagodas Pass: textiles, sandals, bicycles and medical supplies go out to Burma, in return for cattle and highly profitable teak logs – the felling of which has been illegal in Thailand since 1989. Over the last fifty years, the Mon, the Karen and the Burmese government have vied with each other constantly for supremacy at the pass, the rebels relying on the tax on smuggled goods to finance their insurgency campaigns, the government desperate to regain its foothold in rebel territory. However, since 1990, the pass has remained under the control of the Burmese government.

It must be the romantic image of a hilltop smuggling station that attracts the few foreign tourists to the 1400-metre-high pass, because there's nothing substantial to see here. The **pagodas** themselves are diminutive whitewashed structures, said to have been erected in the eighteenth century by the kings of Burma and Thailand as a symbolic peace gesture (during the Ayutthayan period, Burmese troops would regularly thunder through here on elephant-back on their way to attack the capital). Each king supposedly built a chedi on his own side of the border and, at the foot of the central, borderline pagoda, the two kings signed an agreement never to war with each other again. Another interpretation holds that the pagodas represent the three strands of Buddhism – the Buddha, the Dharma (teaching) and the Sangha (monkhood) – and were erected here to boost the morale of Thai soldiers going to and from battle in Burma.

All three pagodas are now on Thai soil, at the edge of **BAN CHEDI SAM ONG**, a tiny village comprising not much more than a market, a few food-stalls and a wat. Burmese land starts 50m away, at the village of Payathonzu, but, at the time of writing, foreign nationals are only allowed to get about 1km **across the border** (daily 6am–6pm) here. Even to make this rather pathetic trip you need to arrive at the border with a permit issued by the immigration office in Sangkhlaburi (see opposite) and US$10 in cash. All of which means it's hardly worth the effort and expense (and some would argue, the US$10 to the Burmese government) – especially as the market on the Thai side of the border post is full of interesting Burmese goods; items worth looking for include the distinctive brightly coloured Karen trousers and jackets, sarongs made of Burmese batik, Burmese face powder – applied as protection against the elements – cheroots, and all manner of teak artefacts and furniture. One worthwhile reason for crossing the border into Burma is the chance to visit the magnificent **Wat Sao Roi Ton**, Temple of One Hundred Teakwood Posts. Commissioned by Ban Waeng Ka's revered Mon abbot Pa Uttama, it is a stately two-storey structure, built in Burmese style and designed around its eponymous one hundred polished-wood pillars. The wat is a ten-minute walk from the border, or a B10 motorbike-taxi ride.

As somewhere to hang out for a few days, Three Pagodas Pass doesn't compare to the more scenic and essentially more congenial Sangkhlaburi, but it is possible to **stay** on the Thai side of the border, at *Three Pagodas Resort* (Ⓣ01 922 6231, Ⓕ02 412 4159; ❸–❹), whose polished teakwood fan and air-con bungalows are set round a pretty garden, under the lip of a limestone cliff on the edge of Ban Sam Phra Chedi Ong.

Ayutthaya and the Chao Phraya basin

Bisected by the country's main artery, the **Chao Phraya River**, and threaded by a network of tributaries and canals, the fertile plain to the north of the capital retains a spectrum of attractions from just about every period of the country's history. The monumental kitsch of the nineteenth-century palace at **Bang Pa-In** provides a sharp contrast with the atmospheric ruins at the former capital of **Ayutthaya**, where ancient temples, some crumbling and overgrown, others alive and kicking, are arrayed in a leafy, riverine setting. **Lopburi**'s disparate remains, testimony to more than a millennium of continuous settlement, are less compelling, but you'll get a frenetic, noisy insight into Thai religion if you visit the nearby **Wat Phra Phutthabat** (Temple of the Buddha's Footprint), still one of Thailand's most popular pilgrimage sites after three and a half centuries.

Each of the attractions of this region can be visited on a day-trip from the capital – or, if you have more time to spare, you can slowly work your way through them before heading north or northeast. **Trains** are the most useful means of getting around, as plenty of local services run to and from Bangkok (note that the State Railway's standard English-language timetables do not list all the local services – phone the railway's hotline on Ⓣ1690 or Hualamphong Station on Ⓣ02 225 0300 for more comprehensive information). The line from the capital takes in Bang Pa-In and Ayutthaya before forking at Ban Phachi: the northern branch heads for Lopburi and goes on to Phitsanulok and Chiang Mai; the northeastern branch serves Isaan. **Buses** between towns are regular but slow, while Bang Pa-In and Ayutthaya can also be reached on scenic but usually expensive **boat** trips up the Chao Phraya.

Bang Pa-In

Little more than a roadside market, the village of **BANG PA-IN**, 60km north of Bangkok, has been put on the tourist map by its extravagant and rather surreal **Royal Palace** (daily 8.30am–5pm, ticket office closes 3.45pm; visitors are asked to dress respectfully, so no vests, shorts or sandals; B100), even though most of the buildings can be seen only from the outside. King Prasat Thong of Ayutthaya first built a palace on this site, 20km downstream from his capital, in the middle of the seventeenth century, and it remained a popular country residence for the kings of Ayutthaya. The palace was abandoned a century later when the capital was moved to Bangkok, only to be revived in the middle of the nineteenth century when the advent of steamboats shortened the journey time upriver. Rama IV (1851–68) built a modest residence here, which his son Chulalongkorn (Rama V), in his passion for westernization, knocked down to make room for the eccentric melange of European, Thai and Chinese architectural styles visible today.

Set in manicured grounds on an island in the Chao Phraya River, and based around an ornamental lake, the palace complex is flat and compact – a free brochure from the ticket office gives a diagram of the layout. On the north side of the lake stand a two-storey, colonial-style residence for the royal relatives and the Italianate **Warophat Phiman** (Excellent and Shining Heavenly Abode), which housed Chulalongkorn's throne hall and still contains private apartments where the present royal family sometimes stays. A covered bridge links this outer part of the palace to the **Pratu Thewarat Khanlai** (The King of the Gods Goes Forth Gate), the main entrance to the inner palace, which was reserved for the king and his immediate family. The high fence that encloses half of the bridge allowed the women of the harem to cross without being seen by male courtiers. You can't miss the photogenic **Aisawan Thiphya-art** (Divine Seat of Personal Freedom) in the middle of the lake: named after King Prasat Thong's original palace, it's the only example of pure Thai architecture at Bang Pa-In. The elegant tiers of the pavilion's roof shelter a bronze statue of Chulalongkorn.

In the inner palace, the **Uthayan Phumisathian** (Garden of the Secured Land), recently rebuilt by Queen Sirikit in grand, neo-colonial style, was Chulalongkorn's favourite house. After passing the **Ho Withun Thasana** (Sage's Lookout Tower), built so that the king could survey the surrounding countryside, you'll come to the main attraction of Bang Pa-In, the **Phra Thinang Wehart Chamrun** (Palace of Heavenly Light). A masterpiece of Chinese design, the mansion and its contents were shipped from China and presented as a gift to Chulalongkorn in 1889 by the Chinese Chamber of Commerce in Bangkok. You're allowed to take off your shoes and feast your eyes on the interior, which drips with fine porcelain and embroidery, ebony furniture inlaid with mother-of-pearl and fantastically intricate woodcarving. This residence was the favourite of Rama VI, whose carved and lacquered writing table can be seen on the ground floor.

The simple marble **obelisk** behind the Uthayan Phumisathian was erected by Chulalongkorn to hold the ashes of Queen Sunandakumariratana, his favourite wife. In 1881, Sunanda, who was then 21 and expecting a child, was taking a trip on the river here when her boat capsized. She could have been rescued quite easily, but the laws concerning the sanctity of the royal family left those around her no option: "If a boat founders, the boatmen must swim away; if they remain near the boat [or] if they lay hold of him [the royal person] to rescue him, they are to be executed." Following the tragedy, King Chulalongkorn became a zealous reformer of Thai customs and strove to make the monarchy more accessible.

Turn right out of the main entrance to the palace grounds and cross the river on the small cable car, and you'll come to the greatest oddity of all: **Wat Nivet Dhamapravat**. A grey Buddhist viharn in the style of a Gothic church, it was built by Chulalongkorn in 1878, complete with wooden pews and stained-glass windows.

Practicalities

Bang Pa-In can easily be visited on a day-trip from Bangkok or Ayutthaya. The best way of getting to Bang Pa-In **from Bangkok** is by **train** from Hualamphong station; the journey takes just over an hour. All trains continue to Ayutthaya, with half going on to Lopburi. From Bang Pa-In station (note the separate station hall built by Chulalongkorn for the royal family) it's a two-kilometre hike to the palace, or you can take a motorbike taxi for about B30. Slow **buses** leave Bangkok's Northern Terminal roughly every half-hour and stop at Bang Pa-In market, a motorbike-taxi ride from the palace.

Every Sunday, the Chao Phraya Express Boat company based at Tha Maharat (Ⓣ02 623 6001–3) and Mitchaopaya based at Tha Chang (Ⓣ02 623 6169) run river tours to Bang Pa-In, taking in Wat Phailom, a breeding ground for open-billed storks escaping the cold in Siberia, from November to June (during the rest of the year they visit Wat Chalerm Phra Kiat in Nonthaburi instead – see p.169), plus a shopping stop at Bang Sai folk arts and handicrafts centre. The boats leave their respective piers in Ratanakosin at 8am, and return at 6pm; tickets, available from the piers, are B350 (B250 one-way), not including lunch and admission to the palace and the handicrafts centre (B100). Luxury cruises to Ayutthaya (see p.255) also stop at Bang Pa-In.

From Ayutthaya, large songthaews leave Thanon Naresuan roughly every hour for the thirty-minute-plus journey to Bang Pa-In market; irregular trains from Ayutthaya's inconveniently located station are quicker (15min) but probably less useful for this short hop.

Ayutthaya

In its heyday as the booming capital of the Thai kingdom, **AYUTTHAYA**, 80km north of Bangkok, was so well endowed with temples that sunlight reflecting off their gilt decoration was said to dazzle from three miles away. Wide, grassy spaces today occupy much of the atmospheric site, which now resembles a graveyard for temples: grand, brooding red-brick ruins rise out of the fields, satisfyingly evoking the city's bygone grandeur while providing a soothing contrast to the brashness of modern temple architecture. A few intact buildings help form an image of what the capital must have looked like, while three fine museums flesh out the picture.

The core of the ancient capital was a four-kilometre-wide **island** at the confluence of the Lopburi, Pasak and Chao Phraya rivers, which was once encircled by a twelve-kilometre wall, crumbling parts of which can be seen at the

Phom Phet fortress in the southeast corner. A grid of broad roads now crosses the island, with recent buildings jostling uneasily with the ancient remains; the hub of the small, grim and lifeless modern town rests on the northeast bank of the island around the corner of Thanon U Thong and Thanon Chao Phrom, although the newest development is off the island to the east.

Ayutthaya comes alive each year for a week in mid-December, when a **festival** is organized to commemorate the town's listing as a **World Heritage Site** by UNESCO on December 13, 1991. The highlight of the celebrations is the nightly *son-et-lumière* show, a grand historical romp featuring fireworks and elephant-back fights and the like, staged at Wat Phra Si Sanphet, Wat Phra Ram or one of the other ancient sites.

Some history

Ayutthaya takes its name from the Indian city of Ayodhya (Sanskrit for "invincible"), the legendary birthplace of Rama, hero of the *Ramayana* epic (see p.127). It was founded in 1351 by U Thong – later **Ramathibodi I** – after Lopburi was ravaged by smallpox, and it rose rapidly through exploiting the expanding trade routes between India and China. Stepping into the political vacuum left by the decline of the Khmer empire at Angkor and the first Thai kingdom at Sukhothai, by the mid-fifteenth century Ayutthaya controlled an empire covering most of the area of modern-day Thailand. Built entirely on canals, few of which survive today, Ayutthaya grew into an enormous amphibious city, which by 1685 had one million people – roughly double the population of London at the same time – living largely on houseboats in a 140-kilometre network of waterways.

Ayutthaya's great wealth attracted a swarm of **foreign traders**, especially in the seventeenth century. At one stage around forty different nationalities, including Chinese, Portuguese, Dutch, English and French, were settled here, many of whom lived in their own ghettos and had their own docks for the export of rice, spices, timber and hides. With deft political skill, the kings of Ayutthaya maintained their independence from outside powers, while embracing the benefits of their cosmopolitan influence: they employed foreign architects and navigators, used Japanese samurai as royal bodyguards, and even took on outsiders as their prime ministers, who could look after their foreign trade without getting embroiled in the usual court intrigues.

In 1767, this 400-year-long **golden age** of stability and prosperity came to an abrupt end. After more than two centuries of recurring tensions, the Burmese captured and ravaged Ayutthaya, taking tens of thousands of prisoners back to Burma with them. With even the wats in ruins, the city had to be abandoned to the jungle, but its memory endured: the architects of the new capital on Ratanakosin island in Bangkok perpetuated Ayutthaya's layout in every possible way.

Practicalities

The best way of getting to Ayutthaya **from Bangkok** is by **train** – there are about twenty a day, concentrated in the early morning and evening; trains continue on to the north and Chiang Mai, and to Nong Khai and Ubon Ratchathani in the northeast. To get to the centre of town from the station on the east bank of the Pasak, take the ferry from the jetty 100m west of the station (last ferry 7pm; B2) across and upriver to Chao Phrom pier; it's then a five-minute walk to the junction of Thanon U Thong and Thanon Chao Phrom (if you're going to stay or eat at *Bann Kun Pra*, take the other ferry from

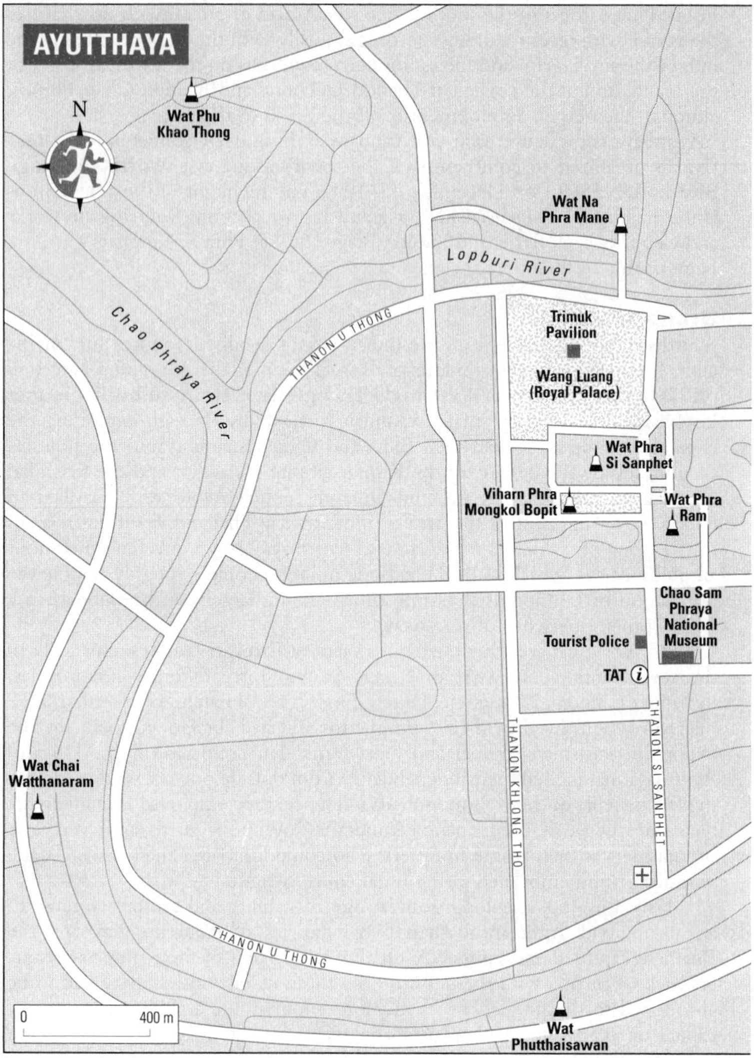

the neighbouring jetty, which runs directly across the river and back). The station has a useful left-luggage service (supposedly 24hr; B10/piece/day). Though frequent, **buses** to Ayutthaya are slower and less convenient, as they depart from Bangkok's distant Northern Terminal. Most buses from Bangkok pull in at the bus stop on Thanon Naresuan, just west of the centre of Ayutthaya, though some, mainly those on long-distance runs, will only stop at Ayutthaya's Northern Bus Terminal, 2km to the east of the centre by the *Ayutthaya Grand Hotel* on Thanon Rojana. Private, air-con minibuses from Bangkok's Victory Monument and Southern Bus Terminal finish their route

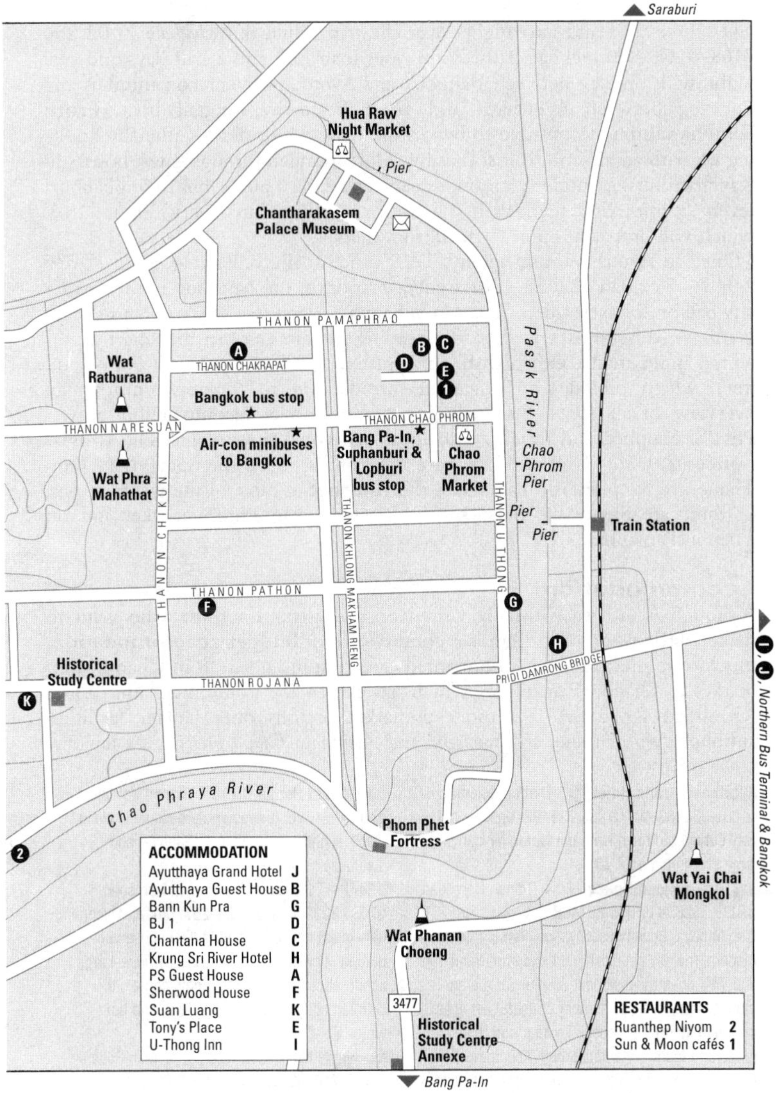

opposite the Thanon Naresuan bus stop (every 30min during daylight hours; 1–2hr depending on traffic). It's also possible to get here by scenic **boat tour** on the Chao Phraya River from Bangkok via Bang Pa-In Palace: River Sun Cruises (ⓣ02 266 9125–6 or 02 266 9316, ⓦwww.riversuncruise.com) based at River City, for example, runs swanky day-trips for B1600 per person, including buffet lunch, with one leg of the journey, whether up to Ayutthaya or back to Bangkok, completed in a coach or air-con minibus. A couple of plushly converted teak rice barges do exorbitantly priced overnight **cruises** to Bang Pa-In and Ayutthaya: the *Manohra 2* (ⓣ02 477 0770, ⓦwww.manohracruises.com)

takes three days and two nights over the trip, while the *Mekhala* (Ⓣ02 256 7168–9, Ⓦwww.mekhalacruise.com) does it in one and a half days and one night, with one leg between Bangkok and Ayutthaya by air-con minibus and one leg between Ayutthaya and Bang Pa-In by longtail boat. **From Kanchanaburi**, it's possible to bypass the Bangkok gridlock, either by hooking up with an air-con tourist minibus (2hr; arranged through guest houses in Kanchanaburi) or, under your own steam, by taking a public bus to Suphanburi (every 30min; 2hr), then changing to an Ayutthaya bus (every 30min; 1hr), which will drop you off at Chao Phrom market.

Once in Ayutthaya, the helpful **TAT** office (daily 8.30am–4.30pm; Ⓣ035 246076–7 or 035 322730–1, Ⓔtatyutya@tat.or.th) can be found in the former city hall on the west side ofThanon Si Sanphet, opposite the Chao Sam Phraya National Museum. It's well worth heading upstairs here to the smartly presented multi-media **exhibition** on Ayutthaya (daily except Wed 9am–5pm; free), which provides an engaging introduction to the city's history, an overview of all the sights, including a scale-model reconstruction of Wat Phra Si Sanphet, and insights into local traditional ways of life. The **tourist police** (Ⓣ035 242352 or 1155) have their office just to the north of TAT on Thanon Si Sanphet. You can access the **Internet** at most of the guest houses, or there are plenty of Internet cafés around Chao Phrom market and on Thanon Pamaphrao.

Accommodation

Although Ayutthaya is usually visited on a day-trip, for those who want to make a little more of it there is a good choice of **budget accommodation**, much of it ghettoized on an unnamed lane, running north from Chao Phrom market to Thanon Pamaphrao, which has earned the ironic nickname "Little Khao San Road". A few more upmarket options offer fancier facilities, although two of these, *U-Thong Inn* and *Ayutthaya Grand Hotel*, are a fair distance from town.

Ayutthaya Grand Hotel 75/5 Thanon Rojana Ⓣ035 335483–91, Ⓕ035 335492. Upscale but way out east of town, with hot water, air-con and a large swimming pool. ❻

Ayutthaya Guest House 12/34 Thanon Naresuan Ⓣ035 232658 or 035 251468, Ⓔayutthaya_guesthouse@yahoo.com. Large, modern, friendly establishment encompassing *Toto* and *TMT* guest houses next door under the same management, with all manner of useful services including Internet access, bike and motorbike rental and tours to Kanchanaburi. Accommodation is in clean, wooden-floored rooms with hot-water bathrooms, either shared or en suite, ranging from B80 dorm beds to air-con en suites. ❷–❸

Bann Kun Pra Thanon U Thong, just north of Pridi Damrong Bridge Ⓣ035 241978, Ⓦwww.bannkunpra.cjb.net. Airy, very attractive rooms (some with river-view balconies), tastefully furnished with simple four-posters, armchairs, antiques and paintings, and sharing plentiful cold-water bathrooms, in a rambling, nineteenth-century riverside teak house with a large, comfy sitting room and balcony. ❸, dorms B150.

BJ 1 Guest House NG 16/7 Thanon Naresuan Ⓣ035 251526. Characterful, reasonably clean place, slightly cramped and shabby – and justifiably cheap. ❶

Chantana House 12/22 Thanon Naresuan Ⓣ035 323200 or 098 850257. Smart, welcoming new guest house in an attractive house with garden opposite *Ayutthaya Guest House*. Large, spotlessly clean, en-suite rooms come either with fan and cold water or air-con and hot water. ❸–❹

Krung Sri River 27/2 Moo 11, Thanon Rojana Ⓣ035 244333–7, Ⓕ035 243777. Ayutthaya's most upmarket accommodation is a grand affair, with swanky lobby, gym and attractive pool, occupying a prime, but noisy, position at the eastern end of the Pridi Damrong Bridge. ❼

PS Guest House 23/1 Thanon Chakrapat Ⓣ066 446331 or 035 242394. Quiet, homely and sociable spot run by a very helpful retired English teacher. Most of the large, clean and simple rooms share bathrooms, though en suite and air-con are available, and there's a balcony overlooking the pleasant garden. Note that at the time of writing *PS* was planning to move to a similar place just round the corner on the east side of Thanon Chikun, overlooking Wat Ratburana. 2–3

Sherwood House (MM Swimming Pool) 21/25 Thanon Pathon (Dechawut) ⓣ06 666 0813, ⓔsherwoodmm@hotmail.com. Western-run guest house of small, concrete fan or air-con bedrooms with shared hot-water bathrooms, whose main draw is the decent-sized swimming pool (B40/day non-guests). A little way from the centre of town, but fairly handy for the historical sites. Bar-restaurant with Internet access, cable TV, and Thai and Western food; bike and motorbike rental available. 3

Suan Luang Thanon Rojana ⓣ & ⓕ035 245537. This training ground for hotel and catering students at Rajabhat College, next to the Historical Study Centre, offers functional, bright, spacious and very clean rooms with fridge, TV, air-con and cold-water bathrooms, in a quiet location handy for TAT and the museums. 4

Tony's Place 12/18 Thanon Naresuan ⓣ035 252578. Sociable, welcoming spot with a diverse set of bedrooms in a sprawling wooden house, ranging from basic digs sharing a bathroom to a large air-con room with an en-suite hot-water bathroom with a small terrace. Internet, pool table, regular live music, big-screen sports and outdoor tables in the bar-restaurant downstairs. 1–4

U-Thong Inn 210 Thanon Rojana ⓣ035 242236–9, ⓕ035 242235. Hot water, satellite TV and air-con in all rooms, and a swimming pool. Similar to, and as far out of town as, *Ayutthaya Grand Hotel*, but not as good value. 6

Eating and drinking

The main travellers' hangout in the evening is the small, laid-back *Moon Café*, on the same lane as the *Ayutthaya Guest House*, which serves good Western and Thai **food** and occasionally has live music; serving the same menu, the adjacent *Sun* is more of a daytime café, with a book exchange, espresso coffee and speciality teas such as Thai mulberry. For bargain-basement Thai dining head for the Hua Raw night market, near the northernmost point of Thanon U Thong, or during the day Chao Phrom market. Many riverside restaurants in Ayutthaya are slightly expensive and disappointing: the best bets are the atmospheric terrace at *Bann Kun Pra* (see opposite), which specializes in reasonably priced fish and seafood, notably prawns; and the congenial *Ruanthep Niyom*, Thanon U Thong on the south side of town, where, on river bank terraces or a moored boat with views of Wat Phutthaisawan's white prang, you can dine on such delicacies as royal tofu with wild mushrooms, crab, cashew nuts and prawns. Around the central ruins are a few pricey restaurants if you need air-conditioning with your lunch.

The City

The majority of Ayutthaya's ancient remains are spread out across the western half of the island in a patchwork of parkland: **Wat Phra Mahathat** and **Wat Ratburana** stand near the modern centre, while a broad band runs down the middle of the parkland, containing the **Royal Palace (Wang Luang)** and temple, the most revered Buddha image, at **Viharn Phra Mongkol Bopit**, and the two main **museums**. To the north of the island you'll find the best-preserved temple, **Wat Na Phra Mane**, and **Wat Phu Khao Thong**, the "Golden Mount", while to the southeast lie the giant chedi of **Wat Yai Chai Mongkol** and **Wat Phanan Choeng**, still a vibrant place of worship.

Busloads of tourists descend on the sights during the day, but the area covered by the old capital is large enough not to feel swamped. Distances are deceptive, so it's best not to walk everywhere: **bicycles** (B30–50/day) can be hired at the guest houses, at a few of the shops in front of the train station or from the tourist police. If even that sounds too much like hard work, some of the guest houses and outlets in front of the station rent small **motorbikes** (B250/day). Otherwise there are plenty of **tuk-tuks** around: their set routes for sharing passengers are more useful for locals than for tourists, but a typical journey in town on your own should only cost B20–30. **Motorbike taxis** charge around B10–15 for short journeys. If you're pushed for time you could hire a tuk-tuk for a whistle-stop tour of the old city for B200 an hour (the current going rate set by the tourist police), either from the train station or from Chao Phrom market.

Tour **boats**, generally accommodating up to eight passengers and charging around B700 for a two-hour trip, can be chartered from the pier outside the Chantharakasem Palace, or through guest houses. *PS Guest House* puts together recommended trips for B150 per person. A typical tour takes in Wat Phanan Choeng (see p.262), **Wat Phutthaisawan**, built around a gleaming white prang by Ramathibodi I in 1353, only two years after the city's foundation, and the recently restored **Wat Chai Watthanaram**, which was built by King Prasat Thong in 1630 to commemorate his victory over Cambodia, taking as its model the imposing symmetry of the Baphuon temple at Angkor. It's also possible to take a twenty-minute **elephant-ride** (B400/person) around the central ruins from behind the TAT office off Thanon Pathon. (You're quite likely to spot these photogenically caparisoned animals in the early evening as they rumble across to the northeast side of town to their home in the restored sixteenth-century kraal, into which wild elephants were formerly driven for capture and taming.)

Wat Phra Mahathat and Wat Ratburana

Heading west out of the new town centre along Thanon Chao Phrom (which becomes Thanon Naresuan), after about 1km you'll come to the first set of ruins, a pair of temples on opposite sides of the road. The overgrown **Wat Phra Mahathat**, on the left (daily 8am–6pm; B30), is the epitome of Ayutthaya's nostalgic atmosphere of faded majesty. The name "Mahathat" (Great Relic Chedi) indicates that the temple was built to house remains of the Buddha himself: according to the royal chronicles – never renowned for historical accuracy – King Ramesuan (1388–95) was looking out of his palace one morning when ashes of the Buddha materialized out of thin air here. A gold casket containing the ashes was duly enshrined in a grand 38-metre-high prang. The prang later collapsed, but the reliquary was unearthed in the 1950s, along with a hoard of other treasures, including a gorgeous marble fish, which opened to reveal gold, amber, crystal and porcelain ornaments – all now on show in the Chao Sam Phraya National Museum (see p.260).

You can climb what remains of the prang to get a good view of the broad, grassy complex, with dozens of brick spires tilting at impossible angles and headless Buddhas scattered around like spare parts in a scrapyard – and look out for the serene head of a stone Buddha that has become nestled in the embrace of a bodhi tree's roots. To the west you'll see a lake, now surrounded by a popular park, where Ramathibodi I discovered an auspicious conch shell, symbol of victory and righteousness, which confirmed his choice of site for his new city, and the slender prang of **Wat Phra Ram**, built in the late fourteenth century on the site of Ramathibodi's cremation by his son and successor as king, Ramesuan.

Across the road from Wat Phra Mahathat, the towering **Wat Ratburana** (daily 8am–6pm; B30) was built in 1424 by King Boromraja II to commemorate his elder brothers, Ay and Yi, who managed to kill each other in an elephant-back duel over the succession to the throne, thus leaving it vacant for Boromraja. Here, four elegant Sri Lankan chedis lean outwards as if in deference to the main prang, on which some of the original stucco work can still be seen, including fine statues of garudas swooping down on nagas. It's possible to descend steep steps inside the prang to the crypt, where on two levels you can make out fragmentary murals of the early Ayutthaya period. Several hundred Buddha images were buried down here, most of which were snatched by grave robbers, although some can be seen in the Chao Sam Phraya Museum (see p.260). They're in the earliest style that can be said to be distinctly Ayutthayan – an unsmiling Khmer expression, but on an oval face and elongated body that show the strong influence of Sukhothai.

Wat Phra Si Sanphet and the Wang Luang (Royal Palace)

Nearly a kilometre west of Wat Ratburana is **Wat Phra Si Sanphet** (daily 8am–6pm; B30), built in 1448 by King Boromatrailokanat as his private chapel. Formerly the grandest of Ayutthaya's temples, and still one of the best preserved, it took its name from one of the largest standing metal images of the Buddha ever known, the **Phra Si Sanphet**, erected here in 1503. Towering 16m high and covered in 173kg of gold, it did not survive the ravages of the Burmese, though Rama I rescued the pieces and placed them inside a chedi at Wat Pho in Bangkok. The three remaining grey chedis in the characteristic style of the old capital were built to house the ashes of three kings, and have now become the most hackneyed image of Ayutthaya.

The site of this royal wat was originally occupied by Ramathibodi I's wooden palace, which Boromatrailokanat replaced with the bigger **Wang Luang** (Royal Palace; same hours and ticket as Wat Phra Si Sanphet), stretching to the Lopburi River on the north side. Successive kings turned the Wang Luang into a vast complex of pavilions and halls, with an elaborate system of walls designed to isolate the inner sanctum for the king and his consorts. The palace was destroyed by the Burmese in 1767 and plundered by Rama I for its bricks, which he needed to build the new capital at Bangkok. Now you can only trace the outlines of a few walls in the grass and inspect an unimpressive wooden replica of an open pavilion – better to consult the model of the whole complex in the Historical Study Centre (see p.260).

Viharn Phra Mongkol Bopit and the cremation ground

Viharn Phra Mongkol Bopit (Mon–Fri 8.30am–4.30pm, Sat & Sun 8.30am–5.30pm; free), on the south side of Wat Phra Si Sanphet, attracts tourists and Thai pilgrims in about equal measure. The pristine hall – a replica of a typical Ayutthayan viharn, with its characteristic chunky lotus-capped columns around the outside – was built in 1956, with help from the Burmese to atone for their flattening of the city two centuries earlier, in order to shelter the revered **Phra Mongkol Bopit**, one of the largest bronze Buddhas in Thailand. The powerfully austere image, with its flashing mother-of-pearl eyes, was cast in the fifteenth century, then sat exposed to the elements from the time of the Burmese invasion until its new home was built. During restoration, the hollow image was found to contain hundreds of Buddha statuettes, some of which were later buried around the shrine to protect it.

The car park in front of the viharn used to be the **cremation site** for Ayutthayan kings and high-ranking members of the royal family. Here, on a propitious date decided by astrologers, the embalmed body was placed on a towering *meru* (funeral pyre), representing Mount Meru, the centre of the Hindu-Buddhist universe. These many-gabled and pinnacled wooden structures, which had all the appearance of permanent palaces, were a miracle of architectural technology: the *meru* constructed for King Phetracha in 1704, for example, was 103m tall and took eleven months to raise, requiring thousands of tree trunks and hundreds of thousands of bamboo poles. The task of building at such great heights was given to *yuan-hok*, a particular clan of acrobats who used to perform at the top of long poles during special festivals. Their handiwork was not consigned to the flames: the cremation took place on a pyramid erected underneath the central spire, so as not to damage the main structure, which was later dismantled and its timber used for building temples. The cremation ground is now given over to a picnic area and a clutch of souvenir and refreshment stalls.

The museums

A ten-minute walk south of the viharn brings you to the largest of the town's three museums, the **Chao Sam Phraya National Museum** (Wed–Sun 9am–4pm; B30; Ⓦwww.thailandmuseum.com), where most of the moveable remains of Ayutthaya's glory – those that weren't plundered by treasure-hunters or taken to the National Museum in Bangkok – are exhibited. The museum itself was funded by a Fine Arts Department sale of the Buddhist votive tablets excavated from Wat Ratburana in the late 1950s, and given the original name (Chao Sam Phraya) of King Boromraja II, who built the wat.

Apart from numerous Buddhas and some fine woodcarving, the museum is bursting with **gold treasures** in all shapes and sizes – the original relic casket from Wat Mahathat, betel-nut sets and model chedis, a royal wimple in gold filigree, a royal sword and scabbard and a crouching elephant, both dripping with gems and both found in the crypt of the main prang of Wat Ratburana. A second gallery, behind the main hall, explores foreign influences on Thai art and is particularly good on the origins of the various styles of Buddha images. This room also contains skeletons and artefacts from the site of the Portuguese settlement founded in 1540 just south of the town on the banks of the Chao Phraya River. The Portuguese were the first Western power to establish ties with Ayutthaya, when in 1511 they were granted commercial privileges in return for supplying arms.

The **Historical Study Centre** (daily 9am–4.30pm; B100), five minutes' walk away along Thanon Rotchana, is the town's showpiece, with a hefty admission charge. The visitors' exhibition upstairs puts the ruins in context, dramatically presenting a wealth of background detail through videos, sound effects and reconstructions of temple murals, along with model ships, a peasant's wooden house and a small-scale model of the Royal Palace that all build up a broad social history of Ayutthaya. The centre's **annexe** (same times and ticket), 500m south of Wat Phanan Choeng on the road to Bang Pa-In, also merits a visit despite its remoteness. Built with Japanese money on the site of the old Japanese settlement, it tells the fascinating story of Ayutthaya's relations with foreign powers, using similar multi-media effects as well as maps, paintings and documents prised from venerable museums around the world.

In the northeast corner of the island, the **Chantharakasem Palace Museum** (Wed–Sun 9am–4pm; B30; Ⓦwww.thailandmuseum.com) was traditionally the home of the heir to the Ayutthayan throne. The Black Prince, Naresuan, built the first *wang na* (palace of the front) here in about 1577 so that he could guard the area of the city wall that was most vulnerable to enemy attack. Rama IV (1851–68) had the palace rebuilt and it now displays many of his possessions, including a throne platform overhung by a white *chat*, a ceremonial nine-tiered parasol that is a vital part of a king's insignia. The rest of the museum features beautiful ceramics and Buddha images, and a small arsenal of late Ayutthaya and early Bangkok period cannon and musketry.

Wat Na Phra Mane

Wat Na Phra Mane (daily 8am–5pm; B20), on the north bank of the Lopburi River opposite the Wang Luang, is Ayutthaya's most rewarding temple, as it's the only one from the town's golden age that survived the ravages of the Burmese. The story goes that when the Burmese were on the brink of capturing Ayutthaya in 1760, a siege gun positioned here burst, mortally wounding their king and prompting their retreat; out of superstition, they left the temple standing when they came back to devastate the city in 1767.

The main **bot**, built in 1503, shows the distinctive features of Ayutthayan architecture – outside columns topped with lotus cups, and slits in the walls instead of windows to let the wind pass through. Inside, underneath a rich red-and-gold coffered ceiling that represents the stars around the moon, sits a powerful six-metre-high Buddha in the disdainful, over-decorated royal style characteristic of the later Ayutthaya period.

In sharp contrast is the dark-green **Phra Khan Thavaraj** Buddha, which dominates the tiny viharn behind to the right. Seated in the "European position", with its robe delicately pleated and its feet up on a large lotus leaf, the gentle figure conveys a reassuring serenity. It's advertised as being from Sri Lanka, the source of Thai Buddhism, but more likely is a seventh- to ninth-century Mon image from Wat Phra Mane at Nakhon Pathom.

Wat Phu Khao Thong

Head 2km northwest of Wat Na Phra Mane and you're in open country, where the fifty-metre chedi of **Wat Phu Khao Thong** rises steeply out of the fields. In 1569, after a temporary occupation of Ayutthaya, the Burmese erected a Mon-style chedi here to commemorate their victory. Forbidden by Buddhist law from pulling down a sacred monument, the Thais had to put up with this galling reminder of the enemy's success until it collapsed nearly two hundred years later, when King Borommakot promptly built a truly Ayutthayan chedi on the old Burmese base – just in time for the Burmese to return in 1767 and flatten the town. This "Golden Mount" has recently been restored and painted toothpaste-white, with a colossal equestrian statue of King Naresuan, conqueror of the Burmese, to keep it company. You can climb 25m of steps up the side of the chedi to look out over the countryside and the town, with glimpses of Wat Phra Si Sanphet and Viharn Phra Mongkok Bopit in the distance. In 1956, to celebrate 2500 years of Buddhism, the government placed on the tip of the spire a ball of solid gold weighing 2500g, of which there is now no trace.

Wat Yai Chai Mongkol

To the southeast of the island, if you cross the suspension bridge over the Pasak River and the rail line, then turn right at the major roundabout, you pass through Ayutthaya's new business zone and some rustic suburbia before reaching the ancient but still functioning **Wat Yai Chai Mongkol**, about 2km from the bridge (daily 8am–5pm; B20). Surrounded by formal lawns and flowerbeds, the wat was established by Ramathibodi I in 1357 as a meditation site for monks returning from study in Sri Lanka. King Naresuan put up the celebrated **chedi** to mark the decisive victory over the Burmese at Suphanburi in 1593, when he himself had sent the enemy packing by slaying the Burmese crown prince in a duel. Built on a colossal scale to outshine the Burmese Golden Mount on the opposite side of Ayutthaya, the chedi has come to symbolize the prowess and devotion of Naresuan and, by implication, his descendants right down to the present king. By the entrance, a **reclining Buddha**, now gleamingly restored in white, was also constructed by Naresuan; elsewhere in the grounds, the wat maintains its contemplative origins, with some highly topical maxims pinned to the trees, such as "Cut down the forest of passion, not real trees".

Wat Phanan Choeng

In Ayutthaya's most prosperous period, the docks and main trading area were located near the confluence of the Chao Phraya and Pasak rivers, to the west of Wat Yai Chai Mongkol. This is where you'll find the oldest and liveliest working temple in town, **Wat Phanan Choeng** (daily 8am–5pm; B20) – as well as the annexe to the Historical Study Centre (see p.260). The main viharn is often filled with the sights, sounds and smells of an incredible variety of merit-making activities, as devotees burn huge pink Chinese incense candles, offer food and rattle fortune sticks. It's even possible to buy tiny golden statues of the Buddha to be placed in one of the hundreds of niches that line the walls, a form of votive offering peculiar to this temple. If you can get here during a festival, especially Chinese New Year, you're in for an overpowering experience.

The nineteen-metre-high Buddha, which almost fills the hall, has survived since 1324, shortly before the founding of the capital, and tears are said to have flowed from its eyes when Ayutthaya was sacked by the Burmese. However, the reason for the temple's popularity with the Chinese is to be found in the early eighteenth-century shrine by the pier, with its image of a beautiful Chinese princess who drowned herself here because of a king's infidelity: his remorse led him to build the shrine at the place where she had walked into the river.

Lopburi and around

Mention the name **LOPBURI** to a Thai and the chances are that he or she will start telling you about monkeys – the central junction of this drab provincial capital, 150km due north of Bangkok, swarms with them. So beneficial are the beasts to the town's tourist trade that a local hotelier treats six hundred of them to a sit-down meal at Phra Prang Sam Yod temple every November, complete with menus, waiters and napkins, as a thank you for their help. In fact, the monkeys can be a real nuisance, but at least they add some life to the town's central **Khmer buildings**, which, though historically important, are rather unimpressive. More illuminating is the **Narai National Museum**, housed in a partly reconstructed seventeenth-century palace complex, and distant **Wat Phra Phutthabat**, a colourful eye-opener for non-Buddhists. Lopburi's main feast days are the three days of the **King Narai Reign Fair** in February, featuring costumed processions and a *son-et-lumière* show at Phra Narai Ratchanivet.

Originally called Lavo, Lopburi is one of the longest-inhabited towns in Thailand, and was a major centre of the Mon (Dvaravati) civilization from around the sixth century. It maintained a tenuous independence in the face of the advancing Khmers until as late as the early eleventh century, when it was incorporated into the empire as the provincial capital for much of central Thailand. Increasing Thai immigration from the north soon tilted the balance against the Khmers, and Lopburi was again independent from some time early in the thirteenth century until the rise of Ayutthaya in the middle of the fourteenth. Thereafter, Lopburi was twice used as a second capital, first by King Narai of Ayutthaya in the seventeenth century, then by Rama IV of Bangkok in the nineteenth, because its remoteness from the sea made it less vulnerable to European expansionists. Rama V downgraded the town, turning the royal palace into a provincial government office and museum; Lopburi's modern role is as the site of several huge army barracks.

Practicalities

As it's on the main line north to Chiang Mai, Lopburi is best reached by **train**. Fifteen trains a day, concentrated in the early morning and evening, run here from Bangkok's Hualamphong station (3hr) via Ayutthaya (1hr 30min): a popular option is to arrive in Lopburi in the morning, leave your bags at the conveniently central **station** while you look around the town, then catch one of the night trains to the north. Within walking distance of the station, to the west of the rail line, lie most of the hotels and just about everything of interest in town. **Buses** from Ayutthaya (every 20min) take around two hours to reach Lopburi, from Bangkok (every 20min) around three hours. If you happen to be coming here from Kanchanaburi, it's possible to bypass Bangkok by taking a public bus to Suphanburi (every 30min; 2hr), then changing to a Lopburi bus (hourly; 3hr). The long-distance bus **terminal** is on the south side of the huge Sakeo roundabout, 2km east of the town centre: a blue city bus or red songthaew heading west on Thanon Narai Mahathat to Narai's Palace will save you the walk. **TAT** has an office in a restored, wooden, colonial-style building on

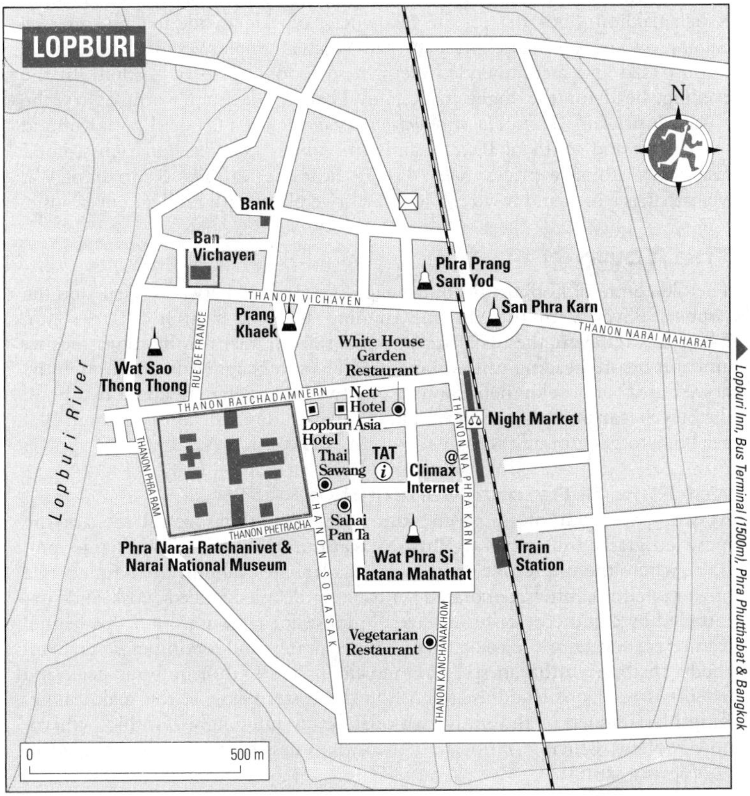

the north side of Wat Phra Si Ratana Mahathat (daily 8.30am–4.30pm; ⓣ036 422768–9, ⓔtatlobri@tat.or.th), and **Internet access** is available just around the corner on Thanon Na Phra Karn at Climax Internet.

Lopburi's choice of **accommodation** is poor, and not helped by Thanon Na Phra Karn, a minefield of seedy budget hotels in front of the train station. By far the best option in the heart of town is the clean and friendly *Nett Hotel*, 17/1–2 Soi 2, Thanon Ratchadamnern (ⓣ036 411738 or 036 421460; ❷–❹), offering recently renovated, en-suite fan or air-con rooms, the latter with hot water, TV and fridge. The town's most prominent hotel, the *Lopburi Asia*, opposite the entrance to Narai's palace, has also recently been refurbished, but still comes in a distant second, with a choice of rooms with fan and bathroom, or with air-con, TV and hot water (ⓣ036 427419; ❷–❹). A long trek east of the centre, the air-conditioned rooms at the recommended *Lopburi Inn*, 28/9 Thanon Narai Maharat (ⓣ036 412609, ⓕ036 412457; ❺), are as posh as Lopburi town gets; if money is no object and you have your own transport, head out of town to its sister establishment, the *Lopburi Inn Resort*, off the Saraburi road, an overblown complex of Mediterranean-style buildings with a large swimming pool, gym and sauna (ⓣ036 421453, ⓦwww.lopburiinn resort.com; ❻).

Lopburi's **restaurants** present an even sorrier selection than its hotels. In the mornings (not Sun), cheap vegetarian food is served up at an unnamed restaurant on the south side of Wat Phra Si Ratana Mahathat on Thanon Kanchanakhom (look out for the yellow flags outside), while the air-con *Thai Sawang*, on Thanon Sorasak near the palace, offers simple Western breakfasts, as well as Thai and recommended Vietnamese food, until 8 or 8.30pm. In the evening, head for the night market on Thanon Na Phra Karn, or try the classier, open-air *White House Garden Restaurant* on Thanon Praya Kumjud (parallel to and south of Ratchadamnern), which specializes in rich seafood dishes at reasonable prices. *Sahai Pan Ta*, near the northwest corner of Wat Mahathat, is a dark and rowdy Wild-West-style place, with food and live music.

The Town

The old centre of Lopburi sits on an egg-shaped island between canals and the Lopburi River, with the rail line running across it from north to south. **Thanon Vichayen**, the main street, crosses the rail tracks at the town's busiest junction before heading east – now called Thanon Narai Maharat through the newest areas of development towards Highway 1. If you're tempted by one of the bicycle **samlors** that hang around the train station, it'll cost you about B80 per hour to get around the sights.

Wat Phra Si Ratana Mahathat

As you come out of the train station, the first thing you'll see are the sprawled grassy ruins of **Wat Phra Si Ratana Mahathat** (daily 6am–6pm; B30), where the impressive centrepiece is a laterite prang in the Khmer style of the twelfth century, decorated with finely detailed stucco work and surrounded by a ruined cloister. Arrayed in loose formation around this central feature are several more rocket-like Khmer prangs and a number of graceful chedis in the Ayutthayan style, among them one with a bulbous peak and faded bas-reliefs of Buddhist saints. On the eastern side of the main prang, King Narai added to the mishmash of styles by building a "Gothic" viharn, now roofless, which is home to a lonely, headless stone Buddha, draped in photogenic saffron.

Phra Narai Ratchanivet (King Narai's palace)

The imposing gates and high crenellated walls of the **Phra Narai Ratchanivet**, a short walk northwest of the wat, might promise more than the complex delivers, but the museum in its central courtyard is worth a look, and the grounds are a green and relaxing spot. King Narai, with the help of French architects, built the heavily fortified palace in 1666 as a precaution against any possible confrontation with the Western powers, and for the rest of his reign he was to spend eight months of every year here, entertaining foreign envoys and indulging his love of hunting. After Narai's death, Lopburi was left forgotten until 1856, when Rama IV – worried about British and French colonialism – decided to make this his second capital and lavishly restored the central buildings of Narai's palace.

The outer courtyard

The main **entrance** to the palace complex is through the Phayakkha Gate on Thanon Sorasak (the gate is open daily 7am–5.30pm, giving access to the palace grounds, but during museum opening hours – see below – the admission fee is collected here). You'll see the unusual lancet shape of this arch again and again in the seventeenth-century doors and windows of Lopburi – just one aspect of the Western influences embraced by Narai. Around the **outer courtyard**, which occupies the eastern half of the complex, stand the walls of various gutted buildings – twelve warehouses for Narai's treasures, stables for the royal hunting elephants, and a moated reception hall for foreign envoys. With their lily ponds and manicured lawns, these well-shaded grounds are ideal for a picnic or a siesta.

The central courtyard and the Narai National Museum

Straight ahead from the Phayakkha Gate another arch leads into the **central courtyard**, where the typically Ayutthayan **Chanthara Phisan Pavilion** contains a fascinating exhibition on Narai's reign – check out the pointed white cap typical of those worn by noblemen of the time, which increased their height by no less than 50cm.

To the left is the colonial-style Phiman Mongkut Hall, now the **Narai National Museum** (Wed–Sun 8.30am–4.30pm; B30; Ⓦwww.thailandmuseum.com), whose exhibits concentrate on the period following the Khmer subjugation of Lopburi in the eleventh century. Inevitably there's a surfeit of Buddhas, most of them fine examples of the Khmer style and the distinctive **Lopburi style**, which emerged in the thirteenth and fourteenth centuries, mixing traditional Khmer elements – such as the conical *ushnisha*, or flame on the crown of the Buddha's head – with new features such as a more oval face and slender body. On the top floor is **King Mongkut's bedroom**, filled with his furniture and assorted memorabilia of his reign, including his very short and uncomfortable-looking bed and eerie painted statues of his equally vertically challenged near-contemporaries, Napoleon and Queen Victoria.

On the south side of the museum lies the shell of the **Dusit Sawan Hall**, where foreign dignitaries came to present their credentials to King Narai. Inside you can still see the niche, raised 3.5m above the main floor, where the throne was set; beneath the niche, a modern plaque showing Narai receiving the French envoy, the Chevalier de Chaumont, in 1685, is revered as an icon of the king, with offerings of gold leaf, joss sticks and garlands. The whole building is divided in two around the throne: the front half has "foreign" doors and windows with pointed arches; the rear part, from where the king would have made his grand entrance, has traditional Thai openings. The hall used to be lined with French mirrors in imitation of Versailles, with Persian carpets and a pyramidal roof of golden glazed tiles rounding off the most majestic building in the palace.

The private courtyards

King Narai's private courtyard, through whose sturdy walls only the trusted few were admitted, occupied the southwest corner of the complex. During Narai's time, hundreds of lamps were placed in niches around the walls of this courtyard by night, shedding a fairy-like light on the palace. Now there's not much more than the foundations left of his residence, the **Sutha Sawan Hall**, and its bathing ponds and artificial grotto.

Rama IV's private courtyard was built to house his harem in the northwest corner of the grounds, behind the present site of the museum. In what used to be the kitchen there's now a small folk museum of central Thai life, containing a loom and various pieces of farming and fishing equipment. In front, you can consult a crude model of the palace as it looked in Narai's time.

Wat Sao Thong Thong and Ban Vichayen

The north gate (now closed) to the palace is called the Vichayen Gate after **Constantine Phaulkon**, a Greek adventurer who had come to Ayutthaya with the English East India Company in 1678. It leads directly to the aptly named Rue de France, the approach to the remains of his grand residence. Halfway along this road, set back on the left, you'll pass a building whose plain terracotta roof tiles and whitewashed exterior give it a strangely Mediterranean look. This is in fact the viharn of **Wat Sao Thong Thong**, and is typical of Narai's time in its combination of Thai-style tiered roof with "Gothic" pointed windows. Erected as either a Christian chapel or a mosque for the Persian ambassador's residence, it was later used as a Buddhist viharn and has now been tastefully restored, complete with brass door-knockers and plush red carpet. Inside there's an austere Buddha image of the Ayutthaya period and, in the lamp niches, some fine Lopburi-style Buddhas.

The complex of **Ban Vichayen** (daily 7am–6pm; B30) had been built by Narai as a residence for foreign ambassadors, with a Christian chapel incongruously stuccoed with Buddhist flame and lotus-leaf motifs. Though now just a nest of empty shells, it still conjures up the atmosphere of court intrigue and dark deeds which, towards the end of Narai's reign, centred on the colourful figure of its chief resident, Phaulkon. He entered the royal service as interpreter and accountant, rapidly rising to the position of Narai's *ookya vichayen* (prime minister). It was chiefly due to his influence that Narai established close ties with Louis XIV of France, a move that made commercial sense but also formed part of Phaulkon's secret plan to turn Narai and his people to Christianity, with the aid of the French. Two missions were sent from Versailles, but both failed in their overt aim of signing a political alliance and their covert attempt at religious conversion. (It was around this time that the word for Westerner, *farang*, entered the Thai language, from the same derivation as *français*, which the Thais render *farangset*.) In 1688, a struggle for succession broke out, and leading officials persuaded the dying Narai to appoint as regent his foster brother, Phetracha, a great rival of Phaulkon's. Phetracha promptly executed Phaulkon on charges of treason, and took the throne himself when Narai died. Under Phetracha, Narai's open-door policy towards foreigners was brought to a screeching halt and the Thai kingdom returned to traditional, smaller-scale dealings with the outside world.

Prang Khaek, Phra Prang Sam Yod and San Phra Karn

Near the northeast corner of the palace, the junction of Thanon Vichayen and Thanon Sorasak is marked by an unusual traffic island, on which perch the three stubby red-brick towers of **Prang Khaek**, a well-preserved Hindu shrine, possibly to the god Shiva, and dating from as early as the eighth century. The nearby **Phra Prang Sam Yod** (daily 7am–6pm; B30), at the top of Thanon Na Phra Karn, seems also to have been a Hindu temple, later converted to Buddhism under the Khmers. The three chunky prangs, made of dark laterite with some restored stucco work, and symbolizing the Hindu triumvirate of Brahma, Vishnu and Shiva, are Lopburi's most photographed sight, though they'll only detain you for a minute or two – at least check out some carved figures of seated hermits at the base of the door columns. The shrine's grassy knoll is a good spot for monkey-watching – they run amok all over this area, so keep an eye on your bags and pockets. Across the rail line at the modern red-and-gold shrine of **San Phra Karn**, there's even a monkey's adventure playground for the benefit of tourists, beside the base of what must have been a huge Khmer prang.

Wat Phra Phutthabat (Temple of the Buddha's Footprint)

Seventeen kilometres southeast of Lopburi along Highway 1 stands the most important pilgrimage site in central Thailand, **Wat Phra Phutthabat**, which is believed to house a footprint made by the Buddha. Any of the frequent **buses** to Saraburi or Bangkok from Lopburi's Sakeo roundabout will get you there in thirty minutes. The souvenir village around the temple, which is on the western side of Highway 1, includes plenty of foodstalls for day-trippers.

The **legend** of Phra Phutthabat dates back to the beginning of the seventeenth century, when King Song Tham of Ayutthaya sent some monks to Sri Lanka to worship the famous Buddha's footprint of Sumankut. To the monks' surprise, the Sri Lankans asked them why they had bothered to travel all that way when, according to the ancient Pali scriptures, the Buddha had passed through Thailand and had left his footprint in their own backyard. As soon as Song Tham heard this he instigated a search for the footprint, which was finally discovered in 1623 by a hunter named Pram Bun, when a wounded deer disappeared into a hollow and then emerged miraculously healed. The hunter pushed aside the bushes to discover a foot-shaped trench filled with water, which immediately cured him of his terrible skin disease. A temple was built on the spot, but was destroyed by the Burmese in 1765 – the present buildings date from the Bangkok era.

A staircase flanked by nagas leads up to a marble platform, where a gaudy mondop with mighty doors inlaid with mother-of-pearl houses the **footprint**, which in itself is not much to look at. Sheltered by a mirrored canopy, the stone print is nearly 2m long and obscured by layers of gold leaf presented by pilgrims; people also throw money into the footprint, some of which they take out again as a charm or merit object. The hill behind the shrine, which you can climb for a fine view over the gilded roofs of the complex to the mountains beyond, is covered in shrines. The small bot, which elsewhere would be the centrepiece of a temple, is where pilgrims go for a nap.

During the dry season in January, February and March, a million pilgrims from all over the country flock to the **Ngan Phrabat** (Phrabat Fair), when other pilgrims are making their way to the other major religious sites at Doi

Suthep, Nakhon Si Thammarat and That Phanom. During the fair, which reaches its peak in two week-long lunar periods, one at the beginning of February, the other at the beginning of March, stalls selling souvenirs and traditional medicines around the entrance swell to form a small town, and traditional entertainments, magic shows and a Ferris wheel are laid on. The fair is still a major religious event, but before the onset of industrialization it was the highlight of social and cultural life for all ages and classes; it was an important place of courtship, for example, especially for women at a time when their freedom was limited. Another incentive for women to attend the fair was the belief that visiting the footprint three times would ensure a place in heaven – for many women, the Phrabat Fair became the focal point of their lives, as Buddhist doctrine allowed them no other path to salvation. Up to the reign of Rama V (1868–1910) even the king used to come, performing a ritual lance dance on elephant-back to ensure a long reign.

The northern plains

Heading north from Lopburi, road and rail plough through Thailand's "rice bowl", a landscape of lurid green paddies interrupted only by the unwelcoming sprawl of **Nakhon Sawan**, located at the confluence of the Ping, Wang, Yom and Nan rivers, which merge here to create the Chao Phraya. A prosperous city of about 100,000 predominantly Chinese inhabitants, Nakhon Sawan plays a vital role as the region's main market and distribution centre for rice, but is of interest to tourists only as a place to change buses for Kamphaeng Phet or Phitsanulok. The bus station is in the town centre and there are a couple of passable budget hotels close by as a last resort. All Bangkok–Chiang Mai trains stop in Nakhon Sawan, but as the station is 10km out of town, with skeletal local transport and no station hotels, breaking your journey 130km further north at Phitsanulok makes much more sense. The one time the city deserves a special visit is during **Chinese New Year** (between late January and mid-February, see Basics p.63), which is celebrated here with more vigour than anywhere else in the country. The place gets transformed for the three-day festival, decked out with Chinese lanterns and decorative arches, as visitors from all over Thailand gather to watch the Chinese dragons and lion-dancers snaking through the streets. Chinese opera troupes, an international lion-dance competition, fireworks and countless food stalls complete the scene.

Many tourists bypass the lush northern reaches of the central plains, fast asleep in an overnight train from Bangkok to Chiang Mai, yet it was here, during the thirteenth, fourteenth and fifteenth centuries, that the kingdom of Thailand first began to cohere and assume its present identity. Some of Thailand's finest buildings and sculpture were produced in **Sukhothai**, once the most powerful city in Thailand. Abandoned to the jungle by the sixteenth century, it has now been extensively restored, the resulting historical park making an attractive open-air museum. Less complete renovations have made Sukhothai's satellite cities of **Si Satchanalai and Kamphaeng Phet** worth visiting, both for their relative wildness and lack of visitors.

The nearest hills in which to clear the cobwebs are in **Ramkhamhaeng National Park** near Sukhothai; further west, the Burmese border town of **Mae Sot** is the departure point for the **Umphang** region, which offers excellent trekking and whitewater-rafting.

Phitsanulok stands at the hub of an efficient **transport** network that works well as a transit point between Bangkok, the far north and Isaan. Nearly every Bangkok–Chiang Mai train stops here, and assorted buses head east towards the Isaan towns of Loei and Khon Kaen. It's also possible to fly in and out of the northern plains via the tiny airstrips at Phitsanulok, Sukhothai and Mae Sot.

Phitsanulok

Well equipped with upmarket hotels and pleasantly located on the east bank of the Nan River, **PHITSANULOK** makes a handy base for exploring the historical centres of Sukhothai and Kamphaeng Phet, but boasts only a couple of unmissable sights of its own. Chief of these is the country's second most important Buddha image, enshrined in historic Wat Mahathat and the focus of pilgrimages from all over Thailand; complementing this sacred sight is one of the best ethnology collections in Thailand, at the Folklore Museum. Though these attractions are unlikely to occupy you for more than a day, there are several potentially rewarding national parks within an hour or two's drive, and TAT has produced a sketch map outlining car and motorbike routes to some of them. **Phu Hin Rongkla National Park**, about 100km northeast of Phitsanulok via Highway 12, was the notorious stronghold of the insurgent Communist Party of Thailand from 1967–1982 and still contains some relics from that period, though its short trails through montane forests and natural rock gardens are now its main point of interest. Or consider organizing a day's mountain-biking in **Thung Salaeng Luang National Park**, 82km east of Phitsanulok off Highway 12. Thung Salaeng is famous for the flowers that carpet its grasslands after the end of the rainy season (the flower meadows are only open from October 23 into December) and has two designated mountain-bike trails as well as rafting opportunities: see Listings on p.275 for details of the mountain-bike rental and rafting outlet in Phitsanulok.

Phitsanulok hosts two lively food **festivals** every year, once during the Western new year period (December 25 to January 1) and again at Songkhran, the Thai new year (April 9–15); almost every restaurant in town participates, selling their trademark dishes from special stalls set up along the east bank of the river. Entertainment includes performances of traditional Thai dance. Later in the year, on the third weekend of September, traditional longboat races are staged on the Nan River, in front of Wat Mahathat.

Arrival, information and transport

Phitsanulok **train station** (Ⓣ055 258005) is in the town centre, but to get into town from the regional **bus station** (Ⓣ055 242430), 2km east on Highway 12, you'll need to catch local bus #1, #2 or #8 (see below). The private **air-con buses** to and from Bangkok, Chiang Mai and Chiang Rai, operated by Win Tour (Ⓣ055 243222) and Yan Yon Tour (Ⓣ055 258647), drop off and pick up passengers at their offices near the train station on Thanon Akkathasaroth (Ekathosarot) in town. You can also fly to Phitsanulok from Bangkok and Chiang Mai; the **airport** is on the southern edge of town, about ten minutes' drive from the train station, and has a tour operators' desk, as well as Avis (Ⓣ055 258062, Ⓦwww.avisthailand.com) and Budget (Ⓣ055 258556, Ⓦwww.budget.co.th) car-rental outlets. Minibuses sent by the upmarket hotels meet all incoming flights, as do Thai Airways "limousine" share taxis, which charge B50 per person to any Phitsanulok accommodation; or you can walk 100m left outside the airport gates and take city bus #4 from the shelter on Thanon Sanambin (see below). The helpful and well-informed **TAT** office (daily 8.30am–4.30pm; Ⓣ055 252742, Ⓔtatphs@loxinfo.co.th) is on the

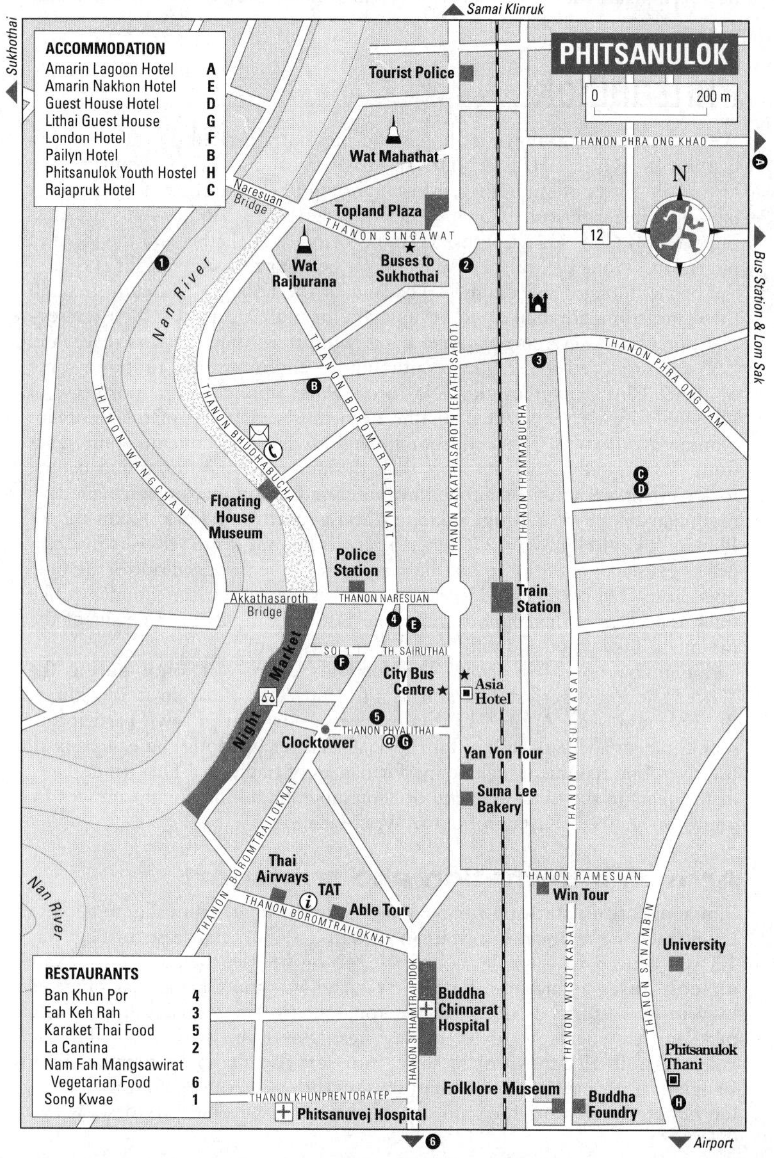

eastern arm of Thanon Boromtrailoknat (known to local taxi drivers as Surasi Trade Centre).

If you've arrived at Phitsanulok train station and want to make an immediate **bus connection to Sukhothai**, you have two choices. The fastest option is to pick up a Sukhothai-bound bus as it passes the Topland Plaza shopping centre on Thanon Singawat – B30 by samlor, or you can use northbound local buses #5, #8 and #11 (see below) as far as the Topland Plaza roundabout and then walk west to the bus stop. Alternatively, take a samlor or city bus to the regional bus station on the eastern edge of town – quite a lengthy ride because of the one-way system – where all Sukhothai-bound buses originate (daily 5.30am–6pm; every 30min; 1hr).

Several local city **bus routes** crisscross the city, connecting the regional bus terminal, the railway station and the major sights. In the town centre, many of them run via the city bus stands on Thanon Akkathasaroth, 150m south of the train station, where southbound buses pick up outside the *Asia Hotel*, and northbound ones from across the road. Most city buses cost a standard B5, except air-conditioned ones, which cost B7. The most useful city bus routes include: #1, from the regional bus station via the *Amarin Lagoon Hotel* to the train station and Wat Mahathat; #4, from the train station to *Phitsanulok Youth Hostel* and the airport; #5 and #11, from the train station to Topland Plaza (for Sukhothai buses) and Wat Mahathat; #6, from the regional bus station to the train station and *Pailyn Hotel*; and #8, from the regional bus station to the Folklore Museum, train station, Topland Plaza (for Sukhothai buses) and Wat Mahathat.

Accommodation

Phitsanulok's budget **accommodation** is nowhere near as inviting as Sukhothai's, but the town does have a better selection of upmarket options.

Amarin Lagoon Hotel 52/299 Thanon Phra Ong Khao ⓣ055 220999, ⓕ055 220944. The poshest place in Phitsanulok, this low-rise hotel is prettily set in landscaped gardens and has attractively furnished rooms with air-con and TV, plus a swimming pool, sauna, Internet access and three restaurants. It's 3km east of the town centre, but there's a hotel shuttle-bus service, and city buses #1 and #2 (for the regional bus station, railway station and Wat Yai) run past the entrance. ❼

Amarin Nakhon Hotel 3/1 Thanon Chaophraya ⓣ055 219069, ⓕ055 219500. Very central and good-value tourist-oriented hotel, offering well-maintained air-con rooms of a good standard; those on the uppermost of the hotel's eleven floors enjoy fine panoramic views of the city. ❹

Guest House Hotel Just east of Thanon Wisut Kasat at 99/9 Thanon Phra Ong Dam ⓣ055 259203, ⓕ055 212737. Misleadingly named, this place is a scaled-down version of the adjoining *Rajapruk Hotel*, offering shabby but passable hotel-style fan rooms with attached bathroom and use of next door's pool. ❷

Lithai Guest House 73/1–5 Thanon Phayalithai ⓣ055 219629, ⓕ055 219627. Centrally located, and sharing the Lithai Building with an Internet café, travel agency and restaurant, this is a recommended lower- to mid-range option, offering big, clean, bright rooms with fan or air-con. ❷–❹

London Hotel 21–22 Soi Buddhabucha (Phuttabucha) 1 ⓣ055 225145. Though cell-like and basic, the cheapest rooms in this converted family home are painted a funky lime-green and yellow and can't be beaten on price. A few equally well-priced en-suite rooms with air-con are also available. ❶–❸

Pailyn Hotel 38 Thanon Boromtrailokanat ⓣ055 252411, ⓦwww.pailynhotel.phitsanulok.com. Popular, long-running tourist hotel where many of the sizeable rooms in the thirteen-storey tower offer river views; all have air-con and TV. It's handy for Wat Mahathat, and there's free transport to the airport and bus and train stations. Also has two good restaurants and nightly live music. Served by city bus #6 (for the regional bus terminal and train station). ❻

Phitsanulok Youth Hostel 38 Thanon Sanambin ⓣ055 242060, ⓦwww.tyha.org. Set in a large, attractive compound full of shade-giving greenery and masses of salvaged antique wooden doors, panels and shutters, this lovely oasis makes a great retreat and is the most traveller-oriented place in town. The charming fan rooms are uniquely designed with wood panelling, antique furniture and idiosyncratic bathrooms; air-con versions are slightly less characterful. There's a B120 dorm as well, plus plenty of tourist information, bicycle, motorbike and car rental, free breakfasts and a streetside café. Youth-hostel membership is not required. The hostel is a 1.5km walk from the centre: take bus #4 from the train station and get off outside the *Phitsanulok Thani Hotel* next door; from the regional bus station take any bus to the train station, then a #4. ❸–❹

Rajapruk Hotel Just east of Thanon Wisut Kasat at 99/9 Thanon Phra Ong Dam ⓣ055 258477, ⓕ055 212737. Well-equipped but rather soulless rooms, all with air-con, hot water and fridge. Only worth considering for its swimming pool. ❺

The Town

Typically for a riverside town, "Phi-lok" is long and narrow, and – while the centre is small enough to cover on foot – its two main sights lie at opposite extremities. Huge swathes of the town were destroyed by fire in 1957, but Phitsanulok's history harks back to a heyday in the late fourteenth and early fifteenth centuries when, with Sukhothai waning in power, it rose to prominence as the favoured home of the crumbling capital's last rulers. After supremacy was finally wrested by the emerging state of Ayutthaya in 1438, Phitsanulok was made a provincial capital, subsequently becoming a strategic army base during Ayutthaya's wars with the Burmese, and adoptive home to Ayutthayan princes. The most famous of these was Naresuan, a notoriously courageous warrior who was governor of Phitsanulok before he assumed the Ayutthayan crown in 1590. The ruins of Naresuan's Phitsanulok palace are currently under excavation in the grounds of a former school northwest of the bridge that bears his name.

Wat Mahathat

Officially called **Wat Phra Si Ratana Mahathat** (and known locally as Wat Mahathat or Wat Yai), this fourteenth-century temple was one of the few buildings miraculously to escape Phitsanulok's great 1957 fire. Standing at the northern limit of the town on the east bank of the Nan River (and served by city buses #1, #5, #8 and #11), it receives a constant stream of worshippers eager to pay homage to the highly revered Buddha image inside the viharn. Because the image is so sacred, a **dress code** is strictly enforced here – shorts and skimpy clothing are definitely forbidden – and there's an entrance fee of B10.

Delicately inlaid mother-of-pearl doors mark the entrance to the viharn, opening onto the low-ceilinged interior, painted mostly in dark red and black and dimly lit by narrow slits along the upper walls. In the centre of the far wall sits the much-cherished **Phra Buddha Chinnarat**: late Sukhothai in style and probably cast in the fourteenth century, this gleaming, polished-bronze Buddha is one of the finest of the period and, for Thais, second in importance only to the Emerald Buddha in Bangkok. Tales of the statue's miraculous powers have fuelled the devotion of generations of pilgrims – one legend tells how the Buddha wept tears of blood when Ayutthayan princes arrived in Phitsanulok to oust the last Sukhothai regent. The Phra Buddha Chinnarat stands out among Thai Buddha images because of its *mandorla*, the flame-like halo that frames the upper body and head like a chair-back, tapering off into nagas at the arm rests, which symbolizes extreme radiance and makes any reproductions immediately recognizable. Not surprisingly, the image has spawned several copies, including an almost perfect replica commissioned for Bangkok's Marble Temple by Rama V in 1901. Every February, Phitsanulok honours the Phra Buddha Chinnarat with a week-long **festival**, which features *likay* folk-theatre performances and dancing.

Behind the viharn, the gilded mosaic **prang** houses the holy relic that gives the wat its name (Mahathat means "Great Relic Chedi") – though which particular remnant lies entombed here is unclear – and the cloister surrounding both structures contains a gallery of Buddha images of different styles.

The east bank

South of Wat Mahathat and Naresuan Bridge, **the east bank** of the Nan River has been landscaped into a pleasant riverside park that runs all the way down to Akkathasaroth (Ekathosarot) Bridge. There are no unmissable sights along its course, but you may want to make a stop at **Wat Rajburana**, just south of Naresuan Bridge and across the road from the river, which also survived the 1957 fire. Recognizable by the dilapidated brick-based chedi that stands in the compound, the wat is chiefly of interest for the *Ramayana* murals (see p.127) that cover the interior walls of the bot. Quite well preserved, they were probably painted in the mid-nineteenth century. The most attractive feature of the riverside park is the **Floating House Museum** (open all hours; free), about 500m south of Wat Rajburana and close by the post office. Understated in style, and completely empty, but beautifully fashioned from teak wood, it replicates a traditional river home, comprising three *salas* connected by a roofed walkway, walls of split reeds, carved window frames and elegant wood-panelled interiors. The house floats in a lily pond beside the road, high above the river. Akkathasaroth Bridge marks the riverside park's southern boundary, beyond which the bank is dominated by the permanent stalls of the **night bazaar** and **night market**, *the* place for locals and tourists to congregate in the evening for a spot of bargain-hunting and a choice selection of good cheap food.

The Folklore Museum and Buddha Foundry

Across town on Thanon Wisut Kasat, southeast of the train station, the **Sergeant Major Thawee Folklore Museum** (Tues–Sun 8.30am–4.30pm; B50) puts a different slant on the region's culture; its fascinating look at traditional rural life makes this one of the best ethnology museums in the country. Local bus #8 will drop you close by. The collection, which is housed in a series of wooden pavilions, belongs to former sergeant major Dr Thawee, who has pursued a lifelong personal campaign to preserve and document a way of life that's gradually disappearing. Highlights include the reconstructed kitchen, veranda and birthing room of a typical village house, known as a "tied house" because its split bamboo walls are literally tied together with rattan cane, and an exceptionally comprehensive gallery of traps – dozens of specialized contraptions designed to ensnare everything from cockroaches to birds perched on water buffaloes' backs. The weaving and natural dyes exhibition is also worth dwelling on, as is the blow-by-blow account – complete with photos – of the routine castration of bullocks and water buffalo.

Cross the road from the museum and walk south about 50m for a rare chance to see Buddha images being forged at the **Buranathai Buddha Bronze-Casting Foundry**, located behind a big green metal gate at 26/43 Thanon Wisut Kasat. The foundry, which also belongs to Dr Thawee, is open during working hours and anyone can drop in to watch the stages involved in moulding and casting a Buddha image. It's a fairly lengthy procedure and best assimilated from the illustrated explanations inside the foundry. Images of all sizes are made here, from thirty-centimetre-high household icons to mega-models destined for wealthy temples. The Buddha business is quite a profitable one: worshippers can earn a great deal of merit by donating a Buddha statue, particularly a precious one, to their local wat, so demand rarely slackens.

Eating

In the evening, the place to head for is the lively **night market** that sets up from about 6pm along the east bank of the river, south of Akkathasaroth Bridge. Fish and mussels are a speciality, but the most famous dish is "**flying vegetables**", in which strong-tasting morning-glory (*phak bung*) is stir-fried before being tossed flamboyantly in the air towards the plate-wielding waiter or customer. Several stallholders at the night market do the honours – look out for the specially adapted, stationary two-tiered trucks – as do a few restaurants around the *Rajapruk Hotel* on Thanon Phra Ong Dam. For calmer eats at bargain prices, go to Thanon Phayalithai, where you'll find several very cheap curry shops.

Ban Khun Por Opposite the *Amarin Nakhon* hotel on Thanon Chao Phraya, just south off Thanon Naresuan. This cosy, parlour-style dining room is full of curios (sepia-tinted royal photos, old telephones, collectors' porcelain) and serves an impressively long mid-priced menu. The focus is on Thai food, with lots of spicy *yam* salads – wing-bean, glass-noodle and ear-mushroom to name a few – masses of seafood and stir-fries, chicken in pandanus leaves, plus a selection of royal Thai desserts. Japanese dishes, including sashimi, also feature prominently. Moderate.

Fah Keh Rah Just east of the railway line on Thanon Phra Ong Dam. A small, family-run Muslim restaurant that specializes in lassi yoghurt drinks and thick *roti* breads served with ladlefuls of the daily curry. Shuts around 7pm. Inexpensive.

Karaket Thai Food Thanon Phaylithai. Tasty Thai curry shop, where you make your selection from the metal trays set out on the pavement trestle, then eat in air-conditioned comfort inside. Very popular for family takeaways. Shuts around 8.30pm. Inexpensive.

La Cantina Southeast corner of the Topland Plaza intersection. Just 100m east of the Sukhothai bus stop, this is a good place to pep yourself up with a mug of fresh coffee before continuing your journey.

Nam Fah Mangsawirat Vegetarian Food Thanon Sithamtraipidok, about 150m south of the Thanon Khunprentoratep junction, or 100m north of the *Indra Hotel*. Typical workaday vegetarian canteen where you pay just B15 for a plate of brown rice plus two servings from the array of veggie stir-fries and curries. Sat–Thurs 6am–2pm.

Song Kwae Thanon Wangchan. One of several long-running floating restaurants on the west bank of the river, this place has a nice atmosphere, pleasing river views and a decent menu of fresh fish and seafood, plus standard Thai-Chinese dishes accompanied by rice. Moderate.

Listings

Airline The Thai Airways office is near TAT on Thanon Boromtrailokanat ☎055 258020; tickets also available from the tour operators listed below.

Car rental Budget and Avis both have desks at the airport (see p.269), and Avis has another office inside the youth hostel compound on Thanon Sanambin ☎055 242060. For hiring a car with a driver, see "Tour operators" below.

Emergencies For all emergencies, call the tourist police on the free 24hr phoneline ☎1155, or contact them at their office north of Wat Mahathat on Thanon Akkathasaroth ☎055 245358.

Exchange There are banks with money-changing facilities and ATMs on Thanon Naresuan and Thanon Boromtrailokanat. The exchange booth on the corner of Naresuan and Chao Phraya roads opens daily 8am–8pm.

Hospitals Inter Medical Hospital, Thanon Boromtrailokanat ☎055 284228–32; Phitsanuvej Hospital, 211/95 Thanon Khunprentoratep ☎055 219941–50; and the government-run Buddha Chinnarat Hospital, Thanon Sithamtraipidok ☎055 219844–52.

Internet access Catnet terminals inside the telephone office on Thanon Bhudhabucha (daily 8am–6pm) and at several private Internet centres in town (see map).

Left luggage At the train station (daily 7am–11pm; B10/item).

Mail The GPO is near the river on Thanon Bhudhabucha.

Motorbike rental At Lady Motorcycle for Rent, near the *Pailyn Hotel*, at 43/12 Thanon Bhudhabucha ☎055 242424; around B200 per day.

Telephones The CAT overseas telephone office is next to the GPO on Thanon Bhudhabucha (daily 8am–6pm).

Tour operators Able Tour and Travel (Mon–Fri 8am–6pm, Sat 8am–4.30pm; ⓣ055 242206, ⓔabletour_phs@yahoo.com), near the TAT office on Thanon Boromtrailokanat, sells air tickets and can arrange B1200 minivans to Sukhothai or Kamphaeng Phet (plus B1000 for optional guide). For mountain-bike and rafting trips in Thung Salaeng Luang National Park, contact the Samai Klinruk bike shop and Nature Camp tour office (ⓣ& ⓕ055 213541) at 193/6 Mu 5 Tambon Hua Ro, which is about 1.5km north of Topland Plaza on the east side of Thanon Akkathasaroth, opposite a big sports complex.

Sukhothai

For a brief but brilliant period (1238–1376), the walled city of **SUKHOTHAI** presided as the capital of Thailand, creating the legacy of a unified nation of Thai peoples and a phenomenal artistic heritage. Now an impressive assembly of elegant ruins, **Old Sukhothai**, 58km northwest of Phitsanulok, has been designated a historical park and has grown into one of Thailand's most visited ancient sites.

There are only a few accommodation options near the historical park, and not many other facilities, so most travellers stay in so-called **NEW SUKHOTHAI**, a modern market town 12km to the east, which has good travel links with the Old City and is also better for restaurants and long-distance bus connections. Straddling the Yom River, it's a small, friendly town, used to seeing tourists but by no means overrun with them. Easy to explore on foot, New Sukhothai offers a couple of outstanding guest houses as well as several other inviting options, which make it a pleasant place to hang out for a few days. The new town also makes a peaceful and convenient base for visiting Ramkhamhaeng National Park, as well as the outlying ruins of Si Satchanalai and Kamphaeng Phet.

Old Sukhothai is the most famous place in Thailand to celebrate **Loy Krathong**, the festival of light, and the ruins are the focus of a spectacular nine-day festival every October/November (see box on p.284). All accommodation gets packed out during the festival, so book in advance unless you're willing to sleep sardine-style on a guest-house floor. Once Loy Krathong is over, a mini version of the Loy Krathong **sound-and-light show** is staged on the last Saturday of every month from November through April at Wat Sra Sri in Old Sukhothai; check ⓦwww.grandfestivalthailand and ask at guest houses for details.

Arrival, information and transport

New Sukhothai has direct **bus** connections with many major provincial capitals. All buses use the Sukhothai **bus terminal**, located about 3km west of New Sukhothai's town centre, just off the bypass, from where there are several ways of getting to accommodation in New Sukhothai. Despite what obstructive samlor drivers might tell you, it is possible to **walk** to *Number 4*, *J&J* and *99* guest houses: from the restaurant at the front of the bus station turn left to follow a narrow track through the fields and within a few hundred metres you'll see signs for *Number 4*; it should take about five minutes to get to *Number 4* and about ten minutes to reach *J&J* or *99*. For transport to other guest houses the cheapest option is the purple #1 **songthaew** (about every 20min from 6am–6pm; B5) that runs from the bus station into town – depending on where you're staying, either get off at the bus stop for the Old City, just before crossing the river, or in front of Wat Ratchathani, just after crossing the river. None of the New Sukhothai guest houses is more than ten minutes' walk from the river. A purple #1 air-con **minibus** also runs between the bus station and town, but it goes the long way round and costs more. If you're heading straight from the bus station to Old Sukhothai, take the #1 songthaew as far as the Old City bus stop, then change to an Old City songthaew (see below). Note, however, that if you're arriving by bus **from Mae Sot or Tak** you will pass via the Old City before reaching New Sukhothai's bus terminal, so get off there if you're intending to stay in the Old City. **Taxi** prices from New Sukhothai bus station should be fixed at B30 for a ride into New Sukhothai or B80 into the Old City.

A more comfortable, though not necessarily faster, option is to take the **train** from Bangkok, Chiang Mai or anywhere in between as far as Phitsanulok and then change onto one of the half-hourly buses to New Sukhothai, which take about an hour; for details see p.271. This bus service also makes Sukhothai feasible as a day-trip from Phitsanulok, and vice versa.

You can also **fly** to Sukhothai from Bangkok and Chiang Mai with Bangkok Airways; the airport is about 15km north of town, and shuttle buses transfer passengers to hotels and guest houses for B80 per person. Bangkok Airways also operates flights from Sukhothai to Louang Phabang in Laos, though not in the reverse direction due to lack of immigration facilities in Sukhothai; see p.19 for more details on travelling from Thailand into Laos. Passengers departing from Sukhothai Airport are subject to a B100 tax (as this is a privately run airport). The local Bangkok Airways office (ⓣ055 647224) is located here, though you can also buy air tickets from the more central Sukhothai Travel Agency (see p.287).

For **local transport**, frequent songthaews shuttle between New Sukhothai and the historical park 12km away, departing from a signed depot west of the river on Thanon Charodvithitong (every 15min during daylight hours; 15min). **Cycling** is also a good way of getting around, and bikes are available for rent in both New and Old Sukhothai, see Listings on p.287 for details.

Although there's a government-run **tourist information** office beside the bridge on Thanon Charodvithitong, it keeps random hours: staff at the best of the guest houses are much better sources of traveller-oriented information.

Accommodation

New Sukhothai has a very good selection of guest-house **accommodation**, but if you want a deluxe hotel you should consider staying in Phitsanulok (see p.271). Though most travellers opt to commute to the Old City for sightseeing, staying in Old Sukhothai makes it easy to revisit the ruins at sunrise and sunset, even if it is a songthaew ride away from the best restaurants, markets and shops.

New Sukhothai

Ban Thai Guest House 38 Thanon Pravetnakorn ⓣ055 610163, ⓦwww.geocities.com/guesthouse_banthai, ⓔguesthouse_banthai@yahoo.com. Set in a garden on the west bank of the Yom River, this comfortable budget option comprises several attractive wood-panelled rooms with shared bathroom in a small purpose-built house with a terrace out front, plus some nice, idiosyncratic wooden bungalows with private bathroom and the option of air-con. The Belgian manager is a great source of information on the area and he also leads small-group bicycle tours (see p.285). Home-made yoghurt is a breakfast favourite, and there's a long menu of Thai and Western main courses too. ❶–❸

Cocoon House 86/1 Thanon Singhawat ⓣ055 612081, ⓕ055 622157. Set way back off the street behind *Dream Café*, this collection of delightful rooms and bungalows is the brainchild of the woman behind *Dream Café* and her artistic stamp is everywhere, from the individually decorated

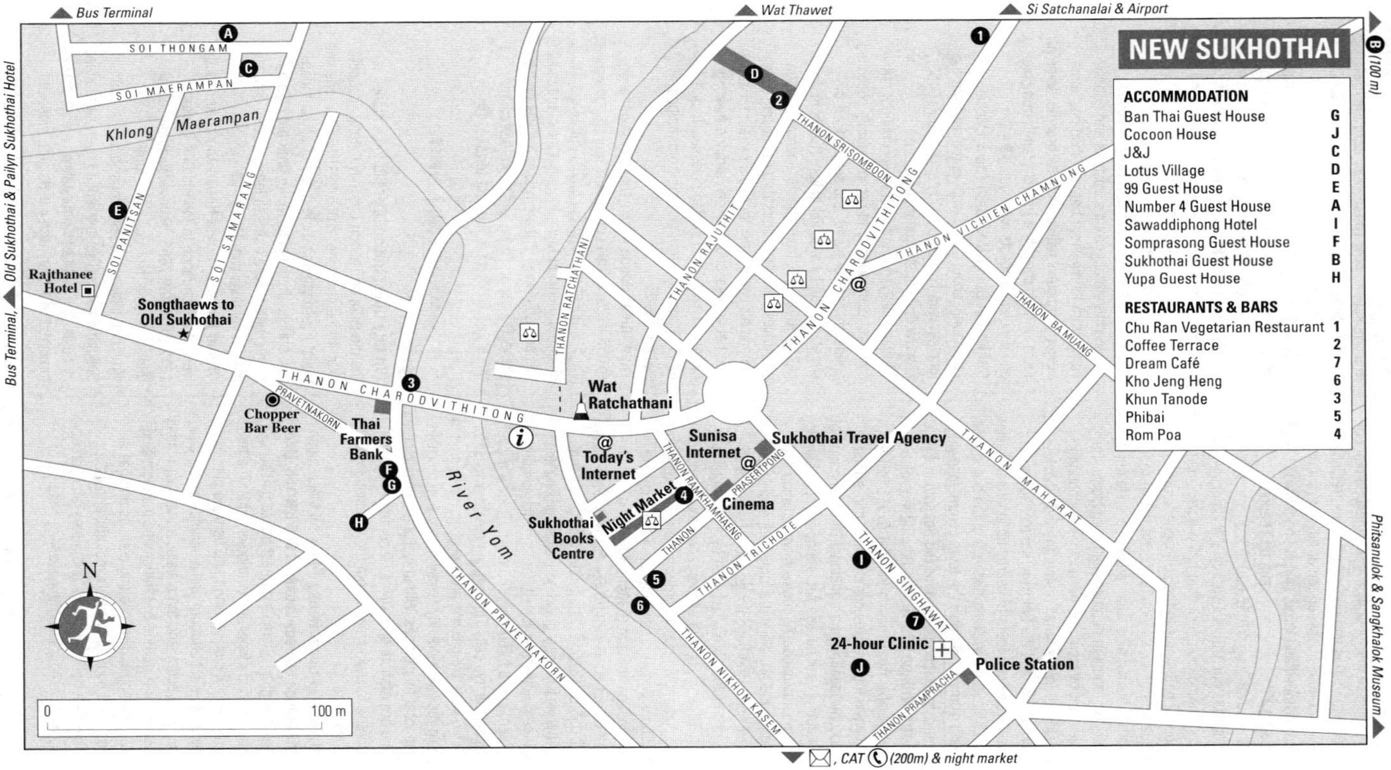

NEW SUKHOTHAI
ACCOMMODATION
Ban Thai Guest House G
Cocoon House J
J&J C
Lotus Village D
99 Guest House E
Number 4 Guest House A
Sawaddiphong Hotel I
Somprasong Guest House F
Sukhothai Guest House B
Yupa Guest House H
RESTAURANTS & BARS
Chu Ran Vegetarian Restaurant 1
Coffee Terrace 2
Dream Café 7
Kho Jeng Heng 6
Khun Tanode 3
Phibai 5
Rom Poa 4
Bus Terminal
Wat Thawet
Si Satchanalai & Airport
B (100 m)
Bus Terminal, Old Sukhothai & Pailyn Sukhothai Hotel
Phitsanulok & Sangkhalok Museum
, CAT (200m) & night market
SOI THONGAM
SOI MAERAMPAN
Khlong Maerampan
SOI PANITSAN
SOI SAMARANG
Rajthanee Hotel
Songthaews to Old Sukhothai
THANON CHARODVITHITONG
PRAVETNAKORN
Chopper Bar Beer
Thai Farmers Bank
THANON RATCHATHANI
Wat Ratchathani
Today's Internet
River Yom
Sukhothai Books Centre
Night Market
THANON RAMKHAMHAENG
Sunisa Internet
PRASERTPONG
Cinema
Sukhothai Travel Agency
THANON
THANON TRICHOTE
THANON RAJUTHIT
THANON SRISOMBOON
THANON VICHIEN CHAMNONG
THANON BAMUANG
THANON MAHARAT
THANON SINGHAWAT
24-hour Clinic
Police Station
THANON PRAMPRACHA
THANON NIKHON KASEM
THANON PRAVETNAKORN
N
0
100 m

interiors to the romantically designed garden dotted with curios and caged birds and prettily lit at night. Choose between fan or air-con rooms in a small house and large, stylish bungalows. ❸–❺

J&J 122/1 Soi Maerampan, off Thanon Charodvithitong ⓣ055 620095, ⓔjjguest@hotmail.com. Offers a variety of inexpensive accommodation, including half a dozen rooms with shared bathrooms in the atmospheric upstairs quarters of an old wooden house; a two-room family house; plus some pricier en-suite fan and air-con rooms in purpose-built bungalows. The pleasant terrace area overlooks neighbouring fields, there's a small restaurant and a book exchange, and the Belgian-Thai managers run well-reviewed tours to nearby national parks (see p.285). Within walking distance of the bus station, or a 10min walk from the town centre, following signs from the bus stop for Old Sukhothai. ❷

Lotus Village 170 Thanon Ratchathani, also accessible from Thanon Rajuthit ⓣ055 621484, ⓦwww.lotus-village.com. Stylish, mid-priced accommodation in a traditional Thai compound of beautiful teak houses set around a tropical garden with lotus ponds. All rooms have polished teak floors and are elegantly furnished; some are in self-contained bungalows, and a few have air-con. Rates include breakfast. Run by a well-informed Thai-French couple who organize tours around the region and let guests browse their fine collection of books on Asian and African art and culture. Reception shuts at 9.30pm. ❺–❻

99 Guest House 234/6 Soi Panitsan (Panichsan) ⓣ055 611315, ⓔninetynine_gh@yahoo.com. Tiny, very homely guest house comprising just three double rooms (with fan and shared bathroom) and a three-bed B80 dorm. There's a lovely, spacious, typically Thai seating area downstairs, filled with axe pillows, and guests are welcome to join the twice-weekly family meals. Run by clued-up local tour guides. Within walking distance of the bus station, or a 10-min walk from the town centre, following signs from the bus stop for Old Sukhothai. ❷

Number 4 Guest House 140/4 Soi Maerampan, off Thanon Charodvithitong ⓣ055 610165. Laid-back, slightly alternative guest house that's wreathed in plants and overlooks fields. The ten charming, if simple, wood and bamboo bungalows each have a bathroom and a veranda (some also have daybeds), and there's also a two-room family house for rent. Run by charismatic manager Sud, who organizes Thai cooking courses and has an excellent book of local DIY motorbike tours. There's a book exchange and a pleasantly breezy upstairs restaurant. Within walking distance of the bus station, or a 10min walk from the town centre, following signs from the bus stop for Old Sukhothai. ❷

Sawaddiphong Hotel 56/2–5 Thanon Singhawat ⓣ055 622113, ⓕ055 612268. Decent enough mid-range hotel-style accommodation that's of most interest for the smart air-con rooms in the new wing; the cheaper air-con and fan rooms don't compare so favourably. ❸–❺

Somprasong Guest House 32 Thanon Pravetnakorn ⓣ055 611709. Large wooden house with sizeable rooms upstairs and good views from its riverfront balcony. Also has some newer bungalows with private bathrooms, some of them with air-con. It's a friendly, family-run place and welcomes guests with kids. ❶–❸

Sukhothai Guest House 68 Thanon Vichien Chamnong, about 200m walk northeast from the junction with Thanon Ba Muang ⓣ055 610453, ⓦwww.thai.net/sukhothaiguesthouse, ⓔsukhogh@yahoo.com. This welcoming if rather compact compound of terraced rooms – cocooned amidst masses of plants and set back off the street – is run by a genial Indian-Thai family and gets rave reviews from guests. Accommodation comprises several clusters of terraced, en-suite, fan and air-con rooms; there's a restaurant and Internet access, and staff can arrange massages, motorbike rental and cooking classes. Phone (until 10pm) for a free pick-up from the bus station. ❸–❺

Yupa Guest House 44/10 Thanon Pravetnakorn ⓣ055 612578. This converted family home was the first guest house in Sukhothai and offers the cheapest rooms in town, though it lacks the facilities and efficiency of more recent arrivals on the scene. Rooms are large and share bathrooms, there's a B50 dorm and a roof terrace. ❶

Old Sukhothai and around

Old City Guest House Opposite the entrance to the museum on Thanon Charodvithitong, just outside the central zone ⓣ055 697515. Thai-oriented guest house offering a big range of accommodation options, from small, rather dark but cheap rooms with shared baths to large, quite plush, air-con versions with TV. ❶–❹

Orchid Hibiscus Guest House About 2km southwest of the entrance to the Old City, on Route 1272 ⓣ01 962 7698, ⓦwww.asiatravel.com/thailand/orchid_hibiscus/index.html, ⓔorchid_hibiscus_guest_house@hotmail.com. Delightful Italian-Thai-managed haven surrounded by fields. The eight brick bungalows are attractively furnished with four-poster beds (and mosquito nets) and ranged around a pretty tropical flower garden and swimming pool. Also has one family house for rent. Rates include breakfast. ❺

Pailyn Sukhothai Hotel 4km east of the old city at 10/1 Thanon Charodvithitong ⓣ055 633336, ⓕ055 613317. Upmarket, package-oriented hotel where all rooms are air-conditioned and comfortably equipped, and there's a swimming pool, sauna and disco on site. However, although you're right on the songthaew route, you're still very much between two places, 4km from the historical park and 8km west of the new city. ❻

Vitoon Guest House Opposite the entrance to the museum on Thanon Charodvithitong, just outside the central zone ⓣ055 697045, ⓕ055 633397. Sprucely kept, very clean rooms with fan and bath in a rather characterless purpose-built little block, plus a separate building containing more appealing, wood-panelled, air-con rooms with TV. Rents bicycles and runs tours to Si Satchanalai. ❸–❹

Old Sukhothai (Muang Kao Sukhothai)

In its prime, **OLD SUKHOTHAI** boasted around forty separate temple complexes and covered an area of about 70 square kilometres between the Yom River and the low range of hills to the west. At its heart stood the walled royal city, protected by a series of moats and ramparts. **Sukhothai Historical Park**, or **Muang Kao Sukhothai** (daily 6am–6pm), covers all this area and is divided into five zones: all of the most important temples lie within the central zone, as does the Ramkhamhaeng Museum; the ruins outside the city walls are spread out over a sizeable area and divided into north, south, east and west zones. There's an official entrance gate for the central zone, but in the other zones you generally buy your ticket at the first temple you visit. **Entry** to the central zone (excluding the museum, which charges a separate admission fee) is B40, plus B10 for a bicycle, B20 for a motorbike, B30 for a samlor or B50 for a car; all other zones cost B30 each, including your vehicle. Also available are single tickets (B150), valid for one month, covering entry to all five zones plus the museum and the ruins of Si Satchanalai (see p.287).

With the help of UNESCO, the Thai government's Fine Arts Department has restored the most significant ruins and the result reveals the original town planners' keen aesthetic sense, especially their astute use of water to offset and reflect the solid monochrome contours of the stone temples. Nevertheless, there is a touch of the too perfectly packaged theme park about the central zone, and while some critics have detected an overly liberal interpretation of the thirteenth-century design, it takes a determined imagination to visualize the ancient capital as it must once have looked. Noticeably absent are the houses and palaces that would have filled the spaces between the wats: like their Khmer predecessors, the people of Sukhothai constructed their secular buildings from wood, believing that only sacred structures merited such a durable and costly material as stone.

Some history

Prior to the thirteenth century, the land now known as Thailand was divided into a collection of petty principalities, most of which owed their allegiance to the Khmer empire and its administrative centre Angkor (in present-day Cambodia). With the Khmers' power on the wane, two Thai generals joined forces in 1238 to oust the Khmers from the northern plains, founding the kingdom of **Sukhothai** ("Dawn of Happiness" in Pali) under the regency of one of the generals, Intradit. In short order they had extended their control over much of present-day Thailand, as well as parts of Burma and Laos.

The third and most important of Sukhothai's eight kings, Intradit's youngest son **Ramkhamhaeng** (*c.*1278–99) laid the foundations of a unique Thai identity by establishing Theravada (Hinayana) Buddhism as the common faith and introducing the forerunner of the modern Thai alphabet; of several inscriptions attributed to him, the most famous, found on what's known as Ramkhamhaeng's

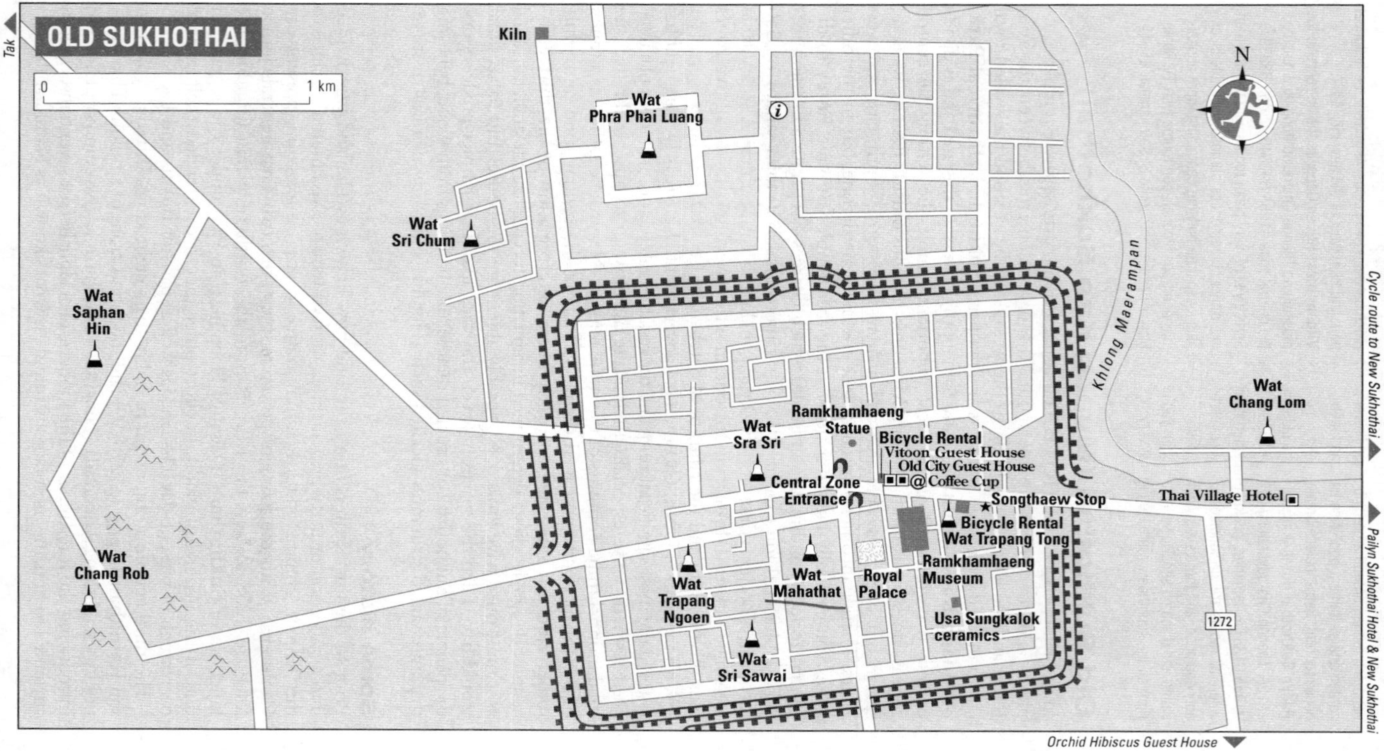
OLD SUKHOTHAI
0
1 km
N
Tak
Kiln
Wat
Phra Phai Luang
Wat
Sri Chum
Wat
Saphan
Hin
Wat
Chang Rob
Khlong Maerampan
Wat
Chang Lom
Cycle route to New Sukhothai
Pailyn Sukhothai Hotel & New Sukhothai
Thai Village Hotel
1272
Orchid Hibiscus Guest House
Ramkhamhaeng
Statue
Wat
Sra Sri
Bicycle Rental
Vitoon Guest House
Old City Guest House
@ Coffee Cup
Songthaew Stop
Central Zone
Entrance
Bicycle Rental
Wat Trapang Tong
Ramkhamhaeng
Museum
Usa Sungkalok
ceramics
Royal
Palace
Wat
Mahathat
Wat
Trapang
Ngoen
Wat
Sri Sawai

Stele and housed in Bangkok's National Museum, tells of a utopian land of plenty ruled by a benevolent monarch. Ramkhamhaeng turned Sukhothai into a vibrant spiritual and commercial centre, inviting Theravada monks from Nakhon Si Thammarat and Sri Lanka to instruct his people in the religion that was to supplant Khmer Hinduism and Mahayana Buddhism, and encouraging the growth of a ceramics industry with the help of Chinese potters. By all accounts, Ramkhamhaeng's successors lacked his kingly qualities and so, by the second half of the fourteenth century, Sukhothai had become a vassal state of the newly emerged kingdom of Ayutthaya; finally, in 1438, it was forced to relinquish all vestiges of its independent identity.

Practicalities

Songthaews from New Sukhothai (every 15min; 15min) stop about 300m east of the museum and central zone entrance point. Alternatively you can **cycle from New Sukhothai** to the Old City along a peaceful canalside track. To pick up the track, start from the bridge in New Sukhothai, cycle west along the main road to the Old City for about 3km until you reach a temple on the right-hand side. A narrow track between this temple and the adjacent Caltex petrol station takes you via a small bridge to a track that runs along the north bank of Khlong Maerampan, nearly all the way to the Old City. It's an easy ride of about 14km, through very pleasant, and frequently shaded, traditional canal-side neighbourhoods. Near the end of the ride you cross a major road to pick up the final stretch of track; then, after reaching the elephant statues at the ruins of Wat Chang Lom (see p.284), cross the bridge on your left to regain the main road into the Old City, about 1.5km away. Any New Sukhothai guest house can help you with bicycle rental, and both *Number 4 Guest House* and *Ban Thai* can provide maps of the khlong route.

Even if you don't arrive at the Old City on a bicycle, it's a good idea to **rent a bicycle** there for touring the ruins: numerous outlets near the songthaew stop rent them out for B20. Alternatively, you could hop onto the **trolley bus** that starts from near the museum and takes groups round the central zone for B20 per person.

There's a **currency exchange** booth (daily 8.30am–12.30pm) inside the park, next to the museum. For **eating**, either try the stalls near the museum, or stop at one of the small restaurants around *Old City* and *Vitoon* guest houses on the main road: *Coffee Cup* serves Thai and Western food and also has **Internet** terminals. For details of accommodation close to the park, see p.278. Several shops just outside the park entrance sell reproduction antique furniture and ceramics, but for a better range of **traditional style ceramics**, especially copies of historic Sangkhalok and Sukhothai designs and glazes, visit the Usa Sungkalok Sukhothai ceramics factory, which is located outside the central zone on the narrow road that runs between the museum and Wat Trapang Tong.

The Sukhothai Buddha

The classic Buddha images of Thailand were produced towards the end of the Sukhothai era. Ethereal, androgynous figures with ovoid faces and feline expressions, they depict not a Buddha meditating to achieve enlightenment – the more usual representation – but an already **enlightened Buddha**: the physical realization of an abstract, "unworldly" state. Though they produced mainly seated Buddhas, Sukhothai artists are renowned for having pioneered the **walking Buddha**, one of four postures described in ancient Pali texts but without precedent in Thailand.

The central zone

Only four of the eleven ruins in the **central zone** are worth dwelling on, and of these Wat Mahathat should definitely not be missed. The zone covers three square kilometres so a bike is recommended, but not essential.

Just outside the entrance to the central zone, the **Ramkhamhaeng National Museum** (daily 9am–4pm; B30) has a collection of locally found but fairly uninspiring artefacts, but if you haven't already seen King Ramkhamhaeng's famous stele in Bangkok, you might want to look at the copy kept here. A modern **statue** of the great man sits to the right just inside the zone entrance: cast in bronze, he holds a palm-leaf book in his right hand – a reference to his role as founder of the modern Thai alphabet. Close by stands a large bronze **bell**, a replica of the one referred to on the famous stele (also reproduced here), which told how the king had the bell erected in front of his palace so that any citizen with a grievance could come by and strike it, whereupon the king himself would emerge to investigate the problem.

Wat Mahathat

Turn left inside the gate for Sukhothai's most important site, the enormous **Wat Mahathat** compound, packed with the remains of scores of monuments and surrounded, like a city within a city, by a moat. This was the spiritual focus of the city, the king's temple and symbol of his power; successive regents, eager to add their own stamp, restored and expanded it so that by the time it was abandoned in the sixteenth century it numbered ten viharns, one bot, eight mondops and nearly two hundred small chedis.

Looking at the wat from ground level, it's hard to distinguish the main structures from the minor ruins. Remnants of the viharns and the bot dominate the present scene, their soldierly ranks of pillars, which formerly supported wooden roofs, directing the eye to the Buddha images seated at the far western ends.

The one component you can't overlook is the principal chedi complex, which houses the Buddha relic: it stands grandly – if a little cramped – at the heart of the compound, built on an east–west axis in an almost continuous line with two viharns. Its elegant centrepiece follows a design termed **lotus-bud chedi** (after the bulbous finial ornamenting the top of a tower), and is classic late Sukhothai in style. This lotus-bud reference is an established religious symbol: though Sukhothai architects were the first to incorporate it into building design – since when it's come to be regarded as a hallmark of the era – the lotus bud had for centuries represented the purity of the Buddha's thoughts battling through the clammy swamp and finally bursting out into flower. The chedi stands surrounded by eight smaller towers on a square platform decorated with a procession of walking Buddha-like monks, another artistic innovation of the Sukhothai school, here depicted in stucco relief. Flanking the chedi are two square mondops, built for the colossal standing Buddhas still inside them today.

The grassy patch across the road from Wat Mahathat marks the site of the former palace, of which nothing now remains.

Around Wat Mahathat

A few hundred metres southwest, the triple corn-cob-shaped prangs of **Wat Sri Sawai** make for an interesting architectural comparison with Wat Mahathat. Just as the lotus-bud chedi epitomizes Sukhothai aspirations, the prang represents Khmer ideals – Wat Sri Sawai was probably conceived as a Hindu shrine several centuries before the Sukhothai kingdom established itself here. The stucco reliefs decorating the prangs feature a few weatherworn figures from

Around New Sukhothai

Though Old Sukhothai is the main draw for visitors to New Sukhothai, there are enough other attractions in the area to make it worth staying on for a couple of extra days. Many of these places – such as Si Satchanalai (see p.287) and Kamphaeng Phet (see p.290) – can be fairly easily reached by public transport, but you'll need to **rent your own transport** (see p.287) for trips to Wat Thawet and Ramkhamhaeng National Park.

Lotus Village guest house does **day-trips** to Kamphaeng Phet historical park and to Si Satchanalai's ruins, textile museum and gold workshop (B1800 for the group, excluding fuel and guide), and can arrange return transport for anyone wanting to climb Khao Luang in Ramkhamhaeng National Park (B600/car). Ronnie at *Ban Thai Guest House* leads very enjoyable two-hour **bicycle tours** around local villages and farmland most afternoons from 4pm (B120 including bike) and can also provide route maps for his guests. *Number 4 Guest House* keeps a resource book full of information on interesting motorbike and bicycle routes through the area, including via the canal track to the Old City, and to Thung Luang pottery village. *J&J* guest house runs unusual overnight B1500 excursions to the caves, waterfalls and lakeside accommodation of Si Satchanalai National Park (as distinct from Si Satchanalai Historical Park), as well as half-day trips to Tham Kham Khao National Park for a swim in the lake and a chance to watch the millions of bats streaming out of a nearby cave at dusk (B500).

Sangkhalok Museum

If you have a serious interest in ceramics you'll probably enjoy the Sukhothai-era exhibits at the **Sangkhalok Museum** (Mon–Fri 10am–6pm, Sat & Sun 10am–8pm; B100, children B50), a couple of kilometres east of New Sukhothai on Highway 101, close to the junction with Highway 12, the road to Phitsanulok. A samlor ride from central New Sukhothai should cost no more than B40.

The ground floor of the museum displays artefacts from twelfth- to sixteenth-century Sukhothai, including some very fine bowls with scalloped rims and bluish-green patterns and lots of the characteristically expressive figurines; unusually, many of the works are signed by the potter. This style of pottery has become known as **Sangkhalok**, after the prosperous city of Sawankhalok, near Si Satchanalai, which was part of the kingdom of Sukhothai at that time (see p.289 for a description of the Sangkhalok kilns in Si Satchanalai). Also on show are ceramics from twelfth-century Burma, China and Vietnam, all of which were found in the area and so show who the citizens of Sukhothai were trading with at that time. The upstairs exhibition presents some of the most exquisite ceramics that were produced in northern Thailand during the Lanna era (thirteenth to sixteenth centuries),

Wat Thawet

Famous for its one hundred different brightly painted concrete statues depicting morality tales and Buddhist fables, **Wat Thawet** is quite a popular sight for Thai tourists, though some farangs find it a bit tacky. The temple **sculpture park** was conceived by a local monk in the 1970s, with the aim of creating a "learning garden", where visitors could learn about the Buddhist ideas of hell and karmic retribution. For example, people who have spent their lives killing animals are depicted here with the head of a buffalo, pig, cock or elephant, while those who have been greedy and materialistic stand naked and undernourished, their ribs and backbones sticking out. Then there's the alcoholic who is forced to drink boiling liquids that literally make his concrete guts explode on to the ground.

Part of the appeal of Wat Thawet is that it makes a good focus for a very pleasant **bicycle** trip from Sukhothai, a sixteen-kilometre round-trip that is almost entirely along peaceful canalside tracks. From New Sukhothai, follow riverside Thanon Ratchathani north beyond *Lotus Village* until you hit the bypass. Cross the bypass and take the concrete path from the west edge of the bridge. Stay on this calm, scenic track for the next 8km, passing typical wooden houses, several banana plantations, a wooden suspension bridge and, about 1km before the temple, going beneath a major flyover; Wat Thawet is beside the second wooden suspension bridge.

Ramkhamhaeng National Park, Khao Luang and Thung Luang Pottery Village

The forested area immediately to the southwest of Sukhothai is protected as **Ramkhamhaeng National Park** (currently still charging only B20 entry, unlike most other national parks) and makes a pleasant day-trip on a motorbike, with the possibility of a challenging mountain climb at the end of it. To get to the main park entrance from New Sukhothai, follow Highway 101 towards Kamphaeng Phet for 19km, then take side road 1319, signed to Khao Luang, for the final 16km to park headquarters. Any Kamphaeng Phet-bound bus will take you as far as the junction, but you'll have trouble hitching into the park from here. You can rent national park **bungalows** (B500 for up to four people) at the park's headquarters.

The headquarters stands at the foot of the eastern flank of the highest peak, **Khao Luang** (1185m), which can be climbed in around four hours, but only safely from November through February. Several very steep trails run up to the summit from here, but they are not very clearly marked; the first couple of kilometres are the worst, after which the incline eases up a little. From the top you should get a fine view over the Sukhothai plains. If you want to camp on the summit, simply alert the rangers at park headquarters, and they will arrange for their colleague at the summit to rent you a tent; you need to take your own food and water up, however.

En route to or from Ramkhamhaeng National Park you could make a detour to **Thung Luang pottery village**, signed 16km out of New Sukhothai on Highway 101, where nearly every household is involved in the production of earthenware pots, vases and statuary. Once you've turned off the main road, drive past a school and two temples to enter the heart of the pottery neighbourhoods.

Eating and drinking

One of the best places to **eat** in New Sukhothai is the **night market**, which sets up every Wednesday and Thursday near the post office on the southeastern end of Thanon Nikhon Kasem. There's another smaller, nightly, gathering of hot-food stalls and streetside tables in front of Wat Ratchathani on Thanon Charodvithitong and a permanent covered area for night market-style restaurants on the soi between Thanon Ramkhamhaeng and Thanon Nikhon Kasem. A fun place for dawdling over a few beers is the string of pavement tables and chairs between the *Chinawat* and *River View* hotels on Nikhon Kasem; some of these small bar-cafés have karaoke too.

Chu Ran Vegetarian Restaurant Next to the temple on Thanon Charodvithitong. No English-language name-board, but look for the sign that proclaims "Eat 'J' One Meal, Ten Thousand Lives Escaped". Typical reasonably nutritious veggie curry shop, where you get a plate of brown rice plus a couple of servings of vegetable and/or meat-substitute curries and stir-fries for B20 or less. Daily 7am–3pm. Inexpensive.

Coffee Terrace At the entrance to *Lotus Village* on Thanon Rajuthit. Cute garden restaurant serving fresh coffee and ice creams, as well as a fairly pricey range of savouries, including baked spare-ribs with pineapple, seafood soup, various spicy *yam* salads and Chinese-style baked rice with olives. Moderate–expensive.

Dream Café 88/1 Thanon Singhawat. A cosy, cool, dark, coffee-shop atmosphere, with walls and windowsills full of curios and Thai antiques, twenty different ice-cream sundaes on the menu and a range of stamina-enhancing herbal drinks. Among its more substantial, fare are authentically fiery Thai curries, fresh Vietnamese-style spring rolls, deep-fried banana-flower fritters, seafood – and gin-and-tonics. Moderate.

Kho Jeng Heng Thanon Nikhon Kasem. This restaurant specializes in duck dishes, some cooked to Chinese recipes, such as the stewed and mildly spiced *pet phalo*, or the roasted *pet yang*, and others to Thai specifications, as in the thick *kaeng pet* curries. Moderate.

Khun Tanode Beside the bridge on Thanon Charodvithitong. Recommended little eating place that makes the most of its breezy riverside location and is prettily illuminated at night. The atmosphere is laidback; try the local speciality – crispy-fried chicken drumsticks in Sukhothai sauce – or mussels cooked in a herb sauce. Inexpensive.

Phibai Corner of Thanon Prasertpong and Thanon Nikhon Kasem. Very well patronized DIY barbecue restaurant where B100 gets you six different kinds of meat and fish to cook in a steamboat at your own table, accompanied by salad and vegetables. Or pile your plate as high as you like from the choice of ready-cooked buffet dishes, for B89. Good value – unless you're vegetarian.

Rom Poa At the edge of the covered night market between Thanon Ramkhamhaeng and Thanon Nikhon Kasem. Popular, place that serves spicy jelly-thread noodle salads (*yam wun sen*), curries, lots of seafood dishes, fruit shakes and a decent vegetarian selection. Inexpensive–moderate.

Listings

Banks and exchange There are several banks with money-changing facilities and ATMs on Thanon Singhawat.

Bicycle rental Most guest houses offer mountain bikes for B50–80 and Chinese bicycles for B30 per day. There are plenty of bicycle-rental places in Old Sukhothai too.

Books A few English-language books are available at Sukhothai Books Centre on Thanon Nikhon Kasem.

Cookery courses Two-day courses at *Number 4 Guest House* (B1500 including all ingredients and two meals); shorter, cheaper courses at *Ban Thai* and *Sukhothai* guest houses.

Emergencies For all emergencies, call the tourist police on the free, 24hr phoneline ⓣ1155, or go to the local police station on Thanon Singhawat.

Hospital The government-run Sukhothai Hospital (ⓣ055 611782) is west of New Sukhothai on the road to Old Sukhothai; there's a more central 24hr clinic on Thanon Singhawat.

Internet access There are currently around a dozen competitively priced Internet centres in New Sukhothai, including Sunisa Internet on Thanon Prasertpong, and Today's Internet on Thanon Charodvithithong; the CAT phone office on Thanon Nikhon Kasem has public Catnet terminals (Mon–Fri 8.30am–4.30pm, Sat 8.30am–noon). In Old Sukhothai, there's Internet access across from the museum at *Coffee Cup* restaurant.

Mail The GPO is on Thanon Nikhon Kasem, 200m southeast from the junction with Thanon Prampracha.

Motorbike rental Motorbikes can be rented through almost any guest house for B200 per day.

Telephones The CAT overseas phone centre (Mon–Fri 8.30am–4.30pm, Sat 8.30am–noon) is next to the post office on Thanon Nikhon Kasem, 200m southeast from the junction with Thanon Prampracha.

Travel agent Domestic and international air tickets from Sukhothai Travel Agency, 10–12 Thanon Singhawat ⓣ055 613075, ⓔsukhothaitravel service@yahoo.com. They can also organize a minivan plus driver for local sightseeing (B1800).

Si Satchanalai and around

In the mid-thirteenth century, Sukhothai cemented its power by establishing several satellite towns, of which the most important was **SI SATCHANALAI**, 57km upriver from Sukhothai on the banks of the Yom. Now a historical park, the restored ruins of **Muang Kao Si Satchanalai** have a quieter ambience than the grander models at Old Sukhothai, and the additional attractions of the riverside wat in nearby **Chalieng**, the **Sangkhalok pottery kilns** in Bang Ko Noi, and the **Sathorn Textile Museum** in New Si Satchanalai combine to make the area worth exploring.

Si Satchanalai is to all intents and purposes a day-trip from Sukhothai, as local accommodation is thin on the ground. Don't attempt to do the ruins of Si Satchanalai and Sukhothai in a single day: several tour outfits offer this option, but seeing so many dilapidated facades in seven or eight hours is mind-numbing.

Half-hourly **buses** bound for Si Satchanalai depart from the bus station in New Sukhothai and take about an hour. The last conveniently timed bus back to New Sukhothai leaves Old Si Satchanalai at 4.30pm; if you miss that one you'll have to wait till about 8pm. Most buses drop passengers on Highway 101 at the signpost for Muang Kao Si Satchanalai, near to a bicycle-rental place and about 2km from the entrance to the historical park. Some buses drop passengers 500m further south, in which case you should follow the track southwest over the Yom River for about 500m to another bicycle-rental place, conveniently placed at the junction for the historical park (1.5km northwest) and Chalieng (1km southeast); the kilns are a further 2km north of the park. **Bikes** cost B20 to rent for the day and are much the best way of seeing the ruins; besides the places already mentioned, there's an outlet at the park entrance. Alternatively, you could either rent a motorbike in New Sukhothai or join a tour from there.

The historical park stands pretty much on its own, with only a couple of hamlets in the vicinity, where you can buy cold drinks but won't get much in the way of food or a place to stay. If you're really determined to see Muang Kao Si Satchanalai on your way elsewhere (like Phrae or Lampang, for example), you could stay at *Wang Yom Resort*, also known as *Suwanthanas* (Ⓣ055 631380; ❻–❼), which has a range of rather pricey fan and air-con **bungalows** (and a crafts centre) set around an attractive garden 300m south of the park entrance, beside the Yom River and west off Highway 101. Alternatively, if you proceed to the old city's modern counterpart at New Si Satchanalai, 11km north along Highway 101 and the terminus of the Sukhothai buses, you'll find basic but inexpensive accommodation at the *Kruchang Hotel* (❷) near the Bangkok Bank in the town centre.

Muang Kao Si Satchanalai

Muang Kao Si Satchanalai (daily 8am–4pm; B40 plus B10–50 surcharge depending on your vehicle, or free if you have a combined Sukhothai–Si Satchanalai ticket) was built to emulate its capital, but Si Satchanalai is much less hyped than Sukhothai, sees fewer tourists and, most significantly, has escaped the sometimes overzealous landscaping of the more popular site. It's also a lot more compact, though lacking in the watery splendour of Sukhothai's main temples.

The ruins are numbered and it makes sense to do them in order. Begin with the elephant temple of **Wat Chang Lom**, whose centrepiece is a huge, Sri Lankan-style, bell-shaped chedi set on a square base studded with 39 life-sized elephant buttresses. Many of the elephants are in good repair, with most of their stucco flesh still intact; others now have their laterite skeletons exposed.

Across the road from Wat Chang Lom, **Wat Chedi Jet Taew**'s seven rows of small chedis are thought to enshrine the ashes of Si Satchanalai's royal rulers, which makes this the ancient city's most important temple. One of the chedis is a scaled-down replica of the hallmark lotus-bud chedi at Sukhothai's Wat Mahathat; some of the others are copies of other important wats from the vicinity.

Following the road a short way southeast of Chedi Jet Taew you reach **Wat Nang Phya**, remarkable for the original stucco reliefs on its viharn wall, which remain in fine condition; stucco is a hardy material that sets soon after being first applied, and becomes even harder when exposed to rain – hence its ability to survive seven hundred years in the open. The balustraded wall has slit windows and is entirely covered with intricate floral motifs. To the right on the way back to Wat Chang Lom, **Wat Suan Utayan Noi** contains one of the few Buddha images still left in Si Satchanalai.

North of Chang Lom, the hilltop ruins of Wat Khao Phanom Pleung and Wat Khao Suan Khiri afford splendid aerial views of different quarters of the ancient city. The sole remaining intact chedi of **Wat Khao Phanom Pleung** sits on top of the lower of the hills and used to be flanked by a set of smaller chedis built to entomb the ashes of Si Satchanalai's important personages – the ones who merited some special memorial, but didn't quite make the grade for Wat Chedi Jet Taew. The temple presumably got its name, which means "mountain of sacred fire", from the cremation rituals held on the summit. **Wat Khao Suan Khiri**'s huge chedi, which graces the summit 200m northwest, has definitely seen better days, but the views from its dilapidated platform – south over the main temple ruins and north towards the city walls and entrance gates – are worth the climb.

Chalieng

Before Sukhothai asserted control of the region and founded Si Satchanalai, the Khmers governed the area from **Chalieng**, just over 2km to the east of Si Satchanalai. Cradled in a bend in the Yom River, all that now remains of Chalieng is a single temple, **Wat Phra Si Ratana Mahathat**, the most atmospheric of all the sites in the Sukhothai area. Left to sink into graceful disrepair, the wat has escaped the perfectionist touch of restorers and now serves both as playground to the kids from the hamlet across the river and as grazing patch for their parents' cows.

Originally a Khmer temple and later adapted by the kings of Sukhothai, Wat Phra Si Ratana Mahathat forms a compact complex of two ruined viharns aligned east–west each side of a central chedi. Of the western viharn only two Buddha images remain, seated one in front of the other on a dais overgrown with weeds, and staring forlornly at the stumps of pillars that originally supported the roof over their heads: the rest has long since been buried under grass, efficiently grazed by the cows. A huge standing Buddha, similar to the two in Sukhothai's Wat Mahathat, gazes out from the nearby mondop. The more important viharn adjoins the central Sri Lankan-style chedi to the east, and is surrounded by a sunken wall of laterite blocks. Entering it through the semi-submerged eastern gateway, you pass beneath a sizeable carved lintel, hewn from a single block of stone. The seated Buddha in the centre of the western end of the viharn is typical Sukhothai style, as is the towering stucco relief of a walking Buddha to the left, which is regarded as one of the finest of its genre.

The Sangkhalok kilns

Endowed with high-quality clay, the area around Si Satchanalai – known as Sawankhalok or Sangkhalok during the Ayutthaya period – commanded an international reputation as a ceramics centre from the mid-fourteenth to the end of the fifteenth century, producing pieces still rated among the finest in the world. More than two hundred **kilns** have been unearthed in and around Si Satchanalai to date, and it's estimated that there could once have been a thousand in all. Two kilometres upstream of Muang Kao Si Satchanalai in **Ban Ko Noi**, the **Sangkhalok Kiln Preservation Centre** (daily 9am–noon & 1–4pm; B30) showcases an excavated production site, with a couple of kilns roofed over as museum pieces.

Unfortunately, there are few English signs to explain how the kilns worked, though a small display of **Sangkhalok ceramics** gives an idea of the pieces that were fired here. Works fall into three broad categories: domestic items such as pots, decorated plates and lidded boxes; decorative items like figurines, temple sculptures and temple roof tiles; and items for export, particularly to Indonesia and the Philippines, where huge Sangkhalok storage jars were used as burial urns. Most Sangkhalok ceramics were glazed – the grey-green celadon, probably introduced by immigrant Chinese potters, was especially popular – and typically decorated with fish or chrysanthemum motifs. Several of Thailand's major museums feature collections of ceramics from both Si Satchanalai and Sukhothai under the umbrella label of Sangkhalok, and there's a dedicated collection of Sangkhalok wares just outside New Sukhothai, described on p.285.

The Sathorn Textile Museum

Eleven kilometres north of the Si Satchanalai ruins, modern Si Satchanalai is worth visiting for the **Sathorn Textile Museum**, located at the northern end of the ribbon-like new town, on the east side of Highway 101. The museum houses the private collection of Khun Sathorn, who also runs the adjacent textile shop, and he or his staff open up the one-room exhibition for anyone who shows an interest. *Lotus Village* guest house in New Sukhothai includes a visit to the museum on its Si Satchanalai day-trip, or you can come here on the bus from New Sukhothai, getting off in modern Si Satchanalai rather than at the ruins.

Most of the **textiles** on show come from the nearby village of Hat Siew, whose weavers have long specialized in the art of *teen jok*, or hem embroidery, whereby the bottom panel of the sarong or *phasin* (woman's sarong) is decorated with a band of supplementary weft, usually done in exquisitely intricate patterns. Some of the textiles here are almost a hundred years old and many of the *teen jok* **motifs** have symbolic meaning showing what the cloths would have been used for – a sarong or *phasin* used for a marriage ceremony, for example, tends to have a double image, such as two birds facing each other. Elephants also feature quite a lot in Hat Siew weaving, and this is thought to be a reference to the village custom in which young men who are about to become monks parade on elephants to their ordination ceremony at the temple. The tradition continues to this day and elephant parades are held at the mass ordination ceremony every year on April 7 and 8. Modern Hat Siew textiles are sold at the adjacent Sathorn shop and at other outlets further south along the main road.

Kamphaeng Phet

KAMPHAENG PHET, 77km south of Sukhothai, was probably founded in the fourteenth century by the kings of Sukhothai as a buffer city between their capital and the increasingly powerful city-state of Ayutthaya. Its name, which translates as "Diamond Wall", refers to its role as a garrison town.

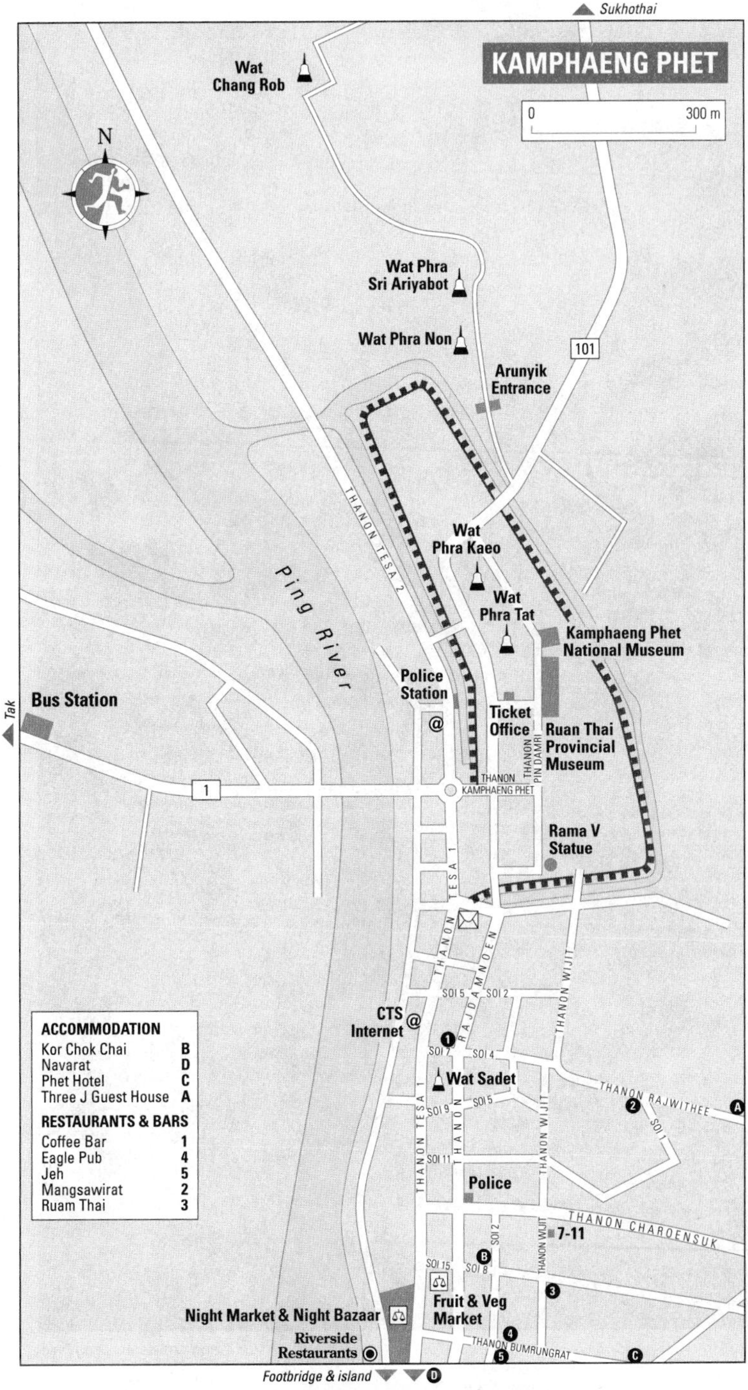
KAMPHAENG PHET
Sukhothai
0 300 m
N
Wat Chang Rob
Wat Phra Sri Ariyabot
Wat Phra Non
101
Arunyik Entrance
THANON TESA 2
Ping River
Wat Phra Kaeo
Wat Phra Tat
Kamphaeng Phet National Museum
Police Station
Ticket Office
THANON PIN DAMRI
Ruan Thai Provincial Museum
Bus Station
Tak
1
THANON KAMPHAENG PHET
Rama V Statue
TESA 1
THANON RAJDAMNOEN
THANON WIJIT
SOI 5
SOI 2
CTS Internet
SOI 7
SOI 4
Wat Sadet
THANON RAJWITHEE
SOI 9
SOI 5
SOI 1
THANON TESA 1
SOI 11
Police
THANON CHAROENSUK
7-11
SOI 2
SOI 15
SOI 8
Night Market & Night Bazaar
Fruit & Veg Market
Riverside Restaurants
THANON BUMRUNGRAT
Footbridge & island
ACCOMMODATION
Kor Chok Chai B
Navarat D
Phet Hotel C
Three J Guest House A
RESTAURANTS & BARS
Coffee Bar 1
Eagle Pub 4
Jeh 5
Mangsawirat 2
Ruam Thai 3

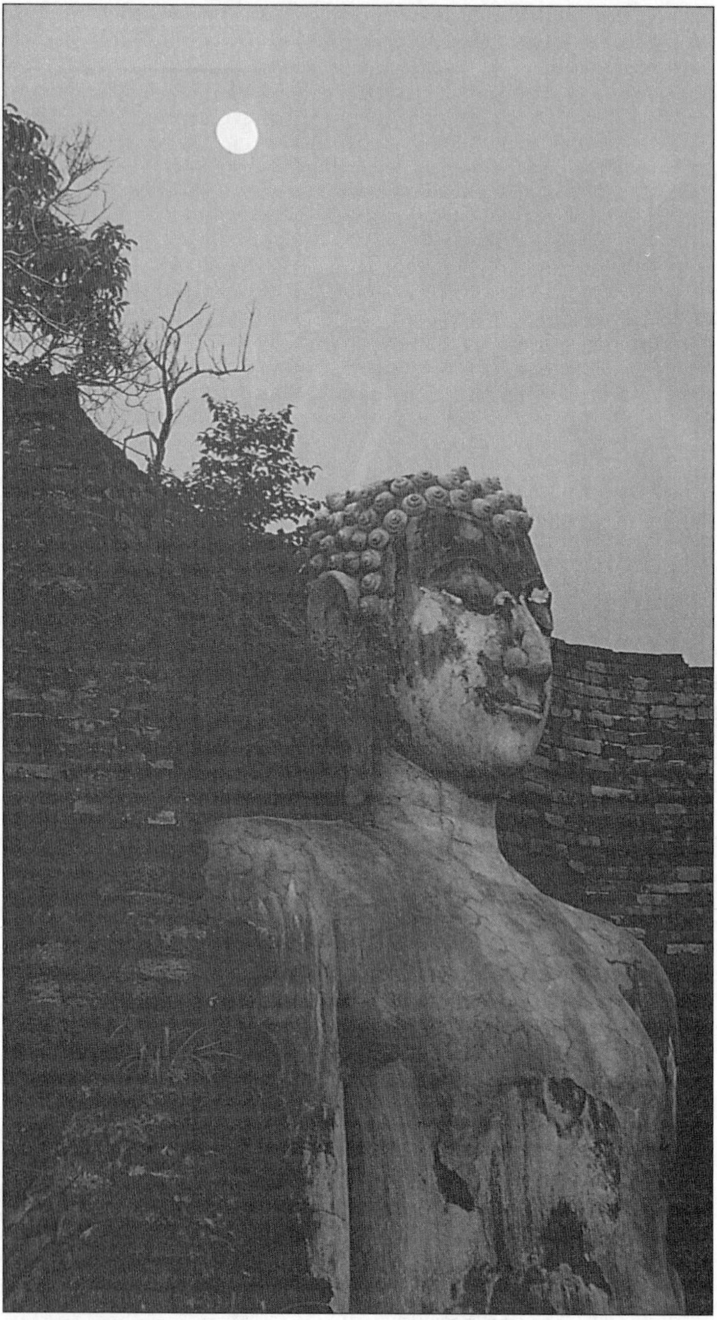

△ Muang Kao Kamphaeng Phet

Strategically sited 100m from the east bank of the Ping, the ruined old city has, like Sukhothai and Si Satchanalai before it, been partly restored and opened to the public as a historical park. The least visited of the three, it should nevertheless rival Si Satchanalai for your attention, mainly because of the eloquently weathered statues of its main temple. A new city has grown up on the south-eastern boundaries of the old, the usual commercial blandness offset by a riverside park, plentiful flowers and a fair number of traditional wooden houses. You can even swim off an island in the middle of the river, accessible via a footbridge near Soi 21, a few hundred metres south of the night market. Should you decide to linger for a few days, *Three J Guest House* not only makes a pleasant base but can also arrange rafting and bird-watching trips in nearby national parks.

The town is served by direct **buses** from Bangkok, Chiang Mai and Tak, but most travellers come here on a day-trip from Sukhothai or Phitsanulok.

Muang Kao Kamphaeng Phet

Ruins surround modern Kamphaeng Phet on all sides, but **Muang Kao Kamphaeng Phet** (daily 8am–5pm; B40 plus B10/bicycle, B20/motorbike and B30/car) takes in the two most interesting areas: the oblong zone inside the old city walls and the forested area just north of that. A tour of both areas involves a five-kilometre round-trip, so the best option is to rent a **bicycle** or **motorbike** from *Three J Guest House* in the new town, though you could also strike a deal with a samlor driver. If you are coming on a day-trip from Sukhothai or Phitsanulok, consider hiring your own transport there. The ruins that dot the landscape across the Ping River, west of the Thanon Tesa roundabout, belong to the even older city of Nakhon Chum, but are now too tumbledown to be worth the effort.

Inside the city walls

Parts of the **city walls** that gave Kamphaeng Phet its name are still in good condition, though Highway 101 to Sukhothai now cuts through the enclosed area and a few shops have sprung up along the roadside, making it hard to visualize the fortifications as a whole. Approaching from the Thanon Tesa roundabout, you can either head up Thanon Pin Damri and start your tour at Wat Phra That and the Provincial Museum, or you enter the compound from the western gate and come in at the back end of **Wat Phra Kaeo**. Built almost entirely of laterite and adorned with laterite Buddhas, this was the city's central and most important structure, and given the name reserved for temples that have housed the kingdom's most sacred image: the Emerald Buddha, now in the wat of the same name in Bangkok, is thought to have been set down here to rest at some point. Seven centuries later, the Buddha images have been worn away into attractive abstract shadows, often aptly compared to the pitted, spidery forms of Giacometti sculptures, and the slightly unkempt feel to the place makes a perfect setting. The statues would originally have been faced with stucco, and restorers have already patched up the central tableau of one reclining and two seated Buddhas. The empty niches that encircle the principal chedi were once occupied by statues of bejewelled lions.

Adjoining Wat Phra Kaeo to the east are the three chedis of **Wat Phra That**. The central bell-shaped chedi, now picturesquely wreathed in lichen and stray bits of vegetation, is typical of the Sri Lankan style and was built to house a sacred relic. Just east of Wat Phra That, **Kamphaeng Phet National Museum** (Wed–Sun 9am–4pm; B30) displays the artistic and archeological heritage of Kamphaeng Phet. The exhibition on the ground floor looks at the historical development of the city, while upstairs is given over to a display of sculptures found in the locality. The prize exhibit up here is the very fine bronze standing Shiva: cast in the sixteenth century in Khmer-Ayutthayan style, the statue has had a chequered history – including decapitation by a keen nineteenth-century German admirer. Also on this floor is an unusual seventeenth- or eighteenth-century Ayutthayan-style standing Buddha in wood, whose diadem, necklace and even hems are finely carved.

When you're at the National Museum you can't fail to see the alluring group of recently built traditional-style teak-wood *salas* in the adjacent compound which, though unsigned in English, are in fact the **Kamphaeng Phet Ruan Thai Provincial Museum** (Wed–Sun 9am–4pm; free). Inside, exhibits and scale models labelled in English and Thai introduce the history, traditions and contemporary culture of Kamphaeng Phet province.

The arunyik temples

The dozen or so ruins in the forested area north of the city walls – east 100m along Highway 101 from behind Wat Phra Kaeo, across the moat and up a road to the left – are all that remains of Kamphaeng Phet's **arunyik** (forest) temples, built here by Sukhothai-era monks in a wooded area to encourage meditation. It's an enjoyable area to explore if you have your own wheels, with the dilapidated structures peeking out of the thinly planted groves that line the access road; the road winds around a fair bit before eventually rejoining the Sukhothai–Kamphaeng Phet highway to the north of the walled city.

Once you're through the entrance, the first temple on the left is **Wat Phra Non**, otherwise known as the Temple of the Reclining Buddha, though little remains of the enormous Buddha figure save for a few chunks helpfully labelled "neck", "head" and the like. Gigantic laterite pillars support the viharn that houses the statue; far more ambitious than the usual brick-constructed jobs, these pillars were cut from single slabs of stone from a nearby quarry and would have measured up to 8m in height.

A relic's throw to the north, the four Buddha images of **Wat Phra Sri Ariyabot** are in better condition. With cores of laterite and skins of stucco, the restored standing and walking images tower over the viharn, while the seated (south-facing) and reclining (north-facing) Buddhas remain indistinct blobs. The full-grown trees rooted firmly in the raised floor are evidence of just how old the place is.

Follow the road around the bend to reach **Wat Chang Rob**, crouched on top of a laterite hill 1km from the entrance gate. Built to the same Sri Lankan model as its sister temples of the same name in Sukhothai and Si Satchanalai, this "temple surrounded by elephants" retains only the square base of its central bell-shaped chedi. Climb one of its four steep staircases for a view out over the mountains in the west, or just for a different perspective of the 68 elephant buttresses that encircle the base. Sculpted from laterite and stucco, they're dressed in the ceremonial garb fit for such revered animals; floral reliefs can just be made out along the surfaces between neighbouring elephants – the lower level was once decorated with a stucco frieze of flying birds.

Practicalities

Arriving by bus from Sukhothai or Phitsanulok, you'll enter Kamphaeng Phet from the east and should get off either inside the old city walls or at the Thanon Tesa roundabout rather than wait to be dumped across the river at the **terminal** 2km west of town on Highway 1. If you are coming from the bus terminal, you'll need to hop on a red town **songthaew** (B6), which will take you to the Thanon Tesa roundabout just east of the river (the most convenient disembarkation point for the ruins), or further into the town centre for most of the hotels and restaurants. From the roundabout, songthaews generally do a clockwise circle around the new town, running south along Thanon Rajdamnoen (get off at the intersection with Rajdamnoen Soi 4 for *Three J Guest House*), then west along Bumrungrat, north up Thanon Tesa 1 and west out to the bus station. There's a **bank** with an exchange counter and ATM close to the roundabout and several more banks on Thanon Charoensuk. The main **post office** is on Thanon Tesa 1, about 200m south of the roundabout; it has a Catnet **Internet** terminal and there are a couple of other Internet centres further south on Thanon Tesa 1.

Accommodation and eating

The most traveller-oriented **place to stay** in Kamphaeng Phet is *Three J Guest House*, located 600m east of the main drag, Thanon Rajdamnoen, at 79 Thanon Rajwithee (Ⓣ055 713129, Ⓔthreejguest@hotmail.com; ❷–❹). Run by an enthusiastic bank-worker and his family, it's a pleasant, secluded home-stay with ten comfortable bungalows built from rough-cut logs and set in a Chinese-style rock garden at the back of the family home. All rooms have cosy verandas; the cheapest options share bathrooms and the priciest have air-con. There's bicycle and motorbike rental, Internet access, and tours to national parks at weekends. The main budget alternative is *Kor Chok Chai* (Ⓣ055 713532; ❸), with its fan and air-con rooms, east of the fruit and veg market on Rajdamnoen Soi 8; the hotel is unsigned but recognizable by its red lanterns. Most of Kor Chok Chai's customers are salespeople, so there's some call-girl activity after hours, but it's clean enough and fine for a night. A better option would be the mid-range *Navarat* (Ⓣ055 711211, Ⓕ055 711961; ❹–❺) on Tesa Soi 21, also known as Soi Prapan, 300m south of the night market at the far southern edge of the new town. Staff here speak English, there's a decent restaurant downstairs, and the all air-con rooms are comfortable, if a bit shabby at the cheaper end. On the southeastern edge of town at the eastern end of Thanon Bumrungrat, the *Phet Hotel* (Ⓣ055 712810, Ⓕ055 712816; ❺) is a little more upmarket and popular with tour groups; it has a swimming pool and night club as well as decent air-con rooms.

The huge range of cheap noodles, stir-fries and over-rice dishes served at *Ruam Thai*, south of the Charoensuk intersection on Thanon Wijit, make this very popular, unpretentious **restaurant** a reliable choice as any time of day, but after dark the night market is the most enjoyable place to eat. It sets up in a covered area in the southern part of the new town, between the river and Thanon Tesa 1; try asking here for the special local noodle dish, *kway tiaw cha kang rao*, made with cow peas and pork. There are a couple of vegetarian restaurants in town, both of them typical cheap canteens that open daily from about 7am to 2pm and offer very good deals of rice plus a couple of stews, curries or stir-fries for B15–20: *Mangsawirat* (no English sign but look for the red Chinese character for "vegetarian" against a yellow background) is on Thanon Rajwithee, at the junction with Soi 1, about 300m east of Thanon Rajdamnoen and 300m west of *Three J Guest House*; *Jeh* (flagged only by the Thai letter for "Jeh" in red against yellow) is right next to a formal dress shop just off Thanon Bumrungrat on Soi 2 at 68/3. For fresh coffee, cappuccinos, espressos – and green tea lattés – the place to head for is the cute little open-fronted *Coffee Bar* just across Thanon Rajdamnoen from Soi 4, but if you're after beer, whisky and live music (from 9pm), the *Eagle Pub*, one block south and east of *Kor Chok Chai* on Thanon Bumrungrat, is one of the livelier spots in town.

West of Sukhothai

Highway 12 heads west from Sukhothai, crossing the westernmost reaches of the northern plains before arriving at the provincial capital of **TAK** (79km), on the east bank of the Ping River. Historically important as the birthplace of King Taksin of Thonburi (who attached the name of his hometown to the one he was born with), Tak is of little interest to tourists except as a place to change **buses** for continuing north to Lampang and Chiang Mai, south to Kamphaeng Phet and Bangkok, or west to Mae Sot and the Burmese border; Tak **bus station** is about 3km east of the town centre. **TAT** has a regional office in the town centre at 193 Thanon Taksin (daily 8.30am–4.30pm; Ⓣ055 514341, Ⓔtattak@tat.or.th). If you need a hotel in Tak, try the *Mae Ping*, across the road from the fruit and veg market at 231 Thanon Mahattai Bamroong (Ⓣ055 511807; ❷–❸), which has faded but inexpensive fan and air-con rooms. The slightly pricier, slightly better *Sa Nguan Thai* (Ⓣ055 511153; ❷–❹) is a couple of blocks north of the market at 619 Thanon Taksin and easily identifiable by its red lanterns hanging outside; you can choose between fan and air-con rooms with or without TV. The town's best hotel is the small, comfortably

Refugees from Burma: the Karen

With a population of five to seven million, the **Karen** are Burma's largest ethnic minority, but their numbers have offered no protection against persecution by the Burmese. This mistreatment has been going on for centuries, and entered a new phase after World War II, when the Karen remained loyal to the British. As a reward, they were supposed to have been granted a special settlement when the British left, but were instead left to fend for themselves. Fifteen years after the British withdrawal, the **Burmese army** took control, setting up an isolationist state run under a bizarre ideology compounded of militarist, socialist and Buddhist principles. In 1988, opposition to this junta peaked with a series of pro-democracy demonstrations that were suppressed by the slaughter of thousands.

The army subsequently felt obliged to hold elections, which resulted in an overwhelming majority for the **National League for Democracy** (NLD), led by **Aung San Suu Kyi**, recipient of the 1991 Nobel Peace Prize. In response, the military placed Aung San Suu Kyi under house arrest (where she has remained on and off ever since) and declared all opposition parties illegal. The disenfranchised MPs then joined the thousands of ordinary citizens who, in the face of the savagery of the Burmese militia against the country's minorities, had fled east to jungle camps along the Thai border and beyond, into Thailand itself.

Armed wings of Burma's numerous minority groups have been fighting from their jungle bases ever since and, although many factions have reached temporary ceasefire agreements with the Burmese junta, **persecution** of minority peoples continues. The Karen, whose homeland state of Kawthulay borders northwest Thailand from Mae Sariang down to Three Pagodas Pass, have been particularly vulnerable: their soldiers, the Karen National Union (KNU), were the last major rebel group to continue fighting, though, at the time of writing, they too were considering engaging in peace talks with the junta. Common tactics employed by the Burmese army against the Karen and other minority groups include the forcible razing and relocation of villages, systematic murder, rape and robbery, and the rounding-up of slave labour: according to the International Confederation of Free Trade Unions, on any given day several hundred thousand men, women, children and elderly people are subjected to forced labour in Burma, mainly for the building of roads, railways and military projects, and as porters for the Burmese army.

furnished *Viang Tak 2* (ⓣ055 511910, ⓕ055 512687; ❺), one block southwest of the fruit and veg market at 236 Thanon Chumphon; it has a swimming pool, and some rooms have nice river views.

Most travellers ignore Tak, however, and go straight **on to Mae Sot**, reached by either of two roads through the stunning western mountain range that divides the northern plains from the Burmese border. **Highway 105**, the more direct route, is served by fast and frequent, if cramped, government minibuses between Tak and Mae Sot. If following this route with your own transport, there are a couple of attractions en route, beginning at kilometre-stone 12, 20km west of Tak, with **Lansang National Park** (dawn to dusk; B200), which has trails and waterfalls and is reached via a three-kilometre side road off Highway 105; some Mae Sot tour operators run trips here too. This region is home to Lisu, Lahu and Maew hill tribes, many of whom live on the cool slopes of 840-metre-high Doi Muser where they grow coffee, fruit and vegetables that they trade, along with hill-tribe crafts, at the **hill-tribe market** alongside the highway between kilometre-stones 28 and 29.

Rickety but roomy ordinary buses take twice as long to ply **Route 1175** between Tak and Mae Sot, which follows a winding and at times hair-raising

As a result of these ongoing atrocities, an estimated one thousand Burmese flee across the Thai border every month, the majority of them Karen. Of the 115,000 registered refugees living at the nine **refugee camps** along the Thailand–Burma border in September 2003, 95,000 were Karen. One of the biggest camps near Mae Sot is the village-like Umpium, on the road to Umphang, which is home for about 16,000 Karen.

Registered refuges are by no means the whole story, however, as for many years **Thai government policy** has been to admit only those refugees who are fleeing active fighting, not human rights violations. The hundreds of thousands who have left their homeland because of politically induced economic hardship – forced labour, theft of their land and livestock, impossibly high taxation and corruption, among other factors – are therefore obliged either to try and enter the refugee camps illegally, or to attempt to make a living as **migrant workers**. Without refugee status, Burmese exiles are extremely vulnerable to abuse, both from corrupt officials and from exploitative employers. In Mae Sot, for example, where Burmese migrants are a mainstay of the local economy, many of them are paid as little as B20 a day (less than twenty percent of Thailand's minimum wage) to work in the worst jobs available, in gem and garment factories, and as prostitutes. Demands for better wages and improved conditions nearly always result in deportation.

Reactions in the **Thai press** to the Burmese refugee issue are mixed, with humanitarian concerns tempered by economic hardships in Thailand and by high-profile cases of illegal Burmese workers involved in violent crimes and drug-smuggling (Burma is now one of the world's leading producers and smugglers of methamphetamines, also known as *ya baa*, or Ice, much of which finds its way into Thailand). Relations between the neighbours have been volatile ever since the Burmese razed Ayutthaya in 1767, and there are still occasional high-level political spats today, but Thailand's politicians are conscious above all of Burma's potential as a lucrative trading partner. As well as acting as peace broker between the junta and some ethnic minority groups, the Thai government has also made a show of cracking down on Burmese dissidents and deporting thousands of migrant works back to Burma.

For recent **news** and archive reports on the situation in Burma and on its borders, see ⓦwww.irrawaddy.org. For information on how to offer **support** to refugees from Burma, see p.298 and Basics pp.82–83.

course across the thickly forested range, affording great views over the valleys on either side and passing through makeshift roadside settlements built by hill tribes. The road eventually descends into the valley of the **Moei River** – which forms the Thai-Burmese border here – and joins the northbound section of Highway 105 at the lovely, traditional village of **Mae Ramat** before continuing south to Mae Sot. Highway 105 carries on north, reaching Mae Sariang (see p.377) after a five-hour songthaew ride – a bumpy but scenic journey through rugged border country.

Mae Sot and the border

Located 100km west of Tak and only 6km from the Burmese border, **MAE SOT** enjoys a rich ethnic mix of Burmese, Karen, Hmong and Thai residents (plus a lively injection of committed NGO expats), a thriving trade in gems and teak, and a laid-back atmosphere. There's little to see in the small town, apart from several glittering Burmese-style temples, but it's a relaxed place to hang out, with a burgeoning number of good restaurants. The short ride to the border market provides additional, if low-key, entertainment (though you can't travel into Burma from here), and there are several caves and waterfalls within day-tripping distance.

Mae Sot's greatest attraction, however, is as a stopover point on the way to **Umphang** (see p.302), a remote village 164km further south, which is starting to get a name as a centre for interesting rafting and trekking adventures. The journey to Umphang takes about four hours in a bumpy songthaew, so it's usually worth staying the night in Mae Sot; you can also organize treks to Umphang through Mae Sot tour operators. If you need to change money for the trip, you should do so in Mae Sot (see "Listings", p.302) as there are no exchange facilities anywhere in Umphang.

The Burmese influence in Mae Sot is palpable in everything from food to fashions, and many of the guest houses are run by Burmese staff, who often speak good English. Over the last two decades the **Burmese population** of Mae Sot and its environs has swelled enormously, as thousands of political and economic refugees have fled across the border to escape the intolerably repressive policies of the Burmese military regime (see the box on p.296). There are currently nine refugee camps along the border to the north and south of Mae Sot, and Mae Sot itself is the headquarters for several related international **aid projects**; many of these organizations welcome donations of clothes and medicines, which can be left at *Ban Thai* guest house, and at *Krua Canadian* and *Bai Fern* restaurants. One of the most famous organizations in Mae Sot is the **Mae Tao clinic** (Ⓦwww.burmachildren.org), which provides free medical care for around 30,000 Burmese refugees a year, focusing on those who fall outside the remit of the refugee camps and cannot use the Thai health system. The clinic was founded in 1989 by a Karen refugee, Dr Cynthia, who has won several prestigious international awards for her work; her clinic also trains and equips "backpack teams" of mobile medics who spend months travelling through the Burmese jungle providing healthcare to internally displaced peoples.

Arrival and information

Mae Sot has pretty good bus connections with towns in the central plains and in the north, including half-hourly direct government minibuses to and from Tak, and songthaews to the border towns of Mae Ramat (every 30min; 45min) and Mae Sariang (hourly 6am–midday; 5hr). If you're arriving on a government **minibus**, you should be dropped off at your chosen guest house.

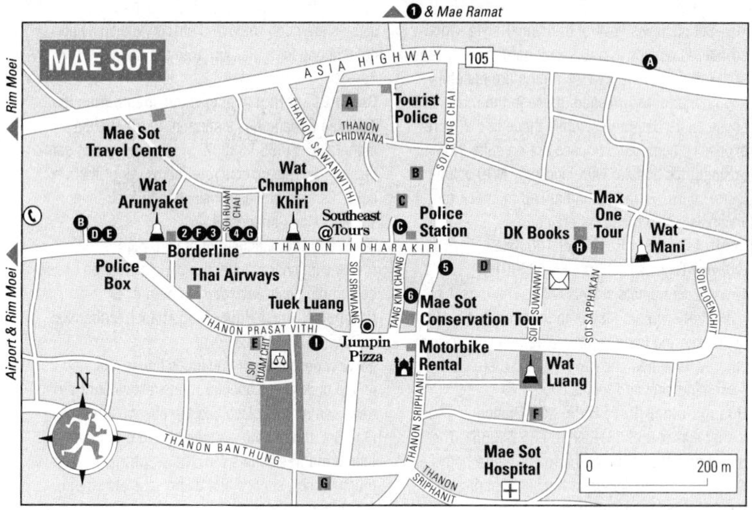

ACCOMMODATION

Bai Fern	F
Ban Thai	B
Central Mae Sot Hill	A
Duang Kamol (D.K.) Hotel	H
Fortune	D
Green Guest House	C
Mate's Place	G
Number 4 Guest House	E
Siam	I

RESTAURANTS AND BARS

Bai Fern	3
Crocodile Tear	4
Khao-Mao Khao-Fang	1
Khun's	2
Krua Canadian Restaurant	5
Pim Hut	6

TRANSPORT

Buses to Bangkok	A
Minivans to Tak	B
Songthaews to Mae Sariang, Mae Ramat & Mae Salid	C
Buses to Chiang Mai, Chiang Rai, Mae Sai, Lampang & Lamphun	D
Songthaews to Rim Moei	E
Songthaews to Umphang	F
Songthaews & minibuses to Pha Charoen, KM 48, Phitsanulok and Sukhothai	G

Otherwise, buses currently use a variety of different **terminals** around town (see the map for details), though at the time of writing a new bus station is under construction east of town near the Highway 105/1090 intersection, and this will be used for the Bangkok service and possibly some others as well. For information on transport between Mae Sot and Umphang, see p.302. Several Air Andaman/Thai **flights** a week connect Mae Sot's tiny airstrip, 3km west of town on the Asia Highway, with Bangkok; to get into town from the airport, either walk out of the airport gates and flag down a west-bound songthaew to the Thanon Prasat Vithi terminus, or take a motorbike taxi. If you're leaving by plane, contact the airline office in Mae Sot (Ⓣ055 531730) to arrange for transport to the airport (B30).

There is no TAT office here, but both *Bai Fern* and *Khrua Canadian* restaurants are good sources of local **information**, and the best guest houses should also be able to help.

Accommodation

Mae Sot's guest houses offer simple **rooms** and information on the area; the hotels are generally more comfortable but less friendly.

Bai Fern 660/2 Thanon Indharakiri Ⓣ055 533343, Ⓔrungrapee@hotmail.com. Very friendly little guest house that's attached to one of the town's best restaurants. Rooms share bathrooms and are dark, quite noisy and altogether pretty basic, but the location is good and staff are welcoming and enthusiastic. ❷

Ban Thai 740 Thanon Indharakiri Ⓣ055 531590, Ⓦwww.mountain-designs.com/banthai/banthai.html. The most appealing guest house in

Mae Sot occupies several traditional-style, wooden-floored houses in a peaceful garden compound at the west end of town. All rooms are tastefully and comfortably furnished; those in the main house share bathrooms, while those in the more expensive compound houses are en suite. Not surprisingly, it's popular with long-stay NGO volunteers, so it's worth phoning ahead to check for vacancies. Also runs cookery courses. ❸–❹

Central Mae Sot Hill Hotel 100 Asia Highway/Highway 105 ⓣ055 532601, ⓦwww.centralhotelsresorts.com. The most upmarket accommodation in the area, but a 10min drive from the town centre. All rooms are air-con, smartly furnished and have TV, and there's a swimming pool and tennis courts. ❼

Duang Kamol (D.K.) Hotel 298 Thanon Indharakiri ⓣ055 531699, ⓕ055 542651. The nicest and best value of the town-centre hotels is set above the bookshop of the same name, and has huge clean rooms, many of them with little balconies and some with air-con and TV. ❸–❹

Fortune 738/1 Thanon Indharakiri ⓣ055 536392, ⓔfortune-maesod@hotmail.com. Clean, bright single, double and triple rooms in a purpose-built guest house run by an eager Burmese family at the west end of town. Some of the en-suite rooms could be noisy as they're close to the road, but the singles are good value and air-con is also available. Phone for a pick-up from the bus terminal. ❷–❸

Green Guest House Across the stream from the Tak/Mae Sariang bus station at 406/8 Thanon Indharakiri ⓣ055 533207. Small, lime-green complex of nice, clean, concrete rooms, all of them en suite. Central, and especially handy for transport to Tak and Mae Sariang. ❷

Mate's Place Thanon Indharakiri. Nice, simple rooms with shared bath in a big old wooden house behind the posh *Salakthai* restaurant. ❷

Number 4 Guest House 736 Thanon Indharakiri ⓣ & ⓕ055 544976, ⓦwww.geocities.com/no4guesthouse. Located in an old teak house about 15min walk west of the town centre, this place has the cheapest rooms in Mae Sot, though there's nothing more to them than a mattress and a fan. The emphasis is very much on self-service and doing your own thing, which can make it hard to get information or service. Runs well-reviewed treks (see box on p.305) and rents out bicycles. ❶

Siam 185 Thanon Prasat Vithi ⓣ055 531176, ⓕ055 531974. Typical Thai-Chinese town hotel, centrally located among the gem and jade shops and with decent enough fan and air-con rooms. ❸

Around Mae Sot

There are several minor caves and waterfalls **around Mae Sot**, which are easy enough to explore if you have your own transport (see Listings on p.302 for rental outlets), but if you've been to Umphang's Thi Lor Su Falls you're unlikely to be that impressed.

Heading north out of Mae Sot, along Highway 105 towards Mae Ramat, take a side road at around kilometre-stone 13 for 7km to reach the three-tiered **Mae Kasa Falls** (rainy season only) and hot springs. Much further north, just after kilometre-stone 95 on Highway 105, a sign directs you the 2km off the highway to the enormous 800-metre-deep bat-cave, **Tham Mae Usu** (inaccessible from July to October because of flooding). South out of town, off Route 1090 to Umphang, the 97 tiers of **Pha Charoen Falls** are 41km from Mae Sot. A couple of kilometres on from the falls, Highland Farm **Gibbon Sanctuary** (ⓦwww.members.tripod.com/highlandfarm) cares for pet gibbons who have been rescued from abusive owners and are unable to live in the wild; the sanctuary welcomes visitors and is located beside the road at kilometre-stone 42.8. To get to the falls or the sanctuary (known as Baan Farang), take a songthaew bound for kilometre-stone 48 from the depot on the southern edge of Mae Sot.

Eco-conscious Mae Sot Conservation Tour, at 415/17 Thanon Tang Kim Chang ⓣ055 532818, ⓔmaesotco@cscoms.com, runs interesting sounding trips to the upland jungle around Mae Lamao, home to Karen and Hmong hill tribes, about 25km east of Mae Sot off Highway 105. The jungle-craft day-trip includes an interpretative two-hour trek and whitewater-rafting (B2100, minimum four people); the overnight version adds a stay in a Karen village plus a side-trip to the gibbon sanctuary (B3500). Max One Tour, based in the *D.K. Hotel* plaza at 296/1 Thanon Indharakiri ⓣ055 542942, ⓦwww.maxontour.com, offers a one-day tour that covers the hot springs, Rim Moei border market, Pha Charoen Falls and the gibbon sanctuary for B1200 (minimum two people), or B1800 if you want to see Mae Usu cave as well.

Shopping and Rim Moei border market

Mae Sot is a good place to buy jewellery: the **gem and jade shops** clustered around the *Siam* hotel on Thanon Prasat Vithi offer a larger and less expensive selection than the stalls at the Rim Moei border market, and even if you don't intend to buy, just watching the performance-like haggling is half the fun. A number of places in town sell **Karen crafts**, including the Borderline Shop next to Wat Arunyaket on Thanon Indharakiri, which is an outlet for shoulder-bags, sarongs and other items made by Karen women living in refugee camps along the border. For fashions, Burmese sarongs and daily necessities, you can't beat the temptingly well-stocked day market that runs south off Thanon Ruamchit.

Frequent songthaews ferry Thai traders and a meagre trickle of tourists the 6km from Mae Sot to the border at **RIM MOEI**, where a large and thriving market for Burmese goods has grown up along the high street and beside the banks of the Moei River. It's a bit tacky, and the gems and jade on display are pricier than those in town, but it's not a bad place to pick up Burmese **handicrafts**, particularly wooden artefacts like boxes and picture frames, woven Karen shoulder-bags and checked *longyis*. The best buys are chunky teak tables and chairs, most of them polished up to a fine golden brown sheen.

The Asia Highway zips straight through Rim Moei and into Burma, via the Thailand–Burma Friendship Bridge. At the time of writing, access to the Burmese village of **Myawaddy** on the opposite bank of the Moei River is open to any foreign national for a fee of B500, payable at the bridge, though foreign visitors are allowed no further into Burma than this, and must return to Thailand on the same day. When coming back through Thai customs (daily 6am–6pm) you will automatically be given a new one-month Thai visa on the spot, which is handy if your existing visa is running out, but not so great if you've still got the best part of a sixty-day visa (you may be able to pre-empt this problem: see p.409 for advice).

Eating and drinking

Thanon Prasat Vithi is well stocked with noodle-shops and night-market stalls, though the more unusual restaurants are mainly found on the town's other main thoroughfare, Thanon Indharakiri.

Bai Fern 660/2 Thanon Indharakiri. This highly recommended restaurant, attached to the guest house of the same name, serves some of the best and most imaginative food in the region. The menu includes pepper steaks served with a variety of unusual sauces, authentic Italian carbonara, traditional Thai curries and lots of vegetarian options, as well as brownies, apple pie, chocolate cake and mixed-grain bread. Moderate.

Crocodile Tear Thanon Indharakiri. Dishes out cocktails and draught beer and hosts live performances of blues, Latin and folk music every night from around 9pm.

Khao-Mao Khao-Fang Out of town, 2km north towards Mae Ramat up Highway 105. This is a garden restaurant extraordinaire, where the artfully landscaped cascades, rivers, lianas, rock features and mature trees make you feel as if you're sitting in a primeval forest film set, especially at night when sea-green lighting adds to the effect. A popular spot for dates and VIP lunches, it serves food that's nothing special, but the cocktails are fun and as one of Mae Sot's most famous attractions, it's worth the hassle to get here. During the day you could use the Mae Ramat/Mae Sariang songthaew service, but after dark you'll need your own transport. Moderate–expensive.

Khun's Thanon Indharakiri. Characterful bar-restaurant that serves delicious, Thai food, including recommended snakehead orange curry, rice with Chiang Mai sausage, and morning-glory tempura, plus great-value margaritas. Sit at the low-slung tables and chairs outdoors or play pool and ponder the arty table-displays inside. Moderate.

Krua Canadian Restaurant Near the police station, just off Thanon Indharakiri. Delicious food at this unpretentious, family-run eatery whose menu includes such local specialities as stir-fried frog and bird curry, mango catfish salad and *matsaman* curries. Also serves several blends of local hill-tribe coffee, plus a long menu of veggie dishes. DVD screenings in the evening. Inexpensive.

Pim Hut 415/12 Thanon Tang Kim Chang. Popular with locals as well as Thai and farang tourists, and offers a big range of Thai and Western food at reasonable prices – everything from green curries to pizzas. Inexpensive.

Listings

Airlines The office for Thai and Andaman Airways is in the town centre at 76/1 Thanon Prasat Vithi ⓣ055 531730. You can also buy domestic and international air tickets at Mae Sot Conservation Tour, 415/17 Thanon Tang Kim Chang, and at Southeast Tours Internet centre and travel agent on Thanon Indharakiri.

Banks and exchange There are several banks with money-changing facilities and ATMs on Thanon Prasat Vithi.

Bicycle, car and motorbike rental *Ban Thai* and *Number 4* guest houses have rental bicycles for guests. *Bai Fern* restaurant rents cars (B1200) and motorbikes (B200), and motorbike rental is also possible from a bike-repair shop near the Bangkok Bank on Thanon Prasat Vithi.

Books A few English-language books are on sale at D.K. Books on Thanon Indharakiri.

Cookery lessons Available through *Ban Thai* guest house (B500).

Emergencies For all emergencies, call the tourist police on the free, 24hr phoneline ⓣ1155, or contact them at their booth near the main terminal for buses to Bangkok ⓣ055 532960. The main police station is in the town centre on Thanon Indharakiri.

Massage Herbal massage at Tuek Luang Yellow House, opposite *Siam* hotel on Thanon Prasat Vithi. Herbal saunas (3–7pm; men only) at Wat Mani, on Thanon Indharakiri.

Hospitals Mae Sot Hospital is on the southeastern edge of town and Pha Wawa Hospital is on the southwestern edge.

Immigration office At Rim Moei border crossing.

Internet access At Southeast Tours on Thanon Indharakiri.

Language lessons Thai lessons through *Krua Canadian* Restaurant, just off Thanon Indharakiri.

Telephone International calls from the government telephone office at the far west end of Thanon Indharakiri.

Umphang

Even if you don't fancy doing a trek, consider making the spectacular trip 164km south from Mae Sot to the village of **UMPHANG**, both for the stunning mountain scenery you'll encounter along the way, and for the buzz of being in such an isolated part of Thailand. Umphang-bound songthaews leave Mae Sot from a spot two blocks south of Thanon Prasat Vithi, departing every hour between 7.30am and 3.30pm and costing B100, or B150 if you're lucky enough to get the front seat. The drive generally takes about four hours and for the first hour proceeds in a fairly gentle fashion through the maize, cabbage and banana plantations of the Moei valley. The fun really begins when you start climbing into the mountains and the road – accurately dubbed the "**Sky Highway**" – careers round the edges of endless steep-sided valleys, undulating like a fairground rollercoaster (there are said to be 1219 bends in all). The views are glorious, but if you're prone to car-sickness, take some preventative tablets before setting out, as this journey can be very unpleasant, not least because the songthaews get so crammed with people and produce that there's often no possibility of distracting yourself by staring out of the window. Karen, Akha, Lisu and Hmong people live in the few hamlets along the route, many growing cabbages along the cleared lower slopes with the help of government incentives (part of a national campaign to steer upland farmers away from the opium trade). The Hmong in particular are easily recognized by their distinctive embroidered jackets and skirts edged in bright pink,

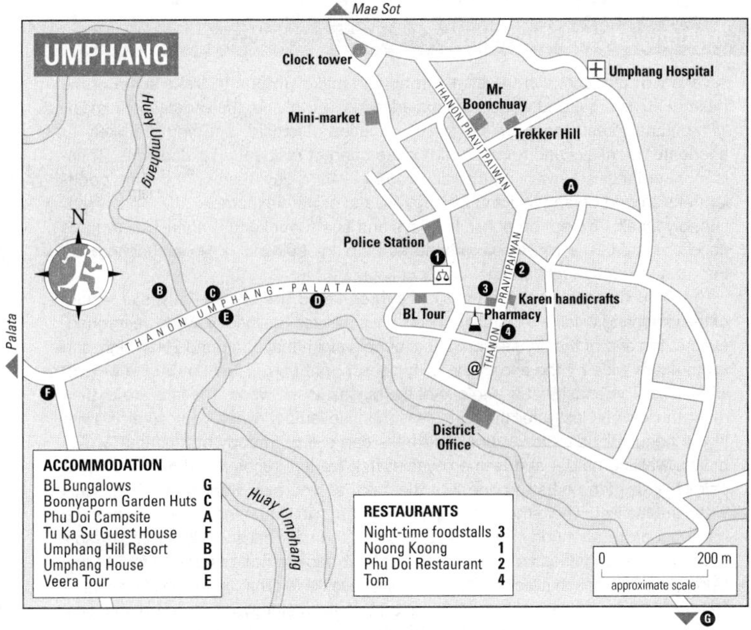

red and blue bands (see p.838). In 2000, the local Karen population grew by 16,000 when three refugee camps from the Rim Moei area were relocated to the purpose-built village of Umpium alongside the Sky Highway midway between Mae Sot and Umphang, just beyond the checkpoint (see the box on p.296 for more on Karen refugees from Burma). In fact the Umphang region was inhabited by Karen hill tribes before the Thais came to settle in the area in the early twentieth century; later when the Thais began trading in earnest with their neighbours across the Burmese border, the Karen traders from Burma used to carry their identification documents into Thailand in a bamboo container which they called an "umpha" – this is believed to be the origin of the name Umphang.

Surrounded by mountains and situated at the confluence of the Mae Khlong and Umphang rivers, Umphang itself is small and very quiet, made up of little more than a thousand or so wooden houses and a wat. It won't take long to explore the minute grid of narrow roads that dissects the village, but independent tourists are still relatively rare here, so you should get a friendly reception. Bring some warm clothes as it can get pretty cool at night and in the early mornings – and the songthaew ride from Mae Sot is often windy.

Practicalities

Mountain bikes can be rented from *Tu Ka Su Guest House* for B40 per hour or B200 per day; there's no official motorbike rental, but some guest-house owners will oblige. When it comes to public transport, Umphang is effectively a dead end, so the only way to travel on from here is to go back to Mae Sot first. **Songthaews** to Mae Sot leave hourly until mid-afternoon; if you tell your guest house when you want to leave they'll arrange for the songthaew to pick you up. There is an **Internet** centre (daily 8am–8pm) to the south of the temple on Thanon Pravitpaiwan, a **pharmacy** near the temple on Thanon Pravitpaiwan, and a basic **hospital** on the northeast edge of town.

Trekking around Umphang

A variety of attractions in the area combine to make **Umphang treks** some of the most genuine organized wilderness experiences in Thailand; the vegetation is mainly montane forest, there are numerous varieties of orchid, and you are likely to encounter monkeys and hornbills, if not the band of resident wild elephants. There is more emphasis on walking (usually around 3–4hr a day) than on the more popular treks around Chiang Mai and Chiang Rai, and as yet the number of visitors is reasonably small – except on public holidays and some weekends, when Thai trippers flood the area. The most comfortable **season** for trekking is November through February, though nights can get pretty chilly.

The focus of most Umphang treks is the three-tiered **Tee Lor Su Falls**, star feature of the Umphang Wildlife Sanctuary, which, unusually for Thailand, flows all year round, even at the end of the dry season. Local people claim that at around 200m high, and up to 400m wide by the end of the rainy season, not only is Tee Lor Su the biggest waterfall in Thailand, but it is also one of the biggest in the world. The falls are at their most thunderous just after the rainy season in November, when you can also swim in the beautifully blue lower pool, but trails can still be muddy at this time, which makes walking harder and less enjoyable; trek leaders recommend that you buy a pair of Wellington boots to cope with the mud, so you may want to anticipate this when in Mae Sot, where the selection is bigger than in Umphang. One stretch of the route becomes so muddy during and just after the rainy season that it's impassable to human feet and needs to be done on elephant-back, a ride of three to four hours. During the dry season (Dec–April), it's usually possible to climb up to one of the waterfall's upper tiers, mud permitting. Access to the falls is strictly controlled by national park rangers, who forbid visitors from taking food or plastic water bottles beyond the ranger station and campsite, which is 1.5km from the falls. Trekkers reach Tee Lor Su Falls via a fairly challenging combination of rafting and walking, but from December 1 to April 30 the **4WD road** to the ranger station is opened to the public, which means you only have to walk the 1.5km route to the falls. During this period some tour operators offer this car-plus-hike option as a day-trip from Umphang, usually throwing in a rafting session as well.

A **typical trek** lasts three days and follows something like the following itinerary. Day one: rafting down the Mae Khlong River via Tee Lor Jor Falls and some impressively honeycombed cliffs; camp overnight at hot springs or beside the river. Day two: a three- to four-hour jungle trek to Tee Lor Su Falls; camp near the falls. Day three: a three-hour trek to a Karen village; a two-hour elephant-ride; return to Umphang. Longer or shorter treks are possible.

Although Tee Lor Su is the most famous destination in the Umphang area, a couple of other programmes that emphasize whitewater-rafting are also becoming popular. From June through October there is whitewater-rafting from the Karen village of **Umphang Khi** via the forty-plus rapids of the Umphang River, which can also include a fairly long trek and a night in the village. Alternatively, there are one- and two-day rafting trips to **Thi Lor Leh Falls**, which involve four to eight hours' rafting (depending on water levels) via a series of cataracts along the Mae Khlong River, and the possibility of a seven-hour trek on the second day.

It's possible to **arrange your trek** in Mae Sot, or even in Bangkok, but the best place to set up a trip is in Umphang itself. Not only are trips from here usually cheaper and better value (you don't waste half a trek day getting to Umphang), but trek leaders are more flexible and happy to take small groups and to customize itineraries. They are experts on the area, and your custom helps boost the economy of the village. The best time to contact trek leaders at the smaller outfits is often after about 4pm, when they've returned from their last trip. Guides should provide tents, bedrolls, mosquito nets and sleeping bags, plus food and drinking water; trekkers may be asked to help carry some of the gear.

Mae Sot trekking operators

In addition to the specialist agencies listed below, you can also try asking at *Fortune* guest house and at *Bai Fern* and *Krua Canadian* restaurants.

Khun Om C/o *Number 4 Guest House*, 736 Thanon Indharakiri Ⓣ & Ⓕ 055 544976, Ⓦwww.geocities.com/no4guesthouse. The treks run by the taciturn Khun Om get rave reviews. He offers a four-day Tee Lor Su programme for B4500 and – his *pièce de résistance* – a seven-day expedition all the way down to Sangkhlaburi for US$400 per person. Although it can be hard to elicit information from the staff at *Number 4*, full details of the treks are given on their informative website; book ahead if possible.

Mae Sot Conservation Tour Next to *Pim Hut* at 415/17 Thanon Tang Kim Chang Ⓣ055 532818, Ⓔmaesotco@cscoms.com. This eco-conscious outfit offers the four-day Tee Lor Su option for B5500.

Max One Tour In the *D.K. Hotel* plaza at 296/1 Thanon Indharakiri Ⓣ055 542942, Ⓦwww.maxonetour.com. One of two Mae Sot outlets for the efficient, Umphang-based Umphang Hill trek operator (see below); the other branch is SP Tour Ⓣ055 531409 at the Mae Sot Travel Centre on the northern outskirts of town at 14/21 Asia Highway (Highway 105). Prices start at B5500 per person (minimum two people) for three days and two nights to Tee Lor Su if departing from Mae Sot, or B3500 if you make your own way to Umphang. Their three-day trek with rafting on the Umphang River costs B5550 from Mae Sot or B3800 from Umphang. See Umphang Hill below for full details.

Umphang trekking operators

The main English-speaking trek leaders operating out of Umphang at the time of writing are listed below, but you can also arrange treks through staff at *Phu Doi*, *Umphang House* and *Tu Ka Su Guest House*. Note that there are **no exchange facilities** in Umphang so you must bring enough cash to cover the cost of your trek.

BL Tour 1/438 Thanon Umphang-Palata Ⓣ055 561021, Ⓕ055 561322. Enthusiastic and well-informed guides. As well as the standard three- and four-day trips to Tee Lor Su (from B3500), BL also runs two-day rafting and trekking programmes to Thi Lor Leh Falls (B3500/person for four people, B4500 if two people) and one- and two-day options to Umphang Khi. Five-day combination trips are also possible.

Mr Boonchuay 500m west of the wat at 360 Thanon Pravitpaiwan Ⓣ055 561020, Ⓕ055 561470. Umphang-born and bred, Mr Boonchuay knows the area well and has a good reputation; though his English is not perfect, he has English-speaking guides. He does three-day treks for B3700 per person and four-day treks for B4000 (minimum two). Trekkers can stay in the basic concrete rooms for B100 a night.

Trekker Hill 700m northwest of the wat, off Thanon Pravitpaiwan Ⓣ055 561090, Ⓕ055 561328. Mr Tee and his "jungle team" of five guides get good reviews. Runs three- and four-day treks to Tee Lor Su (B3500/B4500); dry season drive-trek-and-raft tours to Tee Lor Su (B2000); one-day raft trips around Umphang Khi (B2000); day-trips to view sunrise over the Doi Hua Mot range, famous for its misty panoramas and its flowering shrubs, plus the Tham Ho Bi cave (B2000). Offers accommodation for trekkers in simple, en-suite double bungalows at B200.

Umphang Hill At *Umphang Hill Resort* on Thanon Umphang-Palata, but can also be booked through Max One Tour in Mae Sot Ⓣ055 561063, Ⓦwww.umphanghill.com. Efficiently run, this place often undercuts rival outfits and has English-speaking staff at the office throughout the day. They do eleven different itineraries in the Umphang area (see website), and tailor-made permutations; most treks are led by local Karen guides. Three-day treks cost B3500; four days B4000 (minimum two people; prices drop with larger groups). From Dec–May, with advance notice, they can also arrange a challenging seven-day trek to Sangkhlaburi (B8000/person, minimum six people).

Accommodation and eating

Most of the **accommodation** in Umphang is geared either towards groups of trekkers accompanied by Thai guides, or towards independent travellers who are overnighting just before or after their trek. Because of this, many places charge per person rather than per room; the categories listed below are for two people sharing a room, so expect to pay half if you're on your own. If you've organized a trek from Bangkok or Mae Sot, accommodation should be included in your package; independent trekkers can usually stay in accommodation at their trek leader's home for about B100 per person (see box on p.304).

Most of the guest houses will at least serve breakfast to their guests. The most popular places for other **meals** are located on Thanon Pravitpaiwan: *Phu Doi Restaurant* (closed Sundays) has an English-language menu of curries and meat-over-rice dishes; *Tom* does very cheap noodle soup, *phat thai* and fried rice; and at dusk night-time foodstalls set up close by the temple and the pharmacy. *Noong Koong* is another cheap noodle shop one block to the west. A bit further out, on Thanon Umphang-Palata, the riverside restaurant at *Umphang Hill Resort* has no English-language menu but serves good authentic Thai restaurant food and features karaoke in the evenings. Nearby *Boonyaporn Garden Huts* has a pleasantly situated riverside bar.

BL Bungalows 2km east of Umphang, bookable through the central tour office at 1/438 Thanon Umphang-Palata ⓣ055 561021, ⓕ055 561322. Nice, simple, en-suite bungalows in a stunning spot a couple of kilometres east of town, surrounded by fields and with fine hill views. There's a restaurant here, but most guests are either doing treks with BL or have their own transport. ❷

Boonyaporn Garden Huts 450m west of the wat at 106 Thanon Umphang-Palata, ⓣ & ⓕ055 561093. A spread of accommodation options, set around a riverside garden, ranging from simple rattan huts with mosquito nets and shared bathrooms to quite attractive wooden en-suite bungalows with decks overlooking the river. Not much English spoken. ❶–❹

Phu Doi Campsite About 500m northwest of the wat at 637 Thanon Pravitpaiwan ⓣ055 561049, ⓦwww.phudoi.com. Decent set of comfortable rooms in a couple of wooden houses with verandas overlooking a pond. All rooms have private bathrooms and there's free tea and coffee. ❸

Tu Ka Su Guest House 300m west up the hill from the river at 129 Thanon Umphang-Palata ⓣ & ⓕ055 561295. In a pretty garden with expansive views over the river, fields and mountains, this quite stylish place offers nicely designed en-suite wooden cabins, with TV. Mountain bikes are available for rent. ❹

Umphang Hill Resort 500m west of the wat at 99 Thanon Umphang-Palata ⓣ055 561063, ⓦwww.umphanghill.com. Attractively set in a flower garden on a slope leading down to the river, with views of the surrounding mountains. Large, basic chalets with veranda, air-con, TV and hot water, plus some trekkers' rooms with B50 mattresses if you come in a group. ❷

Umphang House Thanon Umphang-Palata ⓣ & ⓕ055 561073. Large, pretty well-furnished bungalows, all with bathroom and veranda, around a well-tended garden. Not much English spoken. ❸

Veera Tour Thanon Umphang-Palata ⓣ055 561239, ⓔveeratour@hotmail.com. Decent enough if rather dark rooms with mattresses and shared bathrooms in a large timber house. Not much English spoken. ❷

Travel details

Trains

Ayutthaya to: Bangkok Hualamphong Station (20 daily; 1hr 30min); Chiang Mai (6 daily; 12hr); Lopburi (15 daily; 1hr–1hr 30min); Nong Khai (3 daily; 9hr 30min); Phitsanulok (9 daily; 4hr 30min–5hr 30min); Ubon Ratchathani (7 daily; 8hr 30min–10hr).

Kanchanaburi to: Bangkok Thonburi (2 daily; 3hr); Nakhon Pathom (2 daily; 2hr); Nam Tok (3 daily; 2hr–2hr 30min).

Lopburi to: Ayutthaya (15 daily; 1hr–1hr 30min);

Bangkok Hualamphong Station (15 daily; 2hr 30min–3hr); Chiang Mai (6 daily; 11hr); Phitsanulok (9 daily; 3hr–5hr 15min).
Nakhon Pathom to: Bangkok Hualamphong (11 daily; 1hr 40min); Bangkok Thonburi (3 daily; 1hr 10min); Chumphon (11 daily; 5hr 45 min–8hr 30min); Hat Yai (5 daily; 12hr 15min–16hr); Hua Hin (12 daily; 2hr 15min–3hr 15min); Kanchanaburi (2 daily; 1hr 30min); Nakhon Si Thammarat (2 daily; 15hr); Nam Tok (2 daily; 3hr 30min); Phetchaburi (10 daily; 1hr 20min–2hr 20min); Sungai Kolok (2 daily; 18hr 30min–20hr); Surat Thani (10 daily; 8hr–11hr 30min); Trang (2 daily; 14–15hr).
Nam Tok to: Bangkok Thonburi (2 daily; 5hr).
Phitsanulok to: Ayutthaya (8 daily; 4hr 30min–5hr 30min); Bangkok Hualamphong (10 daily; 5hr 40min–8hr), via Don Muang Airport (4hr 50min–7hr); Chiang Mai (6 daily; 5hr 50min–7hr 40min); Lamphun (6 daily; 5hr 40min–7hr 20min); Lopburi (9 daily; 3hr–5hr 15min).

Buses

Ayutthaya to: Bangkok (every 15min; 2hr); Chiang Mai (12 daily; 8hr); Lopburi (every 20min; 2hr); Phitsanulok (9 daily; 4–5hr); Suphanburi (every 30min; 1hr).
Bang Pa-In to: Bangkok (every 30min; 2hr).
Damnoen Saduak to: Bangkok (every 20min; 2hr).
Kamphaeng Phet to: Bangkok (7 daily; 6hr 30min); Sukhothai (hourly; 1hr–1hr 30min); Tak (hourly; 1hr).
Kanchanaburi to: Bangkok (every 15min; 2hr–3hr); Erawan (every 50min; 1hr 30min–2hr); Nam Tok (every 30min; 1hr 30min); Ratchaburi (every 15min; 2hr); Sai Yok (every 30min; 2hr 30min); Sangkhlaburi (11 daily; 3–6hr); Suphanburi (every 20min; 2hr); Thong Pha Phum (every 30min; 3hr).
Lopburi to: Bangkok (every 20min; 3hr), via Wat Phra Phutthabat (30min); Khorat (9 daily; 3hr 30min); Suphanburi (hourly; 3hr).
Mae Sot to: Bangkok (10 daily; 8hr 30min); Chiang Mai (4 daily; 6hr 30min–7hr 30min); Chiang Rai (2 daily; 11hr); Mae Ramat (every 30min; 45min); Mae Sai (2 daily; 12hr); Mae Sariang (7 daily; 5hr); Phitsanulok (7 daily; 3hr 15min–5hr); Sukhothai (6 daily; 2hr 30min–3hr); Tak (every 30min; 1hr 30min–3hr); Umphang (9 daily; 4hr).
Nakhon Pathom to: Bangkok (every 10min; 40min–1hr 20min); Damnoen Saduak (every 20min; 1hr); Kanchanaburi (every 10min; 1hr 45min).
Nam Tok to: Sangkhlaburi (4 daily; 3hr 30min).
Phitsanulok to: Bangkok (up to 19 daily; 5–6hr); Chiang Mai (up to 18 daily; 5–6hr); Chiang Rai (17 daily; 6–7hr); Kamphaeng Phet (hourly; 3hr); Khon Kaen (10 daily; 5–6hr); Khorat/Nakhon Ratchasima (21 daily; 6–7hr); Loei (15 daily; 5hr); Lomsak (hourly; 2hr); Mae Sot (7 daily; 3hr 15min–5hr); Phrae (7 daily; 2–3hr); Sukhothai (every 30min; 1hr); Tak (every 30min; 2–3hr); Ubon Ratchathani (7 daily; 12hr); Udon Thani (5 daily; 7hr).
Sukhothai to: Bangkok (up to 17 daily; 6–7hr); Chiang Mai (up to 16 daily; 5–6hr); Chiang Rai (4 daily; 8–9hr); Kamphaeng Phet (hourly; 1hr–1hr 30min); Khon Kaen (7 daily; 6–7hr); Mae Sot (7 daily; 2hr 30 min–3hr); Nan (2 daily; 6hr); Phitsanulok (every 30min; 1hr); Si Satchanalai (every 30min; 1hr); Tak (every 90min; 2hr).
Tak to: Bangkok (13 daily; 7hr); Chiang Mai (3 daily; 4–6hr); Kamphaeng Phet (hourly; 1hr); Mae Sot (every 30min; 1hr 30min–3hr); Phitsanulok (every 30min; 2–3hr); Sukhothai (hourly; 1hr 30min).

Flights

Mae Sot to: Bangkok (4 weekly; 1hr 20min).
Phitsanulok to: Bangkok (3 daily; 45min); Chiang Mai (3 weekly; 1hr).
Sukhothai to: Bangkok (daily; 1hr 10min); Chiang Mai (daily; 40min); Louang Phabang (Laos; 5 weekly; 1hr 10min).

3

The north

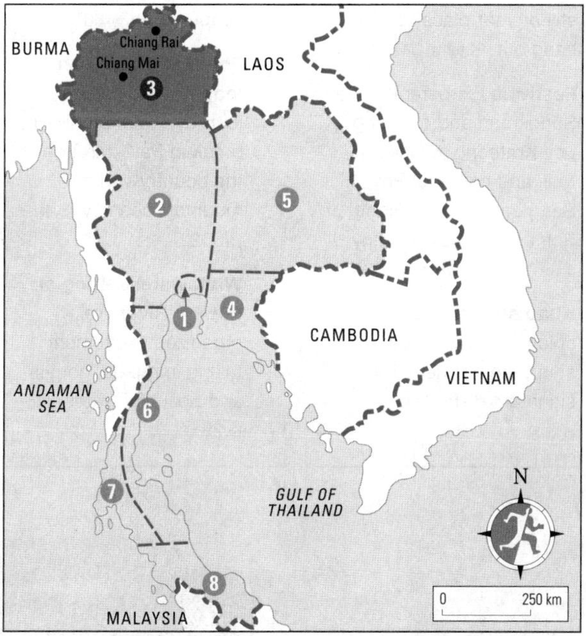
BURMA
Chiang Rai
Chiang Mai
3
LAOS
2
5
1
4
CAMBODIA
VIETNAM
ANDAMAN SEA
6
7
GULF OF THAILAND
8
MALAYSIA
N
0
250 km

CHAPTER 3

Highlights

* **Hill-tribe trekking** A chance to visit these fascinating peoples and explore the dramatic countryside. See p.315
* **Chiang Mai** Old-town temples, cookery courses, the best of Thai crafts, fine restaurants – still a great place to hang out. See p.318
* **Festivals** Exuberant Songkhran and glittering Loy Krathong in Chiang Mai, and colourful Poy Sang Long in Mae Hong Son are the pick of many. See p.335 and p.385
* **Khao soi** Delicious, spicy, creamy noodle soup, the northern Thai signature dish. See p.341
* **Wat Phra That Doi Suthep** Towering views from this stunning example of temple architecture. See p.348
* **Nan** An underrated all-rounder, offering beautiful temple murals, handicrafts and landscapes. See p.366
* **The Mae Hong Son loop** A roller-coaster journey – with a chill-out break in Pai – through the country's wildest mountain scenery. See p.372
* **Whitewater-rafting on the Pai River** Well-organized excitement taking in rapids, gorges and beautiful waterfalls. p.391

△ Mae Sariang

3

The north

Travelling up through the central plains, there's no mistaking when you've reached the **north** of Thailand: somewhere between Uttaradit and Den Chai, the train slows almost to a halt, as if approaching a frontier post, to meet the abruptly rising mountains, which continue largely unbroken to the borders of Burma and Laos. Beyond this point the climate becomes more temperate, nurturing the fertile land which gave the old kingdom of the north the name of **Lanna**, "the land of a million rice fields". Although only one-tenth of the land can be used for rice cultivation, the valley rice fields here are three times more productive than those in the dusty northeast, and the higher land yields a great variety of fruits, as well as beans, groundnuts and tobacco.

Until the beginning of the last century, Lanna was a largely independent region. On the back of its agricultural prosperity, it developed its own styles of art and architecture, which can still be seen in its flourishing temples and distinctive handicraft traditions. The north is also set apart from the rest of the country by its exuberant way with festivals, a cuisine which has been heavily influenced by Burma and a dialect quite distinct from central Thai. Northerners proudly call themselves *khon muang*, "people of the principalities", and their gentle sophistication is admired by the people of Bangkok, whose wealthier citizens build their holiday homes in the clean air of the north's forested mountains.

Chiang Mai, the capital and transport centre of the north, is a great place just to hang out or to prepare for a journey into the hills. For many travellers, this means joining a trek to visit one or more of the **hill tribes**, who comprise one-tenth of the north's population and are just about clinging onto the ways of life which distinguish them from one another and the Thais around them. For those with qualms about the exploitative element of this ethnological tourism, there are plenty of other, more independent options. To the west, the trip to **Mae Hong Son** takes you through the most stunning mountain scenery in the region into a land with its roots across the border in Burma, with the option of looping back through **Pai**, a laid-back hill station for travellers. Bidding to rival Chiang Mai as a base for exploring the countryside is **Chiang Rai** to the north; above Chiang Rai, the northernmost tip of Thailand is marked by the fascinating, schizophrenic border town of **Mae Sai**, and the junction of Laos and Burma at **Sop Ruak**. Fancifully dubbed the "Golden Triangle", Sop Ruak is a must on every bus party's itinerary – you're more likely to find peace and quiet among the ruins of nearby **Chiang Saen**, set on the leafy banks of the Mekong River. Few visitors backtrack south from Chiang Mai, even though the towns of **Lamphun**, **Lampang** and **Phrae** are packed with artistic and historical goodies. Further out on a limb to the east, **Nan** is even less popular, but combines rich mountain scenery with eclectic temple art.

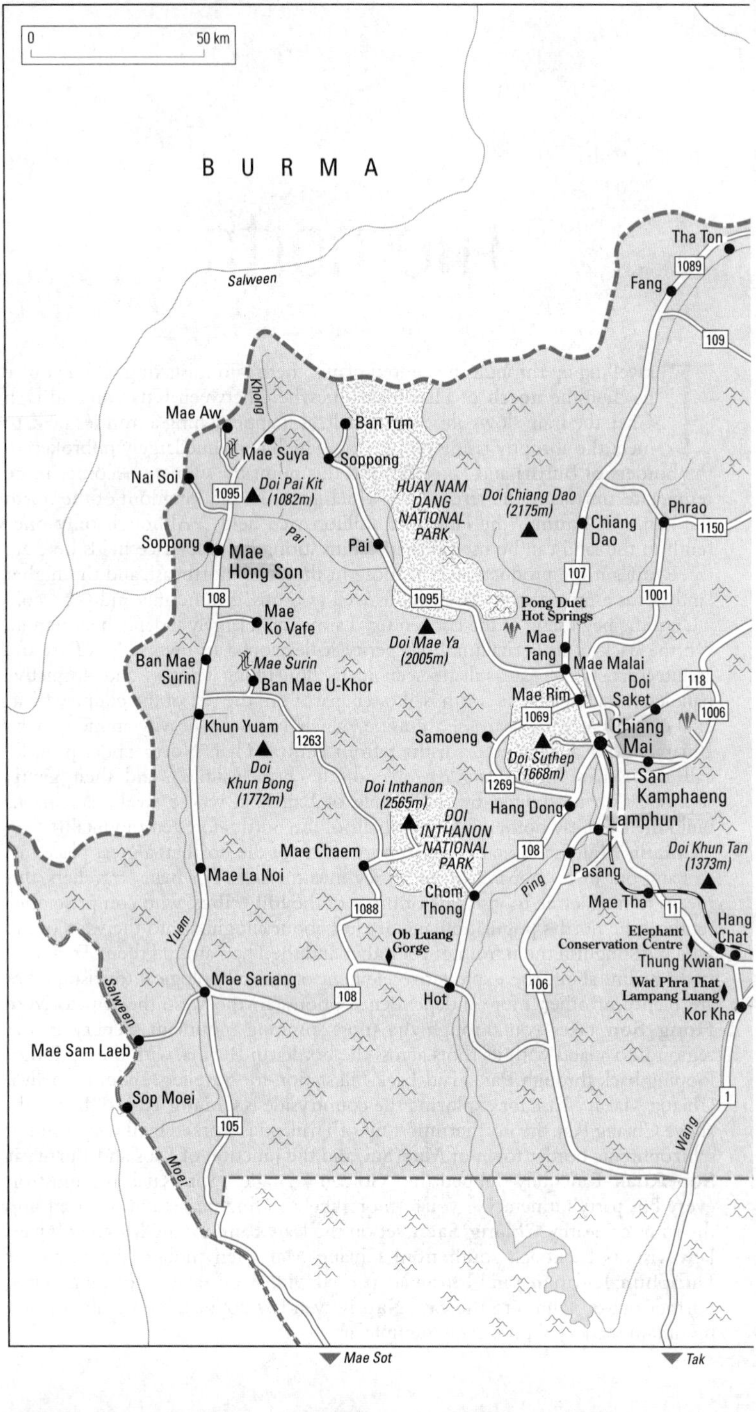
0
50 km
BURMA
Salween
Tha Ton
1089
Fang
109
Khong
Mae Aw
Ban Tum
Mae Suya
Soppong
Nai Soi
1095
Doi Pai Kit (1082m)
HUAY NAM DANG NATIONAL PARK
Doi Chiang Dao (2175m)
Chiang Dao
Phrao
1150
Pai
Soppong
Mae Hong Son
Pai
107
1001
108
1095
Pong Duet Hot Springs
Mae Ko Vafe
Doi Mae Ya (2005m)
Mae Tang
Ban Mae Surin
Mae Surin
Mae Malai
Doi Saket
118
Ban Mae U-Khor
Mae Rim
1006
1069
Khun Yuam
Chiang Mai
Samoeng
1263
Doi Suthep (1668m)
Doi Khun Bong (1772m)
San Kamphaeng
1269
Doi Inthanon (2565m)
Hang Dong
DOI INTHANON NATIONAL PARK
Lamphun
Mae Chaem
108
Doi Khun Tan (1373m)
Mae La Noi
Pasang
Ping
Chom Thong
Mae Tha
11
1088
Hang Chat
Yuam
Ob Luang Gorge
Elephant Conservation Centre
Thung Kwian
Mae Sariang
Wat Phra That Lampang Luang
108
Hot
106
Kor Kha
Salween
Mae Sam Laeb
1
Sop Moei
105
Wang
Moei
Mae Sot
Tak

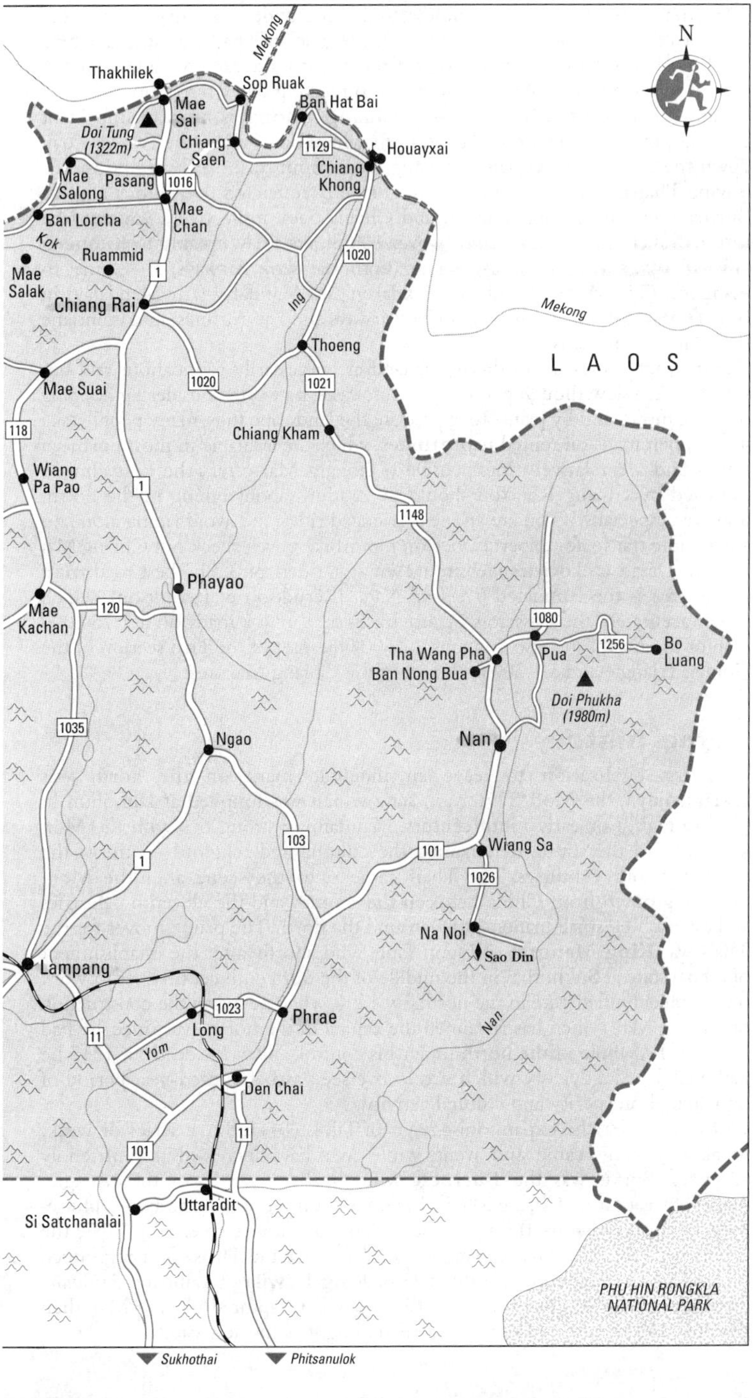
N
Mekong
Thakhilek
Sop Ruak
Mae Sai
Ban Hat Bai
Doi Tung (1322m)
Chiang Saen
1129
Houayxai
Mae Salong
Pasang
1016
Chiang Khong
Mae Chan
Ban Lorcha
Kok
Ruammid
1020
Mae Salak
1
Chiang Rai
Ing
Mekong
Thoeng
LAOS
Mae Suai
1020
1021
118
Chiang Kham
Wiang Pa Pao
1
1148
Phayao
1080
Mae Kachan
120
Tha Wang Pha
Pua
1256
Bo Luang
Ban Nong Bua
Doi Phukha (1980m)
1035
Ngao
Nan
103
101
Wiang Sa
1
1026
Na Noi
Sao Din
Lampang
1023
Phrae
Long
Nan
11
Yom
Den Chai
11
101
Uttaradit
Si Satchanalai
PHU HIN RONGKLA NATIONAL PARK
Sukhothai
Phitsanulok

An attempt by the Thai government to develop trade and tourism across the northern frontiers, forming a "Golden Quadrangle" of Thailand, Burma, China and Laos, has as yet made little progress, the countries so far having had limited success in trying to cajole one another into relaxing entry restrictions. East of Chiang Saen on the Mekong River, **Chiang Khong** is now an important crossing point to Houayxai in Laos, from where boats make the two-day trip down the Mekong to Louang Phabang. Apart from this, overland options for leaving Thailand in this direction are currently restricted to arduous trips to Burma and China, from Mae Sai and Chiang Saen respectively. Chiang Mai International Airport now handles over 100 flights a day, notably to Kunming (Thai Airways), Jinghong and Xi'an (both Bangkok Airways) in China, to Rangoon (Thai Airways and Air Mandalay) and Mandalay (Air Mandalay) in Burma, and to Louang Phabang (Thai Airways and Lao Airlines) and Vientiane (Lao Airlines) in Laos.

Transport routes in northern Thailand are necessarily roundabout and bus services often slow, though frequent: in some cases, it's worth considering hopping over the mountains by plane. To appreciate the landscape fully, many people take to the open roads on rented **motorbikes**, which are available in most northern towns and are relatively inexpensive – Chiang Mai offers the best choice, followed by Chiang Rai. You should be cautious about biking in the north, however, especially if you are an inexperienced rider, and avoid riding alone on any remote trails – for expert advice on motorbike travel, check out Chiang Mai resident David Unkovich's website (ⓦ www.gt-rider.com). The best road **map** of the area is the laminated *Thailand North* (Berndtson & Berndtson), which shows accurately the crisscross of dirt tracks and minor roads on a 1:750,000 map of the north, and also contains a 1:500,000 inset of the Thai section of the Golden Triangle and a 1:300,000 inset of the Chiang Mai area.

Some history

The first civilization to leave an indelible mark on the north was **Haripunjaya**, the Mon (Dvaravati) state which was founded at Lamphun in the late eighth or early ninth century. Maintaining strong ties with the Mon kingdoms to the south, it remained the cultural and religious centre of the north for four centuries. The Thais came onto the scene after the Mon, migrating down from China between the seventh and the eleventh centuries and establishing small principalities around the north. The prime mover for the Thais was **King Mengrai** of Ngon Yang, who, shortly after the establishment of a Thai state at Sukhothai in the middle of the thirteenth century, set to work on a parallel unified state in the north. By 1296, when he began the construction of Chiang Mai, which has remained the capital of the north ever since, he had brought the whole of the north under his control, and at his death in 1317 he had established a dynasty which was to oversee a two-hundred-year period of unmatched prosperity and cultural activity.

However, after the expansionist reign of Tilok (1441–87), a series of weak, squabbling kings came and went, while Ayutthaya increased its unfriendly advances. But it was the **Burmese** who finally snuffed out the Mengrai dynasty by capturing Chiang Mai in 1558, and for most of the next two centuries they controlled Lanna through a succession of puppet rulers. In 1767, the Burmese sacked the Thai capital at Ayutthaya, but the Thais soon regrouped under King Taksin, who with the help of **King Kawila** of Lampang gradually drove the Burmese northwards. In 1774 Kawila recaptured Chiang Mai, then deserted and in ruins, and set about rebuilding it as his new capital.

Kawila was succeeded as ruler of the north by a series of incompetent princes for much of the nineteenth century, until colonialism reared its head. After Britain took control of Upper Burma, **Rama V** of Bangkok began to take an interest in the north – where, since the Bowring Treaty of 1855, the British had established lucrative logging businesses – to prevent its annexation. He forcibly moved large numbers of ethnic Thais northwards, in order to counter the British claim of sovereignty over territory occupied by Thai Yai (Shan), who also make up a large part of the population of Upper Burma. In 1877 Rama V appointed a commissioner over Chiang Mai, Lamphun and Lampang to better integrate the region with the centre, and links were further strengthened in 1921 with the arrival of the railway from Bangkok. Since then the north has built on its agricultural richness to become relatively prosperous, though the economic booms of the last two decades have been concentrated, as elsewhere in Thailand, in the towns, due in no small part to the increase in tourism. The eighty percent of Lanna's population who live in rural areas, of which the vast majority are subsistence farmers, are finding it increasingly difficult to earn a living off the soil, due to rapid population growth and land speculation for tourism and agro-industry.

Hill-tribe treks

Trekking in the mountains of north Thailand differs from trekking in most other parts of the world in that the emphasis is not primarily on the scenery but on the region's inhabitants. Northern Thailand's **hill tribes**, now numbering over 800,000 people living in around 3500 villages, have so far preserved their subsistence-oriented way of life with comparatively little change over thousands of years; see p.836 for more on the tribes themselves. In recent years, the term **mountain people** (a translation of the Thai *chao khao*) is increasingly used as a less condescending way to describe them; since these groups have no chief, they are technically not tribes. While some of the villages are near enough to a main road to be reached on a day-trip from a major town, to get to the other, more traditional villages usually entails joining a hastily assembled guided party for a few days, roughing it in a different place each night. For most visitors, however, these hardships are far outweighed by the experience of encountering peoples of so different a culture, travelling through beautiful tropical countryside and tasting the excitement of elephant-riding and river-rafting.

On any trek you are necessarily confronted by the **ethics** of your role. Over a hundred thousand travellers now go trekking in Thailand each year, the majority heading to certain well-trodden areas such as the Mae Taeng valley, 40km northwest of Chiang Mai, and the hills around the Kok River west of Chiang Rai. Beyond the basic level of disturbance caused by any tourism, this steady flow of trekkers creates pressures for the traditionally insular hill tribes. Foreigners unfamiliar with hill-tribe customs can easily cause grave offence, especially those who go looking for drugs. Though tourism acts as a distraction from their traditional way of life, most tribespeople are genuinely welcoming and hospitable to foreigners, appreciating the contact with Westerners and the minimal material benefits which trekking brings them. Nonetheless, to minimize disruption, it's important to take a responsible attitude when trekking. While it's possible to trek **independently**, the lone trekker will learn very little without a guide as intermediary, and is far more likely to commit an unwitting offence against the local customs, so it's best to go with a sensitive and knowledgeable **guide** who has the welfare of the local people in mind, and follow the basic guidelines on etiquette outlined in the box above. If you don't fancy an organized trek in a group as described below, it's possible to hire a personal guide from an agent, for which rates begin at about B600 per day.

The hill tribes are big business in northern Thailand: in **Chiang Mai** there are over two hundred agencies which between them cover just about all the trekkable areas in the north. **Chiang Rai** is the second-biggest trekking centre, and agencies can also be found in **Mae Hong Son**, **Pai** and **Nan**, which usually arrange treks only to the villages in their immediate area. Guided trekking on a much smaller scale than in the north is available in Umphang (see p.304), Kanchanaburi (see p.235) and Sangkhlaburi (see p.246).

The basics

The right **clothing** is the first essential on any trek. Strong boots with ankle protection are the best footwear, although in the dry season training shoes are adequate. Wear thin, loose clothes – long trousers should be worn to protect against thorns and, in the wet season, leeches – and a hat, and cover your arms if you're prone to sunburn. Antiseptic, antihistamine, anti-diarrhoea **medicine** and insect repellent are essential, and a mosquito net is a good idea. At least two

Trekking etiquette

As the guests, it's up to farangs to adapt to the customs of the hill tribes and not to make a nuisance of themselves. Apart from keeping an open mind and not demanding too much of your hosts, a few **simple rules** should be observed.

❑ Dress modestly, in long trousers or skirt (or at least knee-length shorts if you must) and a T-shirt or shirt.

❑ Loud voices and boisterous behaviour are out of place. Smiling and nodding establishes good intent. A few hill-tribe phrasebooks and dictionaries are available from bookshops and you'll be a big hit if you learn some words of the relevant language.

❑ If travelling with a loved one, avoid displays of public affection such as kissing, which are extremely distasteful, and disrespectful, to local people.

❑ Before entering a hill-tribe village, look out for taboo signs (*ta-laew*), woven bamboo strips on the ground outside the village entrance; these mean a special ceremony is taking place and that you should not enter. Similar signs stuck on the roof above a house entrance or a fresh tree branch mean the same thing. Be careful about what you touch; in Akha villages, keep your hands off cult structures like the entrance gates and the giant swing. Ask first before entering a house, and do not step or sit on the door sill, which is often considered the domain of the house spirits. If the house has a raised floor on stilts, take off your shoes. Most hill-tribe houses contain a religious shrine: do not touch or photograph this shrine, or sit underneath it. If you are permitted to watch a ceremony, this is not an invitation to participate unless asked. Like the villagers themselves, you'll be expected to pay a fine for any violation of local customs.

❑ Some villagers like to be photographed, most do not. Point at your camera and nod if you want to take a photograph. Never insist if the answer is an obvious "no". Be particularly careful with the sick and the old, and with pregnant women and babies – most tribes believe cameras affect the soul of the foetus or new-born.

❑ Taking gifts can be dubious practice. If you want to take something, writing materials for children and clothing are welcome, as well as sewing tools (like needles) for women – ask your guide to pass any gifts to the village headman for fair distribution. However, money, sweets and cigarettes may encourage begging and create unhealthy tastes.

❑ Do not ask for opium, as this will offend your hosts. Getting dressed or changing your clothes in front of villagers is also offensive.

changes of clothing are needed, plus a sarong or towel (women in particular should bring a sarong to wash or change underneath).

If you're going on an organized trek, **water** is usually provided by the guide, as well as a small backpack. **Blankets** or, preferably, a **sleeping bag** are also supplied, but might not be warm enough in the cool season, when night-time temperatures can dip to freezing; you should bring at least a sweater, and buy a cheap, locally made balaclava to be sure of keeping the chill off.

It's wise not to take anything valuable with you; most guest houses in trekking-orientated places like Chiang Mai have safes and left-luggage rooms, but check that the guest house is long-established and has a good reputation before you consider leaving your things, and then make sure you sign an inventory.

Organized treks

Organized treks can be as short as two days or as long as ten, but are typically of three or four days' duration. The standard size of a group is between six and twelve people, with an average size of eight; being part of a small group is preferable, enabling you to strike a more informative relationship with your guides and with the villagers. Everybody in the group usually sleeps on a bamboo floor or platform in the headman's hut, with a guide cooking communal meals, for which some ingredients are brought from outside and others are found locally.

Each trek usually follows a regular itinerary established by the agency, although they can sometimes be customized, especially for smaller groups and with agencies in the smaller towns. Some itineraries are geared towards serious hikers while others go at a much gentler pace, but on all treks much of the walking will be up and down steep forested hills, often under a burning sun, so a reasonable level of fitness is required. Many treks now include a ride on an elephant and a trip on a bamboo raft – exciting to the point of being dangerous if the river is running fast. The typical trek of three days' duration costs about B1800–2000 in Chiang Mai (including transport, accommodation, food and guide), sometimes less in other towns, much less without rafting and elephant-riding.

There are several features to look out for when **choosing a trek**. If you want to trek with a small group, get an assurance from your agency that you won't be tagged onto a larger group. Make sure the trek has at least two guides – a leader and a back-marker; some trekkers have been known to get lost for days after becoming separated from the rest of the group. Ask about transport from base at the beginning and end of the trek; most treks begin with a pick-up ride out of town, but on rare occasions the trip can entail a long public bus ride. If at all possible, meet and chat with the other trekkers, as well as the guides, who should speak reasonable English and know about hill-tribe culture, especially the details of etiquette in each village. Finally, ask what food will be eaten, check how much walking is involved per day and get a copy of the route map to gauge the terrain.

While everybody and their grandmother act as **agents**, only a few know their guides personally, so choose a reputable agent. (Note that many guest houses who offer trekking don't employ their own guides and so on, but just take a commission from outside trekking agents.) When picking an agent, you should check whether they and their guides have licences and certificates from the Tourist Authority of Thailand, which they should be able to show you: this ensures at least a minimum level of training, and provides some comeback in case of problems. Word of mouth is often the best recommendation, so if you hear of a good outfit, try it. Each trek should be **registered** with the tourist police, stating the itinerary, the duration and the participants, in case the party encounters any trouble – it's worth checking with the agency that the trek has been registered with the tourist police before departure.

Independent trekking

The options for **independent trekking** are limited, chiefly by logistics, security risks and poor mapping of the area. A series of green Royal Thai Survey Department 1:50,000 maps are available at Surawong bookshop on Thanon Sri Dornchai in Chiang Mai at B135 each, but each one covers a very limited area. For most independent travellers, the only feasible approach is to use as a base one of the few farang-oriented rural **guest houses** in the north, such as *Wilderness Lodge* near Mae Suya (see p.388), *Cave Lodge* at Ban Tum (see p.389), *Lisu Lodge* near Soppong (see p.322) and *Malee's Nature Lovers Bungalows* near Chiang Dao (see p.396). They're generally set deep in the countryside, within walking range of several hill-tribe villages, about which the owner can give information in English.

If you're confident about finding your way round, it's possible to find **accommodation** in hill-tribe villages themselves. It helps if you speak some Thai, but most villagers, if you hang around for any time, will ask (with the usual "sleep" gesture) if you want to stay. It is usual to stay in the headman's house on a guest platform, but increasingly villages are building small guest houses. Expect to pay at least B50 per night – for this, you will often be offered dinner and breakfast. It's safe to accept plain rice, boiled drinks and food that's boiled or fried in your presence, but you're taking a risk with anything else, as it's not unusual for foreigners to suffer food poisoning. Most villages are safe to stay in; to safeguard yourself against the risk of armed bandits who sporadically rob foreigners, try to check with local guides and the district police in the area where you intend to trek.

Chiang Mai

Although rapid economic progress in recent years – due largely to tourism – has brought its share of problems, not least concern about traffic jams and fumes, **CHIANG MAI** manages to preserve some of the atmosphere of an ancient settlement alongside its modern urban sophistication. It's regarded as the kingdom's second city, with a population of about 250,000, but the contrast with the maelstrom of Bangkok is pronounced: the people here are famously easy-going and even speak more slowly than their cousins in the capital, while the old quarter, set within a two-kilometre-square moat, has retained many of its traditional wooden houses and quiet, leafy gardens. Chiang Mai's elegant temples are the primary tourist sights, but these are no pre-packaged museum pieces – they're living community centres, where you're quite likely to be approached by monks keen to chat and practise their English. Inviting craft shops, good-value accommodation, rich cuisine and riverside bars further enhance the city's allure, making Chiang Mai a place that detains many travellers longer than they expected. Several colourful festivals attract throngs of visitors here too: Chiang Mai is considered one of the best places in Thailand to see in the Thai New Year – Songkhran – in mid-April, and to celebrate Loy Krathong at the full moon in November, when thousands of candles are floated down the Ping River in lotus-leaf boats.

Founded as the capital of Lanna in 1296, on a site indicated by the miraculous presence of deer and white mice, Chiang Mai – "New City" – has remained the north's most important settlement ever since. Lanna's golden age under the Mengrai dynasty, when most of the city's notable temples were founded, lasted until the Burmese captured the city in 1558. Two hundred years passed before the Thais pushed the Burmese back beyond Chiang Mai to roughly where they are now, and the **Burmese influence** is still strong – not just in art and architecture, but also in the rich curries and soups served here. After the recapture of the city, the *chao* (princes) of Chiang Mai remained nominal rulers of the north until 1939, but, with communications rapidly improving from the beginning of the last century, Chiang Mai was brought firmly into Thailand's mainstream as the region's administrative and service centre.

The traditional tourist activities in Chiang Mai are visiting the **temples** and **shopping** for handicrafts, pursuits which many find more appealing here than in the rest of Thailand. These days, increasing numbers of travellers are taking advantage of the city's relaxed feel to indulge in a burst of self-improvement, enrolling for **courses** in **cookery**, **massage** and the like (see box on p.330). However, a pilgrimage to **Doi Suthep**, the mountain to the west of town, should not be missed, to see the sacred temple and the towering views over the valley of the Ping River, when weather permits. Beyond the city limits, a number of other day-trips can be made, such as to the ancient temples of Lamphun or to the orchid farms and elephant shows of the Mae Sa valley – and, of course, Chiang Mai is the main centre for hill-tribe **trekking**.

Arrival, information and city transport

Bounded by a huge ring road, the Superhighway, Chiang Mai divides roughly into two main parts: the **old town**, surrounded by the well-maintained moat and occasional remains of the city wall, where you'll find most of Chiang Mai's traditional wats, and the **new town centre**, between the moat and the Ping River to the east, for hotels, shops, banks and travel agents. The main concentration of guest houses and restaurants hangs between the two, centred on the landmark of **Tha Pae Gate** (*Pratu Tha Pae*) in the middle of the east moat.

Many people arrive at the **train station** (which has a left-luggage office) on Thanon Charoen Muang, just over 2km from Tha Pae Gate on the eastern side of town (☎053 244795 or 053 245363–4), or at the **Arcade bus station** on Thanon Kaeo Nawarat (☎053 242664), 3km out to the northeast. Getting from either of these to the centre is easy by songthaew or tuk-tuk (see "City transport" below). Coming south from Fang or Tha Ton, you'll wind up at the **Chang Phuak bus station** on Thanon Chotana (Thanon Chang Phuak), 500m from the city centre's northern Chang Phuak Gate and 2km northwest of the accommodation concentration around Tha Pae Gate. If you insist on travelling with one of the low-cost private bus companies (see p.36) on Bangkok's Thanon Khao San, find out exactly where you'll be dropped in Chiang Mai before making a booking: many of these companies' buses stop on a remote part of the Superhighway, where they "sell" their passengers to various guest-house touts. There's no obligation to go with the touts, but if you try to duck out you'll have a hard job getting downtown and you'll certainly come in for a lot of hassle. The better guest houses – certainly including those we've listed – don't involve themselves in such shenanigans.

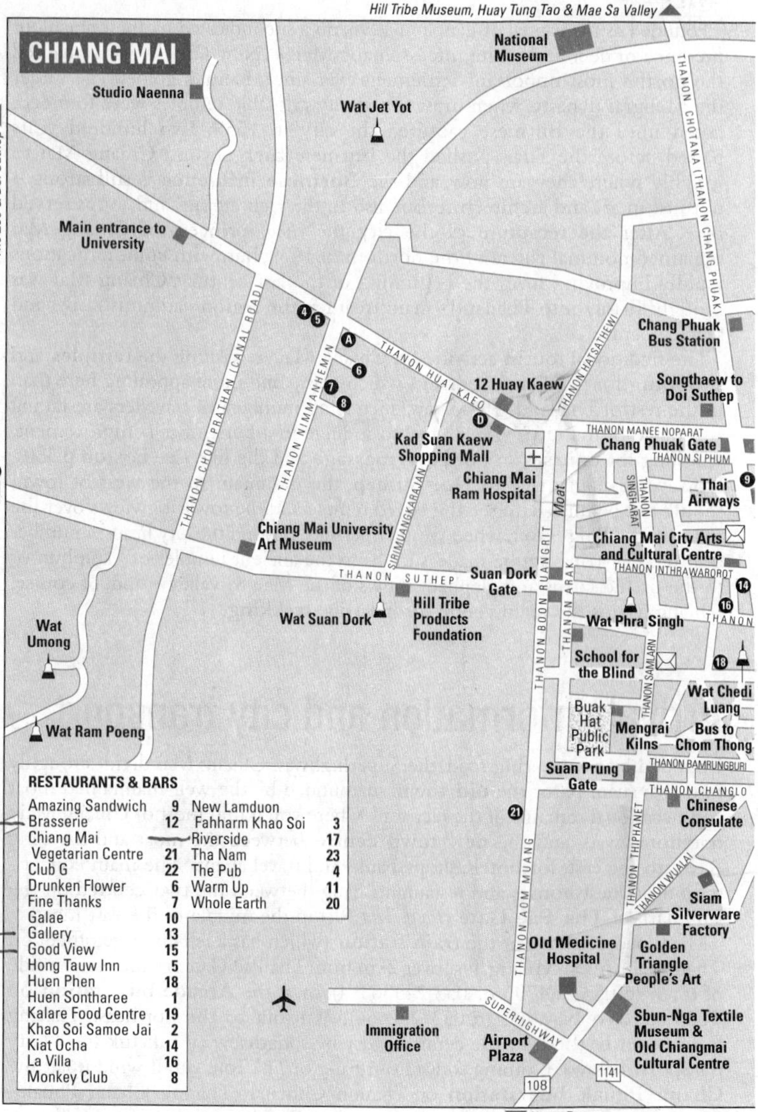

Arriving at the **airport**, 3km southwest of the centre (☎053 270222–34), you'll find currency exchange and left-luggage facilities, a restaurant and a bookshop, an Avis car rental office (☎053 201574), a post office with overseas phone facilities (daily 8.30am–8pm) and a Thai Hotels Association accommodation booking desk (☎053 922129), with prices generally cheaper than rack rates. A well-organized taxi system charges, for example, around B150 for a car to the TAT office in the city centre. If you book accommodation in advance, many hotels and guest houses will pick you up for free from the bus or train station or the airport.

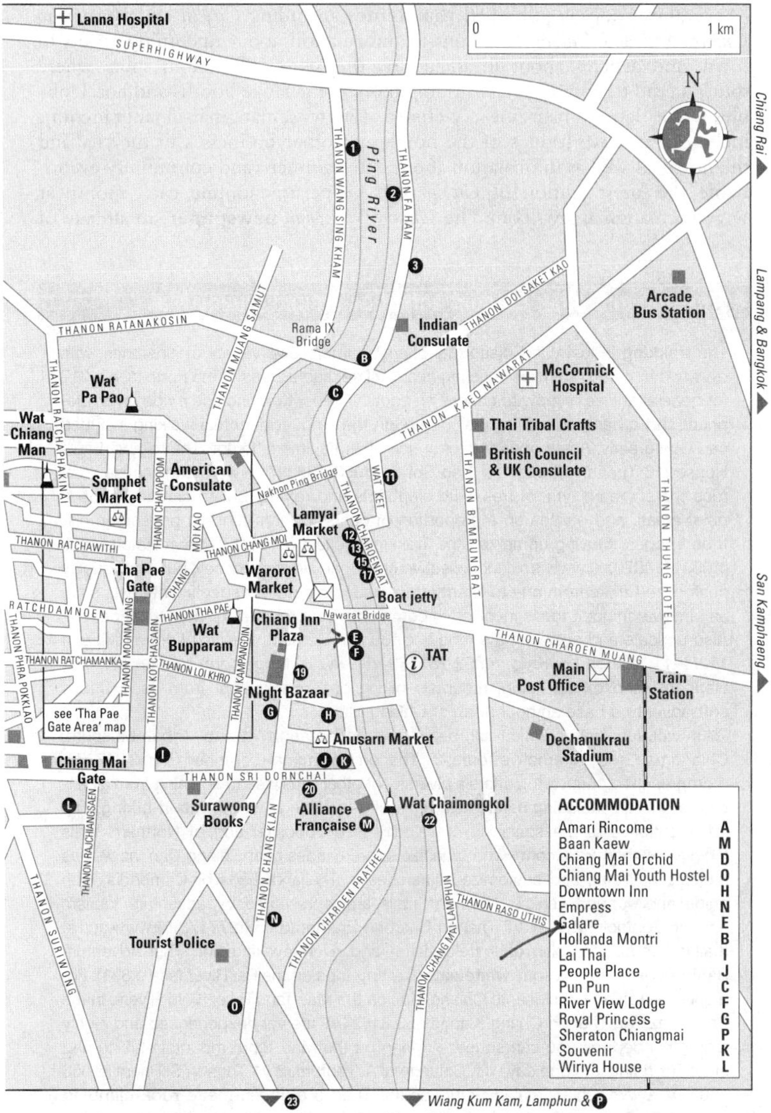

Information

TAT operates out of a swish **information** office (daily 8.30am–4.30pm; ⓣ053 248607 or 053 302500, ⓔtatchmai@tat.or.th) at 105/1 Thanon Chiang Mai–Lamphun, on the east bank of the river south of Nawarat Bridge, where you can pick up handouts and a simple free **map** of the city. *Nancy Chandler's Map of Chiang Mai*, sold in many outlets in the city (B140), is very handy for a detailed exploration: like her brightly coloured Bangkok map, it gives a personal choice of sights, shops, restaurants and various oddities, as well as transport information.

Several free, locally published **magazines**, including *Citylife* and *Welcome to Chiang Mai and Chiang Rai*, contain information about upcoming events in town, and articles about local culture; they're distributed in spots where tourists tend to congregate, including money-exchange booths and hotel lobbies. The latter magazine's **website** (ⓦwww.chiangmai-chiangrai.com), includes extensive listings of the hotels and other businesses in the city and the north, as well as information about entertainment and community events, while the latest edition of *Citylife* can be perused online each month at ⓦwww.chiangmainews.com. The *Chiang Mai Mail* **newspaper**, an affiliate of

Trekking and other outdoor activities around Chiang Mai

The **trekking** industry in Chiang Mai offers an impressive variety of itineraries, with over two hundred agencies covering nearly all trekkable areas of the north (see p.317 for general advice on how to choose an agency). Most treks include a ride on an elephant and a bamboo-raft excursion, though the amount of actual walking included can vary greatly. A few operators offer something a little different. The reliable Eagle House (16 Thanon Chang Moi Kao Soi 3, ⓣ053 235387, ⓦwww.eaglehouse.com) runs the standard type of trek, with elephants and rafting, but to carefully chosen quiet areas, and passes on a proportion of costs towards funding projects in hill-tribe villages. Moving upmarket, the Trekking Collective (25/1 Thanon Ratchawithi, ⓣ053 419079, ⓦwww.trekkingcollective.com) can arrange pricey but high-quality customized treks from one to twenty days and can cater for specific interests such as bird-watching; it too is involved in community programmes to help tribal people. Also upscale and also with a strong eco-tourism element, the *Lisu Lodge* (office at 172/1–11 Thanon Loi Khro, ⓣ053 281789, ⓦwww.lisulodge.com) lays on trekking, elephant- and oxcart-riding, mountain-biking and river-rafting, from its luxurious soft-adventure base an hour north of Chiang Mai.

As well as treks, which all begin with orientation at the Tribal Museum, Chiangmai Green Alternative Tours, 31 Thanon Chiangmai–Lamphun (ⓣ053 247374, ⓔcmgreent@cmnet.co.th), offers a diversity of other trips lasting anything from a half-day to a week, including nature field trips, bird-watching and **mountain-biking**. The last-mentioned is the speciality of Velocity (see opposite) and of Northern Trails (ⓦwww.northerntrails.com), who organize one-day rides near Chiang Dao, as well as multiple day-trips and customized itineraries in Thailand, Laos or Cambodia, with guide and support vehicle. Northern Trails are represented by adventure tourism agency Contact Travel, 73/7 Thanon Charoen Prathet (ⓣ053 277178, ⓦwww.activethailand.com), who also offer treks, lake- and river-kayaking and Thai Adventure Rafting's excellent two-day **whitewater-rafting** trips on the Pai River (see p.391). For a one-day rafting trip closer to Chiang Mai, on the Mae Tang River, Wild Rivers, in the Peak Plaza on Thanon Chang Klan (ⓣ053 818244), are very experienced and highly recommended. Or you can squeeze rafting on the Mae Tang, mountain-biking and elephant-riding into one day with Chiangmai Adventure, 23/1 Thanon Si Phum (ⓣ053 418197, ⓦwww.chiangmaiadventure.co.th). There's a fifteen-metre **rock-climbing** wall at The Peak on Thanon Chang Klan (ⓣ053 820777 or 01 716 4032, ⓦwww.thepeakthailand.com), where you can take three-day courses and arrange one-day trips to Crazy Horse Buttress, a limestone outcrop in the San Kamphaeng area, 50km east of town, which offers highly varied climbing with more than seventy routes, or longer climbing trips to Kiew Lom Reservoir near Lampang, including camping and kayaking. Chiang Mai Rock Climbing Adventures, 55/3 Thanon Ratchaphakinai (ⓣ06 911 1470, ⓦwww.thailandclimbing.com), also lead climbing and caving trips and a wide range of courses to Crazy Horse, with experienced US-trained guides, and offer equipment rental, crag info and a partner-finding service.

the *Pattaya Mail*, is good for local news and entertainment listings, coming out every Saturday. If you expect to stay in Chiang Mai for any length of time, *Exploring Chiang Mai – City, Valley and Mountains* (B495), a **guidebook** by local resident Oliver Hargreave, is a worthwhile investment, as it is packed with useful information about lesser-known temples and attractions, and suggestions for trips out of town.

City transport

Although you can comfortably walk between the most central temples, **bicycles** are the best way of looking round the old town and, with a bit of legwork, getting to the attractions outside the moat. Trusty sit-up-and-beg models and basic mountain bikes are available at many outlets on the roads along the eastern moat for B30–50 a day, while Velocity, 177 Thanon Chang Phuak (Ⓣ053 410665 or 01 595 5975, Ⓔvelocity@thaimail.com), rents (B150/day) and sells better-quality road and mountain bikes and organizes guided cycling tours. If you don't fancy pedalling through the heat and pollution, consider a **motorbike** – there are plenty for rent (from around B100/day; see p.346 for addresses of outlets), though these really come into their own for exploring places around Chiang Mai and in the rest of the north.

Bus services in Chiang Mai come and go, and currently there is only one, not very useful, circular route, covered by purple air-con buses (B10), running from Thanon Wualai past the airport to the west moat, the north moat, Thanon Phra Pokklao, across to Warorot market, down Thanon Chang Klan and back along the south moat. By far the best means of public transport are the red **songthaews** (other colours serve outlying villages), which act as shared taxis within the city, picking up a number of people headed in roughly the same direction and taking each to their specific destination. The charge for an average, popular journey in town, say from Tha Pae Gate to Wat Phra Singh, is currently B10, but it'll naturally cost more to go somewhere off the beaten track or if the driver thinks you want to charter (*mao*) the whole vehicle. Plans have recently been mooted to take old songthaews off the road when they're clapped out and replace them with meter taxis rather than new songthaews.

Chiang Mai is also stuffed with **tuk-tuks**, for which heavy bargaining is expected – allow around B50 for getting from the train station to Tha Pae Gate. They're quick and useful on arrival and departure, and are quite reasonable if you're in a group. The town still has a few **samlors**, which are cheap when used by locals to haul produce home from the market, but not so cheap when chartered by groups of upmarket tourists on sightseeing tours from their hotel.

Accommodation

Chiang Mai is well stocked with all kinds of **accommodation**; usually there are plenty of beds to go around, but many places fill up from December to February and at festival time, particularly during Songkhran (April) and Loy Krathong (November). At these times, you need to book to stay at one of the expensive hotels, and for guest houses it's a good idea to phone ahead – even if you can't book a place, you can save yourself a journey if the place is full.

Many touts at the bus and train stations offer a free ride if you stay at a particular guest house, but you'll probably find that the price of a room is bumped up to pay for your ride – try phoning guest houses, who may pick you up for free to avoid paying commission to the touts. For much of the year there's little need for air-con in Chiang Mai, though the more expensive air-conditioned rooms are usually more spacious and come with hot-water bathrooms, which is a plus in cooler weather. Some places can arrange to switch the air-con option off and charge you the fan-room rate.

Though many guest houses offer use of their safes as a free service, some charge up to B30 per day. Be sure that you can trust the proprietor before you leave valuables in one of the safes or excess baggage in one of the left-luggage rooms while you go off trekking (choose one of the more well-established guest houses, as they're more conscious of the need to maintain their reputation); make a detailed inventory to be signed by both parties, because the hair-raising stories of theft and credit-card abuse are often true.

Inexpensive

In all ways that matter, the choice of **budget guest houses** is better in Chiang Mai than in Bangkok: they're generally friendlier, quieter and more atmospheric and comfortable, and often have their own outdoor cafés. In most budget places you can now get a hot shower, even if it's just in a shared bathroom, while a lot of the more successful places below have developed a few fancier rooms with air-con. Many of the least expensive places make their money from hill-tribe trekking, which can be convenient as a trek often needs a lot of organizing beforehand, but equally can be annoying if you're in Chiang Mai for other reasons and are put under pressure to trek, as can happen at some guest houses; most of the places listed below can arrange trekking, but at none of them should you get this kind of undue hassle.

Most low-cost places are gathered on the surprisingly quiet sois around the eastern side of the old moat and Tha Pae Gate. This puts you between the old town and the new town, in the middle of a larder of Thai and travellers' restaurants.

Chiang Mai Youth Hostel 21/8 Thanon Chang Klan ⓣ053 276737, ⓦwww.chiangmaiyha.com. About 1500m south of the night bazaar. Very clean, quiet and reliable; rooms have en-suite hot showers and fans or air-con. Small discounts for HI members. ❷–❸

Eagle House 1 16 Soi 3, Thanon Chang Moi Kao ⓣ053 235387, ⓦwww.eaglehouse.com; and *Eagle House 2*, 26 Soi 2, Thanon Ratchawithi ⓣ053 210620. Run by an Irishwoman and her Thai husband who are keen to promote ethical eco-tourism, these two friendly, relaxed, well-maintained guest houses have spacious garden terrace areas with good cafés and extensive information boards; phone for a free pick-up. Well-organized treks also on offer, as well as Thai cookery courses at The Chilli Club, based at *Eagle House 2*. Rooms in *Eagle House 1* all have their own bathroom, either with fan, cold water and access to a shared hot shower, or with air-con and hot water; the standard of rooms is higher at the newer *Eagle House 2*, a modern compound with clean, tiled en-suite rooms, some with hot water and some with air-con, as well as a dorm (B80, with shared hot showers). ❶–❸

Fang Guest House 46–48 Soi 1, Thanon Kampangdin ⓣ053 282940. Modern building, with cosy, carpeted rooms, some with air-con, others with fan. Very handy for the night bazaar, but on a fairly quiet lane. ❸

Golden Fern 20 Soi 8, Thanon Phra Pokklao ⓣ053 277665, ⓦwww.goldenfern.com. Welcoming spot in an airy, attractive modern building decorated with plants, near Wat Chedi Luang. Each bright, well-furnished room has a fridge and a bathroom with hot shower, and some stretch to air-con and cable TV. ❸

Hollanda Montri 365 Thanon Charoenrat ⓣ053 242450, ⓔhollandamontri@asia.com. North of the centre by Rama IX Bridge, in a spacious modern building by the river, this Dutch-run guest house has large, clean and attractive fan or air-con rooms with balconies and hot-water bathrooms and a very pleasant riverside bar-restaurant. Good value but a bit far from the action. ❷–❸

Julie Guest House 7/1 Soi 5, Thanon Phra Pokklao ⓣ053 274355, ⓦwww.julieguesthouse.com. Relaxing, laid-way-back place with a variety of rooms with shared or en-suite hot showers and a dorm (B60), in a concrete block. Part-canopied roof terrace with hammocks for hanging out, and downstairs a shady garden café with a pool table. ❶–❷

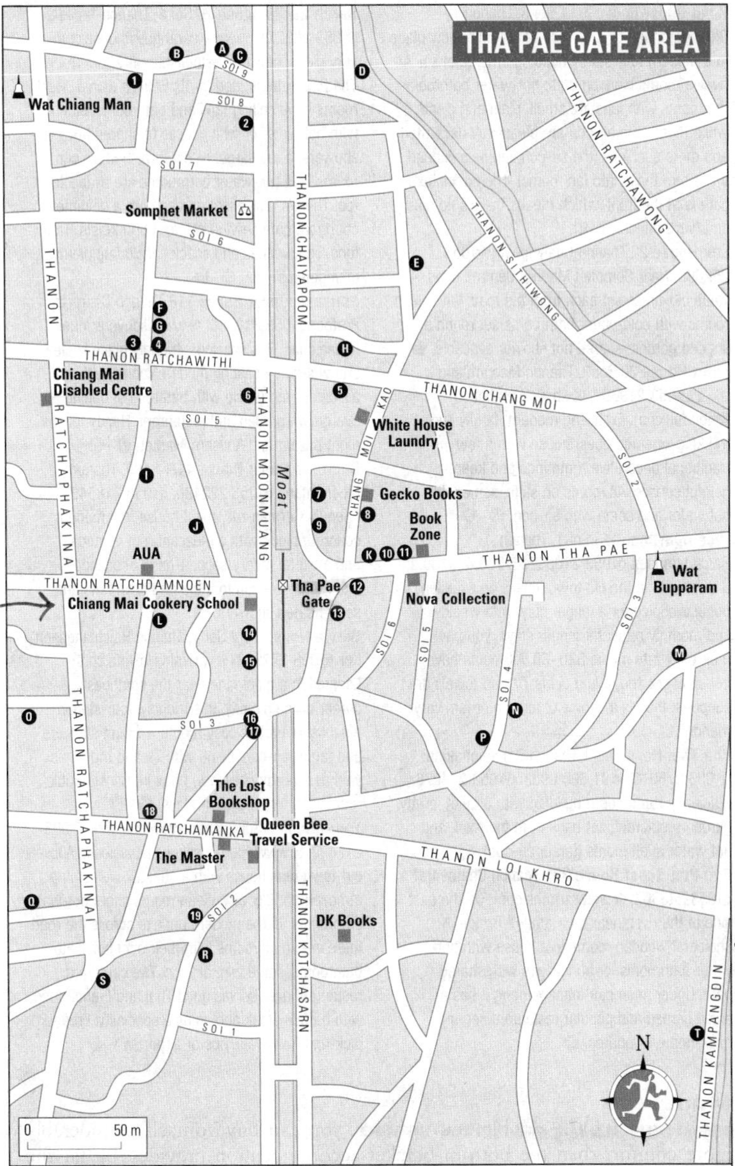

ACCOMMODATION

- Baan Jong Come N
- Eagle House 1 E
- Eagle House 2 G
- Fang M
- Gap's House L
- Golden Fern O
- Imperial Mae Ping Hotel T
- Julie Q
- Kavil I
- Lek House H
- Libra House C
- Marlboro D
- Nice Apartment J
- Pha Thai House S
- Roong Ruang K
- Sarah P
- SK House A
- Supreme B
- Top North Guest House R
- Your House F

RESTAURANTS & BARS

- Art Café 12
- Aum Vegetarian Food 14
- Bierstube 17
- Blue Diamond 1
- Da Stefano 8
- Daret's 9
- The Hemp Collective 13
- The House 2
- Jerusalem Falafel 15
- JJ Coffee Shop 10
- Kafe 6
- Libernard Café 5
- Pinte Blues Pub 16
- Pum Pui 19
- Ratana's Kitchen 11
- Thanom 7
- UN Irish Pub 4
- The Wok 18
- Yoy Pocket 3

Kavil Guest House 10/1 Soi 5, Thanon Ratchdamnoen ⓣ & ⓕ 053 224740. Friendly place in a modern four-storey building on a quiet soi. All twelve rooms have en-suite hot-water bathrooms; the rooms with fans are small, plain and clean, while those with air-con are pleasantly decorated and more spacious (the air-con can be switched off to turn these into fan rooms). The downstairs café is at the front, which means there's no noisy courtyard effect. ❷–❸

Lek House 22 Thanon Chaiyapoom ⓣ 053 252686. Near Somphet Market. Central, good-value old-timer, set back from the road, with clean rooms with cold-water bathrooms set round a shaded garden; shared hot shower available. ❶

Libra House 28 Soi 9, Thanon Moonmuang ⓣ & ⓕ 053 210687, ⓔ libra_guesthouse@hotmail.com. Excellent, modern, family-run, trekking-oriented guest house with a few traditional decorative trimmings and keen, helpful service. All rooms en suite, some with hot water and some with air-con. ❶–❸

Nice Apartment 15 Soi 1, Thanon Ratchdamnoen ⓣ 053 210552, ⓕ 053 419150. In a quiet lane in the old town, this is an excellent, popular choice for a longer stay, with weekly and monthly rates; for longer stays, you pay their daily rate minus B20–80. All rooms have hot showers, fridge and cable TV, and towels are supplied; there's a choice of air-con or fan. Very friendly. ❷–❸

Pha Thai House 48/1 Thanon Ratchaphakinai ⓣ 053 278013 or 01 998 6933, ⓕ 053 274075. Efficiently run modern building with a quiet, pretty garden restaurant, set back from the road, and hot water in all rooms (fan or air-con). ❸

Pun Pun Guest House 321 Thanon Charoenrat ⓣ 053 243362, ⓦ www.armms.com. On the east side of the river, near the Rama IX Bridge. A choice of wooden rooms in a house with hot-water bathrooms, or bungalows with shared bath. Under American management, it has a small garden and popular restaurant serving back-home favourites. ❷

Sarah Guest House 20 Soi 4, Thanon Tapae ⓣ 053 208271, ⓦ www.sarahguesthouse.com. A very clean, peaceful establishment 200m from Tha Pae Gate, named for its English owner. Most rooms have ceiling fans and bathrooms, either with hot water or with access to shared hot showers; a few large, nicely furnished air-con rooms with hot-water bathrooms are available too. There's a pleasant garden with a daytime courtyard café serving Western breakfasts, Thai food, sandwiches and snacks, including plenty of veggie options. ❷–❸

Souvenir Guest House 118 Thanon Charoen Prathet ⓣ 053 818786, ⓦ www.souvenir-guesthouse.com. This spacious, friendly place is clean and well run, boasting modern rooms with air-con or fan (some with bathrooms) behind an overgrown garden and restaurant. Handy for the night bazaar and Anusarn Market. ❷–❸

Supreme Guest House 44/1 Soi 9, Thanon Moonmuang ⓣ 053 222480, ⓕ 053 218545. Friendly German-run guest house in a modern concrete block with a pleasant roof veranda and a useful library/second-hand bookshop. The rooms are comfortable and have fans and solar-heated showers. ❷

Wiriya House 10/4 Soi 1, Thanon Rajchiangsaen Kor ⓣ 053 272948, ⓔ wiriyah@loxinfo.co.th. Located in a quiet lane near the southeast corner of the old city, this friendly, four-storey establishment has cosy rooms with hot showers and fan or air-con, some with TV and fridge, as well as a pretty garden to relax in. Considerable reductions for long-term stays. ❷–❸

Your House 8 Soi 2, Thanon Ratchawithi ⓣ 053 217492, ⓦ www.yourhouseguesthouse.com. A lovely old-town teak house with a suitably welcoming atmosphere. Big, airy, clean rooms share hot-water bathrooms; in the modern annexe across the road there are small rooms with their own hot-water bathrooms, some with air-con. The courtyard restaurant area serves good Thai and French food, with buffalo steak and chips a speciality. Free pick-ups from train, bus or airport. ❷–❹

Moderate

For around B400 a double and upwards, you can buy yourself considerably more comfort than the bottom-bracket accommodation provides. By far the best of these **moderate** places are the upmarket guest houses and lodges, which as well as good facilities (hot water and air-con) often offer decent decor and atmosphere. Chiang Mai also has dozens of bland, no-frills hotels in the same price range.

Baan Jong Come Guest House 47 Soi 4, Thanon Tha Pae ⓣ 053 274823. This family-run place combines modern motel/hotel-style rooms – fan or air-con – with a guest-house atmosphere. The rooms, which are upstairs, are very clean and spacious, with cool tiled floors and big comfortable beds made up with sheets and blankets; bathrooms with hot shower are attached. Below there's a pleasant courtyard with a café. 3–4

Baan Kaew Guest House 142 Thanon Charoen Prathet ⓣ053 271606, ⓔbaankaew_gh @hotmail.com. Set back from the road in a quiet, pretty garden, an attractive modern building with large, simple but well-equipped and maintained rooms with hot water and air-con. 4

Downtown Inn 172/1–11 Thanon Loi Khro ⓣ053 270662, ⓦwww.empresshotels.com. Western-style comforts like mini-bars and TVs without the extras of the big luxury hotels (such as its sister, the *Empress*); quiet considering its central location near the night bazaar. 6

Galare Guest House 7 Soi 2, Thanon Charoen Prathet ⓣ053 818887 or 053 821011, ⓦwww.galare.com. Near Narawat Bridge, a long-standing, well-run upmarket guest house that's justly popular. Air-con rooms, each with hot-water bathroom, TV and fridge, overlook a shady lawn which gives way to a riverside terrace. 6

Gap's House 3 Soi 4, Thanon Ratchdamnoen ⓣ053 278140, ⓦthai-culinary-art.infothai.com. Set around a relaxing, leafy compound strewn with antiques are plush air-con rooms with hot showers. The room price includes a simple breakfast, and a vegetarian buffet is served in the evening; one- or two-day cookery courses available. 4

Lai Thai Guesthouse 111/4–5 Thanon Kotchasarn ⓣ053 271725, 053 271414 or 053 271534, ⓦwww.laithai.com. On the southeast corner of the moat. Frenetic place, very popular with families, who are no doubt attracted by the (small) courtyard swimming pool around which the three floors of this attractive 120-room modern Thai-style building are arranged. Besides hot-water, en-suite bathrooms, the small but clean rooms boast traditional wooden floors, bamboo walls and air-con. 4

Marlboro Guest House 138 Thanon Sithiwongse ⓣ053 232598–9, ⓦwww.infothai.com/mgh. Tastefully furnished rooms in a traditional house, all with hot water, some with air-con, fridge and TV, in convenient location near the northeast corner of the moat. Breakfast included; good deals on single rooms. 3–4

People Place 9 Soi 8, Thanon Charoen Prathet ⓣ053 282487, ⓦwww.infothai.com/people. A compact modern building just a few steps from the night bazaar, with spacious, comfy rooms with en-suite hot-water bathrooms and air-con. 4

Roong Ruang Hotel 398 Thanon Tha Pae ⓣ053 232017–8, ⓕ053 252409. Tucked away off the main road near Tha Pae Gate, this great-value place has attractive rooms, some with air-con and fridge, all with hot water and TV, snuggled around a pretty courtyard. 3–4

SK House 30 Soi 9, Thanon Moonmuang ⓣ053 210690, ⓦwww.sk-riverview.com. Efficient, brick-built high-rise with a ground-floor café and Internet access, a fairly small, shaded swimming pool and a slightly institutional feel. Fan rooms come with hot-water bathrooms, while the air-con rooms are much more colourful and attractive, with satellite TV. 3–5

Top North Guest House 15 Soi 2, Thanon Moonmuang ⓣ053 278900 or 053 278684, ⓕ053 278485, ⓔtopnorth@hotmail.com. Large, modern, unpretentious place with a small swimming pool (B100 for non-guests), in a quiet enclave of guest houses. Fan-cooled and air-con rooms available, all with hot water, some with fridge and satellite TV. 3–4

Expensive

Clustered around the night bazaar, and along Thanon Huai Kaeo, Chiang Mai's **expensive hotels** aren't quite up to Bangkok's very high standards, though room rates are generally more reasonable here; the best hotels lay on all the expected luxuries plus traditional Lanna architectural touches, and breakfast is included at most places. Worth considering in this price range is the *Regent Resort*, out in the Mae Sa valley (see p.353); they'll collect you from the airport and lay on a shuttle bus service into Chiang Mai for guests.

Amari Rincome Hotel 1 Thanon Nimmanheimin ⓣ053 221130, ⓦwww.amari.com. Popular with tour groups, this hotel has an elegant lobby, tastefully furnished rooms, a tennis court and an excellent swimming pool; its *La Gritta* restaurant does a blow-out buffet lunch. Though it's a bit far from the centre, there are lots of restaurants and shops nearby. 9

Chiang Mai Orchid 23 Thanon Huai Kaeo ⓣ053 222091, ⓦwww.chiangmaiorchid.com. Grand, tasteful hotel with efficient service, a swimming pool and a health club, inconveniently located on the northwest side of town. 8

Empress 199 Thanon Chang Klan ⓣ053 270240, ⓦwww.empresshotels.com. Grand international-class hotel with pool, sauna and health centre conveniently placed on the south side of town: within walking distance of the night bazaar, yet far enough removed to get some peace and quiet. ❾

Imperial Mae Ping Hotel 153 Thanon Sri Dornchai ⓣ053 283900, ⓦwww.imperialhotels.com. Central luxury hotel in a fifteen-storey high-rise, with two outdoor pools, a gym, Japanese and Chinese restaurants, and a pleasant beer garden; very convenient for the night bazaar. ❽

River View Lodge 25 Soi 4, Thanon Charoen Prathet ⓣ053 271109–10, ⓦwww.riverviewlodgch.com. Tasteful, well-run and good-value alternative to international-class hotels, with a beautiful riverside garden, a swimming pool and neat decorative touches in the rooms; the most expensive rooms have balconies overlooking the river. ❼

1400

Royal Princess 111 Thanon Chang Klan ⓣ053 281033–40, ⓦwww.royalprincess.com. Tidy, centrally located hotel close to the night bazaar, with elegant rooms, a swimming pool and fitness centre, fine restaurants and impeccable service. ❾

Sheraton Chiangmai Hotel 318/1 Thanon Chiang Mai–Lamphun ⓣ053 275300, ⓦwww.starwood.com. The most luxurious hotel with the most spacious bedrooms in the city is located in one of its tallest buildings, a few kilometres south of town by the river. Facilities include a pool, steam room, business centre and health club as well as several top-class restaurants. ❾

The City

Chiang Mai feels less claustrophobic than most cities in Thailand, being scattered over a wide plain and broken up by waterways. In addition to the moat encircling the temple-strewn old town, the gentle Ping River brings a breath of fresh air to the eastern side of the pungent food markets above Nawarat Bridge, and the modern, hectic shopping area around Thanon Chang Klan. To make the most of the river, take a **boat trip** (1hr 40min; B150; ⓣ01 885 0663 or 01 884 4621) in a converted rice barge from the jetty beside the *Riverside* restaurant, on the east bank just north of Nawarat Bridge. Slow but sturdy, the boats offer a clear view of the surroundings as they take visitors through lush countryside north of town; boats leave every couple of hours, currently at 10am, noon, 2pm, 4pm and 5.30pm. Alternatively, contact Mae Ping River Cruises (ⓣ053 274822), based at Wat Chaimongkol on Thanon Charoen Prathet, who offer pick-up from your hotel and charge B300 per person for a two-hour cruise, usually in a longtail boat; they take you 8km upstream from the centre to a riverside farmhouse for a look around the fruit, herb and flower gardens, plus refreshments and fruit-tasting, before returning to the city.

Wat Phra Singh

If you see only one temple in Chiang Mai it should be **Wat Phra Singh**, perhaps the single most impressive array of buildings in the city, at the far western end of Thanon Ratchdamnoen in the old town. Just inside the gate to the right, the wooden scripture repository is the best example of its kind in the north, inlaid with glass mosaic and set high on a base decorated with stucco angels. The largest building in the compound, a colourful modern viharn fronted by naga balustrades, hides from view a rustic wooden bot, a chedi constructed in 1345 to house the ashes of King Kam Fu, and – the highlight of the whole complex – the beautiful **Viharn Lai Kam**. This wooden gem from the early nineteenth century is a textbook example of Lanna architecture, with its squat, multi-tiered roof and exquisitely carved and gilded pediment: if you feel you're being watched as you approach, it's the sinuous double arch between the porch's central columns, which represents the Buddha's eyebrows.

△ Wat Phra Singh

Courses in Chiang Mai

In recent years there's been a steady increase in the number of visitors who come to Chiang Mai looking to return home with a new skill by taking a self-improvement course. The most popular subject is how to cook Thai food, followed by Thai massage and meditation, but perhaps the most challenging of all, though vital for anyone planning to spend any length of time here, is the Thai language. Other skills to be tackled, besides rock-climbing (see p.322), include: **t'ai chi**, on a ten-day residential programme (twice monthly) at Naisuan House off Thanon Doi Saket Kao (ⓣ01 706 7406, ⓦwww.taichithailand.com); **yoga** courses at the Yoga Centre, 65/1 Thanon Arak (ⓣ053 814253 or 06 192 7375, ⓔyogachiangmai@yahoo.com), or the Hathayoga Centre Chiangmai, 129/79 Chiangmai Villa 1, Pa Daed Intersection (ⓣ053 271555, ⓦwww.hathayogachiangmai.com or www.yoga-therapy-chiangmai.com); joining in the training schedule of a **Thai boxing** camp at Lanna Muay Thai, 64/1 Soi 1, Thanon Huai Kaeo (ⓣ053 892102 or 01 951 3164, ⓦwww.lannamuaythai.com); intensive workshops in **jewellery making** at Nova, 201 Thanon Tha Pae (ⓣ053 273058, ⓦwww.nova-collection.com).

Cookery

There has been an explosion of interest in preparing Thai food, and many Chiang Mai guest houses and cookery schools now offer lessons. The original – and still the best – is the Chiang Mai Thai Cookery School, 1–3 Thanon Moonmuang (ⓣ053 206388, ⓦwww.thaicookeryschool.com) run by Somphon and Elizabeth Nabnian. They offer courses of one to five days (B900–B4200), covering common Thai and one or two traditional Lanna dishes, including the use of substitute ingredients available in the West. Each day begins with either an introduction to Thai ingredients, shopping in the market, making curry pastes or vegetable carving. While the fees might seem expensive, the courses are well worth it, including a first-class lunch, seasonal fruit-tasting and a recipe book. Somphon, an experienced chef himself, also offers pricey evening masterclasses. Courses are held either at *The Wok* restaurant (see p.343) or at the Nabnians' house, a 15min drive out of town (transport provided). Book in advance as the classes are very popular and the number of students is limited (the schedule of courses is given on the website), but you can just turn up and attempt to secure a place. Also recommended is The Master, with an office at 5 Thanon Ratchamanka (ⓣ053 277823, ⓔmasterthaicooking@hotmail.com), who charge B700 for a one-day course, as well as offering half-day and evening classes, two- and three-day courses and dedicated fruit- and vegetable-carving classes. The Chiang Mai Thai Farm Cooking School, whose in-town office is at 10/1 Soi 5, Thanon Ratchadamnoen (ⓣ053 224740, ⓔthaifarmcooking@hotmail.com), offers something slightly different, with the chance to pick your own organic vegetables, herbs and fruits for cooking on their farm thirty minutes' drive from town (transport provided; one- or two-day courses, B800/day).

Thai massage courses

While the best place to study Thai massage in Thailand is considered to be Bangkok's Wat Pho (see p.130), some well-regarded schools make Chiang Mai a popular alternative as a more relaxing base for courses that can run for several weeks. The longest-established centre is the forty-year-old Old Medicine Hospital (aka *Shivagakomarpaj* after the Indian hermit who is said to have founded the discipline over two thousand years ago), off Thanon Wualai opposite the Old Chiang Mai Cultural Center (ⓣ053 275085 or 053 201663, ⓦwww.thaimassageschool.ac.th). Highly respected ten-day courses in English (B4000), under the supervision of the Ministry of Education, are held twice a month, though the group size can get a bit too big at popular times; two-day foot massage courses are held at weekends (B2000).

Also accredited by the Ministry of Education, and highly recommended by past pupils, is the Thai Massage School of Chiang Mai (ⓦwww.1thaimassage.com), which has two locations: TMC1 to the northeast of town on the Mae Jo road, 2km beyond the Superhighway (Ⓣ053 854330); and TMC2 on Thanon Nimmanhemin next to Chiang Mai University's Contemporary Museum (Ⓣ053 907193). Three levels of Thai massage training are on offer, each taking five days, with the foundation course costing B3800 (or you can just do the first three days of this for B2900). Thai foot reflexology is also taught to adults (2 days; B2900) and to children over 12 (4 half-days; B2400). All courses include transportation and lunch.

Massage courses are also offered by the Sunshine Network (Ⓦwww.asokananda.com or www.thaiyogamassage.infothai.com), an international group of practitioners and teachers founded by the highly respected German teacher, Harald Brust, aka Asokananda, who emphasizes the spiritual aspect of what he calls Thai yoga massage or Ayurvedic bodywork. Led either by Asokananda or one of his followers, twelve-day beginners' courses (B9900, including extremely basic accommodation, simple vegetarian rice meals and transportation) are held at a rural retreat in a hill-tribe village between Chiang Mai and Chiang Rai, with optional yoga/t'ai chi classes, Vipassana meditation and discussions on Buddhism. There are also less frequent courses in Keralan Ayurvedic oil massage with hands and feet, the latter involving balancing from a rope (B10,900). For information about the courses in Chiang Mai, ask for Joe or Tom at Goodwill Motorcycles, 26/1 Soi 2, Thanon Chang Moi (Ⓣ053 251186).

Information about having a massage is given on p.346.

Meditation

Northern Insight Meditation Centre, at Wat Ram Poeng (aka Wat Tapotaram) on Thanon Canal near Wat Umong (Ⓣ053 278620 extension 13, Ⓦwww.watrampoeng.cjb.net), holds disciplined Vipassana courses (with a rule of silence, days beginning at 4am, no food after noon and so on), taught by Thai monks with translators. The minimum stay is ten days, with a basic course lasting 26 days, and payment is by donation. The other well-known and respected monastery for meditation retreats in the area is Wat Phra That Chom Thong, 60km southwest of Chiang Mai (see p.374). Once a year, the Sunshine Network (see above) organizes a Vipassana meditation and yoga retreat in the jungle with Asokananda. For more of a soft adventure tour in meditation, contact Sivali (Ⓣ053 464592 or 06 180 1830, Ⓦwww.sivalicentre.com), a rural meditation centre in the foothills of Doi Inthanon, 40km southwest of Chiang Mai, where two changes of white clothing are provided and each person gets his/her own traditional-style hut. The course director's approach to meditation, however, is infused by the ten years she spent as a Buddhist nun, most of it in solitude in forest monasteries throughout Thailand. Five- or ten-day sessions are held twice a month.

For an introduction to meditation and Buddhist culture, go to a talk at Wat Umong on a Sunday afternoon (see p.336) or sign up for one of the free overnight courses run by Mahachulalongkorn Buddhist University, based at Wat Suan Dork (see p.337) on Thanon Suthep. These involve discussions about Buddhism, meditation, walking meditation, chanting, almsgiving and a spot of Thai cooking, and begin at about 2pm on a Saturday or Sunday, before departure to the training centre on Doi Suthep, returning to Wat Suan Dork at 12.30pm the next day. As places are limited you should make contact in advance (Ⓣ09 855 5446 or 053 278967 ext 200, Ⓔthaimonkchat@yahoo.com or monkchat_cm@hotmail.com, Ⓦwww.cmbu.net).

Thai language

The longest-established and best place to learn Thai is the AUA (American University Alumni) Language Centre, 24 Thanon Ratchadamnoen (Ⓣ053 211377 or 053 278407, Ⓦwww.auathailand.org/chiangmai), which is certified by the Ministry of Education. Several levels of classes are offered, starting with spoken Thai for beginners (60hr over about 6 weeks; B3500), with class sizes limited to 5–12 students. Individual and small-group instruction can also be arranged, starting from B250 per hour for 1–2 students.

Inside sits one of Thailand's three **Phra Singh** (or Sihing) Buddha images (see p.631), a portly, radiant and much-revered bronze in a fifteenth-century Lanna style. Its setting is enhanced by the colourful **murals** of action-packed tableaux, which give a window on life in the north a hundred years ago: courting scenes and piggyback fights, merchants, fishermen and children playing. The murals illustrate two different stories: on the right-hand wall is an old folk tale, the *Sang Thong*, about a childless king and queen who are miraculously given a beautiful son, the "Golden Prince", in a conch shell. The murals on the left, which have been badly damaged by water, show the story of the mythical swan Suwannahong, who forms the magnificent prow of the principal royal barge in Bangkok. Incidentally, what look like Bermuda shorts on the men are in fact Buddhist **tattoos**: in the nineteenth century, all boys in the north were tattooed from navel to kneecap, an agonizing ordeal undertaken to show their courage and to enhance their appeal to women. On one side of the wat is a high school for young yellow-sashed novices and schoolboys in blue shorts, who all noisily throng the temple compound during the day. Dally long enough and you'll be sure to have to help them with their English homework.

Wat Chedi Luang

From Wat Phra Singh a ten-minute walk east along Thanon Ratchadamnoen brings you to **Wat Chedi Luang** on Thanon Phra Pokklao, where an enormous chedi, toppled from 90m to its present 60m by an earthquake in 1545, presents an intriguing spectacle – especially in the early evening when the resident bats flit around. You'll need a titanic leap of the imagination, however, to picture the beautifully faded pink-brick chedi, in all its crumbling grandeur, as it was in the fifteenth century, when it was covered in bronze plates and gold leaf, and housed the Emerald Buddha (see p.126) for eighty years. Recent attempts to rebuild the entire chedi to its former glory, now abandoned, have nevertheless led to modern replacements of the elephants at the base, the nagas that line the lengthy staircases, and the Buddha images in its four niches, including an oversized replica of the Emerald Buddha in its old spot on the eastern side. In an unprepossessing modern building (which women are not allowed to enter) by the main entrance stands the city's foundation pillar, the *Inthakin* post, here at the geographical centre of Chiang Mai, sheltered by a stately gum tree which, the story has it, will stand for as long as the city's fortunes prosper. On the north side of the chedi, **Monk Chat** is advertised (Mon–Sat noon–6.30pm), giving you a chance to meet and talk to the monks in English. If you've still got time, pop in on **Wat Pan Tao** next door to see the wonderfully gnarled all-teak viharn, constructed of unpolished panels, supported on enormous pillars and protected by carved wooden bars on the windows, a classic of graceful Lanna architecture.

Chiang Mai City Arts and Cultural Centre

From Wat Chedi Luang, the old town's main commercial street, Thanon Phra Pokklao, heads north past a monument to King Mengrai, the founder of Chiang Mai, set in its own small piazza on the corner of Thanon Ratchdamnoen and supposedly on the site where he was killed by lightning. On Sundays from noon, Thanon Ratchdamnoen becomes a **walking street**, a pedestrianized market with all kinds of shopping and eating, and live music.

A few minutes on up Thanon Phra Pokklao, Mengrai features again in the bronze Three Kings Monument, showing him discussing the auspicious layout of his "new city", Chiang Mai, with his allies, Ramkhamhaeng of Sukhothai and Ngam Muang of Phayao. Behind the monument, the elegant 1920s former provincial office has recently been turned into the **Chiang Mai City Arts and**

climbing wall (see p.322) surrounded by shops and cafés, and traditional dancing at the Kalare Food Centre (see p.342).

During the day, bustling **Warorot market**, along the river immediately north of Thanon Tha Pae, has lots of cheap and cheerful cotton, linen and ceramics for sale on the upper floors. In the heart of the market, you can watch locals buying chilli paste, sausage and sticky rice from their favourite stalls, and maybe even join the queue. There's also a flower market here which is open late at night until the early hours of the morning.

Another place worth knowing about is **Thanon Nimmanhemin**, especially its northern end towards Thanon Huai Kaeo, which savvy locals sometimes tag Chiang Mai's Sukhumvit for its services to well-to-do expats. Here, as well as upmarket clothes shops, you'll find some notable outlets for **contemporary Thai design**, fusing various of the crafts described below with modern, often minimalist elements. On Nimmanhemin's Soi 1, behind the *Amari Rincome Hotel*, Gong Dee is full of wood and lacquer vases, boxes, lamps and bowls, much of it gleaming gold and silver, while Ayodhya opposite sells stylish fabrics as well as funky bowls and boxes covered in dried water-hyacinth stalks, woven liana lampshades and lots of other novel woven accessories and furniture. Over on the east side of the river at 35 Thanon Ratanakosin, Aka Walai shelters thoroughly modern celadon, rich clothes and textiles and cutting-edge home furnishings.

Fabrics and clothes

The **silk** produced out towards San Kamphaeng is richly coloured and hard-wearing, with various attractive textures. Bought off a roll, the material is generally less costly than in Bangkok, though more expensive than in the northeast – prices are around B400–600 a metre for two-ply (for thin shirts and skirts) and B650–750 a metre for four-ply (suitable for suits). Ready-made silk clothes and made-to-measure tailoring, though inexpensive, are generally staid and more suited to formal wear. About 5km out from the centre of Chiang Mai, Piankusol is the best place to follow the silk-making process right from the cocoon. If you've got slightly more money to spend on better quality silk, head for Chiang Mai's oldest silk manufacturer, Shinawatra (7km out, with a shop at 18 Thanon Huai Kaeo; Ⓦwww.shinawatrathaisilk.com), which was once graced by no less a personage than the late Diana, Princess of Wales.

In Chiang Mai you'll find plenty of traditional, pastel-coloured **cotton**, which is nice for furnishings, most of it from the village of Pa Sang southwest of Lamphun. Outlets in the basement of the main Chiang Mai Night Bazaar shopping centre on Thanon Chang Klan have good, cheap selections of this sort of cloth at around B150 per metre, plus hand-painted and batik-printed lengths, and ready-made tablecloths and the like.

A shop worth a root around is Pa Ker Yaw (closed Sun), near the *Downtown Inn* at 180 Thanon Loi Khro, a weather-beaten wooden shophouse stuffed with a selection of rich **fabrics** from Thailand, Laos and Burma, as well as hill-tribe jewellery and basketware and other crafts. For the all-over ethnic look, Classic Lanna Thai, on the first floor of Chiang Mai Night Bazaar, sells classy ready-to-wear **clothes**, made from local fabrics by traditional northern methods. Also upmarket but less obviously ethnic, Paothong, at 66 Thanon Charoenrat, has lovely, elegant garments in silk and cotton, mostly for women. Flower Earring, 6 Soi 1, Thanon Nimmanhemin, specializes in stylish, tastefully chosen women's clothes and traditional fabrics from Northern Thailand, Burma and China, including some gorgeously coloured skirts. If you just need to replenish your rucksack, try Ga-Boutique at 1/1 Thanon Kotchasarn (opposite Tha Pae Gate), which sells ordinary casual clothes of reasonable quality at low prices.

If you're interested in the whole process of traditional fabric production, particularly the use of **natural dyes**, Studio Naenna, 138/8 Soi Changkhian, Thanon Huai Kaeo at the base of Doi Suthep (Ⓦwww.loxinfo.com/naenna), is an excellent place to begin. If you phone for an appointment (Ⓣ053 226042) you can see a demonstration of dyeing, including the plants from which the dyes are extracted; you can then watch the weavers in action (Mon–Fri) and buy the finished products, which consist of top-quality ready-made garments and accessories, in their showroom.

To make sure more of your money goes to those who make the goods, take your custom to one of the **non-profit-making shops** whose proceeds go to the hill tribes. These include the Hill Tribe Products Foundation, on Thanon Suthep in front of Wat Suan Dork, which sells beautiful lengths of cotton and silk, silverware and a variety of hill-tribe gear; Thai Tribal Crafts, 204 Thanon Bamrungrat off Thanon Kaeo Nawarat – *yaam*, the embroidered shoulder bags popular with Thai students, are particularly good here; and Golden Triangle Mountain People's Art and Handicrafts, 137/1 Thanon Nantharam (best to make an appointment on Ⓣ053 276194), which sells mainly high-quality jackets, bags, silver and basketware made by Akha women. The last of these has an excellent library/research centre, the Mountain People Culture and Development Highland Research Institute, specializing in oral history and with useful information in English.

Woodcarving

Chiang Mai has a long tradition of **woodcarving**, which expresses itself in everything from salad bowls to half-size elephants. In the past the industry has relied on the cutting of Thailand's precious teak, but manufacturers are now beginning to use other imported hardwoods, while bemoaning their inferior quality. Carl Bock, who travelled through the region in 1882, observed a habit which is still common today: "The woodcarvers have a quaint taste for inlaying their work with odd bits of coloured glass, tinsel or other bright material: such work will not bear close inspection, but it has a remarkably striking effect when the sun shines on these glittering objects." Wooden objects are sold all over the city, but the most famous place for carving is **Ban Tawai**, a large village of shops and factories where prices are low and you can watch the woodworkers in action. One of Thailand's most important woodcarving centres, Ban Tawai relied on rice farming until thirty years ago, but today virtually every home here has carvings for sale outside and each backyard hosts its own cottage industry. To get there, you'll need your own transport: follow Highway 108 south from Chiang Mai 13km to Hang Dong, then head east for 2km.

Lacquerware

Lacquerware can be seen in nearly every museum in Thailand, most commonly in the form of betel-nut sets, which used to be carried ceremonially by the slaves of grandees as an insignia of rank and wealth (see box on p.523). Betel-nut sets are still produced in Chiang Mai according to the traditional technique, whereby a woven bamboo frame is covered with layers of rich red lacquer and decorated with black details. A variety of other objects, such as trays and jewellery boxes, are also produced, some decorated with gold leaf on black gloss. Lacquerware makes an ideal choice for gifts, as it is both light to carry, and at the same time typically Thai. Just about every other shop in town sells lacquerware: Laitong, 6km out towards San Kamphaeng, is a good place to see the intricate process of manufacture, though prices are lower elsewhere.

Celadon

Celadon, sometimes known as greenware, is a delicate variety of stoneware which was first made in China over two thousand years ago and later produced in Thailand, most famously at Sukhothai and Sawankhalok. Several kilns in Chiang Mai have revived the art, the best of them being Mengrai Kilns at 79/2 Soi 6, Thanon Samlarn. Sticking to the traditional methods, Mengrai produces beautiful and reasonably priced vases, crockery and larger items, thrown in elegant shapes and covered with transparent green and blue glazes.

Umbrellas and paper

The village of **Bo Sang** bases its fame on souvenir **umbrellas** – made of silk, cotton or mulberry paper and decorated with bold, painted colours (from about B75 for a kid's parasol) – and celebrates its craft with a colourful **umbrella fair** every January. The artists who work here can paint a small motif on your bag or camera in two minutes flat. The grainy mulberry (*sa*) **paper**, which makes beautiful writing or sketching pads, is sold almost as an afterthought in many of Bo Sang's shops; it can also be bought from Bang On and Tonpao, in the basement of the Chiang Mai Night Bazaar building, which sell a very wide range of *sa* paper in the form of albums, notepaper and so on (typically ten envelopes and ten pieces of paper for B65).

Silver and jewellery

Of the traditional craft quarters, only the **silversmiths'** area on Thanon Wualai remains in its original location. The oldest factory in Chiang Mai, Siam Silverware on Soi 3, a ramshackle and sulphurous compound loud with the hammering of hot metal, gives you a whiff of what this zone must have been like in its heyday. The end results are repoussé plates, bowls and cups, and attractive, chunky jewellery. Silver is often priced by the gram, with current rates at about B16 per gram, so a thin sterling-silver bracelet costs around B300–350 and a large, chunky bangle around B1100. A good general **jewellery** store is Nova Collection at 210 Thanon Tha Pae, which has some lovely rings and necklaces blending gold, silver and precious stones in striking and original designs, as well as running workshops in jewellery-making (see p.330).

Eating

The main difficulty with **eating** in Chiang Mai is knowing when to stop. All over town there are inexpensive and enticing restaurants serving typically northern food, which has been strongly influenced by Burmese cuisine, especially in curries such as the spicy *kaeng hang lay* (usually translated on menus as "Northern Thai curry"), made with pork, ginger, garlic and tamarind. Another favourite local dish is Chiang Mai *nem*, spicy pork sausage – although the uncooked, fermented varieties are usually too sour for Western palates. At lunchtime the thing to do is to join the local workers in one of the simple, inexpensive cafés that put all their efforts into producing just one or two special dishes – the traditional meal at this time of day is *khao soi*, a thick broth of curry and coconut cream, with egg noodles and a choice of meat. In the evenings, besides Anusarn market (reviewed below), the main **night markets** are along Thanon Bamrungburi by Chiang Mai Gate and at Talat San Pa Khoi, out towards the train station on the south side of Thanon Charoen Muang. Among the **bars** listed below in "Drinking and nightlife", *The Riverside* and *UN Irish Pub* have particularly good reputations for their food.

Little of the Western food in Chiang Mai is top-notch, and it's generally more expensive than Thai, but there's plenty of it, particularly Italian-slanted, and sometimes it's very hard to resist. Probably easier to refuse are the restaurants which lay on touristy **cultural shows** with *khan toke* dinners, a selection of northern dishes eaten on the floor off short-legged lacquer trays. If you are tempted, the Old Chiangmai Cultural Centre, 185/3 Thanon Wualai (☎053 275097; B270), with its show of northern Thai and hill-tribe dancing, has the best reputation – and be sure to make time for the attached Sbun-Nga Textile Museum beforehand (see p.338). **Dinner cruises** on the river are offered by Mae Ping River Cruises (see p.328), nightly at 7pm for B400 per person, and by *The Riverside* (see p.345), at 8pm for an extra B70 per person on top of the cost of the meal.

Thai

Anusarn Market Off Thanon Chang Klan. Happy night-time hunting ground of open-air stalls and restaurants. One-dish operators (serving up *hawy thawt* fried up with great panache, or satay, or very good *phat thai*) square up to each other across a shared courtyard of tables; beyond lie halal restaurants specializing in barbecued chicken with honey, and several good seafood places, including the old favourite *Fatty's*. Inexpensive to moderate.

Aum Vegetarian Food On the corner of Ratchdamnoen and Moonmuang roads. Small and relaxing long-time favourite, now with air-con and lined with used books for sale. Interesting veggie dishes such as *khao soi* and Vietnamese spring rolls, Thai desserts and organic hill-tribe coffee. Inexpensive.

Chiang Mai Vegetarian Centre Thanon Aom Muang. Run by the Santi Asoke group, like the café at Bangkok's Chatuchak Market: a cavernous traditional *sala* serving good veggie dishes on rice, and desserts. Mon–Thurs & Sun 6am–2pm. Inexpensive.

Galae 65 Thanon Suthep. Follow this road to the western end, then climb 200m up the hill to find this relaxing spot on the bank of a small reservoir, where tables are set beneath trees and between bright flowerbeds. With a good, though limited, menu of Thai favourites, it's a useful place to head for after a visit to Wat Umong or the zoo. Moderate.

The Gallery 25 Thanon Charoenrat. Refined restaurant on soothing riverside terraces, behind a gallery for local artists in a century-old teak house. Interesting selection of northern and central Thai food, big portions, slow service, and live traditional northern music nightly. Moderate to expensive.

Hong Tauw Inn 95/17–18 Nantawan Arcade, Thanon Nimmanhemin. Comfortable air-con restaurant done out in "country inn" style, with antiques, plants and old clocks. The reliable menu ranges from rice and noodle dishes such as *khanom jiin*, to central and northern Thai main dishes, and includes a wide range of Thai desserts. Moderate.

Huen Phen 112 Thanon Ratchamanka. Probably Chiang Mai's most authentic northern restaurant, with bags of ambience. The selection of hors d'oeuvres at B85 gives a great taste of all the local specials. Moderate.

Huen Sontharee 46 Thanon Wang Sing Kham. A convivial riverfront restaurant owned by the famous northern Thai folk-singer Sontharee Wechanon, who entertains diners from her balcony-level stage and serves up northern specialities, such as delicious fried Chiang Mai sausage with whole baby garlic. Split levels allow a choice of seating – on a riverside terrace, near the stage or at round low tables on a balcony overlooking the action. Evenings only. Moderate.

Kalare Night Bazaar Food Centre Thanon Chang Klan. A coupon system operates at this open-air collection of northern and central Thai, Indian and veggie foodstalls and bars. It's a good lively place for a break from shopping, a budget meal and a beer, with free shows of traditional dancing on a stage between 8pm and 11pm, making a nice background accompaniment without being too loud or intrusive. Inexpensive.

Khao Soi Samoe Jai Thanon Faham (no English sign). Thick and tasty *khao soi*, delicious satay and other noodle dishes pack the locals in each lunchtime. Daily 9am–3pm. Inexpensive.

Kiat Ocha 41–43 Thanon Inthrawarorot, off Thanon Phra Pokklao (no English sign). Delicious and very popular satay and *khao man kai* – boiled chicken breast served with dipping sauces, broth and rice. This and the surrounding cafés are especially handy if you're looking round the old town. Daily 5am–2.30pm. Inexpensive.

New Lamduon Fahharm Khao Soi 352/22 Thanon Charoenrat. Excellent *khao soi* prepared to a secret recipe. Also satay, waffles and *som tam*. Daily 9am–3pm. Inexpensive.

Ratana's Kitchen 320–322 Thanon Tha Pae. A favourite among locals both for northern specialities like *kaeng hang lay* and *khao soi* and for tasty Western breakfasts, sandwiches and steaks. Inexpensive to moderate.

Tha Nam 43/3 Moo 2, Thanon Chang Klan. Restaurant on the southern edge of town serving good traditional northern and central Thai food in a ramshackle teak house, where the musicians can sometimes be a bit noisy playing their traditional music – it's better to eat on the huge terrace overlooking a quiet green stretch of the river. Moderate to expensive.

Thanom Restaurant 8 Thanon Chaiyapoom, near Tha Pae Gate (no English sign). Great introduction to northern Thai and Burmese-style cooking, in startlingly clean surroundings. The fastidious management aren't over-fond of tourists and expect you to be dressed modestly (so no sleeveless tops or shorts) before they'll let you in, and to eat early: lunch is 11am–1pm, dinner 5–8pm. No alcohol served. Moderate.

Whole Earth 88 Thanon Sri Dornchai. Mostly veggie dishes from Thailand and India, plus a big fish and seafood selection; soothing atmosphere with occasional live mood music in a traditional Lanna house, with verandas overlooking a large garden. Moderate to expensive.

The Wok 44 Thanon Ratchamanka. Centrally located, with a relaxing ambience, and quality guaranteed as it's run by the Chiang Mai Cookery School. Moderate.

European and all-rounders

Amazing Sandwich 252/3 Thanon Phra Pokklao. Situated in the old city near Chang Phuak Gate, this is the place to go if you hanker for a sandwich, bagel or baguette made up to order, or fancy munching on a pie, quiche or salad. Mon–Sat 8.30am–7pm, Sun 11am–3pm. Moderate.

Art Café 291 Thanon Tha Pae. This Italian-run place is a popular farang hangout with a good ambience. All the café favourites (yoghurt and muesli as well as the usual American and continental breakfasts, sandwiches, soups, salads and ice cream) and full meals (pasta and pizza, Thai dishes and a big selection of vegetarian options – but avoid the Mexican menu) are served. A big selection of wines from B80 a glass. Moderate to expensive.

Bierstube 33/6 Thanon Moonmuang. Friendly and efficient service combined with generous portions of German or Thai food at reasonable prices make this place a favourite among locals. The tables outside provide a good people-watching spot, too. Inexpensive to moderate.

Blue Diamond Soi 9, Thanon Moon Muang. Popular travellers' haunt in a quiet neighbourhood of guest houses, serving very good Thai vegetarian food, Western breakfasts, home-made bread, herbal teas and hill-tribe coffee. Mon–Sat 7.30am–9.30pm, Sun 7.30am–2pm. Inexpensive to moderate.

Daret's 4 Thanon Chaiyapoom. The definitive budget travellers' hangout with outdoor trestles and a friendly buzz. Famous fruit shakes, good breakfasts and back-home staples, though the Thai food is rather bland. Inexpensive to moderate.

Da Stefano 2/1–2 Thanon Chiang Moi Kao. Just round the corner from Tha Pae Gate, this has quickly become one of Chiang Mai's most popular Italian restaurants. It's easy to see why: it has a winning combination of tasteful ambience, efficient service and delicious food. Mon–Sat 11.30am–11pm, Sun 5–11pm. The same family own *La Gondola*, with an attractive conservatory and garden by the river in the Rimping Condominium, 201/6 Thanon Charoenrat, by the Nakhon Ping Bridge. Moderate to expensive.

The House 199 Thanon Moon Muang ⓣ053 419011. In an imposing white mansion overlooking the moat, a stylish, new, upmarket restaurant serving very creative and successful fusion cuisine. For gourmets on a budget, the attached tapas bar might be more manageable, offering fairly traditional tapas as well as appetizers and tiny portions of main courses from the restaurant's menu. Evenings only, closed Sun. Very expensive.

Jerusalem Falafel 35/3 Thanon Moonmuang. Small and simple air-con café serving pitta bread, home-made cheeses and yoghurts, and Israeli food right near Tha Pae Gate. Inexpensive to moderate.

JJ Coffee Shop and Bakery Thanon Tha Pae. Very popular with tourists (and local folk too), boasting a bustling, sanitized air-con atmosphere. All kinds of Thai, Western and veggie food, but best for breakfast, with home-baked bread and croissants, great home-made muesli and yoghurt, and brewed coffee. Smaller branch at Chiang Inn Plaza, Thanon Chang Klan. Moderate to expensive.

Kafe 127–129 Soi 5, Thanon Moonmuang. Long-time favourite among locals, with tasty burgers, good Thai food and a wide range of drinks in a warm and welcoming ambience. Inexpensive to moderate.

La Villa 70 Thanon Ratchdamnoen. Relaxing Italian-run restaurant in an attractive traditional wooden house. Good salads, pasta and risotto, the best pizzas in town – baked in a wood-fired oven – and probably the best coffee too. Pool table and live sport on TV. Expensive.

Libernard Café 295–299 Thanon Chang Moi. Small air-con café serving very good coffee in any variety you can think of, made with freshly roasted local beans. Also delicious pancakes and a limited range of simple Thai dishes. Inexpensive to moderate.

Pum Pui 24 Soi 2, Thanon Moonmuang. Trattoria-style Italian-run place where you're guaranteed huge servings; the food is mostly pasta (including an excellent lasagne), but there's pizza too, lots of bruschettas and other antipasti, and the menu has a long vegetarian section. Seating is outside in a tree-filled courtyard off a quiet fume-free lane. Moderate to expensive.

Drinking and nightlife

Although there's a clutch of hostess bars bordering the east moat and along Loi Khro, and several gay bars offering sex shows, Chiang Mai's **nightlife** generally avoids Bangkok's sexual excesses, but offers plenty of opportunities for a wholesome good time. If your heart's set on **dancing**, try the big hotels, some of which have predictable, westernized nightclubs (like Space Bubble at the *Porn Ping* on Thanon Charoen Prathet) which charge about B100 admission, including one drink; for something more adventurous, head for one of the more Thai-style nightclubs such as *Club G*. Some of the places listed here are geared to a relaxing night out, while others get rocking as the night wears on.

Though there are **bars** scattered throughout the city, the main concentrations are on the east bank of the Ping River, around Tha Pae Gate and to the west of town along Thanon Nimmanhemin, which swarms with students from nearby Chiang Mai University. On a patch of open ground that runs from *Eagle House 2* to Thanon Ratchaphakinai, a string of laid-back, mostly open-air bars such as *Rasta Café*, *Roots Rock Reggae* and *Life House* have set up shop. Popular with backpackers and young, music-conscious locals, their playlists are more varied and interesting than their names might suggest.

For a gentle introduction to the city's **gay scene**, check out the small bars such as *Cruise* behind the Chiang Mai Night Bazaar centre on Thanon Chang Klan. There's a bigger concentration in the small roads off the west side of Thanon Chotana (aka Thanon Chang Phuak), including *Adam's Apple*, north of the bus station at 1/21–22 Soi Viengbua (☎053 220380–2), which styles itself as a one-stop entertainment venue for men, with a restaurant, karaoke, minimart, massage and a nightly cabaret show at 11.30pm.

Brasserie 37 Thanon Charoenrat. Good restaurant with pretty riverside terraces, more famous as the venue for some of the city's best live blues and rock. Warms up around 11pm.

Club G 68/2 Thanon Chiang Mai–Lamphun, 500m south of TAT and Narawat Bridge. The latest reincarnation of *Gigi's*, a fun, full-on, sweaty club, packed with young Thais dancing to techno on tables and around their bar stools. No admission charge but pricey drinks.

Drunken Flower (Mao Dok Mai) 295/1 Soi 1, Thanon Nimmanhemin. Tucked away in a lane beside the *Amari Rincome Hotel*, this quirky venue is a favourite among university students. Reasonable prices for Thai and Mexican food, cocktails and other drinks and an eclectic range of background music.

Fine Thanks 119 Thanon Nimmanheimin. Another spot that's popular among Thais, yet welcoming to farangs, an indoor-outdoor pub-restaurant, dimly lit and draped with plants. Thai bands play a mix of Thai and Western pop-rock.

Good View 13 Thanon Charoenrat. An upmarket clone of the neighbouring *Riverside*, this large venue appeals to fashionable Thais with its smart staff, extensive menu of Thai, Chinese, Japanese and Western food, and slick, competent musicians, who play anything from country to jazz.

The Hemp Collective 19/4–5 Thanon Kotchasarn, opposite Tha Pae Gate. Laid-back crusty place, decorated with dayglo paint and paper lanterns, with live bands in the ground-floor bar and an eclectic music choice playing to the floor cushions in the rooftop bar.

Monkey Club 7 Soi 9, Thanon Nimmanhemin. More sophisticated than your average Chiang Mai bar-restaurant, with cool white decor inside, fountains, garden tables and a coffee corner outside. DJs and live bands play Latin, reggae, jazz and pop, and the food is well received.

Pinte Blues Pub 33/6 Thanon Moonmuang. The frontage of this simple bar is so small that you could miss it if you blink, but it is one of the city's longest-standing venues, and an ideal spot for a chat over cheap drinks with blues in the background.

The Pub 189 Thanon Huai Kaeo. Homely, relaxing expat hangout, once rated by *Newsweek* as one of the world's best bars. As the name suggests: draught beer, darts, separate sports bar. Tues–Sun from 5pm.

Riverside 9 Thanon Charoenrat ⓣ053 243239. Archetypal farang bolthole: candlelit terraces by the water, reliable Western and Thai food (moderate to pricey), extensive drinks list and reasonable draught beer. Various soloists and bands perform nightly on two stages, with the tempo increasing as the night wears on.

UN Irish Pub 24/1 Thanon Ratchawithi. Painted green and white, this place is as much a casual, moderately priced café-restaurant as a pub: home-made bread for satisfying breakfasts and sandwiches, jacket potatoes and Irish stew of course, plus pizzas and a good vegetarian selection. Guinness (bottled only), Carlsberg and Heineken (on tap) and reasonably priced wine. Live music Tues & Fri, quiz night Thurs.

Warm Up 60 Thanon Wat Ket. Large indoor-outdoor bar in an old wooden house on the east side of the river, that's hugely popular with students and young locals, with live bands early evening, followed by DJs.

Yoy Pocket 30 Thanon Ratchawithi. The walls here are full of Americana, but the jukebox is just about purely Asian so it's a good spot to listen to some Thai pop music, an essential experience. Packed at night with twenty-something Thais.

Listings

Airlines Air Mandalay, Room 107, Doi Ping Mansion, 148 Thanon Charoen Prathet ⓣ053 818049; Bangkok Airways, Chiang Mai airport ⓣ053 281519; Lao Airlines, Nakornping Condo, 115 Thanon Ratchapruek ⓣ053 223400–1 or 053 404033; Mandarin Airlines, Chiang Mai airport ⓣ053 201268–9; Orient Thai, Chiang Mai airport ⓣ053 922159; Phuket Air, Chiang Mai airport ⓣ053 922118–9; Silk Air, *Mae Ping Hotel*, 153 Thanon Sri Dornchai ⓣ053 276459 or 053 276495; Thai Airways, 240 Thanon Phra Pokklao ⓣ053 210210, 053 211041 or 053 211044–7.

Banks and exchange Dozens of banks are dotted around Thanon Tha Pae and Thanon Chang Klan, and many exchange booths here stay open for evening shoppers.

Books Book Zone at 318 Thanon Tha Pae stocks a wide range of English-language publications, including novels, books about Thailand and maps, while Bookazine on the ground floor of the Chiang Inn Plaza on Thanon Chang Klan carries magazines and books. Two large book stores, Surawong at 54/1 Thanon Sri Dornchai (closed Sun afternoons) and DK Books at 79/1 Thanon Kotchasarn, also have a wide selection; the former's display is the better organized, and it features a newspaper and magazine section, a large stationery shop and a nice little coffee shop. There's an excellent, well-organized array of used and selected new books at the helpful and knowledgeable Gecko Books, 2/6 Thanon Chang Moi Kao, and the Lost Bookshop, 34/3 Thanon Ratchamanka, also has a very good second-hand selection.

Car rental Many outlets in the Tha Pae Gate area rent out cars and four-wheel drives, from as little as B700 a day: reliable companies offering insurance and breakdown recovery include Journey, 283 Thanon Tha Pae ⓣ053 208787, ⓦwww.journeycnx.com; North Wheels, 70/4–8 Thanon Chaiyapoom ⓣ053 874478, ⓦwww.northwheels. com; and Queen Bee, 5 Thanon Moonmuang ⓣ053 275525, ⓦwww.queen-bee.com. The more expensive international chains are represented by Avis, Chiang Mai airport ⓣ053 201798–9, or *Royal Princess Hotel*, 112 Thanon Chang Klan ⓣ053 281033–43; Budget, 201/2 Thanon Mahidol, opposite Airport Plaza ⓣ053 202871–2; and National, *Amari Rincome Hotel*, Thanon Huai Kaeo ⓣ053 210118.

Cinemas Call Movieline ⓣ053 262661, operated by the Raintree Community Centre ⓦwww.rain treecenter.org, or go to ⓦwww.movieseer.com for details of which English-soundtrack or English-subtitled films are showing around town. Cineplexes include Vista (ⓣ053 224333 or 053 894415) at Kad Suan Kaew shopping plaza on Thanon Huai Kaeo, and Major (ⓣ053 283939) at Airport Plaza shopping centre. French-language films with English subtitles are screened at the Alliance Française, 138 Thanon Charoen Prathet (usually Tues 4.30pm & Fri 8pm; ⓣ053 275277). Popular, mostly recent, arthouse films are shown at CMU Art Museum Theatre, near the corner of Suthep and Nimmanhemin roads, every Sun at 3pm (☎053 218280).

Consulates China, 111 Thanon Chang Lo ☎053 276125 or 053 200424; India, 344 Thanon Charoenrat ☎053 243066; US, 387 Thanon Witchayanon ☎053 252629–31 or 053 252644. Honorary consulates include Canada, 151 Chiang Mai–Lampang Superhighway ☎053 850147; and UK, 198 Thanon Bamrungrat ☎053 263015.

Hospitals Lanna, at 103 Superhighway ☎053 357234–53, east of Thanon Chotana, has a 24hr emergency service and dentistry department; McCormick ☎053 241010 or 053 262200–19 is used to farangs and is nearer, on Thanon Kaeo Nawarat; Chiang Mai Ram at 8 Thanon Boonruangrit ☎053 224851–81 also has a very good reputation.

Immigration office On the southern leg of the Superhighway, 300m before the airport, on the left (Mon–Fri 8.30am–4.30pm; ☎053 277510 or 053 201756).

Internet access Most guest houses and hotels offer access to the Internet, and every second shop in town appears to be an Internet café, so you should have no problem getting online. Rates vary from as little as B15 per hour in locations near Chiang Mai University to as much as B120 in downtown areas; B1 a minute is the most typical rate, charged at *Click'n'Drink*, 147 Thanon Chang Klan opposite the *Royal Princess Hotel*, which stays open until 1am and offers a range of coffees. It's well worth taking your business to the Chiang Mai Disabled Centre, 133/1 Thanon Ratchaphakinai (☎053 213941, ⓦwww.infothai.com/disabled), where for B20 per hour, among many other services, your custom will help to support the Foundation to Encourage the Potential of Disabled Persons.

Laundry Most guest houses and hotels have an efficient laundry service; otherwise, try the Chiang Mai Disabled Centre, which also offers sewing repairs and alterations (see "Internet access" above), or White House, 31–35 Thanon Chang Moi Kao (behind Thanon Chaiyapoom), which charges by the kilo and is affordable and dependable. More reliable again is Blue Elephant, which uses filtered water, at 8/5 Thanon Suthep ☎053 279169.

Mail The GPO is on Thanon Charoen Muang near the train station (Mon–Fri 8.30am–4.30pm, Sat & Sun 9am–noon); private packing services operate outside on Thanon Charoen Muang. Poste restante should be addressed to: Chiang Mai Post and Telegraph Office, Thanon Charoen Muang, Chiang Mai 50000. There are also post offices at 43 Thanon Samlarn (Phra Singh PO), and on Thanon Phra Pokklao at the junction with Thanon Ratchawithi (Sri Phum PO), both in the old town, as well as on Thanon Wichayanon near Nawarat Bridge (Mae Ping PO), and at the airport.

Massages and spas The Old Medicine Hospital (see p.330) offers very good massages (B200 for 90min). Traditional massages by extremely competent, blind masseurs can be had (B150/hour) at the School for the Blind, 41 Thanon Arak (☎053 278009), and by disabled masseurs for the same price at the Chiang Mai Disabled Centre (see "Internet access" above). Let's Relax (ⓦwww.bloomingspa.com), with two convenient locations on Thanon Chang Klan, in the Chiang Inn Plaza (☎053 818198) and in the Chiangmai Pavilion opposite the *Royal Princess Hotel* (☎053 818498), is well run and reliable and lays on a wider range of treatments (B300 for a one-hour Thai massage up to B1000 for a facial treatment). Many of the top hotels now have full-service spas, and there are several upmarket stand-alones including: Ban Sabai (ⓦwww.ban-sabai.com), 17/7 Thanon Charoen Prathet in town (☎053 285204–6), with a village branch on the north side of town (☎053 854778–9); and Chiangmai Oasis Spa, 102 Thanon Sirimuangkarajan (☎053 227494, ⓦwww.chiangmaioasis.com).

Motorbike rental Motorbikes of all shapes and sizes are available for rent around Tha Pae Gate, starting from about B100 per day for an 80cc step-through. Among reliable rental outlets, Queen Bee, 5 Thanon Moonmuang ☎053 275525, ⓦwww.queen-bee.com, and Mr Mechanic, 4 Soi 5, Thanon Moonmuang ☎053 214708, who has bikes of all sizes, can also offer limited insurance.

Pharmacy Boots, Thanon Chang Klan, in front of the Chiang Inn Plaza, and at Kad Suan Kaew and Airport Plaza shopping centres.

Swimming Non-guests can use the attractive pool at the *Amari Rincome Hotel* on Thanon Huai Kaeo (daily 8am–7pm; B100); Pong Pot Swimming Pool, 73/22 Soi 4, Thanon Chotana (daily 9am–7pm; B20; ☎053 212812) has one big and one small pool.

Telephones The main office for calling abroad is the Chiang Mai Telecommunication Center (open 24hr), way out on the Superhighway, just south of the east end of Thanon Charoen Muang, but there are plenty of cardphones dotted around town. The GPO and the airport post office have overseas phone services.

Tourist police down a soi behind the *Lanna Palace Hotel*, off Thanon Chang Klan ☎053 278559 or nationwide helpline ☎1699.

Travel agents TransWorld Travel, 259–261 Thanon Tha Pae ☎053 272415, is affiliated with worldwide STA Travel and is reliable for plane tickets, as is Queen Bee, 5 Thanon Moonmuang ☎053 275525, ⓦwww.queen-bee.com, for train and bus tickets.

Around Chiang Mai

You'll never feel cooped up in Chiang Mai, as the surrounding countryside is dotted with day-trip options in all directions. Dominating the skyline to the west, **Doi Suthep** and its eagle's-nest temple are hard to ignore, and a wander around the pastoral ruins of **Wiang Kum Kam** on the southern periphery has the feel of fresh exploration. Further south, the quiet town of **Lamphun** offers classic sightseeing in the form of historically and religiously significant temples and a museum. To the north, the **Mae Sa valley** may be full of tour buses, but its highlights, the elephant camp and the botanic gardens, as well as the nearby lake of **Huay Tung Tao**, merit an independent jaunt. For honest, unabashed commerce, head for the shopping strip which stretches east towards San Kamphaeng (see p.338); about 23km beyond the weaving village, you can relax at some **hot springs**. All the excursions described here can be done in half a day; longer trips are dealt with later in the chapter.

One trip that is much more difficult to categorize but is worth mentioning here is to the **Elephant Nature Park**, in a remote part of Mae Taeng district, about an hour north of Chiang Mai. It's essentially a hospital for sick and injured elephants, but hands-on educational – and recreational – visits by the public are encouraged. On a day-trip from Chiang Mai, you'll get to feed, bathe and learn about the elephants close up (with the optional addition of rubber-rafting), but it's also possible to stay for two or three days (which might also include mountain-biking, rubber-rafting and visits to Akha and Lisu villages), or to sign up as a paying volunteer for a week or two. If you're interested, have a look at their detailed website (Ⓦwww.thaifocus.com/elephant) and contact the park's Chiang Mai office at Gem Travel, Soi 6, Thanon Charoen Prathet (Ⓣ053 272855).

Doi Suthep

A jaunt up **DOI SUTHEP**, the mountain which rises steeply at the city's western edge, is the most satisfying brief trip you can make from Chiang Mai, chiefly on account of beautiful **Wat Phra That Doi Suthep**, which dominates the hillside and gives a towering view over the goings-on in town. This is the north's holiest shrine, its pre-eminence deriving from a magic relic enshrined in its chedi and the miraculous legend of its founding. The original chedi here was built by King Ku Na at the end of the fourteenth century, after the glowing relic of Wat Suan Dork had self-multiplied just before being enshrined. A place had to be found for the clone, so Ku Na put it in a travelling shrine on the back of a white elephant and waited to see where the sacred animal would lead: it eventually climbed Doi Suthep, trumpeted three times, turned round three times, knelt down and died, thereby indicating that this was the spot. Ever since, it's been northern Thailand's most important place of pilgrimage, especially for the candlelit processions on **Maha Puja**, the anniversary of the sermon to the disciples, and **Visakha Puja**, the anniversary of the Buddha's birth, enlightenment and death.

Frequent **songthaews** leave the corner of Manee Noparat and Chotana roads for the sixteen-kilometre trip up to Wat Phra That (B40 to the wat, B70 return, B200 return to include Phuping Palace and Doi Pui village). The road, although steep in places, is paved and well suited for **motorbikes**. At the end of Thanon Huai Kaeo, a statue of Khruba Srivijaya, the monk who organized the gargantuan effort to build the road from here to the wat, points the way to the temple.

Khruba Srivijaya

Khruba Srivijaya, the most revered monk in northern Thailand, was born in 1877 in a small village 100km south of Chiang Mai. His birth coincided with a supernatural thunderstorm and earthquake, after which he was named In Fuan, "Great Jolt", until he joined the monkhood. A generous and tireless campaigner, he breathed life into Buddhist worship in the north by renovating over a hundred religious sites, including Wat Phra That Haripunjaya in Lamphun and Wat Phra That Doi Tung near Mae Sai. His greatest work, however, was the construction in 1935 of the paved road up to Wat Phra That Doi Suthep, which beforehand could only be reached after a climb of at least five hours. The road was constructed entirely by the voluntary labour of people from all over the north, using the most primitive tools. The project gained such fame that it attracted donations of B20 million, and on any one day as many as four thousand people were working on it. So that people didn't get in each other's way, Khruba Srivijaya declared that each village should contribute 15m of road, but as more volunteers flocked to Chiang Mai, this figure had to be reduced to 3m. The road was completed after just six months, and Khruba Srivijaya took the first ride to the temple in a donated car.

When Khruba Srivijaya died in 1938, Rama VIII was so moved that he sponsored a royal cremation ceremony, held in 1946. The monk's relics were divided up and are now enshrined at Wat Suan Dork in Chiang Mai, Wat Phra Kaeo Don Tao in Lampang and at many other holy places throughout the north.

A signpost halfway up is about the only indication that Doi Suthep is a **national park** (B200), though an entry fee is not levied if you are only visiting the wat, Phuping Palace and Doi Pui village. Despite the nearness of the city, its rich mixed forests support 330 species of birds, and the area is a favoured site for nature study, second in the north only to the larger and less disturbed Doi Inthanon National Park. On the higher slopes near park headquarters, about 1km beyond the wat (Ⓣ053 295117), there's a **campsite** and national park **bungalows** (from B400 for two persons).

About 5km from the statue of Khruba Srivijaya, an unpaved road on the right leads 3km to **Mon Tha Than Falls**, a beautiful spot, believed by some to be home to evil spirits. Camping is possible beside the pretty lower cascade, where refreshment stalls are open during the day. The higher fall is an idyllic five-metre drop into a small bathing pool, completely overhung by thick, humming jungle.

Wat Phra That Doi Suthep

Opposite a car park and souvenir village, a flight of three hundred naga-flanked steps – or the adjacent funicular – is the last leg on the way to **Wat Phra That Doi Suthep**. From the temple's **lower terrace**, the magnificent views of Chiang Mai and the surrounding plain, 1000m below, are best in the early morning or late afternoon, though peaceful contemplation of the view is frequently shattered by people sounding the heavy, dissonant bells around the terrace – it's supposed to bring good luck. At the northwestern corner is a two-metre-high statue of the elephant who, so the story goes, expired on this spot.

Before going to the **upper terrace** you have to remove your shoes – and if you're showing a bit of knee or shoulder, the temple provides wraps to cover your impoliteness. This terrace is possibly the most harmonious piece of temple architecture in Thailand, a dazzling combination of red, green and gold in the textures of carved wood, filigree and gleaming metal – even the tinkling of the miniature bells and the rattling of fortune sticks seem to keep the rhythm. A cloister, decorated with gaudy murals, tightly encloses the terrace, leaving room only for a couple of small minor viharns and the altars and ceremonial gold umbrellas which surround the central focus of attention, the **chedi**. This dazzling gold-plated beacon, a sixteenth-century extension of Ku Na's original, was modelled on the chedi at Wat Phra That Haripunjaya in Lamphun – which previously had been the region's most significant shrine – and has now become a venerated emblem of northern Thailand.

A small *hong*, or swan, on a wire stretching to the pinnacle is used to bless the chedi during major Buddhist festivals: a cup in the swan's beak is filled with water, and a pulley draws the swan to the spire where the water is tipped out over the sides of the chedi. Look out also for an old photograph opposite the northwestern corner of the chedi, showing a cockerel which used to peck the feet of visitors who entered with their shoes on.

Beyond the wat

Another 4km up the paved road from the wat, **Phuping Palace** (daily 8.30–11.30am & 1–3.30pm; B50) is the residence for the royals when they come to visit their village development projects in the north (usually Jan–March, when it is closed to the public). There is a viewpoint over the hills to the south, a rose garden and some pleasant trails through the forest, but the buildings themselves are off-limits. About 3km from the palace along a dirt side road and accessible by songthaew, **Ban Doi Pui** is a highly commercialized Hmong village, only worth visiting if you don't have time to get out into the countryside – seeing the Hmong is about all you get out of it.

Wiang Kum Kam

The well-preserved and rarely visited ruins of the ancient city of **WIANG KUM KAM** – traditionally regarded as the prototype for Chiang Mai – are hidden away in the picturesque, rural fringe of town, 5km south of the centre. According to folklore, Wiang Kum Kam was built by King Mengrai as his new capital of the north, but was soon abandoned because of inundation by the Ping River. Recent excavations, however, have put paid to that theory: Wiang Kum Kam was in fact established much earlier, as one of a cluster of fortified satellite towns that surrounded the Mon capital at Lamphun. After Mengrai had conquered Lamphun in 1281, he resided at Kum Kam for a while, raising a chedi, a viharn and several Buddha statues before moving on to build Chiang Mai. Wiang Kum Kam was abandoned sometime before 1750, probably as a result of a Burmese invasion.

About 3km square, the ancient city is best explored on a bicycle or a motorbike, though it's possible to see it by renting a tuk-tuk for half a day (about B300). The best way to approach Wiang Kum Kam without getting lost is from Route 1141, the southern leg of the Superhighway, which links the airport to Highway 11; immediately to the east of the Ping River bridge, take the signposted turning to the south.

About half of Wiang Kum Kam's 22 known temple sites have now been uncovered, along with a stone slab (now housed in the Chiang Mai National Museum) inscribed in a unique forerunner of the Thai script, and a hoard of terracotta Buddha images. It's easiest to head first for **Chedi Si Liam**, reached 1km after the Ping River bridge, which provides a useful landmark: this much-restored Mon chedi, in the shape of a tall, squared-off pyramid with niched Buddha images, was built by Mengrai in memory of his dead wife. Modelled on Wat Kukut in Lamphun, it is still part of a working temple.

Backtracking along the road you've travelled down from Chiang Mai, take the first right turn, turn right again and keep left through a scattered farming settlement to reach, after about 2km, **Wat Kan Thom** (aka Chang Kham), the centre of the old city and still an important place of worship. Archeologists were only able to get at the site after much of it had been levelled by bulldozers building a playground for the adjacent school, but they have managed to uncover the brick foundations of Mengrai's viharn. The modern spirit house next to it is where Mengrai's soul is said to reside. Also in the grounds are a white chedi and a small viharn, both much restored, and a large new viharn displaying fine craftsmanship.

The real joy now is to head off along the trails through the thick foliage of the longan plantations to the northwest of Wat Kan Thom, back towards Chedi Si Liam. On this route, you come across surprisingly well-preserved chedis and the red-brick walls of Wiang Kum Kam's temples in a handful of shady clearings, with only a few stray cows and sprouting weeds for company.

Lamphun

Though capital of its own province, **LAMPHUN** lives in the shadow of the tourist attention (and baht) showered on Chiang Mai, 26km to the north. Yet for anyone interested in history, a visit to this former royal city is a must. The town's largely plain architecture is given some character by the surrounding waterways, beyond which stretch lush rice fields and plantations of *lam yai* (longan); the sweetness of the local variety is celebrated every year in early August at the **Ngan Lam Yai** (Longan Festival), when the town comes alive with processions of fruity floats, a drum-beating competition and a Miss Lam Yai beauty contest. Lamphun also offers a less frantic alternative to Chiang Mai during the Songkhran and Loy Krathong festivals (see box on p.335), the Khuang River being a far less congested place to float your *krathong* than Chiang Mai's Ping River. Though the streets of the town are usually sleepy, the ancient working **temples** of Wat Phra That Haripunjaya and Wat Kukut are lively and worth aiming for on a half-day trip from Chiang Mai. A full-day visit could include Wat Mahawan and the Chama Thevi monument, as well as a stroll round the town's market.

Lamphun claims to be the oldest continuously inhabited town in Thailand, and has a history dating back to the late eighth or early ninth century when the ruler of the major Dvaravati centre at Lopburi sent his daughter, Chama Thevi, to found the Theravada Buddhist state of **Haripunjaya** here. Under the dynasty she established, Haripunjaya flourished as a link in the trade route to Yunnan in southwest China, although it eventually came under the suzerainty of the Khmers at Angkor, probably in the early eleventh century. In 1281, after a decade of scheming, King Mengrai of Chiang Mai conquered Lamphun and integrated it once and for all into the Thai state of Lanna, which by then covered all of the north country.

The Town

Chama Thevi's planners are said to have based their design for the town on the shape of an auspicious conch shell. The rough outcome is a rectangle, narrower at the north end than the south, with the Khuang River running down its kilometre-long east side, and moats around the north, west and south sides. The main street, Thanon Inthayongyot, bisects the conch from north to south, while the road to Wat Kukut (Thanon Chama Thevi) heads out from the middle of the west moat.

One of the north's grandest and most important temples, **Wat Phra That Haripunjaya** has its rear entrance on Thanon Inthayongyot and its bot and ornamental front entrance facing the river. The earliest guess at the date of its founding is 897, when the king of Haripunjaya is said to have built a chedi to enshrine a hair of the Buddha. More certain is the date of the main rebuilding of the temple, under King Tilokaraja of Chiang Mai in 1443, when the present ringed chedi was erected in the then-fashionable Sri Lankan style (later copied at Doi Suthep and Lampang). Clad in brilliant copper plates, it has since been raised to a height of about 50m, crowned by a gold umbrella.

The plain open courtyards around the chedi contain a compendium of religious structures in a wild mix of styles and colours. On the north side, the tiered Haripunjaya-style pyramid of **Chedi Suwanna** was built in 1418 as a replica of the chedi at nearby Wat Kukut. You get a whiff of southern Thailand in the open space beyond the Suwanna chedi, where the **Chedi Chiang Yan** owes its resemblance to a pile of flattened pumpkins to the Srivijayan style. On either side of the viharn (to the east of the main chedi) stand a dark red **bell-tower**, containing what's claimed to be the world's largest bronze gong, and a weather-beaten **library** on a raised base. Just to add to the temple's mystique, an open pavilion at the southwestern corner of the chedi shelters a stone indented with four overlapping **footprints**, believed by fervent worshippers to confirm an ancient legend that the Buddha once passed this way. Next to the pavilion can be seen a small **museum** which houses bequests to the temple, including some beautiful Buddha images in the Lanna style. Finally, beside the back entrance, is the **Phra Chao Tan Jai**, a graceful standing Buddha, surrounded by graphic murals that depict a horrific version of Buddhist hell.

Across the main road from the wat's back entrance, the **Haribhunchai National Museum** (Wed–Sun 9am–4pm; B30) contains a well-organized but not quite compelling collection of religious finds, and occasionally stages some interesting temporary exhibitions. The terracotta and bronze Buddha images here give the best overview of the distinctive features of the Haripunjaya style: large curls above a wide, flat forehead, bulging eyes, incised moustache and enigmatic smile.

Art-history buffs will get a thrill out of **Wat Chama Thevi** (aka Wat Kukut), where two brick chedis, dated to 1218, are the only complete examples not just of Haripunjaya architecture, but of the whole Dvaravati style. Queen Chama Thevi is supposed to have chosen the site by ordering an archer to fire an arrow from the city's western gate – to retrace his epic shot, follow the road along the National Museum's southern wall to the west gate at the city moat, and keep going for nearly 1km along Thanon Chama Thevi. The main chedi – Suwan Chang Kot – is tiered and rectangular, the smaller Ratana Chedi octagonal, and both are inset with niches sheltering beautiful, wide-browed Buddha images in stucco, typical of the Haripunjaya style. Suwan Chang Kot, believed to enshrine Chama Thevi's ashes, lost its pinnacle at some stage, giving rise to the name Wat Kukut, the temple with the "topless" chedi.

On your way back to the town centre from Wat Chama Thevi, you might like to pop in at **Wat Mahawan**, famous for the Buddha image amulets on sale here and located just outside the west gate. The temple has been recently renovated and features some huge and fearsome nagas standing guard at the entrance to the viharn. Following the moat to the south from here brings you in about five minutes to the **Queen Chama Thevi monument**, situated in a large square by the moat in the southwest corner of the city; the monument receives a steady stream of locals making offerings to their heroine. Beside it is the town's main market, which mostly sells fresh produce and buzzes with activity in the morning.

Practicalities

The direct (and scenic) route from Chiang Mai to Lamphun is Highway 106, for much of the way a stately avenue lined by thirty-metre-tall *yang* trees that makes for a pleasant motorbike ride. Otherwise you could catch a blue **songthaew** from the Chiang Mai–Lamphun road, just south of Narawat bridge and opposite the TAT office, or a white **bus** from Chang Puak bus station, via Lamyai flower market, either of which will put you off outside the back entrance of Wat Haripunjaya. If you turn up at Lamphun by **train**, it's a thirty-minute walk or a samlor ride southwest to the town centre.

Among the few **restaurants** in Lamphun with an English-language menu is *Lamphun Ice*, which serves tasty Thai food at reasonable prices; it's conveniently situated at 6 Thanon Chaimongkol, the road that runs along the south wall of Wat Haripunjaya. It's unlikely you'll want to stay overnight in Lamphun, as it makes a perfect day-trip from Chiang Mai and there's not a wide range of **accommodation**. The only decent choice in town is the *Supamit Holiday Inn* on Thanon Chama Thevi opposite Wat Kukut (Ⓣ053 534865–6; ❸–❹), a large modern building with an open-air restaurant on the fourth floor, where bedrooms boast en-suite, hot-water bathrooms and either fan or air-con.

San Kamphaeng hot springs

Thirty-five kilometres east of Chiang Mai, the **San Kamphaeng hot springs**, with their geysers, baths and gardens, as well as a resort, make for a wonderfully indulgent day-trip, easily accomplished by motorbike. The quickest way there, about 45 minutes at a good speed, is to take Highway 11 southeast of Chiang Mai, then turn left onto Route 1317, which heads eastwards as dual carriageway for much of the way before veering north towards Highway 118, the main Chiang Mai–Chiang Rai road (look for the turning on the left after about 35km, signposted "Hot Springs" in English). The slow route, heading east out of the city on Route 1008 through San Kamphaeng (see p.338) before turning north onto Route 1317, allows you to combine mineral bathing with some handicrafts shopping.

The government-run hot springs complex (B20) has pleasantly landscaped gardens and geysers that spout scalding water about 10m high. The best place to enjoy the springs, however, is next door at the *Rong Aroon Hot Springs Resort*, set in its own expansive gardens (Ⓣ053 248475, Ⓕ053 248491). It's perfect for a visit of a few hours, providing a soothing tonic to the general stresses of travel, though options do include staying in **bungalows** (❼), which have hot spring water piped into them. If you're not a guest, the main gate charges B20 admission to the property, and for another B70 you can take advantage of the bath house, which offers hot baths in a private room (towels provided). Massages, mud baths and facials are available at reasonable prices, and there are even Jacuzzi baths and a swimming pool. You can also have a restaurant lunch on the bougainvillea-draped terrace overlooking the hot spring geyser.

Huay Tung Tao and the Mae Sa valley

On the north side of Chiang Mai, Thanon Chotana turns into Highway 107, which heads off through a flat, featureless valley, past a golf course and an army camp, towards the small market town of **Mae Rim** 16km away. With your own transport, you can head off down side roads to the west of Highway 107, either to Huay Tung Tao for a swim and chillout, or to the Mae Sa valley, which despite its theme-park atmosphere has sufficient attractions for an interesting half- or full day out, and some pretty resorts that might even tempt you to spend a night out of Chiang Mai. Without your own vehicle, it's best to visit as part of a tour group as public transport here is at best sporadic – Queen Bee, for example (see p.346), charge B400 for a half-day trip.

About 10km out of Chiang Mai, look for the signpost to the left to **Huay Tung Tao**, a large man-made lake at the base of Doi Suthep, 2km to the west of the turn-off along a dirt road which is easily driven. A great place to cool off during the hot season, the lake is safe to swim in, with canoes and pedaloes to rent, and is also used by anglers and windsurfers. Floating bamboo shelters along the water's edge provide shade from the sun, and you can order simple food such as sticky rice, grilled chicken and *som tam*.

Turn left about 1km after Mae Rim to enter the **Mae Sa valley**, where a good sealed road, Route 1069, leads up into the hills. The main road through the valley passes a menagerie of snake farms, monkey shows, and orchid and butterfly farms, as well as the unspectacular **Mae Sa Waterfall** (B200 national park fee payable), where you can walk up a peaceful trail passing lots of little cascades along the way. Several elephant camps also lie along the route, of which the best is the **Mae Sa Elephant Camp**, 10km along the valley road (with an office at 119/9 Thanon Tha Pae, ⓣ053 206248). Mae Sa offers logging shows at 8am, 9.40am and 1.30pm daily (B80, children B40) and you can take a short ride on an elephant (B80) or a more expensive ride into the countryside (B1000 an hour for two people).

Two kilometres beyond the Mae Sa Elephant Camp, the magnificent **Queen Sirikit Botanic Gardens** (B20, children B10, vehicles B30) are well worth a look, and if you are at all botanically inclined, you could easily spend the whole day here as it covers such a large area, with several nature trails to explore. A vehicle is certainly necessary to get to the upper area where glasshouses display a fantastic array of plants.

Among several **resorts** in the Mae Sa valley, the pick is the *Regent* (ⓣ053 298181–9, ⓦwww.regenthotels.com; ❾), down a side road on the left just 1km after the turning into the valley from Mae Rim. The last word in Lanna luxury, this award-winning resort has superbly appointed pavilions, plush apartments, a swimming pool, a gym and spa, set among beautifully landscaped grounds, and offers top-quality cooking courses among a long menu of activities. Even if you're not staying there, it's a good spot to stop, especially in the late afternoon or early evening, to enjoy a meal or drink on a terrace with a lovely view across hills to the west. Other resorts in the valley are far simpler than the *Regent*, but attractive nonetheless; among these the *Pong Yang Garden Resort* (ⓣ053 879151–2, ⓕ053 879153; ❼) stands out, located a couple of kilometres beyond the botanic gardens on the south side of the road. It boasts well-equipped bungalows as well as a restaurant with a view of an attractive waterfall.

Once you've seen all you want to in the valley, you have the option of retracing your route to Chiang Mai, or continuing west for a scenic drive in the country. For the latter, turn left on to Route 1269 before Samoeng, and follow this road as it swoops up and down over hills, skirting Doi Suthep to join Highway 108 8km south of Chiang Mai, a two-hour drive in all.

East of Chiang Mai

From Chiang Mai, visitors usually head northwest to Mae Hong Son or north to Chiang Rai, but a trip eastwards to the ancient city-states of Lampang, Phrae and Nan can be just as rewarding, not only for the dividends of going against the usual flow, but also for the natural beauty of the region's upland ranges – seen to best effect from the well-marked trails of **Doi Khun Tan National Park** – and its eccentric variety of Thai, Burmese and Laotian art and architecture. Congenial **Lampang** contains Thai wats to rival those of Chiang Mai for beauty – in Wat Phra That Lampang Luang the town has the finest surviving example of traditional northern architecture anywhere – and is further endowed with pure Burmese temples and some fine old city architecture, while little-visited **Phrae**, to the southeast, is a step back in time to a simpler Thailand. Harder to reach but a more intriguing target is **Nan**, with its heady artistic mix of Thai and Laotian styles and steep ring of scenic mountains.

A few major **roads**, served by regular through buses from Chiang Mai, cross the region: Highway 11 heads southeast through Lampang and the junction town of Den Chai before plummeting south to Phitsanulok; from Lampang Highway 1 heads north to Chiang Rai; and from Den Chai Highway 101 carries on northeast through Phrae to Nan, almost on the border with Laos. Route 1148 between Tha Wang Pha and Chiang Kham makes it tempting to continue north from Nan to Chiang Rai, through some spectacular scenery. The northern **rail line** follows a course roughly parallel with Highway 11 through the region, including a stop at Doi Khun Tan National Park, and although trains here are generally slower than buses, the Lampang and Den Chai stations are useful if you're coming up from Bangkok.

Doi Khun Tan National Park

One of three national parks close to Chiang Mai, along with Suthep and Inthanon, **DOI KHUN TAN NATIONAL PARK** (B200) is easily accessible by train from Chiang Mai: the 1352-metre-long rail tunnel, thought to be the longest in Thailand, and completed by German engineers in 1918, actually cuts through the mountain slope. Even so, the park is the least spoilt of the three; a former hill station, it was not declared a national park until 1975 and a lack of tourist infrastructure until recently has meant that it has had few visitors. With food and accommodation now available, it is opening up to tourists: there is a restaurant beside the bungalows, which are spacious and well-appointed log cabins, and there are three campsites. One of the other appeals of Doi Khun Tan National Park is that no road runs through the park itself – it can most easily be reached by **train** from Chiang Mai.

The park

Covering 255 square kilometres, the park's vegetation varies from bamboo forests at an altitude of 350m to tropical evergreen forests between 600 and 1000m; the 1373-metre summit of Doi Khun Tan is known for its wild flowers, including orchids. Most of the small mammal species in the park are squirrels, but you're more likely to see some birds, with over 182 species found here. A leaflet on the park's ecology can sometimes be obtained at the park **headquarters**.

The **trails** are clearly marked. There are short nature trails around the park headquarters (where self-guided maps are available), while three major trails all eventually lead to the summit of **Doi Khun Tan**, the highest summit reachable on self-guided trails in the Chiang Mai area; with impressive views of the surrounding countryside, it's clear how it fulfilled its role as a World War II military lookout. The main 8.3-kilometre trail from the train station to the Doi Khun Tan summit, though steep, is very easy, divided into four quarters of approximately 2km each with each quarter ending at a resting place. While you shouldn't have a problem reaching the summit and returning to the station in a day, a more rewarding option is to do the walk in two days, staying overnight in the bungalows or at one of the campsites along the trail. Alternatively, you can take a circular route to the summit and back, forsaking a large chunk of the main trail for the two subsidiary trails which curve around either side, taking in two **waterfalls**.

Practicalities

Though there are six daily **trains** from Chiang Mai (1hr 30min) which stop at the park, at least three of these arrive after dark, so day-trippers should make a very early start (leaving Chiang Mai at 6.55am and taking the last train back at 7.41pm; check current timetables). Get off at Khun Tan station, from where the park headquarters are 1300m up the summit trail. A **car** or motorbike can also take you to the park headquarters, though no further: follow Highway 11 to the turn-off to Mae Tha and head northeast along a partly paved road, following signs for the park, a further 18km away.

The park is most popular on weekends, when groups of Thai schoolchildren visit, and during the cool season. Park **bungalows** (B1200 for six people, B1800 for nine people), are located just up the main trail from the headquarters, while tents can be hired (B250 sleeping 2–3 people) for the **campsites** (pitching your own costs B30). There is a small **restaurant** just up from the train ticket office, another beside the bungalows, and food is also available at a shop and café near the headquarters.

Lampang and around

A high road pass and a train tunnel breach the narrow, steep belt of mountains between Chiang Mai and **LAMPANG**, the north's second-largest town, 100km to the southeast. Lampang is an important transport hub – Highway 11, Highway 1 and the northern rail line all converge here – and given its undeniably low-key attractions, nearly all travellers sail through it on their way to the more trumpeted sights further north. But unlike most other provincial capitals, Lampang has the look of a place where history has not been completely wiped out: houses, shops and temples survive in the traditional style, and the town makes few concessions to tourism. Out of town, the beautiful complex of Wat Phra That Lampang Luang is the main attraction in these parts, but while you're in the neighbourhood you could also stop by to watch a show at the Elephant Conservation Centre, on the road from Chiang Mai.

Founded as Kelang Nakhon by the ninth-century Haripunjaya queen Chama Thevi, Lampang became important enough for one of her two sons to rule here after her death. After King Mengrai's conquest of Haripunjaya in 1281, Lampang suffered much the same ups and downs as the rest of Lanna, enjoying a burst of prosperity as a **timber** town at the end of the nineteenth

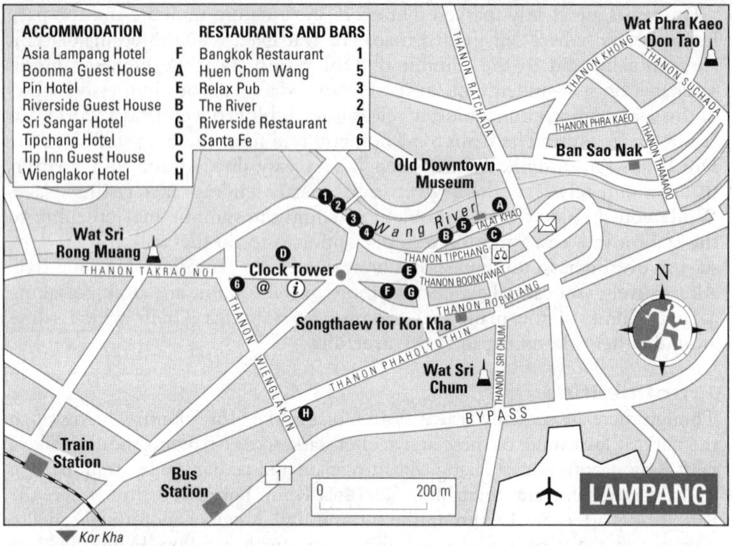

century, when it supported a population of twenty thousand people and four thousand working elephants. Many of its temples are financially endowed by the waves of outsiders who have settled in Lampang: refugees from Chiang Saen (who were forcibly resettled here by Rama I at the beginning of the nineteenth century), Burmese teak-loggers and workers, and, more recently, rich Thai pensioners attracted by the town's sedate charm.

The Town

The modern centre of Lampang sprawls along the south side of the Wang River, with its most frenetic commercial activity taking place along Thanon Boonyawat and Robwiang near Ratchada Bridge. Here, you'll find stalls and shops selling the famous local pottery, a kitsch combination of whites, blues and browns, made from the area's rich kaolin clay. On all street signs around town, and in larger-than-life statues at key intersections, is a white chicken. This symbol of Lampang relates to a legend concerning the Buddha, who sent down angels from Heaven in the form of chickens to wake up the local inhabitants in time to offer alms to the monks at the end of Buddhist Lent. Perhaps the town's image as a laid-back, sleepy place is justified in the light of this legend.

Lampang's few sights are well scattered; the best place to start is on the north side of the river (the site of the original Haripunjaya settlement), whose leafy suburbs today contain the town's most important and interesting temple, **Wat Phra Kaeo Don Tao** (B20). An imposing, rather forbidding complex on Thanon Phra Kaeo, 1km northeast of the Ratchada Bridge, the temple was founded in the fifteenth century to enshrine the Phra Kaeo Don Tao image, now residing at Wat Phra That Lampang Luang (see p.359). For 32 years it also housed the Emerald Buddha (local stories aver this to be a copy of Phra Kaeo Don Tao), a situation which came about when an elephant carrying the holy image from Chiang Rai to Chiang Mai made an unscheduled and therefore auspicious halt here in 1436. The clean, simple lines of the white, gold-capped **chedi**, which is reputed to contain a hair of the Buddha, form a shining backdrop to the wat's most interesting building, a Burmese **mondop** stacked up in extravagantly carved tiers; it was built in 1909 by craftsmen from the local Burmese community, employed for the task by a Thai prince (whose British-style coat of arms can be seen on the ceiling inside). All gilt and gaudy coloured glass, the interior decoration is a real fright, mixing Oriental and European influences, with some incongruously cute little cherubs on the ceiling. The mondop's boyish bronze centrepiece has the typical features of a Mandalay Buddha, with its jewelled headband, inset black and white eyes, and exaggerated, dangling ears, which denote the Buddha's supernatural ability to hear everything in the universe. In front of the Buddha is an image of Khruba Srivijaya, the north's most venerated monk (see box on p.348).

The small, gloomy **museum** diagonally opposite the mondop displays some dainty china among its exhibits, but its main focus is woodcarving, a craft at which Burmese artisans excel. To see a better, though still small, display of ceramics, lacquerware and teak furnishings, make your way to **Ban Sao Nak** ("many pillar house") at 6 Thanon Ratwattana, not far from Wat Phra Kaeo Don Tao (daily 10am–5pm, B30 with free soft drink). This sprawling wooden mansion is supported by a maze of teak pillars and contains some interesting fading photographs of its former occupants, who were local notables.

The Burmese who worked on Wat Phra Kaeo Don Tao were brought to Lampang in the late nineteenth century when, after the British conquest of Upper Burma, timber companies expanded their operations as far as northern Thailand. Fearing that the homeless spirits of fallen trees would seek vengeance, the Burmese logging workers often sponsored the building of temples, most of which still stand, to try to appease the tree spirits and gain merit. Though the spirits had to wait nearly a century, they seem to have got their revenge: due to a short circuit in some dodgy wiring, the viharn of **Wat Sri Chum**, which is the biggest Burmese temple in Thailand as well as the most important and beautiful Burmese temple in town, burnt to the ground in 1992. Now restored to its former glory, with fresh carvings and murals by Burmese craftsmen, it's sited in a small grove of bodhi trees five minutes' walk south of Thanon Robwiang. None of the remaining wats is of outstanding architectural merit, but to get more of a flavour of Burma, try **Wat Sri Rong Muang**, towards the west end of Thanon Takrao Noi, which presents a dazzling ensemble: the crazy angles of its red and yellow roof shelter more Mandalay Buddhas and several extravagantly carved gilt sermon thrones, swimming in a glittering sea of coloured-glass wall tiles.

When you've had your fill of temples, **Thanon Talat Kao**, the "Old Market Street", running behind the south bank of the river, is good for a stroll in the early morning. It has some very old shophouses and mansions, showing a mixture of Burmese, Chinese and European influence, with intricate balconies, carved gables and unusual sunburst designs carved over some of the doors. Some of these lovely structures are now being restored to their former glory, like the **Old Downtown Museum** towards the western end of the road, which features free rotating exhibitions of Northern Thai arts and crafts, though there are no signs in English. Others, like the *Boon Ma Guest House*, offer visitors the chance to stay in an elaborately-designed wooden house on stilts. Small lanes on the north side of Thanon Talat Kao lead down to the Wang River, whose waters are as green as some of its overgrown banks – what used to be the main thoroughfare for trading boats and huge rafts of felled timber has been reduced almost to stagnation by an upriver dam. Unfortunately a large section of the river bank through the main part of town is now stripped of its greenery, and the sandy soil and concrete tiers make for an ugly view.

Though the **Lampang Medicinal Plants Conservation Assembly** (177 Moo 12, Ban Kelangthong, Kanmuang Road, ⓣ054 313128) sounds like the kind of place where botanists might hold seminars, it is in fact a traditional health centre set in a shady compound a few kilometres northeast of town. If you feel like pampering your body, head out here for a herbal sauna, traditional massage, face scrub, mud skin treatment or even a bare-footed health walk over a path of rounded pebbles designed to provide a natural foot massage. The facilities are spotless, the grounds are full of labelled herbs, and a huge range of medicinal plant products is on sale. To get there, a songthaew from the centre of Lampang costs around B50.

Practicalities

Buses from Nawarat Bridge in Chiang Mai run to Lampang every thirty minutes from Thanon Chiang Mai–Lamphun, just south of Narawat bridge, for most of the day, some of which then trundle on up Highway 1 to Phayao and Chiang Rai. Hourly buses also leave from Chiang Mai's Arcade station. Only seven **trains** a day stop here in each direction; the **train and bus stations** lie less than 1km to the southwest of town, and many buses also stop on Thanon Phaholyothin in the centre. The **airport** is located just south of town, and songthaews are on hand for the short ride to the centre. The small, municipal **tourist information** centre (Mon–Fri 8.30am–noon & 1–4.30pm), just east of the clocktower and next to the fire station on Thanon Takrao Noi, can provide a decent map of the town and help with advice on excursions to the elephant training centre and the like. There is cheap and fast **Internet access**, along with coffee and cakes, at N@net in the middle of Thanon Takrao Noi on the south side.

The whole town can be covered on foot without trouble, though to get out to Wat Phra Kaeo Don Tao you might want to employ the services of a **horse-drawn carriage**, which along with white chickens is another prevalent symbol of Lampang (in fact, Thais often refer to the city as *muang rot mah*, or "horse-cart city"). These colourfully decked-out carriages, complete with Stetson-wearing driver, can be hired near the big hotels in centre of town. Standard prices are B150 for 20 minutes, B200 for 30 minutes or B300 for one hour, which is what it would take to get out to Wat Phra Kaeo Don Tao and back. Apart from this quirky mode of transport, there is also a good network of **songthaews** that cruise the streets looking for custom.

Accommodation

As far as accommodation goes, Lampang has several **guest houses** scattered along the quiet banks of the river, among which one place stands out and provides enough reason for a visit to the town in itself. Run by the owners of the restaurant of the same name (see below), the *Riverside Guest House*, 286 Thanon Talat Kao (ⓣ054 227005, ⓕ054 322342, ⓔriversidefamily@yahoo.com; ❸–❹), is a peaceful traditional compound of elegantly decorated rooms, most with en-suite bathrooms; some rooms boast balconies overlooking the river and there is also a motorbike communal relaxing area beside the river. The helpful Belgian owner is a good source of local information and she can rent out motorbikes. A little further west, *Boonma Guest House* at 256 Thanon Talat Kao (ⓣ054 322653; ❶–❸) has a couple of spacious rooms upstairs in a gorgeous, stilted wooden building, and several cramped, less appealing rooms downstairs. Almost opposite *Boonma*, the small and viewless rooms at *Tip Inn Guest House*, 143 Thanon Talad Kao (ⓣ054 221821; ❶–❷) are classic budget travellers' digs.

The town's lowest-priced **hotels** queue up to the west of the centre along Thanon Boonyawat. One of the cleanest of these dismal affairs is *Sri Sangar*, at 213–215 Thanon Boonyawat (Ⓣ054 217070; ❶–❷) where the small, fan rooms are acceptable, but traffic noise could be a problem. For a little more cash, standards improve markedly: the *Pin Hotel*, half a block north at 8 Thanon Suandok (Ⓣ054 221509; Ⓕ054 322286; Ⓔpinhotel@loxinfo.co.th; ❹–❺) has good-sized rooms, all with air-con, TV and hot water, and some with carpets and bathtubs. The rooms at the *Asia Lampang Hotel*, 229 Thanon Boonyawat (Ⓣ054 227844–7, Ⓕ054 224436, Ⓔasiahotel@lampang1.a-net.th; ❹), are also comfortable and good value. There are several top-end hotels in town, among which the *Wienglakor* at 138/35 Thanon Phaholyothin (Ⓣ054 224470; Ⓕ054 316427; ❻–❽) has the most tasteful decor and the cosiest rooms, as well as good views from some of the upper floors. The more tourist-orientated *Tipchang Hotel*, at 54/22 Thanon Takrao Noi (Ⓣ054 226501–6, Ⓕ054 225362; ❻), has its own swimming pool, but otherwise is rather sleazy compared to the *Wienglakor*.

Eating and drinking

A popular place to **eat and drink** is the *Riverside* at 328 Thanon Tipchang, a cosy, relaxing spot on terraces overlooking the water. A wide variety of excellent Thai and Western food (moderate–expensive), including pizza, is served here to the sounds of live music. A quieter ambience prevails at *Huen Chom Wang*, 276 Thanon Talat Kao (no English sign – look for the alley 100m east of the *Riverside Guest House*), where guests are greeted by beautifully arranged blossoms floating in water bowls on the stairway. The sprawling wooden building has fine views of the river and its menu features many northern specialities (moderate–expensive). To the west of the *Riverside*, several other bars have opened recently, including *Relax Pub*, *The River* and *Bangkok Restaurant*, trying to liven up the town's nightlife, though whether they succeed remains to be seen. Among the hotels in town, the *Wienglakor* has a restaurant with an inviting ambience and a good choice of well-prepared dishes. The stretch of Thanon Takrao Noi between the clocktower and Thanon Wienglakon is the liveliest part of town after dark with many simple restaurants and the Atsawin night market running off its side streets to the south. Also along Thanon Takrao Noi are a few Wild West **bars** – Lampang obviously takes its Stetson-wearing image seriously – including *Santa Fe*, near the corner of Thanon Wienglakon. In this area, there are also pubs, discos and karaoke bars that attract the town's youth after dark.

Wat Phra That Lampang Luang

If you've made it as far as Lampang, a visit to **Wat Phra That Lampang Luang**, a grand and well-preserved capsule of beautiful Lanna art and architecture, is a must, one of the architectural highlights of northern Thailand. However, although the wat is a busy pilgrimage site, **getting there** without your own transport isn't always straightforward: some songthaews will take you to the temple direct from outside the Thai Farmers Bank on Thanon Robwiang (B30); otherwise, take one to **Kor Kha**, 10km southwest on Highway 1 (B15), then take another towards **Hang Chat** and get off at the temple entrance. If you're getting there yourself on a motorbike (which can be rented in Lampang from the *Riverside Guest House*) or other transport, cross the bridge over the Mae Nam Wang at Kor Kha and turn right, heading north on a paved road.

The wat was built early in the Haripunjaya era as a *wiang* (fortress), one of a satellite group around Lampang – you can still see remains of the threefold ramparts in the farming village around the temple. A naga staircase leads you up to a wedding cake of a gatehouse, richly decorated with stucco, which is set in the original brick boundary walls. Just inside, the oversized **viharn** is open on all sides in classic Lanna fashion, and shelters a spectacular centrepiece: known as a *ku*, a feature found only in the viharns of northern Thailand, this gilded brick tower looks like a bonfire for the main Buddha image sitting inside, the Phra Chao Lan Thong. If you're over 1.8m tall, mind your head on the panels hanging from the low eaves, which are decorated with attractive, though fading, early-nineteenth-century paintings of battles, palaces and nobles in traditional Burmese gear.

This central viharn is snugly flanked by three others. In front of the murky, beautifully decorated viharn to the left, look out for a wooden *tung chai* carved with flaming, coiled nagas, used as a heraldic banner for northern princes. The battered, cosy **Viharn Nam Tame**, second back on the right, dates back to the early sixteenth century. Its drooping roof configuration is archetypal: divided into three tiers, each of which is divided again into two layers, it ends up almost scraping the ground. Under the eaves you can just make out fragments of panel paintings, as old as the viharn, illustrating a story of one of the exploits of the Hindu god Indra.

Hundreds of rainy seasons have turned the copper plates on the wat's huge central **chedi** into an arresting patchwork of greens, blues and purples: safe inside are supposed to be a hair of the Buddha and ashes from the right side of his forehead and neck. By the chedi's northwest corner, a sign points to a drainage hole in the wat's boundary wall, once the scene of an unlikely act of derring-do: in 1736, local hero Thip Chang managed to wriggle through the tiny hole and free the *wiang* from the occupying Burmese, before going on to liberate the whole of Lampang.

To the south of the chedi, the **Haw Phra Phuttabhat** is a small chamber that acts as a camera obscura. If you close the door behind you, an image of the chedi is projected through a small hole in the door onto a sheet hung on a wall. A gate in the south side of the boundary wall leads to a spreading **bodhi tree** on crutches: merit-makers have donated hundreds of supports to prop up its drooping branches. The tree, with its own small shrine standing underneath, is believed to be inhabited by spirits, and the sick are sometimes brought here in search of a cure.

Don't miss the small, unimpressive viharn to the west of the main complex (go on round beyond the bodhi tree) – it's the home of **Phra Kaeo Don Tao**, the much-revered companion image to Bangkok's Emerald Buddha, and the wat's main focus of pilgrimage. Legend has it that the statuette first appeared in the form of an emerald found in a watermelon presented by a local woman to a venerated monk. The two of them tried to carve a Buddha out of the emerald, without much success, until the god Indra appeared and fashioned the marvellous image, at which point the ungrateful townsfolk accused the monk of having an affair with the woman and put her to death, thus bringing down upon the town a series of disasters which confirmed the image's awesome power. In all probability, the image was carved at the beginning of the fifteenth century, when its namesake wat in Lampang was founded. Peering through the dim light and the rows of protective bars inside the viharn, you can just make out the tiny meditating Buddha – it's actually made of jasper, not emerald – which on special occasions is publicly displayed wearing a headdress and necklace.

Cashing in on Phra Kaeo Don Tao's supernatural reputation, a shop in the viharn sells amulets and Buddha images. Outside the wat, simple snacks, handicrafts and antiques can be bought from market stalls; also available are the small china cows with which devotees make merit, inscribing the models first with their name and the date in black ink and then offering them to the shrine in front of the chedi, making a curious display.

The Thai Elephant Conservation Centre

The **Thai Elephant Conservation Centre** (ⓣ054 229042 or 054 228034; ⓦwww.changthai.com), 37km west of Lampang on Highway 11, is the most authentic place in Thailand to see elephants displaying their skills and, being more out of the way, is less touristy than the elephant showgrounds to the north of Chiang Mai. **Shows** (daily 10am & 11am plus Sat & Sun 1.30pm; bathing at 9.45am and 1.15pm; B50) put the elephants through their paces, with plenty of amusing showmanship and loud trumpeting for their audience. After some photogenic bathing, they walk together in formation and go through a routine of pushing and dragging logs, then proceed to paint pictures and play custom-made instruments. You can buy bananas and sugar-cane to feed them after the show, and if you are impressed by their painting or music you can buy a freshly painted picture or a CD by the Thai Elephant Orchestra. An interpretive centre has exhibits on the history of the elephant in Thailand and **elephant-rides** (B100 for 10min, B200 for 30min or B400 for 1hr) are cheaper here than anywhere else in the north. There is also a **home-stay programme**, on which you spend three days learning how to care for and control elephants for around B1500 a day. For more information, check out their website.

Run by the veterinary section of the Forest Industry Organization, the conservation centre was originally set up in 1969 in another nearby location as a young elephant training centre, the earliest of its kind in Thailand. However, with the high levels of elephant unemployment since the ban on logging (see box on p.362), the new centre, opened in 1992, emphasizes the preservation of the elephant in Thailand. By promoting eco-tourism the centre is providing employment for the elephants and enabling Thai people to continue their historically fond relationship with these animals. Money raised from entrance fees helps to finance the **elephant hospital** here, which cares for sick, abused, ageing and abandoned elephants. Its yearly expenses are 12–14 million baht, with huge expenses incurred from looking after about sixty elephants; the enormous amounts of money the centre needs to feed and care for its elephants mean it is in a permanent funding crisis.

Practicalities

The Thai Elephant Conservation Centre is best visited en route between Chiang Mai and Lampang: ask the bus conductor to stop at the centre. On a day-trip from Lampang, a bus towards Lamphun or Chiang Mai should get you to the entrance gates in around forty minutes, but you'll still have a couple of kilometres to walk from there. If you have your own vehicle, the Thung Kwian **market**, 21km from Lampang on Highway 11, offers not only a useful stop for refreshments near the Elephant Centre, but also a chance to view the panoply of forest products on sale – from wild pigs, squirrels and birds to honeycombs, bugs and creepy crawlies of every description. This is a favourite spot for city Thais to pick up some exotic taste to take back home with them.

Phrae and around

From Lampang, buses follow Highway 11 to the junction town of Den Chai (Bangkok–Chiang Mai trains also stop here), 83km to the southeast, then veer northeastwards on Highway 101 through the tobacco-rich Yom valley, dotted with distinctive brick curing-houses. Frequent songthaews from Den Chai head

The elephant in Thailand

To Thais the **Asian elephant** has profound **spiritual significance**, derived from both Hindu and Buddhist mythologies. Carvings and statues of **Ganesh**, the Hindu god with an elephant's head, feature on ancient temples all over the country and, as the god of knowledge and remover of obstacles, Ganesh has been adopted as the symbol of the Fine Arts Department – and is thus depicted on all entrance tickets to historical sights. The Hindu deity Indra rarely appears without his three-headed elephant mount **Erawan**, and miniature devotional elephant effigies are sold at major Brahmin shrines, such as Bangkok's Erawan shrine. In Buddhist legend, the future **Buddha's mother** was able to conceive only after she dreamt that a white elephant had entered her womb: that is why elephant balustrades encircle many of the Buddhist temples of Sukhothai, and why the rare white elephant is accorded royal status (see p.155) and regarded as a highly auspicious animal.

The **practical** role of the elephant in Thailand was once almost as great as its symbolic importance. The kings of Ayutthaya relied on elephants to take them into battle against the Burmese – one king assembled a trained elephant army of three hundred – and during the nineteenth century King Rama IV offered Abraham Lincoln a male and a female to "multiply in the forests of America" and to use in the Civil War. In times of peace, the phenomenal strength of the elephant has made it invaluable as a beast of burden: elephants hauled the stone from which the gargantuan Khmer temple complexes of the north and northeast were built, and for centuries they have been used to clear forests and carry timber.

The traditional cycle for domestic elephants is to be born in captivity, spending the first three years of their lives with their mothers (who get five years' maternity leave), before being forcibly separated and raised with other calves in training schools. From the age of three each elephant is assigned its own **mahout** – a trainer, keeper and driver rolled into one – who will stay with it for the rest of its working life. Training begins gently, with mahouts taking months to earn the trust of their charge; over the next thirteen years the elephant is taught about forty different commands, from simple "stop" and "go" orders to complex instructions for hooking and passing manoeuvres with the trunk. By the age of sixteen an elephant is ready to be put to work and is expected to carry on working until it reaches 50 or so; it is usually retired at 60, though it can live for another twenty years.

Ironically, the **timber industry** has been the animal's undoing. Mechanized logging has destroyed the wild elephant's preferred river-valley grassland and forest habitats, forcing them into isolated upland pockets. As a result, Thailand's population of wild elephants is now under two thousand. With the 1989 **ban on commercial logging** within Thai borders – after the 1988 catastrophe when the effects of deforestation killed a hundred people and wiped out villages in Surat Thani province, as mudslides swept down deforested slopes carrying cut timber with them – the domesticated population, numbering about three thousand, is becoming less useful. The biggest problem facing these elephants and their mahouts nowadays is **unemployment**. The estimated 250 elephants working on the illegal teak-logging trade are often abused and overworked, while mahouts who can no longer find work for their animals are forced to abandon them since they cannot afford the vast amount of food needed to sustain the creature – about 125kg a day. The discarded animals destroy forests and crops and are often hunted down and killed. In town streets and on beaches, you'll often see those mahouts who keep their elephants charging both tourists for the experience of handfeeding them bananas, and Thais for the chance to stoop under their trunks for good luck. Training schools now concentrate as much on perfecting shows for tourists as on honing the elephants' practical skills, and another lucrative alternative tourist industry is elephant trekking. The Thai Elephant Conservation Centre near Lampang estimates that if drastic measures are not taken, in twenty years' time the elephant could be extinct in Thailand, where the population has dropped by over fifteen thousand since 1984.

for the small city of **PHRAE**, 20km further on, the capital of the province of the same name which is famous for woodcarving and the quality of its *seua maw hawm*, the deep-blue, baggy working shirt seen all over Thailand (produced in the village of Ban Thung Hong, 4km north of Phrae on Highway 101). If you're driving here from Lampang, turn left from Highway 11 at **Mae Khaem** onto Route 1023 and approach the town via Long and some lovely scenery.

The main reason to stop in Phrae is to explore the old city, delineated by an earthen moat, with its lanes filled with traditional teak houses – as in Lampang, the former logging industry attracted Burmese workers and the influence is evident – and to enjoy the old-fashioned and friendly nature of a place still virtually untouched by tourism. Out of town, 18km to the northeast off Highway 101, are the so-called ghost pillars at **Phae Muang Phi**, a geological quirk of soil and wind erosion, which are probably only worth visiting if you are going on through to Nan with your own transport.

The Town

Sited on the southeast bank of the Yom River, Phrae is clearly divided into old and new town; an earthen wall surrounds the roughly oval-shaped old town, with a moat on its southeastern side and the new town centre beyond that. At the centre of the **old town**, a large roundabout is the main orientation point; running northwest–southeast through the roundabout, through Pratuchai (the main gate on the southeastern side of the old town), and into the new town is Thanon Charoen Muang, where several shops sell the trademark deep indigo shirts. The main street in the new town, Thanon Yantarakitkoson, intersects Thanon Charoen Muang about 300m southeast of the old town, and leads northeast to the bus station.

Dotted around the old town, several wats are worth visiting and are easily reached on foot; in fact, a stroll through the area's quiet lanes is recommended, with traditional teak houses to gaze at and a glimpse of local life as extended families congregate sociably outside. You will really find the Thai smile here: people are friendly and will probably try to talk to you with any English they have.

Vongburi House

The white and pink **Vongburi House** (daily 8.30am–5pm; B20) on Thanon Khamlue is a good place to begin an exploration of the old town. Built of teak between 1897 and 1907 in Thai-European style for a wealthy forest concessionary, it's smothered in elaborate, lace-like woodcarving, on all the eaves, gables and balconies, and around doors and windows. Inside the house, exhibits include a howdah, undershirts with magic spells written on them to ward off danger, and various documents such as elephant identity papers and artefacts that shed light on the history of the family, who still live in part of the complex. Fittingly, as this neighbourhood is a traditional silversmithing area, there is also plenty of fine silverware to admire; you can often watch a silversmith at work in the shady grounds, and buy the finished product from the ground-floor souvenir shop.

Wat Luang and Wat Phra Non

Around the corner from the Vongburi House, Phrae's oldest temple complex, **Wat Luang**, dates from the town's foundation around the twelfth century; it contains the only intact original brick entrance gate to the city, though unfortunately it has been closed up and turned into an ugly shrine to Chao Pu, an early Lanna ruler. Apart from the gate, the oldest component of the wat is the crumbling early Lanna-style **chedi** called Chang Kham after the four elephants – now mostly trunkless – which sit at its octagonal base; these alternate with four niches

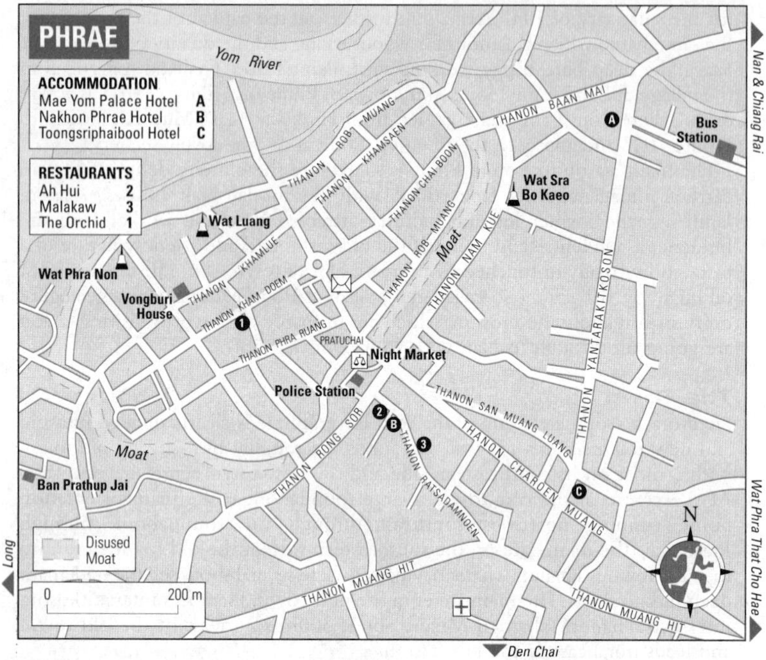

containing Buddha images and some haphazardly leaning gilded bronze parasols. Architectural experts have been called in from Bangkok to plan the restoration of the chedi and the overall complex: unfortunately, over the years, Wat Luang has been added to and parts of it have been quite spoilt in a gaudy modernization process. Until recently, a dishonest monk was even taking down parts of the temple to sell for a profit. Apart from the ruined entrance gate, this meddling is most evident in the **viharn** opposite, where an ugly and very out-of-place laterite brick facade has been placed in front of the original Lanna-style sixteenth-century entrance. Opposite the chedi on the north side of the compound, a **museum** on two floors houses some real treasures, the most important being a collection of sixteenth-century bronze Buddhas and several glass cases containing old manuscripts with beautifully gilded covers, which are located upstairs.

Still within the old city, about a block west of Wat Luang along the boundary road is **Wat Phra Non**, established three centuries ago, whose name comes from the reclining Buddha in a small viharn; look out for the bot's finely carved wooden pediment showing scenes from the *Ramayana*.

Ban Prathup Jai

Signposted among the peaceful lanes out beyond the old town's west gate lies the massive two-storey teak house of **Ban Prathup Jai** (daily 8am–5pm; B20), constructed out of nine old houses in the mid-1980s. A visit here allows you to appreciate the beauty and strength of the wood, even if the overall effect is just too ornate: the lower floor has an impressive interior of 130 pillars of solid teak carved with jungle scenes; huge wooden elephants wander among the columns set against solid teak walls and ornately carved furniture (plus a souvenir shop where you can buy all things wooden). Upstairs has the feel of a traditional house, and the furniture and objects are those that you might find in a well-to-do Thai home: ornately carved cabinets crammed with bowls and other ordinary household objects, tables displaying framed family portraits, wall carvings and even a teak bar.

Wat Sra Bo Kaeo

Just to the east of the old city, near the northern end of Thanon Nam Khue, **Wat Sra Bo Kaeo** is set in a peaceful, shady grove of trees. Its Burmese-style viharn is of no great age, but has an intriguing marble Buddha image and beautiful teak floorboards. The most striking aspect of the temple is the brightly-painted Shan chedi with two unusually attractive guardian figures in flowing robes. Also note the intricate, decorative stucco work on the spire of the bot to the left of the viharn.

Practicalities

Phrae's **bus station**, off Thanon Yantarakitkoson, is 1km northeast of the modern centre. There are usually some **samlors** and **motorbike taxis**, the main forms of transport around town, congregating here, while **songthaews** head for out-of-town routes, including the train station at Den Chai.

Accommodation in Phrae comprises several **hotels** in the new town clustered around Thanon Charoen Muang, Thanon Yantarakitkoson and Thanon Ratsadamnoen In the budget range, the best of these is the *Toongsriphaibool Hotel* at 84 Thanon Yantarakitkoson (Ⓣ054 511011; ❶), near the junction with Thanon Charoen Muang. A large three-storey hotel, it's arranged around a courtyard and so is off the noisy road; the reasonably clean, simply furnished rooms have ceiling fans and attached (cold-water) bathrooms. A popular mid-range hotel, on Thanon Ratsadamnoen close to the Pratuchai gate and the old city, is the *Nakhon Phrae Hotel* (Ⓣ054 511122, Ⓕ054 521937; ❷–❹). It's recently been refurbished, and the fan rooms especially, with parquet floors and hot-water en-suite bathrooms, present very good value; extra baht on an incremental scale secure you air-con, cable TV and fridge. The city's best upmarket hotel is the *Mae Yom Palace* near the bus station at 181/6 Thanon Yantarakitkoson (Ⓣ054 521028–35, Ⓕ054 522904; ❺); a large swimming pool features among its amenities, and **bicycles** (with a suggested route map) can be rented for B100 per day.

For **eating**, you could start with the foodstalls at the lively night market by the Pratuchai gate on Thanon Charoen Muang. Nearby on Thanon Ratsadamnoen around the *Nakhon Phrae Hotel*, there are a few places to choose from including some simple Chinese cafés: the *Ah Hui*, right next to the *Nakhon Phrae Hotel*, serves several tasty rice dishes, though like most eateries in Phrae, it has no English menu. For this luxury, you have to pay slightly higher prices at *Malakaw*, on the opposite side of Thanon Ratsadamnoen about 50m down the road, a popular, rustic-style place serving everything from fried rice and noodles to salads, curries and soups. Phrae's best restaurant is *Ban Fai*, a couple of kilometres south out of town on the main road towards Den Chai, an open-sided barn-like place serving very good Thai food including northern specialities such as *nem* (spiced pork sausages) and the typical Lanna pork curry, *kaeng hang lay*. *The Orchid* on Thanon Kham Doem in the old town is a good place for a drink, with outdoor tables on the pavement and live music in the evenings.

Wat Phra That Cho Hae

Wat Phra That Cho Hae, 9km east of town (1km on from the village of Padang), is an important pilgrimage centre sited on a low hill, led up to by two naga stairways through a grove of teak trees. One staircase leads to a shrine where a revered Buddha image, Phra Chao Tan Chai, is said to increase women's fertility. The small grounds also house a gilded 33-metre-high **chedi**, traditionally wrapped in the yellow satin-like cloth, *cho hae* (which gives the wat its name) in March or April, and a brightly decorated viharn with an unusual cruciform layout. To the north of the main compound, a new viharn houses a shiny Buddha and some well-crafted murals and window carvings. To get to the wat, take a songthaew (around B200 there and back, with a wait) from Thanon Charoen Muang near the Thanon Yantarakitkoson intersection.

Nan

After leaving the Yom, Highway 101 gently climbs through rolling hills of cotton fields and teak plantations to its highest point, framed by limestone cliffs, before descending into the high, isolated valley of the Nan River, one of the two great tributaries of the Chao Phraya. Ringed by high mountains, the small but prosperous provincial capital of **NAN**, 225km east of Lampang, rests on the grassy west bank of the river. This stretch of water really comes alive during the **Lanna boat races**, usually held in late October or early November, when villages from around the province send teams of up to fifty oarsmen here to race in long, colourfully decorated canoes with dragon prows. The lush surrounding valley is noted for its cotton-weaving, sweet oranges and the attractive grainy paper made from the bark of local *sa* (mulberry) trees.

Although it has been kicked around by Burma, Laos and Thailand, Nan province has a history of being on the fringes, distanced by the encircling barrier of mountains. Rama V brought Nan into his centralization programme at the start of the twentieth century, but left the traditional ruling house in place, making it the last province in Thailand to be administered by a local ruler (it remained so until 1931). During the troubled 1970s, communist insurgents holed up in this twilight region and proclaimed Nan the future capital of the liberated zone, which only succeeding in bringing the full might of the Thai Army down on them. The insurgency faded after the government's 1982 offer of amnesty, though there is still a noticeable military presence. Today, energies are focused on development, and the province has become less isolated with the building of several new roads. Nan still has a slight reputation for lawlessness, but most of the bandits nowadays are illegal loggers.

The Town

Nan's centre comprises a disorientating grid of crooked streets, around a small core of shops and businesses where Thanon Mahawong and Thanon Anantaworarichides meet Thanon Sumondhevaraj. The best place to start an exploration is to the southwest at the **National Museum** (daily; 9am–4pm; B30), located in a tidy palace with superb teak floors, which used to be home to the rulers of Nan. Its informative, user-friendly displays give you a bite-sized introduction to Nan, its history and its peoples, the prize exhibit being a talismanic elephant tusk with a bad case of brown tooth decay, which is claimed to be magic black ivory. The tusk was discovered over three hundred years ago and now sits on a colourful wooden *khut*, a mythological eagle. The museum also houses elegant pottery and woodcarving, gorgeously wrought silverware and some rare Lao Buddhas.

Nearby on Thanon Phakwang, **Wat Phumin** will grab even the most over-templed traveller. Its 500-year-old centrepiece is an unusual cruciform building, combining both the bot and the viharn, which balances some quirky features in a perfect symmetry. Two giant nagas pass through the base of the building, with their tails along the balustrades at the south entrance and their heads at the north, representing the sacred oceans at the base of the central mountain of the universe. The doors at the four entrances, which have been beautifully carved with a complex pattern of animals and flowers, lead straight to the four Buddha images arranged around a tall altar in the centre of the building – note the Buddhas' piercing onyx eyes and pointed ears, showing the influence of Laos, 50km away. What really sets the bot apart are the **murals**, whose bright, simple colours seem to jump off the walls. Executed in 1857, though occasionally re-touched, the paintings take you on a whirlwind tour of heaven, hell, the Buddha's previous incarnations, local legends and incidents from Nan's history, and include stacks of vivacious, sometimes bawdy, detail, which provides a valuable pictorial record of that era. Diagonally opposite Wat Phumin, **Wat Chang Kham** is also over 500 years old, though the two viharns that stand side by side are unexceptional in design. The main feature here is a gorgeous, gold-capped chedi, supported by elephants on all sides; those on the corners are adorned with gold helmets. The temple is attached to a school, a reminder that temples were once the only source of education in the country.

Wat Phra That Chae Haeng, on the opposite side of the river 2km southeast of town, is another must, as much for its setting on a hill overlooking the Nan valley as anything else. The wat was founded in 1300, at a spot determined by the Buddha himself when he passed through this way – or so local legend would have it. The nagas here outdo even Wat Phumin's: the first you see of the wat across the fields is a wide driveway flanked by monumental serpents gliding down the slope from the temple. A magnificent gnarled bodhi tree with hundreds of spreading branches and roots guards the main gate, set in high boundary walls. Inside the walls, the highlight is a slender, 55-metre-high golden chedi, surrounded by four smaller chedis and four carved and gilded umbrellas, as well as small belfries and stucco lions. Close competition comes from the viharn roof, which has no fewer than fifteen Laotian-style tiers, stacked up like a house of cards and supported on finely carved *kan tuei* (wood supports) under the eaves.

You can get another great overview of the Nan valley by turning right just after the bridge on Highway 101 to the south of town. Follow the lane a couple of kilometres, and go up the hill to **Wat Phra That Khao Noi**, where you can join a huge image of a standing Buddha in contemplating the lush panorama below.

Crafts and shops

Loyalty to local traditions ensures the survival of several good **handicrafts shops** in Nan, most of which are found on Thanon Sumondhevaraj north of the junction with Anantaworarichides. Traditional lengths of superb **cotton** (much of it *pha sin*, used as wraparound skirts) woven in local villages are sold at Pha Nan, 21/2 Thanon Sumondhevaraj; as the owner is a teacher, the shop has unusual hours (Mon–Fri 5–10pm, Sat & Sun 8am–10pm). The staff are friendly and you can happily browse the huge selection of cloths for hours without hard sell. Jangtragun, at nos. 304–306, also has a good selection of *seua maw hawm*, Phrae's famous blue working shirts, and a few notebooks made from **sa paper**. Hattasin, run by the Thai-Payap Development Association, a **non-profit-making organization** set up to bring extra income to local hill tribes, is a small shop with some gorgeous textiles at 50/10 Thanon Norkham, a small road opposite Wat Hua Wiangtai on Thanon Sumondhevaraj. On sale here are bags, basketware, woodcarving, honey and all manner of fabrics, even Hmong baby-carriers.

A large **silverware** showroom and workshop named Chom Phu Phukha is situated about 2km west of town along the road to Phayao (Route 1091), on the right opposite a petrol station. They stock a wide range of bracelets, necklaces, bowls and trays, priced according to design and weight (about B10–15/gram), and are happy for visitors to look round the workshop, where young hill-tribe people fashion the items. A good variety of local cloth, hand-woven by the hill tribes, is also on sale here.

Practicalities

The bus journey to Nan (B117 non-air-con, B211 air-con, B328 VIP service) from Chiang Mai takes around six hours. The main **bus station** is on Thanon Anantaworarichides on the west side of town, but Bangkok and Phitsanulok services use a smaller station to the east of the centre on Thanon Kha Luang; arriving at either leaves a manageable walk or a samlor ride to the central accommodation area. The **airport** is located to the northwest of town, but there are no flights at present to or from Chiang Mai. For **tourist information** about the town and the province, visit Fhu (see p.370), while for exploring the area, Oversea, at 488 Thanon Sumondhevaraj, rents out decent **bicycles** (B30–50 a day) and **motorbikes** (B150). **Internet outlets** open and close regularly in Nan, but there is usually somewhere offering access near the centre of town, such as the mobile phone shop at 28/6 Thanon Anantaworachides, which has a few online computer terminals.

Accommodation

Despite being a small town with few visitors, Nan has some attractive accommodation options, ranging from family-run guest houses to clean, reasonably priced hotels. The only time of year when finding somewhere to stay might be a problem is when the Lanna boat races take place in town (late Oct or early Nov).

Amazing Guest House 25/7 Thanon Rat Amnuay ⓣ054 710893. About 1km north of the centre, tucked away in a tiny lane to the west of Thanon Sumondhevaraj. Offers clean, simple rooms in a family-style, wooden house with shared bathroom, as well as five bungalows in a shady garden. Gives considerable discounts for longer stays, and bicycles and motorbikes are available for rent. ❶–❷

City Park Hotel 99 Thanon Yantarakitkoson ⓣ054 741343–52, ⓕ054 773135. About 2km from the centre on Highway 101 to Phrae. A smart place with tasteful rooms (all with cable TV) in low-rise buildings that give onto balconies overlooking a large swimming pool. ❻

Dhevaraj Hotel 466 Thanon Sumondhevaraj ⓣ054 710078 or 054 710212, ⓕ054 771365. Rooms at this centrally positioned place are quite plush, with fan or air-con, and cable TV; all are en suite. Though the fan rooms are good value, tour groups here can be noisy. ❸–❹

Doi Phukha Guest House 94/5 Soi 1, Thanon Sumondhevaraj ⓣ054 751517. On the north side of town, this fine guest house occupies a beautiful wooden house in a quiet compound; the simple rooms share hot and cold showers, and there's an informative noticeboard and excellent maps of the province available. ❶

Fahthanin Hotel 303 Thanon Anantaworarichides ⓣ054 757321–4. Carpeted, air-con rooms here come with TV and mini-bar. ❺

Nan Fah Hotel 436–440 Thanon Sumondhevaraj ⓣ054 710284. Next door to the *Dhevaraj Hotel*, this old wooden building looks fine from the outside, but its dozen or so rooms are somewhat characterless. ❸–❹

Nan Guest House 57/16 Thanon Mahaphom ⓣ054 771849. Adequate, if rather basic rooms in a wooden house, separated by rather flimsy partitions. ❶

PK Guest House 33/12 Thanon Prempracharaj ⓣ054 771999, ⓕ054 757099. Despite a different address, this is located in the same lane as *Amazing Guest House*, and offers a range of rooms with varying facilities scattered around a large garden. ❶–❹

Sukkasem Hotel 119–121 Thanon Anantaworarichides ⓣ054 710141. A bargain hotel in the centre, with simple clean rooms just across from the night market. ❷–❸

Eating

Plenty of simple Thai **restaurants** line Thanon Anantaworarichides, among them *Poom Sam*, just next to the *Sukkasem Hotel*. It may look like any other street food outlet, but they prepare excellent Thai and Chinese food with great service at rock-bottom prices. Next to *Poom Sam* is *Tanaya Kitchen*, a tiny, homely café that serves good vegetarian food. Nan's big culinary surprise, however, is *Da Dario* at 37/4 Thanon Rat Amnuay (ⓣ054 750258). Right next door to *Amazing Guest House*, *Da Dario* serves both authentic Italian and Thai food rated by the locals, with moderate to expensive prices. The **night market** includes several good noodle stalls serving up staples like *phat thai* for B20, and for a taste of Isaan food, check out *Suan Issan* at 2/1 Thanon Anantaworarichides, which despite its address is actually in the narrow alley off Thanon Sumondhevaraj, just south of the junction with this road. Cheap and clean, with lots of plants out front, this restaurant has good service, and the fiery Isaan food will have your tongue flapping. Among the hotels, the ground floor restaurant of the *Nan Fah* offers a range of standard Thai dishes at consistent quality. Most shops and restaurants in Nan pull down their shutters by 8pm, but if you're looking for nightlife, check out *Mai Muang* bar on Thanon Prempracharaj, which attracts a fair crowd most nights.

Around Nan

The remote, mountainous countryside around Nan runs a close second to the headlong scenery of Mae Hong Son province, but its remoteness means that Nan has even worse transport and is even more poorly mapped. This does, of course, make it an exciting region to explore, when you may encounter the ethnic minorities of the area – the Thai Lue, the Htin and the little-known Phi Tong Luang.

With or without your own vehicle or motorbike, your best option for exploring this region is to head for the reliable Fhu Travel, the only fixer in Nan at 453/4 Thanon Sumondhevaraj (Ⓣ054 710636, Ⓕ054 775345, Ⓔfhutravel@hotmail.com). Besides organizing popular and enjoyable guided **tours** and trekking trips, Fhu and Ung, his wife, can advise you where to go according to your interests or even arrange customized tours. One- to three-day whitewater-rafting trips cost around B1000 per person a day, depending on group size, and go down the Nam Wa River near Mae Charim to the east of town. One-day tours to Wat Nong Bua, including a visit to the local weavers and views of Doi Phukha from nearby Pua, cost B2000 for two to three people or B600 per person for four to six people, including transport, driver/guide and lunch. Fhu can also arrange home-stays in Ban Don Moon, a small village near Ban Nong Bua, where you can learn more about local agricultural and weaving techniques. Treks (two days B1200/person, three days B1500/person; minimum four people) head west, through tough terrain of thick jungle and high mountains, visiting at least one Phi Tong Luang village (see box) and nearby Hmong and Mien villages where they work, as well as settlements of Htin, an upland Mon-Khmer people, most of whom migrated into Nan province after the Communist takeover of Laos in 1975. For those who want to go it alone, the bus service is sketchy, but Oversea (see p.369) rents out motorbikes.

Sao Din

One of several brief excursions from Nan possible with your own transport, **Sao Din** ("earth pillars"), 60km to the south, provides a more intriguing example of soil erosion than the heavily promoted Phae Muang Phi near Phrae. Here the earth pillars cover a huge area and appear in fantastic shapes, the result of centuries of erosion by wind and rain. The site is almost impossible to reach by public transport, but if you have a motorbike or car, head south on Highway 101 to Wiang Sa, then turn left and follow Route 1026 to Na Noi; a turning on the right just after Na Noi leads into the site. If you visit, take care to wear long trousers and boots, especially in the cool season, as a thorny plant which grows in the region can cause discomfort.

Ban Nong Bua

The easiest and most varied day-trip out of Nan is to the north, heading first for **BAN NONG BUA**, site of a famous muralled temple of the same name. If you're on a bike, ride 40km up Route 1080 to the southern outskirts of the town of **Tha Wang Pha**, where signs in English point you left across the Nan River to Wat Nong Bua, 3km away. Buses from Nan's main bus station on Thanon Anantaworarichides make the hour-long journey to Tha Wang Pha roughly hourly, or you can take a songthaew there from in front of the petrol station by the night market on the same road – then either hire a motorbike taxi in the centre of Tha Wang Pha, or walk the last 3km.

Wat Nong Bua stands behind the village green on the west side of the unpaved through road. Its beautifully gnarled viharn was built in 1862 in typical Lanna style, with low, drooping roof tiers surmounted by stucco finials – here you'll find horned nagas and tusked makaras (elephantine monsters), instead of the garuda finial which invariably crops up in central Thai temples. The viharn enshrines a pointy-eared Laotian Buddha, but its most outstanding features are the **murals** which cover all four walls. Executed between 1867 and 1888, probably by the Wat Phumin painters, they depict with much humour and vivid detail scenes from the *Chanthakhat Jataka* (the story of one of the Buddha's previous incarnations, as a hero called Chanthakhat). This is a particularly long and complex jataka (although a leaflet, available from the monks in return for a small donation to temple funds, outlines the story in English), wherein our hero gets into all kinds of scrapes, involving several wives, other sundry liaisons, some formidably nasty enemies and the god Indra transforming himself into a snake. The crux of the tale comes on the east wall (opposite the Buddha image): in the bottom left-hand corner, Chanthakhat and the love of his life, Thewathisangka, are shipwrecked and separated; distraught, Thewathisangka wanders through the jungle, diagonally up the wall, to the hermitage of an old woman, where she shaves her head and becomes a nun; Chanthakhat travels through the wilderness along the bottom of the wall, curing a wounded naga-king on the way, who out of gratitude gives him a magic crystal ball, which enables our hero to face another series of perils along the south wall, before finally rediscovering and embracing Thewathisangka in front of the old woman's hut, at the top right-hand corner of the east wall.

Ban Nong Bua and the surrounding area are largely inhabited by **Thai Lue** people, distant cousins of the Thais, who've migrated from China in the past

Spirits of the Yellow Leaves

Inhabiting the remote hill country west of Nan, the **Phi Tong Luang** – "Spirits of the Yellow Leaves" – represent the last remnant of nomadic hunter-gatherers in Thailand, and their way of life, like that of so many other indigenous peoples, is rapidly passing. Believing that spirits will be angered if the tribe settles in one place, grows crops or keeps animals, the Phi Tong Luang build only temporary shelters of branches and wild banana leaves, moving on to another spot in the jungle as soon as the leaves turn yellow; thus they earned their poetic Thai name, though they call themselves Mrabri – "Forest People". Traditionally they eke out a hard livelihood from the forest, hunting with spears, trapping birds and small mammals, digging roots and collecting nuts, seeds and honey.

Recent deforestation by logging and slash-and-burn farming has eaten into the tribe's territory, however, and many of the Phi Tong Luang have been forced to sell their labour to Hmong and Mien farmers (the spirits apparently do not get angry if the tribe settles down and works the land for other people). They are paid only in food – because of their docility and their inability to understand and use money, they often get a raw deal for their hard work. They are also particularly ill-equipped to cope with curious and often insensitive tourists, although one of the American missionaries working with the tribe believes that occasional visits help the Phi Tong Luang to develop by teaching them about people in the outside world. The future doesn't look bright: they number only about 100–200 members; their susceptibility to disease (especially malaria) is high and life expectancy low.

150 years. They produce beautiful cotton garments in richly coloured geometric patterns; walk 200m behind the wat and you'll find weavers at work under the stilted sky-blue house of Khun Janthasom Prompanya, who sells the opulent fabrics in the shop behind. The quality of design and workmanship is very high here, and prices, though not cheap, are reasonable for the quality.

Doi Phukha National Park

East of Tha Wang Pha, Route 1080 curves towards the town of **Pua**, on whose southern outskirts Route 1256, the spectacular access road for **Doi Phukha National Park** begins its journey eastwards and upwards. It's difficult to get into the park on public transport, and you'll have to stay the night. Songthaews from Thanon Anantaworarichides or hourly buses from Nan's main station both run to Pua, from where infrequent songthaews (usually only one a day between 8am and 9am) serve the handful of villages along Route 1256. The trip is most exciting if tackled on a bike (though watch out for loose chippings on the bends). The road climbs up a sharp ridge, through occasional stands of elephant grass and bamboo, towards Doi Dong Ya Wai (1939m), providing one of the most jaw-droppingly scenic drives in Thailand. Across the valleys to north and south stand rows of improbably steep mountains (including the 1980-metre Doi Phukha itself, far to the south), covered in lush vegetation with scarcely a sign of human habitation.

At park headquarters, 24km up the road, **accommodation** ranges from a campsite (B250 to rent a tent sleeping 2-3 people, B30 to pitch your own) to large bungalows sleeping six (B1200) and smaller ones sleeping two (B250). In case they are full, it's best to book in advance through the Forestry Department in Bangkok (see p.46). There are several trails within the park but they're not well marked, so it's best to hire a **guide** at headquarters (B300/day). The guides, who unfortunately don't speak English, lead visitors up the arduous slope to the nearest summit, Dong Khao (1305m). You can arrange to have **meals** cooked for you at the headquarters, though the menu is limited and if you are part of a big group, it's best to call in advance and make sure they have enough supplies.

The Mae Hong Son loop

Two roads from Chiang Mai head over the western mountains into Mae Hong Son, Thailand's most remote province, offering the irresistible prospect of tying the highways together into a six-hundred-kilometre loop. The towns en route give an appetizing taste of Burma to the west, but the journey itself, winding over implausibly steep forested mountains and through tightly hemmed farming valleys, is what will stick in the mind.

The southern leg of the route, Highway 108, first passes **Doi Inthanon National Park**, with its lofty views over half of northern Thailand and enough waterfalls to last a lifetime, then **Mae Sariang**, an important town for trade across the Burmese border. The provincial capital, **Mae Hong Son**, roughly at the midpoint of the loop, makes the best base for exploring the area's mountains, rivers and waterfalls, though it can become frantic with tour groups in the cool season. The northern leg, Route 1095, heads northeast out of Mae Hong Son into an area of beautiful caves and stunning scenery around **Mae Suya** and **Soppong**: staying at one of the out-of-the-way guest houses here will enable you to trek independently around the countryside and the local hill-tribe villages. Halfway back towards Chiang Mai from Mae Hong Son is **Pai**, a cosy, cosmopolitan travellers' hangout with plenty of activities and some gentle walking trails in the surrounding valley.

We've taken the loop in a clockwise direction here, in part because Doi Inthanon is best reached direct from Chiang Mai and in part because this dispenses with the straight, fast and boring section of the journey (Chiang Mai–Hot) at the beginning. These considerations apart, you could just as easily go the other way round. Travelling the loop is straightforward, although the mountainous roads go through plenty of bends and jolts. Either way, Mae Hong Son is about eight hours' travelling time from Chiang Mai by air-con or ordinary **bus**, although services along the shorter but even more winding northern route are now augmented by faster **air-con minibuses**, which cover the ground via Pai four times a day in about six hours. The 35-minute Chiang Mai–Mae Hong Son **flight** is surprisingly inexpensive (B765), and is worth considering for one leg of the journey, especially if you're short on time. Above all, though, the loop is made for **motorbikes** and **jeeps**: the roads are generally quiet (but watch out for huge, speeding trucks) and you can satisfy the inevitable craving to stop every five minutes and admire the mountain scenery. A useful piece of equipment for this journey is the 1:375,000 **map** of the Mae Hong Son Loop, with useful insets of Pai's and Mae Hong Son's environs, published by Golden Triangle Rider (Ⓦwww.gt-rider.com) and available in local bookshops at B175.

Highway 108: Chiang Mai to Mae Hong Son

Bus drivers on **Highway 108** are expected to have highly sharpened powers of concentration and the landlubber's version of sea legs – the road negotiates almost two thousand curves in the 349km to Mae Hong Son, so if you're at all prone to travel sickness plan to take a breather in Mae Sariang. Buses to Mae Sariang and Mae Hong Son depart from Chiang Mai's Arcade bus station; services to Chom Thong (for Doi Inthanon National Park) leave from the southern end of Thanon Phra Pokklao (Chiang Mai Gate).

Doi Inthanon National Park

Covering a huge area to the southwest of Chiang Mai, **DOI INTHANON NATIONAL PARK**, with its hill-tribe villages, dramatic waterfalls and panoramas over rows of wild, green peaks to the west, gives a pleasant, if sanitized, whiff of northern countryside, its attractions and concrete access roads kept in good order by the Thai Forestry Department. The park, named after the highest mountain in the country and so dubbed the "Roof of Thailand", is geared mainly to wildlife conservation but also contains a hill-tribe agricultural project producing strawberries, apples and flowers for sale. Often shrouded in mist, Doi Inthanon's temperate forests shelter a huge variety of flora and fauna, which make this one of the major destinations for naturalists in Southeast Asia. The park supports about 380 bird species, the largest number of any site in Thailand

– among them the ashy-throated warbler and a species of the green-tailed sunbird, both unique to Doi Inthanon – as well as, near the summit, the only red rhododendrons in Thailand (in bloom Dec–Feb) and a wide variety of ground and epiphytic orchids. The waterfalls, birds and flowers are at their best in the cool season, but night-time temperatures sometimes drop below freezing, making warm clothing a must.

The gateway to the park is **CHOM THONG**, 58km southwest of Chiang Mai on Highway 108, a market town with little to offer apart from the attractive **Wat Phra That Si Chom Thong**, whose impressive brass-plated chedi dates from the fifteenth century. The nearby bo tree has become an equally noteworthy architectural feature: dozens of Dalí-esque supports for its sagging branches have been sponsored by the devoted in the hope of earning merit. Inside the gnarled sixteenth-century viharn, a towering, gilded *ku* housing a Buddha relic just squeezes in beneath the ceiling, from which hangs a huge, sumptuous red and green umbrella. Weaponry, gongs, umbrellas, thrones and an elephant-tusk arch carved with delicate Buddha images all add to the welcoming clutter. The temple is now famous for its **meditation retreats**, based in the administration buildings at the back of compound. The abbot, Ajaan Tong Sirimangalo, is a revered teacher (and teacher trainer), who is in charge of Vipassana meditation for the whole of northern Thailand. With foreign monks and lay people teaching, a basic course here lasts around 21 days (donations to temple and teacher suggested); call as far as possible in advance to book a place (ⓣ053 826869, ⓦwww.sirimangalo.org). Two doors up from the wat, *Watjanee* is a simple but clean and well-run vegetarian **restaurant**.

The main road through the park turns west off Highway 108 1km north of Chom Thong, winding generally northwestwards for 48km to the top of Doi Inthanon, passing the park headquarters about 30km in. A second paved road forks left 10km before the summit, reaching the riverside market of **Mae Chaem**, southwest of the park, after 20km. Sticking to public transport, you can reach the park headquarters using one of the **songthaews** that shuttle between Chom Thong market (about 100m south of the temple) and Mae Chaem, along the mountain's lower slopes; to get to the summit however, you'll have to hitch from the Mae Chaem turn-off (generally manageable), unless you want to charter a whole songthaew from Chom Thong's temple for around B700 to the peak and back (about 4–5hr). By **motorbike** or **jeep**, you could do the park justice in a day-trip with an early start from Chiang Mai, or treat it as the first stage of a longer trip to Mae Hong Son, either following Route 1088 south from Mae Chaem to pick up Highway 108 again towards Mae Sariang or taking Route 1088 north then Route 1263 to Khun Yuam.

The park

Three sets of waterfalls provide the main roadside attractions on the way to the park headquarters: overrated **Mae Klang Falls**, 8km in, which with its picnic areas and food vendors gets overbearingly crowded at weekends; **Vachiratharn Falls**, the park's most dramatic, with a long, misty drop down a granite escarpment 11km beyond; and the twin cascades of **Siriphum Falls**, backing the park headquarters a further 11km on. With your own wheels you could reach a fourth and much more beautiful cataract, **Mae Ya**, which is believed to be the highest in Thailand – the winding, fourteen-kilometre paved track to it heads west off the main park road 2km north of Highway 108. A rough unpaved side road offers a roundabout but culturally more enlightening route to the headquarters, leaving the main road 3km beyond Vachiratharn Falls, taking in three traditional and unspoilt Karen villages before rejoining the main road at the more developed Hmong village of **Ban Khun Klang**, 500m before the headquarters.

For the most spectacular views in the park, continue 11km beyond the headquarters along the summit road to the sleek, twin chedis looming incongruously over the misty green hillside: on a clear day you can see the mountains of Burma to the west from here. Built by the Royal Thai Air Force, the chedis commemorate the sixtieth birthdays of the Thai king and queen; the king's monument, **Napamaytanidol Chedi** (1987), is brown to the more feminine lilac of the queen's **Napapolphumsiri Chedi** (1992). Starting a short distance up the road from the chedis, the rewarding **Kew Mae Pan Trail**, a two-hour circular walk, wanders through sun-dappled forest and open savanna as it skirts the steep western edge of Doi Inthanon, where violent-red rhododendrons (Dec–Feb) are framed against open views over the canyoned headwaters of the Pan River, when the weather allows. To walk the trail, you have to hire a guide from headquarters (B200).

Doi Inthanon's **summit** (2565m), 6km beyond the chedi, is a big disappointment – from the car park you can see little beyond the radar installation. For many people, after a quick shiver and a snapshot in front of a board proclaiming this the highest point in Thailand, it's time to hop in the car and get back to warmer climes. A small, still-revered stupa behind this board contains the ashes of King Inthanon of Chiang Mai (after whom the mountain was renamed): at the end of the nineteenth century he was the first to recognize the importance of this watershed area in supplying the Ping River and ultimately the Chao Phraya, the queen of Thailand's rivers. One hundred metres back down the road, it's an easy walk to the bog which is the highest source of these great waterways, and one of the park's best bird-watching sites. The cream and brown sphagnum mosses which spread underfoot, the dense ferns that hang off the trees and the contorted branches of rhododendrons give the place a creepy, primeval atmosphere.

The paved **Mae Chaem road** skirts yet another set of waterfalls, 7km after the turning off the summit road: look for a steep, unpaved road to the right, leading down to a ranger station and, just to the east, the dramatic long drop of **Huai Sai Luaeng Falls**. A circular two-hour trail from the ranger station takes in creeks and small waterfalls as well as **Mae Pan Falls**, a series of short cascades in a peaceful, shady setting. Continuing southwest, the paved road affords breathtaking views as it helter-skelters down to the sleepy valley of **Mae Chaem**. With your own transport it's possible to take on a remote, paved route towards Mae Hong Son from here, heading north up Route 1088 then west along Route 1263 (past the Buatong Fields and Mae Surin Waterfall – see p.379), joining Highway 108 just north of Khun Yuam. To rejoin the classic Mae Hong Son loop, however, take the southern 45-kilometre stretch of Route 1088, which joins Highway 108 25km west of Hot.

Practicalities

A checkpoint by Mae Klang Falls collects **entrance fees** of B200 for foreigners, plus B20 per motorbike, and B30 per car. For information on the park, stop at the **visitor centre** (daily, roughly 8am–5pm), 1km beyond the checkpoint, which puts on a fairly interesting slide show with English commentary about the park (just ask to see it). Information is also available at the **park headquarters**, a further 22km on, where you need to stop if you plan to stay overnight or to pick up a guide to walk the Kew Mae Pan trail. Two hundred metres beyond the headquarters on the left, the **Birding Visitor Centre** has a useful logbook and information in English for birders to consult, and sells a primitive map of birding sites.

Accommodation and eating

Accommodation in the national park comes in the standard log-cabin or concrete varieties. Three- to twelve-berth bungalows (B800–3000; bookings at the park on ⓣ053 268550, or in Bangkok – see p.46), set among dense stands of pine near the headquarters, come with hot-water bathrooms, electricity, mattresses or beds and bedding. They are often fully booked at weekends and national holidays, but at other times you should be all right turning up on the day. Elsewhere, the *Little Home Guest House and Restaurant*, 7km from Chom Thong and one of several along this stretch of the main park road (ⓣ01 287 6242 or 07 185 2889; ❹–❺), has clean, breeze-block huts, either fan-cooled or air-conditioned, and with inside bathrooms, most with hot water. The *Navasoung Resort*, just before reaching Mae Chaem from Doi Inthanon (ⓣ & ⓕ053 828477; ❺) offers small, cosy chalets with hot water and fan, set in a colourful garden with pleasant views across the valley that are shared by its restaurant.

Camping, an often chilly alternative, is permitted on a site about 500m from the park headquarters and another site at Huai Sai Luaeng Falls (B30/person/night). Fully equipped two-person tents can be rented at headquarters for B250 per night.

Foodstalls operate in the daytime at Mae Klang, Vachiratharn and Mae Ya falls and also through the evening beside park headquarters and near Mae Pan Falls. The Birding Visitor Centre serves up cheap but tasty dishes, and there's a popular canteen with a reasonable variety of food by the twin chedis. All these places will prepare food to take away if you need a packed lunch.

West to Mae Sariang and Mae Sam Laeb

South from Chom Thong, there are several weaving villages bordering Highway 108, and the **Pa-Da Cotton Textile Museum** at Ban Rai Pai Ngarm (on the east side of the road at kilometre-stone 68) is well worth a look. The museum is dedicated to the work of Saeng-da Bansiddhi, a local woman who started a co-operative practising traditional dyeing and weaving techniques using only natural products. Saeng-da died in the late 1980s, and the museum, which displays some of her personal effects as well as looms, fabrics and plants used in dyeing, was established to honour her efforts to revive these disappearing skills. It is situated on the upper floor of a large wooden building, while on the ground floor weavers can be seen busy at work. Bolts of cloth and a small range of clothes are on sale at reasonable prices.

Highway 108 parallels the Ping River downstream as far as **Hot**, a dusty, forgettable place 27km from Chom Thong, before bending west and weaving through pretty wooded hills up the valley of the Chaem River. Four kilometres west of town, the *Hod Resort* (ⓣ & ⓕ053 461070; ❹) has well-appointed chalets and rooms with hot water, some air-conditioned, and a riverside restaurant which serves tasty food at moderate prices.

Another 13km brings you to **Ob Luang Gorge National Park** (B200), billed with wild hyperbole as "Thailand's Grand Canyon". A wooden bridge over the short, narrow channel lets you look down on the Chaem River bubbling along between sheer walls 50m below. The park is also tagged "Land of Prehistoric Human" because of the discovery of Bronze Age graves here, containing seashell bracelets and other decorative items, as well as rock paintings of elephants and human figures. Upstream from the bridge near park headquarters, you can relax at the roadside foodstalls and swim in the river when it's not too fast, and the shady river bank shelters a **campsite**

(B30/person, plus B250 to hire a three-person tent and blankets). At headquarters you can arrange one-hour, five-kilometre **whitewater-rafting** trips on the river, which cost from B1500 for 2 people up to B2000 for 6–8 people, including guides, transport, life jackets and helmets. Two hundred metres west of the park entrance, *Khao Krairaj Resort* (ⓣ053 384542–3, ⓕ053 865181; ❹–❻) offers a variety of rustic rooms and bungalows with fan or air-con and hot water in shady grounds. West of Ob Luang, the highway gradually climbs through pine forests, the road surface bad in patches and the countryside becoming steeper and wilder.

Mae Sariang

After its descent into the broad, smoky valley of the Yuam River, Highway 108's westward progress ends at **MAE SARIANG**, 183km from Chiang Mai, a quietly industrious market town showing a marked Burmese influence in its temples and its rows of low wooden shophouses. Halfway along the southern route between Chiang Mai and Mae Hong Son, this is an obvious place for a stopover. From here you can make an intriguing day-trip to the trading post of Mae Sam Laeb on the border with Burma and out onto the Salween River, and it's also possible to strike off south on a bone-rattling journey to Mae Sot.

Apart from soaking up the atmosphere, there's nothing pressing to do in this border outpost, which is regularly visited by local hill tribes and dodgy traders from Burma. If you want something more concrete to do, stroll around a couple of temples off the north side of the main street, whose Burmese features provide a glaring contrast to most Thai temples. The first, **Wat Si Boonruang**, sports a fairy-tale bot with an intricate, tiered roof piled high above. Topped with lotus buds, the unusual *sema* stones, which delineate the bot's consecrated area, look like old-fashioned street bollards. The open viharns here and next door at **Wat Uthayarom** (aka Wat Jong Sung) are mounted on stilts, with broad teak floors that are a pleasure to get your feet onto. Both wats enshrine Burmese-style Buddhas, white and hard-faced.

Practicalities

Buses enter Mae Sariang from the east along the town's main street, Thanon Wiang Mai, and pull in at the **terminal** on Thanon Mae Sariang, one of two north–south streets; the other, Thanon Laeng Phanit, parallels the Yuam River to the west. **Motorbikes** (B200/day) for exploring local temples and Karen villages can be hired from Pratin Kolakan, a small outlet opposite the bus terminal, or from the *See View* and *Northwest* guest houses (see below); these two guest houses also rent **bicycles** (B50). One- to three-day **treks** into the countryside northeast of Mae Sariang or along the border can be arranged at *River Side Guest House*, taking in Karen, Hmong, Lawa and Kuomintang villages, caves and waterfalls, and typically cost B2000 for three days including rafting and elephant-riding. As well as organizing **boat trips from Mae Sam Laeb** (see below), *See View Guest House* can offer one-day **jeep treks** to the southeast of town, visiting hill tribes, waterfalls and caves.

When it's time for **food**, don't be put off by the basic appearance of the *Inthira Restaurant* on Thanon Wiang Mai – it's the locals' favourite, and dishes up excellent Thai dishes at moderate prices. *Renu Restaurant*, opposite, is less highly favoured but specializes in "wild food" such as nuthatch curry and wild boar. **Internet access** is available, for example, at Eyecom, just east of the *Inthira Restaurant* on Thanon Wiang Mai. For such a tiny town, Mae Sariang has a good range of **accommodation**, the best of which is listed below.

Mae Sariang Resort ☎053 682344–5. Go 2km out towards Chiang Mai, then turn left before the bridge and follow the minor road for a further 1km. Large, wood and bamboo chalets with hot-water bathrooms and verandas in an idyllic riverside garden. No restaurant. ❸

Northwest Guest House 81 Thanon Laeng Phanit ☎053 681956. Clean, friendly spot where you sleep on a mattress on the floor in a tidy, polished-wood room, and share smart hot-water bathrooms; good reductions for singles. ❷

River House Hotel 77 Thanon Laeng Phanit ☎053 621201, ⓔriverhouse@hotmail.com. Uncomplicatedly stylish rooms with fine river views, verandas, air-con, en-suite hot-water bathrooms and TVs; Internet access available. ❺

River Side Guest House 85 Thanon Laeng Phanit ☎053 681188, ⓕ053 681353. Along with the *See View*, this is one of Mae Sariang's long-standing travellers' hangouts, offering basic bedrooms (mattress only) in an old-fashioned wooden house with shared hot-water bathrooms, or low-ceilinged concrete rooms with hot water en-suite and river-side terraces, some with air-con and TV. The pretty terrace restaurant occupies a choice position above the curving river. ❷–❹

See View ☎053 681556 or 09 552 7616, ⓦwww.thai.net/seeviewguesthouse.com. Just across the river from the town centre, but they meet buses from Chiang Mai and Mae Hong Son and songthaews from Mae Sot. The best budget place to stay in town, with a choice of big, comfortable, concrete rooms, each with a hot-water bathroom, one with air-con, or wood and concrete A-frames in the garden, where there's also a cosy restaurant. Their enthusiastic and helpful owner, Aekkasan, is a mine of local information. ❷–❸

Mae Sam Laeb

Some 46km southwest of Mae Sariang, **MAE SAM LAEB** lies on the mighty Salween (or Salawin) River, which, having descended from Tibet through Burma, forms the Thai-Burmese border for 120km here, before emptying into the Andaman Sea. Mae Sam Laeb is no more than a row of bamboo stores and restaurants, but with its Thai, Chinese, Karen and Burmese inhabitants, it has a classic frontier feel about it. Morning songthaews from Mae Sariang market are sporadic, but your best bet is to sign up for one of the highly recommended one-day **boat trips** organized and guided by Aekkasan at *See View Guest House*, which include transport out to Mae Sam Laeb. The boat (with life jackets provided) cruises down the Salween through idyllic countryside to the small unspoilt Karen village of Sop Moei, right on the confluence of the Moei River with the Salween, where lunch is taken before sailing back to Mae Sam Laeb; the cost is B600–1000 according to the number of people on the trip.

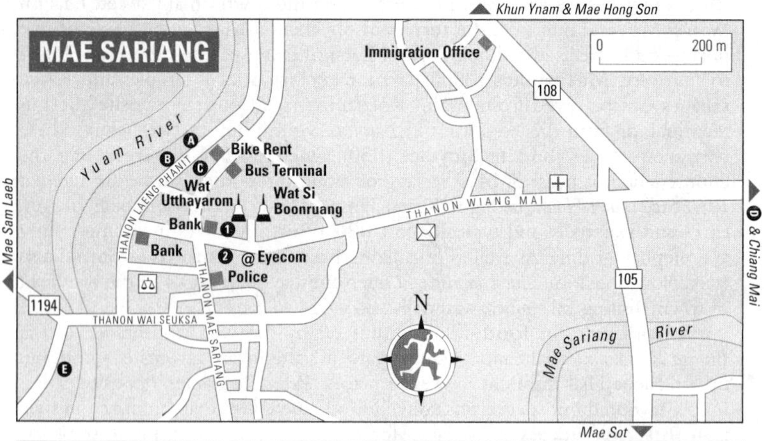

ACCOMMODATION						RESTAURANTS	
Mae Sariang Resort	D	River House	B	See View Guest House	E	Inthira	2
Northwest Guest House	C	River Side Guest House	A			Renu	1

South from Mae Sariang: Highway 105 to Mae Sot

Highway 105, which drops south for 230km to Mae Sot (see p.298), makes a scenic and quiet link between the north and the central plains, though it has some major drawbacks. Setting off through the Yuam valley, the road winds over a range of hills to the Burmese border, formed here by the Moei River, which it then hugs all the way down to Mae Sot. Along the way, you'll pass through traditional Karen villages which still keep some working elephants, and dense forests with occasional forlorn stands of teak.

The major deterrent against travelling this way is the standard of public transport: though the route is paved, it's covered only by **songthaews** (7 daily), with a journey time of about six hours – really too much on a rattling bench seat – at a cost of B160 per person. In the past, this remote border area was the scene of occasional skirmishes between the Burmese army and opposition freedom fighters, but at the time of writing there hasn't been any fighting for at least six years.

North to Mae Hong Son

North of Mae Sariang, wide, lush valleys alternate with tiny, steep-sided glens – some too narrow for more than a single rice paddy – turning Highway 108 into a winding roller coaster. The market town of **KHUN YUAM**, 95km from Mae Sariang, is a popular resting spot, especially for those who've taken the direct route here (Route 1263) over the mountains from Mae Chaem. There's not much here in the way of attractions, though the **World War II Museum**, on the left of the main thoroughfare, Thanon Rajaburana, opposite Wat Muai Tor at the north end of town, has a curious collection of rusting relics from the Japanese World War II occupation – old trucks, rifles, water canisters and uniforms. Lining the walls, hundreds of black-and-white photos document this period, when after their retreat from Burma in 1944, some of the Japanese rested here with the sick and wounded for two years and longer.

The *Ban Farang* **guest house** (ⓣ053 622086 or 07 178 2496; ❸), north again from the museum and well signposted just off Thanon Rajaburana, can put you up in fine style. Each of its smart, very clean rooms has duvets and a hot-water bathroom; the restaurant serves up good Thai and Western food, at reasonable prices. Cheaper rooms can be had at the *Mithkhoonyoum Hotel*, 115 Thanon Rajaburana (ⓣ053 691057; ❶–❹), with large, airy and very simple rooms in the wooden building at the front, some with en-suite cold-water bathrooms, and more expensive rooms with hot-water bathrooms, some with air-con, in the comfy new building behind.

Just north of Khun Yuam, Route 1263 branches off to the east over the hills towards Mae Chaem; after about 20km, a side road leads north up to the **Buatong fields** on the slopes of Doi Mae U-Khor, where Mexican sunflowers make the hillsides glow butter-yellow in November and early December. Much of the roadside elsewhere is bordered by these same flowers at this time of year, but the sheer concentration of blooms at Mae U-Khor, combined with sweeping views over endless ridges to the west, make it worth sharing the experience with the inevitable tour groups. Around 15km further down the same road from the Hmong village of Ban Mae U-Khor, **Mae Surin Waterfall** in Nam Tok Mae Surin National Park (B200) is arguably the most spectacular waterfall in the whole country, the waters hurtling over a cliff and plunging almost 100m before crashing on huge boulders and foaming down a steep gorge. The kind topography of the region allows a great view of the falls from directly in front, but the best view, from below, requires a steep and at times precarious three-hour hike down and back from the well-appointed **campsite**. Basic food is available from a stall at the campsite (Nov–Feb). To reach the park without your own transport, join a tour from Mae Hong Son (see p.384).

Back on the main road, 35km north of Khun Yuam, a right turn leads up to **Mae Ko Vafe** – a Thai rendition of "microwave", referring to the transmitters that grace the mountain's peak; the paved road climbs for 10km to a Hmong village, where the fantastic view west stretches far into Burma. Around 15km beyond this turn-off Highway 108 climbs to a roadside **viewing area**, with fine vistas, this time to the east, of the sheer, wooded slopes and the Pha Bong Dam in the valley far below. Subsequently the road makes a dramatic, headlong descent towards Mae Hong Son, passing the **Ban Pha Bong** hot springs, 7km north of the viewing area (11km before Mae Hong Son). These have been turned into a small spa complex, with private rooms with hot spring-water baths, traditional masseurs and a restaurant.

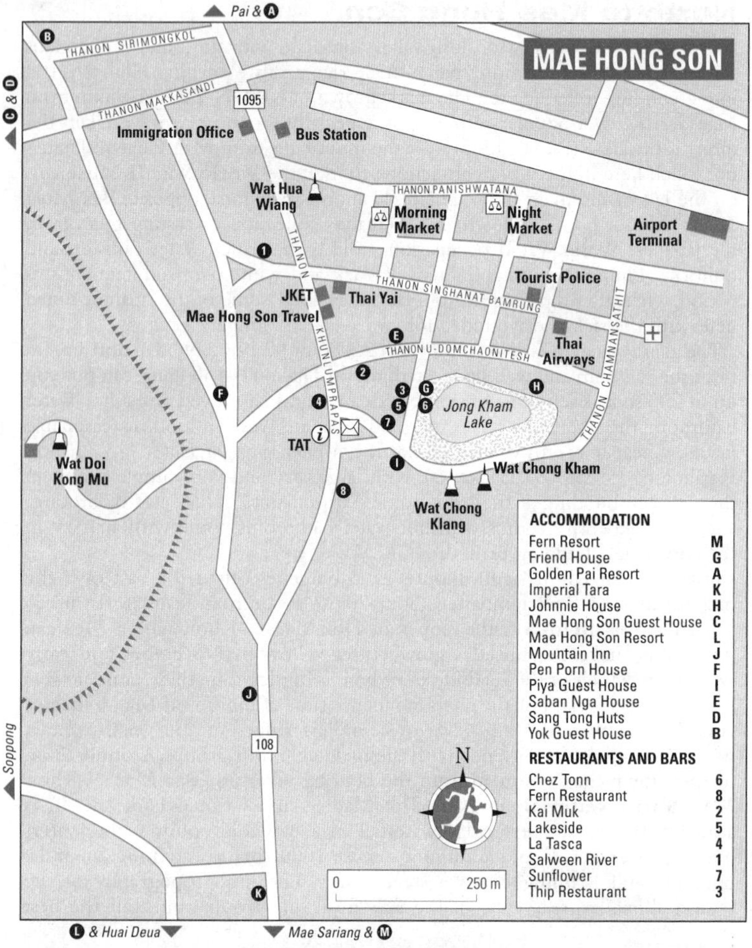

Mae Hong Son and around

MAE HONG SON, capital of Thailand's northwesternmost province, sports more nicknames than a town of just under ten thousand people seems to deserve. In Thai, it's Muang Sam Mok, the "City of Three Mists": set deep in a mountain valley, Mae Hong Son is often swathed in mist, the quality of which differs according to the three seasons (in the hot season it's mostly composed of unpleasant smoke from burning fields). In former times, the town, which wasn't connected to the outside world by a paved road until 1968, was known as "Siberia" to the troublesome politicians and government officials who were exiled here from Bangkok. Nowadays, thanks to its mountainous surroundings, it's increasingly billed as the "Switzerland of Thailand": eighty percent of Mae Hong Son province is on a slope of more than 45 degrees.

To match the hype, Mae Hong Son has become one of the fastest-developing tourist centres in the country, sporting, alongside dozens of backpacker guest houses, several luxury hotels for Thai and farang package tourists who like their city comforts. Most backpackers come here for **trekking** (see p.386) and day-hiking in the beautiful countryside, others just for the cool climate and lazy upcountry atmosphere. The town is still small enough and sleepy enough to hole up in for a quiet week, though in the high season (Nov–Feb) swarms of minibuses disgorge tour groups who hunt in packs through the souvenir stalls and fill up the restaurants.

Mae Hong Son was founded in 1831 as a training camp for elephants captured from the surrounding jungle for the princes of Chiang Mai (Jong Kham Lake, in the southeastern part of the modern town, served as the elephants' bathing spot). The hard work of hunting and rearing the royal elephants was done by the **Thai Yai** (aka Shan), who account for half the population of the province and bring a strong Burmese flavour to Mae Hong Son's temples and festivals. The other half of the province's population is made up of various hill tribes (a large number of Karen, as well as Lisu, Hmong and Lawa), with a tiny minority of Thais concentrated in the provincial capital.

The latest immigrants to the province are **Burmese refugees**: as well as rural Karen, driven across the border when the Burmese army razed their villages (see box on p.296), many urban students and monks, who formed the hard core of the brutally repressed 1988 uprising, fled to this area to join the resistance forces. The refugee camps between Mae Hong Son and the border generally do not encourage visitors as they've got quite enough on their plates without having to entertain onlookers.

Arrival, information and accommodation

Running north to south, Mae Hong Son's main drag, Thanon Khunlumprapas, is intersected by Thanon Singhanat Bamrung at the traffic lights in the centre of town. Arriving at Mae Hong Son's **bus station**, towards the north end of Thanon Khunlumprapas, puts you within walking distance of the guest houses. Tuk-tuks (B50) run from the **airport** to the centre, though if you're already booked into a resort or hotel, a car or minibus should pick you up. Motorbike taxis also operate in and around the town: the local transport hub is the north side of the morning market.

TAT have a helpful office (Mon–Fri 8.30am–4.30pm, plus Sat & Sun same times in high season; ⓣ053 612982–3, ⓦwww.travelmaehongson.org) opposite the post office on Khunlumprapas. In the same building is a government-sponsored shop selling some attractive fabrics (including bags and clothes), local teas and other foodstuffs, while the Tourism Volunteer Centre booth outside (☎053 612800) claims to stay open 24 hours. The **tourist police** are on Thanon Singhanat Bamrung (☎053 611812 or 1155).

Accommodation

At the lower end of the accommodation spectrum, Mae Hong Son has a healthy roster of **guest houses**, most of them being good-value, rustic affairs built of bamboo or wood and set in their own quiet gardens; many have ranged themselves around Jong Kham Lake in the southeast corner of town, which greatly adds to their scenic appeal. If you've got a little more money to spend, you can get out into the countryside to one of several self-contained **resorts**, though staying at one of these is not exactly a wilderness experience – they're really designed for weekending Thais travelling by car. Finally, several **luxury hotels**, notably the *Imperial Tara* on the southern edge of town, have latched onto the area's meteoric development, offering all the usual international-standard facilities.

Guest houses

Friend House 21 Thanon Pradit Jongkham ☎053 620119. Smart and clean modern teak and concrete house with upstairs balcony giving views of the lake. Larger rooms have hot-water bathrooms, smaller ones share hot showers. ❶–❸

Johnnie House Thanon U-Domchaonitesh ☎053 611667. In a small compound by the lake, this clean, friendly place has sturdy, airy wooden rooms which share hot showers, as well as bright, concrete affairs with en-suite hot-water bathrooms. ❶–❸

Mae Hong Son Guest House 295 Thanon Makkasandi ☎053 612510 or 09 635 7045. Relaxing old-timer in the suburbs with a view over the town from its pleasant garden. You'll get an en-suite hot-water bathroom, either in a large attractive bungalow or in one of the simpler rooms. ❸–❹

Pen Porn House 16/1 Thanon Padunomuaytaw ☎ & ℱ053 611577. Smart, clean, well-maintained, motel-like doubles with fans and hot showers, round a small, shady garden. ❸

Saban Nga House 14 Thanon U-Domchaonitesh ☎053 612280. Clean and central; choose between the airy, rattan-walled main block, with mattresses and shared hot showers, and the plain concrete rooms with en-suite bathrooms. ❷–❸

Sang Tong Huts Down a small lane opposite *Mae Hong Son Guest House* off Thanon Makkasandi ☎053 620680, Ⓦwww.sangtonghuts.com. Upmarket, German-run guest house, offering tasteful rustic chic on a steep, jungly slope on the edge of town. Roofed with traditional, thatched *tong teung* leaves, and decorated with rugs and tapestries, the "huts" have verandas, mosquito nets on the beds and large, attractively tiled bathrooms with hot water. Home-baked bread and cakes are served in a simple, open-sided seating area around an open fire. ❺

Yok Guest House Thanon Sirimongkol ☎053 611532 or 09 635 3441. Quiet and welcoming place in a small walled compound on the northwest side of town, offering functional but clean and good-value concrete rooms with fans and en-suite hot-water bathrooms. ❸

Resorts

Fern Resort 6km south of town on Highway 108, then signposted 2km east on paved minor road ☎053 686110–1, Ⓦwww.fernresort.info. The best resort around Mae Hong Son, an eco-friendly place employing local villagers as far as possible. In a peaceful, shady valley, a brook runs through the beautiful grounds, past stylish cottages with hot water, air-con and verandas (no phones or TV). There's an attractive swimming pool, and nature trails in the surrounding Mae Surin National Park; regular free shuttle bus to the *Fern Restaurant* in town. ❼

Golden Pai Resort 6km north of town, signposted to the left of the road towards Pai ☎053 612265–6, ℱ053 612265. Clean, well-appointed, air-con chalets arranged around a smart swimming pool in pleasant grounds, with mud treatments, mineral baths and saunas available at their nearby Pooklon spa. ❻

Mae Hong Son Resort 6km south of town, on the road to Huai Deua ☎053 613138, ℱ053 612086. In a relaxing spot by the Pai River, a friendly and quietly efficient place, with riverside chalets or rooms in the grounds behind. Price includes cooked breakfast. ❺

Hotels

Imperial Tara Hotel 149 Moo 8, Tambon Pang Moo ☎053 611021–4, Ⓦwww.imperialhotels.com. On the south side of the town by the turn-off for Huai Deua, this grand building is set in pretty landscaped gardens, overlooked by spacious rooms featuring satellite TV and mini-bar; there's a swimming pool, sauna and fitness centre, too. ⑨

Piya Guest House 1/1 Thanon Khunlumprapas ⓣ053 611260, ⓕ053 612308. Despite its name, this friendly, well-run place is more like a hotel, boasting spacious rooms with hot-water bathrooms, TV and air-con in a lush garden, with a restaurant overlooking the lake. ⑤

Mountain Inn 112 Thanon Khunlumprapas ⓣ053/612283, ⓕ053 612284. Large, neat and tasteful rooms with air-con, hot-water bathrooms, carpeting and TV, set round a flower-strewn garden. ⑥

The Town

Beyond the typical concrete boxes in the centre, Mae Hong Son sprawls lazily across the valley floor and up the lower slopes of Doi Kong Mu to the west, trees and untidy vegetation poking through at every possible opportunity to remind you that open country is only a stone's throw away. Plenty of traditional Thai Yai buildings remain – wooden shophouses with balconies, shutters and corrugated-iron roof decorations, homes thatched with *tong teung* leaves and fitted with herringbone-patterned window panels – though they take a severe beating from the weather and may eventually be replaced by inexpensive, all-engulfing concrete. Mae Hong Son's classic picture-postcard view is its twin nineteenth-century Burmese-style temples from the opposite, north shore of Jong Kham Lake, their gleaming white and gold chedis and the multi-tiered roofs and spires of their viharns reflected in the water. In the viharn of **Wat Chong Kham** is a huge, intricately carved sermon throne, decorated with the *dharmachakra* (Wheel of Law) in coloured glass on gold; the building on the left has been built around the temple's most revered Buddha image, the benign, inscrutable Luang Pho To. Next door, **Wat Chong Klang** is famous for its paintings on glass, which are said to have been painted by artists from Mandalay over 100 years ago; they're displayed over three walls on the left-hand side of the viharn. The first two walls behind the monks' dais (on which women are not allowed to stand) depict *Jataka* stories from the Buddha's previous incarnations in their lower sections, and the life of the Buddha himself in their upper, while the third wall is devoted entirely to the Buddha's life. A room to the left houses an unforgettable collection of **teak statues**, brought over from Burma in the middle of the nineteenth century. The dynamically expressive, often humorous figures are characters from the *Vessantara Jataka*, but the woodcarvers have taken as their models people from all levels of traditional Burmese society, including toothless emaciated peasants, butch tattooed warriors and elegant upper-class ladies.

The town's vibrant, smelly **morning market**, just south of the bus station, is worth dragging your bones up at dawn to see. People from the local hill tribes often come down to buy and sell, and the range of produce is particularly weird and wonderful, including, in season, porcupine meat, displayed with quills to prove its authenticity. Next door, the many-gabled viharn of **Wat Hua Wiang** shelters, under a lace canopy, one of the most beautiful Buddha images in northern Thailand, the **Chao Palakeng**. Copied from a famous statue in Mandalay, the strong, serene bronze has the regal clothing and dangling ears typical of Burmese Buddhas. Though the town is generally quiet during the day while visitors are out exploring the hills, the main streets come alive in the evening as **handicraft stalls** display colourful bolts of cloth, lacquerware, Burmese puppets, ceramics and jewellery.

For a godlike overview of the area, drive or climb up to **Wat Doi Kong Mu** on the steep hill to the west. From the temple's two chedis, which enshrine the ashes of respected nineteenth-century Thai Yai monks, you can look down on the town and out across the sleepy farming valley north and south. Behind the chedis, the viharn contains an unusual and highly venerated white marble image of the Buddha, surrounded in gold flames. If you've got the energy, trek up to the bot on the summit, where the view extends over the Burmese mountains to the west.

Around Mae Hong Son

Once you've exhausted the few obvious sights in town, the first decision you'll have to grapple with is whether to visit the "**long-neck**" **women**. Our advice is don't, though many travellers do. Less controversial, **boat and raft trips** on the babbling Pai River are fun, and the roaring **Pha Sua Falls** and the Kuomintang village of **Mae Aw** make a satisfying day out. If all that sounds too easy, Mae Hong Son is now Thailand's third-largest centre for **trekking**. Other feasible targets include the hot springs at Ban Pha Bong (see p.382) and, further out, Mae Surin Waterfall (see p.380) and Tham Lot (see p.389).

Local transport, in the form of songthaews from the morning market, is thinly spread and unreliable, so for all of these excursions it's best to rent your own vehicle or join an organized tour through your guest house or a travel agent. Among the many **tour agents** clustered around the main traffic lights, Mae Hong Son Travel on Thanon Khunlumprapas (ⓣ053 620644, ⓦwww.maehongsontravel.com) are long-established and helpful, or check out nearby JKET's more alternative, community-based offerings (see p.386). Thai Yai at 20 Thanon Singhanat Bamrung rents out **motorbikes** for B180, and several places on the main street rent out **four-wheel drives**, though the most reliable – and expensive – place is Avis at the airport (ⓣ053 620457–8; B2000/day).

Nai Soi

The original and largest village of long-neck Padaung women (see p.388) in the Mae Hong Son area, **NAI SOI**, 28km northwest of town, has effectively been turned into a human zoo for snap-happy tourists, with an entrance fee of B250 per person. The "long necks" pose in front of their huts and looms, every now and then getting it together to stage a good-luck song – all a visitor can do is stand and stare in embarrassed silence or click away with a camera. All in all it's a disturbing spectacle, offering no opportunity to discover anything about Padaung culture. At least, contrary to many reports, the "long necks" are not held as slaves in the village: the entrance fee is handled by the Karenni National Progressive Party, a Kayah (Karenni) rebel group to whom the Padaung, in their precarious plight as refugees, have offered their services (the KNPP is fighting for the independence of Burma's Kayah state, where the Padaung come from). Much of the fee is used to support the KNPP, and some goes to help improve conditions in the village and the adjacent Kayah refugee settlement, while the "long necks" themselves are each paid a living wage of about B1500 per month.

Without your own transport, you have to hitch up with an expensive tour (about B800/person, including entrance fee) from a travel agent in town. By motorbike or jeep, head north along Route 1095 for 2km and turn left after the police box; cross the bridge over the Pai River, turn left at the next village, Ban Sop Soi, and continue for another 10km.

Trips on the Pai River

Scenic **boat trips** on the Pai River start from Huai Deua, 7km southwest of town near the *Mae Hong Son Resort*. There's no need to go on an organized tour: take a motorbike taxi, tuk-tuk or one of the infrequent songthaews from

Poy Sang Long

Mae Hong Son's most famous and colourful festival is **Poy Sang Long**, held at the beginning of April, which celebrates the ordination into the monkhood, for the duration of the schools' long vacation, of Thai Yai boys between the ages of seven and fourteen. Similar rituals take place in other northern Thai towns at this time, but the Mae Hong Son version is given a unique flavour by its Thai Yai elements. On the first day of the festival, the boys have their heads shaved and are anointed with turmeric and dressed up in the gay colours of a Thai Yai prince, with traditional accessories: long white socks, plenty of jewellery, a headcloth decorated with fresh flowers, a golden umbrella and heavy face make-up. They are then announced to the guardian spirit of the town and taken around the temples. The second day brings general merry-making and a spectacular parade, headed by a drummer and a richly decorated riderless horse, which is believed to carry the town's guardian spirit. The boys, still in their finery, are each carried on the shoulders of a chaperone, accompanied by musicians and bearers of traditional offerings. In the evening, the novices tuck into a sumptuous meal, waited on by their parents and relatives, before the ordination ceremony in the temple on the third day.

Mae Hong Son market to Huai Deua and approach the owners at the boat station. Twenty minutes downriver from Huai Deua (B500, plus B250 admission charge to the village) will get you to **Ban Nam Phiang Din**, where a dozen or so "long-neck" women display themselves in a setup similar to that at Nai Soi. You're better off enjoying the river for its own sake, as it scythes its way between cliffs and forests towards the nearby Burmese border, or travelling upriver to **Soppong** (B500), a pretty, quiet Thai Yai village 5km due west of Mae Hong Son (not to be confused with the Soppong on Route 1095, northeast of Mae Hong Son). **Elephant-rides** into the surrounding jungle, for B400–500 per hour for two people, can be arranged next to the boat station.

A small stretch of the Pai River between **Sop Soi**, 10km northwest of Mae Hong Son, and Soppong is clear enough of rocks to allow safe clearance for bamboo **rafts**. The journey takes two hours at the most, as the rafts glide down the gentle river, partly hemmed in by steep wooded hills. Most of Mae Hong Son's travel agents can fix this trip up for you, including travel to Sop Soi and from Soppong, charging around B800 per raft (two passengers).

Pha Sua Falls and Mae Aw

North of Mae Hong Son, a trip to Pha Sua Falls and the border village of Mae Aw takes in some spectacular and varied countryside. Your best options are to rent a motorbike or join a tour – agents typically charge around B600 per person for a one-day excursion, which includes a city tour and a visit to the highly overrated Fish Cave – as there are only occasional songthaews to Mae Aw from the market in the morning, and no guarantees for the return journey to Mae Hong Son. Under your own steam, the best route is to head north for 17km on Route 1095 (ignore the first signpost for Pha Sua, after 10km) and then, after a long, steep descent, turn left onto a side road, paved at first, which passes through an idyllic rice valley and the Thai Yai village of **Ban Bok Shampae**. About 9km from the turn-off you'll reach **Pha Sua Falls**, a wild, untidy affair, which crashes down in several cataracts through a dark, overhung cut in the limestone. The waterfall is in full roar in October after the rainy season, but has plenty of water all year round. Take care when swimming, as several people have been swept to their deaths here.

Trekking around Mae Hong Son

There's no getting away from the fact that **trekking** up and down Mae Hong Son's steep inclines is tough, but the hill-tribe villages are generally unspoilt and the scenery is magnificent. To the west, trekking routes tend to snake along the Burmese border, occasionally nipping over the line for a quick thrill, and can sometimes get a little crowded as this is the more popular side of Mae Hong Son. Nearly all the hill-tribe villages here are Karen, interspersed with indigenous Thai Yai (Shan) settlements. To the east of Mae Hong Son the Karens again predominate, but by travelling a little further you'll also be able to visit Hmong, Lisu and Lahu; many villages here are very traditional, having little contact with the outside world. If you're very hardy, you might want to consider the five- to six-day route to Pai, which by all accounts has the best scenery of the lot.

About a dozen guest houses and travel agencies run treks out of Mae Hong Son. Among the reliable operators, *Mae Hong Son Guest House* charges from B1500 per person for a three-day trek in a group of 6–8 people. Or you could take your money to Jor Koe Ecotrek (JKET), 18/1 Thanon Singhanat Bamrung (though actually round the corner on Thanon Khunlumprapas, next to the optician's; ⓣ053 612877, ⓦwww.jket.org). This community-based tourism agency was set up by a small Thai NGO, Project for Recovery of Life and Culture, and among other things, employs village guides and offers home-stays, always with their own guide-translators. A five-day trek, for example, costs B7000 per person, a two-day home-stay in a Thai Yai village B3300, and a one-day trip to a Karen village, including lunch there and a short walk to some caves and a waterfall, costs B1400; specific requests such as bird-watching and botany can also be accommodated. Shorter activities such as boat trips, rafting, elephant-riding and horse-riding are also on offer.

Above the falls the paved road climbs precipitously, giving glorious, broad vistas of both Thai and Burmese mountains, before reaching the unspectacular half-Hmong, half-Thai Yai village of **Naphapak** after 11km. A decent, largely flat stretch covers the last 7km to **MAE AW** (aka Ban Ruk Thai), a settlement of Kuomintang anti-Communist Chinese refugees (see p.406), right on the Burmese border. In the past, this area saw fighting between the Kuomintang and the army of Khun Sa, the opium warlord who, having been kicked out of the Mae Salong area by the Thai army in 1983, set up base somewhere in the uncharted mountains across the border northeast of Mae Aw. The road up here was built by the Thai military to help the fight against the opium trade and all has been quiet for several years. Mae Aw is the highest point on the border which visitors can reach, and provides a fascinating window on Kuomintang life. The tight ring of hills around the village heightens the feeling of being in another country: delicate, bright-green tea bushes line the slopes, while Chinese ponies wander the streets of long, unstilted bamboo houses. In the central marketplace on the north side of the village reservoir, shops sell great bags of Oolong and Chian Chian teas, as well as dried mushrooms.

Eating and drinking

Nobody comes to Mae Hong Son for the **food** – the available options are limited, although a few good restaurants have sprung up in order to cater specifically to foreigners. There's a small **night market** on Thanon Panishwatana, along from the day market.

Chez Tonn Next to *Friend House* near the lake. Small, open-sided restaurant strewn with plants, serving tasty Thai and Western food (especially breakfast favourites and sandwiches). Inexpensive.

Fern 87 Thanon Khunlumprapas. A big, showy, tourist-oriented eating place, with a nice candlelit terrace and a good reputation for its Thai food. Moderate to expensive.

Kai Muk Thanon U-Domchaonitesh. Attractive, efficient and popular, with a huge variety of excellent Thai dishes on its menu. Moderate.

Lakeside Bar 2/3 Thanon Khunlumprapas. A good place for a drink accompanied by some tasty Thai dishes. Here you can relax to the sounds of a live band playing Western and Thai pop and folk music, on a terrace overlooking Jong Kham Lake and the fairy lights on the temples behind. Moderate.

La Tasca Thanon Khunlumprapas. Reasonably authentic Italian restaurant for home-made pizzas and a long menu of familiar pasta dishes, including home-made gnocchi, fettuccini and lasagne. Moderate to expensive.

Salween River Just west of the main traffic lights off Thanon Khunlumprapas. English- and Thai-run restaurant and bar, dishing up a wide variety of western faves, such as soups, jacket potatoes, good burgers and chicken cordon bleu, as well as some delicious Thai food. Moderate.

Sunflower 116/115 Soi 3, Thanon Khunlumprapas. A small, quiet, indoor-outdoor café with a relaxing fountain, serving a few Thai favourites and good Western food including excellent breakfasts with home-made bread and filter coffee. Moderate.

Thip Restaurant Next to *Lakeside Bar*. Wide range of tasty Thai food, including northern specialities and local freshwater food, though service can be a bit sloppy. Great views of the lake, the temples and the mountains behind at lunchtime. Moderate.

Listings

Airline The Thai Airways office is at 71 Thanon Singhanat Bamrung ⓣ053 611367 or 053 612220.

Airport For flight information, call ⓣ053 612057, ext 188.

Exchange The airport has a bank currency exchange (daily 10am–5pm). There are also several banks and exchange booths along Thanon Khunlumprapas.

Immigration office On Thanon Khunlumprapas (Mon–Fri 8.30am–4.30pm, plus some Sat & Sun; ⓣ053 612106).

Internet access Several nameless cybercafés cluster around the post office on Thanon Khunlumprapas.

Mail and telephones The post office is on Thanon Khunlumprapas, with cardphones outside and at the 7–11 supermarket across the road where you can buy the phonecards.

Route 1095: Mae Hong Son to Chiang Mai

Route 1095, the 243-kilometre northern route between Mae Hong Son and Chiang Mai, is every bit as wild and scenic as the southern route through Mae Sariang – if anything it has more mountains to negotiate, with a greater contrast between the sometimes straggly vegetation of the slopes and the thickly cultivated valleys. Much of the route was established by the Japanese army to move troops and supplies into Burma after its invasion of Thailand during World War II. The labour-intensive job of paving every hairpin bend was completed in the 1990s, but ongoing repair work can still give you a nasty surprise if you're riding a motorbike. If you're setting off along this route from Chiang Mai by public transport, catch one of the four daily buses to Mae Hong Son via Pai from the Arcade station.

Long-neck women

The most famous – and notorious – of the Mae Hong Son area's spectacles is its contingent of **"long-neck" women** (see p.384), members of the tiny Padaung tribe of Burma who have come across to Thailand to escape Burmese repression. Though the women's necks appear to be stretched to 30cm and more by a column of brass rings, the "long-neck" tag is a technical misnomer: a *National Geographic* team once X-rayed one of the women and found that instead of stretching out her neck, the pressure of eleven pounds of brass had simply squashed her collarbones and ribs. Girls of the tribe start wearing the rings from about the age of six, adding one or two each year up to the age of sixteen or so. Once fastened, the rings are for life, for to remove a full stack would eventually cause the collapse of the neck and suffocation – in the past, removal was a punishment for adultery. Despite the obvious discomfort, and the laborious daily task of cleaning and drying the rings, the tribeswomen, when interviewed, say that they're used to their plight and are happy to be continuing the tradition of their people.

The **origin** of the ring-wearing ritual remains unclear, despite an embarrassment of plausible explanations. Padaung legend says that the mother of their tribe was a dragon with a long, beautiful neck, and that their unique custom is an imitation of her. Tour guides will tell you the practice is intended to enhance the women's beauty. In Burma, where it is now outlawed as barbaric, it's variously claimed that ring-wearing arose out of a need to protect women from tiger attacks or to deform the wearers so that the Burmese court would not kidnap them for concubines.

In spite of their handicap (they have to use straws to drink, for example), the women are able to carry out some kind of an ordinary life: they can marry and have children, and they're able to weave and sew, although these days they spend most of their time posing like circus freaks for photographs. Only half of the Padaung women now lengthen their necks; left to its own course, the custom would probably die out, but the influence of tourism may well keep it alive for some time yet.

Mae Suya

The first stretch north out of Mae Hong Son weaves up and down the west face of Doi Pai Kit (1082m), giving great views over the lush valley to the north of town. Beyond the turn-off for Mae Aw (see p.386) and the much-touted but unspectacular Fish Cave, the highway climbs eastward through many hairpin bends before levelling out to give tantalizing glimpses through the trees of the Burmese mountains to the north, then passes through a hushed valley of paddy fields, surrounded by echoing crags, to reach the Thai Yai/Kuomintang village of **MAE SUYA**, 40km from Mae Hong Son. Take the left turning by the police box, 3km east of the village to reach *Wilderness Lodge* after a further 1km of dirt road. Set in wild countryside, the friendly, laid-back guest house offers primitive bungalows (❶) and dorm beds (B70) in the barn-like main house, and does a wide range of vegetarian and meat-based Thai food.

The owner of the lodge can give you directions and maps for cave exploration and beautiful wilderness day walks through the mountains to hill-tribe villages. Two hours' walk to the north, **Tham Pha Daeng** is a pretty, 1600-metre-long cave (open Nov–May) with, like Tham Lot (see opposite), ancient coffins; apart from a few low crawls, the journey through the cave is relatively easy. To the south beyond Route 1095, **Tham Nam Lang**, one of the most capacious caves in the world, has a towering entrance chamber which anyone can appreciate, although the spectacular 9km beyond it demands full-on caving, again in the dry season only, and the proper equipment.

Soppong, Tham Lot and Ban Nam Rin

The small market town of **SOPPONG**, 68km from Mae Hong Son in the district of Pang Ma Pha (which is sometimes used on signposts), gives access to the area's most famous cave, **Tham Lot**, 9km north in **BAN TUM** (or Ban Tham). There's no public transport along the gentle paved forest road to the village, so if you haven't got your own wheels, you'll have to hitch, walk or rent a motorbike taxi (B60) or songthaew (B200).

Turn right in the village to find the entrance to the **Tham Lot Nature Education Station** set up to look after the cave, where you have to hire a local guide with lantern for B100 (1–4 people). A short walk through the forest brings you to the entrance of Tham Lot, where the Lang River begins a 600-metre subterranean journey through the cave. Access to the various parts of the cave depends on the time of year and how much rain there has been, and may involve hiring a bamboo raft for some or all of your journey: for most of the year you'll need to raft from Doll to Coffin Cave (B100/group of one to four), while at the driest times it may be possible to wade, and at the highest water levels it may be necessary to walk around to the exit and get to the last part, Coffin Cave, from there. Normally two hours should allow you enough time for travelling through the broad, airy tunnel, and for the main attraction, climbing up into the sweaty caverns in the roof – be sure not to touch any of the cave formations.

The first of these, **Column Cavern**, 100m from the entrance on the right, is dominated by a twenty-metre-high cave stalagmite snaking up towards the ceiling. Another 50m on the left, bamboo ladders lead up into **Doll Cave**, which has a glistening, pure white wall and a weird red and white formation shaped like a Wurlitzer organ; deep inside, stalagmites look like dolls. Just before the vast exit from the cave, wooden ladders on the left lead up into **Coffin Cave**, named after the remains of a dozen crude log coffins discovered here, one of them preserved to its full length of 5m. Hollowed out from tree trunks, they are similar to those found in many of the region's caves: some are raised 2m off the ground by wooden supporting poles, and some still contained bones, pottery and personal effects when they were discovered. These are now on display in a small museum by the main entrance. The coffins are between 1200 and 2200 years old, and local people attribute them to *phi man*, the cave spirits. A twenty-minute nature trail will bring you back to the main entrance, but it's worth hanging round the cave's exit at sunset, when hundreds of thousands of tiny black chirruping swifts pour into the cave in an almost solid column, to find their beds for the night.

Ban Tum and Soppong practicalities

Cave Lodge (Ⓣ053 617203, Ⓦwww.cavelodge.com; ❶–❸), on the other side of Ban Tum from the cave, makes an excellent and friendly base for exploring the area. The owners have plenty of useful information about Tham Lot and some of the two hundred other **caves** in the region, and organize **guided trips** through the more interesting ones when there's enough demand. They also offer **kayaking** trips through Tham Lot, plus 6km of fun rapids, at B490 for a couple of hours, and three-day trips on the Pai River in the dry season. Maps for self-guided walking from the lodge to local Karen, Lahu and Lisu villages are available, as well as four local licensed guides for full-on **trekking** (typically B1700 for 3 days, minimum 4 people). At a nearby Karen village, renowned for its traditional weaving, you can arrange elephant-riding or bamboo-rafting or hire a guide to take you to one of the local caves.

There is a swimming hole right in front of the lodge, a funky communal area for eating and hanging out, and the kitchen bakes its own bread, pizza and cakes. Dorm beds here are B60, and the wooden rooms and bungalows, some with shared hot showers and others with their own bathrooms, are scattered over the overgrown hillside. Also congenial is *Lang River Guest House* (❷, dorm B60), in a lush riverside setting by the main entrance to the cave. Simple bamboo huts, at the lower end of this price code, share toilets and hot showers, the restaurant serves Thai food, Western breakfasts and snacks, and four-wheel-drive and motorbike tours can be arranged.

On the main road at the western end of Soppong, *Jungle Guest House* (Ⓣ053 617099; ❶–❷) is the most popular of several places in town, and can give advice on local walks to caves and Lisu villages or organize inexpensive trekking trips to Lisu, Lahu and Karen settlements further to the south. Accommodation here is in simple bamboo huts with shared bathrooms (hot showers in winter), or some sturdier teak bungalows with hot-water bathrooms attached; the food, including northern Thai and Western specialities and home-made bread and jam, is great. A short walk east of Soppong's bus stop and a little upmarket, *Little Eden Guest House* (Ⓣ053 617054, Ⓦwww.littleeden-guesthouse.com; ❸) has neat, sturdy bungalows with their own hot-water bathrooms, in a pretty garden with a decent-sized swimming pool, sloping down to the Lang River and a relaxing riverside pavilion; plenty of services such as motorbike rental, Internet access and tours and treks are on offer. Note that there are no banks in Soppong.

Ban Nam Rin

About 9km east of Soppong on Highway 1095, 34km from Pai, the Lisu village of **BAN NAM RIN** has been put on the tourist map by the easy-going *Lisu Lodge* (Ⓣ09 953 4243; ❶–❸), run by a Lisu woman and her German husband. On a pretty, shady slope at the west end of the village stand A-frame bamboo huts with shared hot showers and smart, en-suite, brick-built cottages, as well as a restaurant serving Thai food, Western breakfasts and Lisu communal dinners. The owners can advise on trekking in the area, either on your own or with a guide from the village, with the possibility of staying over at other hill-tribe villages (a letter of introduction can be provided if necessary); the most ambitious trip would be the five-day DIY walk to Mae Hong Son including three nights in the jungle.

Pai

Beyond Ban Nam Rin, the road climbs through the last of Mae Hong Son province's wild landscape before descending into the broad, gentle valley of **PAI**, 43km from Soppong. Once treated as a stopover on the tiring journey to Mae Hong Son, Pai is now a destination in its own right, and travellers settle into the town's laid-back, New-Agey feel for weeks or even months. There's nothing special to see in Pai, but you can partake of all manner of outdoor activities, courses and holistic therapies – even retail therapy at the art studios, bookstores, leather and jewellery shops – and the guest houses and restaurants have tailored themselves to the steady flow of travellers who make the four-hour bus journey out from Chiang Mai. The small town's traditional buildings spread themselves liberally over the west bank of the Pai River, but everything is within walking range of the bus station at the north end. On the town's main drag, Thanon Rungsiyanon, an odd mix of hill-tribe people, shrouded Thai Muslims and Westerners mingle together.

Several undemanding **walks** can be made around Pai's broad, gently sloping valley. The easiest – one hour there and back – takes you across the river bridge on the east side of town and up the hill to Wat Mae Yen, which commands a great view over the whole district On the way to the wat, you'll pass the town's large open-air **swimming pool** (daily 10.30am–8.30pm; B50), with food and drink available, as well as a pool table. To the west of town, an unpaved road (accessible by motorbike) heads out from Pai hospital, passing, after 3km, Wat Nam Hu, whose Buddha image has an unusual hinged top-knot containing holy water, before gradually climbing through comparatively developed Kuomintang, Lisu and Lahu villages to **Mo Pang Falls**, with a pool for swimming, about 10km west of Pai.

Pai makes a good base for **trekking**, which can be arranged for around B500 per day (plus around B250 each for rafting and elephant-riding) through the guest houses or trekking agents, among which *Duang Guest House* and Back Trax at 17 Thanon Chaisongkhram (Ⓣ053 699739, Ⓔbacktraxinpai@yahoo.com) are reliable. Karen, Lisu and Lahu villages are within range, and the terrain has plenty of variety: jungles and bamboo forests, hills and flat valleys, caves and waterfalls. The area north of town, where trekking can be combined with bamboo-rafting and elephant-riding, can get a little touristy, but the countryside to the south is very quiet and unspoilt, with a wider range of hill tribes; hardened walkers could arrange a trek to Mae Hong Son, five days away to the southwest. If you just fancy a bit of **bamboo rafting** without the trekking, Back Trax and plenty of other agents can arrange transport and a two-and-a-half-hour trip down the Pai River for around B500 per person.

Among several **elephant camps** around town, Joy, 5km from Wat Mae Yen on the minor road towards the hot springs, with an office on Thanon Chaisongkhram opposite the bus station (Ⓣ01 881 3923, Ⓔcchiamchit@hotmail.com), offers something slightly different. You can go for an elephant ride (from B250/hour), which includes going into the river with the elephant and feeding it, as well as a free bathe in a hot spring pool, or you can volunteer to work at the camp, fetching the elephants from the jungle in the morning, cutting banana trees to feed them and swimming with them in the river; accommodation is available in simple bamboo bungalows in the pretty grounds, and there's a restaurant serving vegetarian and meaty Thai, Vietnamese and Western food.

With a little more cash to spare, you could strike up with the reliable and experienced French-run Thai Adventure Rafting (Ⓣ053 699111, Ⓦwww.activethailand.com/rafting; not to be confused with the imitative Pai Adventure Rafting), in an office next to *Chez Swan* on Thanon Rungsiyanon, for a **rubber-raft trip** down the Pai River to Mae Hong Son, through gorges and class 3–4 rapids, and taking in waterfalls and hot springs. The journey takes two days, including a night at a comfortable jungle camp by the river, and costs B2000 per person; the season runs from July to the end of January, with the highest water from August to early September, and participants must be able to swim.

Accessible from the minor road south from Wat Mae Yen, 2km beyond Joy Elephant Camp, or by turning left off the main Chiang Mai road straight after the bridge over the Pai River, the **hot springs**, with one or two very hot, rough pools, aren't up to much, though there is an attractive valley campsite here. Better to go to one of the nearby **spas**, which put the piped hot water from the springs to much more productive use. Thapai Spa Camping (Ⓣ09 557 6079), down a side road about 1km north of the springs, has a large and shady pool (B50) and offers massages, mud spas and various other accompanying

PAI

Siam Used Books

Bus Station

E
●1

Aya Service

THANON CHAISONGKHRAM

●3 **●4** **F**
Bank **H** Back Trax **G** **●6**

I

●5 **●6**

THANON KHETKALANG

THANON RUNGSIYANON

THANON RATCHADAMNOEN

K

L

Pai River

J

Wat Mae Yen

Swimming Pool

Siam Used Books

●7

N

●M

0 approximate 100 m
scale

ACCOMMODATION

Baan Krating	A	Pairadise	D
Baan Nam Pai	G	Rainbow House	K
Belle Villa	B	River Pai Lodge	L
Charlie's	I	Shan	M
Duang	F	Sipsong Panna	C
Golden Hut	E	Spa Exotic Home	N
Mr Jan's	H	Sun Hut	J

RESTAURANTS AND BARS

All About Coffee	2
Baan Benjarong	8
Be-Bop	9
Chez Swan	7
Edible Jazz	1
Marmalade	5
Pai Blues	4
Rim Nam	6
Tea Room	3

▲ **A**, **B**, **C** & Mae Hong Son ▲ **D**

◄ Wat Nam Hu & Mo Pang Falls

3

▼ Tourist Police & Chiang Mai Joy Elephant Camp, Hot Springs & **N** ▼

●9 ●8

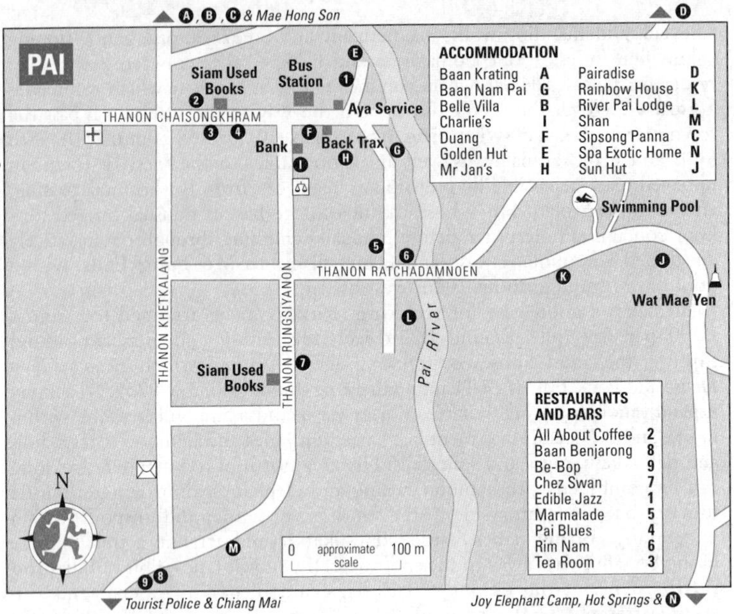

treatments. They also offer rooms with spa-water bathrooms (as well as tents to rent), but for accommodation you're better off going to the more congenial and attractive *Spa Exotic Home* nearby (see below); the latter also has tiled outdoor spa tubs (B40) for non-guests.

Practicalities

Pai's **bus station** is near the junction of Thanon Rungsiyanon and Thanon Chaisongkhram; motorbike **taxis** are available on the junction itself, air-con minibus taxis on the east side of the bus station. The most reliable place to rent **motorbikes** is Aya Service, a travel agency on Chaisongkhram (☎053 699940), which charges from B80 a day, including insurance; Pai Mountain Bike Tours, a couple of doors away on the same street (☎053 699384), and *Duang Guest House* rent **mountain bikes** (B80), the former – home of "Pai Bike Society" – providing a map and information for touring.

Massages are available at several spots around town as well as at *Thapai Spa Camping* near the hot springs (see above). *Mr Jan's Guest House* is famous for its Thai and Burmese/Shan massages (B150/hour) and saunas (B50), while Herbal House in Pai, near the market on Thanon Rungsiyanon (☎053 699964, ℮tiger_healing@hotmail.com), offers massages for B180 an hour, as well as aromatherapy, foot massage and body scrubs. A government-certified massage training centre, Herbal House also lays on **massage courses** of one, three, five and seven days (B800/day), including training in Ayurvedic herbal treatment, as well live-in courses of three, five or seven days (B2000/day) at a retreat just outside of town, which also feature meditation and yoga practice and herbal detoxes. Pai Traditional Thai Massage (PTTM), off Thanon Ratchadamnoen next to *Marmalade* (☎053 699121, ℮pttm2001@hotmail.com), also has a good reputation for traditional massages (B150/hour), as well as foot, face, oil and hand massages (B200/hour) and saunas (B60), and runs three-day massage courses (B2000). Bebe's Wok'n'Roll, based near the tourist police at the south end of town (ⓣ09 953 0205, ⓔthom_bebe@yahoo.com; or go to Eyecom near *Duang Guest House* on Thanon Chaisongkhram for more info), holds Thai **cooking courses** of one (B750) or two (B1350) days, including a trip to the market to learn about ingredients.

At the **post office** at the southern end of Thanon Khet Kalang, you can make international calls. Several shops near the intersection of Thanon Rungsiyanon and Thanon Ratchadamnoen offer **Internet access**. The **tourist police** (ⓣ1155) are just south of town, on the road to Chiang Mai. Among several **bookshops** in Pai, the orderly, Irish-run Siam Used Books has a good selection across two branches, one on Rungsiyanon, the other on Chaisongkhram, while the choice at The Bookshop at *Mr Jan's Guest House* is more eclectic, with a distinct spiritual bent.

Accommodation

Coinciding with the town's soaring popularity, **guest houses** are springing up all the time. There are now forty or so within town, as well as several options in the countryside around Pai, useful for escaping the growing bustle downtown. Several upmarket **resorts** have also sprung up in the countryside, catering largely for Thai weekenders with their own transport.

Baan Krating About 1km north of town, signposted to the right off the Mae Hong Son road, just beyond *Belle Villa* ⓣ053 698255–6. Welcoming upmarket place with a swimming pool, set amidst rice and garlic fields and mango and longan trees. Similar luxury to *Belle Villa* with a more traditional feel: bright, airy bungalows with verandas, bamboo cladding and roofs covered with *tong teung* leaves. ⑧

Baan Nam Pai South off Thanon Chaisongkhram near the river. Well-maintained, friendly guest house in a quiet location, with simple bamboo huts spread around a jungle-like setting, as well as six smart bungalows on stilts with hot water en-suites. ①–⑤

Belle Villa About 1km north of town, signposted to the right off the Mae Hong Son road ⓣ053 698226–7, ⓦwww.bellevillaresort.com. Elegant luxury bungalows on stilts with verandas and large, airy, "rock garden" bathrooms, as well as DVDs, mini-bars and safes. Traversed by a stream and decorated with ricefields, the grounds sport a stylish pool overlooking a lotus pond. Free transfers to town. ⑧

Charlie's Guest House 9 Thanon Rungsiyanon ⓣ053 699039. Offers a variety of rooms, with en-suite or shared hot showers, set around a lush garden, all of them clean (Charlie is the district health officer); it also has B60 dorm beds. ①–②

Duang Guest House 5 Thanon Rungsiyanon ⓣ053 699101, ⓕ053 699581. Opposite the bus station, this is a clean and reliable place to stay, with a good restaurant, though in a rather cramped compound; the best rooms have an en-suite hot-water bathroom, fridge and TV. ①–④

Golden Hut On the river bank, northeast of the bus station ⓣ053 699949. Quiet, shady and congenial guest house offering airy rooms and bungalows, mostly of bamboo-clad concrete, the best of them with riverside balconies; hot showers are either shared or en suite, and there's a tree-house and a B50 dorm. Good Western and Thai food daytime and evenings, including home-made pizzas, as well as home-made bread, jam and yoghurt for breakfast. ①–④

Mr Jan's Thanon Sukhaphibun 3 ⓣ053 699554. On one of a mess of small streets behind and to the east of *Charlie's*, quiet, simple bamboo bungalows and dorms (B60), with access to hot herbal showers, and recommended massages and saunas available, all set in a delightfully overgrown and fragrant medicinal herb garden. ①

Pairadise About 10min walk out on the east side of town, across the Pai River, then first left (signposted) ⓣ09 838 7521, ⓦwww.pairadise.com. Smart, stylish and bright cabins, of brick and polished wood, with hot water bathrooms en suite. Small artificial lake for swimming and lofty views over the valley. Home-baked bread for breakfast. Phone for free pick-up. ④

Rainbow House A short way over the Pai River bridge on the right ⓣ01 289 8409, ⓔrainbowhousepai@hotmail.com. Homely and welcoming family-run place with lots of local info. Large, very clean bamboo-clad bungalows, with comfortable beds and en-suite or shared hot showers, round a small, pretty garden and pond. ②

River Pai Lodge Down a lane on the south side of the main bridge. Helpful budget establishment, offering mostly bamboo stilted huts around a large lawn, priced according to distance from the river, with smart shared toilets and hot showers. ❶–❷

Shan Guest House Thanon Rungsiyanon ⓣ053 699162. Almost in open countryside at the southern end of town, this is a friendly establishment in large pretty grounds, around a pond with a bar on stilts in the middle; old bamboo and wood bungalows with cold-water bathrooms are slowly being replaced by large, smart cottages with hot water en suite. ❶–❷

Sipsong Panna Guest House On the Pai River north of town ⓣ053 698259, ⓔsipsongpanna33@hotmail.com. Head 1km north from town on the Mae Hong Son road, then turn right for another kilometre to the village of Wieng Neua and follow the signs. Airy Thai-style rooms with mosquito nets and stylish, hot-water bathrooms on the river, and a good vegetarian café, they also have a small art studio and offer Thai vegetarian cooking courses. ❸

Spa Exotic Home 6km south of Wat Mae Yen, off the minor road to the hot springs ⓣ053 698088. In a shady, attractive garden by the Pai River that features circular bath tubs filled with hot water piped from the nearby springs, cosy bungalows with polished-wood floors and airy spring-water bathrooms, and a pretty restaurant and sitting area. ❺

Sun Hut 10min out on the road heading east from town just before Wat Mae Yen on the right ⓣ053 699730, ⓔthesunhut1999@yahoo.com. In one of the nicest locations of the out-of-town guest houses, set by a stream with a view over rice paddies to the western hills. Quiet, well-run and friendly place with lots of nice touches such as flowers, candles and hammocks. The compound consists of a treehouse and sturdy bungalows, some sharing hot-water bathrooms and others en suite, arranged around a pond and a communal, open-sided lounging area. ❷–❹

Eating and drinking

As with the guest-house scene, new **restaurants** are opening practically every week, ever more sophisticated and cosmopolitan, as reflected in the recommendations below. In the evening, a popular spot for travellers to congregate is *Be-Bop*, at the south end of town opposite the landmark *View Pai Hotel*, a large, well-designed **bar** with a pool table which hosts live music. A mellower spot for a drink (with a limited food menu including sushi, which has to be ordered the day before) is *Edible Jazz*, a garden café and bar on a quiet, leafy lane off Chaisongkhram that plays "jazzy, funky, groovy music".

All About Coffee Thanon Chaisongkhram. Superb coffee in any variety you might want, in an atmospheric wooden shophouse hung with contemporary art (for sale). Also great breakfasts with home-made bread, a daily selection of home-made cakes, sandwiches and teas, hot chocolate and juices. Moderate.

Baan Benjarong South end of town, opposite the landmark *View Pai Hotel*. In a town where you can get everything from sushi to falafel, finally a very good Thai restaurant, offering a wide variety of authentic dishes – the banana flower salad (*yam hua pree*) is especially delicious. The setting isn't bad either, open-sided and airy with a small terrace at the back. Moderate.

Chez Swan Thanon Rungsiyanon. Good, traditional French dishes, cheeses and wines in attractive old wooden shophouse. Moderate to expensive.

Marmalade Just off the north side of Thanon Ratchadamnoen by the bridge. Small Australian-run café-restaurant with an extensive blackboard menu of excellent, inventive pastas, salads and sandwiches, as well as porridge and other breakfasts. Huge range of healthy shakes, juices and smoothies. Moderate.

Pai Blues Thanon Chaisongkhram. Easy-going, candlelit restaurant where, as well as a wide variety of pancakes and other Western dishes, you can sample tasty Shan cuisine such as fried aubergine with tofu and pumpkin curry. Inexpensive to moderate.

Rim Nam Thanon Ratchadamnoen. Decent versions of standard Thai dishes in a pleasant spot by the bridge on the east side of town, with a covered terrace raised over the river. Moderate.

Tea Room Thanon Chaisongkhram. Bohemian kind of place where you can hang out and maybe play chess. Dozens of teas to choose from, as well as sandwiches, shakes and a limited range of Thai food. Ask about their Cinema Pairadiso a couple of doors away, where you can watch DVDs. Moderate.

From Pai to Chiang Mai

Once out of the Pai valley, Route 1095 climbs for 35km of hairpin bends, with beautiful views north to 2175-metre Doi Chiang Dao near the top. In the cool season, with your own transport, you can witness – if you get started from Pai an hour before dawn – one of the country's most famous views of the sun rising over a sea of mist at **Huay Nam Dang National Park** (B200). The viewpoint is signposted on the left 30km out of Pai; take this turning and go on 6km to the park headquarters. Once over the 1300-metre pass, the road steeply descends the south-facing slopes in the shadow of Doi Mae Ya (2005m), before working its way along the narrow, more populous lower valleys. After 55km (at kilometre-stone 42), a left turn leads 6.5km over some roller-coaster hills to **Pong Duet hot springs**, where scalding water leaps up to four metres into the air, generating copious quantities of steam in the cool season. A few hundred metres downstream of the springs, a series of pools allow you to soak in the temperature of your choice. The last appealing detour of the route is to **Mokfa Falls** (part of Doi Suthep National Park; B200), where a cascade tumbles about 30m into a sand-fringed pool that is ideal for swimming, making an attractive setting for a break – it's 2km south of the main road, 76km from Pai. Finally, at **Mae Malai**, turn right onto the busy Highway 107 and join the mad, speeding traffic for the last 34km across the wide plain of rice paddy to Chiang Mai.

Chiang Rai and the borders

The northernmost tip of Thailand, stretching from the Kok River and **Chiang Rai** to the border, is a schizophrenic place, split in two by Highway 1, Thailand's main north–south road. In the western half, rows of wild, shark's-tooth mountains jut into Burma, while to the east, low-lying rivers flow through Thailand's richest rice-farming land to the Mekong River, which forms the border with Laos here. In anticipation of Burma and Laos throwing open their frontiers to tourism, the region is well connected and has been thoroughly kitted out for visitors. Chiang Rai now has well over two thousand hotel rooms, catering mostly to upmarket fortnighters, who plough through the countryside in air-conditioned Scenicruisers in search of quaint, photogenic primitive life. What they get – fairground rides on boats and elephants, a sanitized presentation of the Golden Triangle's opium fields and colourfully dressed hill people performing artificial folkloric rituals – generally satisfies expectations, but has little to do with the harsh realities of life in the north.

Chiang Rai itself pays ever less attention to independent travellers, so although you will probably have to pass through the provincial capital, you should figure on spending most of your time in the border areas to the north, exploring the dizzy mountain heights, frenetic border towns and ancient ruins. If you're coming up **from Chiang Mai**, the quickest and most obvious route to Chiang Rai is Highway 118, a fast, 185-kilometre road that swoops through rolling hill country. A much more scenic approach, however, is to follow

Highway 107 to **Tha Ton** and then complete the journey by longtail boat or bamboo raft down the **Kok River**.

Tha Ton and the Kok River

Set aside at least two days for this road and river journey along the **Kok River**, allowing for the almost inevitable overnight stay in Tha Ton. Buses between Chiang Mai's northern Chang Phuak bus station and Tha Ton take about four hours; it's best to leave the longtail-boat trip to Chiang Rai until the following afternoon.

Chiang Mai to Fang

From Chiang Mai the route heads north along Highway 107, retracing the Mae Hong Son loop in the early going and, after 56km, passing an **elephant-training centre** on the right, which puts on logging shows daily at 9am and 10am (B60); it's a more attractive setting than the Mae Sa valley camps, especially good for elephant rides and bamboo-rafting. Around kilometre-stone 72 **Chiang Dao**, an oversized market village, stretches on and on along the road as the dramatic crags and forests of Thailand's third-highest peak, Doi Chiang Dao (2175m), loom up on the left.

A road, served by yellow songthaews and motorbike taxis, heads northwest of the village for 5km to an extensive complex of interconnected caverns, **Tham Chiang Dao**, with an attached monastery (the caves were given religious significance by the local legend of a hermit sage who is said to have dwelt in them for a millennium). Several of the caverns can be visited; a couple have electric light but others need the services of a guide with a lantern. Admission to the caves is B10 and guides ask around B100 for a tour of about forty-five minutes, during which they point out unusual rock formations. About 1500m further north along the road from the caves, the secluded *Malee's Nature Lovers Bungalows* (Ⓣ053 456426 or 01 961 8387, Ⓦwww.maleenature.com; ❸–❹) is a cosy compound delightfully set in the shadow of the mountain. Good food and half a dozen comfy en-suite bungalows of varying size, as well as dorm accommodation with shared hot showers (B100) and camping facilities (B50/person), are available here. They can arrange treks and bird-watching trips, rafting and elephant-trekking, or just point birders in the right direction; bicycle and motorbike rental is available.

Back on Highway 107, the road shimmies over a rocky ridge marking the watershed separating the catchment areas of the Chao Phraya River to the south and the Mekong River ahead, before descending into the flat plain around Fang and the Kok River. Branching off to the left some 60km from Chiang Dao, a steep and winding 25-kilometre road, Route 1249, leads up to **Doi Angkhang** (1928m). Besides a royal agricultural project here that produces peaches, raspberries and kiwis in the cool climate, the mountain is home to the eco-friendly **Angkhang Nature Resort** (Ⓣ053 450110, Ⓦwww.amari.com/angkhang; ❽), where the luxurious teak pavilions have balconies with great views, and bird-watching or trekking, mule-riding or mountain-biking to nearby hill-tribe villages are the main activities.

En route to Tha Ton on public transport, you may have to change buses in the ugly frontier outpost of **Fang**, 153km from Chiang Mai, but you're far better off pushing on to Tha Ton for somewhere to stay. With your own transport, you can give Fang a miss altogether by branching west on a bypass signposted to Chiang Rai.

△ Elephant and mahout near Chiang Rai

Tha Ton

The tidy, leafy settlement of **THA TON**, nearly 180km north of Chiang Mai, huddles each side of a bridge over the Kok River, which flows out of Burma 4km to the west upstream. Life in Tha Ton revolves around the bridge – buses and boats pull up here, and most of the accommodation is clustered nearby. The main attractions here are longtail-boat and bamboo-raft rides downstream to Chiang Rai, but on the south side of the bridge the over-the-top ornamental gardens of **Wat Tha Ton**, endowed with colossal golden and white Buddha images and an equally huge statue of Chao Mae Kuan Im, the Chinese goddess of mercy, are well worth the short climb. From any of the statues, the views up the narrow green valley towards Burma and downstream across the sun-glazed plain are heady stuff.

Thip's Traveller House (Ⓣ053 459312, Ⓦwww.thiptravel.com; ❷), on the south side of the bridge, is a convenient and cheap **place to stay**, with decent en-suite rooms in a crowded compound, and good food. The formidable Mrs Thip is a great source of information and organizes rafting packages to Chiang Rai (see opposite) as well as scenic longtail-boat trips to the Burmese border (20min). Another good-value place is *Apple Guesthouse* (Ⓣ053 459315; ❷), a quiet, shady, flower-filled compound of clean, en-suite A-frame bamboo bungalows. To reach the guest house, head 200m south from the bridge, then walk 150m up the first lane on the left. *Apple* also operates a smarter, newer, chalet-style hotel – also called *Apple* – right in front of the boat landing, with attractive rooms, all with hot water, some with TV, above a good restaurant (Ⓣ053 373144; ❹). On the north side of the river, *Garden Home Nature Resort* (Ⓣ053 373015, Ⓕ053 459325; ❷–❻), 300m west from the bridge, is a very appealing option, with attractive en-suite bungalows (some with hot water and air-con) sheltering under an orchard of lychees and mangoes, and bikes available for rent.

With its own gardens and a choice of three restaurants and two bars, about half a kilometre east of the bridge on the south bank of the river, the family-friendly *Mae Kok River Village Resort* (Ⓣ053 459355–6, Ⓦwww.track-of-the-tiger.com; ❽) is Tha Ton's best **upmarket** choice. Well-designed, air-con suites and family villas are set around a pool, and the owner, Shane Beary, also runs Track of the Tiger, which offers a wide variety of **soft adventure tours**, taking visitors off the well-trodden trekking trails in a measure of luxury. Tour options include a motorized river barge which can take people downstream to Chiang Rai via their riverfront jungle camp (with bamboo bungalows and hot showers), as well as (guided or self-guided) mountain-biking, canoeing and bamboo-rafting. At this multi-dimensional resort – which also includes an organic farming and vocational skills school for the disadvantaged – visitors can sign up for courses in Thai cooking or massage, meditation or rock-climbing.

Beyond Tha Ton, Route 1089 heads east towards Mae Chan and Highway 1; about 20km out of town, at Ban Kew Satai, an exciting roller coaster of a side road leads north to Mae Salong (see p.404). There's no direct public transport from Tha Ton to Mae Salong: take one of the yellow songthaews which leave a few hundred metres north of the bridge in Tha Ton, and change songthaew at the Ban Kew Satai turn-off. However you're travelling, it's worth breaking your journey about 1km west of Kew Satai on Route 1089 at **BAN LORCHA**. As part of a community-based tourism development project, owned and managed by the villagers, with technical assistance from the PDA in Chiang Rai (see p.403), this Akha settlement has been opened to visitors, who pay an entrance fee of B40 (income goes into a village development fund). A guide leads you on a one-kilometre walk through the village, which is strategically dotted with interesting display boards in English, and you'll get a chance to have a go on an Akha swing, see a welcome dance and watch people weaving and tool-making, for example.

Along the Kok River

Travelling down the hundred-kilometre stretch of the **Kok River** to Chiang Rai gives you a chance to soak up a rich diversity of typical northern landscapes, which you never get on a speeding bus. Heading out of Tha Ton, the river traverses a flat valley of rice fields and orchards, where it's flanked by high reeds inhabited by flitting swallows. After half an hour, you pass the 900-year-old **Wat Phra That Sop Fang**, with its small hilltop chedi and a slithering naga staircase leading up from the river bank. Beyond the large village of **Mae Salak**, 20km from Tha Ton, the river starts to meander between thickly forested slopes. From among the banana trees and giant wispy ferns, kids come out to play, adults to bathe and wash clothes, and water buffalo emerge simply to enjoy the river. About two hours out of Tha Ton the hills get steeper and the banks rockier, leading up to a half-hour stretch of small but feisty rapids, where you might well get a soaking. Beyond the rapids, crowds of boats suddenly appear, ferrying camcorder-toting tour groups from Chiang Rai to the Karen village of **Ruammid**, 20km upstream, for elephant-riding. From here on, the landscape deteriorates as the bare valley around Chiang Rai opens up.

The best time of year to make this trip is in the cool season (roughly Nov–Feb), when the vegetation is lushest and the rapids most exciting. Canopied **longtail boats** (B250/person, motorbikes B300) leave from the south side of the bridge in Tha Ton every day at 12.30pm for the trip to Chiang Rai, which takes around four rather noisy hours. The slower, less crowded journey upriver gives an even better chance of appreciating the scenery – the longtails leave Chiang Rai at 10.30am. If you can get a group of up to six people together (more in the rainy season), it's better to charter a longtail from the boat landing in Tha Ton (B1700; ⓣ053 459427), which will allow you to stop at the hill-tribe villages and hot springs en route.

If you have more time, the peaceful **bamboo rafts** which glide downriver to Chiang Rai in two days almost make you part of the scenery. Rafts, which leave at about 8–9am, generally take four paying passengers – there are usually plenty of travellers to hitch up with during the high season, when you shouldn't have to wait more than a day for a full complement; the price includes mats, sleeping bags, mosquito nets, soft drinks and food. Each party is accompanied by two steersmen who dismantle the rafts in Chiang Rai and bring the bamboo back to be recycled in Tha Ton. *Mrs Thip's* guest house (see opposite) is a good place to organize the standard two-day, one-night raft trips (B1500/person, B1300 if no elephants), with a night spent at the hot springs at Huai Mak Leam and a one-hour elephant ride at Ruammid.

Mae Kok River Village Resort (see above) offers upmarket rafting and barge trips on this stretch of river, while Lost Valley in Chiang Rai runs rubber-rafting excursions (see p.405). Passengers departing from Tha Ton boat landing are required to sign the log book at the adjacent **tourist police** booth. Between Mae Salak and Ruammid, a couple of peaceful **guest houses** – from either of which you can go walking (guided or self-guided) – might tempt you to break your river journey. At *My Dream* in the Karen village of Ban Khaew Waaw Dam, on the north bank of the Kok (ⓣ01 672 0943; ❷), clean, comfortable bungalows with verandas are set among banana trees in a pretty garden and overlook the river; there are also dorm rooms in the house (B100). Downstream and on the opposite side of the Kok, 3km on foot from the riverside hot springs near Huai Kaeo waterfall, *Akha Hill House* (ⓣ053 718957 or 01 4607450; ⓦwww.akhahill.com; ❶–❸) offers lofty views, comfortable rooms and bungalows, some with en-suite hot showers, and free transport daily to and from Chiang Rai.

Chiang Rai

Having lived in the shadow of Chiang Mai for all but thirty years of its existence, **CHIANG RAI** – sprawled untidily over the south bank of the Kok River – is now trying to make a challenge as an upmarket tourist centre, with all the hype and hustle that goes with it. The long arm of the package-tour industry has reached this northern outpost, bringing snap-happy bus-bound tourists and well-heeled honeymooners, who alight for a couple of days of excursions and then shoot off again. Paradoxically, this leaves the town to get on with its own business during the day, when the trippers are out on manoeuvres, but at night the neon lights flash on and souvenir shops and ersatz Western restaurants are thronged. Meanwhile, the town keeps up its reputation as a dirty-weekend destination for Thais, a game given away by just a few motels and carports – where you drive into the garage and pay for a discreet screen to be pulled across behind you. Budget travellers have been sidelined, but they still turn up for the trekking, day-trips and other outdoor activities (see p.405).

Chiang Rai is most famous for the things it had and lost. It was founded in 1263 by King Mengrai of Ngon Yang who, having recaptured a prize elephant he'd been chasing around the foot of Doi Tong, took this as an auspicious omen for a new city. Tradition has it that Chiang Rai prevailed as the capital of the north for thirty years, but historians now believe Mengrai moved his court directly from Ngon Yang to the Chiang Mai area in the 1290s. Thailand's two holiest images, the Emerald Buddha (now in Bangkok) and the Phra Singh Buddha (now perhaps in Bangkok, Chiang Mai or Nakhon Si Thammarat, depending on which story you believe), also once resided here before moving on – at least replicas of these can be seen at Wat Phra Kaeo and Wat Phra Singh.

Arrival, information and transport

Arriving at the **bus station** on Thanon Phaholyothin on Chiang Rai's south side leaves a long walk to most of the guest houses, so you might want to bundle into a tuk-tuk (around B30–50) or a songthaew, the two main forms of transport around town. Longtails from Tha Ton dock at the **boat station,** northwest of the centre on the north side of the Mae Fah Luang bridge. Thai Airways (at the airport ⓣ053 793084, on Thanon Phaholyothin ⓣ053 711179) **fly** to Chiang Rai from Bangkok, Phuket Air (at the airport ⓣ053 798255–6) from Chiang Mai; taxis run into town from the **airport**, 8km northeast, for B200.

TAT has a helpful office at 448/16 Thanon Singhakai near Wat Phra Singh (daily 8.30am–4.30pm; ⓣ053 717433 or 053 744874, ⓔtatchrai@tat.or.th) with some useful free maps and information brochures. From here they look after Chiang Rai, Nan, Phrae and Phayao provinces, as well as organizing the Mekong Challenge, a nine-day mountain bike trip through China and Laos every October. Gare Garon, 869/18 Thanon Phaholyothin, has a small range of new and used **books** in English, as well as handicrafts and drinks for sale. The **tourist police** (ⓣ1155) are on Thanon Phaholyothin next to the *Golden Triangle Inn*.

Songthaews, which have no set routes, cost locals B10–20 for short hops; you can flag them down and arrange a price for other trips. Most guest houses offer motorbike and **car rental** though **bicycles** can be a little more difficult to find. Both mountain bikes (B100/day) and motorbikes (B150–200) are for hire at the ever-reliable Soon Motorbikes, 197/2 Thanon Trairat (☎053 714068). Pricy, full-service car rental is available through Budget at the *Golden Triangle Inn* (☎053 740442–3), and Avis at the airport (☎053 793827) and the *Dusit Island Resort*, while cheaper local agencies like P.D. Tour, 869/108 Thanon Pemavipat, near the *Wangcome Hotel* (☎053 712829), rent jeeps for B800 per day.

Accommodation

Chiang Rai is overstuffed with **accommodation** in all categories, but much of it offers poor quality for the price; that said, one or two guest houses compare with Chiang Mai's best, and in the *Dusit* it boasts one of the north's finest hotels. Much of the more expensive accommodation is clustered around the commercial centre on Thanon Phaholyothin, while the guest

CHIANG RAI

0 500 m

Kok River

Lak Muang &
Wat Phra That
Doi Tong

THANON KAISORNRASIT

TAT
Wat Phra Kaeo
Wat Phra Singh

THANON SINGHAKAI

THANON UTTARAKIT

Statue of
King Mengrai

Hill Tribe
Museum & Shop

THANON RATBAT
THANON NGAM MUANG

THANON TANALAI

Soon Motorbikes

THANON RATTANAKHET
THANON WISETWIANG

THANON PHAHOLYOTHIN

THANON RATCHAYOTA

THANON BANPHAPRAKAN

Clock
Tower

Tourist Police

Gare Garon Bookshop
Thai Airways
Night Bazaar

Lost Valley

THANON SANAMBIN

THANON JET YOT

THANON PHAHOLYOTHIN

Bus Station

Chiang Mai ▼

Mae Fah Luang Bridge & Boat Station. ◄

Highway 1211 ◄

Airport, Mae Sai & Chiang Saen ►

RESTAURANTS AND BARS

Baan Chivit Mai	4
Bierstube	6
Chiangrai Coffee Co.	3
La Cantina	2
Muang Thong	5
Salungkhum	1

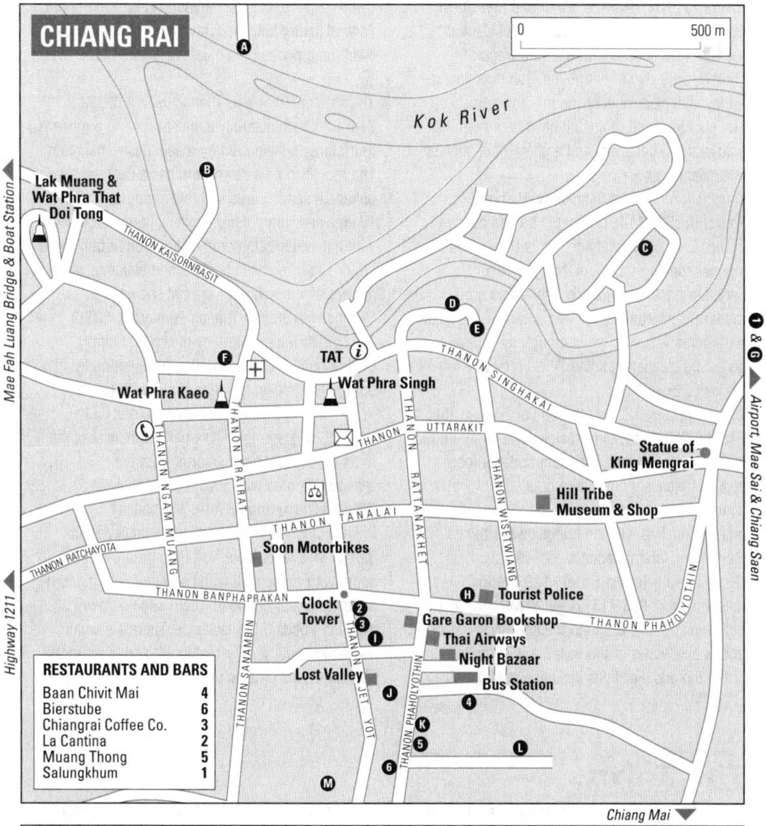

ACCOMMODATION

Baan Bua		Chian House	C	Mae Hong Son	E	Wangcome	I
Baan Worabordee	L	Dusit Island Resort Hotel	B	Rim Kok Resort	A	Wiang Inn	K
Bow Ling	D	Golden Triangle Inn	H	Tourist Inn	M	YMCA	G
Chat House	F

houses, most of which offer tours and treks, can be found along the south bank of the river and on the fringes.

Baan Bua Guest House 879/2 Thanon Jet Yot ⓣ053 718880, ⓔbaanbua@yahoo.com. Congenial and well-run establishment arrayed around a surprisingly large, quiet and shady garden, set back off the road. The very clean and attractive concrete rooms all come with hot-water en-suite bathrooms and some have air-con. ❷–❸

Baan Worabordee 59/1 Moo 18, Thanon Sanpanard ⓣ053 754488, ⓔbaan_warabordee@hotmail.com. Well-appointed, good-value new place down a quiet lane off the main street. Comfortable, clean, attractively decorated rooms with small balconies, hot-water bathrooms, cable TV and fan or air-con. ❸–❹

Bow Ling Guest House Off Thanon Singhakai ⓣ053 712704; near the *Mae Hong Son Guest House*. A cute, peaceful place in a residential soi with tiny, concrete rooms off a fragrant courtyard filled with pot plants. Run by a young family, this place is very friendly and homely. The six functional rooms all have their own cold-water bathrooms, and a shared hot shower is available. ❷

Chat House 3/2 Soi Sangkaew, Thanon Trairat ⓣ053 711481. Located behind its own garden café on a quiet soi, this is Chiang Rai's longest-running travellers' hangout, with a very laid-back atmosphere. The rooms are modern, colourfully decorated and have en-suite bathrooms with hot water, though they could be a little cleaner; satellite TV is on nightly in the café. ❷–❸

Chian House 172 Thanon Koh Loy ⓣ & ⓕ053 713388. In a lively, ramshackle compound around a small swimming pool; accommodation here includes pleasant en-suite rooms (all hot water, some with air-con) and spacious, clean and nicely furnished wooden bungalows with cool tiled floors. Internet access. ❶–❸

Dusit Island Resort Hotel 1129 Thanon Kaisornrasit ⓣ053 715777–9, ⓦwww.dusit.com. Set on a ten-acre island in the Kok River, with unbeatable views of the valley, this is the top of the top end. Facilities include a health club, tennis courts, swimming pool and children's playground, with high standards of service. ❾

Golden Triangle Inn 590 Thanon Phaholyothin ⓣ053 711339, ⓦwww.goldenchiangrai.com. Large, comfortable, tastefully decorated rooms with air-con and hot water in a garden compound in the heart of town. ❺

Mae Hong Son Guest House 126 Thanon Singhakai ⓣ053 715367. This friendly establishment, in a quiet local street, comprises wooden buildings arranged around a very green, shady courtyard with neat bar and café. Very pleasant rooms – some en suite (hot water), others sharing hot showers. ❶–❷

Rim Kok Resort 6 Moo 4, Thanon Chiang Rai–Tha Ton ⓣ053 716445–54, ⓦwww.rimkokresort.com. Palatial luxury hotel in sprawling grounds with a swimming pool on the quiet north side of the river. ❼

Tourist Inn 1004/4–6 Thanon Jet Yot ⓣ053 714682. Clean hotel-style guest house in a modern four-storey building run by a Japanese-Thai team. The reception area downstairs has a European-style bakery, a seating area with big comfy armchairs, TV area and library, while bright, light rooms all come with hot-water bathrooms and air-con or fan. There are cheaper rooms in an attached building, which are not as modern but have hot showers. ❷–❸

Wangcome 869/90 Thanon Pemavipat ⓣ053 711800, ⓔwangcome@loxinfo.co.th. Chintzy, central hotel with a swimming pool, not quite up to international five-star standards. ❼

Wiang Inn 893 Thanon Phaholyothin ⓣ053 711533–5, ⓔwianginn@samart.co.th. Across the main road and slightly smarter than the *Wangcome*, also with a swimming pool. ❼

YMCA International Hotel 70 Thanon Phaholyothin ⓣ053 713785–6, ⓔymcawf@loxinfo.co.th. Ever reliable, with comfortable rooms, some with air-con, all with hot water, in a modern building far out on the northern edge of town, and dorm beds (B90) available. There's a small swimming pool, a café-restaurant and a non-profit handicraft and organic products shop. ❹

The Town

A walk up to **Doi Tong**, the hummock to the northwest of the centre, is the best way to get your bearings and, especially at sunset, offers a fine view up the Kok River as it emerges from the mountains to the west. On the highest part of the hill stands the most interesting of Chiang Rai's few sights, a kind of phallic Stonehenge centred on the town's new **lak muang**, representing the Buddhist layout of the universe. Historically, the erection of a *lak muang* marks the official founding of a Thai city, precisely dated to January 26, 1263 in the case of Chiang Rai; the new *lak muang* and the elaborate stone model around it were erected 725 years later to the day, as part of the celebrations of King Bhumibol's sixtieth birthday. The *lak muang* itself represents Mount Sineru (or Meru), the axis of the universe, while the series of concentric terraces, moats and pillars represent the heavens and the earth, the great oceans and rivers, and the major features of the universe. Sprinkling water onto the garlanded *lak muang* and then dabbing your head with the water after it has flowed into the basin below brings good luck.

The old wooden *lak muang* can be seen in the viharn of **Wat Phra That Doi Tong**, the city's first temple, which sprawls shambolically over the eastern side of the hill. Look out for the small golden prang, the old-fashioned wooden spirit house and the Chinese shrine, with which the wat shares the hillside in a typically ecumenical spirit.

The Emerald Buddha, Thailand's most important image, was discovered when lightning cracked open the chedi (since restored) at **Wat Phra Kaeo** on Thanon Trairat. A beautiful replica, which was carved in China from 300kg of milky green jade and presented by a Chinese millionaire in 1991, can now be seen here in the Hor Phra Yok, a tiny, Lanna-style pavilion situated to the right behind the viharn. At 47.9cm wide and 65.9cm high, the replica is millimetres smaller than the Emerald Buddha, as religious protocol dictated that it could not be an exact copy of the original. The whole complex has recently been renovated and the decorative trimmings show a high level of craftsmanship, including those on the large wooden building to the left of the viharn, which houses ancient religious objects and texts.

The **Hill Tribe Museum and Handicrafts Shop** at 620/25 Thanon Tanalai stocks an authentic selection of tasteful and well-made hill-tribe **handicrafts**. The shop, on the second floor, was started by the country's leading development campaigner, Meechai Viravaidya, under the auspices of the PDA (Population and Community Development Association) and all proceeds go to village projects. The museum (Mon–Fri 9am–6pm, Sat & Sun 10am–6pm; B50) is a great place to learn about the hill tribes before going on a trek, and includes a slick, informative slide show (25min). You can donate old clothes or money for jumpers and blankets, and they also organize treks and tours themselves (see p.405). All sorts of handicrafts, some of good quality and competitively priced, are on sale at the **night bazaar** which is set up off Thanon Phaholyothin next to the bus station, and it might at least give you something to do in the evening.

Eating and drinking

Chiang Rai's **restaurants**, including a growing number of Western places, congregate along Jet Yot and Phaholyothin roads, with some good Thai options in the moderate range scattered around. There's a **food centre** in the night bazaar with lots of delicious snacks and a beer garden too, where you can catch a free performance of transvestite cabaret, local folk-singers or traditional dancers. On Thanon Jet Yot south of the clocktower, several Western-style **bars** offer a relaxed atmosphere, with satellite TV, music or just drinks and a chat.

Baan Chivit Mai 172 Thanon Pra Soop Sook, opposite the bus station. Scandinavian bakery run by a Swedish charity that helps children in Chiang Rai and Bangkok slums (ⓦwww.thailandsbarn.com for more info). Very clean, air-con café serving excellent sandwiches, cakes, cinnamon buns, croissants, coffees and teas. Mon–Sat 7am–9pm, Sun 2–9pm. Inexpensive to moderate.

Bierstube South of the *Wiang Inn* at 897/1 Thanon Phaholyothin. A well-run and easy-going watering hole, with good German food, including steaks and a wide range of sausages with potato salad or French fries. Moderate to expensive.

Cabbages and Condoms Hill Tribe Museum (see p.403). Proudly proclaiming "our food is guaranteed not to cause pregnancy", this restaurant covers its walls with paraphernalia devoted to birth control, including pictures of Meechai Viravaidya, who began this organization to promote family planning and HIV/AIDS prevention. The delicious menu of Thai food, including some traditional northern dishes, is well described in English, with a few dishes suitable for vegetarians. Daily 11am–midnight. Moderate.

Chiangrai Coffee Company 1025/38 Thanon Jet Yot. Simple café-restaurant serving diverse styles of coffee made from local beans, as well as many teas, Belgian waffles, good, varied breakfasts and Western dishes such as chicken breast with orange sauce. Moderate.

La Cantina 1025/40 Thanon Jet Yot. The Italian owner rustles up a long menu of good pastas (some home-made), pizzas and veggie options, as well as good-value set breakfasts. Moderate to expensive.

Muang Thong On the corner of Thanon Phaholyothin, just south of the *Wiang Inn Hotel*. Does a wide range of Thai and Chinese dishes supposedly 24hr a day, and displays a huge selection of ingredients outside its open-sided eating area. Popular among Thais and foreigners alike. Inexpensive to moderate.

Salungkhum 843 Thanon Phaholyothin, between King Mengrai's statue and the river. Justifiably rated by locals as serving the best Thai food in town, with a garden for evening dining; there's no sign in English, but look out for the Cosmo petrol station on the opposite side of the road. Moderate.

North of Chiang Rai

At a push, any one of the places described in this section could be visited on a day-trip from Chiang Rai, but if you can devote three or four days, you'd be better off moving camp to make a circuit of **Mae Salong**, a mountain-top Chinese enclave, the intriguing border town of **Mae Sai**, and **Chiang Saen**, whose atmospheric ruins by the banks of the Mekong contrast sharply with the commercialism of nearby **Sop Ruak**. Given more time and patience, you could also stop over on the way to Mae Sai at **Doi Tung** to look down over Thailand, Laos, Burma and China, and continue beyond Chiang Saen to **Chiang Khong** on the banks of the Mekong, which is now a popular crossing point to Laos.

For hopping around the main towns here by **public transport**, the setup is straightforward enough: frequent buses to Mae Sai run due north up Highway 1; to Chiang Saen, they start off on the same road before forking right onto Highway 1016; for most other places, you have to make one change off these routes onto a songthaew.

Mae Salong (Santikhiri)

Perched 1300m up on a ridge with commanding views of sawtoothed hills, the Chinese Nationalist outpost of **MAE SALONG** lies 36km along a roller coaster of a road that ploughs into the harsh border country west of Highway 1. Songthaews make the dizzying ninety-minute journey when full, starting from **Ban Pasang**, 32km north of Chiang Rai on Highway 1. A few marginally interesting attractions might tempt you to hop off en route, notably the **Hill Tribe Culture Centre**, 12km from Ban Pasang, where there's a handicrafts shop, and a couple of Mien and Akha souvenir villages.

Mae Salong is the focal point for the area's fourteen thousand **Kuomintang**, who for two generations now have held fast to their cultural identity, if not their political cause. The ruling party of China for 21 years,

Tours and trekking from Chiang Rai

Communities from all the hill tribes have settled around **Chiang Rai**, and the region offers the full range of terrain for **trekking**, from gentle walking trails near the Kok River to tough mountain slopes further north towards the Burmese border. The river is deep enough for rafts both to the west and the east of the town, and elephant-riding is included in most treks. However, this natural suitability has attracted too many tour and trekking agencies, and many of the hill-tribe villages, especially between Chiang Rai and Mae Salong, have become weary of the constant to-ing and fro-ing. Some of the trek agencies in Chiang Rai have recently widened their net to include the rest of the province, such as Chiang Khong, where there's a large population of Hmong and Mien. Sizes of group treks from Chiang Rai tend to be smaller than those from Chiang Mai, often with just two or three people, with a maximum of about seven in a group. The rate guidelines set by Chiang Rai TAT are rather high at the moment; an average three-day, two-night trek with an elephant ride typically costs B2500–3000 each for two to five people. Nearly all guest houses in Chiang Rai can fit you up with a trek – *Chat*, *Chian* and *Mae Hong Son* are responsible and reliable.

More expensive treks are offered by several non-profit foundations promoting community-based tourism that are based in Chiang Rai. The Hill Area and Community Development Foundation has set up Natural Focus, 129/1 Moo 4, Thanon Pa-Ngiw (Ⓣ053 715696, Ⓦwww.naturalfocusecotour.com), which offers one- to fifteen-day tours to learn about mountain life, as well as youth, workstay and volunteer skills programmes and craft workshops. Akha-run Dapa Tours, 115 Moo 2, Tambon Rimkok (Ⓣ053 711354, Ⓦwww.dapatours.com) runs one- to three-day treks, as well as all manner of sightseeing tours, with profits going to the Development Agriculture and Education Project for Akha. The development agency PDA (Ⓣ053 740088, Ⓦwww.pda.or.th/chiangrai; see p.403) offers one- to four-day jungle treks, including elephant trekking and a longtail-boat ride. They also offer one-day **mountain-biking trips** up the Kok River, including fishing, meals and a guide/mechanic (B2200), as well as tours to Mae Salong and other places of interest.

Most of the guest houses can arrange sightseeing tours, boat trips and elephant rides; *Mae Hong Son Guest House* and *Chian* also offer motorbike trekking and the latter can lay on horse-riding. With Lost Valley on Thanon Jet Yot (Ⓣ053 752252, Ⓦwww.lostvalleyadventure.com), you can gently paddle a **rubber raft** down the Kok River to the west of town, typically paying B1800 for a two-day trip with one night camping on the river bank or staying in a hill-tribe village; one- and three-day options are also available, which can feature trekking and elephant-riding.

the Kuomintang (Nationalists) were swept from power by the Communist revolution of 1949 and fled in two directions: one group, under party leader Chiang Kai-shek, made for Taiwan, where it founded the Republic of China; the other, led by General Li Zongren, settled in northern Thailand and Burma. The Nationalists' original plan to retake China from Mao Zedong in a two-pronged attack never came to fruition, and the remnants of the army in Thailand became major players in the heroin trade.

Over the last twenty years, the Thai government has worked hard to "pacify" the Kuomintang by a mixture of force and more peaceful methods, such as crop programmes to replace opium. Around Mae Salong at least, its work seems to have been successful, as evidenced by the slopes to the south of the settlement, which are covered with a carpet of rich green tea bushes. Since its rehabilitation, Mae Salong is now officially known as **Santikhiri** (Hill of Peace).

Drugs and the Golden Triangle

A variety of circumstances have led to North Thailand being notorious for the production of **illegal drugs**, especially **opium**, which comes from the resin that oozes from the seed heads of the opium poppy when slit. Though opium is associated with the Far East in the popular imagination, the opium poppy actually originated in the Mediterranean. It arrived in the East, however, over twelve centuries ago, and was later brought to Thailand from China with the hill tribes who migrated from Yunnan province.

Opium growing has been illegal in Thailand since 1959, but during the 1960s and 1970s rampant production and refining of the crop in the lawless region on the borders of Thailand, Burma and Laos earned the area the nickname **"the Golden Triangle"**. Two main "armies" operated most of the trade within this area. The **Shan United Army** (SUA), set up to fight the Burmese government for an independent state for the Shan people, funded itself from the production of **heroin** (a more refined form of opium). Led by the notorious warlord Khun Sa, the SUA attempted to extend their influence inside Thailand during the 1960s, where they came up against the troops of the **Kuomintang** (KMT). These refugees from China, who fled after the Communist takeover there, were at first befriended by the Thai and Western governments, who were pleased to have a fiercely anti-Communist force patrolling this border area. The Kuomintang were thus able to develop the heroin trade, while the authorities turned a blind eye.

Since the 1980s, the danger of Communist incursion into Thailand has largely disappeared, and the government has been able to concentrate on the elimination of the crop. The Kuomintang in the area around Mae Salong have been put on a determined "pacification" programme, though it appears they still play an important role as drugs middlemen. In 1983 the Shan United Army was pushed out of its stronghold at nearby Ban Hin Taek (now Ban Therd Thai), over the border into Burma, and in 1996, Khun Sa

The Town and beyond

Though it has temples, a church and a mosque, it's the details of Chinese life in the back streets – the low-slung bamboo houses, the pictures of Chiang Kai-shek, ping-pong tables, the sounds of Yunnanese conversation – that make the village absorbing. Mae Salong gets plenty of Thai visitors, especially at weekends, who throng the main street's souvenir shops to buy such delicacies as sorghum whisky (pickled with ginseng, deer antler and centipedes) and locally grown Chinese tea, coffee and herbs. It's worth braving the dawn chill to get to the **morning market**, held in the middle of town near *Shin Sane Guest House* from around 5am to 7am, which pulls them in from the surrounding Akha, Lisu and Mien villages.

Towering above the town on top of the hill, the **Princess Mother Pagoda**, a huge, gilt-topped chedi, stands beside a small cruciform viharn and is so distinctive that it has quickly become the town's proud symbol. It is a long and steep climb to get there, but with a rented vehicle you can follow the road to the Tha Ton end of town, and branch right opposite the evening market on a road that carries you heavenward, revealing some breathtaking views on the way.

The Kuomintang live up to their Thai nickname – *jiin haw*, meaning "galloping Chinese" – by offering **treks on horses**, a rare sight in Thailand. Trips to Akha, Lahu and other Chinese villages can be arranged at the *Shin Sane Guest House* (see below) from B400 for four to five hours, but it's worth meeting your guide and checking out the itinerary and the horses before you hand over any money. Armed with a sketch map from one of the guest houses, it would be possible to walk to some of the same villages yourself.

Beyond Mae Salong, paved roads let you nip the back way to Tha Ton, past cut a deal with the corrupt Burmese military dictatorship. The man once dubbed the "Prince of Death" now lives under Burmese army protection in a comfortable villa in Rangoon and has turned his attention to supposedly legitimate business ventures.

The Thai government's concerted attempt to eliminate opium growing within its borders has succeeded in reducing the size of the crop to an insignificant amount. However, Thailand still has a vital role to play as a conduit for heroin; most of the production and refinement of opium has simply moved over the borders into Burma and Laos, where opium yields are second only to post-Taliban Afghanistan.

The destruction of huge areas of poppy fields has had far-reaching repercussions on the hill tribes. In many cases, with the raw product not available, opium addicts have turned to injecting heroin from shared needles, leading to a devastating outbreak of AIDS. It has been necessary for the Thai government to give the hill tribes an alternative livelihood through the introduction of more legitimate cash crops, yet these often demand the heavy use of pesticides, which later get washed down into the lowland valleys, incurring the wrath of Thai farmers.

The dangers of the heroin trade have in recent years been eclipsed by a flood tide of **methamphetamines** or *ya baa* ("crazy medicine"), that is infiltrating all areas of Thai society, but most worryingly the schools. Produced in vast quantities in factories just across the Burmese border, mostly by former insurgents, the United Wa State Army, *yaa ba* is the main objective of vehicle searches in border areas, with perhaps a billion tablets smuggled into Thailand each year. The government estimates that three million Thais are methamphetamine users, prompting them into a fierce crackdown in the first half of 2003 which, much to the consternation of human rights watchers, led to 2000 extra-judicial deaths and 51,000 arrests.

the interesting Akha village of Ban Lorcha (see p.398); songthaews, with a change at Ban Kew Satai, cover the distance in ninety minutes. North of Mae Salong lies **Ban Therd Thai**, although to get to it by road you'd have to backtrack down the main road 12km to Sam Yaek and then make your own way up a paved side road a further 13km into the hills. In its former incarnation as Ban Hin Taek, this mixed village was the opium capital of the notorious Khun Sa (see box above): the Thai army drove Khun Sa out after a pitched battle in 1983, and the village has now been renamed and "pacified" with the establishment of a market, school and hospital.

Practicalities

The best of Mae Salong's budget **accommodation** is *Shin Sane Guest House* (Ⓣ053 765026; ❶–❸), a friendly place on the west side of the main road, which has small bedrooms with shared bathrooms in a funky wooden building and smart bungalows (with hot showers) in the yard behind; motorbikes can be rented for B350 a day. Right next door are the simple but tidy and spacious rooms, with shared hot showers, of the *Akha Guest House* (Ⓣ053 765103; ❶), the polished-wood two-storey home of a Christianized Akha family. The best of the upmarket places is *Mae Salong Villa* (053 765114–9, Ⓦwww.chiangmaimall.com/maesalong; ❻–❼), on the main road towards the eastern end of the village, with a choice of functional rooms or comfy wooden bungalows with balconies facing the Princess Mother Pagoda and Burmese mountains, all with hot-water bathrooms, TVs and fridges. A cheaper alternative is the *Mae Salong Central Hills Hotel* (Ⓣ053 765113, Ⓕ053 765349; ❹), on the right in the middle of town. Also with expansive views, the small, functional rooms are carpeted and reasonably clean, and all have hot water and TV.

The terrace **restaurant** of *Mae Salong Villa* shares the same views and cooks up the best food in town, including delicious but expensive Chinese specialities like *het hawm* (wild mushrooms) and *kai dam* (black chicken). A string of decent, cheaper eateries can be found on the main road beyond *Shin Sane Guest House*. *Salema* cooks up both Thai *khao soi* and Chinese noodle soup, while *Mini*, a little further on the same side, offers Chinese, Thai and Western food, including pancakes, fruit shakes and sandwiches, as well as a motorbike for rent (B200 a day). Beyond on the opposite side of the main road, a bakery sells a small range of cakes and pies.

Doi Tung

Steep, wooded hills rise abruptly from the plains west of Highway 1 as it approaches the Burmese border. Crowned by a thousand-year-old wat, the central peak here, 1300-metre **DOI TUNG**, makes a worthwhile outing just for the journey. A broad, new road runs up the mountainside, beginning 43km north of Chiang Rai on Highway 1, just before **Ban Huai Khrai**. It's best to have your own vehicle or go on a tour from Chiang Rai, though you will also find lilac songthaews in Ban Huai Khrai ferrying villagers up the mountain, usually in the morning and at weekends (about B80 one way). The only other options are to hitch (easy at weekends), hire a motorbike taxi (about B100 to the temple) or charter a whole songthaew for B500.

The old road to the mountain from the centre of Ban Huai Khrai passes after a kilometre or so the **Cottage Industry Centre and Outlet**, where you can watch crafts such as paper making from the bark of the *sa* (mulberry) tree in progress. The centre was set up by the Princess Mother, who had her country seat at Doi Tung until her death in 1995 (the mother of the present king, she was never queen herself, but was affectionately known as *Mae Fa Luang*, "great mother of mankind"). The **Royal Villa**, the **Princess Mother Commemorative Hall** and **Mae Fa Luang Garden**, 12km up the main summit road past Thai Yai, Chinese, Akha and Lahu villages, then left up a side road, are well worth a visit (daily 7am–5/6pm, longer on busy days, villa closed if royals in residence; garden B80, villa B70, commemorative hall B30, all three B150). Regular guided tours take visitors round parts of the largely Swiss-style building that was the country home of the Princess Mother in her later years, passing the Grand Reception Hall, where constellations have been embedded in the ceiling, as well as the positions of the planets at the time of her birth in 1900, then her living room, bedroom and study, all left as when she lived there. The swanky commemorative hall is really for royal watchers, though it does include some of the intricate screens from her funeral *that* (tower). Below, the immaculate ornamental gardens throng with snap-happy day-trippers at weekends. The Princess Mother's hill-tribe project has helped to develop local villages by introducing new agricultural methods: the slopes which were formerly blackened by the fires of slash-and-burn farming are now used to grow teak and pine, and crops such as strawberries, macadamia nuts and coffee, which, along with pottery, *sa* paper, rugs and clothes. are sold in the shops by the entrance to the gardens. There's also a Doi Tung coffee shop, an excellent restaurant and self-service café, and in the woods below the royal villa, upmarket accommodation at *Baan Ton Nam 31*, with air-con, hot water, balcony, TV and fridge (Ⓣ053 767015–7, Ⓦwww.doitung.org; ❽).

Beyond the turn-off for the royal villa, the main summit road shimmies over a precarious saddle with some minor temple buildings 2km before the top, and finally climbs through a tuft of thick woods to **Wat Phra That Doi**

Tung. Pilgrims to the wat earn themselves good fortune by clanging the rows of dissonant bells around the temple compound and by throwing coins into a well, which are collected for temple funds. For non-Buddhist travellers, the reward for getting this far is the stunning view out over the cultivated slopes and half of northern Thailand. The wat's most important structures are its twin **chedis**, erected to enshrine relics of the Buddha's collarbone in 911. When the building of the chedis was complete, King Achutaraj of Ngon Yang ordered a giant flag (*tung*), reputedly 2km long, to be flown from the peak, which gave the mountain its name.

A very steep, paved **back road** runs along the border with Burma to Mae Sai (22km), via the Akha village of Ban Pha Mee, beginning at the saddle beneath the peak. This area has been the scene of conflict among the Kuomintang, the hill tribes and others involved in the drugs trade, but is now safe to travel in with the development of Doi Tung under the Princess Mother's project, though it remains a little intimidating, with two checkpoints en route to Mae Sai. After about 4km of asphalt, you reach the delightful **arboretum** (B50) at the pinnacle of **Doi Chang Moob** (1509m), a landscaped garden planted with rhododendrons, azaleas, orchids and ferns and furnished with fantastic terrace viewpoints, east to Chiang Saen, the Mekong and the hills of Laos beyond, and west to the mountains around Mae Salong. For the most awesome view, however, continue a short way up the Mae Sai road to the Thai military checkpoint, to gaze at the opposing Burmese camp and seemingly endless layers of Burmese mountain stacked up to the north.

Mae Sai and around

MAE SAI, with its bustling border crossing and hustling tourist trade, can be an intriguing place to watch the world go by, though most foreigners only come here on a quick visa run. Thailand's most northerly town lies 61km from Chiang Rai at the dead end of Highway 1, which forms the town's single north–south street. Wide enough for an armoured battalion, this ugly boulevard still has the same name – **Thanon Phaholyothin** – as at the start of its journey north in the suburbs of Bangkok. Buses, however, are no longer allowed to complete the journey, stopping 4km short of the frontier at the **bus station**, from where frequent songthaews shuttle into town.

Thanon Phaholyothin ends at a short but commercially important **bridge** over the Mae Sai River, which forms the border with Burma. During daylight hours (6.30am–5.30pm), Thais have long been allowed to cross over to **Thakhilek**, the Burmese town opposite (though the frontier is sporadically closed during international disputes between the two countries), but this dubious pleasure is now also open to foreigners. If you want to get a new thirty-day entry stamp for Thailand, you'll need first to get stamped out at the **Mae Sai immigration office** (Ⓣ053 731008), inconveniently located 2km south of the bridge on Thanon Phaholyothin but with extended hours (daily 8am–5pm) for Burma day-trippers; on the other side of the bridge, you pay B250 to Burmese immigration for a one-day stay; and on your return to Thailand, you'll automatically be given your new thirty-day entry stamp at the Thai immigration office at the bridge. If, however, you don't want to affect your existing visa (if, say, you have most of a sixty-day tourist visa left), it's still possible to go to Thakhilek for the day: photocopy the relevant pages of your passport at one of the handy copying booths by the frontier, leave your passport at Thai immigration at the bridge, and pay the Burmese B250 for a one-day stamp on the photocopies. Armed with a Burmese visa from their embassy in Bangkok, it's also now possible to make a longer trip from Mae Sai to Kengtung and Mongla, on the border with China – though not, apparently, to cross the Chinese border.

Thakhilek's handful of temples have next to nothing of architectural interest, the town's big draw being – for foreigners and for the hundreds of Thai day-trippers who crowd the narrow streets – a frenzy of **shopping**. The huge market on the right after the bridge is an entrepôt for a bizarre diversity of goods from around the world – from Jacob's Cream Crackers, through CDs and DVDs, to bears' paws and tigers' intestines – but its main thrust is to cater to the everyday demands of Thai customers, with a selection of ordinary, cheap clothes and bedding. The array of Burmese handicrafts – tatty Pagan lacquerware and crude woodcarving – is disappointing.

Shopping is the main activity in Mae Sai, too: from the central morning market crowded with purposeful Burmese, to the stores around the bridge which hawk "Burmese" handicrafts – mostly made in the factories of Chiang Mai, though slightly better quality than in Thakhilek – and coloured glass posing as gems. Village Product, 51/24 Moo 10, Thanon Muang Daeng (about 500m south of the border, turn left near the 7–11, then 200m on your right) offers more interesting stuff, such as hill-tribe fabric and clothes from both Thailand and Burma.

For a better perspective on the town, climb up to the chedi of **Wat Phra That Doi Wao**, five minutes' walk from the bridge (behind the *Top North Hotel*). As well as Doi Tung to the south and the hills of Laos in the east, you get a good view up the steep-sided valley and across the river to Thakhilek. There is a market in the grounds with Burmese and Chinese stuff sold, running from about 5am to 6pm, or later if it's busy.

Practicalities

A handful of mostly ropey **guest houses** are strung out along the river bank west of the bridge. By far the best of these is the furthest away: *Mae Sai Guest House* (Ⓣ053 732021; ❷–❹) is a pretty, relaxing place to stay with a wide variety of well-maintained bungalows, all with en-suite hot-water bathrooms, wedged between a steep hill and the river, fifteen minutes from the main road. The only other guest house in Mae Sai currently worth recommending is *Chad Guest House* on Soi Wiangpan – look out for the signpost on the left, 1km before the bridge – which scores low for location but is the classic travellers' rest (Ⓣ053 732054, Ⓕ053 642496; ❶): the family is welcoming, with plenty of information and local maps for guests, the food is good, there are shared hot showers, and it's an easy place to meet people. The *Wang Thong*, on the east side of the bridge at 299 Thanon Phaholyothin (Ⓣ053 733388–95, Ⓕ053 733399; ❼), is Mae Sai's best **hotel**, with a huge, ornate lobby, a pool and mini-bar, TV, hot water and air-con in every room. Much less pretentious is the *Mae Sai Hotel* at 125/5 Thanon Phaholyothin (Ⓣ053 731462; ❷–❹), which has simple, clean rooms, some with hot showers and air-conditioning.

A popular **eating** place is *Rabieng Kaew*, a cosy, air-con restaurant opposite the Krung Thai Bank on Thanon Phaholyothin, serving a wide choice of excellent Thai cuisine. The terrace of the *Rim Nam* (*Riverside*), under the western side of the bridge, is crowded during the day with tourists watching the border action, while *JoJo*, well back from the bridge at 233 Thanon Phaholyothin (daytime only), serves up decent Western breakfasts, Thai fast food and fancy ice creams at a price.

There's a **tourist police** booth (Ⓣ1155) hard by the frontier bridge. For getting around the local area, **motorbikes** can be rented from Pon Chai, opposite the Bangkok Bank on Thanon Phaholyothin, for B150 a day. You can access the **Internet** at Prasit in the Maesai Plaza near the *Wang Thong Hotel*.

Sop Ruak

The **Golden Triangle**, which was coined to denote a huge opium-producing area spreading across Burma, Laos and Thailand (see p.406), has, for the benefit of tourists, been artificially concentrated into the precise spot where the borders meet, 70km northeast of Chiang Rai. Don't come to the village of **SOP RUAK**, at the confluence of the Ruak and Mekong rivers, expecting to run into sinister drug-runners, addicts or even poppy fields – instead you'll find souvenir stalls, pay-toilets, two opium museums and lots of signs saying "Golden Triangle" which pop up in a million photo albums around the world.

Under the auspices of the Mae Fa Luang Foundation based at Doi Tung (see p.408), the ambitious **Hall of Opium** at the Mae Sai end of the village (currently Thurs–Sun 10am–3.30pm, but longer hours planned; B300; Ⓦwww.goldentrianglepark.org) took B400 million and nine years to research and build, with technical assistance from the People's Republic of China. It provides a well-presented, largely balanced picture, in Thai and English, of the use and abuse of opium, and its history over five thousand years, including its spread from Europe to Asia and focusing on the nineteenth-century Opium Wars between Britain and China. Dioramas, games and audiovisuals are put to imaginative use, notably in a reconstruction of a nineteenth-century Siamese opium den, playing the interactive "Find the Hidden Drugs", and, most movingly, watching the personal testimonies of former addicts and their families.

The Hall of Opium is worth the high admission fee, but if you baulk at the expense, you might be better off at the small **Opium Museum** in the centre of town (daily 7am–7pm; B20). All the paraphernalia of opium growing and smoking, accompanied by an English commentary, is housed in several display cases, including beautifully carved teak storage boxes, weights cast from bronze and brass in animal shapes and opium pipes.

The meeting of the waters is undeniably monumental, but to get an unobstructed view of it you need to climb up to **Wat Phra That Phu Khao**, a 1200-year-old temple perched on a small hill above the village: to the north, beyond the puny Ruak (Mae Sai) River, the mountains of Burma march off into infinity, while eastwards across the mighty Mekong spread the hills and villages of Laos. This pastoral scene has now been transformed, however, by the appearance of a Thai luxury hotel, the *Golden Triangle Paradise* (Ⓣ053 652111; ❽) over on the uninhabited strip of Burmese land immediately upstream of the confluence. The attached casino bypasses Thai laws against gambling, and the usually strict border formalities are waived for visitors coming from Thailand. For B400, you can have the thrill of stepping on Laotian soil. A longtail **boat** from the pier in the centre of the village will give you a kiss-me-quick tour of the "Golden Triangle", including a stop at a market on the Laos side (B20 admission).

Practicalities

From Mae Sai, songthaews make the 45-minute trip to Sop Ruak from the side of the *Sri Wattana Hotel* on Thanon Phaholyothin (they leave when they're full). **From Chiang Saen** you can go by regular songthaew (departing from the west side of the T-junction) or rented bike (an easy 10-km ride on a paved road, though not much of it runs along the river bank).

There's nowhere decent to **stay** in Sop Ruak for budget travellers, but for those willing to splurge, one of the north's finest hotels, the *Anantara Resort and Spa* (Ⓣ053 784084, Ⓦwww.anantara.com; ❾), tastefully designed in a blend of traditional and contemporary styles and set in extensive grounds, is located at the Mae Sai end of the village. The balconies of all its rooms and its swimming pool offer great views over the countryside to the Mekong, Burma and Laos. Among many amenities available to guests are a northern Thai cookery school and an elephant camp where you can take a basic three-day training course as a mahout. Somewhat cheaper rooms, furnished with fridge, TV, hot water and air-con, are also available in the Hall of Opium complex (Ⓣ053 652151; ❽). Among the many riverfront **restaurants** in Sop Ruak, head for *Sriwan* in front of the *Imperial Golden Triangle Hotel*, which offers a wide range of well-prepared Thai dishes and great views of the Mekong.

Chiang Saen

Combining tumbledown ruins with sweeping Mekong River scenery, **CHIANG SAEN**, 60km northeast of Chiang Rai, is a rustic haven and a good base camp for the border region east of Mae Sai. The town's focal point, where the Chiang Rai road (Thanon Phaholyothin) meets the main road along the banks of the Mekong, is a lively junction thronged by buses, songthaews, longtails and cargo boats from Laos and China. Turning left at this junction soon brings you to Sop Ruak, and you may well share the road with the tour buses that sporadically thunder through. Very few tourists turn right in Chiang Saen along the road to Chiang Khong, even though this is the best way to appreciate the slow charms of the Mekong valley.

Originally known as Yonok, the region around Chiang Saen seems to have been an important Thai trading crossroads from some time after the seventh century. The city of Chiang Saen itself was founded around 1328 by the successor to the renowned King Mengrai of Chiang Mai, Saen Phu, who gave up his throne to retire here. Coveted for its strategic location guarding the Mekong, Chiang Saen passed back and forth between the kings of Burma and Thailand for nearly three hundred years until Rama I razed the place to the ground in 1804. The present village was established only in 1881, when Rama V ordered a northern prince to resettle the site with descendants of the old townspeople mustered from Lamphun, Chiang Mai and Lampang.

The Town

The layout of the old, ruined city is defined by the Mekong River running along its east flank; a tall rectangle, 2.5km from north to south, is formed by the addition of the ancient ramparts, now fetchingly overgrown, on the other three sides. The grid of leafy streets inside the ramparts is now too big for the modern town, which is generously scattered along the river road and across the middle on Thanon Phaholyothin. For serious temple explorers, the Fine Arts Department has an **information centre** (Mon–Sat 8.30am–4pm), opposite the National Museum, devoted to the architecture and conservation of the city.

The **National Museum** (Wed–Sun 8.30am–4.30pm; B30; Ⓦwww.thailandmuseum.com) makes an informative starting point, housing some impressive Buddha images and architectural features rescued from the surrounding ruins, with good labelling in English. The art of northern Thailand was once dubbed "Chiang Saen style" because the town had an important school of bronze-casting. The more appropriate name "Lanna style" is now preferred, though you'll still come across the traditional term. As in many of Thailand's museums, the back end is given over to exhibits on folk culture, one of many highlights being the beautiful wooden lintel carved with *hum yon* (floral swirls representing testicles), which would have been placed above the front door of a house to ward off evil. **Wat Phra That Chedi Luang**, originally the city's main temple, is worth looking in on next door for its imposing octagonal chedi, now decorated with weeds and a huge yellow ribbon, while handicraft stalls in the grounds sell Thai Lue cloths among their wares.

Beyond the ramparts to the west, **Wat Pa Sak**'s brick buildings and laterite columns have been excavated and restored by the Fine Arts Department, making it the most accessible and impressive of Chiang Saen's many temples (daily 8am–6pm; B30). The wat's name is an allusion to the hundreds of teak trees which Saen Phu planted in the grounds when he built the chedi in 1340 to house some Indian Buddha relics. The central chedi owes its eclectic shape largely to the grand temples of Pagan in Burma: the square base is inset with niches housing alternating Buddhas and *deva* (angels) with flowing skirts, and above rises the tower for the Buddha relic, topped by a circular spire. Beautiful carved stucco covers much of the structure, showing intricate floral scrolls and stylized lotus patterns as well as a whole zoo of mythical beasts.

The open space around modern Chiang Saen, which is dotted with trees and another 140 overgrown ruins (both inside and outside the ramparts), is great for a carefree wander. A spot worth aiming for is the gold-topped, crooked chedi of **Wat Phra That Chom Kitti**, which gives a good view of the town and the river from a small hill outside the northwest corner of the ramparts.

Practicalities

Buses from Chiang Rai and **songthaews** from Sop Ruak stop just west of the T-junction of Thanon Phaholyothin and the river road, a short walk or a samlor ride from Chiang Saen's main guest houses, while songthaews from Chiang Khong stop on the river road to the south of the T-junction. **Longtail boats** for tours of the "Golden Triangle" (B300/person) and for Chiang Khong congregate just south of the T-junction. To get around the ruins and the surrounding countryside, **bicycles** (B70/day), **motorbikes** (B180/day) and **four-wheel drives** (B900 per/day) can be rented at *Gin's Guest House* (see below), while motorbikes are available for the same price in the centre of town from Tham Thong, on Thanon Phaholyothin opposite the **immigration office**. There's an **Internet** shop (closed Sun) on the same side as the immigration office.

Gin's Guest House can also arrange passage on **cargo boats to Jing Hong** in China. For B2700 per person, you get a bedroom and three meals a day on board on this two-day, one-night trip, as well as a night beforehand at *Gin's*; the period after the rainy season (Oct–Jan) is the most reliable time for the voyage. It's best to get your Chinese visa yourself in Bangkok or Chiang Mai, but *Gin's* can arrange this if necessary in five days (B1800).

Accommodation

Chiang Saen has one **hotel** and just a few **guest houses**, the best of which are listed below. The most convenient are along the riverfront, but though they have great views across the massive Mekong, they can also be very noisy with roaring trucks, whining speedboats and wailing nightclub singers trying to outdo each other.

Ban Suan Near Wat Phrathat Chom Kitti on the town's western bypass ⓣ & ⓕ 053 650907. Large, well-designed rooms with solar-heated water ranged around a sloping garden. Some have air-con, TV and fridge, others just fans. ❹

Chiang Saen Guesthouse Just a block north of the main junction ⓣ 053 650196. Basic, slightly tatty rooms, with shared cold-water bathrooms or en-suite hot showers, and a riverfront café selling Western fare such as banana pancakes. ❶–❸

Gin's Guest House Outside the ramparts, 2km north of the T-junction ⓣ 053 650847. At this attractive guest house which serves good food, there's a choice between large A-frame bungalows in a lychee orchard, or pricier spacious, well-furnished rooms in the main house, with polished wood floors, all with access to hot water; the owner organizes local trekking and all manner of tours. Internet access. ❷–❹

JS Guest House In a lane leading north from the post office ⓣ053 777060. A cheap but clean option near the museum and main temples, where you'll get a hot shower, either shared or en suite. ❷

River Hill South of the T-junction and a block back from the river road ⓣ053 650826–9, ⓕ053 650828. This hotel sets a high standard in a modern four-storey brick building with some traditional touches. Pleasant, friendly and well run, it's sited in a quiet rustic street; the rooms, all of which have air-con, TV, fridge and hot-water bathrooms, are very nicely done out right down to the Thai cushion seats on the floor. ❻

Eating

Food in Chiang Saen is nothing special; you could do worse than try the street stalls, which set up low pavement tables in the evening along the riverfront by the cargo pier. During the day (closes 7pm), *Samying* on Thanon Phaholyothin opposite the Caltex petrol station is popular with locals, a clean, well-run restaurant serving river fish in various preparations and a good *tom yam*. For pleasant service and crisply clean and colourful surrounds, the moderate-to-expensive restaurant at the *River Hill Hotel* is worth a try.

East to Chiang Khong

Several routes lead **from Chiang Saen to Chiang Khong**, 70km downriver, the only other town on the Mekong before it enters Laos; once a peaceful backwater, it is now frequently visited as a crossing point to Laos. The most scenic way to get to Chiang Khong is by **motorbike**, following the northward kink in the river for two hours along winding, scenic roads. An exciting but expensive alternative is to run the rapids on a hired **longtail boat**, which takes about three hours and costs around B1300. There are plenty of **songthaews** between the two towns, though if you leave it until later in the day you may have to change songthaew at Ban Hat Bai. If you're going straight to Chiang Khong **from Chiang Rai**, note that direct **buses** follow three different routes taking two hours, two and a half hours or three hours; be sure to ask for the quickest time, *sawng chua mohng*. Because of the popularity of the border crossing at Chiang Khong, there are now direct **air-con minibuses from Chiang Mai** (2 daily; 5hr; B190), available through guesthouses and travel agents such as Queen Bee (see p.346).

Heading out of Chiang Saen by the river road, you pass through tobacco fields and, after 3km, the tall, brick gate of **Wat Phra That Pha Ngao** on the right. The supposedly sixth-century temple contains a supposedly miraculous chedi perched on top of a large boulder, but the real attraction is the new chedi on the hillside above: take the one-kilometre track which starts at the back of the temple and you can't miss the gleaming, white-tiled Phra Borom That Nimit, designed by an American with attractive modern murals and built over and around a ruined brick chedi. From here, though you have to peer through the trees, the views take in Chiang Saen, the wide plain and the slow curve of the river. To the east, the Kok River, which looks so impressive at Chiang Rai, seems like a stream as it pours into the mighty Mekong. On the way down from the chedi, have a look at the new Lao-style bot, which was inaugurated by Princess Sirindhorn in 1999 and is covered from tip to toe in beautiful woodcarving.

Twenty-three kilometres from Chiang Saen at Ban Mae Ngoen, turn left off Route 1129 to follow the course of the Mekong, reaching the Thai Lue settlement of **Ban Hat Bai** after 9km. Signposts will lead you to

Sukhawadee in the heart of the village, a small unkempt shop selling a wide selection of the beautifully coloured cotton for which the Thai Lue are famous; you can see women of the village weaving in a white building further down the street on the pretty banks of the Mekong. Beyond Hat Bai, the hills close in and the river enters a stretch of rocky rapids, forcing the road to climb up the valley side and making for some dramatic vantage points.

Chiang Khong

CHIANG KHONG is currently one of only five places in Thailand where it's possible for foreigners to **cross to Laos**, and word has clearly got around about the pleasures of the Mekong boat journey to Louang Phabang, and about the availability of fifteen-day **visas** on arrival (US$30 or B1500; see p.19 for information about other means of getting a Lao visa), as the small town these days is constantly bustling with foreigners. At the north end of town is Chiang Khong's main pier, **Hua Wiang**, the departure point for frequent passenger ferries (B20, plus B20 "overtime" payment to Lao immigration at lunchtime and after 4pm) to **Houayxai** across the border, from where the Louang Phabang boats leave. For fishing boats, the port is **Ban Hat Khrai**, just south of town. In between the two ports, Chiang Khong is strung out along a single, roughly north–south street, Thanon Sai Klang, on a high, steep bank above the river. Once you've admired the elevated view of the traffic on the Mekong and the turrets of the French-built Fort Carnot across in Houayxai, there's little to do (if you're not crossing to Laos) but relax and enjoy the fact that none of the hustle is directed at you.

If you do decide to cross over into Laos, there are several possibilities for onward travel once over the border. From Houayxai, passenger boats leave every morning, gliding down the scenic Mekong and taking two days – with an overnight and a change of boat at Pak Beng – to reach Louang Phabang (B460–500). Cramped and noisy speedboats cover the same stretch in six to seven hours for B1100 per person, but these are not recommended as fatalities occur regularly despite the requirements for passengers to wear helmets and life jackets.

Giant catfish

The **giant catfish** (*pla buk*), found only in the Mekong, is the largest scaleless freshwater fish in the world, measuring up to 3m and more in length and weighing in at 300kg. Chiang Khong has traditionally been the catfish capital of the north, attracting fish merchants and restaurateurs from Chiang Rai, Chiang Mai and Bangkok – the mild, tasty meat of the *pla buk* is prized for its fine, soft texture and can fetch more than B500 a kilo. The catfish season is officially opened at the port of Ban Hat Khrai on April 18 with much pomp, including an elaborate ceremony to appease Chao Por Pla Buk, the giant catfish god. The season's haul used to be between thirty and sixty fish all told, but recent years have been so disappointing that Thailand's Fishery Department has begun an artificial spawning programme. Indeed no fish have been caught at Chiang Khong since 2000, when the total for the year was only two. Giant catfish are still caught on a regular basis in Cambodia, but it's now feared that they are going to disappear from Thailand completely, a fear heightened by the imminent blasting of the rapids and whirlpools between Chiang Saen and Chiang Khong – used as a spawning ground by the fish – to improve navigation. There was more bad news for giant catfish fans when a B10 million museum devoted to the species at Ban Hat Khrai collapsed a week before its scheduled opening, when water was put into its aquarium.

If you have time to spare and want to explore the area around Chiang Khong, try a trip to **Thung Na Noi**, a Hmong village 8km west.You can get there by renting a bike from *Ban Tam-Mi-La* guest house, for example (get directions from the proprietor), or taking a songthaew (daily from about 9am; B15) from Soi 8,Thanon Chai Klang, near the post office. First go to the village school, where you will be given a student guide and taken around the village; contribute at least a B20 donation to the school for lunch for the students. Ask the teacher for a guide (B100) to take you on the 3km walk to the attractive Huai Tong waterfall, or even about a two-day trek to Chiang Saen.

Practicalities

Most buses stop on the main road at the southeast end of town, though a few pull into the town centre itself. If you need to get from the bus to the ferry, or anywhere else about town, the local version of a **tuk-tuk**, a converted motorbike, should take you there for B15–20. For exploring the local area, good **mountain bikes** (B150 per/day) can be rented from Wat at *Ban Tam-Mi-La*, who sometimes leads sunset cycling tours around Chiang Khong (otherwise, he can provide sketch maps and info for touring); **motorbikes** (B200 per/day) can be hired through *Ban Tam-Mi-La* and other guest houses. **Internet** access is available, for example, at Tawan, opposite Soi 2 near *Ban Tam-Mi-La*, while Traveller Corner two doors up has a small selection of new and used **books**.

Chiang Khong supports a high-quality batch of **guest houses**, of which the best is *Ban Tam-Mi-La*, at 113 Thanon Sai Klang (Ⓣ & Ⓕ053 791234, Ⓔbaantammila@hotmail.com; ❷–❸), signposted down a lane in the middle of town among a cluster of small restaurants. The staff are helpful and the shady, riverfront atmosphere is easy-going and restful; the place has tasteful, well-designed wooden bungalows and rooms with en-suite bathrooms, some with hot water, and sells good hammocks (Ⓦwww.siamhammock.com). Among the twenty or so other guest houses in town, *Ban Fai* to the south at 27 Thanon Sai Klang (Ⓣ053 791394; ❶) provides clean rooms with shared hot showers in an attractive wooden house. On a jungly slope on the north side of town, the congenial *Bamboo Riverside Guest House* (Ⓣ053 791621, Ⓦwww.arriveat.com/bamboo; ❷–❸) offers attractive, clean bamboo bungalows with shared hot showers or en-suite, wood and brick versions, as well as dorm beds (B70). Motel-like *Chiang Khong Hotel* at 68/1 Thanon Sai Klang (Ⓣ053 791182, Ⓕ053 655640; ❷–❸) has large rooms set back off the street with hot showers and fan or air-con.The swankiest place in town is the *Ruanthai Sopaphan Resort* (Ⓣ053 791023, Ⓔp_darasawang@hotmail.com; ❷–❺), right next to *Ban Tam-Mi-La*; all the comfy rooms within this large teak house have access to hot water, and the best have good views of the river and cable TV. Breakfast is included in the price, and there's Internet access.

Ban Tam-Mi-La has an excellent daytime **restaurant** with a sweeping view of the river and lots of vegetarian options. *Bamboo* has a similar terrace, which is popular for breakfast and dinner, with home-made wholewheat bread, pizzas and Mexican food. Between the two on Thanon Sai Klang, *Orchid* dishes up good-value Thai food such as fried rice, noodles, curries, soups and salads, as well as unpretentious Western main courses, and you could do worse than finish off the night with a drink at *Teepee*, a laid-back **bar** filled with esoteric bric-a-brac opposite *Ban Tam-Mi-La*.

Travel details

Trains

Chiang Mai to: Bangkok (7 daily; 12–14hr).
Den Chai to: Bangkok (9 daily; 9hr); Chiang Mai (7 daily; 4hr).
Doi Khun Tan to: Bangkok (5 daily; 12hr); Chiang Mai (5 daily; 1hr 15min).
Lampang to: Bangkok (7 daily; 10–12hr); Chiang Mai (7 daily; 2hr).
Lamphun to: Bangkok (6 daily; 12–14hr); Chiang Mai (6 daily; 20–30min).

Buses

Chiang Khong to: Bangkok (10 daily; 13–14hr); Chiang Mai (3 daily; 6hr); Chiang Rai (hourly; 2–3hr).
Chiang Mai to: Bangkok (19 daily; 10–11hr); Chiang Khong (3 daily; 6hr); Chiang Rai (every 30min; 3–6hr); Chiang Saen (2 daily; 5hr); Chom Thong (every 30min; 1hr); Fang (every 30min; 3hr 30min); Khon Kaen (10 daily; 12hr); Khorat (12 daily; 12hr); Lampang (every 20min; 2hr); Lamphun (every 15min; 1hr); Mae Hong Son (6 daily via Mae Sariang, 4 daily via Pai; 8hr); Mae Sai (12 daily; 4–5hr); Mae Sot (2 daily; 6hr); Nan (11 daily; 6–7hr); Pai (4 daily; 4hr); Phitsanulok (5 daily; 6hr); Phrae (15 daily; 4hr); Rayong (7 daily; 15–17hr); Sukhothai (11 daily; 5–6hr); Tha Ton (6 daily; 4hr); Ubon Ratchathani (6 daily; 16–17hr); Udon Thani (5 daily; 12hr).
Chiang Rai to: Bangkok (16 daily; 12hr); Chiang Khong (hourly; 2–3hr); Chiang Mai (every 30min; 3–6hr); Chiang Saen (every 15min; 1hr 30min); Khon Kaen (5 daily; 12hr); Khorat (5 daily; 13hr); Lampang (every 20min; 5hr); Mae Sai (every 15min; 1hr 30min); Mae Sot (2 daily; 11hr); Nakhon Phanom (4 daily; 16hr); Nan (1 daily; 6–7hr); Pattaya (4 daily; 16hr); Phitsanulok (4 daily; 7hr); Sukhothai (4 daily; 6hr); Udon Thani (4 daily; 13hr).
Lampang to: Bangkok (10 daily; 8hr); Chiang Mai (every 20min; 2hr); Chiang Rai (every 20min; 5hr); Nan (10 daily; 5hr).
Mae Hong Son to: Bangkok (2 daily; 18hr); Chiang Mai via Mae Sariang (6 daily; 8hr); Chiang Mai via Pai (4 daily; 8hr).
Mae Sai to: Bangkok (8 daily; 13hr); Chiang Mai (12 daily; 4–5hr); Chiang Rai (every 15min; 1hr 30min); Fang, via Tha Ton (1 daily; 2hr).
Nan to: Bangkok (13 daily; 13hr); Chiang Mai (11 daily; 6–7hr); Chiang Rai (1 daily; 6–7hr); Den Chai (5 daily; 3hr); Phrae (13 daily; 2hr–2hr 30min).
Pai to: Chiang Mai (4 daily; 4hr); Mae Hong Son (4 daily; 4hr).
Phrae to: Chiang Mai (15 daily; 4hr); Nan (13 daily; 2hr–2hr 30min).

Flights

Chiang Mai to: Bangkok (14–17 daily; 1hr); Chiang Rai (2 daily; 45min); Jinghong (China; 3 weekly; 2hr 30min); Kunming (China; 2 weekly; 2hr 30min); Louang Phabang (Laos; 6 weekly; 1hr); Mae Hong Son (5 daily; 35min); Mandalay (Burma; 1 weekly; 50min); Phuket (daily; 2hr); Rangoon (Yangon in Burma; 3–5 weekly; 40min); Sukhothai (1 daily; 40min); Vientiane (Laos; 3 weekly; 2hr 10min); Xi'an (China; 3 weekly; 4hr).
Chiang Rai to: Bangkok (5 daily; 1hr 15min); Chiang Mai (2 daily; 45min).
Lampang to: Bangkok (1–2 daily; 1hr).
Nan to: Bangkok (1 daily; 1hr 40min).
Phrae to: Bangkok (1 daily; 2hr 40min).

4

The east coast

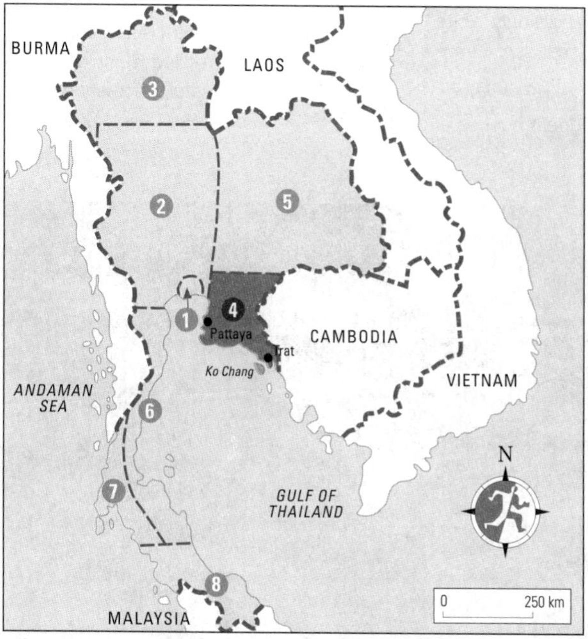

CHAPTER 4

Highlights

* **Ko Si Chang** Tiny, barely touristed island with craggy coastlines, glorious views, and an appealingly laid-back ambience. See p.423

* **Ko Samet** Pretty (and popular) little island fringed with dazzlingly white beaches. See p.438

* **Trat** Welcoming guest houses and an atmospheric old quarter make for a worthwhile stopover. See p.452

* **Ko Chang** Head for Lonely Beach if you're in the mood to party, or to Hat Khlong Phrao for a more tranquil scene. See p.456

* **Ko Mak** Lovely, lazy, palm-filled island with peaceful white-sand beaches. See p.469

△ Ko Chang

4

The east coast

Located within easy reach of the capital, the **east coast** resorts and islands attract a mixed crowd of weekending Bangkokians, pleasure-seeking expats and sybaritic tourists. Transport connections are good, prices are generally more reasonable than at the biggest southern resorts and, if you're heading overland to Cambodia, the east-coast beaches provide the perfect chance to indulge yourself en route before adventuring into more challenging territory across the border. You'll find the whitest beaches on the offshore islands: the five-hundred-kilometre string of mainland strands are disappointingly grey and the resorts here cater more for Thai groups than solitary horizon-gazing farangs. In addition, the discovery of oil and natural gas fields in these coastal waters has turned pockets of the first hundred-kilometre stretch into an unsightly industrial landscape of refineries and depots, sometimes referred to as the Eastern Seaboard. Offshore, however, it's an entirely different story, with island beaches as glorious as many of the more celebrated southern retreats.

The first worthwhile stop comes 100km east of Bangkok at the town of **Si Racha**, which is the point of access for tiny **Ko Si Chang**, whose dramatically rugged coastlines and low-key atmosphere make it a restful haven. In complete contrast, **Pattaya**, just half an hour south, is Thailand's number-one package-tour destination, its customers predominantly middle-aged Western and Chinese males enticed by the resort's sex-market reputation and undeterred by its lacklustre beach. Things soon look up, though, as the coast veers sharply eastwards towards Ban Phe, revealing the island of **Ko Samet**, the prettiest of all the beach resorts within comfortable bus-ride range of Bangkok.

East of Ban Phe, the landscape starts to get more lush and hilly as the coastal highway nears **Chanthaburi**, the dynamo of Thailand's gem trade and one of only two provincial capitals in the region worth visiting. The other appealing inland city is **Trat**, 68km further along the highway and an important departure point for **Ko Chang**, a large, increasingly tourist-oriented island with long, fine beaches and plentiful accommodation. A host of smaller, less-developed islands constitutes the Ko Chang archipelago, including beautiful **Ko Whai**, **Ko Mak** and **Ko Kud**. East of Ko Chang, the Cambodian border post of Hat Lek is one of this region's two main points – the other being Aranyaprathet, a little way north – where it is currently legal to **cross overland into Cambodia**.

Highway 3 extends almost the entire length of the east coast – beginning in Bangkok as Thanon Sukhumvit, and known as such when it cuts through towns – and hundreds of **buses** ply the route, connecting all major mainland destinations. Buses from Bangkok's Eastern (Ekamai) Bus Terminal serve all the provincial capitals and tourist spots; there are a few services here from Bangkok's Northern (Mo Chit) Bus Terminal as well, and tourist minibuses

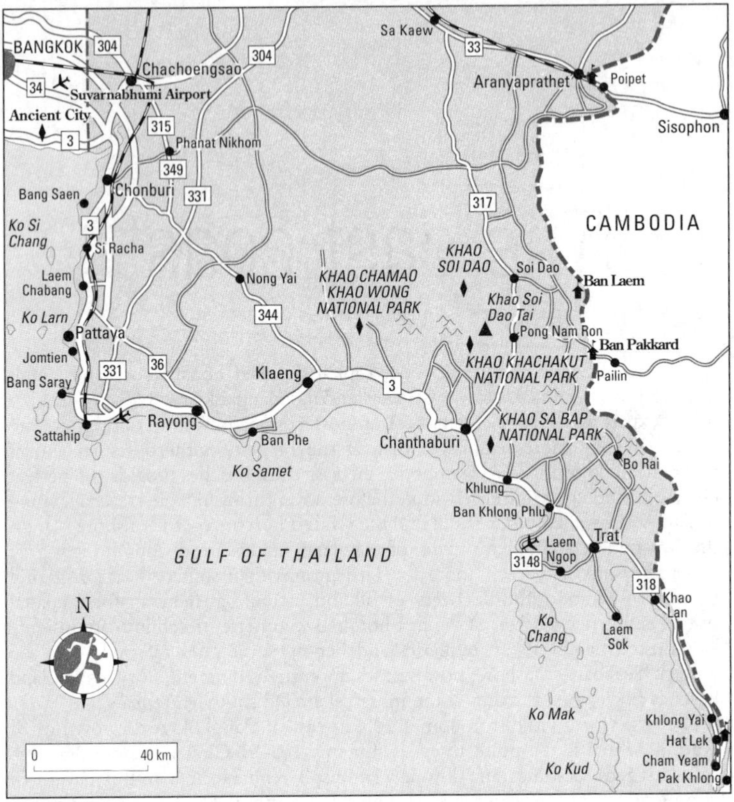

run direct from Banglamphu in Bangkok to the ferry piers for Ko Samet and Ko Chang. It's also possible to travel between the east coast and the northeast without doubling back through the capital: the most direct routes into **Isaan** start from Pattaya, Rayong and Chanthaburi. There are two **airports** along the east coast: at U-Tapao naval base, midway between Pattaya and Rayong, which is served by Bangkok Airways flights to and from Ko Samui and Phuket; and just outside Trat, for Bangkok Airways flights to Bangkok and Ko Samui. Though a rail line connects Bangkok with Si Racha and Pattaya, it is served by just one slow **train** a day in each direction.

Si Racha and Ko Si Chang

Almost 30km southeast of Bangkok, Highway 3 finally emerges from the urban sprawl at the fishing town of Samut Prakan, location of the impressive Muang Boran Ancient City open-air museum, described on p.170. It then continues via the provincial capital of **Chonburi**, whose only real attraction is its annual October bout of buffalo-racing, before reaching **Si Racha**, departure point for the island of **Ko Si Chang**.

Si Racha

Access to Ko Si Chang is from the fishing port and refinery town of **SI RACHA**, famous throughout Thailand as the home of *nam phrik Si Racha*, the orange-coloured, chilli-laced ketchup found on every restaurant and kitchen table in the country. You'll probably only find yourself staying here if you miss the last boat to the island, though the idiosyncratic seafront hotels make this an unexpectedly enjoyable experience, and the town is not without charm, especially at twilight, when the brightly painted fishing boats load up with ice and nets before setting off into the night. The "island temple" of **Wat Ko Loi**, at the end of the very long causeway 400m north of the Ko Si Chang pier, is the main sight in town.

Buses to Si Racha leave frequently from both Bangkok's Eastern (Ekamai) Bus Terminal and the Northern (Mo Chit) Bus Terminal. Air-conditioned buses stop at various points along Thanon Sukhumvit (Highway 3) in Si Racha's town centre, from where you can take a samlor or tuk-tuk to the Ko Si Chang pier; some ordinary buses stop nearer the waterfront, on Thanon Chermchompon (also spelt Thanon Jermjompol), within walking distance of the pier. There are also direct buses between Si Racha and Rayong (for Ban Phe and Ko Samet), Pattaya, and Trat (for Ko Chang). White songthaews from Naklua, the northern suburb of Pattaya, run around twice an hour to Si Racha, dropping passengers near the clocktower on the southern edge of town. One **train** a day in each direction connects Si Racha with Bangkok, departing the capital at 6.55am; the **train station** is on the eastern edge of the town and is most easily reached by tuk-tuk.

Strung out along the wooden jetties are the simple, cabin-like rooms of several waterfront **hotels**, all of which are on Thanon Chermchompon, within five minutes' walk of the Ko Si Chang pier, which is located at the end of Soi 14. The best is the farang-friendly *Sri Wattana* (Ⓣ038 311037; ❷–❸), with a range of decent en-suite rooms and a pleasant sea-view terrace; it's on the (unmarked) Soi 8, directly across Thanon Chermchompon from Thanon Si Racha Nakhon 3, a few metres' walk to the left of the mouth of Soi 14 and the pier. If you need air-con, opt instead for the pokier and less inviting *Samchai*, at the end of the signposted Soi 10, also just a short walk left from Soi 14 (Ⓣ038 311134; ❸). For **eating**, Thanon Si Racha Nakhon 3 is a good place to browse, lined with restaurants and night-time foodstalls. Alternatively, try any of the seafood restaurants along Thanon Chermchompon between sois 8 and 14, or the night-market stalls by the clocktower further south down the road. There's a good bakery across Thanon Chermchompon from Soi 10.

Ko Si Chang

The unhurried pace and the absence of consumer pressures make tiny, rocky **KO SI CHANG** an engaging place to hang out for a few days. Unlike most other east-coast destinations, it offers no real beach life – though the water can be beautifully clear and there are opportunities to dive and snorkel – and there's little to do here but explore the craggy coastline by kayak or ramble up and down its steep contours on foot or by motorbike. The island is famous as the location of one of Rama V's summer palaces (now under renovation), and for its rare white squirrels, who live in the wooded patches inland.

Arrival and information

Ferries to Ko Si Chang leave from the pier at the end of Si Racha's Soi 14, off Thanon Chermchompon, and run approximately hourly from 7am to 8pm

(40min; B20). On **arrival**, you'll probably dock at Ko Si Chang's Tha Bon, the more northerly of the two piers on the east coast, though some boats pull in at Tha Lang. A samlor ride from either pier to most guest houses costs B30, or B80 to Hat Tham Pang. The first boat back to the mainland leaves Tha Lang at 6am and the last at 6pm – the same boats depart Tha Bon about fifteen minutes earlier.

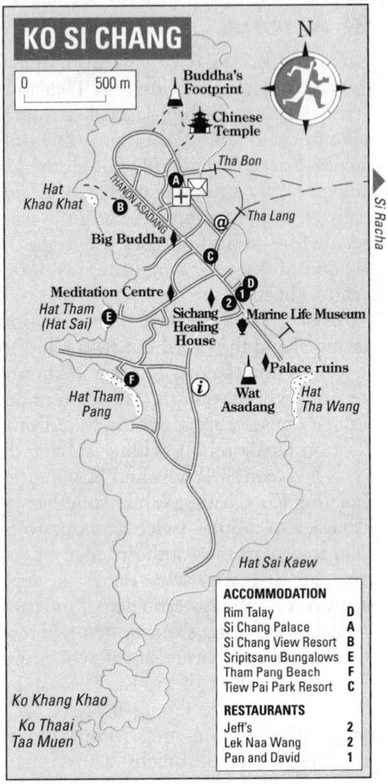

Both piers connect with Thanon Asadang, a small ring road on which you'll find the market, shops and most of the island's houses. Much of the rest of the island is accessible only by paths and tracks. In town it's easy enough to walk from place to place, but to really enjoy what Ko Si Chang has to offer you'll need to either rent a motorbike – from *Sripitsanu Bungalows* (B300/day) or the restaurant at *Tiew Pai Park Resort* (B60/hour or B250/day) – or hire one of the island's trademark bizarrely elongated 1200cc motorbike **samlors** for the day. As there are probably fewer than a dozen private cars on Ko Si Chang, these contraptions virtually monopolize the roads, and a tour of the island will only set you back around B250, stretching to include time out on the beach or at a restaurant; some of the drivers speak good English and staff at any guest house or restaurant can contact one for you.

There are **exchange facilities** and an ATM at the bank between the two piers, and **Internet access** is available at a shop on the approach road to Tha Lang, as well as via Catnet terminals inside the post office, near Tha Bon. The hospital is also near Tha Bon. For a fee of B50, non-guests can use the **swimming pool** at *Si Chang Palace* hotel. The exceptionally charming Sichang Healing House (daily 8am–6pm; ⓣ038 216467) offers various **spa**, massage and herbal-healing treatments (from B400) at its stylishly designed little garden retreat; to get there follow the signs south off the road to the old palace. For **information** on Ko Si Chang look for the locally produced brochure *Island Welcome*, available from some hotels and restaurants, which offers a good overview of the island's attractions and carries adverts for accommodation; the website ⓦwww.ko-sichang is another useful resource, as is its compiler, David, who can be found at *Pan and David Restaurant*. At the time of writing, a tourist information centre was under construction on the perimeter of the Rama V Palace grounds.

Ko Si Chang is just starting to get a reputation for decent **snorkelling** and **diving** around the tiny islands off its southern tip. The best snorkelling spots are off the north coast of Ko Khang Khao, while diving is most rewarding off the southeast and southwest coasts of its diminutive neighbour Ko Thaai Taa Muen. You can arrange dive trips through *Pan and David Restaurant* (B2500 including equipment and three tanks; minimum five people; book two days ahead) or rent snorkelling gear (B100/hour) and a kayak (B300/hour) from Uncle Juk on Hat Tham Pang and paddle out there yourself in about forty minutes; fishing boats with a skipper can be chartered from the piers for B1500 per day.

Accommodation

West-coast **accommodation** enjoys the best views, while Thanon Asadang and east-coast options are less scenic but more convenient for restaurants and shops. Booking ahead is advisable for weekends and public holidays. For the very finest sea views, nothing can beat **camping** on your chosen spot: the cliffs at Hat Khao Khat are a particularly popular site, though quite exposed. You can rent tents for B100 from Uncle Juk on Hat Tham Pang (ⓣ01 822 5540), but phone ahead to reserve one for weekends.

Rim Talay On the east-coast road to the old palace, unsigned, but in front of *Pan and David Restaurant* ⓣ038 216116. Has some standard issue rooms in a block, plus three more interesting bungalows fashioned from converted old wooden Si Racha passenger ferries (the resort owner also runs one of the island's shipping lines). ④–⑥

Si Chang Palace Across from Tha Bon on Thanon Asadang ⓣ038 216276, ⓕ038 216030. The most upmarket place on the island and rather ostentatious, but facilities include a pool, and all rooms have air-con and TV. Price depends on whether or not you want a sea view. ⑤–⑥

Si Chang View Resort Hat Khao Khat ⓣ038 216210, ⓕ038 216211. Attractive fan and air-con accommodation in a pretty tropical garden set in a prime cliffside spot on the west coast, though sadly you can't see the rugged coastline clearly from the rooms. ④–⑤

Sripitsanu Bungalows Hat Tham ⓣ038 216336. Stunningly located place whose ten comfortable, if rather haphazardly maintained, rooms sit almost right at the edge of the cliff – some are actually built into the rockface. It's a gorgeous spot, with unsurpassed views and the possibility of swimming at low tide, though you'll need transport or a samlor driver to get anywhere, and there's not much English spoken. Food is good and served on the panoramic terrace, and some bungalows have their own cooking facilities. Recommended. ④–⑤

Tham Pang Beach Hat Tham Pang ⓣ038 216179. The busiest west-coast accommodation, whose twenty concrete bungalows – all with bathroom, fan, veranda and partial sea view – are stacked in tiers up the cliffside behind the eponymous strand, Ko Si Chang's only real beach. There's a restaurant here, too. ④

Tiew Pai Park Resort Thanon Asadang ⓣ038 216084, ⓔTom_tiewpai@hotmail.com. Very central, and most backpackers' first choice. Rooms and bungalows are set in a wooded garden and range from simple singles with shared bathrooms to air-con ones with private facilities. ③–⑤

Around the island

The most famous site on the island is the ruins of **Rama V's Palace**, Phra Judhadhut, near pebbly Hat Tha Wang beach on the southeast coast. Built here in the 1890s as a sort of health resort where sickly members of the royal family could recuperate in peace, King Chulalongkorn's teak-wood palace formed the heart of a grand and extensive complex comprising homes for royal advisers, quarters for royal concubines and administrative buildings. By the turn of the twentieth century, however, the king had lost interest in his island project and so in 1901 his golden teak palace was moved piece by piece to Bangkok, and reconstructed there as Vimanmek Palace (see p.154). The other buildings were left to disintegrate: aside from the stone steps and balustrades that still cling to the shallow hillside, the only structure on the site to survive intact is the circular **Wat Asadang**, right at the top and surmounted by a chedi. The palace complex is now undergoing major renovations, due to be completed in 2006, and the elegant design of the grounds is emerging once more, centred around an elaborate labyrinth of fifty interlinked ponds, shaded by frangipani trees and dotted with colonial-style villas. It's an enjoyable place to explore and can be reached on foot from *Tiew Pai* in about half an hour – passing the colonnaded palace pier and the new Marine Life Museum (due to open in 2005) en route – or from an entry near the planned tourist information centre.

The main beach on the west coast, and the most popular one on the island, is **Hat Tham Pang**, a kilometre-long stretch of sand complete with deckchairs and beach umbrellas for rent, as well as Uncle Juk's watersports stall, which rents out kayaks, inner tubes, snorkels, fishing rods and tents. A samlor to this beach costs B80 from either pier. North of Hat Tham Pang, and also accessible via a fork off Thanon Asadang opposite *Tiew Pai*, you'll find the Tham Yai Prik temple and meditation centre, which is open to interested visitors and holds frequent retreats, and the dramatically situated *Sripitsanu Bungalows*, both located above a pretty, rocky cove known as **Hat Tham** or Hat Sai, which is only really swimmable at low tide.

Back down on the ring road, continuing in a northwesterly direction, you'll pass beneath the gaze of a large yellow Buddha before reaching the rocky northwest headland of **Khao Khat**, a few hundred metres further along Thanon Asadang. The uninterrupted panorama of open sea makes this a classic sunset spot, and there's a path along the cliffside.

From here the road heads east to reach the gaudy, multi-tiered Chinese temple, **Saan Chao Paw Khao Yai** (Shrine of the Father Spirit of the Great Hill), stationed at the top of a steep flight of steps and commanding a good view of the harbour and the mainland coast. Established here long before Rama V arrived on the island, the shrine was dedicated by Chinese seamen who saw a strange light coming out of one of the **caves** behind the modern-day temple. The caves, now full of religious statues and offertory paraphernalia, are visited by boatloads of Chinese pilgrims, particularly over Chinese New Year. Continue on up the cliffside to reach the small pagoda built for Rama V and enshrining a **Buddha's Footprint**. Two very long, very steep flights of stairs give access to the footprint: the easternmost one starts at the main waterfront entrance to the Chinese temple and takes you past a cluster of monks' meditation cells, while the westerly one rises further west along the ring road and offers the finest lookouts. It's well worth the vertiginous ascent, not least for the views out over Thailand's east coast; looking down you'll see a congestion of river barges bringing tonnes of rice, sugar and tapioca flour from the Central Plains to the international cargo boats anchored off Ko Si Chang's lee shore, and behind them, the tiny island of Ko Khram.

Eating and drinking

One of the most enjoyable **places to eat** on the island is *Pan and David Restaurant* (closed Tues) on the east-coast road to the old palace, which is run by a sociable and well-informed American expat and his Thai wife. The long and delicious menu includes authentically fiery *som tam*, seafood spaghetti, filet steak, Thai curries, a good vegetarian selection and home-made fresh strawberry ice cream. Other good options include *Jeff's* and *Lek Naa Wang*, both located across the road from *Pan and David*, and both of which do good seafood; *Tiew Pai*, which serves travellers' food; and *Si Chang View Resort*, whose speciality is its seafood served in one of several clifftop pavilions, especially popular at sunset, though be prepared for slow service and a fairly hefty bill.

Pattaya

With its streets full of high-rise hotels and touts on every corner, **PATTAYA** is the epitome of exploitative tourism gone mad, but most of Pattaya's two million annual visitors don't mind that the place looks like the Costa del Sol because what they are here for is sex. The town swarms with male and female **prostitutes**, spiced up by a sizeable population of transvestites (*katoey*), and plane-loads of Western men flock here to enjoy their services in the rash of go-go bars and massage parlours for which "Patpong-on-Sea" is notorious. The ubiquitous signs trumpeting "Viagra for Sale" say it all. Pattaya also has the largest **gay scene** in Thailand, with several exclusively gay hotels and a whole area given over to gay sex bars.

Pattaya's evolution into sin city began with the Vietnam War, when it got fat on selling sex to American servicemen. When the soldiers and sailors left in the mid-1970s, Western tourists were enticed to fill their places, and as the seaside Sodom and Gomorrah boomed, ex-servicemen returned to run the sort of joints they had once blown their dollars in. These days, almost half the bars and restaurants in Pattaya are Western-run. More recently, there has been an influx of criminal gangs from Germany, Russia and Japan, who reportedly find Pattaya a convenient centre for running their rackets in passport and credit-card fraud, as well as child pornography and prostitution; expat murders are a regular news item in the *Pattaya Mail*.

Yet Pattaya does have its good points, even if you don't fit the lecherous profile of the average punter, as attested by the number of **families** and older couples who choose to spend their package fortnights here. Although very few people swim off Pattaya's shore, the beach itself is kept clean so lots of tourists make use of the deckchairs that line its length. Pattaya's watersports facilities are among the best in the country, and there are plenty of tourist-oriented theme parks and golf courses within day-tripping distance. Holidaying here is not cheap (with no cheap huts for backpackers, and few bargain foodstalls), but travellers on a modest budget can find good accommodation at relatively low cost.

Orientation

Pattaya comprises three separate bays. At the centre is the four-kilometre **Pattaya Beach**, the noisiest, most unsightly zone of the resort, crowded with yachts and tour boats and fringed by a sliver of sand and a paved beachfront walkway. Known by its English name, and signed as such, **Pattaya Beach Road** (Thanon Hat Pattaya) runs the length of the beach and is connected to the parallel Pattaya 2 Road (Thanon Pattaya Sawng) by a string of sois numbered from 1 in the north to 17 in the south. The core of this block, between sois 6 and 13, is referred to as **Central Pattaya** (Pattaya Klang) and is packed with hotels, restaurants, bars, fast-food joints, souvenir shops and tour operators. During the day this is the busiest part of the resort, but after dark the neon zone south of Soi 13/2 – **South Pattaya** – takes over. Known locally as "the strip", this is what Pattaya's really about, with sex for sale in go-go bars, discos, massage parlours and open-sided "bar-beers". The town's enclave of gay sex bars is here too, focused mainly on the interlinked network of small lanes known as **Pattayaland** sois 1, 2 and 3 (or Boyz Town), but actually signed as sois 13/3, 13/4 and 13/5, between the Royal Garden Plaza and Soi 14. Pattaya Beach Road continues south from its junction with South Pattaya Road (Thanon Pattaya Tai) all the way down to the *Siam Bayshore Hotel*; this stretch

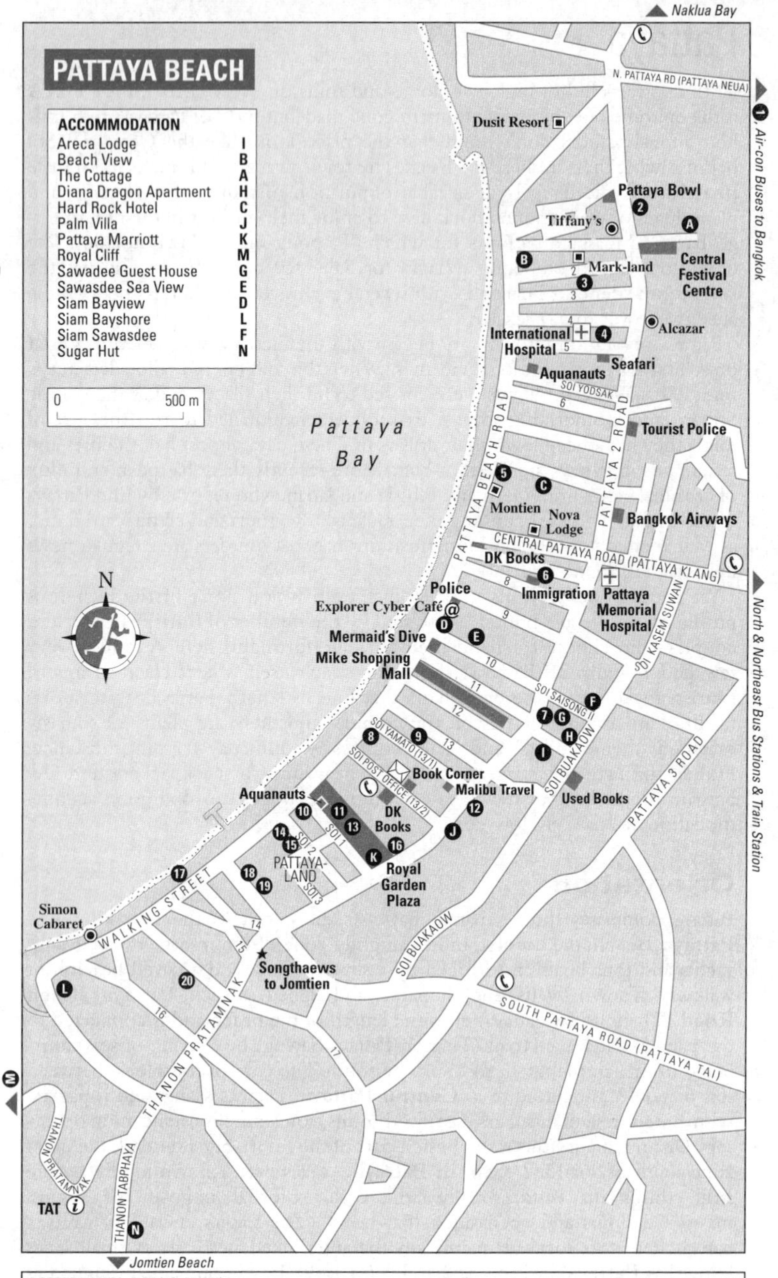

RESTAURANTS, BARS & CLUBS

Bamboo Bar	19	Green Bottle	7	Kum Pun	3	PIC Kitchen	4	Shenanigans	16
Baywatch	10	Hard Rock Café	5	Lobster Pot	17	Pig & Whistle	6	Thai House	1
Benihana	11	Hopf Brew House	8	Marine Disco	20	Rice Mill	11	Tip's	14
Café New Orleans	15	Fra Pattaya	18	Pattaya Palladium	2	Seaview Food Court	13	Vientiane	12
								Yamato	9

of road is also known as **Walking Street** because it's pedestrianized every evening from 7pm. **North Pattaya**, between Central Pattaya Road (Thanon Pattaya Klang) and North Pattaya Road (Thanon Hat Pattaya Neua), also has its "bar-beers", but is a slightly more upmarket district.

The southerly bay, **Jomtien Beach**, is also fronted by enormous high-rises, many of which are condominiums, though there are some low-rise, mid-priced hotels along the beachfront road, Jomtien Beach Road (Thanon Hat Jomtien), as well. Fourteen kilometres long, it is safer and a little cleaner than Pattaya Beach, and is considered Thailand's premier windsurfing spot. The far northern tip of Jomtien, beyond the end of the road, is mainly a gay cruising beach. Though the atmosphere in Jomtien is not as frantic as in Pattaya, the resort suffers from the same excess of bar-beers and shops peddling beachwear and tacky souvenirs.

Naklua Bay, around the northerly headland from Pattaya Beach, is the quietest of the three enclaves, and has managed to retain its fishing harbour and indigenous population despite the onslaught of condominiums, holiday apartments and expat homes. Most of the accommodation here is in time-shared condos.

Arrival and information

Most people **arrive** in Pattaya direct **from Bangkok**, either by public **bus** from the Eastern or Northern bus terminals, or by air-conditioned tour bus from a Bangkok hotel or Don Muang Airport (3 daily; 2hr 30min). Air-con buses to and from Bangkok and the airport use the bus station on North Pattaya Road, from where share-taxis charge B40 per person for hotel transfers. Non-air-con buses use the Baw Kaw Saw government bus station on Thanon Chaiyapruk in Jomtien. Coming **from Si Racha**, **Rayong** or **Trat** you'll probably get dropped just east of the resort on Thanon Sukhumvit, from where songthaews will ferry you into town; if heading on to these towns, you need to pick up your bus from one of the *sala* on Thanon Sukhumvit. Malibu Travel on Soi 13/1 (ⓣ038 723546) offers a fast B150 **minibus service** between Pattaya and the Ban Phe pier (for Ko Samet), and between Pattaya and Ko Chang (B500 including ferry); tickets can be booked through most tour agents. It's also possible to get to Pattaya direct **from Isaan and the north** – Nakorn Chai buses to and from Chiang Mai, Chiang Rai, Khorat and Ubon use a terminus on Thanon Sukhumvit, across from the Central Pattaya Road intersection (ⓣ038 424871); other bus services to the northeast use the Northeastern Bus Station on Central Pattaya Road, just east of the Pattaya 3 Road intersection.

Pattaya is on a branch line of the eastern rail line, and there is one **train** a day in each direction between the resort and Bangkok; the station is on Thanon Sukhumvit, about 500m north of the Central Pattaya Road intersection. Pattaya's U-Tapao **airport** (ⓣ038 601185) is located at the naval base near Sattahip, about 25km south of the resort, and runs Bangkok Airways flights to and from Ko Samui and Phuket. Taxis from Pattaya to Bangkok's **Don Muang** Airport cost about B800 and can be booked through most hotels and tour agents.

The **TAT** office is inconveniently located at 609 Thanon Pratamnak (sometimes referred to as Cliff Road) between South Pattaya and Jomtien (daily 8.30am–4.30pm; ⓣ038 428750, ⓔtatpty@chonburi.ksc.co.th). The *Pattaya Mail* prints local news stories and entertainment listings; it comes out every Friday and is available at most newsstands and bookstores.

Transport

The easiest way to get around Pattaya is by **songthaew** – though on all routes beware of being overcharged. Most follow a standard anticlockwise route up Pattaya 2 Road as far as North Pattaya Road and back down Pattaya Beach Road, for a fixed fee of B10 per person. Never jump in a parked songthaew, as you'll be charged for chartering the whole vehicle: just flag down one that's passing. Songthaews **to Jomtien** start from the junction of Pattaya 2 Road and South Pattaya Road and cost B10 to *KFC* or up to B30 to Thanon Boonkanjana. Songthaews **to Naklua** set off from the junction of Pattaya 2 Road and Central Pattaya Road and cost B10 to Naklua Soi 12.

The alternative is to rent your own transport: Pattaya Beach Road is full of touts offering motorbikes and jeeps for rent. **Motorbike rental** costs from B150 to B700 per day depending on the bike's size; beware of faulty vehicles, and of scams – some people have reported that rented bikes get stolen from tourists by touts keen to keep the customer's deposit, so you may want to use your own lock. Avis **car rental** (Ⓣ038 361627, Ⓦwww.avisthailand.com) have an office inside the *Dusit Resort Hotel* in North Pattaya, Budget (Ⓣ038 710717, Ⓦwww.budget.co.th) has an office on Beach Road, between sois 10 and 11, and many of the motorbike touts also rent out jeeps for about B1000 per day.

Accommodation

Really cheap **hotels** are almost impossible to find in Pattaya and Jomtien. Only a couple of the "inexpensive" hotels listed below have rooms for under B250, but nearly everywhere else offers air-con rooms and a swimming pool at least; prices in all categories plummet by up to fifty percent whenever demand is slack. Advance reservations are advisable to stay in the best-value hotels.

Bear in mind that the sex industry ensures that all rooms have beds large enough for at least two people; rates quoted here are for "single" rooms with one big double bed (a "double" room will have two big double beds and cost more). Another effect of the sex industry is that hotel guests are often assumed to be untrustworthy, so when checking in you're likely to be asked for a deposit against the loss of your room key and against the use of your mini-bar and phone.

Pattaya

Inexpensive and moderate

Areca Lodge 198/21 Soi Diana Inn, Central Pattaya Ⓣ038 424702, Ⓦwww.arecalodge.com. Unusually stylish place for Pattaya, with pleasantly furnished air-con rooms built around a pool, all of them with balconies. ❼

Beach View Between sois 1 and 2, Pattaya Beach Rd, North Pattaya Ⓣ038 422660, Ⓔbeachvw@loxinfo.co.th. Medium-sized mid-range high-rise with swimming pool just across the road from the beach. Many rooms have sea view and all have air-con. Very reasonable for its class. ❺

The Cottage Off Pattaya 2 Rd, North Pattaya Ⓣ038 425660, Ⓔthe_cottage2002@yahoo.com. Good-value, well-appointed air-con bungalows, attractively designed and pleasantly located in a pretty garden compound a good distance off the main road. Convenient for the shops and restaurants in the Central Festival Centre complex. Facilities include two small swimming pools, a bar and a restaurant. Recommended. ❺

Diana Dragon Apartment 198/16 Soi Diana Inn, opposite Soi 11, Central Pattaya Ⓣ038 423928, Ⓕ038 411658. Enormous fan and air-con rooms with fridge, and use of the pool at *Diana Inn*, 100m away; favoured by long-stay tourists. Good value. ❸–❹

Palm Villa 485 Pattaya 2 Rd, opposite Soi 13/2, Central Pattaya Ⓣ & Ⓕ038 429099. Peaceful haven close to the nightlife, with small garden, a swimming pool, and sizeable fan and air-con rooms. ❸–❹

Sawasdee Guest House 502/1 Soi Saisong II (aka Soi Honey Inn), Pattaya 2 Rd, Central Pattaya Ⓣ038 425360, Ⓦwww.sawasdee-hotels.com. The cheapest branch of the ubiquitous Sawasdee chain of budget hotels has some of the most inexpensive rooms in Pattaya, decently if spartanly outfitted (some have no window) and available with fan or air-con. ❷–❸

Sawasdee Sea View 302/1 Soi 10, Central Pattaya ⓣ038 710566, ⓦwww.sawasdee-hotels.com. Occupying a great location in a still quiet soi just a few dozen metres off the beachfront road, this place offers large and quite modishly decorated rooms, all with air-con and TV but none enjoying a real sea view. ❺

Siam Sawasdee Corner of Soi Saisong II and Soi Buakaow, Central Pattaya ⓣ038 720330, ⓦwww.sawasdee-hotels.com. The swimming pool makes this place decent value and the 206 big, comfortable rooms all come with air-con, TV and fridge. ❹

Expensive

Hard Rock Hotel Pattaya 429 Pattaya Beach Rd, just north of the intersection with Central Pattaya Rd, Central Pattaya ⓣ038 428755, ⓦwww.hardrockhotelpattaya.com. The most contemporary and trendy of Pattaya's upper-bracket hotels, this is a fun place to stay – neither too pretentious nor overly cool, though it helps if you're a music fan as the place is stuffed with rock hall-of-fame memorabilia. Rooms are stylish and there's a huge freeform pool, weekly "foam parties", a spa, kids' club and rock-climbing wall. ❾

Pattaya Marriott Resort and Spa 218 Pattaya Beach Rd, Central Pattaya ⓣ038 412120, ⓦwww.marriotthotels.com/pyxmc. Located right in the heart of the resort, across the road from the beach and within easy reach of bars and shops, but pleasingly secluded within a tropical garden, this well-equipped hotel has very comfortable top-notch rooms, a huge pool, a spa, floodlit tennis courts, mountain-bike rental and a kids' club. ❾

Royal Cliff Beach Resort and Spa 353 Thanon Pratamnak (Cliff Rd), South Pattaya ⓣ038 250140, ⓦwww.royalcliff.com. Pattaya's top hotel is a huge complex of over 1000 rooms in four differently styled wings, all of them set in landscaped grounds on a cliff overlooking a small bay. Facilities are very good and include five pools, two kids' pools, a spa, tennis courts and ten restaurants. ❾

Siam Bayshore 559 Pattaya Beach Rd ⓣ038 428678, ⓦwww.siamhotels.com. At the far southern end of the South Pattaya strip, set in a secluded wooded spot overlooking the beach, this popular hotel comprises 270 rooms spread over twelve wings and is set in exceptionally lush tropical gardens. Many rooms have balconies offering uninterrupted sea views, and there are two pools as well as tennis courts and snooker, table-tennis and badminton facilities. ❾

Siam Bayview Pattaya Beach Rd, on the corner of Soi 10, Central Pattaya ⓣ038 423871, ⓦwww.siamhotels.com. Very centrally located upscale hotel that has smart, good-sized rooms, many of them with ocean views. Good value considering its location and facilities, which include two swimming pools, tennis courts, snooker and several restaurants. ❽

Sugar Hut 391/18 Thanon Tabphaya, midway between South Pattaya and Jomtien ⓣ038 251686, ⓦwww.sugarhut.co.th. The most unusual, least corporate accommodation in Pattaya comprises a charming collection of 33 Ayutthaya-style traditional wooden bungalows set in a fabulously lush garden with three swimming pools. The bungalows are in tropical-chic style, with low beds, open-roofed shower rooms, mosquito nets and private verandas; the more expensive ones have a sitting room as well. It's an appealingly laid-back place, but best visited with your own transport as it's nowhere near the restaurants, shops or sea. Published rates start at B6700. ❾

Jomtien Beach

DD Inn Just back from the beach, on a tiny soi opposite *KFC* at the far north end of Beach Rd ⓣ038 232995, ⓔddinnguesthouse@hotmail.com. Friendly, good-value guest-house-style little hotel in an ideal spot just a few metres from the beach. Rooms with balconies are slightly pricier, but all rooms come with air-con and TV. ❹

Grand Jomtien Palace 365 Beach Rd, at the corner of Thanon Wat Boonkanjana (aka Wat Bun) ⓣ038 231405, ⓕ038 231404. Upmarket high-rise hotel where many of the comfortable, air-con rooms have a decent sea view. Facilities include three swimming pools, a beer garden and restaurant, and a small shopping arcade. ❻–❼

JB Guest House 75/14 Soi 5 (Soi Post Office), off Beach Rd ⓣ038 231581. Exceptionally good-value rooms in this small, friendly, Bangkok-style guest house. All rooms have TV and hot water; you pay slightly more for air-con. ❸

Mermaid Beach Resort 75/102 Soi 7, off Beach Rd ⓣ038 232210, ⓕ038 231908. Nicely appointed, mid-range, low-rise hotel that's smartly furnished and well maintained. There's a swimming pool, dive centre and restaurant, and all 120 rooms have air-con and TV. Price depends on whether you want a view of the pool or the street. ❻–❼

Silver Sand Villa Next to Soi White House at the northern end of Beach Rd ⓣ038 231288, ⓔsweetsea@cbi.cscom.com. The huge, nicely furnished air-con rooms in the old wing are good value, but you need to book ahead for a view of the pool (rather than a wall); most of the rooms are wheelchair-accessible. Rooms in the new wing are more expensive; though plainly furnished, they all have balconies and pool views. Two swimming pools and restaurant. ❺–❻

Surf Beach Hotel Between sois 5 and 7 at the north end of Beach Rd ⓣ038 231025, ⓕ038 231029. Popular mid-range place across from the beach. Rooms are a bit faded, but all have air-con and TV, and some have a sea view. ❹

Daytime activities

Most tourists in Pattaya spend the days recovering from the night before: not much happens before midday, breakfasts are served until early afternoon, and the hotel pool generally seems more inviting than a tussle with water-skis. But the energetic are well catered for, with a decent range of dive centres, water-sports facilities, golf courses and theme parks.

Snorkelling and scuba-diving

Snorkelling and scuba-diving are popular in Pattaya, though if you've got the choice between diving here or off the Andaman coast (see p.671), go for the latter – the reefs there are a lot more spectacular. The big advantage of Pattaya is that it can be dived year-round. The main destinations for local **dive trips**

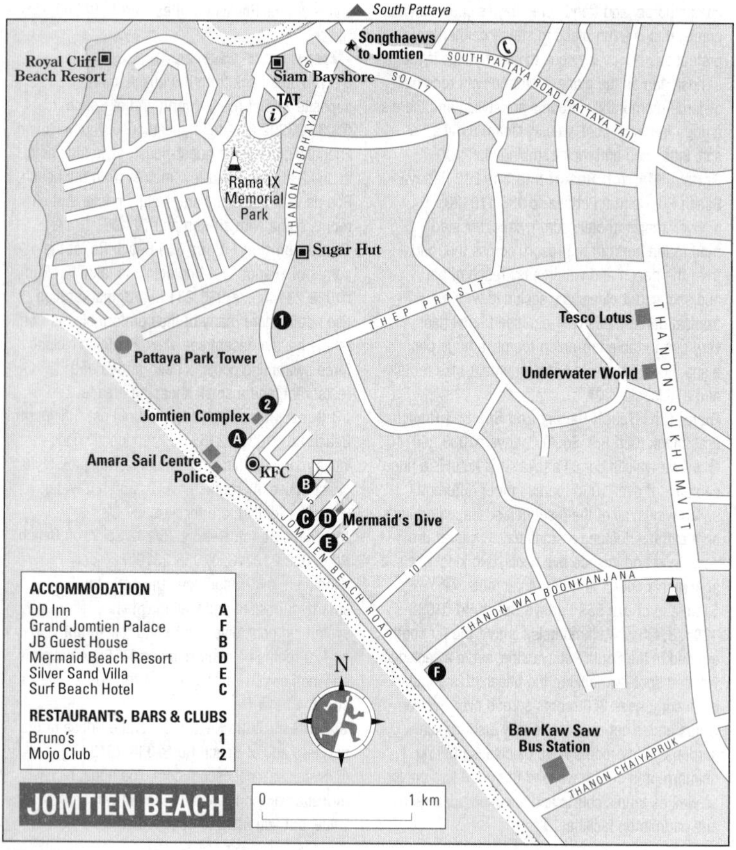

are the group of "outer islands" about 25km from shore, which include Ko Rin, Ko Man Wichai and Ko Klung Badaan, where you have a good chance of seeing big schools of barracuda, jacks and tuna, as well as moray eels and blue-spotted stingrays. There are also three rewarding wreck dives in the Samae San/Sattahip area: the 21-metre-deep freighter *Phetchaburi Bremen*, which went down in the 1930s; the 64-metre-long cargo ship *Hardeep*, which was sunk during World War II and can be navigated along the entire length of its interior; and the HMS *Khram*, which was sunk deliberately by the Thai navy in 2003 to make a new artificial reef. A one-day dive trip including two dives, equipment and lunch generally costs around B3000, with accompanying snorkellers paying B800. Several companies along Pattaya Beach Road run **snorkelling** trips to nearby Ko Larn and Bamboo Island, though mass tourism has taken its toll on these two islands and their coral.

Pattaya is also an easy place to learn to dive: one-day Discover scuba-diving courses start at about B3000, and four-day Openwater **courses** average out at B12,000. Be careful when signing up for a dive course or expedition: unqualified instructors and dodgy equipment are a fact of life in Pattaya, and it's as well to question other divers about all operators, PADI-certified or not (see p.73 of Basics for more guidelines). The local **recompression chamber** is at the Apakorn Kiatiwong Naval Hospital (℗038 601185) in Sattahip, 26km south of Pattaya; it's open 24 hours. Dive shops that run diving expeditions and internationally certificated courses include:

Aquanauts Soi Yodsak, Central Pattaya ℗038 361724, ⓦwww.aquanautsdive.com; and Pattayaland Soi 1, South Pattaya ℗038 710727. British-run PADI Five-Star Instructor Development Centre.

Mermaid's Dive Centre Soi White House, Jomtien ℗038 232219, ⓦwww.mermaiddive.com; and between sois 10 and 11 on Beach Rd, Central Pattaya. PADI Five-Star Instructor Development Centre.

Paradise Scuba Divers *Siam Bay View Hotel*, corner Soi 10, Pattaya Beach Rd, Pattaya ℗038 710567, ⓔls@tauchenthailand.de. PADI Five-Star dive centre.

Seafari Sports Center 359/2 Soi 5, Pattaya Beach Rd, North Pattaya ℗038 429060, ⓦwww.seafari.co.th. Long-running PADI Five-Star Instructor Development Centre; American management.

Watersports and golf

Both Pattaya and Jomtien are full of beachfront stalls organizing **water-skiing** (B1000/hour), **jet-skiing** (B900/hour) and **parasailing** (B400/round), though for **windsurfing** you'll need to go to Jomtien (B500/hour). *Deutsches House* restaurant on Soi 4, North Pattaya (℗038 428725), runs day-long **deep-sea fishing** expeditions for about B2000 per person; you could also try asking about fishing trips at the *Shamrock* bar on Pattayaland Soi 2 (Soi 13/4) in Central Pattaya.

There are currently eighteen international-standard **golf courses** within easy reach of Pattaya, some of them designed by famous golfers. Visitors' green fees start at B900 on a weekday, B1300 on a weekend, plus B200 for a caddy, and a set of clubs can usually be rented for about B350. One popular option is to join a golf **package** to one of the top courses organized by East Coast Travel (℗038 300927, ⓦwww.pattayagolfpackage.com); weekday rates start at B1850 including everything except club rental. The following courses are all less than an hour's drive from Pattaya, with the closest listed first and the furthest last; for directions, either call the course or ask at your hotel. Phoenix Golf and Country Club (27 holes; ℗038 239391); Siam Country Club (18 holes; ℗038 249381); Laem Chabang International Country Club (27 holes; ℗038 338351); Eastern Star Golf Course (18 holes; ℗038 630410); St Andrew's 2000 (18 holes; ℗038 893838).

Theme parks and other attractions

One of the most enjoyable attractions in the resort is **Ripley's Believe It Or Not** (daily 11am–11pm; B370, kids B270), located on the third floor of the Royal Garden Plaza shopping centre on Pattaya Beach Road. It's part of a worldwide chain of curiosity museums inspired by the bizarre collections of the early twentieth-century American cartoonist and adventurer Robert Leroy Ripley, and displays lots of outlandish objects (including fetishes, torture contraptions and tribal masks), and real-life novelties from Thailand and further afield (such as models of the world's tallest, smallest and fattest men), as well as an exhibition on sharks.

Advertised as the only one of its kind in the world, the **Museum of Bottle Art** (daily 11am–8pm; B100), 100m south of the bus station on Thanon Sukhumvit, contains three hundred pieces of miniature art in bottles, all of them painstakingly assembled by Dutch expat Pieter Bij de Leij. The collection includes Dutch windmills, Thai temples, a Saudi mosque and a British coach and horses. To see them, take an eastbound songthaew along Central Pattaya Road, get off as soon as you reach Thanon Sukhumvit, and walk 200m south.

The hugely ambitious **Sanctuary of Truth**, also known as **Wang Boran** and **Prasat Mai** (daily 8am–6pm; B500; ⓣ038 225407), is also a kind of replica, but on a 1:1 scale. Conceived by the man behind the Muang Boran Ancient City complex near Bangkok (see p.170), it's a huge temple-palace designed to evoke the great ancient Khmer sanctuaries of Angkor and built entirely of wood. It was begun in 1981 but is still a work-in-progress. The sanctuary is located behind imposing crenellated walls off the west end of Naklua Soi 12, close to the *Garden Sea View* hotel; from Central Pattaya, take a Naklua-bound songthaew as far as Soi 12, then a B10 motorbike taxi. Built in a fabulously dramatic spot beside the sea, the temple rises to 105m at its highest point and fans out into four gopura (entrance pavilions), each of which is covered in symbolic woodcarvings. The **carvings** on the north (seaside) gopura are inspired by Cambodian mythology, and include a tower above the gopura that's crowned with an image of the four-headed Hindu god Brahma, plus a lotus flower and two three-headed elephants; those on the east gopura refer to China, so the Mahayana Buddhist bodhisattvas have Chinese faces; the carvings on the west gopura evoke India and include scenes from the Hindu epic the *Mahabarata*; and the southern entrance has images from Thailand, such as scenes from the Hindu tale, the *Ramayana*. For more on the symbolism of Hindu and Buddhist sculptures, see the piece on Art and Architecture in "Contexts", p.799.

There are several theme parks, "culture villages" and wildlife parks on the outskirts of Pattaya, all well signed off the main roads. **Mini Siam**, just north of the North Pattaya Road/Thanon Sukhumvit intersection, is just what it sounds like: the cream of Thailand's most precious monuments reconstructed to 1:25 scale, plus miniature replicas of international icons such as the Sydney Opera House and the Statue of Liberty; call ⓣ038 421628 to arrange transport. **Nong Nooch Village**, 18km south of Pattaya off Thanon Sukhumvit, serves up life-sized Thai culture in the form of traditional dancing and elephant-rides against the backdrop of an attractively landscaped park. It's a popular feature of many tour-operators' programmes (B450 half-day; ⓣ038 249321), but it's also worth coming here if you're into flowers: the **orchid garden** is said to be the world's largest. The **Elephant Village**, 7km northeast of Pattaya, offers ninety-minute elephant "treks" round its park for B800, plus the option of doing some whitewater-rafting as well (B1500); there's also an elephant-training show every afternoon (2.30pm; B450). For details and transport, call ⓣ038 249818, or visit ⓦwww.elephant-village-pattaya.com. **Underwater World**, close to Tesco Lotus just south of the Thep Prasit junction with Thanon Sukhumvit (B360, kids B180 or free if under 90cm tall), is a small, expensive, but rather beautiful aquarium comprising a trio of long fibreglass tunnels that transport you through three different marine worlds; easiest access by songthaew would be to try and hail one travelling from Jomtien along Thanon Thep Prasit.

Shopping

Pattaya is not a bad place for **shopping**, especially at the two main shopping plazas – the Central Festival Centre on Pattaya 2 Road in North Pattaya, and Royal Garden Plaza in South Pattaya – which both have tempting arrays of fairly classy shops, ranging from designer clothes boutiques to smart gift and handicraft outlets, as well as branches of Boots the Chemist.

Pattaya boasts some of Thailand's best English-language **bookshops** outside Bangkok. DK Books (daily 8am–11pm) on Soi 13/2 (Soi Post Office) stocks a phenomenal range of books on Asia, and has a smaller branch north up Beach Road, on the corner of Central Pattaya Road. Bookazine, on the first floor of the Royal Garden Plaza in South Pattaya, also has an impressive selection of titles, plus novels and stacks of maps, but is best known for its unrivalled international magazine section. Book Corner on Soi 13/2 (Soi Post Office) is another rewarding place to browse for Southeast Asian titles. Used Books, at 210/6 Soi Buakaow (between Soi Diana Inn and Soi Saisong II) keeps a small stock of inexpensive second-hand novels and non-fiction titles.

Eating

Overall, **food** in Pattaya is expensive and pretty dire, but there are still a few classy gems worth nosing out. Most hotels offer fairly good-value all-you-can eat breakfast buffets for around B100 per head, the majority of which are open to non-guests as well. For inexpensive Thai food, hunt out the curry and noodle vendors on Soi Kasem Suwan. At the other end of the scale, the cavernous *Thai House Restaurant* on North Pattaya Road stages nightly performances of classical Thai dance for diners.

Baywatch Pattaya Beach Rd, between Pattayaland sois 1 and 2 (sois 13/3 and 13/4), Central Pattaya. Open 24hr, this is a good joint for your all-day breakfast, complete with sea view and sidewalk vantage point. Cappuccinos, filter coffees, burgers, sandwiches and pancakes. Moderate.

Benihana 2nd floor, Royal Garden Plaza, Pattaya Beach Rd, Central Pattaya. Lively Japanese eatery that's renowned for its sizzling *teppanyaki* specials, cooked at your own hot-plate table. Also offers authentic sushi and sashimi. Expensive.

Bruno's 306/63 Chateau Dale Plaza, Thanon Tabphaya, Jomtien. A Pattaya institution that's a favourite with expats celebrating special occasions. The food is classy European – Provencal-style rack of lamb, sirloin steak, dark-chocolate mousse – and there's a cellar of some 150 wines. Expensive.

Café New Orleans Pattayaland Soi 2 (Soi 13/4), Central Pattaya. Specializing in Cajun and Creole dishes, with especially recommended baby back ribs and all-you-can-eat lunchtime deals on weekends. Moderate.

Fra Pattaya South Pattaya Rd, South Pattaya. Big menu of staple Thai and Chinese dishes; authentic taste and workaday atmosphere. Inexpensive to moderate.

Lobster Pot Opposite Soi 14, Walking St, South Pattaya. Enormous seafront restaurant specializing in fresh seafood, in particular tiger prawns and giant lobsters. Moderate.

PIC Kitchen Soi 5, North Pattaya. One of Pattaya's finest traditional Thai restaurants, set in a stylish series of teak buildings. Mouth-watering menu of elegantly presented curry, seafood, rice, noodle and vegetarian dishes. Nightly live jazz in the adjacent Jazz Pit. Moderate to expensive.

Rice Mill 2nd floor, Royal Garden Plaza, Pattaya Beach Rd, Central Pattaya. Upmarket Cantonese restaurant that's especially popular at weekends for its all-you-can-eat *dim sum* buffets (Sat & Sun noon–2pm; B249). Expensive.

Seaview Food Court Top floor of the Royal Garden Plaza, Pattaya Beach Rd, Central Pattaya. Lots of hot-food stalls serving specialities from different parts of Thailand, plus Japanese and Italian options too. Not exactly haute cuisine, but fast, hassle-free and fairly inexpensive for Pattaya. Decide what you want and then charge your food card to the right value. Inexpensive to moderate.

Sugar Hut 391/18 Thanon Tabphaya, midway between South Pattaya and Jomtien. Attached to the delightful tropical hotel described on p.431, this restaurant gives you the chance to soak up the ambience and enjoy the tropical gardens without shelling out for a bungalow. Food is served in an open-sided *sala* and is mainly classy (and expensive) traditional Thai; recommendations include fried catfish in coconut milk and chilli, and chicken baked with pineapple. Worth the splurge.

Tip's 22/10 Pattaya Beach Rd, between Pattayaland sois 2 and 3 (sois 13/4 and 13/5), South Pattaya. Long-running Pattaya institution offering over a dozen different set breakfasts. Inexpensive.

Vientiane Between sois 13/1 and 13/2 on Pattaya 2 Rd. Specializes in Southeast Asian food, including Lao-inspired curries and some Indonesian dishes. Moderate.

Yamato Soi 13/1 (Soi Yamato), Central Pattaya. Good-value Japanese fare including sushi, *soba* and *udon* dishes, *tempura* and sashimi. Open evenings only during the week, and for lunch and dinner at weekends. Moderate.

Drinking and nightlife

Entertainment is Pattaya's *raison d'être* and the **nightlife** is what most tourists come for, as do oilfield workers from the Arabian Gulf and US marines on R&R. Of the five hundred-odd **bars** in Pattaya, the majority are the so-called "bar-beers", relatively innocent open-air drinking spots staffed by hostesses whose primary job is to make you buy beer not bodies. However, sex makes more money than booze in Pattaya – depending on who you believe, there are between six thousand and twenty thousand Thais working in Pattaya's sex industry, a workforce that includes children as young as 10. It's an all-pervasive trade: there are hundreds of go-go bars in town, and even the uninspiring discos – such as the huge and sleazy *Marine Disco*, off the southern end of Walking Street, and the enormous *Pattaya Palladium*, just north of the intersection of Soi 1 and Pattaya 2 Road in North Pattaya – depend more on prostitutes than on ravers.

Bars

Pattaya's often nameless outdoor "**bar-beers**" group themselves in clusters all over North, Central and South Pattaya. The setup is the same in all of them: from mid-afternoon the punters – usually lone males – sit on stools around a brashly lit circular bar, behind which the hostesses keep the drinks, bawdy chat and well-worn jokes flowing. Beer is generally quite inexpensive at these places, the atmosphere low-key and good-humoured, and couples as well as single women drinkers are almost always made welcome.

Drinks are a lot more expensive in the bouncer-guarded **go-go bars** on Walking Street in South Pattaya, where near-naked hostesses serve the beer and live sex shows keep the boozers hooked through the night. The scene follows much the same pattern as in Patpong in Bangkok, with the women dancing on a small stage in the hope they might be bought for the night – or the week. Go-go dancers, shower shows and striptease are also the mainstays of the **gay scene**, centred on Pattayaland Soi 3 (Soi 13/5), South Pattaya.

There's not a great deal of demand for **bars** where the emphasis is on simple companionable drinking, but those listed below are comparatively low-key and welcoming.

Bamboo Bar Seafront end of South Pattaya Rd. An exuberant in-house band pulls in a sizeable crowd to this large streetside lounge-style bar.

Green Bottle Adjacent to *Diana Inn*, Pattaya 2 Rd, Central Pattaya. A cosy, air-con, pub-style bar that has forged a studiously unsleazy atmosphere. Serves food.

Hard Rock Café Just north of Central Pattaya Rd on Pattaya Beach Rd, Central Pattaya. Fairly standard franchise of the international chain, with nightly entertainment from a DJ and house band adept at covering classic pop and rock hits. Large cocktail menu plus a selection of burgers and salads to soak up the alcohol.
Hopf Brew House Between sois 13/1 (Yamato) and 13/2 (Post Office), Pattaya Beach Rd, Central Pattaya. Cavernous air-con pub, designed like a German beer hall around an internal courtyard, with a stage for the nightly live music. Attracts a youngish crowd, including vacationing couples, and serves bar snacks as well as beer.
Kum Pun Soi 2, North Pattaya. Typically Thai take on a country-and-western bar (lots of wood and the occasional buffalo head) that's known for its live bands who play nightly sets of authentic Thai folk music as well as soft rock.
Mojo Club Near Jomtien Complex, off Thanon Thep Prasit, North Jomtien (see map on p.432). Laid-back bar run by a couple of jazz musicians, with live jazz and blues nightly.
Pig and Whistle Soi 7, Central Pattaya. Homely English-style pub that serves fish and chips, hosts twice-weekly quiz nights (Mon & Thurs) and shows all the major international sports events on its giant screen.
Shamrock Pattayaland 2 (Soi 13/4), South Pattaya. This British-run bar is a good place to catch local expat gossip. The manager sometimes entertains customers on his banjo, and his collection of folk-music tapes is also worth listening out for. On the edge of the gay district, but attracts a mixed crowd.
Shenanigans Next to the Royal Garden Plaza, Pattaya 2 Rd, Central Pattaya. An Irish pub that serves Guinness and Kilkenny Bitter and hosts frequent theme nights with appropriate food. The big screen shows major sports events, and there are nightly sets from a roster of live bands who start playing around 11pm.

Cabarets

Tour groups – and families – constitute the main audience at Pattaya's three **transvestite cabarets**. Glamorous and highly professional, these shows are performed three times a night at Alcazar, opposite Soi 4 on Pattaya 2 Road in North Pattaya; at Tiffany's, north of Soi 1 on Pattaya 2 Road in North Pattaya; and also at Simon Cabaret on Walking Street in South Pattaya. Each theatre has a troupe of sixty or more transvestites who run through twenty musical-style numbers in fishnets and crinolines, ball gowns and leathers, against ever more lavish stage sets. All glitz and no sleaze, the shows cost from B500 per person.

Listings

Airlines Bangkok Airways, 75/8 Pattaya 2 Rd, Central Pattaya ⓣ038 412382; Thai Airways, inside the *Dusit Resort*, North Pattaya ⓣ038 420995.
Cinemas Central Cineplex, on the top floor of the Central Festival Centre on Pattaya 2 Rd in North Pattaya, runs four English-language shows a day at each of its four screens. There's also a three-screen cinema on the top floor of Royal Garden Plaza in South Pattaya. Tickets from B70. Both cineplexes also have a 3D screen.
Cookery classes At the *Royal Cliff Beach Resort*, Royal Cliff Bay, 353 Thanon Pratamnak ⓣ038 250421, between South Pattaya and Jomtien. Call ahead to reserve; B990.
Dentists At the Bangkok-Pattaya Hospital ⓣ038 427777 on Thanon Sukhumvit, about 400m north of the intersection with North Pattaya Rd; and at Pattaya International Hospital on Soi 4 ⓣ038 428374–5.
Emergencies For all emergencies, call the tourist police on the free, 24hr phone line ⓣ1155, contact them at their booth on Pattaya 2 Rd, just south of Soi 6, Central Pattaya ⓣ038 429371, or call in at the more central police station on Beach Rd, just south of Soi 9.
Exchange There are numerous exchange counters and ATMs, particularly on Pattaya Beach Rd and Pattaya 2 Rd.
Hospitals The best-equipped hospital is the Bangkok-Pattaya Hospital ⓣ038 427777 on Thanon Sukhumvit, about 400m north of the intersection with North Pattaya Rd. Other central private hospitals include the Pattaya International Hospital on Soi 4 ⓣ038 428374–5, and Pattaya Memorial Hospital on Central Pattaya Rd ⓣ038 429422–4.
Immigration office Opposite *Flipper Lodge* on Soi 8 (Mon–Fri 8.30am–4.30pm; ⓣ038 429409). Many travel agents offer cheap visa-renewal day-trips to Cambodia: check advertisements and local press for details.
Internet access At dozens of Internet centres throughout the resort, including the very efficient,

24hr *Explorer Cyber Café*, between sois 9 and 10 on Pattaya Beach Rd; Catnet at the small public CAT phone office on Soi 13/2.

Mail The post office is, not surprisingly, on Soi Post Office in Central Pattaya, though the road has now officially been re-signed as Soi 13/2.

Telephones The main CAT international telephone office is on South Pattaya Rd, just east of the junction with Pattaya 3 Rd, and there's a smaller, more central branch on Soi 13/2 (Post Office) in Central Pattaya. There are lots of private international call centres in the resort.

Rayong

Few farang travellers choose to stop for longer than they have to in the busy provincial capital of **RAYONG**, 65km southeast of Pattaya, but it's a useful place for **bus connections**, particularly if you're travelling between the east coast and the northeast, or if you're trying to get to Ko Samet; Ban Phe, the ferry pier for Ko Samet (see p.440), is about 17km east and served by frequent songthaews from Rayong bus station (every 30min; 30min). Rayong is famous for producing the national condiment *nam plaa* – a sauce made from decomposed fish – and for the pineapples and durian grown in the provincial orchards, but there's nothing much for tourists here. The **TAT office** (Ⓣ038 655420, Ⓔtatryong@tat.or.th) for the Rayong region and Ko Samet is inconveniently located 7km east of Rayong town centre at 153/4 Thanon Sukhumvit (Highway 3), on the way to Ban Phe; any Ban Phe-bound bus or songthaew will drop you at its door. There's a bank with **exchange** counter opposite the access road to Rayong's bus station on Thanon Sukhumvit. If you get stuck in town overnight, you can rent cheap, no-frills fan and air-con **rooms** at the *Asia Hotel,* just east of the bus station and north off Thanon Sukhumvit at no. 962/1 (Ⓣ038 611022; ❶–❸), or there's better, comfier accommodation at the *Burapa Palace*, 100m east of the bus station on the south side of Thanon Sukhumvit at no. 69 (Ⓣ038 622946; ❸–❺).

Ko Samet

Attracted by its proximity to Bangkok and its powdery white sand, backpackers, package tourists and Thai families flock to the island of **Ko Samet**, 80km southeast of Pattaya, whose former name, Ko Kaew Phitsadan, means "the island with sand of crushed crystal". Only 6km long, Ko Samet was declared a **national park** in 1981, but typically the ban on building has been ignored and there are now over thirty bungalow operations here, with owners paying rent to the Royal Forestry Department. Inevitably, these developments have had a huge impact on the island's resources: waste water from many bungalows is dumped into the sea, you quite often stumble across piles of rotting rubbish, and the grounds of most cheaper bungalows are poorly landscaped. The dazzling white beaches, however, remain breathtakingly beautiful, lapped by pale blue water.

As the island gets increasingly upmarket, it is becoming more difficult to find a bungalow for under B400 in high season, but the most backpacker-friendly **beaches** are Ao Hin Kok, Ao Phai and Ao Tub Tim, where you can still find a few simple bamboo huts; Ao Hin Kok and Ao Phai are also quite lively in the evenings. Ao Phrao, Ao Wong Duan and Hat Sai Kaew are mainly dominated by upmarket accommodation and attract families and package tourists as well as Bangkok trendies. In accordance with national park rules, **camping** is permissible on any of the beaches, despite what you might be told.

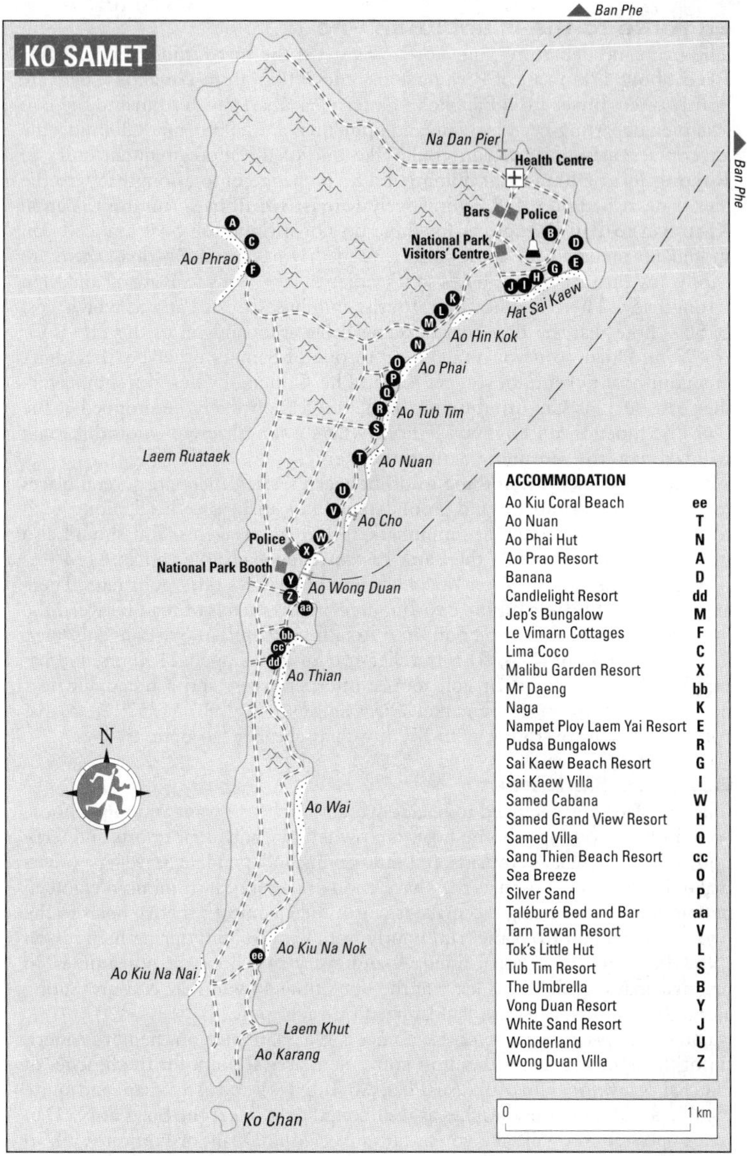

All beaches get packed on **weekends** and national holidays: you could try phoning ahead to reserve a room, though not every place accepts bookings. Many bungalow managers raise their rates by sixty percent during peak periods and sometimes for weekenders as well: the rates quoted here are typical high-season rates.

En route to the island: Ban Phe

The mainland departure-point for Ko Samet is the tiny fishing port of **BAN PHE**, about 17km east of Rayong and some 200km from Bangkok. There are hourly direct **buses** from Bangkok's Eastern (Ekamai) Bus Terminal to the Ban Phe pier, departing between 7am and 5pm, then at 6.30pm and 8.30pm (some air-con services; 3hr), or you could take one of the more frequent buses to **Rayong** (every 40min; 2hr 30min) and then change onto a songthaew to the pier as described on p.438. Alternatively, **tourist minibuses** run from Thanon Khao San to Ban Phe; prices for these do not include the boat fare and you should be prepared for some fairly crazed driving. From **Pattaya**, there are hardly any direct Ban Phe buses so it's easier to take a bus to Rayong and then a songthaew. There are, however, tourist minibuses from Pattaya, which cost B150 – note that the B60 boat ticket available as an add-on to this fare is for Ao Wong Duan, so if you want to go to one of Samet's other beaches, don't buy your boat ticket until you get to Ban Phe. Coming by bus from points further east, such as **Chanthaburi** or **Trat**, you'll most likely be dropped at the Ban Phe junction on Highway 3, from where a songthaew or motorbike taxi will take you the remaining 5km to the pier.

If you get stuck with nothing to do between ferries, there are several places to check your **email** on and around Ban Phe's main pier-head, along with traveller-oriented restaurants, minimarkets and travel agents. You should also stock up on money here – the **bank** has currency exchange and an ATM – as there's no bank nor ATM on Ko Samet, and bungalows offer poor rates. There are a couple of **hotels** on the two-hundred-metre stretch of road between the main Saphaan Nuan Tip pier and the Ao Phrao (Saphaan Sri Ban Phe) pier. *TN Place* (Ⓣ038 651824; ❸) is traveller-friendly, stays open 24 hours, and has simple en-suite fan and air-con rooms, Internet access and a restaurant next door. The slightly more upmarket *Diamond Hotel* (Ⓣ038 651757; ❸–❹) has comfortable air-con rooms with TV, as well as cheaper fan options.

Boats to Ko Samet

Once in Ban Phe, you need to decide which beach you want and then choose your **boat** accordingly. Some boats are owned by individual resorts and ferry both pre-paid package tourists and fare-paying independent travellers; others make the crossing as soon as they have enough passengers (minimum eighteen people) or sufficient cargo to make it worth their while. In theory, boats to the two main piers on Ko Samet run hourly from 8am to 5pm during high season (Nov–Feb) and on national holidays, and every two hours at other times. In practice, many of the boats leave at the same time, so you may end up waiting a couple of hours. Fares are standardized on each route.

The easiest place to get to on Ko Samet is **Na Dan pier** on the northeastern tip of the island, which is the most convenient arrival point for the beaches of Hat Sai Kaew, Ao Hin Kok, Ao Phai, Ao Tub Tim and Ao Nuan, and quite feasible for all the other beaches as well; songthaews meet the boats at Na Dan (see opposite) and will take you as far as Ao Wong Duan, or you can walk to your chosen beach. Boats to Na Dan leave from Ban Phe's Saphaan Nuan Tip pier, opposite the 7–11 shop; they take thirty minutes to get to Samet and charge B50 one way.

There are equally frequent boats to **Ao Wong Duan** (40min; B60), which is also convenient for the nearby beaches of Ao Cho and Ao Thian. Some boats go to Wong Duan direct from Ban Phe's Saphaan Nuan Tip pier, others stop at Na Dan first. Some of the bungalow resorts on the smaller beaches also run boats from Ban Phe direct to their beach – see the individual beach accounts for details.

Leaving Ko Samet

Four **scheduled boats** leave Ko Samet's Na Dan pier every day, currently at about 7am, 8am, noon and 5pm, and there are usually a few extra ones in between; times are posted at the pier, but if you have a plane to catch you should allow for boat delays. There are also regular departures from Ao Wong Duan, every two hours between 8.30am and 4.30pm and, in high season, you'll find at least one Ban Phe boat a day from Ao Cho and Ao Phrao.

Arriving at Ban Phe, you can pick up **buses** to Bangkok, Chanthaburi or Trat, or a songthaew to Rayong, from where buses to all these destinations, plus Pattaya and Si Racha, are far more frequent (see p.438). The Ban Phe bus and songthaew stop is 400m east of the 7–11, though most buses and songthaews pass the pier-head and will pick up passengers there. If you're heading straight back to Bangkok's Thanon Khao San, to Don Muang Airport or to Pattaya, your easiest (and most expensive) option is to buy a direct **minibus** ticket from one of Ko Samet's numerous tour operators; these tickets don't include the boat fare, but departure times from Ban Phe are arranged to coincide with boat arrivals. You can also book tourist minibuses at the tour operators' offices in Ban Phe on the little soi beside the 7–11 shop, across from the main pier, though they may not always have room for last-minute bookings. Travelling to **Ko Chang**, it takes just two and a half hours by tourist minibus from Ban Phe to the Laem Ngop pier, though it's expensive at B230 plus the boat fare; the alternative route by ordinary bus can take all day and often entails changing buses at Chanthaburi and then getting onto a Laem Ngop-bound songthaew in Trat, though it works out at half the price.

Island practicalities

Foreign visitors are charged the B200 national-park **entrance fee** on arrival (B100 for children under 14 or free for the under-3s), payable either at the checkpoint between the Na Dan pier and Hat Sai Kaew (where there is a national park visitor centre, with displays on Ko Samet's marine life); at the booth near the Ao Wong Duan pier; or on the beach at Ao Phrao. There is a sporadic **songthaew** service on Ko Samet, but you shouldn't rely on it as a way to travel between beaches. Songthaews start at Na Dan pier and drive as far as Wong Duan, down the potholed track that runs along the centre of the island; fares are posted at Na Dan pier and range from B10 to Hat Sai Kaew (or B100 if you charter the whole songthaew) to B50 to Ao Kiu (B500 to charter). There are **motorbikes** for rent on every beach (B100/hour or B400/day), but the tracks are pretty rough so not ideal for inexperienced riders.

Ko Samet's **health centre** and **police station** are in Na Dan, and the island's **post office** is run by *Naga Bungalows* on Ao Hin Kok; they offer a poste restante service as well as basic postal facilities (see p.445 for details). There are **international phone services** and **Internet access** at *Naga*, and at the bigger bungalow operations on every main beach. The biggest bungalows also **change money**, though rates are less favourable than on the mainland. In Na Dan and on Hat Sai Kaew, Ao Phai, Tub Tim and Ao Wong Duan, small shops sell basic travellers' necessities, again at higher prices than in Ban Phe and Rayong. CP Travel (Ⓣ038 644208) on Hat Sai Kaew, beside the main track on the edge of the *White Sand* complex, sells domestic and international **air tickets** as well as minibus tickets and package tours.

Samet has no fresh **water**, so water is trucked in from the mainland and should be used sparingly; **electricity** in many places is rationed for evening consumption only.

Around the island

Most of the islanders not associated with the tourist trade live in the **northeast** of the island, near Na Dan, where there are a few shops and foodstalls, as well as the island's only school, health centre and wat. Samet's best **beaches** are along the **east coast**, and this is where you'll find nearly all the bungalow resorts. A rough track connects some of them; otherwise it's a question of walking along the beach at low tide or over the low, rocky points at high water. Long stretches of the **west coast** are well-nigh inaccessible, though at intervals the coastal scrub has been cleared to make way for a track. The views from these clifftop clearings can be magnificent, particularly around sunset, but you can only safely descend to sea level at Ao Phrao, near the northwest headland. A few narrow tracks cross the island's forested central ridge to link the east and west coasts, but much of the **interior** is dense jungle, home of hornbills, gibbons and spectacular butterflies.

Samet has no decent coral reefs of its own, so you'll have to take a boat trip to the islands of Ko Kudi, Ko Thalu and Ko Mun, off the northeast coast, to get good **snorkelling** and **fishing**. Trips cost from B500 to B1000 including equipment, and depart from all the main beaches. Some places also offer full-day boat trips around Samet itself for about B400. Despite the lack of great reefs (it's hard coral only around here) there are a couple of **dive operators** on Samet: Ploy Scuba (Ⓣ06 143 9318) on Hat Sai Kaew, and Ao Prao Divers (Ⓣ038 644100, Ⓔaopraodivers@hotmail.com), at *Ao Prao Resort* on Ao Phrao. Four-day Openwater courses cost B12,000 and day-trips with two tanks cost about B2500.

Hat Sai Kaew

Arriving at **Na Dan** pier, a ten-minute walk south along the track brings you to **HAT SAI KAEW**, or Diamond Beach, named for its long and extraordinarily beautiful stretch of luxuriant sand, so soft and clean it squeaks underfoot – a result, apparently, of its unusually high silicon content, which also makes it an excellent raw material for glass-making. Songthaews from Na Dan to Hat Sai Kaew cost B10 per person, or B100 when chartered.

The most popular – and congested – beach on Samet, Hat Sai Kaew's shore is lined with bungalows, restaurants, beachwear stalls, deckchairs and parasols; the northern end is usually slightly more peaceful than the southern. Holidaying Thais and farangs flock here in pretty much equal numbers, especially at weekends, but big groups of day-tripping package tourists make stretches of the beach almost unbearable from around 11am to 4pm.

At night, you have the option of enjoying a leisurely dinner at one of the large, pricey seafront seafood **restaurants**, watching videos at one of the bungalow cafés, hanging out at the beachside *Reggae Bar*, or heading up the track that connects Hat Sai Kaew with the pier at Na Dan, where you'll find congenial little drinking dens such as *Blue Bar* and *Island Bar*. Another pleasant place to while away the evening is *The Umbrella* bungalows behind the wat, whose delightful restaurant is set beside a lotus pond and serves Thai dishes and cocktails.

There is **Internet access** at several places on the beach, and you can arrange **dive** trips through Ploy Scuba.

Accommodation

Such is the popularity of this beach that most of the **accommodation** here is crammed uncomfortably close together and in high season it's impossible to

△ Phra Abhai Mani's mermaid on Ao Hin Kok

find a room by the sea for under B500. However, if you ask at the little bars on the track in from Na Dan pier, between the police station and the national park visitors' centre, you may be able to rent one of their urban guest-house style rooms for a more affordable price (❷).

Banana ⓣ02 438 9771, ⓦwww.aopraoresort.com. Part of the *Sai Kaew Beach Resort*, but on its own secluded patch of coast and in a style class of its own, this is the most desirable accommodation on Hat Sai Kaew, if not the entire island. The vibe is funky-beach chic, with contemporary colour schemes, garden bathrooms, and a swing on every deck. The bungalows occupy their own grassy haven in front of a pretty but unswimmable shoreline and are only a few minutes' walk from the beach in front of *Sai Kaew Beach*. ❾

Nampet Ploy Laem Yai Resort ⓣ038 644077. Decent, comfortable wooden bungalows with fan or air-con occupy one of the prettiest spots on the beach, under the Laem Yai headland at the nicest, far northern end of Hat Sai Kaew. ❻–❽

Sai Kaew Beach Resort ⓣ02 438 9771, ⓦwww.aopraoresort.com. Distinctive and very stylish blue-and-white bungalows, thoughtfully designed, and a cut above everywhere else on this beach except sister outfit *Banana*. All bungalows have phones, TV and air-con and the priciest have uninterrupted sea views. ❾

Sai Kaew Villa ⓣ038 644144, ⓦwww.saikaew.com. Set in attractively landscaped gardens, this large and efficiently run place comprises a dozen smart, clean rooms with fan or air-con in a hotel-like block, plus some prettier, more expensive bungalows. The price drops a little for every night you stay. Also has Internet access. ❺–❽

Samed Grand View Resort ⓣ09 244 1382, ⓕ038 644219. Bungalows here are built to an unimaginative standard concrete-and-tile design but are at least widely spaced around a garden. Though they're nothing exceptional, the fan rooms are the cheapest on the beach; air-con costs twice as much. ❹–❻

The Umbrella ⓣ038 644221, ⓦwww.theumbrella.net. An inviting, arty little hotel, located inland, behind *Banana* and the wat, but just a couple of minutes' walk from the beach. Run by a Thai artist, the two-storey bungalows are a modern take on traditional Thai design, with sleeping quarters upstairs and a living area and bathroom at entry level. Also has a charming bar-restaurant. ❺–❼

White Sand Resort ⓣ038 644000. This huge complex of standard-issue bungalows in a garden set back from the shorefront dominates the southern end of the beach. Rooms here are unexciting but relatively well priced for this beach, and there's a choice between fan or air-con. ❺–❻

Ao Hin Kok

Separated from Hat Sai Kaew by a low promontory on which sits a mermaid statue – a reference to Sunthorn Phu's early nineteenth-century poem, *Phra Abhai Mani* (see box on p.446) – **AO HIN KOK** is smaller and less cluttered than its neighbour, and has more of a travellers' vibe. There are three congenial bungalow outfits here, overlooking the beach from the slope on the far side of the track. **Songthaews** from Na Dan will drop you at Ao Hin Kok for B20 per person (or B150 when chartered), or you can walk here in about fifteen minutes.

The English-run *Naga Bungalows* (ⓣ038 644167; ❷–❹) has the cheapest **accommodation** on Ko Samet, in the shape of simple plank huts with decks, mosquito nets, platform beds and shared facilities; it also has pricier concrete bungalows with their own adjacent bathroom. It's extremely popular, and has a library as well. Next door, the unusual blue-painted bungalows at *Tok's Little Hut* (ⓣ038 644072; ❸–❺) are built high on stilts up the slope and so all enjoy some kind if view from their verandas; they're en suite and comfortable inside and rate as pretty good value for Samet – price depends on whether you want fan or air-con. *Jep's Bungalow* (ⓣ038 644112, ⓦwww.jepbungalow.com; ❺–❼) has the most upmarket accommodation, much of it in smart wooden chalets with air-con, though some cheaper fan rooms are available.

Ao Hin Kok is a particularly good beach for food, with all three bungalows offering exceptional fare at their **restaurants**. *Naga* is especially recommended for its vegetarian dishes, cocktails and home-made bread and cakes; it also stages regular pool competitions and puts on fire-juggling shows. *Tok's Little Hut* is known for its seafood, but *Jep's* is deservedly the most popular of the three, serving up a great menu of authentic Thai curries, seafood, home-made pizzas, brownies and other travellers' fare at its tables on the beach, prettily decorated with lights in the trees and given extra atmosphere by mellow music. A nearby cappuccino stall does various fresh and liqueur coffees.

Ko Samet **post office** is run out of *Naga Bungalows* and offers a parcel-packing, phone, fax and **Internet** service as well as poste restante; letters are kept for three months and should be addressed c/o Poste Restante, Ko Samet Post Office, Naga Bungalows, Ko Samet.

Ao Phai

The presence of a couple of small bars around the next collection of rocks, on **AO PHAI**, and the frequent parties held on the beach here at *Silver Sand*, make this one of Ko Samet's livelier places to stay, though the beach itself is narrow and the accommodation patchy at best. There's a minimarket on the beach, and *Sea Breeze* has a small library, sells boat trips and minibus tickets, rents out windsurfing equipment and offers overseas telephone and money-exchange facilities. **Songthaews** from Na Dan cost B20 per person to Ao Phai (or B150 when chartered), or you can walk it in twenty minutes.

Ao Phai Hut (ⓣ038 644075; ❸–❼) sits on the rocky divide between Ao Phai and Hin Kok and offers a big range of rather variable **huts**, the more basic ones set in a scruffy area among the trees, the pricier options, some of them with air-con, occupying a more scenic spot overlooking the rocky end of the shore; electricity is only available in the evenings. *Sea Breeze* (ⓣ038 644124, ⓕ038 644125; ❹–❺) is the largest set of bungalows on the beach, offering primitive wooden huts, more solid concrete ones and bigger versions with air-con; as they're built up an unappealingly sparse wooded slope, none has a sea view. The adjacent *Silver Sand* (ⓣ01 996 5720; ❹–❻) has decent, well-maintained bungalows with nice bathrooms, the price depending on distance from the sea (the cheapest ones are quite far back, with no view and some unsightly rubbish nearby), and whether or not you want air-con. The sturdy chalet-style bungalows at the well-appointed *Samed Villa* (ⓣ01 494 8090, ❺–❽) are scenically sited along the rocks and up the slope behind the restaurant, so most have a sea view; they are all comfortably and quite stylishly designed inside and the price depends on whether or not you want air-con.

Ao Tub Tim

Also known as Ao Pudsa, **AO TUB TIM** is a small white-sand bay sandwiched between rocky points, partly shaded with palms and backed by a wooded slope. It has just two bungalow operations and feels secluded, but is only a short stroll from Ao Phai and the other beaches further north, so you get the best of both worlds. *Pudsa Bungalows* organizes boat trips, and has Internet access and money-exchange facilities. **Songthaews** will bring you here from Na Dan pier for B20 per person (or B150 when chartered), or you can walk it in about thirty minutes.

The smaller, more welcoming of the two **places to stay** on Tub Tim, *Pudsa Bungalows* (ⓣ038 644030; ❹–❺) offers a range of pretty nice, large and sturdy huts, especially the priciest ones, which sit alongside the track and enjoy direct sea views. The restaurant here occupies an appealing site on the sand, with several tables fixed under the palm trees. Next door, the sprawling *Tub Tim Resort* (ⓣ038 644025, ⓦwww.tubtimresort.com; ❹–❻) comprises around

Sunthorn Phu and Phra Abhai Mani

Over thirty thousand lines long and written entirely in verse, the nineteenth-century romantic epic **Phra Abhai Mani** tells the story of a young prince and his adventures in a fantastical land peopled not only by giants and mermaids, but also by gorgeous women with whom he invariably falls in love. Seduced by an ogress who lives beneath the sea, and kept captive by her for several months, Phra Abhai Mani pines for dry land and eventually persuades a mermaid to help him escape. Naturally, the two fall in love, and decide to spend some time together on the nearby island of Ko Samet (hence the mermaid statue on Ao Hin Kok). But the prince soon tires of the mermaid's charms, and leaps aboard a passing ship in pursuit of another ill-fated affair, this time with a princess already engaged to someone else. And so it goes on.

Widely considered to be one of Thailand's greatest-ever poets, **Sunthorn Phu** (1786–1856) is said to have based much of his work on his own life, and the romantic escapades of *Phra Abhai Mani* are no exception. By all accounts, the man was a colourful character – a philandering commoner alternately in and out of favour at Bangkok's Grand Palace, where he lived and worked for much of his life. By the time Rama II ascended the throne in 1809, he was well established as the court poet, acting as literary aide to the king. However, he took to the bottle, was left by his wife and participated in a drunken fight that landed him in jail. It was during this stint inside (estimated to be around 1821) that he started work on *Phra Abhai Mani*. The poem took twenty years to complete and was rented out in instalments to provide the poet with a modest income – necessary as royal patronage was withdrawn during the reign of Rama III (1824–51), whose literary efforts Sunthorn Phu had once rashly criticized, and only revived when Rama IV was crowned in 1851.

Aside from authoring several timeless romances, Sunthorn Phu is remembered as a significant **poetic innovator**. Up until the end of the eighteenth century, Thai poetry had been the almost exclusive domain of high-born courtiers and kings, written in an elevated Thai incomprehensible to most of the population, and concerned mainly with the moral Hindu epics the *Mahabarata* and the *Ramayana* (see p.127). Sunthorn Phu changed all that by writing of love triangles, thwarted romances and heartbreaking departures; he also composed travel poems, or *nirat*, about his own journeys to well-known places in Thailand. Most crucially, he wrote them all in the common, easy-to-understand language of vernacular Thai. Not surprisingly, he's still much admired. In the province of Rayong, he's the focus of a special memorial park, constructed, complete with statues of his most famous fictional characters, on the site of his father's home in Klaeng.

sixty bungalows of various sizes and comfort, from small, scruffy wooden huts at the back through to palatial air-conditioned wooden chalets by the sea.

Ao Nuan

Clamber up over the next headland (which gives you a panoramic take on the expanse of Hat Sai Kaew) to reach Samet's smallest beach, the secluded **AO NUAN**. Although not brilliant for swimming, the rocky shore reveals a good patch of sand when the tide withdraws, and the better beach at Ao Tub Tim is only five minutes' walk away. The best way to get to Ao Nuan from the pier is to take a **songthaew** from Na Dan for B20 per person (B150 when chartered).

The atmosphere here is relaxed and much less commercial than the other beaches, and the mellow restaurant of the friendly *Ao Nuan* has some of the best veggie food on the island. Because it's some way off the main track, the beach gets hardly any through traffic and so feels quiet and private. The huts are idiosyncratic (❸–❺), each built to a slightly different design (some circular, some A-frame, some thatched), and dotted across the slope that drops down to the bay; a few are built right over the beach. They're all spartanly furnished – the cheapest have just a mattress on the floor and a mosquito net, and all share bathrooms; price depends on the size and the location.

Ao Cho

A five-minute walk south along the track from Ao Nuan brings you to **AO CHO**, a fairly wide stretch of beach with just a couple of bungalow operations plus a pier, a minimarket and motorbikes for rent. Despite being long and partially shaded, this beach seems less popular than the others, so it may be a good place to try if you want a low-key atmosphere, or if the bungalows on other beaches are packed out. There's some coral off the end of the pier, and you can rent snorkelling gear on the beach. It's also possible to arrange night-time trips on a squid boat, available through *Wonderland* for B5000 per boat (up to about twenty passengers). *Tarn Tawan* rents motorbikes for B100 per hour or B500 per day. The easiest way to get to Ao Cho is to take a **boat** to Ao Wong Duan and then walk here, or you could take the normal boat to Na Dan and then hang around for a songthaew (B30).

Wonderland (Ⓣ & Ⓕ038 644168; ❷–❽) has some of the cheapest **bungalows** on Ko Samet which, though small and basic and away from the shore, do have fans and private bathrooms; they also have lots of better bungalows with air-con and sea views. Adjacent *Tarn Tawan Resort* (Ⓣ038 644070; Ⓔisland tour1999@hotmail.com; ❸–❻) is a much more characterful place to stay: the charming, well-priced, whitewashed bungalows here are set around a peaceful lawn and decorated with shell mobiles and pale-blue-and-pink paintwork; you pay more for a direct sea view. They also have some cheap fan and poor-value air-con rooms in an ugly block at the back.

Ao Wong Duan

The horseshoe bay of **AO WONG DUAN**, round the next headland, is dominated by mid-range and upmarket bungalow resorts and is popular with package tourists, older couples and sophisticated Bangkokians. Although the beach is fairly long and broad, it suffers from revving jet-skis and an almost continual stream of day-trippers, the shorefront is fringed with a rash of beach bars and tourist shops, and the main stretch of beach almost disappears at high tide. Facilities include minimarts, motorbike rental, money exchange, Internet access and overseas telephone services. There's a national-park booth on the beach, where you must pay your B200 entry fee if alighting from a Ban Phe boat, and a police box. At least four direct **boats** a day should run from Na Dan to Wong Duan (see p.440 for details), and vice versa. Alternatively, take a boat to Na Dan, then a B30 ride in a songthaew (or a B200 taxi ride). If you're in a hurry to get to the mainland you can charter a seven-person speedboat from the Wong Duan pier to Ban Phe for B1000.

Accommodation

Malibu Garden Resort Ⓣ038 644020, Ⓦwww.malibu-samet.com. Huge, efficiently run, package-oriented outfit whose white-washed concrete bungalows are set round a shady tropical garden with a small swimming pool. The rooms are uninspiring but decent enough and all come with air-con and TV. ❼–❾

Samed Cabana Ⓣ01 838 4853. Large wood and concrete bungalows reasonably well spaced around the shorefront at the northern end of the beach, many enjoying a decent sea view. All bungalows have a fan and bathroom. ❹–❺

Taléburé Bed and Bar Ⓣ01 862 9402, Ⓔtalebure@hotmail.com. One of Samet's new breed of contemporary-chic boutique-style bungalows, bringing a Bangkok vibe to the beach. The look here is minimalist, with bungalows constructed from whitewashed timbers and kitted out with dark-wood floors and Japanese-style platform beds and low-seating. The most deluxe options are nicest, being large, detached and enjoying fine views. There's an attractive restaurant deck jutting out over the water. ❼–❽

Vong Duan Resort ⓣ038 651777, ⓕ038 651819. The bungalows here are attractively designed inside and out, all have air-con, and stand around a pretty tropical garden. Price depends on proximity to the sea. ❻–❾

Wong Duan Villa ⓣ038 652300, ⓕ038 651741. This is a fun place to stay, with lots of character, if not quite pristine. The white-plank huts are built on stilts and have picture windows, decks (some with sea view), modern furnishings and contemporary style low beds. Choose between fan or air-con, though electricity is only available at night. ❺–❼

Ao Thian (Candlelight Beach)

AO THIAN (also known as Candlelight Beach) has none of the commerce of Wong Duan, a couple of minutes' walk over the hill, though its lovely, scenic shorefront is fronted by an unbroken line of bungalows and little restaurants. The narrow, white-sand bay is dotted with wave-smoothed rocks and partitioned by larger outcrops that create several distinct beaches; as it curves outwards to the south you get a great view of the island's east coast. The best way to get here is to take a boat from Ban Phe to Ao Wong Duan and then walk.

At the northern end, *Sang Thien Beach Resort* (ⓣ01 295 9567; ❺–❻) offers compact but attractive brick **bungalows** with big glass windows (though no real view) and comfy interiors with fan or air-con. Across the track, and for the most part built high on the slope and so affording decent outlooks, *Mr Daeng* (or *Candlelight Beach*; ⓣ01 762 9387; ❺) has a handful of cosy little fan rooms. Further down the shore, the plain but decent bungalows belonging to *Candlelight Resort* (ⓣ01 153 3813; ❺) are strung out in a long line, with each one facing the water.

Ao Kiu

You have to really like the solitary life to plump for Samet's most isolated beach, **AO KIU**, over an hour's walk south of Ao Thian through unadulterated wilderness – the track begins behind *Vong Duan Resort* and can be joined at the southern end of Ao Thian. It's actually two beaches: Ao Kiu Na Nok on the east coast and Ao Kiu Na Nai on the west, separated by a few hundred metres of scrub and coconut grove. The bungalows here belong to *Ao Kiu Coral Beach* (ⓣ038 652561; ❸–❺), and most are set among the palms on the east shore, although a couple look down on the tiny west-coast coral beach; you can also rent tents here for B300.

The most convenient way of **getting here** is by direct boat from the mainland; during high season at least one *Coral Beach* boat makes the run daily – call to check departure times. Songthaews here from Na Dan cost B50 per person or B500 to charter.

Ao Phrao (Paradise Bay)

Across on the west coast, the rugged, rocky coastline only softens into beach once – at **AO PHRAO**, also known as Paradise Bay, on the northwestern stretch, some 4km north of Ao Kiu Na Nai. This is Samet's most exclusive beach, dominated by two exceptionally elegant – and expensive – resorts, with only one slightly more affordable option available. If you're only visiting for the day, the most direct route from the east-coast beaches is via the inland track from behind *Sea Breeze* on Ao Phai, which takes about twenty minutes on foot, though the track from the back of *Tub Tim* on Ao Tub Tim will also get you there. If staying here, your hotel will arrange **boat** transfers from Ban Phe's private Sri Ban Phe pier, or you can come by songthaew from Na Dan for B30 per person, or B200 on charter.

Ao Prao Resort (Ⓣ02 438 9771, Ⓦwww.aopraoresort.com; ⑨) boasts some of the most luxurious **accommodation** on the island, with comfortable wooden chalets set in a mature tropical garden that slopes down to the beach. All chalets have air-con, TVs and balconies overlooking the sea; rooms are discounted on weekdays, but advance booking is advisable for any time of the week. There's a dive centre here (see p.442), Internet access and an overseas phone service, as well as a serenely sited restaurant that juts out over the water. The even more indulgent *Le Vimarn Cottages* (Ⓣ02 438 9771, Ⓦwww.aopraoresort.com; ⑨) is owned by the same company and comprises charming and gorgeously furnished cottages, a delightful spa and a swimming pool; prices start from B7000. *Lima Coco* (Ⓣ09 105 7080, Ⓦwww.limacoco.com; ⑧) caters for slightly more modest budgets and comprises pleasant air-con bungalows built up the side of a small slope, most with sea views.

Chanthaburi

For over five hundred years, the seams of rock rich in sapphires and rubies that streak the hills of eastern Thailand have drawn prospectors and traders of all nationalities to the provincial capital of **CHANTHABURI**, 80km east of Ban Phe. Many of these hopefuls established permanent homes in the town, particularly the Shans from Burma, the Chinese and the Cambodians. Though the veins of precious stones have now been all but exhausted, Chanthaburi's reputation as a gem centre has continued to thrive and this is still the most famous place in Thailand to trade in gems (most of them now imported from Sri Lanka and elsewhere), not least because Chanthaburi is as respected a cutting centre as Bangkok, and Thai lapidaries are considered among the most skilled – not to mention most affordable – in the world.

Chanthaburi's largest ethnic group are Catholic refugees from Vietnam, vast numbers of whom arrived here in the wake of the recurrent waves of religious persecution between the eighteenth century and the late 1970s. The French, too, have left their mark: during their occupation of Chanthaburi from 1893 to 1905, when they held the town hostage against the fulfilment of a territorial treaty on the Lao border, they undertook the restoration and enlargement of the town's Christian cathedral. This cultural diversity makes Chanthaburi an engaging place, even if there's less than a day's worth of sights here. Built on the wiggly west bank of the Maenam Chanthaburi, the town fans out westwards for a couple of kilometres, though the most interesting parts are close to the river, in the district where the **Vietnamese families** are concentrated. Here, along Thanon Rim Nam, the narrow road running parallel to the river, the town presents a mixture of pastel-painted, colonial-style housefronts and traditional wooden shophouses, some with finely carved latticework.

Continuing south along this road, you'll reach a footbridge on the other side of which stands Thailand's largest **cathedral**: the Church of the Immaculate Conception. There's thought to have been a church on this site ever since the first Christians arrived in town, though the present structure was revamped in French style in the late nineteenth century. West of the bridge, the **gem dealers' quarter** begins, centred around Trok Kachang and Thanon Sri Chan (the latter signed in English as "Gem Street") and packed with dozens of gem shops. Most of the shops lie empty during the week, but on Fridays, Saturdays and Sunday mornings they come alive as local dealers arrive to sift through mounds of tiny coloured stones, peering at them through microscopes and classifying them for resale to the hundreds of buyers who drive down from Bangkok.

Chanthaburi has a reputation for high-grade fruit too, notably durian, rambutan and mangosteen, all grown in the orchards around the town and sold in the daily **market**, a couple of blocks northwest of the gem quarter. Basketware products made from woven reeds are also a good buy here, mostly made by the Vietnamese.

West of the market and gem quarter, the landscaped **Taksin Park** is the town's recreation area and memorial to King Taksin of Thonburi, the general who reunited Thailand between 1767 and 1782 after the sacking of Ayutthaya by the Burmese. Chanthaburi was the last Burmese bastion on the east coast – when Taksin took the town he effectively regained control of the whole country. The park's heroic bronze statue of Taksin is featured on the back of the B20 note.

Practicalities

Even if you're not planning a visit to Chanthaburi, you may find yourself stranded here for a couple of hours between **buses**, as this is a major transit point for east-coast services (including most Rayong–Trat buses) and a handy terminus for buses to and from the northeast. Eight daily buses make

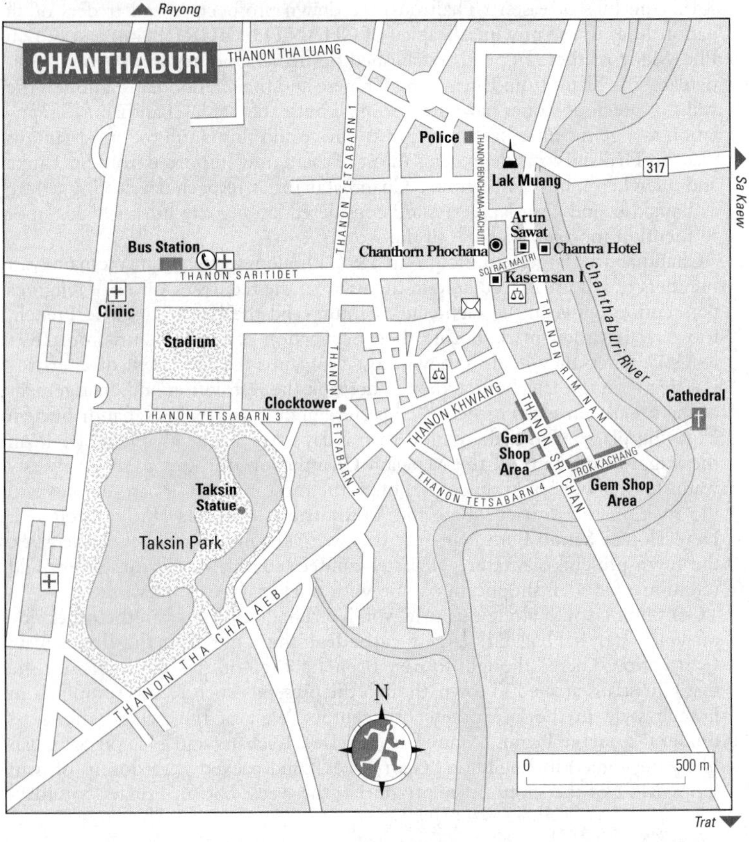

the scenic six-hour Chanthaburi–Sa Kaew–Khorat journey in both directions, with Sa Kaew being a useful interchange for buses to **Aranyaprathet and the Cambodian border** (see box below for details of this border-crossing and two other crossings in Chanthaburi province). Buses to and from all these places, as well as Bangkok's Eastern (Ekamai) and Northern (Mo Chit) stations, use the Chanthaburi **bus station** (Ⓣ039 311299) on Thanon Saritidet, about 750m northwest of the town centre and market. There are several **banks** with ATMs on Thanon Khwang, and some **Internet** centres along Thanon Tetsabarn 2.

The best-located **accommodation** options are near the river. The main hotel here is *Kasemsan 1* (Ⓣ & Ⓕ039 312340; ❷–❺), less than ten minutes' walk east of the bus station at 98/1 Thanon Benchama-Rachutit; choose between the sizeable, clean rooms with fan and bathroom on the noisy street side, and the similar but more expensive air-con ones in the quieter section. Down by the river, the small and basic but friendly *Arun Sawat* (Ⓣ039 311082; ❶–❷) has cell-like en-suite rooms with fan or air-con and is in the heart of the Vietnamese part of town; across the road, the similar *Chantra Hotel* (Ⓣ039 312310; ❶–❸) has the edge because some of its rooms offer river views. The most traveller-friendly **restaurant** in this area is *Chanthorn Phochana*, just north of the Saritidet

Overland into Cambodia via Aranyaprathet–Poipet and Chanthaburi province

The most commonly used **overland crossing into Cambodia** is at **Poipet**, which lies just across the border from the Thai town of **Aranyaprathet**. The border here is open daily from 7am to 8pm and officials will issue thirty-day Cambodian **visas on arrival** (see Basics p.18 for details, and Ⓦwww.talesofasia.com/cambodia-overland-bkksr-self.htm for a very detailed description of the crossing). Once through the border, you face a gruelling eight- to twelve-hour journey in the back of a pick-up to cover the 150km of potholed road between Poipet and Siem Reap. If you need a **hotel** in Aranyaprathet, try either the comfortable fan and air-con rooms at *Inter Hotel* on Thanon Chatasingh (Ⓣ037 231291; ❸–❺), or the cheaper *Aran Garden II* at 110 Thanon Rat Uthit (❷–❹).

Travelling to Poipet from east-coast towns, the easiest route is to take a bus **from Chanthaburi** to the town of **Sa Kaew**, 130km to the northeast, and then change to one of the frequent buses for the 55-kilometre ride east to Aranyaprathet. **From Bangkok**, the easiest way to get to Aranyaprathet is by **train**: there are two services a day, which take about six hours; you'll need to catch the one at 5.55am to ensure reaching the border before 5pm; the other leaves at 1.05pm. Return trains depart Aranyaprathet at 6.35am and 1.35pm. Tuk-tuks will take you the 4km from the train station to the border post. Alternatively, take a **bus** from Bangkok's Northern (Mo Chit) Bus Terminal to Aranyaprathet (4 daily until 5.30pm; 4hr 30min), then a tuk-tuk from the bus station to the border. The last Aranyaprathet–Bangkok bus leaves at 5pm. It's also possible to buy a **through ticket to Siem Reap** from Bangkok from almost any travel agent in Banglamphu for about B1600; transport is by minibus to the border and then by pick-up to Siem Reap.

There are also two less-used crossings in **Chanthaburi province**, giving access to the Cambodian town of **Pailin**, just east of the border. Daung Lem Border Crossing at **Ban Laem** is 88km northeast of Chanthaburi and the Phsa Prom border crossing is at **Ban Pakkard** (aka Chong Phakkat), 72km northeast of Chanthaburi. Both border points are accessible by chartered songthaew from the town of **Pong Nam Ron**, 42km north of Chanthaburi on Highway 317. Songthaews from Chanthaburi to Pong Nam Ron take about ninety minutes. The borders are open daily from 7am to 8pm, but at the time of writing do not issue **visas** on arrival.

intersection on Thanon Benchama-Rachutit, which has an English-language menu listing its mouthwatering range of spicy *yam* salads, curries and stir-fries; the restaurant also has a decent vegetarian section and features local Chateau de Klaeng wine. Otherwise, check out the foodstalls in the market and along the riverside soi for Vietnamese spring rolls (*cha gio*) served with sweet sauce, and for the locally made Chanthaburi rice noodles (*kway tiaw Chanthaburi*).

Trat and around

Most travellers who find themselves in or around the provincial capital of **Trat** are heading either for the island of Ko Chang, via the nearby port at **Laem Ngop**, or for Cambodia, via the border at **Hat Lek**, 91km southeast of town. But Trat itself has a certain charm and lots of welcoming guest houses to tempt you into staying longer, so it's no great hardship to be stuck here between connections.

Trat

The small and pleasantly unhurried market town of **TRAT**, 68km east of Chanthaburi, is the perfect place to stock up on essentials, extend your visa, or simply take a break, before striking out for Ko Chang, the outer islands, or Cambodia. Though there are no real sights in town, the historic neighbourhood down by Khlong Trat, where you'll find most of the guest houses and traveller-oriented restaurants, is full of characterful old wooden shophouses and narrow, atmospheric sois. The covered market in the heart of town is another fun place to wander, though for focused explorations rent a bicycle and ride out to the attractively ornate seventeenth-century Wat Buppharam, 2km west of Trat Department Store.

Trat is famous across Thailand for the **yellow herbal oil** mixture, *yaa luang*, invented by one of its residents, Mae Ang Ki, and used by Thais to treat many ailments: sniff it for travel sickness or rub it on to relieve mosquito and sandfly bites, ease stomach cramps, or sterilize wounds. Ingredients include camphor and aloe vera. You can buy the oil in lip-gloss-size bottles at the market and at Tratosphere bookshop (B80–100); there are now several imitations, but Mae Ang Ki's original product has a tree logo to signify that it's made by royal appointment.

Transport and information

Trat is served by lots of **buses** from Bangkok's Eastern (Ekamai) Bus Terminal (5–6hr), and by some from Bangkok's Northern (Mo Chit) Bus Terminal as well (4hr 30min), and also has useful bus connections with Ban Phe (for Ko Samet), Chanthaburi, Pattaya and Si Racha. All buses drop passengers somewhere on the central four-hundred-metre stretch of Thanon Sukhumvit, mostly at the relevant bus office as shown on the map opposite. Buses also depart from these different spots. Songthaews **to Laem Ngop**, the departure point for ferries to **Ko Chang** and the outer islands, leave from the east side of Thanon Sukhumvit, near the covered market; for details on getting to Laem Ngop see p.455 and for transport to Ko Chang see p.456. Minibuses to **Hat Lek** and the **Cambodian border** also leave from near the covered market on Thanon Sukhumvit: see the box on p.455 for details.

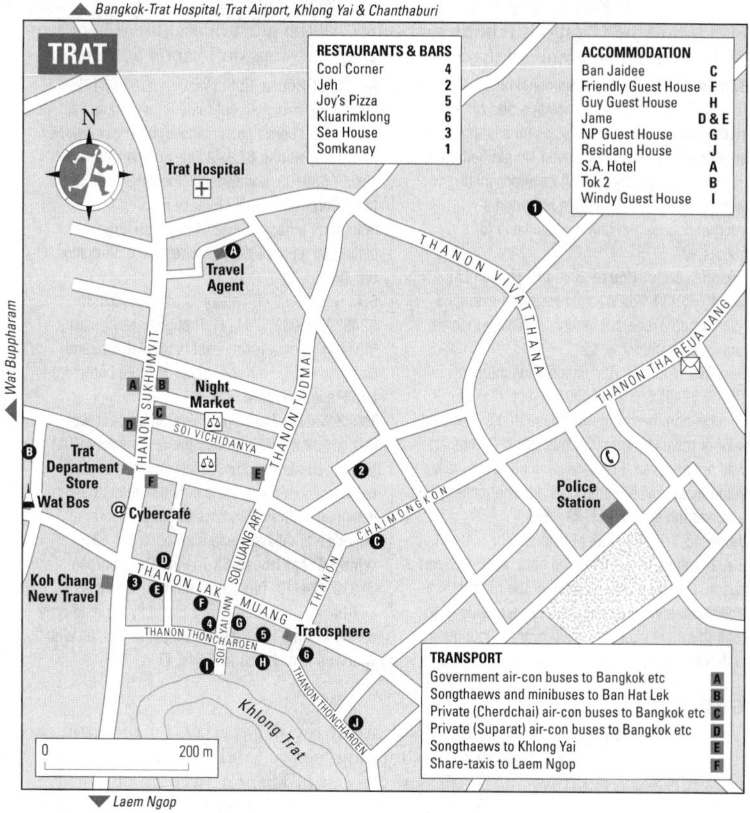

Tiny Trat **airport** (☎039 525767) is served by Bangkok Airways flights to and from Bangkok and Ko Samui. The airport is just 16km from the Ko Chang piers at Laem Ngop and there's a taxi service direct from the airport to Ko Chang hotels for B180–230 per person, including ferry ticket. Trat town is a thirty-minute, B120 taxi ride from the airport. Note that when flying out of Trat, there's a B200 domestic departure tax because it's a private airport. The Bangkok Airways office (☎039 525299) is on the northern edge of town, just beyond the Highway 317 turn-off to Khlong Yai, across from the Bangkok-Trat Hospital.

Trat's official **TAT** office is in Laem Ngop (see p.456), but any guest house will help you out with local **information**. Alternatively, drop by the Tratosphere bookshop at 23 Soi Kluarimklong for tips from the knowledgeable owner and a copy of the free quarterly, *Koh Chang, Trat and the Eastern Islands*, or visit *Cool Corner* restaurant (see p.454) for a browse through the legendary travellers' comment books.

Accommodation

Guest houses in Trat are small, friendly and inexpensive places, most of them very much traveller-oriented and run by well-informed local people who are used to providing up-to-date information on transport to Ko Chang, the outer islands, and the Cambodian border crossings. All the guest houses listed here are within ten minutes' walk of the bus and songthaew stops on Thanon Sukhumvit.

Ban Jaidee 67 Thanon Chaimongkon ⓣ039 520678. Very calm, inviting and rather stylish guest house with a pleasant seating area downstairs and just seven simple bedrooms upstairs, the nicest of which have polished wood floors. All rooms share bathrooms. Internet access and bicycles available for guests. ❶

Friendly Guest House 106–110 Thanon Lak Muang ⓣ039 524053. Rooms in the extended home of an exuberant family; all have windows and share bathrooms. ❶

Guy Guest House 82 Thanon Thoncharoen ⓣ039 524556, ⓔguy_gh2001@hotmail.com. Popular, commercial guest house that sweeps up a lot of travellers from the bus stops. Rooms are well priced, even if they do have plyboard walls; some have private bathrooms. Internet access and a restaurant downstairs. ❶–❷

Jame 45/1 Thanon Lak Muang ⓣ039 530458. Eleven rooms, all with shared bath, split between two houses on opposite sides of the road. At the traditional-style house on the northern side of the road there are cooking facilities and a lounge area with a VCD player. ❶

NP Guest House 10 Soi Yai Onn ⓣ039 512270. Friendly, with simple but fair enough rooms with shared bathrooms; not all of them have windows. ❶

Residang House 87/1–2 Thanon Thoncharoen ⓣ039 530103. Comfortably appointed if slightly faded three-storey place that's more of a small hotel than a guest house. Rooms are large and clean and all have thick mattresses; bathrooms are shared. ❷

S.A. Hotel Just off Thanon Sukhumvit ⓣ039 524572, ⓕ039 524411. Though hardly deluxe, the best hotel in town is set in a quiet spot and comprises large air-con rooms, all with bathrooms and French windows. ❹

Tok 2 West of Trat Department Store, near Wat Bos ⓣ039 511793. One of the few places in Trat to offer en-suite rooms, which makes it a good-value option. Rooms are comfy if a little strangely designed, with no windows but glass doors. There's a small bar-restaurant out front. ❷

Windy Guest House 63 Thanon Thoncharoen ⓣ039 524419. Tiny wooden house with a very laid-back atmosphere that's perfectly situated right on the khlong. Has just five simple rooms, all with windows and shared facilities. ❶

Eating

Two of the best **places to eat** in Trat are at the day market, on the ground floor of the Thanon Sukhumvit shopping centre, and the night market, between Soi Vichidanya and Soi Kasemsan, east of Thanon Sukhumvit. For live music of an evening, try *Somkanay*, a Thai-style pub just off Thanon Vivatthana.

Cool Corner On the corner of Soi Yai Onn and Thanon Thoncharoen. Run almost single-handedly by a local writer/artist, this funky place has lots of personality, both in its cute blue-and-white decor, and in its traveller-oriented menu of wholewheat pasta dishes, home-made bread, real coffee, veggie specials and breakfast combos. A good place to while away an extra hour, listening to the mellow music and perusing the travellers' comment books that are full of first-hand info on Ko Chang, Ko Mak, Ko Whai and the Cambodia border crossings. Moderate.

Jeh No English sign, but follow the soi near *Ban Jaidee*, off Thanon Chaimongkon. Typical very cheap Thai vegetarian place, where you choose two portions of veggie curry, stir-fry or stew from the trays laid out on the counter, and pay about B25 including rice. Shuts about 2pm. Inexpensive.

Joy's Pizza Thanon Thoncharoen. Great range of home-made pizzas served in a chilled-out dining area furnished with low tables and groovy artwork. Expensive.

Kluarimklong Soi Kluarimklong. More Bangkok than Trat in its style and menu, this unexpectedly classy little place has both an indoor and a courtyard dining area and serves delicious, upmarket Thai food. The main focus is on seafood, along with lots of spicy *yam* salads and *tom yum* soups. Moderate.

Sea House On the corner of Thanon Lak Muang and Thanon Sukhumvit. Decked out with seashells fostering an invitingly artsy-folksy atmosphere, this place serves a standard range of Thai food and beer. Moderate.

Listings

Banks and exchange There are several banks along the central stretch of Thanon Sukhumvit.

Bookshops The French-Thai run Tratosphere, at 23 Soi Kluarimklong, buys and sells second-hand books and is a good source of local info; you can also buy curios from all over Thailand here, and

hammocks. Cybercafé near Trat Department Store on Thanon Sukhumvit stocks a few new books on Thailand.
Emergencies For all emergencies, call the tourist police on the free, 24hr phone line ⓣ1155, or contact the local police station off Thanon Vivatthana ⓣ039 511239.
Hospital The best hospital is the Bangkok-Trat Hospital ⓣ039 532735, on the Sukhumvit Highway, 1km north of Trat Department Store; it also offers dental care services.
Immigration office Located on the Trat–Laem Ngop road, 3km northeast of Laem Ngop pier (Mon–Fri 8.30am–4.30pm; ⓣ039 597261).
Internet access At many guest houses, at Cybercafé on Thanon Sukhumvit, and at the CAT overseas telephone office on Thanon Vivatthana.
Mail At the GPO on Thanon Tha Reua Jang.
Massage Ask at *Cool Corner*, Tratosphere, or any guest house for advice on where to go for a massage treatment or lesson.
Telephones The CAT overseas telephone office is on Thanon Vivatthana on the eastern edge of town (daily 7am–4.30pm).
Travel agencies International and domestic flights can be booked at Koh Chang New Travel on Thanon Sukhumvit ⓣ01 687 1112, and at the agency next to *S.A. Hotel*.

Laem Ngop

Ferries to Ko Chang and some of the outer islands currently leave from three different piers west along the coast from the port of **LAEM NGOP** (sometimes signed as Ngop Cape), 17km southwest of Trat. The only way to get to Laem Ngop by public transport is by share-taxi (**songthaew**) from Trat (see p.452). Songthaews leave Trat from the central stretch of Thanon Sukhumvit every half-hour or so; rides can take anything from twenty to forty minutes, excluding the time taken to gather a full complement of passengers, so leave plenty of time

Overland into Cambodia via Hat Lek–Koh Kong

Many travellers use the **Hat Lek–Koh Kong border crossing** (daily 7am–8pm) for overland travel into Cambodia, not least because thirty-day **visas on arrival** are issued here (see Basics p.18) and Koh Kong has reasonable transport connections to Sihanoukville and, via Sre Ambel, Phnom Penh. For a comprehensive guide to the crossing and to the various transport options on both sides of the border, see ⓦwww.talesofasia.com/cambodia-overland-bkkpp.htm, and check the travellers' comment books at *Cool Corner* restaurant in Trat (see opposite).

The only way to get to **Hat Lek** is by minibus from Trat, 91km northwest. **Minibuses** leave Trat approximately every 45 minutes between 6am and 5pm (1hr–1hr 30min; B100) from near the market on Thanon Sukhumvit. In the reverse direction, the timetable is almost the same.

Hat Lek (on the Thai side) and Koh Kong (in Cambodia) are on opposite sides of the Dong Tong River estuary, but a bridge connects the two banks. If you want to reach **Sihanoukville** in one day, you'll need to catch the 6am minibus from Trat, which should give you just enough time to catch the daily 8am **boat** to Sihanoukville from **Koh Kong** (sometimes referred to as Krong Koh Kong) across on the eastern bank of the estuary. To reach Koh Kong pier, you need to take a motorbike or car taxi from the Hat Lek immigration post, across the bridge, to Koh Kong on the east bank of the estuary. Shortly after leaving Koh Kong, the Sihanoukville boat makes a brief stop at **Pak Khlong** (aka Bak Kleng) at the (western) mouth of the estuary, which you can reach from the immigration post without having to go via Koh Kong. However, this involves taking a taxi-boat across open sea all the way down to the mouth of the estuary, and is reportedly not very safe as the boats – available for hire from the pier near the Hat Lek immigration post – are old.

If you leave Trat later in the day and need to overnight in Koh Kong, simply follow the route described above to Koh Kong pier. For a thorough guide to Koh Kong and how to reach it from both sides of the border, visit ⓦwww.kohkong.com/kohkong/overland.html.

to catch the boat. The usual songthaew fare is B20 per person with a full load or about B30 with a minimum of eight people; be sure to board a songthaew with people in it already, otherwise you'll find you've chartered your own taxi for B100. Songthaews will probably drop you first at the ferry-ticket offices in Laem Ngop, which are near the TAT office, at the old pier-head. Once you've bought your ticket you'll be driven to the correct pier: the passenger-ferry pier (for foot-passengers to Ko Chang, Ko Whai, Ko Mak and Ko Kham), which is known as Laem Ngop Monument Pier, or Tha Kromaluang Chumphorn, is a fifteen-minute walk from here. For details of **boat services** to Ko Chang, see p.458, and for boat services to the outer islands, see pp.469–471.

The Trat and Ko Chang **TAT office** (daily 8.30am–4.30pm; ⓣ039 597259, ⓔtatrat@ksc.th.com) is close by the ferry-ticket offices at the old pier-head and provides independent advice on the islands as well as current boat times (staff will also email you the latest schedules on request). You can change money at the Thai Farmers' Bank (usual banking hours), five minutes' walk back down the main road from TAT.

Ko Chang

The focal point of a national marine park archipelago of 52 islands, **KO CHANG** is Thailand's second-largest island (after Phuket), measuring 30km north to south and 8km across, and is mainly characterized by a chain of long, white-sand beaches and a broad central spine of jungle-clad hills, the highest of which, **Khao Salak Pet**, tops 740m. Until fairly recently the domain of just a few thousand fishing families and the odd adventurous tourist, Ko Chang has seen massive development in the last few years, with real estate going through the roof in 2001 when the government poured mega-bucks into the island, financing road-building projects and the construction of several upmarket resorts. As a result Ko Chang is now very much a mainstream destination – with prices to match – and in places still resembles a building site. Despite this, the hilly backbone and its waterfalls are protected as a national park, there has been some attempt to force hotels to apply for planning permission and to install water-treatment plants, and the island is very nearly encircled by a good road.

Ko Chang's west coast has the prettiest **beaches** and is the most developed, with **Hat Sai Khao** (White Sand Beach) drawing the biggest crowds to its mainly mid-range and upmarket accommodation; smaller, congested **Hat Kai Bae** is catching up fast. Most backpackers opt for **Hat Tha Nam**, known as **Lonely Beach**, with its choice of inexpensive beach huts and established party scene; travellers in search of quiet choose **central Hat Khlong Phrao** or the remote beaches at **Ao Bai Lan** and **Hat Bang Bao**. **Laem Chaichet** makes an appealing mid-range alternative. During **peak season**, accommodation on every beach tends to fill up very quickly, so it's often worth booking ahead; the island gets a lot quieter (and cheaper) from May to October, when fierce storms batter the huts and can make the sea too rough to swim in.

Transport to Ko Chang

All **boats** to Ko Chang depart from the Laem Ngop coast, about 17km southwest of the provincial capital of Trat. If you're coming by public transport from Bangkok, Pattaya, Ko Samet, the northeast or Cambodia you'll need to travel via Trat first. For information about Trat see p.452, and for details on getting to Laem Ngop see p.455. If travelling via Trat airport, you can get a

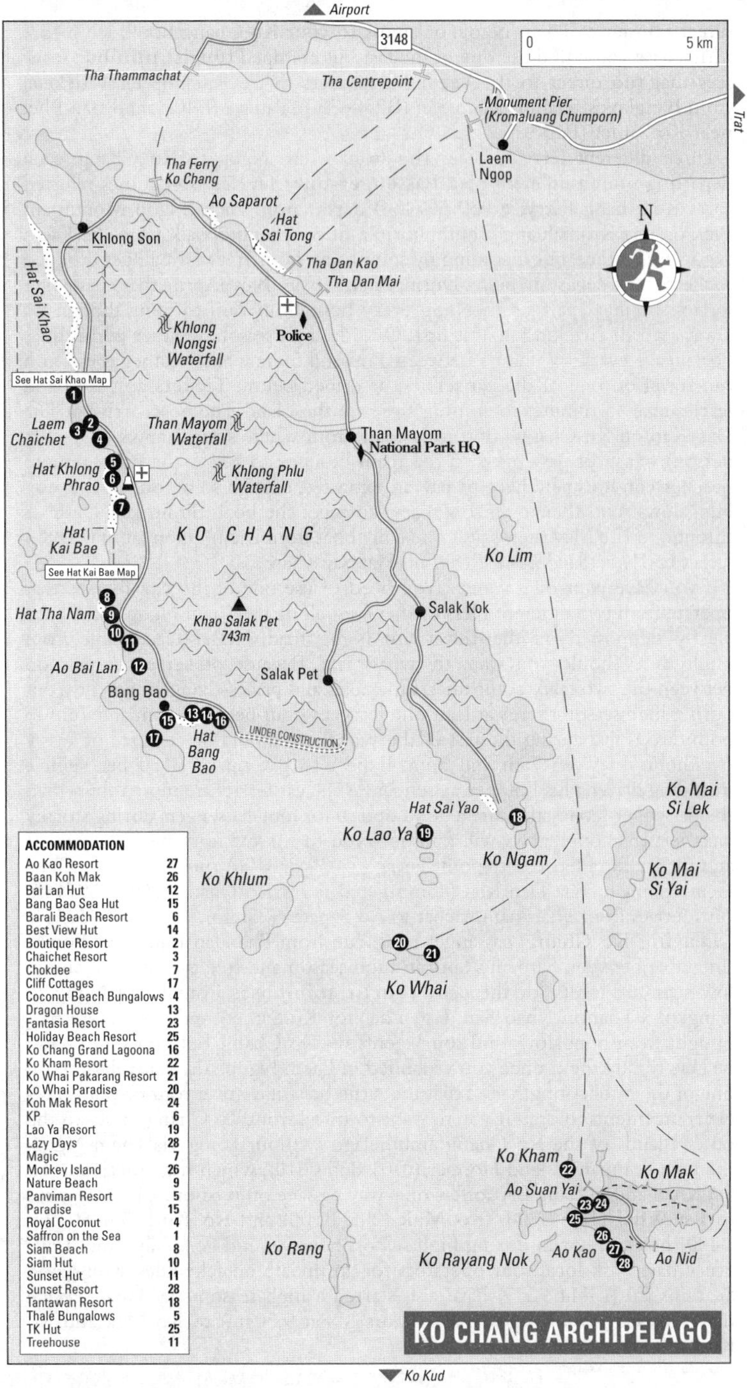
Airport
3148
0
5 km
Tha Thammachat
Tha Centrepoint
Monument Pier (Kromaluang Chumporn)
Trat
Laem Ngop
Tha Ferry Ko Chang
Ao Saparot
Hat Sai Tong
Tha Dan Kao
Tha Dan Mai
N
Khlong Son
Hat Sai Khao
Khlong Nongsi Waterfall
Police
See Hat Sai Khao Map
Laem Chaichet
Than Mayom Waterfall
Than Mayom
National Park HQ
Hat Khlong Phrao
Khlong Phlu Waterfall
Hat Kai Bae
KO CHANG
Ko Lim
See Hat Kai Bae Map
Hat Tha Nam
Khao Salak Pet 743m
Salak Kok
Ao Bai Lan
Salak Pet
Bang Bao
Hat Bang Bao
UNDER CONSTRUCTION
Ko Mai Si Lek
Hat Sai Yao
Ko Lao Ya
Ko Ngam
Ko Khlum
Ko Mai Si Yai
Ko Whai
Ko Kham
Ko Mak
Ao Suan Yai
Ko Rang
Ko Rayang Nok
Ao Kao
Ao Nid
ACCOMMODATION
Ao Kao Resort 27
Baan Koh Mak 26
Bai Lan Hut 12
Bang Bao Sea Hut 15
Barali Beach Resort 6
Best View Hut 14
Boutique Resort 2
Chaichet Resort 3
Chokdee 7
Cliff Cottages 17
Coconut Beach Bungalows 4
Dragon House 13
Fantasia Resort 23
Holiday Beach Resort 25
Ko Chang Grand Lagoona 16
Ko Kham Resort 22
Ko Whai Pakarang Resort 21
Ko Whai Paradise 20
Koh Mak Resort 24
KP 6
Lao Ya Resort 19
Lazy Days 28
Magic 7
Monkey Island 26
Nature Beach 9
Panviman Resort 5
Paradise 15
Royal Coconut 4
Saffron on the Sea 1
Siam Beach 8
Siam Hut 10
Sunset Hut 11
Sunset Resort 28
Tantawan Resort 18
Thalé Bungalows 5
TK Hut 25
Treehouse 11
KO CHANG ARCHIPELAGO
Ko Kud

direct transfer to Laem Ngop, or across to your Ko Chang hotel; see p.453. Otherwise you could use one of the fast but cramped **tourist minibus** services that run direct to the Laem Ngop piers (prices exclude ferry tickets) from Bangkok's Thanon Khao San (B250–350), Pattaya (B400), and Ban Phe, near Ko Samet (B230).

Three different ferry services run from Laem Ngop to Ko Chang, each departing from a different pier. **Passenger-only ferries** (sometimes referred to as Ko Chang Ferry; ⓣ039 597434) depart from Laem Ngop Monument Pier, or Tha Kromaluang Chumphorn, a fifteen-minute walk from the Laem Ngop TAT office, but if coming by songthaew from Trat you will get dropped at the correct departure point. During high season (Nov–April), these passenger ferries should depart Laem Ngop every hour from 7am to 5pm, though it's always worth checking in Trat first. Outside high season, weather permitting, boats leave every two hours between 7am and 5pm; if the weather is bad you can travel on one of the car ferries, described below. **Tickets** cost B50 and ferries take 45 minutes to an hour to reach the island. The boats arrive at Tha Dan Kao on Ko Chang's northeast coast, from where **songthaews** (B30–70/person) transport passengers to the main beaches; to get to the more remote beaches you'll usually have to pay an extra fee, though some out-of-the-way bungalows send their own songthaew to meet the boats. From late October through to late May there's also one daily boat from Laem Ngop (at 3pm; B80) direct to *White Sand Beach Resort* on Hat Sai Khao.

If you have your own vehicle, you need to use one of the **car ferries** that operate from two different piers further west along the Laem Ngop coast, both clearly signposted off the Trat–Laem Ngop road, but also accessible from Highway 3 should you want to bypass Trat. Because of fierce competition between the two ferry companies, timetables and prices change frequently, but during high season there's at least one ferry an hour between 7am and 7pm in both directions; during the rest of the year there should be at least one every two hours between 7am and 5pm. Expect to pay up to B150 per vehicle including driver, plus B30 per passenger. As the car ferries are more robust than the passenger ferries, they are a good option for foot-passengers during stormy weather: Trat songthaews will transport you to the car ferry piers on request and for an extra fee. Centrepoint Ferry (ⓣ039 538196) runs ferries from Tha Centrepoint to Tha Dan Mai (45min); and Ferry Ko Chang (ⓣ039 597143) runs ferries from Tha Thammachat to Ao Saparot (25min).

Leaving Ko Chang, passenger boats run from Tha Dan Kao to an hourly timetable between 8am and 6pm in high season and to a two-hourly one in low season. Tickets for the daily **tourist minibuses** from Laem Ngop to Bangkok's Thanon Khao San, Ban Phe (for Ko Samet) and Pattaya are best bought from bungalows and tour agents on Ko Chang, but you should also be able to buy them once you've landed in Laem Ngop. Alternatively, hop on one of the public songthaews that meet the boat and make your onward travel arrangements in Trat. If you're want to travel from Ko Chang direct to the outer islands of the Ko Chang archipelago without going via Laem Ngop, the boat company Island Hopper (ⓣ01 865 0610), which has offices on Hat Sai Khao and in Bang Bao, offers one-way passage on its snorkelling day-trips to **Ko Whai** (1hr; B200), **Ko Mak** (2hr; B300) and **Ko Kud** (3hr 30min; B400) boats only run during high season however and generally don't leave every day – ask local tour operators for an update on schedules. Koh Kood Seatrans (ⓣ01 444 9259) have also started a high-season speedboat service that runs via Ko Chang (departs Thurs & Sat 9.30am) to Ko Mak and Ko Kud (B800).

Diving and snorkelling around Ko Chang

The **reefs** of the Ko Chang archipelago are nowhere near as spectacular as Andaman coast dive sites, but they're decent enough and – a major advantage – not too crowded. Local **dive sites** range from the beginners' reefs at the Southern Pinnacle, with lots of soft corals, anemones, myriad reef fish and the occasional moray eel at depths of 4–6m, to the more challenging 31-metre dive off Ko Rang, where you're likely to see snapper and possibly even a whale shark. The best coral is found around the islets off Ko Mak (see p.469): in particular at Ko Rayang, Ko Kra and Ko Rang; the coral around Ko Yuak, off Ko Chang's Hat Kai Bae, is mostly dead, though some operators still sell trips there.

All the main beaches have at least one **dive shop** (see relevant beach accounts for details), but nearly all dive boats depart from Bang Bao on the south coast (see p.467). Waves permitting, the dive shops run trips to reefs off Ko Chang's more sheltered east coast during the **monsoon season** from June through September, though visibility is unlikely to be very rewarding during that period. Prices for dive trips should include two dives, transport and lunch, and be in the range of B1800 to B2700 depending on the operator and the destination; accompanying snorkellers generally pay B400–800 including lunch and equipment. All dive centres also offer PADI **dive courses**: the introductory Discover Scuba averages B3000, the four-day Openwater B9000–10,000, and the two-day Advanced B7000–8000. The nearest **recompression chamber** is at the Apakorn Kiatiwong Naval Hospital in Sattahip (☎038 601185), 26km south of Pattaya. See p.73 in Basics for a general introduction to diving in Thailand and for advice on what to look for in a dive centre.

Tour operators and bungalows on every beach can arrange **snorkelling** and **fishing trips** to nearby islands, typically charging B400 per person, including equipment. In addition, Island Hopper (☎01 865 0610), which has offices on Hat Sai Khao and in Bang Bao, runs snorkelling day-trips to Ko Whai (B600) and Ko Mak (B800).

Island practicalities

A wide road runs almost all the way round the island, served – between Tha Dan Kao and Hat Kai Bae – by frequent public **songthaews**; you can also rent cars, motorbikes and mountain bikes on most beaches, and should be able to arrange a motorbike taxi from the same places if necessary. The road can be quite dangerous in places, with steep hills and sharp, unexpected bends, so drive carefully – accidents are not uncommon.

Most of the island's facilities are centred in Hat Sai Khao, including several **ATMs**, currency exchange, a **post office**, an international **clinic** (which will transfer seriously ill patients to its parent hospital, Bangkok-Trat Hospital, in Trat), a **police** box, **Internet** access (B2/minute), plus a number of minimarkets, clothes stalls and souvenir shops. Most of the other main beaches also offer currency exchange, Internet access and small minimarkets, and the **tourist police** have an office on central Hat Khlong Phrao (see p.464).

Though mosquitoes don't seem to be much in evidence, Ko Chang is one of the few areas of Thailand that's still considered to be **malarial**, so you may want to start taking your prophylactics before you get here, and bring repellent with you – refer to p.32 of Basics for more advice on this. Staff at the Ko Chang International Clinic on Hat Sai Kao, however, say that the risk is minimal and advise against taking prophylactics, presumably in an attempt to stop the island mosquitoes developing a resistance to the drugs. Sandflies can be more of a problem on the southern beaches, but there's not a lot you can do about them except soothe your bites with locally made yellow oil (see p.452) or calamine; apart from that, watch out for **jellyfish**, which plague the west coast in April and May, and for **snakes** sunbathing on the overgrown paths into the interior. The other increasing hazard is **theft** from rooms and bungalows: use your own padlock on bags (and doors where possible) or, better still, make use of hotel safety boxes.

The free quarterly magazine, *Koh Chang, Trat and the Eastern Islands* (Ⓦwww.whitesandsthailand.com) is a handy source of **information** on Ko Chang and carries advertisements for dive shops and tour companies; the website Ⓦwww.koh-chang.com is another useful introduction, and provides an accommodation-booking service.

Hat Sai Khao (White Sand Beach)

Framed by a broad band of fine white sand at low tide, a fringe of casuarinas and palm trees and a backdrop of forested hills, **Hat Sai Khao** (White Sand Beach) is the island's longest beach and its most commercial, with over thirty different bungalow operations squashed in between the road and the shore, an increasing number of upmarket hotel developments on the beachfront, plus dozens of shops, travel agents, bars and restaurants lining the inland side of the road. The vibe is more laidback and traveller-oriented at the northern end of the beach, however, beyond *Yakah*, and this is where you'll find the most budget-priced accommodation, some of it pleasingly characterful and nearly all of it enjoying its own sea view. In addition, the road is well out of earshot of most of the bungalows up here, and there's hardly any passing pedestrian traffic, so it can be quite peaceful. Wherever you stay on Hat Sai Khao, be careful when swimming as the **currents** are very strong here and there's no lifeguard service.

Practicalities

Songthaews take about 25 minutes to drive from Tha Dan Kao to Hat Sai Khao and cost B30. If you want the bungalows at *Star Beach*, *Rock Sand* or *White Sand Beach Resort*, get off as soon as you see the sign for *KC Grande*, and then walk along the beach. For bungalows further south, the songthaew should drop you right outside. In high season there's also a daily **boat** from Laem Ngop direct to *White Sand Beach Resort*; see p.458 for details.

You can rent **motorbikes** at several roadside stalls on Hat Sai Khao for B50 an hour or B350 a day. The same places will sometimes act as a **taxi** service, charging about B60 for a ride to Khlong Phrao or B100 to Kai Bae, but **songthaews** are cheaper at about B20 to Hat Khlong Phrao and B30 to Hat Kai Bae. *Ban Nuna* restaurant rents out mountain bikes.

There are **ATMs** near *Ko Chang Lagoon*, near *Ban Pu Ko Chang Hotel* and near *Apple* bungalows, plus a number of outlets offering **money-exchange**, **Internet** access and international phone service. Small shopping plazas are dotted along the road through Hat Sai Khao, containing minimarkets, tour operators, souvenir shops and tailors' outlets. The Ban Pu minimarket complex sells new and second-hand books. The **post office** is at the far southern end of the resort, near *Saffron on the Sea*. There's a **pharmacy** just north of *Oodie's Place* restaurant; the **Ko Chang International Clinic** (daily 9am–8pm, Ⓣ039 551151; 24hr Ⓣ01 863 3609), across the road from *Ban Pu Ko Chang Hotel*, deals with minor injuries and will transport serious cases to Trat. Paradise Scuba Divers (Ⓣ01 291 4732, Ⓦwww.tauchenthailand.de) is one of several **dive shops** on Hat Sai Khao; see box on p.459 for details on diving in Ko Chang.

Accommodation

Central and southern Hat Sai Khao are mainly the province of mid-range and upmarket **accommodation**, a lot of which charges above the odds for decent but unexceptional rooms. Most of the cheaper, better-value options are in northern Hat Sai Khao, though even here it's hard to find anything under ❸ in high season.

Northern Hat Sai Khao

KC Grande Resort ⓣ01 833 1010, ⓦwww.kckohchang.com. One of the most popular budget places on Hat Sai Khao, and deservedly so, *KC* has almost fifty simple bamboo huts that are strung out under the palm trees over a long stretch of beach so that each hut feels a little bit private and has a view of the sea. Huts all have mosquito nets and some have attached bathrooms. As well as the old-style huts, *KC* also offers much larger, more modern wooden and concrete bungalows (some with air-con) set in landscaped gardens near the restaurant, but these are very pricey and not particularly good value. ❸–❾

Rock Sand ⓣ039 551165. Just seventeen simple, idiosyncratic huts perched up on a rocky ledge; price depends on size and amenities, with the cheapest providing just a mattress and a mosquito net, and the better ones having en-suite bathrooms and a good view. Very laid-back atmosphere and a travellers' favourite. ❷–❹

Star Beach ⓣ01 940 2195, ⓔstarbeachbungalows@hotmail.com. Very similar to neighbouring *Rock Sand*, with just eight basic, rickety, plywood huts, some with private facilities, built into the cliff-face and enjoying nice high-level sea views. ❸–❹

White Sand Beach Resort ⓕ039 597300 ⓦwww.whitesandbeachresort.com. Located in a secluded, very attractive spot at the far north end of the beach (about 10min walk along the sand from the next set of bungalows at *Rock Sand*), *White Sand* offers a big range of nicely spaced huts, many of them enjoying uninterrupted sea views. Most of the huts are pretty basic affairs, with or without private bathrooms, but there are also some posher, sturdier ones. The *White Sand* boat comes here once a day from late October through May, departing Laem Ngop at 3pm and costing B80. ❸–❻

Central Hat Sai Khao

Apple ⓣ01 374 0944. Just a handful of good, old-style wooden bungalows, all with mosquito nets and bathrooms, set in a row facing some newer, overpriced, air-con versions. ❹–❼

Bamboo Bungalow ⓣ01 945 4106. Pretty smart but pricey air-con bungalows built in a line, but no proper sea views. ❼

Ban Pu Ko Chang Hotel ⓣ01 863 7314, ⓕ039 551237. Upmarket accommodation comprising a low-rise hotel block and spacious wooden bungalows with unusual, open-roofed bathrooms built around a pretty tropical garden and a small swimming pool. All rooms have sea view, air-con, TV and a veranda. ❽

Cookie ⓣ039 551106. One of the most popular of the mid-range places on this beach, this efficiently run outfit offers smart, thoughtfully designed fan and air-con bungalows, all with small verandas and tiled bathrooms. The main drawback is that they're set very close together, but only those in the third row have no sea view. Also has a hotel block across the road from the beach, where the (all air-con) rooms have large picture-windows and sea-view balconies. ❺–❽

Ko Chang Lagoon ⓣ039 551201, ⓔlagoon@kohchang-hotels.de. Large, resort-style two-storey hotel complex with comfortably furnished air-con rooms and huge two-storey bungalows right on the sand. ❽

Yakah ⓣ01 643 3571. This collection of basic, old-style bamboo huts is crowded together under the trees and furnished with mattresses, bathrooms and mosquito nets; some have beach views, others back on to the road. The pricier ones have air-con. ❸–❻

Southern Hat Sai Khao and beyond

Ko Chang Grand View Resort ⓣ01 863 7802, ⓦwww.grandviewthai.com. Efficiently run place with a range of accommodation set in one garden beside the shore and another across the road. The beachfront garden drops down to a rocky part of the beach, but the sand is just a few steps away. The cheapest accommodation is in fairly basic huts across the road and the most expensive options are air-con bungalows by the sea. ❹–❽

Moonlight ⓣ01 861 7672, ⓔmoonlightresort@yahoo.com. Varying sizes of simple, en-suite bungalows widely spaced above an attractively rocky part of the beach (though just a few metres from sand), most of them with sea view; also has some air-con bungalows. Across the road from a string of bar-beers. ❸–❼

Plaloma Cliff Resort ⓣ01 863 1305, ⓔplalomacliff@hotmail.com. Upmarket air-con bungalows on the lawn and plush air-con rooms in a hotel block with panoramic coastal views. As it's built on a rocky point there's no direct access to the sea from here. ❼–❽

Saffron on the Sea About 1km south of *Plaloma Cliff Resort* ☎ 09 802 4913, ⓦ www.saffrononthesea.com. Charming boutique hotel whose seven idiosyncratically designed fan and air-con bungalows are some of the most stylish on Hat Sai Khao. The best bungalows are

circular and have large picture windows, but all are prettily decorated and set in a garden on a rocky headland to the south of Hat Sai Khao that's fine for swimming but has no beach. Over 1km from the central bar and restaurant area. ❻–❼

Eating and drinking

All the bungalow operations on Hat Sai Khao have **restaurants**, most of which offer very passable European food and standard Thai fare. Many of them do fish barbecues at night as well: the freshly caught barracuda, shark, tuna, king prawns, crab and squid are usually laid out on ice-shavings for you to select yourself, and many places set out candlelit tables on the beach; *Cookie* runs one of the most popular. Across the road from the beach, *Tonsai* is a very pleasant place for an evening meal: seating is Thai-style on cushions set around a circular platform wedged between half a dozen trees, and the reasonably priced, predominantly vegetarian menu includes Thai curries, pastas, Vietnamese sausage and around fifty cocktails. *Hippo Café* in central Hat Sai Khao serves a good range of home-made bread, sandwiches and cakes; the nearby *Food Centre* serves very cheap night-market-style Thai food, including noodle soups, fried noodles and satays, at exceptionally cheap prices; and *Ban Nuna* specializes in German food, as well as pizzas.

After sundown, one of the most popular places for a **drink** on the beach is *Sabay Bar*, where you can either sit beside low tables on mats laid over the sand and work your way through the huge menu of cocktails, or take to the small dance-floor, which pumps out European rave music till the early hours. A few hundred metres further south down the beach, *Tantawan* draws in decent crowds with its nightly live music from the house cover band, as does *Oodie's Place*, a music-bar

HAT SAI KHAO

ACCOMMODATION	
Apple	J
Bamboo Bungalow	I
Ban Pu Ko Chang Hotel	K
Cookie	F & G
KC Grande Resort	D
Ko Chang Grand View Resort	L & M
Ko Chang Lagoon	H
Moonlight	N
Plaloma Cliff Resort	O
Rock Sand	B
Saffron on the Sea	P
Star Beach	C
White Sand Beach Resort	A
Yakah	E

0 500 m

Ao Saparot & Tha Dan Kao

Police box

Pharmacy

ATM

ATM

Clinic

Bookshop

Minimart

RESTAURANTS AND BARS	
Banana Beach	1
Ban Nuna	9
Bar-beers	10
Food Centre	8
Hippo Café	7
Oodie's Place	4
Sabay Bar	5
Tantawan	6
Tonsai	3
Zurich Bar	2

Laem Chaichet & Hat Khlong Phrao ▼ ❼ & ✉

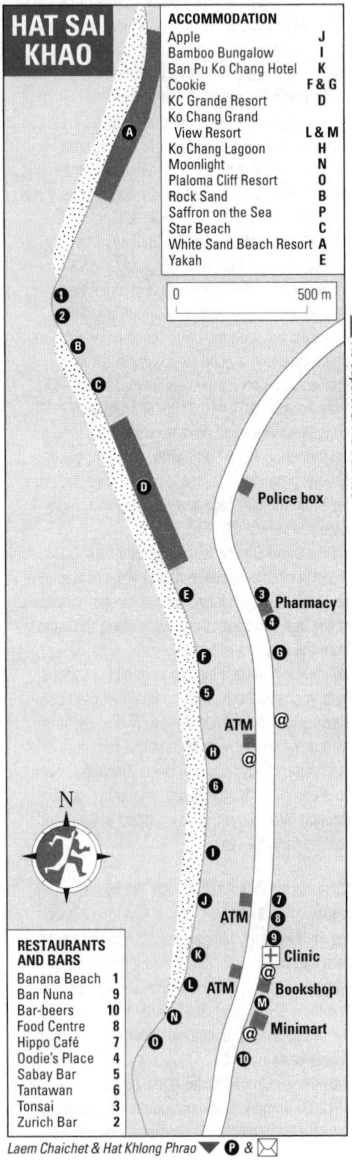

and restaurant beside the road. The alternative party scene happens up on northern Hat Sai Khao, around *Rock Sand* and *Star Bungalows*, site of several cheap 'n' funky little beach bars including *Banana Beach* and *Zurich Bar*. The cluster of bar-beers inland from *Plaloma Cliff Resort* are more middle-of-the-road, Pattaya-style establishments.

Laem Chaichet and northern Hat Khlong Phrao

Four kilometres south of southern Hat Sai Khao, **LAEM CHAICHET** is a small cape whose rocky headland curves round into a secluded casuarina-fringed bay to make an attractive and peaceful setting. There are currently just four bungalow operations on this little stretch of coast, and so far the shops, restaurants and tour operators have been confined to the main road, giving the beach here a much nicer, less congested atmosphere than at Hat Sai Kao and Hat Kai Bae. You can rent **motorbikes** (B60/hour or B400/day) and arrange boat and kayak trips here, and there's Internet access at a centre on the roadside, opposite *Boutique*.

Ten minutes' walk south along the beach from *Coconut*, or a five-minute drive along the main road, brings you to the northern stretch of **HAT KHLONG PHRAO**. The beach here gets a fair bit of flotsam washed up, but is long and never gets crowded. The southern end is defined by quite a wide khlong, which is only wadeable (up to your thighs) at low tide; if you want to get to the central stretch of Hat Khlong Phrao on the other side of the khlong (see p.464), you're better off going via the road. Accommodation options on this northern stretch are oriented towards package-tourists and conferences and not especially interesting.

Songthaews take about ten minutes to reach Laem Chaichet and northern Hat Khlong Phrao from Hat Sai Khao (B20), fifteen minutes from Hat Kai Bae, or 35 minutes from Tha Dan Kao.

Accommodation

Set within a delightful secluded tropical garden just back from the road, less than 100m walk from the beach at Laem Chaichet, *Boutique Resort and Health Spa* (Ⓣ039 551050, Ⓦwww.koh-chang.com/boutique; ❽) comprises eleven comfortable air-con bungalows, an attractive spa and a restaurant. The tall, thatched bungalows are styled like traditional Indonesian rice barns and have wood-panelled interiors and a deck from which to enjoy the garden. Down on the beach itself, the pleasant *Coconut Beach Bungalows* (Ⓣ039 551272, Ⓦwww.webseiten.thai.li/coconut; ❹–❽) has row upon row of seafront accommodation, from simple and mid-range wooden huts to upmarket concrete versions with air-con and TV; some bungalows in all categories have direct sea views and there are also some plush air-con rooms in a low-rise hotel block. Next door, the almost indistinguishable *Royal Coconut* (Ⓣ039 551175; ❺–❻) also has decent fan and air-con bungalows on the seafront, plus some air-con rooms in a small block. Overlooking the scenic little harbour at the northern end of the bay, with impressively long views down to Hat Khlong Phrao, *Chaichet Resort* (Ⓣ01 862 3430, Ⓔchaichet_bl@hotmail.com; ❺–❻) offers a range of options, including large, comfortable air-con bungalows whose decks give out onto the northern coast of the cape and whose design evokes that of a ship, complete with porthole-style windows and hull-shaped roofs.

Khlong Phlu Falls and central Hat Khlong Phrao

The khlong that severs northern from central Hat Khlong Phrao is Khlong Phlu, whose waters tumble into the island's most famous cascade, **Khlong Phlu Falls** (Nam Tok Khlong Phlu), a couple of kilometres east off the main road. Signs lead you inland to a car park and knot of hot-food stalls, where you pay your national park entry fee (B200, kids B100) and walk the final 500m to the waterfall – at twenty metres high it's pretty impressive and plunges into an invitingly clear pool defined by a ring of smooth rocks.

As the long, rather appealing stretch of beach that constitutes **central HAT KHLONG PHRAO** lies between two khlongs it's effectively only accessible by road from northern or southern Hat Khlong Phrao; a **songthaew** ride here from Hat Sai Khao costs B30. Partially shaded by casuarinas and backed in places by a huge coconut grove that screens the beach from the road, it retains an appealingly mellow atmosphere despite the presence of several upmarket resorts alongside the two long-running traveller-oriented options. There is a **clinic** and a fuel station on the main road, about 500m inland, across from Wat Khlong Phrao, as well as the office of Ko Chang's **tourist police** (ⓣ01 982 8381).

The northern stretch of central Hat Khlong Phrao is occupied by the primitive wooden-plank **huts** of the determinedly old-style *Thalé Bungalows* (ⓣ01 926 3843; ❷–❸), whose land runs right up to the khlong. This is one of the cheapest places to stay on Ko Chang: none of the huts here have private bathrooms, but all have mosquito nets and some have a deck too; otherwise price depends on the size. Less basic but still very much traveller-oriented, the popular *KP* (ⓣ01 863 7262; ❸–❺) has fifty fairly simple wooden huts attractively scattered through a coconut grove just a few steps from the beach. The simplest versions share bathrooms; you pay a bit extra to sleep upstairs in one of the two-storey bungalows; and there are larger en-suite huts, some of them designed for families. The management rents out mountain bikes (B150/day), motorbikes (B250/day) and kayaks (B150/hour), and organizes snorkelling and fishing day-trips as well as a three-day sea-safari to Ko Kud. Just south of *KP*, *Barali Beach Resort* (ⓣ039 551238, ⓦwww.baraliresort.com; ❾) is the most elegant spot on the beach, comprising forty tastefully designed, Balinese-style rooms, furnished with four-poster beds, sunken baths and lots of polished wood, and set around a beachfront tropical garden with an infinity-edge swimming pool. It's a much more attractive set-up than the ostentatious *Panviman Resort* (ⓣ039 551290, ⓦwww.panviman.com; ❾), located between *Thalé* and *KP*, whose rather gaudy temple-style architecture and formal service is off-putting. Rooms are perfectly pleasant, however, and extremely well appointed, with wooden floors, four-poster beds and miniature waterfalls in the bathrooms; there's a swimming pool and posh restaurant here too.

Southern Hat Khlong Phrao

South across the next khlong from central Hat Khlong Phrao (again, impassable except by swimming) and round a headland, **southern HAT KHLONG PHRAO** is effectively a completely different little white-sand bay: palm-fringed, secluded and peaceful. There are various options to choose from at *Magic* (ⓣ01 861 4829; ❸–❼), which stands right on the beach, including good, cheap no-frills A-frame huts, plus some less interesting, and pricier, en-suite fan bungalows, as well as air-con versions. The adjacent *Chokdee* (ⓣ01 910 9052, ⓦwww.koh-chang.ch.vu; ❺–❽) sits on a rocky promontory but of course has access to the sand in front of *Magic*; bungalows here are reasonable value and nearly all have a sea view – the price depends on whether or not you want air-con. Inland from *Magic*, on the main road, there's an Internet centre and a few bars, restaurants and tour operators.

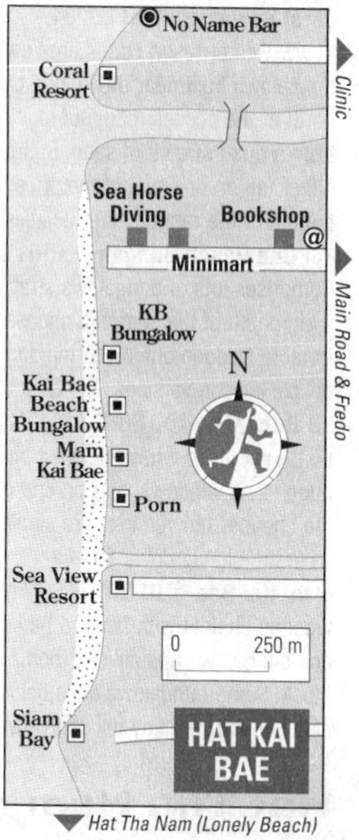

Hat Kai Bae

A couple of kilometres south along the coast from *Chokdee*, narrow, once pretty, little **HAT KAI BAE** has been almost ruined by breakneck development. The nicest stretch of the beach is in front of *KB Bungalows*, which also happens to be the most appealing place to stay on Kai Bae, but much of the rest of the white-sand shore feels claustrophobic under the weight of so many bungalows. North of the main access road to the beach, the shore becomes very rocky, loses the beach completely as it's dissected by a lagoon-like khlong and a shrimp farm, and then re-emerges as a sandy mangrove-fringed strand a bit further on; *Coral Resort* makes the most of this surprisingly charming khlong-side setting.

Big chunks of Kai Bae's beach completely disappear at high tide, so you might prefer to seek out the wider and more swimmable bay about twenty minutes' walk further south – just follow the path south from *Siam Bay* restaurant at the southernmost end of Kai Bae. If you carry on even further, the path takes you to Hat Tha Nam (Lonely Beach), described on p.466, thirty minutes' walk south of *Siam Bay*.

Practicalities

You should have no problem getting a **songthaew** to Kai Bae from Tha Dan Kao (50min; B50) or Hat Sai Khao (25min; B30). Several places on Hat Kai Bae rent out motorbikes, canoes and boats.

On the access road into Hat Kai Bae you'll find a well-stocked **minimart**, a couple of places offering **Internet** access, a bookshop, and several little bars and restaurants. *Kai Bae Beach* **changes money**. There's a **clinic** on the main road, as well as several popular **restaurants**, including the French *Fredo*, a Mexican restaurant, a vegetarian café, and several small bars. All bungalows on Hat Kai Bae offer **snorkelling** outings to local reefs and islands, and Sea Horse Diving (Ⓣ01 996 7147, Ⓦwww.ede.ch/seahorse) organizes **diving** trips in the area: see the box on p.459 for details.

Accommodation and eating

All the Kai Bae bungalows have restaurants, but the best **food** on the beach is served up by *Coral Resort*, whose restaurant occupies a gorgeous breezy spot on the coral rocks north of the access road. The menu includes specialities from Isaan like *som tam* and minced pork *larb*, as well as Thai curries and consistently good barbecued seafood, not to mention decent pizzas. For a few relaxed **beers**, you could do worse than drop in at the ultra-laid-back *No Name Bar*, a few metres further north.

Coral Resort ⓣ09 911 2284, ⓦwww.coral-resort.com. Large concrete and wood bungalows built near the khlong on the coral rocks north of the access road, but only a 5min walk from a quiet stretch of sand. Bungalows come with either fan or air-con, but the pricey rooms at the bottom of the range share facilities. ❹–❽

Kai Bae Beach Bungalow ⓣ01 940 9420. Comprises lots of bungalows stretching over quite a big patch of the seafront: choose between comfortable wooden ones with fan and bathroom, and deluxe air-con versions. ❹–❼

KB Bungalow ⓣ01 862 8103. Attractive, upmarket place whose poshest bungalows have huge glass windows, air-con and comfy interiors; the cheaper fan versions are similar but don't have the big windows. ❺–❼

Mam Kai Bae ⓣ01 757 5870. Fairly standard wooden chalets with fan and bathroom, plus air-con bungalows and air-con rooms in a small hotel block. Some bungalows have been built up the cliffside and so enjoy full sea views. ❹–❽

Porn ⓣ01 949 6052. Laid-back, long-running travellers' hangout that's now the only cheap place to stay on this beach. Has both old-style bamboo huts with shared facilities and more comfortable en-suite wooden bungalows, as well as an attractive shoreside eating area full of cushions and low tables, and a bar. ❸

Sea View Resort and Spa ⓣ039 521661, ⓦwww.seaviewkohchang.com. The most upmarket place on the beach, *Sea View* is set in a tropical flower garden and has a table-tennis table under the palm trees, a swimming pool and spa, and a currency exchange desk. The air-con hotel rooms and bungalows are large, light and airy, and fairly luxuriously furnished; all of them have decks or verandas and some have garden bathrooms. Price mainly depends on the view. ❽–❾

Siam Bay ⓣ01 859 5529. Set right at the southern end of the beach, *Siam Bay* has a beautifully sited restaurant overlooking the rocks, and standard mid-range fan and air-con bungalows on the shore. ❹–❻

Hat Tha Nam (Lonely Beach)

HAT THA NAM – dubbed **Lonely Beach** before it became the backpackers' mecca, and still known as such – is one of the nicest beaches on the island. The long curve of white-sand bay is broad even at high tide and bungalow developments are set at a decent distance from the shoreline. Be extremely careful when swimming here, however, especially around *Siam Beach* at the northern end, as the steep shelf and dangerous current result in a sobering number of **drownings** every year – twenty in 2003; do your swimming further south and don't go out at all when the waves are high.

Nearly all the accommodation on Hat Tha Nam is aimed at budget travellers, so prices are among the cheapest on Ko Chang. The youthful crowd means this is also the island's main party beach: though there are just a handful of **bars**, they crank it up loud and late, so this is not the beach to head for if you want to be lulled to sleep by the sounds of the sea. Behind *Nature Beach*, Ko Chang Dive Point (ⓣ07 142 2948, ⓔarnhelm@gmx.de) organizes **diving** trips and courses (see box on p.459) and has **Internet** access; Internet access is also available at *Siam Beach*. **Songthaews** from Tha Dan Kao take about an hour to Hat Tha Nam and cost B70.

Accommodation

Nature Beach Central beach area ⓣ01 803 8933. Friendly, deservedly popular place whose best bungalows are well priced and attractively furnished with wooden beds and nice bathrooms, plus a partial sea view. Cheaper options are simpler, but en suite, and have mattresses and mosquito nets. ❸–❹

Siam Beach At the far north end of the beach ⓣ09 833 2640. Big place that lacks atmosphere, but has large, simple, decent enough bungalows with fan and bath, set back from the shore. ❸–❹

Siam Hut Central beach area ⓣ09 833 4747. Rows and rows of fairly cheap, primitive, split-bamboo huts, all of them en suite. ❸

Sunset Hut Beyond *Treehouse* at the far southern end of the beach ⓣ01 818 7042. Stilted huts beside the sea with or without bathrooms. Has a good restaurant with lots of veggie options, a water-bottle refill service and a bar. ❷–❸

Treehouse Southern end of the beach ⓣ01 847 8215. Set on the rocky headland at the southern end of the bay, this

German-Thai-managed place is the one that put this beach on the map and is the most chilled and characterful spot on Hat Tha Nam. Its forty cute, trademark, shaggy-thatched huts come in various designs, but they're all very simply equipped, with a mattress, a mosquito net and a paraffin lamp (there's no electricity in the huts, so no fans either) and all of them share bathrooms. Huts are scattered around a pretty garden and there's an inviting seaside deck area with hammocks and floor cushions for the restaurant and bar. Also has a book exchange. ❷–❸

Ao Bai Lan

About one kilometre south of Hat Tha Nam, **AO BAI LAN** accommodates the non-partying refugees from Lonely Beach – though on a really big night, with the wind in the wrong direction, you can still hear the music down here. There's no beach, just rocks, reef, and invitingly clear water, but you can still swim, snorkel and fish and the vibe is ultra laidback. *Bai Lan Hut* (Ⓣ07 028 0796; ❷) comprises a handful of no-frills huts on stilts, some of them right beside the sea, others in the palm-filled garden, plus a lovely seating and eating area, decorated with shell-and-driftwood artwork, on a deck that extends right over the water.

Bang Bao village and Hat Bang Bao

Picturesque **BANG BAO VILLAGE** about 4km south of Ao Bai Lan on Ko Chang's southern coast, is a popular and enjoyable focus for organized day-trips around Ko Chang, and is the departure point for snorkelling and diving trips to the outer islands. The village is built on stilts off one long jetty that extends out into the sheltered fishing harbour and is full of tourist-oriented seafood restaurants, **dive shops** – including BB Divers (Ⓣ06 155 6212, Ⓦwww.bbdivers.com) and The Dive Adventure (Ⓣ07 137 3261, Ⓔmichelangelo4@hotmail.co.uk), see box on p.459 for diving information – and tour operators like Jer Poo Dee Banyang, who run snorkelling trips (B450/person) and **night-fishing** expeditions (Nov–end April; 6pm–1am; B350 including barbecue). Once the day-trippers have left, it's quite an interesting **place to stay**: there are a couple of very simple guest houses on the main jetty, including the no-frills rooms at *Paradise* (❷), as well as the very attractive *Bang Bao Sea Hut* (Ⓣ01 285 0570; ❽), whose fourteen tasteful, octagonal stilted huts overlook the harbour and are connected to the main jetty by a series of walkways.

If you prefer to **stay on the beach**, however, there are a couple of seafront places within walking distance of the village, and a couple a bit further east, all of which describe themselves as being on **HAT BANG BAO**. Just to the west of the jetty village, about fifteen minutes' walk around the shoreline, low-key *Cliff Cottages* (Ⓣ01 864 1471; ❷) occupies the cape that protects Bang Bao's harbour and offers access to a rocky beach as well as stunning views out to sea. The 45 clifftop huts are scattered up a steep incline amongst the trees – you'll need plenty of mosquito repellent here – and are simply furnished with mattresses and mozzie nets. East of the village, a kilometre or so's walk along the road brings you to the small, friendly *Dragon House* (Ⓣ01 982 5815; ❷–❸), which also occupies a rocky shore but is within walking distance of the nice sandy beach further east. Accommodation here is in typical beach huts and the price depends on whether you want a fan and your own bathroom. *Dragon House* rents out bicycles (B120/day) and motorbikes (B250/day) and runs snorkelling trips to nearby reefs (B400/person). Sandy Hat Bang Bao proper is 2km east of the village and effectively the province of the fifty simple, en-suite, rough-hewn wooden huts at *Best View Hut* (Ⓣ06 045 8670, Ⓔbest_view_hut@hotmail.com; ❸–❺). The view in question takes in the striking profiles of Ko Khlum and Ko Whai, which lie directly ahead. Chief among this beach's charms is its emptiness and the fact that its shore is still fringed with palms, mangroves and high grass. *Best View* does a four-island snorkel trip to Ko Rang, Ko Lom, Ko Yak and Ko Whai for B400 per person. East along the shore from *Best View*, set around a lagoon and its own private bay, the *Ko Chang Grand Lagoona* (Ⓣ039 501065, Ⓦwww.grandlagoona.com; ❾) is a bizarre amalgam of converted teak-wood river barges and an enormous old seven-decked cruise liner. Almost everything here floats in the lagoon – including the specially constructed swimming pool. Rooms in the barges and liner are air-con and reasonably deluxe, but the place mainly appeals to conference groups; visitors are charged B100 to look around the sprawling complex and the fee includes a bicycle, a drink and use of the beach.

The east coast

The mangrove-fringed **east coast** is less inviting than the west, and there are hardly any places to stay here. South of the piers at Ao Saparot and Tha Dan Kao, the road runs through long swathes of rubber and palm plantations, with jungle-clad hills to the west and bronze-coloured beaches to the east, passing the national park office and bungalows at **Than Mayom** before reaching the little fishing port of **Salak Pet** on the south coast. At the moment Salak Pet is a quiet spot that's best known for its excellent seafood restaurants, but when the new road between Salak Pet and Hat Bang Bao is completed, thereby encircling the whole island, the area looks set to become a lot busier.

If you fork off the Salak Pet road near the tiny fishing settlement of **Salak Kok**, you can drive almost all the way down to the tip of the southeastern headland, though as yet the road hasn't reached **Hat Sai Yao** (also known as Long Beach), the prettiest beach on this coast, which is currently still only accessible by boat, either from Salak Pet, or by taking the 3pm Ko Whai boat from Laem Ngop during high season and asking to be dropped at Long Beach. Hat Sai Yao is good for swimming and has some coral close to shore. Depending on the sea conditions, some boats will take you directly into Hat Sai Yao, while others will drop you just around a small promontory close to *Tantawan Resort* (❷), an appealingly local, family-run place with just a dozen basic huts in a rocky spot that's good for fishing and just ten minutes' walk from the sands of Long Beach.

The Ko Chang archipelago

South of Ko Chang lies an **archipelago** of 51 islands, a number of which support at least one set of tourist accommodation. All the islands are pretty much inaccessible during the rainy season, but from November through May the main islands of **Ko Whai**, **Ko Mak** and **Ko Kud** are served by regular boats from Laem Ngop and Ko Chang. For the latest information on boat times and weather conditions, ask at any guest house in Trat or Ko Chang, or at the TAT office near the pier in Laem Ngop.

Ko Whai and Ko Lao Ya

Lovely, peaceful little **KO WHAI** (or Ko Wai), which lies about 10km off Ko Chang's southeastern headland, is the perfect place to escape the commercial chaos of Ko Chang. It's only about 3km long and 1.5km wide and has no facilities at all except for a couple of **places to stay** (Nov–April): the inviting, very laid-back *Ko Whai Paradise* (Ⓣ039 597031; ❶–❷), which has cheap and basic bamboo huts on the western end of the island; and the more comfortable *Ko Whai Pakarang Resort* (☎01 945 4383; ❸–❹), which has forty bungalows across towards the eastern headland. **Boats** to Ko Whai depart Laem Ngop's passenger-boat pier, Tha Kromaluang Chumphorn (see p.458), once a day at 3pm (Nov–April; 2hr 30min; B150). Or you can make use of the Island Hopper boats (☎01 865 0610), which run several times a week during high season from Ko Chang (1hr; B200), Ko Mak (1hr; B200) and Ko Kud (2hr 30min; B300): ask locally for the current schedule.

Petite **KO LAO YA**, which sits just off Ko Chang's southeastern headland, halfway to Ko Whai, is a package-tour island. Graced with pretty waters and white-sand beaches, it takes about two and a half hours to reach by tour boat from Laem Ngop. **Accommodation** at the *Lao Ya Resort* (☎02 390 0111) is in air-conditioned bungalows and the all-inclusive price, for boat transfers, two nights' accommodation and six meals, is B3800 per person. Contact the resort for details and times of boats.

Ko Mak and Ko Kham

Many travellers are so seduced by the peaceful pace of life on **KO MAK** (sometimes spelt "Maak"), 20km southeast of Ko Chang, and by the genial welcome they receive, that they wind up staying much longer than they intended. Home to no more than a few hundred people, most of whom either fish or live off the coconut and rubber plantations that dominate the island, Ko Mak measures just sixteen square kilometres and is traversed by a couple of narrow concrete roads and a network of sandy tracks that cut through the trees. The island is shaped like a cross, with fine white-sand beaches along the southwest coast at **Ao Kao** and the northwest coast at **Ao Suan Yai**; the pier is on the southeast coast, at **Ao Nid**. The tiny island of **Ko Kham** lies just off Ao Suan Yai and supports only one small resort. There's decent **diving and snorkelling** at reefs within an hour's boat ride of Ko Mak, particular at Ko Yak and Hin Yak, which have up to thirty different species of coral, and at the 28-metre-deep Hin Gor, where you've a good chance of encountering rays, black-tip sharks, white-tip sharks and leopard sharks. There are dive shops on both beaches: prices average B1800 for two fun dives, B8500 for the four-day Openwater course, and B400 for a day's snorkelling.

There is as yet no major commercial development on the island and no bank, just a couple of local shops at Ao Nid, and a minimarket on Ao Suan Yai. Bungalows on both beaches will change money, there's **Internet access** at *Ao Kao Resort* on Ao Kao and at *Koh Mak Resort* on Ao Suan Yai, a **post office** at *Koh Mak Resort*, and a small **clinic** on the cross-island road (for anything serious a speedboat will whisk you back to the mainland). Electricity on the island is only available from 10am to 2am. Bring some yellow oil with you from Trat (see p.452) to alleviate the inevitable sandfly bites, or slather yourself in locally produced coconut oil, sold at many bungalows. Ko Mak gets lashed by wind and rain from early June through September, so there's no guaranteed ferry service during this period and some bungalows close for the duration. There's no public **transport** on the island and hardly any traffic of any sort, so most travellers either walk or rent a bicycle, though there are also some motorbikes available for rent; apparently it's possible to walk, wade and swim around the entire perimeter of the island in ten hours.

From November to April, there's one **boat** a day from Laem Ngop's passenger-boat pier, Tha Kromaluang Chumphorn (see p.458), to Ao Nid on Ko Mak's southeastern coast (departs 3pm; 3hr 30min; B210); the return boat leaves Ao

Nid daily at 8am. During the rest of the year the boat runs only if the weather permits. Bungalow staff meet the boats. Travelling to or **from Ko Chang** (2hr; B300), **Ko Whai** (1hr; B200) or **Ko Kud** (1hr 30min; B200), you can make use of the Island Hopper boats (ⓣ01 865 0610), which run several times a week during high season to *Ko Mak Resort* on the northwest coast – ask locally for the current schedule; if you're not staying at one of the Ao Suan Yai bungalows, you may have to phone your Ao Kao bungalow for a pick-up. Koh Kood Seatrans (ⓣ01 444 9259) have also started a high-season speedboat service from Laem Ngop (departs Thurs & Sat 9am) to Ko Kud via Ko Chang (9.30am) and Ko Mak (10.30am).

Ao Kao

Ko Mak's longest and most popular beach is **AO KAO** on the southwest coast, a pretty arc of sand that's overhung with lots of stooping palm trees and backed in places by mangroves. The beach is divided by a low rocky outcrop that's straddled by *Ao Kao Resort* – the pretty little southern bay is the domain of *Ao Kao Resort*, *Lazy Days* and *Sunset Resort* (which occupies the far southern headland), while the long western beach is shared by half a dozen other sets of bungalows. From October through May, Bamboo Divers at *Lazy Days* and Paradise Divers at *Ao Kao* both run dive trips and courses. During high season, *Baan Ko Maak* runs a daily boat across to Ko Rayang Nok, which lies less than a couple of kilometres off the western shore and has decent snorkelling (B60/person). All the bungalows have **restaurants**: *Lazy Days* has a good veggie selection and *TK Hut* makes delicious home-made ice cream; the small restaurant next to *TK* is famous across the island for its great *som tam*.

Accommodation

Ao Kao Resort Southern beach ⓣ039 501001, ⓔkhunrano@yahoo.com. This long-running and efficient outfit drops down to the prettiest part of the beach and has a big range of accommodation, including simple rattan huts with shared facilities, similar huts with private bathrooms, and large, comfortable en-suite timber bungalows. Has Internet access and a dive shop, rents motorbikes and bicycles and will cash traveller's cheques. ❷–❺

Baan Koh Mak Central western beach ⓣ09 895 7592, ⓦwww.baan-koh-mak.com. The most sophisticated accommodation on the island, with eighteen contemporary beach-chic-style bungalows, comfortable beds, hammocks on the verandas and a good restaurant. Also rents bicycles. ❺

Holiday Beach Resort Far western end of western beach ⓣ01 902 3179. A dozen wooden chalets, all with shared bathrooms. ❷

Lazy Days Southern beach ⓣ09 099 7819, ⓔblacktip24@hotmail.com. Deservedly popular, very congenial and traveller-oriented British-run accommodation where you can choose between characterful thatched tepees and huts with or without private bathrooms. Has a good restaurant, a dive shop, book exchange, currency exchange, bicycles and canoes for rent. Closed from early June through September. ❶–❸

Monkey Island Central western beach ⓣ09 926 8355, ⓔmonkeyshock_1995@hotmail.com. Of the forty bungalows here, the best value are the large, thatched wooden bungalows with big glass doors; the basic huts with shared facilities are way overpriced. Also has one family apartment with two bedrooms, two bathrooms and air-con. ❹–❻

Sunset Resort Far southern headland ⓣ01 875 4517. Built on a rocky point to the south of *Lazy Days*, this a laid-back place with a handful of fairly basic wooden bungalows with shared bathrooms and a reputation for good food. You'll need to walk to *Lazy Days* for the beach, but swimming is OK here and there's a pleasant deck extending out over the water. ❷

TK Hut Central western beach ⓣ06 111 4378. Decent, well-priced bungalows, with or without private facilities. Also has a good seafront bar and restaurant, plus bicycle and moped rental.

Ao Suan Yai

Long, curvy **Ao Suan Yai** is not as pretty a beach as Ao Kao, but is nonetheless a very nice place to hang out, with a couple of pleasant **places to stay**, both of them run by the same company. At the end of the main cross-island road, *Koh Mak Resort* (Ⓣ039 501013, Ⓦwww.kohmakresort.com; ❹–❼) has a range of good-sized bungalows with fan and private bathroom in a couple of rows along the shorefront, plus some with air-con. West a few hundred metres along the shore, the inviting and deservedly popular *Fantasia Resort* (Ⓣ039 501013, Ⓦwww.kohmakresort.com; ❶–❺) has huge, very comfortable en-suite octagonal bungalows built alongside a small lagoon, plus some simpler A-frame huts among the palm trees; it's closed from June through September. The **food** at *Fantasia* is particularly good, with specialities including home-made bread, pastas and pizzas; at night the place is atmospherically lit with fairylights, with chill-out music and low tables enhancing the mood. *Cabana* restaurant at *Koh Mak Resort* does fabulous *tom yam kung*.

Koh Mak Resort has lots of facilities, including **Internet** access, **currency exchange** and Visa card cash advance, a taxi service, motorbike rental, and **diving** and **windsurfing**. *Fantasia* runs boats across to Ko Kham for snorkelling (B60 return).

Ko Kham

The miniature island of **KO KHAM** lies almost within swimming distance of Ko Mak's Ao Suan Yai, and has room for just twenty simple bamboo bungalows and a restaurant at *Ko Kham Resort* (Ⓣ039 597181; ❷–❹). There's little to do here except swim, sunbathe and enjoy the peace. From November through May a daily **boat** sails from Laem Ngop's passenger-boat pier, Tha Kromaluang Chumphorn (see p.458), to Ko Kham at 3pm (3hr; B210); the return boat leaves Ko Kham at around 8am daily. Or you can get a taxi-boat across from Ao Suan Yai on Ko Mak.

Ko Kud

The second-largest island in the archipelago after Ko Chang, forested **KO KUD** (also spelt Ko Kut and Ko Kood), some 20km south of Ko Mak, measures 25km long and 12km wide and is known for its sparkling white sand and exceptionally clear turquoise water, particularly along the casuarina-shaded west coast. The interior is graced with several waterfalls, including the pretty three-tiered **Nam Tok Khlong Chao**, which tumbles down into a refreshing pool. Most islanders make their living from fishing and growing coconut palms and rubber trees. To date Ko Kud has been the province of upmarket hotels where guests are obliged to stay on full board, with speedboat transfers from the mainland (usually via Laem Sok, due south of Trat) arranged to suit. However, this looks set to change in the near future, following the introduction of **ferry services** aimed at the independent traveller. From November through May, Koh Kood Seatrans (Ⓣ01 444 9259) is running a speedboat service from Laem Ngop (departs Thurs & Sat 9am) to Ko Kud (2hr 30min) via Ko Chang (9.30am) and Ko Mak (10.30am), for B800. The return boat leaves Ko Kud every Friday and Sunday at 9am. Travelling to or **from Ko Chang** (3hr 30min; B400), **Ko Whai** (2hr 30min; B300) or **Ko Mak** (1hr 30min; B200), you can make use of the Island Hopper boats (Ⓣ01 865 0610), which run to Ko Kud several times a week during high season: ask locally for the current schedule.

The main problem with turning up on spec on Ko Kud is that outside weekends it can be hard to find food near your **accommodation**, and unless pre-booked the package hotels generally won't open their kitchens for walk-in guests. For the moment, then, it's the package hotels that dominate the options: except where stated, all the following charge around B4000 per person for a three-day, two-night package, including speedboat transfers, accommodation and all meals, and must be booked in advance; all operate only from November through May. On the **west coast**, at Ao Ta Pho, *Ko Kood Cabana* (ⓣ02 923 2645, ⓦwww.kohkoodcabana.ne) has standard wooden bungalows with fan or air-con in a seafront garden full of palms. About 5km south, and set amongst the mangroves beside the Khlong Chao inlet (which runs down from Khlong Chao Falls), just inland from the pretty beach at Ao Khlong Chao, *Peter Pan Resort* (ⓣ02 966 1800, ⓦwww.captainhookresort.com) comprises elegant wooden chalets, with minimalist furnishings and garden bathrooms. North across the inlet sits tiny, inviting, and very inexpensive *Doy's Guest House* (❷), which has just three simple rooms and is only 300m from the beach; food here is also only generally provided if rooms are reserved in advance. At the most southerly bay, *Ko Kut Ao Phrao Beach* (ⓣ039 525211, ⓦwww.kokut.com) has comfortable, thatched fan and air-con bungalows on the beach at Ao Phrao. Across on the northeast coast, *Kood Island Resort* (ⓣ02 375 6188, ⓦwww.koodresort.com) comprises bungalows on stilts standing right over the bay at Ao Yai Kerd, as well as some less interesting concrete versions on land.

Travel details

Trains

Aranyaprathet to: Bangkok (2 daily; 5hr 15min–5hr 30min).
Pattaya to: Bangkok (1 daily; 3hr 20min); Si Racha (1 daily; 25min).
Si Racha to: Bangkok (1 daily; 3hr); Pattaya (1 daily; 25min).

Buses

Aranyaprathet to: Bangkok (10 daily; 4hr 30min).
Ban Phe to: Bangkok (12 daily; 3hr); Chanthaburi (6 daily; 1hr 30min); Rayong (every 30min; 30min); Trat (6 daily; 3hr).
Chanthaburi to: Bangkok (Eastern Bus Terminal; 18 daily; 4–5hr); Bangkok (Northern Bus Terminal; 5 daily; 3hr); Khorat (8 daily; 6hr); Rayong (8 daily; 2hr); Sa Kaew (for Aranyaprathet; 8 daily; 3hr); Trat (every 1hr 30min; 1hr 30min).
Pattaya to: Bangkok (Don Muang Airport; 3 daily; 2hr 30min); Bangkok (Eastern Bus Terminal; every 30min; 2–3hr 30min); Bangkok (Northern Bus Terminal; every 30min; 2–3hr); Chanthaburi (6 daily; 3hr); Chiang Mai (6 daily; 12hr); Khorat (4 daily; 5–6hr); Nong Khai (7 daily; 12hr); Rayong (every 30min; 1hr 30min); Trat (6 daily; 4hr 30min); Ubon Ratchathani (7 daily; 10hr).
Rayong to: Bangkok (Eastern Bus Terminal; every 40min; 2hr 30min); Bangkok (Northern Bus Terminal; 2 daily; 2hr 30min); Ban Phe (for Ko Samet; every 30min; 30 min); Chanthaburi (every 30min; 2hr); Khorat (18 daily; 4hr).
Si Racha to: Bangkok (Eastern Bus Terminal; every 30min; 2hr); Bangkok (Northern Bus Terminal; every 30min; 2hr); Chanthaburi (6 daily; 3hr 30min); Pattaya (every 20min; 30min); Rayong (for Ban Phe and Ko Samet; every 30min; 2hr); Trat (6 daily; 5hr).
Trat to: Bangkok (Eastern Bus Terminal; at least hourly; daily; 5–6hr); Bangkok (Northern Bus Terminal; 5 daily; 4–5hr); Chanthaburi (hourly; 1hr 30min); Hat Lek (for the Cambodian border; every 45min; 1hr–1hr 30min); Pattaya (6 daily; 4hr 30min); Rayong (for Ko Samet; 6 daily; 3hr 30min); Si Racha (6 daily; 5hr).

Ferries

Ban Phe to: Ko Samet (4–18 daily; 30min).
Laem Ngop to: Ko Chang (hourly; 25min–1hr); Ko Kham (Nov–April 1 daily; 3hr); Ko Mak (Nov–April 1 daily; 3hr 30min); Ko Whai (Nov–April 1 daily; 2hr 30min).
Si Racha to: Ko Si Chang (hourly; 40min).

Flights

Pattaya (U-Tapao) to: Ko Samui (1 daily; 1hr); Phuket (1 daily; 2hr 30min).
Trat to: Bangkok (2 daily; 50min); Ko Samui (1 daily; 1hr).

5

The northeast: Isaan

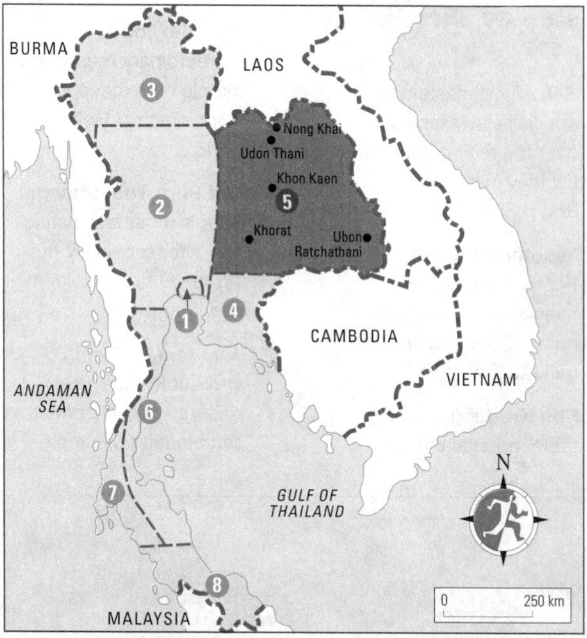

CHAPTER 5

Highlights

- **Khao Yai National Park** Fifteen trails, lots of birds, several waterfalls and night safaris. See p.478
- **Khmer ruins** Exquisite Angkor Wat-style temples at Phimai, Phanom Rung and Khao Phra Viharn. See p.490, p.496 and p.505
- **Silk** A northeastern speciality, available all over the region but particularly in Khon Kaen. See p.523
- **Yasothon Rocket Festival** Bawdy rain-making ritual involving ornate home-made rockets. See p.518
- **Phu Kradung** Teeming table mountain, the most dramatic of the region's national parks. See p.532
- **The Mekong** The best stretch in Thailand for gentle exploration of the mighty riverscape is between Chiang Khan and Nong Khai. See p.536
- **Wat Phu Tok** Extraordinary meditation temple on a steep sandstone outcrop. See p.548
- **Wat Phra That Phanom** Isaan's most fascinating holy site, especially during the February pilgrimage. See p.550
- **Som tam, kai yang and sticky rice** The Isaan classic, a perfect combination of simple

△ Mekong River

5

The northeast: Isaan

Bordered by Laos and Cambodia on three sides, the tableland of **northeast Thailand** – known as **Isaan**, after the Hindu god of death and the northeast – comprises a third of the country's land area and is home to nearly a third of its population. This is the least-visited region of the kingdom, and the poorest: over seventy percent of Isaan villagers earn less than the regional minimum wage of B135 a day. Farming is the livelihood of virtually all northeasterners, despite appallingly infertile soil (the friable sandstone contains few nutrients and retains little water) and long periods of drought punctuated by downpours and intermittent bouts of flooding. In the 1960s, government schemes to introduce hardier crops set in motion a debt cycle that has forced farmers into monocultural cash-cropping to repay their loans for fertilizers, seeds and machinery. For many families, there's only one way off the treadmill: each January and February, Bangkok-bound trains and buses are crammed with northeasterners leaving in search of seasonal or short-term work; of the twenty million who live in Isaan, an average of two million seasonal economic refugees leave the area every year, and northeasterners now make up the majority of the capital's lowest-paid workforce.

Most northeasterners speak a dialect that's more comprehensible to residents of Vientiane than Bangkok, and Isaan's historic allegiances have tied it more closely to Laos and Cambodia than to Thailand. Between the eleventh and thirteenth centuries, the all-powerful **Khmers** covered the northeast in magnificent stone temple complexes, the remains of which constitute the region's most satisfying tourist attractions. During subsequent centuries the territories along the Mekong River changed hands numerous times, until the present border with Laos was set at the end of World War II. In the 1950s and 1960s, **Communist insurgents** played on the northeast's traditional ties with Laos; a movement to align Isaan with the Marxists of Laos gathered some force, and the Communist Party of Thailand, gaining sympathy among poverty-stricken northeastern farmers, established bases in the region. At about the same time, major US air bases for the **Vietnam War** were set up in Khorat, Ubon Ratchathani and Udon Thani, fuelling a sex industry that has plagued the region ever since. When the American military moved out, northeastern women turned to the tourist-orientated Bangkok flesh trade instead, and nowadays the majority of prostitutes in the capital come from Isaan.

These cities, like Isaan's other major population centres, are chaotic, exhausting places, with precious little going for them apart from accommodation and onward transport. For tourists, Isaan's prime sights are its **Khmer ruins**, and the trails through **Khao Yai National Park**. Four huge northeastern **festivals** also draw massive crowds: in May, Yasothon is the focus for the bawdy rocket festival;

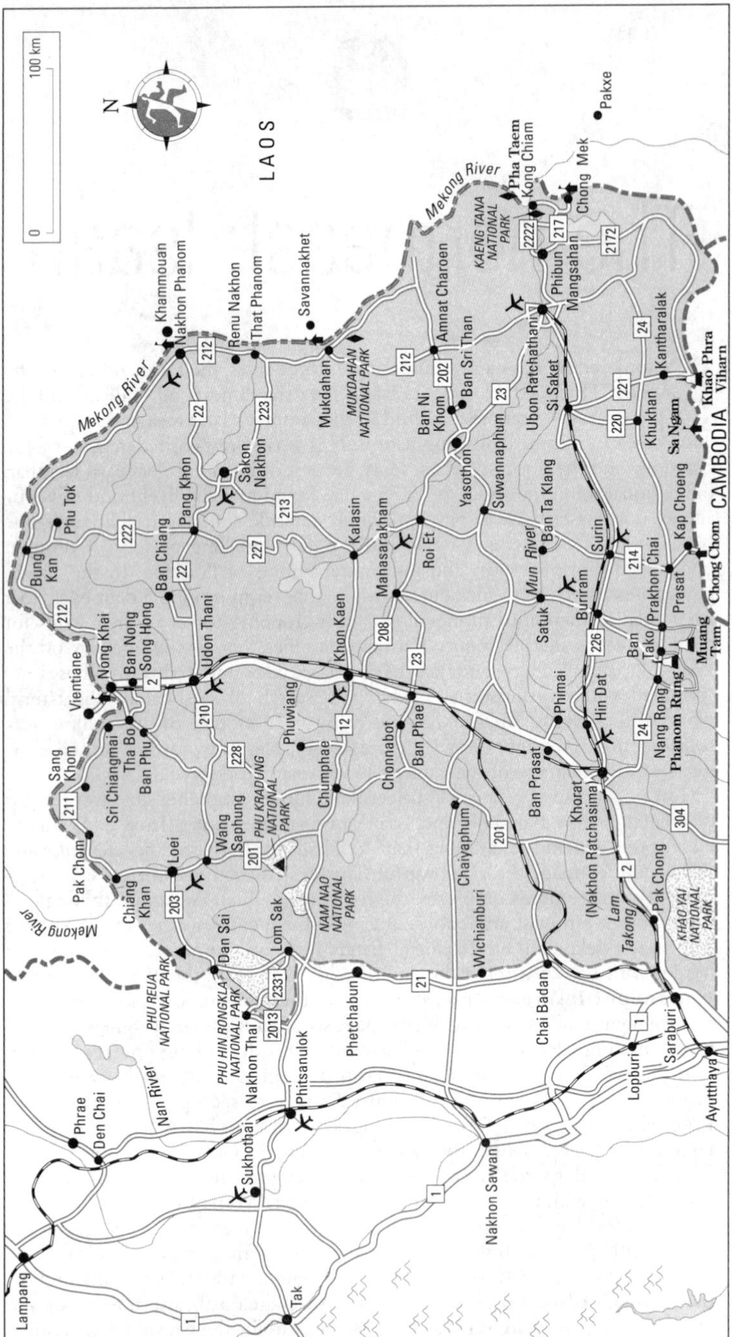
100 km
0
N
LAOS
CAMBODIA
Mekong River
Mun River
Nan River
Lam Takong
Khammouan
Nakhon Phanom
Renu Nakhon
That Phanom
Savannakhet
Mukdahan
MUKDAHAN NATIONAL PARK
Amnat Charoen
KAENG TANA NATIONAL PARK
Pha Taem
Kong Chiam
Chong Mek
Pakxe
Phibun Mangsahan
Ubon Ratchathani
Si Saket
Ban Sri Than
Ban Ni Khom
Yasothon
Suwannaphum
Kantharalak
Khao Phra Viharn
Khukhan
Sa Ngam
Kap Choeng
Chong Chom
Prasat
Prakhon Chai
Surin
Ban Ta Klang
Buriram
Satuk
Ban Tako
Muang Tam
Phanom Rung
Nang Rong
Hin Dat
Phimai
Khorat
(Nakhon Ratchasima)
Ban Prasat
Pak Chong
KHAO YAI NATIONAL PARK
Saraburi
Ayutthaya
Lopburi
Chai Badan
Wichianburi
Chaiyaphum
Chonnabot
Ban Phae
Roi Et
Mahasarakham
Kalasin
Khon Kaen
Phuwiang
Chumphae
PHU KRADUNG NATIONAL PARK
NAM NAO NATIONAL PARK
Lom Sak
Phetchabun
Wang Saphung
Loei
Dan Sai
PHU REUA NATIONAL PARK
PHU HIN RONGKLA NATIONAL PARK
Nakhon Thai
Phitsanulok
Chiang Khan
Pak Chom
Sang Khom
Sri Chiangmai
Tha Bo
Ban Phu
Vientiane
Nong Khai
Ban Nong Song Hong
Udon Thani
Ban Chiang
Bung Kan
Phu Tok
Pang Khon
Sakon Nakhon
Sukhothai
Phrae
Den Chai
Lampang
Tak
Nakhon Sawan
1
2
12
21
22
23
24
201
202
203
208
210
211
212
213
214
217
220
221
222
223
226
227
228
304
2013
2172
2222
2331

the end of June or beginning of July sees the equally raucous rain-making festival of Phi Ta Kon in Dan Sai near Loei; in July, Ubon Ratchathani hosts the extravagant candle festival; while the flamboyant, though inevitably touristy, "elephant round-up" is staged in Surin in November.

Isaan's only mountain range of any significance divides the uninspiring town of **Loei** from the central plains and offers some stiff walking, awesome scenery and the possibility of spotting unusual birds and flowers in the **national parks** that spread across its heights. Due north of Loei, the **Mekong River** begins its leisurely course around Isaan with a lush stretch where a sprinkling of guest houses has opened up the river countryside to travellers. Marking the eastern end of this upper stretch, the border town of **Nong Khai** is surrounded by possibly the most outlandish temples in Thailand. The grandest and most important religious site in the northeast, however, is **Wat Phra That Phanom**, way downstream beyond **Nakhon Phanom**, a town which affords some of the finest Isaan vistas.

The other big draw for travellers are Isaan's four **border crossings into Laos**, at each of which you can now get a Lao visa on arrival. The most popular of these is at Nong Khai, a route that provides easy road access to the Lao capital, Vientiane; the others are Nakhon Phanom, Mukdahan and Chong Mek (see p.19 for a full run-down on overland travel into Laos). You can get a Lao visa in advance from the consulate in the central Isaan town of Khon Kaen, where there's also a Vietnamese consulate issuing visas for Vietnam. It is now also possible to travel **overland between Isaan and Cambodia** through two different border crossings: via the Thai town of Kap Choeng, in Surin province, to O'Smach, which has transport to Anlong Veng and then on to Siem Reap (see p.501 for details); and via Sa Ngam in the Phusing district of Si Saket province to Choam in Anlong Veng. See p.18 for a roundup of overland crossings on the Thai-Cambodia border.

Many travellers approach Isaan from the north, either travelling directly from Chiang Mai to Loei, or going via Phitsanulok, in the northern reaches of the central plains, to Khon Kaen, but you can also take direct **buses** to Khorat from the east-coast towns of Pattaya, Rayong and Chanthaburi. All major northeastern centres have direct bus services from Bangkok. Two **rail** lines cut through Isaan, providing useful connections with Bangkok, Don Muang Airport and Ayutthaya. Thai Airways operates regular **flights** between Bangkok and the major northeastern cities. All major towns and cities in Isaan are connected by public transport, as are many of the larger villages, but compared to many other regions of the country, northeastern roads are fairly traffic-free, so renting your own vehicle is also a good option.

Southern Isaan

Southern Isaan more or less follows one of two branches of the northeastern rail line as it makes a beeline towards the eastern border, skirting the edge of **Khao Yai National Park** before entering Isaan proper to link the major provincial capitals of **Khorat**, **Surin** and **Ubon Ratchathani**. The rail line is handy enough for entering the region, but once here it's as well to follow a route that takes in smaller towns and villages wherever possible, which means switching to buses and songthaews. It is in these smaller places that you'll learn most about Isaan life, particularly if you head for the exceptionally welcoming **guest houses** in Surin, Nang Rong, Phimai and Kong Chiam. For even more of an immersion into a rural community, consider booking yourself onto the **home-stay** programme in the village of **Ban Prasat**.

Even if your time is limited, you shouldn't leave this part of Isaan without visiting at least one set of Khmer ruins: **Prasat Hin Phimai** is the most accessible of the region's top three sites, but it's well worth making the effort to visit either **Prasat Hin Khao Phanom Rung** or **Khao Phra Viharn** as well, both of which occupy spectacular hilltop locations. Relics of an even earlier age, prehistoric cliff paintings also draw a few tourists eastwards to the town of **Kong Chiam**, which is prettily set between the Mekong and Mun rivers and is well worth a visit in its own right. Nearby **Chong Mek** is best known as a legal entry point into Laos, but is also the site of an enjoyable Thai–Lao border market.

Khao Yai National Park

About 120km northeast of Bangkok, the cultivated lushness of the central plains gives way to the thickly forested Phanom Dangkrek mountains. A 2168-square-kilometre chunk of this sculpted limestone range has been conserved as **KHAO YAI NATIONAL PARK**, one of Thailand's most rewarding reserves, and certainly its most popular. Spanning five distinct forest types and rising to a height of 1341m, the park sustains over three hundred bird and twenty large land-mammal species, and offers a plethora of waterfalls and several undemanding walking trails.

With your own transport, Khao Yai could just about be done as a long day-trip from Bangkok or Ayutthaya, but there's camping and basic accommodation in the park itself, and plenty of more comfortable options just beyond the perimeter and in the nearby town of **Pak Chong**. It's quite easy to trek around the park by yourself, as long as you stick to the official trails, but as some of Khao Yai's best features – its waterfalls, caves and viewpoints – are as much as 20km apart, you might get more satisfaction from joining a tour (see box on p.480). Try to avoid visiting at weekends and holidays, when the trails and waterfalls get ridiculously crowded and the animals make themselves scarce. Even at quiet times, don't expect it to be like a safari park – patience, a soft tread and a keen-eyed guide are generally needed, and it's well worth bringing your own binoculars if you have them. Be prepared for patches of fairly rough terrain, and pack some warm clothes, as the air can get quite cool at the higher altitudes in the park, especially at night.

Should you tire of wildlife-spotting, there are a number of popular **golf courses** within easy reach of the park, including Mission Hills (Ⓣ044 297258, Ⓦwww.golfmissionhills.com), which is signed off the park road at kilometre-stone 20, and The Country Club (Ⓣ044 249025), near kilometre-stone 23; hotels on the park road can arrange transport.

Practicalities

Whether you decide to see Khao Yai on your own or as part of a tour, your first port of call has to be the small market town of **PAK CHONG**, 37km north of Khao Yai's visitor centre and major trailheads, and served by trains and buses from lots of major towns. One of the three recommended Khao Yai tour leaders operates from Pak Chong, and there are a couple of places to stay in town too, should you decide to base yourself outside the park. If, on the other hand, you want to head straight up to Khao Yai, you need to get a songthaew from Pak Chong's town centre.

Thanon Tesaban cuts right through the middle of Pak Chong, and small side roads (sois) shoot off it in parallel lines to the north and south; the sois to the north are odd-numbered in ascending order from west to east (Soi 13 to Soi 25) and the sois on the south side of the road have even numbers, from west to east (from Soi 8 to Soi 18). The heart of the town is on the north side, between the train station on Soi 15 and the footbridge a few hundred metres further east, and this is where you'll find the **day market**. Beyond the footbridge is the **post office**, on the corner of Soi 25, and the **CAT international phone office** on the other side of Thanon Tesaban. West of the train station on Thanon Tesaban are a couple of Internet centres and an ATM; there's a **currency-exchange** counter (bank hours) on the south side of the main road between the footbridge and Soi 18, a supermarket about 200m further west, and a **medical centre** between sois 8 and 10.

Getting to Khao Yai and back

Pak Chong **train station** is on Soi 15 (☎044 311534), one short block north of Thanon Tesaban. The **bus station** is towards the west end of town, one block south off the main road between sois 8 and 10, but most long-distance buses also stop in the town centre, beside the footbridge on the main road.

The cheapest way to get **from Pak Chong to Khao Yai** is to take a public **songthaew** from outside the 7–11 shop, 200m west of the footbridge on the north side of the main road (every 30min 6.30am–5pm, less frequently on Sun; 30min; B20). Public songthaews, however, are not allowed to enter the park itself, so you'll be dropped at the park checkpoint, about 14km short of the Khao Yai visitor centre, park headquarters and most popular trailheads. At the checkpoint (where you pay the B200 national-park entrance fee, or B100 for kids), park rangers will flag down passing cars and get them to give you a ride up to the visitor centre; this is normal practice and quite safe. The whole journey from Pak Chong to Khao Yai visitor centre takes about an hour. Note that if you are not planning to stay the night inside the park but want to make two or more day-trips into the park, you'll have to pay the park entry fee every time you come through the checkpoint.

A less time-consuming but pricier option is to **charter a songthaew** from Pak Chong: chartered songthaews count as private vehicles and are allowed inside the park. They can be chartered from the corner of Soi 21, just west of the 7–11 shop, and cost around B500 for the ride from Pak Chong to Haew Suwat Falls, or about B1200 for a return trip, including several hours in the park.

Coming back from the park is often easier, as day-trippers will usually give lifts all the way back down to Pak Chong. Otherwise, get a lift as far as the checkpoint, or walk to the checkpoint from the visitor centre – it's a pleasant three- to four-hour, walk along the fairly shaded park road, and you'll probably spot lots of birds and some macaques, gibbons and deer as well. At the checkpoint you can pick up a songthaew to Pak Chong: the last one usually leaves here at about 5pm.

Khao Yai tours and guides

Tours of Khao Yai are reasonably priced and cater primarily for independent tourists rather than big groups. Not only do you get to be accompanied by an expert wildlife spotter, but you also get transport around the park, so you don't have to backtrack along trails and can see the waterfalls without having to hitch a ride. On the downside, you probably won't be able to choose which trails you cover, and may find the amount of walking unsatisfactorily slight; in addition it's usual, though not compulsory, to stay in the tour operator's own accommodation. An alternative would be to hire a park ranger to be your personal **guide** on the more remote trails; you can arrange this at the park headquarters, but don't expect to get transport as well as a guide. There's no set fee, but a fair rate would be B300 for a few hours, or around B500 for the whole day; organize your guide the night before and be sure to specify a start time.

In recent years, Khao Yai has unfortunately been plagued with unscrupulous tour operators, and readers have reported a number of horror stories, including drunk and unpleasant guides and the theft of travellers' cash and credit cards. As it's not possible to keep track of all fly-by-night operators in Pak Chong and Khao Yai, we are recommending only three reputable tour outfits. If your time is limited, it's worth contacting your chosen tour operator in advance, especially if you're on your own, as prices quoted are for a minimum of two trekkers, and solo travellers will have to pay more if there's no one else to join up with. Advance booking is essential for overnight expeditions in the park.

In Pak Chong, the recommended tour operator is **Wildlife Safari** (ⓣ09 628 8224, ⓔwildlifesafari@bigfoot.com), which emphasizes plant-spotting and animal observation rather than hearty hikes. The standard one-and-a-half day programme features walks along one or two trails, depending on the season and on recent sightings, a swim in Haew Suwat Falls, and a night safari; it costs B1150 per person,

Accommodation and eating

You have several options when it comes to **accommodation** in and around Khao Yai, but note that if you decide to do a tour, it's usual to stay in the lodgings run by your tour guide.

Staying in the park

If you're intending to do several days' independent exploring in the park, the most obvious places to stay are the **national park lodges and tents** in the heart of Khao Yai. Unfortunately, this involves making an advance reservation through the Royal Forestry Department office in Bangkok (ⓣ02 561 4292–3; see Basics p.46 for details) and bringing your receipt to the Khao Yai accommodation office (daily 6am–9pm), next to the visitors' centre, when you arrive. There are half a dozen two-person **lodges** (④) in three locations around the park, and another twenty that cater for groups of four to thirty people. There are also some much cheaper **dorms** (B30–100/person) behind the visitor centre, but Khao Yai's current policy is to only rent these out to huge groups. The cheapest way of staying in the park is to rent one of the **tents**, with or without mats and bedding, pitched at the two park campsites, both of which have showers and toilets. *Pha Kluai Mai* campground (aka *Orchid Camp*) is about 4km east of the park headquarters, on the road to Haew Suwat Falls, and *Lam Takong* campsite is scenically set beside the river near the old golf course, about 5km from HQ, and has a restaurant. Fully equipped tents are only available at *Lam Takong* (from B250 inclusive), while unequipped tents are available at both sites (from B80); advance bookings are not essential for camping, but are advisable at weekends. You can pitch your own tent at either site for B30. For including the B200 park entry fee. Tailor-made and overnight programmes can also be arranged. Wildlife Safari is based about 2km north of Pak Chong train station at 39 Thanon Pak Chong Subsanun, Nong Kaja (call ahead to arrange free transport from Pak Chong); their accommodation here features a range of spacious and comfortably furnished rooms in the garden of the family home, some with private bathrooms and air-con (❷–❹).

The large, efficient and well-established **Khao Yai Garden Lodge** (Ⓣ044 365178, Ⓦwww.khaoyai-garden-lodge.com) is based at kilometre-stone 7 on the road that runs from Pak Chong into the park. It runs a variety of programmes, including half-day visits (B350 plus B200 park entry fee) and one-day outings (B650 plus B200), as well as the popular one-and-a-half day programme (B950/person plus B200), which includes a trip to the bat cave at dusk, plus a full day of trail hikes, a swim at one of the waterfalls and a night safari. It also offers more taxing overnight expeditions into the park at B2000 per person per day, including food, guides, porters, tents and hammocks. For details of *Garden Lodge*'s accommodation, see below.

Green Leaf Guest House and Tour (Ⓣ044 365073 or 09 424 8809, Ⓔbirdman_nine@hotmail.com) is a smaller and newer outfit than the other two, but its owner and main trek leader, Nine, gets very good reviews, particularly as a bird-spotter. It's based at kilometre-stone 7.5 on the park road and is not to be confused with Green Leaf Travel Service, which has an office in front of the train station in Pak Chong and mainly acts as an agent for *Garden Lodge*. *Green Leaf Guest House and Tour* offers the usual one-and-a-half-day programme of trails (with an emphasis on bird-watching), waterfalls and a night safari for the standard price of B1150 including park entry, and can do personalized tours as well. Accommodation is available at the family guest house (see below).

specific queries about Khao Yai accommodation you could try calling the park headquarters on Ⓣ09 424 7698.

There's no need to bring all your food and water supplies with you as there are half a dozen **foodstalls** serving hot food from about 6am to 6pm in the cafeteria complex opposite the park headquarters, where you'll also find a small shop that sells drinking water, beer, snacks, and boil-in-the-bag camping food (the accommodation office rents out stoves). There are also **restaurants** at Haew Suwat Falls and *Lam Takong* campsite.

The park road

The 23-kilometre road that runs from Pak Chong up to the park checkpoint (Thanon Thanarat) is dotted with luxurious "**lodges**", whose predominantly Thai guests nearly always arrive by car, though most lodges can arrange transport from Pak Chong; the Pak Chong songthaew will also bring you here. Addresses are determined by the nearest kilometre-stone on Thanon Thanarat.

The cheapest place to stay on the park road is *Green Leaf Guest House and Tour* (Ⓣ044 365073, Ⓔbirdman_nine@hotmail.com; ❷), a friendly, family-run outfit 12.5km out of Pak Chong, at kilometre-stone 7.5, with just half a dozen undistinguished, en-suite rooms, a good, cheap restaurant and guided treks into the national park (see above). Half a kilometre south of *Green Leaf*, at kilometre-stone 7, *Khao Yai Garden Lodge* (Ⓣ044 365178, Ⓦwww.khaoyai-garden-lodge.com; ❷–❻) is a large, well-designed and very popular bungalow resort set in a landscaped garden, complete with a swimming pool, ponds and an aviary. It offers a few simple rooms with shared facilities as well as various better-appointed en-suite ones, some of which have air-con and extra beds for kids.

Garden Lodge runs tours of the park (see p.481) as well as day-trips to the Khmer temples and other sights of Isaan. There's a restaurant here, and Internet access. *Juldis Khao Yai Resort* (Ⓣ044 297297, Ⓦwww.khaoyai.com; ❼), at kilometre-stone 17, offers good-value upmarket accommodation in its large, comfortably furnished air-conditioned rooms and has three swimming pools, several tennis courts, mountain-bike rental, a not very interesting restaurant and a pub.

Pak Chong

The obvious drawback to basing yourself in Pak Chong itself is that it's about an hour's journey from the Khao Yai trailheads, but if you make an early start you can take the songthaew there and back.

Pak Chong's most acceptable budget **hotel** is the *Phubade Hotel* (Ⓣ044 314964; ❷–❸), located just 50m south down Tesaban Soi 15 from the train station. Coming from the bus station, cross to the north side of the main road, walk 400m east and then turn left up Tesaban Soi 15. The hotel is spartan and shabby but fairly clean, and has both fan and air-conditioned rooms, all with bathrooms. Smarter and more appealing, but not as central, the good-value *Rim Tarn Inn* (Ⓣ044 313364, Ⓕ044 312933; ❹–❺) is on the south side of the main road, about 300m west of the bus station; it has large, pretty luxurious rooms, all with air-con, hot water and TV, and there are a swimming pool, restaurant and beer garden on the premises. You should be able to get a good discount on a week night.

Pak Chong has several evening-only roadside **restaurants** near the *Rim Tarn Inn*, but the cheapest and most popular place to eat after dark is the night market, which sets up along the north edge of the main road, between Tesaban sois 17 and 19. If you're looking for somewhere to have a beer, the *Riverside* **bar** and restaurant, signed off the southern end of Tesaban Soi 8, stages live music most nights, as does *Crossroads*, close by the bus station at the mouth of Soi 10.

The park

During the daytime you're bound to hear some of the local wildlife, even if you don't catch sight of it (see Contexts pp.816–826 for more on many of the following species). Noisiest of all are the **white-handed (lar) gibbons**, which hoot and whoop from the tops of the tallest trees, and the **pileated (capped) gibbons**, whose call is more of a bubbling trill. Gibbons generally avoid contact with the ground, but this is not the case with the hard-to-miss **pig-tailed macaques**, many of whom gather at favoured spots on the road through the park. **Hornbills** also create quite a racket, calling attention to themselves by flapping their enormous wings; Khao Yai harbours large flocks of four different hornbill species, which makes it one of the best places in Southeast Asia to observe these creatures. The great hornbill in particular is an incredibly beautiful bird, with brilliant yellow and black undersides; the magnificent oriental pied hornbill boasts less striking black and white colouring, but is more commonly seen at close range because it swoops down to catch fish, rats and reptiles. You might also see red-headed trogons, orange-breasted trogons, silver pheasants, woodpeckers and Asian fairy-bluebirds and, if you're lucky, the fire-back pheasant, endemic only to Thailand and western Cambodia. From November to March Khao Yai hosts several species of **migrant birds**, including the dramatically coloured Siberian thrush and the orange-headed thrush.

A herd of about two hundred Asian **elephants** lives in the park, and its members are often seen at night – it's the only place in Thailand where you have much likelihood of spotting wild elephants. Khao Yai is also home to an ever-dwindling number of **tigers**, currently estimated at fifteen, sightings of which are rare, though not mythical. You're almost certain to spot **civets**, and you might come across a **slow loris**, while barking **deer** and sambar deer are less nervous after dark. **Wrinkle-lipped bats** assemble en masse at sunset, especially at the cave entrance on Khao Luuk Chang (Baby Elephant Mountain), 6km north of the north (main) gate into the park, which every evening disgorges millions of them on their nightly forage.

Exploring the park

Fifteen well-worn **trails** – originally made by elephants and other park species, and still used by these animals – radiate from the area around the visitor centre and park headquarters at kilometre-stone 37, and a few more branch off from the roads that traverse the park. The main trails are numbered and should be easy to follow: a few are signposted en route or marked with coloured flashes. The **visitor centre** (daily 8am–6pm) sells photocopied park sketch maps with brief trail descriptions, as well as a more detailed park guidebook (B140) that includes a so-so topographical map, trail outlines and descriptions of the main mammals and their tracks. Rangers sometimes alter the course of a trail and, confusingly, they also sometimes renumber them, so ask at headquarters before you set off. Wear good boots, be prepared for some wading through rivers, and take a hat and plenty of water. If you don't fancy walking, you can rent **mountain bikes** from outside the visitors' centre (B40/hr or B300/day).

Snacks, bottled water, hot meals and mosquito repellent can be bought in the cafeteria complex opposite the visitor centre. You will probably be glad of a strong repellent to deter not just the usual insects but also **leeches**, which can be quite a problem during and just after the rainy season. If you've only got shorts, consider buying a pair of leech socks (canvas gaiters) from the shop opposite the visitor centre. The most effective way to get leeches off your skin is to burn them with a lighted cigarette, or douse them in salt; oily suntan lotion or insect repellent sometimes makes them lose their grip and fall off.

The trails

The shortest and least taxing of the park's trails is the one-kilometre-long **Kong Kaew Nature Trail (trail 14)**, which starts just behind the visitor centre. It's paved all the way and takes just thirty minutes in each direction; if it's not too crowded, you could see gibbons, woodpeckers and kingfishers en route.

Of the more adventurous hikes that begin from the park headquarters, the most popular is **trail 5,** which runs from just uphill of the visitor centre restaurant to **Nong Pak Chee observation tower** in the west of the park. This is a fairly easy walk through forest and grassland that culminates at an observation tower built next to a lake. En route you'll hear (if not see) white-handed gibbons in the tallest trees, and might spot barking deer in the savanna. If you stay at the tower long enough you could see needletails dive-bombing the lake; elephants and gaurs sometimes come to drink here, too, and you may even glimpse a tiger. The walk takes about two and a half hours to the observation tower (4.5km), from where it's another 900m down a dirt track which meets the main road between kilometre-stones 35 and 36. From the road, you can walk or hitch back either to the headquarters (2km) or down to the checkpoint (12km) and then travel on to Pak Chong. If you just want to spend a few hours at the observation tower and forget the main part of the walk, stop beside the main road between kilometre-stones 35 and 36 (before reaching the park headquarters) and walk the kilometre down the access track to the tower.

Trails 6 and 7 both branch off trail 5 into slightly shorter alternatives. **Trail 6**, from the park headquarters to **Wong Cham Pi (Wang Jumpee)**, is a two- to three-hour 4.4-kilometre hike that ends on the main road just 1.5km north of the headquarters at kilometre-stone 36. **Trail 7**, from the headquarters to **Mo Sing To,** is about a two-hour 2.7-kilometre route and goes through a different stretch of grassland and past a small lake.

Another good focus for walks is the area around **Haew Suwat Falls**, east of the visitor centre. These 25-metre-high falls are a great place for an invigorating shower, and they featured in the 1999 film *The Beach*. To get to the falls from the park headquarters, either follow trail 1 (see below), or walk, drive or hitch the six-kilometre road beyond the headquarters to Haew Suwat – it's a popular spot, so there should be plenty of cars.

Trail 1 runs from the visitor centre (8km one way; 3–4hr), beginning on the Nature Trail (trail 14) behind the visitor centre, then veering off it, along a path marked with red flashes, to **Haew Suwat**. En route to Haew Suwat you'll pass a turn-off to **trail 2** (which goes to *Pha Kluai/Orchid* campsite and waterfall; 6.1km from the park headquarters; see below); about forty minutes before reaching Haew Suwat is a signed trail off to the left that leads to nearby Haew Pratun Falls; twenty minutes further down trail 1 you may hear Haew Sai Falls in the distance, though these are easier to reach from Haew Suwat itself.

Day-trippers often do the shorter walk from Haew Suwat waterfall to **Pha Kluai/Orchid campsite (trail 3)**, which is paved most of the way and takes two hours at most (3.1km). You've a good chance of spotting gibbons and macaques along this route, as well as kingfishers and hornbills. The area around nearby Pha Kluai Falls is famous for its impressive variety of orchids. **Trail 4**, from Haew Suwat Falls to the **Khao Laem ranger post**, is a more strenuous undertaking; its main attractions are the waterfall, the wide expanse of grassland near Khao Laem and the impressive view of Khao Laem hill itself. You should ask permission from the park headquarters before setting out on this trail, and don't attempt it in the rainy season, as the river gets too high to cross. The trail 4 walk starts just upstream of the falls, from where it's about two hours to Khao Laem (4km) and the same back (along the same route).

Night safaris

A much-touted park attraction are the hour-long **night safaris** – officially known as "night-lightings" – which take truckloads of tourists round Khao Yai's main roads in the hope of catching some interesting wildlife in the glare of the specially fitted searchlights. Regular night-time sightings include deer and civets, and elephants and tigers are sometimes spotted as well. However, opinions differ on the quality of the night-lighting experience: some people find it thrilling just to be out on the edges of the jungle after dark, others see it as rather a crass method of wildlife observation, especially at weekends when the park can feel like a town centre, with four or five trucks following each other round and round the main roads. Whatever your conclusion, you will enjoy the outing a lot more if you take warm clothes with you – Khao Yai is quite high and gets very chilly after sunset.

The night-lighting trucks leave the park headquarters every night at 7pm and 8pm (they can pick you up from the campsite if requested). All night-lightings are run by the park rangers, so tour operators sometimes join forces to hire a truck with ranger and searchlights. If you're on your own, you'll probably need to accompany one of these groups, as the trucks cost B330 to rent and can take up to eight people: book your place at the national park accommodation office, next to the visitor centre.

Khorat (Nakhon Ratchasima) and around

Beyond Pak Chong, Highway 2 and the rail line diverge to run either side of picturesque Lam Takong Reservoir, offering a last taste of undulating, forested terrain before gaining the largely barren Khorat plateau. They rejoin at **KHORAT** (officially known as **Nakhon Ratchasima**) – literally, "Frontier Country" – which is still considered the gateway to the northeast.

If this is your first stop in Isaan, it's not a particularly pleasant introduction: home to around 430,000 people, Khorat is Thailand's second-largest city (after Bangkok), its streets are far too narrow for the traffic they're expected to cope with, and there's nothing here you could call a genuine "tourist attraction". It can also be a confusing place to get to grips with: the **commercial centre** used to be contained within the old city moat, at the eastern end of town, but it has spilt over westwards and there are shops and markets as well as hotels and restaurants in both areas. But Khorat is at the centre of a good **transport network** and is within striking distance of the **Khmer ruins** at Phimai, Phanom Rung and Muang Tam, as well as the archeological remains of **Ban Prasat**. Aside from serving Bangkok and all the main centres within Isaan, Khorat's bus network extends south along Highway 304 to the east coast, enabling you to travel directly to Pattaya, Rayong and Chanthaburi without going through the capital.

Arrival, information and city transport

There are two bus terminals in town. **Bus Terminal 2** (ⓣ044 256006–9), situated on the far northern edge of the city on Highway 2, is the main one and is the arrival and departure point for regular and air-con buses serving regional towns such as Pak Chong (for Khao Yai), Pak Tong Chai and Phimai, as well as long-distance destinations such as Bangkok (24-hr service), Ban Tako (for Phanom Rung), Chiang Mai, Khon Kaen, Nong Khai, Pattaya, Rayong (for Ko Samet) and Surin. The easiest way to get to and from Bus Terminal 2 is by tuk-tuk (B50 to the train station or nearby hotels), but city bus #15 also runs between Terminal 2 and the night bazaar area on Thanon Manat, from where city bus/songthaew #1 runs west along Thanon Chumphon to the train station and beyond (see below for details). **Bus Terminal 1** (ⓣ044 268899), which is more centrally located just off Thanon Suranari, also runs both fan and air-con buses to Bangkok, via Pak Thong Chai and Pak Chong, but the service from Terminal 2 is more frequent. The **train station** on Thanon Mukkhamontri (ⓣ044 242044) is served by city bus routes #1, #2 and #3, described below. It's still currently possible to fly to Khorat from Bangkok, though the service is random and expensive; the **airport** is 20km east of town on Highway 226 (ⓣ044 254834), and all planes are met by taxis and hotel minibuses, which charge B80 for the trip into town.

The **TAT office** (daily 8.30am–4.30pm; ⓣ044 213666, ⓔtatsima@tat.or.th) on the western edge of town gives out free maps of the convoluted city bus network and is reached from the city centre by city bus #2 or #3, as described below.

Flat-fare **songthaews** (B5) and air-conditioned **city buses** (B7) travel most of the main roads within town. The most useful routes are the yellow **#1** (served by both buses and songthaews), which heads west along Thanon Chumphon, goes past the train station and then along Thanon Suebsiri to *Doctor's Guest House* (on its return journey it travels east via Thanon Yommarat instead of Thanon Chumphon); **#2** (buses only), which runs between the main TAT office in the west, via the train station, along Thanon Suranari and Thanon

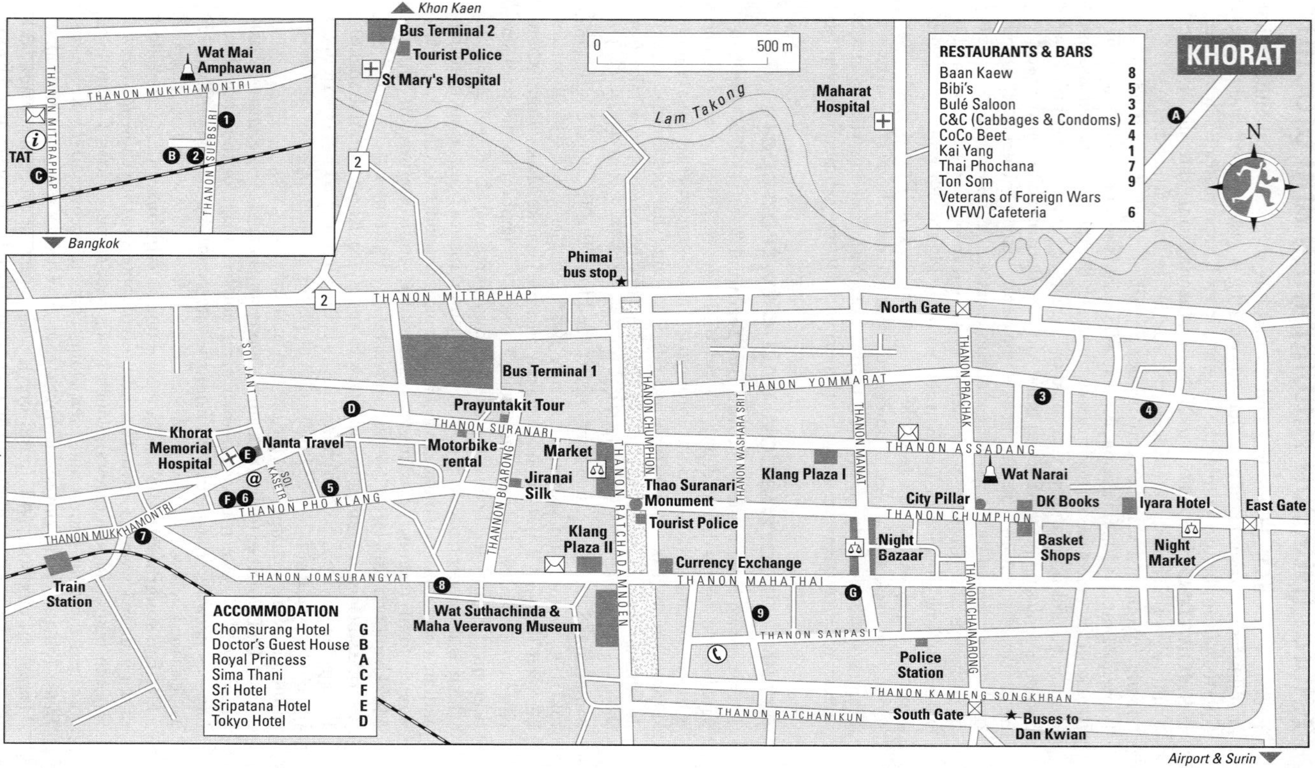
KHORAT
N
0
500 m
RESTAURANTS & BARS
Baan Kaew 8
Bibi's 5
Bulé Saloon 3
C&C (Cabbages & Condoms) 2
CoCo Beet 4
Kai Yang 1
Thai Phochana 7
Ton Som 9
Veterans of Foreign Wars (VFW) Cafeteria 6
ACCOMMODATION
Chomsurang Hotel G
Doctor's Guest House B
Royal Princess A
Sima Thani C
Sri Hotel F
Sripatana Hotel E
Tokyo Hotel D
Khon Kaen
Bangkok
See inset map
Airport & Surin
Bus Terminal 2
Tourist Police
St Mary's Hospital
Maharat Hospital
Lam Takong
Phimai bus stop
Wat Mai Amphawan
THANON MUKKHAMONTRI
THANON SUEBSIRI
THANON MITTRAPHAP
TAT
North Gate
East Gate
South Gate
Bus Terminal 1
Prayuntakit Tour
Khorat Memorial Hospital
Nanta Travel
Motorbike rental
Market
Jiranai Silk
Klang Plaza II
Thao Suranari Monument
Tourist Police
Currency Exchange
Klang Plaza I
Wat Narai
City Pillar
DK Books
Iyara Hotel
Night Bazaar
Basket Shops
Night Market
Police Station
Buses to Dan Kwian
Train Station
Wat Suthachinda & Maha Veeravong Museum
SOI JANT
SOI KASETR
THANON SURANARI
THANON PHO KLANG
THANNON BUARONG
THANON RATCHADAMNOEN
THANON CHUMPHON
THANON WASHARA SRIT
THANON YOMMARAT
THANON MANAT
THANON PRACHAK
THANON ASSADANG
THANON MAHATHAI
THANON SANPASIT
THANON CHAINARONG
THANON KAMIENG SONGKHRAN
THANON RATCHANIKUN
THANON JOMSURANGYAT

Assadang to beyond the *lak muang* (city pillar) in the east; **#3** (buses only), which also runs right across the city, via Mahathai and Jomsurangyat roads, past the train station, to the TAT office in the west; and **#15** (buses only), which runs between Bus Terminal 2 and the night bazaar area on Thanon Manat.

Accommodation

Many of the city's budget **hotels** are noisy and not that cheap, so if you're planning a visit to Phimai, consider staying in the atmospheric old guest house there rather than commuting from Khorat.

Chomsurang Hotel 2701/2 Thanon Mahathai ⓣ044 257088, ⓦwww.chomsurang.com. With expansive views over the city, this is one of Khorat's affordable best, and the usual choice of businesspeople and better-off tourists. All rooms have air-con; the pricier ones have TV and mini-bar, and there's a swimming pool. ❺

Doctor's Guest House 78 Soi 4, Thanon Suebsiri ⓣ044 255846. The most peaceful place in town, with a quaint B&B atmosphere, just five rooms with shared bathrooms, and a garden seating area, though it's currently managed by a couple who don't speak much English. A ten-minute ride west from the city centre: local yellow bus/songthaew #1 stops opposite the soi entrance (ask for "*thanon Suebsiri soi sii*"), while #2 passes the Thanon Suebsiri junction, so get off at the huge "American Standard" billboard across from the ornate Wat Mai Amphawan. Buses from Bangkok or Khao Yai can drop you outside the *Sima Thani* hotel, from where it's a 10min walk east. ❷

Royal Princess 1137 Thanon Suranari ⓣ044 256629, ⓦwww.royalprincess.com. Part of the *Royal Princess* chain, this top-notch hotel is out on the northeastern fringes of town and has 186 comfortable air-con rooms and two restaurants, plus a large swimming pool, a jogging track and a business centre. ❽

Sima Thani Thanon Mittraphap ⓣ044 213100, ⓦwww.simathani.co.th. One of the city's most upmarket hotels, with smart air-con rooms, a swimming pool, three restaurants and a babysitting service. There's a relaxed feel to the place despite its popularity with businesspeople, and the rooms are good value. Its location beside Highway 2 (the Bangkok–Nong Khai road) makes it very convenient for drivers, and buses from Bangkok or Khao Yai can drop you at the door en route to Bus Terminal 2, but it's too far to walk from the hotel to the town centre. Good discounts nearly always available. ❽

Sri Hotel 688–690 Thanon Pho Klang ⓣ044 242831. Less than a 10min walk from the train station, the *Sri* is more central than *Doctor's* and a recommended alternative for budget travellers. The en-suite fan and air-con rooms are surprisingly quiet and spacious (though don't expect a view), and there are some cheaper ones near the road. The friendly management can arrange minibuses to Phimai (B900 for up to three people). ❷–❸

Sripatana Hotel 346 Thanon Suranari ⓣ044 255349, ⓕ044 251655. Reasonably priced for the facilities, which include air-con in all rooms and a swimming pool on site. Significant discounts often available. ❸–❹

Tokyo Hotel 256–258 Thanon Suranari ⓣ044 242788, ⓕ044 252335; a 5min walk from Bus Terminal 1, or #15 from the train station. Good value, conveniently located traveller-friendly option that's both clean and friendly. Rooms are large and en suite, and some have air-con. ❷–❸

The City

Sights are thin on the ground in Khorat, but if you spend more than a couple of hours in the city you're bound to come across the landmark statue at the western gate of the old city walls. This is the much-revered **Thao Suranari Monument**, erected to commemorate the heroic actions of the wife of the deputy governor of Khorat, during an attack by the kingdom of Vientiane – capital of modern-day Laos – in 1826. Some chronicles say she organized a feast for the Lao army and enticed them into bed, where they were then slaughtered by the Thais; another tells how she and the other women of Khorat were carted off as prisoners to Vientiane, whereupon they attacked and killed their guards with such ferocity that the Lao retreated out of fear that the whole Thai army had arrived. At any rate, Thao Suranari saved the day and is still feted by the citizens of Khorat, who lay flowers at her feet, light incense at her shrine and even dance around it. At the end of March, the town holds a week-long **festival** in her honour, with parades through the streets and the usual colourful trappings of Thai merry-making. The **Maha Veeravong Museum** (Wed–Sun 9am–4pm; B10) houses a small and unexceptional collection of predominantly Dvaravati- and Lopburi-style Buddha statues found at nearby sites; it's in the grounds of Wat Suthachinda, on Thanon Ratchadamnoen.

Tourist shops and crafts outlets don't really feature in Khorat, but if you're not going further east to Surin, this is a good place to buy **silk**, much of which is produced in Pak Tong Chai, an uninteresting and over-exploited town 32km south of Khorat on Highway 304. The specialist shops along Thanon Chumphon sell lengths of silk at reasonable prices, but for the best and most exclusive selection visit Jiranai Silk, on the corner of Thanon Buarong and Pho Klang. Across the road from DK Books on Thanon Chumphon is a cluster of shops selling traditional **basketware** goods – though the sticky-rice baskets, fish traps and rice winnowers are sold as functional items, many are so deftly made that they make attractive souvenirs. The **night bazaar** that sets up at dusk every evening along Thanon Manat deals mainly in bargain-priced fashions and doesn't sell handicrafts.

Eating and drinking

The night bazaar on Thanon Manat includes a few hot-food stalls, but there's a bigger selection of **night-market**-style foodstalls, with some streetside tables, about 800m further east near the *Iyara Hotel* on Thanon Chumphon.

Baan Kaew 105/17–19 Thanon Jomsurangyat. Huge Thai-Chinese restaurant that's famous for its seafood dishes and roast-duck curry. Moderate.

Bibi's 300m east of *Sri Hotel* at 520 Thanon Pho Klang. Basic Muslim foodshop serving halal curries and standard one-dish Thai meals. Closes about 6pm. Inexpensive.

Bulé Saloon Thanon Yommarat. Wild-West-style pub and beer garden that stages live music (mainly soft rock) every night. Evenings only.

C&C (Cabbages & Condoms) Next to the Soi 4 intersection at 86/1 Thanon Suebsiri. Typical Thai fare at this restaurant managed along the same lines as its sister operation in Bangkok, with all proceeds going to the Population and Community Development Association of Thailand (PDA). Moderate.

CoCo Beet Thanon Yommarat. Air-con bar featuring nightly sets from bands that play Thai and Western pop. Evenings only.

The Emperor Inside the *Sima Thani* hotel on Thanon Mittraphap. Khorat's best Chinese restaurant, with a long menu of high-quality Chinese standards. Expensive.

Kai Yang Thanon Suebsiri. Popular place for lunchtime fried chicken with sticky rice. Inexpensive.

Thai Phochana 142 Thanon Jomsurangyat. Centrally located air-con restaurant known for its duck curries (*kaeng pet*) and Khorat-style noodles cooked with coconut cream (*mii khorat*). Also has several vegetarian options. Moderate.

Ton Som 125–129 Thanon Washara Srit. Long-running, fairly upmarket restaurant serving classical Thai cuisine that includes seasonal dishes such as *khao chae*, chilled jasmine rice served with up to seven different condiments, plus Chinese and Western standards. Moderate to expensive.

Veterans of Foreign Wars (VFW) Cafeteria Next to the *Sri Hotel* on Thanon Pho Klang. Cheap 'n' cheerful no-frills diner, complete with booths, which was set up by and for the GIs who've settled in the city. Dishes up hearty helpings of steak and fries, Polish sausage, pizzas and sandwiches (drinks only after about 7pm) and is a good place for US and European breakfasts, served from 8am. Inexpensive.

Listings

Bookshops DK Books, east of the *lak muang* on Thanon Chumphon, sells a few cheap Penguin Classics upstairs and a couple of English-language books about Thailand.

Car and motorbike rental From Nanta Travel on Thanon Suranari (see below). Motorbikes only from the repair shop about 200m further east along the same road.
Hospitals The private St Mary's Hospital is at 307 Thanon Mittraphap (Highway 2), near Bus Terminal 2 ☎044 261261; the government Maharat Hospital is on the northeast edge of town ☎044 254990–1.
Internet access Opposite *Sripatana Hotel* on Thanon Suranari, and a few hundred metres west of the train station on Thanon Mukhamontri, as well as (expensively) at the *Sima Thani* and *Royal Princess* hotels.
Mail There are post offices next to TAT on Thanon Mittraphap, inside the city walls on Thanon Assadang, and just west of the city walls on Thanon Jomsurangyat.
Telephones The CAT overseas telephone office is inside the city walls on Thanon Sanpasit.
Tourist police For all emergencies, call the tourist police on the free, 24hr phone line ☎1155, or contact them at one of their booths in town: their main office is opposite Bus Terminal 2 on Highway 2 ☎044 341777–9, and there's a more central booth beside the Thao Suranari Monument on Thanon Chumphon.
Tours and travel agents Nanta Travel Service, located a couple of doors east of the *Sripatana Hotel* on Thanon Suranari (daily 8am–8pm; ☎044 251339, ⓦwww.nantatravel.com), sells bus and air tickets (domestic and international), is an outlet for Budget car rental, and offers a big programme of day-trips to local sights, including to Phanom Rung (B790/person, minimum two people). *Siri Hotel* organizes inexpensive trips for up to three people to Phimai (B900/minibus) or Phanom Rung (B1400). Prayuntakit Tour on Thanon Suranari (cnr Thanon Buarong, ☎044 257211) sells Air Andaman tickets to Bangkok.

Dan Kwian

Some of the most sought-after modern pottery in Thailand is produced by the potters of **DAN KWIAN**, a tiny village 15km south of Khorat on Route 224. To get there, take local bus #1307 (destination Chok Chai; every 30min; 30min) from Bus Terminal 2, or pick it up at Khorat's southern city gate; get off as soon as you see the roadside pottery stalls, which display the whole range of goods, from inexpensive sunbaked clay necklaces to traditional urn-shaped water jars.

The local clay, dug from the banks of the Mun River, has a high iron content, which when fired in wood-burning kilns combines with ash to create the unglazed metallic finish that is characteristic of **Dan Kwian pottery**. The geometrical latticework pattern is also typical, and is incorporated into everything from incense burners and ashtrays to vases and storage jars. Dan Kwian potters also produce ceramic tiles and large-scale religious and secular murals, which make popular decorations in modern wats and city homes.

First settled by Mon in the mid-eighteenth century, Dan Kwian has always been a convenient rest spot for travellers journeying between the Khorat plateau and Cambodia – hence its name, which means "Cart Place" or "Wagon Station". The tag still applies, as the village is now home to a **cart museum** (always open; free), a ramshackle outdoor collection of traditional vehicles and farming implements assembled at the back of the pottery stalls. Look out for the monster machine with two-metre wheels, designed to carry two tons of rice, and the covered passenger wagons with their intricately carved shafts. The exhibits aren't all as archaic as they look – Isaan farmers still use some of the sugar-cane presses on display, and the fish traps and lobster pots are a common sight in this part of the country.

Ban Prasat

The quintessentially northeastern village of **BAN PRASAT** has become a source of great interest to archeologists following the discovery in the 1990s of a series of **burial grounds** within its boundaries, some of which date back 3000 years. The skeletons and attendant artefacts have been well preserved in the mud, and many of the finds are now on public display in Ban Prasat; the village has made extra efforts to entice tourists with low-key craft demonstrations and a home-stay programme. It's also a pleasant village in its own right, a traditional community of stilt houses set beside the Tarn Prasat River, which rises in Khao Yai National Park; water from Tarn Prasat, one of the nine most sacred rivers in Thailand, was used in the religious ceremonies for the king's 72nd birthday celebrations in 1999.

There are currently three **excavation pits** open to the public, each clearly signed from the centre of the village and informatively labelled. From these pits archeologists have surmised that Ban Prasat was first inhabited about 1000 BC and that its resident rice farmers traded their wares with coastal people, from whom they received shell jewellery, among other goods. Each pit contains bones and objects from different eras, buried at different depths but also with the head pointing in different directions, suggesting a change in religious or superstitious precepts. **Artefacts** found and displayed alongside them include stone discs, or *chakra,* believed to date back to 1000 BC, lots of wide-lipped or "trumpet-rim" earthenware vessels decorated with patterns applied in red slip, glazed Khmer-style pottery, and glass and bronze bangles. There are additional exhibits at the **Ban Prasat Museum** beside the car park, though its opening hours seem rather erratic.

Signs in the village direct you to local family-run projects, such as the household of **silk-weavers**, where you should be able to see several stages of the sericulture process (see box on p.503 for more on the Thai silk industry) and buy some cloth. Other village crafts include the weaving of floor mats from locally grown bulrushes, and the making of household brooms.

Ban Prasat is located just off Highway 2, 46km north of Khorat and 17km southwest of Phimai. Any Khorat–Phimai bus (#1305 from Khorat's Bus Terminal 2; every 30min; about 1hr from Khorat or 20min from Phimai) will drop you at the Highway 2 junction, from where motorbike taxis will ferry you the 2km to the village. There are no hotels or restaurants in the village, but there is a **home-stay** programme, which is a great opportunity to savour typical village life. Home-stays cost B400 per person per night, including two meals, and should be arranged at least a week in advance by contacting Khun Teim Laongkarn of the Eco-tourism Society, 282 Mu 7, Tambon Tarn Prasat, Amphoe Non Sung, Nakhon Ratchasima 30420 (Ⓣ044 367075). Alternatively, staff at the Khorat TAT office may be able to help (Ⓣ044 213666, Ⓔtatsima@tat.or.th).

Phimai

Hemmed in by its rectangular old city walls and encircled by tributaries of the Mun River, the small modern town of **PHIMAI**, 60km northeast of Khorat, is completely dominated by the charmingly restored Khmer temple complex of **Prasat Hin Phimai**. No one knows for sure when the prasat was built or for whom, but as a religious site it probably dates back to the reign of the Khmer king Suriyavarman I (1002–49); the complex was connected by a direct road to Angkor and orientated southeast, towards the Khmer capital. Over the next couple of centuries Khmer rulers made substantial modifications, and by the end of Jayavarman VII's reign (1181–1220), Phimai had been officially dedicated to Mahayana Buddhism. Phimai's other claim to fame is **Sai Ngam** (Beautiful Banyan), reputedly the largest banyan tree in Thailand, still growing a couple of kilometres beyond the temple walls.

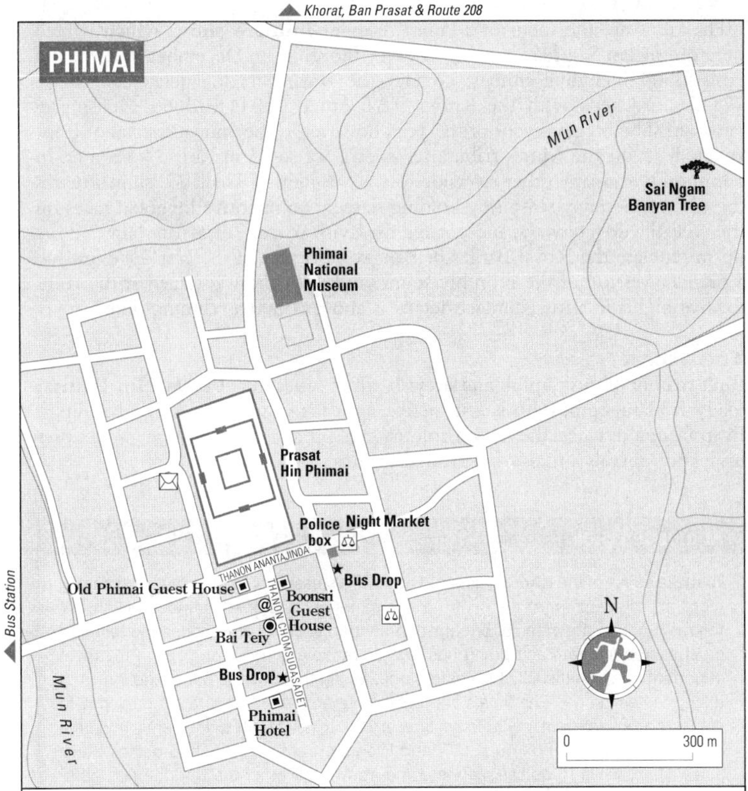

PRASAT HIN PHIMAI

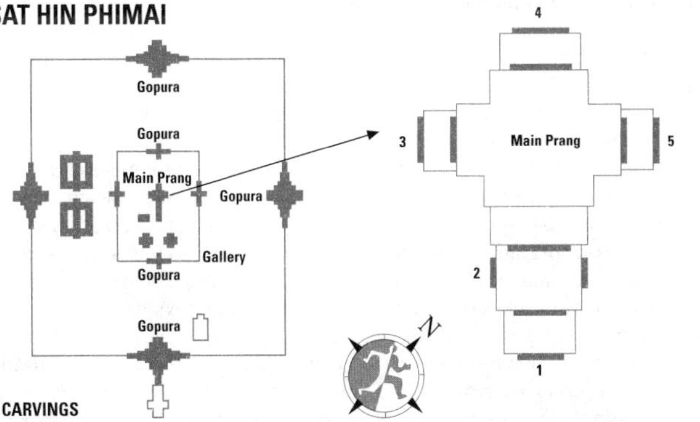

PHIMAI CARVINGS

1 Exterior: The dance of Shiva.
Interior: Buddha sheltered by a naga.

2 Exterior: Krishna lifting Mount Govadhana. Rama and his brother Lakshaman bound with serpentine ropes.

3 Exterior: Battle scene from the *Ramayana*; Rama and his monkeys build a bridge by hurling mountains into the sea.
Interior: Buddha beneath trees; dancers and musicians embellish Buddha's sermons.

4 Exterior: *Ramayana* battle; Vishnu holding conch shell, lotus, club and chakri disc.
Interior: Five Vajarasatvas, each with six hands and three faces.

5 Exterior: The God of Justice pronounces on the Rama/Ravana dispute; Rama kills the giant Viradha.
Interior: Boddhisatva Trailokayavicha with his left foot suspended over Ignorance.

The ruins are the focus of a "mini" **son-et-lumière show**, which is held here on the last Saturday evening of every month from December to April and costs B500 including dinner; contact the organizers for details on ⓣ044 471121, or check with the Khorat TAT office (ⓣ044 213666, ⓔtatsima@tat.or.th). The biggest event of the year, however, is the annual festival of **boat races**, held on the Mun's tributaries over a weekend in early November. In common with many other riverside towns throughout Thailand, Phimai marks the end of the rainy season by holding fiercely competitive longboat races on the well-filled waterways, and putting on lavish parades of ornate barges done up to emulate the Royal Barges of Bangkok. As part of the boat-race festival, a grander version of the monthly sound-and-light show is staged at the ruins for five nights in a row; contact details as above (B500, excluding dinner).

The ruins

Built mainly of dusky pink and greyish white sandstone, **Prasat Hin Phimai** (daily 7.30am–6pm; B40) is a seductive sight for so solemn a set of buildings. Even from a distance, the muted colours give off a far from austere glow; closer inspection reveals a mass of intricate carvings.

Khmer temples

To make sense of the **Khmer ruins** of Thailand, it's essential to identify their common architectural features. At the centre of the rectangular temple compound is always the main prang, a pyramidal or corn-cob-shaped tower built to house the temple's most sacred image. Each prang has four entrance chambers or gopura, the most important of which (usually the eastern one, facing the dawn) is often extended into a large antechamber. The lintels and pediments above the gopura are carved with subjects from relevant mythology: typical Hindu reliefs show incidents from the *Ramayana* epic (see box on p.127) and lively portraits of the Hindu deities Shiva and Vishnu, while Buddhist scenes come from the lives of the Buddha and other bodhisattvas. Antefixes on the roof of the prang are often carved with the Hindu gods of direction, some of the most common being Indra on the three-headed elephant (east); Yama on a buffalo (south); Varuna on a naga or a *hamsa*, a sacred goose (west); Brahma on a *hamsa* (north); and Isaana on a bull (northeast).

Originally, the prang would have sheltered a **shiva lingam**, continuously bathed by lustral water dripping from a pot suspended over it; the water then flowed out of the inner chamber by means of a stone channel, a process which symbolized the water of the Ganges flowing from the Himalayan home of Shiva. In most prasats, however, the lingam has disappeared or been replaced with Hindu or Buddhist statues.

One or two **minor prangs** usually flank the main prang: often these were added at a later date to house images of less important gods, though in some cases they predate the main structure. Concentric sets of walls shield these shrines within an inner courtyard. In many temples, the innermost wall – the **gallery** – was roofed, either with wood (none of these roofs has survived) or stone. Many of the stone blocks used to build the temple walls have **small round holes** in them; these were either fitted with pegs that enabled blocks to be moved with ropes, or were used to fit poles for leverage. At their cardinal points some galleries have gopuras with carved lintels and pediments, which are usually approached by staircases flanked with **naga balustrades**; in Khmer temples, nagas generally appear as symbolic bridges between the human world and that of the gods. Most prangs enclose ponds between their outer and inner walls, and many are surrounded by a network of moats and **reservoirs**: historians attribute the Khmers' political success in part to their skill in designing highly efficient irrigation systems (see p.782 for the history of the Khmers in Thailand).

From the main southeastern gate, a staircase ornamented with classic naga balustrades leads to a gopura in the **outer walls**, which are punctuated on either side by false balustraded windows – a bit of sculptural sleight-of-hand to jazz up the solid stonework without piercing the defences. A raised pathway bridges the space between these walls and the inner gallery that protects the prangs of the **inner sanctuary**. The minor prang to the right, made of laterite, is attributed to the twelfth-century Buddhist king Jayavarman VII, who engaged in a massive temple-building campaign during his reign. Enshrined within is a statue of him; it's a copy of the much more impressive original, which was found in the same location and is now housed in the Phimai National Museum. The pink sandstone prang to the left, which is connected to a Brahmin shrine where seven stone linga were found, was probably built around the same time.

After more than twenty years of archeological detective work and painstaking reassembly, the magnificent white sandstone **main prang** has now been restored to its original cruciform groundplan and conical shape, complete with an almost full set of carved lintels, pediments and antefixes, and capped with a stone lotus bud. The **carvings** around the outside of the prang depict predominantly Hindu themes. Shiva – the Destroyer – dances above the main entrance to the southeast antechamber: his destruction dance heralds the end of the world and the creation of a new order, a supremely potent image that warranted this position over the most important doorway. For more on these legends, see "Art and Architecture" in Contexts (p.802). Most of the other external carvings pick out momentous episodes from the *Ramayana* (see box on p.127), starring heroic Rama, his brother Lakshaman and their band of faithful monkeys in endless battles of strength, wits and magical powers against Ravana, the embodiment of evil. Inside, more sedate Buddhist scenes give evidence of the conversion from Hindu to Buddhist faith, and the prasat's most important image, the Buddha sheltered by a seven-headed naga, sits atop a base that once supported a Hindu Shiva lingam.

Phimai National Museum

Much of the ancient carved stonework discovered at Phimai but not fitted back into the renovated structure can be seen at the **Phimai National Museum** (daily 8.30am–4pm; B30), where it's easier to appreciate, being at eye-level, well labelled and contextualized. The museum stands between one of the old Khmer reservoirs and the Mun River, just inside the old city walls to the northeast of the ruins. It's an easy walk from the ruins, but if you're here for the day from Khorat, you can save your legs a bit as the Khorat–Phimai bus will stop outside the museum if requested. The museum's pièce de résistance is the exceptionally fine sandstone statue of Jayavarman VII that was found in Phimai's laterite prang; seated and leaning slightly forward, he's lost his arms and part of his nose, but none of his grace and serenity. Elsewhere in the galleries, displays take you through the religious and cultural history of the Phimai region, featuring prehistoric items from Ban Prasat (see p.489) as well as some exquisite Buddha statues from more recent times.

Sai Ngam

Two kilometres northeast of the museum – get there by bicycle (see below) or samlor – **Sai Ngam** is a banyan tree so enormous that it's reputed to cover an area about half the size of a soccer pitch (approximately 2300 square metres). It might look like a grove of small banyans, but Sai Ngam is in fact a single *ficus bengalensis* whose branches have dropped vertically into the ground, taken root and spawned other branches, so growing further and further out from its central trunk. Banyan trees are believed to harbour animist spirits, and you can make merit here by releasing fish into the artificial lake that surrounds Sai Ngam. The tree is a popular recreation spot, and several restaurants have sprung up alongside it.

Practicalities

Phimai's **bus station** is inconveniently located 1.5km southwest of the ruins, on the bypass, but nearly everybody gets on and off in the town centre, either near the night-market area or in front of the *Phimai Hotel*. Regular **bus** #1305 runs direct to Phimai from Khorat's Bus Terminal 2, with a pick-up point near the Thanon Mittraphap/Ratchadamnoen junction (every 30min until 6.30pm, then sporadically until 10pm; 1hr 30min); the last return bus departs Khorat at 7pm. The bus passes the turn-off to Ban Prasat (see p.489), so if you get up early you can combine the two places on a day-trip from Khorat. If travelling from Khon Kaen, Udon Thani or Nong Khai, take any Khorat-bound bus along Highway 2 as far as the Phimai turn-off (Highway 208), then change onto the Khorat– Phimai service for the last 10km; the same strategy works in reverse. It's also feasible, if a bit of an effort, to visit Phimai en route to points east or west without having to pass through Khorat. You can do this by taking a **train** to the tiny station of **Hin Dat**, which is about an hour and forty minutes' train ride west of Surin, or about 55 minutes' ride east of Khorat. Hin Dat is 25km south of Phimai, so from here you should either wait for one of the infrequent songthaews to Phimai, splash out on an expensive motorbike taxi or try hitching. Songthaews back to Hin Dat from Phimai are generally timed to link up with east-bound trains; check with the *Old Phimai Guest House*, for current timetables.

Once in Phimai, the best way to get about is by **bicycle**, although this isn't permitted inside the ruins. *Bai Teiy* restaurant has bicycles for rent and issues free maps of cycling routes around town, while *Old Phimai Guest House* has bicycles for guests only. Aside from the ride out to Sai Ngam, the area just west of the ruins, beyond the post office, is especially atmospheric – many of the traditional wooden houses here double as workshops, and you'll often see householders weaving cane chairs in the shade beneath the buildings. There is **Internet** access inside the Agfa photo shop on Thanon Chomsudasadet, near the *Old Phimai*, and the post office has a Catnet terminal.

Accommodation and eating

Though most people visit the ruins as a day-trip, Phimai has two inexpensive **places to stay** as well as an unpretentious hotel, and makes a much more attractive and peaceful overnight stop than Khorat. Your first choice should be the laid-back *Old Phimai Guest House* (Ⓣ & Ⓕ 044 471918; ❷–❸), an old wooden house with a roof terrace, just off Thanon Chomsudasadet and only a couple of minutes' walk from the ruins; YHA members get a ten-percent discount on room rates, and there are also B80 dorm beds available. The rooms are large and some are air-conditioned, but they all share bathrooms. The *Old Phimai* is an excellent source of information and also runs day-trips to Phanom Rung at B380 per person (minimum four people). Equally central, and offering huge, immaculate rooms, *Boonsri Guest House* (Ⓣ 044 471159; ❸) occupies the upper floors of the proprietor's home, above her duck restaurant on Thanon Chomsudasadet; doubles here are en suite and very spruce, or a dorm mattress costs B120. More upmarket, the friendly *Phimai Hotel*, next to the bus drop (Ⓣ 044 471306, Ⓦ www.khorat.in.th/phimaihotel/eindex.htm; ❸–❹), has large, good-quality rooms with fan or air-con.

Bai Teiy on Thanon Chomsudasadet, the town's most popular **restaurant**, serves tasty Thai dishes, including fresh fish from the river; it also acts as an informal tourist information service and can help with bus and train timetables. If you prefer a meal with a view, head out to the string of pricier restaurants alongside Sai Ngam. The night market sets up at dusk on the eastern stretch of Thanon Anantajinda, just southeast of the ruins, and is a good place to sample genuine local fare at genuine local prices.

Phanom Rung and Muang Tam

East of Khorat the bleached plains roll blandly on, broken only by the occasional small town and, if you're travelling along Highway 24, the odd tantalizing glimpse of the smoky Phanom Dangkrek mountain range above the southern horizon. That said, it's well worth jumping off the Surin-bound bus for a detour to the fine Khmer ruins of **Prasat Hin Khao Phanom Rung** and **Prasat Muang Tam**. Built during the same period as Phimai, and for the same purpose, the temple complexes form two more links in the chain that once connected the Khmer capital with the limits of its empire. Sited dramatically atop an extinct volcano, Phanom Rung has been beautifully restored, and the more recently renovated Muang Tam lies on the plains below.

Practicalities: Ban Tako, Nang Rong and Buriram

To get to the ruins, you first need to take a **bus** to the small town of **BAN TAKO**, located on Highway 24 about 115km southeast of Khorat or 83km southwest of Surin. Bus #274 travels between the two provincial capitals, leaving every thirty minutes around the clock and taking 2 hours 25 minutes from Khorat or 1 hour 45 minutes from Surin. From Ban Tako it's 12km south to Phanom Rung and another 8km southeast along a side road to Muang Tam, and as there's no public transport direct to the ruins most people rent an expensive **motorbike taxi** here, which usually costs B300 per person for the round-trip to Phanom Rung, Muang Tam and back to Ban Tako. Alternatively you could try **hitching** – a time-consuming option during the week (so you should take a very early bus from Khorat or Surin), but a lot easier at weekends. The best place to hitch from is a small village south of Ban Tako called **Ban Don Nong Nae**, which you can reach from Ban Tako by taking a ten-minute songthaew ride. Alternatively, rent your own motorbike from *Honey Inn* in Nang Rong (see below), or join one of the inexpensive **day-tours** organized from Phimai by the *Old Phimai Guest House* (B380/person; see opposite), or from Khorat (see p.489). There are two car parks and two **entrances** to the Phanom Rung complex; if you have your own transport, ignore the Gate 2 (west) entrance, signed off the access road, and carry on to the main, Gate 1 (east), entrance and car park – the drama of the site is lost if you explore it back-to-front. Motorbike taxis should take you to the main entrance. There are cheap foodstalls outside the Gate 1 entrance, and a restaurant in its car park area.

Most people do the ruins as a day-trip from Khorat or Surin, but an increasingly popular option is to **stay** in the town of **NANG RONG**, on the #274 bus route, 14km west of Ban Tako on Highway 24. Here, the welcoming guest house *Honey Inn* (ⓣ044 622825, ⓦhoneyinn.com; ❷), at 8/1 Soi Sri Koon, offers rooms with and without bathroom, motorbike rental, meals with the family and Internet access. To get to *Honey Inn* from the Nang Rong bus terminal, either take a B20 samlor ride or walk north about 100m onto

Highway 24, cross the highway, turn right and walk east along the highway for about 300m, passing a PTT petrol station after about 200m. Turn left at the *Honey Inn* sign and it's about 100m further on. The alternative is to stay in the provincial capital of **BURIRAM**, 50km northeast of Nang Rong and served by frequent buses between the two (1hr), as well as by all Bangkok–Ubon trains, and (currently) by Air Andaman flights between Bangkok's Don Muang Airport and **Buriram Airport** (ⓣ044 680132), 30km from town. About 200m south of the train station along the main drag, Thanon Romburi, the *Thai Hotel* (ⓣ044 611112, ⓕ044 612461; ❷–❸), at 38/1, has decent air-con rooms, or there's more comfortable, upmarket accommodation at the *Vongthong Hotel* (ⓣ044 612540, ⓔvongthong@isan.sawadee.com; ❹–❺), a few minutes' walk west of the bus terminal, off Thanon Buladmuan at 512/1 Thanon Jira, which offers large rooms with air-con and TV.

Prasat Hin Khao Phanom Rung

Prasat Hin Khao Phanom Rung stands as the finest example of Khmer architecture in Thailand, graced with innumerable exquisite carvings and with its sandstone and laterite buildings so perfectly aligned that on the morning of the fifteenth day of the waxing moon in the fifth month of the lunar calendar you can stand at the westernmost gopura and see the rising sun through all fifteen doors. This day (usually in April: check dates with TAT) is celebrated with a day-long **festival** of huge parades all the way up the hill to the prasat – a tradition believed to go back eight hundred years. As at most Khmer prasats, **building** at Phanom Rung was a continuous process that spanned several reigns: the earliest structures are thought to date to the beginning of the tenth century and final additions were probably made three hundred years later, not long before it was abandoned. The heart of the temple was constructed in the mid-twelfth century, in early Angkorian style, and is attributed to local ruler Narendraditya and his son Hiranya. A lintel inside the temple is thought to depict Narendraditya's investiture as ruler. Narendraditya was a follower of the Shivaite cult, a sect which practised yoga and fire worship and used alcohol and sex in its rituals, and carved depictions of all these practices decorate the temple. Restoration work at Phanom Rung was begun in 1971 and lasted seventeen years: the results are impressive and give the most complete picture of Khmer architecture in Thailand.

Awesome as the temple complex is, its appeal is greatly enhanced if you can make sense of the layout and symbolism, so it's well worth spending twenty minutes in the excellent, museum-like **Phanom Rung Tourist Information Centre** inside the Gate 1 car park (daily 9am–4pm; free) before entering. A series of clear display boards provide an outstanding introduction to the temple's construction, iconography and restoration. The exhibition also includes small displays on Muang Tam and other nearby Khmer ruins, and there's a separate children's room with related puzzles and activity ideas.

Exploring the temple

The approach to **Prasat Hin Khao Phanom Rung** (daily 6am–6pm; B40) is one of the most dramatic of its kind. Symbolic of the journey from earth to the heavenly palace of the gods, the ascent to the inner compound is imbued with metaphorical import: by following the 200-metre-long avenue, paved in laterite and sandstone and flanked with lotus-bud pillars, you are walking to the ends of the earth. Ahead, the main prang, representing Mount Meru, home of the gods, looms large above the gallery walls, and is accessible only via the first of three **naga bridges**, a raised cruciform structure with sixteen naga balustrades, each naga having five heads. Once across the bridge you have traversed the abyss between earth and heaven. A series of stairways ascends to the eastern entrance of the celestial home, first passing four small ponds, thought to have been used for ritual purification. A second naga bridge crosses to the **east gopura**, entrance to the inner sanctuary, which is topped by a lintel carved with Indra (god of the east) sitting on a lion throne. The gopura is the main gateway through the **gallery**, which runs right round the inner compound and has one main and two minor entranceways on each side. Part of the gallery has been restored to its original covered design, with arched stone roofs, small chambers inside and **false windows**; real windows wouldn't have been strong enough to support such a heavy stone roof, so false ones, which retained the delicate pilasters but backed them with stone blocks, were an aesthetically acceptable compromise. The chambers may have been used for exhibiting as well as storing artefacts.

Phanom Rung is surprisingly compact, so the east gopura leads almost directly into the **main prang**, separated from it only by a final naga bridge. A dancing Shiva, nine of his ten arms intact, and a lintel carved with a relief of a **reclining Vishnu** preside over the eastern entrance to the prang. The Vishnu image has a somewhat controversial history: stolen from the site in the early 1960s, it mysteriously reappeared as a donated exhibit in the Art Institute of Chicago; for over ten years the curators refused to return it to Thailand, but as restoration work on Phanom Rung neared completion in 1988, the Thai public took up the cause and the Institute finally relented. The relief depicts a common Hindu creation myth, known as "Reclining Vishnu Asleep on the Milky Sea of Eternity", in which Vishnu dreams up a new universe, and Brahma (the four-faced god perched on the lotus blossom that springs from Vishnu's navel) puts the dream into practice. On the pediment above this famous relief is a lively carving of **Shiva Nataraja**, or Shiva's Dance of Destruction, which shows him dancing on Mount Kailash in front of several others gods, including Ganesh, Brahma and Vishnu (see p.802 for more on the Hindu legends). Labels highlight the most interesting narrative lintels in the prang, one of which is the supposed investiture of Phanom Rung builder Narendraditya, above the second (inside) southern doorway. Of the other recurring figures decorating the prang, one of the most important is the lion head of Kala, also known as Kirtimukha, symbolic of both the lunar and the solar eclipse and – because he's able to "swallow" the sun – considered far superior to other planetary gods. Inside the prang kneels an almost life-sized statue of Shiva's vehicle, the bull Nandi, behind which stands the all-powerful **Shiva lingam**, for which the prang was originally built; the stone channel that runs off the lingam and out of the north side of the prang was designed to catch the lustral water with which the sacred stone was bathed.

Two rough-hewn laterite libraries stand alongside the main prang, in the northeast and southeast corners, and there are also remains of two early-tenth-century brick prangs just northeast of the main prang. The unfinished **prang noi** (little prang) in the southwest corner now contains a stone Buddha footprint, which has become the focus of the merit-making that underlies the annual April festivities, thus neatly linking ancient and modern religious practices.

Prasat Muang Tam

Down on the well-watered plains 8km to the southeast of Phanom Rung and accessed via a scenic minor road that cuts through a swathe of ricefields, the small but elegant temple complex of **Prasat Muang Tam** (daily 7.30am–6pm; B30) is sited behind a huge kilometre-long *baray* (Khmer reservoir), which was probably constructed at the same time as the main part of the temple, in the early eleventh century. Like Phanom Rung, Muang Tam was probably built in stages between the tenth and thirteenth centuries, and is based on the classic Khmer design of a central prang flanked by minor prangs and encircled by a gallery and four gopura. Muang Tam's history is presented in brief at the **tourist information centre** (daily 9am–4pm; free) in the temple car park, where a short English-language video gives a reasonable introduction to the complex, backed up by a few photographic displays.

The approach to Muang Tam is nothing like as grand as at Phanom Rung but, once through the main, eastern gopura in the outside wall, it's a pretty scene, with the central gallery encircled by four **L-shaped ponds** – such important features that they are referred to in a contemporary inscription that states "this sanctuary is preserved by sacred water". The shape of the ponds gives the impression that the prasat is set within a moat that's been severed by the four entrance pathways at the cardinal points. Each pond is lined with laterite brick steps designed to enable easy access for priests drawing sacred water, and possibly also for devotees to cleanse themselves before entering the central sanctuary. The rims are constructed from sandstone blocks that form naga, the sacred water serpents.

The rectangular central **gallery** was probably roofed with timber (long since rotted away) and so could be punctuated with real windows, rather than the more load-bearing false versions that had to be used at Phanom Rung. Inside, the **five red-brick towers** of the inner sanctuary are arranged on a laterite platform, with three prangs in the front (eastern) row, and two behind. The main, central, prang has collapsed, leaving only its base, but the four other towers are merely decapitated and some have carved **lintels** intact. The lintel above the doorway of the front right tower is particularly lively in its depiction of the popular scene known as Ume Mahesvara (Uma and her consort Shiva riding the bull Nandi). There are interesting details in the temple complex, including recurrent motifs of foliage designs and Kala lion-faces, and figures of ascetics carved into the base of the doorway pillars on the eastern gopura of the outer wall.

Surin and around

Best known for its much-hyped annual elephant round-up, the provincial capital of **Surin**, 197km east of Khorat, is an otherwise typical northeastern town, a good place to absorb the easy-going pace of Isaan life, with the bonus of some atmospheric Khmer ruins nearby. The elephant tie-in comes from the local Suay people, whose prowess with pachyderms is well known and can sometimes be seen first-hand in the nearby village of **Ban Ta Klang**. Thais, Lao and Khmers make up the remainder of the population of Surin province – the Khmers have lived and worked in the region for over a thousand years, and their architectural legacy is still in evidence at the ruined temples of Ta Muean and Ban Pluang. The local Khmer population was boosted during the Khmer Rouge takeover of Cambodia in the 1970s, when many upper-class Cambodians fled here. Three decades on and, with a slightly more stable political situation in Cambodia, it is now possible for foreigners **to cross overland between Thailand and Cambodia** via Surin province's Chong Chom checkpoint near Kap Choeng.

△ Prasat Muang Tam

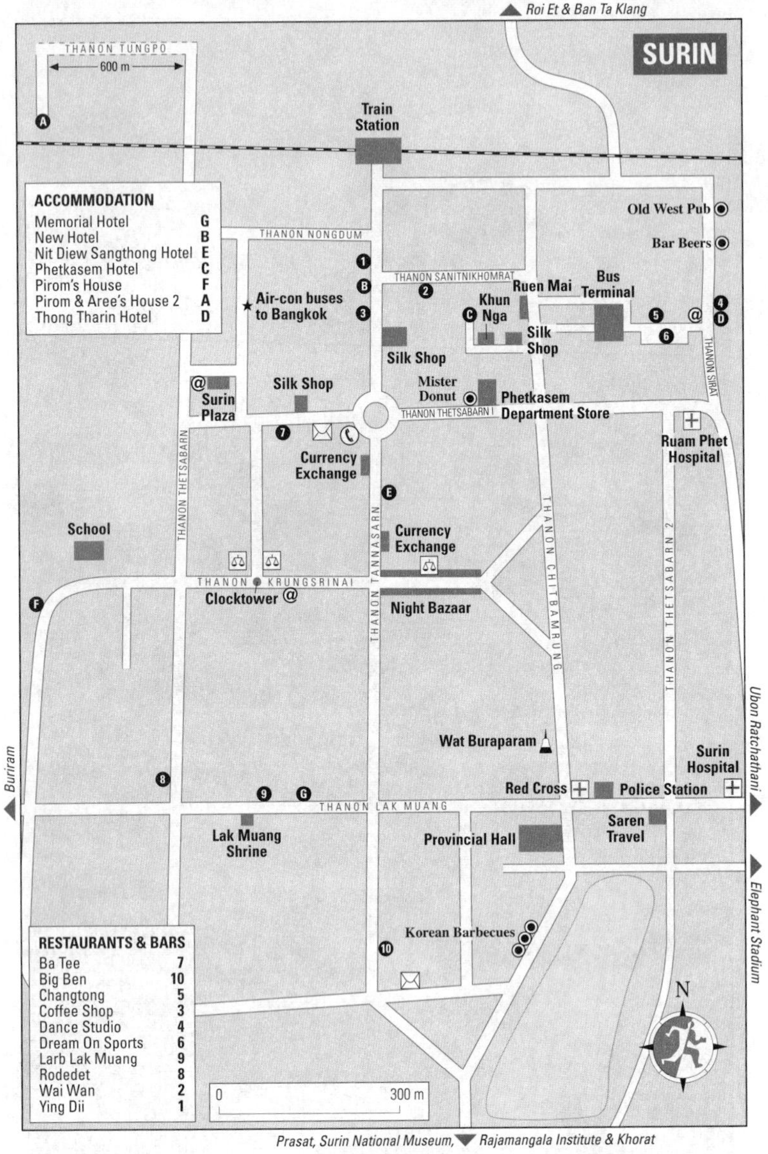

Arrival, information and transport

Several trains a day make the Bangkok–Surin connection, stopping at the **station** (☎044 511295) on the northern edge of town. The **bus terminal** (☎044 511756) off Thanon Chitbamrung runs frequent services to and from Bangkok, to major northeastern towns, and to Pattaya, Rayong, Phitsanulok, Lampang and Chiang Mai. If you're planning to cross **overland into**

Cambodia, buses leave Surin approximately once an hour from dawn until 4.30pm for the one-and-a-half-hour journey via Prasat to Kap Choeng's Chong Chom border pass. Cambodian visas are issued on arrival at the Chong Chom–O'Smach checkpoint (daily 7am–8pm; US$20 or B1000), from where you can get transport to Anlong Veng and then on to Siem Reap, which is 150km from the border crossing. Arriving from Cambodia, songthaews and motorbike taxis ferry travellers from the border checkpoint to the bus stop for Prasat and Surin. For travellers' accounts of the border crossing, see ⓦtalesofasia.com/cambodia-overland-osm-reports.htm; for details on other overland routes into Cambodia, see p.18.There is a tiny **airport** in Surin (ⓣ044 538595), served by irregular Air Andaman flights to and from Bangkok.

Accommodation

During the elephant round-up, room rates in Surin double, and **accommodation** fills up weeks in advance, so book well ahead and make use of the accommodation-booking websites listed in Basics on p.46. During the rest of the year you'll have no trouble finding a place to stay.

Memorial Hotel 186 Thanon Lak Muang ⓣ044 511288, ⓕ044 519344. Average mid-range place, with lacklustre service and karaoke downstairs; some rooms have air-con and TV. ❸–❹

New Hotel 22 Thanon Tannasarn ⓣ044 511341, ⓕ044 538410. Clean enough, if rather worn, rooms with fan and shower, plus some with air-con. ❶–❸

Nit Diew Sangthong Hotel 155–161 Thanon Tannasarn ⓣ044 512099, ⓕ044 514329. The best of the budget hotels, this place is friendly and well run. All rooms are en suite, and some have air-con and TV. ❷–❸

Phetkasem Hotel off Thanon Chitbamrung ⓣ044 511274, ⓔpkhotel@cscoms.com. One of Surin's best hotels, offering good-value, sizeable air-con rooms with TV, and a swimming pool. ❺

Pirom's House 242 Thanon Krungsrinai ⓣ044 515140 or 09 355 4140. Pirom and Aree's teak-wood home is one of the friendliest guest houses in Isaan, and a reason in itself to stop off in Surin. Rooms are simple and have shared facilities, and there's a B70 dorm. As the tenancy on their current home is under threat, Pirom has constructed a new guest house, *Pirom & Aree's House 2*, amidst the rice fields off Thanon Tungpo, northwest of the railway, but for the foreseeable future guests should still head for the original place, though it's probably wise to phone first. ❷

Thong Tarin Hotel 60 Thanon Sirat ⓣ044 514281, ⓕ044 511580. The poshest hotel in town, with upmarket rooms equipped with air-con and TV, plus a swimming pool on the premises and the enormous Dance Studio nightlife complex next door. Discounts often available. ❺

The Town

Surin has no special sights of its own, but the **Surin National Museum** (Wed–Sun 8.30am–4.30pm; B30), inconveniently located about 5km south of town on Highway 214 (any Khorat-bound bus will drop you outside), is the place to get a handle on the province's diverse cultural roots and its major attractions, including the Suay elephant-handlers, nearby Khmer ruins and the local silk industry.

Surin's **silk** weave is famous for its variety: seven hundred designs are produced in Surin province alone, many of them of Cambodian origin, including the locally popular rhomboid pattern. Not surprisingly, Surin is one of the best places in the country to buy silk: in high season, there are usually four or five women selling their cloth around the Tannasarn-Krungsrinai intersection, or you can try Khun Nga's **shop** just outside the *Phetkasem Hotel* off Thanon Chitbamrung; nearby Ruen Mai, at 52 Thanon Chitbamrung, which has a superb selection of silks as well as readymade silk jackets, bags and accessories, silver jewellery and axe pillows; or any of several shops on the western arm of

Thanon Thetsabarn 1. Though it is possible to visit the nearby **villages** where women weave most of Surin's silk and cotton, you'll need to go with a guide to get a more behind-the-scenes look at the process, like how the silkworms are bred and how thread is extracted (see opposite for a summary of the process); *Pirom's House*, listed on p.501, should be able to arrange a guide for you. The best months to visit are between November and June, when the women aren't required to work day and night in the fields.

Surin's **elephant round-up**, held every year on the third weekend of November, draws some forty thousand spectators to watch elephants play soccer, engage in tugs of war and parade in full battle garb. These shows last about three hours and give both trainers and animals the chance to practise their skills, but however well controlled the elephants appear, you should always approach them with caution – in the past, frightened and taunted elephants have killed tourists. Tickets cost B200 (for a seat with no shade) or B500 (a seat in the shade plus English commentary), and the easiest way to book them is through Saren Travel (see p.504), who can also arrange accommodation and transport if you contact them three months ahead; the Bangkok TAT office (see p.98) should also be able to help, or you could join one of the overnight packages organized by Bangkok travel agencies. If you miss the Surin show, you could take a trip out to Ban Ta Klang (see p.504) or book your own elephant ride (see "Listings" p.504).

One of the best reasons for coming to Surin aside from the elephant round-up is to take one of the excellent **local tours** organized from *Pirom's House* (see p.501). Pirom is a highly informed former social worker whose day-trips give tourists an unusual chance to see glimpses of rural northeastern life as it's really lived. Tours cost from B550 per person, with prices depending on the destination and the number of people (minimum two). The village tours feature visits to local silk-weavers and basket-makers, as well as to Ban Ta Klang elephant trainers' village (see p.504), and it's also possible to do overnight village trips, including one that takes in Khao Phra Viharn (see p.505), Kong Chiam (p.515) and Pha Taem (p.515). Tours to ancient Khmer ruins cover prasats at Ban Pluang and in the Ta Muean group close to the Cambodian border.

Eating and drinking

Aside from a reasonable range of local **restaurants**, Surin boasts one of Isaan's best **night bazaars**, which occupies the eastern end of Thanon Krungsrinai and offers a large and tasty selection of local food (including roasted crickets and barbecued locusts when in season), as well as stalls selling fashions and toys. For beer, whisky and music, most people head across to Thanon Sirat, where you can't miss the enormous Dance Studio **nightlife** complex, comprising the cavernous Studio 2000 disco hall, a snooker club and beer garden. Wander a little further north up the road to find a string of open-air bar-beers, and the *Old West Pub*, decked out with wagon wheels and wooden benches.

Ba Tee (Pae Ti) 40–42 Thanon Thetsabarn 1 (no English sign, but enter via the shopfront with all the Jack Daniels posters). Huge place that serves the best, and priciest, Chinese food in Surin, including lots of seafood. Moderate to expensive.

Big Ben Southern end of Thanon Tannasarn (no English sign, but easily recognizable from its barbecue-hot-plate tables). One of several newly fashionable Korean barbecue places (there are a cluster of similar ones opposite the lake on Thanon Chitbamrung), where you select your meat and cook it at your own table. Prices include vegetable dishes and rice. Open nightly 4–11pm. Inexpensive to moderate.

Silk production

Most hand-woven **Thai silk** is produced by Isaan village women, some of whom oversee every aspect of sericulture, from the breeding of the silkworm through to the dyeing of the fabric. A principal reason for Isaan's pre-eminence in the silk industry is that its soils are particularly suitable for the growth of mulberry trees, the leaves of which are the **silkworms'** favoured diet. The cycle of production begins with the female silk-moth, which lives just a few days but lays around 300–500 microscopic eggs in that time. The eggs take about nine days to hatch into tiny silkworms, which are then kept in covered rattan trays and fed on mulberry leaves three or four times a day. The silkworms are such enthusiastic eaters that after three or four weeks they will have grown to about 6cm in length (around ten thousand times their original size), ready for the cocoon-building **pupal** stage.

The silkworm constructs its **cocoon** from a single white or yellow fibre that it secretes from its mouth at a rate of 12cm a minute, sealing the filaments with a gummy substance called sericin. The metamorphosis of the pupa into a moth may take as few as two days or as many as seven, but the sericulturist must anticipate the moment at which the new moth is about to break out of the cocoon in order to prevent the destruction of the precious fibre – which at this stage is often 900m long. At the crucial point the cocoon is dropped into boiling water, killing the moth (which is often eaten as a snack) and softening the sericin, so that the unbroken filament can be unravelled. The fibres from several cocoons are "reeled" into a single thread, and two or three threads are subsequently twisted or "thrown" into the yarn known as **raw silk** (broken threads from damaged cocoons are worked into a second-rate yarn called "spun silk"). In most cases, the next stage is the "de-gumming process", in which the raw silk is soaked in soapy water to dissolve the sericin entirely, reducing the weight of the thread by as much as thirty percent and leaving it soft and lustrously semi-transparent.

Extremely absorbent and finely textured, reeled silk is the perfect material for **dyeing**; most silk producers now use chemical dyes, though traditional vegetable dyes are making a bit of a comeback. Once dyed, the silk is ready for **weaving**. This is generally done during slack agricultural periods, for example just after the rice is planted and again just after it's harvested. Looms are usually set up in the space under the house, in the sheltered area between the piles, and most are designed to produce a sarong length of around 1m x 2m. Isaan weavers have many different weaving techniques and can create countless patterns, ranging from the simplest single-coloured plain weave for work shirts to exquisitely complex wedding sarongs that may take up to six weeks to complete.

Changtong At the back of the bus terminal, off Thanon Sirat. Despite its unprepossessing location, this is a rather snooty air-con restaurant, serving good Thai food, including *tom yam* and various seabass dishes. Moderate.

Coffee Shop Thanon Tannasarn. Real coffee, milk shakes, a few cakes and white-bread sandwiches. Daily until 9pm. Inexpensive.

Dream On Sports (Farang Connection) At the back of the bus terminal, off Thanon Sirat. The place to come for beer, big-screen TV sports, darts and the chance to meet local expats. Moderate.

Larb Lak Muang A couple of shops west of *Memorial Hotel* on Thanon Lak Muang (no English sign). The best place in town for the northeastern speciality, *larb* – a spicy salad made with minced meat or fish, dry-roasted rice and lots of lime and chilli. Inexpensive.

Rodedet Thanon Thetsabarn, the last restaurant on the west side before the junction with Thanon Lak Muang (no English sign). Locally renowned for its trademark dish, pork noodle soup. Lunch only. Inexpensive.

Wai Wan 44–46 Thanon Sanitnikhomrat. Foreigner-friendly restaurant serving American breakfasts, steak and fries, seafood dishes plus some spicy *yam* salads. Inexpensive to moderate.

Ying Dii Thanon Tannasarn (no English sign). Decent-sized portions of Thai standards served with or over rice. Lunch only. Inexpensive.

Listings

Banks and exchange Several banks along Thanon Tannasarn have ATMs and currency exchange.
Hospitals Ruam Phet Hospital, on the eastern arm of Thanon Thetsabarn 1 ⊕044 513638 & 044 513192; and the government-run Surin Hospital on Thanon Lak Muang ⊕044 511006 & 044 511757.
Internet access At several locations, including next to Surin Plaza off the north end of Thanon Thetsabarn, opposite the market on Thanon Krungsrinai, and across from the *Thong Tarin* hotel on Thanon Sirat. There's a Catnet terminal in the telephone office (Mon–Fri 8.30am–4.30pm).
Mail The post office is at the Thanon Thetsabarn 1 roundabout.
Telephones The CAT overseas telephone office is at the Thanon Thetsabarn 1 roundabout.
Tours and travel agents Saren Travel (Mon–Sat 8am–7pm; Sun 8am–noon; ⊕044 513599, ⓔsarentour@yahoo.com), located at the Lak Muang/Thetsabarn 2 junction and with a desk inside *Thong Tarin* hotel, sells air tickets and arranges airport transfers, is an outlet for Budget car rental, and arranges minivan with driver, day-trips and elephant-show tickets. They can also organize elephant rides, at any time of year, in the grounds of Surin's Rajamangala Institute of Technology, for B450 per person.

Ban Ta Klang

Fifty-eight kilometres north of Surin, the "elephant village" of **BAN TA KLANG** is the main settlement of the Suay people and training centre for their elephants. One out of every two Ta Klang families owns its own elephant, occasionally using it as a Western farmer would a tractor, but otherwise treating it as a much-loved pet (see box on p.362 for an introduction to the role of the elephant in Thailand). Traditionally regarded as the most expert hunters and trainers of elephants in Thailand, the **Suay** tribe (also known as the Kui people) migrated to the region from Central Asia before the rise of the Khmers in the ninth century. It was the Suay who masterminded the use of elephants in the construction of the great Khmer temples, and a Suay chief who in 1760 helped recapture a runaway white elephant belonging to the king of Ayutthaya, earning the hereditary title "Lord of Surin". Surin was governed by members of the Suay tribe until Rama V's administrative reforms of 1907.

Now that elephants have been replaced almost entirely by modern machinery in the agricultural and logging industries, there's little demand for the Suay mahouts' skills as captors and trainers of wild elephants, but they do occasionally still get called upon by foreign governments with elephant trouble, and so the Suay still get the chance to observe some of their traditional pre-hunting rituals, including the use of sacred ropes and magic clothing and the keeping of certain taboos. There's an insight into this mysterious aspect of Suay life at the **Centre for Elephant Studies** in Ban Ta Klang (daily 8.30am–4.30pm; free), which also looks closely at the zoology of a wild elephant, its anatomy, its historical relationship with humans and the traditional dress and rituals used in sacred elephant ceremonies.

There are currently around sixty **elephants** registered as living in Ban Ta Klang, but because there's not much for them to do around Surin they spend a lot of the year travelling through Thailand with their mahouts, charging curious urbanites for the pleasure of feeding them or even walking under their trunk or belly for good luck (pregnant women who do this are supposedly guaranteed an easy birth). It's not unheard of for a Suay mahout to walk his elephant the 450km from Surin to Bangkok, charging around B20 per limbo en route and earning up to B20,000 a month for his troubles. This doesn't always go down well: town officials view them as a traffic menace, and animal rights' activists see it as cruel.

All of which means you're unlikely to turn up and find Ban Ta Klang teeming with elephants. Mahouts and their elephants do however return to Ban Ta

Klang every November to help with the rice harvest and to prepare for the annual elephant show in Surin on the third weekend of November (see p.502). In addition, every year on the first weekend of November, the elephants compete in **swimming races**, held further up the Mun River in the town of Satuk, 30km west of Ta Klang. A more authentic local elephant spectacle is the annual **monks' ordination ceremony**, held in Ban Ta Klang as part of the preparations for the beginning of Khao Pansa (Buddhist Lent, which usually takes place in May), when young men ride to the temple on ceremonially clad elephants. At other times of the year you might turn up at Ban Ta Klang and not find a single elephant, though you have a better chance if you come on a tour (see opposite). If there are enough tourists, villagers stage a miniature hour-and-a-half-long version of the November show in Ban Ta Klang on Saturday mornings (9.30am; B200), but it's probably best to enquire at *Pirom's House* or Saren Tour to be certain. Local **buses** to Ban Ta Klang depart approximately hourly from the Surin terminal and take about two hours. If driving yourself, head north along Highway 214 for 36km, turn left at the village of Ban Nong Tad and continue for 22km until you reach Ban Ta Klang.

Khao Phra Viharn, Si Saket and Kantharalak

Perched atop a 547-metre-high spur of the Dangkrek mountains right on the Thai–Cambodian border, about 140km southwest of Ubon Ratchathani and 220km southeast of Surin, the ninth- to twelfth-century Khmer ruins of **KHAO PHRA VIHARN** (also known as Preah Vihear) surpass even the spectacularly set Phanom Rung. A magnificent avenue over 500m long rises to the clifftop sanctuary, from where you get breathtaking views over the jungle-clad hills of Cambodia. The temple buildings themselves, built of grey and yellow sandstone, retain some fine original carvings and have been sufficiently restored to give a good idea of their original structure. Constructed over a three-hundred-year period, Khao Phra Viharn was dedicated to the Hindu god Shiva and is thought to have served both as a retreat for Hindu priests – hence the isolated site – and an object of pilgrimage, with the difficulty of getting there an extra challenge for devotees. The large complex would have also been inhabited by a big cast of supporting villagers who took care of the priests and the pilgrims – hence the presence of several large reservoirs on the site.

An added attraction for modern-day tourists is that the whole complex was only reopened to visitors in 1998, following almost a century of **territorial dispute** between Thailand and Cambodia over who owned the site. The situation was further complicated by Cambodia's civil war, with the Khmer Rouge taking control of the temple in 1975 and laying mines around it, making the temple far too dangerous to visit. Although the ruins have now been de-mined, there are skull-and-cross-bones signs in the vicinity, which should be heeded. It's now accepted that the central sanctuary of the Khao Phra Viharn complex stands on Cambodian land (though that didn't prevent another recent neighbourly spat, resulting in the site being closed to everyone from 2001 to 2003), but the temple is very difficult to reach from the Cambodian side of the border, so most visitors arrive via the northern cliffside-staircase, which starts just inside Thailand's southern border. For the tourist, this dual ownership means having to pay both parties to get into the ruins: there's a B200 National Park

entry fee payable to the Thai authorities about 12km north of the temple car park, at the barrier near the Ban Phum Saron junction (where you have to relinquish your passport); a B5 fee for an "ID check"; and another B200 entry fee at the base of the temple steps, which goes to the Cambodians. In addition to the expense involved, Khao Phra Viharn is very difficult to get to without your own **transport** (see "Practicalities", opposite) – and when you do get there you have to contend with large crowds of tourists and a big gaggle of very persistent hawkers. But, if you can ignore the hassle, the ruins are worth the effort.

The temple car park is lined with souvenir stalls and a score of cheap restaurant shacks. From here it's about 1km to the base of the temple steps – if you can't face the walk, wait for the **shuttle-bus** which ferries people to and fro continuously throughout the day for B5. En route you'll pass the beginning of the path up to the **Pha Mo I Daeng viewpoint**, from where you get a good view of the temple cliff and can just about make out the Khao Phra Viharn complex on its summit. There's not much information on the temple available at the site, so if you have a serious interest in the ruins, buy a copy of the excellent *Preah Vihear* **guidebook** before you come; published by River Books, it's available from most Bangkok bookshops. For a brief guide to the main architectural features and symbolism of Khmer ruins in Thailand see the box on p.492.

The ruins

The approach to the **temple complex** (daily from 8.30am; last entry 3.30pm; total entry fee B405) begins with a steep stairway and continues up the cliff-face via a series of pillared causeways, small terraces with naga balustrades and four cruciform-shaped **gopura** (pavilions), each built with doorways at the cardinal points, and decorated with carved reliefs of tales from Hindu mythology. Beyond the first gopura, as you walk along the first of the pillared causeways, you'll see to the left (east) one of the temple's biggest **reservoirs**, a large stone-lined tank sunk into the cliff and guarded by statues of lions.

As you pass through the last, southernmost, doorway of the second gopura, look back at the door to admire the pediment carving, which depicts the Hindu creation myth, the **Churning of the Sea of Milk**, in which Vishnu appears in his tortoise incarnation and, along with a naga and a sacred mountain (here symbolized by the churning stick), helps churn the cosmic ocean and thereby create the universes, as well as the sacred nectar of immortality; see p.802 for the full story. The third gopura is much larger than the others and is extended by east and west wings. Its central doorways are all decorated with clearly discernible carvings; a particularly eye-catching one above the outside of the northern doorway shows an episode from the Hindu epic the *Mahabarata*, in which the god **Shiva fights with the heroic Arjuna** over who gets the credit for the killing of a wild boar – in fact the carving here looks as if they are enjoying an affectionate embrace. A causeway flanked with two naga balustrades links the third gopura to the fourth; the buildings on either side of the fourth gopura are thought to have been libraries.

The ascent of the cliff-face finally reaches its climax at the **central sanctuary**, built on the summit and enclosed within a courtyard whose impressive colonnaded galleries are punctuated by windows to the east and west. Cambodian monks tend the modern Buddha image inside the sanctuary, keeping a fire burning and selling offertory garlands and incense to tourists. The pediment above the northern entrance to this shrine is carved with an image of the multi-armed **dancing Shiva**, whose ecstatic dance brings about the destruction of the existing world and the beginning of a new epoch (see p.803). Climb through one of the gallery windows to walk across to the cliff edge, from where you get far-reaching views of Cambodia, and can appreciate just how isolated the temple must have been. A look back at the temple complex shows that though the sanctuary's southernmost wall is punctuated by a couple of beautifully carved false doors, there are no genuine south-facing doors or windows – experts assume that this was a deliberate design feature to stop priests being distracted by the clifftop panorama.

Practicalities: Kantharalak and Si Saket

Khao Phra Viharn is not served by public **transport**, so by far the easiest way of getting to the ruins is to rent a car (with or without driver) or motorbike from Ubon Ratchathani (see p.513), Surin (see p.504) or Si Saket (see below), all of which have a decent range of hotels and good long-distance transport connections. Alternatively, you could take a motorbike taxi to the temple from the nearest sizeable town to Khao Phra Viharn, Kantharalak, or from the road junction and national park barriers at Ban Phum Saron.

Kantharalak

KANTHARALAK is located just off the Khao Phra Viharn–Si Saket road (Highway 221), 36km north of the temple. There is an hourly **bus** service here from Ubon Ratchathani (1hr 30min), which departs from a terminus just across the Mun River in the Warinchamrab suburb of Ubon, and a half-hourly bus service from Si Saket; buses arrive at Kantharalak **bus station** (Ⓣ045 661486), 50m from the market on the main street, Thanon Sinpradit.

There is no **songthaew** service from Kantharalak to the temple, but occasional songthaews do connect Kantharalak with **Ban Phum Saron**, the junction near the national-park barrier 12km north of Khao Phra Viharn, from where you can get a **motorbike taxi** to the temple; you can also get a motorbike taxi all the way from Kantharalak to Khao Phra Viharn (about B100 each way).

Kantharalak is a two-street town, with the best of the budget **hotels**, the friendly, English-speaking *Kantharalak Hotel* (Ⓣ045 661085; ❷–❸), on the main street at 131/35–36 Thanon Sinpradit, about 1km off Highway 221; its rooms, scruffy but serviceable (the better ones are upstairs), are set back off the road, all with en-suite bathrooms and TV, and some with air-con.

Si Saket

The quiet provincial capital of **SI SAKET** is a more enjoyable place to base yourself than Kantharalak, with a better choice of hotels, a good night market, a tourist service centre and decent transport connections; however, it is 98km from Khao Phra Viharn. Si Saket **train station** (Ⓣ045 611525) is in the centre of the town; the **bus station** (Ⓣ045 612500) is in the southern part of town and connects Si Saket with Ubon Ratchathani, Phibun Mangsahan, Chong Mek, Surin and Bangkok, but there are no buses from here to Khao Phra Viharn, so you have to get the #523 to Kantharalak (hourly; 2hr) and make onward arrangements from there. You should also be able to get buses from here to Sa Ngam for access to the Cambodian border crossing to Choam (for Anlong Veng and Siem Reap).

Si Saket sees very few tourists, but there is a **Tourism Service Centre** (Mon–Fri 8.30am–4.30pm; Ⓣ045 611574), in front of the Provincial Hall on Thanon Lak Muang. Staff here don't speak much English but can arrange a **car and driver** to take you to Khao Phra Viharn and other nearby ruins

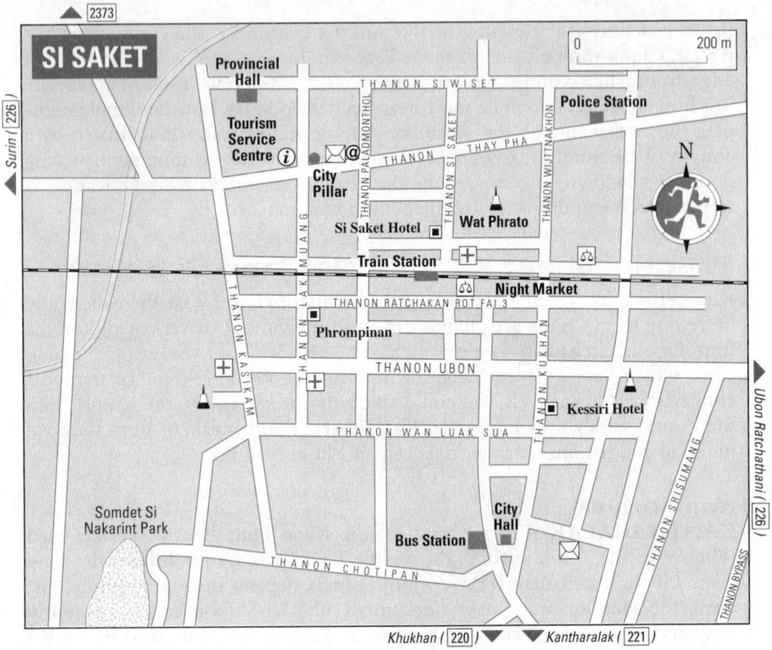

(approximately B1200/day). About 50m east of the Tourism Centre on Thanon Thay Pha is a **post office** and, just east of that, an **Internet** centre.

There are three reasonable **hotels** within easy walking distance of the train station. The *Si Saket Hotel* at 384/5 Thanon Si Saket (Ⓣ045 611846; ❷) offers basic en-suite rooms; at the slightly better *Phrompinan* (Ⓣ045 612677, Ⓕ045 612696; ❸), at 849/1 Thanon Lak Muang, the ground-floor fan rooms are grotty and to be avoided, though the upstairs air-con ones are much more comfortable and reasonable value; and the *Kessiri Hotel*, at 1102–5 Thanon Kukhan (Ⓣ045 614007, Ⓕ045 614008; ❺), is the most comfortable place in town, with good (frequently discounted) rooms, all furnished with TV and air-con, and a restaurant downstairs.

The best place to **eat** in town is the lip-smackingly diverse night market, which sets up around a small plaza along the southern edge of the rail line. Otherwise there are half a dozen small Thai-Chinese restaurants on Thanon Kukhan, between the *Kessiri Hotel* and the rail line; along this road you'll also find several handicraft shops selling locally produced lengths of silk and triangular axe pillows.

Ubon Ratchathani

East of Si Saket, the provincial capital of **UBON RATCHATHANI** (almost always referred to simply as Ubon – not to be confused with Udon, aka Udon Thani, to the north) is Thailand's fifth-largest city but holds little in the way of attractions beyond a couple of wats and a decent museum. It's only really worth visiting in order to make trips out: east to Kong Chiam beside the Mekong

City bus and songthaew routes

Ubon is fairly well served by a fleet of numbered and differently coloured **city buses and songthaews**, which charge a flat fare of B5. They are especially useful for getting to the train station and regional bus depots in Warinchamrab. The following are some of the most useful routes for hotels, sights and transport terminals – not all pass the front door, but should leave you with no more than a five-minute walk; buses cover the same routes in reverse.

#1 (grey/white): Thanon Jaengsanit–Thanon Sumpasit–Thanon Buraphanai–Thanon Phromthep–Thanon Upparat–Nakorn Chai Bus Terminal–Warinchamrab.

#2 (white): Main Bus Terminal–Thanon Chayangkun (for Wat Nong Bua and *Tokyo Hotel*)–Thanon Phichitrangsarn–Thanon Luang (for post office)–Thanon Khuenthani (for TAT, hotels and museum)–Thanon Upparat–Nakorn Chai Bus Terminal–*River Moon Guest House* –Warinchamrab train station.

#3 (pink): Main Bus Terminal–Thanon Chayangkun (for Wat Nong Bua)–Thanon Sumpasit–Thanon Luang (for post office)–Thanon Khuenthani (for TAT, hotels and museum)–Thanon Phromthep–Nakorn Chai Bus Terminal–Talat Warinchamrab (for Kong Chiam and Chong Mek buses).

#6 (pink): Thanon Sumpasit west–Thanon Phichitrangsam west–Thanon Chayangkun (for *Tokyo Hotel*)–Thanon Upparat (for museum, Thanon Khuenthani hotels and TAT)–Nakorn Chai Bus Terminal–Warinchamrab.

River (see p.515) and the Lao border market at Chong Mek (see p.517), or southwest to the Khmer ruins of Khao Phra Viharn (see p.505).

If you're near Ubon in early July, however, you should definitely consider coming into town for the local **Asanha Puja** festivities, an auspicious Buddhist holiday celebrated all over Thailand to mark the beginning of Khao Pansa, the annual three-month Buddhist retreat. Ubon's version of this festival is the most spectacular in the country: each of the city's temples makes a huge wooden or plaster sculpture, coats it in orange beeswax and then carves intricate decorations in the wax. The sculptures are mounted on floats around enormous candles and paraded through the town – hence the tourist name for the celebrations, the **Ubon Candle Festival** – before being judged and then returned to the temple, where the candle is usually kept burning throughout the retreat period. The end of the retreat, **Awk Pansa** (early to mid-Oct), is also exuberantly celebrated with a procession of illuminated boats along the Mun River, each representing one of the city's temples, as well as parades and *likay* theatre shows in Thung Si Muang Park, and lots of fireworks throughout the city. Traditional longboat races are staged on the river in the days following Awk Pansa.

Arrival, information and city transport

Thai Airways operates at least two **flights** a day between Ubon and Bangkok, and the airport (☎045 244073) is just north of the town centre. Ubon's **train** station (☎045 321004) is in the suburb of **Warinchamrab** (Warin Chamrap), south across the Mun River from central Ubon. White city bus #2 meets all trains at Warinchamrab and takes passengers into central Ubon, passing along Thanon Khuenthani, location of several hotels and the TAT office. City buses #1 (grey/white), #3 (pink) and #6 (pink) also cross the river into Ubon; see box above for an outline of the main city bus and songthaew routes. For details of travel agents selling train and air **tickets**, see "Listings" on p.513.

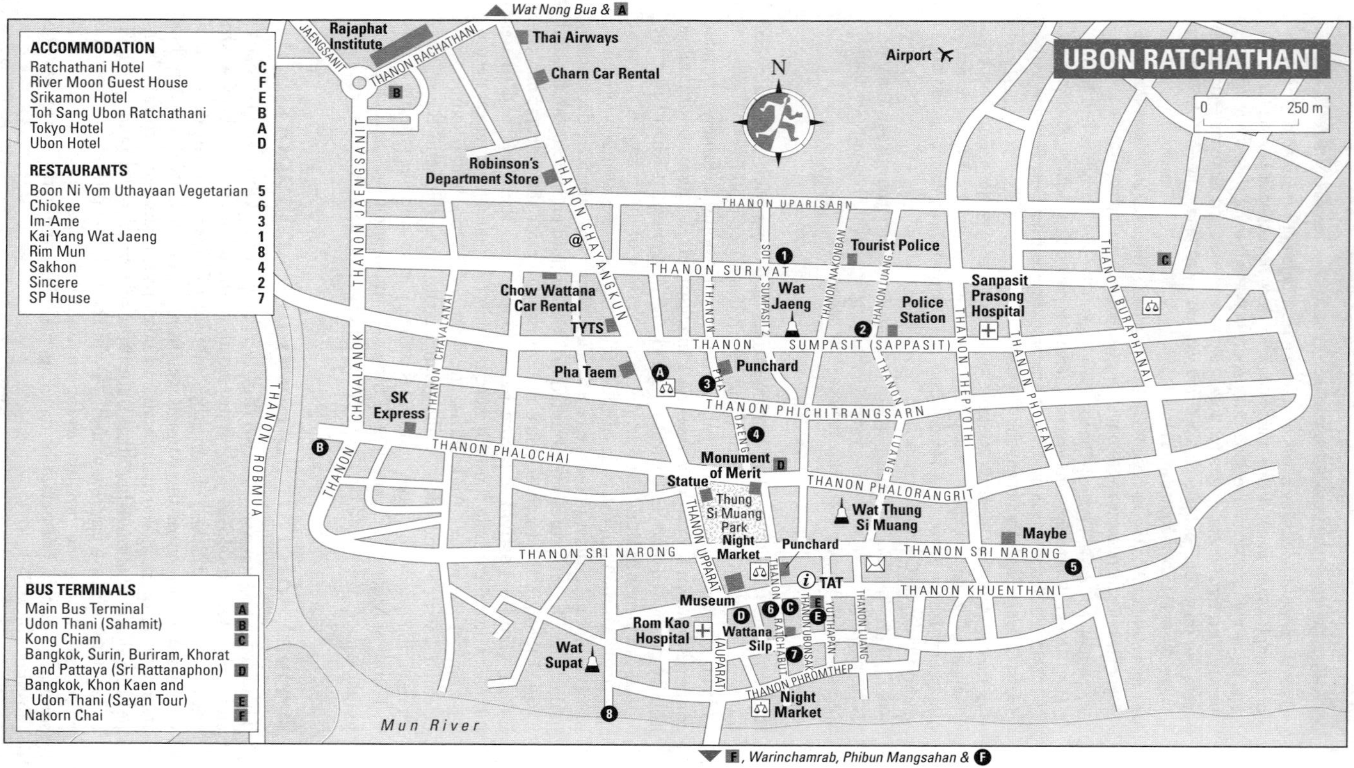
UBON RATCHATHANI
0 250 m
N
Wat Nong Bua & A
F, Warinchamrab, Phibun Mangsahan & F
ACCOMMODATION
Ratchathani Hotel C
River Moon Guest House F
Srikamon Hotel E
Toh Sang Ubon Ratchathani B
Tokyo Hotel A
Ubon Hotel D
RESTAURANTS
Boon Ni Yom Uthayaan Vegetarian 5
Chiokee 6
Im-Ame 3
Kai Yang Wat Jaeng 1
Rim Mun 8
Sakhon 4
Sincere 2
SP House 7
BUS TERMINALS
Main Bus Terminal A
Udon Thani (Sahamit) B
Kong Chiam C
Bangkok, Surin, Buriram, Khorat and Pattaya (Sri Rattanaphon) D
Bangkok, Khon Kaen and Udon Thani (Sayan Tour) E
Nakorn Chai F
Rajaphat Institute
Thai Airways
Charn Car Rental
Airport
Robinson's Department Store
Chow Wattana Car Rental
TYTS
Pha Taem
Punchard
Wat Jaeng
Tourist Police
Police Station
Sanpasit Prasong Hospital
SK Express
Monument of Merit
Statue
Thung Si Muang Park
Night Market
Wat Thung Si Muang
Maybe
Punchard
TAT
Museum
Rom Kao Hospital
Wattana Silp
Wat Supat
Night Market
Mun River
JAENGSANIT
THANON RATCHATHANI
THANON JAENGSANIT
THANON CHAYANGKUN
THANON UPARISARN
THANON SURIYAT
SOI SUMPASIT 2
THANON NAKONBAN
THANON LUANG
THANON SUMPASIT (SAPPASIT)
THANON THEPYOTHI
THANON PHOLFAN
THANON BURAPHANAI
THANON CHAVALANAI
THANON CHAVALANOK
THANON PHA DAENG
THANON PHICHITRANGSARN
THANON PHALOCHAI
THANON PHALORANGRIT
THANON ROBMUA
THANON SRI NARONG
THANON UPPARAT (AUPARAT)
THANON KHUENTHANI
THANON RATCHABUT
THANON UBONSAK
YUTTHAPAN
THANON LUANG
THANON PHROMTHEP

Confusingly, several different companies run long-distance bus services in and out of Ubon, each with their own drop-off and pick-up points, but nearly all services pass through the **main bus terminal** on Thanon Chayangkun, on the northwest edge of town, which is served by city buses #2 and #3. The government Baw Kaw Saw bus company (☎045 241831) is based at the main terminal and covers Bangkok, Buriram, Khorat, Roi Et, Si Saket, Surin and Yasothon; the big, nationwide private air-con bus company Nakorn Chai (☎045 269385), which runs a nonstop service to Bangkok as well as routes to and from Buriram, Chiang Mai, Khorat, Pattaya, Phitsanulok, Rayong, Si Saket and Surin, has its terminal just south of the Mun River, on the road to Warinchamrab, which is served by city buses #1, #2, #3 and #6; and Sahamit (☎045 241319), located in the northwest of town off Thanon Ratchathani, runs air-con services to Sakon Nakhon and Udon Thani. For the locations of other bus company depots, see the map opposite.

If you're travelling between Ubon and Kong Chiam or Chong Mek you'll need to change buses at Phibun Mangsahan. Most regular local buses and songthaews to and from Phibun Mangsahan (see p.514), as well as those to and from Si Saket, use the terminal near the **Talat Kao marketplace in Warinchamrab**, southeast of the river and served by city bus #3 from Ubon, but there's also a frequent Phibun-bound service out of Ubon's main bus terminal. Buses to Kantharalak (for Khao Phra Viharn) also leave from Warinchamrab. For a faster and less restrictive way of visiting Kong Chiam and the cliff paintings, consider renting a **motorbike** (B200–500/day) or **car** (B1200/day with or without driver) from one of the outlets detailed in "Listings" on p.513.

Staff at the **TAT office** (daily 8.30am–4.30pm; ☎045 243770) on Thanon Khuenthani can help you with specific queries on all bus and train departures.

Accommodation

Ubon's choice of **hotels** is fair enough, but as there's not much of a travellers' scene in the city there's just one guest house, *River Moon*, south of the river in Warinchamrab. Prices shoot up during the Candle Festival, when you'll need to book a room as far ahead as possible.

Ratchathani Hotel 229 Thanon Khuenthani ☎045 244388, Ⓕ045 243561. Very central and popular city hotel, offering reasonable-value fan and air-con rooms, all with hot water and TV, if rather spartan furnishings. ④–⑤

River Moon Guest House 21 Thanon Si Saket 2, Warinchamrab ☎045 286093, Ⓔ Phanth_Boonjob@yahoo.com. Ubon's only guest house is run by the charismatic and well-travelled Phan and comprises a group of five old houses, each with a couple of basic fan rooms upstairs and shared bathrooms downstairs. There's plenty of info, Internet access, and a small restaurant. From the train station in Warinchamrab walk straight ahead for 200m, turn left down Thanon Si Saket 2, and it's 200m further, opposite the fire station. Or take city bus #2 from the main bus terminal in Ubon across the Mun River to the guest house or train station in Warinchamrab. ①

Srikamon Hotel 22 Thanon Ubonsak ☎045 241136, Ⓕ045 243792. Comfortable air-con rooms right in the heart of downtown Ubon; a good upper- to mid-range option. ⑥

Toh Sang Ubon Ratchathani 251 Thanon Phalochai ☎045 245531, Ⓦwww.tohsang.com. The poshest hotel in town, with comfortable air-con rooms in a peaceful but rather inconvenient location 1km west of Thanon Chayangkun or about 2km from TAT. City songthaews #4 and #8 pass the door. Significant discounts are usually available. ⑧

Tokyo Hotel 178 Thanon Chayangkun ☎045 241739, Ⓕ045 261262. About a 5min walk north of the museum, this is the best and friendliest of central Ubon's budget hotels. Fan and air-con rooms in the old block are adequate, if a little shabby, while those in the new wing are nicer; nearly all rooms come with cable TV and there's a breakfast café on site. ②–④

Ubon Hotel 333 Thanon Khuenthani ☎045 241045, Ⓕ045 209020. Centrally located place offering unremarkable but well-priced and decent enough rooms with fan or air-con. ③

The City

Central Ubon is easy enough to negotiate, with the main accommodation and eating area confined to a fairly compact rectangle between Thanon Sumpasit (Sappasit) in the north and the Mun River in the south. The centrepiece of this area is **Thung Si Muang Park** and its unmissable landmark, the 22-metre-high **Candle Sculpture**, an enormous yellow-painted replica of the wax sculptures that star in the annual Candle Festival. This particular sculpture was inspired by a story written by the King and features a boat with an enormous garuda figurehead that's ploughing past various figures who are apparently being devoured by sea monsters. In the northeast corner of the park stands a much more unassuming memorial in the shape of a three-metre-high obelisk. Known as the **Monument of Merit**, it was erected by a group of POWs who wanted to show their gratitude to the people of Ubon for their support during World War II. Despite the real threat of punishment by the Japanese occupiers, between 1941 and 1943 Ubon citizens secretly donated food and clothes to the POWs imprisoned in a nearby camp.

South from the park across Thanon Sri Narong and also accessible from Thanon Khuenthani, **Ubon Ratchathani National Museum** (Wed–Sun 9am–4pm; B30) is airily designed around a central courtyard and offers a good overview of the history, geology and culture of southern Isaan, with well-labelled displays on everything from rock formations to folk crafts and musical instruments. Especially notable are a couple of very fine Khmer sculptures: a ninth-century statue of Ganesh and, in the same room, an eleventh-century lintel carved with nine little archways containing nine Hindu deities astride their nine different vehicles, each figure just 20cm high. Elsewhere you'll find examples of the star-embroidered fabric that is a speciality of Ubon, and a pre-fourth-century bronze bell and ceremonial drum found in the vicinity.

Of the city's eight main wats, **Wat Thung Si Muang**, a few hundred metres east of Thung Si Muang Park, along Thanon Sri Narong, is the most noteworthy, mainly for its unusually well-preserved teak library – or *ho trai* – which is raised on stilts over an artificial pond to keep book-devouring insects at bay. The murals in the bot, to the left of the library, have also survived remarkably well: the lively scenes of everyday life in the nineteenth century include musicians playing *khaen* pipes and devotees performing characteristic Isaan merit-making dances, as well as conventional portraits of city life in Bangkok.

Off Thanon Chayangkun near the main bus terminal at the northern edge of town, the much more modern **Wat Nong Bua** (city bus #2 or #3) is modelled on the stupa at Bodh Gaya in India, scene of the Buddha's enlightenment; the whitewashed replica is carved with scenes from the *Jataka* and contains a scaled-down version of the stupa covered in gold leaf. Of more interest, especially if you don't happen to be here during the Candle Festival, is the wax float kept in a small building behind the chedi.

Silk, cotton and silverware are all good buys in Ubon. The biggest selection of clothes made from the stripey rough **cotton** weaves peculiar to the Ubon area is at Maybe, on the eastern end of Thanon Sri Narong; Pha Taem Collection, opposite the *Tokyo Hotel* on Thanon Chayangkun, also uses local cotton weaves for its more fashionable readymade clothing. You'll find cotton tableware and clothes made to local designs, as well as Ubon's best collection of **northeastern crafts**, at Punchard, which has one branch at 128–130 Thanon Ratchabut, 50m east of the museum, and another on Thanon Pha Daeng. Both shops specialize in fine-quality regional goods, like triangular axe pillows (*mawn khwaan*) and lengths of **silk**, and also deal in antique farm and household implements. The **silver handicrafts** shop Wattana Silp on Thanon Ratchabut (just north of the *SP House* restaurant) stocks a good selection of Lao-style silver filigree belts and accessories, as well as lots of other jewellery.

Eating

Ubon is a good place for sampling local Isaan specialities, which you can enjoy either in air-conditioned comfort at one of the restaurants listed below, or at one of the city's **night markets**. The largest and liveliest of these markets sets up on the north bank of the Mun River and serves especially good *hawy thawt* (omelette stuffed with mussels). There are smaller night markets on Thanon Ratchabut (north off Thanon Khuenthani), and on the sidewalk next to the *Tokyo Hotel*.

Boon Ni Yom Uthayaan Vegetarian Restaurant and Centre Thanon Sri Narong; no English sign but its barn-like, open-sided wooden structure is unmistakeable. Famous, canteen-style veggie place that's run by members of a Buddhist organization who grow, sell and cook their own produce. All sorts of meat substitutes and tasty veg and tofu dishes are on offer here at very cheap per-plate prices. Open Tues–Sun 6am–2pm. Inexpensive.

Chiokee Thanon Khuenthani. Friendly, café-style place serving a large menu of Thai and Western staples. Especially popular at breakfast time, when Westerners come for the ham and eggs, local office workers for rice gruel. Inexpensive.

Im-Ame Thanon Pha Daeng (no English sign). Air-con place that's renowned for its Isaan specialities, but also serves dishes from other parts of Thailand. Moderate.

Kai Yang Wat Jaeng Thanon Suriyat, close to the junction with Soi Sumpasit (Sappasit) 2. This simple streetside restaurant is famous across town for its signature barbecued chicken (*kai yang*), which it serves at lunchtime only. Inexpensive.

Rim Mun On the river bank near Wat Supat. Floating restaurant that makes the most of the breeze from the river and specializes in fish dishes. Moderate.

Sakhon 66–70 Thanon Pha Daeng. Another of Ubon's top northeastern restaurants, particularly recommended for its more unusual dishes, like *tom yam* with fish eggs and red ant eggs. Moderate.

Sincere 126/1 Thanon Sumpasit. Highly regarded, predominantly French menu, with an emphasis on steaks and classic sauces. Closed Sun. Expensive.

SP House Thanon Ratchabut. Local outlet of the chain of bakery and ice-cream shops that's a reliable source of coffee, cakes and sundaes and is usually packed out with schoolkids. Moderate.

Listings

Airline The Thai Airways office is at 364 Thanon Chayangkun ☎045 263916, in the north part of town.

Car, motorbike and bicycle rental Cars, motorbikes and bicycles from Chow Wattana at 39/8 Thanon Suriyat, opposite Nikko Massage ☎045 242202; cars only from Charn Car Rental, opposite *Pathumrat Hotel* on Thanon Chayangkun ☎045 313337, ©srikamol@cscoms.com; Budget car rental through SK Express, near the *Toh Sang* hotel on Thanon Phalochai ☎045 264712; car plus driver through Sakda Travel at 150/1 Thanon Kantharalak in Warinchamrab ☎045 321937, ⓦwww.sakdatravel.com, ©sdtravel@hotmail.com.

Exchange At several banks and ATMs, including next to TAT on Thanon Khuenthani and on Thanon Ratchabut.

Hospitals Rom Kao Hospital, near the museum on Thanon Upparat (☎045 244658), is well regarded and has English-speaking staff, or there's Phyathai Ubon Hospital, north of the city at 512/3 Thanon Chayangkun ☎045 284001.

Immigration office In the town of Phibun Mangsahan (see below), 45km east of Ubon (Mon–Fri 8.30am–4.30pm; ☎045 441108).

Internet access At the CAT telephone office, next to the GPO on the Thanon Sri Narong/Thanon Luang intersection and at various small Internet centres around town (see map on p.510).

Mail The GPO is centrally located at the Thanon Sri Narong/Thanon Luang intersection.

Telephones The CAT telephone office is next to the GPO on the Thanon Sri Narong/Thanon Luang intersection.

Tourist police For all emergencies, call the tourist police on the free, 24hr phone line ☎1155, or contact them at their office on Thanon Suriyat ☎045 244941.

Travel agents TYTS Travel Agent on Thanon Chayangkun, near the Sumpasit junction in the city centre (☎045 243601), sells domestic and international flights and train tickets; SK Express, near the *Toh Sang* hotel on Thanon Phalochai (☎045 264712), sells air tickets and is an outlet for Budget car rental; and Sakda Travel at 150/1 Thanon Kantharalak in Warinchamrab (☎045 321937, Ⓦwww.sakdatravel.com, Ⓔsdtravel@hotmail.com), sells air tickets, does guided tours around Isaan and into Laos, and offers car plus driver from B1200 per day.

Around Ubon

On the whole, the area **around Ubon** is a good deal more interesting than the metropolitan hub, particularly if you venture eastwards towards the appealing Mekong riverside town of **Kong Chiam**, the prehistoric paintings at **Pha Taem** and the Lao border market at **Chong Mek**. Nearly all the routes detailed on the following pages can be done as a day-trip from Ubon – most comfortably with your own transport, but manageable on buses and songthaews if you set off very early in the morning – though there's a lot to be said for taking things more slowly and spending a night or two in the rural reaches of Ubon Ratchathani province.

Phibun Mangsahan

There are several routes east out of Ubon, but they nearly all begin with Highway 217, which starts in Ubon's southern suburb of Warinchamrab and then follows the Mun River east for 45km before splitting into two at the town of **PHIBUN MANGSAHAN**. From here, Highway 217 continues southeast to the border at Chong Mek, while the northeasterly fork out of Phibun, called Route 2222, follows the course of the Mun to its confluence with the Mekong at Kong Chiam.

Sited at a turbulent point of the Mun called Kaeng Saphue (*kaeng* means rapids), Phibun Mangsahan (known locally as Phibun) has little more to it than a central bus station and a sprawling market, but for travellers it's an inevitable interchange on any eastbound journey. In April, Ubon celebrates the Thai New Year festival of Songkhran by staging performances of Isaan folk music and dance beside the Kaeng Saphue rapids; these **Maha Songkhran** festivities run from April 12 to 15. Phibun's one exceptional sight, **Wat Phokakaew**, stands on the western outskirts of town, 1km before you get to the town limit, and is signposted off Highway 217. An unusually attractive modern temple, it's worth a look for its exceptionally elegant proportions, eye-catchingly tiled exterior and fine naga-encircled platform from where you can see the hills of Laos on the horizon. The wat's interior walls are decorated with reliefs of twelve of Thailand's most revered temples, including the Golden Mount in Bangkok and Nakhon Pathom's monumental chedi. The space under the temple has been converted into a serene meditation hall.

To get to Phibun from Ubon, either begin from Ubon's main bus station or take city bus #3 across the river to the Warinchamrab bus station near Talat Kao. Phibun-bound buses depart several times an hour from both places until 4.30pm. In Phibun, buses terminate at the **bus station** behind the market in the town centre, where you can change onto the songthaews that run to Chong Mek. Kong Chiam songthaews leave from **Kaeng Saphue bridge**, a short tuk-tuk ride or ten-minute walk from Phibun's bus station: exit the bus station through the market to the main road, turn right and walk the few hundred metres to the main highway (passing currency exchange and Internet facilities on the way), then turn left to reach the river and the songthaew stop.

Kong Chiam and the Pha Taem paintings

The riverside village of **KONG CHIAM** (pronounced Kong Jiem) is a popular destination for day-tripping Thais, who drive out here to see the somewhat fancifully named "two-coloured river" for which the village is nationally renowned. Created by the merging of the muddy brown Mun with the muddy brown Mekong at "the easternmost point of Thailand", the water is hardly an irresistible attraction, but the village has a certain appeal and makes a very pleasant stopover point. Comprising little more than a collection of wooden houses, the requisite post office, school and police station, a few guest houses, several restaurants and two wats, Kong Chiam feels like an island, with the Mun defining its southern limit and the Mekong its northern one. A paved walkway runs several hundred metres along the banks of the Mekong, passing the district office and running down to the large *sala* that's built right over the confluence and affords uninterrupted views. Behind the *sala*, **Wat Kong Chiam** is the more charming of the village's two temples and has an old wooden bell tower in its compound; the cliffside **Wat Tham Khu Ha Sawan**, located near the point where Route 2222 turns into Kong Chiam, is unprepossessing, with a huge modern Buddha image staring down on the villagers below.

Kong Chiam's sights are thin on the ground, but you can rent motorbikes from *Apple* and *Mongkhon* guest houses (see below) and explore the area, or charter a **longtail boat** for a trip up the Mekong River, taking in the Pha Taem cliff-paintings on the way (B700/boat). Even though Laos is just a few hundred metres away from Kong Chiam, on the other bank of the Mekong, foreigners are not supposed to cross the border here, though if you're keen to step on to Lao soil you can usually persuade boatmen to take you there and back for B300 per boat, with a quick stop at the bankside village of Ban Mai; the official border crossing is further downstream at Chong Mek (see p.517).

Pha Taem cliff-paintings

The most popular outing from Kong Chiam is a visit to the **Pha Taem cliff-paintings**, contained within Pha Taem National Park (daily 5am–6pm; B200, kids B100), which cover a 170-metre stretch of cliff-face 18km up the Mekong. Clear proof of the antiquity of the fertile Mekong valley, these bold, childlike paintings are believed to be between 3000 and 4000 years old, the work of rice-cultivating settlers who lived in huts rather than caves. Protected from the elements by an overhang, the red paint – a mixture of soil, tree gum and fat – has kept its colour so well that the shapes and figures are still clearly discernible; human forms, handprints and geometric designs appear in groups alongside massive depictions of animals and enormous fish – possibly the prized catfish still caught in the Mekong.

Pha Taem (Taem Cliff) is clearly signposted from Kong Chiam, but try to avoid coming here on a weekend when the place gets swamped with scores of tour buses. It's an especially popular spot at sunrise, this being the first place in Thailand to see the sun in the morning – a full eighteen minutes ahead of Phuket, the westernmost point. If you're lucky, you might get a ride on one of the infrequent Ubon-bound buses as far as the Pha Taem turn-off, from where you can try and hitch the rest of the way (about 8km), but otherwise, unless you rent a motorbike, you'll have to hitch all the way or charter a tuk-tuk or taxi from the village – ask at *Apple Guest House* for advice. The road passes a group of weird, mushroom-shaped sandstone rock formations known as **Sao Chaliang** before reaching the Pha Taem car park, site of several foodstalls and the visitor centre, on top of the cliff. From the car park, follow the path that's signed "Pha Taem Loop 3km", which runs down the cliff-face and along the shelf in the rock to the paintings. If you continue along the path past the paintings, you'll eventually climb back up to the top of the cliff again, via the **viewpoint** at Pha Mon, taking in fine views of the fertile Mekong valley floor and glimpses of hilly western Laos. It's about 1700m from Pha Mon back to the car park, along a signed trail across the rocky scrub. Should you feel inclined to stay and catch the sunrise, you can rent national park **bungalows** (B1300 for up to ten people) and tents (B30/person) near the national-park checkpoint at Sao Chaliang, about 2km before the car park; these must be booked in advance on ⓣ045 249780.

Practicalities

Kong Chiam is 30km northeast of Phibun, along Route 2222, or 75km from Ubon. Kong Chiam-bound **songthaews** leave Phibun Mangsahan's Kaeng Saphue bridge (see p.514) every half-hour throughout the morning and then hourly until 3.30pm, and take an hour to an hour and a half. A few **buses** go directly from Ubon to Kong Chiam, leaving in the morning from a spot on the eastern end of Ubon's Thanon Suriyat, but these are painfully slow, taking a convoluted back-road route and stopping for long breaks along the way. Two daily buses run from Kong Chiam all the way to Bangkok. Songthaews and buses terminate at the Kong Chiam **bus station** at the west end of Thanon Kaewpradit, Kong Chiam's main drag, a few metres' walk from *Mongkhon Guest House*. If you have your own transport, Kong Chiam combines well with visits to Chong Mek (just 27km away) and Kaeng Tana National Park; *Apple* and *Mongkhon* guest houses rent motorbikes for B200 per day. There's a small **minimarket** and a **pharmacy** on Thanon Kaewpradit, along with a bank that has an **exchange** facility, but no ATM.

Accommodation

Kong Chiam has a nice range of reasonably priced guest houses and "resorts", which is a good incentive to stay over in this pleasant, slow-paced village.

Apple Guest House Opposite the post office on Thanon Kaewpradit, but also accessible from Thanon Phukamchai ⓣ045 351160. About a 5min walk from the bus station and the Mekong. The most traveller-oriented place in Kong Chiam, this is a convivial setup with decent en-suite rooms around a yard, as well as a restaurant, motorbike rental and a useful noticeboard. The pricier rooms have air-con. ❷–❸

Araya Resort Towards the eastern end of Thanon Phukamchai, 10min walk from the bus station ⓣ045 351191. Good-value set of steeply roofed, whitewashed, chalet-style bungalows, built around a garden with several ponds; the rooms are comfortable and have air-con, hot water and TV. Price depends on the view, as the best look straight ahead over trees to distant Lao hilltops. ❹–❺

Ban Kiang Nam Resort Towards the eastern end of Thanon Kaewpradit ⓣ045 351374. Immaculate, prettily painted set of terraced rooms and detached chalet-style bungalows, all furnished in cosy fashion and featuring air-con and TV. ❹–❻

Ban Rim Khong Resort 37 Thanon Kaewpradit ⓣ045 351101. Also has another entrance one block north on the road in front of the Mekong River, between the district office and the wat. Great-looking little resort with half a dozen timbered chalets wreathed in bougainvillea and ranged round a lawn, plus a couple of fabulous riverside ones (#1 and #2, worth phoning ahead to reserve) with huge verandas overlooking the Mekong. The interiors are nothing special but all are spacious and have air-con, TV and fridge. Discounts for stays of more than one night. ❺

Mongkhon Guest House 595 Thanon Kaewpradit, about 10m east of the bus station ⓣ01 718 3182. Good-value and nicely kept rooms behind the wooden family home: cosy decor in all, and some have air-con and fridge. Bicycle and motorbike rental. ❷–❸

Toh Sang Kong Chiam On the south bank of the Mun ⓣ045 351174, ⓦwww.tohsang.com. Romantically located upmarket resort where all rooms have balconies overlooking the river and are very comfortably, if a little kitschly furnished. There's a swimming pool, table-tennis room, spa, Internet access and bicycle and kayak rental, plus a couple of restaurants and boat trips to Pha Taem and other riverside sights. Well-priced (discounts are often available), but inaccessible by public transport and about 10km from Kong Chiam; with your own wheels, follow Highway 2134 south past Kong Chiam bus station, cross the river, take the first left and then continue for 7km, following signs for Ban Woen Buk. ❽

Eating

The most popular places to eat are, not surprisingly, the two **floating restaurants**, *Araya* and *Nam Poon*, moored on the Mekong in front of the district office. Both are unsigned in English, but there's little to choose between them as both serve fairly pricey menus of Thai-Chinese dishes and of course plenty of fish. It's always worth asking if they have any *pla buk*, the giant catfish that used to be a local speciality (see box on p.415). There are a string of cheaper, less flashy little restaurants on the river bank behind the floating restaurants, including the friendly *Rim Khong*, next to the two riverside *Rim Khong* bungalows, along with a few food vendors. Away from the river, opposite *Mongkhon Guest House* on Thanon Kaewpradit, the (unsigned) restaurant-shack *Tuk Tik Tham Mua* serves up good local dishes at good cheap prices: spicy papaya (*som tam*) and green bean salads (*yam thua fak yao*) and grilled fish (*ping plaa*) and chicken (*ping kai*), all served with individual baskets of sticky rice.

To Chong Mek and the Lao border

Nine kilometres east out of Phibun, Route 2172 forks south off the main Highway 217 and heads straight to the so-called **Emerald Triangle**, the spot where Thailand, Laos and Cambodia meet (the name echoes the more famous border area in north Thailand, the Golden Triangle, where Thailand, Laos and Burma meet). A further 10km along Highway 217, the road begins to run alongside one of the largest reservoirs in Isaan (measuring some 43km north to south), held back by the **Sirindhorn dam**, and dotted with permanent fishing-net platforms. Thirteen kilometres later, Route 2296 veers north off Highway 217 to take traffic across the Mun River via the **Pak Mun dam** (whose construction and ill-thought-out design continues to cause controversy more than a decade after its completion in 1994) and on to Kong Chiam. **Kaeng Tana National Park** (B200; kids B100) is signed just off the dam road, but offers only a couple of short trails through predominantly scrubby vegetation to waterfalls and caves.

Chong Mek and crossing into Laos

Disregarding all deviations, Highway 217 finally ends at the village of **CHONG MEK** on the Lao border, 44km east of Phibun Mangsahan and site of a busy Thai-Lao market and one of the legal border crossings for foreigners. Large pale-blue **songthaews** leave approximately hourly between 7am and 3.30pm from Phibun Mangsahan bus station, taking about an hour and a half to reach Chong Mek. There is also a long-distance **bus** service between Chong Mek and Bangkok run by Siriratanaphon bus company (☎045 441848): two air-con buses a day depart from Chong Mek market at 4pm and 5pm, arriving at Mo Chit Northern Bus terminal about twelve hours later.

It is now possible to get a Lao **visa** on arrival at Chong Mek **border crossing**, but you'll be charged US$30 and will only receive a fifteen-day visa – half the time-period of the cheaper visas issued at the Laos consulate in Khon Kaen (see p.525); you'll also need two passport photos. If you get an advance visa from Khon Kaen or elsewhere, it must specify Chong Mek as the entry point (see Basics p.19 for information). Whichever option you choose, once at

Chong Mek you first need to get the Thai exit stamp from the office hidden behind the market on the Thai side (daily 8.30am–noon & 1–4.30pm); having crossed over to the Lao side of the market, Vangtao, you pass via the Lao immigration office (official hours: Mon–Fri 8am–4pm; "surcharge" hours, Mon–Fri 4–6pm, Sat, Sun & hols 8.30am–6pm), where you need to pay US$1 if you arrive during "surcharge" hours and an extra B20 (B50 during "surcharge" hours) for an entry stamp. A songthaew service runs from Vangtao to the city of Pakxe, 40km away (until about 5pm). In reverse, you simply pay the Lao exit tax (B20/50) and get your Thai visa on arrival for free.

Even if you're not planning to cross into Laos, the **border market** at Chong Mek is good for a browse, especially at weekends when it's at its liveliest. Few tourists visit the market, and there's plenty of good-humoured bargaining here without the hassle of more touristed places. The market on the Thai side of the border is full of stuff brought from Bangkok for Lao shoppers, especially fashions, jeans, combat gear and sarongs, but you'll also find traditional herbalists flogging pieces of bark, weirdly shaped roots and bits of dried vegetable and animal matter; lots of basketware sellers; plus plenty of restaurant shacks serving both Thai and Lao goodies. Foreign shoppers can cross over to the Lao-side market in Vangtao simply by paying B5 at the checkpoint across from the duty free shop (no visa required). Descend into the market area beside the café selling fresh Lao coffee for a huge selection of sarongs, as well as cheap VCDs and foreign whisky.

Yasothon, Ban Sri Than and Roi Et

By the beginning of May, Isaan is desperate for rain; there may not have been significant rainfall for six months and the rice crops need to be planted. In northeastern folklore, rain is the fruit of sexual encounters between the gods, so at this time villagers all over Isaan hold the bawdy **Bun Bang Fai** – a merit-making **rocket festival** – to encourage the gods to get on with it. The largest and most public of these festivals takes place in the provincial capital of **YASOTHON**, 98km northwest of Ubon, on a weekend in mid-May. Not only is the fireworks display a spectacular affair, but the rockets built to launch them are superbly crafted machines in themselves, beautifully decorated and carried proudly through the streets before blast-off. Up to 25 kilograms of gunpowder may be packed into the nine-metre-long rockets and, in keeping with the fertility theme of the festivities, performance is everything. Sexual innuendo, general flirtation and dirty jokes are essential components of Bun Bang Fai; rocket-builders compete to shoot their rockets the highest, and anyone whose missile fails to leave the ground gets coated in mud as a punishment. At other times of the year, Yasothon has little to tempt tourists other than a handful of unremarkable wats and a few evocative old colonial-style shopfronts near **Wat Singh Tha** at the west end of Thanon Srisonthoon.

The most interesting attraction in the surrounding area is the village of **BAN SRI THAN**, 21km east of Yasothon, where nearly every household is employed in the making of the famous *mawn khwaan* triangular **axe pillows**. These pillows (*mawn*), so named because their shape supposedly resembles an axe-head (*khwaan*), have been used in traditional Thai homes for centuries, where it's normal to sit on the floor and lean against a densely stuffed *mawn khwaan*. The design has been slightly adapted so it's now also possible to get *mawn khwaan* with up to four flat cushions attached, making lying out more comfortable. The price depends on the number of triangular pods that make up the pillow: in Ban

Sri Than, a stand-alone ten-triangle pillow costs B100, or B370 with three attached cushions – around a third of what it'll cost in Bangkok or Chiang Mai. A good place to see villagers at work, often in the space under their stilted houses, is on Thanon Koson Thammarat, though you're unlikely to find any English-speakers here. If you're driving to Ban Sri Than from Yasothon, follow Route 202 northeast towards Amnat Charoen as far as kilometre-stone 18.5km, then turn south (right) off the highway for 3km to reach the village. Coming by public transport, take a **songthaew** (half-hourly until noon) or **bus** (approximately hourly throughout the day) from Yasothon bus station to **Ban Ni Khom** on Route 202, then a motorbike taxi to cover the last 3km to the village.

Practicalities

All Khon Kaen-bound **buses** from Ubon stop in Yasothon, at the bus station on Thanon Rattanakhet. The nearest airports are in Ubon (see p.509) and Roi Et (see below). If you want to stay here during festival time, book your **hotel** well in advance and be prepared to pay double the normal prices quoted here. *Yot Nakhon*, one block north then west of the market and two blocks north then west of the bus station at 141–143 Thanon Uthai-Ramrit (Ⓣ045 711481, Ⓕ045 711476; ❷–❸) has plenty of decent fan and air-conditioned rooms, all of them en suite; or try the cheaper, less salubrious *Varothon Hotel* (Ⓣ045 712826; ❶–❸), two blocks south and west of the bus station at 604–612 Thanon Chaeng Sanit, the main north–south artery through town. The best hotel in town is the comfortable and good-value *JP Emerald*, which has large, attractive air-con rooms close to the provincial hall on the far north edge of town at 36 Thanon Pha Pa (Ⓣ045 724848, Ⓕ045 724655; ❺). The most rewarding place to **eat** is at the covered **night bazaar**, which runs east off the central section of Thanon Chaeng Sanit; some of the (numbered) stalls here also open during the day, including the vegetarian one at #5 (6am–2pm only). Thanon Chaeng Sanit is where you'll find all the main **banks**, with ATMs and currency exchange, plus the **post office**, a couple of blocks north of the night bazaar. The **travel agent** inside the *JP Emerald* hotel sells domestic and international air tickets.

If Yasothon's booked out, you might want to commute there from either Ubon (see p.508) or **ROI ET**, a pleasant if unarresting town 71km further northwest and also on the Ubon–Khon Kaen bus route. Roi Et's **bus station** (Ⓣ043 511939) is way out beyond the western fringes of town on Thanon Chaeng Sanit, so you need to take a samlor or tuk-tuk to the town centre hotels. Roi Et **airport** (Ⓣ043 518246), 13.5km out of town on the way to Khon Kaen, is currently served by Thai Airways (Ⓦwww.thaiairways.com) and PB Air (Ⓣ043 518572, Ⓔpbairroi@pbair.co.th), which between them run almost daily flights to and from Bangkok. Just off the eastern shore of Roi Et's artificial lake, Beung Phlan Chai, the centrally located *Banchong* **hotel**, at 81 Thanon Suriyadet Bamrung (Ⓣ043 511235; ❷), has reasonable enough fan rooms, while the nearby *Sai Thip* at 95 Thanon Suriyadet Bamrung (Ⓣ043 511742; ❷–❸) is also convenient and has both fan and air-con rooms. On the northern edge of town at 404 Thanon Kolchapalayuk, *Petcharat Garden Hotel* is a standard mid-range option with air-con rooms, a swimming pool and restaurant (Ⓣ043 519000-7, Ⓕ043 519008; ❹); more luxurious accommodation is available at the *Roi Et Thani* (Ⓣ043 520387, Ⓕ043 520401, Ⓔroietthani@isan.sawadee.com; ❻) at 78 Thanon Ploenchit, on the eastern edge of town, which offers a swimming pool, business centre and gym as well as large comfortable rooms. The night market sets up two blocks east of the *Banchong* hotel and is an enjoyable **place to eat**, or there's more upmarket dining at the restaurants around the edge of the lake.

Central Isaan

The more northerly branch of the northeastern rail line bypasses Khorat, heading straight up through **central Isaan** to the Lao border town of Nong Khai via Khon Kaen and Udon Thani, paralleling Highway 2 most of the way. West of these arteries, the smaller Highway 201 is shadowed by the thickly wooded Phetchabun hills and Dong Phaya Yen mountain range, the westernmost limits of Isaan, chunks of which have been turned into the **national parks** of Phu Kradung, Phu Reua, Phu Hin Rongkla (see p.269) and Nam Nao. But hills play only a minor part in central Isaan's landscape, most of which suffers from poor-quality soil that sustains little in the way of profitable crops and, quite apart from what it does to the farmers who work it, makes for drab views from the bus or train window.

Nevertheless, there are a handful of towns worth stopping off at: **Khon Kaen**, for its museum of local history, its textiles and its excellent handicraft shops; **Udon Thani**, a departure point for the Bronze Age settlement of **Ban Chiang**; and **Loei**, for its access to the mountainous national parks. Trains connect only the larger towns, but **buses** link all the above centres, also conveniently serving the town of Phitsanulok (see p.269) – the springboard for a tour of the ruins of Sukhothai and a junction for onward travel to Chiang Mai – via a spectacularly hilly route through the rounded contours of Phetchabun province.

Khon Kaen and around

Geographically at the virtual centre of Isaan, **KHON KAEN** is the wealthiest and most sophisticated city in the northeast, seat of a highly respected university as well as the Channel 5 television studios. Considering its size and importance, the city is surprisingly uncongested and spacious, and there's a noticeably upbeat feel to the place, underlined by its apparently harmonious combination of traditional Isaan culture – huge markets and hordes of street vendors – and flashy shopping plazas and world-class hotels. Its location, 188km northeast of Khorat on the Bangkok–Nong Khai rail line and Highway 2, makes it a convenient resting point, even though a startling modern temple and the provincial museum are just about the only sights here. The foreigners staying in the city tend to be businesspeople or university teachers rather than tourists, though an increasing number of travellers are stopping here for **Lao and Vietnamese visas**, now that both nations have consulates in Khon Kaen.

Arrival, information and city transport

Khon Kaen is well served as a transport hub: the **train station** (Ⓣ043 221112) is on the southwestern edge of town, about fifteen minutes' walk from the main hotel area; the non-air-conditioned **bus station** (Ⓣ043 237300) is a five-minute walk northwest of the Thanon Klang Muang hotels; and the air-con bus terminal (Ⓣ043 239910) is right in the town centre. Khon Kaen **airport** (Ⓣ043 246305), 10km northwest of the city centre, runs daily Thai Airways **flights** to and from Bangkok and has Avis and Budget car-rental desks (see

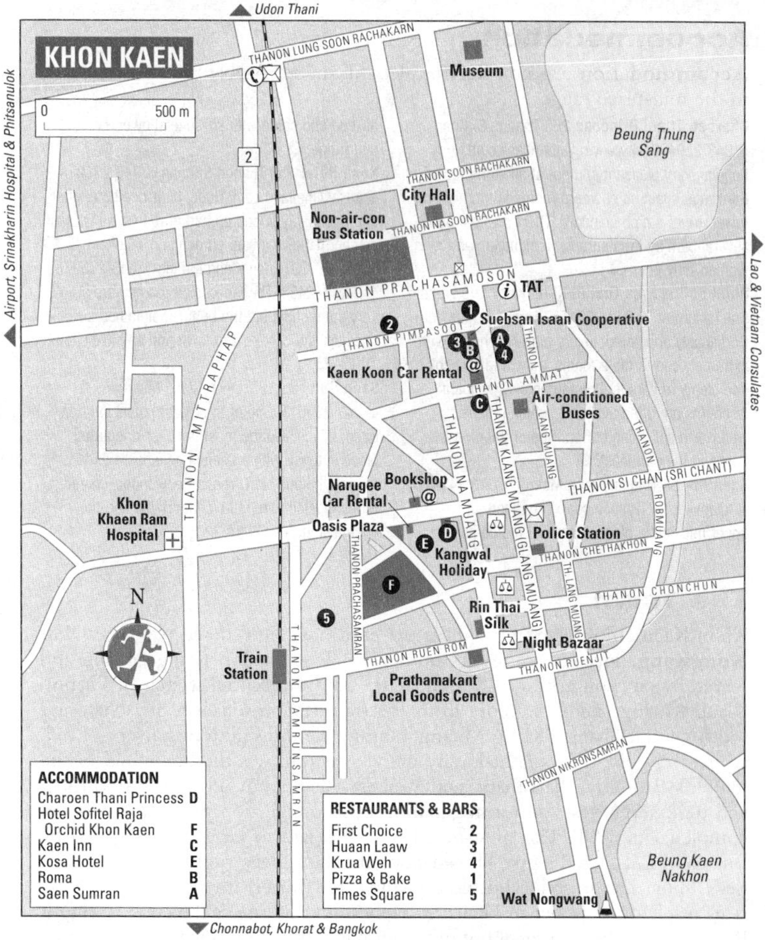

p.525 for details); hotel minibuses meet all flights. The **TAT** office (daily 8.30am–4.30pm; ☎043 244498) is on Thanon Prachasamoson, about five minutes' walk east of the non-air-con bus station.

Local buses and songthaews ply Khon Kaen's streets from 5am to 8pm, charging a standard fare of B5, or B6 for air-con journeys. Khon Kaen TAT publishes a handy map showing the colour-coded routes of all 22 city routes, of which the most useful include: **#3** (yellow), which connects the train station and the regular bus terminal; **#11** (red), which connects the train station, the air-con bus terminal, via Thanon Si Chan, and TAT; **#8** (light blue) and **#9** (light blue), which both connect the regular bus terminal with the air-con bus terminal and continue south down Thanon Klang Muang; and **#15** (yellow) and **#21** (brown), which both run up and down Thanon Klang Muang at least as far as Thanon Chonchun. A short **tuk-tuk** ride within the city should cost you B30, while the minimum fare in a **samlor** is B15. For **car, motorbike and bicycle rental** outlets see "Listings" on p.525.

Accommodation

Accommodation in Khon Kaen is plentiful and reasonably priced, particularly in the mid-price range.

Charoen Thani Princess 260 Thanon Si Chan ⓣ043 220400, ⓦwww.royalprincess.com. Popular, very pleasant and not at all stuffy top-of-the-range chain hotel where rooms in the high-rise tower are of a high standard. There's also a pool, several bars and restaurants, a nightclub and a women-only floor. ❻

Hotel Sofitel Raja Orchid Khon Kaen 9/9 Thanon Prachasamran ⓣ043 322155, ⓦwww.sofitel.com. Gorgeously appointed, luxury high-rise hotel, with extremely comfortable rooms, a swimming pool and plenty of bars and restaurants. Significant discounts are often available, which makes it well worth splashing out on. One of the nicest hotels in the northeast. ❾

Kaen Inn 56 Thanon Klang Muang ⓣ043 245420, ⓔkaeninnhotel@yahoo.com. Very good-value upper mid-range place, where all rooms have air-con and come with en-suite shower, TV and fridge. ❺

Kosa Hotel 250 Thanon Si Chan ⓣ043 225014, ⓔkosa@thailand.com. Huge, high-rise hotel offering reasonably priced upmarket rooms, all with air-con and TV, plus a beer garden and snooker hall. ❻

Roma 50/2 Thanon Klang Muang ⓣ043 236276, ⓕ043 242458. The fan-cooled rooms here aren't very interesting, but the better-maintained air-con ones are the cheapest in town and all have cable TV. ❷–❹

Saen Sumran 55 Thanon Klang Muang ⓣ & ⓕ043 239611. One of the oldest hotels in Khon Kaen, this is also the most traveller-orientated place in town, with a useful noticeboard and friendly, helpful staff. The large, wooden-floored rooms upstairs are quite comfortable and the cheapest in the city. ❷

The Town

Khon Kaen's most arresting sight is the enormous nine-tiered pagoda at **Wat Nongwang,** located at the far southern end of Thanon Klang Muang and served by city songthaews #8 (light blue) from the central stretch of Thanon Klang Muang and #14 (blue) from the train station, Thanon Sri Chan and south-central Thanon Klang Muang. Unmissable in its glittering livery of red, white and gold, this breathtakingly grand structure was the brainchild of the temple's famously charismatic and well-travelled abbot, Phra Wisuttikittisan, and took seven years and a huge amount of foreign donations before it was completed in 1997. The nine-tiered design is said to have been inspired by Burma's most sacred stupa, Shwedagon, but the gallery running around each tier is more Lao in style, and the crowning *that* (tower) is typically Thai. Nine is an auspicious number in Thailand, triply so in this case as the current king is Rama IX and the current abbot of the temple is the ninth since the wat's foundation in 1789. Inside the pagoda, the walls of the first tier are painted with modern murals that depict the founding of Khon Kaen. Each tier has its different purpose, with the first used for assemblies, the second for monks' residences, the third for a scripture library and so on. Climb the staircase all the way up to the ninth tier for views north across the city and east to nearby **Beung Kaen Nakhon**, an artificial lake that you can reach on foot from the temple compound in about fifteen minutes. It takes an hour and a half to walk the perimeter of the lake, but aside from a couple of minor temples and a fine view of Wat Nongwang and its watery reflection, there's nothing much to keep you here, though the lakeside foodstalls and restaurants are popular.

In keeping with its status as a university town, Khon Kaen has several fine collections in its **museum** on Thanon Lung Soon Rachakarn (Wed–Sun 9am–4pm; B30). To get there by local bus, catch #21 (brown) from anywhere on Thanon Klang Muang, #12 (green) or #45012 (yellow) from anywhere on Thanon Na Muang, or #17 (blue) from Thanon Lang Muang, and you'll be dropped outside the museum. The star attraction on the ground floor of the museum is a *sema* carved with a sensuous depiction of Princess Bhimba wiping the Buddha's feet with her hair on his return to Kabilabasad after years of absence in search of enlightenment. In the same room, the scope of the **Ban Chiang** collection of reassembled pots, bronze tools and jewellery rivals those held in Bangkok's National Museum and at Ban Chiang itself (see p.528), and is put into context by a map showing the distribution of contemporaneous settlements in the region. The display of **folk craft** in one of the smaller ground-floor galleries includes traditional fish traps and animal snares, and a selection of **betel trays** that run the gamut of styles from crude wooden vessels carved by Isaan farmers to more intricate silver sets given by the better-off as a dowry. Upstairs, the displays of Buddha sculptures feature the most perfect small bronze Lanna-style images outside of northern Thailand.

Shopping

Khon Kaen is great for **shopping**, its stores boasting a huge range of regional **arts and crafts**, including high-quality Isaan **silk** of all designs and weaves. One of the best outlets is the cavernous Prathamakant Local Goods Centre (daily 9am–8.30pm) at the southern end of town at 81 Thanon Ruen Rom. Although aimed squarely at tourists, the selection here is quite phenomenal: hundreds of gorgeous *mut mee* (see p.542) cotton and silk weaves, as well as clothes, furnishings, triangular axe pillows, *khaen* pipes and silver jewellery. To get to Prathamakant from the north part of town, take almost any local bus down Thanon Na Muang to the Ruen Rom junction. Rin Thai Silk on Thanon Na Muang stocks a smaller range of Isaan silk, but will tailor clothes too. Itinerant vendors, who wander the main streets with panniers stuffed full of silk and cotton lengths, also offer competitive prices, and though the choice is restricted you can be sure most of the money will go to the weavers; they often gather on the steps of the *Kaen Inn* and along the stretch of Thanon

Betel

Betel-chewing is a habit indulged in all over Asia, and in Thailand nowhere more enthusiastically than in the northeast, where the three essential ingredients for a good chew – betel leaf, limestone ash and areca palm fruit – are found in abundance. You chew the coarse red flesh of the narcotic fruit (best picked when small and green-skinned) first, before adding a large heart-shaped betel leaf, spread with limestone ash paste and folded into manageable size; for a stronger kick, you can include tobacco and/or marijuana at this point. An acquired and bitter taste, betel numbs the mouth and generates a warm feeling around the ears. Less pleasantly, constant spitting is necessary: in traditional houses you spit through any hole in the floorboards, while in more elegant households a spittoon is provided. It doesn't do much for your looks either: betel-chewers are easily spotted by their rotten teeth and lips stained scarlet from the habit.

When travelling long distances, chewers carry basketloads of the ingredients with them; at home, guests are served from a betel set, comprising at least three small covered receptacles, and sometimes a tray to hold these boxes and the knife or nutcracker used to split the fruit. Betel-chewing today is popular mainly with elderly Thais, particularly northeastern women, but it used to be a much more widespread social custom, and a person's betel tray set was once a Thai's most prized possession and an indication of rank: royalty would have sets made in gold, the nobility's would be in silver or nielloware, and poorer folk wove theirs from rattan or carved them from wood. Betel sets still feature as important dowry items in Isaan, with tray-giving processions forming part of northeastern engagement ceremonies.

Klang Muang just north of the hotel. Weavers from across the province congregate in the city to display and sell their fabrics at the annual **Silk Festival** (Nov 29–Dec 10), which takes place at the City Hall on Thanon Na Soon Rachakarn. Another fair-trade outlet for local craftspeople is the Suebsan Isaan Cooperative shop at 16 Thanon Klang Muang, which sells textiles fabricated from bamboo fibre and water hyacinth, as well as more usual *mut mee* silks and cottons, basketware, herbal cosmetics and other traditional products. Nearby on this stretch of Thanon Klang Muang, just north of *Roma Hotel*, Neam Lap La is the place to buy local food specialities such as spicy sausages, sugar-coated beans and other Khon Kaen delicacies.

Eating, drinking and entertainment

Khon Kaen has a reputation for very **spicy food**, particularly sausages, *sai krog isaan*, which are served with cubes of raw ginger, onion, lime and plenty of chilli sauce, at stalls along Thanon Klang Muang to the north of the *Kaen Inn*. These and other local favourites – such as pigs' trotters, roast duck and shellfish – can also be sampled at the stalls along the northern edge of the lake Bueng Kaen Nakhon. Foodstalls pop up all over other parts of town at dusk, with a particular concentration at the **night bazaar** on the eastern end of Thanon Ruen Rom.

Nightlife in Khon Kaen is mainly focused in and around the *Charoen Thani*, *Kosa* and *Sofitel* hotels. The *Charoen Thani* flagship is *Zolid*, a three-floor nightclub which hosts live bands and cabarets nightly, has enormous music-video screens, and is said to be the biggest disco in the northeast, while the *Sofitel* competes with its *Wow Club*, offering much the same fare. The *Kosa Hotel*'s outdoor beer garden is a more convivial place for a beer and chat, or you could venture over to the nearby neon nightmare that is *Times Square*, an outdoor eating and drinking plaza whose small bar-restaurants employ either hostesses or musicians to draw in the punters.

Baker's Basket Lobby of the *Hotel Sofitel*. Can't be beaten for its delicious selection of cakes and pastries. Expensive.

First Choice 18/8 Thanon Pimpasoot. Another tourist-friendly restaurant, offering air-conditioned premises and an English-language menu offering Thai, Western and Japanese options, plus a sizeable vegetarian selection and decent breakfasts. Daily 7am–11pm. Moderate.

Huaan Laaw 39 Thanon Pimpasoot (no English sign). Located inside an elegant modern wooden home decorated with crafts and antiques, this is a conducive place in which to enjoy Thai and Lao dishes. Moderate.

Krönen Brauhaus In the basement of the *Hotel Sofitel*. Cosy, dimly lit microbrewery bar where the German-style beer flows strong and dark.

Krua Weh Vietnamese Food Next door but one to the *Saen Sumran* hotel on Thanon Klang Muang. Very popular air-con place that serves mainly Vietnamese food from its pictorial menu (no English translations), plus some northeastern standards. One of their specialities is *yam kai weh*, spicy chicken salad made with mint. Daily 11am–9.30pm. Moderate.

Pizza & Bake 6/5 Thanon Klang Muang. Tempts the Western palate with real coffee, American breakfasts, pancakes, sandwiches and a salad bar. The more adventurous can try Vietnamese pizzas and spring rolls. Daily 7.30am–11pm. Moderate.

Underground In the basement of the *Hotel Sofitel*. Basement food and drink complex with half a dozen small restaurant concessions, including a surprisingly authentic pizzeria as well as a sushi bar and a Chinese restaurant. Expensive.

Listings

Airline The Thai Airways office is inside the *Hotel Sofitel* on Thanon Prachasumran ⓣ043 227701.

Banks and exchange There's a currency-exchange booth in front of the Bangkok Bank on Thanon Si Chan, between the *Charoen Thani* and *Kosa* hotels (daily 9am–5pm), plus plenty of ATMs on southern Thanon Na Muang and north-central Thanon Klang Muang.

Bookshop The bookshop opposite the *Charoen Thani* on Thanon Si Chan stocks a reasonable selection of English-language titles published by Asia Books, plus some novels and a good range of Thai maps and road atlases.

Car, motorbike and bicycle rental Avis ⓣ043 344313, ⓦwww.avis.com and Budget ⓣ043 345460, ⓦwww.budget.co.th both have desks at the airport, and Budget also has a desk inside the *Kaen Inn*. Cars, with or without driver, and motorbikes are also available from: Narugee Car Rental, next to Oasis Plaza department store and the *Kosa Hotel* off Thanon Si Chan ⓣ043 224220; cars only from Kaen Koon Car Rental at 54/1–2 Thanon Klang Muang ⓣ043 239458. Bicycles from *First Choice* restaurant at 18/8 Thanon Pimpasoot.

Consulates The Lao consulate is located some way east of TAT at 171 Thanon Prachasamoson (Mon–Fri 8am–noon & 1–4pm; ⓣ043 242856–8); city songthaew #11 (red) runs right past the consulate from the train station, via Thanon Si Chan and the Thanon Klang Muang air-con bus terminal, as does city songthaew #10 (blue), en route from the non-air-con bus station and TAT, then continuing all the way down Thanon Klang Muang via the air-con bus station. Thirty-day visas usually take three working days to process (B1050) or can be done in 15min for B1350. For more details on travel into Laos, see p.19. There's also a Vietnamese consulate in Khon Kaen (Mon–Fri 8.30am–4pm; ⓣ043 242190), south of the Lao consulate and about 1.5km from the TAT office, off Thanon Prachasamoson at 65/6 Thanon Chaiaphadung; city songthaew #10 (blue) runs right past it: see above for details. Thirty-day Vietnamese visas are issued here within 24hr and cost B1800.

Hospitals Khon Kaen Ram Hospital, on the far western end of Thanon Si Chan, is the main private hospital in town ⓣ043 333900–3, or there's the Srinakarin Hospital, attached to Khon Kaen University, north of town on Highway 2 ⓣ043 242331–44.

Internet access Available at the shop next to the *Roma Hotel* on Thanon Klang Muang and opposite the *Charoen Thani* on Thanon Si Chan.

Mail The most centrally located post office is on Thanon Si Chan, and there's another branch next to the phone centre on Thanon Lung Soon Rachakarn.

Pharmacies Several along north-central Thanon Klang Muang, plus a Boots the Chemist outlet on the ground floor of Oasis Plaza on Thanon Si Chan.

Telephones The CAT international telephone centre is in the north of town on Thanon Lung Soon Rachakarn.

Tourist police For all emergencies, call the tourist police on the free, 24hr phone line ⓣ1155, or contact them at the TAT office on Thanon Prachasamoson ⓣ043 236937.

Travel agents Domestic and international air tickets are available from Kaen Koon Car Rent at 54/1–2 Thanon Klang Muang ⓣ043 239458, ⓔkaenkoontravel@yahoo.co.uk; and Kangwal Holiday, on the *Charoen Thani* approach road on Thanon Si Chan ⓣ043 227777, ⓔkangwal_holiday@yahoo.com.

Around Khon Kaen

The outer reaches of Khon Kaen province hold a couple of places that are worth exploring on **day-trips**. If you're looking for other things to occupy yourself, don't be duped by the TAT brochure on the "tortoise village" in the village of Ban Kok, about 5km west of Chonnabot, which is both duller and more depressing than the tourist literature implies.

Chonnabot

Khon Kaen makes a reasonable base from which to explore the local silk-weaving centre of **Chonnabot**, about 54km southwest of the city. Traditionally a cottage industry, this small town's **silk production** has become centralized over the last few years, and weavers now gather in small workshops in town, each specializing in just one aspect of the process. You can walk in and watch the women (it's still exclusively women's work) at their wheels, looms or dye vats, and then buy from the vendors in the street out front. For more details on silk-weaving processes, see the box on p.503. To get to Chonnabot from Khon Kaen, take any ordinary Khorat-bound bus to **Ban Phae** (every 30min), then a songthaew for the final 10km to Chonnabot.

Phuwiang National Park: Dinosaurland

Khon Kaen hit the international headlines in 1996 when the oldest-ever fossil of a tyrannosaur **dinosaur** was unearthed in Phuwiang National Park, about 90km northwest of Khon Kaen. Estimated to be 120 million years old, it measures just 6m from nose to tail and has been named *Siamotyrannus isanensis* – Siam for Thailand, and Isaan after the northeastern region of Thailand. Before this find at Phuwiang, the oldest tyrannosaur fossils were the 65-million- to 80-million-year-old specimens from China, Mongolia and North America. These younger fossils are twice the size of the *Siamotyrannus*; the latter's age and size have therefore established the *Siamotyrannus* as the ancestor of the *Tyrannosaurus rex*, and confirmed Asia as the place of origin of the tyrannosaur genus, which later evolved into various different species.

The fossil of this extraordinary dinosaur – together with eight moderately interesting paleontological finds – is on show to the public at Dinosaurland in **Phuwiang National Park** (daily 8am–4.30pm; B10). The **Dinosaurland** tag is a little misleading as there are no theme-park attractions here, just nine quarries and a small visitor centre. Nearly all the information is in Thai, so it's worth picking up the informative English-language brochure on Dinosaurland from Khon Kaen's TAT office before you come.

The *Siamotyrannus isanensis* is displayed in **Quarry #9**, which is accessible via the 1.5-kilometre track that starts across the road from the visitor centre; from the car park at the end of the track, it's a five-hundred-metre walk to the quarry. The fossil is an impressive sight, with large sections of the rib cage almost completely intact. **Quarry #1** contains the other displays, as well as two previously undiscovered species. The theropod *Siamosaurus sutheethorni* (named after the paleontologist Warawut Suteehorn) is set apart from the other, carnivorous, theropods by its teeth, which seem as if they are unable to tear flesh; the fifteen- to twenty-metre-long *Phuwiangosaurus sirindhornae* (named in honour of Thailand's Princess Royal) is thought to be a new species of sauropod.

Though it's possible to take a non-air-con bus from Khon Kaen to Phuwiang town, you then need to hire a motorbike taxi to continue to Dinosaurland and back, so it's easier to hire your own wheels in Khon Kaen. To **get to the park**, head west out of Khon Kaen on Highway 12, following the signs for Chumpae as far as kilometre-stone 48, where you'll see an unmissable dinosaur statue beside the road. Turn right off the main road here, and continue for another 38km along Highway 2038, passing through the small town of Phuwiang and following signs all the way for Dinosaurland. There's a **food** and drink stall at the car park in front of Quarry #3, which is about one kilometre's drive north of the visitor centre.

Udon Thani and Ban Chiang

Economically important but charmless, **UDON THANI** looms for most travellers as a misty, early-morning sprawl of grey cement seen from the window of the overnight train to Nong Khai. The capital of an arid sugar-cane and rice-growing province, 137km north of Khon Kaen, Udon was given an economic shot in the arm during the Vietnam War with the siting of a huge American military base nearby, and despite the American withdrawal in 1976, the town has maintained its rapid industrial and commercial development. The only conceivable reason to alight here would be to satisfy a lust for

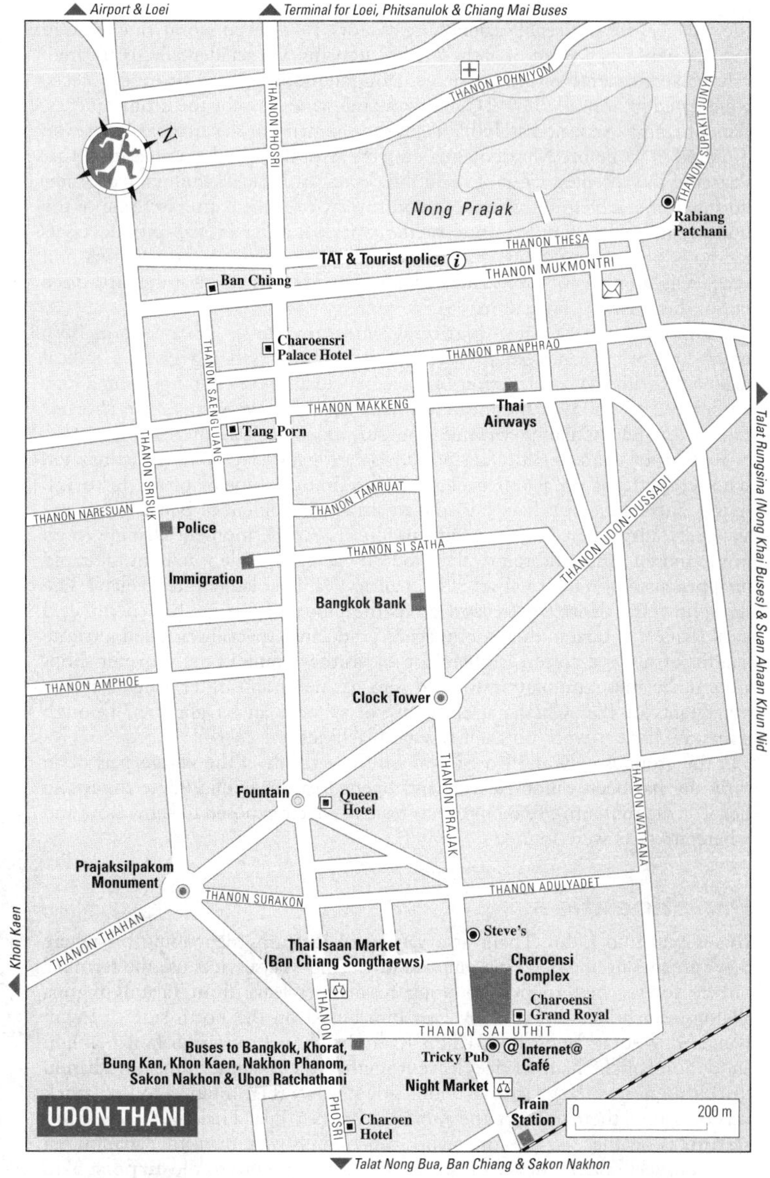

archeology at the excavated Bronze Age settlement of **BAN CHIANG**, 50km to the east in sleepy farming country, though plenty of travellers avoid spending time in Udon by visiting Ban Chiang on a day-trip from the much preferable base of Nong Khai (see p.540) or by staying in the village itself.

Listed as a UNESCO World Heritage site in 1992, the village of Ban Chiang is unremarkable nowadays, although its fertile setting is attractive and the villagers are noticeably friendly to visitors. It achieved worldwide fame in 1966, when a rich seam of archeological remains was accidentally discovered: clay pots, uncovered in human graves alongside sophisticated **bronze** objects, were dated to around 3000 BC, implying the same date for the bronze pieces. Ban Chiang was immediately hailed as the vanguard of the Bronze Age, seven hundred years before Mesopotamia's discovery of the metal – a revelation that shattered the accepted view of mainland Southeast Asia as a cultural backwater during that era. Despite continuing controversy over the dating of some of the finds, Ban Chiang stands as one of the world's earliest bronze producers; its methods of smelting show no signs of influence from northern China and other neighbouring bronze cultures, which suggests the area was the birthplace of Southeast Asian civilization.

The present village's fine **National Museum** (daily 8.30am–5pm; B30; hours and price may change after the renovation) is being given a radical makeover, with the construction of three new exhibition buildings, which may be finished by 2005. In the meantime you can still view some of the choicest finds from Ban Chiang's Bronze Age culture, as well as the country's best collection of characteristic late-period Ban Chiang clay pots, with their red whorled patterns on a buff background – although not of prime historical significance, these pots have become an attractive emblem of Ban Chiang, and are freely adapted by local souvenir producers. At the moment a single room in the museum is dedicated to the modern village; the tale it tells, of the rapid disappearance of traditional ways, is an all-too-familiar lament in Thailand. The story, however, doesn't quite end there: the influx of tourists has encouraged local farmers to turn to their looms again, producing especially rich and intricate lengths of silk and cotton *mut mee*, for sale as they come in the souvenir shops around the museum, or transformed into garments and other articles by the inhabitants of Ban Chiang itself, many of whom can be glimpsed through doorways hard at work on their sewing machines.

In the grounds of **Wat Pho Si Nai**, on the east side of the village, part of an early dig has been canopied over and opened to the public (same times and ticket as the museum). Two burial pits have been left exposed to show how and where artefacts were found.

Practicalities

Buses pull into Udon Thani at a variety of locations, depending on where they've come from: Loei, Phitsanulok and Chiang Mai services use the terminal on the town's western bypass; Nong Khai buses leave from Talat Rungsina (Rungsina market, also used by Ban Phu buses) on the north side of town; Bangkok, Khorat, Bung Kan, Khon Kaen, Nakhon Phanom, Sakon Nakhon and Ubon Ratchathani services leave from the other main terminal on Thanon Sai Uthit; nearby, Ban Chiang-bound songthaews (big, multi-coloured truck versions) base themselves at the morning market, Talat Thai Isaan. The **train station** is on the east side of town, a ten-minute walk from the Thanon Sai Uthit bus terminal. Minibuses from the big hotels run out to the **airport**, 3km southwest of the centre, to meet incoming flights, charging non-guests B100 per person to drop them anywhere in town. Alternatively, both Avis (ⓣ042 244770) and Budget (ⓣ042 246805) have **car-rental** desks at the airport.

Udon's **TAT office** (daily 8.30am–4.30pm; ⓣ042 325406–7, ⓔtatudon@tat.or.th) also covers Nong Khai, Nong Bua Lamphu and Loei provinces; with an adjoining **tourist police** office, it's housed at 16/5 Thanon Mukmontri on the south side of Nong Prajak, a landscaped lake and park to the northwest of the centre. Numbered **songthaews** ply set routes around town for B5 per person (a rough map is available from TAT); among the more useful routes, #15 connects the Thanon Sai Uthit bus terminal with the terminal on the western bypass, while #6 runs the length of Thanon Udon-Dussadi to Talat Rungsina. Alternatively, there are plenty of **skylabs**, Udon's version of tuk-tuks, for hire (from B20 for a short journey). There's **Internet access** at Internet@Café (daily 9am–10pm), off Thanon Prajak opposite the Charoensi Complex shopping centre and Robinson department store.

To **get to Ban Chiang** from Udon, either take a direct songthaew from Talat Thai Isaan (Mon–Sat every 30min or so until about 1.30pm) or catch a Sakon Nakhon-bound bus (every 20min) to Ban Palu and then a motorized samlor (B30/person) for the last 5km or so from the main road to the village. Heading back to Udon the same day by songthaew is not possible as the service runs only until about 9am, so you'll have to make do with a samlor and bus combination.

Accommodation and eating

It's possible to **stay overnight in Ban Chiang** at the excellent *Lakeside Sunrise Guesthouse* (ⓣ042 208167, ⓔalexovenden696@hotmail.com; ❷), and in fact many guests linger for a few days; rates, which are at the lower end of this price code, can be reduced for longer stays. Run by Australian Alex Ovenden and his wife Tong, the guest house is just a few minutes' walk from the museum (where Tong works): facing the museum, head left then turn right at the first intersection and look for a large Western-style wooden two-storey house. Guests here sleep in clean first-floor rooms with fans and mosquito screens and can relax on a huge balcony – equipped with a helpful noticeboard and small library – overlooking an artificial lake; there are shared cold-water showers downstairs, though hot water can be brought to you for a small fee. Bicycles are available for exploring the surrounding countryside, or Alex can arrange motorbike rental; there's a bird and animal sanctuary 6km away, and a couple of interesting forest wats closer to the village, all marked on Alex's useful hand-drawn map of the area. There are half a dozen simple **restaurants** in the village – the place directly opposite the museum does an excellent *raht nah* (noodles in a thick gravy) – and a small night market just east of the museum.

Among **Udon's accommodation** options, the centrally located *Queen Hotel* at 6–8 Thanon Udon-Dussadi (ⓣ042 221451; ❶–❷) is the best budget bet, with decent fan-cooled and air-con rooms and a friendly owner who speaks some English; the *Tang Porn*, 289/1 Thanon Makkeng (ⓣ042 221032; ❶), also has a reasonable location and clean rooms. In the middle of the range, the excellent-value *Charoensri Palace Hotel*, 60 Thanon Phosri (ⓣ042 242611–3, ⓕ042 242612; ❹), is a popular businessmen's haunt that offers large, clean bedrooms with air-con and hot water. Further up the scale, the *Charoen Hotel* at 549 Thanon Phosri (ⓣ042 248155, ⓕ042 241093, ⓔcharoen@edtech.co.th; ❺) has air-con rooms with hot showers and TVs, and a swimming pool outside, but better still are *Ban Chiang* at 5 Thanon Mukmontri (ⓣ042 327911–20, ⓕ042 223200, ⓔbchiang@udon.ksc.co.th; ❻) and the luxury *Charoensri Grand Royal*, next to the Charoensi Complex at 277/1 Thanon Prajak (ⓣ042 343555, ⓕ042 343550, ⓔcharoensri@pantip.co.th; ❽) – both centrally located, with health club, pool and karaoke bar among their offerings.

Delicious *kai yaang* (barbecued chicken) and *khao niaw* (sticky rice) are served at several inexpensive **restaurants** around the junction of Thanon Prajak and

Thanon Pranphrao. For a greater variety of low-priced comestibles – Thai, Chinese and Vietnamese – head for the night market on the west side of the train station. At lunchtime, probably the best deal in Udon is the buffet at the *Charoen Hotel*, a huge, all-you-can-eat selection of Thai, Japanese and Western food, with salads, desserts and coffee, for B150 per person. One of Udon's most popular restaurants is the *Rabiang Phatchani*, northeast of the centre in Nong Prajak Park, with a large menu of Thai and Chinese dishes and outdoor seating on a leafy terrace overlooking the lake. For a real culinary treat, head out into the northern suburbs to the very clean and friendly *Suan Ahaan Khun Nid*, which is famous far and wide among Thai gourmets for its carefully prepared Isaan food, such as spiced, salted and grilled snakehead fish, deep-fried land crab, deep-fried sun-dried beef and a wide variety of northeastern salads. It's on Soi 9 (Soi Nonniwate), Thanon Udon-Dussadi (☎042 246128): to get there, take a skylab or catch songthaew #6 up Udon-Dussadi, then walk ten minutes west along the soi past the temple and it's on the left at the end of a short alley (no English sign). Fast food of the *Pizza Company* and *KFC* ilk is eagerly consumed by the locals at the Charoensri Complex; around the complex, there's a cluster of decent eating and drinking options, including the air-con *Tricky Pub* opposite and *Steve's*, an English-run pub and restaurant round the corner at 254/26 Thanon Prajak.

Loei and around

Most people carry on from Udon Thani due north to Nong Khai (see p.540), but making a detour via **LOEI**, 147km to the west, takes you within range of several towering national parks and sets you up for a lazy tour along the Mekong River. The capital of a province renowned for the unusual shapes of its stark, craggy mountains, Loei is, more significantly, the crossroads of one of Thailand's least-tamed border regions, with all manner of illegal goods coming across from Laos. This trade may be reined in – or perhaps spurred on – by current plans for a 3km-long bridge across the Heuang River, a tributary of the Mekong, to Xainyabouli province in Laos. Despite its frontier feel, the town, lying along the west bank of the small Loei River, is friendly and offers legitimate products of its own, such as tamarind paste and pork sausages, which are sold in industrial quantities along Oua Thanon Aree (off Thanon Charoenrat, Loei's main street, which runs roughly parallel to the Loei River).

One reason to make a special trip to this region is to attend the unique rain-making **festival of Phi Ta Kon**, or Bun Phra Wet, held over three days either at the end of June or the beginning of July in the small town of **Dan Sai**, 80km southwest of Loei. In order to encourage the heavens to open, townsfolk dress up as spirits in patchwork rags and fierce, brightly painted masks (made from coconut palm fronds and the baskets used for steaming sticky rice), then rowdily parade the town's most sacred Buddha image round the streets while making fun of as many onlookers as they can, waving wooden phalluses about and generally having themselves a whale of a time. Top folk and country musicians from around Isaan are attracted to perform in the evenings during Phi Ta Kon; the afternoon of the second day of the festival sees the firing off of dozens of bamboo rockets, while the third day is a much more solemn affair, with Buddhist sermons and a purification ceremony at Wat Phon Chai. The carnival can be visited in a day from Loei, though rooms are hard to come by at this time.

Practicalities

Beyond its meagre attractions, Loei is really only useful as a transport hub and a base for the nearby national parks. **Buses** run here from Udon Thani every twenty minutes and from Khon Kaen every thirty minutes, from Phitsanulok in the central plains five times a day and from Bangkok (via Chaiyaphum) eighteen times a day. Half-hourly songthaews and buses link the town to Chiang Khan, an hour to the north at the start of the Mekong River route, while buses run hourly in the mornings to Sang Khom (3hr, bypassing Chiang Khan) and all the way to Nong Khai (6–7hr); if you come this way in the afternoon, you'll have to change buses in Pak Chom. If you're going straight from Loei to Nong Khai, it's quicker but far less scenic to catch a bus to Udon and change. All of these arrive at and depart from the **bus terminal** on Thanon Maliwan, the main through north–south road (Highway 201), about 2.5km south of the centre.

The TAT **tourist office** (Mon–Fri 8.30am–4.30pm; ⓣ042 812812) is in the old district office on Thanon Charoenrat on the south side of the centre. Keen nature-lovers might want to ask here – or through the Forestry Department in Bangkok (see p.75) – about cool-season tours into the fragile **Phu Luang Wildlife Sanctuary**, to the southwest of Loei. For **Internet access**, PA Computer is a little nearer the centre at 139 Thanon Charoenrat (daily 9am–midnight).

Accommodation and eating

Unless it's festival time, finding a decent **place to stay** in Loei shouldn't be a problem. The town boasts an outstanding guest house in a quiet residential area, five minutes' walk from the top of Thanon Charoenrat on the north side of the centre, *Sugar Guest House*, 4/1 Soi 4, Thanon Wisuttitep (ⓣ042 812982, ⓔsugarnamtan@hotmail.com; ❷–❸). Bright, colourful, sparkling-clean rooms are either fan-cooled with shared hot-water bathrooms, or air-con with TV and en-suite hot-water bathrooms. Bicycles (B30) and motorbikes (B200) can be rented, and the friendly, informative owners can arrange day-trips in a car with driver (B1400) to, for example, Phu Reua or the relaxing Huay Krating, where bamboo rafts are towed out onto the reservoir and you can eat lunch delivered to you by longtail boat. Comfortable and centrally placed, *Thai Udom Hotel*, at 122/1 Thanon Charoenrat (ⓣ042 811763, ⓕ042 830187; ❷–❸), has rooms with fan or air-con, all with hot-water bathrooms. The quieter and smarter *Sun Palace Hotel*, south of the centre at 191/5 Thanon Charoenrat (ⓣ042 815714, ⓕ042 815453; ❹), offers similar facilities but with the benefit of a recent renovation. Some of its rooms on the higher floors offer good mountain views. Out on its own at the top of the range is the *Loei Palace Hotel*, 167/4 Thanon Charoenrat (ⓣ042 815668–74, ⓦwww.amari.com; ❽), a shining white landmark that actually stands across the Loei River from Thanon Charoenrat, in the city park on the southeast side of the centre. Attractive, international-standard rooms enjoy fine garden views, and there's a large swimming pool and fitness centre.

The **food** at the *Nawng Neung Restaurant* is delicious and very economical – *khao man kai*, *khao muu daeng* and noodle soup with duck or pork are the specialities – but it's only open until 3pm; find it by the Thai Military Bank towards the western end of Thanon Ruamjai (no. 8/22), the main east–west street between Thanon Charoenrat and Thanon Maliwan. During the evening the central night market, on the east side of Thanon Charoenrat, serves up the usual budget eats, as well as Isaan specialities such as *larb*, *som tam* and *kai yaang* and the distinctly uncommon local delicacy, *khai ping* – barbecued eggs on skewers, which taste like coarse, salty soufflés. The clean *Sor Ahan Thai*, 100m west of the clocktower on Thanon Nok Kaew (an east–west street to the south of Ruamjai), offers a large range of moderately priced Thai dishes on its English-language menu and outdoor seating, while the nearby *Suan Pak*, 17/26 Thanon Nok Kaew, is an excellent little daytime vegetarian place (closed Sun) dishing up everything from *phat thai* and *som tam* to trays of curries and daily specials such as Vietnamese spring rolls. At the simple, open-air *Kungsee*, slightly south of the centre at 167/1 Thanon Charoenrat by the bridge to the *Loei Palace Hotel*, you can tuck into noodles or fried rice on a terrace with pretty views over the river and the thickly forested hills beyond.

Phu Kradung National Park

The most accessible and popular of the parks in Loei province, **PHU KRADUNG NATIONAL PARK**, about 80km south of Loei, protects a grassy 1300-metre plateau whose temperate climate supports a number of tree, flower and bird species not normally found in tropical Thailand. Walking trails crisscross much of sixty-square-kilometre Phu Kradung (Bell Mountain), and you ought to reckon on spending three days here if you want to explore them fully – at a minimum you have to spend one night, as the trip from Loei to the top of the plateau and back can't be done comfortably in a day. The park is closed during the rainy season (June–Sept), owing to the increased risk of mud-slides and land-slips, and is at its busiest during weekends in December and January, when the summit headquarters is surrounded by a sea of tents.

Access and accommodation

To get to the park, take any **bus** between Loei and Khon Kaen and get off at the village of Phu Kradung (1hr 30min), then hop on a B20 **songthaew** for the remaining 7km to the well-organized **Sri Taan Visitor Centre** (Oct–May daily 7am–2pm) at the base of the plateau, where you can pick up a trail map and pay the B200 admission fee. You can also leave your gear at the visitor centre, or hire a porter to tote it to the top for you. Up on the plateau at the **Wang Kwang Visitor Centre**, 8km from the Sri Taan Visitor Centre, there are ten national park **bungalows** sleeping from eight people upwards (B200/person); at busy times it is best to reserve in advance, either at the park itself (ⓣ042 871333) or through the Forestry Department in Bangkok (see p.46). There are also tents for rent (B200) or you can pitch your own for B30; blankets (essential on cool-season nights) and pillows both go for B10 each. Simple **restaurants** at park headquarters compete with several at the rim of the plateau, all of which can rustle up inexpensive, tasty food from limited ingredients, so there's no need to bring your own provisions. On the plain beneath the plateau a private concern with its own restaurant, *Phu Kradung Resort*, operates 2–3km from the Sri Taan Visitor Centre towards Phu Kradung village (ⓣ042 871076; ❸–❺); its en-suite bungalows, with either fan and cold water or air-con and hot water, sleep up to five people.

The park

The challenging main **trail** leads from the visitor centre 5.5km up the eastern side of Phu Kradung, passing occasional refreshment stalls, and becoming steeper and rockier on the last 1km, with wooden steps over the most difficult parts; most people take at least three hours, including rest stops. The main trail is occasionally closed for maintenance, when a parallel 4.5-kilometre trail is opened up in its place. At the end of the climb, the unbelievable view as your head peeps over the rim more than rewards the effort: flat as a playing field, the broad plateau is dotted with odd clumps of pine trees thinned by periodic lightning fires, which give it the appearance of a country park. Several feeder trails fan out from here, including a 9.5-kilometre path along the precipitous southern edge that offers sweeping views of Dong Phaya Yen, the untidy range of mountains to the southwest that forms the unofficial border between the northeast and the central plains. Another trail heads along the eastern rim for 2.5km to Pha Nok An – also reached by a two-kilometre path east from the Wang Kwang Visitor Centre – which looks down on neat rice fields and matchbox-like houses in the valley below, an outlook that's especially breathtaking at sunrise.

The attractions of the mountain come and go with the **seasons**. October is muddy after the rains, but the waterfalls that tumble off the northwestern edge of the plateau are in full cascade and the main trail is green and shady. December brings out the maple leaves; by February the waterfalls have disappeared and the vegetation on the lower slopes has been burnt away. April is good for rhododendrons and wild roses, which in Thailand are only found at such high altitudes as this.

Among the park's **wildlife**, mammals such as elephants, sambar deer and gibbons can be seen very occasionally, but they generally confine themselves to the evergreen forest on the northern part of the plateau, which is out of bounds to visitors. In the temperate pines, oaks and beeches that dot the rest of the plateau you're more likely to spot resident **birds** such as jays, sultan tits and snowy-browed flycatchers if you're out walking in the early morning and evening.

Nam Nao National Park

Amongst the undulating sandstone hills of the Phetchabun range, the flat-topped summit of Phu Phajit (1271m), **Nam Nao National Park**'s highest peak, can be seen to the southwest from nearby Phu Kradung National Park. At just under a thousand square kilometres, Nam Nao is larger and more ecologically valuable than its neighbour, with a healthy population of possibly over a hundred mammal species, including large animals such as forest elephant, banteng and a handful of tigers, and more often-seen barking deer, gibbons and leaf monkeys, as well as over two hundred bird species. These creatures thrive in habitats ranging from tropical bamboo and banana stands to the dominant features of dry evergreen forest, grasslands, open forest and pine stands that look almost European. Though the park was established in 1972, it was regarded as unsafe for visitors, remaining a stronghold for guerillas of the Communist Party of Thailand until the early 1980s; still much less visited than Phu Kradung, it can provide a sense of real solitude. The range of wildlife here also benefited from a physical isolation which stopped abruptly in 1975, when Highway 12 was cut through the park and poachers could gain access more easily. However, as the park adjoins the **Phu Khieo Wildlife Sanctuary**, there is beneficial movement by some species between the two areas.

The turn-off to the park headquarters is on Highway 12; look out for the sign at kilometre-stone 50, 147km west of Khon Kaen and 160km by road from Loei. Several **buses** a day run through at irregular times from Khon Kaen, Phitsanulok and Loei – all about two- to three-hour journeys. Once you've paid the B200 admission fee, walk or hitch the 2km down the pot-holed road past the park HQ to the **visitor centre** (☎056 729002), where you can pick up an English-language brochure that contains a rough sketch map of the park. **Accommodation** here consists of ten bungalows (from B800 for a four-person unit), and a campsite where two-person tents can be rented (B50/person) or you can pitch your own (B30/person). Stalls near headquarters sell simple **meals**.

A good network of clearly marked circular forest **trails** begins near the park headquarters, ranging from a one-kilometre nature trail teeming with butterflies to a six-kilometre track known for occasional elephant sightings; another 3.5-kilometre trail climbs through mixed deciduous forest to the Phu Kor outlook, with its sweeping views across to Phu Phajit. Other trails can be accessed directly from Highway 12, most of them clearly signposted from the road: at kilometre-stone 39, a steep climb up 260 roughly hewn steps leads to the Tham Pha Hong viewpoint, a rocky outcrop offering stunning panoramas of the park; at kilometre-stone 49, there's a four-kilometre nature trail taking in Suan Son Dang Bak viewpoint; and at kilometre-stone 67, a seven-hundred-metre trail leads to the beautiful Haew Sai waterfall, best seen during or immediately after the rainy season. Experienced walkers can reach the top of Phu Phajit along a rugged trail which begins from kilometre-stone 69; you need to hire a guide from the visitor centre (best booked in advance) for the steep six-hour climb. Most people camp on top, bringing their own gear and supplies, before making the descent the next day.

Phu Reua National Park

About 50km west of Loei, the 120-square-kilometre **Phu Reua National Park** gets the name "Boat Mountain" from its resemblance to an upturned sampan, with the sharp ridge of its hull running southeast to northwest. The highest point of the ridge, Yod Phu Reua (1365m), offers one of the most spectacular panoramas in Thailand: the land drops away sharply on the Laos side, allowing views over toy-town villages to countless green-ridged mountains spreading towards Louang Phabang. To the northwest rises Phu Soai Dao (2102m) on Laos' western border; to the south are the Phetchabun mountains. If you happen to be driving yourself here from the west along Highway 203, it might be worth breaking your journey 10km from the Phu Reua turn-off at the **Château de Loei vineyard**, for the novelty value if nothing else: you can drive for 6km around the vast, seemingly incongruous fields of vines, taste a variety of wines and brandy, and get something to eat at the simple restaurant.

Access and accommodation

The nine-kilometre paved road north from Ban Pachan Tom on Highway 203 to the summit means the park can get crowded at weekends, though during the week you'll probably have the place to yourself. The snag is that there's no organized **public transport** up the steep summit road – regular Lom Sak and Phitsanulok buses from Loei can drop you at the turn-off to the park on Highway 203, but then you'll have to walk/hitch or charter a songthaew to fill up (B400–500). The easiest option would be to **rent a motorbike** at the *Sugar Guest House* in Loei (see p.531). Once on the summit road, you have to pay B200 admission at a checkpoint, before reaching the **headquarters** and **visitor centre 1** (☎042 801716) after 4km, which has a trail map, a large, simple restaurant, and, in the pretty, pine-shaded grounds, five standard-issue, five- to six-berth national park **bungalows** (B1000–1200/bungalow). **Visitor centre 2** (Phuson), a three-kilometre walk or 5.5-kilometre drive further up the mountain near Hin Sam Chan waterfall, boasts several restaurants and is at the heart of the mountain's network of paths. At both visitor centres, a variety of **tents** can be rented and pitched: all with bedrolls and pillows, they cost B250–500 for two to six people; there's a B30 charge per person if you bring your own tent. Warm clothes are essential on cool-season nights – the lowest temperature in Thailand (-4°C) was recorded here in 1981 – and even by day the mountain is usually cool and breezy.

There are also plenty of **private accommodation** options, both on Highway 203 around Ban Pachan Tom and on the summit road itself. *Song Pee Nong* (☎042 899399; ❹), at the east end of the village, 1km towards Loei from the turn-off to the national park, offers decent, spacious chalets with fans and en-suite hot water, or you could stay 800m up the summit road at *Phupet Guesthouse* (☎042 899157 or 01 320 2874; ❺), in one of their large, attractive rooms with hot water, air-con and TV.

The park

A day's worth of well-marked trails fan out over the meadows and pine and broad-leaved evergreen forests of Phu Reua, taking in gardens of strange rock formations, the best sunrise viewpoint, Loan Noi, and, during and just after the rainy season, several waterfalls. The most spectacular **viewpoint**, Yod Phu Reua (Phu Reua Peak), is an easy one-kilometre stroll from the top of the summit road where the songthaews drop you. The park's population of barking deer, wild pigs and pheasants has declined over recent years – rangers' attempts to stop poaching by local villagers have been largely unsuccessful and have resulted in occasional armed clashes – but you may be lucky enough to spot one of 26 bird species, which include the crested serpent-eagle, green-billed malkoha, greater coucal, Asian fairy-bluebird, rufescent prinia and white-rumped munia, as well as several species of babbler, barbet, bulbul and drongo.

Along the Mekong

The **Mekong** is the one of the great rivers of the world, the third longest in Asia, after the Yangtse and the Yellow River. From its source 4920m up on the east Tibetan plateau it roars down through China's Yunnan province – where it's known as Lancang Jiang, the "Turbulent River" – before snaking its way a little more peaceably between Burma and Laos, and then, by way of the so-called "Golden Triangle", as the border between Thailand and Laos. After a brief shimmy into rural Laos via Louang Phabang, the river reappears in Isaan to form 750km of the border between Thailand and Laos. From Laos it crosses Cambodia and continues south to Vietnam, where it splinters into the many arms of the Mekong delta before flowing into the South China Sea, 4184km from where its journey began.

This dramatic stretch around Isaan is one of the more accessible places to observe the mighty river, and as Laos opens further border crossings to visitors, the Mekong is slowly becoming more of a transport link and less of a forbidding barrier. The guest houses along the upper part of this stretch, east from **Chiang Khan**, are geared towards relaxation and gentle exploration of the rural way of life along the river bank. **Nong Khai**, the terminus of the rail line from Bangkok and the principal jumping-off point for trips to the Lao capital of Vientiane, is the pivotal town on the river, but has lost some of its restful charm since the building of the massive Thai-Australian Friendship Bridge and the ensuing increase in cross-border trade. East of Nong Khai you're into wild country; here the unique natural beauty of **Wat Phu Tok** is well worth the hefty detour, and your Mekong journey wouldn't be complete without seeing **Wat Phra That Phanom**, a place of pilgrimage for 2500 years. Sights get sparse beyond that, although by continuing south through **Mukdahan** you can join up with the southern Isaan route at Ubon Ratchathani (see p.508).

A road, served by very slow **buses** and **songthaews**, runs beside or at least parallel to the river as far as Mukdahan. If you've got the time (allow at least a week to do it any sort of justice) you could make the entire marathon journey described in this section, although realistically you'll probably start in Nong Khai and work your way either upstream or downstream from there. **Motorbike** and **car rental** may provide another incentive to base yourself in Nong Khai (though they're also available, on a smaller scale, in Chiang Khan): having your own transport will give you more freedom of movement in this region, and the roads are quiet and easy to negotiate, though often in a state of disrepair. There's no official long-distance **boat** transport along this stretch of the river, at least from the Thai side, though if you're willing to spend the money it's possible to arrange private charters downstream from Chiang Khan all the way to Nong Khai.

Chiang Khan to Nong Khai

Rustic "backpackers' resorts" – and the travelling between them – are the chief draw along the reach of the Mekong between **Chiang Khan** and Nong Khai. Highway 211 covers this whole course: songthaews take you from Chiang Khan to **Pak Chom**, from where buses complete the journey, stopping at all towns en route.

Chiang Khan

The Mekong route starts promisingly at **CHIANG KHAN**, a friendly town that happily hasn't been entirely converted to concrete yet. Rows of shuttered wooden shophouses stretch out in a two-kilometre ribbon parallel to the river, which for much of the year runs red with what locals call "the blood of the trees": rampant deforestation on the Lao side causes the rust-coloured topsoil to erode into the river. The town has only two streets – the main through route (Highway 211, also known as Thanon Sri Chiang Khan) and the quieter Thanon Chai Khong on the waterfront – with a line of sois connecting them numbered from west to east.

Arguably the most enjoyable thing you can do here is to hitch up with other travellers for a **boat-trip** on the river, organized through *Rimkong* (see below) or one of the other guest houses. If you opt to go **upstream**, you'll head west towards the lofty mountains of Khao Laem and Khao Ngu on the Thai side and Phu Lane and Phu Hat Song in Laos, gliding round a long, slow bend in the Mekong to the mouth of the Heuang River tributary, 20km from Chiang Khan, which forms the border to the west of this point; stops can be arranged to share the fine views with Phra Yai, a twenty-metre-tall golden Buddha standing on a hilltop at the confluence, and at Hat Sai Kaew, a sandy beach for swimming, fishing and picnicking. Upstream trips cost around B250 per person and take three hours or so. A ride **downstream to Pak Chom** will take you through some of the most beautiful scenery on the Thai Mekong: hills and cliffs of all shapes and sizes advance and recede around the winding flow, and outside the rainy season, the rapids are dramatic without being dangerous (best between December and April), and the shores and islands are enlivened by neat grids of market gardens. This jaunt costs around B1500 for the boat, and takes around six hours, including an hour in Pak Chom, if you go both ways. Private charters all the way **downstream to Nong Khai** will set you back around B8500 for the boat (maximum of twenty people); the journey takes around eight hours. Most guest houses also offer a one-hour **sunset on the Mekong** cruise for about B150 per person.

It's also worth taking a walk towards the eastern end of the river road to **Wat Tha Khok**, by Soi 20, for its unobstructed view across the majestic Mekong. The Lao viharn shows some odd French influences in its balustrades, rounded arches and elegantly coloured ceiling. Continuing another 2km east along the main highway, a left turn back towards the river will bring you to **Wat Tha Khaek**, a formerly ramshackle forest temple which, on the back of millions of bahts' worth of donations from Thai tourists, has embarked on an ambitious but slow-moving building programme in a bizarre mix of traditional and modern styles. One kilometre further along this side road lies the reason for the influx of visitors: at this point, the river runs over rocks at a wide bend to form the modest rapids of **Kaeng Kut Khu**. Set against the forested hillside of imaginatively named Phu Yai (Big Mountain), it's a pretty enough spot, with small restaurants and souvenir shops shaded by trees on the river bank. If you're feeling brave, try the local speciality *kung ten*, or "dancing shrimp" – fresh shrimp served live with a lime juice and chilli sauce. Boats can be hired at Kaeng Kut Khu, costing from B300 for a half-hour pootle around the rapids. With your own transport you could continue your explorations to **Phu Thok**, an isolated hill topped by a communications mast to the south of here. On Highway 211 just east of the turn-off to Wat Tha Khaek and Kaeng Kut Khu, a small signpost will point you down 3km of rough paved road, before you fork right and climb steeply for nearly 2km to the summit. From there, you'll be rewarded with splendid views of Chiang Khan, the Mekong and the striking patchwork of fields in the broad valley to the south, especially at sunset.

Practicalities

Songthaews from Loei (every 30min) and Pak Chom (hourly in the morning, twice only in the afternoon) and **buses** from Loei (every 30min) stop at the west end of town near the junction of Highway 201 (the road from Loei) and Highway 211. Many of the guest houses rent out **bicycles** for B50 a day. There's **Internet access** at the northern end of Soi 10, near the junction with Highway 211, but currently there are **no banks** nor ATMs in Chiang Khan – the nearest are in Loei. You can extend your visa at the **immigration office** (Mon–Fri 8.30am–4.30pm; ⓣ042 821911 or 042 821175), a ten-minute walk east along Thanon Chai Khong from the *Rabieng* restaurant.

When it comes to **accommodation**, there are several very good guest houses strung out along the riverside Thanon Chai Khong. Opposite Soi 8 on the Mekong side of the road at no. 294, *Rimkong Pub and Guesthouse* (ⓣ042 821125; ❶–❸) is run by a helpful Thai-French couple who have lived in Chiang Khan for over ten years and are a great source of information on the area; a wide variety of wooden rooms with fans and mosquito screens share clean hot-water bathrooms, and there's a small terrace on the top floor. Boat trips, massages and a huge range of tours can be arranged here, as well as bicycle and motorbike rental (B200/day). The *Tonkhong Guest House* at no. 299/3, a little further east between sois 9 and 10 (ⓣ042 821547, ⓔtonkhong@hotmail.com; ❷–❸), is run by a welcoming Thai couple and has eight clean rooms – some en suite, one with air-con – and a first-floor terrace overlooking the river, perfect for lounging; the popular restaurant downstairs serves a good range of Thai dishes, including plenty of veggie options, as well as Western breakfasts. Extras on offer include traditional massage (B130/hour), herbal steam baths (B170/hour), motorbike rental, boat trips, occasional local day-trips, cooking courses and Internet access. Opposite at no. 300, the *Uro (Friendship) Guest House* (ⓣ042 822052 or 01 263 9068; ❷) has eight decent-sized wood-panelled rooms with clean shared hot-water bathrooms in a lovely fifty-year-old teak house; alongside the usual boat trips, massages and bike and motorbike rental, the owners can arrange car rental.

A more traditional hotel is the *Souksomboon* (ⓣ042 821064; ❷–❸), in an old-fashioned wooden building around a courtyard on Thanon Chai Khong, between sois 8 and 9; its best rooms overlook the river with attached cold-water bathrooms, or there are cheaper share-bathroom options. For more in the way of luxury, the *Chiang Khan Hill Resort* (ⓣ042 821285, ⓦwww.chiangkhanhill.com; ❺) offers a swimming pool and a variety of air-con bungalows, all with hot-water bathroom, TV and fridge, in a pretty garden overlooking the river at Kaeng Kut Khu.

One of the most fruitful hunting grounds for **food** is the market on the south side of Thanon Sri Chiang Khan between sois 9 and 10, which opens in the morning (at its best before 7am) and from 4.30 to 8pm. For a hearty *phat thai* in the evening, head for *Lom Look* on the east side of Soi 9. The best restaurant in town, with peaceful water views and inexpensive Chinese and Thai dishes, is *Rabieng*, nearby at the T-junction with Soi 9 and the river road.

Pak Chom, Sang Khom and on towards Nong Khai

Hourly songthaews from Chiang Khan cover the beautiful, winding route to **PAK CHOM**, 41km downriver, where you can pick up a bus from Loei (7 daily) to continue your journey towards Nong Khai via Sang Khom. Pak Chom used to be the site of a refugee camp for fifteen thousand Lao Hmong, who were moved in 1992 to Chiang Rai province and then dispersed to all parts of the globe, and its array of largely redundant administrative buildings has something of the air of a ghost town. There's little incentive to stay apart from the *Pak Chom Guest House* (ⓣ042 881332 or 09 276 5854; ❶–❷), on Soi 1 at the west end of town, which is set in leafy grounds with peerless views of the Mekong. Bungalows are either primitive affairs on stilts, or smart and wooden with verandas, fans and en-suite cold-water bathrooms, and extras are laid on such as boat trips (B70/person/hour), massages (B100/hour) and a communal Thai-Lao dinner (B80).

Beyond Pak Chom, the road through the Mekong valley becomes flatter and straighter. After 50km, a sign in English points down a side road to **Than Tip Falls**, 3km south, which is well worth seeking out. The ten-metre-high waterfall splashes down into a rock pool overhung by jungle on three sides; higher up, a bigger waterfall has a good pool for swimming, and if you can face the climb you can explore three higher levels.

Staying in quiet, tree-shaded **SANG KHOM**, 63km east of Pak Chom, puts you in the heart of an especially lush stretch of the river within easy biking distance of several backroad villages and temples. *Bouy Guest House* (ⓣ042 441065 or 06 356 5319; ❶) enjoys a particularly choice location: decent

△ Mekong sunset, Sang Khom

bamboo huts, with beautiful views out over the river, are set in a spacious compound on a spit of land reached by a wooden bridge over a small tributary. The obliging owners can arrange day-trips to Ban Phu, for instance, and boat trips on the Mekong, or if that sounds too strenuous, you can settle for a massage (B150/hour) or just relax in the hammocks strung from the veranda of each hut. Good food is available on a deck overlooking the stream (most of it also in vegetarian versions), and you can access the Internet, make international phone calls and rent bicycles (B50/day). Next door, just upstream of *Buoy*, the *New TXK (Mama's) Guest House* is the oldest guest house in Sang Khom, but isn't a patch on its neighbours. You can rent bicycles (B50/day) and motorbikes (B200–300/day) at *River Huts* (ⓣ042 441012, ⓔriverhuts @hotmail.com; ❶), which occupies a patch of shady river bank, with bungalows that run to tables, chairs and verandas. The establishment also offers good Thai and Western food and Internet access.

Another 19km east on Route 211, midway between Sang Khom and Sri Chiangmai, **Wat Hin Maak Peng** is a famous meditation temple, popular with Thai pilgrims and rich donors. The long white boundary wall and huge modern buildings are evidence of the temple's prosperity, but its reputation is in fact based on the asceticism of the monks of the Thammayut sect, who keep themselves in strict poverty and allow only one meal a day to interrupt their meditation. The flood of merit-makers, however, proved too distracting for the founder of the wat, Luang Phu Thet, who before his death in 1994 decamped to the peace and quiet of Wat Tham Kham near Sakon Nakhon. Visitors have the opportunity to stroll around the immaculate gardens and to revere no fewer than three effigies of the great monk, one in his chedi-like mausoleum, another in a *sala* overlooking a lake, and the third in a lifelike attitude of meditating near the river.

Nong Khai and around

The major border town in these parts is **NONG KHAI**, still a relative backwater but developing fast since the construction of the huge **Thai-Australian Friendship Bridge** over the Mekong on the west side of town in 1994. Occupying a strategic position at the end of Highway 2 and the northeastern rail line, and just 24km from Vientiane, Nong Khai acts as a conduit for goods bought and sold by Thais and Lao, who are allowed to pass between the two cities freely for day-trips. For the souvenir markets that have sprung up around the main pier, **Tha Sadet**, and the slipway to the bridge, the Lao bring across silver, wood and cane items, and sundry goods from the old Soviet bloc; they return with noodles, ketchup, toilet rolls and the like.

As with most of the towns along this part of the Mekong, the thing to do in Nong Khai is just to take it easy, enjoying the riverside atmosphere and the peaceful settings of its guest houses, which offer good value. Before you lapse into a relaxation-induced coma, though, try joining an evening river tour, or make a day-trip out to see the sculptures and rock formations in the surrounding countryside.

Nong Khai celebrates the generic Thai and Isaan festivals with due gusto, but in recent years a peculiarity of this stretch of the Mekong River has begun to attract celebrants from Bangkok and beyond. Every year in or around October, silent and vapourless **naga fireballs** appear from the river, small, pink, fiery balls that float vertically up to heights of as much as 150m, then disappear. This strange occurrence has now been consolidated into the festival of **Bang Fai Phaya Nak**, held over two days around the fifteenth day of the waxing moon in the eleventh lunar month. A tentative scientific theory proposes that the balls are methane gas from the mud on the bottom of the river, which reaches a certain temperature at that time of the year and is released; romantics will prefer the local belief that the nagas or *naks* (serpents) of the river breathe out the fireballs to celebrate the Buddha's return to earth at the end of Buddhist Lent.

The Town

Nong Khai lays itself out along the south bank of the Mekong in a four-kilometre band which is never more than 500m deep. Running from east to west, Thanon Meechai dominates activity: the main shops and businesses are plumb in the middle around the post office and Tha Sadet, with more frenetic commerce to the east at the Po Chai morning market by the bus station, and to the west at Chaiyaporn market in the afternoons. Although most of the buildings have been replaced by concrete boxes, a few weather-beaten wooden houses remain, their attractive balconies, porticoes and slatted shutters showing the influence of colonial architecture, which was imported from across the river before the French were forced out of Laos in 1954.

The most pleasant place for a stroll, however, is the riverside area. Although built-up in the centre around Tha Sadet, it becomes rustic and leafy around the fringes, which are often busy with people bathing, washing their clothes and fishing, especially in the early morning and evening. If you're lucky, you might also catch sight of a sunken chedi at the far eastern end of town, **Phra That Nong Khai**, which slipped into the river in 1847 and has since subsided so far that it's only visible in the dry season; this is thought to be a particularly good spot to see naga fireballs (see above), said to be produced by the naga that guards the relic in the chedi. To catch the best of life on the river, take the **boat trip** that sets out from the *Ruenpae Haisoke* floating restaurant behind the temple at the top of Thanon Haisoke every evening at 5.30pm. At B30, it's the

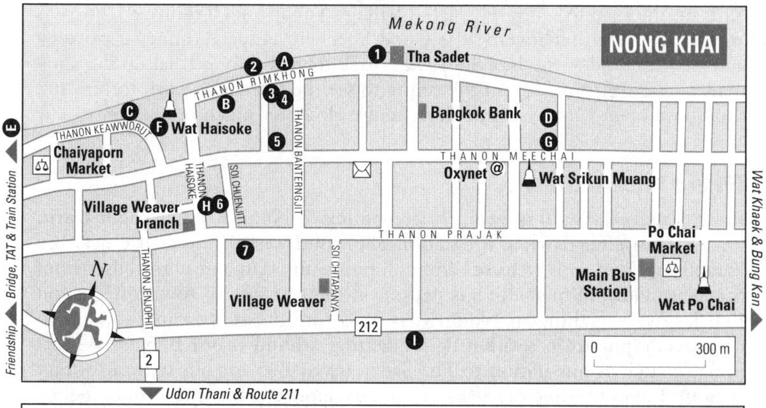

ACCOMMODATION				RESTAURANTS & BARS			
Esan Guest House	D	Nongkhai Grand Thani Hotel	I	Daeng Naem-Nuang	4	Nobbi's Restaurant	3
K. C. Guesthouse	F	Pantawee	H	Danish Baker	5	Thai Thai Restaurant	7
Mekong Guest House	A	Royal Mekhong Nongkhai	E	Meeting Place	6	Udomrod	1
Mut Mee	C	Ruan Thai Guest House	B	Nam Tok Rim Khong	2		
		Sawasdee Guest House	G				

least expensive way of getting onto the Mekong in Thailand, and runs up and down the length of Nong Khai for an hour and a half, sticking to the Thai side. Reasonably priced drinks can be ordered from the bar; the food is not particularly recommended and has to be ordered twenty minutes before the boat leaves. There's no stunning scenery, but plenty of activity on both river banks as the sun sets behind the Friendship Bridge.

The main temple of the region is **Wat Po Chai** off the east end of Thanon Prajak. The cruciform viharn, with its complex and elegant array of Lao tiers, shelters a venerated golden image, the Phra Sai Buddha. Prince Chakri, the future Rama I, is said to have looted the image from Vientiane, along with the Emerald Buddha, but the boat which was bringing back the Phra Sai overturned and sank in the Mekong. Later, the statue miraculously rose to the surface and the grateful people of Nong Khai built this great hangar of a viharn to house it, where the present king, Chakri's descendant, comes every year to pay his respects. It's worth a visit for the Buddha's stagy setting, in front of a steep, flame-covered altar, dazzlingly lit from above and below. The solid gold head is so highly polished that you have to peer carefully to make out the Sukhothai influence in its haughty expression and beaked nose.

Fifteen minutes' walk west of Wat Po Chai at 1151 Soi Chitapanya, just off Thanon Prajak, **Village Weaver Handicrafts** (daily 8am–5pm; ⓣ042 411236, ⓦwww.thaivillageweaver.com) specializes in **mut mee** (literally "tied strings"), the northeastern method of tie-dyeing bundles of cotton thread before hand-weaving, which produces geometrical patterns on a coloured base; Village Weaver also has a branch shop (daily 8am–7pm) slightly nearer the centre at 1020–1020/1 Thanon Prajak, on the corner of Thanon Haisoke. Through a self-help project initiated in 1982 to help local rural women earn cash, the work is produced in nearby villages and in the yard behind the main shop, where you can watch the weaving process (daily except Sun). White on indigo is the simplest, most traditional form, but the shop also carries a wide range of more richly patterned lengths of silk and cotton (tailoring available), as well as ready-made clothes, wall hangings, bags and axe pillows; they offer a very reasonable and professional posting and packing service back to your home country, and it's also possible to order by email. Seven kilometres south of Nong Khai on the road to Udon Thani, the **Village Vocational Training Centre** is another self-help initiative by the Good Shepherd Sisters, producing **pottery** and weaving sold at the Isan Shop, 3km back towards Nong Khai on the same road; you're welcome to visit the centre to see the artisans at work (centre and shop both open Mon–Sat 8am–5pm, centre closes for lunch noon–1pm).

Practicalities

From Bangkok, you'll most likely be coming to Nong Khai by night **train**, arriving just after dawn at the station 3km southwest of the centre near the Friendship Bridge. Day **buses** from all points in Isaan and night buses from further afield pull in at the bus station on the east side of town off Thanon Prajak. As everything in Nong Khai is so spread out, you might want to consider hopping on a **tuk-tuk** for getting around (from B15 for a short journey such as bus station to Tha Sadet, up to B45 for bus station to train station). To get to some of the area's remoter spots, **motorbikes** can be rented (from B200/day) on Thanon Keawworut in front of the *Mut Mee Guest House* and at *The Meeting Place* (see below). Village Weaver Handicrafts (see above) offers **four-wheel drives** for around B1000 per day including insurance, and there's a branch of **Budget** at the *Pantawee Hotel* (ⓣ1800-BUDGET,

Crossing to Laos from Nong Khai

When crossing to Laos, you can now get a fifteen-day tourist **visa on arrival** at Nong Khai's **Thai-Australian Friendship Bridge** for US$30, plus two photos (full details of the visa options for Laos are given on p.19). It's possible to pay in baht at the bridge, though it's over the odds at B1500; Monday to Friday after 4pm and at weekends, there's an "overtime" surcharge of US$1/B50. Foreigners have to use the bridge here (daily 6am–10pm), as the ferry service from Tha Sadet is now reserved for Thais and Lao. From downtown Nong Khai, take a tuk-tuk to the foot of the bridge (about B45–50), then a minibus (every 20min until 9.30pm; B10, plus B10 "overtime" Mon–Fri noon–1pm and after 4pm, and all day at weekends) across the span itself. On the other side you can catch a taxi (about B200 one-way, B500 for a one-day tour), tuk-tuk (about B100) or bus (B10) to Vientiane, 24km away.

Ⓦwww.budget.co.th). For local exploration, **bicycles** are available on Thanon Keawworut in front of the *Mut Mee Guest House* (B30/day), while *Mut Mee* itself has mountain bikes (see below).

There's a small **TAT information booth** (daily 8.30am–4.30pm; Ⓣ & Ⓕ042 467844) at the Tha Udom market on the road leading up to the Friendship Bridge. If time's running out on your Thai visa, you can get an extension at the **immigration office** (Mon–Fri 8.30am–4.30pm; Ⓣ042 420242) further south on the same road – though at current prices for extensions, you might as well treat yourself to a day in Vientiane and get a free thirty-day Thai entry stamp on your way back.

There are plenty of places offering **Internet access**, including Oxynet, 569/2 Thanon Meechai, the *Mekong Guest House*, and the Hornbill Bookshop, on the funky little lane leading to *Mut Mee Guest House*, where you can also send faxes and make international calls. The shop stocks an excellent selection of new and second-hand **books** in English, as well as postcards and batik hangings.

Accommodation

Nong Khai has an excellent choice of inexpensive **places to stay**, the best and most reliable among which are *Mut Mee* and *Sawasdee*. In the wake of the Friendship Bridge has come a rash of luxury developments, of which more are to be expected.

Esan Guest House 538 Soi Srikunmuang, Thanon Meechai Ⓣ01 262 6996, Ⓔguyfernback@hotmail.com. Welcoming, English-run place in a quiet spot near the river and just round the corner from *Sawasdee*. Clean, well-kept rooms with fans and shared hot-water bathrooms occupy an airy traditional wooden house looking onto a neat ornamental garden and shady café. ❷

K.C. Guest House 1018 Thanon Keawworut, Ⓣ07 238 4533, Ⓔinchuta06@yahoo.com; next to Hornbill Bookshop on lane leading to *Mut Mee*. This two-storey all-wooden guest house is a cheaper, more intimate alternative to *Mut Mee*, and just nearby so you can still hang out/eat there, as *K.C.* itself offers no food. Sharing hot-water bathrooms, the simple, clean rooms have mosquito screens, shutters and fans; friendly, easy-going management. ❷

Mekong Guest House 519 Thanon Rimkhong near Tha Sadet Ⓣ042 460689. A fallback when other places are full: good for watching the bustle at the pier from the pleasant riverside restaurant/bar, but fairly noisy and warren-like. Recently refurbished, with tiled-floor rooms, some air-con, in the new block downstairs, and slightly battered wood-built rooms upstairs; hot-water bathrooms, both en suite and shared. The nicest rooms overlook the river. ❷–❺

Mut Mee Guest House 1111 Thanon Keawworut Ⓕ042 460717, Ⓔmutmee@nk.ksc.co.th. The attractive riverside terrace is a magnet for travellers; well-kept rooms, all fitted with fans and screens, sprawl around it. Bathrooms with cold or hot water are either shared or en suite, and three-bed dorms are available (dorm bed B80). With helpful, well-informed staff and a good riverside restaurant, it's also home to yoga, reiki and astrology sessions. Mountain bikes are available for rent at a rate of B42 a day (ask for their map of local sights). ❷–❹

Nongkhai Grand Thani Hotel 589 Moo 5, Nongkhai–Phonpisai road ⓣ042 420033, ⓦwww.nongkhaigrand.com. On the southern bypass, a luxury hotel with high standards of service, a swimming pool and an open-air rooftop restaurant offering Isaan specialities and panoramic views over Nong Khai and Laos. ❽

Pantawee Hotel 1049 Thanon Haisoke ⓣ042 411568–9, ⓦwww.nongkhaihotel.com. A good mid-range choice, with a colourful, brazenly lit frontage, that's surprisingly comfortable for the price: immaculately clean rooms nearly all come with hot-water bathroom, TV and fridge – some with fan, others with air-con. They also have motel-like fan or air-con bungalows on the opposite side of Thanon Haisoke. ❷–❹

Royal Mekong Nongkhai 222 Thanon Panungchonprathan ⓣ042 420024, ⓦwww.welcome.to/royal_mekong. In riverside grounds west of town, 200m past the Friendship Bridge and next to the dry-season beach at Hat Jommanee, an international-standard hotel with a large swimming pool where all two hundred bedrooms have views of the Mekong and Laos. ❻

Ruan Thai Guest House 1126 Thanon Rimkhong ⓣ042 412519. Newly renovated wooden houses in a quiet garden compound with attractive, well-maintained rooms that run the gamut of facilities from shared cold-water bathrooms to air-con, hot-water en suites. Internet access is available and there's a smart outdoor café serving a range of teas and coffees. ❶–❹

Sawasdee Guest House 402 Thanon Meechai ⓣ042 412502, ⓕ042 420259. A well-restored, grand old wooden shophouse round a pleasant courtyard, with helpful management: luggage storage and showers available for those catching a night train or bus. Fan-cooled rooms sharing bathrooms (try to avoid those overlooking the noisy main road), with hot showers available, and air-con rooms with en-suite hot-water bathrooms. ❶–❸

Eating

Among local people and tourists alike, the most popular **restaurants** in Nong Khai are the handful of moderately priced riverside terraces clustered around the pier on Thanon Rimkhong, though these compete with travellers' fare at guest houses and some excellent Vietnamese places.

Daeng Naem-Nuang 1062/1–2 Thanon Banterngjit. Delicious Vietnamese food at this immaculately clean, popular and airy place: the speciality here is *nam nueng* – make-it-yourself fresh spring rolls with barbecue pork. The obliging owner will demonstrate how to build the rolls using fresh soft rice wrappers, pork, vermicelli noodles, lettuce, mint, lemony *chat moong* leaves, chopped starfruit, green banana, cucumber, garlic, chilli and a rich peanut sauce. Takeaways also available. Closes at 7pm. A more upmarket branch is being built around the corner on Thanon Rimkhong. Inexpensive.

The Danish Baker Thanon Meechai. Congenial bar/restaurant with a few pavement tables on the busy main road for people-watching. An extensive Thai menu, plus good Western set breakfasts and a wide range of other dishes such as sausages with potato salad and pizzas. Moderate.

Meeting Place 1117 Soi Chuenjitt. Friendly farang-run bar/restaurant serving very good Cumberland sausage and mash, fish and chips, all-day breakfasts and Sunday roasts, plus Thai food and beer on tap. The decor is bright and neat, with some pleasant outdoor tables, and there's a pool table to help while away the evenings. Moderate.

Mut Mee Guest House 1111 Thanon Keawworut. This relaxed riverfront eatery under bamboo shelters is deservedly popular: good Thai dishes, particularly vegetarian versions, vie with tasty Western efforts including marinated pork or chicken steaks with french fries, French bread and home-made yoghurt and tzatziki. Inexpensive.

Nam Tok Rim Khong Thanon Rimkhong. Simple but very popular restaurant with an attractive balcony overlooking the river, specializing in *nam tok*, spicy hot beef salad, as well as other Isaan delicacies such as dried beef, sausages and soups. Closes at 8pm. Inexpensive.

Nobbi's Restaurant 997 Thanon Rimkhong. Run by a German-Thai couple, this bright and busy restaurant is popular with expats for its all-day Western breakfasts, German sausages, smoked ham, tasty pizzas and beer on tap. Books, newspapers and board-games are welcome extras. Happy hour 3–6pm. Moderate.

Thai Thai Restaurant 1155/8 Thanon Prajak. The place to come for honest, inexpensive Thai food; the menu in English is limited, but will get you as far as fried rice or noodles, soups and curries, or you can point out anything else you fancy on the colourful display counter.

The similar *Dee Dee Pochana Restaurant* next door is also very popular. Daily 3pm–2am. Inexpensive.

Udomrod Thanon Rimkhong. Particularly good food and atmosphere at this riverside terrace restaurant, hard by Tha Sadet and good for watching the Mekong traffic. It specializes in *paw pia yuan* (Vietnamese spring rolls), river prawns and fish, and northeastern dishes such as *larb*, *kai yaang* and *som tam*. Moderate.

Around Nong Khai

By far the easiest and most popular day-trip out of Nong Khai takes in **Sala Kaeo Kou**, with its surreal sculptures, a short songthaew hop to the east. To the southwest of town and also fairly easy to get to, **Wat Phra That Bang Phuan** offers classic temple sightseeing, while the natural rock formations at **Ban Phu** require much more effort and a full day out. Some of the sights upstream along the Mekong described on the previous pages, as well as Wat Phu Tok described below, are also within day-tripping distance, and it's quite possible to get to Ban Chiang and back in a day, changing buses at Udon Thani.

Sala Kaeo Kou

Just off the main highway 5km east of Nong Khai, **Sala Kaeo Kou** (aka Wat Khaek; daily 7am–6pm; B10) is best known for its bizarre sculpture garden, which looks like the work of a giant artist on acid. The temple was founded by the late **Luang Phu Boonlua Surirat**, an unconventional Thai holy man who studied under a Hindu guru in Vietnam and preached in Laos until he was thrown out by the Communists in the late 1970s. His charisma – those who drank water offered by him would, it was rumoured, give up all they owned to the temple – and heavy emphasis on morality attracted many followers among the farmers of Nong Khai. Luang Phu's popularity suffered, however, after his eleven-month spell in prison for insulting King Bhumibol, a crime alleged by jealous neighbours and probably without foundation; he died aged 72 in August 1996, a year after his release.

Arrayed with pretty flowers and plants, the **sculpture garden** bristles with Buddhist, Hindu and secular figures, all executed in concrete with imaginative abandon by unskilled followers under Luang Phu's direction. The religious statues, in particular, are radically modern. Characteristics that marked the Buddha out as a supernatural being – tight curls and a bump on the crown of the head called the *ushnisha* – are here transformed into beehives, and the *rashmis* on top (flames depicting the Buddha's fiery intellect) are depicted as long, sharp spikes. The largest statue in the garden shows the familiar story of the kindly naga king, Muchalinda, sheltering the Buddha, who is lost in meditation, from the heavy rain and floods: here the Buddha has shrunk in significance and the seven-headed snake has grown to 25m, with fierce, gaping fangs and long tongues.

Many of the statues illustrate **Thai proverbs**. Near the entrance, an elephant surrounded by a pack of dogs symbolizes integrity, "as the elephant is indifferent to the barking dogs". The nearby serpent-tailed monster with the moon in his mouth – Rahoo, the cause of eclipses – serves as an injunction to oppose all obstacles, just as the people of Isaan and Laos used to ward off eclipses by banging drums and firing guns. In the corner furthest from the entrance, you enter the complex Circle of Life through a huge mouth representing the womb, inside which a hermit, a policeman, a monk, a rich man and a beggar, among others, represent different paths in life. A man with two wives is shown beating the older one because he is ensnared by the wishes of the younger one, and an old couple who have made the mistake of not having children now find they have only each other for comfort.

The disturbingly vacant, smiling faces of the garden Buddhas bear more than a passing resemblance to Luang Phu himself, whose picture you can see in the **temple building**, a huge white edifice with mosque-like domes – he's the one with the bouffant hairdo, dressed in white. Don't leave Sala Kaeo Kou without feeding the fish, an activity that's immensely popular with Thais and farangs alike; you can buy bags of food from the stalls near the garden's small lake. If you're heading over to Laos, the **Xiang Khouan** sculpture garden – Sala Kaeo Kou's precursor, 25km from downtown Vientiane on the Mekong River – shouldn't be missed; Luang Phu spent twenty years working on the sculptures there before his expulsion.

Wat Phra That Bang Phuan

More famous as the site of a now concealed 2000-year-old Indian chedi than for its modern replacement, rural **Wat Phra That Bang Phuan** remains a highly revered place of pilgrimage. The wat is in the hamlet of **Ban Bang Phuan**, southwest of Nong Khai on Highway 211; buses from Nong Khai to Pak Chom and Loei pass this way (though not buses to Tha Bo, which use the minor road west along the river bank from Nong Khai), or it might be quicker to take an Udon-bound service 12km down Highway 2 to Ban Nong Song Hong, then change onto an Udon–Sri Chiangmai bus for the remaining 12km. On the way to or from Wat Phra That Bang Phuan, it would be well worth breaking your journey up at the Village Vocational Training Centre and shop, between Nong Khai and Ban Nong Song Hong on Highway 2 (see p.542).

The original **chedi** is supposed to have been built by disciples of the Buddha to hold 29 relics – pieces of breastbone – brought from India. A sixteenth-century king ofVientiane piously earned himself merit by building a tall Lao-style chedi over the top of the previous stupa; rain damage toppled this in 1970, but it was restored in 1977 to the fine, gleaming white edifice seen today. The unkempt compound also contains a small museum, crumbling brick chedis and some large open-air Buddhas.

Ban Phu

Deep in the countryside 61km southwest of Nong Khai, the wooded slopes around **BAN PHU** are dotted with strangely eroded sandstone formations, which have long exerted a mystical hold over people in the surrounding area. Local wisdom has it that the outcrops, many of which were converted into small temples from around the ninth century onwards, are either meteorites – believed to account for their burnt appearance – or, more likely, were caused by glacial erosion. Together with a stupa enshrining a Buddha footprint that is now an important pilgrimage site (especially during its annual festival, held between March 11 and 15), the rock formations have been linked up under the auspices of fifty-square-kilometre **Phu Phra Bat Historical Park** (daily dawn–dusk; B30). The **information centre** (daily 8am–4.30pm; ⓣ042 910107 or 910702) by the park entrance contains fairly interesting displays on the red prehistoric paintings of animals, humans, hands and geometric patterns that are found on the rock formations, and on the tale of Ussa and Barot (see below). **Bungalows** (❸) with en-suite hot-water bathrooms can be rented here, though there's nowhere in the park to get food. Around the information centre, a well-signposted network of **paths** has been cleared from the thin forest to connect 25 of the outcrops, each of which has a helpful English-language information board attached. It would take a good five hours to explore the whole park, but the most popular circuit, covering all the sights listed below, can be completed in an ambling two hours.

On **public transport**, the easiest way of getting there from Nong Khai is to take the 7.15am bus to Ban Phu; if you leave any later you won't have time to see the park properly, as the whole journey takes a couple of hours and the last bus back to Nong Khai leaves at around 3.30pm. From Ban Phu, it's another 14km west to the historical park; take a songthaew for the first 10km to the Ban Tiu intersection; from here a motorbike taxi will bring you the final 4km up to the main park entrance and information centre. If you happen to be coming from Udon Thani, it's best to catch a bus from Talat Rungsina towards either Nam Som or Na Yung, which will drop you off at Ban Tiu.

Among the most interesting of the outcrops are **Tham Wua** and **Tham Khon**, two natural shelters whose paintings of oxen and human stick figures suggest that the area was first settled by hunter-gatherers two to three thousand years ago. A legend that's well known in this part of Thailand and Laos accounts for the name of nearby **Kok Ma Thao Barot** (Prince Barot's Stable), a broad platform overhung by a huge slab of sandstone. A certain Princess Ussa, banished by her father to these slopes to be educated by a hermit, sent out an SOS which was answered by a dashing prince, Barot. The two fell in love and were married against the wishes of Ussa's father, prompting the king to challenge Barot to a distinctly oriental sort of duel: each would build a temple, and the last to finish would be beheaded. The king lost. Kok Ma Thao Barot is celebrated as the place where Barot kept his horse when he visited Ussa.

The furthest point of the circuit is the viewpoint at **Pha Sadej**, where the cliff drops away to give a lovely view across green fields and forest to the distant mountains. More spectacular is **Hor Nang Ussa** (Ussa's Tower), a mushroom formed by a flat slab capping a five-metre-high rock pillar. Under the cap of the mushroom, a shelter has been carved out and walled in on two sides. The *sema* found scattered around the site, and the square holes in which others would have been embedded, indicate that this was a shrine, probably during the ninth to eleventh centuries in the Dvaravati period. Nearby, a huge rock on a flimsy pivot miraculously balances itself against a tree at **Wat Por Ta** (The Father-in-Law's Temple); the walls and floor have been evenly carved out to form a vaguely rectangular shrine, with Dvaravati Buddha images dotted around.

The left fork on the way to the park entrance leads to **Wat Phra Bat Bua Bok**: a crude *that* built in imitation of Wat Phra That Phanom (see p.550), it's decorated with naive bas-reliefs of divinities and boggle-eyed monsters, which add to the atmosphere of simple, rustic piety. In a gloomy chamber in the tower's base, the only visible markings on the sandstone **Buddha footprint** show the Wheel of Law. Legend has it that the Buddha made the footprint here for a serpent that had asked to be ordained as a monk, but had been refused because it was not human. Higher up the slope, a smaller *that* perches on a hanging rock that seems to defy gravity.

Downstream to Mukdahan

East of Nong Khai, the land on the Thai side of the Mekong becomes gradually more arid, while jagged forest-covered mountains loom on the Laos side. Few visitors make it this far, to the northeast's northeast, though the attractions are surprisingly varied, ranging from painterly riverscapes to Isaan's major religious site, **Wat Phra That Phanom**. **Transport** along Highway 212 out of Nong Khai is fairly straightforward: fourteen buses a day from Nong Khai run to Bung Kan, 137km away, five of which continue to Nakhon Phanom, where you have to change onto one of the hourly buses to get to That Phanom and Mukdahan.

Wat Phu Tok

The most compelling destination in the area to the east of Nong Khai is the extraordinary hilltop retreat of **Wat Phu Tok**. One of two sandstone outcrops that jut steeply out of the plain 35km southeast of Bung Kan, Phu Tok has been transformed in the past few years into a meditation wat, its fifty or so monks building their scattered huts on perches high above breathtaking cliffs. The outcrop comes into sight long before you get there, its sheer red face sandwiched between green vegetation on the lower slopes and tufts of trees on the narrow plateau above. As you get closer, the horizontal white lines across the cliffs reveal themselves to be painted wooden walkways, built to give the temple seven levels to represent the seven stages of enlightenment.

In an ornamental garden at the base, reflected in a small lake, an elegant, incongruously modern marble chedi commemorates **Phra Ajaan Juen**, the famous meditation master who founded the wat in 1968 and died in a plane crash ten years later. Within the chedi, the monk's books and other belongings, and diamond-like fragments of his bones, are preserved in a small shrine.

The first part of the ascent of the outcrop takes you to the third level up a series of long, sometimes slippery, wooden staircases, the first of many for which you'll need something more sturdy than flip-flops on your feet. A choice of two routes – the left fork is more interesting – leads to the fifth and most important level, where the **Sala Yai** houses the temple's main Buddha image in an airy, dimly lit cavern. The artificial ledges that cut across the northeast face are not for the fainthearted, but they are one way of getting to the dramatic northwest tip here on level five: on the other side of a deep crevice spanned by a wooden bridge, the monks have built an open-sided Buddha viharn under a huge anvil rock (though the gate to the viharn is usually locked). This spot affords stunning **views** over a broad sweep of countryside and across to the second, uninhabited outcrop. The flat top of the hill forms the seventh level, where you can wander along overgrown paths through thick forest.

Practicalities

Getting to Wat Phu Tok isn't easy – the location was chosen for its isolation, after all – but the journey out gives you a slice of life in remote countryside. It's quite possible to do the trip with your own transport in a day from Nong Khai, but it's a real slog by public transport: change buses at Bung Kan, catching one of the half-hourly buses south along Route 222 towards Pang Khon; get off after 25km at **Ban Siwilai** from where songthaews make the hour-long, twenty-kilometre trip east to Phu Tok either when they gather a full complement of passengers (more likely in the morning) or under charter (around B200).

It's not possible to **stay** at Wat Phu Tok or in the attached village, though **food** is available: just outside the grounds, a collection of foodstalls and a simple restaurant dish up the usual noodles and grilled chicken. Ban Siwilai has a couple of very basic hotels if you get really stuck, or you might want to break your journey in **Bung Kan**, a dusty but reasonably prosperous riverside settlement which supports a **guest house**: the *Mekong Guest House*, on the riverfront at 202 Moo 1, Thanon Chansin (Ⓣ042 491341, Ⓦwww.danishbaker.dk/bungkan; ❸), offers neat, decent-sized rooms with en-suite hot-water bathrooms, some with air-con, fridge and balcony overlooking the water. The attached *Joy's* is a smartly turned out restaurant with a few outdoor tables overlooking the river, dishing up mainly Isaan and central Thai food alongside a few Western dishes, including breakfast.

Nakhon Phanom

Beyond Bung Kan, the river road rounds the hilly northeastern tip of Thailand before heading south through remote country where you're apt to find yourself stopping for water buffalo as often as for vehicles. The Mekong can only be glimpsed occasionally until you reach **NAKHON PHANOM** (meaning "City of Mountains"), 313km from Nong Khai, a clean and prosperous town, which affords the finest view of the river in northern Isaan, framed against the giant ant hills of the Lao mountains opposite.

The town makes a pleasant place to hang out, its quiet broad streets lined with some grand old public buildings, colonial-style houses and creaking wooden shophouses. During the Indochina wars, Nakhon Phanom was an important gateway for thousands of Vietnamese refugees, whose influence can be seen in the dilapidated and atmospheric hybrid, **Wat Or Jak**, opposite the pier for Laos. The **ferry** from this pier crosses to **Khammouan (Tha Khaek) in Laos** usually every half-hour or so (depending on demand; B50 one-way), and fifteen-day **Lao visas** can be bought on arrival for US$30 (see p.19). If you're not crossing the border, you'll have to **hire a boat** from the pier for an hour (B1000 for up to fifteen people) to get the best perspective on the beautiful riverscape. Walking around town, you'll see several lit-up boat shapes around the place, a reminder of Nakhon Phanom's best-known festival, the **illuminated boat procession,** which is held on the river every year, usually in October at the end of the rainy season. The week-long celebrations – marking the end of the annual three-month Buddhist Rains Retreat – also feature colourful dragon-boat races along the Mekong, pitting Thai and Lao teams against each other.

Practicalities

The main **bus station** is about 2km west of the centre on Highway 22. You can fly to Nakhon Phanom from Bangkok with PB Air (Ⓦwww.pbair.com); the airline's limousine from the **airport** costs B70 per person. **TAT** has an impressive office at 184/1 Thanon Suntorn Vichit, corner of Thanon Salaklang (daily 8.30am–4.30pm; Ⓣ042 513490–1, Ⓔtatphnom@tat.or.th), 500m north of the pier for Laos; they also cover Sakon Nakhon and Mukdahan provinces. Ask here if you're interested in visiting the house where the Vietnamese national hero, Ho Chi Minh, lived in the early 1920s, when he was forced to go underground during the struggle for independence from France; at the time of writing the simple wooden house, 5km southwest of Nakhon Phanom at Ban Na Joke, was being turned into a museum. The efficient North by Northeast Tours (Ⓣ042 513572, Ⓦwww.thaitourism.com), situated underneath the *Mae Namkhong Grand View Hotel* on Highway 212, is a US-Thai-run outfit which offers tailor-made itineraries and a range of **tours** around the Mekong region, ranging from boat trips and one-day Lao trips, through three-day eco-tours of rural Laos, to a grand five-country Southeast Asian loop. There's **Internet access** at the J-Net Cybercafé, 203–207 Thanon Suntorn Vichit, just north of the pier.

Accommodation and eating

The best of Nakhon Phanom's budget **hotels** is the friendly four-storey *Grand Hotel* at 210 Thanon Sri Thep (Ⓣ042 511526, Ⓕ042 511283; ❷–❸), a block back from the river just south of the passenger ferry and market, with bright modern rooms, all en suite with TV, ranging from fan and cold-water rooms (with access to a shared hot shower) to hot-water and air-con. Less central, but excellent value and well worth a splurge is the friendly *Mae*

Nam Kong Grand View, on Highway 212 at the southern edge of town (Ⓣ042 513564, Ⓕ042 511037; ④); the international-standard rooms here come with en-suite hot-water bathrooms and the nicest have balconies with river views. At the luxury end, the best option is the eight-storey *Nakhonphanom River View* (Ⓣ042 522333–40, Ⓔriverview@cscoms.com; ⑥), a few hundred metres south of the *Mae Namkhong Grand View*, with tasteful rooms boasting facilities ranging from cable TV to bathtubs, as well as an outdoor swimming pool overlooking the river.

Among a few small riverside **restaurants** clustered around the passenger pier and the old clocktower, at the corner of Suntorn Vichit and Sri Thep roads, the *Golden Giant Catfish*, specializing in Mekong giant catfish dishes, is both reasonable and reliable. To the south of the centre, the popular terrace restaurant attached to the *Mae Nam Kong Grand View Hotel* serves up excellent Thai food and fresh fish in a lovely riverside setting. There are a couple of good Vietnamese eateries along Thanon Sri Thep: *Dararat*, 50m north of the *Grand Hotel* at no. 91, has tasty *nam nueng* (unfried spring rolls) on offer, while the *Phorn Thep* at no. 344 is a popular spot for breakfast – *khai krata* (eggs, Vietnamese sausages and French bread) is available until around 9am. Thanon Fueng Nakhon, running west from the old clocktower, has a choice of several simple eateries and is a lively spot at **night**, while several simple Isaan restaurants on stilts line the river bank to the south of the *Mae Nam Kong Grand View Hotel*.

That Phanom and around

Fifty kilometres south of Nakhon Phanom, **THAT PHANOM**, a small, green and friendly town of weather-beaten wooden buildings, sprawls around Isaan's most important shrine. Popularly held to be one of the four sacred pillars of Thai religion (the other three are Chiang Mai's Wat Phra That Doi Suthep, Wat Mahathat in Nakhon Si Thammarat, and Wat Phra Phutthabat near Lopburi), **Wat Phra That Phanom** is a fascinating place of pilgrimage, especially at the time of the ten-day Phra That Phanom festival, usually in February, when thousands of people come to pay homage and enjoy themselves in the traditional holiday between harvesting and sowing; pilgrims believe that they must make the trip seven times during a full moon before they die.

This far-northeastern corner of Thailand may seem like a strange location for one of the country's holiest sites, but the wat used to serve both Thais and Lao, as evidenced by the ample boat landing in the village, now largely disused; since the Pathet Lao took over in 1975, Lao have only been allowed to cross the river for the Ngan Phra That Phanom and the fascinating Monday and Thursday morning waterfront **market**, where Lao people offer for sale such items as wild animal skins, black pigs and herbal medicines, alongside the usual fruit and veg. The temple reputedly dates back to the eighth year after the death of the Buddha (535 BC), when five local princes built a simple brick chedi to house bits of his breastbone. It's been restored or rebuilt seven times, most recently after it collapsed during a rainstorm in 1975; the latest incarnation is in the form of a Lao *that*, 57m high, modelled on the That Luang in Vientiane.

The best approach to the temple is from the river: a short ceremonial way leads directly from the pier, under a Disneyesque victory arch erected by the Lao, through the temple gates to the **chedi** itself, which, as is the custom, faces water and the rising sun. A brick-and-plaster structure covered with white paint and gold floral decorations, the chedi looks like nothing so much as a giant, ornate table leg turned upside down. From each of the four sides, an eye forming part of the traditional flame pattern stares down, and the whole thing is surmounted by an umbrella made of 16kg of gold, with precious gems and gold rings embedded in each tier. The chedi sits on a gleaming white marble platform, on which pilgrims say their prayers and leave every imaginable kind of offering to the relics. Look out for the brick reliefs in the shape of four-leaf clovers above three of the doorways in the base: on the northern side, Vishnu mounted on a garuda; on the western side, the four guardians of the earth putting offerings in the Buddha's alms bowl; and above the south door, a carving of the Buddha entering Nirvana. At the corners of the chedi, brick plaques, carved in the tenth century but now heavily restored, tell the stories of the wat's princely founders.

That Phanom is only an hour away from Nakhon Phanom, Sakon Nakhon and Mukdahan, and served by frequent **buses** from each (with the Nakhon Phanom route also served by frequent songthaews), which stop on Thanon Chayangkun, near the wat. The centre of the village is 200m due east of here, clustered around the pier on the Mekong.

Practicalities

That Phanom's outstanding **accommodation** choice is the welcoming *Niyana Guest House*, two blocks north of the pier just off the riverfront road, at 110 Moo 14, Thanon Rimkhong (☎042 541450; ❷). The effusive owner, Niyana, is a fund of local information, and rustles up excellent Thai and Western vegetarian and meaty food (breakfast and dinner only), as well as renting out bicycles (B40/day) and organizing occasional tours of Mukdahan National Park (see p.553). The pleasant rooms (including good-value singles) in her quiet, wooden two-storey house are decorated with her own paintings and share hot-water bathrooms. Niyana has a sideline selling unstuffed axe pillows, rarely available unfilled elsewhere in Thailand, and much cheaper to post home. If Niyana can't put you up, try the *Chaivon Hotel*, a basic but characterful old place on Thanon Phanom Phanarak on the north side of the victory arch (☎042 541391; ❶).

For somewhere to **eat**, there are a few simple restaurants around the victory arch, the best of these being *That Phanom Pochana*, on the north side of the arch, a big, clean airy place which is good for a *phat thai* or a choice of Isaan, Thai and Chinese dishes. There are several **banks** with ATMs on Thanon Chayangkun near the wat, and a few **Internet** places scattered around town, including e-Tech Computer Centre opposite the *That Phanom Pochana* restaurant.

Around That Phanom

From That Phanom the weaving village of **Renu Nakhon**, 15km northwest, can be reached by regular songthaews to the Renu junction, then 8km north by tuk-tuk. The wat at the centre of the village has a smaller, stubbier imitation of the Phra That Phanom, crudely decorated with stucco carvings and brown paint, and an attached cultural centre where local dance performances are sometimes held. Around the wat, shops – augmented by dozens of stalls on market day, Wednesday – sell a huge variety of reasonable cotton and silk, much of it in simple, colourful *mut mee* styles.

An interesting cycle ride from That Phanom (bikes can be hired from *Niyana Guest House*; see above) takes the road following the river – a mixture of deteriorating paved road and red dirt – through green countryside and a couple of villages 18km south to the **Kaeng Kabao rapids**. Here Thai tourists gather to watch the white water; their numbers are catered for with bamboo *salas* overlooking the river where they can picnic, and many stalls and restaurants selling simple food such as barbecued chicken or pork.

Continuing 3km south of the rapids along the river road, you'll be met with the incongruous sight of a very lavish Catholic church, **Our Lady of the Martyrs of Thailand Shrine** (called Wat Songkhon in Thai), which was blessed and dedicated in December 1995. It's situated on an idyllic stretch of the Mekong, with manicured lawns looking across a few river islands and some longtail-boat activity to Laos. Many of the people who live along the stretch of the river between That Phanom and Mukdahan are Catholic, and in the 1950s some were accused of being Communist sympathisers and were killed by the Thai authorities; at the rear of the church, seven glass coffins hold models of the bodies of the Thais who have been declared martyrs by the Catholic Church. The minimalist modern complex is surrounded by a terracotta-coloured laterite circular wall with Stations of the Cross, and the square glass-walled church comes complete with a gold-coloured floating Jesus; note that, just as with Buddhist temples in Thailand, it's customary to take off your shoes before going inside. To get there from Mukdahan, head north up Highway 212, then 9km east, then look out for a sign of the cross at a turning and head the final 5km north.

Mukdahan and beyond

Fifty kilometres downriver of That Phanom, **MUKDAHAN** is the last stop on the Mekong trail before Highway 212 heads off inland to Ubon Ratchathani, 170km to the south. You may feel as if you're in the Wild East out here, but this is one of the fastest-developing Thai provinces, owing to increasing friendship between Laos and Thailand and the proximity of **Savannakhet**, the second-biggest Lao city, just across the water. Though the Mekong is particularly wide here, at nearly 2km, construction of a bridge across the river 7km north of Mukdahan is planned to begin in 2004; further into the future, a new train line linking Mukdahan with the existing Thai rail network at Ubon Ratchathani has also been discussed. Very few farang visitors make it this far, though Mukdahan–Savannakhet is an officially sanctioned crossing to Laos, with fifteen-day tourist visas available for US$30 on arrival (see p.19 for further details).

In the heart of town, the main river **pier** serves the cross-border trade, which accounts for a large part of the local economy. By the pier, the promenade overlooking Savannakhet is swamped by the daily **Indochina Market**, which is especially busy at weekends. On sale here are household goods and inexpensive ornaments, such as Vietnamese mother-of-pearl and Chinese ceramics, brought over from Laos; the market is also good for local fabrics like lengths of coarsely woven cotton in lovely muted colours, and expensive but very classy silks. At the southern edge of town rises the 65-metre-high **Mukdahan Tower** (daily 8am–6pm; B20), a modern white edifice that looks somewhat out of place in the low-rise outskirts. Built to commemorate the fiftieth anniversary of the king's accession to the throne in 1996, the tower houses an interesting array of historic artefacts from the Mukdahan area, including traditional Isaan costumes, pottery, coins, amulets, vicious-looking weaponry and fossils. The highlight of the tower, however, is the expansive view from the sixth floor – 50m high to reflect fifty years of Rama IX – over Mukdahan and the Mekong into Laos. On the smaller floor above is a much-revered, Sukhothai-style silver Buddha image, the Phra Phuttha Nawaming Mongkhon Mukdahan, fronted by the bone relics of famous monks in small glass containers.

Practicalities

Half-hourly buses from That Phanom and Ubon Ratchathani stop at the **bus terminal** about 2km northwest of the centre on Highway 212. **Ferry** services for Savannakhet leave Mukdahan seven times a day Monday–Friday, with four on Saturday and two on Sunday. There's **Internet access** at, for example, Blue Planet in the small complex of shops in front of the *Ploy Palace Hotel* on Thanon Pitakpanomkhet.

The best budget **accommodation** option is the *Ban Thom Kasem* at 25–25/2 Thanon Samut Sakdarak (ⓣ042 611235 or 612223; ❶–❸). Centrally located, this four-storey hotel offers basic, wood-floored rooms with fan and en-suite cold-water bathrooms, or much smarter air-con rooms with hot water; there's an attached clean and pleasant café serving simple rice dishes, too. If you want a little more comfort, turn south off the main east–west street, Thanon Pitakpanomkhet, at the town's largest traffic circle, onto Thanon Phitak Santirat, where you'll find the motel-like *Saensuk Bungalows* (ⓣ042/611214; ❸) at no. 136, 100m down on your right: clean air-con rooms, all with hot water, are ranged around a tidy courtyard. Further west, at 40 Thanon Pitakpanomkhet, *Ploy Palace Hotel* (ⓣ042 631111, ⓦwww.hotelthailand.com/mukdahan/ploypalace; ❼), a grand pink edifice with an overblown marbled lobby and tasteful bedrooms, is the best of Mukdahan's luxury options, with good service and a rooftop swimming pool, sauna and gym.

Of the **restaurants** that dot the riverside promenade, Thanon Somranchaikhong, the best – and priciest – is the popular *Riverview*, 1km south of the pier, which serves excellent food on a pretty bougainvillea-covered terrace built out over the Mekong. En route you'll pass a couple of cheaper places on the same street, including the friendly *Wine, Wild, Why*, a tiny restaurant bar with a wooden terrace overlooking the river and a good range of Thai meals, notably salads. Alternatively, you can eat on the river itself: standard Thai food is served on board the *Morris*, a slightly ramshackle former French riverboat permanently moored just south of the main pier and lit up with coloured bulbs, so you can't miss it. The emphasis here is more on drinking, which is no bad thing, sitting on the top deck and watching the moon rise. For breakfast, the *Pith Bakery*, one block north of *Saensuk Bungalows* on the same road, opposite the police station, is a good bet, with Western-style cakes and breakfasts, fresh juices and thirteen different varieties of coffee beans.

Mukdahan National Park

If you're tired of concrete Isaan towns, stretch your legs exploring the strange rock formations and beautiful waterfalls of **Mukdahan National Park** (aka Phu Pha Terp; B200), down a minor road along the Mekong southeast of Mukdahan. Regular songthaews pass the turning for the park 14km out of town, and from there it's just over a one-kilometre walk uphill to the park headquarters. Just above the headquarters is a hillside of bizarre rocks, eroded into the shapes of toadstools, camels and crocodiles, which is great for scrambling around. The hillside also bears two remnants of the area's prehistory: the red finger-painting under one of the sandstone slabs is reckoned to be 4000 years old, while a small cage on the ground protects a 75-million-year-old fossil. Further up, the bare sandstone ridge seems to have been cut out of the surrounding forest by a giant lawnmower, but from October to December it's brought to life with a covering of grasses and wildflowers. A series of ladders leads up a cliff to the highest point, on a ridge at the western end of the park (a two-kilometre walk from the park headquarters), which affords a sweeping view over the rocks to the forests and paddies of Laos. Nearby, at least from July to November, is the park's most spectacular waterfall, a thirty-metre drop through thick vegetation, and a cave in which villagers have enshrined scores of Buddha images.

The park, which can be readily visited on a day-trip from Mukdahan or That Phanom, has no official accommodation, but you can camp with your own gear free of charge. The simple **foodstalls** near headquarters will keep you going with fried rice and noodles.

Travel details

Trains

Buriram to: Ayutthaya (9 daily; 4hr 30min–7hr 45min); Bangkok (10 daily; 6hr–9hr 30min), via Don Muang Airport (5hr 30min–8hr 30 min); Khorat (10 daily; 1hr 30min–2hr 40min); Pak Chong (10 daily; 2hr 30min–5hr); Si Saket (7 daily; 1hr 45min–3hr 20min); Surin (10 daily; 35–65min); Ubon Ratchathani (7 daily; 2hr 30min–4hr 15min).
Khon Kaen to: Ayutthaya (5 daily; 6hr–8hr 20min); Bangkok (5 daily; 7hr 30min–10hr 20min), via Don Muang Airport (6hr 45min–9 hr 20min); Khorat (1 daily; 2hr 30min); Nong Khai (3 daily; 2hr 25min–3hr); Udon Thani (5 daily; 1hr 35min–2hr 15min).
Khorat to: Ayutthaya (7 daily; 3hr 30min); Bangkok (9 daily; 4–5hr); Khon Kaen (1 daily; 2hr 30min); Pak Chong (11 daily; 1hr 30min–2hr); Si Saket (7 daily; 4hr–5hr 30min); Surin (7 daily; 2hr 5min–3hr 40min); Ubon Ratchathani (7 daily; 5hr–6hr 40min); Udon Thani (1 daily; 4hr).
Nong Khai to: Ayutthaya (4 daily; 9–11hr); Bangkok (4 daily; 11hr 30min–12hr 30min); Khon Kaen (10 daily; 2–3hr); Udon Thani (4 daily; 1hr).
Pak Chong (for Khao Yai) to: Ayutthaya (11 daily; 2hr–2hr 45min); Bangkok (11 daily; 3hr 30min–4hr 45min) via Don Muang Airport (2hr 50min–4hr); Khorat (10 daily; 1hr 30min–2hr); Si Saket (7 daily; 4hr 20min–7hr 30min); Surin (10 daily; 3hr 10min–5hr 15min); Ubon Ratchathani (7 daily; 6hr 50min–8hr 40min).
Prachinburi to: Aranyaprathet (2 daily; 2hr 20min); Bangkok (7 daily; 2hr 30min).
Surin to: Ayutthaya (9 daily; 5hr 10min–9hr); Bangkok (10 daily; 7–10hr), via Don Muang Airport (6hr 30min–9hr); Buriram (10 daily; 35–65min); Khorat (10 daily; 2hr–3hr 15min); Pak Chong (10 daily; 3hr 30min–5hr 30min); Si Saket (7 daily; 1hr 35min–2hr 10min); Ubon Ratchathani (7 daily; 2hr 30min–3hr 30min).
Ubon Ratchathani to: Ayutthaya (7 daily; 7–12hr); Bangkok (7 daily; 8hr 30min–14hr), via Don Muang Airport (8–13hr); Buriram (7 daily; 2hr 30min–4hr 15min); Khorat (7 daily; 5hr–6hr 40min); Si Saket (7 daily; 1hr 10min); Surin (7 daily; 2hr 30min–3hr 30min).
Udon Thani to: Ayutthaya (5 daily; 8–10hr); Bangkok (5 daily; 9–12hr 30min); Khon Kaen (5 daily; 1hr 30min–2hr); Khorat (1 daily; 4hr); Nong Khai (4 daily; 1hr); Pak Chong (1 daily; 6hr).

Buses

Bung Kan to: Bangkok (4 daily; 8hr); Nakhon Phanom (6 daily; 4hr); Nong Khai (14 daily; 2hr); Sakon Nakhon (hourly; 3hr); Udon Thani (hourly; 4hr).
Chiang Khan to: Bangkok (4daily; 9–11hr); Khorat (9 daily; 7hr); Loei (every 30min; 1hr); Pak Chom (hourly by songthaew; 1hr).
Chong Mek to: Bangkok (2 daily; 12 hr); Phibun Mangsahan (every 30min; 90min).
Khon Kaen to: Bangkok (23 daily; 6–7hr); Chiang Mai (11 daily; 11–12hr); Khorat (hourly; 2hr 30min–3hr); Loei (every 30min; 4hr); Nong Khai (10 daily; 2–3hr); Phitsanulok (6 daily; 5–6hr); Rayong (13 daily; 10–12hr); Sri Chiangmai (6 daily; 3hr); Surin (hourly; 4hr 30min–6hr); Ubon Ratchathani (15 daily; 4–6hr); Udon Thani (every 30min; 1hr 30min–2hr).
Khorat to: Bangkok (every 20min; 4–5hr); Ban Tako (for Phanom Rung; every 30min; 2hr); Buriram (every 30min; 3hr); Chanthaburi (every 30min; 6–8hr); Chiang Mai (7 daily; 12–14hr); Chiang Rai (5 daily; 14–16hr); Dan Kwian (every 30min; 30min); Khon Kaen (hourly; 2hr 30min–3hr); Lopburi (11 daily; 3hr 30min); Nakhon Phanom (3 daily; 8hr); Nong Khai (7 daily; 6–8hr); Pak Tong Chai (every 30min; 45min); Pattaya (8 daily; 6–8hr); Phimai (every 30min; 1hr–1hr 30min); Phitsanulok (7 daily; 7–9hr); Rayong (for Ko Samet; every 30min; 6–8hr); Sri Chiangmai (6 daily; 6hr 30min); Surin (every 30min; 4–5hr); Ubon Ratchathani (7 daily; 5–7hr); Udon Thani (hourly; 3hr 30min–5hr).
Loei to: Bangkok (18 daily; 10hr); Chiang Khan (every 30min; 1hr); Chiang Mai (4 daily; 9–12hr); Chiang Rai (4 daily; 9–11hr); Khon Kaen (every 30min; 4hr); Nong Khai (hourly via Pak Chom; 6–7hr); Pak Chom (every 30min; 2hr 30min); Phitsanulok (5 daily; 4hr); Sang Khom (hourly; 3hr); Udon Thani (every 20min; 3–4hr).
Mukdahan to: Bangkok (13 daily; 11hr); Nakhon Phanom (hourly; 2hr); That Phanom (every 30min; 1hr 20min); Ubon Ratchathani (every 30min; 2–3hr); Udon Thani (5 daily; 4hr–4hr 30min).

Nakhon Phanom to: Bangkok (17 daily; 12hr); Bung Kan (6 daily; 4hr); Chiang Rai (4 daily; 16hr); Khon Kaen (6 daily; 4–5hr); Khorat (20 daily; 8hr); Mukdahan (hourly; 2hr); Nong Khai (5 daily; 6hr); Phitsanulok (4 daily; 10hr); That Phanom (hourly; 1hr); Ubon Ratchathani (7 daily; 4hr); Udon Thani (9 daily; 5–7hr).
Nong Khai to: Bangkok (17 daily; 10hr); Bung Kan (14 daily; 2hr); Loei (hourly via Pak Chom; 6–7hr); Nakhon Phanom (5 daily; 6hr); Rayong (7 daily; 12hr); Sang Khom (hourly; 3–4hr); Udon Thani (every 20min; 1hr).
Pak Chom to: Chiang Khan (hourly by songthaew; 1hr); Loei (every 30min; 2hr 30min); Nong Khai (hourly; 5hr).
Pak Chong to: Bangkok (every 15min; 3hr); Khorat (every 20min; 1hr 30min).
Sang Khom to: Loei (hourly; 3hr); Nong Khai (hourly; 3–4hr).
Surin to: Bangkok via Don Muang Airport (up to 20 daily; 8–9hr); Ban Tako (every 30min; 2hr); Chiang Mai (6 daily; 13hr 30min–14hr 30min); Kap Choeng (13 daily; 1hr 30min); Khon Kaen (8 daily; 4hr 30min–6hr); Khorat (every 30min; 4–5hr); Pattaya (9 daily; 9–11hr); Rayong (for Ko Samet; 9hr 30min–11hr 30min); Roi Et (12 daily; 3hr–3hr 30min); Si Saket (at least 12 daily; 1hr 30min–3hr); Ta Klang (hourly; 2hr); Ubon Ratchathani (at least 12 daily; 2hr 30min–3hr); Yasothon (hourly; 2–3hr).
That Phanom to: Bangkok (4 daily; 12hr); Mukdahan (every 30min; 1hr 20min); Nakhon Phanom (hourly; 1hr); Ubon Ratchathani (10 daily; 3–4hr); Udon Thani (4 daily; 4–5 hr).
Ubon Ratchathani to: Bangkok (19 daily; 10–12hr); Chiang Mai (6 daily; 16–18hr); Kantharalak (8 daily; 1hr 30min); Khon Kaen (16 daily; 4–6hr); Khorat (17 daily; 5–7hr); Pattaya (9 daily; 11hr 30min–13hr 30min); Phibun Mangsahan (every 25min; 1hr); Rayong (9 daily; 12–14hr); Roi Et (16 daily; 3hr); Si Saket (at least 12 daily; 45min–1hr); Surin (at least 12 daily; 2hr 30min–3hr); Udon Thani (11 daily; 5–7hr); Yasothon (18 daily; 1hr 30min–2hr).
Udon Thani to: Ban Chiang (every 30min until 1.30pm by songthaew; 1hr 30min); Bangkok (every 15min; 9hr); Ban Phu (every 45min; 1hr); Bung Kan (hourly; 4hr); Chiang Mai (4 daily; 11–13hr); Chiang Rai (4 daily; 12–14hr); Khon Kaen (every 30min; 1hr 30min–2hr); Khorat (hourly; 3hr 30min–5hr); Loei (every 20min; 3–4hr); Mukdahan (5 daily; 4hr–4hr 30min); Nakhon Phanom (9 daily; 5–7hr); Nong Khai (every 20min; 1hr); Phitsanulok (2 daily; 7hr); Rayong (7 daily; 12hr); Sakon Nakhon (every 30min; 3hr); That Phanom (4 daily; 4–5hr); Ubon Ratchathani (7 daily; 5–7hr).
Yasothon to: Khon Kaen (hourly; 3hr–3hr 30min); Roi Et (hourly; 1hr).

Flights

Buriram to: Bangkok (daily; 40min).
Khon Kaen to: Bangkok (5 daily; 55min); Chiang Mai (1 daily; 50min–1hr 30min).
Khorat to: Bangkok (2 daily; 50min).
Loei to: Bangkok (4 weekly; 1hr 20min).
Nakhon Phanom to: Bangkok (daily; 1hr 5min).
Roi Et to: Bangkok (7 weekly; 1hr).
Ubon Ratchathani to: Bangkok (2 daily; 1hr 5min); Chiang Mai (3 weekly; 1hr 50min); Khon Kaen (3 weekly; 40min).
Udon Thani to: Bangkok (3 daily; 1hr); Chiang Mai (3 weekly; 1hr 30min).

6

Southern Thailand: the Gulf coast

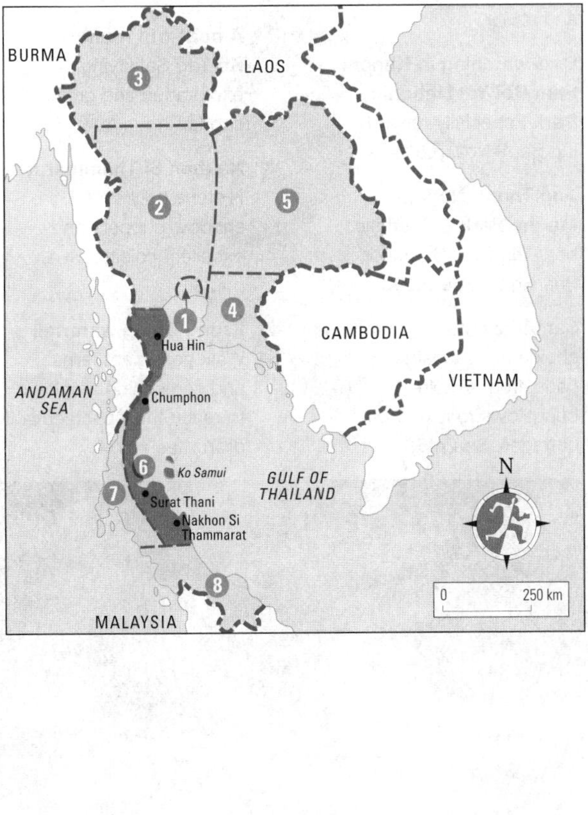

CHAPTER 6 **Highlights**

* **Phetchaburi** Charming historic town, boasting several fine old working temples. See p.561
* **Leisurely seafood lunches** At the squid-pier restaurants in Hua Hin or under the trees at Ban Krud. See p.572 and p.579
* **Bird-watching in Khao Sam Roi Yot National Park** Especially rewarding Sept–Nov. p.575
* **Ang Thong National Marine Park** A dramatic boat-trip from Samui or Pha Ngan. See p.593
* **Samui resorts** A great choice of beachside pads, from simple bungalows to luxurious cottages. See p.589
* **Full moon at Hat Rin** DIY beach parties draw ravers in their thousands. See p.611
* **Ao Thong Nai Pan on Ko Pha Ngan** Beautiful, secluded bay with good accommodation. See p.617
* **A boat-trip round Ko Tao** Satisfying exploration and great snorkelling. p.624
* **Nakhon Si Thammarat** Historic holy sites, shadow puppets and excellent cuisine. See p.628
* **Krung Ching waterfall** Walk past giant ferns and screeching monkeys to reach this spectacular drop. See p.634

△ Ko Nang Yuan, Ko Tao

6

Southern Thailand: the Gulf coast

The major part of southern Thailand's **Gulf coast**, gently undulating from Bangkok to Nakhon Si Thammarat, 750km away, is famed above all for the Samui archipelago, three small idyllic islands lying off the most prominent hump of the coastline. This is the country's most popular seaside venue for independent travellers, and a lazy stay in a Samui beachfront bungalow is so seductive a prospect that most people overlook the attractions of the mainland, where the sheltered sandy beaches and warm clear water rival the top sunspots in most countries. Added to that you'll find scenery dominated by forested mountains that rise abruptly behind the coastal strip, especially impressive in **Khao Sam Roi Yot National Park**, which is one of Thailand's most rewarding bird-watching spots, and a sprinkling of historic sights – notably the crumbling temples of ancient **Phetchaburi**. Though not a patch on the islands further south, the stretch of coast around **Cha-am** and **Hua Hin** is popular with weekending Thais escaping the capital and is crammed with condos, high-rise hotels, bars and restaurants, not to mention a large population of foreign tourists. The scene at the sophisticated little beach resort of **Pak Nam Pran**, just a short distance further south, is much quieter, and there's only slightly more development at **Ban Krud**. Though the provincial capital of **Chumphon**, 150km further down the coast, has little to offer in its own right, it is the convenient departure point for direct boats to Ko Tao.

Southeast of Chumphon lies **Ko Samui**, by far the most naturally beautiful of the islands, with its long white-sand beaches and arching fringes of palm trees. The island's beauty has not gone unnoticed by tourist developers of course, but this at least means you can buy a little luxury if you've got the cash. In recent years the next island out, **Ko Pha Ngan**, has drawn increasing numbers of backpackers away from its neighbour: its bungalows are generally simpler and cost less than Ko Samui's, and it offers a few stunning beaches with a more laid-back atmosphere. **Hat Rin** is the distillation of all these features, with back-to-back white sands, relaxed resident hippies and t'ai chi classes – though after dusk it swings into action as Thailand's dance capital, a reputation cemented by its farang-thronged full moon parties. The furthest inhabited island of the archipelago, **Ko Tao**, has taken off as a **scuba-diving** centre, but despite a growing nightlife and restaurant scene, still has the feel of a small, rugged and isolated outcrop.

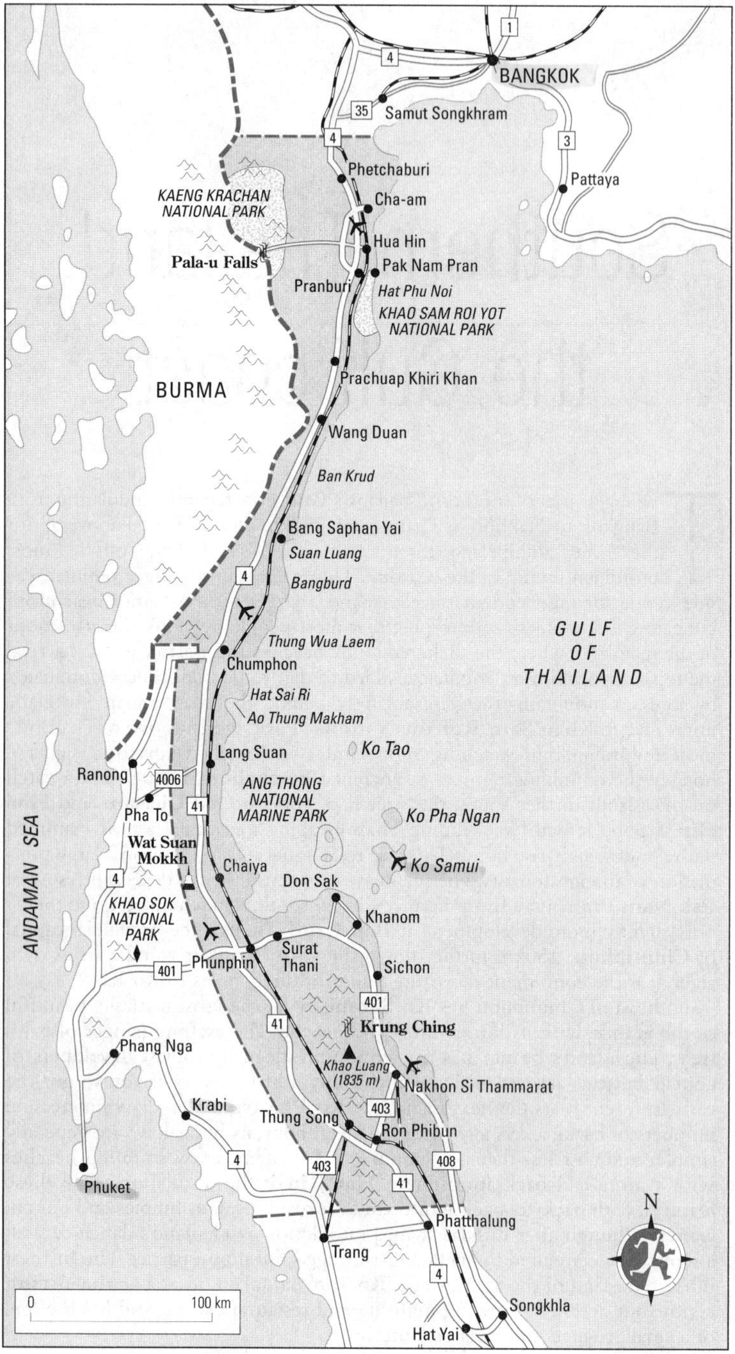
BANGKOK
Samut Songkhram
Pattaya
Phetchaburi
Cha-am
Hua Hin
Pak Nam Pran
Pranburi
Hat Phu Noi
KHAO SAM ROI YOT NATIONAL PARK
KAENG KRACHAN NATIONAL PARK
Pala-u Falls
BURMA
Prachuap Khiri Khan
Wang Duan
Ban Krud
Bang Saphan Yai
Suan Luang
Bangburd
Thung Wua Laem
Chumphon
Hat Sai Ri
Ao Thung Makham
GULF OF THAILAND
Lang Suan
Ko Tao
ANG THONG NATIONAL MARINE PARK
Ko Pha Ngan
Ko Samui
Ranong
Pha To
Wat Suan Mokkh
Chaiya
Don Sak
Khanom
ANDAMAN SEA
KHAO SOK NATIONAL PARK
Phunphin
Surat Thani
Sichon
Krung Ching
Phang Nga
Khao Luang (1835 m)
Nakhon Si Thammarat
Krabi
Thung Song
Ron Phibun
Phuket
Phatthalung
Trang
Songkhla
Hat Yai
0
100 km
N
1
4
35
3
4006
41
401
403
408

Tucked away beneath the islands, **Nakhon Si Thammarat**, the cultural capital of the south, is well worth a short detour from the main routes through the centre of the peninsula – it's a sophisticated city of grand old temples, delicious cuisine and distinctive handicrafts. With its small but significant Muslim population, and machine-gun dialect, Nakhon begins the transition into Thailand's deep south.

The **train** from Bangkok connects all the mainland towns, including a branch line to Nakhon, and **bus** services, along highways 4 (also known as the Phetkasem Highway, or, usually, Thanon Phetkasem when passing through towns) and 41, are frequent. From Bangkok, Thai Airways **flies** to Surat Thani and Nakhon Si Thammarat, Air Andaman to Chumphon, and Bangkok Airways runs a variety of popular routes to Ko Samui's airport. Daily boats run to the islands from two jumping-off points: **Surat Thani**, 650km from Bangkok, has the best choice of routes, but the alternatives from **Chumphon** get you straight to the tranquillity of Ko Tao.

The Gulf coast has a slightly different **climate** to the Andaman coast and much of the rest of Thailand, being hit heavily by the northeast monsoon's rains, especially in November, when it's best to avoid this part of the country altogether. Most times during the rest of the year should see pleasant, if changeable, weather, with some mild effects of the southwest monsoon felt on the islands between May and October. Late December to April is the driest period, and is therefore the region's high season, which also includes July and August. **Jellyfish** can be a problem on the Gulf coast, particularly just after a storm. Fatalities are very rare, but two travellers on Ko Pha Ngan died from (unidentified) jellyfish stings in August 2002. Ask for local advice before swimming, and scour the shore for dead jellyfish, which are a sign that they're in the area; see p.33 for more on jellyfish and how to deal with stings.

Phetchaburi

Straddling the Phet River about 120km south of Bangkok, the provincial capital of **PHETCHABURI** has been settled ever since the eleventh century, when the Khmers ruled the region, but only really got going six hundred years later, when it began to flourish as a trading post between the Andaman Sea ports and Burma and Ayutthaya. Despite periodic incursions from the Burmese, the town gained a reputation as a cultural centre – as the ornamentation of its older temples testifies – and after the new capital was established in Bangkok it became a favourite country retreat of Rama IV, who had a hilltop palace built here in the 1850s. Today the town's main claim to fame is as one of Thailand's finest sweet-making centres, the essential ingredient for its assortment of *khanom* being the sugar extracted from the sweet-sapped palms that cover Phetchaburi province. This being very much a cottage industry, modern Phetchaburi has lost relatively little of the ambience that so attracted Rama IV: the central riverside area is hemmed in by historic wats in varying states of disrepair, and wooden rather than concrete shophouses still line the river bank.

Despite the obvious attractions of its old quarter, Phetchaburi gets few overnight visitors as most people do it on a day-trip from Bangkok, Hua Hin or Cha-am. It's also possible to combine a day in Phetchaburi with an early-morning expedition from Bangkok to the floating markets of Damnoen Saduak, 40km north (see p.216); budget tour operators in Bangkok's Thanon Khao San area offer this option as a day-trip package for about B600 per person.

Arrival, information and transport

Arriving by **bus**, you are likely to be dropped in one of three places. The main station for **non-air-con buses** is on the southwest edge of Khao Wang, about thirty minutes' walk or a ten-minute songthaew ride from the town centre. However, non-air-con buses to and from **Cha-am and Hua Hin** use the small terminal in the town centre, less than ten minutes' walk from the Chomrut Bridge accommodation. The **air-con bus terminal** is also about ten minutes' walk from Chomrut Bridge, just off Thanon Rajwithi. Phetchaburi **train station** is on the northern outskirts of town, about 1500m from the main area of sights.

There is no TAT office in town, but *Rabieng Rimnum Guest House* is a good source of local **information**; there is Internet access at the CAT **phone office** (daily 8.30am–4.30pm), which is next to the **GPO** on Thanon Rajwithi. The branch of Bangkok Bank 150m east of Wat Mahathat on Thanon Phra Song does **currency exchange** and has an ATM.

To see the major temples in a day and have sufficient energy left for climbing Khao Wang, you might want to hire a **samlor** for a couple of hours, at about B100 per hour. Alternatively make use of the public **songthaews** that circulate round the town and charge B6, or **rent a bicycle** (B120/day) **or motorbike** (B240/day) from *Rabieng Rimnum Guest House*.

Accommodation

Most travellers **stay** at the *Rabieng Rimnum (Rim Nam) Guest House*, centrally located at 1 Thanon Chisa-in, on the southwest corner of Chomrut Bridge (Ⓣ032 425707, Ⓕ032 410983; ❷). Occupying a century-old house next to the Phet River and, less appealingly, a noisy main road, the guest house offers nine

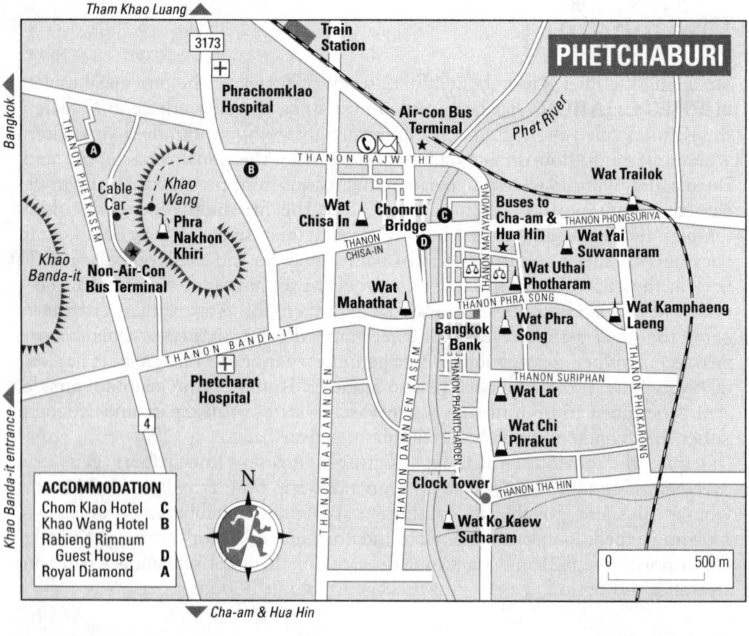

simple rooms with shared bathrooms, lots of local info and the best restaurant in town; it also rents out bicycles and motorbikes and organizes day-trips and overnight visits to Kaeng Krachan National Park for bird-watching and hiking (from B1200/person). Less traveller-oriented, but quieter and cheaper, is the friendly *Chom Klao* hotel across on the northeast corner of Chomrut Bridge at 1–3 Thanon Phongsuriya (ⓣ032 425398; ❶–❷); it's not signed in English, but is easily recognized by its pale-blue doors and riverside location. Some of the rooms give out onto the riverside walkway and you can choose whether or not you want an en-suite bathroom; all rooms have fans. Across on the other side of town, near the eastern base of Khao Wang, the slightly seedy *Khao Wang Hotel*, 174/1–3 Thanon Rajwithi (ⓣ032 425167; ❷–❸), has both fan and air-con rooms, all with TV, but don't expect immaculate decor or furnishings. West of Khao Wang, on the outskirts of town, is Phetchaburi's most upmarket option, the *Royal Diamond* (ⓣ032 411062, ⓕ032 424310; ❺), which has comfortable air-con rooms and is located on Soi Sam Chao Phet, just off the Phetkasem Highway.

The Town

The pinnacles and rooftops of the town's thirty-odd wats are visible in every direction, but only a few are worth stopping off to investigate; the following description takes in the top three, and can be done as a leisurely two-hour circular walk beginning from Chomrut Bridge.

Of all Phetchaburi's temples, the most attractive is the still-functioning seventeenth-century **Wat Yai Suwannaram** on Thanon Phongsuriya, about 700m east of Chomrut Bridge. The temple's fine old teak *sala* has elaborately carved doors, bearing a gash said to have been made by the Burmese in 1760 as they plundered their way towards Ayutthaya. Across from the *sala* and hidden behind high whitewashed walls stands the windowless Ayutthaya-style bot. The bot compound overlooks a pond, in the middle of which stands a small but well-preserved scripture library, or *ho trai*: such structures were built on stilts over water to prevent ants and other insects destroying the precious documents. Enter the walled compound from the south and make a clockwise tour of the cloisters filled with Buddha statutes before entering the bot itself via the eastern doorway (if the door is locked, one of the monks will get the key for you). The bot is supported by intricately patterned red and gold pillars and contains a remarkable, if rather faded, set of murals, depicting Indra, Brahma and other lower-ranking divinities ranged in five rows of ascending importance. Once you've admired the interior, walk to the back of the bot, passing behind the central cluster of Buddha images, to find another Buddha image seated against the back wall: climb the steps in front of this image to get a close-up of the left foot, which for some reason was cast with six toes.

Fifteen minutes' walk east and then south of Wat Yai, the five tumbledown prangs of **Wat Kamphaeng Laeng** on Thanon Phra Song mark out Phetchaburi as the probable southernmost outpost of the Khmer empire. Built to enshrine Hindu deities and set out in a cruciform arrangement facing east, the laterite corncob-style prangs were later adapted for Buddhist use, as can be seen from the two that now house Buddha images. There has been some attempt to restore a few of the carvings and false balustraded windows, but these days worshippers congregate in the modern whitewashed wat behind these shrines, leaving the atmospheric and appealingly quaint collection of decaying prangs and casuarina topiary to chickens, stray dogs and the occasional tourist.

Continuing west along Thanon Phra Song from Wat Kamphaeng Laeng, across the river you can see the prangs of Phetchaburi's most fully restored and important temple, **Wat Mahathat**, long before you reach them. Boasting the "Mahathat" title only since 1954, when the requisite Buddha relics were donated by the king, it was probably founded in the fourteenth century, but suffered badly at the hands of the Burmese. The five landmark prangs at its heart are adorned with stucco figures of mythical creatures, though these are nothing compared with those on the roofs of the main viharn and the bot. Instead of tapering off into the usual serpentine *chofa*, the gables are studded with miniature *thep* and *deva* figures (angels and gods), which add an almost mischievous vitality to the place. In a similar vein, a couple of gold-embossed crocodiles snarl above the entrance to the bot, and a caricature carving of a bespectacled man rubs shoulders with mythical giants in a relief around the base of the gold Buddha, housed in a separate mondop nearby.

Leaving Wat Mahathat, it's a five-minute walk north up Thanon Damnoen Kasem to Thanon Phongsuriya and another few minutes east to Chomrut Bridge, but if you have the time, backtrack a little and return via the **market**, which lines Thanon Matayawong and spills over into the alleyways on either side – there are enough stalls selling the locally famous *khanom* to make it worth your while.

Khao Wang and Khao Banda-It

Dominating the western outskirts, about thirty minutes' walk from Wat Mahathat, stands Rama IV's palace, a stew of mid-nineteenth-century Thai and European styles scattered over the crest of the hill known as **Khao Wang.** During his day, the royal entourage would struggle its way up the steep brick path to the summit, but now there's a **cable car** (daily 8.15am–5.15pm; B50, kids under 90cm tall go free), which starts from the western flank of the hill off Highway 4, quite near the non-air-con bus terminal. To get to the base of the hill from the town centre, take a white local **songthaew** from Thanon Phongsuriya and ask for Khao Wang. If you want to walk to the summit, get off as soon as you see the pathway on the eastern flank of the hill, just across from the junction with Thanon Rajwithi; for the cable car, stay put until you've passed the last of the souvenir stalls on Highway 4, then walk south about 700m. If you do walk up the hill, you'll have to contend with the hundreds of aggressive monkeys who hang out at its base and on the path to the top.

Up top, the wooded hill is littered with wats, prangs, chedis, whitewashed gazebos and lots more, in an ill-assorted combination of architectural idioms – the prang-topped viharn, washed all over in burnt sienna, is particularly ungainly. Whenever the king came on an excursion here, he stayed in the airy summer house, **Phra Nakhon Khiri** (daily 9am–4pm; B40, kids B10), with its Mediterranean-style shutters and verandas. Now a museum, it houses a moderately interesting collection of ceramics, furniture and other artefacts given to the royal family by foreign friends. Besides being cool and breezy, Khao Wang also proved to be a good star-gazing spot, so Rama IV had an open-sided, glass-domed observatory built close to his sleeping quarters. The king's amateur astronomy was not an inconsequential recreation: in August 1868 he predicted a solar eclipse almost to the second, thereby quashing the centuries-old Thai fear that the sun was periodically swallowed by an omnipotent lion god.

If you've got energy to spare, the two cave wats out on the western edges of town make good time-fillers. **Khao Banda-it**, a couple of kilometres west of Khao Wang, comprises a series of stalactite caves filled with Buddha statues and a 200-year-old Ayutthaya-style meditation temple. Five kilometres north of Khao Wang, the dramatic, partially roofless cave **Tham Khao Luang** is filled with assorted Buddha images and chedis, including a huge reclining Buddha statue.

Eating

Phetchaburi's best **restaurant** is the *Rabieng Rimnum (Rim Nam*; daily 8am–1am*)*, which is attached to the guest house of the same name and occupies a traditional wooden house beside the Chomrut Bridge, overlooking the Phet River. It offers a long and interesting menu of inexpensive Thai dishes, from banana-blossom salad to spicy crab soup, and is deservedly popular with local diners.

Almost half the shops in the town centre stock Phetchaburi's famous **sweet snacks**, as do many of the souvenir stalls crowding the base of Khao Wang, vendors at the day market on Thanon Matayawong, and the shophouses on the soi behind the Bangkok Bank. The most famous local speciality is *khanom maw kaeng*, a baked sweet egg custard made with mung beans and coconut and sometimes flavoured with lotus seeds, durian or taro. *Khanom taan* is another Phetchaburi classic: small, steamed, saffron-coloured cakes made with local palm sugar, coconut and rice flour, and wrapped in banana-leaf cases.

Cha-am and around

Forever in the shadow of its more famous neighbour, Hua Hin, the beach resort of **CHA-AM**, 41km south of Phetchaburi, picks up the overspill from Hua Hin and positions itself as a more sedate alternative. It used to be a typically Thai resort, with accommodation catering mainly to families and student groups from Bangkok and an emphasis on shorefront picnics rather than swimming and sunbathing, but that's beginning to change as the Europeans and expats move in, bringing with them package-holiday high-rises and Western-style restaurants. The most developed bit of Cha-am's coastal strip stretches about 3km along Thanon Ruamchit (sometimes spelt Ruamjit), from the *Mark Land Hotel* in the north to the *Santisuk* bungalows in the south. The beach here is pleasantly shaded, though rather gritty and very narrow at high tide, and the water is perfectly swimmable, if not pristine. During the week the pace of life in Cha-am is slow and peaceful, and it's easy to find a solitary spot under the casuarinas, particularly up at the northerly end of the beach, but that's rarely possible at weekends, when prices shoot up and traffic thickens considerably. Away from the seafront there's not much to do here, but there are several **golf courses** within striking distance (see p.571) and buses shuttle between Cha-am and Hua Hin (25km south) every half-hour, taking just 35 minutes.

Practicalities

Nearly all ordinary and air-con **buses** use the bus station (Ⓣ032 425307) in the town centre on Thanon Phetkasem (Highway 4), close to the junction with Thanon Narathip, 1km west of the beach. The **train station** (Ⓣ032 471159) is a few short blocks west of this junction. Thanon Narathip is the most useful of the side roads linking Thanon Phetkasem and the beachfront, and ends at a small seaside promenade and **tourist police** booth (Ⓣ032 471000) on Thanon Ruamchit, roughly halfway down the three-kilometre strip of beachfront development. To get down to the beach from Thanon Phetkasem, either walk or take a B20 motorbike taxi. Some private air-con buses to and from Bangkok use the depot at the little plaza on the beachfront Thanon Ruamchit, just south of the Ruamchit/Narathip junction.

Thanon Ruamchit is where you'll find most of the hotels and restaurants, as well as a few tourist-oriented businesses. **Addresses** on Thanon Ruamchit are determined by whether they are north or south of the Thanon Narathip junction, and the sois running off the beachfront road are labelled accordingly, eg Soi Cha-am North 1 is the first lane off Ruamchit to the north of the Narathip junction, while Soi Cha-am South 1 is the first minor road to the south. The landmark *Mark Land Hotel* at the northern end of the main beachfront sits alongside Soi Cha-am North 8, while *Santisuk* bungalows near the southern end of the beach is next to Soi Cha-am South 4.

The small Thanon Ruamchit **post office** is just north of Soi Cha-am North 5 and has one Catnet Internet terminal; there are more Catnet terminals inside the CAT **phone office**, which is 200m north up Thanon Narathip from the seafront. Several travel agents offer **Internet** access with more user-friendly hours, including Suthatinee Tours and Travel (ⓣ032 471984, ⓔsuthatineetours@hotmail.com), located between Soi Cha-am North 8 and 9. They also rent out motorbikes (B280/day), act as an agent for Budget car rental, sell airline, ferry and bus tickets, as well as minibus tickets to Bangkok's Don Muang Airport, and organize golf packages and day-trips. Several other smaller places along the beachfront also rent **motorbikes** as well as **tandems** and three-person **pushbikes** (B20). Cha-am's main business district occupies the small grid of streets west of Thanon Phetkasem, between the bus drop and the train station, and this is where you'll find the market, most of the shops, the **police station** (ⓣ032 471323), the **GPO** and banks with **exchange** facilities and ATMs. The local **TAT** office (daily 8.30am–4.30pm; ⓣ032 471005, ⓔtatphet@tat.or.th) is on Highway 4, about 1km south of the centre.

Accommodation

Most of the cheaper accommodation is concentrated on **central Cha-am Beach**, set along the west side of beachfront Thanon Ruamchit. There are no obvious backpacker-oriented guest houses in Cha-am: instead you'll find mainly small, mid-range hotels. The more expensive accommodation occupies the 25km of coastline **between Cha-am and Hua Hin**, where resorts are able to enjoy what are in effect private beaches, though guests without transport have to rely on hotel shuttles or public buses to get to the shops and restaurants of Cha-am or Hua Hin. Many Cha-am hotels give a fifteen- to thirty-percent discount from Sunday to Thursday.

Central Cha-am Beach

Kaen Chan Beach Hotel North of Soi Cha-am North 7 241/3 Thanon Ruamchit ⓣ032 471314, ⓦwww.kaenchanbeachhotel.com. Characterful and stylish mid-sized hotel, with a papaya-coloured facade, a sixth-floor swimming pool and appealing, sleekly furnished rooms, all with air-con, TV and sea view. ❻

Mark Land Hotel Just south of Soi Cha-am North 8 at 208/14 Thanon Ruamchit ⓣ032 433821, ⓕ032 433834. Good-value high-rise where the nicely appointed deluxe rooms all have a balcony, most of which afford a partial, long-distance, seaview. All rooms are equipped with air-con, and TV, and there's a swimming pool. Fifty-percent discounts during the week. ❽

Memory House Next to Soi Cha-am North 2 on Thanon Ruamchit ⓣ032 472100, ⓔcha_ammemory@yahoo.com. Good-value and well-kept little hotel whose cute fan and air-con rooms are decked out in a shell and seashore theme. ❸–❹

Nirandorn 3 Just south of the Narathip junction on Thanon Ruamchit ⓣ032 470300, ⓕ032 470303. Clean, well-maintained hotel rooms with fan or air-con and TV – the best ones are on the upper floors and have sea views. Plus some less interesting and more expensive two-room motel-style bungalows for B2000. ❹

Scandy Resort North of Soi Cha-am North 5 at 274/32–33 Thanon Ruamchit ⓣ 032 471926, ⓦwww.scandyresort.thethai.com. Small, mid-market guest house above a restaurant offering huge, good-value rooms, all with air-con and TV, and most with balconies and good sea views. ❺

Between Cha-am and Hua Hin

Beach Garden Hotel About 7km south of Cha-am at 949/21 Soi Suan Loi, off Thanon Phetkasem ⓣ032 508234, ⓦwww.beachgarden chaam.com. Set in a lush tropical garden that runs down to the sea, accommodation in this good-value resort is in either attractive, comfortably furnished cottages or a less characterful but smart hotel block. Has a swimming pool, games room, tennis courts, windsurfing and other watersports facilities. ❽

Dusit Resort and Polo Club 14km south of Cha-am and 9km north of Hua Hin at 1349 Thanon Phetkasem ⓣ032 520009, ⓦhuahin.dusit.com. One of the most luxurious and elegant spots on this stretch of coast, boasting four restaurants, a huge pool and children's pool, all manner of sporting facilities – including a polo field, riding and sailing lessons and squash courts – and cultural entertainments; there's an Avis car-rental desk here too. ❾

Regent Cha-am About 8km south of Cha-am at 849/21 Thanon Phetkasem ⓣ032 451240, ⓦwww.regent-chaam.com. Well-regarded upmarket resort set in appealing gardens that run down to a nice stretch of beach. Rooms are comfortably furnished; facilities include three swimming pools, squash and tennis courts, a fitness centre and horse-riding on the beach. ❽–❾

Eating and drinking

The choice of **restaurants** in Cha-am is not a patch on the range you get in Hua Hin, but for a change from hotel food you might want to drop by the *Tipdharee* on Thanon Ruamchit, north of Soi Cha-am North 5 and next to *Scandy Resort*, which has a huge menu of mid-priced Thai dishes, including lots of seafood, curries and one-plate dishes. *Poom*, about 150m north of Soi Cha-am North 5 at 274/1 Thanon Ruamchit, serves a good, if pricey selection of Thai-style seafood dishes, including recommended shrimps with garlic, on its sea-view terrace. *Baan Plang Pub and Restaurant* on Thanon Narathip opens nightly from 7pm to 2am and stages live music.

Phra Ratchaniwet Marukhathaiyawan

Ten kilometres south of Cha-am, on the way to Hua Hin, stands the lustrous seaside palace of Rama VI, **Phra Ratchaniwet Marukhathaiyawan** (daily 8am–4pm; B90), a rarely visited place, despite the easy access; the half-hourly Cha-am–Hua Hin buses stop within a couple of kilometres' walk of the palace at the sign for Rama VI Camp – just follow the road through the army compound.

Designed by an Italian architect and completed in just sixteen days in 1923, the golden teak building was abandoned to the corrosive sea air after Rama VI's death in 1925. Restoration work began in the 1970s, and today most of the structure looks as it once did, a stylish composition of verandas and latticework painted in pastel shades of beige and blue, with an emphasis on cool simplicity. The spacious open hall in the north wing, hung with chandeliers and encircled by a first-floor balcony, was once used as a theatre, and the upstairs rooms, now furnished only with a few black-and-white portraits from the royal family photo album, were given over to royal attendants. The king stayed in the centre room, with the best sea view and access to the promenade, while the south wing contained the queen's apartments.

Hua Hin

Thailand's oldest beach resort, **HUA HIN** used to be little more than an overgrown fishing village with one exceptionally grand hotel, but the arrival of mass tourism, high-rise hotels and farang-managed hostess bars has made a serious dent in its once idiosyncratic charm. With the far superior beaches of Ko Samui, Krabi and Ko Samet so close at hand, there's little here to draw the dedicated sunseeker, but it's nonetheless a convivial place in which to drink and enjoy fine seafood and, if you can afford it, stay in the atmospheric former *Railway Hotel*. In addition, the town makes a convenient base for day-trips to Khao Sam Roi Yot National Park, 63km south, and there are half a dozen golf courses in the area, plus a couple of exceptionally indulgent hotel spas. If none of that appeals, you might consider stopping by for Hua Hin's well-respected **jazz festival** in June (check Ⓦwww.huahinjazzfestival.com for details), or for the rather more unusual **elephant polo tournament**, held every September (Ⓦwww.anantara.com/elephantpolo).

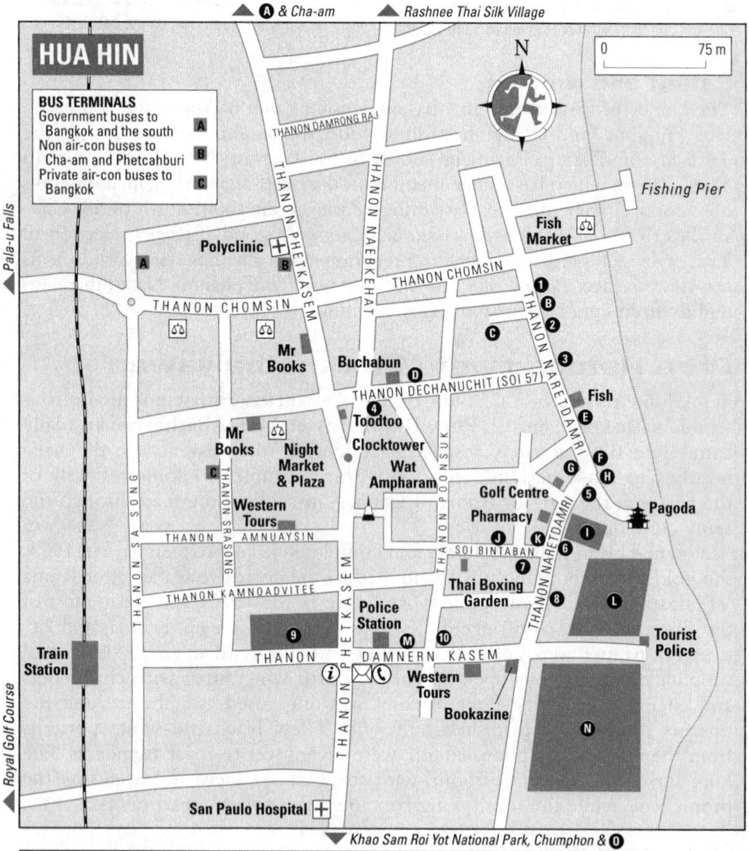

ACCOMMODATION

All Nations D
Anantara Resort A
Bird H
Central Village Hua Hin L
Chiva-Som Resort O
City Beach Resort M
Fresh Inn K
Fu-Luay Guest House E
Hilton Hua Hin I
Hotel Sofitel Central N
K Place G
Karoon Hut B
Mod Guest House F
Pattana Guest House C
Phuen Guest House J

RESTAURANTS AND BARS

Brasserie de Paris 1
Chao Lay 3
Gene Pub 7
Hua Hin Brewing Company 6
La Villa 10
Montri Restaurant 8
Satukarn Square 9
Som Moo Joom 4
Thanachote 2
World News Coffee 5

The **royal family** were Hua Hin's main visitors at the start of the twentieth century, but the place became more widely popular in the 1920s, when the opening of the Bangkok–Malaysia rail line made short excursions to the beach much more viable. The Victorian-style *Railway Hotel* was built soon after to cater for the leisured classes, and in 1926 Rama VII had his own summer palace, Klai Klangwon (Far from Worries), erected at the northern end of the beach. It was here, ironically, that Rama VII was staying in 1932 when the coup was launched in Bangkok against the system of absolute monarchy. The current king lives here most of the time now, apparently preferring the sea breezes to the traffic fumes of the capital.

Arrival, information and transport

Hua Hin is on the Bangkok–Surat Thani rail line, but journeys tend to be slow (3hr 30min–4hr from Bangkok), and inconveniently timetabled. You can also get from Kanchanaburi to Hua Hin by train, but you need to change trains at Ban Pho (not listed on English-language timetables). Famously photogenic Hua Hin **train station** (Ⓣ032 511073) is at the west end of Thanon Damnern Kasem, about ten minutes' walk from the seafront.

Hua Hin's **bus** service is more useful. Non-air-con Cha-am and Phetchaburi buses arrive and depart from a spot just north of the junction of Thanon Phetkasem and Thanon Chomsin, while government buses to and from Bangkok (Southern Bus Terminal), Chumphon and the south use the depot further west off Thanon Chomsin. The private air-con buses to southern destinations beyond Chumphon, such as Phuket (B650), Krabi (B600) and Ko Tao (B650 including ferry), all leave from various spots around town in the late evening; for details and tickets contact tour agents (see p.573). Tiny Hua Hin **airport** (Ⓣ032 520343) is 6km north of town, beside the Phetkasem Highway, but at the time of writing flights to Bangkok and Ko Samui had been suspended because of a lack of customers. Many of Hua Hin's bigger hotels offer minibus transfers direct to and from Bangkok's **Don Muang Airport** (about 3hr).

The **tourist information** desk at the local government office (daily Dec-Feb 8.30am–4.30pm, Mon–Fri only March–Nov; Ⓣ032 532433), on the corner of Thanon Damnern Kasem and Thanon Phetkasem, offers advice on getting to Khao Sam Roi Yot National Park and sells bus tickets for southern destinations.

Hua Hin has plenty of **samlors** and **motorbike taxis**, but many tourists rent cars and motorbikes to explore the area by themselves. Avis (Ⓣ032 512021, Ⓦwww.avis.com) has desks inside the *Hotel Sofitel*, and at *Chiva-Som* and the *Dusit Resort* outside Hua Hin (see p.567); several Hua Hin tour agencies also act as agents for Budget (Ⓦwww.budget.co.th). The transport touts outside the *Hotel Sofitel* and across from the tourist information office rent out 150cc bikes for around B200 a day.

Accommodation

A night or two at the former *Railway Hotel* (now the *Sofitel*) is reason in itself to visit Hua Hin, but there are plenty of other **places to stay**. The most unusual guest houses are built on converted squid piers, with rooms strung out along wooden jetties so you can hear and feel the waves beneath you, even if you can't afford a room with a window overlooking them. Rooms at jetty guest houses are fairly inexpensive, the only drawback being the rather strong aroma of seashore debris at low tide. These squid-pier hotels are currently under threat, however, as the local government considers them an encroachment on public land (the sea) and wants to demolish them. Room rates can drop significantly from Mondays to Thursdays, so don't be afraid to ask for a discount. Resorts beyond the northern fringes of Hua Hin, on the stretch of coast between Hua Hin and Cha-am, are described on p.567.

Inexpensive and moderate

All Nations 10 Thanon Dechanuchit ⓣ032 512747, ⓔcybercafehuahin@hotmail.com. Large, comfortable double rooms, many of them with balconies, some with air-con, and most with bathrooms shared between two rooms. Single rooms are a bit more cramped. Also has a roof terrace. Good value for Hua Hin. ❸–❹

Bird 31/2 Thanon Naretdamri ⓣ032 511630. A classic friendly little jetty guest house, with smallish but very clean en-suite rooms (some with air-con) set over the water, plus a nice breezy sea-view terrace at the end. Phone ahead as it's very popular. ❹

Fresh Inn 132 Thanon Naretdamri ⓣ032 511389, ⓕ032 532166. Small Italian-run hotel with a friendly, cosy atmosphere; all rooms are spacious and comfortable and have air-con and TV. A swimming pool is on the cards. ❺

Fu-Lay Guest House and Hotel 110/1 Thanon Naretdamri, guest house ⓣ 032 513145, hotel ⓣ032 513670, ⓔfulayhuahin@hotmail.com. A well-appointed jetty guest house with some cheap cell-like fan rooms plus a high standard of air-con rooms with nice en-suite bathrooms and TV. Friendly staff, plus the characteristic breezy seating area set right over the water. Air-con rooms in the small hotel wing across the road are equally good. ❸–❺

Karoon Hut 80 Thanon Naretdamri ⓣ032 530242, ⓕ032 530737. Friendly jetty guest house, with decent fan- and air-con rooms (no cells) and a nice big open-air seating area at the end of the pier. Well priced for Hua Hin. ❸–❹

K Place 116 Thanon Naretdamri ⓣ032 511396, ⓔkplaceus@yahoo.com. Large, comfortable and well-appointed rooms, all with air-con and TV, make this small place a good-value mid-range option. ❺

Mod Guest House 116 Thanon Naretdamri ⓣ032 512296. Jetty guest house with some good rooms (a few with air-con), others fairly basic but very cheap (for Hua Hin), plus a seafront seating area. Call ahead to secure a room. ❷–❹

Pattana Guest Home 52 Thanon Naretdamri ⓣ032 513393, ⓔhuahinpattana@hotmail.com. Cosy, comfortable, inexpensive rooms in an appealingly traditional teak-wood house, quietly located at the end of a small soi. Some rooms have private bathrooms, others also have air-con. ❸–❹

Phuen Guest House Soi Bintaban (also spelt Binthabat) ⓣ032 512344. Traditional wooden house in a busy street of bars, crammed with lots of small, basic, en-suite rooms, a few of them air-conditioned. ❷–❸

Expensive

Anantara Resort and Spa 5km north of Hua Hin at 43/1 Thanon Phetkasem ⓣ032 520250, ⓦwww.anantara.com. Set in effusive, beautifully designed tropical gardens that run right down to the shore, this is a lovely resort-style idyll just out of town. Accommodation is in a series of Thai-style pavilions, whose stylishly appointed rooms use plenty of wood. It has three restaurants, two free-form pools, a charming spa and its own stretch of beach. ❾

Central Village Hua Hin Thanon Damnern Kasem ⓣ032 512036, ⓦwww.centralhotelsresorts.com. Like its sister operation, the *Sofitel*, the *Central Village*, comprised of 41 cream-painted wooden villas set in a seafront garden, has a distinctive old-fashioned charm. All the villas have large verandas, and some have two rooms and an uninterrupted sea view, though they're not exactly the last word in contemporary luxury. There's a pool and a restaurant on the premises, and guests can also use the facilities at the *Sofitel* over the road. ❾

Chiva-Som International Health Resort South of Hua Hin at 73/4 Thanon Phetkasem ⓣ032 536536, ⓦwww.chivasom.com. Super-deluxe spa and health resort that's a favourite with A-list celebs and is famous for its personalized holistic health treatments, detox programmes, fitness plans and psycho-spiritual consultations. Accommodation comprises just 57 exclusive bungalows and hotel rooms set in tropical beachfront gardens. Published rates for full board start at about US$345 per person per day, or from US$1750 for a week's full board with treatments. ❾

City Beach Resort 16 Thanon Damnern Kasem ⓣ032 512870, ⓦwww.citybeach.co.th. Reasonably priced, centrally located high-rise hotel with comfortable, well-equipped rooms, all with air-con and TV and most enjoying a sea view from the balcony. Has a swimming pool and a couple of restaurants. ❽

Hilton Hua Hin 33 Thanon Naretdamri ⓣ032 512888, ⓦwww.hilton.com. Set bang in the centre of Hua Hin's beachfront, the *Hilton's* high-rise profile disfigures the local skyline, but the facilities are extensive and the views excellent. Has an impressive stepped swimming pool right on the seafront, a spa, and a stunning indoor-outdoor water garden in the lobby. Rooms are comfortable though not exciting; published rates start at US$165. ⑨

Hotel Sofitel Central Hua Hin 1 Thanon Damnern Kasem ⓣ032 512021, ⓦwww.sofitel.com. The former *Railway Hotel* remains a classic of colonial-style architecture, with high ceilings, polished wood panelling, wide sea-view balconies and a garden full of topiary animals. All is much as it was in 1923, except for the swimming pools and tennis courts, which were built especially for the filming of *The Killing Fields* – the *Railway Hotel* stood in as Phnom Penh's plushest hotel. Also has a spa. Published rates start at B6150; weekends get booked out several weeks in advance. ⑨

The resort

The prettiest part of Hua Hin's five-kilometre-long **beach** is the patch in front of and to the south of the *Sofitel*, where the sand is at its softest and whitest. North of here the shore is crowded with tables and chairs belonging to a string of small restaurant shacks, beyond which the beach ends at a Chinese-style pagoda atop a flight of steps running down to Thanon Naretdamri. The coast to the north of the pagoda is dominated by the jetties and terraces of guest houses and seafood restaurants, but if the local government has its way the jetties may soon be demolished and the seafront banked by a new esplanade. South of the *Sofitel*, upmarket hotels and condos overshadow nearly the whole run of beach down to Khao Takiab (Chopstick Hill), 8km further south.

Pala-u Falls and other excursions

Hua Hin is well placed for **excursions** to Khao Sam Roi Yot National Park (described on p.575), Phetchaburi (see p.563), Damnoen Saduak floating markets (see p.216) and the old summer palace of Phra Ratchaniwet Marukhathaiyawan (see p.567). The fifteen-tiered **Pala-u Waterfall** is another popular destination within day-tripping distance and, though the falls themselves are hardly exceptional, the route there takes you through lush, hilly landscape and past innumerable pineapple plantations. The falls are 63km west of Hua Hin, close to the Burmese border and within Kaeng Krachan National Park (daily 8am–4.30pm; B200). There's no public transport to the falls, but every tour operator features them in its programme (about B900/person). To get there under your own steam, follow the signs from the west end of Thanon Chomsin along Highway 3218. Once inside the park you'll see hundreds of butterflies and may also catch sight of monitor lizards and hornbills. A slippery and occasionally steep path follows the river through the fairly dense jungle up to the falls, passing the (numbered) tiers en route to the remote fifteenth level, though most people opt to stop at the third level, which has the first pool of any decent depth (full of fish but not that clear) and is a half-hour walk from the car park.

Golf courses

The Thai enthusiasm for **golf** began in Hua Hin in 1924, with the opening of the Royal Hua Hin Golf Course behind the train station, and now there are another five courses of international standard in the Hua Hin/Cha-am area. Visitors' green fees range from B800 to B2500 on a weekday, B1200 to B2500 on a weekend, plus about B200 for a caddy. Some clubhouses also rent sets of clubs for B500, or you can ask at the Hua Hin Golf Centre (daily noon–10pm; ⓣ032 530119, ⓦwww.huahingolf.com) on Thanon Naretdamri across from the *Hilton*, which also sells and repairs clubs and organizes trips to local courses. Several other general tour operators also offer golf packages, which include transfers and green fees.

The historic eighteen-hole Royal Hua Hin Golf Course (Ⓣ032 512475), established in 1924, is the most centrally located of the **courses**, easily reached on foot by simply crossing the railway tracks to the west side of Hua Hin Railway Station. All the others are outside town and all have eighteen holes except where noted: Bangkok Golf Milford (Ⓣ032 572441; 15km south of Hua Hin near Pak Nam Pran); Imperial Lake View (27 holes; Ⓣ032 456233; 15km north of Hua Hin); Majestic Creek Country Club (Ⓣ032 520162; 20km west of Hua Hin); Palm Hills Golf Resort (Ⓣ032 520800, Ⓦwww.palmhills-golf.com; 8km north of Hua Hin); Springfield Royal Country Club, designed by Jack Nicklaus (Ⓣ032 593223, Ⓦwww.springfieldresort.com; 22km north of Hua Hin, just to the south of Cha-am).

Eating, drinking and entertainment

Hua Hin is renowned for its **seafood**, and some of the best places to enjoy the local catch are the seafront restaurants along Thanon Naretdamri. Fish also features heavily at the large and lively **night market**, which sets up at sunset along the western end of Thanon Dechanuchit. The biggest concentration of **bars** is along Soi Bintaban; many of these places are so-called "bar-beers", with lots of seating round a large oval bar and hostesses dispensing beer and flirtation through the night.

Montri Restaurant on Thanon Naretdamri (Ⓣ032 532128) stages free classical **Thai dance** performances for diners every Wednesday at 8pm, and again on Saturdays at 8pm in high season. Tuesdays and Fridays are fight nights at the **Thai Boxing Garden** off Thanon Poonsuk (Ⓣ032 515269), with programmes starting at 9pm and featuring five different fights (B250); it's owned by local *muay Thai* champion Khun Chop, who also runs Thai boxing classes most days at 5pm.

Brasserie de Paris 3 Thanon Naretdamri. Refined French restaurant that's known for its seafood and has an appealing terrace over the water. Specialities include crab Hua Hin, *coquilles St Jacques* and *filet à la Provençal*. Expensive.

Chao Lay Thanon Naretdamri. Hua Hin's most famous jetty restaurant is deservedly popular, serving up a simple menu of high-quality seafood, including rock lobster, blue crab, scallops, cottonfish and mixed seafood platters. Moderate to expensive.

Gene Pub 4 Soi Bintabat. The rustic, wood-beamed exterior of *Gene Pub* stands out on this soi full of bar-beers and gives a hint of what goes on inside: nightly sets from Thai country music bands, and a low-key presence from hostesses. Moderate.

Hua Hin Brewing Company In front of the *Hilton* on Thanon Naretdamri. Cavernous, half-timbered pub-restaurant that attempts to recreate the feel of a fisherman's tavern. There's live music nightly, plus a seafood-dominated menu, but the real attractions are the special beers produced by the in-house microbrewery: Sabai Sabai wheat beer, Elephant Tusk dark ale and Dancing Monkey lager. Nightly 5pm–2am. Moderate.

La Villa Thanon Poonsuk. Long-established and highly regarded Italian place that serves famously delicious home-made ice creams as well as a typical selection of pizzas and pastas. Moderate.

Satukarn Square At the Thanon Phetkasem/Damnern Kasem junction. Take your pick from the twenty or so little restaurants in this partially open-air plaza, where the choice includes Italian, Indian, German and seafood outlets. Nightly from around 6pm. Moderate.

Som Moo Joom 51/6 Thanon Dechanuchit (corner of Thanon Naebkehat); no English sign. Exceptionally good seafood at very cheap prices makes this one of the most popular places with Thai holidaymakers. The trademark dish is sukiyaki-style shrimp and seafood soups, but the menu also covers the range of standard seafood dishes. Decor is bare bones and indoor seating is available only from 6pm to 9pm nightly, after which it's pavement tables only. Cheap.

Thanachote 11 Thanon Naretdamri. Atmospheric seafood restaurant, set on its own pier over the sea and serving great fish dishes. Moderate.

World News Coffee Thanon Naretdamri. The place to come for skinny lattes, sun-dried tomato bagels, cheesecakes, fresh vegetable juices, UK and US newspapers, Internet access – and a very large bill. Expensive.

Shopping

Among the resort's myriad souvenir **shops**, Buchabun, at 22 Thanon Dechanuchit (Mon–Fri 5–10pm), stands out for its eclectic range of unusual antique crafts and for its modern ceramics, while Fish, at 27 Thanon Naretdamri, sells gorgeous handmade clothes in local cotton and silk fabrics. Other fun places to shop for clothes and souvenirs (after 6pm only) are the stalls at the night market on the west end of Thanon Dechanuchit, the more upmarket little shops in the Night Plaza that runs off it, and the handful of little shops selling handicrafts and clothes among the restaurants in Satukarn Square at the Thanon Phetkasem/Thanon Damnern Kasem crossroads. There's a small outlet for the high-quality Jim Thompson silk and clothing franchise in the lobby area of the *Hilton* hotel on Thanon Naretdamri, but the most rewarding place to start any serious silk shopping is the **Rashnee Thai Silk Village** (daily 9am–6pm) at 18 Thanon Naebkehat, about ten minutes' walk north from the town-centre clocktower. Every visitor to the "village" (actually a series of open-air workshop pavilions and an air-conditioned shop) is given a free and well-explained guided tour of the entire silk production process, after which you are encouraged to pop in to the Rashnee tailors' shop and get yourself suited up.

Listings

Banks and exchange There are currency-exchange counters all over the resort, especially on Thanon Damnern Kasem and Thanon Naretdamri; most of the main bank branches with ATMs are on Thanon Phetkasem.

Books English-language books at the excellent Bookazine, on the corner of Damnern Kasem and Naretdamri; at several branches of Mr Books, on Thanon Phetkasem and Thanon Dechanuchit; and in the minimarkets on Thanon Damnern Kasem.

Cookery classes One-day courses (B1000) can be arranged through the Buchabun handicrafts shop at 22 Thanon Dechanuchit (Mon–Fri 5–10pm; ⓣ01 857 5727, ⓦwww.buchabun.com); call to check when the next class is scheduled, or drop by the shop.

Emergencies For all emergencies, call the tourist police on the free, 24hr phoneline (ⓣ1155), or contact them at their office opposite the *Sofitel* at the beachfront end of Thanon Damnern Kasem (ⓣ032 515995). The Hua Hin police station is further west on Damnern Kasem (ⓣ032 511027).

Horse-riding On the beach in front of the *Sofitel*.

Hospitals The best private hospital in Hua Hin is the San Paulo, 222 Thanon Phetkasem (ⓣ032 532576–8), south of the tourist information office, but for minor ailments there's also the reputable Hua Hin International Polyclinic (daily 8am–9pm; ⓣ032 51624–5) beside the Thai Farmers Bank on Thanon Phetkasem, which also offers dental services.

Internet access Available at several outlets in the resort, including on Thanon Phetkasem and, cheapest of all, at the CAT international phone office on Thanon Damnern Kasem (daily 8am–11pm).

Mail The GPO is on Thanon Damnern Kasem.

Pharmacy Several in the resort, including the very well-stocked Medihouse (daily 9am–10pm) opposite the *Hilton* on Thanon Naretdamri.

Spas Plenty of options, from the numerous cheap day-spa shops that offer foot massages and Thai massages in several town-centre locations on Thanon Naretdamri and Thanon Phetkasem, to the artfully designed luxury havens at Hua Hin's top hotels, notably the *Chiva-Som* (see p.570) and the *Anantara* (see p.570).

Telephones The CAT overseas telephone office (daily 8am–11pm) is on Thanon Damnern Kasem, next to the GPO.

Tour operators Both Toodtoo Tours, inside the Apilat Plaza on Thanon Phetkasem (ⓣ032 530553, ⓦwww.toodtoo.com), and Western Tours, at 11 Thanon Damnern Kasem (ⓣ032 533303, ⓦwww.westerntourshuahin.com) and on Thanon Amnuaysin (ⓣ032 521171), sell bus and air tickets, golf packages, and day-trips (B900/person) to Khao Sam Roi Yot National Park, Pala-u Falls and the rest. Sunseeker Tours, based inside the *Hilton* on Thanon Naretdamri (ⓣ032 533666), offers cruises to local beaches on its yacht for around B1500 per person.

Pak Nam Pran

The stretch of coast between Hua Hin and Chumphon barely registers on most foreign tourists' radar, but many better-off Bangkokians have favourite beaches in this area, the nicest of which is the delightfully sophisticated **PAK NAM PRAN**. Just 33km south of Hua Hin, Pak Nam Pran used only to cater for families who owned beach villas here, but in the last few years the beach homes have been joined by a handful of enticing, if pricey, boutique hotels, and signs are there's more development to come. As yet there are still no tour agents, cafés, souvenir shops or car-rental outlets to mar the peaceful ambience, just a couple of small fish restaurants and the possibility of organizing day-trips to nearby Khao Sam Roi Yot National Park (see opposite) through hotel staff. As along much of the Gulf coast, the beach itself is not exceptional (it has hardly any shade and is suffering from erosion in parts), but it is long and sandy, and nearly always empty. During the rainy season you're quite likely to see dolphins playing within sight of the shore.

Practicalities

Pak Nam Pran beach begins just south of the Pran River estuary and its eponymous town and runs south for around five kilometres to Khao Kalok headland and the tiny Thao Kosa Forest Park. Easiest **access** is via the town of **Pranburi**, which straddles Highway 4 some 23km south of Hua Hin and runs a frequent bus service to and from Hua Hin (every 20min; 40min) from close by the town centre's main intersection. There's no public transport from Pranburi to Pak Nam Pran beach, but hotels can arrange transfers, any Pranburi songthaew driver will taxi you there, or you could rent your own car or motorbike from Hua Hin. If making your own way, turn east off Highway 4 at Pranburi's town-centre traffic lights and then take minor road 3168 down to the sea (about 10km in all), picking up the relevant sign for your hotel. All the hotels are south of the little town of Pak Nam Pran: the *Evason* is the northernmost (about 2km southeast of Pak Nam Pran town), and the rest are spread over a two-kilometre stretch of the beachfront road, starting about 2km south of the *Evason*.

Accommodation

Aside from one notable exception, all Pak Nam Pran's **hotels** comprise just a handful of rooms; because of their unusual layout some aren't suitable for kids. Breakfast is generally included in the price of the room. During weekends in high season (Nov–July) you'll need to book ahead.

Aleenta Central Pak Nam Pran beach, ⓣ032 570194, ⓦwww.aleenta.com. This stunningly designed tiny hotel is the sleekest outfit on the beach, comprising three gorgeous circular bungalows, each with an uninterrupted sea view, a deck and personal plunge pool, plus half a dozen other very tasteful villa-style rooms. The feel is modernist chic, with elegantly understated local furnishings and huge glass windows, but no phones or TVs. There's a small rooftop pool, a spa and restaurant, plus a couple of family villas available for rent. ⑨

Evason Hua Hin Resort and Spa Far northern Pak Nam Pran beach, ⓣ032 632111, ⓦwww.evasonhuahin.com. With 185 rooms and a distinct resort atmosphere, the *Evason* is the biggest, best-known and most expensive hotel in Pak Nam Pran, but as accommodation is divided into discrete village areas and screened by graceful gardens, the feel is quite private and small-scale. Rooms are attractively cool and contemporary and all have big balconies, TV and air-con. Facilities include a huge pool, a spa complex, three restaurants, a kids' club and Internet access. Published rates start at B5750. ⑨

Huaplee Lazy Beach Central Pak Nam Pran beach, ⓣ032 631854, ⓦwww.huapleelazybeach.com. This exceptionally cute collection of eight idiosyncratic white-cube rooms is the work of the architect-interior designer owners. It's a delightfully characterful place with whimsical interiors done out with white-painted wood floors, blue-and-white colour schemes and funky shell and driftwood decor. All rooms are air-con and all but one has a sea view from its terrace/balcony. ⑧

Jamsawang Resort Northern Pak Nam Pran beach, ⓣ032 570050. Just half a dozen pale-blue concrete bungalows widely spaced around a garden across the road from the beach. All have air-con and TV. ⑥

Pran Havana Central Pak Nam Pran beach, ⓣ032 570077, ⓔpran_havana@mweb.co.th. More white-cube architecture right next to *Huaplee* at this slightly bigger but equally charming beachfront accommodation, where the warren of individually furnished rooms is accessed by a series of whitewashed steps and sea-view terraces. Interiors are all seaside-chic and the price depends on the size of the room (some are huge) and the view. ⑨

Eating

Within walking distance of most accommodation, the (unsigned) shack-like shorefront **restaurant** *J Tim*, at the far southern end of Pak Nam Pran beach, about 1km south of *Huaplee*, *Pran Havana* and *Aleenta*, has an extensive menu of very good seafood dishes; mosquitoes are a problem here, so take repellent. On the edge of Pak Nam Pran town, about 2km north of the *Evason*, *Krua Jao* (daily 9am–9pm) offers an enormous, mid-priced menu of 120 mostly fish and seafood dishes, including very good crab curry and pork with garlic. The restaurant is on the seafront road but accessible only via Pak Nam Pran town: from the main road through Pak Nam Pran head east down (signed) Soi Pasukvanich 16, which is opposite a gate in a large walled temple compound; when the soi emerges at the sea you'll find the restaurant immediately to your left – it's unsigned in English but you can't miss it.

Khao Sam Roi Yot National Park

With a name that translates as "The Mountain with Three Hundred Peaks", **KHAO SAM ROI YOT NATIONAL PARK** (daily 6am–6pm; B200), 28km south of Pak Nam Pran beach or 63km south of Hua Hin, encompasses a small but varied coastal zone of just 98 square kilometres. The dramatic limestone crags after which it is named are the dominant feature, looming up to 650m above the gulf waters and the forested interior, but perhaps more significant are the mud flats and freshwater marsh which attract and provide a breeding ground for thousands of migratory birds. **Bird-watching** at Thung Khao Sam Roi Yot swamp is a major draw, but the famously photogenic Phraya Nakhon Khiri cave is the focus of most day-trips, while a few decent trails and a couple of secluded beaches provide added interest.

The park

Khao Sam Roi Yot's most-visited attraction is the surprisingly worthwhile **Tham Phraya Nakhon** cave system, hidden high up on a cliffside above **Hat Laem Sala**, an unremarkable sandy bay at the base of a headland that's inaccessible to vehicles but has a park checkpoint, a restaurant and some national park bungalows. The usual way to get to Hat Laem Sala is by a five-minute boat-ride from the knot of food stalls behind Wat Bang Pu on the edge of **Ban Bang Pu** fishing village (6km from the park's northern checkpoint). Boat prices are fixed at B100 per person for the round-trip visit to

Hat Laem Sala, or B200 if you also want to go swimming off a nearby island. It's also possible to walk over the headland from behind Wat Bang Pu to Hat Laem Sala, along a signed, but at times steep, five-hundred-metre-long trail. From Hat Laem Sala, another taxing though shaded trail runs up the hillside to the Tham Phraya Nakhon caves and takes around thirty minutes.

The huge twin **caves** are hung with stalactites and stalagmites and wreathed in lianas and gnarly trees, but their most dramatic features are their partially collapsed roofs, which allow the sunlight to stream in and illuminate the interiors, in particular beaming down on the famous royal pavilion, Phra Thi Nang Khua Kharunhad, which was built in the second cave in 1890 in honour of Rama V. A three-hour trek south from Tham Phraya Nakhon brings you to **Tham Sai**, a genuinely dark and dank limestone cave, complete with stalactites, stalagmites and petrified waterfalls. The trek offers some fine coastal views, but a shorter alternative is the twenty-minute trail from **Ban Khung Tanot** village (accessible by road, 8km on from the Ban Bang Pu turn-off), where you can rent an essential flashlight.

Another enjoyable activity is to charter a boat (B300/hour for up to ten people) from beside Wat Khao Daeng in the southern part of the park (1.5km from park HQ) and take a trip along the mangrove-fringed **Khao Daeng canal**. You can scramble up **Khao Daeng** itself, a 322-metre-high outcrop that offers good summit views over the coast, from a thirty-minute trail that begins close by the park headquarters. The park's two official **nature trails** also start from close by HQ – the "Horseshoe Trail" takes in the forest habitats of monkeys, squirrels and songbirds, while the "Mangrove Trail" leads through the swampy domiciles of monitor lizards and egrets, with the chance of encountering longtailed (crab-eating) macaques.

The park hosts up to three hundred species of **bird** and between September and November the mud flats are thick with migratory birds from Siberia, China and northern Europe. Khao Sam Roi Yot also contains Thailand's largest freshwater marsh, **Thung Khao Sam Roi Yot**, which is near the village of **Rong Jai** (Rong Che) in the north of the park, and accessed not from the main park road, but by turning east off Highway 4 200m north of kilometre-stone 276 and continuing 9km to the wetlands. This is an excellent place for observing **waders** and **songbirds**, and is one of only two places in the country where the **purple heron** breeds; rangers rent out boats here for bird-watching excursions (B100/person/hour).

Practicalities

Like most of Thailand's national parks, Khao Sam Roi Yot is very hard to explore by public transport. From Hua Hin, you need to take a local **bus** (every 20min; 40min) to Pranburi (23km) and then charter either a songthaew or a motorbike taxi (B150–250) into the park. Or you can make use of the limited local **songthaew** service, which runs hourly from 6am to noon from Pranburi market to the village of **Ban Bang Phu**, the access point for boats to Hat Laem Sala and the Phraya Nakhon Khiri cave – but note that the last return songthaew leaves Ban Bang Phu at 1pm and this option is only feasible if you're not interested in visiting any of the other sights in the park, all of which are spread too far apart to walk between. It's much easier either to join a one-day **tour** from Hua Hin (see p.573), Pak Nam Pran (see p.574) or Hat Phu Noi (see below) or to rent your own transport from Hua Hin. With your own wheels, take Highway 4 south to Pranburi, turn east at Pranburi's main intersection (kilometre-stone 254) and then follow the national-park signs to the **northern park checkpoint** 23km further south. All the main attractions are well signed from the main road through the park: it's 6km from the northern checkpoint to the departure point for boats to Hat Laem Sala and Phra Nakhon Khiri, and 14km to the **park headquarters** (Ⓣ032 619078), **trail heads**, **visitors' centre** and **southern park checkpoint** near the village of Khao Daeng. If coming from the south, turn off Highway 4 into the park at kilometre-stone 286.5, following signs to the southern park checkpoint, HQ, etc 13km further east. Rangers hand out rather sketchy **park maps** when you pay your entrance fee at the checkpoint.

Accommodation: Hat Phu Noi

The park's **accommodation** sites are near the headquarters at Khao Daeng, at Sam Phraya Beach, and at Laem Sala; at all these locations it's a choice between camping, at B40 per person, or staying in one of the national park bungalows (from B700), which sleep up to twenty people – advance reservation is essential (Ⓣ032 603751). Most people prefer to stay a few kilometres outside the park entrance at the more appealing, family-friendly hotels on the long, golden-sand beach of **HAT PHU NOI**. Hat Phu Noi is clearly signed off the road into the park, 4km before the northern checkpoint, and is at the end of a two-kilometre side road; hotels can arrange transfers from Pranburi or Hua Hin. At the northern end of Hat Phu Noi, the long-running, UK-managed, *Dolphin Bay Resort* (Ⓣ032 559333, Ⓦwww.dolphinbayresort.com; ❻) has about eighty comfortable air-con rooms and bungalows ranged around a couple of swimming pools, plus a big restaurant with a bar, pool table and Internet access. The adjacent *Phu Noi Beach Bungalows* (Ⓣ032 559359, Ⓕ032 559334; ❺) is also British-run and has similar, equally good rooms and facilities, but is much smaller, with only twenty air-con bungalows. Both these hotels organize excursions into the park, as well as dolphin-watching, sailing, snorkelling and fishing trips. A few hundred metres further south along the beach, next to *Sam Roi Yot Resort*, *Khun At* (the sign reads simply "Rooms for Rent"; Ⓣ032 559261, Ⓦwww.geocities.com/khun_at; ❸–❹) offers basic rooms with a fan and a mattress on the floor, plus some better ones with beds and air-con.

South to Chumphon

Most foreign tourists zip through the region immediately south of Khao Sam Roi Yot en route to the more obvious delights of the Ko Samui archipelago, but the unexpectedly charming seaside town of **Prachuap Khiri Khan** and the small beach resorts at **Ban Krud** and **Suan Luang** are worth investigating if you're happy to substitute good seafood and laid-back Thai hospitality for full-on resort facilities. Twenty-two kilometres south of Prachuap, Highway 4 passes through Wang Duan, where a sign announces the fact that this is the narrowest part of Thailand: just 10.96km of Thai land separates the Gulf of Thailand from the Burmese border at this point.

Prachuap Khiri Khan

Despite lacking any must-see attractions, the tiny provincial capital of **PRACHUAP KHIRI KHAN**, 67km south of Pranburi and 90km from Hua Hin, exudes a genuine small-town charm and makes a pleasant place to break any journey up or down the coast; if nothing else, it's a great spot for a seafood lunch with a view. The town is contained in a small grid of streets that runs just 250m east to west, between the sea and the train station, and around 500m north to south, from the Khao Chong Krajok hill at the northern end to the airforce base in the south.

Monkey-infested **Khao Chong Krajok** is Prachuap's main sight: if you climb the 417 steps from Thanon Sarachip to the golden-spired chedi at the summit you get a great perspective on the scalloped coast below and west to the mountainous Burmese border, just 12km away. At the far southern end of town, the long sandy beach at **Ao Manao** is the best place in the area for swimming and sunbathing. The bay is on the base belonging to the 4th Air Division, so you usually need to sign in at the airforce checkpoint two kilometres north of the beach itself. To get there, just head south down the town centre's Thanon Sarachip for about 4km until you get to the 4th Air Division sign and checkpoint. A tuk-tuk to the beach should cost around B50, or about B25 for a motorbike taxi. On weekdays you're likely to have the beach almost to yourself, but it's a very popular spot with Thai families on weekends, and there are plenty of facilities on the beachfront road. At low tide you can walk out from Ao Manao along a sandy spit to an outcrop known as Khao Lommuak, where a memorial commemorates the battle that took place here between Thai and Japanese forces in World War II.

Practicalities

Prachuap **train station** (ⓣ032 611175) is on the west edge of town at the western end of Thanon Kong Kiat, which runs east down to the sea and the main pier. The **non-air-con bus station**, for services to Chumphon, Pranburi and Hua Hin, is one block east of the train station and two blocks north, on Thanon Phitak Chat. **Air-con buses** to Hua Hin, Phetchaburi and Bangkok leave from two offices about 100m further south along the same road. There's a small **tourist information** office (daily 8.30am–4.30pm, ⓣ032 611491) at the far northern end of town in a little compound of municipal offices that sits between Thanon Susuek (Sooseuk) and beachfront Thanon Chai Thaleh, about 200m northeast of the non-air-con bus terminal, or 350m from the train station. The **post and telephone office**, directly behind the *Hadthong Hotel* on Thanon Susuek has a couple of Catnet **Internet** terminals upstairs (Mon–Fri 8.30am–4.30pm, Sat & Sun 8.30am–noon), or there's a private Internet place one block west and around the corner on Thanon Sarachip, which keeps longer hours. There's currency exchange on Thanon Kong Kiat, between the train station and the sea, and several ATMs on the main stretch of Thanon Phitak Chat.

The cheapest and most traveller-oriented **place to stay** in town is the friendly *Prachuapsuk Hotel* at 69 Thanon Susuek (ⓣ032 611019, ⓕ032 601711; ❷–❸), where the en-suite rooms are simple but large and come with either fan or air-con. It's 50m south of the post office or about 300m southeast of the train station. If you've got more money to play with it's well worth splashing out on one of the good-value places with a sea view: the cheaper of these is the very clean, well-run *Suksant Hotel*, at 11 Thanon Susuek, but also accessible from the beachfront road (ⓣ032 611145, ⓕ032 601208; ❸), where good fan rooms on the third and fourth floors come with balconies and fine sea views. Nearby *Hadthong Hotel*, at 21 Thanon Susuek, but also with an entrance on the beachfront road (ⓣ032 601050, ⓦwww.hadthong.com; ❺), is a more deluxe variation on the same theme, with bigger balconies, equally nice sea views, air-con and a swimming pool.

Prachuap's famously good seafood is most cheaply sampled at the town's two particularly good **night markets**, one in the town centre, across from the *Inthira Hotel* on Thanon Phitak Chat, and the other in a great location just north of the pier on seafront Thanon Chai Thaleh. Otherwise there are several well-regarded seafood **restaurants** along Thanon Chai Thaleh, including *Pan Pochana*, south of the pier and next to the *Suksant Hotel*, where dishes range from shrimp and crab salads to fried sea asparagus and plenty of squid, and the shady terrace commands a perfect bay view. The dining area at *Sai Tong*, further north along Thanon Chai Thaleh near the tourist information, is less inviting but the food is popular with office-workers at the nearby municipal centre.

Ban Krud

Graced with a tranquil, five-kilometre sweep of white sand, pale-blue sea and swaying casuarinas, **BAN KRUD** (Ban Krut), 70km south of Prachuap, is scenic and quite popular. A dozen or so fairly upmarket bungalow outfits and seafood restaurants line the central stretch of beachfront road, whose northern headland, **Khao Thongchai**, is dominated by the fourteen-metre-high Phra Phut Kitti Sirichai Buddha image and its sparkling modern temple, Wat Phra Mahathat Phraphat. Crowned with nine golden chedis, the temple displays an impressive fusion of traditional and contemporary features, including a series of charming modern stained-glass windows depicting Buddhist stories; reach it via a 1500-metre-long road that spirals up from the beachfront. Other than a visit to the temple and possibly a snorkelling trip to nearby Ko Lamla (B300–450/person), the main pastime in Ban Krud is sitting under the trees and enjoying a long **seafood lunch** or dinner (the casuarinas are lit with fairylights at night).

Most southbound **buses** drop passengers at the Ban Krud junction on Highway 4, from where motorbike taxis cover the twelve kilometres down to the beach. Ban Krud **train** station is about 3km from the beach. *Bann Kruit Youth Hostel* (Ⓣ01 839 6857, Ⓦwww.thailandbeach.com; ❺–❼), north of the Big Buddha headland, about 2.5km from the central area, is one of the best, and priciest, youth hostels in the country, occupying an effectively private chunk of very good beach, and offering air-con, two-person **bungalows** right on the shore, plus a range of other garden-view, fan bungalows and air-con dorms as well. YH members get a B200 discount on two-person bungalows or B50 off a B350 dorm mattress, and there's a swimming pool and bicycle rental. Cheaper and more central is the friendly and clued-up *Sala Thai* (Ⓣ032 695182, Ⓦwww.resortinthai.com; ❺) in the main beach area, whose forty wooden bungalows with air-con and TV are spread under the coconut trees just across the road from the beach; they also rent out B150 two-person tents with mats (or B250 for bigger tents). Another popular option is the German-run *Baanklangaow Beach Resort* (Ⓣ032 695123, Ⓦwww.baan-klang-aow.co.th; ❼), a big compound of 48 wooden chalets set in a mature tropical garden across the road from the sea and located 2km south of the central resort. Facilities here include two swimming pools, a restaurant, Internet access, bicycle rental and the UK-Danish dive outfit Absolut Wreck (Ⓦwww.absolutwreck.com).

Suan Luang

Thirty kilometres south down the coast from Ban Krud, the beach at **SUAN LUANG** is scruffy and has a slight air of abandonment, but for some this is part of its appeal, and there are a couple of pleasant places to stay here. About 750m before you hit the coast, laid-back, traveller-oriented *Suan Luang Resort* (Ⓣ032 691663; ❸–❹) has fourteen fan and air-con bungalows widely spaced around a peaceful garden, a very good restaurant, pool and table-tennis tables, motorbike rental (B200/day), and masses of information on the local area. Down on the beach, tiny *Wharee Bungalows* (no phone; ❷–❸), next to makeshift *Coco Bar*, has just four basic huts with fan and bath, but the biggest outfit here is the French-run mini-resort *Coral Hotel* (Ⓣ032 691667, Ⓦwww.coral-hotel.com; ❼–❽), which offers very good facilities, including a huge pool, sauna, games room and fitness centre, Internet access, two restaurants and a range of spacious rooms and bungalows, all with air-con and TV; full- and half-board packages are also available. *Coral* runs a big programme of day-trips, adventure-sports activities and diving excursions. Access to Suan Luang is by **train** or bus to Bang Saphan Yai, about 7km from Suan Luang; hotels will collect guests on request.

Chumphon and around

South Thailand officially starts at **CHUMPHON**, where the main highway splits into west- and east-coast branches, and inevitably the provincial capital saddles itself with the title "gateway to the south". Most tourists take this tag literally and use the town as nothing more than a transport interchange between the Bangkok train and **boats to Ko Tao** (see p.582), so the relaxed and friendly town is well equipped to serve these passers-through, offering clued-up travel agents, efficient transport links and plenty of Internet cafés. As for reasons to stick around, there are average beaches north and south of town and a few offshore reefs worth diving and snorkelling, but perhaps the most rewarding direction for day-trippers is inland, through Chumphon province's famously abundant fruit orchards.

Arrival, information and transport

Chumphon **train station** (Ⓣ077 511103) is on the northwest edge of town, less than ten minutes' walk from most guest houses and hotels. The centrally located main **bus terminal** (Ⓣ077 502725) on Thanon Tha Tapao is used by all non-air-con buses as well as by most air-con services, including those to and from Bangkok, Phetchaburi, Hua Hin, Ranong, Phuket, Surat Thani and Hat Yai. There are also several private **air-con bus and minibus** services that leave from other parts of town: air-con minibuses to Surat Thani leave from Thanon Komluang Chumphon every half-hour; hourly air-con minibuses to Ranong leave from Thanon Tha Tapao; Chokeanan Tour air-con buses to Bangkok (4 daily; Ⓣ077 511480) leave from just off Thanon Pracha Uthit. Chumphon **Airport** (Ⓣ077 591068), 35km north of town, is served by Air Andaman **flights** to Bangkok (Ⓣ077 591267, Ⓦwww.airandaman.com).

There is a municipal **tourist information** service centre near the post office on Thanon Paramin Manka (Mon–Fri 8.30am–4.30pm, Ⓣ077 511024 ext 120) but the town's league of **travel agents** – most of them conveniently located on Thanon Tha Tapao – are more used to answering independent travellers' questions. As well as flogging Ko Tao boat tickets, they all sell bus, train and air tickets, and many also book accommodation on Ko Phayam, near Ranong off the Andaman coast (see p.649), offer day-trip programmes, and will store luggage free of charge; some also offer free showers and video shows to travellers awaiting onward connections. Long-established agents include Songserm Travel (24hr; Ⓣ077 506205), which lets travellers kip down on the office floor while waiting for the boat; and Infinity Travel (daily 6am–11pm, Ⓣ077 501937) and *Ban's Diving Pub* (daily 8am–10pm, Ⓣ077 570751), both of which have Internet access and a restaurant, and offer free showers and video shows.

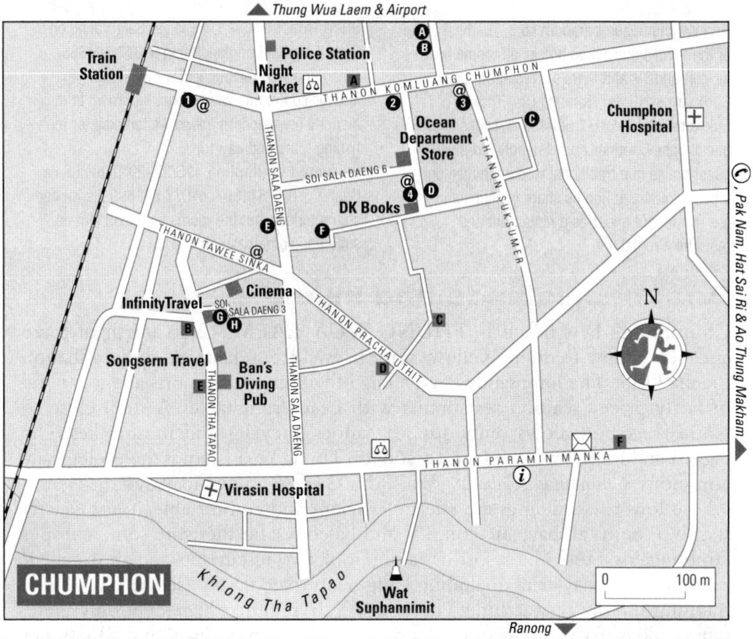

ACCOMMODATION

Infinity Travel Guest House	A
Jansom Chumphon	D
Mayaze's Resthouse	H
New Chumphon Guest House	B
Paradorm Inn	F
Sooksamer Guest House	C
Suda Guest House	G
Suriwong Chumphon	E

RESTAURANTS

Fame	4
Montana	3
Papa	2
Puen Jai	1

BUS TERMINALS

Air-con minibuses to Surat Thani	A
Air-con minibuses to Ranong	B
Chokeanan Tour buses to Bangkok	C
Songthaews to Thung Wua Laem	D
Main Bus Station	E
Songthaews to Pak Nam, Hat Sai Ri & Ao Thung Makham Noi	F

Accommodation

Chumphon's **guest houses** are well used to accommodating Ko Tao-bound travellers, so it's generally no problem to check into a room for half a day before catching the night boat; some guest houses also offer shower services to non-guests for B20–30.

Infinity Travel Check in through their office on Thanon Tha Tapao ☎077 501937. *Infinity* has three rooms above its travel agency office on Thanon Tha Tapao, and another eight rooms in a characterful old wooden house on Soi 1, Thanon Komluang Chumphon. All rooms share bathrooms, and the old house has a nice seating area downstairs plus motorbike rental. ❷

Jansom Chumphon Off Thanon Sala Daeng ☎077 502502, Ⓦwww.sawadee.com/chumphon/jansom. Chumphon's top hotel offers comfortable if rather faded rooms with air-con and TV. ❹–❺

Mayaze's Resthouse Off Thanon Sala Daeng at 111/35 Soi 3 (aka Soi Bangkok Bank) ☎077 504452, Ⓔmayazes@hotmail.com. Small, welcoming guest house with comfortable fan and air-con rooms, all of which share bathrooms. Plenty of local information and free tea and coffee. ❸

New Chumphon Guest House (aka *Miao*) Soi 1, Thanon Komluang Chumphon ☎077 502900. Popular place on a quiet, residential soi with a pleasant outdoor seating area and an interesting programme of treks and day-trips. Rooms all share facilities and the price depends on the size of the room. ❷

Paradorm Inn 180/12 Thanon Paradorm, east off Thanon Sala Daeng ☎077 511598,

Ⓦwww.chumphon-paradorn.com. The best value of the town's mid-range hotels: all rooms have air-con and TV, and there's a restaurant. ④

Sooksamer Guest House 118/4 Thanon Suksumer Soi 8 Ⓣ077 502430, Ⓔsooksamer guesthouse@hotmail.com. Friendly old-style guest house in a traditional wooden house on a peaceful street. Rooms share facilities and are simple but fine. Has a restaurant and motorbike rental. ②

Suda Guest House Off Thanon Sala Daeng on Soi 3 (aka Soi Bangkok Bank) Ⓣ077 504366. Clean and well maintained, with just four fan and air-con rooms with shared bathroom in the owner's own modern house. Motorbikes for rent, fishing tours and day-trips. ②–③

Suriwong Chumphon 125/27–29 Thanon Sala Daeng Ⓣ077 511397, Ⓕ077 502699. Large and characterless, but the rooms are clean and en suite and some have air-con. ③–④

Beaches, islands and inland

Chumphon's best beach is **THUNG WUA LAEM**, 12km north of town and served by frequent yellow songthaews from halfway down Thanon Pracha Uthit. The long sandy stretch has a few bungalow resorts and a handful of fairly pricey seafood restaurants with beachfront tables. A shop close to *Clean Wave* bungalows rents out sea canoes, bicycles and motorbikes. The biggest and most popular **place to stay** on Thung Wua Laem is the ecologically conscious *Chumphon Cabana* (Ⓣ077 560245, Ⓦwww.cabana.co.th; ⑤–⑧), whose low-rise buildings are energy-efficient and comfortable, if not exactly stylish. Rooms all have air-con, TV and balcony, and there are some cheaper fan bungalows too. The resort has a big pool, two restaurants and an excellent programme of day-trips, including Lang Suan river-rafting (see below), squid-trapping and firefly-watching. There's also a **dive centre** (Jan–Sept only) here, which does trips to nearby islands for B1800 per diver and B650 per snorkeller, openwater courses for B11,500 or B13,500 including five nights' accommodation and full board, and live-aboards to Ko Tao (B5900 excl. equipment; 2 days) and Ang Thong (B1115,000 excl. equipment; 3 days). *Chumphon Cabana* runs shuttle buses between the resort and their Chumphon office, which is next to Infinity Travel on Thanon Tha Tapao. Cheaper places to stay include the fan rooms and large air-con bungalows set round a garden

Boats to Ko Tao

There are currently five different **boat services from Chumphon to Ko Tao**. Tickets for all boats are sold by all travel agents and most guest houses in town and the 7am boat tickets all include free transfers from Chumphon to the port area. The fastest service is **Lomlahk Speedboat** (daily at 7am; 1hr 30min; B400; Ⓣ077 558212), which departs from the pier beside *MT Resort* at Ao Thung Makham Noi (see opposite), 25km south of Chumphon, but cannot run in windy weather. Three other fairly fast services also depart at 7am, all of them from Pak Nam port, 14km southeast of Chumphon: **Songserm express** (Jan–Oct only at 7am; 3hr; B400 one-way, B750 return, also does through-tickets to Ko Pha Ngan; Ⓣ077 506205); **Ko Tao Cruiser** (daily at 7am; 2hr 30min; B400; Ⓣ09 587 4107); and **Ekawin Speed Ferry** (daily at 7am; 2hr 30min; B400; Ⓣ077 501821). A Songserm bus meets all the morning trains arriving from Bangkok and takes passengers to their office in town, from where there's onward transport to the ferry at about 6.20am; they will also pick up from guest houses in town. Ko Tao Cruiser and Ekawin also pick up passengers from town-centre guest houses at about 6.20am. The cheapest option is the **slow boat** (daily at midnight; 6hr; B200; Ⓣ077 521615), which departs from the Tha Reua Ko Tao pier (aka the Tha Thai and Seafood pier) in Pak Nam and runs in all but the very worst weather. To get to Tha Reua Ko Tao you'll need to take the taxi-vans offered by guest houses, which leave town at about 10pm and cost B50 per person.

at *Clean Wave* (☎077 560151; ❸–❺), halfway down the beach, while at *New Miao House* you can rent a whole five-person house, or one of the rooms inside it (❷), if you contact *New Chumphon Guest House* in town (see p.581).

About 25km south of town, peaceful, palm-fringed **AO THUNG MAKHAM NOI** is one half of a double bay, with its larger twin, Ao Thung Makham Yai (site of Wat Pong Pang and its cave containing a large Buddha image), visible just over the headland to the south. Waters are calm here, making it a good place to wait out bad weather if you're trying to get to Ko Tao, and there's hardly any development save for *MT Resort*, sometimes known as *Mother Hut* (☎077 558153, Ⓦwww.thaisouth.com/mt; ❸), which is the most appealing and traveller-oriented beach accommodation in the Chumphon area. Just nine simple bamboo huts, all with fan and bath, are set around a beachside garden and restaurant, and room rates include free use of kayaks. There's plenty of local info available, plus motorbike rental, snorkelling trips (B500) and fishing outings. The Lomlahk speedboat pier for the fastest service to Ko Tao (see opposite) is just a few metres from *MT*. To get to Ao Thung Makham Noi from Chumphon, either take one of the songthaews from Thanon Paramin Manka or arrange transport through *Mayaze's Resthouse*.

Nearly all Chumphon's beach hotels offer snorkelling trips to nearby **islands**, and *Chumphon Cabana* on Thung Wua Laem also organizes diving trips. The reefs and underwater caves around **Ko Ngam Yai** and **Ko Ngam Noi**, about 18km offshore, are particularly good for divers, who are likely to see hawksbill turtles, large rays and nudibranchs. More rewarding for snorkellers is the shallower kilometre-long reef at **Ko Lawa**, about half an hour by longtail from Ao Thung Makham Noi.

Though Chumphon province may not be renowned for its beaches and islands, its reputation as a major **fruit-growing** region is well established, and a great way to appreciate this is to head inland for some gentle **rafting on the Lang Suan River** near Pha To. *Chumphon Cabana* on Thung Wua Laem runs good-value day-trips here (B750), or you can do it with your own transport by heading south down Highway 41 for 71km and then continuing west along Highway 4006 for 26km until you reach Pha To. Highway 4006 winds its exceptionally scenic way through endless plantations of trees bearing papayas, mangosteens, durians, bananas, rambutans, pomelos and coconuts, plus the occasional *robusta* coffee field as well (over fifty percent of Thailand's *robusta* coffee crop is grown in Chumphon). At **PHA TO**, about 300m west of the roadside Pha To post office, a left turn takes you into the tiny town centre, where Malin Rafting (☎077 539053), easily spotted from the dozens of life-jackets outside, offers rafting trips, including transport, local lunch at a fruit farm, and a couple of hours' floating down the pretty if not spectacular Lang Suan River, for B470 per person (minimum six people, book the day before). There are plenty of chances to swim in the river, and it's good fun for kids too.

Eating and drinking

One of the liveliest **places to eat** dinner is the huge, open-sided *Papa* on Thanon Komluang Chumphon, which has an extensive menu of fresh seafood priced by weight, plus plenty of Western standards. *Puen Jai*, an upmarket garden restaurant across from the train station, serves pizza, has Internet access, and singing girls in the evening. The much cheaper **night market** sets up along both sides of Thanon Komluang Chumphon and is an enjoyable place to munch your way through a selection of fried noodles, barbecued chicken and sticky, coconut-laced sweets. For live music with your beer, head down to the wood-fronted, country-style pub *Montana*, at the north end of Thanon Suksumer (nightly 6pm–1am). For a decent cup of coffee, try either the coffee stall on the third floor of the Ocean department store, which stocks eight different blends; the similarly well-endowed coffee bar next to *Tha Tapao Hotel*; or the coffee stand inside the *Suriwong Chumphon*. *Fame* (11.30am–7am), at the eastern end of Soi Sala Daeng 6, serves a small but tasty menu of cheap travellers' food.

Listings

Banks and exchange The main banks, with exchange counters and ATMs, are on Thanon Sala Daeng and Thanon Pracha Uthit.

Books DK Books, opposite the *Jansom Chumphon* hotel, has a stand of English-language books upstairs, and sells the *Bangkok Post*.

Emergencies For all emergencies, call the tourist police on the free, 24hr phoneline ☎1155, or contact the Chumphon police station on the north end of Thanon Sala Daeng (☎077 511505).

Hospitals The private Virasin Hospital (☎077 503238–40) is off the southern end of Thanon Tha Tapao, and the government Chumphon Hospital (☎077 503672–4) is on the northeast edge of town.

Internet access Available at lots of places on Thanon Tha Tapao, several places on Thanon Komluang, as well as inside the Freshmart minimarket on Thanon Tawee Sinka (access also through the *Surwiwong Hotel*; daily 7am–midnight) and at *Fame* restaurant, opposite the *Jansom Thara* hotel (daily 11.30am–7am).

Mail The GPO is on the southeastern edge of town, on Thanon Paramin Manka.

Motorbike rental For B150 per day from *Suda Guest House*, *New Chumphon Guest House* and Infinity Travel.

Pharmacy On Thanon Sala Daeng.

Telephones The main CAT overseas phone centre is on the far southeastern edge of town, several hundred metres east of the GPO on Thanon Paramin Manka: any Paramin Manka songthaew will drop you outside. The more central *Fame* restaurant, opposite the *Jansom Thara* hotel, also offers overseas phone and fax services.

Chaiya and around

About 140km south of Chumphon, **CHAIYA** was the capital of southern Thailand under the Srivijayan empire, which fanned out from Sumatra between the eighth and thirteenth centuries. Today there's little to mark the passing of the Srivijayan civilization, but this small, sleepy town has gained new fame as the site of **Wat Suan Mokkh**, a progressively minded temple whose meditation retreats account for the bulk of Chaiya's foreign visitors. Unless you're interested in one of the retreats, the town is best visited on a day-trip, either as a break in the journey south, or as an excursion from Surat Thani.

Chaiya is 3km east of Highway 41, the main road down this section of the Gulf coast: **buses** running between Chumphon and Surat Thani will drop you off on the highway, from where you can catch a motorbike taxi or walk into town; from Surat Thani's Talat Kaset I bus station, hourly local buses take an hour to reach Chaiya. The town also lies on the main Southern Rail Line, though many **trains** from Bangkok arrive in the middle of the night.

The Town

The main sight in Chaiya is **Wat Phra Boromathat** on the western side of town, where the ninth-century chedi – one of very few surviving examples of Srivijayan architecture – is said to contain relics of the Buddha himself. Hidden away behind the viharn in a pretty, red-tiled cloister, the chedi looks like an oversized wedding cake surrounded by an ornamental moat. Its unusual square tiers are spiked with smaller chedis and decorated with gilt, in a style similar to the temples of central Java.

The **National Museum** (Wed–Sun 9am–4pm; B30; Ⓦwww.thailandmuseum.com), on the eastern side of the temple, is a bit of a disappointment. Although the Srivijaya period produced some of Thailand's finest sculpture, much of it discovered at Chaiya, the finest pieces have been carted off to the National Museum in Bangkok. Replicas have been left in their stead, which are shown alongside fragments of some original statues, two intricately worked 2000-year-old bronze drums, found at Chaiya and Ko Samui, and various examples of Thai handicrafts. The best remaining pieces are a calm and elegant sixth- to seventh-century stone image of the Buddha meditating from Wat Phra Boromathat, and an equally serene head of a Buddha image, Ayutthayan-style in pink sandstone, from **Wat Kaeo**, an imposing ninth- or tenth-century brick chedi on the south side of town. Heading towards the centre from Wat Phra Boromathat, you can reach this chedi by taking the first paved road on the right, which brings you first to the restored base of the chedi at Wat Long, and then after 1km to Wat Kaeo, enclosed by a thick ring of trees. Here you can poke around the murky antechambers of the chedi, three of which house images of the Buddha subduing Mara.

Wat Suan Mokkh

The forest temple of **Wat Suan Mokkh** (Garden of Liberation), 6km south of Chaiya on Highway 41, was founded by **Buddhadasa Bhikkhu**, southern Thailand's most revered monk until his death in 1993 at the age of 87. His back-to-basics philosophy, encompassing Christian, Zen and Taoist influences, lives on and continues to draw Thais from all over the country to the temple, as well as hundreds of foreigners. It's not necessary to sign up for one of the wat's retreats to enjoy the temple, however – all buses from Surat Thani to Chaiya and Chumphon pass the wat, so it's easy to drop by for a quiet stroll through the wooded grounds.

The layout of the wat is centred on the Golden Hill: scrambling up between trees and monks' huts, past the cremation site of Buddhadasa Bhikkhu, you'll reach a hushed clearing on top of the hill, which is the temple's holiest meeting-place, a simple open-air platform decorated with images of Buddha and the Wheel of Law. At the base of the hill, the outer walls of the Spiritual Theatre are lined with bas-reliefs, replicas of originals in India, which depict scenes from the life of the Buddha. Inside, every centimetre is covered with colourful didactic painting, executed by resident monks and visitors in a jumble of realistic and surrealistic styles.

Meditation retreats

Meditation retreats are led by Western and Thai teachers over the first ten days of every month at the International Dharma Heritage, a purpose-built compound 1km from the main temple at Wat Suan Mokkh. Large numbers of foreign travellers, both novices and experienced meditators, turn up for the retreats, which are intended as a challenging exercise in mental development – it's not an opportunity to relax and live at low cost for a few days. Conditions imitate the rigorous lifestyle of a *bhikkhu* (monk) as far as possible, each day beginning before dawn with meditation according to the Anapanasati method, which aims to achieve mindfulness by focusing on the breathing process. Although talks are given on Dharma (the doctrines of the Buddha – as interpreted by Buddhadasa Bhikkhu) and meditation technique, most of each day is spent practising Anapanasati in solitude. To aid concentration, participants maintain a rule of silence, broken only by daily chanting sessions, although supervisors are available for individual interviews if there are any questions or problems. Men and women are segregated into separate dormitory blocks and, like monks, are expected to help out with chores.

Each course has space for about one hundred people – turn up at the information desk in Wat Suan Mokkh by 4pm on the last day of the month to enrol. The fee is B1200 per person, which includes two vegetarian meals a day and accommodation in simple cells. Bring a flashlight (or buy one outside the temple gates) and any other supplies you'll need for the ten days – participants are encouraged not to leave the premises during the retreat. For further information, go to Ⓦwww.suanmokkh.org or telephone Ⓣ077 431661–2 or 077 431596–7.

Surat Thani

Uninspiring **SURAT THANI**, 60km south of Chaiya, is generally worth visiting only as the jumping-off point for the Samui archipelago. Strung along the south bank of the Tapi River, with a busy port for rubber and coconuts near the river mouth, the town is experiencing rapid economic growth and paralysing traffic jams. It might be worth a stay, however, when the Chak Phra Festival (see box opposite) is on, or as a base for seeing the near-by historic town of Chaiya.

Practicalities

Buses to Surat Thani arrive at three different locations, two of which are on Thanon Taladmai in the centre of town, at Talat Kaset I on the north side of the road (local buses) and opposite at Talat Kaset II (many long-distance buses, including those from Krabi, Phang Nga, Phuket, Ranong, Nakhon Si

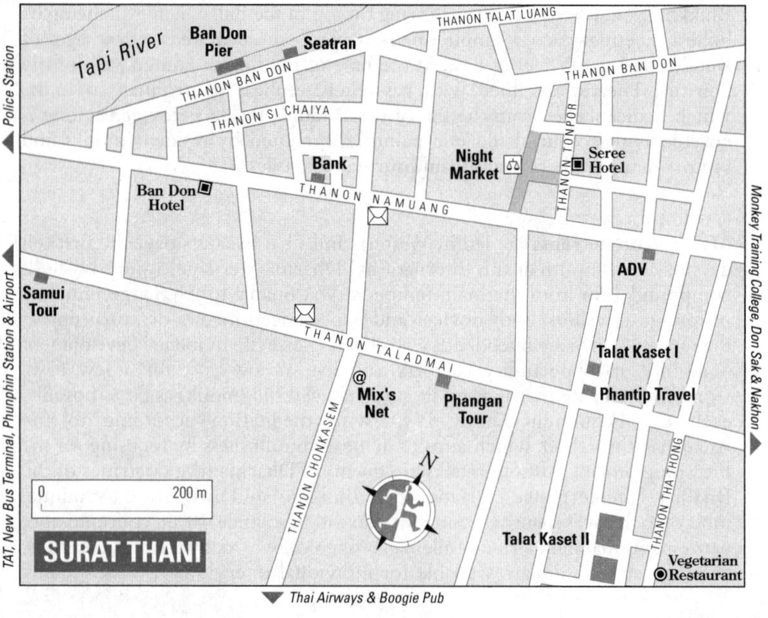

The Chak Phra Festival

At the start of the eleventh lunar month (September or October) the people of Surat Thani celebrate the end of Buddhist Lent with the **Chak Phra Festival** (Pulling the Buddha), which symbolizes the Buddha's return to earth after a monsoon season spent preaching to his mother in heaven. On the Tapi River, tugboats pull the town's principal Buddha image on a raft decorated with huge nagas, while on land sleigh-like floats bearing Buddha images and colourful flags and parasols are hauled across the countryside and through the streets. As the monks have been confined to their monasteries for three months, the end of Lent is also the time to give them generous offerings in the *kathin* ceremony, of which Surat Thani has its own version, called Thot Pha Pa, when the offerings are hung on tree branches planted in front of the houses before dawn. Longboat races, between teams from all over the south, are also held during the festival.

Thammarat and Hat Yai). The new bus terminal, 2km southwest of the centre on the road towards Phunphin, handles mostly services from Bangkok; Talat Kaset II buses going to or from places to the west such as Krabi and Phuket also make a stop here. Arriving by **train** means arriving at **Phunphin**, 13km to the west, from where buses run into Surat Thani every ten minutes between around 6am and 8pm, while share-taxis charge B100 to charter the whole car into town; many buses heading west out of Surat also make a stop at Phunphin station, which might save you a journey into town and out again. It's also possible to buy through-tickets to Ko Samui and Ko Pha Ngan from the train station for the same price as they would be from Surat Thani town, including a connecting bus to the relevant pier. If you're planning to leave by train, booking tickets at Phantip Travel, in front of Talat Kaset I at 293/6–8 Thanon Taladmai (Ⓣ077 272230 or 077 272906), will save an extra trip to Phunphin.

Details of **boats** to **Ko Samui**, **Ko Pha Ngan** and **Ko Tao** are given in the account of each island – see p.591, p.609 and p.622. Phunphin and the bus stations are teeming with touts, with transport waiting to escort you to their employer's boat service to the islands – they're generally reliable, but make sure you don't get talked onto the wrong boat. If you manage to avoid getting hustled, you can buy tickets direct from the boat operators: Seatran, on Thanon Ban Don near the night-boat pier (Ⓣ077 275060–2; Ⓦwww.seatranferry.com), has fast boats to Samui and Pha Ngan and vehicle ferries to Samui (with connecting buses), both sailing from Don Sak, 68km east of Surat; Samui Tour, 326/12 Thanon Taladmai (Ⓣ077 282352), handles buses to Ko Samui via the Raja vehicle ferries from Don Sak; Phangan Tour, also on Thanon Taladmai (Ⓣ077 205799), handles buses to Ko Pha Ngan via the Raja vehicle ferries from Don Sak; tickets for Songserm Express Boats to Samui, Pha Ngan and Tao (and from there to Chumphon) from the pier at Pak Nam Tapi, on the east side of Surat town itself, can be bought at ADV on Thanon Namuang (Ⓣ077 205418–9 or 077 287124). The night boats to Ko Samui, Ko Pha Ngan and Ko Tao line up during the day at Ban Don Pier in the centre of Surat; as they're barely glorified cargo boats, it's worth going along there as early as you can, as the first to buy tickets get the more comfortable upstairs mattresses.

Arriving by **air**, you can take a B70 Phantip minibus for the 27-kilometre journey south from the airport into Surat Thani, or a combination ticket to Ko Samui (B280) or Ko Pha Ngan (B420); if you're flying out of Surat, you can catch the minibus from town to the airport at the Phantip Travel office in front of Talat Kaset I (see above). Budget (ⓣ077 441166) have an outlet at the airport for **car rental**. **Thai Airways** have an office in town at 3/27–28 Thanon Karoonrat, off Thanon Chonkasem (ⓣ077 272610).

If you're coming from points south by **air-conditioned minibus** or **share-taxi**, you should be deposited at the door of your destination. For **moving on**, share-taxis and air-con minibuses tend to congregate around Talat Kaset II. Beware, however, that there have been many reports of **scams** on the private, tourist-oriented minibus and bus services out of Surat, notably those heading for Khao Sok National Park (see p.653): travellers have been obliged to stay at a particular guest house at Khao Sok; or have bought a minibus-and-accommodation "package", which has earned them only blank looks when they arrived at the Khao Sok guest house in question. These and other problems are bad enough that TAT (see below) are now recommending that travellers should catch a public bus bound for Phuket from Talat Kaset II to get to Khao Sok; or if they want to buy a package, should contact TAT for a list of recommended travel agents. Particular problems have also occurred concerning private minibus journeys to Malaysia, with travellers being told that they have to pay a fee for a visa – not needed – or that they have to buy a certain amount of ringgit (at terrible rates of exchange) before entering Malaysia – again not needed. Generally, as in most places in Thailand, you're better off making your own way to the public bus terminal, which, for most journeys from Surat, is bang in the centre of town.

TAT's office at the western end of town at 5 Thanon Taladmai (daily 8.30am–4.30pm; ⓣ077 288817–9, ⓔtatsurat@tat.or.th) covers Surat Thani, Chumphon and Ranong provinces and has an adjacent branch of the **tourist police** (ⓣ1155 or 077 421281). Small **share-songthaews** buzz around town, charging around B10 per person. You can access the **Internet** at Mix's Net on Thanon Chonkasem, just south of Thanon Taladmai.

Accommodation and eating

Most budget **accommodation** in Surat Thani is noisy, grotty and overpriced – you may consider yourself better off on a night boat to one of the islands. If you do get stuck here, head for the recently refurbished *Ban Don Hotel*, above a restaurant at 268/2 Thanon Namuang (ⓣ077 272167; ❷–❸), where most of the very clean rooms with en-suite bathrooms and fans or air-con are set back from the noise of the main road. At similar prices but not as good value, *Seree Hotel*, 2/2–5 Thanon Tonpor (ⓣ077 272279; ❷–❸), is reasonably clean and quiet, with fan and air-con rooms. On the western side of the centre by the TAT office, *Wangtai Hotel*, 1 Thanon Taladmai (ⓣ077 283020–39, ⓔwangtai@loxinfo.co.th; ❻), was for a long time Surat Thani's only luxury option, and is still very good value, with large, smart rooms around a swimming pool and a highly recommended breakfast buffet; challengers include the slightly more modern *Diamond Plaza*, Thanon Sriwichai (ⓣ077 205333–52, ⓦwww.diamondplazahotel.com; ❻), which has a large, attractive pool but is 3km further west of the centre – at least it's handy, if you're driving, for a quick getaway on Highway 41.

For tasty, inexpensive Thai and Chinese **food** in large portions, head for the restaurant on the ground floor of the *Ban Don Hotel*. The night market between Thanon Si Chaiya and Thanon Ban Don displays an eye-catching range of dishes; a smaller offshoot by Ban Don pier offers less choice but is handy if you're taking a night boat. During the day, simple restaurants around Talat Kaset II bus station serve noodles, dim sum and Thai-style fast food, while one block east on Thanon Tha Thong, an unnamed restaurant offers a wide selection of cheap and delicious tray food or fried dishes, mostly vegetarian, though with some fish (look for the yellow flags outside and a sign saying "vegetarian food"; closes 7pm). For more upmarket food, you could do a lot worse than the *Wangtai Hotel*, which at various restaurants and times of the day can offer buffet breakfasts, dim sum and tasty Thai and Western food, with friendly service and fierce air-conditioning. If you're stranded in Surat for the night, your best bet for a **drink** is the *Boogie Pub*, a typical Wild West-style bar with regular live music; it's a ten-minute walk from Thanon Taladmai down Thanon Chonkasem, then take the first left and it's on your left.

Ko Samui

An ever-widening cross-section of visitors, from globetrotting backpackers to suitcase-toting fortnighters, come to southern Thailand just for the beautiful beaches of **KO SAMUI**, 80km from Surat – and at 15km across and down, Samui is generally large enough to cope with this diversity, except during the rush at Christmas and New Year. The paradisal sands and clear blue seas have to a surprising extent kept their good looks, which are enhanced by a thick fringe of palm trees that gives a harvest of three million coconuts each month. However, development behind the beaches – which has brought the islanders far greater prosperity than the crop could ever provide – speeds along in a messy, haphazard fashion with little concern for the environment. A local bye-law limits new construction to the height of a coconut palm (usually about three storeys), but the island's latest hotel complexes bask in the shade of some suspiciously lofty trees, rumoured to have been brought in from northern Thailand.

For most visitors, the days are spent indulging in a few watersports or just lying on the beach waiting for the next drinks' seller, hair-braider or masseur to come along; some even have the energy to make it to one of Samui's many spas, whether independent or attached to one of the posh hotels, for further pampering. For something more active, you should not miss the almost supernatural beauty of the **Ang Thong National Marine Park**, which comprises many of the eighty islands in the Samui archipelago (speedboat day-trips to Ko Tao are also available all over the island, but they cost a lot of money – from around B1300 – for a matter of hours on the island). A day-trip by rented motorbike or car on the fifty-kilometre round-island road will throw up plenty more fine beaches, or you could hook up with a **round-island tour**, such as those organized by Mr Ung's Magical Safari Tours (Ⓣ077 230114 or 01 895 5657, Ⓦwww.ungsafari.com; from B1200), which will at least get you up the rough tracks of the mountainous interior to some spectacular viewpoints. Night-time entertainment is provided by a huge number of beach bars, tawdry bar-beers and clubs, and Samui now plays host to a three-day Caribbean-style carnival once a year in late July – the first event in 2003 was great fun, though it remains to be seen how far it will take off. Buffalo-fighting, once a common sport on the island, is now generally restricted to festivals such as Thai New Year; the practices and rituals are much the same as those of bullfighting in Hat Yai (see p.764).

The island's most appealing beach, **Chaweng**, has seen the heaviest, most crowded development and is now the most expensive place to stay, though it does offer by far the best range of amenities and nightlife. Its imperfect cousin, **Lamai**, lags a little behind in terms of looks and top-end development, but retains large pockets of backpacker bungalow resorts. The other favourite for backpackers is **Maenam**, which though generally less attractive again, is markedly quiet, with plenty of room to breathe between the beach and the round-island road. **Choeng Mon**, set apart in Samui's northeast corner, offers something different again: the small, part-sandy, part-rocky bay is quiet and pretty, the seafront between the handful of upmarket hotels is comparatively undeveloped, and Chaweng's nightlife is within easy striking distance.

Accommodation on the island is generally in bungalow resorts, from the basic, through the comforts of the ever-growing mid-range, to the very swish: at the lower end of the scale, there are very few places left for under B250, but nearly all bottom-end bungalows now have en-suite bathrooms, constant electricity and fans; for the most upmarket places you can pay well over B3000 for the highest international standards. The price codes on the following pages are based on high-season rates, but out of season (roughly April–June, Oct & Nov) dramatic reductions are possible.

No particular **season** is best for coming to Ko Samui. The northeast monsoon blows heaviest in November, but can bring rain at any time between October and January, and sometimes makes the sea on the east coast too choppy for swimming. (The north coast is generally calm enough for swimming all year round.) January is often breezy, March and April are very hot, and between May and October the southwest monsoon blows mildly onto Samui's west coast and causes some rain.

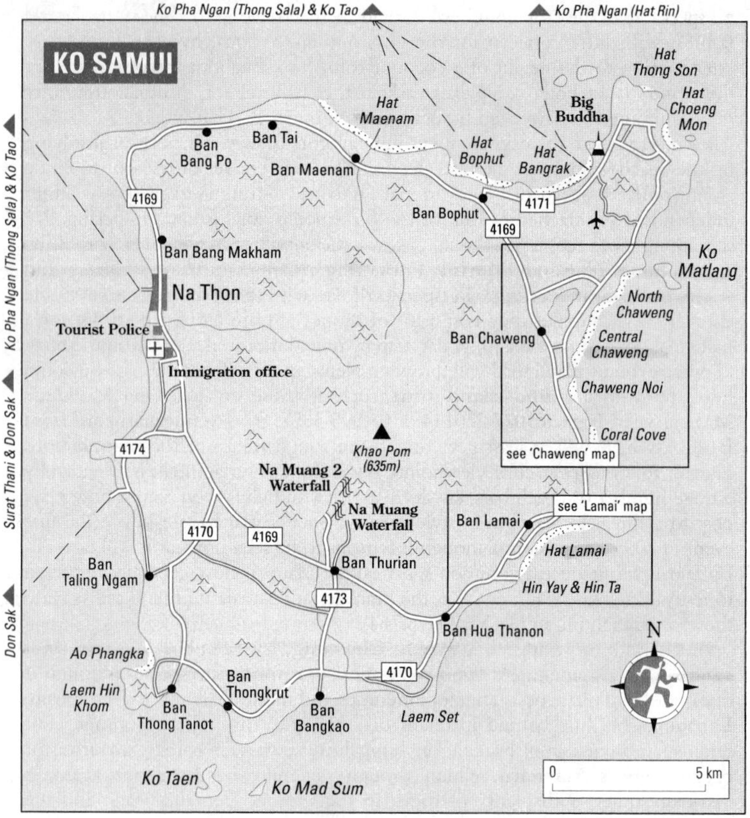

TAT runs a small but helpful office (daily 8.30am–noon & 1–4.30pm; ⓣ077 420504 or 077 420720–2, ⓔtatsamui@tat.or.th), tucked away on an unnamed side road in Na Thon (north of the pier and inland from the post office). Another useful source of **information** is ⓦwww.samui.sawadee.com, a website set up by a German based at Lamai, which handles, among other things, direct bookings at a range of hotels on the island.

Ko Samui has around a dozen **scuba-diving** companies, offering trips for qualified divers and a wide variety of courses throughout the year, and there's a **recompression chamber** at Bangrak (ⓣ077 427427, ⓦwww.sssnetwork.com). Although the coral gardens at the north end of Ang Thong National Marine Park offer good diving between October and April, most trips for experienced divers head for the waters around Ko Tao (see p.622), which contain the best sites in the region; a day's outing costs around B3000, though if you can make your own way to Ko Tao, you'll save money and have more time in the water. The range of courses is comparable to what's on offer at Ko Tao, though prices are generally higher. Established and reliable PADI Five-Star Dive Centres include, each with several branches around the island, Samui International Diving School (ⓦwww.planet-scuba.net), which has its head office at the *Malibu Resort* towards the north end of Central Chaweng (ⓣ077 422386); and Easy Divers (ⓦwww.thaidive.com), which has its head office next to *Sandsea Resort*, towards the north end of Lamai (ⓣ077 231190).

Getting to the island

The most obvious way of getting to Ko Samui is on a boat from the Surat Thani area. Services fluctuate according to demand and extra boats are often laid on in high season, but the longest-established ferry is the night boat that leaves **Ban Don** pier in Surat Thani itself for **Na Thon** – the main port on Samui – at 11pm every night (7hr); tickets (B120) are sold at the pier on the day of departure.

From **Pak Nam Tapi** pier, on the east side of Surat town, one so-called Express Boat a day, handled by Songserm Travel (on Ko Samui ⓣ077 421316–9) runs to Na Thon (2hr 30min; B150 including transport from Surat or Phunphin train station to the pier). Seatran vehicle ferries run every two hours from **Don Sak** pier, 68km east of Surat, to the new pier at Na Thon (1hr 30min; B80, or B150 including air-con bus from Surat or Phunphin; on Ko Samui ⓣ077 426000–2). Twice a day, Seatran's fast boat, the Seatran Express (passengers only), covers the same route in 45 minutes (B200 including air-con bus from Surat or Phunphin). Raja vehicle ferries run hourly between Don Sak and **Thong Yang**, 8km south of Na Thon (1hr 30min; B69; on Samui ⓣ077 415230–3); every two hours to coincide with alternate boats, Samui Tour (see p.587) runs fan or air-con buses from Surat or Phunphin to Don Sak and from Thong Yang to Na Thon, costing B150. Note that the total journey time (from Surat Thani) using the vehicle ferries from Don Sak is much the same as on the Songserm Express Boat from Pak Nam Tapi; only Seatran's fast boat will cut down the total journey time significantly.

From Bangkok, the State Railway does train/bus/boat packages through to Ko Samui that cost a little less than if you organized the parts independently – about B550 if you travel in a second-class bunk. Overnight bus and boat packages from the government-run Southern Terminal cost around B450 air-con, B650 VIP, and are far preferable to some of the cheap deals offered by private companies on Thanon Khao San (around B370), as the vehicles used on these latter services are often substandard and many thefts have been reported.

At the top of the range, you can get to Ko Samui direct **by air** on Bangkok Airways (in Bangkok ⓣ02 265 5555; at Samui airport ⓣ077 245601–8;

Ⓦwww.bangkokair.com); around fifteen flights a day leave Bangkok, and there are even daily flights from Phuket, Krabi, U-Tapao (near Pattaya) and Singapore, with routes from Trat and Kuala Lumpur planned. Air-con minibuses meet incoming flights (and connect with departures) at the **airport** in the northeastern tip of the island, charging B100 to Chaweng for example. As well as bar and restaurant facilities, the quaint, rustic terminal has a reservations desk handling most of the island's moderate and expensive hotels, sometimes with very good discounts on rack rates. There are also currency-exchange facilities and an ATM, a post office with international telephones (daily 8am–noon & 1–7pm), a tourist police booth (Ⓣ1155 or 077 425611) and Budget car rental (Ⓣ077 427188).

For information about boats from Ko Samui to **Ko Pha Ngan** see p.610, and to **Ko Tao** see p.623; all offer the same service in the return direction.

Island transport

Songthaews, which congregate at the car park between the two piers in Na Thon, cover a variety of set routes during the daytime, either heading off clockwise or anti-clockwise on Route 4169, to serve all the beaches; destinations are marked in English and fares for most journeys range from B30 to B50. In the evening, they tend to operate more like taxis and you'll have to negotiate a fare to get them to take you exactly where you want to go. Ko Samui now also sports a handful of **air-con taxis**, whose drivers hang out at the same car park and will ferry you to Chaweng for about B300; you'll also see some **motorbike taxis** buzzing about the island: they charge from B30 for a local drop, up to B150 from Na Thon to Chaweng. You can **rent a motorbike** from B150 in Na Thon, but it's hard to find a decent new bike in the capital, so it's probably safer, and more convenient, to rent at one of the main beaches. Dozens are killed on Samui's roads each year, so proceed with caution, and wear a helmet – apart from any other considerations, you can be landed with an on-the-spot B500 fine by police for not wearing one.

Na Thon

The island capital, **NA THON**, at the top of the long western coast, is a frenetic half-built town which most travellers use only as a service station before hitting the sand: although most of the main beaches now have post offices, currency-exchange facilities, supermarkets, travel agents and clinics, the biggest and best concentration of amenities is to be found here. The town's layout is simple: the two piers come to land at the promenade, Thanon Chonvithi, which is paralleled first by narrow Thanon Ang Thong, then by Thanon Taweeratpakdee, aka Route 4169, the round-island road; the main cross-street is Thanon Na Amphoe, by the more northerly of the piers.

Practicalities

All of Na Thon's supermarkets and department stores are geared up for beachside needs, while some of the **banks** have ATMs, late-night opening and safe-deposit boxes. At the northern end of the promenade, there's a **post office** (Mon–Fri 8.30am–4.30pm, Sat & Sun 9am–noon) with poste-restante and packing services and an international telephone service upstairs, including Catnet **Internet access**, that's open daily from 7am to 10pm. Nathon Book Store, on Thanon Na Amphoe, is the best second-hand English-language **bookshop** in this part of Thailand.

For emergencies, the main police station is on Thanon Taweeratpakdee just north of Thanon Na Amphoe (Ⓣ077 421095), or better still contact the

tourist police (Ⓣ1155 or 077 421281), who are based 1km south of town on Route 4169; private **clinics** operate on Thanon Ang Thong and Thanon Taweeratpakdee, while the recently upgraded state **hospital** (Ⓣ077 421230–2) is 3km south of town off Route 4169. Tourist visas may be extended at the **immigration office**, also south of town, 2km down Route 4169 (Mon–Fri 8.30am–4.30pm; Ⓣ077 421069). Finally, on a more soothing note, the Garden Home Health Center, 2km north along Route 4169 in Ban Bang Makham (Ⓣ077 421311), dispenses some of the best traditional Thai **massages** (B250/hr) on the island, along with herbal saunas (B300), though note that it closes at sunset.

Accommodation and eating

If you really need a **place to stay** in Na Thon, your best bets are the *Nathon Residence* (Ⓣ077 236058; ❹), on Thanon Taweeratpakdee next to Siam City Bank and near the market, a well-run place with a café downstairs and large, plain but spotless tiled rooms with air-con, cable TV and en-suite bathrooms upstairs; and *Jinta Residence* towards the south end of Thanon Chonvithi (Ⓣ077 420630–1, Ⓕ077 420632, Ⓦwww.tapee.com; ❹), with smart, bright bungalows (some with en-suite hot-water bathrooms, air-con and TV) and its own **Internet café**.

Several stalls and small cafés purvey inexpensive Thai **food** around the market on Thanon Taweeratpakdee and on Thanon Chonvithi (including a lively night market by the piers), and there are plenty of Western-orientated places clustered around the piers. Justifiably popular, especially for breakfast, is cheerful and inexpensive *RT (Roung Thong) Bakery*, with one branch opposite the piers and another on Thanon Taweeratpakdee, which supplies bread to bungalows and restaurants around the island and also serves Thai food. For lunch, head for the modern block of shops behind the large Samui Mart department store towards the south end of Thanon Taweeratpakdee: here you can choose between *Zheng Teck*, a neat and simple Chinese-run veggie restaurant, and *Hia Meng (Starfish)*, a popular, well-run café serving duck or pork on rice.

Ang Thong National Marine Park

Even if you don't get your buns off the beach for the rest of your stay, it's worth taking at least a day out to visit the beautiful **ANG THONG NATIONAL MARINE PARK**, a lush, dense group of 42 small islands strewn like dragon's teeth over the deep-blue Gulf of Thailand, 31km west of Samui. Once a haven for pirate junks, then a Royal Thai Navy training base, the islands and their coral reefs, white-sand beaches and virgin rainforest are now preserved under the aegis of the National Parks Department. Erosion of the soft limestone has dug caves and chiselled out fantastic shapes that are variously said to resemble seals, a rhinoceros, a Buddha image and even the temple complex at Angkor.

The surrounding waters are home to dolphins, wary of humans because local fishermen catch them for their meat, and *pla thu* (short-bodied mackerel), part of the national staple diet, which gather in huge numbers between February and April to spawn around the islands. On land, long-tailed macaques, leopard cats, common wild pig, sea otters, squirrels, monitor lizards and pythons are found, as well as dusky langurs, which, because they have no natural enemies here, are unusually friendly and easy to spot. Around forty bird species have had confirmed sightings, including the white-rumped shama, noted for its singing, the brahminy kite, black baza, little heron, Eurasian woodcock, several species of pigeon, kingfisher and wagtail, as well as common and hill mynah; island caves shelter swiftlets, whose homes are stolen for bird's nest soup (see box on p.725).

The largest land mass in the group is **Ko Wua Talab** (Sleeping Cow Island) where the park headquarters shelter in a hollow behind the small beach. From there it's a steep 430-metre climb (about 1hr return; bring walking sandals or shoes) to the island's peak to gawp at the panorama, which is especially fine at sunrise and sunset: in the distance, Ko Samui, Ko Pha Ngan and the mainland; nearer at hand, the jagged edges of the surrounding archipelago; and below the peak, a secret cove on the western side and an almost sheer drop to the clear blue sea to the east. Another climb from the beach at headquarters, only 200m but even harder going (allow 40min return), leads to Tham Buabok, a cave set high in the cliff-face. Some of the stalactites and stalagmites are said to resemble lotuses, hence the cave's appellation, "Waving Lotus". If you're visiting in September, look out for the white, violet-dotted petals of **lady's slipper orchids**, which grow on the rocks and cliffs.

The feature that gives the park the name Ang Thong, meaning "Golden Bowl", and that was the inspiration for the setting of cult bestselling novel, *The Beach*, is a landlocked saltwater lake, 250m in diameter, on **Ko Mae Ko** to the north of Ko Wua Talab. A well-made path (allow 30min return) leads from the beach through natural rock tunnels to the rim of the cliff wall that encircles the lake, affording another stunning view of the archipelago and the shallow, blue-green water far below, which is connected to the sea by a natural underground tunnel.

Practicalities

Apart from chartering your own boat at huge expense, the only way of **getting to Ang Thong** is on an organized day-trip; boats leave Na Thon every day at 8.30am, returning at 5.30pm. In between, there's a two-hour stop to explore Ko Wua Talab (just enough time to visit the viewpoint, the cave and have a quick swim, so don't dally), lunch, some cruising through the archipelago, a visit to the viewpoint over the lake on Ko Mae Ko and a snorkelling stop (snorkel hire is an extra B50). Tickets cost B550 per person (or B650 with pick-up from your accommodation; add on B200 entry to the national park), available from Highway Travel (ⓣ077 421290) by Na Thon pier and through agencies on Samui's main beaches. Similar trips run from Ban Bophut on Ko Samui (contact Air Sea Tour on ⓣ077 422262–3) and from Ko Pha Ngan and Ko Tao, but less frequently; *Seaflower*, at Ao Chaophao on Ko Pha Ngan's west coast, does three-day "treks" (see p.619). Several companies on Samui do speedboat day-trips to Ang Thong: Lom Prayah, based at Maenam (ⓣ077 247401, ⓦwww.lomprayah.com), for example, charge B1800 all-in.

Most of these boats now carry a few desultory kayaks on board, but if you want to make the most of the park's beautiful scenery of strange rock formations and hidden caves, it's best to go to one of the two dedicated **kayaking** operators, Sea Canoe (see p.604) and Blue Stars. The latter is based at Gallery Lafayette near the *Full Circle* nightclub on Chaweng (ⓣ077 413231, ⓦwww.bluestars.info) and has native English speakers as guides. For a one-day trip, taking in the lake at Ko Mae Ko and kayaking and snorkelling among the islands in the northern part of the park, they charge B1990, including all transfers, a light breakfast, buffet lunch, snorkelling gear and national-park entrance fee. A two-day trip, which also comprises camping on a beach at Ko Sam Sao and kayaking to Ko Wua Talab, costs B4750.

If you want to **stay at Ko Wua Talab**, the National Parks Department maintains simple four- to fifteen-berth bungalows (B400–1200) at the headquarters. To book accommodation, contact the Ang Thong National Marine Park Headquarters (ⓣ077 420225 or 077 286025), or the Forestry Department in Bangkok (see p.46). Camping is also possible in certain specified areas: if you bring your own tent, the charge is B50 per night, or two-person tents can be rented for B100 a night. If you do want to stay, you can go over on a boat-trip ticket – it's valid for a return on a later day. For getting around the archipelago from Ko Wua Talab, it's possible to charter a motorboat from the fishermen who live in the park; the best snorkelling is off Ko Thai Plao. The limited canteen at park headquarters is open only during the daytime.

Maenam

The most westerly of the bays on the north coast is **MAENAM**, 13km from Na Thon and Samui's most popular destination for shoestring travellers. The exposed four-kilometre bay is not the island's prettiest, being more of a broad dent in the coastline, and the sloping, white-sand beach is relatively narrow and slightly coarse by Samui's high standards. But Maenam features the lowest rates for bed and board on the island, unspoilt views of fishing boats and Ko Pha Ngan, and good swimming. Despite the recent opening of several upmarket developments on the shoreline and a golf course in the hills behind, this is still the quietest and most laidback of the major beaches, with very little in the way of nightlife – though if you want to go on the razzle, there are late-night songthaews to and from Chaweng and Lamai. The main road is set back far from the beach among the trees, and runs through the sizeable fishing village of **Ban Maenam**, in the centre of the bay, one of the few places on Samui where there's more to life than tourism.

Practicalities

Most visitors to Maenam **eat** in their hotel or resort restaurant, though a few unaffiliated places stand out. At the west end of the bay, signposted on a lane that runs from *Shangrilah* west towards Wat Na Phra Larn and *Home Bay*, *Sunshine Gourmet* is worth hunting down for its warm welcome and keen prices; it does a bit of everything, from cappuccino and home-made yoghurt for all-day breakfast, through own-baked pies, sandwiches and cakes, to international, especially German, main courses, seafood and other Thai dishes. *Gallery Pizza* in Ban Maenam on the pier road (closes 8.30pm; ⓣ077 247420) dishes up delicious, authentic pizza from a wood-fired oven to take away. *Angela's Bakery*, opposite the **police station** on the main through-road to the east of the pier, is a popular, daytime-only expat hangout, offering a wide choice of sandwiches, cakes, pies and salads, plus delicacies such as home-made chocolates and Western meats and cheeses to stock up on. Further east, beyond the access road to *Cleopatra's Palace*, is a **post office** with poste restante, while Triple S, near *Gallery Pizza* on the pier road, provides **Internet access**. For **watersports**, windsurfers are available from *Santiburi Dusit Resort* and *Moonhut*, which also has jet-skis.

Accommodation

As well as one or two upmarket resorts, Maenam has over twenty inexpensive bungalow complexes, most offering a spread of accommodation. There's little to choose between these places, although the best of the bunch are at the far eastern end of the bay.

Cleopatra's Palace At the eastern end of the bay, 1km from the village ⓣ077 425486, ⓔorasa@hotmail.com. A variety of clean wooden and concrete bungalows, all with fans and bathrooms, stand in a slightly cramped compound; the Thai and Western food is recommended. ❸–❹

Friendly About 500m east of *Cleopatra's Palace* ⓣ077 425484. Easy-going place with helpful staff. All the bungalows are very clean and have their own bathrooms, though the place feels exposed, with no trees to provide shade. ❷–❸

Harry's At the far western end, near *Home Bay* ⓣ077 425447, ⓔharrys@samart.co.th. Set back about 150m from the beach amidst a secluded tropical garden complete with swimming pool and waterfall, this place offers clean, spacious en-suite bungalows, with either fan or air-con. ❹–❺

Home Bay At the far western end of Maenam ⓣ077 247214 or 077 247241, ⓕ077 247215. Has a grandiose-looking restaurant overlooking its own large stretch of untidy beach, tucked in beside a small cliff; sleeping options range from small wooden bungalows with mosquito screens, fans and en-suite cold-water bathrooms, through larger concrete affairs with hot water, to beach-side, air-con cottages. ❸–❻

Maenam Resort 500m west of the village, just beyond *Santiburi Dusit Resort* ⓣ & ⓕ077 425116. A moderately priced beachfront resort in tidy grounds, with a clean restaurant. The rooms and large bungalows, with verandas and air-con, offer good-value comfort. ❺–❻

Moonhut Near the village, just east of the pier ⓣ077 425247, ⓦkohsamui.com/moonhut. Quiet, welcoming farang-run place on a large, sandy plot, with colourful, substantial and very clean bungalows; all have verandas, mosquito screens, wall fans and en-suite bathrooms, some have hot water and some have air-con. ❸–❻

Morning Glory Next door to *Friendly* at the eastern end of the bay. Laid-back old-timer (formerly *Rose*) that has resisted the urge to upgrade: basic thatched-roofed wooden huts in a shady compound have mosquito nets and bathrooms but no fans, and the electricity still comes from a generator (lights out 11.30pm). ❷

Naplarn Villa At the far western end, off the access road to *Home Bay* ⓣ077 247047. Good value if you don't mind a 5min walk to the beach: nice welcome, excellent food and clean, quiet, well-furnished, en-suite wooden bungalows with ceiling fans, mosquito screens and verandas, arrayed around a pleasant garden. ❷–❹

Santiburi Dusit Resort 500m west of the village ⓣ077 425031–8, ⓦwww.dusit.com. Luxury hotel in beautifully landscaped grounds spread around a huge freshwater swimming pool and stream. Accommodation is mostly in Thai-style villas, inspired by Rama IV's summer palace at Phetchaburi, each with a large bathroom and separate sitting area, furnished in luxurious traditional design. Facilities include watersports on the private stretch of beach, tennis courts and golf course, a spa, car rental, and an excellent "royal" cuisine restaurant, the *Sala Thai*; also on offer are day-trips and sunset cruises on a 60-year-old wooden sailing boat. ❾

Shangrilah West of *Maenam Resort*, served by the same access road ⓣ077 425189, ⓦwww.geocities.com/pk_shangrilah. A friendly place in a flower-strewn compound that sprawls onto the nicest, widest stretch of sand along Maenam. Accommodation is in a variety of smart, well-maintained en-suite bungalows with verandas, decent furniture and mosquito screens; the cheapest have ceiling fans, the most expensive air-con and hot water. The restaurant serves good Thai food. ❸–❻

SR At the far eastern end of the bay ⓣ077 427529–31. A quiet, welcoming place with a very good restaurant. Accommodation is in decent beachfront bungalows with bathrooms, verandas and chairs. ❸

Bophut

The next bay east along from Maenam is **BOPHUT**, which has a similar look to Maenam but shows a marked difference in atmosphere and facilities. The quiet, two-kilometre beach attracts a mix of young and old travellers, as well as families, and **Ban Bophut** (now sometimes tagged "Fisherman's Village"), at the east end of the bay, is well geared to meet their needs with a bank currency-exchange booth and ATM, several scuba-diving outlets, a small second-hand bookstore, travel agents and supermarkets crammed into its two narrow streets. However, it mostly maintains a sleepy village feel, momentarily jostled when the speedboats to Ko Tao (see p.623) offload and pick up passengers. The part of the beach that stretches from *Peace* to *Zazen* bungalows, at the west end of the bay, is the nicest, but again the sand is slightly coarse by Samui's standards.

Practicalities

Active pursuits are amply catered for, with jet-skis available just to the west of the village, and sailboards, canoes and water-skiing, as well as windsurfing and sailing lessons, offered by former Asian windsurfing champion, Sa-ard Panyawan (Ⓣ01 979 2713), at *Samui Palm Beach Resort*. Samui Go-kart, a **go-karting** track (daily 9am–9pm; Ⓣ077 425097; from B300 for 10min) on the main road 1km west of the village, offers everyone the chance to let off steam without becoming another accident statistic on the roads of Samui.

Besides a branch of *Angela's Bakery* (see p.595), the best **place to eat** in Ban Bophut itself is *Happy Elephant*: service is good, there's an attractive beachside terrace, and a good choice of mostly Thai food, including a few unusual dishes and reasonably priced seafood. At the far western end of the beach on the main road, *Eddy's* is very popular for its delicious, well-presented food that covers all the bases. Among Western dishes, burgers are the speciality, among Thai, it's seafood; there's a two-person set menu in the evenings, a great two-course lunch deal, and breakfast and brunch are excellent value. For party folk, the beach **bar** at *Gecko* hosts DJ sessions every Sunday, and full moon warm-up parties (see p.611) every month, followed by speedboats across to Hat Rin (B400).

Accommodation

There's very little ultra-cheap accommodation left among Bophut's twenty or so resorts. Most establishments are well spaced out along the length of the beach, though a handful of places cluster together on the west side of Ban Bophut.

Cactus Towards the west end of the beach beyond *Samui Palm Beach Resort* Ⓣ077 245565, Ⓔcactusbung@hotmail.com. Welcoming place where ochre cottages with attractive bed platforms, small verandas and well-equipped bathrooms stand in two leafy rows running down to the beach; the cheapest have fans and cold water, the most expensive hot water, air-con and TV. Pool table, Internet access. ❺–❽

Eddy's At the far west end of Bophut back towards Maenam Ⓣ077 245221, Ⓔed_samui@ksc.th.com. Poor location on the main road, but only a 2min walk to the beach and good value for the facilities: large, stylish rooms above a landmark restaurant with verandas, TVs, mini-bars and hot water (some rooms with air-con) and helpful staff; discounts for longer stays and in low season. ❻–❼

The Lodge Towards the western end of the village Ⓣ077 425337, Ⓦwww.apartmentsamui.com/lodge. Apartment-style block with immaculately clean and tastefully decorated modern rooms, all with balconies looking over the water, and boasting air-con, ceiling fan, mini-bar, satellite TV, plus spacious bathrooms with tubs to soak in. There's a waterfront bar downstairs where you can get breakfast. ❼

Peace At the mid-point of the beach Ⓣ077 425357, Ⓦwww.peaceresort.com. This large, well-run, friendly concern has shady and attractive lawned grounds, and being well away from the main road, lives up to its name. Spotless, tasteful bungalows, all with air-con, mini-bars, hot water and verandas, are brightly decorated and thoughtfully equipped. There's a beautiful pool with Jacuzzi and children's pool, a spa, a library, Internet access, and a beachside restaurant serving good Thai and European food. ❽

Samui Palm Beach Resort West of *Peace*, from which it's next door-but-two Ⓣ077 425494 or 077 425495, Ⓦwww.samuipalmbeach.com. Expensive but reasonable value, with frequent large discounts, especially at the airport (it's owned by Bangkok Airways). Cottages are elegant – though some are a little frayed at the edges – with air-con, satellite TV, fridges and hints of southern Thai architecture, and there are two attractive swimming pools in the spacious grounds, as well as a wide range of watersports on offer (see above). ❾

Smile House Across the road from *The Lodge*, at the western end of the village Ⓣ077 425361, Ⓦwww.smilehouse-samui.com. Firmly in the moderate range, *Smile* has a reliable set of chalets grouped around a small, clean swimming pool. At the bottom end of the range you get a clean bathroom, mosquito screens and a fan; at the top, plenty of space, hot water, fridge, TV, breakfast and air-con. ❹–❼

Zazen At the west end of the beach near *Eddy's* Ⓣ077 425085, Ⓦwww.samuizazen.com. Stylish bungalows clustered round a cute pool and lotus pond, furnished with traditional Thai tables, wardrobes and cabinets, as well as satellite TV, DVD and music station, and mini-bar; many sport a tropical-style open-air bathroom with rockery and fountain. Other facilities include a recommended international restaurant, table-tennis, pool table and the like, and Internet access. ❽

Bangrak

Beyond the sharp headland with its sweep of coral reefs lies **BANGRAK**, sometimes called **Big Buddha Beach** after the colossus that gazes sternly down on the sun worshippers from its island in the bay. The beach is no great shakes, especially during the northeast monsoon, when the sea retreats and leaves a slippery mud flat, but Bangrak still manages to attract the watersports crowd. Every Sunday, Bangrak sees the family-friendly **Secret Garden Festival**, with barbecues, drink and live music from 5 to 11pm.

The **Big Buddha** (*Phra Yai*) is certainly big and works hard at being a tourist attraction, but is no beauty. A short causeway at the eastern end of the bay leads across to a messy clump of souvenir shops and foodstalls in front of the temple, catering to day-tripping Thais as well as foreigners. Here you can at least get a decent cup of coffee or tea, or a sandwich at *Big Buddha Coffee*. Ceremonial dragon-steps then bring you up to the covered terrace around the Big Buddha, from where there's a fine view of the sweeping north coast. Look out for the B10 rice-dispensing machine, which allows you symbolically to give alms to the monks at any time of the day.

Bangrak's **bungalows** are squeezed together in a narrow, noisy strip between the road and the shore, underneath the airport flight path. By far the best of a disappointing bunch is *Shambala* (Ⓣ077 425330, Ⓦwww.samui-shambala.com; ④–⑤), a farang-run place that's well spread out in a lush garden; the large, smart bungalows all have verandas, en-suite bathrooms and fans, and some of the newer, beachside ones have hot water. Bangrak also supports one noteworthy **restaurant**, *The Mangrove*, a short way down the airport access road (Ⓣ077 427584; daily from 5.30pm; closed last three days of month), serving pricey but high-quality French-influenced food in a quiet, friendly and informal alternative to big hotel restaurants.

Choeng Mon

After Bangrak comes the high-kicking boot of Samui's northeastern cape, with its small, rocky coves overlooking Ko Pha Ngan and connected by sandy lanes. Songthaews run along the paved road to the largest and most beautiful bay, **CHOENG MON**, whose white sandy beach is lined with casuarina trees that provide shade for the bungalows and upmarket resorts.

Accommodation

The tranquillity and prettiness of Choeng Mon have attracted two of Samui's most expensive hotels and a handful of bungalows and beach restaurants, but on the whole the shoreline is comparatively underdeveloped and laidback.

Boat House Hotel South side of Choeng Mon Ⓣ077 425041–52, Ⓦwww.imperialhotels.com. Run by the reliable Imperial group, *Boat House* is named after the two-storey rice barges that have been converted into suites in the grounds. It also offers luxury rooms in more prosaic modern buildings, often filled by package tours. Beyond the garden pool and the beachside boat-shaped pool, the full gamut of watersports is drawn up on the sands, plus there's a spa and a fitness room. ⑨

Island View Tucked in beside the *Boat House Hotel* Ⓣ077 245031. Smart, good-value chalets with either fan and en-suite cold-water bathroom or air-con, hot water and fridge, in a spacious and lively compound with a supermarket, dive shop and beachfront bar. ④–⑥

Ô Soleil Next door to *PS Villas* Ⓣ & Ⓕ077 425232, Ⓔosoleil@loxinfo.co.th. A lovely, orderly place in a pretty garden, with sturdy, pristine wooden bungalows. The most basic have fans and en-suite bathrooms, while the best have hot water, TV, fridge and air-con. ②–⑦

PS Villas Next door to *White House* Ⓣ077 425160, Ⓕ077 425403. Friendly place in large, beachfront grounds, offering a range of spacious, attractive fan-cooled or air-con bungalows with verandas and mosquito screens. ❹–❼

The Tongsai Bay Cottages and Hotel North side of Choeng Mon ⓣ077 425015–28, ⓦwww.tongsaibay.co.th. The island's finest hotel, an easy-going establishment with the unhurried air of a country club and excellent service. The luxurious hotel rooms, red-tiled cottages and large villas command beautiful views over the spacious, picturesque grounds, the private beach (with plenty of non-motorized watersports), a freshwater and a vast saltwater swimming pool and the whole bay; all of them also sport second bathtubs on their secluded open-air terraces, so you don't miss out on the scenery while splashing about. The hotel's very fine restaurants include *Chef Chom's*, which specializes in improvising Thai dishes from the day's freshest ingredients, and there's a tennis court, a gym and a delightful health spa. ❾

White House Next door to *Choeng Mon Bungalows* ⓣ077 245315–7, ⓕ077 245318. Swiss-managed luxury hotel with narrow beach frontage and correspondingly cramped grounds around a small swimming pool and pretty courtyard garden. What it lacks in space it makes up for in style, with plants and beautiful traditional decor in the common areas and rooms. ❾

Chaweng

For looks alone, none of the other beaches can match **CHAWENG**, with its broad, gently sloping strip of white sand sandwiched between the limpid blue sea and a line of palm trees. Such beauty has not escaped attention of course, which means, on the plus side, that Chaweng can provide just about anything the active beach bum demands, from thumping nightlife to ubiquitous and surprisingly diverse watersports.The negative angle is that the new developments are ever more cramped and expensive, building work behind the palm trees and repairs to the over-commercialized main drag are always in progress – and there's no certainty that it will look lovely when the bulldozers retreat.

The six-kilometre bay is framed between the small island of Ko Matlang at the north end and the 300-metre-high headland above Coral Cove in the south. From **Ko Matlang**, where the waters provide some colourful snorkelling, an often exposed coral reef slices southwest across to the mainland, marking out a shallow lagoon and **North Chaweng**.This S-shaped part of the beach is comparatively peaceful, though it has some ugly pockets of development; at low tide it becomes a wide, inviting playground, and from October to January the reef shelters it from the worst of the northeast winds. South of the reef, the idyllic shoreline of **Central Chaweng** stretches for 2km in a dead-straight line, the ugly, featureless and seemingly endless strip of amenities on the parallel main drag largely concealed behind the treeline and the resorts. Around a low promontory is **Chaweng Noi**, a little curving beach in a rocky bay, which is comparatively quiet in its northern part, away from the road.

South of Chaweng, the road climbs past **Coral Cove**, a tiny, isolated beach of coarse sand hemmed in by high rocks, with some good coral for snorkelling. It's well worth making the trip to the *Beverly Hills Café*, towards the tip of the headland dividing Chaweng from Lamai, for a jaw-dropping view over Chaweng and Choeng Mon to the peaks of Ko Pha Ngan (and for some good, moderately priced food, notably seafood).

Samui Ocean Sports, on the beach in front of the *Chaweng Regent* at the bottom end of North Chaweng (ⓣ01 940 1999, ⓦwww.samui.sawadee.com/watersports), **rents windsurfers** (B400/hr) and **kayaks** (one-person B150/hr; two-person B200/hr), as well as offering **sailing** lessons, trips and charters. For a break from the beach, you could take one of the highly recommended **Thai cookery courses** at the Samui Institute of Thai Culinary Arts (SITCA; ⓣ077 413172, ⓦwww.sitca.net), on Soi Colibri, a small lane at the south end of Central Chaweng opposite the landmark *Central Samui Beach Resort*. A ninety-minute morning class costs B995, two hours in the afternoon B1400, and

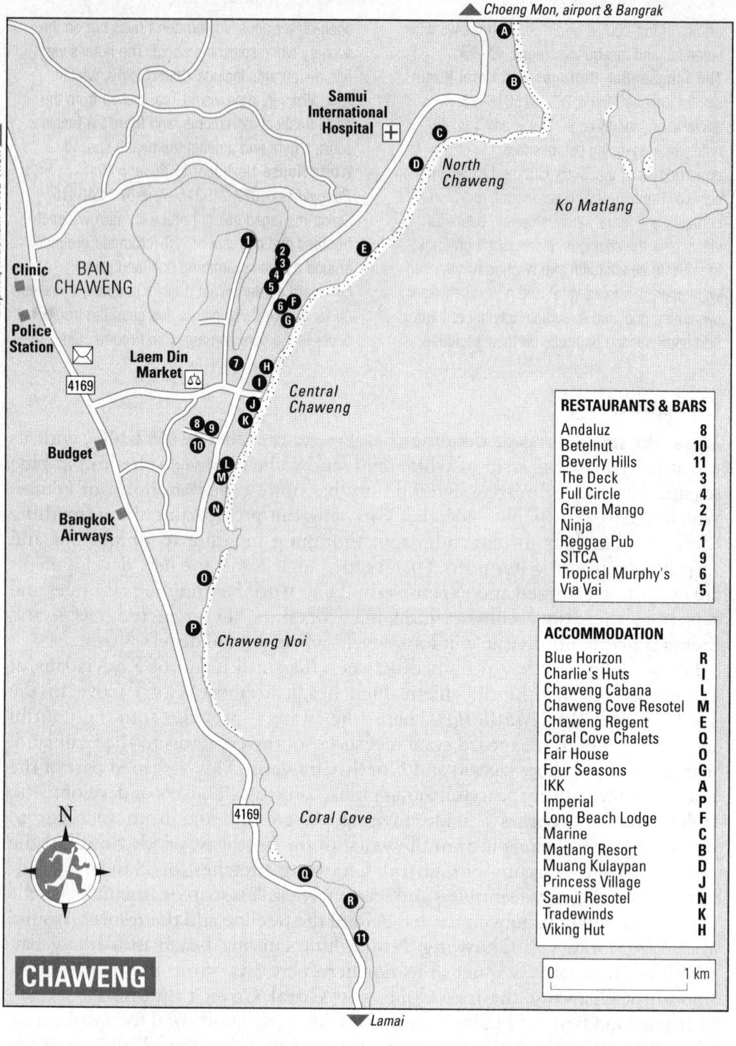

you get to eat what you've cooked with a friend afterwards. They also run fruit- and vegetable-carving courses (2hr/day for 3 days; B2995), and have a culinary shop selling Thai cooking accessories, ingredients and cookbooks, and a fine dining room (see p.603).

Practicalities

Banks with ATMs, **Internet** outlets and **supermarkets** can be found at many locations along the main drag, as can **rental motorbikes** (from B150/day) and **four-wheel drives** (from B800/day); if reliability is your main priority, contact Budget in Ban Chaweng (Ⓣ077 413384, Ⓦwww.budget.co.th; pick-ups from B900 a day). English-run Travel Solutions, at the north end of Central Chaweng Beach near *Samui Mandalay Resort* (Ⓣ077 230203,

Ⓦwww.travelsolutions.co.th), is a reliable and knowledgeable all-round **travel agent**, offering worldwide air-ticketing, Thai train tickets and local services. Several small **clinics** on the main drag cater specifically to tourists, while the private Samui International **hospital** on North Chaweng (Ⓣ077 230781–2, Ⓦwww.sih.co.th) provides, among other things, 24-hour emergency services, house calls and a dental clinic. Boots has a **pharmacy** in the middle of Central Chaweng, just up the road from *Tropical Murphy's* pub, which is flanked on its other side by Bookazine, selling English-language **books**, newspapers and magazines. There's a **tourist police** booth (Ⓣ1155) to the north of here, just up the road from *Chawengburi Resort* in the heart of Central Chaweng. To the south, on Soi Colibri opposite *Betelnut* restaurant, Bubbles (Ⓣ077 230715) is a dependable, English-run **laundry**.

The original village of **Ban Chaweng**, 1km inland of Central Chaweng beach on the round-island road, has a **police station**, a **post office** with poste-restante and packing service, and a branch of Bangkok Airways (Ⓣ077 422512–9).

Accommodation

Over fifty **bungalow resorts** and **hotels** at Chaweng are squeezed into thin strips running back from the beachfront at right angles. In the ever-diminishing inexpensive and moderate range, prices are generally over the odds; as well as being reasonably quiet, North Chaweng is probably the best hunting ground in this range. More and more expensive places are sprouting up all the time, offering sumptuous accommodation at top-whack prices.

Inexpensive to moderate

Blue Horizon Above Coral Cove Ⓣ077 422426, Ⓔbluehorizon@samuitourism.com. One of several resorts clinging to the steep hillside, this is a friendly, well-ordered place, where some of the sturdy, balconied bungalows have air-con and hot water. ❻

Charlie's Huts In the heart of Central Chaweng Ⓣ077 422343 or 077 230285. Some of the cheapest accommodation options left on Chaweng are the wooden huts with shared bathrooms, mosquito nets and fans in *Charlie's* grassy compound; en-suite and air-con bungalows also available here and in the slightly shadier grounds of the now-incorporated *Viking Huts* next door, but no hot water in any of them. ❷–❺

Chaweng Cove Resotel South end of Central Chaweng Ⓣ077 422509–10, Ⓦwww.samuiresotel.com. Welcoming, reliable place that offers all the mod cons (air-con, hot water, mini-bar, TV), though little character, at reasonable prices. At the back towards the road, hotel rooms with balconies; towards the beach, a good-sized pool and tightly packed wooden bungalows with thatched roofs and verandas. ❻–❽

Four Seasons At the top end of Central Chaweng Ⓣ077 422238, Ⓕ077 422411. Secluded among dense trees in what used to be *Dew Drop Huts*, large, wooden bungalows on high stilts with verandas, mosquito screens, ceiling fans and en-suite bathrooms, now joined by some upgraded pads with hot water, air-con and fridges on the beach; there are also plans to build a spa here. ❹–❽

IKK Around the point at the far north end of North Chaweng Ⓣ077 413281, Ⓦwww.ikksamui.com. Comfortable bungalows with fans and en-suite, cold-water bathrooms in an immaculately kept flower garden, giving onto a broad, shady and peaceful stretch of sand. ❹

Long Beach Lodge Towards the north end of Central Chaweng Ⓣ & Ⓕ077 422372. An unusually spacious and shady sandy compound. All the orderly, clean bungalows are a decent size and have fans and en-suite bathrooms; the larger, more expensive ones have hot water, fridge, TV and air-con. ❺–❽

Marine Towards the north end of North Chaweng Ⓣ077 422416. Plenty of variety and value here, with small but cheap en-suite, fan-cooled bungalows as well as reasonably priced air-con ones. They've also taken over an old favourite, *Lazy Wave*, next door: the large, attractive wooden bungalows are showing their age a bit, but have fridges, hot water, big beds and verandas, on a spacious, tree-clad slope. ❸–❺

Matlang Resort At the far north end of North Chaweng Ⓣ077 230468–9, Ⓔmatlang@loxinfo.co.th. A decent fallback: the en-suite wooden bungalows, all with verandas and mosquito screens, some with air-con, are a little bit battered, but are scattered around a very pleasant, shady flower garden facing a broad stretch of beach. ❹–❻

Samui Resotel (Munchies) At the south end of Central Chaweng ⓣ077 422374, ⓦwww.samuiresotel.com. Under the same ownership as *Chaweng Cove Resotel*, with a similar concept of no-frills luxury, but marginally cheaper and with a smaller pool. All rooms with hot water, air-con, mini-bar and TV: choose between hotel rooms at the back by the road, and squat chalets increasing in price towards the beach. ❻–❽

Expensive

Chaweng Cabana South end of Central Chaweng ⓣ077 422377, ⓦwww.chawengcabana.com. Reliable, well-run option, popular with families, with a smallish swimming pool; tightly packed bungalows in a lush garden with bland but tasteful decor, come with air-con, hot water, cable TV and fridge. ❽

Chaweng Regent At the bottom end of North Chaweng ⓣ077 422389–90, ⓦwww.chawengregent.com. Elegant bungalows and rooms with all mod cons around lotus ponds, two pools, a fitness centre, sauna and spa, though conditions are a little cramped. ❾

Coral Cove Chalets Above Coral Cove ⓣ077 422260–1, ⓦwww.coralcovechalet.com. Especially good-value and stylish place with bright, tasteful bungalows and rooms, each with air-con, balcony, TV and mini-bar, grouped around an attractive pool and Jacuzzi. ❽

Fair House North end of Chaweng Noi ⓣ077 422255–6, ⓕ077 422373. A great location on a lovely stretch of beach, with extensive, lush gardens and two pools. The colourfully decorated bungalows are preferable to the large hotel rooms, which have good facilities but lack style. Towards the lower end of this price bracket. ❾

Imperial On a small rise above Chaweng Noi ⓣ077 422020–36, ⓦwww.imperialhotels.com. The longest-established luxury hotel on Samui is a grand but lively establishment with a Mediterranean feel, set in sloping, landscaped gardens; features include two pools (one sea water, one fresh with a Jacuzzi), a spa, tennis court, Thai cookery classes and all kinds of watersports. ❾

Muang Kulaypan North Chaweng ⓣ077 230036, ⓦwww.kulaypan.com. Original, stylish boutique hotel arrayed around a large, immaculate garden with a black-tiled swimming pool and an excellent beachside restaurant (see below). Rooms – each with their own private balcony or garden – combine contemporary design with traditional Thai-style comforts. Towards the lower end of this price bracket. ❾

Princess Village Central Chaweng ⓣ077 422216, ⓦwww.samuidreamholiday.com. Traditional Ayutthaya-style houses on stilts set in plenty of space around beautiful lotus ponds. Decorated with carved wooden panels and traditional silk and cotton fabrics, blended stylishly with the Western-style bathrooms, mini-bars and air-con. ❾

Tradewinds Next door to *Princess Village*, Central Chaweng ⓣ077 230602–4, ⓦwww.tradewinds-samui.com. A cheerful, well-run place of characterful bungalows (all with air-con, hot water, mini-bar and balcony) with plenty of room to breathe in colourful tropical gardens. The resort specializes in sailing, with its own catamarans (instruction available), as well as offering kayaks and croquet. ❽

Eating

Chaweng offers all manner of foreign **cuisines**, from Italian to Korean, much of it of dubious quality. Amongst all this, it's quite hard to find good, reasonably priced Thai food – setting aside the places recommended below, it would be worth exploring the cheap and cheerful night-time food stalls at Laem Din market, which are popular with local workers, on the middle road between Central Chaweng and Highway 4169.

Andaluz Soi Colibri, Central Chaweng. Small, elegant tapas bar under the same ownership as *Betelnut* opposite. Sangria and lots of irresistible offerings, such as beautifully presented paella and delicious Andalucian sausages fried with apples. Expensive.

Betelnut Soi Colibri, a small lane at the south end of Central Chaweng opposite the landmark *Central Samui Beach Resort* ⓣ077 413370. By far Samui's best restaurant, serving exceptional Californian-Thai fusion food, with prices to match. Few tables, so reservations highly recommended. Expensive.

Budsaba Restaurant At the *Muang Kulaypan Hotel* ⓣ077 230036. This charming beachfront restaurant fully justifies the journey up to North Chaweng: you get to recline in your own seaside *sala* or open-sided hut on stilts while tucking into unusual and excellent Thai dishes such as banana-flower and shrimp salad. Expensive.

The Deck Central Chaweng, just north of the *Full Circle* club. Good, reasonably priced all-rounder where you're bound to find something to satisfy from the wide-roaming menu: Western and Thai main courses with good vegetarian and vegan options, hearty baguettes, very good espresso coffees, and various set menus (all-day breakfast, early-bird, five-dish Thai meal). Moderate.

The Dining Room at SITCA Soi Colibri, Central Chaweng ☎077 413172. Some of the best Thai food on Samui, at very reasonable prices, above the renowned cookery school (see above). Try the pomelo salad with peanuts, dried shrimp and giant prawns or the deep-fried fish in red curry. All dishes can be spiced to order, there's an unusually wide range of Thai desserts to leave room for, and appetizers and sweetmeats with green tea are free. Evenings only. Moderate to expensive.

Ninja Near *Charlie's Huts* on Central Chaweng. Popular, well-run, very basic restaurant, serving simple Thai faves such as *tom yam*, *som tam* and *phat thai*, as well as crepes, breakfasts and other Western food. Open 24hr. Inexpensive.

Via Vai Near *Swensen's*, Central Chaweng. Two Neapolitan brothers have built an authentic wood-fired brick oven here to produce great thin-crust pizzas such as Delicata with asparagus and blue cheese. The pasta menu includes several home-made varieties and sauces such as smoked salmon and mascarpone, and there are twenty varieties of home-made ice cream to look forward to. Moderate to expensive.

Drinking and nightlife

Avoiding the raucous bar-beers and English theme pubs on the main through road, the best place to **drink** is on the beach: at night dozens of resorts and dedicated bars lay out small tables and candles on the sand, especially towards the north end of Central Chaweng and on North Chaweng. One theme pub is worth singling out: with draught Guinness and Kilkenny, big-screen sports, quiz nights and decent food, Irish-run *Tropical Murphy's*, on the main drag opposite McDonald's, has turned itself into a popular landmark and meeting place.

Bang in the heart of Central Chaweng but set well back from the beach, *The Reggae Pub* is Chaweng's oldest **nightclub**, a venerable Samui institution with a memorabilia shop to prove it. It does time now as an unpretentious, good-time, party venue, with plenty of drinking games, but shows its roots with a rasta party on Wednesday and a dancehall party on Saturday. Chaweng's other long-standing dance venue, *Green Mango* at the north end of Central Chaweng, occupies a similarly huge shed combining an industrial look with that of a tropical greenhouse, complete with fountain, fairylights and ornamental garden. The title of Samui's best club, however, goes to *Full Circle*, a hip, stylish place done out in minimalist metal with splashes of primary colours, which pulls in local and foreign DJs to play everything from acid jazz to garage; it's set amid a forest of bar-beers on North Chaweng (look out for flyers or ask about regular beach parties the club hosts at Rocky Bay or Ko Som on the island's northeastern cape).

Lamai

Samui's nightlife is most tawdry at **LAMAI** (though Chaweng is fast catching up): planeloads of European tourists are kept happy here at women's Thai boxing and mud-wrestling shows and dozens of open-air hostess bars, sinking buckets of booze while slumped in front of music videos. The action is concentrated into a farang toytown of bars and Western restaurants that has grown up behind the centre of the beach, interspersed with supermarkets, clinics, banks, ATMs, dive shops and travel agents. Running roughly north to south for 4km, the white palm-fringed beach itself is, fortunately, still a picture, and generally quieter than Chaweng, with far less in the way of watersports and a lighter concentration of development – it's quite easy to avoid the boozy mayhem by staying at the peaceful extremities of the bay, where the backpackers' resorts have a definite edge over Chaweng's. At the northern end, the spur of land that hooks eastward into the sea is perhaps the prettiest spot, though it's beginning to attract some upmarket development: it has more rocks than sand, but the shallow sea behind the coral reef is protected from the high seas of November, December and January.

The original village of **Ban Lamai**, set well back at the northern end, remains surprisingly aloof, and its wat contains a small museum of ceramics, agricultural tools and other everyday objects. Most visitors get more of a buzz from **Hin Yay** (Grandmother Rock) and **Hin Ta** (Grandfather Rock), small rock formations on the bay's southern promontory, which never fail to raise a giggle with their resemblance to the male and female sexual organs. To cool off, you might want to head for Sea Canoe (ⓣ077 230484 or 01 893 1220, ⓦwww.samuiseacanoe.com), on Highway 4169 opposite *Weekender Villa*, who run **kayaking trips**, primarily to Ang Thong National Marine Park (see

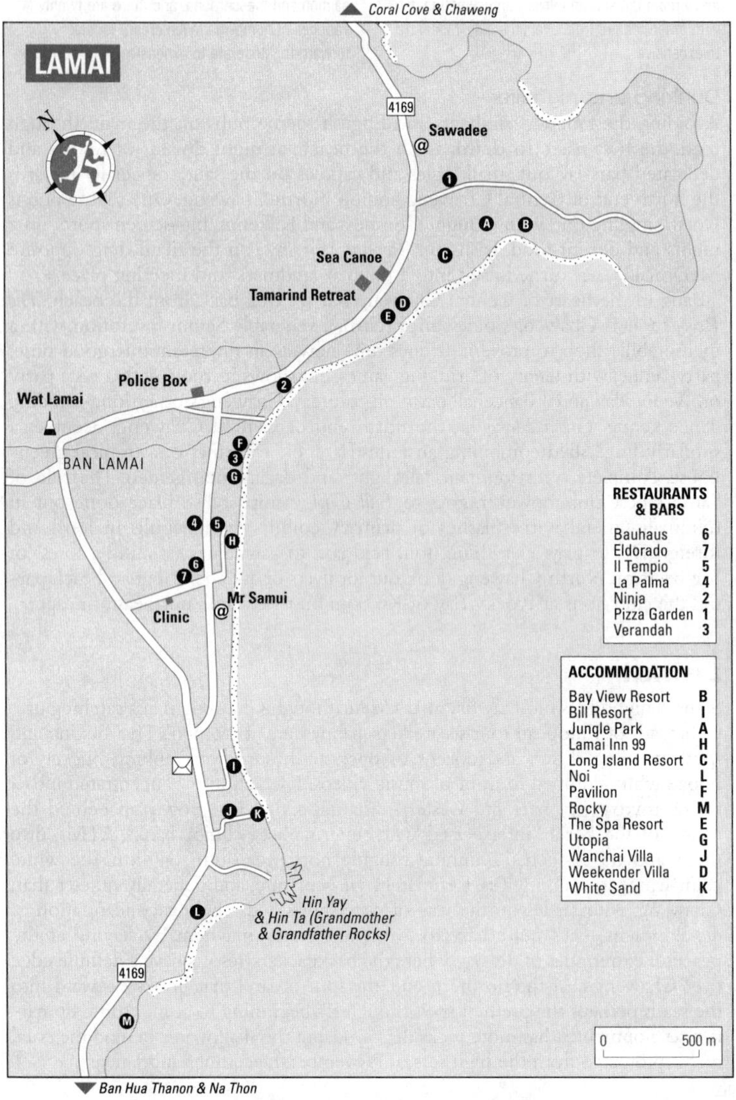

p.593). Small-group day-trips with knowledgeable guides, taking in Ko Wua Talab and Ko Mae Ko, a seafood lunch and snorkelling, cost B2300, while overnights, either camping or staying in national park bungalows, go for B5500. They also organize paddles around Ko Taen and Ko Mad Sum, islands off Samui's south coast, for B1500 including lunch and snorkelling (minimum 4 people), and offer two-person **kayak rental** (B150/hr).

Lamai boasts two of Samui's longer-standing and better **spas**. The oldest, *The Spa Resort* (see p.606) at the far north end of the beach, now covers everything from Thai massage (B250/hour) and herbal saunas (B250/hour) to rejuvenating cleansing and fasting programmes (US$260/week). Also on offer are a wide range of other massages, facials, body wraps, reflexology and yoga and meditation sessions. In similar vein, but much more upmarket, is Tamarind Retreat (Ⓣ077 230571 or 077 424436, Ⓦwww.tamarindretreat.com), set in a beautiful, secluded coconut grove just north of *Spa Resort* off the main road; here a herbal sauna and two-hour Thai massage, for example, costs B1900. Other massages, such as head, foot and face, are also available, activities include yoga and t'ai chi classes, and there are luxury villas on the site to rent.

Practicalities

Several places on the main beachside drag offer **rental motorbikes** (from B150/day) and **four-wheel drives** (from B800/day). A couple of **Internet cafés**, among dozens of options on Lamai, stand out. *Mr Samui's* art gallery and café, just south of the central crossroads, is a congenial choice offering good espresso coffee, or you could head for the unmissable, shiny headquarters of Sawadee.com at the north end of the bay, which contains a smart, new Internet café. There's a **police box** in Ban Lamai, and the **post office**, with poste restante, is on the way out south on Highway 4169.

Accommodation

Lamai's **accommodation** is generally less cramped and slightly better value than Chaweng's, though it presents far fewer choices at the top end of the market. The far southern end of the bay towards the Grandparent Rocks has the tightest concentration of budget bungalows.

Bay View Resort On the bay's northern headland Ⓣ & Ⓕ077 418429, Ⓦwww.bayviewsamui.com. Neat, stylish bungalows with verandas and en-suite hot-water bathrooms in an extensive, flower-bedecked compound; the poshest come with air-con, mini-bar and cable TV. Offers a friendly welcome and great sunset views of the beach from the attractive restaurant. ❺–❽

Bill Resort At the far southern end of the bay Ⓣ077 424403, Ⓔbillresort@hotmail.com. An efficient and orderly setup, crammed into a fragrant, overgrown garden on a rocky stretch of beach and up the hill behind; clean rooms and bungalows with en-suite hot-water bathrooms, mini-bars and verandas, most with air-con. ❹–❼

Jungle Park On the bay's northern headland Ⓣ077 418034–7, Ⓦwww.jungle-park.com. Next door to *Bay View Resort*. Lives up to its name with spacious grounds full of shady trees. Notable here are the large swimming pool and the attractive bar-restaurant sandwiched between it and the beach. All the reliable, well-maintained rooms and bungalows have air-con, mini-bar and hot water; more expensive bungalows are beachfront and have TVs. ❼–❾

Lamai Inn 99 On the beach near the tourist village's main crossroads Ⓣ077 424427, Ⓦwww.kohsamui.net/lamaiinn. Surprisingly roomy for its central location, and offering a variety of bungalow styles and sizes, some with hot water, air-con, fridge and TV. If you want to be near the throbbing heart of Lamai's nightlife, this is your place. ❹–❻

Long Island Resort At the far north end of the beach Ⓣ077 424202 or 077 418456, Ⓦwww.sawadee.com/samui/longisland. A self-styled "boutique resort" with elegant but cosy bungalows (all with hot water, the cheapest with fans, the priciest with air-con, cable TV and mini-bars), an attractive pool, a spa offering massages, steam and various other treatments, a fitness room, a good Thai and Western restaurant and beds in the bar so you can kick back and enjoy the view. ❺–❾

Noi Just beyond the headland, at the far southern end of the bay ⓣ077 424562, ⓔgaborwan@hotmail.com. The compound is small and cramped, but it's tidy and well run, right on the beach and with a friendly and mellow atmosphere. Clean bungalows run from shared bathrooms to air-con with en-suite hot water. ❷–❺

Pavilion On the central stretch of Lamai, north of the crossroads ⓣ077 232083–7, ⓦwww.pavilionsamui.com. Lamai's best upmarket choice, just far enough from the pubs and clubs to get some peace; the atmosphere is friendly and lively, and there's a spa and a good beachside pool and restaurant. Most of the accommodation is in attractive, contemporary Thai-style rooms, but if your purse will stretch that far, go for one of the spa junior suites, each boasting a private courtyard with Jacuzzi and day bed. ❽–❾

Rocky Beyond the headland, at the far southern end of the bay ⓣ077 418367, ⓦwww.rockyresort.net. Squeezes as much as it can into its beachside strip: a small swimming pool, a restaurant and a wide choice of rooms and bungalows, all with bathrooms, some with hot water and air-con. ❺–❾

The Spa Resort At the far north end of the beach next to *Weekender Villa* ⓣ077 230855, ⓦwww.spasamui.com. A wide variety of cosy, well-constructed rooms – the cheapest with fan, mosquito net and en-suite cold-water bathroom the priciest with air-con, hot water and mini-bar – though they're often full with people being rejuvenated (see p.605); delicious veggie and non-veggie food. A generally more upmarket branch, *Village Spa*, has opened in the hills above Lamai, linked by regular shuttle buses with *Spa Resort*. There's a swimming pool and fine views up here, and all bungalows have hot water, TV and fridge, and some have air-con. ❸–❾

Utopia On the central stretch of Lamai, north of the crossroads ⓣ077 233113, ⓔjim_utopia@hotmail.com. Good-value, welcoming place on a narrow strip of land teeming with flowers. The cheapest bungalows have mosquito screens, fans and en-suite bathrooms, while those at the top of the price range boast air-con, hot water, TV and fridge. Good coffee and breakfasts, and plenty of free beach equipment. ❹–❼

Wanchai Villa On the access road to *White Sand*, at the far southern end of the bay ⓣ077 424296, ⓔwanchai_villa@hotmail.com. Quiet, spacious, family-run operation set back from the beach, offering a range of very clean, simple bungalows with fans and verandas (some with en-suite bathrooms) among the palm trees, and excellent, cheap food; grand, air-con bungalows were being added at the time of writing. ❷–❸

Weekender Villa Between the main road and the beach to the east of Ban Lamai ⓣ077 424116, ⓔweekendervilla@samui2002.com. Despite its location, this very well-maintained, German-run establishment is quiet enough; the staff are friendly and the large, en-suite wooden bungalows (some with hot water) shelter under the coconut trees in a smart, spacious compound. The attractive beachside bar-restaurant sports a pool table, satellite TV and nice touches like check tablecloths. ❹–❺

White Sand At the far southern end of the bay ⓣ077 424298. Long-established and laid-back budget place with around two dozen simple beachside huts, some en suite, which attract plenty of long-term travellers. ❶–❷

Eating and drinking

There are far fewer eating options on Lamai than on Chaweng to tempt you away from your guest-house kitchen. Besides the **restaurants** recommended below, you could try any one of several decent Italian places, such as *Il Tempio* and *La Palma*, a short way north of the tourist village's main crossroads. Lamai's **nightlife** is all within spitting distance of the central crossroads and even less inspiring. Apart from the hostess bars, *Bauhaus* is the main draw, a barn-like entertainment complex with pool, big screens showing satellite sport and a dance floor (foam parties Fridays), as well as a bistro, souvenir shop and travel agent.

Eldorado Just west of the central crossroads. Highly recommended, good-value Swedish restaurant, serving a few Thai favourites, baguettes, salads, steaks and other international main courses, plus one or two indigenous specialities such as herring plate. Cheap draught Carlsberg; all-you-can-eat barbecue Wed. Moderate to expensive.

Ninja On Highway 4169, east of Ban Lamai. A branch of Chaweng's backpacker hotspot, a dependable, simple café serving basic Thai favourites, as well as crepes and other Western food. Inexpensive.

Pizza Garden Northern end of the bay, on the headland above *Jungle Park*. To work up an appetite, walk out to this Austrian-run restaurant (evenings only), which bakes great pizzas, as well as serving up good pastas and Viennese iced coffee. Moderate.

The Spa Resort At the far north end of the beach. Excellent, casual beachside restaurant, serving a huge range of Thai and Western (including Mexican) dishes. The vegetarian "ginger nuts" stir-fry is excellent, omelettes and salads are specialities, but there are also plenty of meat and marine offerings. A long menu of juices, smoothies and tonics includes a delicious lime juice with honey. Moderate.

Verandah At *Mui Bungalows*, a few hundred metres north of the central crossroads. Reliable, German-run place, which serves excellent, well-presented international and Thai food. Moderate to expensive.

The south and west coasts

Lacking the long, attractive beaches of the more famous resorts, the **south and west coasts** rely on a few charming, isolated spots with peaceful accommodation, which can usually only be reached by renting a motorbike or four-wheel drive. Heading south from Lamai, you come first to the Muslim fishing village at **Ban Hua Thanon** and then, about a kilometre or so south and well signposted off Route 4170, the spacious gardens of *Samui Marina Cottage* (ⓣ077 233394–6, ⓦwww.samuimarina.com; ❻), a well-run, welcoming place with a large swimming pool and air-con, hot water, satellite TV and mini-bar in all the bungalows. A couple of kilometres further down the coast, and also well signposted off Route 4170, is one of the island's most secluded hotels: originally founded as a private club on a quiet south-facing promontory, the *Laem Set Inn* (ⓣ077 424393, ⓦwww.laemset.com; ❾) offers a wide range of elegant rooms and suites – some of them reassembled village houses – as well as an excellent restaurant, cookery courses, a spa, plenty of watersports and a scenically positioned swimming pool. The access road to the *Laem Set Inn* takes you past the nearby **Samui Butterfly Garden** (daily 8.30am–5pm; B150, children B80), opposite *Central Samui Village*, where you can wander the hillside overlooking the sea surrounded by dozens of brilliantly coloured lepidopterans.

The gentle but unspectacular coast beyond is lined with a good reef for snorkelling, which can be explored most easily from the fishing village of **Ban Bangkao**. On the west side of the village, the Sundowner Horseranch (ⓣ077 420145 or 06 092 0351) offers **horse-riding** through the jungle and along the beach from B1200 for two hours. Snorkellers rave about the coral around **Ko Taen**, a short way offshore to the south: an all-day tour from, for example, TK Tour (ⓣ077 423258) in the next village to the west, **Ban Thongkrut**, including pick-up from your accommodation, snorkelling equipment and lunch on the neighbouring island of Ko Mad Sum, will set you back B700 per person.

About 5km inland, near **Ban Thurian**, the **Na Muang Falls** make a popular outing as they're not far off the round-island road (each of the two main falls has its own signposted kilometre-long paved access road off Route 4169). The lower fall splashes and sprays down a twenty-metre wall of rock into a large pool, while Na Muang 2, upstream, is a more spectacular, shaded cascade that requires a bit of foot-slogging from the car park (about 15min uphill); alternatively you can walk up there from Na Muang 1, by taking the 1500-metre trail that begins 300m back along the access road from the lower fall. The self-styled "safari camp" at the Na Muang 1 entrance offers forty-minute **elephant-rides**, taking in Na Muang 2 falls, for B700 per person.

At the base of the west coast, **AO PHANGKA** (Emerald Cove) is a pretty horseshoe bay, sheltered by Laem Hin Khom, the high headland that forms Samui's southwestern tip, and by a coral reef which turns it into a placid paddling pool. The beach is poor and often littered with flotsam but, like the whole of the west coast, gives fine views of the tiny offshore islands of Ko Si Ko Ha –

where birds' nests are harvested for the health-giving Chinese soup (see box on p.725) – with the sun setting over the larger Ang Thong archipelago behind. The best budget place to stay here is the laid-back *Seagull* on the north shore of the bay (ⓣ077 423091; ❷–❹), where a wide variety of clean bungalows, all with showers, is spread out on a flowery slope, and there's a good, if slow, restaurant. Across the headland on the south-facing shore of Laem Hin Khom and further upmarket, the quiet *Coconut Villa* (ⓣ & ⓕ077 423151, ⓔcoconutvilla@sawadee.com; ❹–❻) commands stunning views of Ko Mad Sum and its neighbouring islands; the fan-cooled or air-con bungalows all have en-suite bathrooms, the food is recommended, and there's an excellent swimming pool set in attractive gardens by the sea.

Further up the coast, the flat beaches are unexceptional but make a calm alternative when the northeast winds hit the other side of the island. In a gorgeous hillside setting near **Ban Taling Ngam** village, *Le Royal Meridien Baan Taling Ngam* (ⓣ077 429100, ⓦwww.meridien-samui.com; ❾) boasts no fewer than seven swimming pools. The accommodation is in villas or balconied rooms on the resort's steep slopes, luxuriously decorated in traditional style. There's a spa and a Thai cookery school, and the hotel lays on the largest array of sports and watersports facilities on the island.

Ko Pha Ngan

In recent years, backpackers have tended to move over to Ko Samui's little sibling, **KO PHA NGAN**, 20km to the north, but the island still has a simple atmosphere, mostly because the lousy road system is an impediment to the developers. With a dense jungle covering its inland mountains and rugged granite outcrops along the coast, Pha Ngan lacks the huge, gently sweeping beaches for which Samui is famous, but it does have plenty of coral to explore and some beautiful, sheltered bays: **Hat Khuat** (**Bottle Beach**) and **Hat Khom** on the north coast; **Thong Nai Pan** and half a dozen remote, pristine beaches on the east coast; and, on an isolated neck of land at the southeast corner, **Hat Rin**, a pilgrimage site for ravers. Most of Pha Ngan's development, however, has plonked itself along the less attractive south and west sides, linked by the only coastal roads on the island, which fan out from **Thong Sala**, the capital.

Pha Ngan's **bungalows** all have running water and electricity (on the remoter beaches, only in the evenings and from individual generators), and most offer the choice of shared or en-suite bathrooms. There are only a handful of luxury resorts, though a few places now offer air-con, especially on Hat Rin. The three hundred or so resorts generally have more space to spread out than on Ko Samui, and the cost of living is lower; the prices given on the following pages are standard for most of the year, but in slack periods you'll be offered discounts, and at the very busiest times (especially Dec and Jan) Pha Ngan's bungalow owners are canny enough to raise the stakes. As on Ko Samui, nearly all the bungalow resorts have inexpensive, traveller-orientated **restaurants**; at one or two of the cheapest resorts, however, where they make their money from food more than accommodation, owners have been known to kick out guests who don't eat at the in-house restaurant.

There's no TAT office on Ko Pha Ngan, but you might want to take a look at ⓦwww.kohphangan.com, a website with a miscellany of **information** about the island, set up by the owner of Phangan Batik in Thong Sala (see p.610). If you're going to be exploring, well worth picking up from supermarkets on the island is Visid Hongsombud's excellent, regularly updated **map** of Ko Pha Ngan and Ko Tao (B70). The island isn't a great base for **scuba-diving**: getting to the best sites around Ko Tao (see box on p.622) involves time-consuming and expensive voyages, and there aren't as many dive companies here as on Ko Samui or Ko Tao – of those that exist, Easy Divers on Hat Rin (Ⓣ077 375258, Ⓦwww.thaidive.com) and Phangan Divers on Hat Rin, Thong Nai Pan and Hat Yao (Ⓣ077 375117, Ⓦwww.phangandivers.com) are PADI Five-Star Centres.

Getting to Ko Pha Ngan

Boat services to Ko Pha Ngan fluctuate according to demand, the weather and so on, and in high season extra boats may appear. The slowest **ferry** from the Gulf coast leaves Ban Don pier in **Surat Thani** at 11pm every night for Thong Sala (7hr; B200); tickets are available from the pier on the day of departure. From Don Sak to Thong Sala, there are four Raja vehicle ferries a day (2hr 30min; B240; on Ko Pha Ngan Ⓣ077 377452–3) and two Seatran fast boats (1hr 30min; B320; on Ko Pha Ngan Ⓣ077 238130); from Pak Nam Tapi, there's one Songserm Express Boat service a day (4hr; B250; on Ko Pha Ngan Ⓣ077 377046); all the above include bus transport to the pier from Surat Thani.

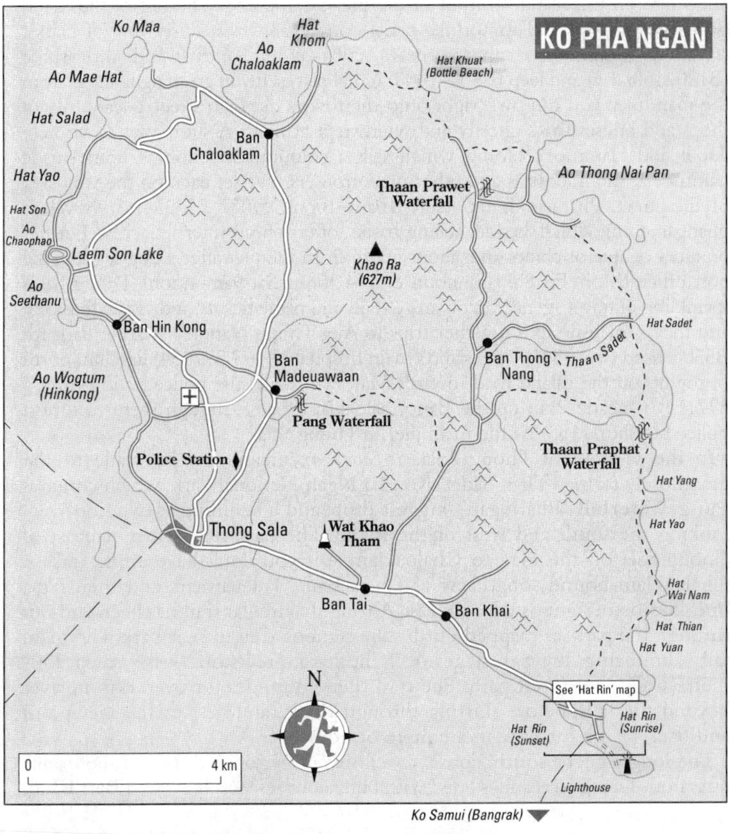

Two Songserm Express Boats a day do the 45-minute trip from Na Thon on **Ko Samui** to Thong Sala (B115), while Seatran does the same voyage twice a day in thirty minutes (B120). Speedboats from Bangrak, Bophut and Maenam on Samui (at least twice a day) and the Lomprayah catamaran from Maenam (twice a day; Ko Samui head office ⓣ077 247401–2) call in at Thong Sala after thirty minutes (B250), on their way to Ko Tao. From Bangrak, three passenger boats a day take an hour to cross to Hat Rin (B100). If the weather's good enough – generally reliable between January and October – one longtail boat a day crosses from Maenam to Hat Rin (B100), before sailing up Ko Pha Ngan's east coast, via Hat Sadet and anywhere else upon demand, to Thong Nai Pan (B200).

Four kinds of vessel currently run between Ko Pha Ngan and **Ko Tao**, though from roughly June to November they are occasionally cancelled due to bad weather: one slow boat (3hr; B180); one Songserm Express Boat a day (2hr; B250); the Lomprayah catamaran twice a day (1hr; B350); and at least two speedboats a day (50min–1hr; B350). **From Bangkok**, bus and train packages similar to those for getting to Ko Samui are available (see p.591).

Thong Sala and the south coast

Like the capital of Samui, **THONG SALA** is a port of entrance and little more, where the incoming ferries are met by touts sent to escort travellers to bungalows elsewhere on the island. In front of the piers, transport to the rest of the island (songthaews, jeeps and motorbike taxis) congregates by a dusty row of banks, travellers' restaurants, supermarkets, scuba-diving outfits and motorbike (B120–150/day) and jeep (B800–1000) rental places. If you go straight ahead from the main pier, you can turn right onto the town's old high street, a leafy mix of shops and houses that's ghostly and windswept at night. A short way down here you'll find Hammock Home, which sells a colourful selection of home-made hammocks, shoulder bags and fishermen's trousers, and, set back on the west side of the street, Phangan Batik (daily 10am–10pm; ⓣ077 377254, ⓦwww.kohphangan.com), which, besides selling batiks, offers cheap Internet access. Further on are a couple of clinics and, about 500m from the pier after a dog-leg left, the post office (Mon–Fri 8.30am–noon & 1–4.30pm, Sat 9am–noon). Thong Sala's sprinkling of travel agents can organize train and plane tickets, and visa extensions, and they sometimes put together trips to Ang Thong National Marine Park for B550 a head (see p.593). The island's main hospital (ⓣ077 377034) lies 3km north of town, on the inland road towards Mae Hat, while the police station (ⓣ077 377114) is nearly 2km up the Ban Chaloaklam road – though there's a tourist police booth(ⓣ1155) by the main pier in Thong Sala.

In the vicinity of Thong Sala, an easy excursion can be made to the grandiosely termed Than Sadet–Ko Pha Ngan National Park, which contains **Pang Waterfall**, Pha Ngan's biggest drop, and a stunning viewpoint overlooking the south and west of the island. The park lies 4km northeast of Thong Sala off the road to Chaloaklam – if you don't have a bike, take a Chaloaklam-bound songthaew as far as Ban Madeuawaan, and then it's a one-kilometre signposted walk east. A roughly circular trail has been laid out through the park, as mapped out by the signboard in the car park. The main fall – bouncing down in stages over the hard, grey stone – is a steep 250-metre walk up a forest path. The trail then continues for over 1km upriver beyond the falls, before skirting through thick rainforest to the viewpoint and back to the car park in a couple of hours.

The long, straight **south coast** is well served by songthaews and motorbike taxis from Thong Sala, and is lined with bungalows, especially around **Ban Khai**, to take the overspill from nearby Hat Rin. It's hard to recommend staying here, however: the beaches are mediocre by Thai standards, and the coral reef that hugs the length of the shoreline gets in the way of swimming. Ban Khai does, however, offer **horse-riding** on the beach through Sunset Horses (ⓣ01 083 0936).

On a quiet hillside above **Ban Tai**, 4km from Thong Sala, **Wat Khao Tham** holds ten-day **meditation retreats** most months of the year (B3500/person to cover food; minimum age 20, with further requirements for under-26s during the high season); the American and Australian teachers emphasize compassionate understanding as the basis of mental development. Space is limited (retreats are especially heavily subscribed Dec–March), so it's best to pre-register either in person or by writing to Wat Khao Tham, PO Box 18, Ko Pha Ngan, Surat Thani 84280. For further information, including full details of rules and requirements and the schedule of retreats, go to ⓦwww.watkowtahm.org.

If you need to **stay** around Thong Sala, walk 800m north out of town to *Siriphun* (ⓣ077 377140, ⓕ077 377242; ❸–❻). The owner is helpful, the food very good and the bungalows are clean and well positioned along the beach; all have showers and mosquito screens on the windows, and an extra wad of baht buys air-con, hot water, fridge, TV and one of the island's few bathtubs. Alternatively, *Charm Beach Resort*, a friendly, sprawling place on the beach only 1500m southeast of Thong Sala (ⓣ077 377165 or 077 377412; ❷–❻), has a wide variety of decent bungalows (some with air-con and hot water), Internet access and good Thai food. The incongruous white high-rise overshadowing Thong Sala's pier is the *Pha Ngan Chai Hotel* (ⓣ & ⓕ077 377068; ❻), which makes a fair stab at international-standard features for visiting businessmen and government officials, with air-con, hot water, TVs and, in some rooms, sea-view balconies.

Hat Rin

HAT RIN is now firmly established as the major rave venue in Southeast Asia, especially in the high season of December and January, but every month of the year people flock in for the **full moon party** – something like *Apocalypse Now* without the war. Note that when the full moon coincides with an important Buddhist festival, the party is moved one night away to avoid a clash; check out ⓦwww.thaisite.com/fullmoonparty for details. There's a more sedate side to Hat Rin's alternative scene, too, with old- and new-age hippies packing out the t'ai chi, yoga and meditation classes, and helping consume the drugs that are readily available. Drug-related horror stories are common currency round here, and many of them are true: dodgy Ecstasy, *ya baa* (Burmese-manufactured methamphetamines), speed punch, diet pills, and special teas containing the local fungus, *hed khi kwai* (buffalo-shit mushrooms), put an average of two farangs a month into hospital for psychiatric treatment. The local authorities have started clamping down on the trade in earnest, setting up a permanent police box at Hat Rin, instigating regular roadblocks and bungalow searches, and drafting in scores of police (both uniformed and plain-clothes) on full moon nights. It doesn't seem to have dampened the fun, only made travellers a lot more circumspect (the police's going rate for escaping a minor possession charge is a B50,000 "fine").

Hat Rin occupies the flat neck of Pha Ngan's southeast headland, which is so narrow that the resort comprises two back-to-back beaches, joined by transverse roads at the north and south ends. The eastern beach, usually referred to as **Sunrise**, or Hat Rin Nok (Outer Hat Rin), is what originally drew visitors here, a classic curve of fine white sand between two rocky slopes; there's still some coral off the southern slope to explore, but the bay sees a lot of boat traffic these days and its waters are far from limpid. This beach is the centre of Hat Rin's action, with a solid line of bars, restaurants and bungalows tucked under the palm trees. **Sunset** beach, or Hat Rin Nai (Inner Hat Rin), which for much of the year is littered with flotsam, looks ordinary by comparison but has plenty of quieter accommodation. Unfortunately, development between the beaches does no justice to the setting: it's ugly, cramped and chaotic, with new low-rise concrete shophouses thrown up at any old angle. Half-hearted attempts to tart up the large body of water in the middle of the headland with a few park benches and lights have been undermined by all-too-accurate signposts pointing to "Hat Rin Swamp".

Practicalities

The awkwardness of **getting to Hat Rin** in the past helped to maintain its individuality, but this has changed now that the road in from Ban Khai has been paved. All the same, it's a winding, precipitous roller-coaster of a route, covered by songthaews and motorbike taxis from Thong Sala – take care if you're driving your own motorbike. The easiest approach of all, however, if you're coming from Ko Samui, or even Surat Thani, is by direct boat from Samui's north coast: three boats a day (departure times have been fixed for some years now at 10.30am, 1pm & 4pm; B100) cross to the pier on Sunset beach from Bangrak in under an hour; and if the weather's good enough – generally reliable between January and October – one longtail boat a day crosses from Maenam to Hat Rin (B100), before sailing up Ko Pha Ngan's east coast to Thong Nai Pan.

The area behind and between the beaches – especially around what's known as Chicken Corner, where the southern transverse road meets the road along the back of Sunrise – is crammed with shops and businesses: there are clinics, a post office (near the pier on Sunset), supermarkets, travel agents, motorbike rental places (from B150/day), overseas phone facilities, dozens of Internet outlets, plenty of ATMs and bank currency-exchange booths, even tattooists, body-piercers and video-game arcades.

There's a cheap self-service **laundry** on the northern transverse, and Hat Rin boasts a couple of good **bookshops**, diagonally opposite each other, north of Chicken Corner near the school: Book Corner carries a decent line of new fiction, guides and books about Thailand and Southeast Asia, and the mostly secondhand Bay's Books also has a good selection to rent, buy or swap. As well as being a **gym**, Jungle Gym (Ⓦwww.junglegym.co.th), near the pier, offers Thai boxing classes, a steam room, yoga and a juice bar, while Chakra, nearby in an alley off the opposite side of the southern transverse, offers the best **massages** in Hat Rin.

Boat trips to Ang Thong National Marine Park (see p.593) are put together by *Big Boom Bar* on Sunrise beach: overnights (B2000/person), staying in the national park bungalows, are preferable, but it is possible to get there and back on a more hurried day-trip (B1200). Plenty of places on Hat Rin, such as Sopin Tour on the northern transverse, organize day-trips up the east coast and back, typically charging B300 (including simple lunch and snorkelling equipment) and taking in Ao Chaloaklam, Hat Khom, Hat Khuat and Thaan Sadet; if the weather is right, some will keep going all the way round the island, via Ao Mae Hat.

Accommodation

For most of the year, Hat Rin has enough bungalows to cope, but on **full moon nights** as many as ten thousand revellers may turn up. Your options are either to arrive a day or more early (especially during the Dec–Jan peak season), to forget about sleep altogether, or to hitch up with one of the many party boats (about B400 return/person) organized by guest houses and restaurants on Ko Samui,

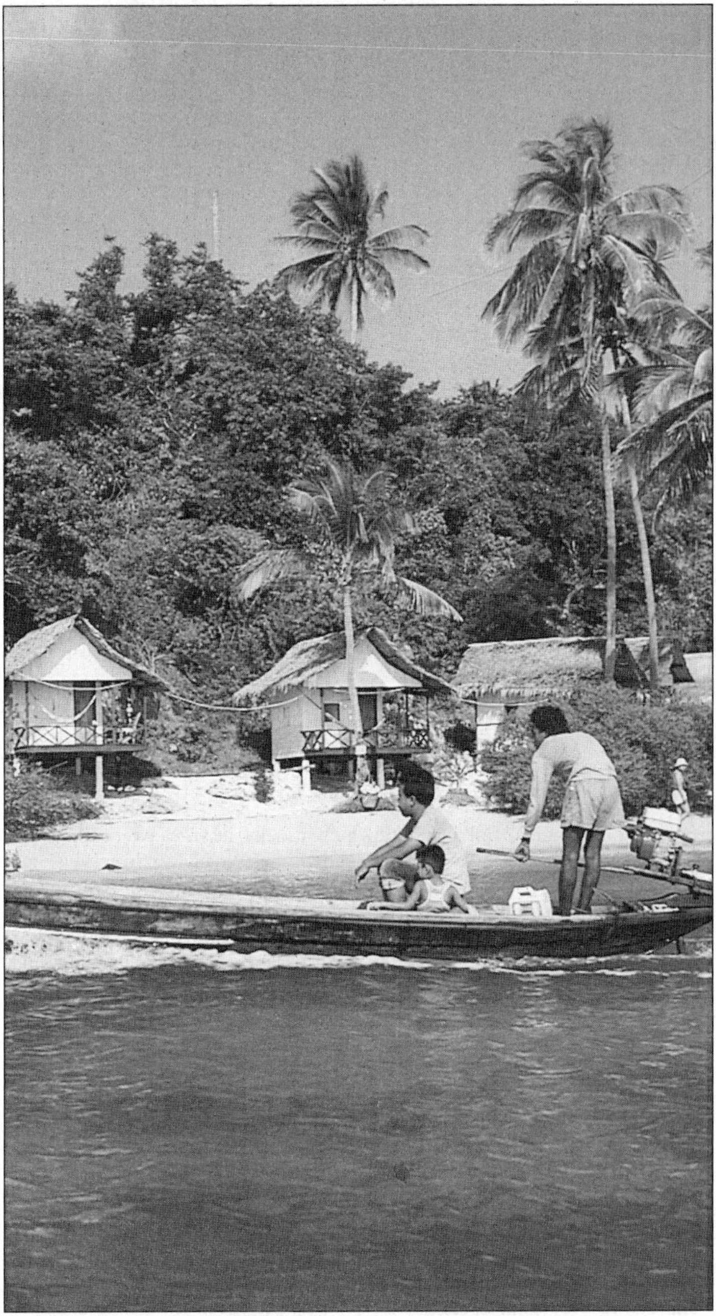

△ Hat Rin

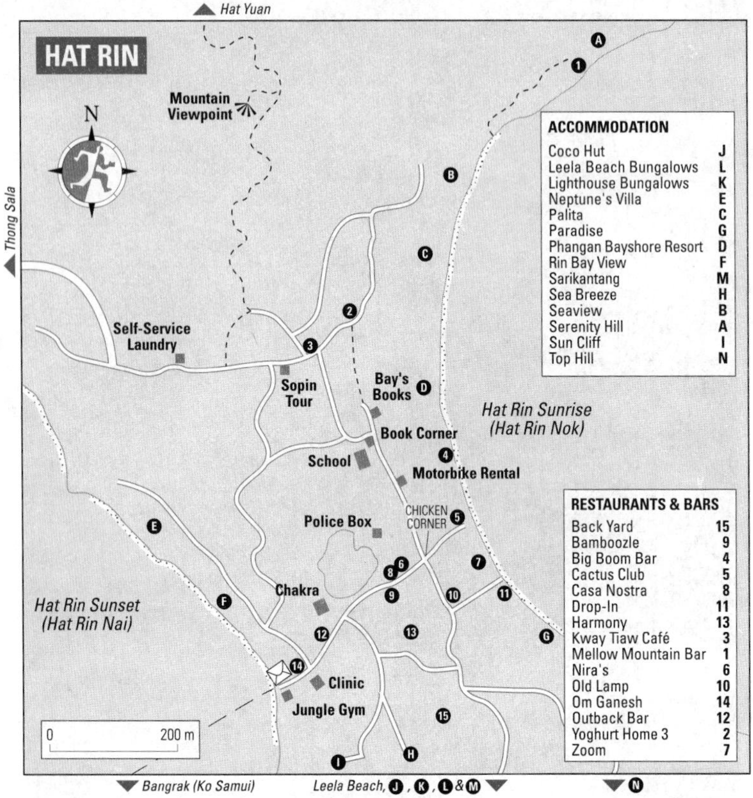

especially at Bangrak and Bophut, which usually leave between 9pm and midnight and return after dawn. Even at other times, staying on **Sunrise** is often expensive and noisy, though a few places can be recommended. On **Sunset**, the twenty or more resorts are laid out in orderly rows, and are especially quiet and inexpensive between April and June and in October. Many visitors choose to stay on the **headland** to the south of the main beaches, especially at white-sand, palm-fringed **Leela Beach**, which is a twenty-minute walk along a well-signposted route from Chicken Corner, on the west side of the headland. At any of the places out here your bungalow is likely to have more peace and space and better views, leaving you a torchlit walk to the night-time action.

Coco Hut Leela Beach ⓣ077 375368, ⓦwww.cocohut.com. On a clean, quiet stretch of beach, this efficiently run place is smart and attractive, painted ochre and with some traditional southern Thai elements in the architecture. On offer is a huge variety of accommodation, from rooms with fans and cold water to beachfront bungalows with air-con and hot water. 3–7

Leela Beach Bungalows Leela Beach ⓣ077 375094 or 01 995 1304, ⓦwww.leelabeach.com. A good budget choice with plenty of space under the palm trees and almost half of the white-sand beach to itself. The no-frills bungalows are sturdy and well built and all have fans, mosquito nets and en-suite bathrooms. Price varies according to whether you are at the back or on the beachfront, where there are also some larger, better-furnished bungalows with ceiling fans. 1–3

Lighthouse Bungalows On the far south-western tip of the headland ⓣ077 375075, ⓔLighthouse_bg@hotmail.com. A 30min walk from Chicken Corner, the last section along a wooden walkway over the rocky shoreline, which can be a bit disconcerting at night. At this friendly haven, wooden and concrete bungalows, sturdily built to withstand the wind and backed by trail-filled jungle, either share bathrooms or have their own. The restaurant food is varied and tasty. 2–4

Neptune's Villa Near the small promontory at the centre of Sunset ⓣ077 375251, ⓔneptune1@thaimail.com. A popular, laid-back place in grassy, shady grounds giving onto the beach. Accommodation is either in simple, fan-cooled wooden clapboard huts with or without their own bathrooms, or in a block of rooms to one side (all with hot-water bathrooms, some with air-con), slightly cramped but attractive enough with small lawns and flowers. 2–6

Palita At the northern end of Sunrise ⓣ077 375170–2 or 01 917 7455, ⓔpalitas9@hotmail.com. Clean, well-run place with smart, white-clapboard air-con bungalows giving onto the beach, and large, simple huts (all with fans and their own bathrooms) among the coconut palms behind. The food gets rave reviews. 3–6

Paradise Spread over the far southern end of Sunrise and up the slope behind ⓣ077 375244–5, ⓦwww.paradisebungalow.com. Well-established place, with two good restaurants – the original full moon party began here, and it's still a party focus once a month. There's a range of rooms and bungalows of different sizes, but all are en suite with fans; those further up the hillside offer fine views over the bay from their verandas. 2–3

Phangan Bayshore Resort In the middle of Sunrise ⓣ077 375227, ⓕ077 375226. An upmarket, well-ordered place, though staff seem somewhat jaded and service is brusque. Big bungalows with spacious verandas, some with hot water and air-con, are set on a green lawn, shaded with palms. 3–7

Rin Bay View Near the pier on Sunset ⓣ077 375188. A decent fallback in a central location, occupying a narrow strip of land, though not too tightly squeezed and ornamented with flowers and trees. The en-suite bungalows with mosquito screens and balconies are a decent size and generally well maintained and clean. Price varies according to size and distance from the beach, and whether they are fan-cooled or air-con, with hot or cold water. 3–5

Sarikantang (*Bumble Bee Lodge*) Leela Beach ⓣ077 375055–6, ⓦwww.sarikantang.com. Boutique resort with a good measure of style, though housekeeping could be improved. Accommodation ranges from rooms or wooden bungalows with fans, verandas and cold-water bathrooms to chic, white-painted "superior" rooms with air-con, hot-water showers and separate outdoor sunken baths. 4–7

Sea Breeze Next to and above *Sun Cliff* ⓣ077 375162. Sprawls a little untidily over the ridge from near the southern transverse all the way to the north end of Leela Beach, so plenty of space and views out to the west. Choose between older en-suite bungalows with fans, and large, smart, new villas on stilts, with air-con, hot water, big decks and great sunset vistas. 3–6

Seaview At the quieter northern end of Sunrise ⓣ077 375160. On a big plot of shady land, this clean, orderly place is a similar setup to *Palita* next door. Simple, en-suite huts at the back, posher bungalows (some air-con) beachside. 3–6

Serenity Hill At the quieter northern end of Sunrise. Attached to the famous *Mellow Mountain Bar* in a scenic spot, its distinctive blue-roofed bungalows are well spread out along the headland's rocky slopes, with balconies to take in the views of the bay. The site is not very well maintained, but the bungalows themselves are decent enough, with mosquito nets, fans and en-suite cold-water bathrooms. 2–3

Sun Cliff High up on the tree-lined slope above the south end of Sunset ⓣ077 375134. Friendly place with great views of the south coast and Ko Samui, and a wide range of bright, well-maintained bungalows, some with large balconies, fridges, hot water and air-con. 2–7

Top Hill About 1km south along the coast from Sunrise ⓣ077 375327 or 01 895 8696. Reached by following signs from Chicken Corner, which take you along a steep but well-maintained path, this is the furthest and highest of several bungalow operations along this stretch, and has the best views. A neat little place with a colourful flower garden and only ten rooms, each with balcony, fan and en-suite bathroom. 3

Eating

As well as good simple Thai fare at some of the bungalows, Hat Rin sports an unnerving choice of world **foods** for somewhere so remote, and vegetarians are unusually well provided for. All-day breakfasts of croissants, cakes and good coffee at *Nira's* 24-hour bakery café near Chicken Corner are especially popular, as well as at *Yoghurt Home 3* behind the north end of Sunrise, which offers home-made yoghurt in many combinations, as well as Thai filter coffee and generous servings of Thai and Western veggie and non-veggie food. On the southern transverse near the pier, *Om Ganesh* is an excellent, relaxing Indian restaurant with good vegetarian and non-vegetarian thalis and cheerful service. Further away from the pier on the same road, *Bamboozle* serves excellent Mexican food in mellow, leafy surroundings – chicken fajitas with all the trimmings are especially delicious. A little further on again, opposite 7–11, and you're in Italy: a small, bright café-restaurant called *Casa Nostra* prepares great pastas – try the spaghetti bolognese – pizzas (whole or by the slice), espresso coffee, salads and plenty of other dishes for vegetarians, such as ravioli stuffed with pumpkin and aubergine. Also worth seeking out are *The Old Lamp*, just south of Chicken Corner, where simple but delicious Western and Thai food is served at relaxing low tables, and a simple *kway tiaw* café on the northern transverse (the sign says "Dong Bar") popular with locals for its noodle soup with pork or beef and *som tam*.

Nightlife

Nightlife normally begins at the south end of Sunrise at venues such as the *Cactus Club* and *Drop-In*, which pump out pop and anthems onto low-slung candlelit tables and mats on the beach. Inland on the southern transverse, *Outback Bar* is a lively meeting place with pool tables, big-screen sports and well-received steak pies and the like. For somewhere to chill, head for *Mellow Mountain Bar*, which occupies a great position up in the rocks on the north side of Sunrise, with peerless views of the beach.

For dancing, a convenient rota of **club** nights is currently in operation. *Harmony*, a stylish, spacious club with a chill-out room upstairs, to the south of Chicken Corner opposite *The Old Lamp* and up behind *Sea Garden Bungalows*, hosts psy-trance Monday, Wednesday and Friday. Much further up the hill behind the southern end of Sunrise, off the path to Leela Beach, *Back Yard*, with a large balcony area overlooking the beach, does progressive house Tuesday and Thursday, psy-trance on Sunday. On the beach, the *Big Boom Bar* brings you house Monday and Friday, *Zoom* psy-trance on Saturday.

On **full moon night**, *Paradise* styles itself as the party host, but the mayhem spreads along most of Sunrise, fuelled by hastily erected drinks stalls and sound systems pumping out everything from psy-trance to drum'n' bass. Next day, *Back Yard* kicks off its funky house and techno afterparty at around ten in the morning, and later in the evening *Harmony* plays psy-trance.

The east coast

North of Hat Rin, the rocky, exposed **east coast** stretches as far as Ao Thong Nai Pan, the only centre of development. No roads run along this coast, only a rough, steep, fifteen-kilometre trail, which starts from Hat Rin's northern transverse road (signposted) and runs reasonably close to the shore, occasionally dipping down into pristine sandy coves with a smattering of bungalows. When the weather's OK – it's generally reliable roughly from January to October – one longtail boat a day runs via the east coast beaches from Hat Rin to Thong Nai Pan (B100), having started its voyage across at Maenam on Ko Samui. Otherwise there are ample longtails on Sunrise that will taxi you up the coast – around B100 to Hat Thian, for example. See p.612 for information about organized day-trips by boat up this coast from Hat Rin.

About ninety minutes up the trail, the adjoining small, sandy bays of **HAT YUAN** and **HAT THIAN** have established a reputation as a quieter alternative to Hat Rin and now sport about a dozen bungalow outfits between them. On the former, *Bamboo Huts* (❶–❸) is a good choice, a friendly place with good food and well-built huts (either sharing bathrooms or en suite) in a pleasant garden. Accommodation on Hat Thian is available at the friendly *Haad Tien Resort* (ⓣ01 229 3919; ❷), with well-built en-suite wood-and-bamboo bungalows on the slope above the beach; and at the *Sanctuary* (ⓣ01 271 3614, ⓦwww.thesanctuary-kpg.com; ❸–❽), which offers a huge range of basic and luxury en-suite bungalows, as well as dorm accommodation (B60), and good vegetarian fare, seafood and home-made bread, cakes and yoghurt. It also hosts courses in yoga, meditation and the like, and provides two diverse kinds of treatment: the Spa does massage, facials and beauty treatments, while the Wellness Centre goes in for fasting and cleansing.

Steep, remote **HAT SADET**, 12km up the trail from Hat Rin, has a handful of bungalow operations, sited here because of their proximity to **Thaan Sadet**, a boulder-strewn brook that runs out into the sea. The spot was popularized by various kings of Thailand who came here to walk, swim and vandalize the huge boulders by carving their initials on them. A rough track has been bulldozed through the woods above and parallel to Thaan Sadet to connect with the unpaved road from Thong Sala to Ao Thong Nai Pan. Best of the bungalows is the welcoming *Mai Pen Rai* (ⓣ077 377414 at their Thong Sala office, ⓦwww.thansadet.com; ❸), which has a variety of attractive, characterful accommodation with airy bathrooms (some with big upstairs terraces), either on the beach at the stream mouth or scattered around the rocks for good views; a jeep taxi leaves Thong Sala for the resort every day at 1pm (B80).

AO THONG NAI PAN is a beautiful, semicircular bay backed by steep, green hills, which looks as if it's been bitten out of the island's northeast corner by a gap-toothed giant, leaving a tall hump of land dividing the bay into two parts. The longer, southern beach has marginally the better sand, but both halves are sheltered and deep enough for swimming, and there's good snorkelling around the central headland and along the outer rim of the bay's southern half. The bay is now developed enough for tourism to support a few shops, dive outfits, bars and stand-alone restaurants. A bumpy nightmare of a dirt road winds its way for 12km over the steep mountains from Ban Tai on the south coast to Thong Nai Pan: jeeps (B80/person) connect with incoming and outgoing boats at Thong Sala every day, though occasionally after heavy rain they don't chance it.

A dozen or so resorts line the southern half of the bay, sometimes called **Ao Thong Nai Pan Yai**, in the centre of which the friendly *Pingjun* (ⓣ077 299004; ❷–❸) has a range of large, en-suite bungalows with verandas and hammocks on a broad stretch of beach. At the far southern end, all the airy, en-suite bungalows at *White Sand* (❸) have nice verandas on the beach. The steep slopes of the central outcrop make a beautiful setting for *Panviman* (ⓣ077 445100–9, ⓦwww.panviman.com; ❼–❽), one of Ko Pha Ngan's few attempts at a luxury resort, comprising air-conditioned cottages and hotel-style rooms with verandas, hot water, satellite TV and mini-bars. For non-guests it's worth making the climb up here for the view from the restaurant perched over the cliff edge.

On the northern beach, or **Ao Thong Nai Pan Noi**, *Star Huts* (ⓣ077 299005, ⓔstar_hut@hotmail.com; ❷–❹) gets the nod as the best budget choice: very clean, well-maintained bungalows, with en-suite or shared bathrooms, line the sand, and the friendly owners dish up good food and can provide information about local walks. Styling itself as "upmarket budget accommodation", *Baan Panburi* (Ⓣ077 238599, Ⓦwww.baanpanburi.bigstep.com; ❸–❽) occupies a long stretch of beach nearby. Attractive, well-designed huts and bungalows, some of them a little cramped together, are set among flowers and come in a variety of sizes and styles, most with ceiling fans and mosquito nets, a few with air-con. The food is great, there's a massage house and spa, and daily activities such as hiking, volleyball and boat trips are laid on. Among restaurants, *Bio's Dynamic Kitchen*, raised on the rocks behind *Baan Panburi*, is worth singling out, a laid-back, cluttered restaurant and bar, serving a short but interesting menu of cheap Thai vegetarian dishes.

The north coast

The village of **BAN CHALOAKLAM**, on Ao Chaloaklam, the largest bay on the **north coast**, has long been a famous R&R spot for fishermen from all over the Gulf of Thailand, with sometimes as many as a hundred trawlers littering the broad and sheltered bay. Nowadays it is also a low-key tourist destination, as it can easily be reached from Thong Sala, 10km away, by songthaew or motorbike taxi along the island's best road. Facilities include travel agencies, motorbike rental, clinics, international phone and Internet services and scuba outfits. The best bit of beach is at **Hat Khom**, a tiny cove dramatically tucked in under the headland to the east, with a secluded strip of white sand and good coral for snorkelling. For **accommodation**, try *Fanta* (Ⓣ077 374132, Ⓔfantaphangan@yahoo.com; ❷–❹) at the eastern end of Ban Chaloaklam, on a wide spread of beach backed by casuarinas with clean, en-suite bungalows and good food. Or walk out to friendly *Coral Bay* (Ⓣ077 374245; ❶–❹), which has plenty of space and great views on the grassy promontory dividing Hat Khom from the rest of Ao Chaloaklam. The sturdy bungalows range from simple affairs with mosquito nets and shared bathrooms to large pads with funky bathrooms built into the rock; snorkelling equipment is available to make the most of Hat Khom's reef.

If the sea is not too rough, longtail boats run three times a day for most of the year from Ban Chaloaklam to isolated **HAT KHUAT** (**Bottle Beach**), the best of the beaches on the north coast, sitting between steep hills in a perfect cup of a bay; you could also walk there along a testing trail from Hat Khom in around ninety minutes. There are four resorts here: *Bottle Beach I* (❶–❸) currently has the cheapest huts, as well as some with en-suite bathrooms on the beach; the setup at *Bottle Beach II* (❶–❸) is similar; all of *Bottle Beach III*'s bungalows (❷–❺) are en suite and arrayed along the beach, and are priced according to size; while *Smile Resort* (❸) has the nicest setting for its en-suite bungalows, on a pretty flower-strewn hillside at the western end of the beach.

The west coast

Pha Ngan's **west coast** has attracted about the same amount of development as the forgettable south coast, but the landscape here is more attractive and varied, broken up into a series of long sandy inlets with good sunset views over the islands of the Ang Thong National Marine Park to the west; most of the bays, however, are sheltered by reefs which can keep the sea too shallow for a decent swim, especially between May and October. The coast road from Thong Sala as far up as Hat Yao is in decent condition, as is the inland road via the hospital, which loops round past Ao Mae Hat to Ban Chaloaklam. However the side roads down to Hat Salad have not as yet been similarly upgraded, and can be testing if you're on a bike. Taxis and sometimes boats cover the whole coast, but motorbike taxis may balk at Hat Salad.

The first bay north of Thong Sala, Ao Wogtum (aka Hinkong), yawns wide across a featureless expanse that turns into a mud flat when the sea retreats behind the reef barrier at low tide. The nondescript bay of **AO SEETHANU** beyond is home to the excellent *Loy Fah* (Ⓣ077 377319 or 077 349022; ❷–❹), a well-run place that commands good views from its perch on top of Seethanu's steep southern cape, and offers decent snorkelling and swimming from the rocks; lodgings range from simple en-suite huts to concrete cottages with verandas and chairs.

Continuing north, there's a surprise in store in the shape of **Laem Son Lake**, a beautiful, tranquil stretch of clear water cordoned by pines, which spread down to the nearby beach. Under the shade of the pines, the rudimentary en-suite huts of *Bovy Resort* (❶) can only be recommended for their beachfront peace and quiet; yoga and meditation classes are currently being offered here. *Seethanu Bungalows* (Ⓣ077 349113, Ⓔole_seetanu@yahoo.com; ❸–❺), actually round the next headland on the small bay of **AO CHAOPHAO**, is a lively spot with a popular restaurant; sturdy, characterful wooden bungalows (all en suite) are arrayed around a colourful garden, with the more expensive options, with air-con and hot water, by the beach. Next door, *Seaflower* (Ⓣ077 349090, Ⓕ077 349091; ❷–❹) is quieter and more congenial, set in a well-tended garden, and the veggie and non-veggie food is excellent. En-suite bungalows with their own bathrooms vary in price according to their size and age: the newer ones – more like cottages – have marble open-air bathrooms and big balcony seating areas. If you're feeling adventurous, ask the owner about the occasional three-day longtail-boat treks to Ang Thong National Marine Park (see p.593), which involve snorkelling, caving, catching your own seafood, and sleeping in tents on the beach (B2200/person, including food and soft drinks). The adjacent *Village Green* pub-restaurant keeps the punters happy with a wide variety of breakfasts, great sandwiches (including the raid-the-pantry DIY option), Thai and Western main courses, pancakes and Thai desserts; occasional DJ nights are washed down with a big choice of drinks and cocktails. Two doors away stands friendly *Haad Chao Phao Resort* (Ⓣ077 349273; ❷): in a shady garden, the ten clean and well-kept en-suite bungalows (all with mosquito nets and verandas) lead down to an attractive patch of beach.

North of Chaophao, *Haad Son Bungalows* (Ⓣ077 349103–4, Ⓦwww.phangan.info/haadson; ❸–❽) have the small, sandy beach of **HAT SON** to themselves. They're spaciously laid out among pretty flowers on a terraced hillside, and vary from the simple, though fan-cooled and en suite are all the same, to the deluxe (air-con, hot water and mini-bar). This popular, family-oriented place also has a very attractive swimming pool with a separate children's pool.

Beyond the next headland, the long, attractive, gently curved beach of **HAT YAO** is gradually and justifiably becoming livelier and more popular, with several stand-alone bars and restaurants, diving outfits, supermarkets and jeep and bike rental. Among a nonstop line of bungalows here, good bets are *Ibiza* (Ⓣ077 349121; ❸–❼), with smart, airy en-suite bungalows in a spacious garden, some with hot water and air-con, and kayaks for rent (B100/hr); and the friendly *Bay View* (Ⓣ077 349235; ❶–❹), which offers good food and views from a wide range of bungalows on the quiet northern headland. To the north of Hat Yao, **HAT SALAD** is another pretty bay, sheltered and sandy, with good snorkelling off the northern tip. Despite poor road access, it has attracted ten or so bungalow outfits in various price categories. Run by a friendly family, *Asia* (Ⓣ077 377288; ❷–❹) is a good option, offering great food and en-suite bungalows, including some larger ones with fridges.

On the island's northwest corner, **AO MAE HAT** is good for swimming and snorkelling among the coral that lines the sand causeway to the tiny islet of Ko Maa. The bay, which is most easily reached by the road west from Ban Chaloaklam, also supports several decent bungalow resorts, including *Island View Cabana* (Ⓣ077 374173; ❶–❸), a popular place with a well-positioned, thatch-roofed restaurant and a variety of well-designed bungalows shaded by casuarina trees.

Ko Tao

KO TAO (Turtle Island) is so named because its outline resembles a turtle nose-diving towards Ko Pha Ngan, 40km to the south. The rugged shell of the turtle, to the east, is crenellated with secluded coves where one or two bungalows hide among the rocks. On the western side, the turtle's underbelly is a long curve of classic beach, Hat Sai Ree, facing Ko Nang Yuan, a beautiful Y-shaped group of islands offshore, also known as Ko Hang Tao (Turtle's Tail Island). The 21 square kilometres of granite in between is topped by dense forest on the higher slopes and dotted with huge boulders that look as if they await some Easter Island sculptor. It's fun to spend a couple of days exploring the network of rough trails, after which you'll probably know all 900 of the island's inhabitants. Ko Tao is now best known as a venue for **scuba-diving**, with a wide variety of dive sites in close proximity; see the box on p.622 for further details.

The island is the last and most remote of the archipelago that continues the line of Surat Thani's mountains into the sea. There were over a hundred sets of **bungalows** at the latest count (still sometimes not enough during the peak season from December to March, when travellers occasionally have to sleep on the beach until a hut becomes free) concentrated along the west and south sides. Some still provide the bare minimum, with plain mattresses for beds, mosquito nets and shared bathrooms, but most places can now offer en-suite bathrooms and a few comforts, and there are even a few upmarket resorts around with such luxuries as air-con, hot water and swimming pools. There's a limited government supply of electricity, so much of it still comes from private generators, and it's usually evenings only, with few places providing 24-hour service. Due to a lack of seasonal rain, Ko Tao suffered severe water shortages in 2002, so visitors are asked to conserve water whenever possible.

If you're just arriving and want to stay on one of the less accessible beaches, it might be a good idea to go with one of the touts who meet the ferries at Mae Hat, with pick-up or boat on hand, since at least you'll know their bungalows aren't full or closed – the former is possible from December to March, the latter from June to August; failing that, call ahead, as even the remotest bungalows now have mobile phones. Some resorts with attached scuba-diving operations have been known to refuse guests who don't sign up for diving trips or courses; on the other hand, some of the bigger dive companies now have their own functional lodgings, which are often included in the price of a dive course. As is the case on Ko Pha Ngan, at some of the cheapest resorts, where they make their money from food more than accommodation, owners have been known to kick out guests who don't eat at the in-house restaurant.

The **weather** is much the same as on Pha Ngan and Samui, but being that bit further off the mainland, Ko Tao feels the effect of the southwest monsoon more: June to October can have strong winds and rain, with a lot of debris blown onto the windward coasts. There isn't a TAT office on Ko Tao, but the regularly updated and widely available free booklet, *Ko Tao Info*, is a useful source of **information**, along with its associated **website**, Ⓦwww.kohtao online.com. If you're going to be exploring, well worth picking up from supermarkets on Ko Tao or Ko Pha Ngan is Visid Hongsombud's excellent, regularly updated **map** of Ko Pha Ngan and Ko Tao (B70).

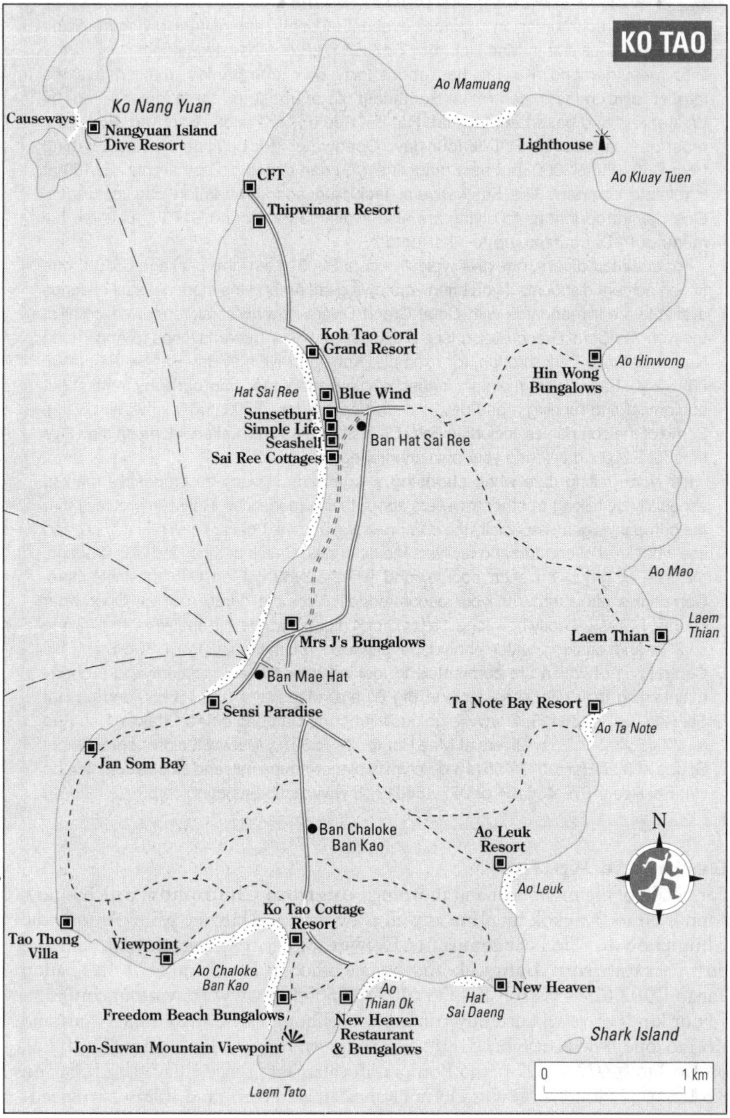

Scuba-diving off Ko Tao

Some of the best **dive sites** in Thailand are found off Ko Tao, which is blessed with outstandingly clear (visibility up to 35m) and deep water close in to shore. On top of that, there's a kaleidoscopic array of coral species and other marine life, and you may be lucky enough to encounter whale sharks, barracudas, leatherback turtles and pilot whales. Diving is possible at any time of the year, with sheltered sites on one or other side of the island in any season – the changeover from southwest to northeast monsoon in November is the worst time, while visibility is best from April to July, in September (usually best of all) and October. Ko Tao now supports a small, one-person recompression chamber, evacuation centre and general diving medicine centre at Badalveda in Mae Hat (Ⓣ077 456664, Ⓦwww.badalveda.com).

To meet demand, Ko Tao has about forty **dive companies**, making this the largest dive-training centre in Southeast Asia; most of them are staffed by Westerners and based at Mae Hat, Hat Sai Ree or Ao Chaloke Ban Kao. By far the most popular **course**, PADI's four-day "Openwater" for beginners costs anything from B6000 to B9000, but as a guideline, you can expect to pay around B7400 at a reliable company like Easy Divers, including accommodation and insurance. One-day introductions to diving are also available for around B1750, as is the full menu of PADI courses, up to "Instructor".

For **qualified divers**, one dive typically costs B800, a ten-dive package B5500, with fifteen percent discounts if you bring your own gear. Among the more unusual offerings available are live-aboards with Coral Grand Divers (Ⓦwww.coralgranddivers.com) at the *Koh Tao Coral Grand Resort* (see p.626), and two- or three-day trips to Ang Thong National Marine Park through, for example, Koh Tao Divers at Ban Hat Sai Ree (Ⓣ06 069 9244). Easy Divers maintain a speciality in **underwater photography**, renting out equipment and running a one-day, two-dive course for B3700 (for Openwater divers). Some of the companies, including Easy Divers, will take **snorkellers** along on their dive trips for B200 a day (bring your own snorkelling equipment).

It's worth taking care when **choosing a company** in such a competitive market, especially by talking to other travellers about their experiences. Reassure yourself that the company's gear, especially the compressors, and the boat are well maintained, and see what level of comfort and facilities the latter has. Check out the kind of instruction, the size of group on each course, and whether you get on with the instructors. Companies often throw in your accommodation for the duration of an Openwater course, but ask exactly how long it's for (3 or 4 nights), where it is and what it's like; free snacks and drinking water should be provided on the boat. PADI Five-Star Dive Centres, all of which are committed to looking after the environment and properly maintaining their dive sites, include Big Blue at Mae Hat Ⓣ077 456050 and on Hat Sai Ree Ⓣ077 456415, Ⓦwww.bigbluediving.com; Carabao on Ao Chaloke Ban Kao Ⓣ077 456402–3; Easy Divers at Mae Hat Ⓣ077 456010, Ⓦwww.thaidive.com; Planet Scuba at Mae Hat Ⓣ077 456110–1, Ⓦwww.planet-scuba.net; and Scuba Junction on Hat Sai Ree Ⓣ077 456164 or 077 456013, Ⓦwww.scuba-junction.com.

Getting to Ko Tao

For details of the night boat and morning boats **from Chumphon**, which is now connected to Bangkok by plane as well as by train and bus, see p.582. Among the Chumphon–Ko Tao boat companies, Ekawin, for example, organizes VIP bus and boat packages **from Bangkok** and has an office in Banglamphu at 42 Thanon Tanao (Ⓣ02 629 4598; on Ko Tao Ⓣ077 456052; Ⓦwww.ekawintour.com).

Four kinds of vessel currently run between Thong Sala on **Ko Pha Ngan** and Ko Tao: one slow boat (3hr; B180); one Songserm Express Boat a day (2hr; B250; on Ko Tao Ⓣ077 456274); the Lomprayah catamaran twice a day (1hr; B350; on Ko Tao Ⓣ077 456176, Ⓦwww.lomprayahcatamaran.com); and at least two speed-

Main dive sites

Ko Nang Yuan Surrounded by a variety of sites, with assorted hard and soft corals and an abundance of fish, which between them cater for just about everyone: the Nang Yuan Pinnacle, a granite pinnacle with boulder swim-throughs; Green Rock, a maze of swim-throughs, caves and canyons, featuring triggerfish, hawksbill turtles and occasional reef sharks, which is fun for advanced divers; Twins, good for beginners, two rock formations covered in corals and sponges; and the Japanese Gardens, on the east side of the sand causeway, which get their name from the hundreds of hard and soft coral formations here and are popular among snorkellers.

White Rock (Hin Khao) Sarcophyton leather coral turns the granite boulders here white when seen from the surface; also wire, antipatharian and colourful soft corals, and gorgonian sea fans. Plenty of fish, including titan triggerfish, butterfly fish, angelfish and morays.

Shark Island Large granite boulders with acropora, wire and bushy antipatharian corals, sea whips, gorgonian sea fans and barrel sponges. Reef fish include angelfish, triggerfish and groupers; leopard and reef sharks and hawksbill turtles may be found as well as occasional whale sharks.

Hinwong Pinnacle Generally for experienced divers, often with strong currents. Similar scenery to White Rock, over a larger area, with beautiful soft coral at 30m depth. A wide range of fish, including blue-spotted fantail stingrays, sweetlips and large groupers, as well as hawksbill turtles.

Chumphon or **Northwest Pinnacle** A granite pinnacle for experienced divers, starting 14m underwater and dropping off to over 36m, its top covered in anemones; surrounded by several smaller formations and offering the possibility of exceptional visibility. Barrel sponges, tree and antipatharian corals at deeper levels; a wide variety of fish, in large numbers, attract local fishermen; barracudas, batfish, whale sharks (seasonal) and huge groupers.

Southwest Pinnacle One of the top sites in terms of visibility, scenery and marine life for experienced divers. A huge pyramid-like pinnacle rising to 6m below the surface, its upper part covered in anemones, with smaller pinnacles around; at lower levels, granite boulders, barrel sponges, sea whips, bushy antipatharian and tree corals. Big groupers, snappers and barracudas; occasionally, large rays, leopard and sand sharks, swordfish, finback whales and whale sharks.

Sail Rock (Hin Bai) Midway between Ko Tao and Ko Pha Ngan, emerging from the sand at a depth of 40m and rising 15m above the sea's surface. Visibility of up to 30m, and an amazing ten-metre underwater chimney (vertical swim-through). Antipatharian corals, both bushes and whips, and carpets of anemones. Large groupers, snappers and fusiliers, blue-ringed angelfish, batfish and juvenile clown sweetlips; occasional whale sharks and mantas.

boats a day (50min–1hr; B350). The speedboats originate at Bangrak, Bophut and Maenam, the Lomprayah catamaran at Maenam, on **Ko Samui** (total journey time to Ko Tao on either 1hr 30min; B550), while the Songserm Express Boat originates at Na Thon (total journey time to Ko Tao 3hr 30min; B345). There's also a night boat from **Surat Thani**, departing at 11pm (9hr; B500).

These services fluctuate according to demand, and in high season extra boats may appear. All voyages to and from Ko Tao are also at the mercy of the weather, especially between June and November; plenty of travellers have missed onward connections through being stranded on the island, so it's best not to plan to visit at the end of your holiday.

Island transport

You can **get around** easily enough on foot, but there are roads of sorts now to most of the resorts, though some are still four-wheel drive only; motorbike taxis and pick-ups (B30–80/person, more late at night), rental mopeds (B150/day) and even a few jeeps (B1000/day) are available in Mae Hat. Longtail-boat taxis are available at Mae Hat or through your bungalow, or you could splash out on your own **round-island boat tour**, allowing you to explore the coastline fully, with stops for snorkelling and swimming (about B1000–1500 for the boat for the day, depending on the number of passengers); alternatively you could hook up with a group tour, again through your resort or at Mae Hat (usually about B450/head). Tao Siam at the southern end of Mae Hat (Ⓣ077 456720–1) charges B550 per person for a round-island tour in a speedboat, as well as organizing occasional **off-island trips** to Ang Thong National Marine Park for the day (B1500/person), or to Hat Rin for the full moon party (B600).

Mae Hat, the west coast and Ko Nang Yuan

All boats to Ko Tao dock at **MAE HAT**, a small, lively village with a few restaurants, clinics and supermarkets. A paved high street heads straight up the hill from the main pier (eventually ending up in Ao Chaloke Ban Kao), with narrower front streets running at right angles, parallel to the seafront. At the crossroads hard by the pier, there's a Krung Thai Bank currency-exchange booth (daily 9am–noon & 1–4pm; cash advances on credit cards available), while Siam City Bank has a branch with an ATM (and Western Union facilities) up the high street on the left (daily 8.30am–4.30pm). On the same side of the street, Prasit Service has a good reputation both as a travel agent and for Internet access, while B-Books across the road sells second-hand and new books. At the top of the village – turn left off the high street – is a post office (Mon–Fri 8.30am–4pm, Sat 8.30am–noon), with phone and poste-restante facilities. Also at the top of the village, on the road out towards Ao Chaloke Ban Kao, there's a gym, Monsoon, which offers yoga classes. MV Sports (Ⓣ07 264 2633 or 06 091 5718), south of the pier on the front street at *Kallaphanga Resort*, is one of several places on the island that rents kayaks (two-person B200/hr, B800/day), as well as offering sailing rental and tuition and water-skiing. If you don't see what you want listed above, don't worry, you'll probably find it at the branch of Mr J's supermarket and travel agency (see opposite), south of the pier near *Kallaphanga Resort*.

Not surprisingly, Mae Hat boasts the pick of the island's **eating and drinking** options. The *Swiss Bakery*, 100m from the pier up the high street, serves good coffee and a wide range of pastries and savouries, including delicious croissants, and now has a smarter-looking French-run rival across the road: *Cappuccino*, which does a mean *pain au chocolat* and coffee, plus gourmet sandwiches and salads. *The Californian* (closed Mon), up the street from the *Swiss Bakery*, serves up great burgers, as well as Mexican food, some interesting pastas, healthy fare such as roast veg and brown rice gratin, and high-energy smoothies. Off the north side of the high street near the pier, *Café del Sol* probably has the biggest choice of expensive Western goodies on the island – this is the place to come if you fancy breadcrumbed fish'n'chips or beef carpaccio with parmesan.

Whitening, a cool bar, restaurant and club 200m south of the pier down the front street, is more of a **nightlife** venue, famous for its Friday night parties, but it does dish up some very tasty and creative Thai and Western food on a great deck overlooking the bay. Other popular bars include *Dragon Bar*, a stylish place on the high street, painted ochre and decorated with elegant bamboo fronds, with regular DJ sessions; and *Sea Monkey*, opposite *Café del Sol*, a mellow spot with a pool table and nightly DJs playing anything from trip-hop to retro. Ask at the latter about Venus Park, Ko Tao's twice-monthly party that attracts DJs and performance artists from Bangkok and abroad.

South of Mae Hat

For somewhere good to stay on the southern edge of Mae Hat, try *Sensi Paradise Resort* (ⓣ077 456244, ⓦwww.kohtaoparadise.com; ❹–❽), whose pretty, flower-covered grounds sprawl over the lower slopes of the headland to the south of the village. It offers some of the best upmarket accommodation on the island, in well-designed wooden cottages with en-suite cold-water bathrooms, some with air-con and some with large terraces and open-air bathrooms.

In this direction, also handy for the village (15min walk) is *Jan Som Bay* (ⓣ09 031 5324; ❹), a characterful place under the palm trees overlooking a rocky beach. In traditional Thai style, the large wooden chalets have only shutters on the windows and slits under the roof to catch the breeze (bed nets rather than screens keep the mosquitoes off), as well as large verandas with deckchairs and tables.

A good way further down the coast (40min walk from Mae Hat or around B100 in a taxi-boat), *Tao Thong Villa* (ⓣ077 456078 or 077 456224; ❶–❸) offers plenty of shady seclusion and good snorkelling and swimming. Sturdy bungalows, some with en-suite bathrooms, are dotted around a rocky outcrop and the slope behind, with a breezy restaurant on the small, sandy isthmus in between.

North of Mae Hat

Five minutes' walk north of Mae Hat, at the top of a small rise opposite the school, you'll find the head office of Ko Tao's all-purpose fixer, Mr J (ⓣ077 456066–7). At the supermarket and travel agency here – and at Mr J's other shops in Mae Hat and Ao Chaloke Ban Kao – you can rent motorbikes (B150/day), sell unwanted air tickets, organize a visa extension, exchange several currencies, recycle batteries, buy and sell second-hand books, even borrow money. The attached café fries up the cheapest *phat thai* on the island, and if you're looking for functional, reliable accommodation, head round the back to *Mrs J's Bungalows* (❷–❸), a sloping terrace of large, clean, bright, mostly en-suite rooms.

To the north beyond a small promontory, you'll find **Hat Sai Ree**, Ko Tao's only long beach. The strip of white sand stretches for 2km in a gentle curve, backed by a smattering of coconut palms and around twenty bungalow resorts. Towards the midpoint of the beach, twenty minutes' walk from Mae Hat, *Sai Ree Cottages* (ⓣ077 456126; ❷–❹) has primitive huts and sturdy bungalows, all en suite and well maintained, in a beautiful, flower-strewn garden, and serves excellent grub. The spacious, tidy compound next door belongs to *Seashell Resort* (ⓣ077 456271, ⓦwww.kohtaoseashell.com), a friendly, well-run place under the tall palm trees; it offers Internet access and traditional massage, as well as very smart, sturdy bungalows, with en-suite showers and mosquito screens, either with fans (❹) or with air-con (❼). A hundred metres or so further up the beach, *Simple Life* (ⓣ077 456142; ❷–❹) makes a good budget choice, with en-suite, fan-cooled bungalows – some of them smart, tiled affairs – and great food. On a narrow but tree-lined strip of land next door is the upmarket *Sunsetburi Resort* (ⓣ077 456266, ⓕ077 456101), with its own large swimming pool and fan-cooled (❺) or air-con (❼), modern, concrete cottages. *Blue Wind* (ⓣ077 456116; ❸), next door but one, is another good choice here: the smart, well-kept bungalows are scattered about a shady compound, and the very good beachside restaurant serves up home-made breads, croissants and cakes, as well as pasta and other Western meals and Thai food; yoga courses are held here.

Around and inland from *Sunsetburi* and *Blue Wind* spreads **BAN HAT SAI REE**, a burgeoning village of supermarkets, clinics, travel agents, boutiques, Internet outlets and a branch of Siam City Bank with an ATM. *New Heaven* is here (closes 8.30pm), a bakery producing great breads, cakes, sandwiches, pies and the like, while *Leaves* combines a second-hand bookshop with café serving good coffee and a wide range of teas, as well as tasty cakes and light meals (closed Mon). Next to *Leaves*, *Suthep* is an expat favourite in the evenings, serving all kinds of Western food, including pasta, pizza and a good vegetarian selection, as well as tasty Thai food. On the beach at *New Way Resort*, *Dry Bar* is a night-time favourite, with regular DJ sessions and parties.

The paved road continues **north of the village** past a new luxury beachfront development, the welcoming *Koh Tao Coral Grand Resort* (Ⓣ077 456431–3, Ⓦwww.kohtaocoral.com; ❼–❾). Sandstone-pink octagonal cottages with hardwood floors and large, attractive bathrooms gather – some a little tightly – around a pretty, Y-shaped pool; most have hot water and air-con, some stretch to TV and mini-bar. North again beyond the end of Hat Sai Ree, another upscale spot, *Thipwimarn Resort* (Ⓣ077 456409, Ⓦwww.thipwimarnresort.com; ❻–❽), tumbles down a steep slope to its own small beach. Dotted around the hillside, smart, thatched, whitewashed villas, some with hot water, air-con and mini-bar, enjoy a fair measure of seclusion, fine sunset views and satellite TV. The road ends at isolated *CFT* (Ⓣ077 456730; ❶–❺) on the rocky northwest flank of the island, which offers cheap shacks or en-suite bungalows, and excellent food; there's no beach here, but you can swim, snorkel or kayak off the rocks (equipment available to rent) and the views over to Ko Nang Yuan are something else. Based at *CFT* is Here and Now (Ⓦwww.hereandnow.be), a respected centre for traditional massages, as well as t'ai chi/chi gong and massage courses.

Ko Nang Yuan

One kilometre off the northwest of Ko Tao, **KO NANG YUAN**, a close-knit group of three tiny islands encircled by a ring of easily accessible coral, provides the most spectacular beach scenery in these parts, thanks to the causeway of fine white sand that joins up the islands. Boats from the Lomprayah pier in Mae Hat, just south of the main pier, run back and forth three times a day (B60 return), but note that rules to protect the environment here include banning visitors from bringing cans and plastic bottles with them, and day-trippers are charged B100 to land on the island. Transfers from and to Mae Hat are free for people staying at the *Nangyuan Island Dive Resort* (Ⓣ077 456088–93, Ⓦwww.nangyuan.com; ❼–❾), which makes the most of its beautiful location, its swanky fan and air-con bungalows spreading over all three islands.

The east coast

The sheltered inlets of the **east coast**, most of them containing one or two sets of bungalows, can be reached by boat, pick-up or four-wheel-drive. The most northerly inhabitation here is at **Ao Hinwong**, a deeply recessed bay strewn with large boulders, which has a particularly remote, almost desolate air. Nevertheless, *Hin Wong Bungalows* (Ⓣ01 229 4856; ❸) is welcoming and provides good, basic accommodation on a steep, grassy slope above the rocks. In the middle of the coast, the dramatic tiered promontory of **Laem Thian** shelters a tiny beach and a colourful reef on its south side. With the headland to itself, *Laem Thian* (Ⓣ077 456477, Ⓔpingpong_laemthian@hotmail.com; ❷–❺) offers comfy bungalows and hotel-style rooms, decent food and a secluded, castaway feel.

Laem Thian's coral reef stretches down towards **Ao Ta Note**, a horseshoe inlet sprinkled with boulders and plenty of coarse sand, with the best snorkelling just north of the bay's mouth. The pick of the half-dozen resorts here is *Ta Note Bay Dive Resort* (Ⓣ077 456757–9; ❸–❺), with well-designed, en-suite wooden bungalows, set among thick bougainvillea, some enjoying large verandas and views out towards Ko Pha Ngan and Ko Samui. The last bay carved out of the turtle's shell, **Ao Leuk**, has a well-recessed beach and is serviced by the en-suite huts at *Ao Leuk Resort* (Ⓣ077 456692; ❷), which enjoy plenty of space and shade in a palm grove. The water is deep enough for good swimming and snorkelling, featuring hard and soft coral gardens and large boulders, which shelter an assortment of fish and green and hawksbill turtles.

The south coast

The southeast corner of the island sticks out in a long, thin mole of land, which shelters the sandy beach of **Hat Sai Daeng** on one side if the wind's coming from the northeast, or the rocky cove on the other side if it's blowing from the southwest. Straddling the headland is *New Heaven* (Ⓣ077 456462, Ⓦwww.newheavenresort.com; ❸), a laid-back, well-equipped place with a good kitchen, a small dive school and kayaks and snorkelling equipment; its pleasantly idiosyncratic en-suite bungalows enjoy plenty of elbow room and good views. Overlooking **Ao Thian Ok**, the next bay along on the **south coast**, *New Heaven* also own a scenic restaurant with bungalows (same phone number and website): on a beautiful deck perched high on the eastern flank of the Laem Tato headland, classic Thai dishes, including seafood specialities, are dished up in the evening, simpler fare at lunchtime; the bungalows (❹), on a tree-covered slope running down to a private sandy beach, feature large, cold-water bathrooms and verandas with great views, and include family and single rooms. The remote hills between Hat Sai Daeng and Ao Thian Ok provide the spectacular location for Ko Tao's first **spa**, *Jamahkiri* (call Ⓣ077 456400–1 for reservation and pick-up; Ⓦwww.jamahkiri.com), which offers saunas, body wraps, facials and massages, as well as a panoramic bar-restaurant.

The deep indent of **Ao Chaloke Ban Kao** is sheltered from the worst of both monsoons, and consequently has seen a fair amount of development, with several dive resorts taking advantage of the large, sheltered bay. There's a branch of Mr J's supermarket and travel agency (see p.625), and **rock-climbing** and bouldering can be organized through the Diving Village (Ⓣ06 038 3341).

Three accommodation options stand out from the crowd here. Run by a friendly, young bunch and home to Big Bubble Diving, *Viewpoint Bungalows* (Ⓣ077 456666 or 077 456777, Ⓔviewpointresort@hotmail.com; ❷–❼) sprawl along the western side of the bay; the best of the well-built, clean, en-suite bungalows have air-con and verandas overlooking the sunset from the headland. *Ko Tao Cottage International Dive Resort* (Ⓣ077 456133–4, Ⓦwww.kotaocottage.com; ❹–❼) makes a fair stab at institutionalized luxury and is worth a splurge, especially if you're considering scuba-diving with its diving school. The cottages, which have verandas and plain, smart decor (some with air-con, hot water, sea views and mini-bars), are ranged around a shady garden and restaurant by the beach, or up the hillside above.

On the east side of the bay, *Freedom Beach Bungalows* (Ⓣ077 456593; ❷–❹) are resolutely old-style, blue-painted huts with sturdy corrugated roofs and small verandas, with or without their own bathrooms; they dot a spacious slope that leads down to the idyllic white sand of Freedom Beach, a secluded palm-lined spot carved out of the **Laem Tato** headland and slung with hammocks.

Rough signposts will lead you beyond the bungalows for a fifteen-minute walk, the last stretch up a steep hillside to **Jon-Suwan Mountain Viewpoint**, which affords fantastic views, especially at sunset, over the neighbouring bays of Chaloke Ban Kao and Thian Ok and across to Ko Pha Ngan and Ko Samui.

Nakhon Si Thammarat and around

NAKHON SI THAMMARAT, the south's second-largest town, occupies a blind spot in the eyes of most tourists, whose focus is fixed on Ko Samui, 100km to the north. Its neglect is unfortunate, for it's an absorbing place, though a bit short on accommodation and other facilities. The south's major pilgrimage site and home to a huge military base, Nakhon is relaxed, self-confident and sophisticated, well known for its excellent cuisine and traditional handicrafts. The stores on Thanon Thachang are especially good for local nielloware (*kruang tom*), household items and jewellery, elegantly patterned in gold or silver often on black, and *yan lipao*, sturdy basketware made from intricately woven fern stems of different colours. Nakhon is also the best place in the country to see how Thai shadow plays work, at Suchart Subsin's workshop.

The town is recorded under the name of Ligor (or Lakhon), the capital of the kingdom of Lankasuka, as early as the second century, and classical dance-drama, *lakhon*, is supposed to have been developed here. Well placed for trade with China and southern India (via an overland route from the port of Trang, on the Andaman Sea), Nakhon was the point through which the Theravada form of Buddhism was imported from Sri Lanka and spread to Sukhothai, the capital of the new Thai state, in the thirteenth century.

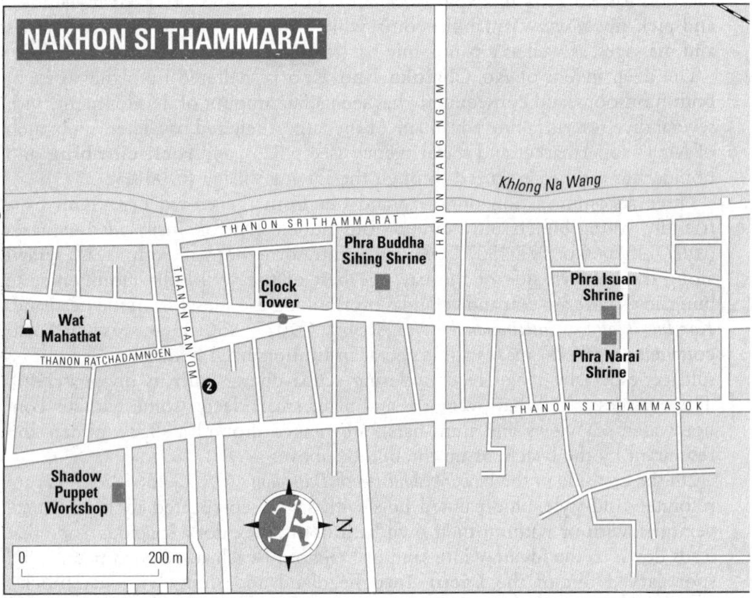

Known as *muang phra*, the "city of monks", Nakhon is still the religious capital of the south, and the main centre for **festivals**. The most important of these are the **Tamboon Deuan Sip**, held during the waning of the moon in the tenth lunar month (either September or October), and the **Hae Pha Khun That**, which is held several times a year, but most importantly on Maha Puja (February full moon – see also p.63) and on Visakha Puja (May full moon – see p.63). The purpose of the former is to pay homage to dead relatives and friends; it is believed that during this fifteen-day period all *pret* – ancestors who have been damned to hell – are allowed out to visit the world, and so their relatives perform a merit-making ceremony in the temples, presenting offerings from the first harvest to ease their suffering. A huge ten-day fair takes place at Sri Nakharin park on the north side of town at this time, as well as processions, shadow plays and other theatrical performances. The Hae Pha Khun That also attracts people from all over the south, to pay homage to the relics of the Buddha at Wat Mahathat. The centrepiece of this ceremony is the Pha Phra Bot, a strip of yellow cloth many hundreds of metres long, which is carried in a spectacular procession around the chedi.

The Town

The **town plan** is simple, but puzzling at first sight: it runs in a straight line for 7km from north to south and is rarely more than a few hundred metres wide, a layout originally dictated by the availability of fresh water. The modern centre for businesses and shops sits at the north end around the train station, with the main day market (to the east of the station on Thanon Pak Nakhon) in this food-conscious city displaying a particularly fascinating array of produce that's best around 8 or 9am. To the south, centred on the elegant, traditional mosque on Thanon Karom, lies the old Muslim quarter; south again is the start of the

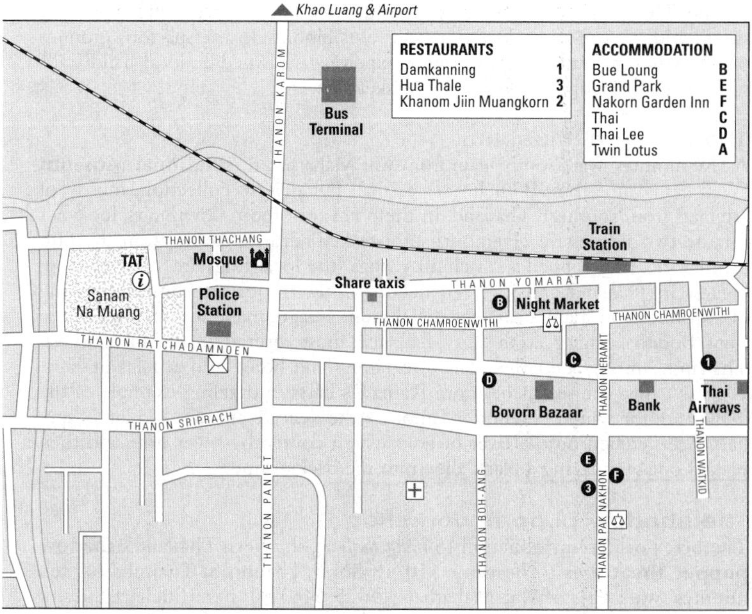

old city walls, of which few remains can be seen, and the historic centre, with the town's main places of interest now set in a leafy residential area.

Wat Mahathat

Missing out **Wat Mahathat** would be like going to Rome and not visiting St Peter's, for the Buddha relics in the vast chedi make this the south's most important shrine. In the courtyard inside the temple cloisters, which have their main entrance facing Thanon Ratchadamnoen, about 2km south of the modern centre, row upon row of smaller chedis, spiked like bayonets, surround the main chedi, the **Phra Boromathat**. This huge, stubby Sri Lankan bell supports a slender, ringed spire, which is in turn topped by a shiny pinnacle said to be covered in 600kg of gold leaf. According to the chronicles, relics of the Buddha were brought here from Sri Lanka two thousand years ago by an Indian prince and princess and enshrined in a chedi. It's undergone plenty of face-lifts since: an earlier Srivijayan version, a model of which stands at one corner, is encased in the present twelfth-century chedi. The most recent restoration work, funded by donations from all over Thailand, rescued it from collapse, although it still seems to be leaning dangerously to the southeast. Worshippers head for the north side's vast enclosed stairway, framed by lions and giants, which they liberally decorate with gold leaf to add to the shrine's radiance and gain some merit.

The **Viharn Kien Museum** (hours irregular, but usually daily 8am–4pm), which extends north from the chedi, is an Aladdin's cave of bric-a-brac, said to house fifty thousand artefacts donated by worshippers, ranging from ships made out of seashells to gold and silver models of the Bodhi Tree. At the entrance to the museum, you'll pass the Phra Puay, an image of the Buddha giving a gesture of reassurance. Women pray to the image when they want to have children, and the lucky ones return to give thanks and to leave photos of their chubby progeny.

Outside the cloister to the south is the eighteenth-century **Viharn Luang**, raised on elegant slanting columns, a beautiful example of Ayutthayan architecture. The interior is austere at ground level, but the red coffered ceiling shines with carved and gilded stars and lotus blooms. In the spacious grounds on the viharn's south side, cheerful, inexpensive stalls peddle local handicrafts such as shadow puppets, bronze and basketware.

The National Museum

A few minutes' walk south again from Wat Mahathat, the **National Museum** (Wed–Sun 9am–4pm; B30) houses a small but diverse collection, mostly of artefacts from southern Thailand. In the prehistory room downstairs, look out for the two impressive ceremonial bronze kettledrums, dating from the fifth century BC and topped with chunky frogs (the local frogs are said to be the biggest in Thailand and a prized delicacy). Next door are some interesting Hindu finds and many characteristic Buddha images made in imitation of the Phra Buddha Sihing at the city hall, the most revered image in southern Thailand. Among the collections of ceramics and household articles upstairs, you can't miss the seat panel from Rama V's barge, a dazzling example of the nielloware for which Nakhon is famous – the delicate animals and landscapes have been etched onto a layer of gold which covers the silver base, and then picked out by inlaying a black alloy into the background.

The shadow puppet workshop

The best possible introduction to *nang thalung*, southern Thailand's **shadow puppet theatre**, is to head for 110/18 Soi 3, Thanon Si Thammasok, ten minutes' walk east of Wat Mahathat (ⓣ075 346394): here Suchart Subsin,

Shadow puppets

Found throughout southern Asia, **shadow puppets** are one of the oldest forms of theatre, featuring in Buddhist literature as early as 400 BC. The art form seems to have come from India, via Java, to Thailand, where it's called *nang*, meaning "hide": the puppets are made from the skins of water buffalo or cows, which are softened in water, then pounded until almost transparent, before being carved and coloured to represent the characters of the play. The puppets are then manipulated on sticks in front of a bright light, to project their image onto a large white screen, while the story is narrated to the audience.

The grander version of the art, **nang yai** – "big hide", so called because the figures are life-size – deals only with the *Ramayana* story (see box on p.127). It's known to have been part of the entertainment at official ceremonies in the Ayutthayan period, but has now almost died out. The more populist version, **nang thalung** – *thalung* is probably a shortening of the town name, Phatthalung (which is just down the road from Nakhon), where this version of the art form is said to have originated – is also in decline now: performances are generally limited to temple festivals, marriages and ordinations, lasting usually from 9pm to dawn. As well as working the sixty-centimetre-high *nang thalung* puppets, the puppet master narrates the story, impersonates the characters, chants and cracks jokes to the accompaniment of flutes, fiddles and percussion instruments. Not surprisingly, in view of this virtuoso semi-improvised display, puppet masters are esteemed as possessed geniuses by their public.

At big festivals, companies often perform the *Ramayana*, sometimes in competition with each other; at smaller events they put on more down-to-earth stories, with stock characters such as the jokers Yor Thong, an angry man with a pot belly and a sword, and Kaew Kop, a man with a frog's head. Yogi, a wizard and teacher, is thought to protect the puppet master and his company from evil spirits with his magic, so he is always the first puppet on at the beginning of every performance.

In an attempt to halt their decline as a form of popular entertainment, the puppet companies are now incorporating modern instruments and characters in modern dress into their shows, and are boosting the love element in their stories. They're fighting a battle they can't win against television and cinemas, although at least the debt owed to shadow puppets has been acknowledged – *nang* has become the Thai word for "movie".

one of the south's leading exponents of *nang thalung*, and his son have opened up their workshop to the public, and, for a small fee (usually around B100), they'll show you a few scenes from a shadow play in the small open-air theatre. You can also see the intricate process of making the leather puppets and can buy the finished products as souvenirs: puppets sold here are of much better quality and design than those usually found on southern Thailand's souvenir stalls.

The Phra Buddha Sihing shrine

In the chapel of the provincial office on Thanon Ratchadamnoen sits the **Phra Buddha Sihing shrine** (Mon–Fri 8.30am–noon & 1–4pm), which according to legend was magically created in Sri Lanka in the second century. In the thirteenth century it was sent by ship to the king of Sukhothai, but the vessel sank and the image miraculously floated on a plank to Nakhon. Two other images, one in the National Museum in Bangkok, one in Wat Phra Singh in Chiang Mai, claim to be the authentic Phra Buddha Sihing, but none of the three is in the Sri Lankan style, so they are all probably derived from a lost original. Although similar to the other two in size and shape, the image in Nakhon has a style unique to this area, distinguished by the heavily pleated flap of its robe over the left shoulder, a beaky nose and harsh features, which sit uneasily on the short, corpulent body. The image's plumpness has given the style the name *khanom tom* – "banana and rice pudding".

Practicalities

Nakhon's **bus terminal** and **train station** are both fairly centrally placed, though the **airport**, served daily by PB Air (at the airport, ⓣ075 313030) and Thai Airways (1612 Thanon Ratchadamnoen, ⓣ075 342491 or 075 343874), is way out to the northwest of the city off the Surat Thani road; air-con minibuses meet arriving flights to ferry passengers to the centre of town. **Share-taxis** congregate towards the south end of Thanon Yomarat, most **air-con minibuses** on Thanon Chamroenwithi; on arrival, both should drop you off right at your destination. For getting around Nakhon, small blue **share-songthaews** ply up and down Thanon Ratchadamnoen for B6 a ride.

TAT has an office in a restored 1920s government officers' club on Sanam Na Muang (daily 8.30am–4.30pm; ⓣ075 346515–6, ⓔtatnakon@nrt.cscoms.com), which also covers the provinces of Trang and Phatthalung. The main **post office** (Mon–Fri 8.30am–4.30pm, Sat & Sun 8.30am–noon) is nearby on Thanon Ratchadamnoen, opposite the police station, and has international phones upstairs. Klickzone in Bovorn Bazaar on Thanon Ratchadamnoen is a good place to access the **Internet**.

Accommodation

Though many of Nakhon's **hotels** are dingy and soulless, there are enough exceptions to get by.

Bue Loung Hotel 1487/19 Soi Luang Muang, Thanon Chamroenwithi ⓣ075 341518, ⓕ075 342977. Central but reasonably quiet; gets the thumbs-up from visiting reps and businessmen, with a choice of fan and cold water or air-con, hot water and cable TV in basic double or twin rooms. ❷–❸

Grand Park Hotel 1204/79 Thanon Pak Nakhon ⓣ075 317666–73, ⓕ075 317674. If you're looking for something more upmarket in the centre of town, this recently established place is worth considering – it's large, stylish and bright, with air-con, hot water, TV and fridge in every room, and staff are cheery and attentive. ❺

Nakorn Garden Inn 1/4 Thanon Pak Nakhon ⓣ075 313333, ⓕ075 342926. A rustic but sophisticated haven in a three-storey, red-brick building overlooking a tree-shaded yard. Large, smart rooms come with air-con, hot water, cable TV and mini-bars. The best moderately priced option in town. ❹

Thai Hotel 1375 Thanon Ratchadamnoen ⓣ075 341509, ⓕ075 344858. Formerly top of the range in Nakhon, this large institutional high-rise can still offer clean, reliable rooms, with fans and cold water or air-con and hot water, all with TV. ❷–❹

Thai Lee Hotel 1130 Thanon Ratchadamnoen ⓣ075 356948. For rock-bottom accommodation, the large, plain and reasonably clean rooms here aren't a bad deal (it's worth asking for a room at the back of the hotel to escape the noise of the main street). ❶

Twin Lotus About 3km southeast of the centre at 97/8 Thanon Patanakarn Kukwang ⓣ075 323777, ⓕ075 323821. Gets pride of place in Nakhon – though not location; sports five restaurants, a large, attractive outdoor swimming pool and a health club. ❼

Eating and drinking

Nakhon is a great place for inexpensive **food**. Most famous, and justifiably so, is the lunchtime-only *Khanom Jiin Muangkorn* on Thanon Panyom near Wat Mahathat: the rough-and-ready outdoor restaurant dishes up one of the local specialities, *khanom jiin*, noodles topped with hot, sweet or fishy sauce served with *pak ruam*, a platter of crispy raw vegetables. Also boasting rock-bottom prices for lunch is *Krua Nakhon* in the Bovorn Bazaar on Thanon

Ratchadamnoen, a big, rustic pavilion with good *khanom jiin* and other local dishes: *kaeng som*, a mild yellow curry; *kaeng tai plaa*, fish stomach curry; *khao yam*, a delicious southern salad of rice and vegetables; and various *khanom wan*, coconut milk puddings.

Also in Bovorn Bazaar, *Hao Coffee* is a good spot for Thai or Western breakfast or lunch, with cakes and a wide selection of teas and coffees, including Thai filter coffee, to wash them down. It's a busy, friendly place, modelled on an old Chinese-style coffee shop, packed full of ageing violins, clocks and other antiques. The busy night market on Thanon Chamroenwithi near the *Bue Loung Hotel* is great for inexpensive food, such as *yam plaa meuk* and *yam kung*, and people-watching. In the old Muslim quarter, stalls near the corner of Thanon Karom and Thanon Ratchadamnoen sell good Muslim food, such as *roti* (sweet pancake – also available at stalls in and around the night market).

The best of Nakhon's more conventional **restaurants** is *Hua Thale* (daily 4–10pm), on Thanon Pak Nakhon opposite the *Nakorn Garden Inn,* renowned among locals for its excellent, inexpensive seafood. Run by a friendly Thai who lived in Los Angeles for many years and who will take your order (no English menu), it's plain and very clean, with the day's catch displayed out front and relaxing patio tables out back. Recommended dishes include whole baked fish and *hoy meng pho op mordin*, large green mussels in a delicious herb soup containing lemon grass, basil and mint. On the corner of Thanon Watkid and Thanon Ratchadamnoen, *Damkanning* is a decent fallback, one of many affordable, popular restaurants with pavement tables in the area.

If you're looking for somewhere to **drink**, head for *Rock 99*, a bar and grill with outdoor tables in the Bovorn Bazaar that's popular with Nakhon's sprinkling of expats, or to Thanon Watkid, where a group of congenial bars with names like *The Voice* offer live music.

Khao Luang National Park

Rising to the west of Nakhon Si Thammarat and temptingly visible from all over town, is 1835-metre-high **Khao Luang**, southern Thailand's highest mountain. A huge national park encompasses Khao Luang's jagged green peaks, beautiful streams with numerous waterfalls, tropical rainforest and fruit orchards, as well as the source of the Tapi River, one of the peninsula's main waterways, which flows into the Gulf of Thailand at Surat Thani. **Fauna** here include macaques, musk deer, civets, binturongs, as well as more difficult to see Malayan tapirs and serows, plus over two hundred bird species. There's an astonishing diversity of **flora** too, notably rhododendrons and begonias, dense mosses, ferns and lichens, plus more than three hundred species of both ground-growing and epiphytic orchids, some of which are unique to the park. The best time to visit is after the rainy season, from January onwards, when there should still be a decent flow in the waterfalls, but the trails will be dry and the leeches not so bad. However, the park's most distinguishing feature for visitors is probably its difficulty of access: main roads run around the 570-square-kilometre park with spurs into some of the waterfalls, but there are no roads across the park and very sparse public transport along the spur roads. Only **Krung Ching Waterfall**, one of Thailand's most spectacular, which features on the back of one-thousand-baht notes, really justifies the hassle of getting there.

Before heading off to Khao Luang, be sure to drop into Nakhon's TAT office for a useful park **brochure**, with a sketch map and sketchy details of the walking routes to Krung Ching waterfall and to the peak itself (for the latter, which begins at Ban Khiriwong on the southeast side of the park and involves at least one night camping on the mountain, ask at TAT about hiring local guides or try phoning the Khiriwong Agrotourism Promotion Centre on ⓣ075 309010 or 01 229 0829). Irregular **songthaews** on the main roads around the park and to Ban Khiriwong congregate on and around Thanon Chamroenwithi near the *Bue Loung Hotel* in Nakhon. The only **rental transport** available in Nakhon are pricey air-conditioned minibuses with drivers from Muang Korn Travel, 1242/67 Thanon Boh-Ang (ⓣ075 356574; B1500–1800/day); otherwise you might try doing a deal with a share-taxi driver at the bottom of Thanon Yomarat to take you to the park.

Krung Ching

A trip to **Krung Ching**, a nine-tier waterfall on the north side of the park, makes for a highly satisfying day out, with a mostly paved nature trail taking you through dense, steamy jungle to the most beautiful, third tier. The easiest way to **get there** from Nakhon with your own transport is to head north on Highway 401 towards Surat Thani, turning west at Tha Sala on to Highway 4140, then north again at Ban Nopphitam on to Highway 4186, before heading south from Ban Huai Phan on Highway 4188, the spur road to Ban Phitham and the Krung Ching park office, a total journey of about 70km. Songthaews will get you from Nakhon to Ban Huai Phan in about an hour, but you'd then have to hitch the last 13km. Four-person bungalows are available at the park office (B300); camping is free if you bring your own tent. There's a sporadically open canteen, and an informal shop selling snacks and drinks.

The shady four-kilometre **trail** to the dramatic main fall is very steep in parts, so you should allow four hours at least there and back. On the way you'll pass giant ferns, including a variety known as *maha sadam*, the largest fern in the world, gnarled banyan trees, forests of mangosteen and beautiful, thick stands of bamboo. You're bound to see colourful birds and insects, but you may well only hear macaques and other mammals. At the end, a long, stepped descent brings you to a perfectly positioned wooden platform with fantastic views of the forty-metre fall; here you can see how, shrouded in thick spray, it earns its Thai name, Fon Saen Ha, meaning "thousands of rainfalls".

Sichon

The coast north from Nakhon is dotted with small, Thai-orientated beach resorts, none of which can match the Ko Samui archipelago, in the Gulf beyond, for looks or facilities. However, if you're searching for a quiet, low-key antidote to Samui's Western-style commercialism, the most interesting of these resorts, **SICHON**, might be just the place.

Buses, air-con minibuses and share-taxis make the 65-kilometre journey north from Nakhon along the Surat Thani road to Talat Sichon, as the town's unpromising modern centre, with a few facilities such as banks and plenty of motorbike taxis, is known. This half-hearted, built-up area sprawls lazily eastwards for 3km to Pak Nam Sichon, a lively and scenic fishing port at the mouth of the eponymous river. Here, when they're not fishing in the bay, brightly coloured boats of all sizes draw up at the docks, backed by low-slung traditional wooden shophouses, the angular hills around Khanom beyond and, in the far distance, Ko Samui. About 1km south of the river mouth, **Hat Sichon** (aka Hat Hin Ngarm) begins, a pretty crescent bay of shelving white sand ending in a tree-tufted, rocky promontory. The beach is home to the best-value accommodation option in the area, *Prasarnsuk Villa* (Ⓣ075 335560–2, Ⓦwww.pssresort.com; ❸–❻), a neatly organized, welcoming place with a good, popular restaurant that stretches to a few tables and umbrellas on the beach. Amid spacious lawns, trees and flowers, bungalows range from decent, fan-cooled, en-suite affairs with verandas to "VIP" suites with air-con, hot water, fridge and TV. The next beach south, **Hat Piti**, is not quite so attractive, a long, straight, deserted stretch of white sand backed by palm trees. But if you want a few more facilities, this is where to come: *Piti Resort* (Ⓣ075 335301–4, Ⓦwww.pitiresort.com; ❻), 2km south of *Prasarnsuk*, can offer a small swimming pool, a fitness room and a tastefully designed beachside restaurant, as well as hot water, air-con, fridge and cable TV in all bungalows and rooms.

Travel details

Trains

Ban Krud to: Bangkok Hualamphong (2 daily; 6hr–7hr 30min); Bangkok Thonburi (2 daily; 7hr 30min); Hua Hin (2 daily; 3hr 30min); Nakhon Pathom (2 daily; 5hr 30min); Phetchaburi (2 daily; 6hr); Prachuap Khiri Khan (2 daily; 30min).
Bang Saphan Yai to: Bangkok Hualamphong (4 daily; 6hr 30min–8hr); Bangkok Thonburi (2 daily; 7hr 40min); Hua Hin (4 daily; 3–4hr); Nakhon Pathom (4 daily; 4hr 35min–6hr); Phetchaburi (3 daily; 4hr–4hr 30min); Prachuap Khiri Khan (4 daily; 20min–1hr).
Cha-am to: Bangkok (12 daily; 3hr 10min–3hr 50min); Chumphon (10 daily; 4–5hr); Hua Hin (11 daily; 25min); Surat Thani (7 daily; 7hr 10min–8hr 25min).
Chumphon to: Bangkok (12 daily; 7hr–9hr 30min); Hua Hin (12 daily; 3hr 30min–5hr); Surat Thani (10 daily; 2hr 15min–4hr).
Nakhon Si Thammarat to: Bangkok (2 daily; 15–16hr); Surat Thani (2 daily; 3hr 30min).
Hua Hin to: Bangkok (12 daily; 3hr 30min–4hr); Chumphon (10 daily; 3hr 30min–5hr 20min); Prachuap Khiri Khan (8 daily; 2hr 40min–3hr 40min); Surat Thani (10 daily; 5hr 40min–8hr).
Phetchaburi to: Bangkok Hualamphong (8 daily; 2hr 45min–3hr 45min); Cha-am (12 daily; 35min); Chumphon (10 daily; 4hr 30min–6hr 30min); Hua Hin (12 daily; 1hr); Prachuap Khiri Khan (8 daily; 3hr 40min–4hr 10min); Surat Thani (9 daily; 6hr 45min–9hr).
Prachuap Khiri Khan to: Bangkok Hualamphong (7 daily; 4hr 15min–7hr 40min); Bangkok Thonburi (2 daily; 6hr 30min); Nakhon Pathom (8 daily; 4hr 15min–5hr 40min).
Surat Thani (Phunphin) to: Bangkok (11 daily; 9–12hr); Butterworth (Malaysia; 1 daily; 10hr 30min); Hat Yai (5 daily; 4–5hr); Nakhon Si Thammarat (2 daily; 3hr 30min); Phatthalung (5 daily; 3–4hr); Sungai Kolok (2 daily; 9hr); Trang (2 daily; 4hr); Yala (4 daily; 6–8hr).

Buses

Cha-am to: Bangkok (every 40min; 2hr 45min–3hr 15min).
Chumphon to: Bangkok (12 daily; 6hr 30min–9hr); Hat Yai (4 daily; 7hr 30min); Hua Hin (every 40min; 3hr 30min–4hr 30min); Phuket (3 daily; 7hr); Ranong (hourly; 2hr); Surat Thani (every 30min; 2hr 45min).
Hua Hin to: Bangkok (every 40min; 3hr 30min); Cha-am (every 30min; 35min); Chumphon (every 40min; 3hr 30min–4hr 30min); Phetchaburi (every 30min; 1hr 30min); Pranburi (every 20min; 40min).
Ko Samui to: Bangkok (Southern Terminal; 5 daily; 15hr); Nakhon Si Thammarat (1 daily; 5hr).
Nakhon Si Thammarat to: Bangkok (Southern Terminal; 11 daily; 12hr); Hat Yai (16 daily; 3hr); Ko Samui (1 daily; 5hr); Krabi (2 daily; 3hr); Phatthalung (7 daily; 3hr); Phuket (7 daily; 7hr); Ranong (1 daily; 6hr); Songkhla (9 daily; 3hr); Surat Thani (13 daily; 3hr); Trang (3 daily; 2–3hr).
Phetchaburi to: Bangkok (every 30min; 2hr); Cha-am (every 30 min; 50min); Chumphon (about every 2hr; 5hr–6hr); Hua Hin (every 30 min; 1hr 30min).

Surat Thani to: Bangkok (Southern Terminal; 7 daily; 10–11hr); Chaiya (hourly; 1hr); Chumphon (every 30min; 2hr 45min); Hat Yai (11 daily; 4–5hr); Krabi (hourly; 4hr); Nakhon Si Thammarat (13 daily; 3hr); Phang-Nga (5 daily; 4hr); Phuket (11 daily; 5–6hr); Phunphin (every 10min; 30min); Ranong (7 daily; 4–5hr); Trang (2 daily; 3hr).

Flights

Chumphon to: Bangkok (3 weekly; 1hr 20min).
Ko Samui to: Bangkok (15 daily; 1hr 20min); Krabi (1 daily; 50min); Phuket (2 daily; 50min); Singapore (1 daily; 1hr 40min); Pattaya (1 daily; 1hr).
Nakhon Si Thammarat to: Bangkok (2–3 daily; 1hr 15min).
Surat Thani to: Bangkok (2 daily; 1hr 10min).

7

Southern Thailand: the Andaman coast

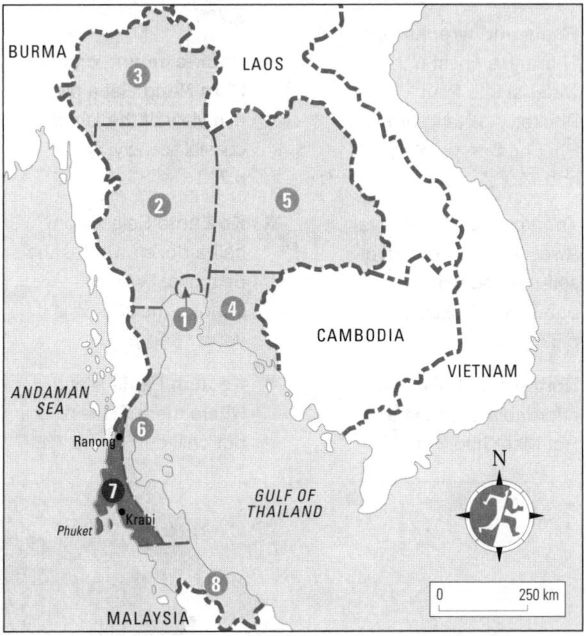

CHAPTER 7

Highlights

- **Khao Sok National Park** Sleep in a treehouse and wake to the sound of hooting gibbons. See p.654

- **Ko Similan** Remote chain of islands with some of the best diving in the world. See p.664

- **Reefs and wrecks** Dive Thailand's finest underwater sights from Phuket, Ao Nang or Ko Phi Phi. See pp.670, 713 and 720

- **The Vegetarian Festival** Awesome public acts of self-mortification on parade in Phuket. See p.675

- **Northwest Phuket** Quiet, affordable beaches at Hat Mai Khao, Hat Nai Thon and Hat Kamala. See pp.676, 678 and 680

- **Sea-canoeing along the Krabi coastline** The perfect way to explore the region's myriad mangrove swamps and secret lagoons. See p.706

- **Rock-climbing on Laem Phra Nang** Get a bird's-eye view of the fabulous coastal scenery. See p.709

- **Ko Lanta** Select from half a dozen white-sand beaches: lively or remote, the choice is yours. See p.726

- **Ko Jum** Petite island where there's little to do but chill out. See p.738

△ Laem Phra Nang

7

Southern Thailand: the Andaman coast

As Highway 4 switches from the east flank of the Thailand peninsula to the **Andaman coast** it enters a markedly different country: nourished by rain nearly all the year round, the vegetation down here is lushly tropical, with forests reaching up to 80m in height, and massive rubber and coconut plantations replacing the rice and sugar-cane fields of central Thailand. In this region's heartland the drama of the landscape is enhanced by sheer limestone crags, topographical hallmarks that spike every horizon and make for stunning views from the road. Even more spectacular – and the main crowd-puller – is the Andaman Sea itself: translucent turquoise and so clear in some places that you can see to a depth of 30m, it harbours the country's largest **coral reefs** and is far and away the top diving area in Thailand.

Unlike the Gulf coast, the Andaman coast is hit by the **southwest monsoon**, which usually gets going by the end of May and lasts into the middle of October. During this period heavy rain and high seas render some of the outer islands inaccessible, but conditions aren't generally severe enough to ruin a holiday on the other islands, or on the mainland, and you're likely to get good discounts on accommodation. Although some bungalows at the smaller resorts shut down entirely during low season, nearly every beach detailed in this chapter keeps at least one place open, and an increasing number of Andaman coast dive shops are leading expeditions year-round as well.

Eager to hit the high-profile beaches of Phuket and Krabi, most people either fly over the first three-hundred-kilometre stretch of the west coast or pass through it on an overnight bus, thereby missing out on the lushly forested hills of **Ranong** province and bypassing several gems: the tiny and still idyllic islands of **Ko Chang** (not to be confused with its larger, more famous namesake off the east coast) and **Ko Phayam**; the **Ko Surin** and **Ko Similan** island chains, whose reefs rate alongside the Maldives and the Great Barrier Reef; the enjoyable **Khao Sok National Park**, where you can stay in a treehouse beneath the shadows of looming limestone outcrops; and the mid-market resort of **Khao Lak**, which hugs the rugged mainland coast on the edge of Khao Lak National Park. Tourism begins in earnest on **Phuket**, Thailand's largest island and a popular place to learn to dive, though the high-rises and consumerist gloss that characterize many of the beaches here don't appeal to everyone. East around the mainland coast from Phuket, the limestone pinnacles that so dominate the landscape of southern

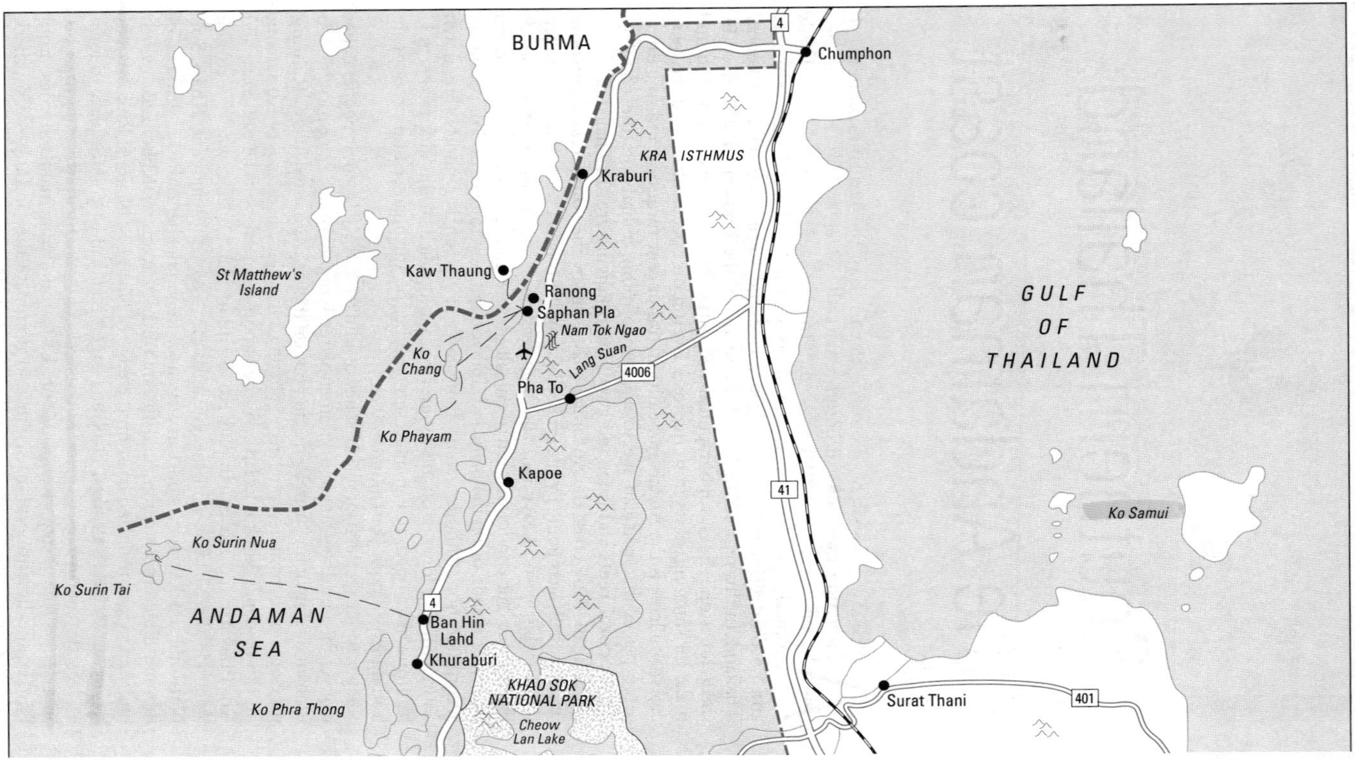
BURMA
Chumphon
KRA ISTHMUS
Kraburi
Kaw Thaung
St Matthew's Island
Ranong
Saphan Pla
Nam Tok Ngao
Lang Suan
Ko Chang
4006
Pha To
Ko Phayam
Kapoe
41
4
GULF OF THAILAND
Ko Samui
Ko Surin Nua
Ko Surin Tai
ANDAMAN SEA
Ban Hin Lahd
Khuraburi
KHAO SOK NATIONAL PARK
Cheow Lan Lake
Ko Phra Thong
Surat Thani
401

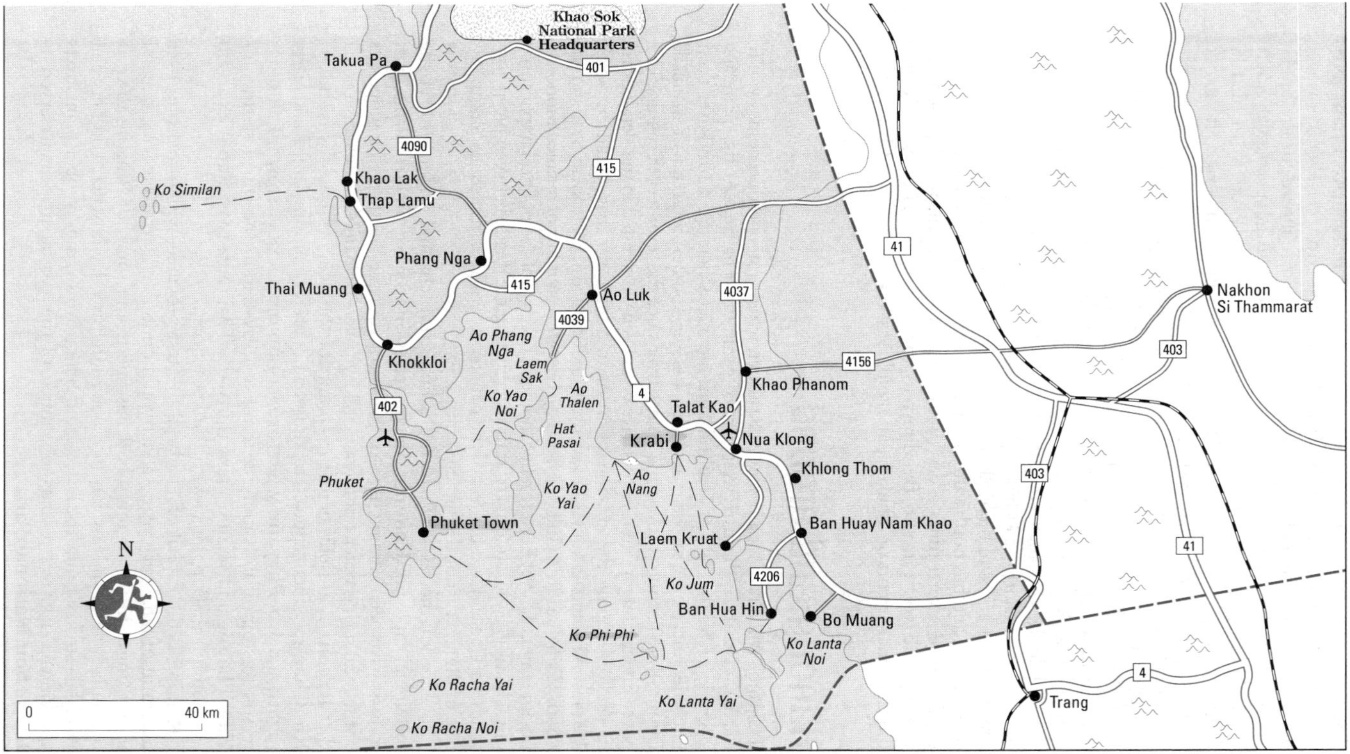
Khao Sok
National Park
Headquarters
Takua Pa
401
4090
415
Ko Similan
Khao Lak
Thap Lamu
Phang Nga
415
Thai Muang
Ao Luk
4039
4037
41
Nakhon
Si Thammarat
Ao Phang
Nga
Laem
Sak
Khokkloi
4156
403
Khao Phanom
4
Ko Yao
Noi
Ao
Thalen
402
Talat Kao
Krabi
Nua Klong
Hat
Pasai
Phuket
Ao
Nang
Khlong Thom
Ko Yao
Yai
403
Phuket Town
Laem Kruat
Ban Huay Nam Khao
41
N
4206
Ko Jum
Ban Hua Hin
Bo Muang
Ko Phi Phi
Ko Lanta
Noi
4
Ko Racha Yai
Ko Lanta Yai
Trang
0
40 km
Ko Racha Noi

Thailand suddenly begin to pepper the sea as well, making **Ao Phang Nga** one of the most fascinating bays in the country. Most travellers, however, head straight for the hub of the region at **Krabi**, springboard for the hugely popular mainland beaches of unexceptional **Ao Nang**, spectacular **Laem Phra Nang** and beautiful but depressingly over-exploited **Ko Phi Phi**. Bigger, better preserved **Ko Lanta Yai** makes a more laid-back alternative, with tiny nearby **Ko Jum** another calm option.

Getting to Andaman coast destinations is made easy by Highway 4, also known as the Phetkasem Highway – and usually called Thanon Phetkasem when it passes through towns. The road runs from Bangkok to the Malaysian border, and frequent **buses** ply this route, connecting all mainland tourist destinations. There is no rail line down the Andaman coast, but many travellers take the **train** from Bangkok to the Gulf coast, enjoy that region's splendours for a while and then nip over to the Andaman coast by bus before proceeding southwards. A less common alternative for access to the Krabi region is to take the train down to Trang, south of Ko Lanta, and bus northwards from there. **Ferries** to the most popular islands usually leave several times a day (with reduced services during the monsoon season), and you can also **fly** direct to the Andaman coast: there's a busy international airport on Phuket, plus useful local ones in Krabi and Ranong.

Ranong and around

Thailand's Andaman coast begins at **Kraburi**, where a signpost welcomes you to the **Kra Isthmus**, the narrowest part of peninsular Thailand. At this point just 22km separates the Gulf of Thailand from the inlet where the Chan River flows into the Andaman Sea, west of which lies the southernmost tip of mainland Burma, Kaw Thaung (aka Victoria Point). Ever since the seventeenth century, Thai governments and foreign investors have been keenly interested in this slender strip of land, envisaging the creation of an Asian Suez canal that would cut some 1500km off shipping routes between the Indian Ocean (Andaman Sea) and the South China Sea (the Gulf of Thailand). Despite a number of detailed proposals, no agreement has yet been reached, not least because of the political implications of such a waterway: quite apart from accentuating the divide between prosperous southern Thailand and the rest of the country, it would vastly reduce Singapore's role in the international shipping industry.

Seventy kilometres south of the isthmus, the channel widens out at the provincial capital of **Ranong**, which thrives on its proximity to Burma. Thai tourists have been coming here for years, to savour the health-giving properties of the local spring water, but foreign holidaymakers have only recently discovered that Ranong is a useful departure-point for the delightful nearby islands of **Ko Chang,** which appeals to those who prefer paraffin lamps and early nights, and **Ko Phayam**, which attracts a more sociable crowd. The other reason to stop off in Ranong is to make a day-trip to the Burmese town of **Kaw Thaung** and acquire a new thirty-day Thai tourist visa into the bargain – an option that's popular with Phuket expats.

Ranong is the capital of Thailand's wettest province, which soaks up over 5000mm of rain every year – a fact you'll undoubtedly experience first hand if you linger in the region. The landscape to the south of Ranong town is particularly lush, and any journey along Highway 4 will whizz you between waterfall-streaked hills to the east and mangrove swamps, rubber plantations and casuarina groves to the west; much of this coastal strip is preserved as **Laem Son National Park**.

Ranong Town

Despite being the wettest town in the whole country, **RANONG** has an enjoyable buzz about it, fuelled in great part by the seemingly amiable mix of Burmese, Thai, Chinese and Malay inhabitants. As with most border areas, however, there's also a flourishing illegal trade operating out of Ranong – in amphetamines, guns and labour, apparently – not to mention the inevitable tensions over international fishing rights, which sometimes end in shoot-outs, though the closest you're likely to get to any of these activities is reading about them in the *Bangkok Post*.

The **geothermal springs** so favoured by Thai tourists are the focus of diminutive Raksawarin Park, about 3km east of the central Thanon Ruangrat market and accessible on songthaew #2 or by motorbike taxi. You can't submerge yourself in the water here, but you can buy eggs to boil in the sulphurous 65°C water, or paddle in the cooler pools that have been siphoned off from the main springs. To properly appreciate the springs you need to soak in public mineral baths at *Jansom Thara Hotel*, five minutes' walk away.

If you haven't had enough of water features, you could make a trip out of town to the impressive **Nam Tok Ngao**, an enormous waterfall 12km south of Ranong, which cascades almost all the way down the eastern hillside in full view of Highway 4. Any south-bound bus will drop you there. Another enjoyable day out would be to head into the interior for a day's organized rafting at Pha To, 51km east of Ranong, off Route 4006 to Chumphon; see p.583 for details.

Practicalities

Phuket Airlines (Ⓣ077 824591, Ⓦwww.phuketairlines.com) operates daily **flights** between Bangkok and Ranong, which arrive at the **airport** 20km south of Ranong on Highway 4; share-taxis meet the flights, charging up to B100 per person, or you can walk out of the airport onto Highway 4 and flag down any north-bound bus. Air tickets can be bought from *Pon's Place* (see below). All west-coast buses travelling between Bangkok or Chumphon and Khuraburi, Takua Pa, Phuket or Krabi stop briefly at Ranong's **bus station** on Highway 4 (Thanon Phetkasem), 1500m southeast of the central market; coming from Khao Sok, you'll probably need to change buses at Takua Pa. **Minibuses** to and from Surat Thani use a more central depot on Thanon Luwan and the terminus for minibuses to and from Chumphon is towards the northern end of Thanon Ruangrat. Several city **songthaews** serve Ranong bus station, including one that runs to the Thanon Ruangrat hotels and day market, and another that shuttles between the bus station and the port area at Saphan Pla, 5km to the southwest, where you pick up boats to Kaw Thaung, Ko Chang and Ko Phayam (see p.645); another songthaew runs direct from the market on Thanon Ruangrat to the Saphan Pla port area. Many songthaews have their destinations written in English on the side, and most charge B7–10 per ride.

There is no official **tourist information** in town, but several hotels carry detailed advertisements for bungalows on Ko Chang and Ko Phayam and you can book most island bungalows through them. *Pon's Place* on Thanon Ruangrat (daily 7am–midnight; Ⓣ077 823344) is both a restaurant and a **tour agency**, and if you book island accommodation here you get free transport to the port; *Pon* also offers various local tours (including a visa run to Burma and back for B600, which also covers the cost of the visa), rents out motorbikes (B200/day) and cars (B1200/day) and sells air, bus and (Chumphon) train tickets. *Kiwi Orchid Guest House*, in the bus station compound on Thanon

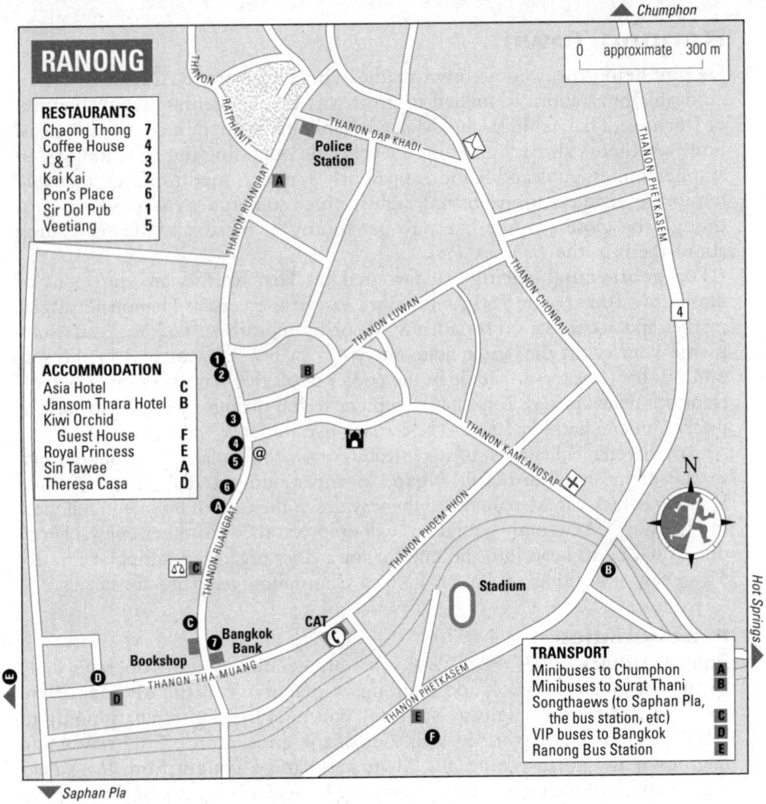

Phetkasem, is another good source of local info: you can buy boat tickets for Ko Surin here (B450–1000), book Khao Sok, Ko Chang and Ko Phayam accommodation, and organize a visa run into Burma. *Kai Kai* restaurant and Internet centre further north on Thanon Ruangrat also rents out motorbikes for B200 per day.

Marking the town centre, Thanon Ruangrat is where you'll find several of the budget hotels and traveller-oriented restaurants, as well as the day and night **markets**. There's a Bangkok Bank with an ATM and an **exchange** counter at the southern end of Thanon Ruangrat, and several other banks with ATMs within a few hundred metres' walk, west of the junction with Thanon Tha Muang. North of the *Sin Tawee* hotel, Thanon Ruangrat has half a dozen places offering **Internet access**, and the CAT **international phone office** (Mon–Fri 8.30am–4.30pm) on Thanon Tha Muang also has Catnet Internet terminals. The **post office** is about 1.5km northeast of the central market, on Thanon Chonrau. English-language books and newspapers are stocked at the **bookstore** diagonally across the road from the Bangkok Bank. The Thonburi-Ranong **hospital** (Ⓣ077 834214) is at 41/142 Thanon Tha Muang. Ranong's **immigration office** is 5km out of town in Saphan Pla; for details on how to extend or renew your visa here see p.646. Ko Phayam's A-One Diving **dive centre** (Ⓣ077 832984, Ⓦwww.a-one-diving.com) has an office in Saphan Pla, near the immigration office.

Accommodation

Most travellers linger in Ranong for just one night, but there's a reasonable spread of accommodation to choose from.

Asia Hotel 39/9 Thanon Ruangrat ⓣ077 811113. Painted pale blue inside and out, this typical Thai-Chinese hotel is the cheapest place in town, offering scruffy but large and decent enough fan and air-con rooms, all of them en suite. Staff speak English and are used to dealing with travellers en route to the islands. Very central. ❷–❸

Jansom Thara Hotel 2/10 Thanon Phetkasem ⓣ077 821611, ⓦwww.jansom-hot-spa-hotel.com. A mid-range hotel that makes the most of its situation out near the hot springs, offering mineral baths, public and private Jacuzzis and a range of pretty comfortable air-con rooms. Also has a swimming pool and several restaurants. ❻–❼

Kiwi Orchid Guest House Located in an unmissable mango-coloured building in the bus station compound on Thanon Phetkasem, some distance from the town centre ⓣ077 889 0473, ⓔerl@Thailand.com. This New Zealand-Thai-run guest house is the most traveller-oriented accommodation in town, offering heaps of local information, various tours, Internet access and luggage storage. There's a pleasant communal seating area on the upstairs veranda and rooms are nice enough, but all share bathrooms and some have no window. ❸

Royal Princess 41/144 Thanon Tha Muang ⓣ077 835240, ⓦwww.royalprincess.com. Modern chain hotel that's the most luxurious in town. As well as standard upmarket air-con rooms, the hotel boasts Jacuzzis with spa water, and a swimming pool. Large discounts often available. ❽

Sin Tawee 81/1 Thanon Ruangrat ⓣ077 811213. Central place, of a similar style to the *Asia Hotel* but with better – and pricier – rooms. There's a choice of en-suite accommodation ranging from small fan rooms to larger versions with TV, and air-con options at the top end. ❷–❹

Theresa Casa Thanon Tha Muang ⓣ077 811135. Comprising just a dozen clean, pleasant rooms set around a small garden and open-sided lobby area, this is a quiet guest house, set behind a bakery shop (which also serves fresh coffee). It's a bit of a walk from the market, but handy for transport to Saphan Pla. All rooms have bathrooms, though not all the cheaper fan rooms have windows; some rooms have air-con and there are also a couple of very comfortable VIP options. ❸–❺

Eating and drinking

Ranong's ethnic diversity ensures an ample range of **eating** options, and a stroll up Thanon Ruangrat will take you past Muslim foodstalls and Chinese pastry shops as well as a small but typically Thai night market.

Chaong Thong 8–10 Thanon Ruangrat. Choose from a long and varied selection of dishes that includes Spanish omelette, shrimp curry and lemon-grass tea, as well as lots of veggie options and hearty breakfasts. Closed Sun. Inexpensive.

Coffee House 173 Thanon Ruangrat. Managed by the same French-Thai family who run *Aow Yai Bungalows* on Ko Phayam, this is the place for filled baguettes, pancakes – and coffee. You can also book accommodation at *Aow Yai Bungalows* here. Inexpensive.

J & T Thanon Ruangrat. Very popular family café serving cheap Thai fare, including stir-fries, soups, salads and over-rice dishes. Inexpensive.

Kai Kai Thanon Ruangrat. Decent selection of typical travellers' fare, plus Thai soups, fried rice and ice creams. Also has Internet access and motorbike rental. Inexpensive.

Pon's Place Thanon Ruangrat. Opens at 7.30am for breakfast – Thai or farang style – and continues dishing out food and travel advice until midnight. Inexpensive.

Sir Dol Pub 301 Thanon Ruangrat. Pool, live music, beer and snacks nightly from 7pm.

Veetiang Thanon Ruangrat. Boasts an extensive menu covering all manner of seafood cooked to Thai and Chinese recipes, as well as standard over-rice dishes. Inexpensive.

Saphan Pla and Kaw Thaung

Ranong's port is 5km southwest of the town centre at **SAPHAN PLA** and gives access to Kaw Thaung in Burma as well as to the islands of Ko Chang and Ko Phayam. Frequent **songthaews** run from Ranong's Thanon Ruangrat and bus station to Saphan Pla (20min; B7 to the main road or B10–15 to the pier). If going to Kaw Thaung, alight from the songthaew at the immigration office on the main road, as described below. If heading for the islands, your songthaew driver might take you down to the pier head; if not, follow the signs to the pier from Saphan Pla's main-road drop-off, a walk of less than 500m. For details of boat times see the relevant island accounts. Any songthaew will take you back from Saphan Pla to Ranong, but if you want to go directly to the bus station, catch a blue one.

Into Burma: Kaw Thaung (Ko Song)

The southernmost tip of Burma – known as **KAW THAUNG** in Burmese, Ko Song in Thai, and Victoria Point when it was a British colony – lies just a few kilometres west of Ranong across the Chan River estuary, and is easily reached by longtail boat from Saphan Pla on the Thai side of the border. So long as you follow the procedures detailed below, it's quite straightforward for foreign tourists to **enter Burma** at this point, and nipping across the border and back is a popular way of getting a new thirty-day Thai tourist visa – though it does mean you're giving your money to the Burmese military regime.

Although there's nothing much to do in Kaw Thaung itself, it's an enjoyable focus for a trip out of Ranong, and sufficiently different from Thai towns to merit an hour or two's visit. Alighting at the quay, the market and tiny town centre lie before you, while over to your right, about twenty minutes' walk away, you can see an eye-catching hilltop pagoda, surmounted by a huge reclining Buddha and a ring of smaller ones. Once you've explored the covered market behind the quay and picked your way through the piles of tin trunks and sacks of rice that crowd the surrounding streets, it's fun to take a coffee break in one of the typically Burmese quayside pastry shops before negotiating a ride in a boat back to Saphan Pla; Thai money is perfectly acceptable in Kaw Thaung.

Practicalities

All non-Thais must first get a Thai exit stamp before boarding a boat to Kaw Thaung, so get out of the songthaew at the Thai **immigration office** (daily 8.30am–4.30pm), across the road from the Thai Farmers Bank on the outskirts of Saphan Pla. Once you've got your stamp you can either accompany the hovering boat boys (in which case you'll probably end up chartering the boat) or continue walking down the road for about fifteen minutes until you reach the PTT petrol station, where you should turn down to the right to find a quayside thick with longtails. There's another small quay a few hundred metres further up the quayside, but the PTT one is busier.

Longtails leave for Kaw Thaung when they have enough custom: the fare should be B50 per person in an already crowded boat, or B150 one way to charter the whole boat. The crossing takes about thirty minutes, but the longtails have to stop en route at a tiny island containing the **Burmese immigration** office, where you buy your Burmese visa: US$5 (or B300) for a one- to three-day pass, or US$36 for thirty days. For stays of more than a day you will need to change US dollars into Foreign Exchange Certificates (FECs): $50 for two to three days, or $300 for thirty days. Legally, you are not allowed to travel beyond Kaw Thaung unless you have already bought a proper visa from a Burmese embassy (see p.18) to supplement the Kaw Thaung passes. If you do have a visa, you can fly to Rangoon from the airport 7km north of Kaw Thaung, but road travel from here to Rangoon is currently forbidden to foreigners.

If you're simply making the trip to get a new Thai visa, you can take the boat straight back to Saphan Pla from the immigration island, though Kaw Thaung is just a few minutes' boat ride further on. If you do visit Kaw Thaung, when you return to Saphan Pla your boat will stop at the Burmese immigration island to collect your passport; once back on Thai soil you must return to the Thai immigration office to get your new Thai thirty-day tourist visa before catching a songthaew back to Ranong.

Ko Chang

Not to be confused with the much larger island of Ko Chang on Thailand's east coast (see p.456), Ranong's **KO CHANG** is a forested little island about 5km offshore, with less than perfect greyish-yellow-sand beaches but a charmingly low-key atmosphere. The beaches are connected by tracks through the trees; there are no cars (just a few motorbikes) and, for the moment at least, only sporadic, self-generated supplies of electricity. Most islanders make their living from fishing and from the rubber, palm and cashew-nut plantations that dominate the flatter patches of the interior. The pace of life on Ko Chang is very slow, and for the relatively small number of tourists who make it here the emphasis is strongly on kicking back and chilling out – bring your own hammock and you'll fit right in. Nearly all the bungalows on Ko Chang **close** down from June until mid- or late October, when the island is subjected to very heavy rain; many bungalow staff relocate to the mainland for this period, so you should phone ahead to check first.

The best of Ko Chang's beaches are on the west coast, and of these the longest, nicest and most popular is **Ao Yai**. Effectively divided in two by a narrow lagoon, the main cross-island track, and the stumps of a long wooden pier, Ao Yai enjoys a fine view of the brooding silhouette of Burma's St Matthew's Island, which dominates the western horizon. The 800-metre-long stretch of Ao Yai that runs north from the lagoon is the most attractive on the island, nice and wide even at high tide, and especially popular with kids. South of the khlong, the beach is very narrow at high tide, but when the water goes out you have to walk a longish distance to find any depth. Southern Ao Yai, which begins just beyond the rocky divide occupied by *Ko Chang Resort*, has greyish sand but is fine for swimming. Further south still, around an impassable rocky headland, tiny secluded gold-sand **Ao Daddaeng** (Tadang) is sandwiched between massive boulders and holds just a few bungalows: reach it via a five-minute footpath from behind *Tadang Bay*. Much further south and accessible either by boat or by a five-kilometre track, remote black-sand **Ao Lek** at Ko Chang's southwestern tip has another couple of bungalow outfits: *Tommy's Garden Bungalows* and *N&X*. Follow the track behind *Eden* on northern Ao Yai to reach *Ko Chang Contex* and *Hornbill*, each in its own little bay – en route, at the top of the hill (currently the best place on the island to get a mobile phone signal), you'll pass the barbed-wire perimeters of a military camp, established here to monitor the fairly frequent skirmishes between Thai and Burmese fishermen.

A narrow concrete road connects central Ao Yai with a mangrove-filled little harbour on the east coast, a distance of around 1700m that can be walked in under half an hour. The western end of the road begins beside the island's only temple, **Wat Pah Ko Chang**, whose bot and monks' quarters are partially hidden amongst the trees beside the beach, with a sign that asks tourists to dress modestly when in the area and not to swim or sunbathe in front of it. About halfway between the two coasts, a crossroads bisects Ko Chang's only **village**, a tiny settlement that is home to most of the islanders and holds just a few shops, restaurants and a clinic. Signs at the crossroads direct you south to Saphan Hin (3km) and Ao Lek (5km); follow the unsigned northern route for a concrete path to the northern pier (the wet-season boat drop).

Practicalities

Longtail **boats** to Ko Chang leave from Ranong's port area, Saphan Pla; see p.645 for details of how to get to the port, but note that some accommodation-booking agents in Ranong offer free transport to the pier for their customers. At the time of writing there was one scheduled daily boat **departure** at 9am, and usually another one at noon, with others likely to be running during high season; ask at Ranong information centres for the current schedule. If there are more than six in your party, you can probably charter your own boat almost immediately. The journey takes about an hour and costs B100 per person; you'll be dropped as close as possible to your intended bungalow. If heading for Saphan Hin or Ao Lek (aka Ao Siad), you'll probably be put on the Ko Phayam boat (see p.650), which stops at those two beaches en route. The Ko Chang boat generally only goes to the main west-coast beach of Ao Yai. If you're travelling to Ko Chang from Ko Phayam and want to stay on Ao Yai, it's generally simpler, though more expensive, to take the boat back to Saphan Pla on the mainland and start again, as it's a long hot walk to Ao Yai from Ao Lek and Saphan Hin. Very few boats travel to Ko Chang during the **rainy months** of June through October, and those that do drop passengers on the island's east coast, a three-kilometre walk from Ao Yai. During the tourist season, there's at least one boat a day from Ko Chang **back to Saphan Pla**, generally in the morning between about 7am and 9am – ask at your bungalows the day before.

To date there is very little commercial activity on Ko Chang, save for a few local **minimarkets** selling basic necessities: at *Golden Bee* and behind the lagoon on Ao Yai, and at *Sunshine Restaurant*, beside the crossroads in the heart of the island. The crossroads is also where you'll find the island **clinic**. **Overseas phone calls** can be made at *Golden Bee* and *Cashew Resort* and you can also buy Ranong–Bangkok air tickets from *Cashew*. The German-run **dive shop** Aladdin Safari (ⓣ077 820472, ⓦwww.aladdindivecruise.de) is based next to *Cashew Resort* and from late October through April runs live-aboards to Ko Surin (3 days; B12,900) and Ko Similan (4 days; B15,400), as well as PADI dive courses (B3900 for the four-day Openwater).

Accommodation and eating

Most of the **bungalow** operations are simple wooden-plank constructions, comprising just a dozen huts and a small restaurant each. Though they nearly all have their own generators (which usually only operate in the evenings), it's a good idea to bring a torch as many bungalow managers bow to customers' preference to stick to candles and paraffin lamps. Except where stated, all bungalows listed here **close** down from June until mid- or late October. Most of the bungalows serve a broadly similar menu of travellers' **food**, but *Cashew Resort* also bakes fresh bread; *Nature View* brews its own mango and papaya wine (but doesn't serve food); *Golden Bee* features lots of veggie options and seafood dishes; and *Mama's* is well known for its home-cooked south-German specialities.

Ao Yai

Cashew Resort North of the lagoon on central Ao Yai ⓣ077 820116. The longest-running set of bungalows on the island, and also the largest, this place is nicely spread out among the cashew trees and has simple wooden huts with shared bathrooms, as well as more solid en-suite versions with glass windows, all of them well spaced and private. Has the most facilities on the island, including foreign exchange and Visa card capability, and an overseas phone service. ❶–❸

Chang Tong South of the lagoon on central Ao Yai ⓣ077 820178. Simple, clean wood and bamboo bungalows, well spaced in two rows. All have mosquito nets and all but the cheapest have bathrooms. ❶–❷

Eden Bungalows Far northern end of Ao Yai Widely spaced en-suite bungalows of varying sizes, nicely secluded amongst the trees. ❶–❷
Full Moon Southern Ao Yai ⓣ077 820130, ⓔfamilymoon99@hotmail.com. Exceptionally friendly place offering cheap huts with or without bathrooms at the back of the shore, wooden en-suite bungalows on the beachfront, and some larger bungalows for up to five people. ❶–❸
Golden Bee Just south of the lagoon on central Ao Yai ⓣ077 820129. Set among the palm trees, this is a welcoming and exuberantly run place. Huts come in various styles but are all fairly simple, ranging from extremely cheap and fairly dilapidated through en-suite options in two sizes. Open all year. ❶–❷
Ko Chang Resort Southern Ao Yai ⓣ077 820176, ⓔsound_of_sea@lycos.com. Occupying a fabulous spot high on the rocks, the en-suite wooden bungalows here have fine sea views from their balconies and are simply but intelligently designed inside. The older ones are set further back and share bathrooms, and there are some newer inland en-suite versions too. There's a stylish restaurant with low tables, cushions and a similarly engaging panorama, and the swimmable beach is just a couple of minutes' scramble to the south. ❶–❷
Nature View Bungalows Far southern Ao Yai ⓔkornelis@mail.com. Occupying a fine elevated position, with views right up the beach, this place comprises just four huge bungalows, all of them with big glass windows and en-suite bathrooms. The bungalows are lit by paraffin lamps, but elsewhere everything's run on solar and wind-powered energy. The Canadian-Thai owners serve drinks but no food in the restaurant area on the first floor of the rather bizarre three-storey structure that's designed to look like a Chinese pagoda. ❷–❸
Sunset Bungalows North of the lagoon on central Ao Yai ⓣ077 820171. Very popular outfit that's set in a rather dark grove of cashew-nut trees on the edge of the beach, comprising decent huts with or without attached bathrooms. Also has a congenial socializing and restaurant area. ❶–❸
Tadang Bay Far southern Ao Yai ⓣ077 820177. Set up on the headland, the en-suite wooden cabins here enjoy nice long views of the whole bay. The price depends on the size of the hut. ❶–❷

The rest of the island

Hornbill North around two headlands from Ao Yai. Simple, unobtrusive bungalows built amongst the trees behind their own little gold-sand bay, just a few minutes' walk north of *Ko Chang Contex*, and within easy reach of Ao Yai. Lives up to its name, as majestic black-and-white hornbills are a common sight here. ❶–❷
Ko Chang Contex About a 10min walk over the hill from *Eden* and Ao Yai. Located in its own peaceful little bay, the handful of huts here is scattered across the rocks above the beach, with just the resident black-and-white hornbills for company. ❶–❷
Lae Tawan Five minutes' walk south over the headland from Ao Yai, on Ao Daddaeng ⓣ077 820179. Fifteen funky, idiosyncratically designed huts, with or without bathroom. Shares the bay with just a couple of other bungalow outfits and enjoys great sunset views. ❶–❸
Mama's Bungalows South over the headland from Ao Yai, on Ao Daddaeng ⓣ077 820180, ⓔmamasbungalows@yahoo.com. German-Thai-run set of just eight attractive bungalows built in a pretty flower garden atop a rocky outcrop that overlooks the bay and affords fine views of St Matthew's Island. Choose between bungalows that share bathrooms and those that have their own nicely designed en-suite facilities. The restaurant occupies an equally appealing spot. Open all year. ❶–❷

Ko Phayam

The diminutive kangaroo-shaped island of **KO PHAYAM** offers fine white-sand beaches and coral reefs and is home to around five hundred people, most of whom either make their living from prawn, squid and crab fishing, or from growing cashew nuts, *sator* beans, coconut palms and rubber trees. Many islanders live in Ko Phayam's only **village**, on the northeast coast, which comprises a pier, a temple and about two dozen shops and businesses and connects to other corners of the island by a network of concrete roads and muddy tracks. A motorbike taxi service plies the more popular routes, but no journey is very great as the island measures just four by seven kilometres at its widest points. Because of the roads, Ko Phayam has a slightly more developed feel to it than neighbouring Ko Chang, underlined by a fledgling though still very low-key bar scene, and the presence of a significant number of young foreigners who choose to spend six or more months here every year. Some expats even take up the rainy-season challenge, staying on through the downpours and rough seas that lash the island from June to October, but many bungalows close down during this time.

Ko Phayam's nicest beach is the three-kilometre-long **Ao Yai** on the southwest coast, a beautiful long sweep of soft white sand that curves quite deeply at its northern and southern ends into rocky outcrops that offer some snorkelling possibilities. The shore is pounded by decent waves that are fun for boogie-boarding and pretty safe; the sunsets are quite spectacular here too. For the moment Ao Yai's bungalow operations are still widely spaced along the shoreline, and much of the forest behind the beach is still intact. You're more than likely to see – and hear – some of the resident black-and-white hornbills at dawn and dusk, and sightings of crab-eating macaques and sea eagles are also very possible.

The northwest coast is scalloped into **Ao Kao Kwai**, a name that's pronounced locally as **Ao Kao Fai** and translates as **Buffalo Bay**; if you stand on the cliffside midway along the bay you'll appreciate how it got its name, as the two halves of the beach curve out into buffalo-like horns. The southern half of Ao Kao Kwai is subject to both very low and very high tides, which makes it unreliable for swimming, but the northern stretch, particularly around *Sai Thong* and *Mr Gao* bungalows, is pretty, with appealing golden sand, decent swimming at any tide, and none of the big waves that characterize Ao Yai. The entire beach affords impressive views of the enormous hilly profile of Burma's St Matthew's Island.

Practicalities

From November to May there's at least one **boat** a day from Ranong's port area, Saphan Pla, to Ko Phayam, departing at 9am and taking two to three hours to reach the village pier on the east coast (B100); there should also be another boat at about 2pm, but check with the information centres in Ranong. See p.645 for details of how to get to the Saphan Pla pier from Ranong, and note that some accommodation-booking agents in Ranong offer free transport to the pier. The boat returns from Ko Phayam to Saphan Pla at about 8am and there is sometimes another departure at 3pm. Boats are less regular during the rainy season, from June to October, when many bungalows close, so call ahead during this period to check first.

There are no cars on the island, and the main mode of transport is motorbikes. **Motorbike taxis** always meet incoming boats at the pier and should be easy enough to find in Ko Phayam village; on the beaches, contact staff at your bungalow. The going rate for a ride between the village and the beaches is B50. The other option is to rent a motorbike in the village or through your bungalow for B150–200 per day: be warned though that many tracks are steep, extremely rough, and pitted with deep holes, and that you'll need to contend with both sand and mud. Many travellers heading into the village from one of the beaches opt to **walk** at least one way: from Ao Yai it's a pleasant five-kilometre, 75-minute stroll along the narrow and fairly shady concrete road, with the possibility of stopping for a breather at the aptly named *Middle Island Restaurant*; from Ao Kao Kwai to the village takes less than an hour.

The **village** has just enough to cater to travellers' needs, including a few tiny general stores, a 24-hour minimarket, a couple of small restaurants and a **clinic**. Most mobile phones can get a signal in the village but not elsewhere on the island. *Oscar's* bar (see below), which is just north of the pier-head, is a good source of island information, rents motorbikes and offers **Internet** access

(B3/minute). A-One Diving (☎077 832984, Ⓦwww.a-one-diving.com), a few metres west of the pier-head, is also useful: it serves as the island **post office** and also offers Internet access, as well as teaching PADI **dive** courses and running live-aboards to Ko Surin (from B9000 for two days) and Ko Similan (from B16,000 for four days) and further afield to Burma Banks and the Mergui archipelago. *Mr Gao* on Ao Kao Kwai (☎077 823995) runs two-day snorkelling trips to Ko Surin at B2500 per person: transport is by speedboat and the price includes food, a round-archipelago tour, and accommodation in national park tents.

Accommodation, eating and drinking

The best of Ko Phayam's **accommodation** is found on the two main beaches, Ao Yai and Ao Kao Kwai. Unless otherwise stated all bungalows close down during the wet season, from June to October. Every set of bungalows has a **restaurant**, and there are several others away from the two beaches, including *Middle Island Restaurant*, on the Ao Yai–village road, which serves very cheap Thai food and drink; and *Oscar's*, in the village. *Oscar's* has no menu, serving anything from breakfasts to shepherds' pie, seafood to Indian curries, depending on availability, but it's most famous for its (mostly open-air) **bar**, which is the focal point of the expat social scene and makes an enjoyable place to while away an afternoon, as well as being a useful source of island information. Customers who stay late and can't get home are invited to crash out at the adjacent *Hangover Hut*. Several bungalow operations on Ao Yai also run tiny beach bars during high season (Dec–Feb).

Ao Yai

Aow Yai Bungalow Gilles and Phatchara At the southern end of the bay ☎077 821753, Ⓦwww.R24.org/travelsmart.net/nst/aowyai, Ⓔgilles_phatchara@hotmail.com. Established by a French-Thai couple, this was the first set of bungalows on the island and remains one of the most popular, with a good travellers' vibe. The bungalows are dotted around a garden of flowers, fruit trees and palms; each has its own washbasin inside, and only the very cheapest share bathrooms. Otherwise you're looking at a range of wood and concrete options, with price depending on size (some sleep four) and whether you want electricity all day. Staff rent boogie boards and can arrange boat trips around the island. During the rainy season it's best to email to check whether it's open. ❶–❹

Bamboo Bungalows In the centre of the bay ☎077 820012. The 25 bungalows here are set under the trees in a well-tended flower garden. They've been built with imaginative use of local materials and all have bathrooms and mosquito nets. At the top of the range, the appealing shell-studded concrete bungalows have verandas and characterful open-air bathrooms; other options include a choice of bamboo and wood huts, with price depending on size. *Bamboo* rents out boogie boards and offers an overseas phone service. It's run by an Israeli-Thai couple and stays opens all year round. ❷–❹

Bann Suan Kayoo Overlooking the rocks at the far northern end of the bay Ⓔbannsuankayoo@yahoo.com. Set in a flower garden, the best of the neat woven-rattan bungalows here all have a deck, a bathroom and a fan, while the split-bamboo huts are of a simpler design, but still en suite. ❷–❸

Coconut Bungalow In the centre of the bay ☎077 820011. Run by a Ko Phayam family, this place offers a range of accommodation, from small bamboo en-suite huts through larger wood or bamboo versions to big concrete bungalows at the top end. Snorkels and a dinghy are available for rent. ❷–❺

Smile Hut In the centre of the bay ☎077 820335, Ⓦwww.thaismilehut.com. Low-key enterprise of simple bamboo huts, all of them with their own bathroom and some of them with upstairs sleeping quarters (but no view); price depends on size and location. Offers Thai massage and lends boogie boards free to its guests. ❷–❸

Ao Kao Kwai (Buffalo Bay)

Kao Kwai Hill (aka **JPR**) In the centre of the bay ☎01 847 6285, Ⓔttrisikkha@hotmail.com. Nine good-quality bamboo, wood and concrete bungalows set amongst the cashew and *sator* trees high up on the rocks. The gorgeously sited restaurant overlooks a pair of eyecatchingly eroded outcrops and affords perfect views of Ao Kao Kwai's trademark "buffalo horn" layout. ❷–❸

Mr Gao Northern part of the bay ☎077 823995. Located on the best stretch of the beach, this is a well-established operation comprising just seven exceptionally well-designed bungalows, in assorted sizes and luxuriousness. All have bathrooms and most have polished wood floors, screened windows and thoughtfully furnished interiors. Mr Gao runs overnight trips to the Surin islands (see p.654) as well as fishing and snorkelling outings to other parts of Ko Phayam. ❶–❹

Sai Thong Bungalows Northern part of the bay ☎077 820466. Friendly, local setup that shares the same pretty stretch of beach with *Mr Gao* and has just five rattan huts, each furnished with an unusually thick mattress, a mosquito net and its own well-appointed bathroom. ❷

Vijit Southern part of the bay ☎077 834082. Though it occupies the least attractive stretch of the beach, this long-running outfit is popular and well priced, with some very cheap en-suite huts and other nicer, more spacious bungalows set between the trees. Runs snorkelling trips to other beaches and is open all year. ❶–❸

Ko Surin and around

The coastal town of **Khuraburi**, 110km south of Ranong on Highway 4, is the closest (though not necessarily the most convenient) departure point for the magnificent national park island chain of **Ko Surin**, a group of five small islands around 60km offshore, just inside Thai waters. Also accessible from Khuraburi is the island of **Ko Phra Thong**, which is exceptionally rewarding for bird-watching and site of a popular eco-resort.

The chao ley

Sometimes called sea gypsies, the **chao ley** or *chao nam* ("people of the sea" or "water people") have been living off the seas around the west coast of the Malay peninsula for hundreds of years. Some still pursue a traditional nomadic existence, living in self-contained houseboats known as **kabang**, but many have now made permanent homes in Andaman coast settlements in Thailand and Malaysia.

Dark-skinned and sometimes with an auburn tinge to their hair, the sea gypsies are thought to be Austronesian or Malay in **origin**, and their migration probably first started west and then north from the Riau-Lingga archipelago, which lies between Singapore and Sumatra. It's estimated that around five thousand *chao ley* now live off the coasts of the Andaman Sea, divided into five groups, with distinct lifestyles and dialects.

Of the different groups, the **Urak Lawoy**, who have settled on Ko Lipe in Ko Tarutao National Park (see p.759) and in Phuket (see p.692), are the most integrated into Thai society. They are known as *Mai Thai*, or "New Thai", and many have found work on coconut plantations or as fishermen. Other groups continue in the more traditional *chao ley* **occupations** of hunting for pearls and seashells on the ocean floor, attaching stones to their waists to dive to depths of 60m with only an air-hose connecting them to the surface; sometimes they fish in this way too, taking down enormous nets into which they herd the fish as they walk along the sea bed. Their agility and courage make them good birds'-nesters as well (see box on p.725), enabling them to harvest the tiny nests of sea swifts from nooks and crannies hundreds of metres high inside caves along the Andaman coast.

The **Moken** of Thailand's Ko Surin islands and Burma's Mergui archipelago are the most traditional of the *chao ley* communities and still lead remote, itinerant lives. They own no land or property, but are dependent on fresh water and beaches to

Ko Surin

The spectacular shallow reefs around **KO SURIN** National Park (B200 entry) offer some of the best snorkelling and diving on the Andaman coast. The most beautiful and easily explored of the reefs are those surrounding the two main islands in the group, Ko Surin Nua (north) and Ko Surin Tai (south), which are separated only by a narrow channel. **SURIN NUA**, slightly the larger at about 5km across, holds the national park headquarters, visitor centre and park accommodation, as well as an interpretative trail and a turtle hatchery. The water is so clear here, and the reefs so close to the surface, that you can make out a forest of sea anemones while sitting in a boat just 10m from the park headquarters' beach. Visibility off the east and west coasts of both islands stretches to a depth of 40m.

Across the channel, **SURIN TAI** is the long-established home of a community of *chao ley* (see below) who divide their time between boat-building and fishing. Every April, as part of the Songkhran New Year festivities, hundreds of *chao ley* from nearby islands (including those in Burmese waters) congregate here to celebrate with a ceremony involving, among other rites, the release into the sea of several hundred turtles, which are a symbol of longevity and especially precious to Thai and Chinese people.

Practicalities

Because the islands are so far out at sea, Ko Surin is effectively out of bounds during the monsoon season, when the sixty-kilometre trip becomes a potentially suicidal undertaking. During the rest of the year, most visitors join an organized live-aboard **dive trip** out of Khao Lak (see p.662), Phuket (see p.670),

collect shells and sea slugs to sell to Thai traders. They have extensive knowledge of the plants that grow in the remaining jungles on Thailand's west-coast islands, using eighty different species for food alone, and thirty for medicinal purposes.

The sea gypsies are **animists**, with a strong connection both to the natural spirits of island and sea and to their own ancestral spirits. On some beaches they set up totem poles as a contact point between the spirits, their ancestors and their shaman. The sea gypsies have a rich **musical heritage** too. The Moken do not use any instruments as such, making do with found objects for percussion; the Urak Lawoy on the other hand, due to their closer proximity to the Thai and Malay cultures, are excellent violin- and drum-players. During community entertainments, the male musicians form a semicircle around the old women, who dance and sing about the sea, the jungle and their families. See the discography on p.830 for details of *chao ley* music on CD.

Building a new boat is the ultimate expression of what it is to be a *chao ley*, and every newly married couple has a *kabang* built for them. But the complex art of constructing a seaworthy home from a single tree trunk, and the way of life it represents, is disappearing. In Thailand, where **assimilation** is actively promoted by the government, the truly nomadic flotillas have become increasingly marginalized, and the number of undeveloped islands they can visit unhindered gets smaller year by year. On Phuket, the Urak Lawoy villages have become sightseeing attractions, where busloads of tourists trade cute photo poses for coins and sweets, setting in motion a dangerous cycle of dependency. In Burma, the continued political instability and repression has further restricted their mobility, and there is a real danger of getting arrested and even forced into slave labour – nothing short of hell on earth especially for a people whose lives have always been determined by the waves and the wind.

Ranong (see p.644), Ko Chang (see p.648) or Ko Phayam (see p.651). Many of these trips also feature other remote reefs such as Richelieu Rock or the Burma Banks and cost from B9000 for two days; *Mr Gao* on Ko Phayam runs overnight **snorkelling** trips to Ko Surin at B2500 per person (see p.652).

If you'd rather travel independently, you'll need to make your way to the Ko Surin pier at **Ban Hin Lahd**, about 6km north of Khuraburi town. Board any bus running along Highway 4 between Phuket, Khao Lak, Takua Pa, Ranong and Chumphon, get off at kilometre-stone 720.7, and then take a motorbike taxi down to the pier. Two different types of **boat** run to Ko Surin from here, but phone ahead to check departure times as these change frequently and can depend on the weather. Speedboats depart Ban Hin Lahd at about 8.30am, return from Ko Surin at 3pm, take one hour and cost B1700 round-trip. Open-deck ferries (which are safer in rough weather) depart Ban Hin Lahd at about 8.30am, return from Ko Surin at about 10am, take three to five hours and cost B900 return. To check times and purchase tickets contact either Greenview Travel (Ⓣ076 421360) or Sabina Tour (Ⓣ076 491585) in Khuraburi, or *Kiwi Orchid Guest House* in Ranong (Ⓣ07 889 0473, Ⓔerl@Thailand.com). Once you're on the islands, you can **charter a longtail** from the *chao ley* to explore the coasts (about B700/day).

If you're making your own way to Ko Surin from Ban Hin Lahd, you could either spend the previous night at a **hotel** in Ranong, a ninety-minute bus ride away, or stay closer to hand, at *Khuraburi Greenview Resort* (Ⓣ076 421360, Ⓦandaman-island-hopping.com/hotels/kuraburigreen.htm; ❼–❽), 12km south of Khuraburi, alongside Highway 4, at kilometre-stone 739. *Greenview's* attractively designed wooden chalets all have air-con, TV and use of the swimming pool, and the hotel sells tickets for speedboats to Ko Surin and can provide transfers to the pier.

For **accommodation on Ko Surin**, you have the choice of renting one of the expensive six-person national park **bungalows** on Surin Nua (B1200), settling for a dorm bed (B100) in the nearby longhouse or opting for a national park tent (from B200). Accommodation gets very booked up, so it's worth reserving a bed in advance by calling Ⓣ076 491378 or 076 419028, or visiting the National Parks website at Ⓦwww.thaiforestbooking.com. Otherwise, you can camp in your own tent in the vicinity of the park buildings. Unless you take your own **food** to the islands, you'll be restricted to the meals served at the restaurant on Surin Nua.

Ko Phra Thong

One kilometre off the Khuraburi coast, **KO PHRA THONG** (Golden Buddha Island) is home to an eco-resort, the *Golden Buddha Beach Resort* (Ⓣ01 892 2208, Ⓦwww.losthorizonsasia.com; ❻) which, as well as renting out kayaks and running a turtle sanctuary, also hosts yoga retreats. Its bungalows have mosquito nets and open-air bathrooms, and are set among the trees beside the main beach, which is 7km long and blessed with fine white sand. Access is via the Ko Surin pier at Ban Hin Lahd; see above for transport information, or contact *Golden Buddha* for transfers from Phuket, Ranong or Khuraburi.

Khao Sok National Park

Most of the Andaman coast's attractions are found, unsurprisingly enough, along the shoreline, but the stunning jungle-clad karsts of **KHAO SOK**

NATIONAL PARK are well worth heading inland for. Located about halfway between the southern peninsula's two coasts and easily accessible from Khao Lak, Phuket and Surat Thani, the park has become a popular stop on the travellers' trail and is furnished with enough guest houses and adventure-trekking possibilities to make a very enjoyable detour. Much of the park is carpeted in impenetrable rainforest, home to gaurs, leopard cats and tigers among others – and up to 155 species of bird. It protects the watershed of the Sok River, is dotted with dozens of waterfalls, and rises to a peak of nearly 1000m. The limestone crags that dominate almost every vista are breathtaking, never more so than in the early morning: waking up to the sound of hooting gibbons and the sight of thick white mist curling around the karst formations is an experience not quickly forgotten.

Practicalities

The park entrance is located at kilometre-stone 109 on Highway 401, which cuts east from the junction town of **Takua Pa**, 40km south of Khuraburi, and is the route taken by most Surat Thani-bound **buses** from Khao Lak and a few from Phuket. It's a spectacular journey through a landscape of limestone crags and jungle, and takes less than an hour from Takua Pa, ninety minutes from Khao Lak, and two hours from Surat Thani. Buses run at least every ninety minutes in both directions; at the park entrance you'll be met by guest-house staff offering free lifts to their accommodation, the furthest of which is 3km from the main road. Coming by bus from Bangkok, Hua Hin or Chumphon, take a Surat Thani-bound bus, but ask to be dropped off at the junction with the Takua Pa road, about 20km before Surat Thani, and then change onto a Takua Pa bus. If coming direct from Surat Thani, think twice about using the tourist **minibus** services to Khao Sok that leave at or after 3pm: many people have complained that, despite advertising a door-to-door service, these minibuses simply dump their passengers at an affiliated guest house on the Khao Sok access road, delaying their arrival until after dark. Onward bus connections from Khao Sok are frequent and guest-house staff will ferry you back to the main road, or you can make use of the various minibus services to the most popular destinations, including Krabi (2hr; B250), Ko Samui (3hr; B350), Trang (4hr 30min; B400) and Penang (12hr; B750).

Despite the area being a national park, a **tourist village** has grown up along the access road to the national park visitor centre and trailheads, and along the main track that bisects it. As well as around twenty sets of bungalows, you'll find half a dozen minimarkets and email centres, a currency exchange (but no ATM), laundry services and the all-important massage centres – a life-saver after a challenging jungle trek. *Bamboo House 2* sells some over-the-counter medicines and rents out **motorbikes** (B200/day); *Treetops River Huts* rents **mountain bikes**; and Khao Sok Diving Connection acts as a booking agent for **diving trips** to Ko Similan out of Khao Lak.

Accommodation and eating

The longest-running and most peaceful of Khao Sok's jungle **guest houses** are situated down the side track that runs alongside the river; the newer ones are located along the main north–south road. Nearly all the guest houses serve food, and there are several independent restaurants as well – including the popular *Nirvana Bar*, across from *Nung House*; more controversially, there are also a growing number of travellers' bars, at least one of which shatters the fairy-light tranquillity by pumping out loud techno music every night.

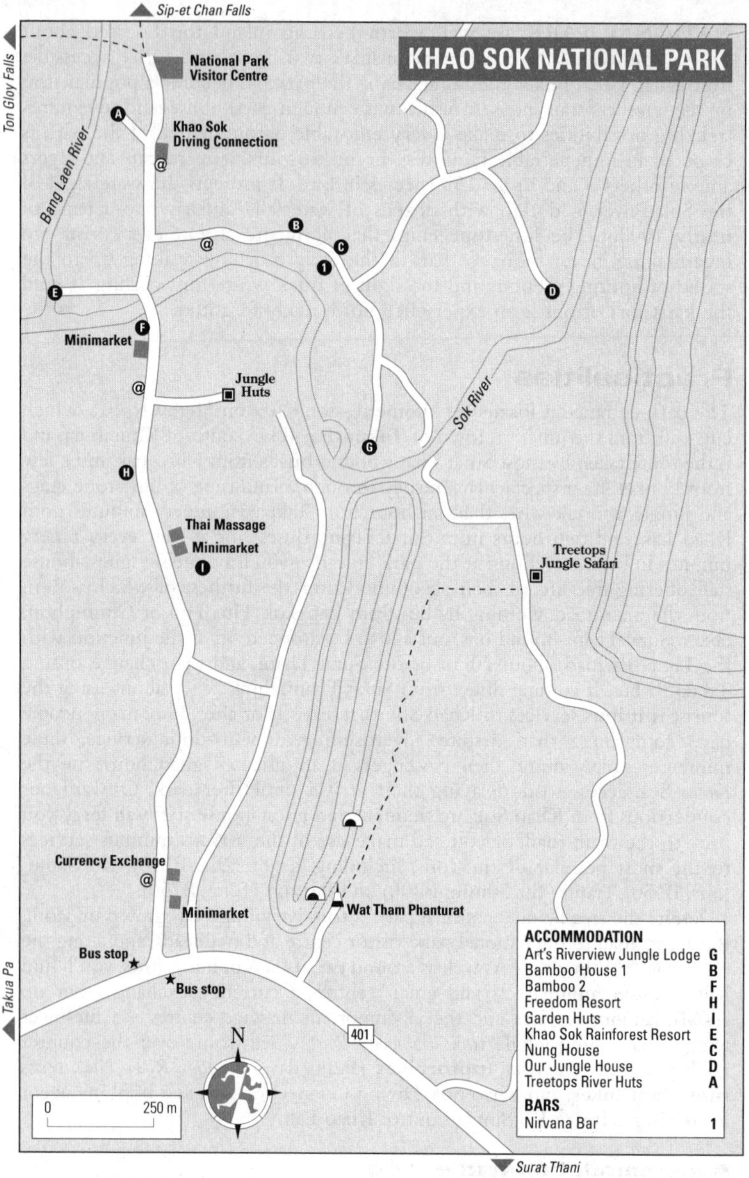

Art's Riverview Jungle Lodge
ⓣ06 282 2677, ⓕ076 421614. One of the longest-running and most popular places to stay in Khao Sok, with 25 bungalows nicely located away from the main fray and mostly enjoying lovely river views. The cheaper bungalows are spacious wooden affairs, with shutters and a deck; the deluxe versions are even bigger and tastefully furnished. Also has a few treetop huts. It's popular with backpackers' tour groups, so advance booking is recommended. 5–7

Bamboo House 1 ⓣ01 787 7484, ⓦwww.krabidir.com/bamboo/index. One of the first guest houses in the park and run by members of the park warden's family, this place offers a range of options, from simple bamboo huts with attached bathrooms to stilted wooden huts, concrete versions, and a couple of treehouses. Also has a swimming platform in the river. ❷–❹

Bamboo 2 ⓣ077 395141. Just a handful of well-appointed wood and concrete bungalows, all with nice tiled bathrooms and most of them overlooking the river – but within earshot of the road. ❹

Freedom Resort ⓣ01 370 1620. Australian-managed place comprising a few sizeable bamboo houses on stilts, with verandas that look straight into a patch of jungle. Standard simply furnished accommodation, with en-suite bathrooms. The adjacent restaurant hosts regular barbecues and plays loud music. ❷–❹

Garden Huts ⓣ07 282 8223. Set well away from the main track and prettily located beside a small pond surrounded by wild flowers, the half-dozen bungalows here are simple bamboo affairs with attached bathrooms, mosquito nets, fans and electricity, and nice views of the karsts. ❷

Khao Sok Rainforest Resort ⓣ077 395135, ⓦwww.vacations.to/rainforest, ⓔkhaosokrainforest@yahoo.com. Run by the relatives of the two most famous jungle guides in Khao Sok, this place has five spectacularly sited "mountain view" bungalows – set high on a jungle slope and affording unsurpassed karst views – plus eight other bungalows at ground level, overlooking the river. Rooms are decent enough if a bit faded and are all en suite. ❹–❺

Nung House ⓣ077 359024, ⓦwww.nunghouse.com. Friendly place with fourteen huts run by the park warden's son and his family. Choose between simple bamboo constructions with en-suite facilities, concrete bungalows, and treehouses. Their attractive restaurant serves good food and has Thai-style seating; you can take cookery courses here, too. ❷–❹

Our Jungle House ⓕ09 909 6814, ⓦwww.losthorizonsasia.com. The most romantically located of Khao Sok's guest houses is set in a secluded riverside spot beneath the limestone cliffs, about a 15min walk beyond *Nung House*. You can choose between beautifully situated treehouses and private cabins by the river, all of them simply but elegantly designed wooden constructions, furnished with mosquito nets and bathrooms. Well managed and deservedly popular, so reserve ahead. ❹–❺

Treetops River Huts ⓣ077 395143, ⓦwww.treetops-riverhuts.com. Located beside the river, very close to the visitor centre and trailheads, with a choice of comfortable accommodation ranging from simple bamboo huts with bathrooms through to en-suite wood or stone ones. ❷–❹

The park

Several trails radiate from the park headquarters and visitor centre, some of them more popular and easier to follow than others, but all quite feasible as day-trips. Take plenty of water as Khao Sok is notoriously humid. The B200 national park entrance fee (B100 for kids) is payable at the checkpoint close to the visitor centre and is valid for three days – you'll need to pay this in addition to the fees for any guided treks or tours. The **visitor centre** (daily 8am–6pm, ⓣ077 395025) gives out a small sketch map of the park and trails, but the best introduction to Khao Sok is the recommended **guidebook**, *Waterfalls and Gibbon Calls* by Thom Henley (B470), which includes lots of information on flora and fauna as well as a full description of the interpretative trail (see below); it's available at Khao Sok minimarkets and some bungalows. If you don't buy the book, you might want to spend a few minutes looking at the exhibition on Khao Sok's highlights inside the visitor centre.

Eight of the park's nine current trails follow the same route for the first 5km. This clearly signed route heads directly west of the park headquarters and follows the course of the Sok River. Its first 3.5km constitute the **interpretative trail** described in *Waterfalls and Gibbon Calls* – a ninety-minute one-way trail along a broad, road-like track that's not terribly interesting in its own right but is greatly enhanced by the descriptions in the book. Most people carry on after the end of the interpretative trail, following signs for **Ton Gloy waterfall**, 7km from headquarters (allow 3hr each way), which flows year-round and tumbles into a pool that's good for swimming. En route to Ton Gloy, you'll pass signs for other attractions including **Bang Leap Nam waterfall** (4.5km from headquarters), which is a straightforward hike; and **Tan Sawan waterfall** (6km from headquarters), a more difficult route that includes a wade along the river bed for the final kilometre and should not be attempted during the rainy season.

The other very popular trail is the one to **Sip-et Chan waterfall**, which shoots off north from the park headquarters and follows the course of the Bang Laen River. Though these falls are only 4km from headquarters, the trail can be difficult to follow and involves a fair bit of climbing plus half a dozen river crossings. You should allow three hours each way, and take plenty of water and some food. With eleven tiers, the falls are a quite spectacular sight; on the way you should hear the hooting calls of white-handed gibbons at the tops of the tallest trees, and may get to see a helmeted hornbill flying overhead.

Guided treks and tours

Even though the signed trails are straightforward and easy to navigate, it's well worth making at least one **guided trek** into the jungle, preferably one that goes off-trail, though joining a guided expedition to Cheow Lan Lake and the nearby caves can also be rewarding. The best jungle guides will educate you in rudimentary jungle craft and open your eyes to a wealth of detail that you'd miss on your own, such as the claw marks left by a sun-bear scaling a tree in search of honey, and the medicinal plants used for malarial fevers and stomach upsets. If you're lucky you might even see the **rafflesia kerrii** in bloom. Officially classified as having the second-biggest flowers in the world, with a diameter of up to 80cm, this rather unprepossessing brown, cabbage-like plant unfurls its enormous russet-coloured petals between January and March, having emitted a disgusting stink in order to attract its pollinator, the green-headed housefly.

Guided treks into the jungle interior can be arranged through most of Khao Sok's guest houses, but the most reputable and long-serving **guides** are to be found at *Khao Sok Rainforest Resort* (whose father-and-son team is highly rated by *Waterfalls and Gibbons* author Thom Henley), and at *Nung House*, *Bamboo House 1* and *Treetops River Huts*. Some Khao Sok guides and tour operators stick to an agreed pricing policy, which is outlined below, and it's likely that any outfit quoting much cheaper rates will employ tour leaders rather than jungle guides; all prices listed below are exclusive of the three-day national park pass.

For between B300 and B550 per person, you can join a trek along the main park trails (usually to Ton Gloy waterfall or Sip-et Chan falls) or to a nearby cave, but the most popular day-trips focus on **Cheow Lan Lake** (also known as Ratchabrapa reservoir), which is studded with countless spectacular karst formations and has three impressive caves near the access trail; it's 65km north of the accommodation area, and is only open to guided treks. A typical day-trip to the lake (B1000–1200) includes a boat ride and swim, with a possible fishing option, plus an adventurous three-hour trek to the Nam Talu cave – which has a river running through it, so you may have to swim in parts. Overnight trips to the lake generally cover the same ground and feature either camping in the jungle (B1800) or accommodation at the national park raft house on the lake (B2200); some guides also offer a two-night lake programme for B3500. Several outfits offer more unusual treks: *Rainforest* does a challenging "Adventurer" trip, featuring about seven hours of off-trail walking and, from December to March, an overnight option too (B725/1400), while *Bamboo 1* will take serious hikers deep into the park, accompanied by armed rangers for protection against poachers.

Most guest houses also do **night safaris** along the main park trails, when you're fairly certain to see civets and might be lucky enough to see some of the park's rarer inhabitants, like elephants, tigers, clouded leopards and pony-sized black-and-white tapirs (B300 for 2hr or B500 for 4hr).

The **Sok River** that runs through the park and alongside many of the guest houses is fun for swimming in and inner-tubing down; tubing and canoeing trips (with tube/canoe and pick-up or drop included) cost around B300/B600. Many guest houses can also arrange **elephant-rides** (2hr; B800).

Khao Lak

Fringed by casuarina and palm trees, the scenic strip of bronze-coloured beach at **KHAO LAK**, about 30km south of Takua Pa, makes a pleasant if slightly congested destination in its own right, though its most obvious appeal is as a departure point for **diving trips** to Ko Similan (see p.664) and Ko Surin (see p.652). The calm, family-oriented atmosphere and strict ban on jet-skis and girlie bars is encouraging an increasing number of Swedish and German package tourists to base themselves here rather than on nearby Phuket, and though there is little for the budget traveller, the presence of dozens of energetic young expat dive instructors means there are enough restaurants and traveller-style bars to inject some life into the place. During the **monsoon**, from June to October, Khao Lak can seem almost wintry; although nearly all dive operators and several bungalow operations close down for the duration an increasing number of places do stay open and offer huge discounts as an enticement.

The area usually referred to as Khao Lak is in fact three separate beaches. The real **Khao Lak** is the southernmost and least developed part, isolated from the heart of the resort by a rocky headland and five-kilometre run of Highway 4, and with just a few places to stay. **Nang Thong** occupies the central stretch and contains the bulk of the accommodation and tourist-oriented businesses; most of the hotels and bungalows are down on the beach, about 500m west of Highway 4, while the main road itself is lined with small restaurants, dive operators, numerous little shopping plazas and a few guest houses. The beach here is nice enough but can get quite crowded. A 45-minute walk north up the beach brings you to **Bang Niang**, whose lovely long stretch of golden sand is for the most part free of rocks and good for swimming between November and April. Much of Bang Niang's beachfront land has been commandeered by hotel developments and the hinterland is also filling up; access to Highway 4 is via a kilometre-long track.

Whichever resort you're based at, once you've had your fill of trips out to the islands, you might want to rent a motorbike and head off to a local **waterfall** – Tong Pling is across from the *Merlin* resort in Khao Lak, Chong Fah Falls are less than 5km east of Bang Niang, and Nam Tok Lumphi is about 20km south of Khao Lak. Several tour operators, including *Bamboo Lodge* (Ⓣ076 420625), behind *Nang Thong Bay Resort 1*, organize **day-tours** to other local attractions. Typical programmes include a boat tour around the karst islands of Ao Phang Nga (B950); trekking; canoeing and elephant-riding in Khao Sok National Park (B1500–2000), with the option of a night on the lake there (B4300);

trekking to waterfalls in nearby Sri Phang Nga National Park (B1200); and a day-trip to Kaw Thaung in Burma (B2000).

Practicalities

Khao Lak is just one hour's B1300 taxi-ride from **Phuket airport** (see p.668). All **buses** running from Phuket to Takua Pa and Ranong (and vice versa), as well as some of its Surat Thani services, pass through Khao Lak; if you're coming from Krabi or Phang Nga you should take a Phuket-bound bus as far as **Khokkloi** bus terminal and switch to a Takua Pa or Ranong bus. Most bus drivers will be familiar with the big-name resorts in Khao Lak and should drop you as near as possible; otherwise, for most Nang Thong beach hotels you should get off as soon as you see the Nang Thong supermarket and walk the 500m down to the beach, while for Bang Niang, alight when you see a cluster of signs for the Bang Niang resorts and either walk the kilometre down the road to the beach, or arrange a motorbike taxi at the roadside. When it comes to moving on, many guest houses and all tour operators can arrange **taxi services** for up to four people to Phang Nga (B800), Khao Sok (B800) and Phuket airport or beaches (B1300).

It's sometimes also feasible to use the Highway 4 buses for **local transport** between the three beaches, particularly if staying at *Poseidon* down in Khao Lak, from where they charge about B10 to Nang Thong or Bang Niang. A fleet of blue songthaews also shuttles up and down Highway 4, running north from Nang Tong's *Ruen Mai* restaurant to Takua Pa (B40), via Bang Niang (B20); the drivers also act as taxi drivers, so be careful you don't end up chartering a whole songthaew (eg B200 to *Poseidon*). Alternatively you can rent **motorbikes** through many hotels, and **cars** through several tour operators; Budget also has at least one agent on the Nang Thong highway (Ⓦwww.budget.co.th).

In Nang Thong, the Nang Thong **supermarket** stocks everything from mosquito repellent and over-the-counter pharmaceuticals to newspapers, snorkels and Danish pastries; the Laguna Night Plaza, near the *Khao Lak Laguna Resort,* has a small bookstore, boutique, restaurant and souvenir outlet as well as car rental and several tour operators. Dotted along the main road you'll also find several tailors' shops. There are two **banks** in Nang Thong, with ATMs and exchange counters: one next to Sea Dragon and the other inside the Laguna Night Plaza. Lots of places on Highway 4 offer **Internet** access, as do several of the beachfront resorts. Most tour agents sell international and domestic air tickets and can arrange train tickets; for day-trip operators, see above. There's a **clinic** at *Krathom Khao Lak* bungalows north of Nang Thong Supermarket (every evening during high season from about 3-9pm; the doctor is on call 24hr; Ⓣ09 868 2034). Bang Niang is less commercial, but has a cluster of businesses beside Highway 4 at the turn-off to the beach, including a tour operator and Internet access, plus a couple of little shopping plazas on the road down to the beach.

Accommodation

The standard of **accommodation** in Khao Lak is high, but so are rates (there's little under B500) and the trend is upmarket, with a burgeoning number of international chain hotels; it's certainly not a budget travellers' resort. Rooms in all categories are best reserved ahead during high season. Unless otherwise stated, all accommodation stays open during the rainy season, from June through October, when they nearly all offer discounts of up to fifty percent on the rates quoted below.

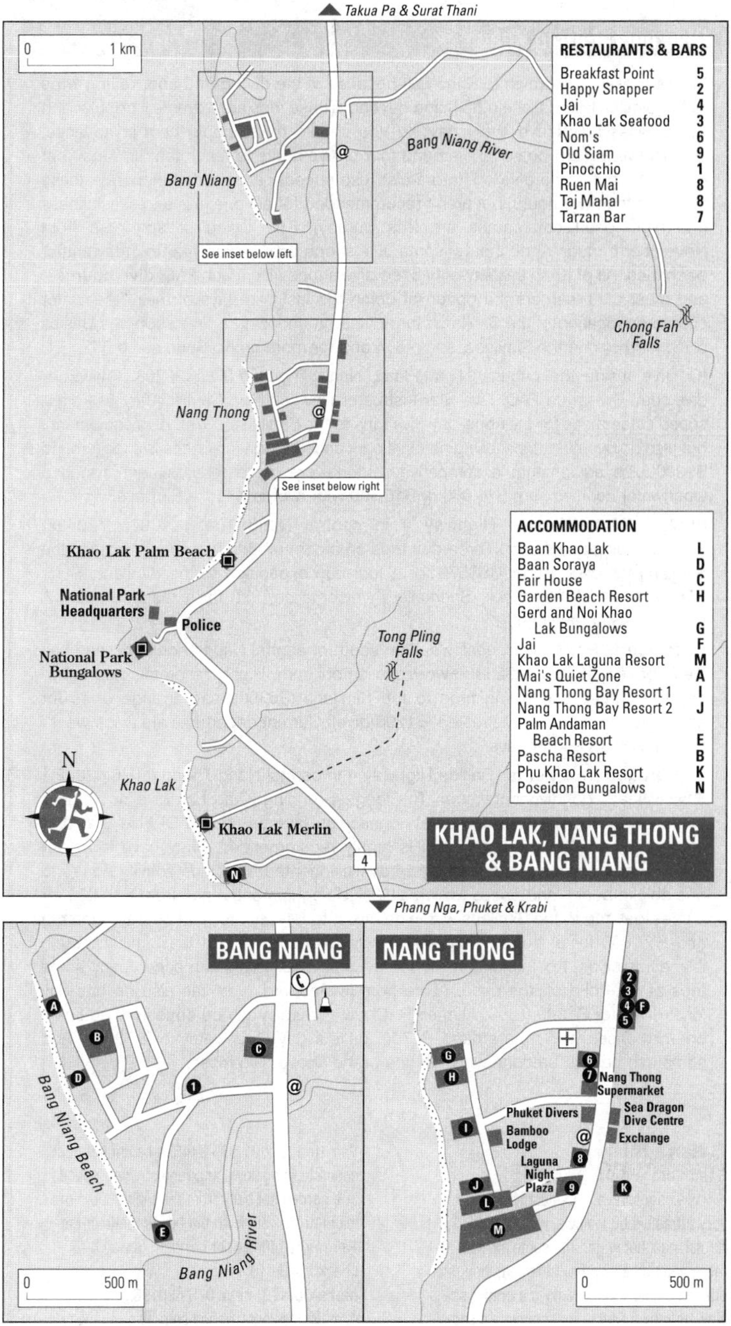
Takua Pa & Surat Thani
0 1 km
RESTAURANTS & BARS
Breakfast Point 5
Happy Snapper 2
Jai 4
Khao Lak Seafood 3
Nom's 6
Old Siam 9
Pinocchio 1
Ruen Mai 8
Taj Mahal 8
Tarzan Bar 7
Bang Niang River
Bang Niang
See inset below left
Chong Fah Falls
Nang Thong
See inset below right
ACCOMMODATION
Baan Khao Lak L
Baan Soraya D
Fair House C
Garden Beach Resort H
Gerd and Noi Khao Lak Bungalows G
Jai F
Khao Lak Laguna Resort M
Mai's Quiet Zone A
Nang Thong Bay Resort 1 I
Nang Thong Bay Resort 2 J
Palm Andaman Beach Resort E
Pascha Resort B
Phu Khao Lak Resort K
Poseidon Bungalows N
Khao Lak Palm Beach
National Park Headquarters
Police
National Park Bungalows
Tong Pling Falls
N
Khao Lak
Khao Lak Merlin
4
KHAO LAK, NANG THONG & BANG NIANG
Phang Nga, Phuket & Krabi
BANG NIANG
Bang Niang Beach
Bang Niang River
0 500 m
NANG THONG
Nang Thong Supermarket
Phuket Divers
Sea Dragon Dive Centre
Bamboo Lodge
Exchange
Laguna Night Plaza
0 500 m

Dive operators in Khao Lak

Most travellers are drawn to Khao Lak because of the **diving and snorkelling trips** to the Similan islands (see p.664) and beyond. These trips are extremely popular and don't necessarily leave every day, so you should try to book them in advance. Normal live-aboard boats take around four or five hours to reach the Similans from Khao Lak, but some dive operators also use speedboats for day-trippers – these take less than two hours, but aren't recommended for anyone prone to seasickness (the high-speed catamarans are less bumpy). The diving season runs from November through April, though some dive shops do run trips year-round, weather permitting. All of Khao Lak's twenty or so dive shops also teach PADI **dive courses**, and most offer learners the option of doing the last two days of their Openwater course on location in the Similans; for advice on choosing a dive shop see Basics p.73; for more on the Similans, see p.664 and for more on Ko Surin see p.652.

IQ Dive Inside the Laguna Night Plaza, Nang Thong ⓣ076 420208, ⓦwww.iq-dive.com. Swiss-run PADI Five-Star Instructor Development Centre. They use high-speed catamarans for their one-day dive trips to the Similans (B3700 plus equipment), but also do overnight trips, using national park accommodation on the islands (around B9000 plus equipment); accompanying snorkellers get a forty percent discount. Openwater courses from B11,000 or B15,500 with two days in the Similans.

Phuket Divers Beside Highway 4 in central Nang Thong, ⓣ076 420628, ⓦwww.phuketdivers.com. Three-day trips on a comfortable live-aboard boat to the Similans for US$440, or US$570 for a four-day expedition to the Similans, Surin islands and Richelieu Rock. Snorkellers welcome on both for a reduced price. A PADI Five-Star dive centre.

Poseidon At *Poseidon Bungalows*, 7km south of central Nang Thong, in Khao Lak (see opposite) ⓣ076 443258, ⓦwww.similantour.com. Highly recommended three-day live-aboard snorkelling trips to the Similans (B6300); can arrange dives for accompanying divers if requested (B1200/dive). Current departures are twice weekly on Tuesdays and Fridays.

Sea Dragon Dive Center Beside Highway 4 in central Nang Thong ⓣ076 420420, ⓦwww.seadragondivecenter.com. The longest-running Khao Lak dive operator is managed by experienced and safety-conscious farangs, is a PADI Five-Star dive centre, has a good reputation and is highly recommended. They have four live-aboard boats – including one budget traveller-oriented boat, one activity boat and one deluxe boat – and prices (which all include equipment) range from B10,800 for a three-day trip to the Similans with nine dives, to B12,800 for a three-day Surin trip and B17,800 for a four-day expedition with thirteen dives on the Similans, Surin islands, Ko Bon, Ko Tachai and Richelieu Rock. Snorkellers can accompany some trips at one-third off the price. Aside from live-aboards you can also do one-day local dives for B1300–1800. All their PADI dive courses can be done in Khao Lak – one-day Discover Scuba around B1700, or four-day Openwater for B7800 – and some can be also be done while on one of the above dive trips.

Bang Niang

Baan Soraya ⓣ076 420192, ⓦwww.baansoraya.com. Just half a dozen very attractive bungalows, with stylish furnishings, hot water and some air-con; a mere hop and a skip from the sea, though only one bungalow actually enjoys a proper sea view. Run by a Dutch-Thai couple. Closed May–Oct. Recommended. ❻

Fair House ⓣ01 895 3445. A handful of neat concrete bungalows and rooms widely spaced in a garden set back from the main road, but a kilometre's walk from the beach. Contact the *Fair House* office right beside Highway 4 to check in. ❹–❺

Mai's Quiet Zone ⓣ076 420196, ⓔmaisquietzone@yahoo.com. Far and away the most characterful place to stay in the

Khao Lak area, with thirty idiosyncratic brick and timber bungalows built to many different designs and clustered together in a feral tropical flower garden beneath palm and casuarina trees. The bungalow interiors are nothing flashy but they're all en suite and have fans; choose between ground-level or upper-storey accommodation. There's also a fabulously sited seafront deck, with a restaurant and yoga and massage area. Reserve ahead by email if possible. Recommended. ❺–❻

Palm Andaman Beach Resort Ⓣ076 420185, Ⓦwww.palmandaman-khaolak.com. A rather stylish and very popular beachfront resort, whose very spacious air-con bungalows are attractively designed and have unusual open-air bathrooms. Also offers some deluxe hotel-block accommodation, has a swimming pool and rents mountain bikes. ❾

Pascha Resort Ⓣ076 420280, Ⓦwww.thaisouth.com/pascha, Ⓔpascha43@hotmail.com. Another nice, affordable upmarket option that's especially popular with families and has a high standard of service. The tastefully designed teak-wood bungalows are each furnished in traditional Thai style and come with air-con, TV and mini-bar, and there's a swimming pool. Within a few metres of the beach. ❽–❾

Nang Thong

Baan Khao Lak Ⓣ076 420199, Ⓦwww.baankhaolak.com. Upmarket collection of 62 cool, unadorned, air-con bungalows and hotel rooms set in a shady tropical garden around a shorefront swimming pool. ❽–❾

Garden Beach Resort Ⓣ076 420121, Ⓔgardenbeachresort@hotmail.com. Well-maintained and unusually well-priced, simple, en-suite brick bungalows, the cheapest of which are the lowest priced in Khao Lak. Those on the beachfront cost more. ❸–❺

Gerd and Noi Khao Lak Bungalows Ⓣ076 420145, Ⓦwww.gerd-noi.com. Large, nicely furnished villas with huge glass windows that look out onto the tropical shorefront garden. All rooms have fans and mosquito nets; price depends on the location. ❺–❼

Jai Ⓣ076 420390. Friendly family-run place offering some of the cheapest accommodation in Khao Lak, comprising good concrete bungalows furnished with mozzie nets and bathrooms, set close to the main road and about 600m from the beach. ❸–❹

Khao Lak Laguna Resort Ⓣ076 420200, Ⓦwww.khaolaklaguna.net. The pick of the crop in Khao Lak, where guests stay in tasteful, traditional *sala*-style villas, equipped with fan or air-con, mini-bar and hot water. There's a swimming pool and a restaurant in the attractively landscaped beachfront grounds and a small shopping plaza beside the road. ❾

Nang Thong Bay Resort 1 Ⓣ076 420088, Ⓔnangthong1@hotmail.com. Efficiently run, popular place that offers a range of very clean, smartly maintained bungalows, with fan or air-con. The most expensive ones are set in a garden that leads right down to the water, the cheaper ones occupy another garden on the other side of the track. Also has some luxurious hotel-style rooms. The restaurant serves good but pricey food and has a book exchange. Recommended. ❹–❼

Nang Thong Bay Resort 2 Ⓣ076 420078, Ⓔnangthong2@hotmail.com. Forty-two bungalows comfortably furnished to a similarly high standard as at its sister resort but located in a slightly quieter spot, around a garden. The cheapest ones have fan and bathroom; the pricier accommodation has air-con and a fridge. Reserve ahead. Recommended. ❺–❼

Phu Khao Lak Resort Ⓣ076 420141, Ⓔphukhaolak@hotmail.com. Diagonally across the main road from the *Laguna*, the spotlessly clean concrete bungalows at this family-run place sit prettily amid a coconut plantation. They're among the cheapest in the resort, though they're a bit of a walk from the beach. Price depends on the size of the bungalow. Recommended. ❹

Khao Lak

Poseidon Bungalows Ⓣ076 443258, Ⓦwww.similantour.com. Seven kilometres south of central Nang Thong, on a wild and rocky shore surrounded by rubber plantations, this Swedish-Thai-run guest house is a lovely place to hang out for a few days and it's also a long-established organizer of snorkelling expeditions to the Similan islands (see opposite). The smaller, cheaper bungalows share facilities, while the more expensive en-suite ones are larger and more comfortable; there's a good restaurant here too. To get here, either ask to be dropped off the bus at the *Poseidon* access road between kilometre-stones 53 and 54, from where it's a walk of 1km; or get off at the bus station in nearby Lam Kaen village (between kilometre-stones 50 and 51), from where it's easy to get a B40 motorbike taxi ride to the bungalows. Motorbikes are available for rent. Closed May–October. ❸–❺

Eating and drinking

Although the handful of tiny beachfront **bars** around *Nang Thong 1* and *Garden Beach* entice some punters to spend their evenings down by the sea, most people gravitate towards the main road **restaurants** after dark. It should be no problem travelling between Nang Thong and Bang Niang in search of dinner, as the blue songthaews cruise up and down that stretch of highway till around 9pm.

Breakfast Point Nang Thong. German-run bakery that earns its name by serving home-made bread, home-made yoghurt and fresh coffee. Also offers a decent selection of imported cheeses, mouthwatering cakes and some more substantial hot dishes. Moderate.

Happy Snapper Nang Thong. This very chilled-out bar and restaurant is popular with dive instructors and makes a pleasant place to while away an evening. Upstairs, it's mainly floor seating in the open-sided *sala* among the Thai and Burmese artefacts, while downstairs there's live music most nights, and the occasional open-mike session for would-be entertainers. The food menu is fairly limited but tasty enough, featuring tacos, pasta and red snapper; the drinks menu runs to 140 different cocktails. Moderate.

Jai Nang Thong. Deservedly popular and unusually well-priced restaurant attached to the bungalows of the same name. Serves lots of different curries, including Penang and *matsaman* versions, as well as plenty of seafood, *tom yam* and the like. Inexpensive to moderate.

Khao Lak Seafood Nang Thong. Very popular, unpretentious place to sample the local catch. Moderate.

Nom's Nang Thong. Home-style cooking: mainly noodle and rice dishes as well as plenty of fresh seafood. Inexpensive.

Old Siam Laguna Night Plaza, Nang Thong. Designed for guests staying at the nearby *Khao Lak Laguna Resort*, with a hotel-style ambience, and a refined menu that features delicious fish cakes, *tom yam kung* and the rest. Moderate.

Pinocchio Bang Niang. Home-made pizzas straight from the wood-fired oven. Moderate.

Ruen Mai Nang Thong. Classy place that serves delicious seafood dishes plus some Thai standards. Moderate.

Taj Mahal Nang Thong. Authentic Indian food, but a bit on the pricey side, at around B200 for a meat dish. Expensive,

Tarzan Bar Nang Thong. Long-running watering hole that's popular with dive-shop staff.

Ko Similan

Rated by *Skin Diver* magazine as one of the world's top ten spots for both above-water and underwater beauty, the nine islands that make up the **KO SIMILAN** National Park are among the most exciting **diving** destinations in Thailand. Massive granite boulders set magnificently against turquoise waters give the islands their distinctive character, but it's the thirty-metre visibility that draws the divers. The underwater scenery is nothing short of overwhelming here: the reefs teem with a host of coral fish, from the long-nosed butterfly fish to the black-, yellow-and-white-striped angel fish, and the ubiquitous purple and turquoise parrot fish, which nibble so incessantly at the coral. A little further offshore, magnificent mauve and burgundy crown-of-thorns starfish stalk the sea bed, gobbling chunks of coral as they go – and out here you'll also see turtles, manta rays, moray eels, jacks, reef sharks, sea snakes, red grouper and quite possibly white-tip sharks, barracuda, giant lobster and enormous tuna.

The **islands** lie 64km off the mainland and are numbered from nine at the northern end of the chain to one at the southern end. In descending order, they are: Ko Bon (number nine), Ko Ba Ngu, Ko Similan, Ko Payoo, Ko Miang (actually two islands, numbers five and four, known collectively as Ko Miang), Ko Pahyan, Ko Pahyang and Ko Hu Yong. Only islands number eight (Ko Ba Ngu) and number four (Ko Miang) are inhabited, with the national park headquarters and accommodation located on the latter; some tour groups are also allowed to camp on island number eight. Ko Similan is the largest island in the chain, blessed with a beautiful, fine white-sand bay and impressive boulders; Ko Hu Yong has an exceptionally long white-sand bay and is used by **turtles** for egg-laying (see box on p.760) from November to February.

Such beauty has not gone unnoticed and the islands are now extremely popular with day-trippers from Phuket and Khao Lak, as well as with divers and snorkellers on longer live-aboard trips. This has caused the inevitable congestion and environmental problems and the Similan reefs have been damaged in places by anchors and by the local practice of using dynamite in fishing. National parks authorities have responded by taking drastic action to protect this precious region, banning fishermen from the island chain (to vociferous and at times violent protest), imposing a three-kilometre ban on sport fishing, enforcing strict regulations for tourist boats, and, at the time of writing, closing off islands one, two and three to all divers, leaving them open only to snorkellers. The whole Similan chain is usually closed to all visitors from May 16 through November 15, when high seas make it almost impossible to reach anyway.

Practicalities

Ko Similan is not really a destination for the independent traveller, but if you have your own diving gear and want to do it on your own, you should head down to **Thap Lamu pier**, which is signed off Highway 4 about 8km south of central Khao Lak. Met Sine Travel and Tours, based at the Thap Lamu pier (Ⓣ076 443276, Ⓦwww.similanthailand.com), runs day-trips by speedboat from here to the Similans (B2300), which depart every day during the season at 8.30am, take two hours and can also be used by independent travellers wanting to stay on the island for a few days.

Limited **accommodation** is available on Ko Miang, in the shape of national park bungalows (B600–2000) and tents (B150), and there's an expensive restaurant. It's definitely worth booking your accommodation in advance, either with the national parks office near Thap Lamu pier (Ⓣ076 595045) or online (Ⓦwww.thaiforestbooking.com/nationalpark-eng.htm), as the place can get crowded with tour groups, especially on weekends and holidays. There's no drinking-water available outside Ko Miang, and campfires are prohibited on all the islands. Inter-island shuttles, the only way of getting from place to place, are expensive, at B250 per person per trip.

Organized snorkelling and diving tours

It's far simpler to do what most people do and join an organized **tour** (usually Nov–May only). Most travel agents in Phuket sell snorkelling **day-trips** to Ko Similan for B2300–3000, the majority of which travel first to Thap Lamu by bus and then take a speedboat, a total journey time of around three hours. IQ Dive in Khao Lak (see box on p.662) also does one-day dive and snorkel trips to the Similans (B3700/27000 excluding equipment), as does Marina Divers on Phuket (B4250/3500; see pp.670 and 671).

Overcrowding is a growing problem at the Similans and the best way to escape this is to join an **overnight** trip to the islands, which means you can visit the best spots before or after the day-tripping boats. Many dive companies sell two- to four-day all-inclusive live-aboard trips, and the best and cheapest of these run out of Khao Lak, the closest mainland resort to the Similans; Phuket is another popular springboard and you can also start live-aboard trips from Ko Chang (see p.648) and Ko Phayam (see p.651). Khao Lak prices start at B10,800 for a three-day live-aboard **diving** trip, with about a forty percent discount for accompanying snorkellers, while a three-day dedicated **snorkelling** live-aboard costs B6300; for full details see p.662. Most of the Phuket-based dive operators (see p.670) only offer four-day live-aboards to the Similans (also featuring Richelieu Rock and a couple of other sites) for B26,000 (excluding equipment); some trips are open to accompanying snorkellers at a slight discount. Met Sine in Thap Lamu (ⓣ076 443276, ⓦwww.similanthailand.com) runs two-day Similan packages (B3700), which include accommodation on Ko Miang and snorkelling equipment, though the route is based on the day-tripping itinerary.

Phuket

Thailand's largest island and a province in its own right, **Phuket** (pronounced "Poo-ket") has been a well-off region since the nineteenth century, when Chinese merchants got in on its tin-mining and sea-borne trade, before turning to the rubber industry. Phuket remains the wealthiest province in Thailand, with the highest per-capita income, but what mints the money nowadays is **tourism**: with an annual influx of foreign visitors that tops one million, Phuket ranks second in popularity only to Pattaya, and the package-tour traffic has wrought its usual transformations. Thoughtless tourist developments have scarred much of the island, particularly along the west coast, whose series of long sandy beaches is punctuated by sheer rocky headlands, and the trend on all the beaches is upmarket, with very few budget possibilities. As mainstream resorts go, however, those on Phuket are just about the best in Thailand, offering a huge range of **watersports** and magnificent **diving** facilities to make the most of the clear and sparkling sea. As with the rest of the Andaman coast, the sea is at its least inviting during the monsoon, from June to October, when Phuket's west-coast beaches in particular become quite rough and windswept. Remoter parts of the island are still attractive, however, particularly the interior: a fertile, hilly expanse dominated by rubber and pineapple plantations and interspersed with wild tropical vegetation. Many inland neighbourhoods are clustered round the local mosque – 35 percent of Phuketians are Muslim, and there are said to be more mosques on the island than Buddhist temples – and, though the atmosphere is generally as easy-going as elsewhere in Thailand, it's especially important to dress with some modesty when not in the main resorts, and to not sunbathe topless on any of the beaches.

Phuket's capital, Muang Phuket or **Phuket town**, is on the southeast coast, 42km south of the Sarasin Bridge linking the island to the mainland. Most people pass straight through the town on their way to the beaches on the **west coast**, where three big resorts corner the bulk of the trade: high-rise **Ao Patong**, the most developed and expensive, with an increasingly seedy nightlife; the nicer, if unexceptional, **Ao Karon**; and adjacent **Ao Kata**, the smallest and least spoilt of the trio. If you're really looking for peace and quiet you should turn instead to some of the beaches on the far northwest coast, such as the seventeen-kilometre-long national park beach of **Hat Mai Khao**, its more developed neighbour **Hat Nai Yang** or the delightful little bays of **Hat Nai Thon** and **Hat Kamala**. Most of the other west-coast beaches have been taken over by upmarket hotels, specifically **Hat Nai Harn**, **Ao Pansea** and **Ao Bang Tao**. In complete contrast, the

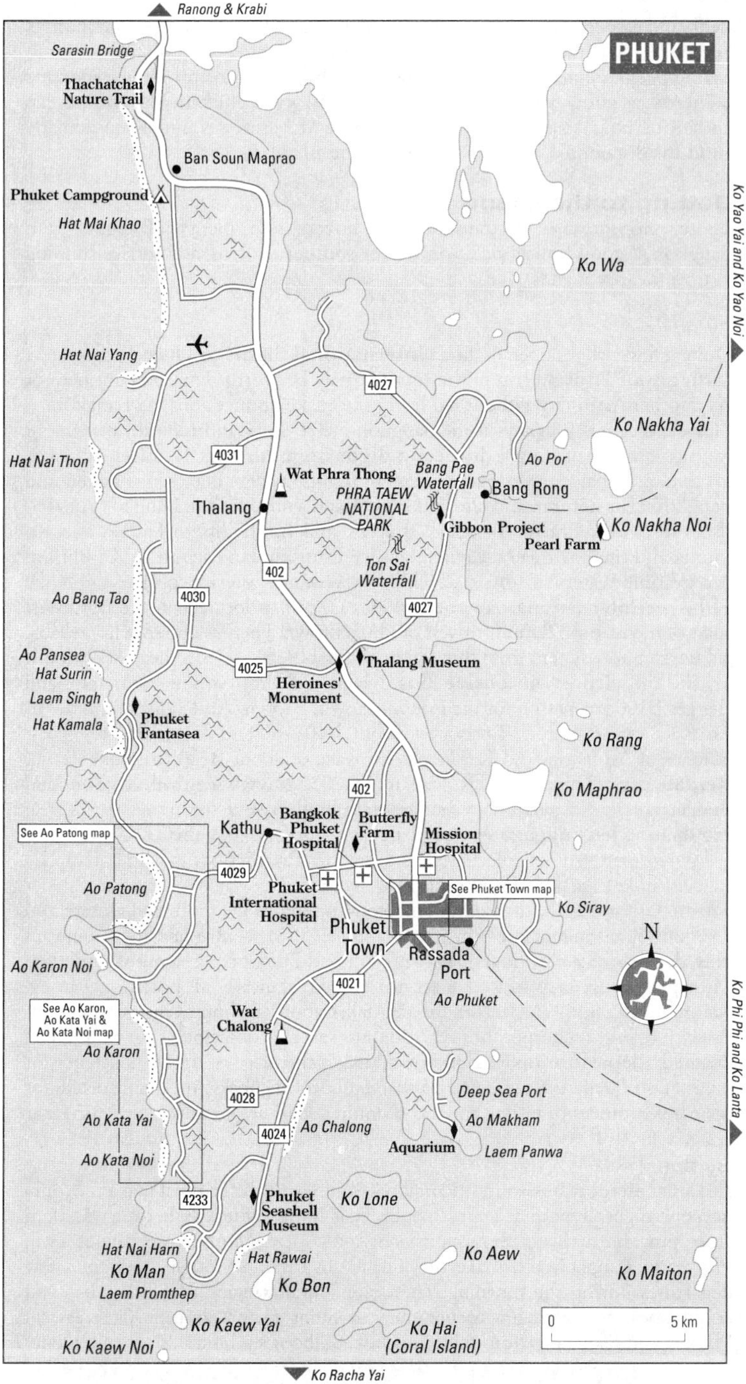
PHUKET
Ranong & Krabi
Sarasin Bridge
Thachatchai Nature Trail
Ban Soun Maprao
Phuket Campground
Hat Mai Khao
Ko Wa
Hat Nai Yang
4027
Ko Nakha Yai
Hat Nai Thon
4031
Ao Por
Wat Phra Thong
Bang Pae Waterfall
Bang Rong
Thalang
PHRA TAEW NATIONAL PARK
Gibbon Project
Ko Nakha Noi
Pearl Farm
402
Ton Sai Waterfall
Ao Bang Tao
4030
4027
Ao Pansea
Hat Surin
4025
Thalang Museum
Heroines' Monument
Laem Singh
Hat Kamala
Phuket Fantasea
Ko Rang
402
Ko Maphrao
Kathu
Bangkok Phuket Hospital
Butterfly Farm
Mission Hospital
See Ao Patong map
4029
Ao Patong
Phuket International Hospital
See Phuket Town map
Ko Siray
Phuket Town
Rassada Port
N
Ao Karon Noi
4021
Ao Phuket
See Ao Karon, Ao Kata Yai & Ao Kata Noi map
Wat Chalong
Ao Karon
4028
Deep Sea Port
Ao Kata Yai
4024
Ao Chalong
Ao Makham
Aquarium
Laem Panwa
Ao Kata Noi
4233
Phuket Seashell Museum
Ko Lone
Hat Nai Harn
Ko Man
Hat Rawai
Ko Aew
Ko Maiton
Laem Promthep
Ko Bon
Ko Kaew Yai
Ko Hai (Coral Island)
0
5 km
Ko Kaew Noi
Ko Racha Yai
Ko Yao Yai and Ko Yao Noi
Ko Phi Phi and Ko Lanta

south and east coasts hold one of Thailand's largest seafaring *chao ley* communities (see p.652), but the beaches along these shores have nothing to offer tourists, having been polluted and generally disfigured by the island's tin-mining industry.

There's a good **website** about Phuket, Ⓦwww.phuket.com, which has numerous links to Phuket tour operators and businesses and is particularly good for discounted accommodation on the island.

Getting to the island

There's no shortage of transport to Phuket, with plenty of flights from Bangkok, a good bus service from major southern towns, and ferries running in from nearby islands.

By air

Quite a few airlines operate direct **international flights** to Phuket, so if you're starting your Thailand trip in the south, it may be worth flying straight here or via another Asian city rather than having to make connections via Bangkok.

Given that bus journeys from Bangkok are so long and tedious, you might want to consider taking a **domestic flight** from the capital – or elsewhere – to Phuket. Thai Airways runs sixteen flights a day between Phuket and Bangkok (1hr 25min), and also links the island with Hat Yai; Bangkok Airways also runs a few Phuket–Bangkok shuttles, and has flights to Pattaya and Ko Samui; and there is a daily seaplane service from Phuket Airport to Ko Phi Phi run by Blue Water Air (Ⓣ076 250538; Ⓦwww.bluewaterair.com).

Phuket International Airport (Ⓣ076 327230) is located on the northwest coast of the island, 32km northwest of Phuket town. There is currently no reliable public transport system from the airport to the beaches, so the cheapest option is to take the **airport limousine bus**, which will drop you at your hotel and charges B100 per person for the ride into town, B150 to Ao Patong and B180 to Ao Kata or Ao Karon. **Taxis** cost about B400–600 to the main west-coast beaches of Ao Patong, Ao Karon and Ao Kata, or about B300 to Phuket town. **Rental car** companies Avis (Ⓣ076 351243, Ⓦwww.avisthailand.com) and Budget (Ⓣ076 205396, Ⓦwww.budget.co.th) both have desks in the arrivals area, and there's a **left-luggage** service (daily 6am–10pm; B40/item/day).

The cheapest way for solo travellers to **get to the airport** is with a company called Phuket Airport Limousine (Ⓣ076 248596), which charges B120 per person. Unfortunately their office and pick-up point is inconveniently located on Thanon Vichitsongkhram, 4km west of Phuket town centre, and their minivans only depart every two hours between 7am and 5pm, taking about 45 minutes. Most people use taxis instead, a service offered by nearly all hotels on Patong, Karon and Kata for B400–600; the trip takes about an hour. One company on Patong offers a cheaper hourly minibus service, described on p.683. The domestic **departure tax** of B30 is included in the price of the air ticket, but for international departures you will be charged B500 at check-in. Contact details for the Phuket offices of international and domestic airlines are given on p.675.

By bus

All direct **air-con buses** from Bangkok's Southern Bus Terminal make the journey overnight, leaving at approximately half-hourly intervals between 5.30pm and 7pm and arriving about fourteen hours later. Most air-con buses from Phuket to Bangkok also make the journey overnight, though there are a few departures during the morning. There is no train service to Phuket, but you could book an overnight sleeper train to Surat Thani, about 290km east of Phuket, and take a bus from there to Phuket (about six hours). There are plenty of ordinary and air-con buses between **Surat Thani** and Phuket, some of which run via **Khao Sok**, **Takua Pa** and **Khao Lak**, and a private minibus service also runs from Phuket's *Montri Hotel* on Thanon Montri to Surat Thani. Takua Pa is a useful interchange for local services to Khuraburi and Ranong, though there are a few direct buses between **Ranong** and Phuket. As for points further south: numerous buses travel between **Krabi** and Phuket, via **Phang Nga**, and there are also frequent services to and from **Trang**, **Nakhon Si Thammarat** and **Hat Yai**. The TAT office in Phuket town (see p.676) keeps up-to-date bus timetables.

Nearly all buses to and from Phuket use the **bus station** (☎076 211977) at the eastern end of Thanon Phang Nga in Phuket town, from where it's a ten-minute walk or a short tuk-tuk ride to the town's central hotel area, and slightly further to the Thanon Ranong departure-point for songthaews to the beaches.

By boat

If you're coming to Phuket from Ko Phi Phi, Ko Lanta or Ao Nang, the quickest and most scenic option is to take the **boat**. During peak season, up to four ferries a day make the trip to and **from Ko Phi Phi** (1hr 30min–2hr 30min), usually docking at Rassada Port on Phuket's east coast; during low season, there's at least one ferry a day in both directions. Travellers from **Ko Lanta** (service available Nov–May only; 1 daily; 4hr 30min) may have to change boats at **Ao Nang** (Nov–May only; 1 daily; 2hr 30min). Minibuses meet the ferries in Phuket and charge B100 per person for transfers to Phuket town and the major west-coast beaches, or B150 to the airport (leave plenty of extra time if you have a flight to catch as boats are notoriously tardy); some ferry agents include the transfer price in their tickets.

Island transport

Although the best west-coast beaches are connected by road, to get from one beach to another by **public transport** you nearly always have to go back into Phuket town; songthaews run regularly throughout the day from Thanon Ranong in the town centre and cost between B15 and B25 from town to the coast. **Tuk-tuks and taxis** do travel directly between major beaches, but charge around B100 from Kata to Karon, B200 between Patong and Karon, and B300 for Karon to Kamala. For transport within resorts, the cheapest option is to make use of the public songthaews where possible, and to hail **motorbike taxis** elsewhere (from B20). However, many tourists on Phuket ride **motorbikes** or mopeds, available for rent on all the main beaches for B200–250 per day (be sure to ask for a helmet, as the compulsory helmet law is strictly enforced on Phuket); alternatively, rent a **jeep** for B800–1200. Be aware though that traffic accidents are legion on Phuket, especially for bikers: some reports put the number of motorbike fatalities on Phuket as high as three hundred per year, many of which could allegedly have been prevented if the rider had been wearing a helmet.

Phuket town

Though it has plenty of hotels and restaurants, **PHUKET TOWN** (Muang Phuket) stands distinct from the tailor-made tourist settlements along the beaches as a place geared primarily towards its residents. Most visitors hang about just long enough to jump on a beach-bound songthaew, but you may find yourself returning for a welcome dose of real life; Phuket town has an enjoyably

Diving and snorkelling off Phuket

The reefs and islands within sailing distance of Phuket rate among the most spectacular in the world, and this is where you'll find Thailand's largest concentration of **dive shops**, offering some of the best-value certificated courses and trips in the country. All the dive centres listed below offer PADI-certificated diving courses and have qualified instructors and dive-masters; we have highlighted those that are accredited PADI Five-Star Centres (the Instructor Development Centres are one step higher than the Five-Star Centres); see p.73 for details. Nonetheless, you should still try to get first-hand recommendations from other divers before signing up with any dive shop, however highly starred, and always check the equipment and staff credentials carefully.

You should also check that the dive shop has membership for one of Phuket's three **recompression chambers**; if yours doesn't, you could take out your own two-week membership with Badalveda (B300), which entitles you to sixty percent discounts on the hourly rate for use of the chamber (down from US$350–$115/hour), though the best dive shops should ensure that their customers never get into a situation that requires recompression. Phuket's recompression centres are: Hyperbaric Services Thailand (HST), 233 Thanon Raja Uthit Song Roi Phi on Ao Patong (Ⓣ076 342518, Ⓦwww.sssnetwork.com); Badalveda Diving Medicine Centre at Bangkok Phuket Hospital, 2/1 Thanon Hongyok Utis, in Phuket town (Ⓣ076 254425, Ⓦwww.badalveda.com); and at Wachira Hospital, Soi Wachira, Thanon Yaowarat, Phuket town (Ⓣ076 211114). All dive shops rent **equipment**, and many of them sell essential items too; for the full range, visit Dive Supply, at 189 Thanon Raja Uthit Song Roi Phi on Ao Patong (daily 9.30am–7pm; Ⓣ076 342511).

A one-day introductory **diving course** averages B1900–2500, and a four-day Openwater course costs between B8400 and B9900, usually including equipment. The price of **day-trips** to local reefs depends on the distance to the dive site, and the operator, but generally falls between B2000 and B3500, including at least two dives, all equipment and food. Nearly all dive centres also offer **live-aboard** cruises: a typical four-day live-aboard trip to Ko Similan (see p.664) and Ko Surin (see p.652) costs US$500, including at least eight dives, all equipment and full board.

Snorkellers are usually welcome to join divers' day-trips (for a discount of about B1000) and can sometimes go on live-aboard cruises at slightly reduced rates. In addition, all travel agents sell mass-market day-trips to Ko Phi Phi, which include snorkelling stops at Phi Phi Leh and Phi Phi Don, an hour's snorkelling (mask, fins and snorkel provided) and a seafood lunch. Transport is on large boats belonging to the main local ferry companies, with prices averaging B1200, or B800 for children. Most of these companies also offer day-trips to Ko Similan, for B2300–3000, depending on the speed of the boat; some companies use boats from Phuket, which take three hours, while other companies bus passengers to Thap Lamu and then use speedboats, which also takes around three hours in total.

Dive shops

All the dive shops listed below offer a variety of itineraries and cruises, with schedules depending on weather conditions and the number of divers. Check out the Phuket Island Access website (Ⓦphuket.com/diving/guide.htm) for links to Phuket dive operators and for some fine underwater pictures.

AO PATONG

Marina Divers Thanon Sawatdirak Ⓦwww.marinadivers.com. Five-Star PADI Instructor Development Centre.

Santana 222 Thanon Thavee Wong Ⓣ076 294220, Ⓦwww.santanaphuket.com. Five-Star PADI Instructor Development Centre.

Scuba Cat Next to Häagen Dazs at 94 Thanon Thavee Wong Ⓣ076 293120, Ⓦwww.scubacat.com. Five-Star PADI Instructor Development Centre.

AO KARON/AO KATA

Andaman Scuba 111/22 Thanon Taina on the Kata/Karon headland ⓣ076 331006, ⓦwww.andamanscuba.com.

Dive Asia 24 Thanon Karon ⓣ076 396199; Kata/Karon headland ⓣ076 330598, ⓦwww.diveasia.com. Five-Star PADI Instructor Development Centre.

Kon-Tiki c/o *Karon Villa* and *Phuket Orchid* hotels, central Karon ⓣ076 396312, ⓦwww.kon-tiki-diving.com. Five-Star PADI Instructor Development Centre.

Marina Divers Next to *Marina Phuket Resort* at 45 Thanon Karon ⓣ076 330272, ⓦwww.marinadivers.com. Five-Star PADI Instructor Development Centre.

Andaman coast dive and snorkel sites

The major **dive and snorkel sites** visited from Andaman coast resorts are listed below. Here you'll find a stunning variety of coral and a multitude of fish species, including sharks, oysters, puffer fish, stingrays, groupers, lion fish, moray eels and more. For more information on marine life see "Flora, Fauna and Environmental Issues" in Contexts, p.821; for ratings and descriptions of Andaman coast dive sites, consult the **handbook** *Diving in Thailand*, by Collin Piprell and Ashley J. Boyd (Asia Books).

Anemone Reef About 22km east of Phuket. Submerged reef of soft coral and sea anemones starting about 5m deep. Lots of fish, including leopard sharks, tuna and barracuda. Usually combined with a dive at nearby Shark Point. Unsuitable for snorkellers.

Burma Banks About 250km northwest of Phuket; only accessible on live-aboards from Khao Lak and Phuket. A series of submerged "banks", well away from any land mass and very close to the Burmese border. Visibility up to 25m.

Hin Daeng and **Hin Muang** 26km southwest of Ko Rok Nok, near Ko Lanta (see box on p.728). Hin Daeng is a highly recommended reef wall, with visibility up to 30m. One hundred metres away, Hin Muang also drops to 50m and is a good place for encountering stingrays, manta rays, whale sharks and silvertip sharks. Visibility up to 50m. Because of the depth and the current, both spots are considered too risky for novice divers who have logged fewer than 20 dives. Unsuitable for snorkellers.

King Cruiser Near Shark Point, between Phuket and Ko Phi Phi. Dubbed the *Thai Tanic*, this became a wreck dive in May 1997, when a tourist ferry sank on its way to Ko Phi Phi. Visibility up to 20m, but hopeless for snorkellers because of the depth.

Ko Phi Phi 48km east of Phuket's Ao Chalong. Visibility up to 30m. Spectacular drop-offs; good chance of seeing whale sharks. See p.720.

Ko Racha Noi and **Ko Racha Yai** About 33km and 28km south of Phuket's Ao Chalong respectively. Visibility up to 40m. Racha Yai (see p.692) is good for beginners and for snorkellers; at the more challenging Racha Noi there's a good chance of seeing manta rays, eagle rays and whale sharks.

Ko Rok Nok and **Ko Rok Nai** 100km southeast of Phuket, south of Ko Lanta (see box on p.728). Visibility up to 18m. Shallow reefs that are excellent for snorkelling.

Ko Similan 96km northwest of Phuket; easiest access from Khao Lak. One of the world's top ten diving spots. Visibility up to 30m. Leopard sharks, whale sharks and manta rays, plus caves and gorges. See p.664.

Ko Surin 174km northwest of Phuket; easiest access from Ko Chang and Ko Phayam and from Khuraburi. Shallow reefs particularly good for snorkelling. See p.652.

Richelieu Rock Just east of Ko Surin (see above). A sunken pinnacle that's famous for its manta rays and whale sharks.

Shark Point (Hin Mu Sang) 24km east of Phuket's Laem Panwa. Protected as a marine sanctuary. Visibility up to 10m. Notable for soft corals, sea fans and leopard sharks. Often combined with the *King Cruiser* dive and/or Anemone Reef; unrewarding for snorkellers.

authentic market and some of the best handicraft shops on the island. If you're on a tight budget, the town is worth considering as a base, as accommodation and food come a little less expensive, and you can get out to all the beaches with relative ease. Bear in mind, though, that the town offers limited nightlife, and as public transport to and from the more lively beaches stops at dusk, you'll have to either rent your own wheels or spend a lot of money on tuk-tuks.

Aside from a market on Thanon Ranong, there's not a great deal to see, though a two-hour wander around the streets will take you past several faded colonial-style **Sino-Portuguese residences** built by Chinese merchants who emigrated from Penang in the late nineteenth century. Recognizable

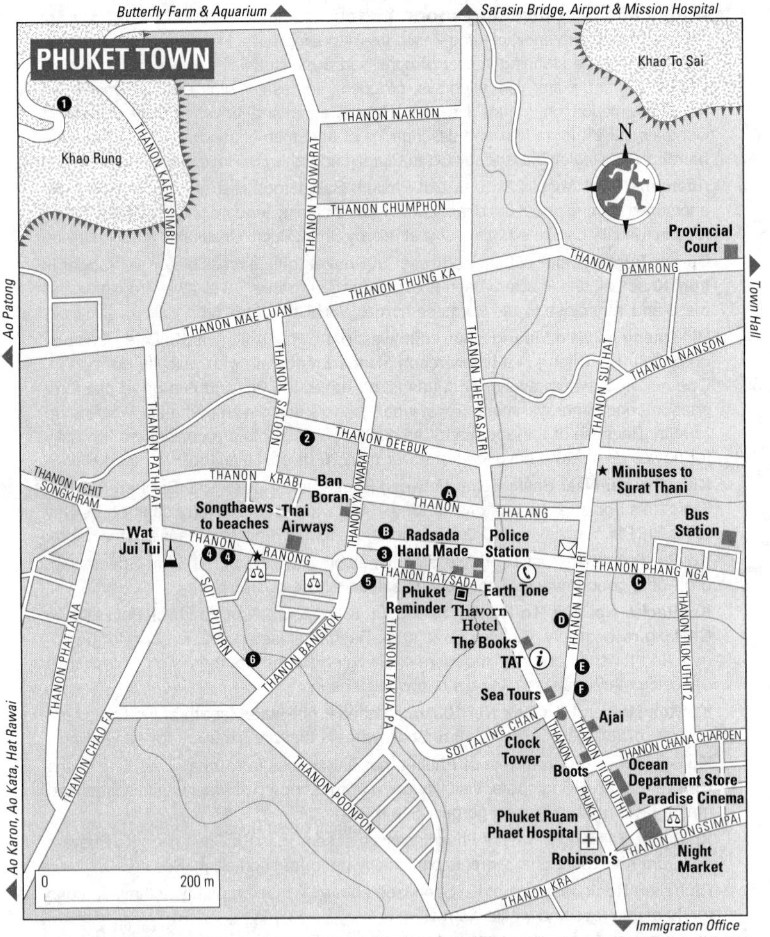

ACCOMMODATION

Crystal Guest House	E	Royal Phuket City	C
Metropole	F	Talang Guest House	A
On On Hotel	B		
Pearl Hotel	D		

RESTAURANTS

The Circle	5	Phuket View Restaurant	1
Dibuk Restaurant	2	Salvatore's	3
Natural Restaurant	6	Vegetarian Restaurants	4

by their doors and shutters painted in pastel pinks, blues and greens, a string of these elegant old mansions lines Thanon Thalang: the carved lintels and brightly painted shutters of the building next door to the Chinese temple are definitely worth an upward glance, as is the intricate wooden fretwork gracing the doors and window shutters of the buildings on the western arm of nearby Thanon Deebuk (Dibuk). You'll find relics of other historical buildings on Thanon Yaowarat, and on Thanon Ranong (where the Thai Airways office is a fine example), Thanon Phang Nga (the *On On Hotel*) and Thanon Damrong, where the town hall, just east of the Provincial Court, stood in for the US embassy in Phnom Penh in the film *The Killing Fields*. Some of these roads are still dominated by traditional businesses and shops: the eastern end of Thanon Thalang, for example, is full of old-style shops selling fabric and dressmaking accessories, including lots of good-value sarongs from Malaysia and Indonesia. There's a much quainter, mustier whiff of the past contained within the wood-panelled lobby of Thanon Rat Sada's *Thavorn Hotel*, whose museum-like reception area and adjacent rooms, signed as the **Phuket History Corner**, are filled with faded photos of historic Phuket, plus a jumble of posters, typewriters and other everyday objects dating from the late nineteenth and early twentieth century, most of it amassed by the Thavorn family. Entry is free and non-guests are welcome to admire the eclectic collection, some of which also spills over into the hotel's streetside *Collector Pub*.

Kids usually enjoy the **Phuket Butterfly Farm and Aquarium** (*Faam Phi Seua*; daily 9am–5pm; B150, kids B60), located a couple of kilometres beyond the northern end of Thanon Yaowarat at 71/6 Soi Paneang in Ban Sam Kong, but though there are heaps of butterflies of various species, and a few reef fish, there's a lack of specific information. There's no public **transport** to the butterfly farm, but a tuk-tuk from the town centre should cost around B80 return. If you have your own vehicle, follow Thanon Yaowarat as far north as you can and then pick up the signs for the farm.

Accommodation

Few tourists choose to stay in Phuket town, but there's a reasonable spread of accommodation to choose from.

Crystal Guest House 41/16 Thanon Montri ⓣ076 222774. One of several good, clean guest houses in the town centre. All rooms have attached bathroom, though the cheapest have no window; the most expensive have air-con, hot water and TV. Internet access in the lobby. ❸–❹

Metropole 1 Thanon Montri ⓣ076 215050, ⓕ076 215990. One of the largest hotels in town, and popular with package tourists and business-people. Rooms are comfortably equipped if not particularly stylish. ❽

On On Hotel 19 Thanon Phang Nga ⓣ076 211154. This attractive, colonial-style 1920s building is a long-running travellers' standby. Rooms have very thin walls and are basic but adequate; the cheapest share bathrooms, the most expensive have air-con. Table tennis and Internet access in the lobby. ❶–❸

Pearl Hotel 42 Thanon Montri ⓣ076 211044, ⓕ076 212911. Large, mid-range hotel favoured by Asian package tourists; facilities include a rooftop restaurant and swimming pool, which make it reasonable value for its class. ❼

Royal Phuket City 154 Thanon Phang Nga ⓣ076 233333, ⓦwww.royalphuketcity.com. Huge chain hotel, with swimming pool, gym, business centre and comfortable rooms. The best in town. ❽

Talang Guest House 37 Thanon Thalang ⓣ076 214225, ⓦwww.talangguesthouse.com. A dozen large fan and air-con rooms in an old wooden house in one of Phuket's most traditional streets. All rooms have attached bathrooms, with soap and towels provided, and a couple of rooms are up on the rooftop, affording unusual panoramic views. A little faded but good value. ❸

Eating

For authentically inexpensive and tasty Thai **food**, check out the night market, which materializes behind Robinson's department store at the southern Thanon Tilok Uthit 1 every evening at about 6pm. Foodstalls are also set up at night opposite the TAT office on Thanon Phuket, but the prices here are inflated because of the English-language menu.

The Circle Beside the roundabout on Thanon Rat Sada. Conveniently located a couple of blocks east of the songthaew stop, and open-fronted for maximum street-view, this place is ideal for a coffee and a snack, serving cappuccinos, real coffees (including hill-tribe blends from north Thailand), delicious cakes, plus a few hot dishes. Moderate.

Dibuk Restaurant 69 Thanon Deebuk. Posh French food – including steaks and *moules* (mussels) – plus some Thai dishes, served in an attractive old Sino-Portuguese building. Expensive.

Natural Restaurant (aka **Thammachat**) 62/5 Soi Putorn (Phoo Thon). Very popular with Phuket residents, this is a rambling, informal eatery whose open-sided dining rooms are wreathed in trailing plants. The food is great and includes fried sea bass with chilli paste, fried chicken with Muslim herbs, soft-shelled crab with garlic and pepper, and spicy Phuket bean salad. Recommended. Inexpensive to moderate.

Phuket View Restaurant On Thanon Kaew Simbu near the top of Khao Rung, the wooded hill on the northwestern outskirts of town. Middle-class Phuketians drive up to this slightly formal restaurant for outdoor seafood with a view. Bring mosquito repellent. Moderate.

Salavatore's 15 Thanon Rat Sada. Cosy Italian joint that's popular with expats. The authentic menu includes crab-meat tagliatelle, spicy penne arrabiata, various steaks and daily specials. Moderate to expensive.

Vegetarian Restaurants Just one minute's walk from the songthaew stop on Thanon Ranong. Two cheap and simple vegan canteens, located almost side by side and staffed by volunteers from the nearby Wat Jui Tui Chinese temple. For B20 you get two main-course servings and a plate of brown rice: choose from the trays of stir-fries and curries, many of them made with soya-based meat substitutes. Daily 7am–8pm. Inexpensive.

Shopping

Phuket town has the best **bookshop** on the island: The Books (daily 9.30am–9.30pm) on Thanon Phuket stocks a phenomenal range of English-language volumes about Thailand plus some modern novels. Ban Boran, at 51 Thanon Yaowarat, specializes in clothes made from the **handspun cotton** of north and northeast Thailand, while Earth Tone, near the police station on Thanon Thepkasatri, sells more modern creations made from natural textiles. If it's high-street **fashions** you're after, however, Robinson's department store on Thanon Tilok Uthit 1 is the place, with nearby Ocean Department Store a reasonable back-up option. The two most fruitful shopping roads for **handicrafts** and **antiques** are Thanon Yaowarat and Thanon Rat Sada. On Thanon Rat Sada, Radsada Hand Made at no.29 and Phuket Reminder at no.85 both sell textiles, carved wooden textile hangers, mango-wood vases and silver jewellery, while both Soul of Asia at no.37 and Touch Wood at no.14 specialize in quality Southeast Asian antiques, fine art and furniture. Ajai on Thanon Tilok Uthit 1 displays a stunning selection of home furnishings made from batik and screen-printed textiles, and Ocean Department Store's more mass-market souvenir stalls are also worth a browse.

Note that if you're planning to buy antiques or religious artefacts and take or send them home, you need to have an **export licence** granted by the Fine Arts Department, which can be obtained through Thalang Museum, located 12km north of Phuket town in Thalang (see p.694; ☎076 311426); see Basics p.23 for more information.

Ngan Kin Jeh: the Vegetarian Festival

For nine days every October or November, at the start of the ninth lunar month, the streets of Phuket are enlivened by **Ngan Kin Jeh** – the Vegetarian Festival – which culminates in the unnerving spectacle of men and women parading about with steel rods through their cheeks and tongues. The festival marks the beginning of **Taoist Lent**, a month-long period of purification observed by devout Chinese all over the world, but celebrated most ostentatiously in Phuket, by devotees of the island's five Chinese temples. After six days' abstention from meat, alcohol and sex, the white-clad worshippers flock to their local temple, where drum rhythms help induce a trance state in which they become possessed by spirits. As proof of their new-found transcendence of the physical world they skewer themselves with any available sharp instrument – fishing rods and car wing-mirrors have done service in the past – before walking over red-hot coals or up ladders of swords as further testament to their otherworldliness. In the meantime there's singing and dancing and almost continuous firework displays, with the grandest festivities held at Wat Jui Tui on Thanon Ranong in Phuket town.

The ceremony dates back to the mid-nineteenth century, when a travelling Chinese opera company turned up on the island to entertain emigrant Chinese working in the tin mines. They had been there almost a year when suddenly the whole troupe – together with a number of the miners – came down with a life-endangering fever. Realizing that they'd neglected their gods somewhat, the actors performed expiatory rites, which soon effected a cure for most of the sufferers. The festival has been held ever since, though the self-mortification rites are a later modification, possibly of Hindu origin.

Listings

Airlines Air Andaman, at the airport ⓣ076 351374; Bangkok Airways, 158/2–3 Thanon Yaowarat ⓣ076 225033; China Airlines, at the airport ⓣ076 327099; Dragon Air, 956/14 Thanon Phang Nga ⓣ076 215734; Lauda Air, at the airport ⓣ076 327329; Malaysia Airlines, 1/8 Thanon Thungka ⓣ076 213749; Silk Air/Singapore Airlines, 183 Thanon Phang Nga ⓣ076 213895; Thai Airways, 78 Thanon Ranong, international ⓣ076 212499, domestic ⓣ076 211195.

American Express c/o Sea Tours, 95/4 Thanon Phuket (ⓣ076 218417, ⓕ076 216979; Mon–Fri 8.30am–5pm, Sat 8.30am–noon). Refunds on lost traveller's cheques are usually available here within the hour, and staff keep poste-restante letters and faxes for at least a month.

Banks and exchange All the main banks have branches on Thanon Phang Nga or Thanon Rat Sada, with adjacent exchange facilities open till at least 7pm and ATMs dispensing cash around the clock.

Cinema The Paradise Multiplex next to Ocean Department Store on Thanon Tilok Uthit 1 shows English-language blockbusters throughout the day and evening.

Dentists At Phuket International Hospital (ⓣ076 249400), on the airport bypass road just west of Phuket town, and at Bangkok Phuket Hospital, on the northwestern edge of town at 2/1 Thaon Hongyok Utis ⓣ076 245421; see map on p.667 for locations.

Hospitals Phuket International Hospital (ⓣ076 249400, emergencies ⓣ076 210935), behind Big C on the airport bypass road just west of Phuket town, at 44 Thanon Chalermprakiat Ror 9, is considered to have Phuket's best facilities, including an emergency department, an ambulance service and private rooms. Other reputable alternatives include Bangkok Phuket Hospital, on the northwestern edge of town at 2/1 Thaon Hongyok Utis ⓣ076 254425, and the Mission Hospital (aka Phuket Adventist Hospital), on the northern outskirts at 4/1 Thanon Thepkasatri ⓣ076 237220–6, emergencies ⓣ076 237227. See map on p.667 for locations.

Immigration office At the southern end of Thanon Phuket, near Ao Makham ⓣ076 212108; Mon–Fri 8.30am–4.30pm.

Internet access At several places on Thanon Rat Sada and elsewhere around town, including at *Crystal Guest House*, 41/16 Thanon Montri; and *On On Hotel*, 19 Thanon Phang Nga. There's Catnet public Internet access at the phone office on Thanon Phang Nga.

Mail The GPO is on Thanon Montri. Poste restante should be addressed c/o GPO Thanon Montri, Phuket 83000 and can be collected Mon–Fri 8.30am–4.30pm, Sat 8.30am–3.30pm.
Pharmacy There's a branch of Boots on Thanon Tilok Uthit 1.
TAT 73–75 Thanon Phuket (daily 8.30am–4.30pm ⓣ076 212213, ⓦwww.phukettourism.org).
Telephones For international calls use the CAT phone office on Thanon Phang Nga (daily 8am–midnight).
Tourist Police For all emergencies, call the tourist police on the free, 24hr phone line ⓣ1155, or contact the police station on the corner of Thanon Phang Nga and Thanon Thepkasatri ⓣ076 355015.

Hat Mai Khao

Phuket's northwest coast kicks off with the island's longest and least-visited beach, the seventeen-kilometre **HAT MAI KHAO**, which starts a couple of kilometres north of the airport and 34km northwest of Phuket town, and remains almost completely unsullied by any touristic enticements, with to date just a couple of discreet budget accommodations hidden behind a sandbank at the back of the shore, plus one super-deluxe development. Together with Hat Nai Yang immediately to the south (see opposite), Hat Mai Khao constitutes **Sirinath National Park**, chiefly because a few giant marine turtles come ashore here between October and February to lay their eggs (see box on p.760). Mai Khao is also a prime habitat of a much-revered but non-protected species – the sea grasshopper or sea louse, a tiny crustacean that's considered a great delicacy. While you're at Mai Khao, you might want to make a trip to the Thachatchai Nature Trail, which also comes under the protection of the Sirinath National Park, but is actually on Phuket's northeast coast, very close to the Sarasin Bridge and about 8km north from the Hat Mai Khao accommodation; it's described on p.695.

If you're looking for peace, solitude and 17km of soft sand to yourself, then the Hat Mai Khao **accommodation** is for you. At the far northern end of the beach, just 3km south of Sarasin Bridge, the very expensive five-star *JW Marriott Phuket Resort and Spa* (ⓣ076 338000, ⓦwww.marriotthotels.com; ❾; prices start at US$200) comprises an enormous low-rise complex of tasteful, upmarket rooms, a couple of pools, a spa complex and several restaurants. Several kilometres further south along the beach, the other two options are much cheaper and more traveller-oriented and are by far the most uncommercialized places to stay on Phuket. Run by members of the same family, they occupy adjacent plots in their own little shorefront enclave, surrounded by coconut plantations 1.5km off the road, with easy access to nearby wetlands and their large bird populations. *Phuket Campground* (ⓣ01 676 4318, ⓦwww.phuketcampground.com) rents out tents with bedding (B150/person), which you can either set up near their small restaurant or move down onto the beach a few metres away beyond the sandbank; it also has three en-suite bungalows (❺). On the other side of a small shrimp-breeding pond, *Mai Khao Beach Bungalows* (ⓣ01 895 1233, ⓔbmaikhao_beach@hotmail.com; ❸–❺) has just a few bungalows with fan and en-suite bathrooms as well as a handful of tiny, tent-like A-frame huts with mattresses, mosquito nets and shared bathrooms. Both places offer an exceptionally warm, home-stay-like welcome, both serve food and can arrange motorbike rental, and both close during the monsoon season (from May–Oct) when wind and rain makes it dangerous to swim.

The easiest way to get to Hat Mai Khao is by long-distance **bus**. All buses travelling between Phuket town bus station and any mainland town (eg Krabi, Phang Nga, Khao Lak or Surat Thani) use Highway 402: just ask to be dropped in **Ban Soun Maprao**, a road junction just north of kilometre-stone 37. (If coming directly here from the mainland you'll waste a good couple of hours if you go into town and then come back out again.) Five songthaews a day also travel this far up Highway 402, but buses are faster and more frequent. The owner of *Phuket Campground* has an office at the bus drop on the east side of the road in Ban Soun Maprao, from where you can arrange transfers to the accommodation, but if the office isn't open you can either phone for a pick-up or walk. From the bus drop, walk 1km west down the minor road until you reach a signed track off to the west, which you should follow for 1.5km to reach the accommodation and the beach. Travelling to Hat Mai Khao from the airport, 15km away, is best done by taxi.

Hat Nai Yang

Despite being part of the Sirinath National Park – and location of the national park headquarters – the long curved sweep of **HAT NAI YANG**, 5km south of Hat Mai Khao and 30km north of Phuket town, has become fairly developed, albeit in a relatively low-key way, with around thirty open-air restaurant-shacks and beach bars set up along the beachfront road and the track that runs off it, and a tiny tourist village of transport rental outlets, minimarkets, an Internet centre and the inevitable tailor's. For the moment though, the developments are fairly unobtrusive and the beach is a pleasant place to while away a few hours, ideally around lunch- or dinner-time when you can browse the restaurant menus at leisure – barbecued seafood and wood-fired pizzas are the local specialities. Eating out here in the shade of the feathery casuarina trees that run the length of the bay is a hugely popular weekend pastime with local Thai families; to avoid the crowds, come during the week. Should you feel a little more energetic, the beach is fairly clean and fine for swimming at the southern end, and there's a reasonable, shallow **reef** about 1km offshore (10min by longtail boat) from the national park headquarters, which are a fifteen-minute walk north of the tourist village. If you're staying here and have your own transport, you could make a trip to the Thachatchai Nature Trail (see p.695).

Practicalities

Accommodation is pleasingly limited on Hat Nai Yang. The cheapest and most peaceful place to stay is at the national park bungalows (ⓣ076 328226, ⓔsirinath_np@yahoo.com; ❸–❺), prettily set out under the trees on a very quiet stretch of beach (unswimmable at low tide) fifteen minutes' walk north from the tourist village. Two-person fan and air-con rooms and bungalows are basic but en suite, and must be booked in advance. Tents are also available for B200 and can be pitched anywhere you like; if you bring your own you must first get permission from the park headquarters or visitor centre (both daily 8.30am–4.30pm). *Nai Yang Beach Resort* (ⓣ076 328300, ⓦwww.naiyangbeachresort.com; ❻–❽) in the heart of the tourist village has a range of comfortable, mid-market bungalows set in a spacious garden on the inland side of the beachfront road, and offers a choice between fan and air-con. Best of the lot is the elegant and luxurious *Pearl Village* (ⓣ076 327006, ⓦwww.phuket.com/pearlvillage; ❾) where hotel rooms and pretty cottages are set in gorgeously landscaped tropical gardens that run down to the southern end of the beachfront road; facilities here include a swimming pool and tennis courts.

Hat Nai Yang is just 2km south of the **airport**, so a taxi ride down to the beach shouldn't cost much. An infrequent **songthaew** service (B30; 1hr 45min) runs between Phuket town and Hat Nai Yang via the airport, or a taxi costs around B350.

Hat Nai Thon

The next bay south down the coast from Hat Nai Yang is the small but perfectly formed **Hat Nai Thon**, currently one of the least commercialized beaches on the island. The five-hundred-metre-long gold-sand bay is shaded by casuarinas and surrounded by fields and plantations of coconut, banana, pineapple and rubber trees, all set against a dazzling backdrop of lush green hills. The access road off Highway 402 winds through this landscape, passing a few villages en route before reaching the shore, and to date there are just a handful of formal places to stay at the beach, plus a couple of homes with rooms for rent, one dive operator, a few rental jeeps and a restaurant attached to each hotel. There's good snorkelling at reefs that are easily reached by longtail, but otherwise you'll have to make your own entertainment. All this might change quite soon, however, as land speculation south along the coast from Nai Thon has been feverish and development is likely to follow. The best way to get to Nai Thon is to take one of the half-hourly **songthaews** (B20; 1hr 30min) from Phuket town to Ao Bang Tao, the next resort south down the coast, and then hire a taxi, which could cost as much as B150.

At the northern end of the shorefront road, across the road from the sea, *Phuket Naithon Resort* (ⓣ076 205233, ⓦwww.phuketnaithonresort.com; ❺–❾) offers big, apartment-style **rooms** in terraced bungalows with the choice between (genuine) mountain views or (less interesting) sea views, and the option of air-con, balcony and TV; the resort also has a small spa. About 100m south down the road, *Naithon Beach Resort* (ⓣ076 205379, ⓕ076 205381; ❻–❼), set in a small garden across the road from the beach, has wooden fan and air-con bungalows with more character but lesser views. The nearby *Tienseng* restaurant (ⓣ06 947 6814; ❹–❺) has rooms upstairs, at the cheapest rates in Nai Thon, though it's worth paying a bit more here to get the rooms with air-con and a sea view.

Ao Bang Tao

The eight-kilometre-long **AO BANG TAO** is dominated by the upmarket *Laguna Resort*, an "integrated resort" comprising five luxury hotels set in extensive landscaped grounds around a series of lagoons. There's free transport between the hotels, and for a small fee all *Laguna* guests can use facilities at any one of the five hotels – which include fifteen swimming pools, thirty restaurants, several children's clubs, a couple of spas and countless sporting facilities ranging from tennis courts to riding stables, windsurfers, and hobie-cats to badminton courts. There's also the eighteen-hole Laguna Phuket golf course, the Quest Laguna outdoor sports centre and a kids' activity centre called Camp Laguna, with entertainments for 8- to 18-year-olds ranging from abseiling and rock-climbing to team games and arts and crafts workshops. Not surprisingly the *Laguna* hotels are exceptionally popular with families, though beware of the undertow off the coast here, which confines many guests to the hotel pools. South and mainly out of sight of the enormous *Laguna* complex, an unsightly jumble of development has been squashed into every remaining inch of Bang Tao's beachfront land, so there's little to recommend staying in this part, unless you choose to base yourself at the one affordable option listed below. Half-hourly **songthaews** (B20; 1hr 15min) cover the 24km from Phuket town to Ao Bang Tao; taxis cost about B200 for the same journey. There are reputable **car-rental** desks at all the hotels, as well as small shopping arcades.

Day-trips and other activities

There are heaps of things to do on Phuket, and tour agents on all the main beaches will be only too happy to fix you up with your activity of choice, or you can arrange it yourself by calling the relevant numbers. Transport from your hotel is usually included in the price of a day-trip. For details of dive operators in Phuket, see p.670.

Activities and days out

Deep-sea fishing Day-trips and overnight charters in custom-built boats from Andaman Hooker ⓣ076 282036, ⓦwww.phuket.com/fishing/andaman.htm; Harry's Fishing ⓣ076 340418, ⓦwww.harrysfishing-phuket.com; and Phuket Sport Fishing Centre ⓣ076 214713.

Golf Phuket has four eighteen-hole courses open to the public, costing B2200 to B3500, with club rental B300–500 and caddies B200: the Blue Canyon Country Club near Hat Nai Yang ⓣ076 328088, ⓦwww.bluecanyonclub.com; the Laguna Phuket Club on Hat Bang Tao ⓣ076 324350, ⓦwww.lagunaphuket.com/activities/golf; the Loch Palm Golf Club in Kathu ⓣ076 321929, ⓦwww.lochpalm.com; and the Phuket Country Club, also in Kathu ⓣ076 321038, ⓦwww.phuketcountryclub.com. You can arrange golf packages through Golf Phuket ⓣ076 280461, ⓦwww.golfphuket.com.

Horse-riding Ride along jungle trails and sandy beaches with Phuket Laguna Riding Club on Hat Bang Tao ⓣ076 324199, or Phuket Riding Club in Rawai ⓣ076 288213.

Sea-canoeing One- and two-day self-paddling expeditions in sea kayaks around the limestone karsts of Phang Nga bay (see p.699), the Krabi coastline (see p.706) or in Khao Sok National Park (see p.654) for around B3000 per person per day. Contact John Gray Sea Canoe ⓣ076 254505, ⓦwww.johngray-seacanoe.com; Santana ⓣ076 294220, ⓦwww.santanaphuket.com; or Sea Canoe Thailand ⓣ076 212172, ⓦwww.seacanoe.net.

Thai cookery courses On request at Pat's Home, near Phuket town, arranged through Phuket Reminder handicraft shop at 86 Thanon Rat Sada, Phuket town (ⓣ076 213765, ⓦwww.phuket.com/dining/index_cooking.htm); and every Saturday and Sunday at *Mom Tri's Boathouse* hotel on Ao Kata Yai (ⓣ076 330015, ⓦwww.boathousephuket.com; B1800 for one day, or B2800 for both days).

Nights out

Phuket Fantasea ⓣ076 385000. Enjoyable spectacular that's staged at the Fantasea entertainments complex just inland of Hat Kamala. The 75-minute show is a slick, hi-tech fusion of high-wire trapeze acts, acrobatics, pyrotechnics, illusionists, comedy and traditional dance – plus a depressing baby elephant circus. Transport is included in the steep ticket price (B1100/800 adults/children), with an optional pre-show dinner (B500). The show starts at 9pm every night except Tuesday; tickets can be bought through any tour operator.

Phuket Simon Cabaret ⓣ076 342114. Famous extravaganza in which a troupe of outrageously flamboyant transvestites perform song-and-dance numbers. It's all very Hollywood – a little bit risqué but not at all sleazy – so the show is popular with tour groups and families. The cabarets are staged twice a night, and tickets can be bought from any tour agent for B500; agents should provide free transport to the theatre, which is south of Patong, on the road to Karon.

Accommodation

All *Laguna Phuket* **hotels** are in the top price bracket: the *Allamanda* and *Laguna Beach* have the cheapest rooms and the *Banyan Tree Phuket* is the most exclusive option on the beach (and the whole island). The below quoted rates are generally discounted a little if you book via the *Laguna Phuket* website

(Ⓦ www.lagunaphuket.com), and rates drop by up to fifty percent during the low season, from May to October.

Allamanda Ⓣ076 324359, Ⓦwww.allamanda.com. Consciously family-oriented hotel comprising 235 apartment-style suites – all with a kitchenette – set round the edge of a lagoon and the fringes of the golf course. There are some special children's suites, children's pools, a kids' club and a babysitting service. Rates from US$160. ❾

Bangtao Lagoon Bungalows Ⓣ076 324260, Ⓦwww.phuket-bangtaolagoon.com. Not part of the *Laguna* complex, but located further south among the cheaper developments. Seventy-one plain but decent enough fan and air-con bungalows set in a beachfront garden. ❻–❽.

Banyan Tree Phuket Ⓣ076 324374, Ⓦwww.banyantree.phuket.com. The most sumptuous and exclusive of the *Laguna* hotels, and considered among the best hotels in the whole of Phuket, with a select 108 villas, all gorgeously furnished and kitted out with private gardens and outdoor sunken baths. Also on site are the award-winning Banyan Tree spa and an eighteen-hole golf course. Rates from US$650. ❾

Dusit Laguna Ⓣ076 324320, Ⓦwww.dusit.com. Located between two lagoons and set amidst lush tropical gardens, all rooms here have private balconies with pleasant views. Facilities include a spa, a couple of swimming pools and a club for kids aged 4 to 12. One child under 15 can share the adults' room for free. ❾

Laguna Beach Resort Ⓣ076 324352, Ⓦwww.lagunabeach-resort.com. Another family-oriented hotel, with a big waterpark, lots of sports facilities, Camp Laguna activities for children, plus a spa and luxury five-star rooms in the low-rise hotel wings. Two children under 11 can share the adults' room for free. Rates from B5660. ❾

Sheraton Grande Laguna Ⓣ076 324101, Ⓦwww.sheraton.phuket.com. Built on its own island in the middle of one of the lagoons, with exceptionally nice five-star rooms, a huge pool featuring a waterfall and children's pool, and nine bars and restaurants. Two children under 11 can share the adults' room for free. Rates from US$255. ❾

Hat Surin and Ao Pansea

South of Ao Bang Tao, **HAT SURIN** proper is packed with ugly condominium developments, but its small northern bay, secluded from the riff-raff and sometimes referred to as **AO PANSEA**, is a favourite haunt of royalty and Hollywood stars, who stay here at one of Phuket's most indulgent resorts, the *Amanpuri* (Ⓣ076 324333, Ⓦwww.amanresorts.com; ❾; rates start at US$650). Part of the super-exclusive, Hong Kong-based Aman chain, the *Amanpuri* comprises a series of private Thai-style pavilions, each of which is staffed by a personal attendant, plus a spa and black marble swimming pool. Also on Ao Pansea are the delightful traditional-style thatched villas at *The Chedi* (Ⓣ076 324017, Ⓦwww.phuket.com/chedi; ❾; rates from US$320) whose published prices are slightly more reasonable. Songthaews travel the 24km between Phuket town and Hat Surin approximately every half-hour and cost B25.

Hat Kamala and Laem Singh

A small, characterful tourist development has grown up along the shorefront of **HAT KAMALA**, sandwiched between the beach and the inland Muslim village of Ban Kamala, about 300m west of the main Patong–Surin road and 26km northwest of Phuket town. With cheerfully painted houses, no high-rises or big hotels, and plenty of greenery, Hat Kamala is one of the most appealingly low-key resorts on Phuket. The one drawback is that almost the entire length of the small beach is taken up with tightly packed lines of sunloungers, a strangely mainstream feature for such a laissez-faire little place. Aside from the accommodation, the little tourist village, which is clustered either side of Thanon Rim Had (also spelt Rim Hat), has several restaurants and bars, transport rental, Internet access, a couple of minimarkets, a health centre, a post office and several tour operators. For anything else you'll need to head a couple of kilometres inland to the faceless shophouse developments on the main road, or continue south around the headland to Ao Patong, just a few kilometres away. The Phuket Fantasea entertainments complex (see box on p.679) is about 1km northeast of Hat Kamala on the main Patong–Surin road. If you look closely you'll see that the shorefront land across the road from the Fantasea is actually a Muslim cemetery – the grass is dotted with small shards of rock indicating the burial plots. A few hundred metres north of the cemetery, a couple of steep paths lead west off the main road and down to **Laem Singh** cape, a pretty little sandy cove that's a picturesque combination of turquoise water and smooth granite boulders; it's nice for swimming and very secluded. The easiest way to get to Hat Kamala is by **songthaew** from Phuket town (every 30min, 1hr 15min; B25).

Accommodation and eating

Hat Kamala is popular with long-stay tourists, and many of the **hotels** offer rooms with kitchenettes; on the whole prices here are reasonable for Phuket. A few of the hotels have **restaurants**, and there are several independent restaurants along Thanon Rim Had, including *Roberta, Charoen Seafood* and *The Beer House*, all of which feature lots of seafood, and *Kamala Coffee House*, whose breezy roof terrace and fresh coffee make this a nice spot for breakfast.

Benjamin Resort 83 Thanon Rim Had, opposite the school at the southerly end of the beachfront road, ⓣ076 385147, ⓕ076 385739. Set right on the beach, this block of thirty air-con rooms lacks character but couldn't be closer to the sea – though views are occluded from all but the most expensive rooms. ❹–❼

Bird Beach Bungalow Central seafront road at 73/3 Thanon Rim Had ⓣ & ⓕ076 279669. Popular, long-running place with well-furnished bungalows set around a courtyard. Rooms are a bit dark but comfortable and reasonable value, with a choice of fan or air-con. ❺–❻

Kamala Beach Estate ⓣ076 279756, ⓦwww.phuket.com/kamala/beach. Stunningly located on Hat Kamala's far southern headland and set around a swimming pool in tropical gardens, this place offers luxury serviced apartments for rent and is favoured by long-term and repeat guests. ❾

Malinee House 75/4 Thanon Rim Had ⓣ076 385094, ⓔmalineehouse@hotmail.com. Very friendly, traveller-oriented guest house with Internet access and the Jackie Lee travel agency downstairs, and large, comfortably furnished air-con rooms upstairs, all of them with balconies. ❹–❻

Papa Crab Guest House Southerly end of the seafront road at 93/5 Thanon Rim Had ⓣ & ⓕ076 385315. Exceptionally stylish decor in this striking, mango-coloured three-storey block, where rooms are outfitted with rattan furnishings and air-con. Try to get one on the top floor if possible. ❻

Phuket Kamala Resort Northern end of the seafront road at 74/8 Thanon Rim Had ⓣ076 385396, ⓔkamalaresort@hotmail.com. Efficiently run hotel with forty rooms in air-con bungalows set either round the swimming pool or in the garden to the rear. All rooms have TVs and some also have a kitchenette. There's a massage centre, a restaurant and tour desk here too. ❼

Seaside Inn Central seafront at 88/6 Thanon Rim Had ⓣ 076 385152 ⓕ076 279894. Fourteen nice bungalows ranged around a pretty garden across the road from the seafront. All rooms have air-con, TV and kitchenette. Big discounts in low season. ❻

Ao Patong

The busiest and most popular of all Phuket's beaches, **AO PATONG** – 5km south of Ao Kamala and 15km west of Phuket town – is vastly over-developed and hard to recommend. A congestion of high-rise hotels, tour agents and souvenir stalls disfigures the beachfront, limpet-like touts are everywhere, and hostess bars and strip joints dominate the resort's nightlife, attracting an increasing number of single Western men to what is now the most active scene between Bangkok and Hat Yai. On the plus side, the broad, three-kilometre-long beach

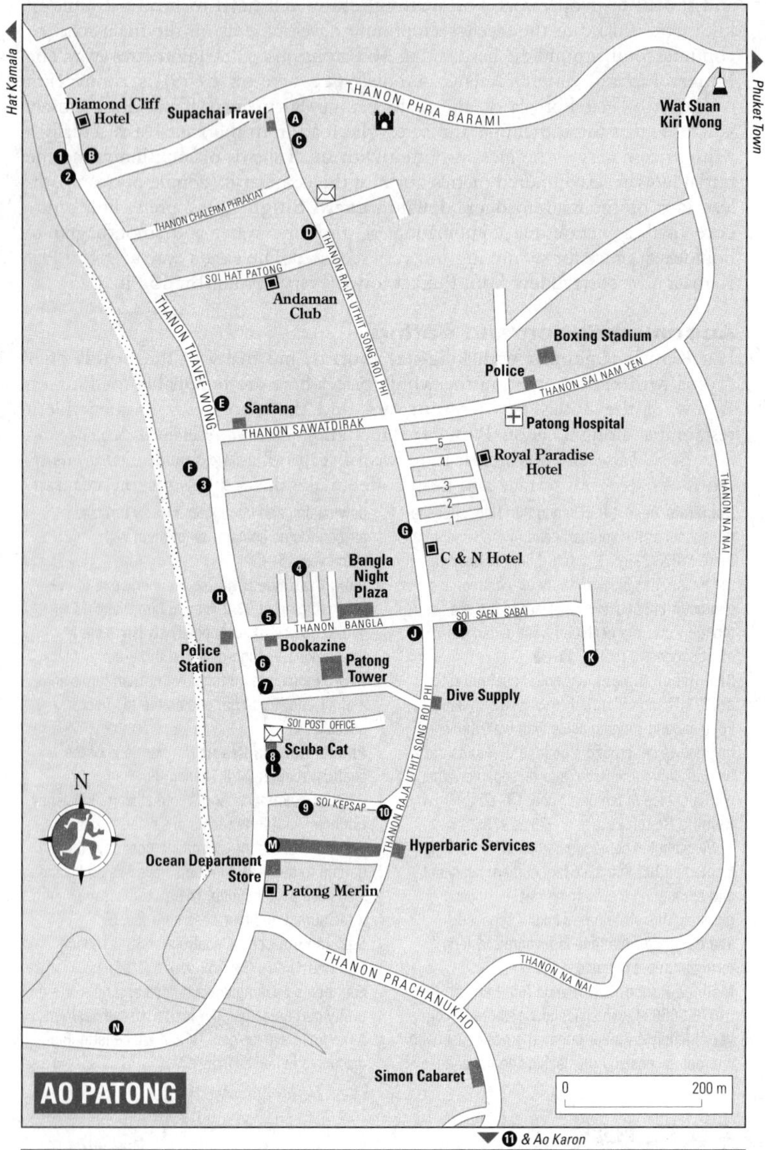

ACCOMMODATION

Amari Coral Beach Resort	N
Baan Sukhothai	J
Casuarina Bungalows	E
Holiday Inn Phuket	M
Impiana Phuket Cabana	F
Neptuna Hotel	G
Novotel Phuket Resort	B
Patong Bay Garden Resort	H
PS2 Bungalow	A
Regent 2002 Guesthouse	D
Sand Inn	I
Sansabai Bungalows	K
Sea Beach Inn	L
Shamrock Park Inn	C

RESTAURANTS & BARS

Baan Rim Pa	2
Baan Sukhothai	J
Baluchi	9
Banana Pub & Disco	7
Da Maurizio	1
Molly Malone's	8
Patong Seafood Restaurant	6
Restaurant 4	4
Safari Disco	11
Sala Bua	3
Scruffy Murphy's	5
Tabeta	10

offers good sand and plenty of shade beneath the casuarinas and parasols, and the resort also boasts the island's biggest choice of watersports and diving centres.

The resort is strung out along the two main roads, **Thanon Thavee Wong** and **Thanon Raja Uthit Song Roi Phi** (sometimes signed as Thanon Raja Uthit 200 Phi), which run parallel to the beachfront, spilling over into a network of connecting sois that in turn have spawned numerous pedestrian-only "plazas". It's along the two major thoroughfares that you'll find most of the accommodation, while **Thanon Bangla**, one of the roads that connects them, forms the heart of the nightlife district.

Practicalities

Songthaews from Phuket town's Thanon Ranong (every 15min from 6am–6pm; 20min) approach Patong from the northeast, driving south along Thanon Thavee Wong as far as the *Patong Merlin*, where they usually wait for a while to pick up passengers for the return trip to Phuket town. A **tuk-tuk** or **taxi** from Patong to Ao Karon will set you back about B200, but a **motorbike taxi** from one part of Patong to another should only cost B20–30 (the main motorbike taxi stand is in front of the *Royal Paradise Hotel* complex on Thanon Raja Uthit Song Roi Phi). SMT/National **car rental** (ⓣ076 340608, ⓦwww.smtrentacar.com) has a desk inside the *Holiday Inn*, or you can rent jeeps or motorbikes from the transport touts who hang out along Thanon Thavee Wong. Every transport and tour agent in Patong can provide a taxi service **to the airport** for about B400, but a cheaper alternative for solo travellers is the hourly minibus service operated by Supachai Travel at 26/1 Thanon Raja Uthit Song Roi Phi (ⓣ076 340046), which does hotel pick-ups between 6am and 6pm and charges B150 per person.

Most of the **tour agents** and **dive operators** have offices on the southern stretch of Thanon Thavee Wong: see the box on p.679 for a roundup of available day-trips and activities, and the box on p.670 for diving details. There are private **Internet** centres every few hundred metres on all the main roads in the resort, which charge much less than the business centres in the top hotels, but the cheapest place to check email is via the Catnet terminals in the telecom centre (daily 8am–11pm) next to the small post office on Thanon Thavee Wong; the main **post office** is at the northern end of Thanon Raja Uthit Song Roi Phi. Bookazine on Thanon Bangla carries a good range of English-language **books** about Asia, plus novels and magazines. The **police station** is on Thanon Thavee Wong, across from the west end of Thanon Bangla.

Accommodation

Moderately priced accommodation on Patong is poor value and during high season it's almost impossible to find a vacant room for less than B800. Some of the best-value, mid-range places are at the far northern end of Thanon Raja Uthit Song Roi Phi, beneath the hill road that brings everyone in from town, a 750-metre walk from the central shopping and entertainment area, but only 100m from the sea itself. Patong's **upmarket** hotels are generally better value, and many occupy prime sites on beachfront Thavee Wong. If you're travelling with **kids**, consider staying at the *Holiday Inn*, which has some specially furnished children's bedrooms and a kids' club as well, or the *Novotel Phuket Resort*, which has some of the most child-friendly facilities on the island.

High season here runs from November to April, but during the crazy fortnight over Christmas and New Year, when rooms should be reserved well in advance, most places add a supplementary charge of 25 percent. Every hotel drops its prices during the low season, when discounts of up to fifty percent on the rates listed are on offer.

Inexpensive and moderate

Casuarina Bungalows 92/2 Thanon Thavee Wong ⓣ076 341197, ⓦwww.travelthailand.com/casuarina. Individual bungalows and rooms in a small block set attractively in tree-covered grounds just across the road from the sea. Swimming pool and sauna. ❼

Neptuna Hotel 82/49 Thanon Raja Uthit Song Roi Phi ⓣ076 340824, ⓦwww.phuket-neptuna.com. Popular collection of air-con bungalows with all the trimmings in a pleasantly manicured if slightly congested garden. Ideal location, protected from the bustle, but only 200m walk from Thanon Bangla. Good value. ❼

PS2 Bungalow 78/54 Thanon Raja Uthit Song Roi Phi ⓣ076 342207, ⓦwww.ps2bungalow.com. Well-managed mini-hotel, with sizeable if slightly scruffy fan and air-con bungalows set around a swimming pool and garden area. At the far northern end of the resort so a fair walk from the main attractions. ❺–❻

Regent 2002 Guesthouse 70 Aroonsom Plaza, Thanon Raja Uthit Song Roi Phi ⓣ076 341664, ⓦwww.phuketdir.com/regent2002. Efficiently run small hotel with sizeable air-con rooms and Internet access in the lobby. ❺

Sand Inn 171 Soi Saen Sabai ⓣ076 340275, ⓦwww.sandinnphuket.com. Clean, well-appointed air-con rooms, a little on the compact side, east off the bar-packed Thanon Bangla. TV in all rooms and a Euro Café bakery downstairs. ❺

Sansabai Bungalows 17/21 Soi Saen Sabai ⓣ076 342948, ⓦwww.phuket-sansabai.com. Plain but comfortable bungalows in a peaceful green oasis of a garden off the far end of the soi; the priciest options have air-con and TV. Close to the nightlife but secluded. Good value for Patong. ❹–❺

Sea Beach Inn 90/1–2 Soi Permpong 2 ⓣ & ⓕ076 341616. Decent rooms, some with large balconies, a stone's throw from the beach and reached by following the signs through the warren of beachwear stalls. Fan and air-con available. Good value for Patong. ❹–❺

Shamrock Park Inn 31 Thanon Raja Uthit Song Roi Phi ⓣ076 342275, ⓔshamrock340991@hotmail.com. Friendly, reasonable value option at the northern end of the resort. Pleasant air-con rooms in a two-storey complex, all with en-suite shower and many with balconies. ❺

Expensive

Amari Coral Beach Resort 104 Thanon Traitrang ⓣ076 340106, ⓦwww.amari.com. Occupies a secluded spot on a cliff at the southernmost end of the beach; supremely luxurious with all facilities, including two swimming pools and a spa as well as tennis courts, a fitness centre and several restaurants. ❾

Baan Sukhothai Eastern end of Thanon Bangla ⓣ076 340195, ⓦwww.phuket-baansukhothai.com. A traditionally styled haven in a road packed with tacky modernity, this low-rise hotel sits in a landscaped garden and is the most characterful setup on Patong. Accommodation is either in upmarket rooms in two-storey blocks or in the much more interesting, and expensive, water-house bungalows, which each occupy their own tiny island. There's a swimming pool, a spa, and a good restaurant. Recommended. ❾

Holiday Inn Phuket 86/11 Thanon Thavee Wong ⓣ076 340608, ⓦwww.phuket.holiday-inn.com. Recommended upmarket option that offers very smart rooms in two differently styled wings, but retains a relaxed and informal atmosphere. The poshest villa rooms have their own interconnected plunge-pools and there are also large pools for each wing, plus several restaurants and an interesting programme of daily activities. Also has some "kidsuites" (bedrooms designed for children) and a kids' club, as well as a self-service laundry. Free for two under-18s sharing the adults' room. ❾

Impiana Phuket Cabana 94 Thanon Thavee Wong ⓣ076 340138, ⓦwww.impiana.com. Gorgeous collection of very tastefully designed bungalows, all equipped with air-con, TV and fridge, and set around a garden swimming pool. Right on the beach and the choice option in its price bracket. ❾

Novotel Phuket Resort Thanon Hat Kalim ⓣ076 342777, ⓦwww.phuket.com/novotel. Luxurious and relaxing chain hotel set on the hillside at the quieter, northern end of the beach. Set in landscaped tropical gardens and offering fine views. Facilities include three restaurants and a multi-level swimming pool. Especially good for families as it offers heaps of sporting activities and runs a free kids' club with games, videos and craft-making. Free for one under-15 sharing the adults' room. ❾

Patong Bay Garden Resort 33 Thanon Thavee Wong ⓣ076 340297, ⓦwww.patongbaygarden.com. Small hotel set right on the beach, with many rooms having French windows that literally open out onto the (rather crowded) sand and others that give out onto the courtyard swimming pool. Rooms are comfortable and well equipped, with air-con and TV. ❽

Eating

Much of the **food** on Patong is dire – low-grade microwaved slop sold at inflated prices. But in among the disastrous little cafés advertising everything from Hungarian to Swedish "home cooking" you'll find a few genuinely reputable, long-running favourites. Phone numbers are given where reservations are advisable.

Baan Rim Pa Across from the *Novotel* at 100/7 Thanon Hat Kalim ⓣ076 340789. Popular, elegant, traditional Thai restaurant, beautifully set in a teak building overlooking the bay. Specializes in classic "Royal Thai" cuisine and unusual contemporary dishes, and has a cellar of more than 270 wines. Live jazz-piano nightly except Mondays. Advance booking advised. Expensive.

Baan Sukhothai Hotel restaurant at the eastern end of Thanon Bangla. Elegant upmarket restaurant, particularly recommended for its fine "Royal Thai" dishes. Expensive.

Baluchi Inside the *Horizon Beach Hotel* on Soi Kepsap. Perhaps the best Indian restaurant in the resort, specializing in North Indian cuisine and tandoori dishes. Moderate to expensive.

Da Maurizio Across from the *Novotel* at 100/9 Thanon Hat Kalim ⓣ076 344079. Superior Italian restaurant in a stunning location set on the rocks overlooking the sea. Authentic pasta and antipastos, fabulous seafood and a good wine list. Reservations advisable. Expensive.

Patong Seafood Restaurant On the central stretch of Thanon Thavee Wong. Cavernous, unatmospheric but very popular open-sided restaurant that serves all manner of locally caught fish and seafood, particularly Phuket lobster, cooked to Thai, Chinese and Western recipes. Moderate.

Restaurant 4 At the back of one of the stall-lined sois running north off Thanon Bangla, clearly signed from the pavement. Pared down to the basics with nothing more than a few tables and chairs and customers' graffiti all over the back wall, this place keeps its prices down and so usually hosts a decent-sized crowd. The menu is all about fresh seafood, at very reasonable prices considering the competition. Inexpensive to moderate.

Sala Bua Thanon Thavee Wong. Fabulously stylish, breezy, beach-view restaurant attached to the equally glamorous *Impiana Phuket Cabana* hotel. The innovative Pacific Rim menu includes ravioli stuffed with mud crabs and rock-lobster omelette. Expensive, but worth it.

Tabeta Thanon Raja Uthit Song Roi Phi, near the mouth of Soi Kepsap. Pay B300 and you're allowed one hour to eat as much sushi as you can from the conveyor belt in front of you. Hopeless for vegetarians but a reasonable deal for anyone else who's hungry.

Nightlife and entertainment

Most of Patong's **nightlife** is packed into Thanon Bangla and the tiny sois that lead off it – a noisy strip of go-go clubs and neon-lit open-air "bar-beers" staffed by flirty, solicitous hostesses. The bars and clubs listed below are the best of the more salubrious options. The **gay** entertainment district is concentrated around the network of small sois and dozens of bar-beers in front of *Paradise Hotel* on Thanon Raja Uthit Song Roi Phi: see ⓦwww.gayphuket.com for reviews, events listings and details of the annual Gay Pride festival, which is held in late January or early February. If you're looking for something else to do with yourself or your kids in the evening, check out the nearby transvestite Simon Cabaret, or the spectacular show at Phuket Fantasea, both described in the box on p.679.

Banana Pub and Disco Inside the *Patong Beach Hotel* complex at 124 Thanon Thavee Wong. Very popular, very central upstairs disco and street-level bar attracting a mixed clientele of Thais, expats and tourists, but a bit of a pick-up joint. Live music. Nightly from 9pm.

Molly Malone's Next to McDonalds on Thanon Thavee Wong. As you'd expect, the resort's original Irish pub serves draught Guinness and Kilkenny beer, dishes out bar food and entertains drinkers with an Irish band every night from 9pm; also shows live TV coverage of international sports. There's a nice beer garden and no overt hostess presence. Daily from 11am.

Safari Pub and Disco Just beyond the southern edge of Patong, between Simon Cabaret and the *Le Meridien* hotel at 28 Thanon Siriat. Decked out to look like a jungle theme park, complete with waterfalls, this is one of the most popular dance venues on Phuket, with two bands playing nightly from around 9pm; the music fuses disco beats from the 1980s with more recent techno sets. There's a restaurant too.

Scruffy Murphy's Thanon Bangla. Like its sister pub, *Molly Malone's*, this is one of the few bars in Patong where you stand a decent chance of not being hassled by hostesses. Here too there's Guinness and Kilkenny on tap, nightly live music from 9pm, sports TV, and some outdoor seating. Daily from 11am.

Ao Karon

Phuket's second resort, after Patong, is **AO KARON**, 5km further south and considerably less congested. With its affordable guest houses and good-value package-tour hotels, Karon attracts young families and mid-budget backpackers looking for a lively but manageable major resort and, though bar-beers are popping up in several locations, it's still a decent place to bring the kids. That said, Karon is not exactly postcard pretty: the long sandy beach may be completely free of developments, but it offers very little in the way of shade, and to the south of the *Phuket Arcadia* the road runs right alongside it; in addition, the sand all but disappears here at high tide. The **undertow** off Ao Karon is treacherously strong during the monsoon season from June to October, so you should heed the warning signs and flags and ask for local advice – fatalities are not uncommon. For the rest of the year, there's plenty of scope for **watersports** on Karon; windsurfing is good all year round, and the reefs around the tiny island of Ko Pu, just off the headland separating Karon from neighbouring Ao Kata Yai to the south, make for enjoyable snorkelling. The tiny bay just north of Ao Karon – known as Karon Noi or Relax Bay – is almost exclusively patronized by guests of the swanky *Le Meridien* hotel, but non-guests are quite welcome to swim and sunbathe here. For inland entertainment, there's the Dino Park **mini-golf** (daily 10am–midnight; B240, kids B180, or B120/90 without the golf), next to *Marina Phuket Resort* on the Kata/Karon headland, which is part of a pseudo-prehistoric theme park comprising a dino restaurant and an erupting "volcano". For theatrical entertainment, try an evening at the nearby transvestite Simon Cabaret or the spectacular show at Phuket Fantasea, both of which are described in the box on p.679.

Some of the posher hotels on Phuket's other beaches offer expensive **spa treatments** to their guests, but on Karon anyone is welcome to the Kata Spa, near *Peach Hill* at 95 Thanon Pakbang (Ⓣ076 330914, Ⓦwww.distinctivespas-phuket.com/kata_spa.htm), where local herbs are used in all massage treatments (B450–1250); Kata Spa also teaches **courses in Thai massage**, lasting anything from half a day to a ninety-hour programme.

Practicalities

Ao Karon is 20km southwest of Phuket town and served by **songthaews** from the Thanon Ranong terminal (every 20min; 30min; B20). They arrive in Karon via Thanon Patak, hitting the beach at the northern end of Ao Karon and then driving south along beachfront Thanon Karon, continuing over the headland as far as *Kata Beach Resort* on Ao Kata Yai. To catch a songthaew back into town, just stand on the other side of the road and flag one down. If you're aiming for accommodation on Thanon Taina, you can save yourself at least ten minutes by getting off at the songthaew drop just north of the post office on Thanon Patak; for Thanon Luang Pho Chuan accommodation, alight just after the *Baan Karon* hotel on Thanon Patak. Avis **rental cars** has a counter at *Le Meridien* (Ⓣ076 340480, Ⓦwww.avis.com), and National/SMT has a desk inside *Karon Royal Wing* (Ⓣ076 396139, Ⓦwww.smtrentacar.com); or try the cheaper vehicles hired out by transport touts throughout the resort.

Karon's main **shopping** and eating areas are grouped around the *Islandia Hotel* on the northern curve of Thanon Patak, around *Phuket Arcadia* and *Phuket Orchid* on Thanon Karon, along Thanon Luang Pho Chuan, and along Thanon Taina (sometimes referred to as Kata Centre). In all these places you'll find **Internet centres**, minimarkets, tailors' shops, beachwear outlets, craft shops, restaurants and bars. There are **currency exchange** facilities, with ATMs, at the Thanon Patak/Karon roundabout; on Thanon Karon just south of the Thanon Luang Poh Chuang turn-off; and on the Thanon Karon corner of Thanon Taina. Karon's best second-hand **bookshop** is hidden away inside the Karon Circle supermarket at the Thanon Patak/Karon roundabout and has thousands of paperbacks in all literary genres. The Good Earth Bookstore (closed Sun) on Thanon Taina has a smaller range. There's a **clinic** on Thanon Luang Pho Chuan and a **police station** on central Thanon Karon.

Accommodation

Karon is less pricey than Patong, but during peak season you'd be lucky to find any **accommodation** in the ❸ category, with most places only dropping their rates below ❹ on weekdays during the monsoon season. The best places to search for budget hotels are along Thanon Taina on the Karon/Kata headland, and on Soi 1, which runs south off Thanon Luang Pho Chuan. High season here runs from November to April, but you'll almost certainly be charged an extra 25 percent over the Christmas and New Year fortnight when everything gets booked up weeks in advance. During the low season, expect to get discounts of up to fifty percent on the rates given below.

Inexpensive and moderate

Casa Brazil Soi 1, Thanon Luang Pho Chuan ⓣ076 396317, ⓦwww.phukethomestay.com. Unusually stylish little hotel, designed in Santa Fe style, with adobe-look walls and funky decor and furnishings. The 21 rooms are comfortable and nearly all have air-con. ❻

Happy Inn Soi 1, Thanon Luang Pho Chuan ⓣ076 396260. Nice assortment of smart bungalows in a small garden that occupies a surprisingly peaceful spot. Price depends on the size of the bungalow and whether it has air-con. ❹–❺

The Little Mermaid 94/25 Thanon Taina, Kata Centre ⓣ076 330730, ⓔmermaid@phuket.ksc.co.th. Exceptionally good bungalow rooms, all with air-con, TV and comfortable furnishings, set round a swimming pool. Also some cheaper, city-style fan and air-con rooms in the central hotel block. Advance booking essential. ❸–❺

Lucky Guest House 110/44–45 Thanon Taina, Kata Centre ⓣ076 330572, ⓔluckyguesthousekata@hotmail.com. Reasonable-value place offering unusually large, bright en-suite rooms in a low-rise block (the best ones have balconies) and some rather plain semi-detached bungalows on land further back. Choose between fan and air-con. ❹–❺

Merit Hill Bungalow 28 Soi 2, Thanon Karon ⓣ076 333300, ⓕ076 330585. Located up a slope across the road from the beach, this is an appealing spot with a range of different accommodation options. The nicest are the apartment-style bungalows, all with air-con, kitchen, living room and a restful view over an adjacent palm grove. Cheaper fan-cooled chalets are also pleasant, while the cheapest of all are rooms in a row without any view. ❹–❻

Prayoon Bungalows Behind the stadium, off Thanon Karon; access via *Andaman Seaview* ⓣ076 396196. Family-run place with just seven smart bungalows, with fan, ranged across a grassy slope a little way off the beach. ❹

Ruam Thep Inn Far southern end of beachfront Thanon Karon ⓣ076 330281. Forty good, fully equipped fan and air-con bungalows, just 20m from the beach. Superbly situated restaurant terrace jutting out over the sea. ❺–❻

Expensive

Karon Villa, Karon Royal Wing Thanon Karon ⓣ076 396148, ⓦwww.karonvilla.com. The most attractive place on Ao Karon: a self-contained village in the central beach area. Bungalows built to several different designs stand in lovely gardens, with even more luxurious accommodation provided in the main "Royal Wing" building. Numerous restaurants and bars, plus a pool and fitness club. ❾

Le Meridien On Ao Karon Noi (also known as Relax Bay), north of Ao Karon ⓣ076 340480, ⓦwww.lemeridien.com. Has the tiny bay all to itself; facilities include nine restaurants, a huge lake-style swimming pool (with islands), a spa, squash and tennis courts and private woods. A good place for kids, with special activities arranged every day for under-14s. Thai cookery classes also available. ❾

Marina Phuket Resort Thanon Karon, far southern end of Ao Karon, on the Karon/Kata headland ⓣ076 330625, ⓦwww.marinaphuket.com. Full range of luxurious cottages in a gorgeous tropical garden that leads right down to the beach. Convenient for bars and restaurants. Advance booking recommended. ❾

Peach Hill 13 Thanon Karon ⓣ076 330520, ⓦwww.peach-hill.com. Popular and stylish but low-key option that's perfectly located on a hill between the Thanon Taina shops and restaurants and the beach. Some rooms are in the hotel wing and others are in private bungalows set in the garden. All rooms have air-con and TV, and there are three pools. Recommended; booking ahead is essential. ❽–❾

Phuket Golden Sand Inn Northern end of Ao Karon ⓣ076 396493, ⓕ076 396117, ⓦwww.phuket.com/goldensandinn. Medium-sized hotel, one of the least costly of its kind, with good-value fan or air-con bungalows, plus pricier rooms in the central block. Popular and friendly. ❽–❾

Phuket Orchid 34 Thanon Luang Pho Chuan ⓣ076 396519, ⓦwww.katagroup.com. Enormous, package-tour-oriented hotel spread over grounds that feature three swimming pools and some Angkor-inspired statuary. Rooms are standard upmarket air-con, and popular with families. Well placed for easy access to bars and restaurants, and just a few metres from the beach. ❾

Eating and drinking

For the cheapest and most authentic Thai **food** you can't beat the carts that dish out noodle soup, satay and fried bananas on Thanon Taina throughout the day. Another very enjoyable place to eat is at the string of half a dozen open-fronted streetside restaurants just north of the stadium on Thanon Karon, whose inexpensive offerings range from king prawns to burgers and *matsaman* curries to spaghetti.

Most of the Thanon Taina **bars** are small, genial places: *Café del Mar* is an inviting, hip little joint serving margaritas and daiquiris as well as other drinks, while *Blue Fin* and *Anchor Bar* are both pleasant places for a beer. Though there are as yet no go-go bars on Karon, the Patong bar scene has made significant inroads, and there are clusters of bar-beers with hostess service in the Karon Centre and around the *Thavorn Palm Beach* on Thanon Karon, on sois off Thanon Luang Pho Chuan, and around the *Islandia Hotel* on Thanon Patak.

Euro Deli Across from *Marina Phuket Resort* on Thanon Karon. Real coffee, fresh brioches, croissants and Danish pastries make this a good place to start the day. Moderate.

Kampong-Kata Hill Restaurant Thanon Taina. Occupies a superb position on a steep slope just off the main road, its winding, flower-lined walkway lit up with fairy lights after dark. As you'd expect, the food is fairly high class, too, with quality Thai dishes a speciality. Moderate to expensive.

Kwong Seafood Shop Thanon Taina. Very popular for its array of freshly caught fish and seafood which can be barbecued or cooked to order. Moderate.

Lemongrass Kata/Karon headland. Pleasant place with classy touches. They specialize in good-quality Thai food (mainly curries, noodles and seafood) at reasonable prices; the shrimp curry is especially delicious. Moderate to expensive.

Ma Now Kata/Karon headland. Quality Thai food and seafood served in fairly classy surrounds. Moderate.

Old Siam In front of the *Thavorn Palm Beach Hotel*, Thanon Karon ⓣ076 396090. Large but fairly elegant teak-wood restaurant with indoor and outdoor dining areas, plus some traditional floor seating; renowned for ts classical Royal Northern Thai cuisine. Stages performances of Thai music and dance (Wed from 8pm) and can feel overly touristy. Call for free transport here. Moderate to expensive.

On the Rock In the grounds of *Marina Phuket Resort*, Kata/Karon headland. Open-air seafood restaurant situated right on the rocks overlooking Ao Karon. Moderate.

PN Restaurant Soi 1, Thanon Luang Pho Chuan. Small, simple, family-run café, in front of the family home, that deserves a mention for determinedly continuing to dish out Thai standards (mainly fried rice and noodle dishes) at exceptionally cheap prices, despite the inflated rates charged by most other similar places. Inexpensive.

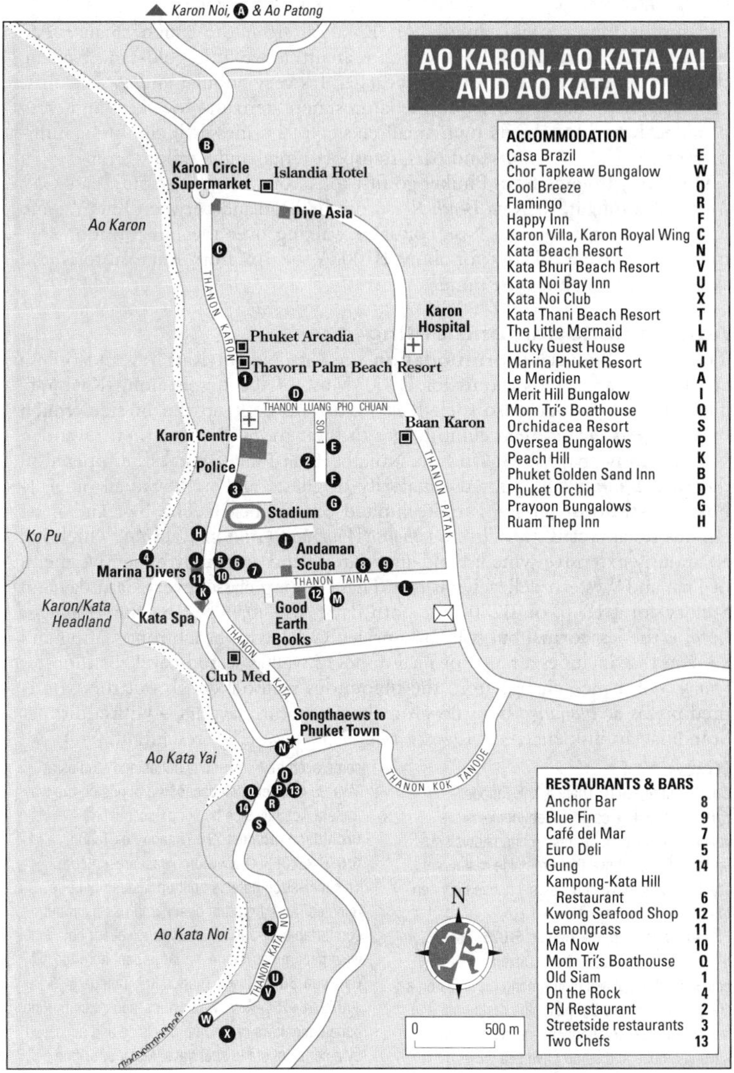

Ao Kata Yai and Ao Kata Noi

Tree-lined **AO KATA YAI** (Big Kata Bay) is only a few minutes' drive around the headland from Karon (17km from Phuket town), but both prettier and safer for swimming, thanks to the protective rocky promontories at either end. The northern stretch of Kata Yai is given over to the unobtrusive buildings of the *Club Med* resort, and then it's a lengthy trek down to the rest of the accommodation at the southern end, where you'll also find the restaurants, bars, minimarkets, tour operators and transport rental outlets. A headland at the southernmost point divides Ao Kata Yai from the much smaller **AO KATA NOI** (Little Kata Bay), which is an attractive little gold-sand bay and the nicest of the three Karon-Kata beaches. It's very popular and so gets quite crowded with deckchairs, but the atmosphere remains low-key and very pleasant. Kata Noi has its own small cluster of businesses including a mini-market, several restaurants and bars, transport rental and a tailor's shop.

Most **songthaews** from Phuket go first to Karon, then drive south past *Club Med* and terminate at *Kata Beach Resort* on the headland between Kata Yai and Kata Noi. To get to Kata Noi, continue walking over the hill for about ten minutes, or take a tuk-tuk for about B100. A tuk-tuk from Kata Yai to Karon should cost you about the same.

Accommodation and eating

There is no budget **accommodation** on Kata Noi or Kata Yai, and only a couple of places with rooms for B600. Most of the hotels along Kata Yai's Thanon Kok Tanode (also spelt Kok Tanot) are built up the hillside, which means guests face a steep climb to get to their rooms, but are then rewarded with expansive bay views. On Kata Noi, the *Kata Thani* and its sister operation the *Kata Bhuri* account for the majority of guests, and as they're all on half-board, **restaurant** choice is quite limited on this beach. The best and most famous restaurant is *Mom Tri's Boathouse Wine and Grill* on Kata Yai, which has a famously extensive wine list and an exquisite and extremely expensive menu of Thai and Western delicacies; it runs Thai cooking classes every Saturday and Sunday for B1800, or B2800 for both days. Also managed by the *Boathouse* hotel is the less formal but still fairly pricey *Gung*, with beachfront seating and a menu that includes a range of Thai dishes as well as seafood and rock lobster (*gung*). For a nice change from the ubiquitous seafood, check out the wood-fired pizzas at *Flamingo* bungalows or the European flavours – with a distinct Scandinavian influence – at *Oversea Bungalows' Two Chefs* restaurant.

Kata Yai

Cool Breeze 35/10 Thanon Kok Tanode ⓣ076 330484, ⓔcoolbreezebungalows@yahoo.com. Sixteen appealing bungalows set up the hillside, above the streetside restaurant. The best ones have sea views; choose between fan and air-con. ❺–❻

Flamingo Thanon Kok Tanode ⓣ076 330776, ⓦwww.flamingo-resort.com. Dozens of prettily positioned bungalows built among the trees on a steep incline above the pale pink restaurant and bar. Fan or air-con bungalows available; most have verandas and some have sea views. Also has a swimming pool and a small spa. ❻

Kata Beach Resort Thanon Kata ⓣ076 330530, ⓦwww.katagroup.com. Huge high-rise hotel with grounds that run down to the white-sand beach. There's also a big swimming pool, a kids' pool and lots of watersports facilities; popular with families. ❾

Mom Tri's Boathouse Thanon Kok Tanode ⓣ076 330015, ⓦwww.boathousephuket.com. Exclusive and very pricey beachfront boutique hotel with just 36 elegantly furnished rooms and a reputation for classy service. Room rates from B7000. Also has some even more luxurious suites and studios at *Villa Royale*, set in landscaped grounds on the way to Kata Noi. Advance booking essential. ❾

Orchidacea Resort 210 Thanon Kok Tanode ⓣ076 284083, ⓦwww.orchidacearesort.com. This mid-sized hotel is built up a steep hill a few minutes' walk from the beach and has plain but comfortable air-con rooms with excellent bay-view panoramas. There's a large pool here too. ❾

Oversea Bungalows Thanon Kok Tanode ⓣ & ⓕ076 284155, ⓦwww.twochefs-phuket.com. Nine huge bungalows ranged up a hillside and accessed by a series of steep stairways. Many offer fine sea views from their wraparound balconies and all have air-con. Run by the same Swedish trio behind the adjacent *Two Chefs* restaurant. Fifty-percent discount May–Oct. ❼

Kata Noi

Chor Tapkeaw Bungalow 18 Thanon Kata Noi ⓣ076 330433, ⓦwww.phuketdir.com/ctabkaew. The best of Kata Noi's cheaper options, whose spacious and fairly comfortably furnished fan and air-con bungalows are ranged up the hillside at the far southern end of the road; the verandas give good sea views and the restaurant is right on the beach. Book ahead as there are only 24 rooms and it's very popular. ❻–❽

Kata Bhuri Beach Resort Thanon Kata Noi ⓣ076 330124, ⓦwww.katathani.com. Sister hotel to the even swankier *Kata Thani*, on the beachfront across the road, this hotel boasts beautifully designed modern interiors, with all rooms done out in sleek contemporary furnishings and each enjoying a balcony with pool view. All accommodation is on a half-board basis (B6300 for two), with six restaurants here and at the *Kata Thani* to choose from. Also has a beachfront pool. ❾

Kata Noi Bay Inn Thanon Kata Noi ⓣ076 333308, ⓦwww.phuket.com/katanoibayinn, ⓔkatanoi_bayinn@hotmail.com. Small, friendly little hotel attached to a seafood restaurant, offering 28 good-value rooms with balconies and, in some cases, a distant sea view. Fan and air-con available. ❺–❻

Kata Noi Club Thanon Kata Noi ⓣ076 284025, ⓔkatanoi_club@yahoo.com. Set in among lots of trees at the far southern end of the beachfront road, this small, 25-room operation has some rather spartan bungalows as well as a few better, pricier air-con ones. ❻–❽

Kata Thani Beach Resort and Spa 14 Thanon Kata Noi ⓣ076 330124, ⓦwww.katathani.com. Occupying about half the beachfront, this is the biggest and poshest outfit on Kata Noi, offering very deluxe sea-view rooms, a spa, three swimming pools, plus tennis courts, a games room, a dive shop and a kids' playground. Accommodation is on a half-board basis (B7700 for two), with six restaurants here and at its sister hotel, the *Kata Thani* to choose from. ❾

Hat Nai Harn and Laem Promthep

Around the next headland south from Kata Noi, **HAT NAI HARN** – 18km southwest of Phuket town – is generally considered to be one of the loveliest beaches on the island, given character by a sparkling saltwater lagoon and dominated by the luxurious hotel, *Le Royal Meridien Phuket Yacht Club* (ⓣ076 380200, ⓦwww.phuket-yachtclub.com; ❾), which is rated among the best on the island. Follow the coastal road 2km south and you'll get to a small bay with coral reefs very close to the shore, though the currents are strong and the sewage pipes uncomfortably close. A further 1km on, you reach the southernmost tip of Phuket at the sheer headland of **Laem Promthep**. Wild and rugged, jutting out into the deep blue of the Andaman Sea, the cape is one of the island's top beauty spots: at sunset, busloads of tour groups get shipped in to admire the scenery – and just to ensure you don't miss the spectacle, a list of year-round sunset times is posted at the viewpoint. Several reefs lie just off the cape, but it's safer to snorkel from a boat rather than negotiate the rocky shore.

Songthaews from Phuket town (every 30min; B25) bypass Laem Promthep and follow the direct inland road between Hat Nai Harn and Hat Rawai instead, so you may have to do the lengthy climb round the promontory on foot.

The east coast and its islands

Shadowed by the mainland, Phuket's **east coast** lacks the fine sandy beaches and resorts of the west coast, and is chiefly the province of docks and harbours for ferries, speedboats and longtails to other **islands**, though Phuketians come for the numerous seafood restaurants along the shore.

Hat Rawai

The eastern side of Laem Promthep curves round into **HAT RAWAI**, Phuket's southernmost beach and the first to be exploited for tourist purposes. Thirty years on, the developers have moved to the softer sands of Kata and Karon and returned Rawai to its former inhabitants, the *chao ley*. Most visitors come either to eat seafood with Phuket's townspeople in one of the open-air seafood restaurants on the beachfront, or to hire a longtail out to the islands offshore, but you may also want to drop by the **Phuket Seashell Museum** (daily 8am–6pm), which displays some two thousand species of shell, including 380 million-year-old fossils, giant clams, and a 140-carat gold pearl. **Songthaews** from Phuket town's Thanon Ranong market pass through Rawai (B20) on their way to and from Nai Harn.

Ko Racha Yai and Ko Hai

Lying just a few kilometres off Hat Rawai, the islands of Ko Racha Yai (Raya Yai), Ko Racha Noi (Raya Noi), Ko Hai (aka Ko Hey or Coral Island) and Ko Khai Nok are all good for snorkelling and diving and are popular day-tripping destinations, though it's also possible to stay overnight on some of them.

The visibility and variety of the reefs around **KO RACHA YAI** in particular compare with those off Ko Similan further up the Andaman coast, and are frequented by Phuket's diving centres (see box on p.670). Longtail boats to Ko Racha Yai (1hr 30min) are easily chartered from Rawai; for a maximum of eight people, a boat should cost around B2000 for a day-trip, including snorkelling time and return transport. Alternatively, from November through April a speedboat leaves Ao Chalong (see below) every morning at about 9am and returns from the island at 3pm (B500 one way). You can stay on Ko Racha Yai at *Ban Raya Resort* (ⓣ076 224439, ⓦwww.phuket.com/banraya; ❼–❽), which has fan and air-con bungalows scattered through a palm grove on a headland, within a few minutes' walk of several lovely beaches.

Longtails to **KO HAI** (**Coral Island**) from Rawai cost around B800 for a half-day snorkelling charter, or B1500 for a day-trip by speedboat from Ao Chalong (sold by all travel agents in west-coast resorts); a one-way transfer from Ao Chalong costs B300 (contact *Coral Island Resort* for details). *Coral Island Resort* (ⓣ076 281060, ⓦwww.phuket.com/coralisland; ❽) has 64 bungalows and a pool set in lush tropical gardens and is within easy reach of several beautiful white-sand beaches.

Ao Chalong, Laem Panwa and Ko Siray

East of Rawai, the sizeable offshore island of Ko Lone protects the broad sweep of **AO CHALONG**, where many a Chinese fortune was made from the huge quantities of tin mined in the bay. These days, Ao Chalong is the main departure point for dive excursions and fishing trips, and for speedboats to other islands, including Ko Racha and Ko Hai. For islanders however, Chalong is important as the site of **Wat Chalong** (8km southwest of Phuket town), Phuket's loveliest and most famous temple, which enshrines the statue of revered monk Luang Pho Cham, who helped quash a violent rebellion by migrant Chinese tin-miners in 1876. Elsewhere in the temple compound, the Phra Mahathat chedi is believed to contain a relic of the Buddha.

Ao Chalong tapers off eastwards into **LAEM PANWA**, at the tip of which you'll find the **Phuket Aquarium** (daily 10am–4pm; B20), 10km south of Phuket town and accessible by frequent songthaews. Run by the island's Marine Research Centre, it's not a bad primer for what you might see on a reef.

Around the other side of Laem Panwa, the island's deep-sea port of **Ao Makham** is dominated by a smelting and refining plant, bordered to the north by **Ao Phuket** and **KO SIRAY** (aka Ko Sire), which just about qualifies as an island because of the narrow channel that separates it from Phuket. Tour buses always stop off at Ko Siray (5km due east of Phuket town) to spy on Phuket's largest and longest-established *chao ley* community, an example of exploitative tourism at its worst. For more on the *chao ley* see p.652. The Ko Siray channel is the departure point for many scheduled **ferries to Ko Phi Phi**, most of which use **Rassada Port**; transfers to and from the port are nearly always included in the price of the boat ticket.

Songthaews to Ao Chalong (B15) and the aquarium (B20) leave approximately every thirty minutes from Thanon Ranong in Phuket town.

Ko Yao Noi

Although officially part of Phang Nga province, not Phuket, the large, scenic islands of Ko Yao Yai and Ko Yao Noi are most easily accessed from Phuket and lie just a few kilometres off Phuket's northeastern shore. **KO YAO NOI** is the smaller but more beautiful of the two, about 10km by 12km at its widest points, and has some tourist accommodation. Most of its four thousand islanders are of Malay or *chao ley* origin and earn their living from fishing, shrimp-farming and coconut plantations. The island is forested and crisscrossed by trails that make for decent mountain-biking and hiking, with a good chance of encountering monkeys and barking deer, not to mention plenty of birds, including majestic oriental pied hornbills. **Kayaking** around the coast is also possible, and the dozens of tiny islands visible from the east coast make enticing destinations for experienced paddlers. Kayaks can be rented through Ko Yao Noi hotels, or you can join an overnight kayaking trip here: Sea Canoe trips (Ⓦwww.seacanoe.net) depart from Phuket (Ⓣ076 212252) and Ao Nang/Krabi (Ⓣ075 637170) and cost B8500 per person. The eastern shore has the best beaches, and most of the **accommodation** is here, on picturesque **Hat Pasai**. *Sabai Corner* (Ⓣ01 892 1827; ❹–❺) is a pleasant low-key little outfit with just a few comfortable bungalows. Similarly appealing is the Thai-Canadian-run *Lom'Lae Bungalows* (Ⓣ01 958 0566, Ⓦwww.geocities.com/lomlae_Thailand; ❹), which rents out split-bamboo bungalows and can arrange boat tours, kayaking and trekking excursions. *Koyao Island Resort* (Ⓣ076 597474, Ⓦwww.koyao.com; ❾) is the plushest place on the island, with fifteen luxurious bungalows set under the palm trees in a beachfront tropical garden.

Regular passenger **boats** run to Ko Yao Noi from Bang Rong on Phuket's northeast coast, departing at noon, 2.30pm and 5pm, and returning from Ko Yao Noi at 7am, 10am and 3pm; the ride costs B50 one way and takes about an hour. Longtails to Ko Yao Noi can be chartered for around B1000. There is a sporadic **songthaew** service from Phuket's Thanon Ranong to Bang Rong (B20), but it usually departs about once an hour, only runs until noon, and takes around ninety minutes. It's also possible to get to Ko Yao Noi from Ao Thalen's Laem Sak pier in Ao Luk, south of Phang Nga: a ferry departs here every morning at noon, and returns from Ko Yao Noi at 7am (1hr; B50).

The interior

If you have your own transport, exploring the lush, verdant **interior** makes a good antidote to lying on scorched beaches. All the tiny backroads – some too small to figure on tourist maps – eventually link up with the arteries connecting Phuket town with the beaches, and the minor routes south of Hat Nai Yang are especially picturesque, passing through monsoon forest that once in a while opens out into spiky pineapple fields or regimentally ordered **rubber plantations**. Thailand's first rubber trees were planted in Trang in 1901, and Phuket's sandy soil proved to be especially well suited to the crop. All over the island you'll see cream-coloured sheets of latex hanging out to dry on bamboo racks in front of villagers' houses.

Thalang and around

North of Ao Karon, Phuket's minor roads eventually swing back to the central Highway 402, also known as Thanon Thepkasatri after the landmark monument that stands on a roundabout 12km north of Phuket town. This **Heroines' Monument** commemorates the repulse of the Burmese army by the widow of the governor of Phuket and her sister in 1785: the two women rallied the island's womenfolk who, legend has it, cut their hair short and rolled up banana leaves to look like musket barrels to frighten the Burmese away. All songthaews to Hat Surin and Hat Nai Yang pass the monument (as does all mainland-bound traffic), and this is where you should alight for the **Thalang Museum** (Wed–Sun 8.30am–4pm; B20), five minutes' walk east of here on Route 4027. Phuket's only museum, it has a few interesting exhibits on the local tin and rubber industries, as well as some colourful folkloric history and photos of the masochistic feats of the Vegetarian Festival (see box on p.675). If you continue along Route 4027 you'll eventually reach the Gibbon Rehabilitation Project, described below.

Eight kilometres north of the Heroines' Monument, just beyond the crossroads in the small town of **THALANG**, stands **Wat Phra Thong**, one of Phuket's most revered temples on account of the power of the Buddha statue it enshrines. The solid gold image is half-buried and no one dares dig it up for fear of a curse that has struck down excavators in the past. After the wat was built around the statue, the image was encased in plaster to deter would-be robbers.

Phra Taew National Park

The road east of the Thalang intersection takes you to the visitor centre of **PHRA TAEW NATIONAL PARK**, 3km away. Several paths cross this small hilly enclave, leading you through the forest habitat of macaques and wild boar, but the most popular features of the park are the Gibbon Rehabilitation Project and the Ton Sai and Bang Pae waterfalls, which combine well as a day-trip. The Gibbon Project is located about 10km northeast of the Heroines' Monument, off Route 4027. **Songthaews** from Phuket town, more frequent in the morning, will take you most of the way: ask to dropped off at Bang Pae (a 40min drive from town) and then follow the signed track for about 1km to get to the project centre. You can get drinks and snacks at the foodstall next to the Rehabilitation Centre, and the route to the waterfalls is signed from here. The **Bang Rong pier** for boats to Ko Yao is a few kilometres northeast of the national park; see p.693 for details.

The Gibbon Rehabilitation Project

Phuket's forests used once to resound with the whooping calls of indigenous white-handed lar gibbons, but because these primates make such charismatic pets there is now not a single wild gibbon at large on the island. The situation has become so dire that the lar is now an endangered species, and in 1992 it became illegal in Thailand to keep them as pets, to sell them or to kill them. Despite this, you'll come across a good number of pet gibbons on Phuket, kept in chains by bar and hotel owners as entertainment for their customers or as pavement photo opportunities for foolish tourists. The **Gibbon Rehabilitation Centre** (daily 10am–4pm, last tour at 3.15pm; donation; Ⓦ www.warthai.org, Ⓔ gibbon@samart.co.th) aims to reverse this state of affairs, first by rescuing as many pet gibbons as they can, and then by resocializing and re-educating them for the wild before finally releasing them back into the forests. It is apparently not unusual for gibbons to be severely traumatized by their experience as pets: not only will they have been taken forcibly from their mothers, but they may also have been abused by their owners.

Visitors are welcome at the project, which is centred in the forests of Phra Taew National Park, close to Bang Pae waterfall, but because the whole point of the rehab project is to minimize the gibbons' contact with humans, you can only admire the creatures from afar. There's a small exhibition here on the aims of the project, and the well-informed volunteer guides will fill you in on the details of each case and on the idiosyncratic habits of the lar gibbon (see Contexts on p.819 for more about Thailand's primates). Should you want to become a project volunteer yourself, or make a donation, you can email the project centre.

Bang Pae and Ton Sai waterfalls

If you follow the track along the river from the Gibbon Project, you'll soon arrive at **Bang Pae Falls**, a popular picnic and bathing spot, ten to fifteen minutes' walk away. Continue on the track for another 2.8km (about 1hr 30min on foot) and you should reach **Ton Sai Falls**: though not a difficult climb, it is quite steep in places and can be rough underfoot, so take plenty of water and wear decent shoes. There are plenty of opportunities for cool dips in the river en route. Once at Ton Sai you can either walk back down to the Phra Taew National Park access road and try to hitch a ride back home, or return the way you came.

Thachatchai Nature Trail

Forty-one kilometres north of the Thalang intersection, just 700m south of the Sarasin Bridge exit to the mainland, a sign east off Highway 402 brings you to the **THACHATCHAI NATURE TRAIL**, part of the Sirinath National Park (which also covers the west-coast beaches of Hat Mai Khao and Hat Nai Yang). Although probably not worth a special trip, the trail does combine nicely with a visit to Hat Mai Khao (see p.676) or Hat Nai Yang (see p.677) – and it's free. Any bus running between Phuket town and the mainland will drop you at the sign (it's across the road from the old headquarters of the Sirinath National Park, now moved to Hat Nai Yang), just be sure to get off before you cross the bridge. There's a visitor centre at the trailhead where you can pick up a leaflet, and a drinks stall next door.

The six-hundred-metre trail runs along a raised wooden walkway that loops through a patch of coastal mangrove swamp. Informative English-language interpretive boards are set at regular intervals to show you what **flora and fauna** to look and listen out for: you can't fail to spot the swarms of fiddler crabs scuttling about in the sand and mud around the roots of the mangrove trees, and with a little patience you might also notice a few of the crabs that you may already have encountered elsewhere, as they're the ones that give the distinctive taste to the green papaya salad, *som tam*. The "bok-bok" sound that you can hear above the roar of the distant highway is the sound the mangrove-dwelling shrimps make when they snap their pincers as they feed. For more on mangroves, see p.704.

Ao Phang Nga

Protected from the ravages of the Andaman Sea by Phuket, **AO PHANG NGA** has a seascape both bizarre and beautiful. Covering some four hundred square kilometres of coast between Phuket and Krabi, the mangrove-lined bay is littered with limestone karst formations up to 300m in height, jungle-clad and craggily profiled. The bay is thought to have been formed about twelve thousand years ago when a dramatic rise in sea level flooded the summits of mountain ranges, which over millions of years had been eroded by an acidic mixture of atmospheric carbon dioxide and rainwater. The most popular way to see it is on an **organized tour** from the town of **Phang Nga** – you can go from Phuket or Krabi, but the Phuket boats are quite expensive and generally too big to manoeuvre in the more interesting areas, and Krabi tours go via Phang Nga anyway.

△ Ao Phang Nga

Phang Nga

All buses from Phuket and Takua Pa to Krabi pass through nondescript little **PHANG NGA** about midway along their routes, dropping passengers at the bus station (☎076 412014) on Thanon Phetkasem. If you want to go straight to the bay, change onto a songthaew bound for **Tha Don**; the pier is 9km to the south. There's no official **tourist information**, but the several tour operators inside the bus station compound are helpful and will store your baggage for a few hours; they also sell bus and boat tickets for onward journeys to Krabi, Ko Phi Phi, Ko Lanta and Ko Samui. Phang Nga has hourly **buses** to Phuket and Krabi, and four air-con departures a day to Surat Thani, with the 11.30am departure timed to link up with the Ko Samui boat, getting you to the island at 5pm. If you're heading to or from Khao Lak or points further north up the west coast, you'll probably find it faster to get a bus to Khokkloi and then change.

All Phang Nga's hotels are within a 250-metre radius of the bus station, which is itself towards the northern end of this long, thin town. This is also where you'll find the main **banks**, with exchange counters and ATMs. Most other municipal facilities are further south down Thanon Phetkasem: the **police station** (☎076 430390) and immigration office (☎076 412011) are about 500m south of the bus station, off Soi Thungchedi, the **telephone office** is another 100m south of them, and Phang Nga Hospital (☎076 412034) and the **post office** are over 2km south of the bus station.

Aside from the bay there are several caves and waterfalls within a short distance of town: all Phang Nga tour operators offer trips to visit them, or you can try and rent a motorbike through the tour outfits, or take motorbike taxis. The most famous is **Tham Phung Chang**, or **Elephant Belly Cave**, a natural 1200-metre-long tunnel through the massive 800-metre-high wooded cliff that towers over the Provincial Hall, about 3km west of the town centre. With a bit of imagination, the cliff's outline resembles a kneeling elephant, and the hollow interior is, of course, its belly. It's possible to travel through the elephant's belly to the other side of the cliff and back on organized two-hour excursions that involve wading, rafting and canoeing along the freshwater stream, Khlong Tham, that has eroded the channel. Any Phang Nga tour operator can arrange this for you, or you can organize it yourself at the desk in the car park in front of the cliff (afternoons are quieter); the price is B500. To get to the cave entrance yourself, exit Phang Nga along the Phuket–Krabi highway and watch for signs – and a large statue of an elephant – on the north side of the road, before the highway forks right for Phuket and left for Krabi.

Accommodation and eating

Phang Nga's best budget **hotels** are all within 100m of each other, on the bus station side of Thanon Phetkasem. First up, on the right-hand side as you turn right out of the bus station, is *Ratanapong Hotel* at no. 111 (☎076 411247; ❷–❸), which probably gets the most custom, offering en-suite fan rooms plus some with air-con, and an informal restaurant at street level. A few doors further on, the modern, well-liked *Phang Nga Guest House* (☎076 144358; ❷–❸) has clean and comfortable en-suite rooms with fan or air-con, while the *Thawisuk Hotel* at no. 77 (☎076 412100; ❷) has large, slightly cheaper fan rooms and a rooftop terrace. The most upmarket accommodation in town is at *Phang Nga Inn* (☎076 411963; ❹–❺), which is clearly signed to the left of the bus station, about 250m away, at 2/2 Soi Lohakji, just off the town's main road. It's the former family home of the people who also run the *Phang Nga Guest House*, and the seventeen rooms here are all attractively furnished and equipped with air-con and TV, the price depending on the size of the room. Down at Tha Don pier, the *Phang Nga Bay Resort* (ⓣ076 412067, ⓕ076 412070; ❻) has a swimming pool and views of the bay.

For **eating**, check out the *Phing Kan Restaurant* under the *Ratanapong Hotel*, where the English-language menu features a variety of noodle and rice standards, or the well-established streetside restaurant nearby, which offers similar fare. There's a also a tiny vegetarian café (*raan ahaan jeh*; daily 6.30am until about 2pm) on Thanon Phetkasem, about 100m walk left out of the bus station, which serves the usual array of exceptionally cheap veggie curries and stir-fries over brown rice.

The bay

On tours, the standard itinerary follows a circular or figure-of-eight route around the bay, passing extraordinary karst silhouettes that change character with the shifting light – in the eerie glow of an early-morning mist it can be a breathtaking experience. Many of the formations have nicknames suggested by their weird outlines – like **Khao Machu**, which translates as "Pekinese Rock", and **Khao Tapu**, or Nail Rock. Others have titles derived from other attributes – **Tham Nak** (or Nark, meaning Naga Cave) gets its name from the serpentine stalagmites inside; and a close inspection of **Khao Kien** (Painting Rock) reveals a cliff wall decorated with paintings of elephants, monkeys, fish, crabs and hunting weapons, believed to be between three thousand and five thousand years old.

Ao Phang Nga's most celebrated feature, however, earned its tag from a movie: the cleft **Khao Ping Gan** (Leaning Rock) is better known as **James Bond Island**, after doubling as Scaramanga's hideaway in *The Man With the Golden Gun*. Every boat stops off here and the rock crawls with trinket vendors.

From Khao Ping Gan most of the boats return to the mainland via the eye-catching settlement of **Ko Panyi**, a Muslim village built almost entirely on stilts around the rock that supports the mosque. Nearly all boat tours stop here for lunch, so the island's become little more than a tourists' shopping and eating arcade. You're best off avoiding the expensive and noisy seafood restaurants out front, and heading towards the islanders' foodstalls around the mosque. The overnight tours, which include an evening meal and dormitory-style accommodation on the island, offer a more tranquil experience and a chance to watch the sun set and rise over the bay, though there's little to do in the intervening hours and you're confined to the village until a boat picks you up after breakfast.

At some point on your trip you should pass several small brick **kilns** on the edge of a mangrove swamp – once used for producing charcoal from mangrove wood – before being ferried beneath **Tham Lod**, a photogenic archway roofed with stalactites and opening onto spectacular limestone and mangrove vistas.

Tours of the bay

The most popular budget tours are the **longtail-boat trips** operated by the handful of small tour operators based inside Phang Nga bus station. Competition between these outfits is fierce and the itineraries they offer are almost identical, so it's best to get recommendations from other tourists fresh from a bay trip, especially as reputations fluctuate with every change of staff. The main operators are Triple Friends Tour (ⓣ076 430195), Sayan Tour (ⓣ076 430348, ⓦwww.sayantour.com) and Mr Kean Tour (ⓣ076 430619). All three offer half-day tours of the bay (daily at 8am & 2pm; 3–4hr) costing B200 per person (minimum four people), as well as full-day extensions, which last until

4pm and cost B500, including lunch. (Take the 8am tour to avoid seeing the bay at its most crowded.) Note that all prices exclude the B200 national park entry fee. All tours include a chance to swim in the bay, and most offer the option of a canoeing session as well, for an extra B300 per hour. The tours leave from the tour operators' offices, but will pick up from the town's hotels if booked in advance; people staying at Tha Don, the departure-point for trips around Ao Phang Nga, can join the tours at the pier.

All tour operators also offer the chance to **stay** overnight on **Ko Panyi**. This can be tacked onto the half- or full-day tour for an extra B250 (departures at 8am, 2pm & 4pm); dinner, accommodation, and morning coffee are included in the price. Triple Friends Tour can add a three-hour canoeing option to its overnight Ko Panyi programme (total B1150), and also offers overnight camps on the national park island of Ko Lava (B1250 plus B300 for optional canoeing).

If you have the money, the most rewarding way to see the bay is by **sea canoe**. Several companies in Phuket (see p.679) and Khao Lak (see p.659) now offer this activity, in which you paddle round the bay in two-person kayaks, exploring the hidden lagoons (*hongs*) inside the karst outcrops (see box on p.706 for more on these), and observing the seabirds, kingfishers and crab-eating macaques that haunt the mangrove-fringed shores – without the constant roar of an engine to scare them away. Most outings also include snorkelling and swimming time, plus lunch on a deserted beach somewhere; some companies offer overnight trips, with the chance to paddle into *hongs* after dark. Everyone gets full paddling instruction and English-speaking guides should always be to hand; some companies have big support boats as well. Prices average B3000 per person (kids B1500).

Krabi

The compact little fishing town of **KRABI** is both provincial capital and major hub for onward travel to some of the region's most popular islands and beaches, including Ko Phi Phi, Ko Lanta, Ao Nang and Laem Phra Nang. So efficient are the transport links that you don't really need to stop here, but it's an attractive spot, strung out along the west bank of the Krabi estuary, with mangrove-lined shorelines to the east, looming limestone outcrops on every horizon, and plenty of welcoming guest houses, so it's both possible and enjoyable to base yourself here and make day-trips to the Krabi beaches (see p.705), 45 minutes' ride away by boat or songthaew. Krabi is at its busiest during high season, from November through February, a period which officially begins with the annual **Andaman Festival**, a week of festivities featuring parades, outdoor concerts, fishing contests, a funfair and lots of street stalls that climaxes at Loy Krathong, the nationwide festival celebrated in late October or early November (see p.284).

Arrival, transport and information

There are several daily **flights** between Bangkok and Krabi (on Thai Airways, Bangkok Airways, Phuket Airlines and PB Air), and Bangkok Airways runs daily shuttles between Ko Samui and Krabi. In addition, Silk Air operates three international flights a week between Singapore and Krabi. Diminutive Krabi **airport** (☎075 691940) is 18km east of town, just off Highway 4. Thai Airways minibuses transport passengers from the airport into town for B60, though these seem often to be commandeered by tour groups, so you may end up getting a taxi for B300 to Krabi or B500 to Ao Nang (maximum four passengers). Budget **car**

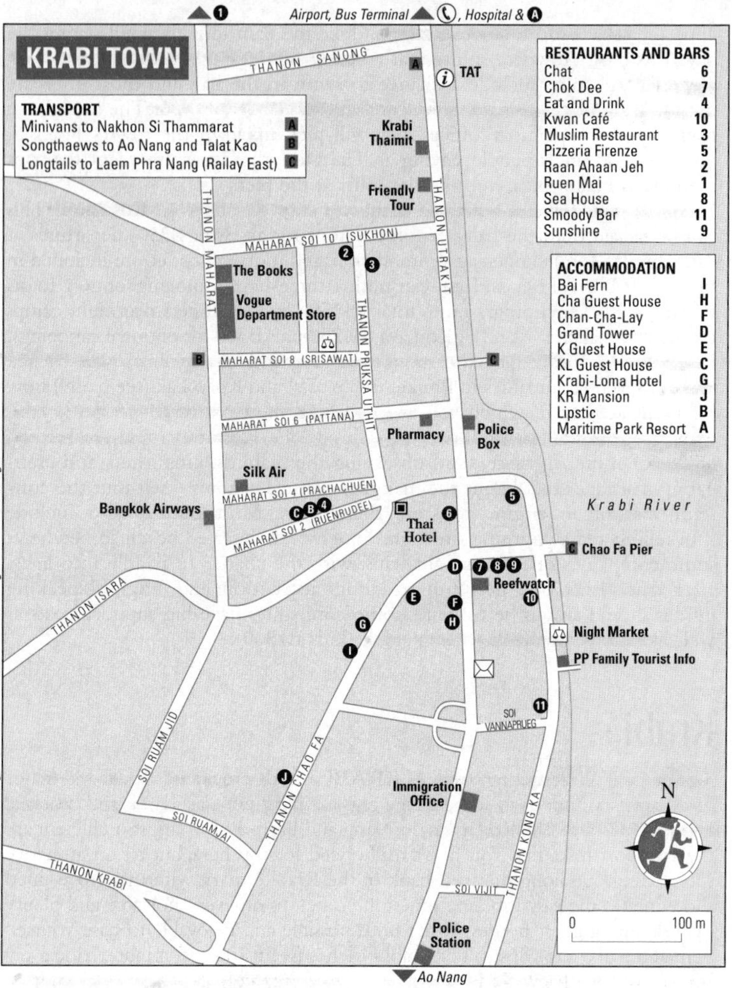

rental has a desk in the airport arrivals area (ⓣ075 691938, ⓦwww.budget.co.th), as does National/SMT (ⓣ075 691939, ⓦwww.smtrentacar.com).

Direct air-con and VIP **buses** from Bangkok leave the Southern Bus Terminal at staggered intervals between 6.30pm and 8pm and take at least twelve hours. Ordinary and air-con buses run hourly to and from Surat Thani (2–3hr), so if you're travelling from Bangkok, you could take an overnight **train** to Surat Thani and then pick up a Krabi bus. There are also hourly buses to and from Phuket via Phang Nga; if travelling to or from Khao Sok or Khao Lak you may have to change buses at Khokkloi. Only a few buses drop their passengers in central Krabi: most pull in at the **bus terminal** 5km north of town in the village of Talat Kao, which stands at the intersection of Thanon Utrakit and Highway 4 (ⓣ075 611804). From here there's a frequent songthaew service to Krabi's Thanon Maharat.

When it comes to moving on from Krabi, you can buy combination bus and train tickets **to Bangkok** via Surat Thani (2 daily; 16hr; B600–850) from any travel agent; these firms also sell tickets on private buses, minibuses and/or boats to **Phuket hotels** (daily; 4hr; B250), **Khao Lak** (2 daily; 2hr 30min; B250), **Khao Sok** (2 daily; 3hr; B250), **Ko Samui** (2 daily; 6hr; B300–370), **Ko Pha Ngan** (2 daily; 6hr; B400), Bangkok's **Thanon Khao San** (daily; 14hr; B450–550), **Penang** (2 daily; 6hr; B400) and **Langkawi** (daily; 12hr; B550). Note that despite the advertising, nearly all buses used by the private tour operators are minibuses, and some are quite dilapidated.

Ferries to Ko Phi Phi and Ko Lanta leave from the **Krabi Passenger Port** outside Krabi town, a couple of kilometres to the southwest. Ferry tickets bought from tour operators in town should include a free transfer from central Krabi or your guest house, though any Ao Nang-bound songthaew will also go via the port if requested (a ride of about ten minutes). All tour operators post the ferry timetables on their walls: at the time of writing, ferries **to Ko Phi Phi** depart daily from November to May at 9.30am, 11am, 1pm, 2.30pm and 4pm, with at least two daily departures guaranteed during the rest of the year (B200–250). Ferries **to Ko Lanta**, via Ko Jum, only run from mid-October to mid-May, departing at 10.30am and 1.30pm (B200); at other times you need to go by songthaew or minibus (see p.729). Longtail boats for **East Railay** on Laem Phra Nang (45min; B70) leave on demand from the town-centre piers at Tha Chao Fa on Thanon Kong Ka and nearby on Thanon Utrakit.

Public **songthaews** to local towns and attractions leave from outside the Vogue Department Store on Thanon Maharat, circulating around town and along Thanon Utrakit before heading out; unless otherwise stated, most run at least twice an hour from dawn till noon, and then less frequently until dusk. Useful destinations include Ao Nang, via Krabi Passenger Port (5.30am–10.30pm; B20); Wat Tham Seua (B15); Hat Nopparat Thara (B20) and Ao Luk (B20).

Information

Krabi's **TAT office** (daily 8.30am–4.30pm, ⓣ075 622163, ⓕ075 622164) is housed in a lone whitewashed hut on Thanon Utrakit at the northern edge of the town centre. Don't confuse this with the tourist information office run by the ferry operator PP Family, which is down on Thanon Kong Ka; you can get information here, but it may be partisan. The town has no shortage of **tour agents**, all of whom will be only too happy to sell you bus, boat and train tickets, and to fix you up with a room on one of the islands – a service that may be worth using for your first night's island or beach accommodation, as Ko Phi Phi especially gets packed out during peak season.

The monthly free, independent, **tourist magazine**, *Flyer*, carries features on local sights and activities and rounds up general transport information in the Krabi, Laem Phra Nang and Ao Nang area; it's available at some restaurants and guest houses. If you're spending some time in this region, it's worth buying a copy of *Krabi: Caught in the Spell – A Guide to Thailand's Enchanted Province*, expat environmentalist Thom Henley's lively and opinionated **book** about Krabi people, islands and traditions, which is packed with enticing photographs and ideas for exploratory day-trips; see "Books" on p.851 for details.

Accommodation

The guest houses and small hotels in Krabi offer a good range of **accommodation** that's mostly a lot better value than equivalent options on nearby beaches.

Bai Fern 24 Thanon Chao Fa ⓣ075 630339. Smart, spruce and sizeable rooms in a three-storey block that's away from the main fray; all rooms have private bathrooms and a balcony and some have air-con. Better than many pricier hotels in town. ❸–❺

Cha Guest House 45 Thanon Utrakit ⓣ075 621125, ⓔchaguesthouse@hotmail.com. Long-standing traveller-oriented place with good rooms in bungalows set round a garden compound behind an Internet centre. Room rates depend on size and whether you want a private bathroom. ❷–❸

Chan-Cha-Lay 55 Thanon Utrakit ⓣ075 620952, ⓦwww.geocities.com/chan_cha_lay, ⓔchancha lay_krabi@hotmail.com. With its stylish blue-and white-theme throughout, funky bathrooms, white-painted wooden furniture and blue shutters, this is the most charming and arty place to stay in Krabi. Choose from rooms with shared bathrooms or en suites with fan or air-con. Reservations essential. Recommended. ❷–❺

Grand Tower Hotel At the corner of Thanon Utrakit and Thanon Chao Fa ⓣ075 621146, ⓕ075 611741. Central, fairly comfortable travellers' hotel with well-furnished rooms, all of them en suite and some with TV and air-con. Can be noisy because of the bar next door. Internet access and a travel agency downstairs. ❸–❹

K Guest House 15–20 Thanon Chao Fa ⓣ075 623166. Deservedly popular spot, whose attractive upstairs rooms are timber-clad inside and out and mostly have streetside balconies. Also offers some cheaper, less interesting rooms with shared bathroom downstairs and at the back. Reservations essential. ❷–❸

KL Guest House 28 Soi 2, Thanon Maharat ⓣ075 612511. No frills, budget option; all rooms have a fan and shared bathroom, but the cheaper ones have no window. ❷

KR Mansion 52 Thanon Chao Fa ⓣ075 612761, ⓦwww.krmansion.com. Traveller-oriented hotel with a range of decent enough rooms, from those with shared bathrooms at the bottom end to air-con en suites at the top. Lots of traveller's information, a nice rooftop bar and a good restaurant. Also offers Internet access, book exchange and bicycle rental. ❷–❺

Krabi-Loma Hotel 20 Thanon Chao Fa ⓣ075 611168, ⓦwww.etccafe.com/krabiloma. The best of the town-centre hotels offers uninspired though perfectly comfortable mid-market air-con rooms, but the main attraction here is the small swimming pool. ❺

Lipstic 20–22 Soi 2, Thanon Maharat ⓣ075 612392, ⓔkayanchalee@hotmail.com. Good budget choice tucked away off the street with nice clean rooms; some have windows and others have private bathrooms, but none have both. ❷

Maritime Park Resort Krabi 2km north of town off Thanon Utrakit ⓣ075 620028, ⓕ075 612992. Beautifully located luxury hotel, set beside the limestone karsts and mangroves of the Krabi River. Rooms are attractive and have fine views. There's a big pool, a spa, a kids' games room and babysitting service. Thirty percent discounts May–Oct. ❾

Eating and drinking

Krabi has plenty of traveller-oriented restaurants, the best of which are detailed below, but for a truly inexpensive Thai meal, go to the riverside **night market**, which sets up around the pier-head on Thanon Kong Ka every evening from about 6pm, or try the inland night market on Soi 10, Thanon Maharat.

Chat Thanon Utrakit. Travellers' café and bar, which stages live music nightly when there are enough punters in town. Inexpensive.

Chok Dee, Sea House and **Sunshine** Thanon Kong Ka. A trio of adjacent, independently run little travellers' restaurants, serving standard Thai and Western dishes, set breakfasts, real coffee, curries and burgers. Inexpensive.

Eat and Drink Soi 2, Thanon Maharat (aka Thanon Ruenrudee). Emphasizes healthy East-West fusion cuisine, serving lots of fish and baking its own bread; also does Thai food and *matsaman* curries, and serves cocktails. Ask about cookery courses. Moderate.

Kwan Café Thanon Kong Ka. Popular place for leisurely breakfasts of pastries, pains chocolats, home-made breads, baguettes, cappuccino and fresh coffees. Moderate.

Maritime Park Resort Krabi 2km north of the town centre off Thanon Utrakit. Fabulous views from the sky lounge on the eighth floor at Krabi's poshest hotel – a great place for a sundowner as you're admiring the riverine landscape of karsts and mangrove swamps.

Muslim Restaurant Thanon Pruksa Uthit. Filling *rotis* (flat fried breads) served with a choice of curry sauces. Inexpensive.

Pizzeria Firenze Thanon Kong Ka. Authentic Italian dishes, including pizzas, pastas, sandwiches and ice creams. Moderate to expensive.

Raan Ahaan Jeh (Vegetarian Café) Thanon Pruksa Uthit. Typical unpretentious Thai veggie café serving meat-substitute curries and stir-fries at B20 for two servings over rice. Daily 6.30am until about 2pm. Inexpensive.

Ruen Mai About 2km north of the town centre on Thanon Maharat. Popular with locals and well regarded, this inviting, artfully planted garden restaurant is worth making the effort to get to, not least for the change from the more touristed options in the town centre. It serves quality Thai dishes, including lots of seafood and *tom yam*. Run by the same man behind *Same Same But Different* restaurant on Ko Lanta. Moderate.

Smoody Bar Thanon Kong Ka. Nightly live music and reasonably priced beer on the waterfront at the edge of the night market.

Tamarind Tree Restaurant attached to *KR Mansion* at 52 Thanon Chao Fa. Does a full range of Thai and Western fare at reasonable prices. It's well worth coming here before sunset to soak up the distant mountain views from the separate rooftop bar (open 4pm–1am) while you work your way through the cocktail menu. Moderate.

Listings

Airlines Any Krabi tour operator can book you a flight, or contact the airlines direct: Bangkok Airways, Thanon Maharat ⓣ075 622955; PB Air, at the airport ⓣ075 692143; Phuket Airlines, at the airport ⓣ075 636393; Silk Air, Soi 4, Thanon Maharat ⓣ075 623370; Thai Airways, beside *Maritime Park Resort Krabi* on Thanon Utrakit ⓣ075 622440.

Banks and exchange All major banks have branches on Thanon Utrakit with exchange counters and ATMs.

Bookshop The Books, next to Vogue Department Store on Thanon Maharat, carries a good range of English-language books about Thailand, plus maps and some novels.

Car rental At Krabi airport (see p.699), and through some guest houses and tour companies, including Friendly Tour at 173 Thanon Utrakit ⓣ075 612558, ⓔkrabifriendly1@hotmail.com; and Krabi Thaimit at 177 Thanon Utrakit ⓣ075 632054, ⓦwww.asiatravel.com/thailand/krabi carrent; both rent jeeps for B1200 per 24hr and cars for B1500, including full insurance.

Cookery classes Available at the Krabi Thai Cookery School, just off the Krabi–Ao Nang road (8am–2pm & 2.30–8pm; B1000 including transport; ⓣ075 695133, ⓦwww.krabidir.com/krthaicookery).

Dive centre Although there are dive centres at all the Krabi beaches, it's possible to organize trips and courses from Krabi town through the British-run Reefwatch Worldwide Dive Operator, 48 Thanon Utrakit (ⓣ075 632650, ⓦwww.reefwatchworldwide.com), a PADI Five-Star dive centre. They charge B10,700 for the four-day Openwater course and run dive trips to local sites (see p.720) for B2100, generally in a longtail boat.

Hospitals Krabi Hospital is about 1km north of the town centre at 325 Thanon Utrakit (ⓣ075 611202) and also has dental facilities, but the better hospital is considered to be the private Muslim hospital, Jariyatham Ruampat Hospital (ⓣ075 611223), which is about 3km north of town and has English-speaking staff.

Immigration office On Thanon Utrakit (Mon–Fri 8.30am–4.30pm; ⓣ075 611097).

Internet access Available at nearly every Krabi guest house. Catnet Internet terminals at the phone office on Thanon Utrakit.

Mail The GPO is on Thanon Utrakit. Poste restante should be addressed c/o GPO and can be collected Mon–Fri 8.30am–4.30pm, Sat 9am–noon.

Motorbike rental Through some guest houses and tour companies for about B250 per day.

Pharmacies There are a couple of town-centre pharmacies between Thanon Utrakit and Maharat Soi 6, and a branch of Boots the Chemist inside Vogue Department Store on Thanon Maharat.

Police For all emergencies, call the tourist police on the free, 24hr phone line ⓣ1155, or contact the police station at the southern end of Thanon Utrakit ⓣ075 611222 or 075 612740.

Telephones For international calls use the CAT phone office about 2km north of the town centre on Thanon Utrakit (Mon–Fri 8am–8pm, Sat & Sun 8.30am–4.30pm), which is easily reached on any songthaew heading up that road, or on foot.

Day-trips from Krabi

With time on your hands you'll soon exhaust the possibilities in Krabi, but there are several trips to make out of town, apart from the popular excursions to Laem Phra Nang (p.707), Hat Nopparat Thara (see p.712), Ao Phang Nga (see p.695) and Ko Phi Phi (see p.716). Alternatively, you could join one of the numerous **organized tours** sold by every Krabi travel agent, for example a kayaking trip around the Krabi coastline (see p.706); a tour of four or five islands, which take in the reefs and beaches around Laem Phra Nang; or a hike through the national park near **Khlong Thom**, home of the turquoise-feathered Gurney's pitta, a rare bird that's endemic to southern Thailand and southern Burma. Tour agencies sell the same basic itineraries, so prices are kept competitive.

The mangroves

Longtail-boat tours of the **mangrove swamps** that infest the Krabi River estuary can be organized directly with the boatmen who hang around Krabi's two piers (about B300/hour for up to six people) or through most tour operators (average B500/person for three hours). All mangrove tours give you a chance to get a close-up view of typical mangrove flora and fauna (see box below), and most will stop off at a couple of riverside caves on the way. The most famous features on the usual mangrove itinerary are the twin limestone outcrops known as **Khao Kanab Nam**, which rise a hundred metres above the water from opposite sides of the Krabi River near the *Maritime Park Resort* and are so distinctive that they've become the symbol of Krabi. One of the twin karsts hides caves, which can be easily explored – many skeletons have been found here over the centuries, thought to be those of immigrants who got stranded by a flood before reaching the mainland.

Even more fun is a self-paddle **kayaking** tour of the mangroves and *hongs*, hidden lagoons found further north up the coast. Every tour operator in Krabi sells these outings; see the box on p.706 for itineraries and prices.

Life in a mangrove swamp

Mangrove swamps are at their creepiest at low tide, when their aerial roots are fully exposed to form gnarled and knotted archways above the muddy banks. Not only are these roots essential parts of the tree's breathing apparatus, they also reclaim land for future mangroves, trapping and accumulating water-borne debris into which the metre-long mangrove seedlings can fall. In this way, mangrove swamps also fulfil a vital ecological function: stabilizing shifting mud and protecting coastlines from erosion and the impact of tropical storms.

Mangrove swamp mud harbours some interesting creatures too, like the instantly recognizable **fiddler crab**, named after the male's single outsized reddish claw, which it brandishes for communication and defence purposes – the claw is so powerful it could open a can of baked beans. If you keep your eyes peeled you should be able to make out a few **mudskippers**. These specially adapted fish can absorb atmospheric oxygen through their skins as long as they keep their outsides damp, which is why they spend so much time slithering around in the sludge; they move in tiny hops by flicking their tails, aided by their extra-strong pectoral fins. You might well also come across **kingfishers** and white-bellied **sea eagles**, but you'd be very lucky indeed to encounter the rare crab-eating macaque. For more on mangrove ecosystems see Contexts, p.818.

Though the Krabi mangroves have not escaped the **environmentally damaging** attentions of the prawn-farming industry (see "Environmental Issues" in Contexts, p.825, for more on this), or the cutting down of the bigger trees to make commercial charcoal, around fifteen percent of the Andaman coastline is still fringed with mangrove forest, the healthiest concentration of this rich, complex ecosystem in Thailand.

Wat Tham Seua

Beautifully set amid limestone cliffs about 10km northeast of Krabi, the tropical forest of **Wat Tham Seua** (Tiger Cave Temple) can be reached by taking one of the infrequent red songthaews from Thanon Maharat or Utrakit (20min; B15), and then walking 2km down the signed track. Alternatively, rent a motorbike and enjoy exploring the scenic backroads and nearby **Huay Toh Falls**, a five-tiered cascade that lies within Khao Phanom Bencha National Park (dawn till dusk; B200 entry), 25km north of Krabi. As Wat Tham Seua is a working monastery, visitors must wear respectable dress (no shorts or singlets for men or women), so bear this in mind before you leave town.

Wat Tham Seua's main **bot** – on the left under the cliff overhang – might come as a bit of a shock: alongside portraits of the abbot, a renowned teacher of Vipassana meditation, close-up photos of human entrails and internal organs are on display – reminders of the impermanence of the body. Any skulls and skeletons you might come across in the compound serve the same educational purpose. The most interesting part of Wat Tham Seua lies beyond the bot, reached by following the path past the nuns' quarters until you get to a couple of steep **staircases** up the 600-metre-high cliffside. The first staircase is long (1272 steps) and very steep, and takes about an hour to climb, but the vista from the summit is quite spectacular, affording fabulous views over the limestone outcrops and out to the islands beyond. There's a small shrine and a few monks' cells hidden among the trees at the top. The second staircase, next to the large statue of the Chinese fertility goddess Kuan Im, takes you on a less arduous route down into a deep dell encircled by high limestone walls. Here the monks have built themselves self-sufficient meditation cells, linked by paths through the lush ravine: if you continue along the main path you'll eventually find yourself back where you began, at the foot of the staircase. The valley is home to squirrels and monkeys as well as a pair of remarkable trees with overground **buttress roots** over 10m high.

Susaan Hoi

Thais make a big deal out of **Susaan Hoi** (Shell Cemetery), 17km west around the coast from Krabi, but it's hard to get very excited about a shoreline of metre-long forty-centimetre-thick beige-coloured rocks that could easily be mistaken for concrete slabs. Nevertheless, the facts of their formation are impressive: these stones are 75 million years old and made entirely from compressed shell fossils. You get a distant view of them from any longtail boat travelling between Krabi and Ao Phra Nang; for a closer look take any of the frequent Ao Nang-bound songthaews from Thanon Maharat or Utrakit (B16).

Krabi beaches

Although the mainland beach areas west of Krabi can't compete with the local islands for underwater life, the stunning headland of **Laem Phra Nang** is accessible only by boat, so staying on one of its four beaches (**Ao Phra Nang, West and East Railay and Ao Ton Sai**) can feel like being on an island, albeit a crowded and potentially rather claustrophobic one. In contrast, a road runs right along the **Ao Nang** beachfront, which has enabled a burgeoning resort to thrive around its rather unexceptional beach. The next bay to the west, **Hat Nopparat Thara**, is long and unadulterated and has some appealingly solitary places to stay at its western end. Swimming and snorkelling conditions deter ... ıches during the rainy season from May to October, so r ... odation drops by up to fifty percent for this period, an ... lown for the duration.

Sea-kayaking in the K...

By far the most rewardinc ... ories of the Krabi coastline is by **sea kayak**. Paddling silently and steal... ...he eerie mangrove swamps and secret lagoons, or *hongs,* hidden inside the limestone karsts is an awesome experience and gives you close-up views of birds, animals and plants that would be impossible in a roaring longtail.

Hongs are the pièce de résistance of south Thailand's coastline – invisible to any passing vessel, these secret tidal lagoons can only be accessed at certain tides in canoes and boats small enough to travel along the narrow tunnels that lead into the karst's central pool. Once inside a *hong* you are completely enclosed by a ring of cliff faces hung with strange plants that nourish a local population of flying foxes and monkeys and support an ecosystem that has remained unchanged for millennia. Like the karsts themselves, the *hong*s have taken millions of years to form, with the softer limestone hollowed out from above by the wind and the rain, and from the side by the pounding waves. Eventually, when the two hollows met, the heart of the karst was able to fill with water via the wave-eroded passageway at sea level, creating a lagoon. At high water these tunnels are filled and so impassable to any human, but when the tide recedes – for about fifty minutes every six hours – some tunnels do become passable to kayaks, enabling people to navigate into the mysterious *hong* at the heart of the karst.

Many companies take tourists kayaking around the karsts and mangrove swamps along the Krabi coastline, to impressive spots such as **Ao Thalen** (aka Ao Talin or Talane), about 25km northwest of Krabi town, where you paddle out to the *hong*s and beaches of **Ko Hong** and **Ko Bileh**. This is the best area for wildlife and general wilderness, but is not always possible to reach because it becomes inaccessible during the daytime for periods of up to ten days at a time. Another 25km north up the Krabi coast, the **Ban Bor Tor** (aka Ban Bho Tho) area of **Ao Luk** bay is famous as much for its caves as for its mangroves and karst landscape, and is another popular destination for kayak trips. The most celebrated cave up here is **Tham Lod**, with a long tunnel hung with stalagmites and stalactites and an entrance that's obscured by vines. The walls of nearby **Tham Phi Hua Toe** display around a hundred prehistoric cave-paintings, as well as some interestingly twisted stalactite formations. Some Ao Luk tours also feature a visit to the inland botanical gardens of **Than Bokkharani**, 1km south of Ao Luk. Called Than Bok for short, the tiny park is a glade of emerald pools, grottoes and waterfalls enclosed in a ring of lush forest; if you want to see them independently, catch an Ao Luk songthaew from Krabi (1hr; B20) and then walk down to the gardens.

Kayaking **trips** to any of the above destinations usually cost about B1700 for a full day or B900 for half a day; the better companies will take groups of two and limit their numbers to fourteen. Timing is obviously crucial in the exploration of these *hong*s, so sea-kayaking tour operators have to arrange their itinerary day by day to coincide with the tide. They can be arranged through any tour operator in Krabi town, Laem Phra Nang or Ao Nang, or directly with reputable kayaking operators such as John Gray Sea Canoe (Ⓣ076 254505, Ⓦwww.johngray-seacanoe.com) and Sea Canoe (Ⓣ075 637170, Ⓦwww.seacanoe.net). Both John Gray and Sea Canoe also do longer trips of up to a fortnight, with two-day excursions costing around B8500. All kayaking tours are priced for self-paddling, and tour leaders should give you full kayaking instruction; if asked, most tour operators can arrange for someone else to paddle you around for an extra B300.

The least attractive of the cape's beaches, **EAST RAILAY** (also sometimes known as Nam Mao, but not to be confused with the Ao Nam Mao proper, immediately to the east) is not suitable for swimming because of its fairly dense mangrove growth, a tide that goes out for miles and a bay that's busy with incoming longtails. Still, there's a greater concentration of less expensive bungalows here, and none is more than ten minutes' walk from the much cleaner sands of West Railay and Ao Phra Nang. To get to East Railay from Ao Phra Nang, follow the walkway from the eastern edge; from West Railay walk through the *Railay Bay* or *Sand Sea* bungalow compounds.

At low tide you can pick your way over the razor-sharp oyster rocks at the northern end of West Railay (beyond the *Railay Beach Club* compound) to reach **AO TON SAI**; at high tide you either need to swim or get a longtail. Ao Ton Sai is the travellers' beach with, to date, plenty of accommodation in the ❷–❹ categories (though a planned upmarket hotel complex may change this) and regular all-night beach parties hosted by some of the shorefront bars. Hardly any of the accommodation here has direct beach access as most of it is well hidden several hundred metres back from the shore, dug in amongst a thickly planted bowl of coconut palms. The beach itself is not one of Krabi's prettiest, disfigured by building detritus and littered with rocks that make it impossible to swim at low tide. But the karst-filled outlook is awesome and Ao Ton Sai's own orange-and-ochre-striped cliffs are equally fabulous confections, dripping with rocky curlicues, pennants and turrets that attract a lot of rock-climbers.

Climbing, kayaking and snorkelling

Given the topography, there's huge potential for **rock-climbing**, abseiling and caving at Laem Phra Nang. There are some six hundred bolted sport-climbing routes on the cape, ranging in difficulty from 4a–8c, and no shortage of places where you can rent equipment and hire guides and instructors. Some of the longest-established climbing outfits include: Cliffsman (ⓣ075 621768, ⓦwww.thaiclimb.com), on East Railay as well as on Ao Ton Sai; King Climbers (ⓣ075 637125, ⓦwww.railay.com/railay/climbing/climbing_intro.shtml), at *Ya Ya* on East Railay, as well as on Ao Ton Sai; Hot Rock (ⓣ075 621771), in Bobo Plaza on West Railay, as well as on Ao Ton Sai; and Tex Climbing (ⓣ01 891 1528, ⓦwww.texrock.com), beyond *Sunrise Tropical* on East Railay. It's a good idea to check with other tourists before choosing a climbing guide, as operators' safety standards vary. All the climbing centres rent out equipment (B1000/day for two people) and offer a range of climbing **courses** and expeditions. A typical half-day introduction for novice climbers costs B800, a one-day climbing outing is B1500, and for B5000 you get a three-day course which should leave you experienced enough to strike out on your own. If you're already self-sufficient, you might want to get hold of the *Route Guide* to the Laem Phra Nang climbs, written by the guys at King Climbers and available from most of the climbing shops. For more information check out ⓦwww.simonfoley.com/climbing and see Basics p.75.

Limestone cliffs and mangrove swamps also make great **kayaking** environments, and several places on East and West Railay rent out kayaks for B100–150 per hour. Some places also offer kayaking tours of spectacular Ao Luk and Ko Hong (see p.706) for B850–900.

All bungalows on Laem Phra Nang organize **snorkelling trips** (B250–400 including equipment) to the nearby islands of Hua Kwan and Ko Poda, and some offer two-night trips to Bamboo Island (B2000).

Practicalities

Laem Phra Nang is only accessible by **boat** from Krabi town, Ao Nang, Ao Nam Mao and Ko Phi Phi. Longtail boats to Laem Phra Nang depart from various spots along the **Krabi** riverfront (45min; B70), leaving throughout the day as soon as they fill up. Depending on the tide, all Krabi boats land on or off East Railay, so you'll probably have to wade; from East Railay it's easy to cut across to West Railay along any of the through-tracks. Krabi boats do run during the rainy season, but it's a nerve-wracking experience, so you're advised to go via Ao Nang instead. **Ao Nang** is much closer to Laem Phra Nang, and longtails run from the beachfront here to West Railay and Ao Ton Sai (10min; B50, or B80 after dark) all year round. During high season there's one direct boat every morning between Laem Phra Nang and **Ko Phi Phi** (2hr).

The three big bungalow operations on West Railay all have tour agencies and shops selling beach gear and postcards. You can **change money** at nearly all the bungalow operations on the cape, but rates can be up to ten percent lower than at the Krabi banks. There is **Internet access** at several places, including *Ya Ya* on East Railay and at Ao Ton Sai; an **overseas phone** service at *Sand Sea* and *Railay Village*, and at *Dream Valley* on Ao Ton Sai; a **clinic** in the *Railay Bay* compound, midway along the access track between East and West Railay; and a small **bookshop** stocked with new and second-hand books at *Railay Village*.

Accommodation, eating and drinking

Accommodation on the Railay beaches tends to be more expensive and less good value than equivalent options on the mainland, and staff at some of the cheaper places can be quite unwelcoming. The cheaper bungalows rarely take bookings, so to get a room for a decent price during high season it's often necessary to arrive early and hang around waiting for people to check out. Prices listed below are for high season, but rates can drop up to fifty percent from May to October. Ao Ton Sai has the best range of cheaper options, though you're unlikely to get a sea view as the hundreds of bungalows here are well camouflaged in the palm groves, several hundred metres from the shoreline.

All the bungalow operations have **restaurants** but their food is generally pricey and unremarkable. There's no shortage of relaxed beachfront **bars**, including *Railay Experience* and the famously chilled-out *Last Bar*, both near *Diamond Cave Bungalows* on East Railay, but the main party beach is Ao Ton Sai, where the beachfront *Freedom Bar* and *Chillout Bar* hold regular all-night events, plus monthly full moon **parties**. Though not as hectic, or large, as the famous Ko Pha Ngan versions, these draw lively crowds and there's boat transport from West Railay and Ao Nang through the night. Further inland on Ao Ton Sai, the *Rawkus Sport Bar* stages regular bouts of Thai boxing.

Ao Phra Nang

Rayavadee Premier ⓣ075 620740, ⓦwww.rayavadee.com. Set in a beautifully landscaped compound bordering three beaches, and the only place with direct access to Ao Phra Nang, this exclusive resort is an unobtrusively designed small village of supremely elegant two-storey pavilions costing a staggering B20,000 a night. The lack of beachfront accommodation is more than compensated for by a swimming pool with sea view. ❾

West Railay

Railay Bay Resort and Spa ⓣ 075 622330, ⓦwww.railaybay-resort.com. A huge range of accommodation on a stretch of land that runs down to both East and West Railay, with a swimming pool and spa centre on site. The cheapest rooms are in small fan-cooled huts, while the top-end bungalows are thoughtfully designed and have sea-view verandas and air-con. Also has some plush air-con rooms in a two-storey hotel block. Some of the huts are closer to East than West Railay. ❻–❾

Railei Beach Club ⓣ075 622582, ⓦwww.raileibeachclub.com. Exclusive, secluded compound of nineteen gorgeous private houses, built of wood in idiosyncratic Thai style and rented out by their owners. One- two- and three-bed houses are available, but must be booked several months in advance. Nearly all houses have kitchen facilities and offer a housekeeping service, and there's a club house. ❾

Railay Village ⓣ075 622578, ⓕ075 622579, ⓦwww.railay.com/railay/accommodation/railay_village.shtml. Attractive fan and air-con bungalows occupying landscaped grounds – with swimming pool – in between the two beaches, with nowhere more than 300m from the West Railay shore. Efficiently run and nicely maintained. ❺–❽

Sand Sea Resort ⓣ075 622170, ⓦwww.krabisandsea.com. Comfortable bungalows with fan and bathroom, plus deluxe air-con versions with big windows and nice furniture. All accommodation is set around a lovely tropical garden, and the place feels peaceful and secluded from the fray. ❼–❾

East Railay

Coco Bungalow ⓣ01 228 4258. The cheapest accommodation on the cape, comprising unadorned but pleasant enough en-suite bamboo huts in a small garden compound. Always fills up fast. ❸

Diamond Cave Bungalows At the far eastern end of the beach ⓣ075 622589, ⓦwww.diamondcaveresort.com. Huge range of rooms, mostly in detached bungalows, impressively located beside several karsts, including Diamond Cave itself. Rooms are plainly but comfortably furnished, some have air-con and TV, and the cheapest ones, which have shared bathrooms, are rented out to climbers at good monthly rates. Has a swimming pool. ❹–❽

Rapala Rock Wood Resort ⓣ075 622586, ⓔrapala@loxinfo.co.th. The best of the cheaper options on Railay has nice wooden huts with mattress-beds and decent bathrooms set in rows around a garden high up above the beach. A popular place, with a travellers' vibe, it also has a tiny hot-tub-sized pool and a lounging area with TV. ❹

Sunrise Tropical Resort ⓣ075 622599, ⓦwww.sunrisetropical.com. The most stylish of the affordable hotels on the cape offers just 28 elegant, spacious, wood-panelled air-con bungalows set around a landscaped tropical garden. ❾

Viewpoint Bungalows ⓣ075 622587, ⓦwww.viewpointresort66.com. Located up above the shore, which means that many of the fan and air-con bungalows enjoy good bay views from the large picture windows; some fan rooms in a hotel block are also available. The terrace restaurant affords great vistas of the mangrove and karst-dotted seascape too, and is worth a visit from non-guests; there's also a pool. ❺–❾

Ya Ya Bungalows ⓣ075 622593. Dozens of huts and three-storey wooden towers jammed into a small area make this place seem a bit claustrophobic and lacking in privacy, and leave the ground-floor rooms rather dark. All rooms have bathrooms and some have air-con. ❹–❻

Ao Ton Sai

Banyan Tree Beach Resort ⓣ075 621684. Offers standard bamboo and wooden bungalows with mosquito nets and bathrooms, plus some especially nice mint-green clapboard chalets with comfortable beds and good bathrooms. ❸–❹

Dream Valley Resort ⓣ075 622583, ⓦwww.krabidir.com/dreamvalresort/index.htm. Nearly eighty bungalows are ranged discreetly amongst the trees here, offering a range of accommodation from split bamboo huts with fan and bathroom through to air-conditioned cabins. ❹–❻

Krabi Mountain View ⓣ075 622610, ⓦwww.krabidir.com/krmtnviewres. One of the more upmarket options on Ao Ton Sai, with nice, clean, whitewashed fan and air-con rooms, all with good wooden beds. ❺–❼

Tonsai Bay Bungalow ⓣ075 622584. Very popular option with simple en-suite bamboo huts in a grove about 200m back from the shore, plus more upmarket concrete options with nicely designed bathrooms and good beds just behind the seafront restaurant. Fills up fast. ❷–❹

Viking 2 Small, primitive huts, with or without bathrooms, and very close to the shore. ❸

Ao Nang and Hat Nopparat Thara

AO NANG (sometimes confusingly signed as Ao Phra Nang), a couple of bays further north up the coast from Laem Phra Nang, is a lively if rather faceless mainland resort that still offers some relatively low-budget accommodation, but is increasingly upmarket in its emphasis. Though it lacks the cape's fine beaches, some people find Ao Nang a friendlier and less claustrophobic place than Laem Phra Nang, and there's a much greater choice of restaurants and bars, plus a wealth of dive shops, tour operators and other typical resort facilities. A road runs right alongside a big chunk of Ao Nang's narrow shore, with the resort area stretching back over 1km along both arms of Highway 4203, meeting Hat Nopparat Thara at the northwestern limit. But you only need to walk about 1km down the track that runs southeast along the beachfront from *Phra Nang Inn*, past the circular villas at *Golden Beach* and along the paved walkway to *The Last Café*, to reach a much prettier part of the beach, backed by a towering karst and sufficiently removed from the roar of incoming longtails. En route you can take your pick of two-dozen massage huts set out under the trees, several of which advertise themselves as Wat Pho-trained, or as specialists in remedial treatments. Around a small headland beyond *The Last Café* lies **Ao Phai Plong**, another bay of fine gold sand that's accessible by swimming or wading; or it's an impressive ten-minute boat ride from the Ao Nang shore to the beaches of Laem Phra Nang (see p.707).

Follow the road northwest past *Krabi Resort* for about 1km and you come to the eastern end of two-kilometre-long **HAT NOPPARAT THARA**. This beach is part of the national marine park that encompasses Ko Phi Phi, and has three sections (see the map on p.707). The far **eastern** end of the beach is the least interesting and has a fairly noisy road running alongside it. With inland development moving fast, eastern Hat Nopparat Thara is rapidly turning into Ao Nang's western suburb; transport between the two is frequent and it takes half an hour or less to cover on foot, and the restaurants, bars and shops of Ao Nang are effectively shared between the two accommodation centres. The **central** stretch of the beach is quieter and more attractive, with no private tourist accommodation, just the park headquarters about two-thirds of the way along the roadside and the **visitor centre** another kilometre further on, secluded amongst the trees beyond the T-junction. At low tide it's almost impossible to swim here, but the sands are enlivened by thousands of starfish and hermit crabs, and from the visitor centre you can walk out to the small offshore island if you tire of the supine life. This area is especially popular with Thai picnickers, who order from the makeshift food stalls that set up around the visitor centre and then settle on the grass mats under the casuarinas and wait to be served.

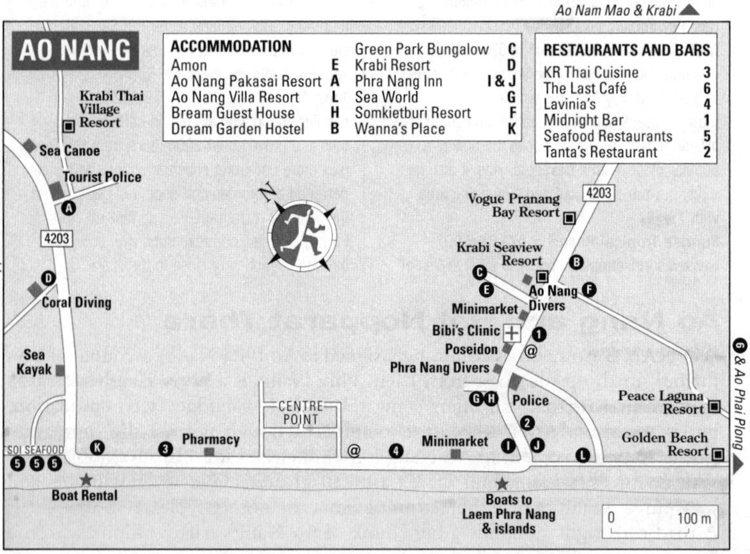

The **western** stretch of Hat Nopparat Thara feels like a different beach as it's separated from the visitor centre and central Hat Nopparat Thara by a khlong, and can only be reached by the longtails which depart from the national park harbour, Tha Hat Nopparat Thara, close by the visitor centre. (There is a 4WD track to the western beach, but it is only really used by experienced bikers and pick-ups.) Sometimes known as Hat Ton Son, western Hat Nopparat Thara currently has just four bungalow operations sharing the long swathe of peaceful casuarina- and palm-shaded shoreline, and is a great place to escape the crowds and commerce of other Krabi beaches. The views of the karst islands are magnificent – and you can walk to some of the nearer ones at low tide, though swimming here is just as tide-dependent as on central and eastern Hat Nopparat Thara. All the bungalow outfits here can arrange snorkelling trips to nearby islands.

Diving, snorkelling and kayaking

Ao Nang is Krabi's main centre for **dive shops**, with about ten outlets on the beach road and up Route 4203, including Ao Nang Divers at *Krabi Seaview* (Ⓣ075 637242, Ⓦwww.aonang-divers.com), Coral Diving at *Krabi Resort* (Ⓣ075 637662, Ⓦwww.coral-diving.com), Phra Nang Divers (Ⓣ075 637064, Ⓦwww.pndivers.com), and Poseidon (Ⓣ075 637263, Ⓦwww.poseidon-krabi.com). Most of the dive operators stick to a price agreement and charge the same rates, and most offer the same programmes. Diving with Ao Nang operators is possible year-round, with some dive staff claiming that off-season diving is more rewarding, not least because the sites are much less crowded. Most one-day **dive trips** head for the area round Ko Phi Phi (see p.720) and include dives at Shark Point and the "King Cruiser" wreck dive (see p.671 for descriptions) for B2500 including two tanks. Two dives in the Ao Nang area – at Ko Poda and Ko Yawasam – average B2500, or B1800 (B1200 for snorkellers) if you opt to go in a longtail rather than a dive boat. PADI dive courses start at B3600 for the introductory Discover Scuba day, or B11,900 for the Openwater. The nearest **recompression chambers** are on Phuket (see p.670); check to see that your dive operator is insured to use one of them. See Basics p.73 for general information on diving in Thailand.

It's quite common to arrange your own **snorkelling trips** with the longtail boatmen who congregate on the Ao Nang beachfront: a typical price would be B200 per person for a four- or five-hour snorkelling trip to Ko Poda, B250 to Chicken Island, or B1500 for a whole boat to Ko Hong. Alternatively, all Ao Nang tour agents sell snorkelling and swimming day-trips such as those advertised as "four-island" tours. Most dive shops rent mask, snorkel and fins for about B150 the set.

Several tour agents in Ao Nang offer **kayaking** expeditions, including the longest-established and highly reputable Sea Canoe (Ⓣ075 637170, Ⓦwww.seacanoe.net), which has an office near the tourist police on the way to Hat Nopparat Thara. For around B1700 they take you on self-paddle trips through the mangrove swamps and caves of Ao Luk or Ao Thalen, just south of Ao Phang Nga. See the box on p.706 for more on kayaking in the Krabi area. Some outlets also rent kayaks at B100–150 per hour.

Practicalities

Access to Ao Nang is easy, as **songthaews** run from Krabi regularly throughout the day, taking about 45 minutes (every 10min 6am–6.30pm; B20; every 30min 6.30pm–10.30pm; B50). During the day, all Krabi–Ao Nang songthaews go via the national park visitor centre (for the harbour and boats to the western beach) and all travel the length of eastern Hat

Nopparat Thara as well. The fare is B20 from Krabi (30min) or B10 from Ao Nang (10–15min); the 6.30–10.30pm Krabi–Ao Nang service takes a different route and doesn't pass any part of Hat Nopparat Thara.

Longtails from Tha Hat Nopparat Thara leave for the **western beach** when full and will drop you beside the closest set of bungalows, *Andaman Inn* (B10), from where you can walk to the accommodation of your choice; at high tide they'll take you further up the beach if asked (B20–30). Frequent longtail boats shuttle back and forth from Ao Nang to West Railay and Ao Ton Sai on **Laem Phra Nang** (10min; B50, or B80 after dark), while from November to May daily boats run to **Ko Phi Phi Don** (2hr), **Ko Lanta** (2hr 30min) and **Phuket** (2hr) from the harbour at Hat Nopparat Thara; transfers from Ao Nang hotels are included in the ticket price.

Bear the songthaew prices in mind before agreeing to the extortionate rates quoted by the dozens of **taxi-touts** loitering on Ao Nang's every corner: it's much cheaper to hire **motorbikes** (B120–200/24hr), or jeeps (B1200/day) from one of the tour operators, or through Budget **car** rental, which has a desk inside *Ao Nang Villa*, on Ao Nang's beachfront (ⓣ075 637913, ⓦwww.budget.co.th).

Ao Nang's shops and businesses can meet most travellers' requirements, with several official **money exchange** counters, lots of **Internet** centres, several minimarkets and pharmacies, a proliferation of beachwear stalls, numerous tour operators, and the inevitable tailors' shops. The local **tourist police** are based next to the *Ao Nang Pakasai Resort* (ⓣ075 637208) and there's a **clinic** at Bibi's (daily 9am–4pm).

Ao Nang's free monthly **tourist magazine**, *Flyer*, is a good source of information on the resort and is available from some hotels and restaurants.

Accommodation

Ultra-low budget **accommodation** is fairly thin on the ground in Ao Nang, and some of the mid-priced places are set within rather cramped confines. Room standards are good, however, and there are decent deals to be had at the upper end of the market if you book online (see Basics p.46 for some online booking agents). For locations of accommodation on eastern and western Hat Nopparat Thara, see the map on p.707: Eastern Hat Nopparat Thara has a couple of enticing budget options, but you'll have to head out to western Hat Nopparat Thara to find the archetypal beach bungalow, most of which have electricity in the evenings only and some of which close up for the rainy season from May to October. The only place to stay on the central beach is at the **national park bungalows**, beside the pier (ⓣ075 637159; ⑤), where you can also rent six-person tents for B300.

Ao Nang and eastern Hat Nopparat Thara

Inexpensive and moderate

Amon Ao Nang ⓣ075 637695. Tiny outfit run by a local Muslim family whose en-suite concrete row-houses have neither views nor a special atmosphere but come at a good price. ③

Bream Guest House Ao Nang ⓣ075 637555. Urban-style guest house offering some of the cheapest rooms in the resort, all with shared bathroom; the slightly pricier options have balconies. ③

Cashew Nut 150m down a track from eastern Hat Nopparat Thara's main beachfront road, about 1.5km from Ao Nang ⓣ075 637200. Good sturdy brick and concrete bungalows with fan and bathroom ranged around a garden of cashew trees. Price depends on the size. ④

Dream Garden Hostel Ao Nang ⓣ075 637338, ⓦwww.krabidir.com/dreamgardenhostel. Squashed into a narrow area behind a shopfront, this place offers two storeys of very good fan and air-con rooms, the only drawback being the wall view (partly obscured by plants). Upstairs rooms are brighter. ⑤–⑥

Green Park Bungalow Ao Nang ⓣ075 637300. Friendly family-run place set in a shady grove of trees and offering bamboo huts with verandas and private bathrooms, slightly sturdier wooden ones, or more expensive concrete versions. Recommended budget option that's traveller-friendly, is a good source of local information and serves a menu of home-cooked food. 3–5

Laughing Gecko 200m down a track from eastern Hat Nopparat Thara's main beachfront road, about 1.5km from Ao Nang ⓣ075 695115. An exceptionally traveller-friendly haven that's run by a Thai-Canadian couple who cultivate an atmosphere of easy-going hospitality. Choose from a range of simple bamboo huts set around a garden dotted with cashew trees: the cheapest beds are in a nine-person dorm (B100), or there are private rooms with shared bathrooms and en-suite huts with platform beds and mosquito nets. Hosts nightly all-you-can-eat Thai buffets for B100, plus occasional live music. 2–4

Sea World Ao Nang ⓣ075 637388, ⓔseaworld_aonang@hotmail.com. Well-priced rooms with bathroom, balcony and some good views, with or without air-con; a few of the cheapest rooms share bathrooms. Internet access downstairs. Very popular so try to reserve ahead. 2–6

Expensive

Ao Nang Pakasai Resort Ao Nang ⓣ075 637777, ⓕ075 637637, ⓦwww.krabi-hotels.com/aonangpakasai. Stylish and luxurious resort, with accommodation scattered up the hillside in steeply landscaped grounds giving fine bay views. The rooms are beautifully furnished and there's a scenically located rooftop swimming pool, table tennis, games room and bicycle hire. Rates from B5900. 9

Ao Nang Villa Resort Ao Nang ⓣ075 637270, ⓦwww.aonangvilla.com. Attractive air-con bungalows and sea-view hotel rooms just across the side road from the quiet, eastern end of the beach. All rooms have air-con, TV and use of the pool. 9

Krabi Resort Ao Nang ⓣ075 637030, ⓦwww.krabiresort.net. Set in a large tropical garden in a tiny bay, this is the oldest resort in Ao Nang, and one of the more old-fashioned. Offers both bungalows and rooms in a low-rise hotel, all of them air-con, plus a pool and tennis courts. 9

Phra Nang Inn Ao Nang ⓣ075 637130, ⓦwww.phrananginn.com. This timber-clad hotel, built in two wings on either side of the road and within a few metres of the sea, looks quaint from the outside, but the interiors have a contemporary feel and plenty of character. The comfortable air-con rooms are painted in bold, modern colours, tastefully furnished and attached to funky bathrooms. The best rooms overlook one of the hotel's three pools (one of which is for kids); there's also a spa and a recreation room. Good value for its class and location. 8–9

Somkietburi Resort Ao Nang ⓣ075 637990, ⓦwww.somkietburi.com. Guests here enjoy one of the most delightful settings in Ao Nang, with rooms and swimming pools surrounded by a feral, jungle-style garden that's full of hanging vines and lotus ponds. Rooms are perfectly pleasant but nothing special; all have air-con and TV, and there's a spa. Good value. 8

Wanna's Place and Andaman Sunset Resort Ao Nang ⓣ075 637322, ⓦwww.wannasplace.com. This two-in-one operation is the most affordable of the few beach-front places, with 47 air-con rooms in a low-rise sea-view hotel block and in bungalows ranged up the steep hill behind. The rooms are all of a good standard, the place is well run, and there's a small swimming pool. It's very popular so reserve ahead. 8

Western Hat Nopparat Thara

Andaman Inn 100m west of the khlong ⓣ01 956 1173. The most commercial option on the western beach, with a huge range of huts, from very simple affairs with shared bathrooms to large en-suite versions. Does day-trips and snorkelling tours. Closes May to early Sept. 1–4

Emerald Bungalows Next to *Andaman Inn* ⓣ01 956 2566, ⓔkumthont@yahoo.com. Offers the most comfortable accommodation on the beach, in big, brightly painted and tastefully furnished wooden bungalows, all with sea views, large decks, private bathroom and fan. Some less interesting air-con options also available. Runs boat trips to nearby islands at B1500 for up to six people. Usually closed May–Aug, but phone to check. 6–8

Long Beach Bungalow and Camp ⓣ09 885 5559, ⓔlongbeachfishcamp@yahoo.com. Laid-back outfit whose simple bamboo huts all come with platform bed and mosquito net; some also have private bathrooms. Also organizes three-day fishing camps to Bamboo Island for B2500 per person. Should be open all year. 2–3

PAN Beach At westernmost end of the beach, about 700m walk from the khlong ⓣ09 866 4373. Ten sturdy wooden bungalows, each with screened windows and bathroom, set just back from the shore. In low season, call to check whether it's open. 3

Eating, drinking and entertainment

Seafood is Ao Nang's best suit, and one of the best places to enjoy it is on so-called Soi Seafood, a cluster of little **restaurants** off the western end of the beachfront road, where you get excellent fish dishes plus an uninterrupted view of the waves; sunset is an especially popular time to dine here. Ao Nang has a big Muslim population and as dusk falls handcarts selling the Muslim **roti** pancakes pop up all over the resort, particularly on the stretch of road between *Phra Nang Inn* and *Bream*: choose from a selection of sweet fillings including condensed milk, banana or chocolate.

The **bar** scene in Ao Nang is focused around the Centre Point complex, behind the front row of shops on the beachfront road, but the German-managed *Midnight Bar* on Route 4203 can also be worth checking out. There's a *muay Thai* **boxing** stadium 1km west out of Ao Nang, near the *Laughing Gecko* guest house on Hat Nopparat Thara (see p.715), which stages regular bouts in high season; check local flyers for details.

KR Thai Cuisine Beachfront road, Ao Nang. Low-key but popular café that serves a huge, well-priced menu of everything from stir-fries to yellow, green and *matsaman* curries, plus seafood, a decent vegetarian selection and cocktails. Inexpensive to moderate.

The Last Café Situated beneath a towering karst at the far eastern end of the beach, this is a perfect, peaceful spot on Ao Nang's prettiest sands. Tables are set under the trees just back from the shore and the menu runs from rice-based dishes and soups through fruit shakes and home-made cakes. To get there, simply follow the shorefront southeast from *Phra Nang Inn* as far as you can go, passing *The Last Fisherman Bar* and massage huts en route – about 1km in all. Inexpensive to moderate.

Lavinia's Beachfront road, Ao Nang. Choose from over twenty thin-crust pizzas or a variety of sandwiches made with ciabatta or dark bread. Also specializes in pasta and home-made ice cream, and has a decent selection of imported wines. Moderate.

Tanta's Restaurant Just north of *Phra Nang Inn* on Route 4203. Large, open-sided restaurant that attracts capacity crowds of diners eager to enjoy the exceptionally tasty, Thai and seafood dishes, not to mention the Penang and *matsaman* curries. Moderate.

Ko Phi Phi

Now well established as one of southern Thailand's most popular destinations, the two islands known as **KO PHI PHI** look breathtakingly beautiful as you approach from the sea, their classic arcs of pure white sand framed by dramatic cliffs and lapped by turquoise water so clear that the banks of cabbage coral and yellow-striped tiger fish are clearly visible from the surface. Things don't look quite so pretty once you land on the larger island, **Ko Phi Phi Don**, however, whose core overflows with dozens of poorly designed bungalow developments and tourist enterprises, and where large swathes of land seem to be permanently under construction, disfigured by building rubble and piles of rotting rubbish. The problem has worsened since uninhabited sister island **Ko Phi Phi Leh** – under national marine park protection on account of its lucrative bird's-nest business (see box on p.725) – gained worldwide attention as the location for the movie *The Beach* in 1999. Since then, businesses on Phi Phi Don have capitalized mercilessly on the islands' increasing popularity, resulting in some of the worst-value accommodation in the whole of Thailand and a less than welcoming atmosphere. There are exceptions of course, particularly on the northern beaches, but be warned that many tourists find Phi Phi a disappointment.

Getting to the islands

During peak season, **ferries** to Ko Phi Phi Don run up to five times daily **from Krabi**, 40km to the north, and two or three times a day from **Phuket**, 48km to the west; ticket prices depend on the speed and comfort of the boat, though be warned that the glassed-in air-con ferries can be far stuffier and more fume-filled than the open-sided ones. In the rainy season the service from both Krabi and Phuket is generally reduced to twice daily. Buying a return ticket offers no advantages and can sometimes be limiting, as some ferries won't take tickets issued by other companies. Return ferries to Krabi leave up to five times a day from Ao Ton Sai, between 8am and 3.30pm, depending on the season; and there should be at least two boats a day back to Phuket, year-round, departing at about 9am and 2.30pm. There is also a daily **seaplane** service between Phuket Airport and Ko Phi Phi run by Blue Water Air (Ⓣ076 250538; Ⓦwww.bluewaterair.com). From November to May, daily ferries run to Phi Phi Don from **Ao Nang** (Tha Hat Nopparat Thara) and **Laem Phra Nang**, returning from Ao Ton Sai at 3.30pm; and to Ko Phi Phi Don from **Ko Lanta Yai**, returning at 8am and 1pm. The only way you can get to Phi Phi Leh is by longtail from Phi Phi Don or as part of a tour.

Because of the accommodation situation, you might prefer to see Phi Phi on a **day-trip**: tour agents in Phuket, Ao Nang, Krabi town and Ko Lanta all organize snorkelling excursions to Phi Phi Don and Phi Phi Leh, with prices starting from around B1200, including lunch and snorkelling equipment, or B800 for under-12s. Alternatively, you could organize your own outing to Phi Phi Don on the scheduled ferries: the return boat to Ko Lanta leaves Phi Phi Don at 1pm, while the last boats to Krabi, Ao Nang and Phuket leave at around 3pm.

Ko Phi Phi Don

KO PHI PHI DON would itself be two islands were it not for the tenuous palm-fringed isthmus that connects the hilly expanses to east and west, separating the stunningly symmetrical double bays of Ao Ton Sai to the south and Ao Loh Dalum to the north. So steep is the smaller western half that the tiny population lives in isolated clusters across the slopes of the densely vegetated eastern stretch, while the tourist bungalows stick mainly to the intervening sandy flats, with a few developments on the beaches fringing the cliffs east and north of the isthmus.

All boats dock at **Ao Ton Sai**, the busiest bay on the island. From here you can catch a longtail to any of the other beaches, or walk – there are a couple of short motorbike tracks but no roads on Phi Phi Don, just a series of paths across the steep and at times rugged interior, at points affording superb views over the bays. **Accommodation** on the island ranges from the exclusive to the ramshackle, but in the "budget" and mid-market categories you could end up paying as much as three times what you'd pay on the mainland. The prices listed below are for high season, which runs from November to April, but most bungalow operators slap on a thirty to fifty percent surcharge during the ridiculously hectic Christmas and New Year period; reservations are absolutely essential over this holiday fortnight, and are strongly recommended throughout high season. From May to October you should be able to negotiate up to fifty percent off the prices listed below. The commercial heart of the island is Ton Sai village, which has all sorts of tourist-oriented **facilities** including exchange counters, Internet access, international telephone centres, postal services and lots of small shops, bars and restaurants.

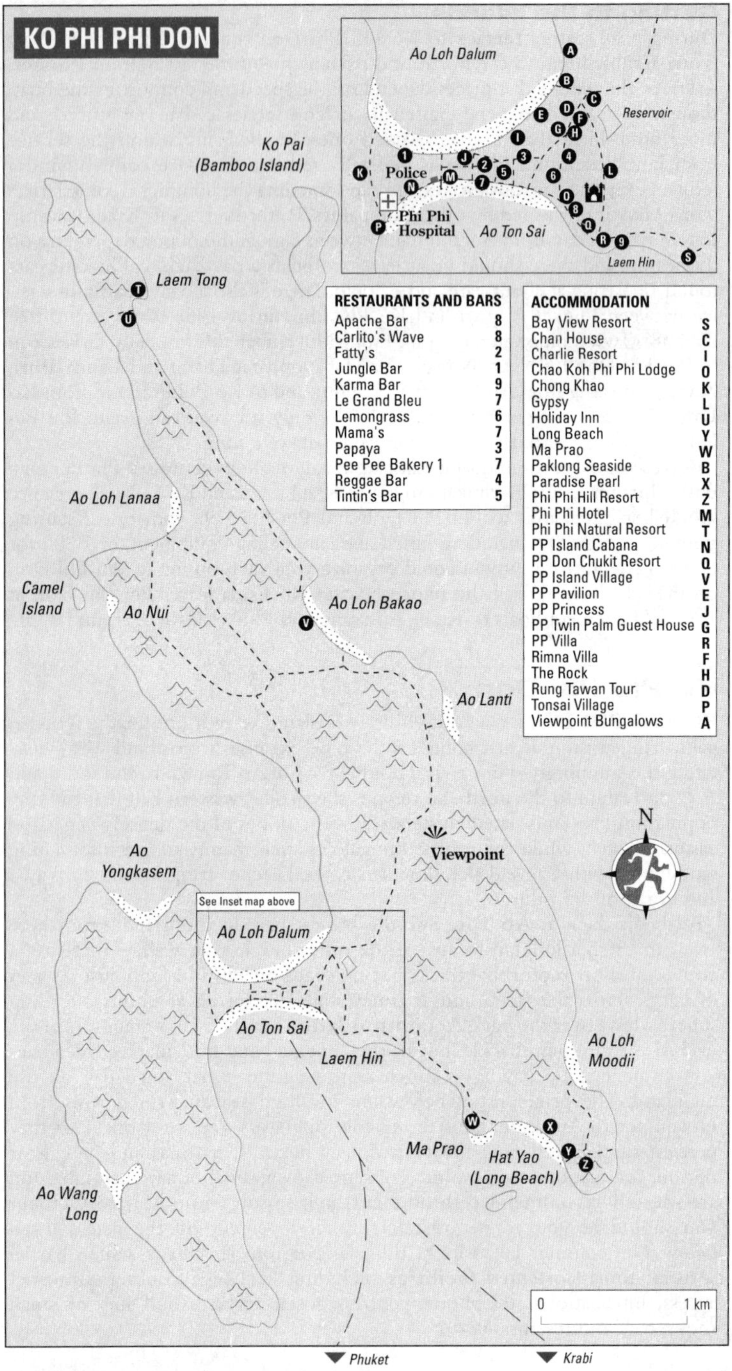
KO PHI PHI DON
Ao Loh Dalum
Reservoir
Police
Phi Phi Hospital
Ao Ton Sai
Laem Hin
RESTAURANTS AND BARS
Apache Bar 8
Carlito's Wave 8
Fatty's 2
Jungle Bar 1
Karma Bar 9
Le Grand Bleu 7
Lemongrass 6
Mama's 7
Papaya 3
Pee Pee Bakery 1 7
Reggae Bar 4
Tintin's Bar 5
ACCOMMODATION
Bay View Resort S
Chan House C
Charlie Resort I
Chao Koh Phi Phi Lodge O
Chong Khao K
Gypsy L
Holiday Inn U
Long Beach Y
Ma Prao W
Paklong Seaside B
Paradise Pearl X
Phi Phi Hill Resort Z
Phi Phi Hotel M
Phi Phi Natural Resort T
PP Island Cabana N
PP Don Chukit Resort Q
PP Island Village V
PP Pavilion E
PP Princess J
PP Twin Palm Guest House G
PP Villa R
Rimna Villa F
The Rock H
Rung Tawan Tour D
Tonsai Village P
Viewpoint Bungalows A
Ko Pai
(Bamboo Island)
Laem Tong
Ao Loh Lanaa
Camel Island
Ao Nui
Ao Loh Bakao
Ao Lanti
N
Viewpoint
Ao Yongkasem
See Inset map above
Ao Loh Dalum
Ao Ton Sai
Laem Hin
Ao Loh Moodii
Ma Prao
Hat Yao (Long Beach)
Ao Wang Long
0
1 km
Phuket
Krabi

Ao Ton Sai

The constantly expanding village at **AO TON SAI** is a full-blown low-rise holiday resort, and it's the liveliest – if not exactly the pleasantest – place to stay on the island. Backpacker-oriented shops, tour operators, restaurants and dive centres line the main walkway that parallels the beachfront and runs east as far as *PP Don Chukit Resort*, while every available inch of land between the Ao Ton Sai shoreline and the resorts on Ao Loh Dalum is crammed with more makeshift stalls, tin-shack guest houses, dive shops, reggae bars, massage centres, souvenir shops and restaurants. If you can ignore the building debris at every turn and the pervasive whiff of sewage, it can be quite a fun place to hang out for a few hours; if not, head up the coast as fast as you can. All the main services are here, including two **exchange** counters run by national banks (daily 7am–10pm), a **post office**, international telephone call centres and scores of little places offering **Internet access**. The island's only health centre, **Phi Phi Hospital** (Ⓣ075 622151), is at the western end of Ton Sai, in the compound of the *PP Island Cabana*, and there's a **police** box at the pier and another one next to the *Apache Bar* on the track to Laem Hin (Ⓣ06 687 8432).

The **beach** itself is most attractive at the western end, under the limestone karsts, but even this stretch gets unbearably crowded in the middle of the day when it plays host to hundreds of day-trippers who snorkel just offshore and then eat lunch at the beachfront restaurants. The central part of the bay is far too busy with ferries and longtails to even consider swimming there, but the eastern stretch, in front of *PP Villa*, is a little quieter.

Accommodation

Most of Ton Sai's **accommodation** is packed between the Ao Ton Sai and Ao Loh Dalum beaches, and at the foot of the hills to the east and west. The cheapest places are the ever-growing number of small guest houses stuffed cheek-by-jowl into extremely rickety shacks that look like a significant fire hazard and are very poor value for money.

Chan House About 100m inland from the eastern end of Ao Loh Dalum; easiest access from the pier is to turn north beside *Chao Koh Phi Phi Lodge* Ⓣ01 970 4122. Welcoming staff but low-grade en-suite rooms in this small, simply designed, nine-room block. ❹

Chong Khao Bungalows Behind *Tonsai Village*, at the western end of the village Ⓣ01 894 1233. Set in a coconut grove, this place has dozens of concrete bungalows squashed every which way into a small patch of land that's midway between Ao Ton Sai and Ao Loh Dalum. Rooms (fan only) are comfortable enough, but the place feels congested and staff are pressed. ❺–❻

Phi Phi Hotel 50m north (inland) from the pier Ⓣ075 611233 Ⓦwww.phiphihotel.com. Low-rise hotel with smart and relatively good-value rooms, each equipped with air-con, TV, phone and mini-bar; the priciest have sea views. Advance booking essential. ❽

PP Island Cabana Hotel Main entrance is just west (left) of the pier, but stretches all the way over to Ao Loh Dalum Ⓣ075 620634, Ⓦwww.phiphicabana-hotel.com. One of the biggest outfits on the island, this place offers direct access to both beaches, comprising cute, mid-range fan bungalows set in a garden fronting the eastern stretch of Ao Ton Sai, plus a central hotel block set round an enormous pool and offering stunning northwards views of Ao Loh Dalum from the priciest air-con rooms. ❽–❾

PP Twin Palm Guest House In the thick of the inland scrum; easiest access from the pier is to turn north beside *Chao Koh Phi Phi Lodge* Ⓣ09 195 3480, Ⓦwww.krabidir.com/pptwinpalmbung. Scrapes by with a handful of dark Bangkok-style en-suite guest-house rooms, plus some slightly nicer bungalows, some of which have air-con. ❹–❼

Rimna Villa About 150m inland from the eastern end of Ao Loh Dalum; easiest access from the pier is to turn north beside *Chao Koh Phi Phi Lodge* Ⓣ01 894 2668, Ⓦwww.krabidir.com/rimnavilla/index.htm. Unusually for cheapish accommodation on Phi Phi, this place offers some high views and

Diving, snorkelling, kayaking and rock-climbing off Ko Phi Phi

More accessible than Ko Similan and Ko Surin, Ko Phi Phi and its neighbouring islands rate very high on the list of Andaman coast **diving and snorkelling** spots, offering depths of up to 35m, visibility touching 30m, and the possibility of seeing white-tip sharks, moray eels and stingrays. At uninhabited **Ko Pai** (or Bamboo Island), off the northeast coast of Phi Phi Don, much of the reef lies close to the surface, and gives you a chance of seeing the occasional turtle and possibly the odd silver-and-black-striped banded sea snake – which is poisonous but rarely aggressive. At the adjacent **Ko Yung** (or Mosquito Island), the offshore reef plunges into a steep-sided and spectacular drop. Off the west coast of Phi Phi Don, **Ao Yongkasem** also has good reefs, as do the tranquil waters at **Ao Maya** on the west coast of Phi Phi Leh. For a description of the other local top sites, see p.670.

Dive shops on Phuket (see p.670) and Ao Nang (see p.713) run daily excursions here, and there are also about twenty centres on Phi Phi itself. The biggest concentration is in Ton Sai village, where there are over a dozen competing outfits, so prices are cheap and some operators cut corners; because of this it's very important to check your operator's credentials and equipment and to try and talk to other divers about their experiences (see Basics p.73 for general advice on diving). Note that the cheaper dive trips are usually by longtail boat rather than the much more comfortable, better-equipped proper dive boats: ask to see a photo of your boat before booking. Also note that, despite what some of the less scrupulous dive shops may say, it is considered risky for a novice diver with fewer than twenty dives under their belt to dive at Hin Daeng and Hin Muang (see p.671), due to the depth and the current. Many dive centres on Phi Phi sell imported dive equipment, and they all rent equipment too. Recommended Ton Sai operators include Moskito, a PADI Five-Star Instructor Development Centre opposite the post office, near *Fatty's* (Ⓣ075 612092, Ⓦwww.moskitodiving.com); Viking Divers, on the cross-island soi beside *Chao Koh Phi Phi Lodge* (Ⓣ01 970 3644, Ⓦwww.vikingdiversthailand.com); and Visa Diving, on the main track to the pier (Ⓣ075 618106, Ⓦwww.phiphidiving.com). There are also small dive centres on Hat Yao, Ao Loh Bakao and Laem Tong. Average prices for **day-trips** including two tanks, equipment and lunch are: B1800 for local reefs off Phi Phi Leh; B2600 for the *King Cruiser* wreck; and B3600 for Hin Daeng and Hin Muang

a fair amount of space and is embraced by a grove of coconut palms. Its bungalows are perched up the side of the slope overlooking a rainwater reservoir (formerly intended as a water-treatment plant) and are connected to each other via a precarious network of rickety wooden walkways. The en-suite bungalows are decent enough, and the price depends on how high up the slope you want to be. ❺

The Rock About 200m inland from the eastern end of Ao Loh Dalum; easiest access from the pier is to turn north beside *Chao Koh Phi Phi Lodge* Ⓣ075 612402. Has the cheapest beds on the island, in a four-bed dorm (B150/bed) and a sixteen-bed dorm (B200/bed). A few single rooms with shared bathrooms also available, but no doubles. ❸

Rung Tawan Tour In the heart of the inland village; easiest access from the pier is to turn north beside *Chao Koh Phi Phi Lodge* Ⓣ01 535 3288. Very rudimentary rooms in a rickety shack divided by plywood walls, only worth considering because they all have private bathrooms. ❹

Tonsai Village Located under a cliff at the far western end of the beach Ⓣ075 621297, Ⓦwww.tonsaivillage.com. The fifty nicely appointed bungalows here are kitted out with air-con, TV and comfortable furnishings, though they're a bit dark and close together. ❽

Eating

Ton Sai is by far the best place to eat on the island – there are dozens of little **restaurants** in the village, ranging from bakeries to Muslim foodstalls, but the (by speedboat). Excalibur Liveaboards (www.thailand-liveaboard.com), which currently runs out of Moskito, organizes live-aboard trips direct from Phi Phi to the Similan and Surin islands (US$640 for four days). **Dive courses** on Phi Phi cost B2500 for the introductory Discover Scuba day, B10,000 for the certificated four-day Openwater course, and B7400 for a two-day Advanced course. If you're short on time, email ahead to reserve a place on a dive course or live-aboard trip. The nearest **recompression chambers** are on Phuket (see p.670); check to see that your dive operator is insured to use one of them.

Nearly all the tour operators and bungalow operations on Phi Phi Don organize day and half-day **snorkelling** trips. Prices range from B400 to B600 for a day-trip, including lunch and snorkelling gear, with the price depending on the size of the boat and number of participants. In the case of snorkelling, the longtails that run from Ko Phi Phi are better than the larger fishing boats and the Phuket cruise ships, which are so popular that you can rarely see the fish for the swimmers. Many dive operators will take accompanying snorkellers on their one-day dives for about B500.

The limestone cliffs and secluded bays of the Phi Phi islands make perfect **kayaking** territory, as the lagoons and palm-fringed coasts are much better appreciated in silence than accompanied by the roar of a longtail or cruise ship. If you rent a kayak for a whole day you can incorporate sunbathing and snorkelling breaks on small, unpopulated bays nearby. Lots of tour operators in the village rent out kayaks at B100–200 per hour or B600–800 per day, depending on size and quality, and there are also kayaks for rent on Hat Yao. Seasports at *PP Princess* on Ao Loh Dalum (01 897 2256, sea_fun@hotmail.com) rent **windsurfing** equipment (B300/hour or B700/half a day) and offer **sailing trips** around Ao Phang Nga or to Langkawi in Malaysia, lasting several days and priced at US$80 per day.

Phi Phi's topography is also a gift for **rock-climbers** and several places in the village offer climbing instruction and equipment rental. Prices average B500 for a two-hour beginners' introduction, and B1500 for a one-day course with full instruction and equipment. The main climbing area is a small beach just to the west of Ao Ton Sai, and includes the Ton Sai Tower and the Drinking Wall, with heights of 15m and 30m respectively. A newer attraction is **cliff-jumping**, offered by several tour agencies and featuring jumps of up to 18m off a Phi Phi Don cliff.

biggest crowd-pullers are the larger eateries serving fresh seafood. Less expensive but just as tasty are the typically Thai curry-and-rice shops in the market area at the heart of the village, and there are always lots of hawkers flogging *rotis* and fried bananas from their hand-carts.

Fatty's North up the soi beside *Mama's* restaurant. Pleasantly spacious European restaurant that's renowned for its hearty portions of western food, especially steaks, goulash, meatballs and schnitzels. Not top of the list for vegetarians. Moderate.

Le Grand Bleu Close by the pier, on the main track. A French place, serving classy menus of the day and lots of fresh seafood. Expensive.

Lemongrass About 20m north up the soi beside *Chao Koh Phi Phi Lodge*. Serves only Thai food on a lengthy menu that includes mussels, red and green curries and some decent veggie options. Moderate.

Mama's On the main track from the pier. French-run eatery that's a long-standing favourite for fresh seafood and good cakes. Moderate to expensive.

Papaya In the market area north of Phi Phi Diving School. One of the best of several hot-food stalls serving cheap and authentic Thai standards to Thais who live and work in the village. Inexpensive.

Pee Pee Bakery 1 On the main track from the pier. The best place for breakfast and takeaway cakes and buns. Real coffee plus a huge selection of freshly baked croissants, Danish pastries, home-made breads, cakes and cookies. Inexpensive to moderate.

Drinking

Small **bars** proliferate in the village, adorned with hand-painted signboards and throbbing to the usual Bob Marley and Euro-pop standards. The scene is youthful and can get quite excessive.

Apache Bar At the eastern end of the village, just beyond *Chao Ko Phi Phi*, on the track to Laem Hin. Huge, multi-tiered bar and dance floor that hosts regular parties (check locally posted flyers) and has a long happy hour.

Carlito's Wave At the eastern end of the village, next to *Chao Ko Phi Phi*, on the track to Laem Hin. Popular seafront joint with a big cocktails menu and easy-going atmosphere.

Jungle Bar Part of the *PP Island Cabana* complex, on the beachfront at the western end of Ao Loh Dalum. Relaxed outdoor place that's nicely decked out with plants and attracts a more mature and less extreme crowd than many Ao Ton Sai bars. Stages live music nightly, with plenty of jazz.

Karma Bar At the eastern end of the village, on the track to Laem Hin, beyond *Chao Ko Phi Phi* and the police box. Very chilled out sea-view place that plays mellow tunes and has cushion-seating and mats on the shore for good views of the regular fire-juggling shows.

Reggae Bar In the heart of the village, on the soi that runs north beside *Chao Koh Phi Phi Lodge*. One of the most excessive of the village bars, where the main pastime is getting totally smashed on Sansom whisky mixed with Red Bull. The bar also stages regular bouts of Thai boxing for its customers.

Tintin's Bar On the soi that runs north of Barakuda dive shop. Similar in its vibe to *Reggae Bar*, not least because the house drink is half-buckets of Sansom whisky mixed with Red Bull and Sprite. Draws a huge crowd of backpackers and its dance floor heaves to techno beats after midnight.

Laem Hin

East along the coast from the pier, about ten minutes' walk down the main track, is the promontory known as **Laem Hin**, beyond which lies a small stretch of beach that's quieter than Ao Ton Sai and better for swimming. Bungalows cover the Laem Hin promontory and beachfront, and they're popular places to stay, being in easy reach of the restaurants and nightlife at Ao Ton Sai but feeling a little less claustrophobic and hectic.

Bay View Resort At the far eastern end of Laem Hin beach and stretching east along the hillside all the way along to *Ma Prao* on Hat Yao ⓣ075 621223, ⓦwww.phiphibayview.com. Nicely furnished air-con bungalows occupying a superb position high on the cliffside, their massive windows affording unbeatable views. Good value considering the competition. ❽–❾

Gypsy Inland, down the track between the mosque and *PP Villa* ⓣ01 229 1674. Twenty-five clean, pleasant, good-value concrete bungalows, all with attached bathroom; set round an unusually spacious lawn about 150m north of the water. Recommended. ❹

PP Don Chukit Resort Just east of the promontory ⓣ075 618126, ⓦwww.chukit.ajndesign.com. Choose between mid-range air-con bungalows, reasonably well spaced around a garden, and similar but pricier (and probably noisier) versions beside the seafront walkway, with uninterrupted sea views. Also has some fan rooms in single-storey blocks. ❺–❼

PP Villa East of the promontory ⓣ075 621524, ⓦwww.krabidir.com/ppvillaresort/index.htm. Huge, deluxe, thatched air-con cottages at the front of a prettily landscaped garden, cheaper options in the middle of the compound, and a few cheaper fan rooms right at the back. ❺–❾

Ao Loh Dalum

Just 300m north across the narrow isthmus from Ao Ton Sai, **AO LOH DALUM** looks astonishingly pretty at high tide, with its glorious curve of powder-white sand beautifully set off by pale blue water. Not surprisingly, the setting draws huge crowds of sunbathers, and guests at the shorefront hotels pay premium rates for a room with a view, particularly at Ao Ton Sai's *PP Island Cabana Hotel* (see p.719), which dominates the most attractive, western end. There are watersports facilities at *PP Pavilion* and *PP Princess*, and Ao Ton Sai's restaurants and bars, including *Jungle Bar* at *PP Island Cabana*, are all within just a few minutes' walk (see opposite). Aside from the sheer number of people packed onto the beach, Ao Loh Dalum's main drawback is that the tide goes out for miles, leaving you with a long trek before you can get a decent dip.

The **viewpoint** that overlooks the far eastern edge of the beach affords a magnificent panorama of both Ao Loh Dalum and Ao Ton Sai: photographers slog up the steep half-hour climb for sunset shots of the two bays, but early morning is an equally good time, and the café at the summit serves simple breakfasts as well as cold drinks. To get there, follow the track inland (south) from beside *Paklong Seaside* and then branch off to the left (eastwards) near the rainwater reservoir. From the viewpoint you can descend the rocky and at times almost sheer path to **Ao Lanti**, a tiny bay on the east coast with choppy surf and a couple of resident *chao ley*. Theoretically, it should also be possible to reach the northeastern bay of Ao Loh Bakao (see p.724) by a path from near the viewpoint, but the two-kilometre route is unsignposted and overgrown.

Charlie Resort In the middle of the beach ⓣ & ⓕ075 620615. Upper-mid-range place with comfortable air-con rooms in a two-storey block at the back of the compound, and pricier, fairly densely packed bungalows nearer the sea. Efficiently managed operation, with a lively bar and restaurant on the beach. ❹–❻

Paklong Seaside At the easternmost end of the beach ⓣ01 978 2474, ⓦwww.krabidir.com/hparklongsea/index.htm. Comfortable guest house right on the shore, with just fourteen decent fan-cooled rooms in three small wooden buildings; price depends on the size of the room. ❻

PP Pavilion At the eastern end of the beach ⓣ075 620677, ⓦwww.krabidir.com/pppavilionresort/index.htm. Fifty attractive upmarket wooden chalets, nicely spaced over the beachfront grounds. Fan bungalows are towards the back and air-con versions stand nearer the sea. ❻–❽

PP Princess Towards the western end of the beach ⓣ075 622079, ⓦwww.ppprincess.com. Accommodation here is fairly plush but quite congested, with the seafront compound taken up with dozens of detached wooden chalets, plus some terraced ones. They're nicely designed though, with big windows, verandas, air-con, TV and mini-bar. Price depends on proximity to shorefront. ❽–❾

Viewpoint Bungalows Up the cliffside at the far eastern end of the beach ⓣ075 622351, ⓦwww.phiphiviewpoint.com. Strung out across the hillside, these attractive but pricey bungalows give great views out over the bay. The most expensive have air-con and TV. ❼–❽

Hat Yao

With its deluxe sand and large reefs packed with polychromatic marine life just 20m offshore, **HAT YAO** (Long Beach) is considered the best of Phi Phi's main beaches, but that can be hard to appreciate, with hundreds of sunbathers pitching up on the gorgeous sand every day and throngs of day-trippers making things even worse at lunchtime. Unperturbed by all the attention, shoals of golden butterfly fish, turquoise and purple parrot fish and hooped angel fish continue to scour what remains of Hat Yao's coral for food, escorted by brigades of small cleaner fish who live off the parasites trapped in the scales of larger species. The Long Beach Dive Shop at *Long Beach* runs day-trips to more extensive local reefs (B1700), rents out diving and snorkelling equipment, and teaches PADI courses (B9700 for the four-day Openwater including free accommodation for the duration at *Long Beach*).

Longtail **boats** do the ten-minute shuttle between Hat Yao and Ao Ton Sai from about 8am to 8pm (B40, or B50 after dark), but it's also possible to **walk** between the two in half an hour. At low tide you can get to Hat Yao along the shore, though this involves quite a bit of clambering over smooth wet rocks – not ideal when wearing a heavy rucksack, nor after a night spent trawling the bars of Ton Sai village (take a torch). The alternative route takes you over the hillside via the steps up from *Bay View Resort* on Laem Hin – with a side track running down to *Ma Prao*'s little bay – and then finally dropping down to Hat

Yao. A different path connects Hat Yao to the tiny bay of **Ao Loh Moodii**, ten minutes' walk to the north: the trail starts behind the last of the bungalows at *Long Beach* and can also be accessed from *Phi Phi Hill*.

Accommodation

Some of the most attractive Hat Yao **accommodation** is tucked away in a little cove west of Hat Yao itself, with easy access via a rocky path. The small, secluded and friendly Belgian-run *Ma Prao* (ⓣ075 622486, ⓦwww.maprao.com; ❸–❻) has 35 characterful wood and bamboo bungalows ranged across the hillside overlooking the sea, and a pleasant eating area out front. The cheapest huts share bathrooms, but some have a terrace; among the more expensive en-suite options, you can choose to have a boat-shaped deck, a rooftop sun-terrace or a bamboo villa set high among the trees; rates are discounted for stays of two or more nights. There's a small dive operation here, you can rent kayaks, and the kitchen produces a long menu that includes eighty different cocktails, and home-made yoghurt. Not surprisingly, it's a popular place, so call the day before to secure a room, or check in somewhere else and put yourself on the waiting list.

Of the two bungalow operations on Hat Yao itself, most budget travellers head first for *Long Beach Bungalows* (ⓣ075 61217; ❸–❹), which covers the eastern half of the beach and part of the hill behind. It's a ramshackle place that's been poorly thought out and under-maintained; some of the cheapest huts here are on the verge of collapse, and the proximity of rubbish dumps makes them no more enticing. On the plus side, they're the cheapest options on Hat Yao, you've a good chance of getting a hut right on the beach, and if you pay a bit extra you get your own bathroom. Neighbouring *Paradise Pearl* (ⓣ075 622100, ⓦwww.ppparadise.com; ❹–❽) is another story entirely, with efficient management, a decent, inviting restaurant, Internet access, international phone service, a tour counter and book exchange. The eighty or so bungalows here are fairly well spaced along the western half of the beach and come in various styles: the older, en-suite fan bungalows are at the back, while those nearer the sea are huge, well furnished, and come with fan or air-con. Be warned that front-row residents get the worst of the noise from incoming longtails.

Occupying a glorious spot high up on the hilltop overlooking the far eastern end of Hat Yao, *Phi Phi Hill Resort* (ⓣ01 734 1570, ⓦwww.phiphihill.com; ❹–❼) offers commanding views and simply furnished fan and air-con accommodation in its fifty mint-green wooden chalets set amongst the palms. With fine sunrise views and plenty of breeze, the only off-putting factor here are the one hundred steps that connect the resort with the beach below (though there is a pulley system for luggage).

Ao Loh Bakao and Laem Tong

Far removed from the hustle of Ao Ton Sai and its environs, a few exclusive resorts have effectively taken over the beautiful, secluded northern beaches of Phi Phi Don. This is primarily package-holiday territory and it's difficult and expensive to get to the other parts of the island, so you should choose your hotel with care. There are no regular boats here from Ao Ton Sai, but resorts offer transfers by speedboat from Phuket or by longtail from Ao Ton Sai. Chartering your own longtail from Ao Ton Sai will cost about B300; the trip takes around an hour to Ao Loh Bakao and a further half-hour north to Laem Tong. To charter a return boat at night, you're looking at B1000 for a round trip including waiting time.

Just over halfway up the coast, the eighty plush, air-conditioned chalets at *Phi Phi Island Village Beach Resort and Spa* (ⓣ076 215014, ⓦwww.ppisland.com; ❾;

rates start at B5500 and rise if you want a sea view) have the gorgeous eight-hundred-metre-long beach of **AO LOH BAKAO** all to themselves. It's a popular honeymoon spot, and a lovely location for anyone looking for a quiet, comfortable break. The wooden bungalows are designed in traditional Thai style and furnished with character and elegance. There's a pool and spa centre in the prettily landscaped tropical gardens, as well as a dive centre, tennis courts and kayak rental. At the northernmost tip, **LAEM TONG** has several upmarket resorts on its shores and views across to nearby Bamboo Island and Mosquito Island. The *Holiday Inn* (Ⓣ076 214654, Ⓦwww.phiphi-palmbeach.com; ⑨; room rates start at B6800) offers luxurious air-conditioned bungalows plus a swimming pool, outdoor Jacuzzi, dive centre and tennis courts, as well as batik and cookery courses and trips to local islands. Up at *Phi Phi Natural Resort* (Ⓣ075 613010, Ⓦwww.phiphinatural.com; ⑨), the upmarket rooms and chalets are scattered around a tropical shorefront garden, and there's a swimming pool and a terrace restaurant offering fine sea views; snorkelling, fishing and dive trips are all available here.

Ko Phi Phi Leh

More rugged than its twin, Ko Phi Phi Don, and a quarter the size, **KO PHI PHI LEH** is home only to the **sea swift**, whose valuable nests are gathered by intrepid *chao ley* for export to specialist Chinese restaurants all over the world. Tourists descend on the island not only to see the nest-collecting caves but also to snorkel off its sheltered bays and to admire the very spot where *The Beach* was filmed; the anchoring of tourist and fishing boats has damaged much of the coral in the most beautiful reefs. Most snorkelling trips out of Phi Phi Don include Phi Phi Leh, which is only twenty minutes south of Ao Ton Sai, but you can also get there by hiring a longtail from Ao Ton Sai or Hat Yao (B500–700/six-person boat). If you do charter your own boat, go either very early or very late in the day, to beat the tour-group rush. Alternatively, why not try paddling yourself in and out of the quiet bays in a kayak – see box on p.720 for details.

Bird's-nesting

Prized for its aphrodisiac and energizing qualities, **bird's-nest soup** is such a delicacy in Taiwan, Singapore and Hong Kong that ludicrous sums of money change hands for a dish whose basic ingredients are tiny twigs glued together with bird's spit. Collecting these nests is a lucrative but life-endangering business: sea swifts (known as edible nest swiftlets) build their nests in rock crevices hundreds of metres above sea level, often on sheer cliff-faces or in cavernous hollowed-out karst. **Nest-building** begins in January and the harvesting season usually lasts from February to May, during which time the female swiftlet builds three nests on the same spot, none of them more than 12cm across, by secreting an unbroken thread of saliva, which she winds round as if making a coil pot. **Gatherers** will only steal the first two nests made by each bird, prising them off the cave walls with special metal forks. Gathering the nests demands faultless agility and balance, skills that seem to come naturally to the *chao ley* (see p.652), whose six-man teams bring about four hundred nests down the perilous bamboo scaffolds each day, weighing about 4kg in total. At a market rate of B20,000–50,000 per kilo, so much money is at stake that a government franchise must be granted before any collecting commences, and armed guards often protect the sites at night. The *chao ley* seek spiritual protection from the dangers of the job by making offerings to the spirits of the cliff or cave at the beginning of the season; in the Viking Cave, they place buffalo flesh, horns and tails at the foot of one of the stalagmites.

Most idyllic of all the bays in the area is **Ao Maya** on the southwest coast, where the water is still and very clear and the coral extremely varied – a perfect snorkelling spot and a feature of most day-trips. Unfortunately the discarded lunch boxes and water bottles of day-trippers threaten the health of the marine life in **Ao Phi Leh**, an almost completely enclosed east-coast lagoon of breathtakingly turquoise water. Not far from the cove, the **Viking Cave** gets its misleading name from the scratchy wall-paintings of Chinese junks inside, but more interesting than these 400-year-old graffiti is the **bird's-nesting** that goes on here: rickety bamboo scaffolding extends hundreds of metres up to the roof of the cave, where the harvesters spend the day scraping the tiny sea-swift nests off the rockface.

Ko Lanta Yai

Although **KO LANTA YAI** can't compete with Phi Phi's stupendous scenery, the thickly forested 25-kilometre-long island does offer plenty of fine sandy beaches and safe seas and is actually a much friendlier place to stay. The majority of its twenty thousand residents are mixed-blood Muslim descendants of Malaysian and *chao ley* peoples and most have traditionally supported themselves by fishing and cultivating the land, though the recent tourist boom has had a big effect on island job opportunities. Traditional *chao ley* rituals are celebrated on Ko Lanta twice a year, when ceremonial boats are set afloat on the full moon nights in June and November (see p.652 for more on the *chao ley*).

The local *chao ley* name for the island is *Pulao Satak*, "Island of Long Beaches", an apt description of the string of silken **beaches** along the western coast, each separated by rocky points and strung out at quite wide intervals. The northernmost one, Hat Khlong Dao, is developed almost to full capacity, but more peaceful spots are easier to find further south and they nearly all offer luxuriously soft sand and clear water. All the bungalow outfits advertise snorkelling trips to the reefs off Ko Lanta's myriad satellite islands, and diving is also a popular and rewarding activity; Ko Lanta's mangrove-fringed east coast is unsuitable for swimming but ideal for kayaking. The same goes for Lanta Yai's sister island of **Ko Lanta Noi**, north across a narrow channel from the port at Ban Sala Dan, which has Ko Lanta's administrative offices and several small villages but no tourist accommodation, and is generally only visited on kayaking tours or in transit if driving to Ko Lanta Yai from the mainland.

Ko Lanta Yai is extremely popular during **high season** (Nov–Feb), when it's well worth either booking your first night's accommodation in advance or taking up the suggestions of the bungalow touts who ride the boats from the mainland. **Accommodation pricing** on Ko Lanta is extremely flexible and alters according to the number of tourists on the island: it's not uncommon, for example, for bungalow rates to triple in the thirty-day period from mid-November to mid-December, while during the **rainy season** between May and October rates are vastly discounted and the seas become too rough for boats to get here from Krabi (some places close for this period). The price range shown in our Ko Lanta accommodation listings are for the beginning and end of high season (generally Nov & March–April). All bungalows increase their rates for the peak months of December and January; most places double their prices for this period, the exceptions being many of the cheapest (❶–❸) places, which can triple or even quadruple their prices, and the most expensive places (❽–❾), which usually add around twenty percent.

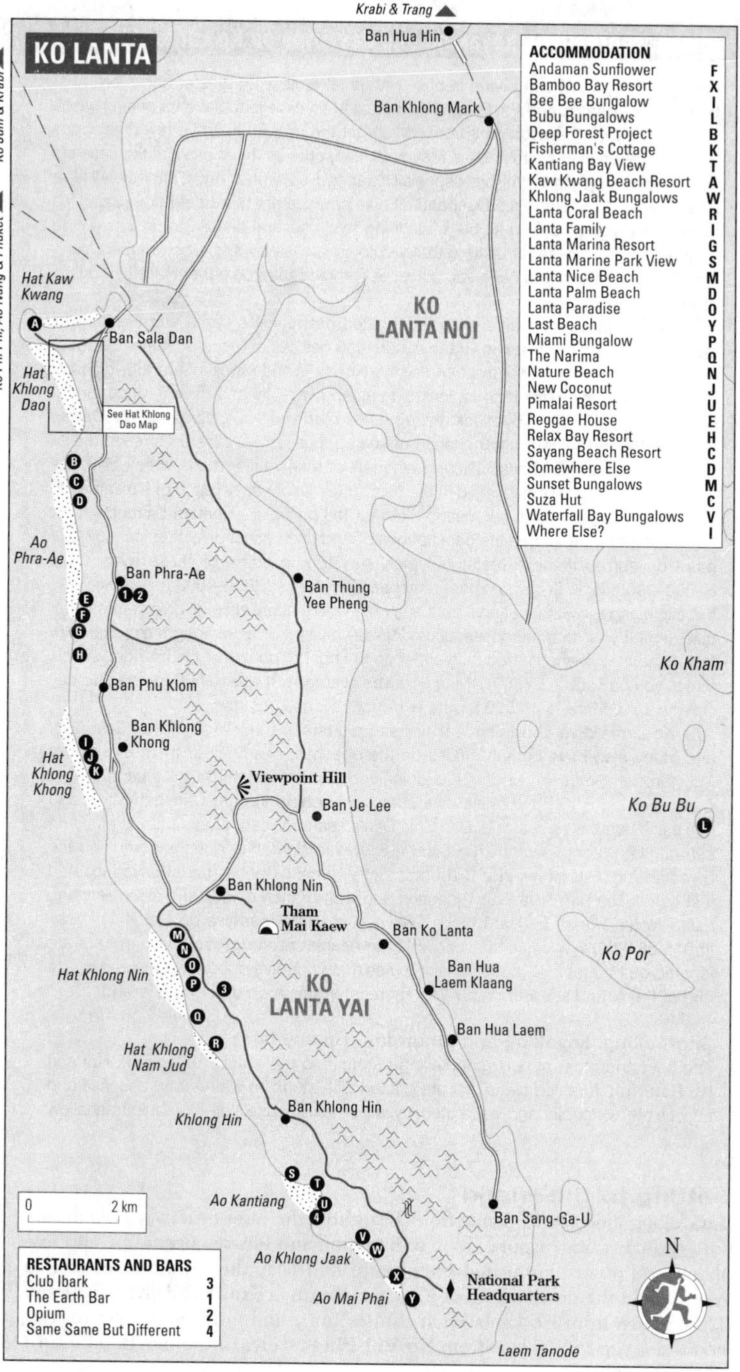
KO LANTA
Krabi & Trang
Ko Jum & Krabi
Ko Phi Phi, Ao Nang & Phuket
ACCOMMODATION
Andaman Sunflower F
Bamboo Bay Resort X
Bee Bee Bungalow I
Bubu Bungalows L
Deep Forest Project B
Fisherman's Cottage K
Kantiang Bay View T
Kaw Kwang Beach Resort A
Khlong Jaak Bungalows W
Lanta Coral Beach R
Lanta Family I
Lanta Marina Resort G
Lanta Marine Park View S
Lanta Nice Beach M
Lanta Palm Beach D
Lanta Paradise O
Last Beach Y
Miami Bungalow P
The Narima Q
Nature Beach N
New Coconut J
Pimalai Resort U
Reggae House E
Relax Bay Resort H
Sayang Beach Resort C
Somewhere Else D
Sunset Bungalows M
Suza Hut C
Waterfall Bay Bungalows V
Where Else? I
RESTAURANTS AND BARS
Club Ibark 3
The Earth Bar 1
Opium 2
Same Same But Different 4
Ban Hua Hin
Ban Khlong Mark
KO LANTA NOI
Hat Kaw Kwang
Ban Sala Dan
Hat Khlong Dao
See Hat Khlong Dao Map
Ao Phra-Ae
Ban Phra-Ae
Ban Thung Yee Pheng
Ban Phu Klom
Ban Khlong Khong
Hat Khlong Khong
Viewpoint Hill
Ban Je Lee
Ko Kham
Ko Bu Bu
Ban Khlong Nin
Tham Mai Kaew
Ban Ko Lanta
Hat Khlong Nin
KO LANTA YAI
Ban Hua Laem Klaang
Ban Hua Laem
Ko Por
Hat Khlong Nam Jud
Khlong Hin
Ban Khlong Hin
Ao Kantiang
Ban Sang-Ga-U
Ao Khlong Jaak
Ao Mai Phai
National Park Headquarters
Laem Tanode
0 2 km
N

Diving, snorkelling, kayaking and day-trips on Ko Lanta

Ko Lanta is a significant diving centre, with local reefs a lot quieter and more pristine than the ones round Phi Phi and Phuket, and an excellent place for seeing whale sharks. The diving season runs from November through April, and a few dive shops continue to run successful trips in May and June; outside these months the seas are usually too rough to travel on, especially during September and October. All dive boats depart from Ban Sala Dan, and all dive courses are taught either in Sala Dan or on Hat Khlong Dao, so if you're planning to do several day dives or take a dive course you will save a lot of time that would otherwise be spent commuting along the atrocious road if you base yourself at accommodation on either Hat Khlong Dao or Ao Phra-Ae.

Some of Lanta's best **dive sites** are located between Ko Lanta and Ko Phi Phi, including the soft coral at **Hin Bidah**, where you get lots of leopard sharks, barracuda and tuna. West and south of Lanta, the **Ko Ha** island group offers four different dives on each of its five islands, including steep drop-offs and caves. Much further south, about four hours' boat ride, there's a fifty-metre wall at spectacular **Hin Daeng** and **Hin Muang**, plus a good chance of seeing tuna, jacks, silvertip sharks, manta rays and even whale sharks. There is also talk of a new tailor-made wreck dive, **the King's Wreck,** being established in the near future within easy reach of Ko Lanta; an old steel fishing boat has been earmarked for the purpose – contact Lanta Diver for the latest information. See the descriptions of Andaman coast dive sites on p.671 for more on some of these reefs. A typical **day-trip** to some of these reefs costs B2500–3000, including equipment rental and two tanks (B800–1000 for snorkellers), but excluding the B200 national park entry fee where applicable; all dive centres offer discounts if you do three consecutive one-day dives. For an overnight expedition to local islands with accommodation either on the boat or on one of the islands, and six tanks, you pay about B7500. Diving **courses** average out at B10,500 for the four-day Openwater course, or B7500 for the two-day Advanced course.

All Ko Lanta **dive shops** have their headquarters in the village of Ban Sala Dan, and many also have branch offices on the beaches; nearly all of them close from May through October. Two of the best include the long-established Ko Lanta Diving Centre, which is run by prolific dive author and photographer Christian Mietz and has its HQ on the west arm of Ban Sala Dan's seafront road, plus a branch office on central Hat Khlong Dao (Ⓣ075 684065, Ⓦwww.kohlantadivingcenter.com); and the Swedish-run, PADI Five-star Instructor Development Centre, Lanta Diver, located just before the Ban Sala Dan T-junction and with branch offices at *Golden Bay* and *Lanta Noble House* on Hat Khlong Dao and at *Lanta Paradise* on Hat Khlong Nin (Ⓣ075 684208, Ⓦwww.lantadiver.com). The nearest **recompression chambers** are located on Phuket (see p.670); check to see that your dive operator is insured to use one of them, and see Basics p.73 for more information on diving in Thailand.

Snorkelling, kayaking and other day-trips by boat

The best and most popular snorkelling outing is to the islands of **Ko Rok Nai** and **Ko Rok Nok**, forested twins that are graced with stunning white-sand beaches and accessible waterfalls and separated by a narrow channel full of fabulous shallow

Getting to the island

If travelling direct to Ko Lanta from **Bangkok**, the easiest gateway is Krabi airport, though Trang airport, Trang train station and Phuket airport are also feasible access points. From mid-October to mid-May there are **ferries** to Ban Sala Dan on the northern tip of Ko Lanta Yai from **Krabi** (2 daily; 2hr 30min; B200; return from Ko Lanta Yai at 8am & 1pm), and from November to May ferries also run to Sala Dan from **Ko Phi Phi** (2 daily; 1hr 30min; B200; return reefs. The islands are 47km south of Ko Lanta and served by speedboats (1hr; B1300) that can be booked through most tour agents, or direct with Lanta Garden Hill Speed Boat (☎075 684042). The other very popular day-trip is to four islands off the Trang coast (see p.750 for island descriptions): the enclosed emerald lagoon on the island of **Ko Mook** (aka Ko Muk), nearby **Ko Hai** (Ko Ngai), **Ko Cheuak** (Ko Chuk) and **Ko Kradan**. Though the islands are beautiful, and the coral passable, these trips are large-scale outings in boats that can hold around a hundred passengers, so the sites get very crowded: tickets cost B850 per person, including snorkelling gear, lunch and national park entry fee. You may find it more rewarding to organize a private longtail-boat tour to the better reefs off the **Ko Ha** island group, described under "diving", above (about two hours' boat ride southwest of Lanta), with snorkelling or fishing as requested: enthusiastic angler Jack, of Ko Lanta Tour at *Lanta Villa* on Hat Khlong Dao (☎01 538 4099), charges B1500/2000 per boat for a half day's snorkelling/fishing trip carrying up to four people, or B3200 for the whole day.

The north coast of Ko Lanta Noi is rich in mangroves and caves, which makes it fun to explore by **kayak**. Kayaking outings generally feature about four hours' kayaking plus a visit to a cave, a trip through the mangroves and a swim. They can be arranged through tour operators in Ban Sala Dan, and on some beaches, for B900–1200 per person, including transport, lunch and kayak; Lanta Sea Kayak in Ban Sala Dan (☎075 684397, Ⓦwww.krabidir.com/lantaseakayak/index.htm) do more adventurous kayaking trips around the caves and islands of Ko Talabeng and Ko Bubu (B1200) and out at Ko Mook (B2000). Mr Yat's Lanta On Beach Travel and Tour, next to *Funky Fish* on Ao Phra-Ae (☎09 021 1924), offers half-day boat tours to see the **mangroves** and go crab-fishing around Ban Thung Ye Pleng on north-eastern Ko Lanta Yai (B450/person) and also runs an interesting-sounding "alternative four-island tour" to **Ko Talabeng**, **Ko Rapu**, **Ko Kham** and **Ko Bubu**, off southeastern Ko Lanta Noi – there's no coral here, but the swimming is good, there are impressive limestone cliffs, stalactites, caves and mangrove swamps to explore, and you're likely to see more bats and monkeys than other tourists.

Day-trips inland

Ko Lanta's biggest inland attraction is the **Tham Mai Kaew caves**, located in the heart of the island, and signposted from the west-coast road at Hat Khlong Nin. There are myriad chambers here, some of which you can only just crawl into, and they boast stalactites and interesting rock formations as well as a creepy cave pool and the inevitable bats. To properly explore the cave system you need to bring your own torch, and you need a guide: the Muslim family who live close to the caves act as caretakers and guides and give two-hour tours for B150 per person if asked. Though it's not much more than a trickle, the **waterfall** inland from Ao Khlong Jaak is another fairly popular spot, and can be reached from the bay by walking along the course of the stream for about two hours. Alternatively join one of the tours that combine visits to the caves and the waterfall in a half-day trip for about B500, or B900 with a ninety-minute **elephant-ride** thrown in.

from Ko Lanta Yai at 8am & 1pm), from Rassada Port on **Phuket** (daily; 4hr 30min; B600; return from Ko Lanta Yai at 1.30pm), and from Tha Hat Nopparat Thara near **Ao Nang** (daily; 2hr 30min; B280; return from Ko Lanta Yai at 1.30pm) via West Railay on **Laem Phra Nang** (2hr; B280). Bungalow touts always meet the boats at Ban Sala Dan and transport you to the beach of your choice. During the rainy season you'll need to arrange **minivan** transport from Krabi with one of the tour agencies, which costs the same and takes a bit longer (2 daily; 3hr). The minivans take the **overland route**, which is also available to anyone with their own car. (If you do come with your own wheels, be warned that Lanta's roads are far from perfect and in the south degenerate into extremely rough tracks.) Overland access is via Ban Hua Hin on the mainland, 75km east of Krabi, from where a small ferry crosses to Ban Khlong Mark on Ko Lanta Noi, after which there's a seven-kilometre drive across to Lanta Noi's southwest tip, then another ferry over the narrow channel to Ban Sala Dan on Ko Lanta Yai; both ferries run approximately every twenty minutes from about 7am to 9pm and cost B50 per car. This is also the route used year-round by minivans from **Trang** (4 daily; 3hr).

Island practicalities

Though a road runs the entire length of Ko Lanta Yai's west coast, becoming pretty rough just after Hat Khlong Nin and finally grinding to a bumpy halt at the far southern tip, **transport** between the beaches is quite difficult as there's no regular songthaew service on the island. Once you're established on your beach you have either to hire a motorbike from your accommodation (about B40/hour, B250/day; B500/day for a big trailbike), or cadge a lift with the bungalow operators when they go and meet the boats at Ban Sala Dan. Tour operators in Ban Sala Dan also rent jeeps (B1200/day) as well as bikes. There's an organized **motorbike taxi** service in Ban Sala Dan, which operates from a stand opposite the 7–11 and posts a list of rates to the beaches: B20–30 to Hat Khlong Dao or B40–50 to Ao Phra-Ae; if you're staying on Hat Khlong Dao it's an easy half-hour walk to the village.

Most bungalows will **change money**, though you'll get the best rates at the bank in Ban Sala Dan. Many bungalows offer international telephone services for guests, and there are **Internet** centres in Ban Sala Dan, and on Hat Khlong Dao and Ao Phra-Ae (B2/min). There's a Thai **cookery school** at *Time for Lime* bungalows on Hat Khlong Dao, described on p.733.

Ban Sala Dan

During high season, direct boats from Krabi and Phi Phi arrive at Lanta's main settlement, the Muslim fishing port and village of **BAN SALA DAN**, located on the northernmost tip of Ko Lanta Yai. It's essentially a T-junction village, with about three dozen shops and businesses, including several minimarkets that sell essentials like mosquito repellent and sunscreen, as well as new and second-hand books, newspapers, beachwear and postcards. There's a Siam City bank with currency **exchange** and a Visa cash advance service (daily 8.30am–4pm), several places offering **Internet** access, a **police** booth and a **health centre**, though for anything serious you'll need to go to Krabi or Phuket. Ban Sala Dan is the best place on the island to arrange a **diving** course or expedition and also has half a dozen tour operators offering **day-trips** (see box above for a guide to diving and day-tripping destinations), as well as bike and jeep rental and boat, bus, train and air tickets.

While you're in the village, it's well worth stopping for a breezy meal at one of the **restaurants** whose dining area juts out on a shaded jetty right over the water, giving enjoyable views of the fishing boats and Ko Lanta Noi. Both *Seaside* and the nearby *Sea View* have good, very inexpensive menus offering authentic Thai dishes from chicken and cashews to fish fried with chilli or garlic. Also here are the similar *Catfish*, which serves bakery items and sells cards and second-hand books, and *Bai Fern*, which does noodles.

Hat Khlong Dao

Lanta Yai's longest and most popular beach is **HAT KHLONG DAO**, the northernmost of the west-coast beaches, about half an hour's walk from Ban Sala Dan, or 2–3km by road. The sand here is soft and golden, the sunsets can be magnificent, and the whole is framed by a dramatic hilly backdrop. Not surprisingly, this is where you'll find the densest collection of bungalows on the island, but though most of the shorefront land has been built on, development is relatively discreet. The beach is long and broad enough never to feel overcrowded and as it's flat and safe for swimming it's very popular with families. The northern curve of Hat Khlong Dao juts out into a rocky promontory known as **Laem Kaw Kwang** (Deer Neck Cape), whose north-facing shore, **Hat Kaw Kwang**, is mainly characterized by mudflats and mangroves and is home to a *chao ley* settlement.

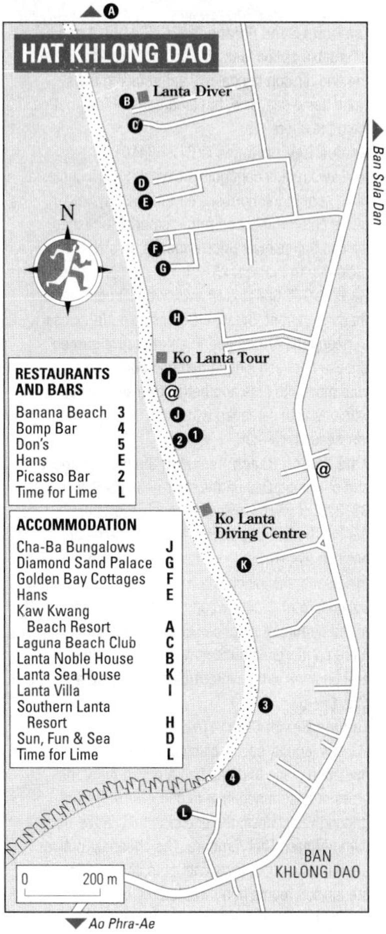

There are a couple of small minimarts on the beach and dive shops at several of the bungalows (see p.728 for dive info). Ko Lanta Tour at *Lanta Villa* does recommended fishing trips as well as other boat tours (see box on p.729); for anything else you'll need to go to Ban Sala Dan. The nicest way to walk to the village (about 30min from *Golden Bay*) is to head to the deer neck at the northern curve of the beach, and then take a right along the mostly shaded track which leads from *Kaw Kwang Beach Resort* to the road into Ban Sala Dan.

Accommodation

Accommodation on Khlong Dao is almost entirely mid-market, with little under the ❺ category and just a couple of options in the ❸ and ❹ brackets. Room standards are high, none of the bungalows in the places listed below is more than 100m from the sea, and an increasing number of places are now adding swimming pools.

Cha-Ba Bungalows and Art Gallery ⓣ075 684118, ⓦwww.krabidir.com/chababungalows/index.htm. Just fifteen cute, brightly painted fan bungalows with lots of character and pretty interiors, plus some air-con options. Set round a small garden alongside the owners' small art gallery. ❹–❺

Diamond Sand Palace ⓣ075 684135. A good, affordable option with sizeable and well-furnished fan and air-con bungalows set in facing rows. None has a sea view, but all are just a few metres from the shore. ❺

Golden Bay Cottages ⓣ075 684161, ⓦwww.krabidir.com/goldenbaycottage. Occupies a good spot in the northern part of the bay, and offers comfortable and rather smartly furnished air-con bungalows; price depends on size and proximity to the sea. ❻–❽

Hans ⓣ075 684152, ⓦwww.krabidir.com/hansrestaurant. Small, inexpensive outfit whose thirteen huts are ranged in an attractive garden. Choose between simple bamboo bungalows with mosquito nets and better-furnished wooden versions with screened windows. Closed during low season. ❸–❹

Kaw Kwang Beach Resort At the northernmost end of Khlong Dao on the deer neck itself ⓣ075 621373, ⓦwww.kawkwangbeachresort.com. Set in a beachfront garden in a nice secluded position away from the other bungalows on this beach, this place has a huge range of options, from decent wood and concrete huts at the bottom of its price list through bigger, more comfortable bungalows to some deluxe air-con ones with uninterrupted sea views and TVs. ❺–❼

Laguna Beach Club ⓣ075 684172, ⓦwww.laguna-beach-club.com. European-managed place that has half a dozen different types of accommodation to choose from, all of it thoughtfully designed and tastefully kitted out with northern Thai furniture. The cheapest options are bamboo bungalows with fans, the priciest are air-con rooms in a three-storey block, where there's even a two-roomed penthouse suite. Also has a swimming pool and dive centre. Closed June–Sept. ❹–❽

Lanta Noble House ⓣ075 684096, ⓔlantanoblehouse@hotmail.com. Swiss-run place where the inviting fan and air-con bungalows have big glass windows and bath tubs. Has the deepest swimming pool on the island, and a dive centre. ❺–❼

Lanta Sea House ⓣ075 684073, ⓔlantaseahouse@hotmail.com. Selection of comfortable wooden chalet-style bungalows set round a swimming pool and seafront garden; all have air-con, but a premium is charged for those with a sea view. ❼–❾

Lanta Villa ⓣ075 684129, ⓦwww.lantavillaresort.com. A big collection of comfortably furnished, decent-sized wooden bungalows, set in a garden running back from the shore, many with air-con and TV, and some with sea view. Also has a swimming pool, Internet access and a good restaurant. ❺–❽

Southern Lanta Resort ⓣ075 684174, ⓦwww.southernlanta.com. One of the biggest hotels on the beach, offering dozens of very spacious air-con bungalows set at decent intervals around a garden of shrubs, clipped hedges and shady trees. There's a good-sized swimming pool too. Good value considering the competition, and popular with families and package tourists. ❼–❽

Sun Fun & Sea ⓣ075 684025, ⓦwww.thailandbungalow.ch. Fifteen prettily furnished bungalows scattered around a garden, all with hot water and some with air-con. ❻–❼

Time for Lime ⓣ075 684590, ⓦwww.timeforlime.net. Just nine charmingly designed bungalows attached to a cooking school at the rocky, far southern end of the beach. The decor is chic – whitewashed interiors given character by interesting fabrics and furnishings – and the price is very good, though there are no views, and the compound is quite close to the road. Closed mid-June–early Nov. ❹

Eating and drinking

All the bungalows have **restaurants** serving travellers' fare and standard Thai dishes, and at night they're lit up with fairy lights and low lanterns, which lends a nice mellow atmosphere to the evenings and makes a welcome change from the neon frenzy at mainland resorts. Most restaurants also offer fresh seafood at night, where you choose your specimen and the cooking method and are charged by its weight: the seafood barbecues at *Lanta Villa* are popular and enjoyable. *Hans*, towards the northern end of the beach, is recommended for its German-style fillet steaks, as well as its creamy coconut curries and barbecued meats. *Banana Beach* also serves very good curries, as well as cocktails and ice creams, and the occasional seafood barbecue. Further south, *Don's Restaurant and Bar* does a good line in steaks and pizzas, as well as Thai soups, and plays an eclectic mix of tunes, from funk to house.

There are several clusters of small **bars** along Hat Khlong Dao. The most northerly group is in the centre of the beach, set back from the shore behind *Cha-Ba Bungalows*, whose artist proprietors also run the *Picasso Bar*. To the south, near *Lanta Garden Home*, you'll find the pleasingly chilled-out *Bomp Bar*, with cushions, deckchairs and low tables spread out on the sand, a campfire, and decent music. Several hundred metres further south, past *Don's* and some other little bar-restaurants, you reach the Norwegian-run *Time for Lime*, which has a beachfront bar but is mainly a **cookery school** (Ⓣ075 684590, Ⓦwww.timeforlime.net); workshops take place in the strikingly modern open-plan kitchen behind the bar (Tues–Sat afternoons and evenings; from B1200 including meal).

Ao Phra-Ae (Long Beach)

A couple of kilometres south of Khlong Dao, **AO PHRA-AE** (also known as **Long Beach**) boasts a beautiful long strip of soft white sand, with calm, crystal-clear water that's good for swimming, some shady casuarinas, and an enjoyably youthful ambience. Traveller-oriented bamboo huts are fairly plentiful (though there's not much in the ultra-budget bracket) and there are some decent little beachfront restaurants as well as lots of beach-shack bars with mats on the sand, especially in the north-central part of the beach, between *Sayang Beach Resort* and *Lanta Palm Beach*. The main stretch of the beach is divided by a shallow, easily wadeable lagoon, with bungalows to north and south of it. *Lanta Marina Resort* marks the far southern end of the beach, and this is also where you'll find the *Lanta Spa* complex, which gives all sorts of massage and spa treatments. All bungalows on Ao Phra-Ae rent out **motorbikes** for around B250 a day and organize boat trips for snorkelling and fishing. Mr Yat at Lanta On Beach Travel and Tour, next to *Funky Fish*, organizes boating and kayaking expeditions: see box on p.729 for details.

Accommodation

Andaman Sunflower At the rocky, far southern end of the beach Ⓣ075 684023. Twenty simple, well-priced bamboo huts of varying sizes but all with mosquito nets and private bathrooms. Closed June–Oct. ❷–❹

Deep Forest Project At the northernmost end of the beach Ⓣ075 684247. Eleven plain, old-style huts, sold at old-style prices, and all equipped with mosquito net, fan and en-suite bathroom. Closed during low season. ❷–❸

Lanta Marina Resort Around the southern headland from the main stretch of Ao Phra-Ae, close to a rocky point Ⓣ075 684168.This place has about thirty large, shaggily thatched wood and split-bamboo bungalows facing the sea, plus a couple of two-storeyed A-frames with beds on the upstairs platform and coral-floored bathrooms down below. ❸–❺

Lanta Palm Beach Ⓣ01 787 9483, Ⓕ075 684406. A busy and very popular spot that has a range of different bungalows, plus Internet access, and is within stumbling distance of the main travellers' bars. Cheapest are the bamboo huts with bathrooms, good beds and mosquito nets – they're set in the remains of a coconut grove and enjoy a full view of the sea. The pricier concrete bungalows sit back from the shore, within a garden of neat clipped hedges, and come with fan or air-con. Or you can pitch a tent here for B50. ❹–❻

Reggae House Half a dozen primitive, almost circular, brick huts next door to the loud and popular *Reggae House* bar and furnished with very skinny mattresses, mosquito nets and bathrooms. One of the cheapest spots on the island. ❶–❷

Relax Bay Resort Ⓣ075 684194, Ⓦwww.relaxbay.com. Set in its own tiny bay south around the next rocky point (and quite a hike) from *Lanta Marina*, the style of this French-managed place is affordable rustic chic. The nicest accommodation is in tastefully simple bamboo and wood bungalows, all of which have large sea-view decks and open-air bathrooms. Also has a few less-interesting concrete air-con bungalows. ❺–❼

Sayang Beach Resort Ⓣ075 684156, Ⓔsayangbeach@hotmail.com. Friendly, family-run operation occupying expansive grounds with huts nicely spaced among the palm trees. All bungalows are built with natural materials and are stylishly decorated with batik furnishings and a tasteful wood and bamboo finish. Price depends on location

△ Ao Phra-Ae

and size, and whether or not you want air-con. Also has some family bungalows. ❺–❽

Somewhere Else ☎01 536 0858. Located in the heart of the liveliest part of Ao Phra-Ae, with beach bars left, right and seaward, this little outfit has just sixteen spacious, nicely designed bungalows made of tightly woven bamboo and with pretty bathrooms. Price depends on the size. Run by the same family as *Where Else?* bungalows on Hat Khlong Khong. ❸–❹

Suza Hut ☎01 370 9710, ⓔsuzahutlanta@hotmail.com. Some of the cheapest accommodation on the beach, in a handful of rudimentary bamboo huts furnished with nothing more than a mattress and a mosquito net; bathrooms are shared. Closed during low season. ❷

Eating and drinking

Ao Phra-Ae has the liveliest after-dark scene on the island, with lots of beach **bars** seating their customers on cushions spread out along the shore and entertaining them with chill-out music or dance hits. There are more bars and restaurants inland, along the main west-coast road.

The Earth Bar On the road, inland from *Reggae House*. Popular bar that plays dance music.

Funky Fish On the beach, next to *Somewhere Else*. One of the most famous bars on the beach: renowned for pizzas, cocktails and a quality sound system. You can get massages here too.

Opium On the road, inland from *Reggae House*. Another of the longer-established and better-known chill-out dance-bars.

The Ozone Bar On the beach, near *Somewhere Else*. Capacious, laid-back beach bar.

Reggae House On the beach, next to *Reggae House* bungalows. Typically laid-back bar where the DJ plays reggae and dub tracks and hosts regular parties, at least once a week, with live music. The bar sometimes stages a reggae festival at the beginning of December, featuring *chao ley* musicians.

Sayang Beach Resort On the beach, at *Sayang Beach Resort*. The kitchen here has a tandoori oven and serves authentic Indian dishes as well as Thai food, plus seafood. Moderate.

Second Home On the beach, next to *Suza Hut*. A good choice for fresh fish – barbecued or fried; the fried red snapper with three-style Thai sauce is especially tasty. Moderate.

Hat Khlong Khong

The lovely long beach at **HAT KHLONG KHONG**, 2km south of Ao Phra-Ae's *Relax Bay Resort*, is peppered with rocks and only really swimmable at high tide, though the snorkelling is good. The shore is crammed with bungalows, many of them reasonably priced, and there are quite a number of bars too, including the laid-back *Feeling Bar* at *Where Else?* bungalows, which is decorated with driftwood sculptures.

Accommodation

Bee Bee Bungalow ☎01 537 9932, ⓔbeebeepiya02@hotmail.com. A great spot that stands out from other places on the beach because of its eleven highly individual huts, each of which is a charmingly idiosyncratic experiment in bamboo architecture. All the bungalows are comfortably furnished and have fans, mosquito nets and open-air bathrooms; some have an upstairs rooms as well. Closed June–Oct. ❸–❹

Fisherman's Cottage At the southern end of the beach ☎01 476 1529, ⓦ www.krabidir.com/fishermanscottage/index.htm. This quiet, low-key place has just nine bungalows, each with big glass windows, characterful furnishings, mosquito nets and decent bathrooms. Closed July–Oct. ❹–❼

Lanta Family ☎075 648310, ⓔdumsupaporn@yahoo.com.sg. Seventeen well-kept en-suite bungalows ranged under the palm trees. The cheapest options are bamboo huts at the back of the compound; larger, pricier versions sit nearer the sea, or you can opt for one of the brick bungalows beside the beach. ❷–❻

New Coconut ☎01 537 7590, ⓔlantamaster@hotmail.com. Twenty comfortable en-suite bungalows, and tents for rent at B100 a double. Also has a pool table and the beachfront *Monkey Bar*. ❷–❸

Where Else? ☎01 536 4870, ⓔwhereelse51@hotmail.com. As you might expect from the name, this charming collection of 22 bungalows has a relaxed, laid-back atmosphere and lots of personality. The bamboo and coconut-wood bungalows all have attractive open-air, coral-floored bathrooms, filled with plants, and there are shell mobiles and driftwood sculptures all over the place. The pricier bungalows are larger and nearer the sea, and some even have sunroofs. ❸–❹

Hat Khlong Nin and Hat Khlong Nam Jud

About four kilometres south of Hat Khlong Khong the road forks, with the left-hand, east-bound arm running across to Ko Lanta Yai's east coast, via **Tham Mai Kaew** caves and **Viewpoint Hill**, where several little cafés capitalize on the spectacular view over the offshore islands. The right-hand fork is the route to the southern beaches and continues southwards along the west coast, quickly degenerating into an unnervingly potholed route that's only partly surfaced and becomes almost impassable after heavy storms.

Just beyond the junction, the west-coast road passes long, sandy **HAT KHLONG NIN**, which is very good for swimming and has several bungalow operations – rather tightly packed at the centre of the beach – and a burgeoning nightlife that revolves around ten little beach bars and a full-on club. You can walk the 3km to the Tham Mai Kaew caves from Khlong Nin in about an hour. *Miami Bungalow* rents **motorbikes** for B250 per day and has an international phone service, and there's a minimarket and **email** centre and several small restaurants located inland, around the east-west junction. The most famous of Khlong Nin's after-dark haunts is **Club Ibark** (Ⓣ01 582 2625 or 09 668 4104, Ⓦwww.ibark-krabi.com), located inland and south a bit from *Sri Lanta* resort, beyond the southern end of the coastal strip; it's a sophisticated Bangkok-by-the-sea-style dance club with an impressive roster of international DJs, regular live music and special club nights, a chill-out lounge, food, and even some rather stylish accommodation (❺) for those trucked in from other beaches. As it's set on a hillside you get great views from the open-air dance floor – and plenty of breeze.

All the **bungalows** on Hat Khlong Nin are open all year. At the far northern end of the beach, *Lanta Nice Beach Resort* (Ⓣ075 697276, Ⓦwww.nice-beach.com; ❹–❼) is located on a broad swathe of sand and offers rows of spacious concrete bungalows, many with sea views and some with air-con, plus a neat arrangement of cheaper bamboo bungalows in a garden across the road from the beach. Next up is *Sunset Bungalows* (Ⓣ01 535 6288; ❸–❺), which has ten whitewashed terraced bungalows set in an L-shape around a small yard on the seafront; the good rooms are all of a decent size, with the most expensive providing air-con and a direct sea view. To the south, *Nature Beach Bungalow* (Ⓣ01 397 0785, Ⓦwww.krabidir.com/lantanaturebeach/index.htm; ❹–❻) isn't very aesthetic but offers a high standard of accommodation in cheapish fan rooms across the road from the beach, and larger concrete villas with air-con on the beachfront. Next door, at the long-running *Lanta Paradise* (Ⓣ09 473 3279, Ⓦwww.lantaparadise.com; ❹–❼), you can choose between old wooden huts and big, concrete air-con bungalows nearer the sea, which are packed rather uncomfortably close together but feel spacious inside; there's a pool here too. The accommodation at neighbouring *Miami Bungalow* (Ⓣ075 697081, Ⓦwww.lantamiami.com; ❺–❼) ranges from simple wooden huts with fans to larger concrete versions, some with air-con and sea view.

Just over 1km south of Hat Khlong Nin, the road passes the two tiny little bays known as **HAT KHLONG NAM JUD**. The northerly one is the domain of *The Narima* (Ⓣ075 607700, Ⓦwww.narima-lanta.com; ❽), an elegantly designed resort of posh but unadorned thatch-roofed bamboo bungalows set in a palm-filled garden. The bungalows all have polished wood floors, verandas with sea view, and fans, as well as air-con; there's also a pool and a spa. Around the headland to the south, the next tiny cove is rocky in parts but enjoys a swimmable beach and one set of bungalows, *Lanta Coral Beach* (Ⓣ075 618073; ❸–❻; closed May–Oct). The twenty good-sized bamboo and concrete huts here are scattered among the palms (some of which are hung with hammocks) and come with fan or air-con; you can rent canoes here too.

Ao Kantiang, Ao Khlong Jaak and Ao Mai Phai

The secluded, almost remote cove of **AO KANTIANG**, some 7km beyond Hat Khlong Nam Jud, is an impressively curved sweep of long, sandy bay backed by jungle-clad hillsides and fronted by just a few bungalows and one large hotel. The beach is good for swimming, there's some coral at the northern end, and snorkelling and fishing trips are easily arranged. The thirty or so bungalows at *Lanta Marine Park View* (Ⓣ01 397 0793, Ⓦwww.krabidir.com/lantampv; ❷–❽) are ranged up the slope at the northern end of the beach, so that some, which are raised even higher on stilts, enjoy fabulous views over the bay. Other accommodation comes in various styles and prices, from bamboo huts with shared baths to plush air-con bungalows just above the water, but it's all pretty good; there's also a small cliffside bar affording great views, plus Internet access and a tour agency. Down at sea level, in the middle of the bay, *Kantiang Bay View Resort* (Ⓣ01 787 6192; ❷–❻) also offers lots of different accommodation options, including plenty of cheap bamboo huts, concrete huts (fan and air-con) and rooms in a small block. The southern end of Ao Kantiang is the province of Ko Lanta's poshest hotel, the *Pimalai Resort and Spa* (Ⓣ075 607999, Ⓦwww.pimalai.com; ❾; rates from B10,500), which spreads over such an extensive area that guests are shuttled around in golf buggies. All rooms are luxuriously and elegantly designed in contemporary style, and there's a delightful spa, a swimming pool and dive centre. Only the more expensive accommodation gets a sea view (the walled bayfront suites are particularly stunning but cost B20,500). Guests are transferred direct to the resort by boat, so avoiding the atrocious road. Wherever you're staying on Ao Kantiang, it's well worth heading down to *Same Same But Different*, a lovely tranquil haven of a **restaurant** to the south of *Pimalai*, where the tables are set beneath a tangled growth of shrubs and vines, surrounded by shell-mobiles and driftwood sculptures; it's run by the man behind the renowned *Ruen Mai* restaurant in Krabi, and the mid-priced menu of mainly Thai and seafood dishes is of a similarly high standard.

The road deteriorates further as you head south from Ao Kantiang, eventually descending into a track that leads to the isolated little **AO KHLONG JAAK**, site of the mid-range *Waterfall Bay Bungalows* (Ⓣ01 836 4877, Ⓦwww.waterfallbaybeach.com; ❹–❽). The 23 huts here are simple but stylish and set peacefully within a grassy, tree-filled garden; those nearer the sea are more expensive, as are those with air-con. The resort has Internet and international phone services, and organizes boat trips and other excursions. Sharing the same bay, *Khlong Jaak Bungalows* (Ⓣ09 866 2768; ❷–❹) has a range of comfortable huts from simple en-suite rooms in a line at the back through to bigger front-row bungalows. There's a restaurant and bar here, which hosts occasional parties, and staff rent out motorbikes and organize snorkelling trips.

An abysmal track continues for 3km south of *Waterfall Bay*, affording good sea views, passing a quiet sandy beach and then coming to a halt at the lighthouse and national park headquarters. Access is pretty tricky for anyone not used to off-road biking, and few drivers will offer to drive you down here, however much you pay them, but if you like the quiet, solitary life it might be worth making the trip to the pretty, white-sand cove of **AO MAI PHAI**, which is extremely peaceful and has good coral close to the shore. At the northern end of the bay, the Danish-Thai run *Bamboo Bay Resort* (Ⓣ075 618240, Ⓦwww.bamboobay.net; ❺–❼) offers 21 bungalows set among the trees up the hillside, all with great sea views and a few with air-con; it also has an ideally sited restaurant and massage platform, and can arrange boat and jungle trips. The wooden huts at nearby *Last Beach* (❷) are simpler and best reached by cadging a lift from Ban Sala Dan with the member of staff who meets the ferries.

Ko Bubu and Ko Jum

Now that Ko Lanta is firmly registered on the beaten track, some travellers have pushed on to a couple of other, smaller, nearby islands. The minuscule **Ko Bubu**, only 7km off Lanta Yai's east coast, is the preserve of just one bungalow outfit, but in contrast to many one-resort islands, this is not an exclusive upmarket operation. North of Ko Lanta, **Ko Jum** has a greater choice of accommodation but still retains a pleasantly low-key ambience.

Ko Bubu

With a radius of not much more than 500m, wooded **KO BUBU** can be circled in less than an hour and has room for just thirty simple, en-suite bungalows and a restaurant at *Bubu Bungalows* (☎075 612536; ❸–❺; closed May–Oct), plus a few tents for rent at B150 a double. The island is twenty minutes' chartered longtail ride (B100) from the small town of **Ban Ko Lanta** on Ko Lanta Yai's east coast and can also be reached direct **from Krabi** by following the rainy-season route for Ko Lanta Yai and taking a longtail from Bo Muang for B150. Most of Krabi's tour agents (see p.701) will book you in for the Ko Bubu bungalow resort and can organize through transport from Krabi.

Ko Jum (Ko Pu)

Situated halfway between Krabi and Ko Lanta Yai, **KO JUM** (also known as **Ko Pu**) is the sort of laid-back and simple spot that people come to for a couple of days, then can't bring themselves to leave. Its mangrove-fringed east coast holds two of the island's three fishing villages – **Ban Ko Pu** sits on the northeast tip and **Ban Ko Jum**, complete with its own beachfront school, is on the southeast tip – while across on the sandy west coast there are a number of small bungalow operations to the south of the third village, **Ban Ting Lai**, plus a few to its north. Much of the north is made inaccessible by the breastbone of forested hills, whose highest peak (395m) is Khao Ko Pu, and the ten-kilometre track that connects the north and south of the island runs around its north-eastern flank. There's little to do on the island except hunt for shells, stroll the kilometre across the island to buy snacks in Ban Ko Jum or roast on the beach and then plunge into the sea. Sandflies can be quite a problem on Ko Jum, so bring insect repellent. If you're feeling more energetic, the Thai-German-run Wildside Tours can organize kayaking, snorkelling, mountain-biking, caving and hiking excursions around the island; they also sell home-made bread and cakes and have a water bottle refilling service. Otherwise, when you tire of bungalow **food**, try the inexpensive and authentic Thai food at *Rimthang* on the track into Ban Ko Jum, or *Mama Cooking*, in Ban Ko Jum itself.

Except where specified, most tourist **accommodation** on Ko Pu closes down from May through October. At the southern end of the island, *New Bungalow* (❶–❸) has just fifteen basic bamboo huts plus a couple of treehouses. Close by *New*, the 35 smart wood and concrete bungalows of the long-running *Joy Bungalows* (☎01 464 6153; ❷–❺) are comfortably equipped with balconies, beds and nets, and the bamboo huts are simple but decent enough. North up the beach a bit, *Woodland Lodge* (☎01 893 5330, Ⓦwww.woodland-koh-jum.tk; ❶–❻) is one of the few places on the island to stay open year round; it has simple en-suite bamboo huts with mattress and mosquito net, plus some sturdier wooden huts and some family bungalows, all set under the trees. In among a palm grove further north up the beach, *Golden Pearl* (❷–❺) makes another inviting option, with a similar choice of bamboo and wooden bungalows close by the shore. Up in the northwest corner of the island, *Bonhomie Beach Cottages* (Ⓣ01 844 9069, Ⓦwww.designparty.com/member/467501/home; ❹–❻) has attractively designed wooden chalets with mosquito nets and private stone-walled bathrooms, and the price depends on whether you opt for sea or mountain view.

During high season, access to Ko Jum is via the Krabi–Ko Lanta **ferries** (1hr 30min from Krabi or about 45min from Ko Lanta; see p.728 for times); Ko Jum bungalows send longtails out to meet the ferries as they pass the west coast. When it comes to moving on, you can charter a longtail from Ko Jum to Ko Phi Phi for about B1000; the trip takes a couple of hours. In the **rainy season** you have to get there overland, first taking a **songthaew** from Krabi to Talat Kao (B10), then changing onto one bound for Nua Klong (B15; though there are occasional songthaews direct from Krabi to Nua Klong in the early morning), where you get another songthaew to **Laem Kruat** (B25), a total journey of about 40km. Several **boats** run from Laem Kruat to Ban Ko Jum in the southern part of the island, including at least three slow boats a day (departing at approximately noon, 1pm and 2pm; B25–40) and one speedboat (departs at 3pm and returns from Ko Jum at 7.30am; B60); from Ban Ko Jum it's an easy walk to the southern bungalows. Unless you're heading for *Bonhomie* in the north, make sure your boat is not going to the northern village of Ban Ko Pu instead, which is around 6km from most of the southern bungalows and will entail getting a very expensive motorbike taxi.

Travel details

Buses

Khao Lak to: Khao Sok (every 90min; 1hr 30min); Phuket (11 daily; 2hr 30min); Ranong (8 daily; 2hr 30min–3hr); Surat Thani (every 90min; 3hr 30min); Takua Pa (every 40min; 30min).
Khao Sok to: Khao Lak (every 90min; 1hr 30min); Surat Thani (every 90min; 2hr); Takua Pa (every 90min; 50min).
Krabi to: Bangkok (8 daily; 12–14hr); Hat Yai (14 daily; 4–5hr); Nakhon Si Thammarat (at least hourly; 3–4hr); Phang Nga (hourly; 1hr 30min–2hr); Phuket (every 30min; 3–5hr); Ranong (5 daily; 6–7hr); Satun (2 daily; 5hr); Sungai Kolok (2 daily; 9hr); Surat Thani (hourly; 4hr); Takua Pa (5 daily; 3hr 30min–4hr 30min); Trang (at least hourly; 2–3hr).
Phang Nga to: Bangkok (4 daily; 11hr–12hr 30min); Krabi (hourly; 1hr 30min–2hr); Phuket (hourly; 1hr 30min–2hr 30min); Surat Thani (4 daily; 4hr).
Phuket to: Bangkok (27 daily; 12–15hr); Hat Yai (16 daily; 6–8hr); Khao Lak (11 daily; 2hr 30min); Khao Sok (at least 2 daily; 3–4hr); Krabi (22 daily; 3–5hr); Nakhon Si Thammarat (26 daily; 7–8hr); Phang Nga (30 daily; 1hr 30min–2hr 30min); Phattalung (2 daily; 6–7hr); Ranong (8 daily; 5–6hr); Satun (2 daily; 7hr); Sungai Kolok (3 daily; 11hr); Surat Thani (20 daily; 4hr 30min–6hr); Takua Pa (17 daily; 3hr); Trang (22 daily; 5–6hr).
Ranong to: Bangkok (12 daily; 8–10hr); Chumphon (every 90min; 2–3hr); Hat Yai (3 daily; 5hr); Khuraburi (8 daily; 1hr 30min–2hr); Krabi (5 daily; 6–7hr); Phang Nga (2 daily; 4–5hr); Phuket (8 daily; 5–6hr); Surat Thani (10 daily; 4–5hr); Takua Pa (8 daily; 2hr 30min–3hr).
Takua Pa to: Bangkok (10 daily; 12–13hr); Krabi (at least 8 daily; 3hr 30min–4hr 30min); Phuket (hourly; 3hr); Ranong (8 daily; 2hr 30min–3hr); Surat Thani (11 daily; 3hr).

Ferries

Ao Nang to: Ko Lanta Yai (Nov–May 1 daily; 2hr 30min).
Khuraburi to: Ko Surin (Nov–May 1–2 daily; 1–5hr).
Ko Lanta Yai to: Ao Nang (Nov–May 1 daily; 2hr 30min); Ko Phi Phi Don (Nov–May 2 daily; 1hr 30min); Krabi (mid-Oct to mid-May 2 daily; 2hr

30min); Phuket (Nov–May 1 daily; 4hr 30min).
Ko Phi Phi Don to: Ao Nang and Laem Phra Nang (Nov–May 1 daily; 2hr); Ko Lanta Yai (Nov–May 2 daily; 1hr 30min); Krabi (2–5 daily; 1hr 30min–2hr); Phuket (2–3 daily; 1hr 30min–2hr 30min).
Krabi to: Ko Jum (mid-Oct to mid-May 2 daily; 1hr 30min); Ko Lanta Yai (mid-Oct to mid-May 2 daily; 2hr 30min); Ko Phi Phi Don (2–5 daily; 1hr 30min–2hr).
Phuket to: Ao Nang (Nov–May daily; 2–2hr 30min); Ko Phi Phi Don (2–3 daily; 1hr 30min–2hr 30min); Ko Lanta Yai (Nov–May 1 daily; 4hr 30min); Ko Similan (mid-Nov to mid-May 1 daily; 1hr 30min); Ko Yao (4 daily; 1hr) .
Ranong to: Ko Chang (Nov–May 1–2 daily; 1hr); Ko Phayam (Nov–May 1–2 daily; 2–3hr).
Thap Lamu (Khao Lak) to: Ko Similan (Nov–May 1 daily; 2hr).

Flights

Krabi to: Bangkok (4 daily; 1hr 20min); Ko Samui (1 daily; 50min).
Phuket to: Bangkok (20 daily; 1hr 25min); Hat Yai (1 daily; 45min); Ko Samui (2 daily; 50min); Pattaya/ U-Tapao (1 daily; 2hr 20min).
Ranong to: Bangkok (1 daily; 1hr 20min).

8

The deep south

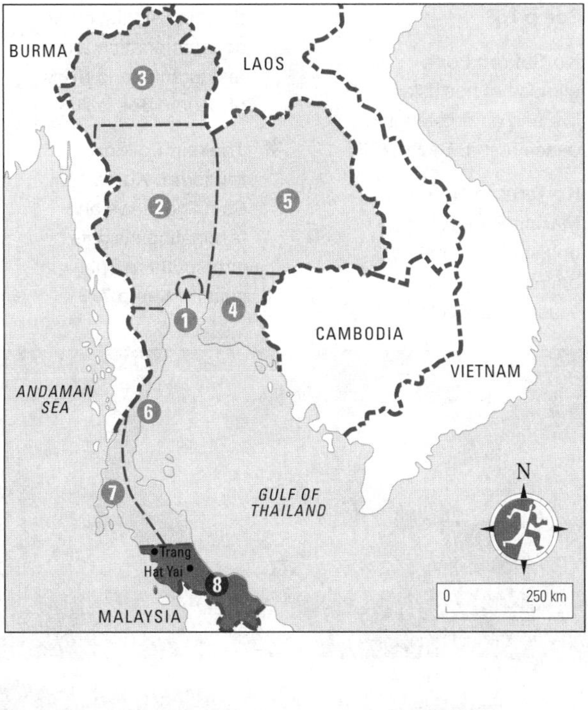

CHAPTER 8

Highlights

* **Thale Noi Waterbird Park** Boating on this fascinating inland lake isn't just for bird-watchers. See p.747
* **Ko Mook** One of the best of the Trang islands, with laid-back resorts and the stunning Emerald Cave. See p.753
* **Ko Sukorn** For a glimpse of how islanders live and an outstanding beach resort. See p.755
* **Ko Tarutao National Marine Park** A largely undisturbed haven of beautiful land- and seascapes. See p.758
* **Ko Lipe** One dazzling beach, fine opportunities for snorkelling and diving, and an appealing rough-and-ready feel. See p.763
* **Songkhla** Reliable all-rounder, with diverting sights, great accommodation and restaurants, and miles of beach. See p.768
* **Thaksin Folklore Museum, Ko Yo** Stunning views and fascinating insights into southern Thai culture. See p.773

△ Ko Tarutao National Marine Park

8

The deep south

The frontier between Thailand and Malaysia carves across the peninsula six degrees north of the equator, but the cultures of the two countries shade into each other much further north. According to official divisions, the southern Thais – the *thai pak tai* – begin around Chumphon, and as you move further down the peninsula you see ever more sarongs, yashmaks and towering mosques, and hear with increasing frequency a staccato dialect that baffles many Thais. In Trang, Phatthalung and Songkhla provinces, the Muslim population is generally accepted as being Thai, but the inhabitants of the four southernmost provinces – Satun, Pattani, Yala and Narathiwat – are ethnically more akin to the Malays: most of the 1.5 million followers of Islam here speak Yawi, an old Malay dialect. To add to the ethnic confusion, the deep south has a large urban population of Chinese, whose comparative wealth makes them stand out sharply from the Muslim farmers and fishermen.

On a journey south, the first thing you might be tempted by is an atmospheric boat trip through the **Thale Noi Waterbird Park** near Phatthalung. The easiest route after that is to hop across to the great natural beauty of the **west coast**, with its sheer limestone outcrops, pristine sands and fish-laden coral stretching down to the Malaysian border. The spread of tourism outwards from Phuket has been inching its way south to the idyllic islands around **Trang**, but for the time being at least these remain more or less unscathed. Further south in the spectacular **Ko Tarutao National Park**, you'll usually still have the beaches all to yourself, although **Ko Lipe** and its beautiful beach of Hat Pattaya have been arousing travellers' interest of late, albeit at a low-key, manageable level.

On the less attractive **east** side of the peninsula, you'll probably pass through the ugly, modern city of **Hat Yai** at some stage, as it's the transport capital for the south and for connections to Malaysia, but a far more sympathetic place to stay is the old town of **Songkhla**, half an hour away on the seashore. The region southeast of here is where you'll experience Malay Muslim culture at its purest, but with the exception of **Narathiwat**, a pleasant stopover on the journey south to the border (though see p.746), it has little to offer the visitor.

As well as the usual bus services, flights (to Trang, Hat Yai and Narathiwat) and the rail line, which forks at Hat Yai to Butterworth and Kuala Lumpur on the Malaysian west coast and Sungai Kolok on the eastern border, the deep south is the territory of **share-taxis**, which connect all the major towns for about twice the fare of ordinary buses. The cars leave when they're full, which usually means six passengers, with, quite possibly, babes-in-arms and livestock. They are a quick way of getting around and you should get dropped off at the door of your journey's end. A more recent – and now more successful –

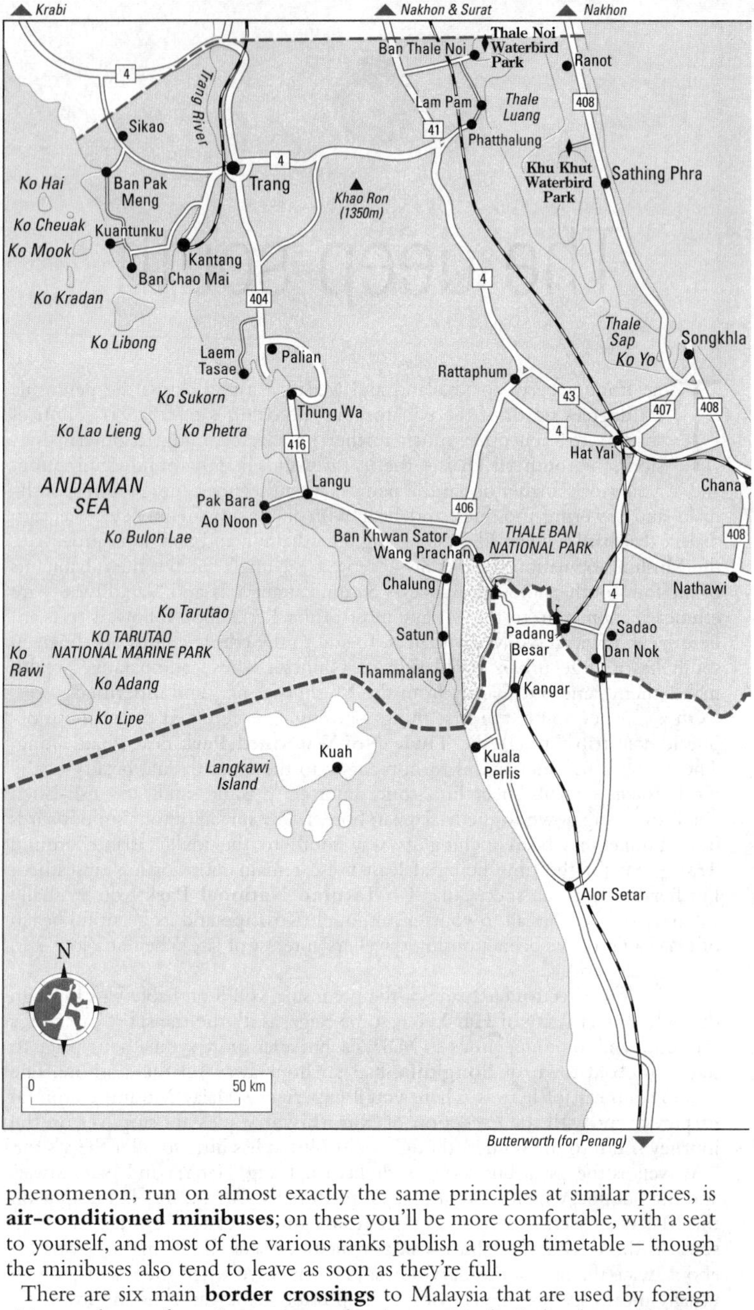

phenomenon, run on almost exactly the same principles at similar prices, is **air-conditioned minibuses**; on these you'll be more comfortable, with a seat to yourself, and most of the various ranks publish a rough timetable – though the minibuses also tend to leave as soon as they're full.

There are six main **border crossings** to Malaysia that are used by foreign visitors – by sea from Satun to Langkawi or to Kuala Perlis, the rest by land from Padang Besar, Sadao, Sungai Kolok and Ban Taba – which are outlined in

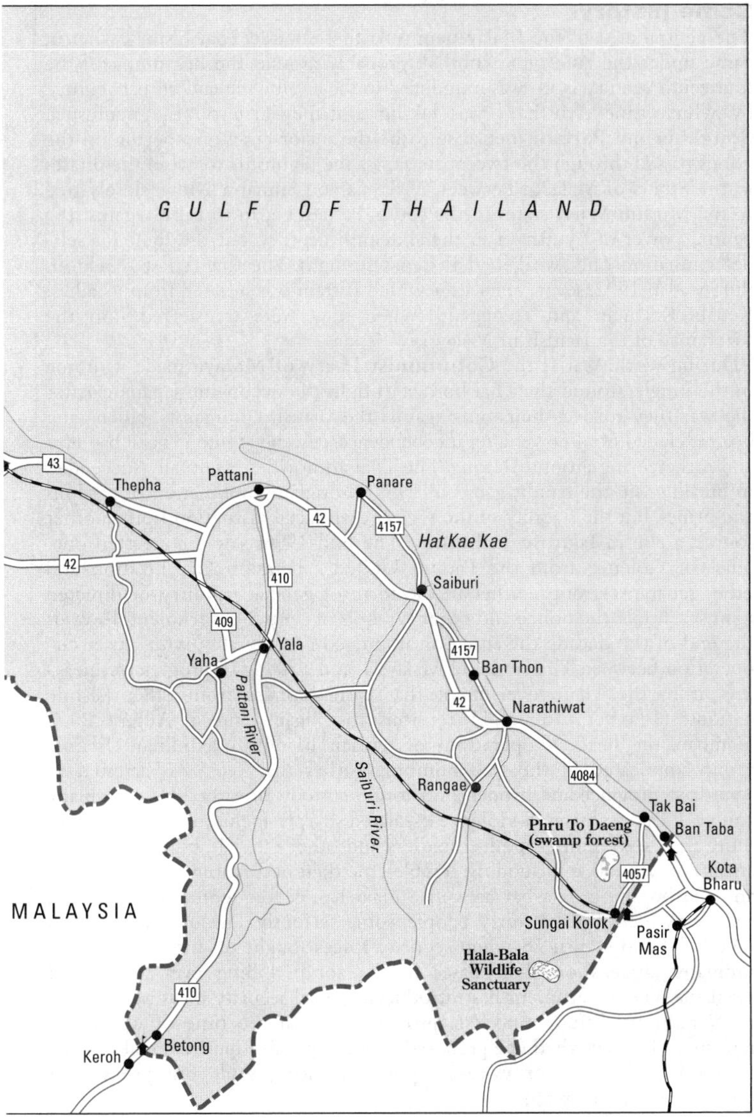

the relevant parts of this chapter. (A seventh, the long, slow route from Yala to the frontier town of Betong, is certainly a quiet and scenic way to enter Malaysia, but otherwise has little to offer.) Remember that Malaysian time is one hour ahead of Thai time. At any of these crossings you can nip across and back to get a thirty-day Thai visa (or to begin a new part of a multiple-entry visa); longer visas can be obtained at the Thai consulates at Penang on the west side of Malaysia and Kota Bharu on the east side (details on p.22 of Basics).

Some history

The central area of the Malay peninsula first entered Thai history when it came under the rule of Sukhothai, probably around the beginning of the fourteenth century. Islam was introduced to the area by the end of that century, by which time Ayutthaya was taking a firmer grip on the peninsula. **Songkhla** and **Pattani** then rose to be the major cities, prospering on the goods passed through the two ports across the peninsula to avoid the pirates in the Straits of Malacca between Malaysia and Sumatra. More closely tied to the Muslim Malay states to the south, Pattani began to **rebel** against the central power of Ayutthaya in the sixteenth century, but the fight for self-determination only weakened Pattani's strength. The town's last rebellious fling was in 1902, seven years after which Pattani was isolated from its allies, Kedah, Kelantan and Trengganu, when they were transferred into the suzerainty of the British in Malaysia.

During World War II the **Communist Party of Malaya** made its home in the jungle around the Thai border to fight the occupying Japanese. After the war they turned their guns against the British colonialists, but having been excluded from power after independence, descended into general banditry and racketeering around Betong. The Thai authorities eventually succeeded in breaking up the bandit gangs in 1989 through a combination of pardons and bribes, but the stability of the region then faced disruption from another source, a rise in **Islamic militancy**. The mid-1990s saw a concerted outburst of violence from the Pattani United Liberation Organization and other separatist groups, either in the form of general banditry, or directed against schools, the police and other symbols of central government. Towards the end of the decade the situation improved considerably, with closer co-operation between Thailand and Malaysia, and a string of progressive measures from the Thai government that earned praise from other Islamic nations. However, after 9/11 tensions rose again, and in August 2002 Hambali, the head of operations of Jemaah Islamiyah, a militant Islamic group implicated in the Bali bombing earlier that year, was arrested in Ayutthaya province and handed over to US custody. In early 2004, criminally and politically motivated violence escalated sharply, including the killings of more than sixty monks, police, soldiers and other officials, bomb and arson attacks on schools and Buddhist temples, the theft of weapons and explosives, and the bombing of a bar area in Sungai Kolok frequented by Malaysian tourists, which injured thirty people, some seriously. The troubles reached new heights on April 28 when security forces fought off fifteen or so co-ordinated attacks on their bases in the south, killing over a hundred assailants. The government has introduced special security measures in parts of Narathiwat, Pattani, and Yala provinces, but at the time of writing, it remains to be seen whether a proposed new softly-softly approach will succeed in defusing tensions – for up-to-the-minute advice, consult your government travel advisory (see p.59).

Phatthalung and Thale Noi

Halfway between Nakhon and Hat Yai, the hot, dusty town of **PHATTHALUNG** is worth a stop only if you're tempted by a boat trip through the nearby Thale Noi Waterbird Park – though even then it's possible to bypass the town altogether, as outlined below. Although its setting among limestone outcrops is dramatic, Phatthalung itself is drab and unwelcoming, its only claim to fame being *nang thalung*, the Thai shadow puppet theatre to which it probably gave its name (see box on p.631).

Phatthalung is on the major rail line, which crosses the main street, Thanon Ramet, in the centre of town. Out of a poor selection of **hotels**, the best value is the friendly *Thai Hotel*, at 14 Thanon Disara Sakarin, behind the Bangkok Bank on Thanon Ramet (ⓣ074 611636; ❸–❹); rooms with attached bathrooms and a choice of fan or air-conditioning are clean and reasonably quiet. *Koo Hoo*, at 9 Thanon Prachabamrung (parallel to and south of Ramet), is an excellent, moderately priced **restaurant** – try the sweet and sour fish or the delicious giant tiger prawns.

Thale Noi Waterbird Park

Thale Noi Waterbird Park isn't just for bird-spotters – even the most recalcitrant city-dweller can appreciate boating through the bizarre freshwater habitat formed at the head of the huge lagoon that spills into the sea at Songkhla. Here, in the "Little Sea" (*thale noi*), which has an average depth of just 1.5m, the distinction between land and water breaks down: the lake is dotted with low, marshy islands, and much of the intervening shallow water is so thickly covered with water vines, lotus pads and reeds that it looks like a field. But the real delight of this area is the hundreds of thousands of birds that breed here – brown teals, loping purple herons, white cattle egrets and nearly two hundred other species. Most are migratory, arriving here from December onwards from as far away as Siberia – March and April provide the widest variety of birds, from October to December you'll generally spot only native species, while June to September is the worst season for spotting. Early morning and late afternoon are the best times to come, when the heat is less searing and when, in the absence of hunters and fishermen, more birds are visible.

To get from Phatthalung to **BAN THALE NOI**, the village on the western shore, take one of the frequent **songthaews** (1hr) from Thanon Nivas, which runs north off Thanon Ramet near the station. If you're coming from Nakhon or points further north by bus, you can save yourself a trip into Phatthalung by getting out at **Ban Chai Khlong**, 15km from Ban Thale Noi, and waiting for a songthaew there. If you're travelling by train, it's also possible to bypass Phatthalung, by getting out at **Ban Pak Khlong** and catching a songthaew for the last 8km to Ban Thale Noi. **Longtail boats** can be hired at the pier in the village: for B200 per person, the boatman will give you a ninety-minute trip around the lake. If you want to get a dawn start, stay in one of the few national park **bungalows** built over the lake (donation required; book on ⓣ074 685230).

Trang province

Trang town, 60km west of Phatthalung, is fast developing as a popular jumping-off point for backpackers, drawn south from the crowded sands of Krabi to the pristine **beaches and islands** of the Trang coast. Inland, too, tourism is beginning to develop, with whitewater-rafting, kayaking and trekking excursions now on offer. So popular is the area becoming that it even has its own website: the excellent ⓦwww.trangonline.com has plenty of well-presented information on attractions, tours and accommodation in the region, including links to some interesting articles about Trang, and allows online bookings.

Trang town

The town of **TRANG** (aka Taptieng), which prospers on rubber, oil palms, fisheries and – increasingly – tourism, is a sociable place whose wide, clean streets are dotted with crumbling, wooden-shuttered houses. In the evening, restaurant tables sprawl onto the main Thanon Rama VI and Thanon Wisetkul, and during the day, many of the town's Chinese inhabitants hang out in the cafés, drinking the local filtered coffee. Trang's Chinese population makes the **Vegetarian Festival** at the beginning of October almost as frenetic as Phuket's (see box on p.675) – and for veggie travellers it's an opportunity to feast at the stalls set up around the temples. Getting there is easy, as Trang is ninety minutes from Phatthalung and well served by buses from all the surrounding provinces.

Practicalities

Thai Airways, with an office on Thanon Wisetkul (ⓣ075 218066), run daily **flights** between Bangkok and Trang airport, which is connected to Trang town by B40 air-conditioned minibuses. Two overnight **trains** from the capital run down a branch of the southern line to Trang, stopping at the station at the western end of Thanon Rama VI. Most **buses** arrive at the terminal on Thanon Huay Yod, to the north of the centre; buses from Satun stop on Thanon Ratsada out on the southeast side of town. **Air-conditioned minibuses** for Hat Yai are based on Thanon Huay Yod near the main bus terminal, those for Nakhon Si Thammarat on Thanon Klong Huai Yang, off Thanon Wisetkul. Those for Ko Lanta (five times daily to Ban Saladan, including the two short boat trips) pick up from several travel agencies and guest houses around town who handle bookings for them, including Sukorn Beach Bungalows and Tours, 22 Thanon Sathanee (ⓣ075 211457, ⓦwww.sukorn-island-trang.com), and *Yamawa Guesthouse*. These establishments also handle minibuses to Pak Bara in high season (roughly Nov–May); at other times of year you have to take a bus to Langu and then a songthaew.

TAT have recently opened a small **tourist office** on Thanon Ruenrom (daily 8.30am–4.30pm; ⓣ075 215867). There's an excellent **bookshop**, Ani's, at 285 Thanon Ratchadamnoen, which stocks a wide range of books in English and other languages, as well as handicrafts, beachwear, bags and hammocks. The owners are a good source of information on the area, and also have several **motorbikes**, which they rent out at B150 for the day (B200/24hr). *Yamawa Guesthouse* rents motorbikes, too, charging B200 for the day, B250 for 24 hours, B1000 for a week. For self-drive **car rental**, Avis (ⓣ075 691941) have a branch at Trang airport. Sukorn Beach Bungalows and Tours (see above) can arrange hire of an air-con minibus with driver, for around B1500 a day. You can connect to the **Internet** at, for example, *The Meeting Point* (see below) and Trang Cyber Computer opposite *Yamawa Guesthouse* on Thanon Wisetkul.

Accommodation

Hotels in Trang are concentrated along Thanon Rama VI and Thanon Wisetkul. The town's outstanding **budget** choice is the *Yamawa Guesthouse* at 94 Thanon Wisetkul (ⓣ075 216617; ❷–❹), whose twelve large rooms, with shared hot-water bathrooms, are beautifully decorated throughout and festooned with plants; some come with air-con and cable TV. There's a bar-restaurant on the ground floor, as well as a leafy roof terrace. The friendly Thai-Belgian family who run the guest house also organize one- to three-day treks in the Trang area from January to May (about B1000/day/person), as well as day-trips by car. If you can't get a room here, a good second best is the *Ko Teng*

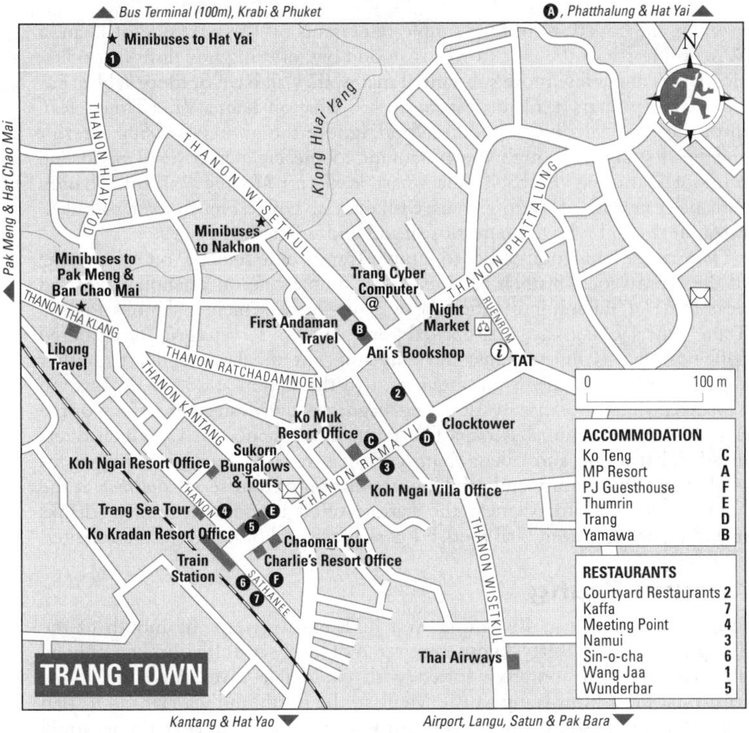

Hotel at 77–79 Thanon Rama VI (☎075 218622; ❷–❸), with smartly renovated, large, clean en-suite rooms, some with cable TV and air-con, above a popular restaurant and coffee shop, serving Thai, Chinese and Western food. The functional, concrete rooms with shared cold showers at *PJ Guesthouse*, 25/12 Thanon Sathanee (☎ & Ⓕ075 217500; ❷), offer poorer value, though the owner is helpful.

There are two good choices in the **moderate** range, the *Trang Hotel*, 134/2–5 Thanon Wisetkul, at the junction with Thanon Rama VI overlooking the clocktower (☎075 218944, Ⓕ075 218451; ❹), which has large, comfortable twin rooms with air-con, hot water and TV, and the *Thumrin Hotel*, on Rama VI near the station (☎075 211011, Ⓕ075 218057; ❹), which offers the same facilities at a slightly cheaper price. The latter used to be the town's only deluxe option, but has been usurped by several **luxury** hotels, among which the *MP Resort Hotel*, about 2km east of the centre on the Phatthalung road (☎075 214230–45, Ⓕ075 211177; ❼), stands out, a grandiose white edifice built to resemble a cruise liner, with a pool, golf driving range, sauna, tennis court and fitness centre.

Eating and drinking

Trang's **food** comes into its own in the early evenings, when the excellent night market opens for business; it's around the back of the city hall on Thanon Ruenrom. Try the *khanom jiin*, soft noodles topped with hot, sweet or fishy sauces and eaten with crispy greens. At any time of the day or evening, the courtyard of four simple restaurants off the west side of Thanon Wisetkul north of the clocktower is a good bet: offering tray dishes, noodles, rice, soups and a few more substantial mains, they all have outdoor tables. For something posher, head for *Namui* at 130 Thanon Rama VI, a large, clean institution specializing in good seafood; ignore the unprepossessing interior and head straight through the restaurant to the creeper-covered patio and outdoor seating at the back. The smart, well-run *Meeting Point* on Thanon Sathanee caters largely to foreigners, with espresso coffee, French toast, pancakes, pasta, steaks and a large menu of seafood and other Thai dishes.

There are several good places to sample Trang's **café** society. You can partake of the typical local brunch at *Wang Jaa*, a simple café on Thanon Huay Yod near the Hat Yai minibus office (daily 5am–2pm), which is famous for the Trang delicacy, *muu yaang* (barbecued pork), but also serves *kopii* (local filtered coffee), *salapao* (Chinese buns) and dim sum. For an all-day coffee fix, either *kopii* or espresso, head for *Sin-o-cha*, next to the station at 25/25–26 Thanon Sathanee, which also serves various teas, baguettes and Western breakfasts, or the slightly more traditional *Kaffa*, a few doors along at no. 25/47, which offers mostly Thai dishes and cakes. Trang even has a farang **bar**, pandering to its small expat community and growing population of tourists: *Wunderbar*, at the bottom end of Rama VI near the station, offers a wide selection of drinks including draught beer, Thai food, burgers, pizzas and other Western favourites.

Around Trang

From Ban Pak Meng, 40km due west of Trang town, to the mouth of the Trang River runs a thirty-kilometre stretch of lovely **beaches**, broken only by dramatic limestone outcrops pitted with explorable caves. Air-conditioned **minibuses** run from Trang to Pak Meng in the north, and via Hat Yao to Ban Chao Mai in the south, but if you want to explore the whole coastline, you'll need to rent a motorbike or car in Trang.

Much nicer than the mainland beaches – and more geared towards foreign tourists – are the fantastic **islands** off the coast. Generally blessed with blinding white beaches, great coral and amazing marine life, these islands have managed, with at most a handful of resorts on each, to cling onto that illusory desert-island atmosphere which better-known places like Phuket and Samui lost long ago. Boat access to the islands is improving all the time, as described in the accounts below, and accommodation, much of which is in the moderate price range, is now often fully booked at peak times. Nearly all the resorts open year round, though in practice many can't be reached out of season (roughly June–Oct) due to treacherous seas. It's sensible to phone ahead, either to the place you want to stay or to its office in Trang town, to check whether they're open or have vacancies, and in many cases to arrange transfers to the resort from Trang.

Besides the specific resort offices (detailed below in the island accounts), there are several **travel agencies in Trang**, such as the helpful Chaomai Tour at 15 Thanon Sathanee (ⓣ075 214742, ⓔjongkolneetrang@hotmail.com) and Trang Sea Tour, 59/9 Thanon Sathanee (ⓣ07 277 8224), which offer a wider range of services. If you just fancy a day exploring the islands, any agent can book you on a **boat trip** (mid-Oct to mid-May only) to the Emerald Cave on Ko Mook, Ko Hai, Ko Cheuak ("Robe Island", so named after its limestone folds) and other small nearby islands for snorkelling, for B800 per person including admission to Hat Chao Mai National Park, packed lunch and soft drinks; snorkelling gear is available and the boat will drop you off at one of the islands if you wish. The well-organized Sukorn Beach Bungalows and Tours (see p.748) offer a similar range of travel agency services – including accommodation booking on any island, boat trips and car rental – in addition to running their own bungalow outfit on Ko Sukorn. The friendly staff are a great source of information on the area, and their office makes a good first stop in town. **Scuba-diving** is available from Ko Hai and Ko Mook, while Paddle Asia (see p.761) run four- to six-day **sea-kayaking** trips around the Trang islands costing US$675–850.

Away from the beach, **inland** Trang Province has plenty to offer too, including **trekking**, **whitewater-rafting** and **canoeing** excursions, most taking in some of the myriad caves and waterfalls that are scattered though the province. Libong Travel, 59/1 Thanon Tha Klang (☎075 217642 or 01 606 8530), offer a particularly wide range of trips, including whitewater-rafting in the rainy season (B850/person day-trip), canoeing through the mangroves near Ban Chao Mai and the caves along the Trang coast (B950 day-trip), and a three-day jungle trek up to the 1200-metre peak of nearby Mount Rutu from Sairoong waterfall (B1700). They also offer a day-trip to three waterfalls and Tham Le (aka Khao Kob), a dramatic inland system of caverns accessed by boat (B600), as well as island tours. *Yamawa Guesthouse* (see p.748) runs trekking trips, which are also offered by Sukorn Beach Bungalows and Tours (see p.748), alongside whitewater-rafting, canoeing and possibly elephant-trekking in the future.

The coast: Pak Meng to Ban Chao Mai

Although it has a fine outlook to the headlands and islands to the west, the beach at **PAK MENG** is certainly not the most attractive on the coast, a rather muddy strip of sand truncated at its northern end by a busy pier and to the south by a promenade and sea wall. However, if it's just a day on the sand you're after, and a meal at one of the many foodstalls and simple eateries that line the back of the beach, it's not at all bad. Getting to Pak Meng takes about an hour on one of the air-con **minibuses** that leave when full (roughly half-hourly; B50) from Thanon Tha Klang in Trang. If you need **to stay**, the nicest place is the *Lay Trang Resort*, a stone's throw from the pier (☎075 274027–8, ⓦwww.laytrang.com; ❹–❺); its smart brick rooms with en-suite bathrooms, ranged around a large, peaceful garden, come with fan and cold water or air-con, TV and hot water, and there's a pleasant, reasonably priced restaurant attached.

Immediately south of Pak Meng's beach is the white sand of **Hat Chang Lang**, famous for its oysters, which shelters at its north end the finest luxury hotel in the province, *Amari Trang Beach Resort* (☎075 205888, ⓦwww.amari.com; ❾). The low-rise blocks of stylish bedrooms with large balconies are set behind a line of casuarina trees, and facilities include a beautiful, large pool, excellent Thai, Italian and international restaurants, a spa and fitness centre, and a wide-ranging watersports and excursion centre. A short way down Hat Chang Lang is the simpler *Chang Lang Resort* (☎075 213369, ⓕ075 291008; ❹–❼), a pleasant resort with attached restaurant, set back from the beach just off the main road; well-built concrete bungalows, some air-conditioned and with hot water, all come with en-suite bathrooms, TVs and their own verandas. A couple of kilometres further on is the turning for the **headquarters** of the **Hat Chao Mai National Park** (entry B200), which covers 230 square kilometres, including the islands of Mook and Kradan and the entire stretch of coastline from Pak Meng down to Ban Chao Mai. At the headquarters, there's a simple café, as well as some rooms in large **bungalows** (B500 for two people), or for B200 a night, you can rent a two-person tent to pitch under the casuarinas at the back of the sandy beach. From HQ a short trail leads to the south end of the beach and a viewpoint part way up a karst pinnacle, from which you can see Ko Mook and occasionally dugong (manatees) in the bay below.

Four kilometres south of Hat Chang Lang, beyond Kuantunku, the pier for Ko Mook, is **Hat Yong Ling**. This quiet and attractive convex beach, which shelters a national park ranger station, is probably the nicest along this stretch of coast, with a large cave which you can swim into at high tide or walk into at low tide. Immediately beyond comes **Hat Yao**, which runs in a broad five-kilometre white-sand strip, backed by casuarina trees and some simple restaurants. Next up is **Hat Chao Mai**, where *Sinchai's Chaomai Resort* (Ⓣ01 396 4838 or 075 203034; ❷–❺) occupies a shady, scenic spot at the western end of the beach. It's very relaxed and friendly, though accommodation is ramshackle, with a choice between very basic huts at the back of the compound, and wooden or concrete rooms or bungalows, some with air-con. The owners rustle up tasty Thai meals, especially seafood, and Western breakfasts, and can arrange boat tours to the nearby islands and caves.

A short walk away from *Sinchai's* is the Muslim village of **BAN CHAO MAI**, a straggle of mostly thatched houses on stilts, which exists on fishing, especially for crabs. Roughly half-hourly air-conditioned **minibuses** (B50) from Thanon Tha Klang (same stand as for Pak Meng) in Trang via Hat Yao take about an hour to reach Ban Chao Mai, from whose harbour boats run regularly across to Ko Libong. By the harbour, the distinctive green tin-roofed *Had Yao Nature Resort* (Ⓣ075 203012 or 01 894 6936, Ⓔnatureresorts@hotmail.com; ❸–❺) is an efficiently run, official HI **hostel**. The same people own the *Libong Nature Beach Resort*, covered on p.755, and a resort on an organic farm off Highway 4 between Trang and Krabi. Dorm beds in the large house cost B150, and there are also some fan-cooled rooms with shared bath, as well as nicer self-contained rooms and bungalows with hot water and air-con, some of which have balconies over the canal. The breezy, waterside **restaurant** serves up Western breakfasts and excellent squid and other seafood dishes; **bikes** can be rented at the hostel for B200 per day. The owners organize trips to the local islands and to **Tham Chao Mai**, a nearby cave which is large enough to enter by boat; inside are impressively huge rock pillars and a natural theatre, its stage framed by rock curtains. Tham Chao Mai can be visited with a longtail and guide (B600 for a half-day trip) or you can rent a **kayak** (B300/day) and guide yourself with a map and torch. Also near Ban Chao Mai's harbour is the office of Bangkok-based adventure travel company, X-Site (Ⓣ075 207518, Ⓦwww.laoliangisland.com), who run three-day **scuba-diving**, **snorkelling** or **rock-climbing** trips from here to **Ko Lao Lieng**, twin desert islands to the south near Ko Sukorn; all-in costs range from B4500 to B5600, including kayaking and fishing in your down time, camping in luxury tents on Lao Lieng and transfers from Trang.

Ko Hai (Ko Ngai)

KO HAI (aka **KO NGAI**), 16km southwest of Pak Meng, is one of the most developed of the Trang islands, though it's still decidedly low-key. The island's action, such as it is, centres on the east coast, where a handful of resorts enjoy a dreamy panorama of jagged limestone outcrops, whose crags glow pink and blue against the setting sun, stretching across the sea to the mainland behind. A two-kilometre-long beach of fine, white sand here has a gentle slope that's ideal for swimming, and there's some good snorkelling in the shallow water off the southeastern tip. For the best snorkelling in the region, *Ko Ngai Resort* and *Fantasy* run boat trips every day in high season (B350/person) to Ko Cheuak, Ko Maa and Ko Waen, just off Ko Hai to the east, where you can swim into caverns and explore a fantastic variety of multi-coloured soft and hard coral; these trips also take in Ko Mook's Emerald Cave.

For getting to Ko Hai, **boats** leave Pak Meng for the one-hour voyage at around 10.30am, charging B150 one way; if you miss the boat, longtails can be chartered for B600. *Ko Ngai Resort* (ⓣ075 206924–6; Trang office at 66/4 Thanon Sathanee, ⓣ075 210317; ⓦwww.kohngai.com; ❻–❽) occupies a sandy cove on the east coast by the island's jetty, to the south of the main beach; besides a good restaurant, it has a spread of upmarket **accommodation** ranging from fan-cooled en-suite rooms to air-conditioned, thatched beachside bungalows with wooden verandas and spacious bathrooms. The resort also has a well-organized **dive shop**, the German-run Rainbow Divers (Nov–April; ⓦwww.rainbow-diver.com). Operated by the same company as *Ko Ngai Resort*, *Fantasy Resort* (ⓣ075 206922–3, ⓦwww.kohngai.com; ❽), a short way north on the main beach, is swankier still, with foot spas outside each bungalow to wash away the sand before you step inside. Its thirty pastel-coloured bungalows with hot water and air-con are set in a pretty garden under coconut palms, and there's a good restaurant too.

Further up the main beach, at *Ko Ngai Villa* (ⓣ075 203263; Trang office at 112 Thanon Rama VI, ⓣ075 210496; ❸–❺), simple, well-organized bamboo bungalows boast verandas and small toilets, or you could opt for a newer concrete bungalow or room in a concrete longhouse, or even a tent (B200). Alone on the short south coast, *Ko Hai Paradise Resort*'s well-designed, en-suite bungalows are sheltered by tall palms in the spacious, grassy grounds (ⓣ075 211260, ⓔkohhaiparadise@yahoo.com; Trang office at *The Meeting Point* – see p.748; ❹). The food's good and the white-sand beach slopes down towards some great coral for snorkelling right in front of the resort. They provide their own longtail transfer from Trang via Kuantunku pier (B250/person).

Ko Mook

KO MOOK, about 8km southeast of Ko Hai, offers some of the best accommodation on the Trang islands. The easiest way to **get there** is to book a minibus-and-boat package through one of the resort offices or travel agents in Trang (B170 to the island village, B200 to Hat Farang). Otherwise, there's a pretty reliable boat (B50) at midday to Ko Mook's village from Kuantunku pier, 8km south of Pak Meng, between Hat Chang Lang and Hat Yong Ling; Ban Chao Mai air-con minibuses from Trang charge B100 to detour to Kuantunku. The island supports a comparatively busy fishing village on its east coast, but its main source of renown is **Tham Morakhot**, the stunning "Emerald Cave" on the west coast, which can only be visited by boat, but shouldn't be missed. An eighty-metre swim through the cave – 10m or so of which is in pitch darkness – brings you to an inland beach of powdery sand open to the sky, at the base of a spectacular natural chimney whose walls are coated with dripping vegetation. Unless you're a nervous swimmer, avoid the organized tours on bigger boats offered by some of the resorts on nearby islands, and charter your own longtail instead: you won't get lifejackets and torches, but the boatman will swim through the cave with you and – if you're lucky – you'll avoid the tours and get the inland beach all to yourself, an experience not to be forgotten.

Hat Farang, south of Tham Morakhot and a thirty-minute walk west from the island village (or B30 on a motorbike taxi), is by far the best beach on Ko Mook, with gently shelving white sand, crystal-clear water that's good for swimming and snorkelling, and beautiful sunsets. With most of the beach to itself, the nicest of the **bungalow** outfits here is *Charlie's* (ⓣ075 203281–2; Trang office at 17 Thanon Sathanee, ⓣ075 217671–2; ⓦwww.kohmook.com; ❺–❽), a well-run establishment offering very smart bamboo huts that share a spotlessly clean shower block, as well as attractive concrete en-suite cottages, some with hot water and air-con. The recommended restaurant serves good coffee and a huge variety of Western and Thai food, including local dishes and plenty of seafood, and there are Internet, exchange and overseas phone facilities. You can rent kayaks, have a massage (a full-service spa is planned) or take a boat trip, either to Tham Morakhot and around Ko Mook or to neighbouring islands (from B300/person). If all that isn't enough for you, there's a **dive shop** offering courses and trips by longtail or speedboat to sites such as Hin Daeng (see p.671), Ko Rok (see p.728) and a sunken Japanese destroyer. Three times a week, *Charlie's* runs speedboat transfers from its sister resort on Ko Phi Phi (B1200).

At the rocky, northern end of the beach, *Sawaddee*'s en-suite bungalows (ⓣ075 207964–5, ⓔsawaddeeresort64@yahoo.com; or contact *Wunderbar* in Trang – see p.750; ❹) are a little more rough and ready, but enjoy plenty of shade and largely uninterrupted sea views. There are also a couple of good places on the attractive, shady slopes just behind the beach: friendly *Hat Farang* (ⓣ07 884 4785; ❷–❸) offers simple but clean en-suite huts and very basic rooms, as well as good food, including Western breakfasts and a *matsaman* curry speciality; and *Rubber Tree* (ⓣ075 203284 or 01 270 4148; ❹) has well-maintained, thatched, en-suite bungalows in a small plantation.

The beaches on the eastern side of the island are disappointing, often reduced to dirty mud flats when the tide goes out. On this coast just north of the village is *Ko Mook Resort* (ⓣ075 203303; Trang office at 45 Thanon Rama VI, ⓣ & ⓕ075 214441; ❷–❹); arrayed on the shady slopes here are basic en-suite bungalows as well as big bamboo and wood versions with verandas. The resort runs free boat transport every day to nicer beaches around Ko Mook.

Ko Kradan

About 6km to the southwest of Ko Mook, **KO KRADAN** is the remotest of the inhabited islands off Trang, and one of the most beautiful. Apart from a Hat Chao Mai National Park ranger station, *Ko Kradan Paradise Beach* (Trang office at 28–30 Thanon Sathanee, ⓣ075 211391; ⓦwww.kradanisland.com; ❺–❼), an uninspiring and rather pricey resort on the east coast, is about Ko Kradan's only sign of life (though rumours about future big-league development of the island abound). Some of the en-suite wooden **bungalows** come with air-con and TV, or there are tents to rent (from B300 for two people). You can swim at the long, narrow beach of steeply sloping, powdery sand in front of the resort – complete with its own coral reef – or at Sunset Beach, in a small bay ten minutes' walk away on the other side of the island. There's more good snorkelling among a great variety of hard coral in the clear waters off the island's northeastern tip, or you could join a boat trip to the neighbouring islands (B450/person). To get there, arrange a transfer from the resort's Trang office (B250/person).

Ko Libong

The largest of the Trang islands, **KO LIBONG**, lies 10km southeast of Ko Mook, opposite Ban Chao Mai on the mainland. Less visited than its northern neighbours, it's known mostly for its wildlife, although it has its fair share of golden beaches too. Libong is one of the most significant remaining refuges in Thailand of the **dugong** (also known as the manatee), a large marine mammal which feeds on sea grasses growing on the sea floor – the sea-grass meadow around Libong is reckoned to be the largest in Southeast Asia. Sadly, dugongs are now an endangered species, traditionally hunted for their blubber (used as fuel) and meat, and increasingly affected by fishing practices such as scooping, and by coastal pollution which destroys their source of food. The dugong has now been adopted as one of fifteen "reserved animals" of Thailand and is the official mascot of Trang province, but it remains to be seen how effective methods of conservation will be, especially with tourist interest in the dugong growing all the time.

Libong is also well known for its migratory **birds**, which stop off here on their way south from Siberia, drawn by the island's food-rich mud flats (now protected by the Libong Archipelago Sanctuary, which covers the eastern third of the island). For those seriously interested in ornithology, the best time to come is during March and April, when you can expect to see crab plovers, great knots, Eurasian curlews, bar-tailed godwits, brown-winged kingfishers, masked finfoots and even the rare black-necked stork, not seen elsewhere on the Thai–Malay peninsula.

Libong Nature Beach Resort runs award-winning, environmentally friendly, day-long **boat trips** (B600/person), which are also available from their sister resort, *Had Yao Nature Resort*. As well as visiting a *chao ley* village, these give you the chance to kayak into the sanctuary to observe the rare birds and to snorkel at the sea-grass beds – with, they reckon, a fifty-fifty chance of seeing a dugong.

Practicalities

Boats depart daily year-round from Ban Chao Mai (see p.752) when full (B20, or B200 to charter the whole boat), arriving twenty minutes later at Ban Phrao on Ko Libong; from here motorbike taxis transport you across to Ban Lan Khao and the island's two **resorts**. Both of these are situated on the long, thin strip of golden sand which runs along the southwestern coast, where at low tide the sea retreats for hundreds of metres, exposing rock pools that are great for splashing about in but not so good for a dip. The *Libong Nature Beach Resort* (Ⓣ075 203012 or 01 894 6936, Ⓔnatureresorts@hotmail.com; ⑤) is run by the same team who operate the *Had Yao Nature Resort* (see p.752). Its neat, brick en-suite bungalows are set slightly back from a secluded stretch of beach, a ten-minute walk south of the fishing village of Ban Lan Khao; there's a good restaurant attached too. At *Libong Beach Resort* (Ⓣ075 281160 or 01 477 8609, Ⓦwww.libongbeach.com; ⑤–⑥), on the opposite, northern, side of Ban Lan Khao, a little closer to the clutter of the village, sturdy and smart en-suite bungalows on stilts come with or without air-con, and there's also a reasonable restaurant.

Ko Sukorn

A good way south of the other Trang islands, low-lying **KO SUKORN** lacks the white-sand beaches and beautiful coral of its neighbours, but makes up for it with its friendly inhabitants, laid-back ambience and one excellent resort; for a glimpse of how islanders live and work, this is the place to come.

The lush interior of the island is mainly given over to rubber plantations, interspersed with rice paddies, banana and coconut palms, while Hat Talo Yai, the island's main **beach** – 500m of gently shelving brown sand, backed by coconut palms – runs along the southwestern shore. It's here you'll find the outstanding *Sukorn Beach Bungalows* (Ⓣ075 207707; Trang office at 22 Thanon Sathanee, Ⓣ075 211457, Ⓦwww.sukorn-island-trang.com; ④–⑥), one of the few Trang resorts that's reliably accessible all year round (discounts of up to sixty percent are available in low season). The clued-up and congenial Thai-Dutch duo who run the place are keen to keep the resort low-key and work with the locals as much as possible, something that's reflected in the friendly welcome you get all over the island. Attractively decorated and well-designed bungalows and rooms – all spotlessly clean and with en-suite bathrooms – are set around a lush garden dotted with deckchairs and umbrellas, and there's an excellent, well-priced **restaurant**. At the resort, you can access the Internet, make overseas calls and get a good massage, and you're free to paddle around in kayaks.

Boat excursions from the resort include trips out to Ko Phetra, Ko Lao Lieng and Ko Takieng, all part of the Mu Ko Phetra National Marine Park, for some excellent snorkelling. These run in high season only, when the sea is calm enough; at other times of year you're restricted to fishing trips – and to looking round the island itself, which, at thirty square kilometres, is a good size for exploring. The resort offers **guided tours** (B250/person), or it has motorbikes (half-day B185) and mountain bikes (half-day B100) for rent, as well as a handy map that marks all the sights, including the seafood market and a 150-metre-high viewpoint.

A songthaew-and-boat **transfer to the island** (B90/person) leaves the resort's office in Trang daily at 11.30am and takes a couple of hours, or you can arrange a private transfer. The resort can also organize pricey longtail-boat transfers to or from any of the nearby islands, and can even put together an all-in island-hopping package, with stays at *Charlie's* on Ko Mook and *Libong Beach Resort*, for B12,000, most of which goes on your private longtail transfers.

If *Sukorn Beach Bungalows* is not your cup of tea, the best of the rest of the island's handful of resorts are the friendly and peaceful *Ko Sukorn Cabana* (Ⓣ09 646 5513, Ⓦwww.sukorncabana.com; ❻), with large, well-appointed log cabins on a secluded beach to the north of Hat Talo Yai; and *Pavena Resort* (❸), run by the local village headman, offering functional en-suite bungalows among pretty bougainvillea, on the sandy southern coast.

Satun province

Satun province, which lies south of Trang and flush against the Malaysian border, provides the first glimpse of Thailand for many travellers on their way up through the Thai-Malay peninsula. The sleepy provincial capital, **Satun**, offers few attractions for the visitor, but makes a good base for the nearby **Thale Ban National Park**, with its caves, waterfalls and luxuriant jungle. The province's main attraction, however, is the **Ko Tarutao National Marine Park**, with pristine stretches of sand and a fantastic array of marine life, which is now served by daily dry-season ferries from Thammalang near Satun town, as well as from the port of **Pak Bara**, further up the coast. North of the national park, the tiny islands of the **Ko Phetra National Marine Park** are much less visited, with the exception of **Ko Bulon Lae**, which has a good selection of privately run bungalows along its long and beautiful beach.

Satun

Nestling in the last wedge of Thailand's west coast, the remote town of **SATUN** is served by just one road, Highway 406, which approaches through forbidding karst outcrops. Set in a green valley bordered by limestone hills, the town is leafy and relaxing but not especially interesting: the boat services to and from Ko Tarutao, Ko Lipe and Malaysia are the main reason for foreigners to come here.

If you find yourself with time on your hands in Satun, it's worth seeking out the **National Museum** (Wed–Sun 9am–4pm; free) on Soi 5, Thanon Satun Thani, on the north side of the centre. It's memorable, as much as anything else, for its setting, in the graceful **Kuden Mansion**, which was built in British colonial style, with some Thai and Malay features, by craftsmen from Penang, and inaugurated in 1902 as the Satun governor's official residence. The exhibits and audiovisuals in English have a distinctive anthropological tone, but are diverting enough, notably concerning Thai Muslims, the *chao ley* on Ko Lipe, and the Sakai, a dwindling band of nomadic hunter-gatherers who still live in the jungle of southern Thailand.

Practicalities

Frequent **buses** depart for Satun from Thanon Ratsada in Trang, and regular buses also come here from Hat Yai and Phatthalung. Buses arrive at the terminal on the north side of Satun on Thanon Satun Thani, the main road into town; share-taxis and air-con minibuses are based in the centre around the junction of Thanon Saman Pradit (the main east–west thoroughfare) and Thanon Buriwanit, which runs parallel to and west of Thanon Satun Thani. There's **Internet access** at Satun CyberNet, 136 Thanon Satun Thani, and at Andaman Trips and Services, 148 Thanon Satun Thani (ⓣ074 725148, ⓔandamantrips@hotmail.com), where friendly **fixer** Bon can also organize motorbike and minivan rental, sea-kayaking trips, cooking classes and ferry tickets.

Just on the west side of the centre at 4 Thanon Saman Pradit, *Rian Thong* (ⓣ074 711036; ❶) is the best budget **hotel** in Satun; the owners are friendly, and some of the clean, large, en-suite rooms overlook the canal. *Amm Guest House* (ⓣ074 724912 or 06 287 5730; closed June–Sept; ❸), 3km south of town on the road to Thammalang pier, offers basic but clean rooms with shared bathrooms in a rustic, riverside setting. In complete contrast, *Pinnacle Wangmai Hotel*, out towards the bus depot at 43 Thanon Satun Thani (ⓣ074 711607–8, ⓦwww.pinnaclehotels.com/satun.html; ❹), is a typical "deluxe" hotel with air-conditioned rooms in a modern concrete building; similar but more central and preferable is the *Sinkiat Thani*, 50 Thanon Buriwanit (ⓣ074 721055–8, ⓔsinkiathotel@hotmail.com; ❺), where large, well-equipped bedrooms offer good views over the surrounding countryside.

A good option for moderately priced Thai and Western **food** is the air-conditioned *Time Restaurant*, which is suitably decorated with nostalgic antiques, next door to the *Pinnacle Wangmai Hotel* on Thanon Satun Thani. For a meal in the evening, try the lively night market, north of the centre on the west side of Thanon Satun Thani, or *Yim Yim*, on Thanon Saman Pradit by the Chinese temple, a clean and popular restaurant which serves good, simple Chinese food.

From **Thammalang** pier, 10km south of Satun at the mouth of the river, longtail **boats** leave when full on regular, thirty-minute trips (B100/person) to **Kuala Perlis** on the northwest tip of **Malaysia**, from where there are plentiful transport connections down the west coast. Six ferry boats a day cross to the Malaysian island of **Langkawi** from Thammalang (50min; B220); you can get information in town from Satun Travel and Ferry Service, opposite the *Pinnacle Wangmai Hotel* at 45/16 Thanon Satun Thani (ⓣ074 711453), or from Thai Ferry Centre at the pier (ⓣ074 730511–2), who both also handle ferries from **Thammalang to Tarutao and Lipe** (see p.760). Frequent songthaews (B20) and motorbike taxis (B30) run to Thammalang from near the junction of Thanon Saman Pradit and Thanon Buriwanit, taking around fifteen minutes. If you are entering Thailand by sea from Malaysia, be sure to have your passport stamped at the **immigration office** at Thammalang pier, otherwise you may have problems on your eventual departure from Thailand. (It's also possible to cross by road into Malaysia from Satun at Thale Ban National Park, but this is only practicable if you have your own transport.)

Thale Ban National Park

Spread over rainforested mountains along the Malaysian border, **THALE BAN NATIONAL PARK** is a pristine nature reserve which shelters a breathtaking variety of wildlife: from tapirs, Malayan sun bears, clouded leopards and barking tree frogs, to butterflies, which proliferate in March, and unusual birds such as bat hawks, booted eagles and flamboyant argus pheasants. Unfortunately for naturalists and casual visitors alike, few trails have been marked out through the jungle, but the lush, peaceful setting and the views and bathing pools of the Yaroy waterfall are enough to justify the trip.

Twice-daily **songthaews** leave from opposite *Rian Thong* hotel in Satun, passing through the village of Wang Prachan and reaching Thale Ban **headquarters** (☎074 722736–7), 2km further on, in an hour. Otherwise, get off any bus along Highway 406 between Satun and Hat Yai at **Ban Khwan Sator**, 19km north of Satun, from where songthaews make the twenty-kilometre journey along Highway 4184 to Thale Ban roughly hourly.

Hemmed in by steep, verdant hills and spangled with red water lilies, the **lake** by the headquarters is central to the story that gives the park its name. Local legend tells how a villager once put his *ban* (headscarf) on a tree stump to have a rest; this caused a landslide, the lake appeared from nowhere, and he, the stump and the *ban* tumbled into it. The water is now surrounded by **bungalows** (B300–1000/night depending on size), a **campsite** (B20/person/night) with showers and toilets, and a decent open-air **canteen**.

One of the easiest trips from park headquarters brings you to **Tham Tondin**, a low, sweaty stalactite cave that gradually slopes down for 800m to deep water. It's about 2km north of headquarters just off the road to Khwan Sator; if you time your visit so that you emerge just before dusk, you'll see hundreds of bats streaming out of the hole for the night. A more compelling jaunt, though, is to **Yaroy waterfall** – bring swimming gear for the pools above the main fall. Take the main road north from the headquarters through the narrow, idyllic valley for 6km (beyond the village of Wang Prachan) and follow the sign to the right. After 700m, you'll find the main, lower fall set in screeching jungle. Climbing the path on the left side, you reach what seems like the top, with fine views of the steep, green peaks to the west. However, there's more: further up the stream are a series of gorgeous shady pools, where you can bathe and shower under the six-metre falls.

The most interesting **jungle walk** heads northeast from the headquarters, then west, approaching Yaroy waterfall from above after 16km – someone at headquarters might be free to guide you for a small fee. If you set out early and at a decent pace, it's possible to complete the walk and get back from Yaroy waterfall to headquarters in a day (a minimum of about 8hr). Along the way, you'll be rewarded with magnificent views that on a clear day stretch as far as the islands of Tarutao and Langkawi, you'll pass old elephant passages and mating playgrounds of argus pheasants, and you'll be unlucky not to spot at least boars, gibbons and bats.

Ko Tarutao National Marine Park

The unspoilt **KO TARUTAO NATIONAL MARINE PARK** is probably the most beautiful of all Thailand's accessible beach destinations. Occupying 1400 square kilometres of the Andaman Sea, the park covers 51 mostly uninhabited islands, of which three are easy to reach from the mainland and offer accommodation for visitors. Site of park headquarters, **Ko Tarutao** offers the widest variety of accommodation and things to do, while **Ko Adang** is much more low-key and a springboard to some excellent snorkelling. Home to a population of around seven hundred *chao ley* (see p.652), **Ko Lipe** is something of a frontier maverick, attracting ever more backpackers with one dazzling beach, ten or so private bungalow resorts and a rough-and-ready atmosphere.

The park's forests and seas support an incredible variety of **fauna**: langurs, crab-eating macaques and wild pigs are common on the islands, which also shelter several unique subspecies of squirrel, tree shrew and lesser mouse deer; among the hundred-plus bird species found here, reef egrets and hornbills are regularly seen, while white-bellied sea eagles, frigate birds and pied imperial pigeons are more rarely encountered; and the park is the habitat of about 25 percent of the world's tropical fish species, as well as marine mammals such as the dugong, sperm whale and dolphins. The islands are also home to dwindling populations of Olive Ridley, green, hawksbill and leatherback **turtles** (see box). Ao Sone is the main nesting beach on Ko Tarutao, especially in January; park rangers try to keep an eye on the nests and are generally happy to share the information with visitors. The park's delicate environment can bear the current level of tourism, but will be disastrously disturbed if proposals to set up regular boat connections with the highly developed Malaysian resort on Langkawi island, 8km from Ko Tarutao, are acted upon.

The park amenities on Tarutao and Adang are officially **closed** to tourists in the monsoon season from mid-May to mid-November (the exact dates vary from year to year). Ko Lipe claims to stay open year-round, though ferry services are reduced during the rains and there are times when storms can make the sea passage too hazardous for any ferries to attempt, especially in September and the first half of October. Accommodation is only likely to get full around the three New Years (Thai, Chinese and Western), when it's best to book national park rooms in advance in Bangkok (see p.46) or at the Pak Bara visitor centre.

In high season, **ferries** currently leave **Pak Bara** at 10.30am and 3pm daily for the roughly ninety-minute voyage to Ao Pante on Ko Tarutao (B200 one way); the 10.30am boat then continues on to Ko Adang (B450 from Pak Bara), 40km and about two hours west of Ko Tarutao, from where it's just a short longtail hop (B30) to any of the beaches on Ko Lipe. There's also a 1.30pm ferry via Ko Bulon Lae (see p.763) to Ko Adang (about 3hr in total; B450). At busy times, there may be additional ferries and speedboats. Call the

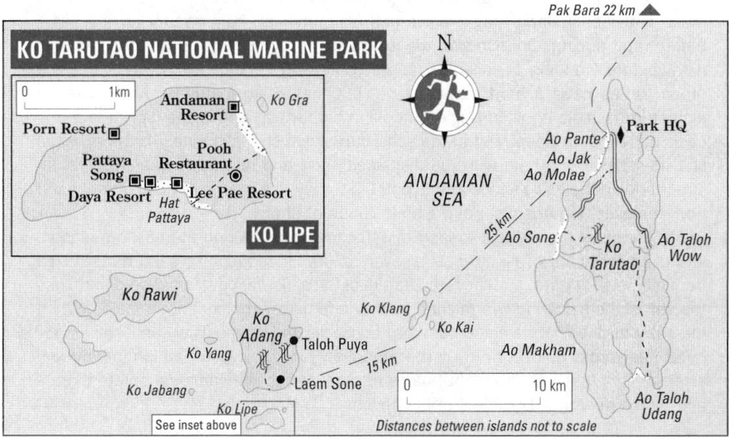

Pak Bara National Park Visitor Centre (☎074 783485 or 074 783597) or one of the ferry operators at the pier, such as Andrew Tour (☎074 783459 or 01 897 8482) or Adang Sea Tour (☎074 783368 or 01 609 2604, ⓔadang_sea_tour@hotmail.com), for up-to-date information. From **Thammalang** pier near Satun town (☎074 730511–2 or 074 711453), the 11am boat calls in at Ao Taloh Wow on the east side of Ko Tarutao (1hr; B250 one way; car to Ao Pante B40/person), before continuing to Ko Lipe (roughly 2hr; B500). Coming back, boats for Pak Bara leave Ko Adang at around 10am, calling in at Ko Tarutao or Bulon Lae; there's also an additional 9am sailing from Ao Pante on Ko Tarutao. The ferry for Thammalang via Ao Taloh Wow leaves Ko Lipe at 2pm. On any of these ferries you'll probably want to buy one-way tickets, so that you can vary

Turtles in Thailand

Thailand is home to four species of **marine turtle**: the green, the leatherback, the Olive Ridley and the hawksbill; the loggerhead turtle also once swam in Thai waters, until the constant plundering of its eggs rendered it locally extinct. Of the remaining four species, the **green turtle** is the commonest, a mottled brown creature named not for its appearance but for the colour of the soup made from its flesh. Adults weigh up to 180kg and are herbivorous, subsisting on sea grass, mangrove leaves and algae. The **leatherback**, encased in a distinctive ridged shell, is the world's largest turtle, weighing in at between 250kg and 550kg; it eats nothing but jellyfish. The small **Olive Ridley** weighs up to 50kg and feeds mainly on shrimps and crabs. Named for its peculiar beak-like mouth, the **hawksbill** is prized for its spectacular carapace (the sale of which was banned by CITES in 1992); it weighs up to 75kg and lives off a type of sea sponge.

The survival of the remaining four species is by no means assured – prized for their meat, their shells and their eggs, and the frequent victims of trawler nets, all types of marine turtle are now **endangered species**. The worldwide population of female turtles is thought to be as small as 70,000 to 75,000, and only around fifty percent of hatchlings reach adulthood. As a result, several of the Thai beaches most favoured by egg-laying turtles have been protected as **marine parks**, and some are equipped with special hatcheries. The breeding season usually starts in October or November and lasts until February, and the astonishing egg-laying ritual can be witnessed, under national park rangers' supervision, on Ko Surin Tai (p.652) and Ko Tarutao.

Broody female turtles of all species always return to the beach on which they were born to lay their **eggs**, often travelling hundreds of kilometres to get there – no mean feat, considering that females can wait anything from twenty to fifty years before reproducing. Once *in situ*, the turtles lurk in the water and wait for a cloudy night before wending their laborious way onto and up the beach: at 180kg, the green turtles have a hard enough time, but the 550kg leatherbacks endure an almost impossible uphill struggle. Choosing a spot well above the high-tide mark, each turtle digs a deep nest in the sand into which she lays ninety or more eggs; she then packs the hole with the displaced sand and returns to sea. Tears often stream down the turtle's face at this point, but they're a means of flushing out sand from the eyes and nostrils, not a manifestation of grief.

Many females come back to land three or four times during the nesting season, laying a new batch of ninety-plus at every sitting. Incubation of each batch takes from fifty to sixty days, and the temperature of the sand during this period determines the sex of the hatchling: warm sand results in females, cooler sand in males. When the **baby turtles** finally emerge from their eggshells, they immediately and instinctively head seawards, guided both by the moonlight on the water – which is why any artificial light, such as flashlight beams or camera flashes, can disorientate them – and by the downward gradient of the beach.

your route back to the mainland, but note that all the operators offer discounts on return tickets to discourage you from doing just that.

The prime **dive sites** in the park are to the west of Ko Tarutao, around Ko Klang, Ko Adang, Ko Rawi and Ko Dong, where encounters with reef and even whale sharks, dolphins, stingrays and turtles are not uncommon. These are now served by two reliable, foreign-run **dive shops** on Ko Lipe, which both offer day-trips to around twenty sites, as well as PADI courses from Openwater to Divemaster: Sabye Sports at *Porn Resort* (Ⓣ074 728026, or 074 734104 in Langu, Ⓦwww.sabye-sports.com); and the slightly cheaper Starfish Scuba at *Lee Pae Resort* (Ⓣ074 728089 or 01 896 9319; Ⓦwww.starfishscuba.com; see also p.763), who also have a custom-made yacht for live-aboards to sites such as Fifty-Mile Rock. **Snorkelling gear** can be rented at Pak Bara visitor centre or on Ko Adang for B50 per day, and is widely available from the private bungalow outfits or dive shops on Ko Lipe. For watery adventures above the surface, Paddle Asia, 9/71 Thanon Rasdanusorn, Phuket (Ⓣ076 240952, Ⓦwww.paddleasia.com), organizes four- to eight-day, small-group **sea-kayaking** trips around the Tarutao islands, costing US$580–1275 per person.

En route to Tarutao and Bulon Lae: Pak Bara

From Trang, Sukorn Beach Bungalows and Tours (see p.748) runs regular direct minibuses to **PAK BARA** in high season; otherwise you'll need to take a Satun-bound bus (2hr 30min) or a share-taxi (1hr 30min) to the inland town of **Langu** and change there to a red songthaew for the ten-kilometre hop to the port. Frequent buses and taxis **from Satun** make the fifty-kilometre trip to Langu. Coming **from Hat Yai**, you can catch a bus from the terminal or the clocktower all the way through to Pak Bara (6 daily; 2hr 30min), or one of the air-con minibuses that leave for Pak Bara roughly every hour from an office just up from the train station off Thanon Rattakan.

Accommodation is available in Pak Bara for people who miss the boats. The best choice is the friendly *Bara Guesthouse* (Ⓣ09 654 2801; ❷), about 500m before the pier, which offers large, tiled, concrete rooms with their own bathrooms in a garden running down to the sea. Another 500m or so from the pier and a short way upmarket, the motel-like *Grand Villa* (Ⓣ074 783499; ❹) provides air-con and TV in its smart, modern, en-suite rooms. There are no banks on the Tarutao islands or Bulon Lae, but Smooth Tours by the pier offers **currency-exchange** facilities, including traveller's cheques, as well as **Internet access**.

Ko Tarutao

The largest of the national park's islands, **KO TARUTAO** offers the greatest natural variety: mountains covered in semi-evergreen rainforest rise steeply to a high point of 700m; limestone caves and mangrove swamps dot the shoreline; and the west coast is lined with perfect beaches for most of its 26-kilometre length.

Boats dock at **Ao Pante**, on the northwestern side of the island, where the admission fee (B200) is collected and where the **park headquarters** (Ⓣ074 729002–3) is situated. Here you'll find the only shop on the island, selling basic supplies, as well as a visitor centre, a library and two restaurants. The **bungalows** (from B1000/bungalow sleeping four, or B600 for a twin room), which are spread over a large, quiet park behind the beach, are for the main part national park standard issue with cold-water bathrooms, but there are also some basic mattress-on-floor four-person rooms in **bamboo longhouses**, sharing bathrooms (B400/room). No mosquito nets are provided here, so come with your own or bring plenty of mosquito repellent. Two- and four-person **tents** can be rented for B100 and B200 respectively per night; campers with their own gear are charged B20 per person per night.

Behind the settlement, the steep, half-hour climb to **To-Boo cliff** is a must, especially at sunset, for the view of the surrounding islands and the crocodile's-head cape at the north end of the bay. A fun one-hour boat trip (B40/person; contact the visitor centre to book) can also be made near Ao Pante, up the canal which leads 2km inland from the pier, through a bird-filled mangrove swamp, to **Crocodile Cave** – where you're unlikely to see any of the big snappers, reported sightings being highly dubious.

A half-hour walk south from Ao Pante brings you to the two quiet bays of **Ao Jak** and **Ao Molae**, fringed by coconut palms and filled with fine white sand; the latter now sports some **bungalows** (from B800 for a twin room) and a small restaurant. Behind the house at the south end of Ao Molae, a road leads over the headland to **Ao Sone** (a 2hr walk from Ao Pante), where a pretty freshwater stream runs past the ranger station at the north end of the bay, making this a good place for peaceful camping – two-person **tents** can be rented for B100 per night and there's a simple restaurant. A favourite egg-laying site for sea turtles, the main part of the bay is a three-kilometre sweep of flawless sand, with a ninety-minute trail leading up to a waterfall in the middle and a mangrove swamp at the far south end.

On the east side of the island, **Ao Taloh Wow** is a rocky bay with a ranger station, restaurant and campsite, connected to Ao Pante by a twelve-kilometre road (B40/person in a car) through old rubber plantations and evergreen forest. If you have a tent, you might want to set off along the overgrown, five-hour trail beyond Taloh Wow, which cuts through the forest to **Ao Taloh Udang**, a sandy bay on the south side where you can set up camp. Here the remnants of a penal colony for political prisoners are just visible: the plotters of two failed coup attempts were imprisoned here in the 1930s before returning to high government posts. The ordinary convicts, who used to be imprisoned at Ao Taloh Wow, had a much harsher time, and during World War II, when supplies from the mainland dried up, prisoners and guards ganged together to turn to piracy. Pirates and smugglers still occasionally hide out in the Tarutao archipelago, but the main problem now is illegal trawlers fishing in national park waters.

Ko Adang

At **KO ADANG**, a wild, rugged island covered in tropical rainforest, the park station is at **Laem Sone** on the southern shore, where the beach is steep and narrow and backed by a thick canopy of pines. There are **rooms** in bamboo longhouses (B400/room sleeping four), as well as three-person rooms in bungalows (B300); two- or four-person **tents** can be rented (B100/B200/night), as well as comfortable two-person tents in thatched shelters by the beach (B200); or campers can pitch their own tents for B20 per person per night. There's a **restaurant** here, too.

The half-hour climb to **Sha-do** cliff on the steep slope above Laem Sone gives good views over Ko Lipe to the south. About 2km west along the coast from the park station, the small beach is lined with coconut palms and an abandoned customs house, behind which a twenty-minute trail leads to the small **Pirate Waterfall**. You can rent **longtail boats** (as well as snorks and masks) through the rangers for excellent snorkelling trips to nearby islands such as Ko Rawi and Ko Jabang (B1000 for 6–8 people).

Ko Lipe

KO LIPE, 2km south of Adang, makes a busy contrast to the other islands. A small, flat triangle, it's covered in coconut plantations and inhabited by *chao ley*, with shops, a school and a health centre in the village on the eastern side. By rights, such a settlement should not be allowed within the national park boundaries, but the *chao ley* on Lipe are well entrenched: Satun's governor forced the community to move here from Phuket and Ko Lanta between the world wars, to reinforce the island's Thai character and prevent the British rulers of Malaya from laying claim to it. Relations with park rangers have been strained in the past, but the park authority is working on a scheme to demarcate village and national park areas, which will hopefully go some way towards both resolving the tensions and preserving some of the island's natural beauty.

There are a growing number of **bungalow** outfits on the island, generally not very well designed and mostly operated by enterprising newcomers from the mainland rather than the indigenous *chao ley*. Several can be found on **Hat Pattaya**, the prettiest beach on Ko Lipe, a shining crescent of squeaky-soft white sand, 1km from the village on the south side of the island; it also has a good offshore reef to explore. Towards the western end of the beach, the slightly institutional *Lee Pae Resort* (Ⓣ074 724336 or 074 723804; ❸–❻) has dozens of serried bungalows, ranging from en-suite bamboo huts to the most expensive beds on the island, concrete cottages with mosquito screens and large glass doors facing the beach. At the far west end of the beach, the Italian-run *Pattaya Song* (Ⓣ074 728034, Ⓦwww.pattayasongresort.com; ❷–❹) has a lovely location: basic, en-suite bamboo or concrete bungalows are strung out behind the beach or up on the steep hillside with great views of the bay. Fishing and snorkelling trips can be arranged, and **sea-kayaks** can be rented for B500 per day. *Daya Resort* next door (Ⓣ074 728030; ❸–❹) offers concrete rooms or bamboo-and-thatch bungalows, some in a great position right on the beach. Their **restaurant** makes itself very popular with candlelit tables on the beach and excellent grub, notably grilled seafood and southern Thai curries. A few beach bars are thinly scattered along Hat Pattaya, while midway along the path that connects the eastern end of Hat Pattaya to the village, *Pooh's* is a popular bar-restaurant-travel agent, serving good Thai and Western food, including a choice of breakfasts and coffees, and providing **Internet** access.

On the northwest side of the island, what's sometimes called "Sunset Beach" is not as postcard-perfect as Hat Pattaya, but *Porn* here is probably the most attractive resort on the island: in a pleasant setting under the trees on the beach are well-kept thatched, bamboo bungalows with verandas and en-suite bathrooms (❸). On the east coast, *Andaman Resort* (Ⓣ074 729200; ❷–❺) has some rock-bottom shacks with shared bathrooms, as well as en-suite bamboo bungalows strung out on a long stretch of sand under casuarina trees and concrete rooms. The beach on this side of the island is nowhere near as nice as Hat Pattaya, though there's rewarding water and a beautiful coral reef around tiny **Ko Gra**, 200m out to sea from the village.

Ko Bulon Lae

The scenery at tiny **KO BULON LAE**, 20km west of Pak Bara, isn't as beautiful as that generally found in Ko Tarutao National Park to the south, but it's not at all bad: a two-kilometre strip of fine white sand runs the length of the casuarina-lined east coast, while *chao ley* fishermen make their ramshackle homes in the tight coves of the rest of the island. A reef of curiously shaped hard coral closely parallels the eastern beach, while **White Rock** to the south of the island has beautifully coloured soft coral and equally dazzling fish. **Snorkelling** gear, as well as boats for trips to White Rock and surrounding islands (B1500/boat seating up to 8 people), can be rented at *Pansand*, the island's largest and best **resort** (ⓣ01 397 0802, ⓔpansand@cscoms.com; ❻–❽), where large, smart, white clapboard cottages come with verandas, cold-water bathrooms and plenty of room to breathe. On the beach side of the shady, well-tended grounds, there's a sociable restaurant serving up good seafood and other Thai dishes; Internet access and massages are also available. To book a room here or find out about boats in the off season, contact the resort directly or First Andaman Travel at 82–84 Thanon Wisetkul in Trang (ⓣ075 218035, ⓕ075 211010). The best of several budget resorts is friendly *Bulone* (ⓣ01 897 9084; ❷–❺), a huge grassy compound under the casuarinas at the north end of the main beach. Choose between airy, bamboo-walled bungalows and larger, white, clapboard affairs, with or without their own bathrooms, and be sure to eat at the restaurant, which features a small selection of tasty Italian faves. On the north coast about ten minutes' walk from *Pansand*, *Bulon Viewpoint* (ⓣ074 728005–6, ⓔbulon_view_satun@hotmail.com; ❷–❺) doesn't quite live up to its name. In a shady garden sloping steeply down to a beach bar and restaurant, simple rooms share equally basic bathrooms, while the large, sturdy, en-suite bungalows come with verandas and chairs.

In high season, **ferries** for Ko Bulon Lae leave Pak Bara (see p.761) daily at about 1.30pm and 3pm (1h–1hr 30min; B200 one way, B300 return); the former continues to Ko Adang (2hr; B300 one way). Boats return from Bulon Lae to Pak Bara at 9am and noon. Services are reduced, sometimes to nothing, during the monsoon season; contact *Pansand* or First Andaman Travel for the latest information.

Hat Yai

HAT YAI, the transport axis of the region, was given a dose of instant American-style modernization in the 1950s, since when it has commercially usurped its own provincial capital, Songkhla. The resulting concrete mess, reminiscent of Bangkok without the interesting bits, attracts over a million tourists a year, nearly all of them Malaysians and Singaporeans who nip across the border to shop and get laid. If the concrete and the sleaze turn you off a protracted stay, remember that Songkhla (see p.768) is only 25km away.

Hat Yai is one of the south's major centres for **bullfighting**, which in its Thai version involves bull tussling with bull, the winner being the one that forces the other to retreat. Fights can last anything from a few seconds to half an hour, in which case the frantic betting of the audience becomes more interesting than the deadlock in the ring. Every weekend, day-long competitions, beginning around 10.30am and featuring thirty or so bouts, are held at various points around the south. Admission is usually B100, and it's best to get there in the early afternoon as the big fights, involving betting of up to one million baht, are lower down the card. It's worth checking with TAT for the latest information but, at the time of writing, the most convenient event is at Noen Khum Thong, 10km out of Hat Yai on the way to the airport, on the first Saturday of the month (charter a songthaew to get there).

Practicalities

On any extended tour of the south you are bound to end up in Hat Yai, and you may as well take the opportunity to call in at the **TAT** office for Songkhla

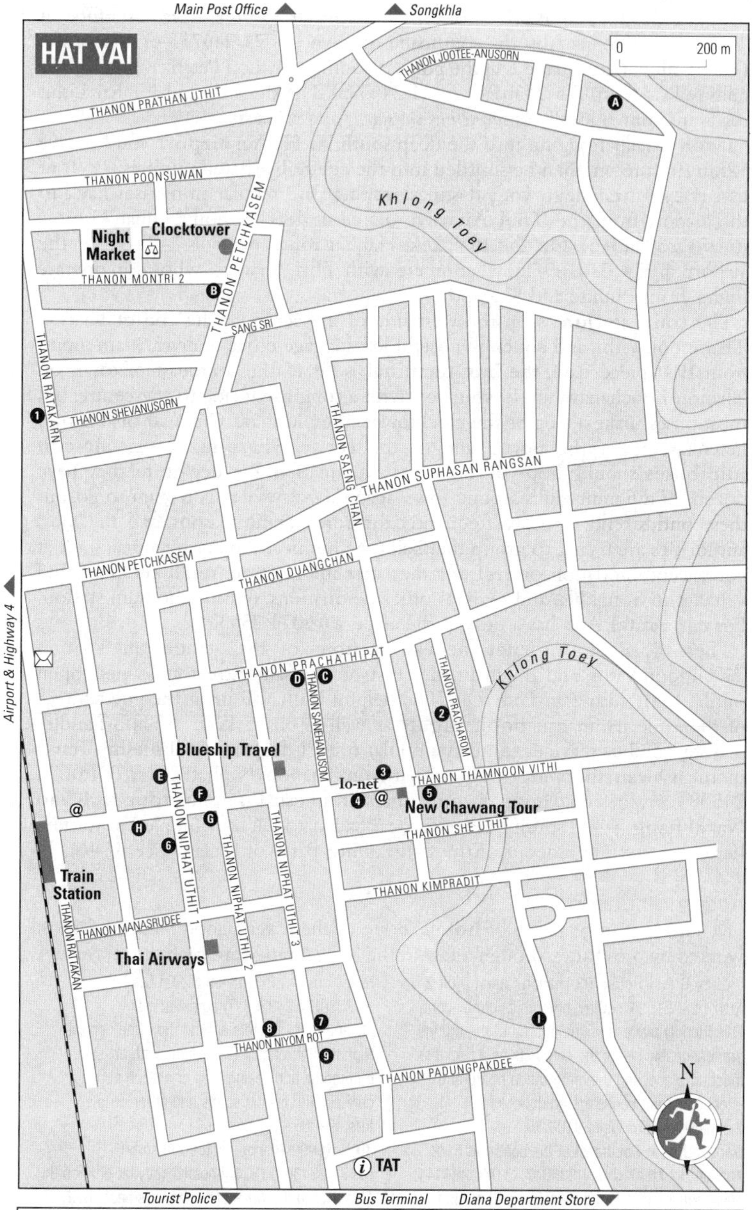

ACCOMMODATION				RESTAURANTS AND BARS			
Cathay Guest House	G	Lee Gardens Plaza Hotel	C	Corazons	2	Pee Lek	7
Garden Home Hotel	I	Louise Guest House	H	Jye Beer and Bakery	1	Post Laser Disc	4
Hok Chin Hin Hotel	E	Novotel Central Sukontha Hotel	D	Mae Thip	9	Sugar Rock	3
JB Hotel	A	Sorasilp Guest House	B	Muslim O-Cha	6	West Side Saloon	5
Laem Thong Hotel	F			Nakorn Nai	8		

and Satun provinces at 1/1 Soi 2, Thanon Niphat Uthit 3 (daily 8.30am–4.30pm; ⓣ074 243747, ⓔtatsgkhl@tat.or.th). The **tourist police** have an office at Thanon Sripoovanart on the south side of town (ⓣ074 246733 or 1155), and the **immigration office** is at the police station on Thanon Petchkasem near the railway bridge (ⓣ074 243019 or 074 246333). The three central Niphat Uthit roads are known locally as *sai neung*, *sai sawng* and *sai saam*.

If you're leap-frogging into the deep south via Hat Yai **airport** you'll arrive 12km from town, then be shuttled into the centre by shared minibus (B60) or taxi (B240) straight to your destination; there are regular minibuses back to the airport from the **Thai Airways office** at 180 Thanon Niphat Uthit 1 (ⓣ074 230445–6). On the Bangkok–Hat Yai route, no-frills 1-2-Go (at the airport ⓣ074 240169) now compete with Thai Airways, who also operate flights from Phuket and Singapore.

The **train station** is on the west side of the centre at the end of Thanon Thamnoon Vithi, and contains a useful left-luggage office (daily 5.30am–6pm; from B10/piece/day); the **bus terminal** is far to the southeast of town on Thanon Kanchanawanit, leaving you with a songthaew ride to the centre, but most buses make a stop at the clocktower (the old Plaza Cinema) on Thanon Petchkasem, on the north side of the centre. **Share-taxis** and **air-con minibuses** should drop you off at your destination. For departure, they have dozens of different ranks around town according to where you want to go, but these stands tend to move frequently for bureaucratic reasons, and the local authorities are trying to group them all together near the bus terminal – ask at your accommodation or TAT for the latest information. You'll certainly find vehicles to Songkhla, and perhaps other destinations, outside the train station. For **car rental**, Avis has a desk at the airport (ⓣ074 250321).

There's central **Internet access** in front of the station on Thanon Thamnoon Vithi, and much further east on the same street at Io-net (open until 11pm), near *Post Laser Disc*. The helpful Cathay Tour, at the guest house of the same name, can **book flights** as well as bus tickets, and also handles private minibus services to many popular tourist destinations. Blueship Travel in the Odean shopping mall car park on Thanon Niphat Uthit 3 (ⓣ074 245086, ⓔblueship@hotmail.com) offers an unusual minibus **tour** to **Khao Namkhang**, 80km south of Hat Yai near Sadao, to see the complex of tunnels here, an erstwhile hideout of the Communist Party of Malaya (see p.746).

Accommodation

Hat Yai has a huge range of **hotels**, none of them very good value and most worked by prostitutes, though a few in the budget range are geared to travellers.

Cathay Guest House 93 Thanon Niphat Uthit 2 ⓣ074 243815, ⓔcathay_ontours@hotmail.com. This friendly place is falling apart, but the fittings are reasonably clean; the café acts as a sociable meeting-place, and the information board and guest comment books are guidebooks in themselves. Dorm beds B100. ❷

Garden Home Southeast of the centre at 51/2 Thanon Hoi Mook ⓣ074 236047, ⓕ074 234444. This pastiche of a grand mansion built around a plant-filled courtyard offers very good value; the large bedrooms show some sense of decor and have a good range of facilities (air-con, hot water, TV and mini-bar). ❹

Hok Chin Hin 87 Thanon Niphat Uthit 1 ⓣ & ⓕ074 243258. The best of many cheap Chinese hotels around the three central Niphat Uthit roads. Clean rooms with en-suite bathrooms and ceiling fans or air-con above a café serving noodle soups and other simple fare. ❷–❸

JB Hotel 99 Thanon Jootee-Anusorn ⓣ074 234300–18, ⓔjbhotel@hadyailoxinfo.co.th. This rival to the *Novotel* as Hat Yai's best hotel is less handily placed, on the edge of the town centre, but accordingly has more room to breathe, with attractive grounds and a large outdoor swimming pool. ❽

Crossing into Malaysia from Hat Yai

Hat Yai is only 50km north of the border with **Malaysia**. The fastest way of getting across here (4–5hr) is to take a **share-taxi** (B250) or a slightly more comfortable **air-con minibus** (B220) to Penang (where you can renew your visa at the Thai consulate). Taxis congregate every morning on Thanon Niphat Uthit 1, while tickets for the minibuses can be bought at Hat Yai travel agents, such as Cathay Tour, underneath the eponymous guest house at 93 Thanon Niphat Uthit 2 (ⓣ074 235044), or New Chawang Tour, 131/1 Thanon Thamnoon Vithi (ⓣ074 233016). These agents also handle minibuses to Sungai Kolok (3hr; B160; see p.776) and Butterworth (4–5hr; B220), and VIP buses to Kuala Lumpur (12hr; B350–400) and Singapore (18hr; B600).

The least expensive but most time-consuming method is to catch a **bus** straight down Highway 4 to Dan Nok (1hr 30min), walk 500m across the frontier to Bukit Kayu Hitam, and take a bus down Malaysia's North–South Highway to Alor Setar (about 1hr) and beyond.

Most comfortable are the **trains**, though they're not very frequent: seven a day run from Hat Yai to Sungai Kolok on the east-coast border, and one a day heads to Butterworth (for the ferry to Penang or trains on to Kuala Lumpur and Singapore) via the frontier at Padang Besar.

Laem Thong 46 Thanon Thamnoon Vithi ⓣ074 352301–5, ⓔlaemthonghotel@yahoo.com. Large and efficient Chinese-run place, with a choice of fan-cooled or air-con rooms, most with hot water. ❸–❹

Lee Gardens Plaza Hotel 29 Thanon Prachatipat ⓣ074 261111, ⓦwww.leeplaza.com. Characterless but good-value and central upmarket option with great views of the city from its comfortable rooms. Facilities include a pool and a 33rd-floor panoramic restaurant. ❻

Louise Guest House By the train station at 21–23 Thanon Thamnoon Vithi ⓣ074 220966. Small, clean Chinese-run place, with fan or air-con rooms all with en-suite, cold-water bathrooms. ❸–❹

Novotel Central Sukontha Hotel 3 Thanon Sanehanusom ⓣ074 352222, ⓦwww.centralhotelsresorts.com. Luxury hotel in a handy central location next to the Central Department Store, with fitness centre, sauna and swimming pool. Offers great views over the city from its four top-notch restaurants. ❾

Sorasilp Guest House 251/7–8 Thanon Petchkasem ⓣ074 232635. On the upper floors of a modern building, with some air-con, beside the clocktower and old Plaza Cinema. Friendly and clean, though a little noisy. ❷–❸

Eating, drinking and nightlife

Hat Yai's **restaurants**, a selection of which are listed below, offer a choice of Thai, Chinese, Muslim and Western food, while the sprawling **night market**, behind the clocktower around Thanon Montri 2, has something for everyone: seafood and beer, Thai curries, deep-fried chicken and the Muslim speciality *khao neua daeng*, tender cured beef in a sweet red sauce.

For a quiet **drink**, head for *Sugar Rock*, 114 Thanon Thamnoon Vithi, a pleasant café-bar with low-volume Western music. Live bands play at *Post Laser Disc* (see below); *West Side Saloon*, on the same road at no. 135/5, a typical Wild West-style place playing Thai pop and "songs for life"; and *Corazons Latin Pub and Restaurant*, a slightly more sophisticated spot at 41 Thanon Pracharom, for jazzy pop and Latin. To get away from it all, the mini-theatres at Diana department store, on Thanon Sripoovanart on the south side of the centre, and at Lee Gardens Plaza underneath the hotel of the same name, show Western **movies** with English soundtracks.

Jye Beer and Bakery Thanon Ratakarn. Good for a bit of a splurge – they do posh Thai and American food in a cosy, rustic atmosphere. Moderate to expensive.

Mae Thip 187/4 Niphat Uthit 3. Good reliable Thai place, popular with locals; also does a few Malay dishes, including satay. Inexpensive to moderate.

Muslim O-Cha 117 Niphat Uthit 1. A simple, clean restaurant that serves small portions of curried chicken and rice, *roti* for breakfast, and other inexpensive Muslim dishes. Daily until 8pm. Inexpensive.

Nakorn Nai 166/7 Niphat Uthit 2. Cool and comfortable, this is a reasonable place for all-day breakfasts, Western food and some interesting Thai dishes. Daily except Wed 8am–8pm. Moderate.

Pee Lek 59 185/4 Niphat Uthit 3, at the junction with Thanon Niyom Rot. This welcoming place, with outdoor seating and an air-con room, gets the thumbs-up for Thai-style seafood – try *gataa rawn*, a sizzling dish of mixed marine life. Moderate.

Post Laser Disc Thanon Thamnoon Vithi. Popular with farangs, this comfy, spacious restaurant-bar has a large Thai and Western menu, cheap drinks, big-screen sport and live music every night. Moderate.

Songkhla and around

Known as the "big town of two seas" because it sits on a north-pointing peninsula between the Gulf of Thailand and the **Thale Sap** lagoon, **SONGKHLA** provides a sharp contrast to Hat Yai. A small, sophisticated provincial capital, it retains many historic buildings – such as the elegant Wat Matchimawat and the Chinese mansion that now houses the National Museum – and its broad main streets are planted with soothing greenery. With some fine restaurants and excellent accommodation, and its proximity to the wonderful Southern Folklore Museum at Ko Yo, Songkhla makes a stimulating place in which to hole up for a few days.

The settlement was originally sited on the north side of the mouth of the Thale Sap, where a deepwater port has now been built, and flourished as a **trading port** from the eighth century onwards. The shift across the water came after 1769, when a Chinese merchant named Yieng Hao was granted permission by the Thai ruler, Taksin, to collect swallows' nests from Ko Si Ko Ha – now part of Khu Khut Waterbird Park. Having made a packet from selling them for their culinary and medicinal properties, he was made governor of Songkhla by Taksin and established the city on its present site. For seven generations the **Na Songkhla dynasty** he founded kept the governorship in the family, overseeing the construction of many of the buildings you see today. The town is now an unhurried administrative centre, which maintains a strong central Thai feel – most of the province's Muslim population live in the hinterland.

The Town

The town which the Na Songkhlas built has expanded to fill the headland, and makes a great place for strolling around. The western side, where the town first developed, shelters a fishing port which presents a vivid, smelly scene in the mornings. Two abrupt hills – **Khao Tung Kuan** and the smaller **Khao Noi** – border the north side of the centre, while in the heart of town lie the main tourist attractions, the **National Museum** and the extravagantly decorated **Wat Matchimawat**. Sitting on the fringe of town at the southern end of **Hat Samila** – the 8km of beach along the eastern shore – **Khao Saen** is an impoverished but vibrant fishing village, whose multi-coloured boats provide Songkhla's most hackneyed postcard image. If you're about on a Sunday, don't miss the hectic **morning market** that fills the streets around the *Uan Khao Tom* restaurant and the old train station.

Khao Tung Kuan, Laem Sai Fort and Hat Samila

To get your bearings, climb up **Khao Tung Kuan** at the northwestern end of town. From Thanon Laem Sai, on the western side of the hill, steps rise past what looks like a red-brick Wendy house – Rama V ordered the pavilion to be built at the height of his westernization programme, but the local artisans clearly couldn't get their heads round the monarch's conception. From the chedi at the top of the hill, you can look south over the town and the fishing port, and west over the Thale Sap to the island of Ko Yo.

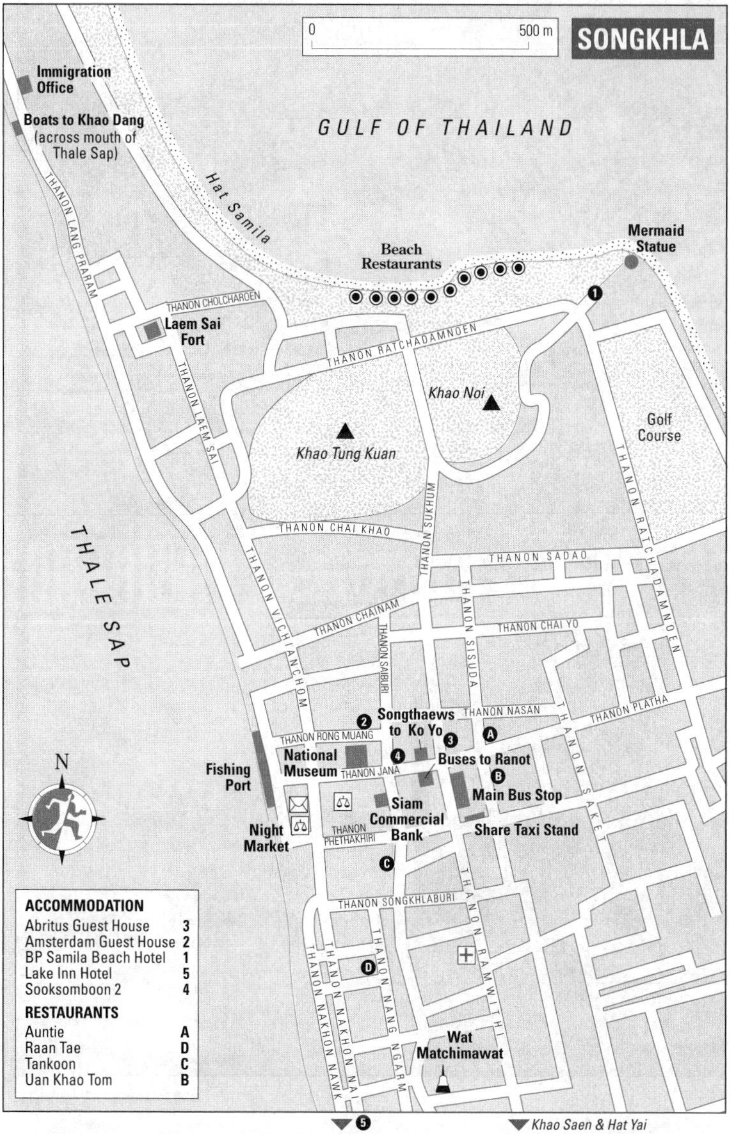

△Songkhla National Museum

Further up Thanon Laem Sai, you can visit **Laem Sai Fort**, with its low walls and cannon, which was built by the French in the seventeenth century, when they held favour with the kings of Ayutthaya. Just beyond lies palm-fringed **Hat Samila**; its famous **mermaid statue**, the symbol of the town, lies a few hundred metres east along the beach in front of the *BP Samila Beach Hotel*.Various bits of **watersports** equipment, such as jet-skis, banana boats and windsurfers, are available along Hat Samila, including at the Navy watersports club near Thanon Thalayluang, roughly around the midpoint of the beach.

Songkhla National Museum

The **Songkhla National Museum** (Wed–Sun 9am–noon & 1–4pm; B30; Ⓦwww.thailandmuseum.com) on Thanon Jana, the main east–west street, is worth a visit for its architecture alone. Built in 1878 in south Chinese style and recently renovated to its original condition, this graceful mansion was first the residence of the governor of Songkhla and Nakhon, then the city hall, and later the local poorhouse before being converted into a museum in the 1970s. Its best side faces the garden at the back: from here you can see how the ornamental staircases and the roof were constructed in shapely curves to disorientate straight-flying evil spirits.

A jumble of folk exhibits, such as *nang thalung* puppets and agricultural implements, are displayed in the garden, while inside the wildly diverse collection includes well-preserved examples of Ban Chiang pottery, early Hindu statues and Mahayana Buddhist images from the Srivijaya period, and a selection of beautiful Chinese ceramics. Upstairs everything is upstaged by overblown Chinese and Thai furniture, all lacquer and mother-of-pearl and bas-relief carving, and the mansion's original doors, carved with extravagant dragons.

Wat Matchimawat

From the museum, you can explore the atmospheric old streets of Nakhon Nai and Nakhon Nawk, which show European influence in their colonnaded pavements and crumbling stucco, on your way south to **Wat Matchimawat**, a grand, attention-grabbing affair set in ornamental grounds on Thanon Saiburi. What stands out most of all is the bot, a florid mixture of Chinese and Thai styles, which was apparently modelled on Wat Phra Kaeo in Bangkok. Fetching stone bas-reliefs decorate the low walls around the bot, depicting leafy scenes from the *Romance of the Three Kingdoms*, a Chinese historical novel which served as a handbook of manners and morals in the middle of the nineteenth century, when the temple was built. Every centimetre of the lofty interior is covered with colourful *Jataka* murals, telling of the previous lives of the Buddha, mixed in with vivacious tableaux of nineteenth-century Songkhla life.The bot is usually locked, but you can get the key from the adjacent informal museum (daily, hours irregular, but generally 1–4pm or later; free), which is cluttered with ceramics, votive tablets and statues of Hindu gods from the province, including an elephant-headed Ganesh in stone that's said to be over a thousand years old and is still much revered with gold leaf. Behind the museum in the temple's northwest corner is the interesting Sala Reusii, a heavily restored, red-brick, open-sided pavilion that's decorated with colourful murals of hermits displaying yoga postures.

Khao Saen

To see the best of the Muslim shanty village of **Khao Saen**, set against a rocky headland on the southern edge of Songkhla's tide of development, visit in the late afternoon, when the boisterous fish market is in full swing. Songthaews from Thanon Platha make the trip in fifteen minutes. The crowded, rotting shacks of the village make a bleak contrast with the objects for which Khao Saen is most celebrated – its decorated prawn-fishing vessels. Drawn up in rows on the beach, these immaculate small boats have dragon prows wrapped in lucky garlands and hulls brightly painted with flags and intricate artwork. These pictures, which mostly depict mosques and idyllic landscapes, are the work of an artist at Saiburi, further down the coast (see p.777), and cost each fisherman a month's income.

Practicalities

Most **buses** arrive at the major junction of Thanon Ramwithi with Jana and Platha roads, though Bangkok services use the terminal at the south end of Thanon Nakhon Nawk. People usually come here straight from Hat Yai, 25km southwest, but buses also run direct from Nakhon. **Taxis** for these towns and places further afield congregate on the south side of the main bus stop, just off Thanon Ramwithi. If the heat gets to you as you stroll around town, catch one of the **songthaews** (B7) or motorbike taxis (B10–20) which cruise the streets. **Mountain bikes** can be rented at the *Abritus Guest House* for B100 per day, and they also have some motorbikes available (B200/day), useful for getting to Songkhla Zoo and Ko Yo. There are several places for **Internet access** around town, including Dot Com next door to the *Abritus*.

On dry season weekends, roughly from November to May and usually at about 5pm, various outdoor **performances** – *manohra* (the southern Thai dance-drama), *nang thalung* puppet shows, classical dance and pop music – are staged at the eastern end of Thanon Thalayluang, near the midpoint of the beach (contact TAT in Hat Yai for details).

Accommodation

Budget travellers are spoilt for choice when it comes to **places to stay** in Songkhla, with a couple of excellent guest houses. For more luxury, the recently refurbished *BP Samila Beach* provides all the creature comforts.

Abritus Guest House 28/16 Thanon Ramwithi ⓣ074 326047, ⓔabritus_th@yahoo.com. Scores high on friendliness; the Bulgarian family who run the place are especially welcoming, and a mine of information on the town. Huge clean rooms with ample shared bathrooms are set above a popular café which dishes up great breakfasts – including home-made yoghurt and filter coffee – as well as salads, omelettes and Bulgarian meatballs. Internet access. ❷

Amsterdam Guest House 15/3 Thanon Rong Muang, on the north side of the museum ⓣ074 314890, ⓕ074 442444. Homely vine-covered place whose rooms, with shared bathrooms, are bright and clean; there's cable TV, and a relaxed downstairs seating area that's well equipped with comfy sofas monopolized by dozing cats. Outside is a small shady patio, and next door an excellent little restaurant serves up beer and fruit juices alongside the Thai and Western food. ❷

BP Samila Beach Hotel 8 Thanon Ratchadamnoen ⓣ074 440222, ⓦwww.bphotelsgroup.com. The best hotel in town, with outdoor swimming pool, a fitness room and the beach right on its doorstep; rooms come with sea or "mountain" view, and breakfast. ❽

Lake Inn Hotel 301 Thanon Nakhon Nawk ⓣ074 321441–2, ⓔlakeinn@hotmail.com. Good hotel 500m south of the centre close by the Thale Sap lagoon; half of the tastefully furnished rooms face the lake and there's a good ground-floor restaurant, also with views of the water. ❹

Sooksomboon 2 18 Thanon Saiburi ⓣ074 323809–10, ⓕ074 321406. Comfortable, modern air-con rooms, all with hot-water bathrooms and TVs, or plain fan rooms with cold-water en-suites in the cavernous old wooden block next door, at this good-value, centrally located hotel. ❷–❹

Eating and drinking

For daytime eating, pull up a deckchair and relax at the shaded beach **restaurants** which congregate at the northern end of Thanon Sukhum and at the east end of Thanon Platha; or saunter down to the quiet and clean *Tankoon Restaurant*, 25/1 Thanon Saiburi (closes 8pm), where you can relax with a beer and some tasty Thai fodder in its peaceful leafy interior; the attached **coffee shop**, *Coffeebucks*, offers delicious speciality coffees and Internet access. Songkhla's most famous restaurant, *Raan Tae*, at 85 Thanon Nang Ngarm (closes 8pm), is spotlessly clean and justly popular, serving especially good seafood – try *sator*, a green vegetable that's a local speciality, served sweet-and-sour with prawns and onions. All manner of Thai dishes, including fish, prawns and the rice porridge of its name, are served at the cheap and popular *Uan Khao Tom*, Talat Rot Fai, where you can relax outdoors on a quiet street (opens 6pm). The **night market**, south of the post office on Thanon Nakhon Nai, is the place for budget-conscious travellers. A sprinkling of westernized **bars** and restaurants, such as *Auntie*, 62/1 Thanon Sisuda, cater to the good ole boys who work on the offshore oil rigs, with American-style food and ice-cold beers, at a price.

Around Songkhla

The excellent **Thaksin Folklore Museum** on Ko Yo is the biggest draw outside Songkhla; a visit there is best combined with lunch at one of the island's renowned restaurants. Slightly further afield, the **Khu Khut Wildlife Sanctuary** is similar to, though not quite as impressive as, Thale Noi Waterbird Park (see p.747) near Phatthalung.

Off the coast, **Ko Losin**, 130km east of Songkhla, offers superb **diving** on a coral-encrusted rock beneath the surface. Visibility is generally excellent, and some of the reef's better sites, along with its inhabitants – blacktip reef sharks, giant manta rays, whale sharks and turtles – can be viewed between 5m and 20m down. Starfish Scuba, at 166 Thanon Phatthalung in Songkhla (Ⓣ074 442170 or 09 466 1130; see also p.761; Ⓦwww.starfishscuba.com), runs live-aboard charters to the island between May and September.

Ko Yo

KO YO, the small island in the Thale Sap to the west of Songkhla, has long been a destination for day-trippers, and the road link with the land on both sides of the lagoon has accelerated the transformation of **Ban Nok** – the island's main settlement – into a souvenir market. Here you'll find durian cakes, an amazing variety of dried and treated seafood, and the high-quality fabrics – mostly cotton, but sometimes with small amounts of silk woven in – for which Ko Yo is famous; if you're around in the morning, take a left fork off the main road in the village to watch the weavers at work in their houses.

The best way of getting there **from Songkhla** is by songthaew (B10), which set off at regular intervals from Thanon Jana, via the main bus stop on Thanon Ramwithi. If you're coming **from Hat Yai**, there's no need to go into Songkhla first: take a Songkhla-bound bus or minibus but get off on the edge of the suburbs at the junction with Highway 408, and catch a songthaew across the bridge to Ko Yo.

The chief appeal of Ko Yo is the Institute for Southern Thai Studies' **Thaksin Folklore Museum** (daily 8.30am–5pm; B60; Ⓦwww.tsu.ac.th), which sprawls over the hillside on the far tip of the island just before the northern bridge. Affording stunning views over the water to Songkhla and of the fishing villages on the western side of the island, the park is strewn with all kinds of boats and wooden reproductions of traditional southern houses, in which much of the collection is neatly set out. The exhibits, such as the shadow-puppet paraphernalia and the *kris* – long knives with intricately carved handles and sheaths – show the strong influences of Malaysia and Indonesia on southern Thailand. Also on show are the elaborate dance costumes for the *manohra*, but probably the most fascinating objects are the *lek kood*, or coconut scrapers, which are set into seat-blocks carved into an offbeat variety of shapes – rabbits, elephants, phalluses, beauty queens. The museum's **shop** has the island's finest selection of fabrics, and there's a pleasant **café** with great views over the museum rooftops to the fishing villages below. Better still are the panoramas from the top of the **viewing tower** in the museum courtyard. A range of **accommodation** is also available, from basic rooms with shared bathrooms to red-brick kiln-like dwellings with air-con, en-suite bathrooms and panoramic views of the Thale Sap (Ⓣ074 331184–9; ❸–❺).

Ko Yo is renowned for its excellent seafood **restaurants**, which line the main road with great views east over the lake towards Songkhla. Alternatively, follow the access road to the museum west around the island for 500m to reach a couple of simpler places right on the water's edge – *Ko Khaeng* and *Korn Thong* – both with great seafood. Or you could ignore your seaside location and head for *Pa Nu*, a foodstall with tables shaded by large trees, just off the main road in the centre of the village. Auntie Nu is justly famous far and wide for her delicious southern Thai speciality, *khao yam*, a mild salad-like dish of rice (marinated black with morente leaves), shredded coconut, shrimp paste and vegetables.

Khu Khut Wildlife Sanctuary

About 40km up Highway 408 from Songkhla near the village of Sathing Phra, a left turn by the police station leads after 2km to the headquarters of **Khu Khut Wildlife Sanctuary**, a conservation area on the Thale Luang where over 140 species of mostly migratory birds are found. Buses from Songkhla (via Ko Yo) bound for Ranot will only drop you off at the junction, from where you can take a motorbike taxi (B20) to reach the park. The best time of year to visit is from November to March, and the birds are at their most active in the early morning and late afternoon. A longtail trip on the shallow lake, weaving between water reeds and crayfish traps to view the birds, costs B250 for about an hour.

Songkhla Zoo

Songkhla's newest attraction, **Songkhla Zoo** (daily 9am–6pm; B30; Ⓦwww.zoothailand.org), home to favourites such as tigers, elephants and chimpanzees and an important breeding centre for tapirs, is situated some 15km south of the city on Highway 408, the Songkhla–Nathawi road. It's a huge place, spread over eleven square kilometres of hills, so making your way around it can be rather tiring (there are plans for some kind of tourist train). The benefit of the elevation, however, especially from the treehouse viewing tower, is the great view it gives over Songkhla and the sea. The easiest way to get here is to rent a motorbike from the *Abritus Guest House* in Songkhla; this gives the added advantage of a means of transport around the zoo itself (for an additional B10 entry fee). Alternatively, take a Chana-bound songthaew from the main bus stop on Thanon Ramwithi (B10).

Narathiwat and around

Capital of one of the least developed provinces of the deep south, **Narathiwat** nevertheless offers a decent range of hotels and restaurants, and the opportunity of a day at the beach and an excursion to the beautiful **Wat Chonthara Sing He**, 30km to the south in Tak Bai. Its most famous sight, however, the **Phra Buddha Taksin Mingmongkon**, touted near and far as the largest seated

Buddha in Thailand, impresses only by virtue of its vital statistics (it's 24m high, 17m knee to knee). For information on the security situation in Narathiwat at the time of writing, see p.746.

Narathiwat town

NARATHIWAT is set on the west bank of the slowly curving Bang Nara River, at the mouth of which, just five minutes' walk north of the centre, sits a shanty fishing village fronted by *korlae* boats (see p.777). Just beyond the fishing village, peaceful deckchair restaurants overlook **Hat Narathat**, a beach too dangerous for swimming. Fortunately, the best beach in the area, boulder-strewn **Ao Manao**, 3km south towards Tak Bai, then 3km left down a paved side road, is within easy reach by motorbike taxi. Known as "lemon bay" due to the long, gentle curve of its coastline, this beautiful stretch is lined with trees and dotted with seafood restaurants.

It's worth getting up early on a Friday morning for the bustling, colourful **market** that sprawls over the north end of Thanon Puphapugdee (the main river-bank road). Local batiks are sold here, as well as all kinds of food, including the local fish sauce, **nam budu**: all around the region you'll see hundreds of concrete and ceramic pots laid out along the roadside containing the fermenting fish that goes to make the paste. Narathiwat's annual **Khong Dee Muang Nara** festival takes place in September every year, coinciding with the royal family's one-month visit to the nearby Taksin Ratchaniwet palace (see p.778); the festival involves *korlae* boat racing along the river, as well as a major **dove-cooing** contest. The breeding of luck-bringing Java doves is an obsession among the Muslim population of the south, where most houses have a bird cage outside and many villages feature fields of metal poles six to eight metres tall on which to hang the cages during the competition season, which is normally March and April. The birds are judged on the pitch, melody and volume of their cooing and on their appearance; the most musical specimens can change hands for as much as two million baht.

Practicalities

Narathiwat's two main streets run north–south: Thanon Puphapugdee and the inland Thanon Pichit Bamrung, where most **buses** make a stop to the south of the clocktower – though the bus terminal is on the southwest side of town. **Air-con minibuses** for Hat Yai are based on Thanon Pichit Bamrung, at the corner of Thanon Jamroonara or down near the clocktower, and for Sungai Kolok and Ban Taba at 308/5 Thanon Pichit Bamrung; **share-taxis** hang around further north on the same road. The **airport**, served by air-con minibuses (B50; B140 to Sungai Kolok), lies 12km north of town; Thai Airways (with an office in town at 322–4 Thanon Puphapugdee; Ⓣ073 511161) fly here daily, Air Andaman (Ⓣ02 229 9555) three times a week. **Trains** on the line to Sungai Kolok stop at **Tanyongmat**, a half-hour songthaew ride from the centre. Narathiwat's **TAT** office (daily 8.30am–4.30pm; Ⓣ073 516144, Ⓔtatnara@cscoms.com) is inconveniently situated a couple of kilometres out of town on the Tak Bai road (take a motorbike taxi). There's an **Internet** shop next door to the *Royal Princess* hotel on Thanon Pichit Bamrung.

Accommodation and eating

One of the best places to **stay** in Narathiwat is the *Baan Burong Riverside Guest House* at 399 Thanon Puphapugdee (Ⓣ073 511027, Ⓕ073 512001, Ⓔnatini@chaiyo.com; ❹). Situated in a sixty-year-old Sino-Portuguese house in

Crossing into Malaysia near Narathiwat

You can cross to Malaysia southeast of Narathiwat at either of two frontier posts, both of which are well connected to **Kota Bharu**, the nearest town on the other side. Frequent songthaews and buses from Narathiwat make the ninety-minute trip to the riverside frontier post of **Ban Taba**, a village 5km beyond Tak Bai. From here boats (B7) shuttle across to the Malaysian town of Pengkalan Kubor, which has frequent buses to Kota Bharu, 20km to the southeast.

If you're coming from points north of Narathiwat, transport connections are likely to draw you inland to **Sungai Kolok**, a seedy brothel town popular with Malaysian weekenders. The longer-established of the border posts, Sungai Kolok is the end of the rail line from Bangkok, its station in the northern part of town a mere 800m west of the frontier bridge; motorbike taxis cover the ground if you can't face the walk. Hat Yai and Narathiwat air-con minibuses are based opposite the station, and most buses stop to set down or pick up there, too. From Rantau Panjang on the other side, frequent buses and share-taxis head for Kota Bharu, 30km away. Kolok boasts dozens of mediocre hotels in all price ranges – many of them doubling as brothels – in case you're really stuck.

a central location overlooking the river, the air-con rooms with shared hot-water bathrooms are nicely decorated and spotlessly clean, and there's a living room with satellite TV, a small book collection and free bread, tea and coffee; cheaper fan rooms, as well as out-of-town riverside bungalows are planned. Guests have free use of bicycles and kayaks (for non-guests, bicycles are B50/day, kayaks B150/day), and **motorbike rental** and **minivan hire** with driver can also be arranged – useful for exploring the nearby coast. The helpful and friendly owner, Natini, can also organize a variety of activities, including batik-making and goat-milking, as well as providing information about local trips, such as to Phru To Daeng, Thailand's last remaining swamp forest, and the Hala Bala tropical rainforest wildlife sanctuary, where ten of the world's twelve species of hornbill can be found.

Much cheaper than the *Baan Burong*, but nowhere near as nice, is the *Narathiwat Hotel*, which occupies a characterful wooden building on the same street at no. 341 (ⓣ073 511063; ❶); overlooking the river, the rooms are clean enough, if rather basic. In a similar price range to *Baan Burong*, the friendly, well-run and comfortable *Tanyong Hotel*, on a cross street towards the north end of town at 16/1 Thanon Sopapisai (ⓣ073 511477–9, ⓕ073 511834; ❹–❺), is highly recommended, with fan or air-con rooms available, all with hot water, TV and mini-bar. Narathiwat's best hotel is the luxury *Royal Princess*, 228 Thanon Pichit Bamrung (ⓣ073 515041–50, ⓦwww.dusit.com; ❼), which offers a swimming pool and other smart international-standard amenities; it's generally booked solid in September when the royal family and their entourage decamp to Taksin Ratchaniwet.

The top **restaurant** in town is the swish *Mankornthong* at 433 Thanon Puphapugdee, with a floating platform at the back; the seafood is pricey but very good. Much simpler, and considerably cheaper, is the spotlessly clean Muslim restaurant *Cheh Seni* at 51–53 Thanon Sopapisai, which specializes in *kai korlae* (chicken in a mild thick curry gravy). At the night market on Pichit Bamrung opposite the *Royal Princess Hotel*, you'll find excellent *roti*, chicken satay and *khao yam*. The clean, air-con *Kopiitiam*, on Puphapugdee opposite and under the same ownership as *Baan Burong Guest House*, dishes up *roti* with syrup or various curries, various reasonably priced Western dishes including sandwiches and breakfast, good cafetière coffees and lots of teas.

Up the coast to Saiburi and beyond

From Narathiwat, a minor road (Route 4157) stretches all the way north up the coast to Panare – with a brief detour inland just before Saiburi – passing dozens of tiny Muslim fishing villages, protected from the winds that batter the coast during the monsoon by sturdy palm-frond windbreaks. Lined with beaches, it's a picturesque route, with goats and sheep straying onto the road and fish laid out to dry on racks by the roadside; note that this is a fervently Muslim area, so women should cover up with a T-shirt on the beach. The best way to make the trip is to rent a **motorbike** or a chauffeured **minivan** from the *Baan Burong Riverside Guest House* in Narathiwat (see p.775); alternatively, local **songthaews** will eventually get you all the way up the coast to Panare.

SAIBURI, 50km from Narathiwat on the bus route to Pattani, is a relaxing, leafy town sprinkled with evidence of its former importance as a trading port – ancient Chinese shophouses, dilapidated wooden mansions and the brick shell of a 400-year-old mosque, Masjid Khao, preserved in landscaped gardens. About 2km from the centre, across the Saiburi River and behind the fishing port, the quiet, tree-lined beach of Hat Wasukri is served by a handful of restaurants.

The best of this area, however, lies further north. The remote riverside village of **Ban Pasey Yawo** (Ban Bon), 2km up the road, is renowned as one of the best centres for the manufacture of **korlae** boats, the beautifully decorated smacks used by Muslim fishermen all along this coast, and visitors are welcome to watch the craftsmen at work in the shade of the village's coconut plantation. The intricacy and extent of their decoration is what makes these boats unique – floral motifs and pastoral scenes cover every centimetre, from the bird-of-paradise figurehead to the *singtoh* lion god at the stern, thought to protect the fishermen from the spirits of the sea. Each boat is entirely handmade, takes four months to complete and sells for over B60,000, although B1000–3000 replicas are produced as a sideline.

About 15km further up towards Panare, you'll come to a turning for **Hat Kae Kae**, an idyllic seaside hamlet among shady palm trees, which gets its onomatopoeic name from the sound the sea makes when it hits the smooth boulders on the small, steeply sloping beach. If you're coming by songthaew, you'll be left with a five-hundred-metre walk over a low rocky rise to reach the seashore, backed by some simple foodstalls.

Wat Chonthara Sing-He and Taksin Ratchaniwet

South of Narathiwat, one of the finest bots in Thailand lies about 30km down the coast in **TAK BAI**. Standing in a sandy, tree-shaded compound by the river, the bot at **Wat Chonthara Sing-He** (aka Wat Chon) was built in the middle of the last century, as an emblem of Thai sovereignty to prove that Narathiwat was an integral part of Thailand, at a time when the British were claiming the area as part of Malaya. The building's brightly coloured fifteen-tiered roof exemplifies the fashion for curvaceous Chinese styles, here mixed with typical southern Thai features, such as the spiky white nagas, to produce an elegant, dynamic structure. Ask a monk for the key and look at the lively, well-preserved murals that completely cover the interior, portraying bawdy love scenes as well as typical details of southern life: bull- and goat-fighting, and men dressed in turbans and long sarongs.

The wat can be visited either as an easy day-trip from Narathiwat or on your way to the border – frequent buses and songthaews for Ban Taba pass through the small town. About 7km into the hour-long trip, you can't miss the **Taksin Ratchaniwet palace**, which stands on a wooded hill overlooking the sea. It is possible to visit the grounds when the king is not in residence (generally Oct–Aug Mon–Fri 8.30am–4pm; free), but you'll need your own transport to get round the extensive estate, and the excursion is only of real interest to devotees of the royal family. If you do make the trip, look out for the **gold-leaf vine** in the grounds; the velvety leaves of this highly prized plant, which is native only to the area around Narathiwat, turn an iridescent pink, then gold, then silver, each year from September to November. Other provinces have attempted to cash in on the vine's money-spinning appeal by planting it in other areas of Thailand – only to find that the leaves remain resolutely green all year round.

Travel details

Trains

Hat Yai to: Bangkok (5 daily; 14–16hr); Butterworth (Malaysia; 1 daily; 5hr 30min); Padang Besar (1 daily; 1hr); Phatthalung (10 daily; 1–2hr); Sungai Kolok (7 daily; 3hr 30min–5hr); Surat Thani (7 daily; 4hr–6hr 30min); Yala (10 daily; 1hr 30min–3hr).
Phatthalung to: Bangkok (5 daily; 12–15hr); Hat Yai (10 daily; 1–2hr).
Sungai Kolok to: Bangkok (2 daily; 20hr); Hat Yai (7 daily; 3hr 30min–5hr); Surat Thani (3 daily; 9–12hr).
Trang to: Bangkok (2 daily; 15–16hr).
Yala to: Bangkok (4 daily; 15–19hr).

Buses

Hat Yai to: Bangkok (21 daily; 12–15hr); Chumphon (6 daily; 8hr 45min); Ko Samui (1 daily; 7hr); Krabi (1 daily; 5hr); Nakhon (every 30min; 3–4hr); Narathiwat (3 daily; 3–4hr); Padang Besar (every 10min; 1hr 40min); Pak Bara (6 daily; 2hr 30min); Phang Nga (1 daily; 6hr 30min); Phatthalung (every 30min; 1hr 40min); Phuket (13 daily; 7–9hr); Ranong (3 daily; 8hr); Satun (every 15min; 1hr 30min–2hr); Songkhla (every 10min; 30min); Sungai Kolok (1 daily; 4hr); Surat Thani (10 daily; 5hr 30min–6hr 30min); Trang (every 30min; 3–4hr).
Narathiwat to: Ban Taba (every 30min; 1hr 30min); Bangkok (4 daily; 17–19hr); Hat Yai (3 daily; 3–4hr); Sungai Kolok (hourly; 1–2hr); Tak Bai (every 30min; 1hr).
Satun to: Bangkok (2 daily; 16hr); Hat Yai (every 15min; 1hr 30min–2hr); Phuket (2–3 daily; 7hr); Trang (every 30min; 3hr).
Songkhla to: Hat Yai (every 10min; 30min); Nakhon Si Thammarat (9 daily; 3hr); Ranot (every 30min; 1–2hr).
Sungai Kolok to: Bangkok (3 daily; 18–20hr); Hat Yai (1 daily; 4hr); Narathiwat (hourly; 1–2hr); Tak Bai (hourly; 30min).
Trang to: Bangkok (8 daily; 12–14hr); Hat Yai (every 30min; 3–4hr); Krabi (hourly; 2hr); Nakhon Si Thammarat (3 daily; 2–3hr); Phatthalung (hourly; 1hr 30min); Phuket (hourly; 4hr 30min); Satun (every 30min; 3hr).

Flights

Hat Yai to: Bangkok (7 daily; 1hr 30min); Phuket (1 daily; 45min); Singapore (1 daily; 1hr 35min).
Narathiwat to: Bangkok (1–2 daily; 1hr 40min–2hr 20min).
Trang to: Bangkok (1–2 daily; 1hr 30min).

Contexts

Contexts

History

As long as forty thousand years ago, Thailand was inhabited by **hunter-gatherers** who lived in semi-permanent settlements and used tools made of wood, bamboo and stone. By the end of the last Ice Age, around ten thousand years ago, these groups had become **farmers**, keeping chickens, pigs and cattle, and – as evidenced by the seeds and plant husks which have been discovered in caves in northern Thailand – cultivating rice and beans. This drift into an agricultural society gave rise to further technological developments: the earliest **pottery** found in Thailand has been dated to 6800 BC, while the recent excavations at **Ban Chiang** in the northeast have shown that **bronze** was being worked at least as early as 2000 BC, putting Thailand on a par with Mesopotamia, which has traditionally been regarded as the earliest Bronze Age culture. By two thousand years ago, the peoples of Southeast Asia had settled in small villages, among which there was regular communication and trade, but they had split into several broad families, differentiated by language and culture. At this time, the ancestors of the Thais, speaking proto-Thai languages, were still far away in southeastern China, whereas Thailand itself was inhabited by Austroasiatic speakers, among whom the Mon were to establish the region's first distinctive civilization, Dvaravati.

Dvaravati and Srivijaya

The history of **Dvaravati** is ill-defined to say the least, but the name is applied to a distinctive culture complex which shared the **Mon** language and **Theravada Buddhism**. This form of religion probably entered Thailand during the second or third centuries BC, when Indian missionaries were sent to Suvarnabhumi, "land of gold", which seems to correspond to the broad swath of fertile land stretching from southern Burma across the north end of the Gulf of Thailand.

From the discovery of monastery boundary stones (*sema*), clay votive tablets and Indian-influenced Buddhist sculpture, it's clear that Dvaravati was an extensive and prosperous Buddhist civilization which had its greatest flourishing between the sixth and ninth centuries AD. No strong evidence has turned up, however, for the existence of a single capital – rather than an empire, Dvaravati seems to have been a collection of city-states, which, at least in their early history, came under the lax suzerainty of **Funan**, a poorly documented kingdom centred in Cambodia. Nakhon Pathom, Lopburi, Si Thep and Muang Sema were among the most important Dvaravati sites, and their concentration around the Chao Phraya valley would seem to show that they gained much of their prosperity, and maintained religious and cultural contacts with India, via the **trade route** from the Indian Ocean over the Three Pagodas Pass.

Although they passed on aspects of their heavily Indianized art, religion and government to later rulers of Thailand, these Mon city-states were politically fragile and from the ninth century onwards succumbed to the domination of the invading Khmers from Cambodia. One northern outpost, the state of **Haripunjaya**, centred on Lamphun, which had been set up on the trade route with southern China, maintained its independence probably until the beginning of the eleventh century.

Meanwhile, to the south of Dvaravati, the shadowy Indianized state of Lankasuka had grown up in the second century, centred on Ligor (now Nakhon Si Thammarat) and covering an area of the Malay peninsula which included the important trade crossings at Chaiya and Trang. In the eighth century, it came under the control of the **Srivijaya** empire, a Mahayana Buddhist state centred on Sumatra, which had strong ties with India and a complex but uneasy relationship with neighbouring Java. Thriving on seaborne trade between Persia and China, Srivijaya extended its influence as far north as Chaiya, its regional capital, where discoveries of temple remains and some of the finest stone and bronze statues ever produced in Thailand have borne witness to the cultural vitality of this crossroads empire. In the tenth century the northern part of Lankasuka, under the name **Tambralinga**, regained a measure of independence, although it seems still to have come under the influence of Srivijaya as well as owing some form of allegiance to Dvaravati. By the beginning of the eleventh century however, peninsular Thailand had come under the sway of the Khmer empire, with a Cambodian prince ruling over a community of Khmer settlers and soldiers at Tambralinga.

The Khmers

The history of central Southeast Asia comes into sharper focus with the emergence of the **Khmers**, vigorous empire-builders whose political history can be pieced together from the numerous stone inscriptions they left. Originally vassal subjects of Funan, the Khmers of **Chenla** – to the north of Cambodia – seized power in the latter half of the sixth century during a period of economic decline in the area. Chenla's rise to power was knocked back by a punitive expedition conducted by the Srivijaya empire in the eighth century, but was reconsolidated during the watershed reign of **Jayavarman II** (802–50), who succeeded in conquering the whole of Kambuja, an area which roughly corresponds to modern-day Cambodia. In order to establish the authority of his monarchy and of his country, Jayavarman II had himself initiated as a *chakravartin*, or universal ruler, the living embodiment of the **devaraja**, the divine essence of kingship – a concept which was adopted by later Thai rulers. Taking as the symbol of his authority the phallic lingam, the king was thus identified with the god Shiva, although the Khmer concept of kingship and thus the religious mix of the state as a whole was not confined to Hinduism: elements of ancestor worship were also included, and Mahayana Buddhism gradually increased its hold over the next four centuries.

It was Jayavarman II who moved the Khmer capital to **Angkor** in northern Cambodia, which he and later kings, especially after the eleventh century, embellished with a series of prodigiously beautiful temples. Jayavarman II also recognized the advantages of the lakes around Angkor for irrigating rice fields and providing fish, and thus for feeding a large population. His successors developed this idea and gave the state a sound economic core with a remarkably complex system of **reservoirs** (*baray*) and water channels, which were copied and adapted in later Thai cities.

In the ninth and tenth centuries, Jayavarman II and his imperialistic successors, especially **Yasovarman I** (889–900), confirmed Angkor as the major power in Southeast Asia. They pushed into Vietnam, Laos, southern China and into northeastern Thailand, where the Khmers left dozens of Angkor-style temple complexes, as seen today at Prasat Phanom Rung and Prasat Hin Phimai. To the west and northwest, Angkor took control over central Thailand, with its most important outpost at Lopburi, and even established a strong presence to the south on the Malay peninsula. As a result of this expansion, the Khmers were masters of the most important trade routes between India and China, and indeed nearly every communications link in the region, from which they were able to derive huge income and strength.

The reign of **Jayavarman VII** (1181–1219), a Mahayana Buddhist who firmly believed in his royal destiny as a *bodhisattva*, sowed the seeds of Angkor's downfall. Nearly half of all the extant great religious monuments of the empire were erected under his supervision, but the ambitious scale of these building projects and the upkeep they demanded – some 300,000 priests and temple servants of 20,000 shrines consumed 38,000 tons of rice per year – along with a series of wars against Vietnam, terminally exhausted the economy.

In subsequent reigns, much of the life-giving irrigation system around Angkor turned into malarial swamp through neglect, and the rise of the more democratic creed of Theravada Buddhism undermined the divine authority which the Khmer kings had derived from the hierarchical Mahayana creed. As a result of all these factors, the Khmers were in no position to resist the onslaught between the thirteenth and fifteenth centuries of the vibrant new force in Southeast Asia, the Thais.

The earliest Thais

The earliest traceable history of the **Thai people** picks them up in southern China around the fifth century AD, when they were squeezed by Chinese and Vietnamese expansionism into sparsely inhabited northeastern Laos and neighbouring areas. The first entry of a significant number of Thais onto what is now Thailand's soil seems to have happened in the region of Chiang Saen, where it appears that some time after the seventh century the Thais formed a state in an area then known as **Yonok**. A development which can be more accurately dated and which had immense cultural significance was the spread of Theravada Buddhism to Yonok via Dvaravati around the end of the tenth century, which served not only to unify the Thais but also to link them to Mon civilization and give them a sense of belonging to the community of Buddhists.

The Thais' political development was also assisted by **Nan-chao**, a well-organized military state comprising a huge variety of ethnic groups, which established itself as a major player on the southern fringes of the Chinese empire from the beginning of the eighth century. As far as can be gathered, Nan-chao permitted the rise of Thai *muang* or small principalities on its periphery, especially in the area immediately to the south known as **Sipsong Panna**.

Thai infiltration continued until, by the end of the twelfth century, they seem to have formed the majority of the population in Thailand, then under the control of the Khmer empire. The Khmers' main outpost, at Lopburi, was by then regarded as the administrative capital of a land called "Syam" (possibly from the Sanskrit *syam*, meaning swarthy) – a mid-twelfth-century bas-relief at Angkor Wat, portraying the troops of Lopburi preceded by a large group of self-confident Syam Kuk mercenaries, shows that the Thais were becoming a force to be reckoned with.

Sukhothai

By the middle of the thirteenth century, the Thais, thanks largely to the decline of Angkor and the inspiring effect of Theravada Buddhism, were poised on the verge of autonomous power. The final catalyst was the invasion by Qubilai Khan's Mongol armies of China and Nan-chao, which began around 1215 and was completed in the 1250s. Demanding that the whole world should acknowledge the primacy of the Great Khan, the Mongols set their hearts on the "pacification" of the "barbarians" to the south of China, which obliged the Thais to form a broad power base to meet the threat.

The founding of the first Thai kingdom at **Sukhothai**, now popularly viewed as the cornerstone of the country's development, was in fact a small-scale piece of opportunism which almost fell at the first hurdle. At some time around 1238, the princes of two small Thai principalities in the upper Chao Phraya valley joined forces to capture the main Khmer outpost in the region at Sukhothai. One of the princes, **Intradit**, was crowned king, but for the first forty years Sukhothai remained merely a local power, whose existence was threatened by the ambitions of neighbouring princes. When attacked by the ruler of Mae Sot, Intradit's army was only saved by the grand entrance of Sukhothai's most dynamic leader: the king's nineteen-year-old son, Rama, held his ground and pushed forward to defeat the opposing commander, earning himself the name **Ramkhamhaeng**, "Rama the Bold".

When Ramkhamhaeng came to the throne around 1278, he saw the south as his most promising avenue for expansion and, copying the formidable military organization of the Mongols, seized control of much of the Chao Phraya valley. Over the next twenty years, largely by diplomacy rather than military action, Ramkhamhaeng gained the submission of most of the rulers of Thailand, who entered the **new empire**'s complex tributary system either through the pressure of the Sukhothai king's personal connections or out of recognition of his superior military strength and moral prestige. To the east, Ramkhamhaeng pushed as far as Vientiane in Laos; by marrying his daughter to a Mon ruler to the west, he obtained the allegiance of parts of southern Burma; and to the south his vassals stretched down the peninsula at least as far as Nakhon Si Thammarat. To the north, Sukhothai concluded an alliance with the parallel Thai states of Lanna and Phayao in 1287 for mutual protection against the Mongols – though it appears that Ramkhamhaeng managed to pinch several *muang* on their eastern periphery as tribute states.

Meanwhile **Lopburi**, which had wrested itself free from Angkor sometime in the middle of the thirteenth century, was able to keep its independence and its control of the eastern side of the Chao Phraya valley. Having been first a major cultural and religious centre for the Mon, then the Khmers' provincial capital, and now a state dominated by migrating Thais, Lopburi was a strong and vibrant place mixing the best of the three cultures, as evidenced by the numerous original works of art produced at this time.

Although the empire of Sukhothai extended Thai control over a vast area, its greatest contribution to the Thais' development was at home, in cultural and political matters. A famous **inscription** by Ramkhamhaeng, now housed in the Bangkok National Museum, describes a prosperous era of benevolent rule: "In the time of King Ramkhamhaeng this land of Sukhothai is thriving. There is fish in the water and rice in the fields … [The King] has hung a bell in the opening of the gate over there: if any commoner has a grievance which sickens his belly and gripes his heart … he goes and strikes the bell … [and King Ramkhamhaeng] questions the man, examines the case, and decides it justly for him." Although this plainly smacks of self-promotion, it seems to contain at least a kernel of truth: in deliberate contrast to the Khmer god-kings, Ramkhamhaeng styled himself as a **dhammaraja**, a king who ruled justly according to Theravada Buddhist doctrine and made himself accessible to his people. To honour the state religion, the city's temples were lavishly endowed: as original as Sukhothai's political systems were its religious **architecture and sculpture**, which, though bound to borrow from existing Khmer and Sri Lankan styles, show the greatest leap of creativity at any stage in the history of art in Thailand. A further sign of the Thais' new self-confidence was the invention of a new **script** to make their tonal language understood by the non-Thai inhabitants of the land.

All this was achieved in a remarkably short period of time. After the death of Ramkhamhaeng around 1299, his successors took their Buddhism so seriously that they neglected affairs of state. The empire quickly fell apart, and by 1320 Sukhothai had regressed to being a kingdom of only local significance.

Lanna

Almost simultaneous with the birth of Sukhothai was the establishment of a less momentous but longer-lasting kingdom to the north, called **Lanna**. Its founding father was **Mengrai**, chief of Ngon Yang, a small principality on the banks of the Mekhong near modern-day Chiang Saen. Around 1259 he set out to unify the squabbling Thai principalities of the region, first building a strategically placed city at Chiang Rai in 1262, and then forging alliances with Ngam Muang, the Thai king of Phayao, and with Ramkhamhaeng of Sukhothai.

In 1281, after ten years of guileful preparations, Mengrai conquered the Mon kingdom of Haripunjaya based at Lamphun, and was now master of northern Thailand. Taking advice from Ngam Muang and Ramkhamhaeng, in 1292 he selected a site for an impressive new capital of Lanna at **Chiang Mai**, which remains the centre of the north to the present day. Mengrai concluded further alliances in Burma and Laos, making him strong enough to successfully resist further Mongol attacks, although he was eventually obliged to bow to the superiority of the Mongols by sending them small tributes from 1312 onwards. When Mengrai died after a sixty-year reign in 1317, supposedly struck by a bolt of lightning, he had built up an extensive and powerful kingdom. But although he began a tradition of humane, reasonable laws, probably borrowed from the Mons, he had found little time to set up sound political and administrative institutions. His death severely destabilized Lanna, which quickly shrank in size and influence.

It was only in the reign of **Ku Na** (1355–85) that Lanna's development regained momentum. A well-educated and effective ruler, Ku Na enticed the venerable monk Sumana from Sukhothai, to establish an ascetic Sri Lankan sect in Lanna in 1369. Sumana brought a number of Buddha images with him, inspiring a new school of art that flourished for over a century, but more importantly his sect became a cultural force that had a profound unifying effect on the kingdom. The influence of Buddhism was further strengthened under **King Tilok** (1441–87), who built many great monuments at Chiang Mai and cast huge numbers of bronze seated Buddhas in the style of the central image at Bodh Gaya in India, the scene of the Buddha's enlightenment. Tilok, however, is best remembered as a great warrior, who spent most of his reign resisting the advances of Ayutthaya, by now the strongest Thai kingdom.

Under continuing pressure both from Ayutthaya and from Burma, Lanna went into rapid decline in the second quarter of the sixteenth century. For a short period after 1546, Chiang Mai came under the control of Setthathirat, the king of Lan Sang (Laos), but, unable to cope with Lanna's warring factions, he then abdicated, purloining the talismanic Emerald Buddha for his own capital at Louang Phabang. In 1558, Burma decisively captured Chiang Mai, and the Mengrai dynasty came to an end. For most of the next two centuries, the Burmese maintained control through a succession of puppet rulers, and Lanna again became much as it had been before Mengrai, little more than a chain of competing principalities.

Ayutthaya

While Lanna was fighting for its place as a marginalized kingdom, from the fourteenth century onwards the seeds of a full-blown Thai nation were being sown to the south at **Ayutthaya**. The city of Ayutthaya itself was founded on its present site in 1351 by U Thong, "Prince Golden Cradle", when his own town, Lopburi, was ravaged by smallpox. Taking the title **Ramathibodi**, he soon united the principalities of the lower Chao Phraya valley, which had formed the western provinces of the Khmer empire. When he recruited his bureaucracy from the urban elite of Lopburi, Ramathibodi set the **style of government** at Ayutthaya – the elaborate etiquette, language and rituals of Angkor were adopted, and, most importantly, the conception of the ruler as *devaraja*. The king became sacred and remote, an object of awe and dread, with none of the accessibility of the kings of Sukhothai: when he processed through the town, ordinary people were forbidden to look at him and had to be silent while he passed. This hierarchical system also provided the state with much-needed manpower, as all freemen were obliged to give up six months of each year to the crown either on public works or military service.

The site chosen by Ramathibodi turned out to be the best in the region for an international port, and so began Ayutthaya's rise to prosperity, based on its ability to exploit the upswing in **trade** in the middle of the fourteenth century along the routes between India and China. Flushed with economic success, Ramathibodi's successors were able to expand their control over the ailing states in the region. After a long period of subjugation, Sukhothai became a province of the kingdom of Ayutthaya in 1438, six years after Boromraja II had powerfully demonstrated Ayutthaya's pre-eminence by capturing the once-mighty Angkor, enslaving large numbers of its subjects and looting the Khmer royal regalia. (The Cambodian royal family were forced to abandon the palace forever and to found a new capital near Phnom Penh.)

Although a century of nearly continuous warfare against Lanna was less decisive, success generally bred success, and Ayutthaya's increasing wealth through trade brought ever greater power over its neighbouring states. To streamline the functioning of his unwieldy empire, **Trailok** (1448–88) found it necessary to make reforms of its administration. His **Law of Civil Hierarchy** formally entrenched the inequality of Ayutthayan society, defining the status of every individual by assigning him or her an imaginary number of rice fields – for example, 25 for an ordinary freeman and 10,000 for the highest ministers of state. Trailok's legacy is found in today's unofficial but fiendishly complex status system, by which everyone in Thailand knows their place.

Ramathibodi II (1491–1529), almost at a loss as to what to do with his enormous wealth, undertook an extensive programme of public works. In the 1490s he built several major religious monuments, and between 1500 and 1503 cast the largest standing metal image of the Buddha ever known, the Phra Si Sanphet, which gave its name to the temple of the royal palace. By 1540, the kingdom of Ayutthaya had grown to cover most of the area of modern-day Thailand.

Burmese wars and European trade

In the sixteenth century recurring tensions with Burma led **Chakkraphat** (1548–69) to improve his army and build brick ramparts around the capital. This was to no avail however: in 1568 the Burmese besieged Ayutthaya with a huge army, said by later accounts to have consisted of 1,400,000 men. The Thais held out until August 8, 1569, when treachery within their own ranks helped the Burmese break through the defences. The Burmese looted the city, took thousands of prisoners and installed a vassal king to keep control.

The decisive character who broke the Burmese stranglehold twenty years later and re-established Ayutthaya's economic growth was **Naresuan** (1590–1605), who defied the Burmese by amassing a large army. The enemy sent a punitive expedition which was conclusively defeated at Nong Sarai near modern-day Suphanburi on January 18, 1593, Naresuan himself turning the battle by killing the Burmese crown prince. Historians have praised Naresuan for his personal bravery and his dynamic leadership, although the chronicles of the time record a strong streak of tyranny – in his fifteen years as king he had eighty thousand people killed, excluding the victims of war. A favoured means of punishment was to slice off pieces of the offender's flesh, which he was then made to eat in the king's presence.

The period following Naresuan's reign was characterized by a more sophisticated engagement in **foreign trade**. In 1511 the Portuguese had become the first Western power to trade with Ayutthaya, and Naresuan himself concluded a treaty with Spain in 1598; relations with Holland and England were initiated in 1608 and 1612 respectively. For most of the seventeenth century, European merchants flocked to Thailand, not only to buy Thai products, but also to gain access to Chinese and Japanese goods on sale there. The role of foreigners at Ayutthaya reached its peak under **Narai** (1656–88), but he overstepped the mark in cultivating close links with Louis XIV of France, who secretly harboured the notion of converting Ayutthaya to Christianity. On Narai's death, relations with Westerners were severely cut back.

Despite this reduction of trade and prolonged civil strife over the succession to the throne whenever a king died – then, as now, there wasn't a fixed principle of primogeniture – Ayutthaya continued to flourish for much of the eighteenth century. The reign of **Borommakot** (1733–58) was particularly prosperous, producing many works of drama and poetry. Furthermore, Thai Buddhism had by then achieved such prestige that Sri Lanka, from where the Thais had originally imported their form of religion in the thirteenth century, requested Thai aid in restoring their monastic orders in 1751.

However, immediately after the death of Borommakot the rumbling in the Burmese jungle to the north began to make itself heard again. Alaunghpaya of Burma, apparently a blindly aggressive country bumpkin, first recaptured the south of his country from the Mons, then turned his attentions on Ayutthaya. A siege in 1760 was unsuccessful, with Alaunghpaya dying of wounds sustained there, but the scene was set. In February 1766 the Burmese descended upon Ayutthaya for the last time. The Thais held out for over a year, during which they were afflicted by famine, epidemics and a terrible fire which destroyed ten thousand houses. Finally, in **April 1767**, the walls were breached and the city taken. The Burmese razed everything to the ground and tens of thousands of prisoners were led off to Burma, including most of the royal family. The king, Suriyamarin, is said to have escaped from the city in a boat and starved to death ten days later. As one observer has said, the Burmese laid waste to Ayutthaya "in such a savage manner that it is hard to imagine that they shared the same religion with the Siamese". The city was abandoned to the jungle, but with remarkable speed the Thais regrouped and established a new seat of power, further down the Chao Phraya River at Bangkok.

The early Bangkok empire

As the bulk of the Burmese army was obliged by war with China to withdraw almost immediately, Thailand was left to descend into banditry. Out of this lawless mess several centres of power arose, the most significant being at Chanthaburi, commanded by **Phraya Taksin**. A charismatic, brave and able general who had been unfairly blamed for a failed counter-attack against the Burmese at Ayutthaya, Taksin had anticipated the fall of the besieged city and quietly slipped away with a force of five hundred men. In June 1767 he took control of the east-coast strip around Chanthaburi and very rapidly expanded his power across central Thailand.

Blessed with the financial backing of the Chinese trading community, to whom he was connected through his father, Taksin was crowned king in December 1768 at his new capital of Thonburi, on the opposite bank of the river from modern-day Bangkok. One by one the new king defeated his rivals, and within two years he had restored all of Ayutthaya's territories. More remarkably, by the end of the next decade Taksin had outdone his Ayutthayan predecessors by bringing Lanna, Cambodia and much of Laos into a huge new empire. During this period of expansionism, Taksin left most of the fighting to Thong Duang, an ambitious soldier and descendant of an Ayutthayan noble family, who became the *chakri*, the military commander, and took the title **Chao Phraya Chakri**.

However, by 1779 all was not well with the king. Being an outsider, who had risen from an ordinary family on the fringes of society, Taksin became paranoid about plots against him, a delusion that drove him to imprison and torture even his wife and sons. At the same time he sank into religious excesses, demanding that the monkhood worship him as a god. By March 1782, public outrage at his sadism and dangerously irrational behaviour had reached such fervour that he was ousted in a coup.

Chao Phraya Chakri was invited to take power and had Taksin executed. In accordance with ancient etiquette, this had to be done without royal blood touching the earth: the mad king was duly wrapped in a black velvet sack and struck on the back of the neck with a sandalwood club. (Popular tradition has it that even this form of execution was too much: an unfortunate substitute got the velvet sack treatment, while Taksin was whisked away to a palace in the hills near Nakhon Si Thammarat, where he is said to have lived until 1825.)

Rama I

With the support of the Ayutthayan aristocracy, Chakri – reigning as **Rama I** (1782–1809) – set about consolidating the Thai kingdom. His first act was to move the capital across the river to Bangkok, a better defensive position against any Burmese attack from the west. Borrowing from the layout of Ayutthaya, he built a new royal palace and impressive monasteries, and enshrined in the palace wat the Emerald Buddha, which he had snatched back during his campaigns in Laos.

As all the state records had disappeared in the destruction of Ayutthaya, religious and legal texts had to be written afresh and historical chronicles reconstituted – with some very sketchy guesswork. The monkhood was in such a state of crisis that it was widely held that moral decay had been partly responsible for Ayutthaya's downfall. Within a month of becoming king, Rama I issued a series of religious laws and made appointments to the leadership of the monkhood, to restore discipline and confidence after the excesses of Taksin's reign. Many works of drama and poetry had also been lost in the sacking of Ayutthaya, so Rama I set about rebuilding the Thais' literary heritage, at the same time attempting to make it more cosmopolitan and populist. His main contribution was the *Ramakien*, a dramatic version of the Indian epic *Ramayana*, which is said to have been set to verse by the king himself, with a little help from his courtiers, in 1797. Heavily adapted to its Thai setting, the *Ramakien* served as an affirmation of the new monarchy and its divine links, and has since become the national epic.

In the early part of Rama I's reign, the Burmese reopened hostilities on several occasions, the biggest attempted invasion coming in 1785, but the emphatic manner in which the Thais repulsed them only served to knit together the young kingdom. Trade with China revived, and the king addressed the besetting problem of manpower by ordering every man to be tattooed with the name of his master and his town, so that avoiding royal service became almost impossible. On a more general note, Rama I put the style of government in Thailand on a modern footing: while retaining many of the features of a *devaraja*, he shared more responsibility with his courtiers, as a first among equals.

Rama II and Rama III

The peaceful accession of his son as **Rama II** (1809–24) signalled the establishment of the **Chakri dynasty**, which is still in place today. This Second Reign was a quiet interlude, best remembered as a fertile period for Thai literature. The king, himself one of the great Thai poets, gathered round him a group of writers including the famous Sunthorn Phu, who produced scores of masterly love poems, travel accounts and narrative songs.

In contrast, **Rama III** (1824–51) actively discouraged literary development – probably in reaction against his father – and was a vigorous defender of conservative values. To this end, he embarked on an extraordinary redevelopment of Wat Po, the oldest temple in Bangkok. Hundreds of educational inscriptions and mural paintings, on all manner of secular and religious subjects, were put on show, apparently to preserve traditional culture against the rapid change which the king saw corroding the country. In foreign affairs, Rama III faced a serious threat from the vassal states of Laos, who in 1827 sent an invading army from Vientiane, which got as far as Saraburi, only three days' march from Bangkok. The king's response was savage: having repelled the initial invasion, he ordered his army to destroy everything in Vientiane apart from Buddhist temples and to forcibly resettle huge numbers of Lao in Isaan. Shortly after, the king was forced to go to war in Cambodia, to save Buddhism and its traditional institutions from the attentions of the newly powerful, non-Buddhist Vietnamese. A series of campaigns in the 1830s and 1840s culminated in the peace treaty of 1845–46, which again established Thailand as the dominant influence in Cambodia.

More significant in the long run was the danger posed by the increase in Western influence which began in the Third Reign. As early as 1825, the Thais were sufficiently alarmed at British colonialism to strengthen Bangkok's defences by stretching a great iron chain across the mouth of the Chao Phraya River, to which every blacksmith in the area had to donate a certain number of links. In 1826 Rama III was obliged to sign a limited trade agreement with the British, the **Burney Treaty**, by which the Thais won some political security in return for reducing their taxes on goods passing through Bangkok. British and American missions in 1850 unsuccessfully demanded more radical concessions, but by this time Rama III was seriously ill, and it was left to his far-sighted and progressive successors to reach a decisive accommodation with the Western powers.

Mongkut and Chulalongkorn

Rama IV, more commonly known as **Mongkut** (1851–68), had been a Buddhist monk for 27 years when he succeeded his brother. But far from leading a cloistered life, Mongkut had travelled widely throughout Thailand, had maintained scholarly contacts with French and American missionaries and, like most of the country's new generation of leaders, had taken an interest in Western learning, studying English, Latin and the sciences. He had also turned his mind to the condition of Buddhism in Thailand, which seemed to him to have descended into little more than popular superstition; indeed, after a study of the Buddhist scriptures in Pali, he was horrified to find that Thai ordinations were probably invalid. So in the late 1830s he set up a rigorously fundamentalist sect called *Thammayutika*, the "Order Adhering to the Teachings of the Buddha", and as abbot of the order he oversaw the training of a generation of scholarly leaders for Thai Buddhism from his base at Bangkok's Wat Bowonniwet, which became a major centre of Western learning.

When his kingship faced its first major test, in the form of a threatening British mission in 1855 led by **Sir John Bowring**, Mongkut dealt with it confidently. Realizing that Thailand was unable to resist the military might of the British, the king reduced import and export taxes, allowed British subjects to live and own land in Thailand and granted them freedom of trade. Of the **government monopolies**, which had long been the mainstay of the Thai economy, only that on opium was retained. After making up the loss in revenue through internal taxation, Mongkut quickly made it known that he would welcome diplomatic contacts from other Western countries: within a decade, agreements similar to the Bowring Treaty had been signed with France, the US and a score of other nations. Thus by skilful diplomacy the king avoided a close relationship with only one power, which could easily have led to Thailand's annexation.

While all around the colonial powers were carving up Southeast Asia amongst themselves, Thailand suffered nothing more than the weakening of its influence over Cambodia, which in 1863 the French brought under their protection. As a result of the open-door policy, foreign trade boomed, financing the redevelopment of Bangkok's waterfront and, for the first time, the building of paved roads. However, Mongkut ran out of time for instituting the far-reaching domestic reforms which he saw were needed to drag Thailand into the modern world.

The modernization of Thailand

Mongkut's son, **Chulalongkorn**, took the throne as Rama V (1868–1910) at the age of only 15, but he was well prepared by an excellent education which mixed traditional Thai and modern Western elements – provided by Mrs Anna Leonowens, subject of *The King and I*. When Chulalongkorn reached his majority after a five-year regency, he set to work on the reforms envisioned by his father. One of his first acts was to scrap the custom by which subjects were required to prostrate themselves in the presence of the king, which he followed up in 1874 with a series of decrees announcing the gradual abolition of slavery. The speed of his financial and administrative reforms, however, proved too much for the "**Ancients**" (*hua boran*), the old guard of ministers and officials inherited from his father. Their opposition culminated in the Front Palace Crisis of 1875, when a show of military strength almost plunged the country into civil war, and, although Chulalongkorn skilfully defused the crisis, many of his reforms had to be quietly shelved for the time being.

An important administrative reform which did go through, necessitated by the threat of colonial expansionism, concerned the former kingdom of Lanna. British exploitation of teak had recently spread into northern Thailand from neighbouring Burma, so in 1874 Chulalongkorn sent a commissioner to Chiang Mai to keep an eye on the prince of Chiang Mai and make sure that he avoided any collision with the British. The commissioner was gradually able to limit the power of the princes and integrate the region more fully into the kingdom.

In the 1880s prospects for reform brightened as many of the "Ancients" died or retired. This allowed Chulalongkorn to **restructure the government** to meet the country's needs: the Royal Audit Office made possible the proper control of revenue and finance; the Department of the Army became the nucleus of a modern armed services; and a host of other departments were set up, for justice, education, public health and the like. To fill these new positions, the king appointed many of his younger brothers, who had all received a modern education, while scores of foreign technicians and advisers were brought in to help with everything from foreign affairs to rail lines.

Throughout this period, however, the Western powers maintained their pressure on the region. The most serious threat to Thai sovereignty was the **Franco-Siamese Crisis** of 1893, which culminated in the French, based in Vietnam, sending gunboats up the Chao Phraya River to Bangkok. Flouting numerous international laws, France claimed control over Laos and made other outrageous demands, which Chulalongkorn had no option but to concede. In 1907 Thailand was also forced to relinquish Cambodia to the French, and in 1909 three Malay states fell to the British. In order to preserve its independence, the country ceded almost half of its territory and forewent huge sums of tax revenue. But from the end of the Fifth Reign, the frontiers were fixed as they are today.

By the time of the king's death in 1910, Thailand could not yet be called a modern nation-state – corruption and nepotism were still grave problems, for example. However, Chulalongkorn had made remarkable advances, and, almost from scratch, had established the political institutions to cope with twentieth-century development.

The end of absolute monarchy

Chulalongkorn was succeeded by a flamboyant, British-educated prince, **Vajiravudh** (1910–25), who was crowned Rama VI. The new king found it difficult to shake the dominance of his father's appointees in the government, who formed an extremely narrow elite, comprised almost entirely of members of Chulalongkorn's family. In an attempt to build up a personal following, Vajiravudh created, in May 1911, the **Wild Tigers**, a nationwide paramilitary corps recruited widely from the civil service. However, in 1912 a group of young army lieutenants, disillusioned by the absolute monarchy and upset at the downgrading of the regular army in favour of the Wild Tigers, plotted a **coup**. The conspirators were easily broken up before any trouble began, but this was something new in Thai history: the country was used to in-fighting among the royal family, but not to military intrigue from men from comparatively ordinary backgrounds.

Vajiravudh's response to the coup was a series of modernizing **reforms**, including the introduction of compulsory primary education and an attempt to better the status of women by supporting monogamy in place of the widespread practice of polygamy. His huge output of writings invariably encouraged people to live as modern Westerners, and he brought large numbers of commoners into high positions in government. Nonetheless, he would not relinquish his strong opposition to constitutional democracy.

When **World War I** broke out in 1914, the Thais were generally sympathetic to the Germans out of resentment over their loss of territory to the French and British. The king, however, was in favour of neutrality, until the US entered the war in 1917, when Thailand followed the expedient policy of joining the winning side and sent an expeditionary force of 1300 men to France in June 1918. The goodwill earned by this gesture enabled the Thais, between 1920 and 1926, to negotiate away the unequal treaties which had been imposed on them by the Western powers. Foreigners on Thai soil were no longer exempted from Thai laws, and the Thais were allowed to set reasonable rates of import and export taxes.

Yet Vajiravudh's extravagant lifestyle – during his reign, royal expenditure amounted to as much as ten percent of the state budget – left severe financial problems for his successor. Vajiravudh died without leaving a son, and as three better-placed contenders to the crown all died in the 1920s, **Prajadhipok** – the seventy-sixth child and last son of Chulalongkorn – was catapulted to the throne as Rama VII (1925–35). Young and inexperienced, he responded to the country's crisis by creating a Supreme Council of State, seen by many as a return to Chulalongkorn's absolutist "government by princes".

Prajadhipok himself seems to have been in favour of constitutional government, but the weakness of his personality and the opposition of the old guard in the Supreme Council prevented him from introducing it. Meanwhile a vigorous community of Western-educated intellectuals had emerged in the lower echelons of the bureaucracy, who were increasingly dissatisfied with the injustices of monarchical government. The final shock to the Thai system came with the Great Depression, which from 1930 onwards ravaged the economy. On June 24, 1932, a small group of middle-ranking officials, led by a lawyer, Pridi Phanomyong, and an army major, Luang Phibunsongkhram, staged a **coup** with only a handful of troops. Prajadhipok weakly submitted to the conspirators, or "Promoters", and 150 years of absolute monarchy in Bangkok came to a sudden end. The king was sidelined to a position of symbolic significance and in 1935 he abdicated in favour of his ten-year-old nephew, **Ananda**, then a schoolboy living in Switzerland.

To the 1957 coup

The success of the 1932 coup was in large measure attributable to the army officers who gave the conspirators credibility, and it was they who were to dominate the constitutional regimes that followed. The Promoters' first worry was that the French or British might attempt to restore the monarchy to full power. To deflect such intervention, they appointed a government under a provisional constitution and espoused a wide range of liberal Western-type reforms, including freedom of the press and social equality, few of which ever saw the light of day.

The regime's first crisis came early in 1933 when **Pridi Phanomyong**, by now leader of the government's civilian faction, put forward a socialist economic plan based on the nationalization of land and labour. The proposal was denounced as communistic by the military, Pridi was forced into temporary exile and an anti-communist law was passed. Then, in October, a royalist coup was mounted which brought the kingdom close to civil war. After intense fighting, the rebels were defeated by Lieutenant-Colonel **Luang Phibunsongkhram** (or Phibun), so strengthening the government and bringing Phibun to the fore as the leading light of the military faction.

Pridi was rehabilitated in 1934 and remained powerful and popular, especially among the intelligentsia, but it was Phibun who became prime minister after the decisive **elections of 1938**, presiding over a cabinet dominated by military men. Phibun encouraged a wave of nationalistic feeling with such measures as the official institution of the name Thailand in 1939 – Siam, it was argued, was a name bestowed by external forces, and the new title made it clear that the country belonged to the Thais rather than the economically dominant Chinese. This latter sentiment was reinforced with a series of harsh laws against the Chinese, who faced discriminatory taxes on income and commerce.

World War II

The outbreak of **World War II** gave the Thais the chance to avenge the humiliation of the 1893 Franco–Siamese Crisis. When France was occupied by Germany in June 1940, Phibun seized the opportunity to invade western Cambodia and the area of Laos lying to the west of the Mekong River. In the following year, however, the threat of a Japanese attack on Thailand loomed. On December 8, 1941, almost at the same time as the assault on Pearl Harbour, the Japanese invaded the country at nine points, most of them along the east coast of the peninsula. The Thais at first resisted fiercely, but realizing that the position was hopeless, Phibun quickly ordered a ceasefire. Meanwhile the British sent a force from Malaysia to try to stop the Japanese at Songkhla, but were held up in a fight with Thai border police. The Japanese had time to establish themselves, before pushing down the peninsula to take Singapore.

The Thai government concluded a military alliance with Japan and declared war against the US and Great Britain in January 1942, probably in the belief that the Japanese would win the war. However, the Thai minister in Washington, Seni Pramoj, refused to deliver the declaration of war against the US and, in co-operation with the Americans, began organizing a resistance movement called **Seri Thai**. Pridi, now acting as regent to the young king, furtively co-ordinated the movement under the noses of the occupying Japanese, smuggling in American agents and housing them in a European prison camp in Bangkok.

By 1944 Japan's final defeat looked likely, and Phibun, who had been most closely associated with them, was forced to resign by the National Assembly in July. A civilian, Khuang Aphaiwong, was chosen as prime minister, while Seri Thai became well established in the government under the control of Pridi. At the end of the war, Thailand was forced to restore the annexed Cambodian and Lao provinces to French Indochina, but American support prevented the British from imposing heavy punishments for the alliance with Japan.

Postwar upheavals

With the fading of the military, the election of January 1946 was for the first time contested by organized political parties, resulting in Pridi becoming prime minister. A new constitution was drafted and the outlook for democratic, civilian government seemed bright.

Hopes were shattered, however, on June 9, 1946, when King Ananda was found dead in his bed, with a bullet wound in his forehead. Three palace servants were hurriedly tried and executed, but the murder has never been satisfactorily explained, and public opinion attached at least indirect responsibility for the killing to Pridi, who had in the past shown strong anti-royalist feeling. He resigned as prime minister, and in April 1948 the military made a decisive return: playing on the threat of communism, with Pridi pictured as a Red bogeyman, Phibun took over the premiership.

After the bloody suppression of two attempted coups in favour of Pridi, the main feature of Phibun's second regime was its heavy involvement with the US. As communism developed its hold in the region, with the takeover of China in 1949 and the French defeat in Indochina in 1954, the US increasingly viewed Thailand as a bulwark against the Red menace. Between 1951 and 1957, when its annual state budget was only about $200 million a year, Thailand received a total $149 million in American economic aid and $222 million in military aid. This strengthened Phibun's dictatorship, while enabling leading military figures to divert American money and other funds into their own pockets.

In 1955, his position threatened by two rival generals, Phibun experienced a sudden conversion to the cause of democracy. He narrowly won a general election in 1957, but only by blatant vote-rigging and coercion. Although there's a strong tradition of foul play in Thai elections, this is remembered as the dirtiest ever: after vehement public outcry, **General Sarit**, the commander-in-chief of the army, overthrew the new government in September 1957.

To the present day

Believing that Thailand would prosper best under a unifying authority – an ideology that still has its supporters – Sarit set about re-establishing the monarchy as the head of the social hierarchy and the source of legitimacy for the government. Ananda's successor, **King Bhumibol** (Rama IX), was pushed into an active role while Sarit ruthlessly silenced critics and pressed ahead with a plan for economic development. These policies achieved a large measure of stability and prosperity at home, although from 1960 onwards the international situation worsened. With the Marxist Pathet Lao making considerable advances in Laos, and Cambodia's ruler, Prince Sihanouk, drawing into closer relations with China, Sarit turned again to the US. The Americans obliged by sharply increasing military aid and by stationing troops in Thailand.

The Vietnam war

Sarit died in 1963, whereupon the military succession passed to **General Thanom**, closely aided by his deputy prime minister, **General Praphas**. Neither man had anything of Sarit's charisma and during a decade in power they followed his political philosophies largely unchanged. Their most pressing problem was the resumption of open hostilities between North and South Vietnam in the early 1960s – the **Vietnam War**. Both Laos and Cambodia became involved on the side of the communists by allowing the North Vietnamese to supply their troops in the south along the Ho Chi Minh Trail, which passed through southern Laos and northeastern Cambodia. The Thais, with the backing of the US, quietly began to conduct military operations in Laos, to which North Vietnam and China responded by supporting anti-government insurgency in Thailand.

The more the Thais felt threatened by the spread of communism, the more they looked to the Americans for help – by 1968 around 45,000 US military personnel were on Thai soil, which became the base for US bombing raids against North Vietnam and Laos, and for covert operations into Laos and beyond.

The effects of the **American presence in Thailand** were profound. The economy swelled with dollars, and hundreds of thousands of Thais became reliant on the Americans for a living, with a consequent proliferation of corruption and prostitution. What's more, the sudden exposure to Western culture led many to question the traditional Thai values and the political status quo.

The democracy movement and civil unrest

At the same time, poor farmers were becoming disillusioned with their lot, and during the 1960s many turned against the Bangkok government. At the end of 1964, the **Communist Party of Thailand** and other groups formed a **broad left coalition** that soon had the support of several thousand insurgents in remote areas of the northeast. By 1967, the problem had spread to Chiang Rai and Nan provinces, and a separate threat had arisen in southern Thailand, involving **Muslim dissidents** and the Chinese-dominated **Communist Party of Malaya**, as well as local Thais.

Thanom was now facing a major security crisis, especially as the war in Vietnam was going badly. In 1969 he held elections which produced a majority for the government party but, still worried about national stability, the general got cold feet. In November 1971 he reimposed repressive military rule, under a triumvirate of himself, his son Colonel Narong and Praphas, who became known as the "Three Tyrants". However, the 1969 experiment with democracy had heightened expectations of power-sharing among the middle classes, especially in the universities. **Student demonstrations** began in June 1973, and in October as many as 500,000 people turned out at Thammasat University in Bangkok to demand a new constitution. King Bhumibol intervened with apparent success, and indeed the demonstrators were starting to disperse on the morning of October 14, when the police tried to control the flow of people away. Tensions quickly mounted and soon a full-scale riot was under way, during which over 350 people were reported killed. The army, however, refused to provide enough troops to suppress this massive uprising, and later the same day, Thanom, Narong and Praphas were forced to resign and leave the country.

In a new climate of openness, **Kukrit Pramoj** managed to form a coalition of seventeen elected parties and secured a promise of US withdrawal from Thailand, but his government was riven with feuding. Meanwhile, the king and much of the middle class, alarmed at the unchecked radicalism of the students, began to support new, often violent, right-wing organizations. In October 1976, the students demonstrated again, protesting against the return of Thanom to Thailand to become a monk at Wat Bowonniwet. Supported by elements of the military and the government, the police and reactionary students launched a massive assault on Thammasat University. On October 6, hundreds of students were brutally beaten, scores were lynched and some even burnt alive; the military took control and suspended the constitution.

General Prem

Soon after, the military-appointed prime minister, **Thanin Kraivichien**, imposed rigid censorship and forced dissidents to undergo anti-communist indoctrination, but his measures seem to have been too repressive even for the military, who forced him to resign in October 1977. General Kriangsak Chomanand took over, and began to break up the insurgency with shrewd offers of amnesty. His power base was weak, however, and although Kriangsak won the elections of 1979, he was displaced in February 1980 by **General Prem Tinsulanonda**, who was backed by a broad parliamentary coalition.

Untainted by corruption, Prem achieved widespread support, including that of the monarchy, which was to prove crucial. In April 1981, a group of disaffected military officers seized government buildings in Bangkok, forcing Prem to flee the capital. However, the rebels' attempt to mobilize the army was hamstrung by a radio message from Queen Sirikit in support of Prem, who was easily able to retake Bangkok. Parliamentary elections in 1983 returned the military to power and legitimized Prem's rule.

Overseeing a period of strong foreign investment and rapid economic growth, Prem maintained the premiership until 1988, with a unique mixture of dictatorship and democracy sometimes called Premocracy: although never standing for parliament himself, Prem was asked by the legislature after every election to become prime minister. He eventually stepped down because, he said, it was time for the country's leader to be chosen from among its elected representatives.

The 1992 demonstrations

The new prime minister was indeed an elected MP, **Chatichai Choonhavan**, a retired general with a long civilian career in public office. He pursued a vigorous policy of economic development, but this fostered widespread corruption, in which members of the government were often implicated. Following an economic downturn and Chatichai's attempts to downgrade the political role of the military, the armed forces staged a bloodless **coup** on February 23, 1991, led by Supreme Commander Sunthorn and General Suchinda, the army commander-in-chief, who became premier.

When Suchinda reneged on promises to make democratic amendments to the constitution, hundreds of thousands of ordinary Thais poured onto the streets around Bangkok's Democracy Monument in **mass demonstrations** between May 17 and 20, 1992. Hopelessly misjudging the mood of the country, Suchinda brutally crushed the protests, leaving hundreds dead or injured. Having justified the massacre on the grounds that he was protecting the king from communist agitators, Suchinda was forced to resign when King Bhumibol expressed his disapproval in a ticking-off that was broadcast on world television.

Chuan, Banharn and Chavalit

In the elections on September 13, 1992, the Democrat Party, led by **Chuan Leekpai**, a noted upholder of democracy and the rule of law, gained the largest number of parliamentary seats. Despite many successes through a period of continued economic growth, he was able to hold onto power only until July

1995, when he was forced to call new elections. Chart Thai and its leader, **Banharn Silpa-archa** – nicknamed by the local press "the walking ATM", a reference to his reputation for buying votes – emerged victorious. Allegations of corruption soon mounted against Banharn and in the following year he was obliged to dissolve parliament.

In November 1996, **General Chavalit Yongchaiyudh**, leader of the New Aspiration Party (NAP), narrowly won what was dubbed the most corrupt election in Thai history, with an estimated 25 million baht spent on vote-buying in rural areas. The most significant positive event of his tenure was the approval of a **new constitution**. Drawn up by an independent drafting assembly, its main points included: direct elections to the senate, rather than appointment of senators by the prime minister; acceptance of the right of assembly as the basis of a democratic society and guarantees of individual rights and freedoms; greater public accountability; and increased popular participation in local administration. The eventual aim of the new charter was to end the traditional system of patronage, vested interests and vote-buying.

The economic crisis

At the start of Chavalit's premiership, the Thai **economy** was already on shaky ground. In February 1997 foreign-exchange dealers began to mount speculative attacks on the baht, alarmed at the size of Thailand's private foreign debt – 250 billion baht in the unproductive property sector alone, much of it accrued through the proliferation of prestigious skyscrapers in Bangkok. The government valiantly defended the pegged exchange rate, spending $23 billion of the country's formerly healthy foreign-exchange reserves, but at the beginning of July was forced to give up the ghost – the baht was floated and soon went into free-fall.

Blaming its traditional allies the Americans for neglecting their obligations, Thailand sought help from Japan; Tokyo suggested the **IMF**, who in August put together a $17-billion **rescue package** for Thailand. Among the conditions of the package, the Thai government was to slash the national budget, control inflation and open up financial institutions to foreign ownership.

Chavalit's performance in the face of the crisis was viewed as inept, more concerned with personal interests and political game-playing than managing the economy properly. In November he resigned, to be succeeded by Chuan Leekpai, who took up what was widely seen as a poisoned chalice for his second term. Chuan immediately took a hard line to try to restore confidence in the economy: he followed the IMF's advice, which involved maintaining cripplingly high interest rates to protect the baht, and pledged to reform the financial system. Although this played well abroad, at home the government encountered increasing hostility. Unemployment, which had been as low as 1 million before the crisis, edged past 2 million by mid-1998, inflation peaked at ten percent, and there were frequent public protests against the IMF.

By the end of 1998, however, Chuan's tough stance was paying off, with the baht stabilizing at just under 40 to the US dollar, and interest rates and inflation starting to fall. Foreign investors slowly began returning to Thailand, and by October 1999 Chuan was confident enough to announce that he was forgoing almost $4 billion of the IMF's planned rescue package.

Thaksin

The year 2000 was dominated by the build-up to the general election in January 2001. It was to be the first such vote held under the 1997 constitution, which was intended to take the traditionally crucial role of money, especially for vote-buying, out of politics. However, this election coincided with the emergence of a new party, **Thai Rak Thai** (Thai Loves Thai), formed by one of Thailand's wealthiest men, **Thaksin Shinawatra**, an ex-policeman who had made a personal fortune from government telecommunications concessions.

Although Thaksin denied the money attraction, over one hundred MPs from other parties, including the ruling Democrats, were drawn to Thai Rak Thai as the dissolution of parliament approached. However, in September, the **National Counter-Corruption Commission** announced an investigation into Thaksin's affairs, citing a failure to disclose fully his business interests, in a declaration of assets when he joined Chavalit's 1997 government (under the new constitution, ministers can hold no more than a five percent stake in a business). The NCCC also wanted to know how members of Thaksin's household – including his maid, nanny, driver and security guard – came to hold over one billion baht's worth of stock in his businesses.

Paying no heed to the NCCC investigation, the voters gave Thaksin the biggest electoral victory in Thai history. After the recently formed **Election Commission** instigated new polls in 62 constituencies where there had been voting irregularities, his final count came to 248 seats out of a possible 500. Thaksin duly entered into a coalition with Chart Thai and New Aspiration, thereby controlling a healthy total of 325 seats.

Instead of a move towards greater democracy, as envisioned by the new constitution, Thaksin's government seemed to represent a full-blown merger between politics and big business, concentrating economic power in even fewer hands. His first cabinet was a motley crew of old-style vested interests, including as deputy premier former PM Chavalit, credited by many with having sparked the 1997 economic crisis. In August 2001, with no good reason given but obviously frightened of sparking a major political crisis, the **Constitutional Court** cleared Thaksin of the charge of filing a false asset statement by a narrow margin of 8–7. Thaksin did, however, live up to his billing as a populist reformer by carrying through nearly all of his controversial election promises. In his first year of government, he issued a three-year loan moratorium for perennially indebted farmers and set up a one-million-baht development fund for each of the country's seventy thousand villages – though many villages just used the money as a lending tool to cover past debts, rather than creating productive projects for the future as intended. To improve public health access, a standard charge of B30 per hospital visit was introduced nationwide.

As part of a wider social order campaign, the PM also fulfilled his hustings promise to wage **war on drugs**. An estimated one billion tablets of *ya baa* (methamphetamines) are being smuggled into Thailand from Burmese laboratories each year, aimed at three million users, many of them in schools and colleges. In a brutal clampdown in the first half of 2003, there were 51,000 arrests and over 2000 extra-judicial killings, much to the consternation of human rights' watchers. In response, the government claimed that only forty or so of these died at the hands of the police – and then only in self-defence – while the remainder were killed by rival drug gangs, or by their own gang leaders to prevent them becoming informants. Thaksin proclaimed a resounding victory, which brought an indirect admonition from the king in his birthday speech, when he pointed out that the war on drugs was far from over and requested a full explanation of all the deaths.

In early 2004, politically and criminally motivated violence in the **Islamic southern provinces** escalated sharply. This has included the killings of more than sixty police, soldiers and even Buddhist monks, the theft of weapons and explosives, the burning of schools, and the bombing of a bar area in Sungai Kolok frequented by Malaysian tourists, injuring thirty people, some seriously. The troubles reached new heights on April 28 when security forces fought off fifteen or so co-ordinated attacks, killing over a hundred assailants. At the time of writing, the Thai authorities seem unsure as to why the violence has accelerated so quickly and who is behind it. Some officials described the attackers as Muslim separatists and hinted at links with Al-Qaeda and Jemaah Islamiyah, but Thaksin dismissed the perpetrators as bandits, bent on stealing and smuggling arms. Nor does the government seem to have made up its mind about whether to get tough, which would appear to be Thaksin's natural instinct, or to adopt a more softly-softly approach towards defusing tensions, which has worked in the past.

The escalation of violence may have dented the aura of invincibility that has built up around Thaksin. In truth, there are few mysteries about this aura. The prime minister has applied commercial and legal pressure, including several lawsuits, to try to silence critics in the media and parliament, and has rejected constitutional reforms designed to rein in his power – famously declaring that "democracy is only a tool" for achieving other goals. Since the 2001 election, Thai Rak Thai has absorbed the New Aspiration and Seritham parties, and now wields such a large majority as to remove the possibility of effective parliamentary opposition. While the opposition have as their new leader Banyat Bantadan, a veteran Southern democrat but widely seen as lacking the charisma to challenge Thaksin, in preparation for an election that is due by early 2005, the prime minister has persuaded Chart Pattana, a minority opposition party, to merge with Thai Rak Thai.

Art and architecture

Aside from pockets of Hindu-inspired statuary and architecture, the vast majority of historical Thai culture takes its inspiration from Theravada Buddhism and, though the country does have some excellent museums, to understand fully the evolution of Thai art you have to visit its temples. For Thailand's architects and sculptors, the act of creation was an act of merit and a representation of unchanging truths, rather than an act of expression, and thus Thai art history is characterized by broad schools rather than individual names. This section is designed to help make sense of the most common aspects of Thai art and architecture at their various stages of development.

The basics

To appreciate the plethora of temples and religious images in Thailand, and the differences in the creations of different eras, you first need a grasp of the fundamental architectural forms and the iconography of Buddhism and Hinduism.

The wat

The **wat** or Buddhist temple complex has a great range of uses, as home to a monastic community, a place of public worship, a shrine for holy images and a shaded meeting-place for townspeople and villagers. Wat architecture has evolved in ways as various as its functions, but there remain several essential components which have stayed constant for some fifteen centuries.

The most important wat building is the **bot** (sometimes known as the *ubosot*), a term most accurately translated as the "ordination hall". It usually stands at the heart of the compound and is the preserve of the monks: lay people are rarely allowed inside, and it's generally kept locked when not in use. There's only one bot in any wat complex, and often the only way to distinguish it from other temple buildings is by the eight **sema** or boundary stones which always surround it. Positioned at the four corners of the bot and at the cardinal points of the compass, these stone *sema* define the consecrated ground and usually look something like upright gravestones, though they can take many forms. They are often carved all over with symbolic Buddhist scenes or ideograms, and sometimes are even protected within miniature shrines of their own. (One of the best *sema* collections is housed in the National Museum of Khon Kaen.)

Often almost identical to the bot, the **viharn** or assembly hall is for the lay congregation. This is the building tourists are most likely to enter, as it usually contains the wat's principal **Buddha image**, and sometimes two or three minor images as well. Large wats may have several viharns, while strict meditation wats, which don't deal with the laity, may not have one at all.

Thirdly, there's the **chedi** or stupa (known as a **that** in the north), a tower which was originally conceived as a monument to enshrine relics of the Buddha, but has since become a place to contain the ashes of royalty – and anyone else who can afford it. Of all Buddhist structures, the chedi has undergone the most changes and as such is often the most characteristic hallmark of each period (see box on p.214).

Less common wat buildings include the small square **mondop**, usually built to house either a Buddha statue or footprint or to contain holy texts, and the **ho trai**, or scripture library; there are good examples of traditional *ho trai* at Wat Rakhang in Bangkok, at Wat Thung Si Muang in Ubon Ratchathani and at Wat Yai Suwannaram in Phetchaburi.

Buddhist iconography

In the early days of Buddhism, image-making was considered inadequate to convey the faith's abstract philosophies, so the only approved iconography comprised doctrinal **symbols** such as the *Dharmachakra* (Wheel of Law, also known as Wheel of Doctrine or Wheel of Life). Gradually these symbols were displaced by **images of the Buddha**, construed chiefly as physical embodiments of the Buddha's teachings rather than as portraits of the man (see p.811 for more on the life of the Buddha). Sculptors took their guidance from the Pali texts which ordained the Buddha's most common postures (*asanha*) and gestures (*mudra*).

Of the **four postures** – sitting, standing, walking and reclining – the **seated Buddha**, which represents him in meditation, is the most common in Thailand. A popular variation shows the Buddha seated on a coiled serpent, protected by the serpent's hood – a reference to the story about the Buddha meditating during the rainy season, when a serpent offered to raise him off the wet ground and shelter him from the storms. The **reclining** pose symbolizes the Buddha entering Nirvana at his death, while the **standing** and **walking** images both represent his descent from Tavatimsa heaven.

The most common **hand gestures** include: *Dhyana Mudra* (Meditation), in which the hands rest on the lap, palms upwards; *Bhumisparsa Mudra* (Calling the Earth to Witness, a reference to the Buddha resisting temptation), with the left hand upturned in the lap and the right-hand fingers resting on the right knee and pointing to the earth; *Vitarkha Mudra* (Teaching), with one or both hands held at chest height with the thumb and forefinger touching; and *Abhaya Mudra* (Dispelling Fear), showing the right hand (occasionally both hands) raised in a flat-palmed "stop" gesture.

All three-dimensional Buddha images are objects of reverence, but some are more esteemed than others. Some are alleged to have displayed human attributes or reacted in some way to unusual events, others have performed miracles, or are simply admired for their beauty, their phenomenal size or even their material value – if made of solid gold or of jade, for example. Most Thais are familiar with these exceptional images, all of which have been given special names, always prefixed by the honorific "Phra", and many of which have spawned thousands of miniaturized copies in the form of amulets. Pilgrimages are made to see the most famous originals.

It was in the Sukhothai era that the craze for producing **Buddha footprints** really took off. Harking back to the time when images were allusive rather than representative, these footprints were generally moulded from stucco to depict the 108 auspicious signs or *lakshanas* (which included references to the sixteen Buddhist heavens, the traditional four great continents and seven great rivers and lakes) and housed in a special mondop. Few of the Sukhothai prints remain, but Ayutthaya-Ratanakosin-era examples are found all over the country, the most famous being Phra Phutthabat near Lopburi, the object of pilgrimages throughout the year. The feet of the famous Reclining Buddha in Bangkok's Wat Po are also inscribed with the 108 *lakshanas*, beautifully depicted in mother-of-pearl inlay.

Hindu iconography

Hindu images tend to be a lot livelier than Buddhist ones, partly because there is a panoply of gods to choose from, and partly because these gods have mischievous personalities and reappear in all sorts of bizarre incarnations. Central to the Hindu philosophy is the certainty that any object can be viewed as the temporal residence, embodiment or symbol of the deity; thus its iconography includes abstract representations (such as the phallic lingam for Shiva) as well as figurative images. Though pure Hinduism receded from Thailand with the collapse of the Khmers, the iconography has endured, as Buddhist Thais have incorporated some

Hindu and Brahmin concepts into the national belief system and have continued to create statues of the three chief Hindu deities – Brahma, Vishnu and Shiva – as well as using lesser mythological beasts in modern designs.

Vishnu has always been especially popular: his role of "Preserver" has him embodying the status quo, representing both stability and the notion of altruistic love. He is most often depicted as the deity, but frequently crops up in other human and animal incarnations. There are ten of these manifestations in all, of which **Rama** (number seven) is by far the most popular in Thailand. The epitome of ideal manhood, Rama is the super-hero of the epic story the *Ramayana* (see box on p.127) and appears in storytelling reliefs and murals in every Hindu temple in Thailand; in painted portraits you can usually recognize him by his green face. Manifestation number eight is **Krishna**, more widely known than Rama in the West, but slightly less common in Thailand. Krishna is usually characterized as a flirtatious, flute-playing, blue-skinned cowherd whose most famous achievement is the lifting of Mount Govadhana (as depicted in relief at Phimai; see box on p.803), but he is also a crucial moral figure in the *Mahabharata*. Confusingly, Vishnu's ninth avatar is the **Buddha** – a manifestation adopted many centuries ago to minimize defection to the Buddhist faith. When represented as **the deity**, Vishnu is generally shown sporting a crown and four arms, his hands holding a conch shell (whose music wards off demons), a discus (used as a weapon), a club (symbolizing the power of nature and time), and a lotus (symbol of joyful flowering and renewal). The god is often depicted astride a **garuda**, a half-man, half-bird. Even without Vishnu on its back, the garuda is a very important beast – a symbol of strength, it's often shown "supporting" temple buildings.

Statues and representations of **Brahma** (the Creator) are very rare. Confusingly, he too has four arms, but you should recognize him by the fact that he holds no objects, has four faces (sometimes painted red), and is generally borne by a goose-like creature called a *hamsa*.

Shiva (the Destroyer) is the most volatile member of the pantheon. He stands for extreme behaviour, for beginnings and endings (as enacted in his frenzied Dance of Destruction, described in the box on p.803), and for fertility, and is a symbol of great energy and power. His godlike form typically has four, eight or ten arms, sometimes holding a trident (representing creation, protection and destruction) and a drum (to beat the rhythm of creation). In his most famous role, as **Nataraja**, or Lord of the Dance, he is usually shown in stylized standing position with legs bent into a balletic position, and the full complement of arms outstretched above his head. Three stripes on a figure's forehead also indicate Shiva, or one of his followers. In abstract form, he is represented by a **lingam** or phallic pillar (once found at the heart of every Khmer temple in the northeast). Primarily a symbol of energy and godly power, the lingam also embodies fertility, particularly when set upright in a vulva-shaped vessel known as a **yoni**. The yoni doubles as a receptacle for the holy water that worshippers pour over the lingam.

Close associates of Shiva include **Parvati**, his wife, and **Ganesh**, his elephant-headed son (the story of how Ganesh came to look as he does is explained in the box on p.803). Depictions of Ganesh abound, both as statues and, because he is the god of knowledge and overcomer of obstacles (in the path of learning), as the symbol of the Fine Arts Department – which crops up on all entrance tickets to museums and historical parks.

The royal, three-headed elephant, **Erawan**, usually only appears as the favourite mount of the god **Indra**, who is rather unremarkable without the beast but generally figures as the king of the gods, with specific power over the elements (particularly rain) – four statues of the god and his mount grace the base of the prang at Bangkok's Wat Arun.

Lesser mythological figures, which originated as Hindu symbols but feature frequently in wats and other Buddhist contexts, include the **yaksha** giants who ward off evil spirits (like the enormous freestanding ones guarding Bangkok's Wat Phra Kaeo); the graceful half-woman, half-bird **kinnari**; and finally, the ubiquitous **naga**, or serpent king of the underworld – often the proud owner of as many as seven heads, whose reptilian body most frequently appears as staircase balustrades in Hindu and Buddhist temples.

The schools

In the 1920s art historians and academics began compiling a classification system for Thai art and architecture which was modelled along the lines of the country's historical periods – these are the guidelines followed below. The following brief overview starts in the sixth century, when Buddhism began to take a hold on the country; few examples of art from before that time have survived, and there are no known earlier architectural relics.

Dvaravati (sixth–eleventh centuries)

Centred around Nakhon Pathom, U Thong and Lopburi in the Chao Phraya basin and in the smaller northern enclave of Haripunjaya (modern-day Lamphun), the **Dvaravati** state was populated by Theravada Buddhists who were strongly influenced by Indian culture.

Hindu legends

Once you've recognized the main characters of the Hindu pantheon, you'll want to know what they're up to in the murals and reliefs that ornament temple walls and ceilings. Of the hundreds of different episodes featured in as many interpretations by painters and sculptors – many taken from the *Ramayana* and *Mahabharata* – the following recur frequently.

The Churning of the Sea of Milk (*in situ* at Khao Phra Viharn, on display at Phimai's National Museum, and in reproduction at Ayutthaya's Historical Study Centre). A creation myth in which Vishnu appears in his second, tortoise, incarnation. The legend describes how the cosmic ocean (or "milk") was churned with a sacred inverted conical mountain to create the universes and all things in them ("the butter"). A naga was used as the churning rope, and the holy tortoise offered his shell to support the mountain – an image which gave rise to the notion of tortoise as the base and foundation stone of the world. The churning also produced a sacred nectar of immortality, which both the gods and the demons were keen to consume. Vishnu craftily encouraged the demons to hold the head-end of the naga rope while helping to make this nectar, giving the gods the tail-end, and encouraging the demons to drink the liquid at its early, alcoholic stage; the friction of the process caused the naga to heat up and breathe fire, burning the demons, who by this stage were so intoxicated that they promptly fell asleep, leaving the distilled nectar for the gods.

Reclining Vishnu Asleep on the Milky Sea of Eternity (the most accessible lintels at Phanom Rung, in the National Museum in Bangkok and at Wat Phra That Narai Cheng Weng near Sakhon Nakhon). Another common creation myth, this time featuring Vishnu as four-armed deity (sometimes referred to as Phra Narai), sleepily reclining on a naga, here representing the Milky Sea of Eternity. Vishnu is dreaming of creating a new universe, shown by the lotus blossoms which spring from his

Only one, fairly late, known example of a Dvaravati-era **building** remains standing: the pyramidal laterite chedi in the compound of Lamphun's Wat Kukut, which is divided into five tiers with niches for stucco Buddha images on each row. Dvaravati-era **artefacts** are much more common, and the national museums in Nakhon Pathom and Lamphun both house quite extensive collections of Buddha images from that period. In an effort to combat the defects inherent in the poor-quality limestone at their disposal, sculptors made their Buddhas quite stocky, cleverly dressing the figures in a sheet-like drape that dropped down to ankle level from each raised wrist, forming a U-shaped hemline – a style which they used when casting in bronze as well. Nonetheless many **statues** have cracked, leaving them headless or limbless. Where the faces have survived, Dvaravati statues display some of the most naturalistic features ever produced in Thailand, distinguished by their thick lips, flattened noses and wide cheekbones.

Nakhon Pathom, a target of Buddhist missionaries from India since before the first century AD, has also yielded a substantial hoard of **dharmachakra**, originating in the period when the Buddha could not be directly represented. These metre-high carved stone wheels symbolize the cycles of life and reincarnation, and in Dvaravati examples are often accompanied by a small statue of a deer, which refers to the Buddha preaching his first sermon in a deer park.

Srivijaya (eighth–thirteenth centuries)

While Dvaravati's Theravada Buddhists were influencing the central plains and, to a limited extent, areas further to the north, southern Thailand was paying

navel, and the four-faced god Brahma who perches atop them; as "Creator", Brahma will be responsible for putting this dream into practice.

Krishna Lifting Mount Govadhana (lintel at Phimai). A story of godly rivalry, in which a community of worshippers suddenly transferred allegiance from the god Indra to the interloping Krishna. Indra, the god of the elements, was so incensed that he attacked the turncoats with a raging storm; they called on Krishna for help, and he obliged by lifting up the mighty Mount Govadhana to provide an enormous umbrella.

Shiva Nataraja: the Dance of Shiva or Shiva's Dance of Destruction (at Phimai, Phanom Rung, Khao Phra Viharn and Wat Phra That Narai Cheng Weng near Sakhon Nakhon). A very powerful and highly symbolic image in which the multi-armed Shiva, as Nataraja, performs a wild, ecstatic dance that brings about the total destruction (through fire) of the extant world and replaces it with a new epoch (as represented by a double-sided drum). In the northeastern Khmer temples this dance is a fairly common subject of stone reliefs, nearly always set as a lintel above a major gateway into the sanctuary.

How Ganesh Came to Have an Elephant's Head. At the time of Ganesh's birth, his father, Shiva, happened to be away from home. On returning to his wife's apartments, Shiva was enraged to find a strange young man in Parvati's boudoir and rashly decapitated the youth. Of course, the boy turned out to be Ganesh, Shiva's own son; full of remorse, the god immediately despatched a servant to procure the head of the first living being he encountered so that his son could be restored to life. The servant returned with an elephant's head, which is why this endearing Hindu god has the pot-bellied body of a child and the head of a young elephant. An alternative version of the tale has Shiva overreacting after his baby son's cries woke him from a particularly pleasant daydream.

allegiance to the Mahayana Buddhists of the **Srivijayan** empire. The key distinction between Theravada and Mahayana strands of thought is that Mahayanists believe that those who have achieved enlightenment should postpone their entry into Nirvana in order to help others along the way. These stay-behinds, revered like saints both during and after life, are called **bodhisattva**, and **statues** of them were the mainstay of Srivijayan art.

The finest Srivijayan *bodhisattva* statues were cast in bronze and show such grace and sinuosity that they rank among the finest sculpture ever produced in the country. Usually shown in the **tribunga**, or hipshot pose, with right hip thrust out and left knee bent, many are lavishly adorned, and some were even bedecked in real jewels when first made. By far the most popular *bodhisattva* subject was **Avalokitesvara**, worshipped as compassion incarnate. Generally shown with four or more arms and with an animal skin over the left shoulder or tied at the waist, Avalokitesvara is also sometimes depicted with his torso covered in tiny Buddha images. Bangkok's National Museum holds the most beautiful Avalokitesvara, found in Chaiya; most of the other best Srivijayan sculptures have been snapped up by Bangkok's curators as well.

As for Srivijayan **temples**, quite a number have been built over, and so are unviewable. The most typical intact example is the Javanese-style chedi at Chaiya's Wat Phra Boromathat, heavily restored but distinguished from contemporaneous Dvaravati structures by its highly ornamented stepped chedi, with mini chedis at each corner.

Khmer and Lopburi (tenth–fourteenth centuries)

By the end of the ninth century the **Khmers** of Cambodia were starting to expand from their capital at Angkor into the Dvaravati states, bringing with them the Hindu faith and the cult of the god-king (*devaraja*). As lasting testaments to the sacred power of their kings, the Khmers built hundreds of imposing stone **sanctuaries** across their newly acquired territory: the top examples are in southern Isaan, at Phimai, Phanom Rung, and Khao Phra Viharn, though there is also an interesting early one at Muang Singh near Kanchanaburi.

Each magnificent castle-temple – known in Khmer as a **prasat** – was constructed primarily as a shrine for a Shiva lingam, the phallic representation of the god Shiva. They followed a similar pattern, centred on at least one towering structure, or **prang**, which represented Mount Meru (the gods' heavenly abode), and surrounded by concentric rectangular enclosures, within and beyond which were dug artificial lakes and moats – miniature versions of the primordial ocean dividing heaven from earth.

The prasats' most fascinating and superbly crafted features, however, are the **carvings** that ornament almost every surface. Usually gouged from sandstone, but frequently moulded in stucco, these exuberant reliefs depict Hindu deities, incarnations and stories, especially episodes from the *Ramayana* (see box on p.127). Towards the end of the twelfth century, the Khmer leadership became Mahayana Buddhist, commissioning Buddhist carvings to be installed alongside the Hindu ones, and simultaneously replacing the Shiva lingam at the heart of each sanctuary with a Buddha or *bodhisattva* image. (See p.492 for more on the architectural details.)

The temples built in the former Theravada Buddhist principality of **Lopburi** during the Khmer period are much smaller affairs than those in Isaan, and are best represented by the triple-pranged temple of Phra Prang Sam Yot. The Lopburi classification is most usually applied to the Buddha statues that emerged at the tail end of the Khmer period, picking up the Dvaravati sculptural legacy. Broad-faced and muscular, the classic Lopburi Buddha wears a diadem or ornamental headband – a nod to the Khmers' ideological fusion of earthly and heavenly power – and the *ushnisha* (the sign of enlightenment) becomes distinctly conical rather than a mere bump on the head. Early Lopburi Buddhas come garlanded with necklaces and ornamental belts; later examples eschew the jewels. As you'd expect, Lopburi National Museum houses a good selection.

Sukhothai (thirteenth–fifteenth centuries)

Capitalizing on the Khmers' weakening hold over central Thailand, two Thai generals established the first real Thai kingdom in **Sukhothai** in 1238, and over the next two hundred years the artists of this realm produced some of Thailand's most refined art. Sukhothai's artistic reputation rests above all on its **sculpture**. More sinuous even than the Srivijayan images, Sukhothai Buddhas tend towards elegant androgyny, with slim oval faces that show little of the humanistic Dvaravati features or the strength of Lopburi statues, and slender curvaceous bodies usually clad in a plain, skintight robe that fastens with a tassel close to the navel (see box on p.281). The sculptors favoured the seated pose, with hands in the *Bhumisparsa Mudra*, most expertly executed in the Phra Buddha Chinnarat image, now housed in Phitsanulok's Wat Si Ratana Mahathat (replicated at Bangkok's Wat Benjamabophit) and in the enormous Phra Sri Sakyamuni, now enshrined in Bangkok's Wat Suthat. They were also the first to represent the **walking Buddha**, a supremely graceful figure with his right leg poised to move forwards and his left arm in the *Vitarkha Mudra*, as seen in the compounds of Sukhothai's Wat Sra Si.

The cities of Sukhothai and nearby Si Satchanalai were already stamped with sturdy relics of the Khmers' presence, but rather than pull down the sacred prangs of their predecessors, Sukhothai builders added bots, viharns and chedis to the existing structures, as well as conceiving quite separate **temple complexes**. Their viharns and bots are the earliest halls of worship still standing in Thailand (the Khmers didn't go in for large public assemblies), but in most cases only the stone pillars and their platforms remain, the wooden roofs having long since disintegrated. The best examples can be seen in the historical park at Sukhothai, with less grandiose structures at the parks in nearby Si Satchanalai and Kamphaeng Phet.

Most of the **chedis**, though, are in much better shape. Many were modelled on the Sri Lankan bell-shaped reliquary tower (symbolizing the Buddha's teachings ringing out far and wide), often set atop a one- or two-tiered square base surrounded by elephant buttresses – Si Satchanalai's Wat Chang Lom is a stylish example. The architects also devised a new type of chedi, as elegant in its way as the images their sculptor colleagues were producing. This was the **lotus-bud chedi**, a slender tower topped with a tapered finial that was to become a hallmark of the Sukhothai era. In Sukhothai both Wat Mahathat and Wat Trapang Ngoen display good examples.

Ancient Sukhothai is also renowned for the skill of its potters, who produced a **ceramic ware** known as Sawankhalok, after the name of one of the nearby kiln towns. Most museum ceramics collections are dominated by Sawankhalok ware, which is distinguished by its grey-green celadon glazes and by the fish and chrysanthemum motifs used to decorate bowls and plates; there's a dedicated Sawankhalok museum in Sukhothai.

Lanna (thirteenth–sixteenth centuries)

Meanwhile, to the north of Sukhothai, the independent Theravada Buddhist kingdom of Lanna was flourishing. Its art styles – known interchangeably as Chiang Saen and Lanna – evolved from an eclectic range of precursors, building on the Dvaravati heritage of Haripunjaya, copying direct from Indian sources and incorporating Sukhothai and Sri Lankan ideas from the south.

△ Wat Sri Sarai, Sukhothai

The earliest surviving Lanna **monument** is the Dvaravati-style Chedi Si Liem in Chiang Mai, built to the pyramidal form characteristic of Mon builders in fairly close imitation of the much earlier Wat Kukut in Lampang. Also in Chiang Mai, Wat Jet Yot replicates the temple built at Bodh Gaya in India to commemorate the seven sites where the Buddha meditated in the first seven weeks after attaining enlightenment – hence the symbolic seven pyramidal chedis, and hence also the name, which means "the temple of seven spires".

Lanna **sculpture** also drew some inspiration from Bodh Gaya: the early Lanna images tend to plumpness, with broad shoulders and prominent hair curls, which are all characteristics of the main Buddha at Bodh Gaya. The later works are slimmer, probably as a result of Sukhothai influence, and one of the most famous examples of this type is the Phra Singh Buddha, enshrined in Chiang Mai's Wat Phra Singh. Other good illustrations of both styles are housed in Chiang Mai's National Museum.

Ayutthaya (fourteenth–eighteenth centuries)

Although the Sukhothai era was artistically fertile, the kingdom had only a short political life and from 1351 Thailand's central plains came under the thrall of a new power centred on **Ayutthaya** and ruled by a former prince of Lopburi. Over the next four centuries, the Ayutthayan capital became one of the most prosperous and ostentatious cities in Asia, its rulers commissioning some four hundred grand wats as symbols of their wealth and power. Though essentially Theravada Buddhists, the kings also adopted some Hindu and Brahmin beliefs from the Khmers – most significantly the concept of *devaraja* or god-kingship, whereby the monarch became a mediator between the people and the Hindu gods. The religious buildings and sculptures of this era reflected this new composite ideology, both by fusing the architectural styles inherited from the Khmers and from Sukhothai and by dressing their Buddhas to look like regents.

Retaining the concentric layout of the typical Khmer **temple complex**, Ayutthayan builders played around with the component structures, most notably the prang, which they refined and elongated into a **corncob-shaped tower**, rounding it off at the top and introducing vertical incisions around its circumference. As a spire they often added a bronze thunderbolt, and into niches within the prang walls they placed Buddha images. In Ayutthaya itself, the ruined complexes of Wat Phra Mahathat and Wat Ratburana both include these corncob prangs, but the most famous example is Bangkok's Wat Arun, which though built during the subsequent Bangkok period is a classic Ayutthayan structure.

Ayutthaya's architects also adapted the Sri Lankan **chedi** so favoured by their Sukhothai predecessors, stretching the bell-shaped base and tapering it into a very graceful conical spire, as at Wat Sri Sanphet in Ayutthaya. The **viharns** of this era are characterized by walls pierced by slit-like windows, designed to foster a mysterious atmosphere by limiting the amount of light inside the building. As with all of Ayutthaya's buildings, few viharns survived the brutal 1767 sacking, with the notable exception of Wat Na Phra Mane. Phitsanulok's Wat Phra Ratana Si Mahathat was built to a similar plan – and in Phetchaburi, Wat Yai Suwannaram has no windows at all.

From Sukhothai's Buddha **sculptures** the Ayutthayans copied the soft oval face, adding an earthlier demeanour to the features and imbuing them with an hauteur in tune with the *devaraja* ideology. Like the Lopburi images, early Ayutthayan statues wear crowns to associate kingship with Buddhahood; as the court became ever more lavish, so these figures became increasingly adorned, until – as in the monumental bronze at Wat Na Phra Mane – they appeared in earrings, armlets, anklets, bandoliers and coronets. The artists justified these luscious portraits of the Buddha – who was, after all, supposed to have given up worldly possessions – by pointing to an episode when the Buddha transformed himself into a well-dressed nobleman to gain the ear of a proud emperor, whereupon he scolded the man into entering the monkhood.

While a couple of wats in Sukhothai show hints of painted decoration, religious **painting** in Thailand really dates from the Ayutthayan era. Unfortunately most of Ayutthaya's own paintings were destroyed in 1767 and others have suffered badly from damp, but several temples in other parts of the country still have some well-preserved murals, in particular Wat Yai Suwannaram in Phetchaburi. By all accounts typical of late-seventeenth-century painting, Phetchaburi's murals depict rows of *thep*, or divinities, paying homage to the Buddha, in scenes presented without shadow or perspective, and mainly executed in dark reds and cream.

Ratanakosin (eighteenth century to the 1930s)

When **Bangkok** emerged as Ayutthaya's successor in 1782, the new capital's founder was determined to revive the old city's grandeur, and the **Ratanakosin** (or Bangkok) period began by aping what the Ayutthayans had done. Since then neither wat architecture nor religious sculpture has evolved much further.

The first Ratanakosin **building** was the bot of Bangkok's Wat Phra Kaeo, built to enshrine the Emerald Buddha. Designed to a typical Ayutthayan plan, it's coated in glittering mirrors and gold leaf, with roofs ranged in multiple tiers and tiled in green and orange. To this day, most newly built bots and viharns follow a more economical version of this paradigm, whitewashing the outside walls but decorating the pediment in gilded ornaments and mosaics of coloured glass. Tiered temple roofs – an Ayutthayan innovation of which few examples remain in that city – still taper off into the slender bird-like finials called *chofa*, and naga staircases – a Khmer feature inherited by Ayutthaya – have become an almost obligatory feature of any major temple. The result is that modern wats are often almost indistinguishable from each other, though Bangkok does have a few exceptions, including Wat Benjamabophit, which uses marble cladding for its walls and incorporates Victorian-style stained-glass windows, and Wat Rajabophit, which is covered all over in Chinese ceramics. The most dramatic chedi of the Ratanokosin era – the tallest in the world – was constructed in the mid-nineteenth century in Nakhon Pathom to the original Sri Lankan style, but minus the elephant buttresses found in Sukhothai.

Early Ratanakosin sculptors produced adorned **Buddha images** very much in the Ayutthayan vein, sometimes adding real jewels to the figures, and more modern images are notable for their ugliness rather than for any radical departure from type. The obsession with size, first apparent in the Sukhothai period, has plumbed new depths, with graceless concrete statues up to 60m high becoming the norm (as in Roi Et's Wat Burapha), a monumentalism made worse by the routine application of browns and dull yellows. Most small images are cast from or patterned on older models, mostly Sukhothai or Ayutthayan in origin.

Painting has fared much better, with the *Ramayana* murals in Bangkok's Wat Phra Kaeo (see p.128) a shining example of how Ayutthayan techniques and traditional subject matters could be adapted into something fantastic, imaginative and beautiful.

Contemporary

Following the democratization of Thailand in the 1930s, artists increasingly became recognized as individuals, and took to signing their work for the first time. In 1933 the first school of fine art (now Bangkok's Silpakorn University) was established under the Italian sculptor Corrado Feroci, designer of the capital's Democracy Monument and, as the new generation experimented with secular themes and styles adapted from the Western Impressionist, post-Impressionist and Cubist movements, later embracing Abstraction and Expressionism, Thai art began to look a lot more "**modern**". Nonetheless, with a few notable exceptions, the leading artistic preoccupation of the past 75 years has been Thailand's spiritual heritage, with nearly every major figure on the contemporary art scene tackling religious issues at some point. For some artists this has meant a straightforward modernization of Buddhist legends or a reworking of particular symbols, while others have sought to dramatize the moral relevance of their religion in the light of political, social and philosophical trends. A number of Thailand's more established contemporary artists have earned the title **National Artist**, an honour that has been bestowed on one or two artists, of any discipline, nearly every year since 1985.

Bangkok has a near-monopoly on Thailand's **art galleries**. While the permanent collections at the National Gallery are disappointing, regular exhibitions of more challenging contemporary work appear at the Silpakorn University Art Gallery, The Queen's Gallery, and the Queen Sirikit Convention Centre, as well as at smaller gallery spaces around the city. The listings magazine *Bangkok Metro* prints details of current exhibitions, and does features on prominent artists too, or there's the bi-monthly free Art Connection calendar of exhibitions, available from galleries. The headquarters of Bangkok's major banks and securities' companies also display works by modern Thai artists both established and lesser known, and in recent years have made a big show of backing substantial art prizes. For a preview of works by Thailand's best modern artists, visit the Rama IX Art Museum Foundation's website at ®www.rama9art.org.

One of the first modern artists to adapt traditional styles and themes was **Angkarn Kalayanapongsa** (b. 1926), whose most public work can be seen in temple murals such as those at Wat Sri Khom Kham in Phayao. Characteristic of this aspect of Angkarn's work is the fusion of the elegant, two-dimensional styles of Ayutthayan mural painting (of which few original examples remain) with a surrealistic, dreamlike quality. Many of his paintings feature casts of *khon*-like figures and flying *thep* in a setting studded with symbols from both Buddhism and contemporary culture. Angkarn was an early recipient of the title National Artist.

Aiming for the more secular environments of the gallery and the private home, National Artist **Pichai Nirand** (b. 1936) rejects the traditional mural style and makes more selective choices of Buddhist imagery, appropriating religious objects and icons and reinterpreting their significance. He's particularly well known for his fine-detail canvases of Buddha footprints, many of which can be seen in Bangkok galleries and public spaces.

Pratuang Emjaroen (b. 1935) is famous for his social commentary, as epitomized by his huge and powerful canvas *Dharma and Adharma; The Days of Disaster*, which he painted in response to the vicious clashes between the military and students in 1973. The 5m x 2m picture depicts images of severed limbs, screaming faces and bloody gun barrels amid shadowy images of the Buddha's face, a spiked *dharmachakra* and other religious symbols. Many of Pratuang's subsequent works have addressed the issue of social injustice, using his trademark strong shafts of light and bold colour in a mix of Buddhist iconography and abstract imagery.

Prolific traditionalist **Chakrabhand Posayakrit** (b. 1943) is also inspired by Thailand's Buddhist culture; he is famously proud of his country's cultural heritage, which infuses much of his work and has led to him being honoured as a National Artist. He is best known for his series of 33 *Life of the Buddha* paintings, and for his portraits, including many of members of the Thai royal family.

More controversial, and more of a household name, **Thawan Duchanee** (b. 1939) has tended to examine the spiritual tensions of modern life. His surreal juxtaposition of religious icons with fantastical Bosch-like characters and explicitly sexual images prompted a group of fundamentalist students to slash ten of his early paintings in 1971 – an unprecedented reaction to a work of Thai art. Since then, Thawan has continued to produce allegorical investigations into the individual's struggles against the obstacles that dog the Middle Way, prominent among them lust and violence, but since the 1980s his street cred has waned as his saleability has mushroomed. Critics have questioned his integrity at accepting commissions from corporate clients, and his neo-conservative image cannot have been enhanced when he was honoured as a National Artist in 2001.

Complacency is not a criticism that could be levelled at **Vasan Sitthiket** (b. 1957), Thailand's most outspoken and iconoclastic artist, whose uncompromising pictures are shown at – and still occasionally banned from – large and small galleries around the capital. A persistent crusader against the hypocrisies of establishment figures such as monks, politicians and military leaders, Vasan's is one of the loudest and most aggressive political voices on the contemporary art scene, expressed on canvas, in multi-media works and in performance art. His significance is well established and he was one of the seven artists to represent Thailand at the 2003 Venice Biennale, where Thailand had its own pavilion for the first time. Some of Vasan's most famous recent work has taken the form of enormous wooden puppets: typical were his grotesque representations of 49 Thai luminaries in his 2000 show What's In our Head, an exhibit that had to be assembled in just a few days following the banning of his original show for being too provocative.

Contemporary women artists tend to be less high profile in Thailand, but **Pinaree Santipak** (b. 1961) is becoming an important name: her mostly multi-media work focuses on gender issues and makes recurrent use of a female iconography. Her Vessels and Mounds show of 2001, for example, featured installations of huge breast-shaped floor cushions, candles and bowls.

Religion: Thai Buddhism

Over ninety percent of Thais consider themselves Theravada Buddhists, followers of the teachings of a holy man usually referred to as the Buddha (Enlightened One), though more precisely known as Gautama Buddha to distinguish him from three lesser-known Buddhas who preceded him, and from the fifth and final Buddha who is predicted to arrive in the year 4457 AD. Theravada Buddhism is one of the two main schools of Buddhism practised in Asia, and in Thailand it has absorbed an eclectic assortment of animist and Hindu elements into its beliefs as well. The other ten percent of Thailand's population comprises Mahayana Buddhists, Muslims, Hindus, Sikhs and Christians.

The Buddha: his life and beliefs

Buddhists believe that Gautama Buddha was the five-hundredth incarnation of a single being: the stories of these five hundred lives, collectively known as the **Jataka**, provide the inspiration for much Thai art. (Hindus also accept Gautama Buddha into their pantheon, perceiving him as the ninth manifestation of their god Vishnu.)

In his last incarnation he was born in Nepal as **Prince Gautama Siddhartha** in either the sixth or seventh century BC, the son of a king and his hitherto barren wife, who finally became pregnant only after having a dream that a white elephant had entered her womb. At the time of his birth astrologers predicted that Gautama was to become universally respected, either as a worldly king or as a spiritual saviour, depending on which way of life he pursued. Much preferring the former idea, the prince's father forbade anyone to let the boy out of the palace grounds, and took it upon himself to educate Gautama in all aspects of the high life. Most statues of the Buddha depict him with elongated earlobes, which is a reference to this early pampered existence, when he would have worn heavy precious stones in his ears.

The prince married and became a father, but at the age of 29 he flouted his father's authority and sneaked out into the world beyond the palace. On this fateful trip he encountered successively an old man, a sick man, a corpse and a hermit, and thus for the first time was made aware that pain and suffering were intrinsic to human life. Contemplation seemed the only means of discovering why this should be so – and therefore Gautama decided to leave the palace and become a **Hindu ascetic**.

For six or seven years he wandered the countryside leading a life of self-denial and self-mortification, but failed to come any closer to the answer. Eventually concluding that the best course of action must be to follow a "Middle Way" – neither indulgent nor over-ascetic – Gautama sat down beneath the famous riverside bodhi tree at **Bodh Gaya** in India, facing the rising sun, to meditate until he achieved enlightenment. For 49 days he sat cross-legged in the "lotus position", contemplating the causes of suffering and wrestling with temptations that materialized to distract him. Most of these were sent by **Mara**, the Evil One, who was finally subdued when Gautama summoned the earth goddess **Mae Toranee** by pointing the fingers of his right hand at the ground – the gesture known as *Bhumisparsa Mudra*, which has been immortalized by hundreds of Thai sculptors. Mae Toranee wrung torrents of water from her hair and engulfed Mara's demonic emissaries in a flood, an episode that also features in several sculptures and paintings, most famously in the statue in Bangkok's Sanam Luang.

Temptations dealt with, Gautama soon came to attain **enlightenment** and so become a Buddha. As the place of his enlightenment, the **bodhi tree** (or bo tree) has assumed special significance for Buddhists: not only does it appear in many Buddhist paintings and a few sculptures, but there's often a real bodhi tree (*ficus religiosa*) planted in temple compounds as well. Furthermore, the bot is nearly always built facing either a body of water or facing east (preferably both).

The Buddha preached his **first sermon** in a deer park in India, where he characterized his Dharma (doctrine) as a wheel. From this episode comes the early Buddhist symbol the **Dharmachakra**, known as the Wheel of Law, Wheel of Doctrine or Wheel of Life, which is often accompanied by a statue of a deer. Thais celebrate this first sermon with a public holiday in July known as Asanha Puja. On another occasion 1250 people spontaneously gathered to hear the Buddha speak, an event remembered in Thailand as Maha Puja and marked by a public holiday in February.

For the next forty-odd years the Buddha travelled the region converting non-believers and performing miracles. One rainy season he even ascended into the Tavatimsa heaven (Heaven of the thirty-three gods) to visit his mother and to preach the doctrine to her. His descent from this heaven is quite a common theme of paintings and sculptures, and the **Standing Buddha** pose of numerous Buddha statues comes from this story. He also went back to his father's palace where he was temporarily reunited with his wife and child: the Khon Kaen museum houses a particularly lovely carving of this event.

The Buddha "died" at the age of eighty on the banks of a river at Kusinari in India – an event often dated to 543 BC, which is why the Thai calendar is 543 years out of synch with the Western one, so that the year 2005 AD becomes 2548 BE (Buddhist Era). Lying on his side, propping up his head on his hand, the Buddha passed into **Nirvana** (giving rise to another classic pose, the Reclining Buddha), the unimaginable state of nothingness which knows no suffering and from which there is no reincarnation. Buddhists believe that the day the Buddha entered Nirvana was the same date on which he was born and on which he achieved enlightenment, a triply significant day that Thais honour with the Visakha Puja festival in May.

Buddhist doctrine

After the Buddha entered Nirvana, his **doctrine** spread relatively quickly across India, and probably was first promulgated in Thailand in about the third century BC. His teachings, the *Tripitaka*, were written down in the Pali language – a derivative of Sanskrit – in a form that became known as Theravada, or "The Doctrine of the Elders".

As taught by the Buddha, **Theravada Buddhism** built on the Hindu theory of perpetual reincarnation in the pursuit of perfection, introducing the notion of life as a cycle of suffering which could only be transcended by enlightened beings able to free themselves from earthly ties and enter into the blissful state of Nirvana. For the well-behaved but unenlightened Buddhist, each reincarnation marks a move up a vague kind of ladder, with animals at the bottom, women figuring lower down than men, and monks coming at the top.

The Buddhist has no hope of enlightenment without acceptance of the **four noble truths**. In encapsulated form, these hold that desire is the root cause of all suffering and can be extinguished only by following the eightfold path or Middle Way. This **Middle Way** is essentially a highly moral mode of life that includes all the usual virtues like compassion, respect and moderation, and eschews vices such as self-indulgence and antisocial behaviour. But the key to it all is an acknowledgement that the physical world is impermanent and ever-changing, and that all things – including the self – are therefore not worth craving. Only by pursuing a condition of complete **detachment** can human beings transcend earthly suffering.

By the beginning of the first millennium, a new movement called **Mahayana** (Great Vehicle) had emerged within the Theravada school, attempting to make Buddhism more accessible by introducing a Hindu-style pantheon of *bodhisattva*, or Buddhist saints, who, although they had achieved enlightenment, nevertheless postponed entering Nirvana in order to inspire the populace. Mahayana Buddhism subsequently spread north into China, Korea, Vietnam and Japan, also entering southern Thailand via the Srivijayan empire around the eighth century and parts of Khmer Cambodia in about the eleventh century. Meanwhile Theravada Buddhism (which the Mahayanists disparagingly renamed "Hinayana" or "Lesser Vehicle") established itself most significantly in Sri Lanka, northern and central Thailand and Burma.

The monkhood

In Thailand it's the duty of the 270,000-strong **Sangha** (monkhood) to set an example to the Theravada Buddhist community by living a life as close to the Middle Way as possible and by preaching the Dharma to the people. A monk's life is governed by 227 strict rules that include celibacy and the rejection of all personal possessions except gifts.

Each day begins with an alms round in the neighbourhood so that the laity can donate food and thereby gain themselves merit (see p.814), and then is chiefly spent in meditation, chanting, teaching and study. Always the most respected members of any community, monks act as teachers, counsellors and arbiters in local disputes, and sometimes become spokesmen for villagers' rights. They also perform rituals at cremations, weddings and other events, such as the launching of a new business or even the purchase of a new car. Although some Thai women do become nuns, they belong to no official order and aren't respected as much as the monks.

Monkhood doesn't have to be for life: a man may leave the Sangha three times without stigma and in fact every Thai male (including royalty) is expected to **enter the monkhood** for a short period at some point in his life, ideally between leaving school and marrying, as a rite of passage into adulthood. So ingrained into the social system is this practice that Thai government departments and some private companies grant their employees paid leave for their time as a monk, but the custom is in decline as young men increasingly have to consider the effect their absence may have on their career prospects. The most popular time for temporary ordination is the three-month Buddhist retreat period – **Pansa**, sometimes referred to as "Buddhist Lent" – which begins in July and lasts for the duration of the rainy season. (The monks' confinement is said to originate from the earliest years of Buddhist history, when farmers complained that perambulating monks were squashing their sprouting rice crops.) **Ordination ceremonies** take place in almost every wat at this time and make spectacular scenes, with the shaven-headed novice usually clad entirely in white and carried about on friends' or relatives' shoulders, or even on elephants as in Hat Siew near Si Satchanalai (see p.290) and Ban Ta Klang near Surin (see p.505). The boys' parents donate money, food and necessities such as washing powder and mosquito repellent, processing around the temple compound with their gifts, often joined by dancers or travelling players hired for the occasion.

Monks in contemporary society

In recent years, some monks have extended their role as village spokesmen to become influential activists: monks played a key role in the fierce campaign against the Pak Mun dam in Isaan (see p.824), for example; Wat Tham Krabok near Lopburi and Wat Nong Sam Pran in Kanchanaburi are among a growing number of temples that have established themselves as successful drug rehabilitation centres; and monks at Wat Phai Lom near Bangkok have developed the country's largest breeding colony of Asian open-billed storks. However, the increasing involvement of many monks in the secular world has not met with unanimous approval.

Far more disappointing to the laity are those monks who **flout the precepts** of the Sangha by succumbing to the temptations of a consumer society, flaunting Raybans, Rolexes and Mercedes (in some cases actually bought with temple funds), chain-smoking and flirting, even making pocket money from predicting lottery results and practising faith-healing. With so much national pride and integrity riding on the sanctity of the Sangha, any whiff of a deeper scandal is bound to strike deep into the national psyche, and everyone was shocked when a young monk confessed to robbing and then murdering a British tourist in 1995. Since then Thai monks have been involved in an unprecedented litany of crimes, including several rapes and murders, and there's been an embarrassment of exposés of corrupt, high-ranking abbots caught carousing in disreputable bars, drug-dealing and even gun-running. This has prompted a stream of editorials on the state of the Sangha and the collapse of spiritual values at the heart of Thai society. The inclusivity of the monkhood – which is open to just about any male who wants to join – has been highlighted as a particularly vulnerable aspect, not least because donning saffron robes has always been an accepted way for criminals, reformed or otherwise, to repent of their past deeds. Interestingly, back in the late 1980s, the influential monk, Phra Bodhirak, was unceremoniously defrocked after criticizing what he saw as a tide of decadence infecting Thai Buddhism and advocating an all-round purification of the Sangha. He now preaches from his breakaway Santi Asoke sect headquarters on the outskirts of Bangkok, but though his ascetic code of behaviour is followed by thousands of devotees across Thailand, it is not sanctioned by the more worldly figures of the Sangha Supreme Council.

Buddhist practice

In practice most Thai Buddhists aim only to be **reborn** higher up the incarnation scale rather than set their sights on the ultimate goal of Nirvana. The rank of the reincarnation is directly related to the good and bad actions performed in the previous life, which accumulate to determine one's **karma** or destiny – hence the Thai obsession with "making merit".

Merit-making (*tham bun*) can be done in all sorts of ways, from giving a monk his breakfast to attending a Buddhist service or donating money to the neighbourhood temple, and most festivals are essentially communal merit-making opportunities. Between the big festivals, the most common days for making merit and visiting the temple are *wan phra* (holy days), which are determined by the phase of the moon and occur four times a month. For a Thai man, temporary ordination is a very important way of accruing merit not only for himself but also for his mother and sisters – wealthier citizens might take things a step further by commissioning the casting of a Buddha statue or even paying for the building of a wat. One of the more bizarre but common merit-making activities involves **releasing caged birds**: worshippers buy one or more tiny finches from vendors at wat compounds and, by liberating them from their cage, prove their Buddhist compassion towards all living things. The fact that the birds were free until netted earlier that morning doesn't seem to detract from the ritual at all. In riverside and seaside wats, birds are sometimes replaced by fish or even baby turtles.

Spirits and non-Buddhist deities

The complicated history of the area now known as Thailand has, not surprisingly, made Thai Buddhism a strangely syncretic faith, as you'll realize when you enter a Buddhist temple compound to be confronted by a statue of a Hindu deity. While regular Buddhist merit-making insures a Thai for the next life, there are certain **Hindu gods and animist spirits** that most Thais also cultivate for help with more immediate problems. Sophisticated Bangkokians and illiterate farmers alike find no inconsistency in these apparently incompatible practices, and as often as not it's a Buddhist monk who is called in to exorcize a malevolent spirit. Even the Buddhist King Bhumibol employs Brahmin priests and astrologers to determine auspicious days and officiate at certain royal ceremonies and, like his royal predecessors of the Chakri dynasty, he also associates himself with the Hindu god Vishnu by assuming the title Rama IX – Rama, hero of the Hindu epic the *Ramayana*, having been Vishnu's seventh manifestation on earth.

If a Thai wants help in achieving a short-term goal, like passing an exam, becoming pregnant or winning the lottery, then he or she will quite likely turn to the **Hindu pantheon**, visiting an enshrined statue of Brahma, Vishnu, Shiva or Ganesh, and making offerings of flowers, incense and maybe food. If the outcome is favourable, devotees will probably come back to show thanks, bringing more offerings and maybe even hiring a dance troupe to perform a celebratory *lakhon chatri* as well. Built in honour of Brahma, Bangkok's Erawan Shrine is the most famous place of Hindu-inspired worship in the country.

Whereas Hindu deities tend to be benevolent, **spirits** (or *phi*) are not nearly as reliable and need to be mollified more frequently. They come in hundreds of varieties, some more malign than others, and inhabit everything from trees, rivers and caves to public buildings and private homes – even taking over people if they feel like it. So that these *phi* don't pester human inhabitants, each building has a special **spirit house** (*phra phum*) in its vicinity, as a dwelling for spirits ousted by the building's construction. Usually raised on a short column to set it at or above eye-level, the spirit house must occupy an auspicious location – not, for example, in the shadow of the main building – so help from the local temple is usually required when deciding on the best position. Spirit houses are generally about the size of a dolls' house and designed to look like a wat or a traditional Thai house, but their ornamentation is supposed to reflect the status of the humans' building, so if that building is enlarged or refurbished, the spirit house should be improved accordingly. Figurines representing the relevant guardian spirit and his aides are sometimes put inside the little house, and daily offerings of incense, lighted candles and garlands of jasmine are placed alongside them to keep the *phi* happy – a disgruntled spirit is a dangerous spirit, liable to cause sickness, accidents and even death. As with any religious building or icon in Thailand, an unwanted or crumbling spirit house should never be dismantled or destroyed, which is why you'll often see damaged spirit houses placed around the base of a sacred banyan tree, where they are able to rest in peace.

Flora, fauna and environmental issues

Spanning some 1650km north to south, Thailand lies in the heart of Southeast Asia's tropical zone, its northernmost region just a few degrees south of the Tropic of Cancer, its southern border running less than seven degrees north of the Equator. As with other tropical regions across the world, Thailand's climate is characterized by high humidity and even higher temperatures, a very fertile combination which nourishes a huge diversity of flora and fauna in a vast range of habitats, from mixed deciduous and dry dipterocarp forests in the mountainous north to wet tropical rainforests in the steamy south. At least six percent of the world's vascular plants are found here, with over 15,000 species so far recorded.

Seventeen percent of Thailand's land mass is protected as **national park**, and it is in these reserves that the kingdom's natural heritage is best appreciated. The most rewarding of the country's national parks, including Khao Yai in the northeast, Doi Inthanon and Doi Suthep in the north, and Khao Sam Roi Yot and Khao Sok in the south, are described in detail in the guide; general practical information on national parks is given in Basics on p.75.

The geography of Thailand

Thailand has a **tropical monsoon climate**. Most rain is brought from the Indian Ocean by the southwest monsoon from May to October, the so-called rainy season. From November to February the northeast monsoon brings a much cooler and drier climate from China, the cold, dry season. However, this northeastern monsoon hits the peninsular east coast after crossing the South China Sea, loading up with moist air and therefore extending this region's rainy season until January or later. The north–south divide is generally considered to lie just north of Ranong (10°N) – the capital of Thailand's wettest province – at the Kra Isthmus (see p.642).

Agriculture plays a significant role in Thailand's economy, and 46 percent of Thais live off the land. Waterlogged rice paddies characterize the central plains; cassava, tapioca and eucalyptus are grown as cash crops on the scrubby plateau of the northeast; and rubber plantations dominate the commercial land-use of the south. Dotted along Thailand's coastline are mangrove swamps and palm forests; the country's coral reefs are discussed under "Wildlife" (see p.822).

Mixed deciduous and dry dipterocarp forests

An estimated 65 percent of Thailand's forests are **deciduous**, occasionally referred to as monsoon forest because they have to survive periods of up to six months with minimal rainfall, so the trees shed their leaves to conserve water. Deciduous forests are often light and open, with canopies ranging from as low as 10m up to a maximum of about 40m. The undergrowth is usually fairly thick. As they are relatively easy to fell, especially with the notorious slash-and-burn technique, a significant proportion of Thailand's deciduous forest has been cleared for both small and commercial cultivation purposes.

The family **Dipterocarpaceae** dominate these forests, a group of tropical hardwoods prized for their timber and, in places, their resin. The name comes from the Greek and means "two-winged fruit". **Teak** was once a common species in northern deciduous forests, but its solid, unwarpable timber is such a sought-after material for everything from floors to furniture that nearly all the teak forests have been felled. Teak trees take around two hundred years to attain their full height of 40m, but artificial cultivation is becoming increasingly widespread in Thailand, and a teak tree's life-span on a plantation can be as short as fifteen years.

Bamboo thrives in a monsoon climate, shooting up at a remarkable rate during the wet season, often in soils too poor for other species; as a result bamboo often predominates in secondary forests (those where logging or clearing has previously taken place, and a new generation of plants has grown up – the majority of Thailand's forest). The smooth, woody, hollow stem characteristic of all varieties of bamboo is a fantastically adaptable material, used by the Thais for constructing everything from outside walls to chairs to water-pipes (in hill-tribe villages) and musical instruments; and the bamboo shoot is an essential ingredient in Thai-Chinese cuisine.

Tropical rainforests

Thailand's **tropical rainforests** occur in areas of high and prolonged rainfall in the southern peninsula, most accessibly in the national parks of Khao Sok, Thale Ban, Tarutao and Khao Luang. Some areas contain as many as two hundred species of tree within a single hectare, along with a host of other flora. Characteristic of a tropical rainforest is the multi-layered series of **canopies**. The uppermost storey of emergent trees sometimes reaches 60m, and these towering trees often have enormous buttressed roots for support; beneath this, the dense canopy of 25–35m is often festooned with climbers and epiphytes such as ferns, lianas, mosses and orchids; then comes an uneven layer 5–10m high consisting of palms, rattans, shrubs and small trees. The forest floor in tropical rainforests tends to be relatively open and free of dense undergrowth, owing to the intense filtering of light by the upper three layers.

Again, members of the Dipterocarpaceae family are dominant, and it is these trees, along with strangling figs, that form some of the most spectacular buttress roots. Though dipterocarps provide little food for fauna, they play an important role as nesting sites for hornbills, as lookout posts for gibbons – and as timber.

Semi-evergreen forests

Semi-evergreen forests are the halfway house between tropical rainforests and dry deciduous forests, showing characteristics of both habitats. It's a classification that includes all lowland and submontane evergreen forests from the plains to about 1000m. Semi-evergreen forests thrive in regions with distinctly seasonal rainfall where the humidity is relatively low; they share many similarities with the southern rainforests, though the canopies are lower and you'll find fewer palms and rattans. Fine examples can be found at Khao Yai and Kaeng Krachang national parks, and all along the Burmese border, all of which are potentially good places to observe large mammals, including elephants, gaurs, tigers and bears.

Hill evergreen (montane) forests

Above 1000m, the canopy of tall trees gives way to **hill evergreen forest** growth, consisting of oaks, chestnuts, laurels and other shorter temperate-zone tree families, many with twisted trunks and comparatively small leaves. Rainfall is frequent and often continuous at these elevations, so moss usually covers the forest floor and the undergrowth seems a lot denser, particularly with epiphytes, rhododendrons and various types of tree fern. These highland forests are exposed to the harshest winds and coolest temperatures, so only the hardiest, sturdiest tree and plant species survive.

Hill evergreen forest can occur within areas dominated by either monsoon forest or tropical rainforest. Good examples can be seen in Doi Inthanon and Phu Kradung national parks, and in parts of Doi Suthep and Khao Yai national parks. In the higher areas of the north not protected as national park, a lot of the primary hill evergreen forest has been cleared for cultivation, especially by local hill tribespeople who favour the slash-and-burn farming technique.

Mangrove swamps and coastal forests

Mangrove swamps are an important habitat for a wide variety of marine life (including 204 species of bird, 74 species of fish and 54 types of crab) but, like much of Thailand's natural heritage, they have fallen victim to destructive economic policies (see "Environmental Issues", p.825). Huge swathes of Thailand's coast used to be fringed with mangrove swamps, but now they are mainly found only along the west peninsular coast, between Ranong and Satun. On Phuket, the Thachatchai Nature Trail leads you on a guided tour through a patch of mangrove swamp, but an even better way of exploring the swamps is to paddle through them in a kayak; several tour operators in Phuket and in the Krabi area can arrange this. At high tide only the upper branches of the thirty or so species of mangrove are visible, thick with glossy, dark green leaves, but as the tide recedes, a tangled mass of aerial roots is exposed. These roots not only absorb oxygen, but also trap water-borne debris brought in by the tides, thus gradually extending the swamp area (reclaiming land from the sea) and simultaneously nurturing fertile conditions for the new mangrove seedlings.

Nipa palms share the mangrove's penchant for brackish water, and these stubby-stemmed palm trees grow in abundance in southern **coastal areas**, though commercial plantations are now replacing the natural colonies. Like most other species of palm indigenous to Thailand, the nipa is a versatile plant, its components exploited to the full – alcohol is distilled from its sugary sap, for instance, while roofs, sticky-rice baskets and chair-backs are constructed from its fronds.

Taller and more elegant, **coconut palms** grace some of Thailand's most beautiful beaches. On islands such as Ko Samui, they form the backbone of the local economy, with millions of coconuts harvested every month, most of them by specially trained pig-tailed macaques, for their milk, their oil, their fibrous husks (used in matting and for brushes and mattress stuffing) and their wood.

Casuarinas also flourish in sandy soils and are common on the beaches of southern Thailand; because they are also fast-growing and attain heights of up to 20m, they are quite often used in afforestation programmes on beaches elsewhere. At first glance, the casuarina's feathery profile makes it look like a pine tree of some kind, but it's actually made up of tiny twigs, not needles.

The wildlife

Before World War II, Thailand's landscapes were virtually unspoiled and were apparently teeming with **wild animals** such as elephants, wild boars, rhinoceroses, bears and deer. So numerous were these species, in fact, that they were regarded as little more than an impediment to economic progress, an attitude which resulted in a calamitous reduction of Thailand's wildlife and its habitats.

Nonetheless, in zoogeographical terms, Thailand lies in an exceptionally rich "transition zone" of the Indo-Malayan realm, its forests, mountains and national parks attracting creatures from both Indochina and Indonesia. In all, Thailand is home to 282 species of mammal (over forty of which are considered to be endangered) and 978 species of bird (145 of them endangered).

Mammals

In the main national parks of Khao Yai, Doi Inthanon, Khao Sok and the like, the animals you're most likely to encounter – with your ears if not your eyes – are **primates**, particularly macaques and gibbons. The latter spend much of their time foraging for food in the higher reaches of the forest canopy, while the former usually seek their sustenance lower down, often descending closer to the ground to rest and to socialize.

The gibbons are responsible for the unmistakable hooting that echoes through the forests of some of the national parks. Chief noise-maker is the **white-handed** or **lar gibbon**, an appealing beige- or black-bodied, white-faced animal whose appearance, intelligence and dexterity unfortunately make it a popular pet. The poaching and maltreating of lar gibbons has become so severe that a Gibbon Rehabilitation Project has been set up in Phuket (see p.694).

Similarly chatty, macaques hang out in gangs of twenty or more. The **long-tailed** or **crab-eating macaque** lives in the lowlands, near the rivers, lakes and coasts of Krabi, Ko Tarutao, Ang Thong and Khao Sam Roi Yot, for example. It eats not only crabs, but mussels, other small animals and fruit, transporting and storing food in its big cheek pouch when swimming and diving. The **pig-tailed macaque**, so called because of its short curly tail, excels at scaling the tall trees of Erawan, Khao Yai, Doi Inthanon and other national parks, a skill which has resulted in many of the males being captured and trained to pick coconuts.

You're almost certain to see deer in areas of protected forest, especially the **barking deer**, a medium-sized loner happy in pretty much any type of woodland (easily seen in Khao Yai, Phu Kradung and Erawan) and the large, dark-brown **sambar deer**, which prefers the deciduous forests of the same parks. The tiny **mouse deer** is less often seen, and at only 20cm from ground to shoulder it's Southeast Asia's smallest hoofed animal. Mouse deer live in the dense undergrowth of forests (Khao Yai, Erawan, Ko Surin) but their reputed tastiness could see them heading for the endangered species list.

Commonly sighted on night treks in Doi Inthanon, Doi Suthep, Khao Yai and Khao Sam Roi Yot national parks, the **civet** – species of which include the common palm and small Indian – is a small mongoose-type animal which hunts smaller mammals in trees and on the ground; it's known in the West for the powerful smell released from its anal glands, a scent used commercially as a perfume base. More elusive is the **Indochinese tiger**, which lives under constant threat from both poachers and the destruction of its habitat by logging interests, both of which have reduced the current population to probably fewer than one hundred; for now Khao Yai and Khao Sok are the two likeliest places for sightings. The medium-sized arboreal **clouded leopard** is also on the endangered list, and is hard to spot anyway as it only comes out to feed on birds and monkeys under cover of darkness, rarely venturing out in moonlight let alone daylight.

The shy, nocturnal **tapir**, an ungulate with three-toed hind legs and four-toed front ones, lives deep in the forest of peninsular Thailand but is occasionally spotted in daylight. A relative of both the horse and the rhino, the tapir is the size of a pony and has a stubby trunk-like snout and distinctive colouring that serves to confuse predators: the front half of its body and all four legs are black, while the rear half is white. Another unusual ungulate is the **gaur**, recognizable by its brown coat, sharp horns, powerful off-white legs and sheer bulk – the largest member of the cattle family, it measures up to 2m at shoulder height and can weigh over a tonne. It feeds mainly at night, and is most frequently spotted at salt licks, for example in Khao Yai.

It's thought there are now as few as two thousand wild **elephants** left in Thailand: small-eared Asian elephants found mainly in Khao Yai and Khao Sok. For more on elephants in the wild and in captivity see the boxes on p.362 and p.155.

Birds

Even if you don't see many mammals on a trek through a national park, you're certain to spot a satisfying range of **birds**. Because of its location at the zoogeographical crossroads of Southeast Asia, Thailand boasts a huge diversity of bird species. The forests of continental Thailand are home to many of the same birds that inhabit India, Burma and Indochina, while the mountains of the north share species with the Himalayas and Tibet, and the peninsular forests are home to birds found also in Malaysia and Indonesia. Khao Yai and Khao Nor Chuchi are prime year-round sites for bird-spotting, and, during the winter, Doi Inthanon is a good place for flycatchers and warblers, and Khao Sam Roi Yot a rewarding area to see migrant waders and waterfowl.

There are twelve species of **hornbill** in Thailand, all equally majestic with massive, powerful wings (the flapping of which can be heard for long distances) and huge beaks surmounted by bizarre horny casques. Khao Yai is the easiest place to spot at least two of the species, the plain black-and-white **oriental pied hornbill** and the flashier **great hornbill**, whose monochromic body and head are broken up with jaunty splashes of yellow; the little islands of Ko Phayam and Ko Chang in Ranong province also have some resident oriental pied hornbills.

The shyness of the gorgeous **pitta** makes a sighting all the more rewarding. Usually seen hopping around on the floor of evergreen forests, especially in Doi Inthanon, Doi Suthep and Khao Yai, these plump little birds – varieties of which include the **rusty-naped**, the **blue** and the **eared** – have dazzling markings in iridescent reds, yellows, blues and blacks. The one pitta you might see outside a rainforest is the **blue-winged** pitta, which occasionally migrates to drier bamboo forests. Thailand is also home to the extremely rare **Gurney's pitta**, found only in Khlong Thom National Park, inland from Ko Lanta.

Members of the pheasant family can be just as shy as the pittas, and are similarly striking. The black-and-white-chevron-marked **silver pheasant**, and the **green peafowl** are particularly fine birds, and the commonly seen **red jungle fowl** is the ancestor to all domestic chickens.

The striking orange-breasted and red-headed **trogons** live mainly in the middle layer of forests such as Khao Yai, as does the **barbet**, a little lime-green relative of the woodpecker. Less dramatic but more frequently sighted forest residents include the **abbot's babbler**, whose short tail and rounded, apparently ineffectual wings mean it spends most of its time on the forest floor; and the distinctive, deeply fork-tailed, glossy black **drongo**. The noisy, fruit-eating **bulbuls** are also commonly spotted; many bulbuls have confusingly similar green and brown colouring, but two easily recognized species are the yellow-chested olive-backed **black-crested bulbul**, and the black, brown and white **red-whiskered bulbul**. The **black-naped oriole**, small groups of which fly from tree to tree in gardens as well as forests, is also easy to single out, both by its loud chirping and by its yellow body, black head and wing markings and reddish beak.

Thailand's **rice fields** also attract a host of different birds, not only for the seeds and grasses but also for the insects, rodents and even fish that inhabit the paddies. Some of the most common rice-field visitors are the various species of **munia**, a chubby relative of the finch, whose chunky, conical beak is ideally suited to cracking the unripened seeds of the rice plant; the aptly named **scaly breasted** munia and the **white-headed** munia are the most recognizable members of the family, although all members are an assortment of browns and whites. **Egrets** and **herons** also frequent the fields, wading through the waterlogged furrows or perching on the backs of water buffaloes and pecking at cattle insects, while from November to April, thousands of **Asian open-billed storks** – so called because of the gap between the upper and lower mandibles – descend on agricultural land as well, building nests in sugar-palm trees and bamboos and feeding on pira snails – each baby stork polishing off at least half a kilo a day.

Coastal areas also attract storks, egrets and herons, and the mud flats of Khao Sam Roi Yot are a breeding ground for the large, long-necked **purple heron**. The magnificent **white-bellied sea eagle** haunts the Thai coast, nesting in the forbidding crags around Krabi, Phang Nga and Ko Tarutao and preying on fish and sea snakes. The tiny **edible nest swiftlet** makes its eponymous nest – the major ingredient of bird's-nest soup and a target for thieves – in the limestone crags, too, though it prefers the caves within these karsts; for more on these swiftlets and their nests see box on p.725.

Snakes

Thailand is home to around 175 different species and subspecies of **snake**, 56 of them dangerously venomous. Death by snakebite is not common, however, but all hospitals should keep a stock of serum, produced at the Snake Farm in Bangkok (see p.162).

Found everywhere and highly venomous, the two-metre, nocturnal, yellow-and-black-striped **banded krait** is one to avoid, as is the shorter but equally poisonous **Thai** or **monocled cobra**, which lurks in low-lying humid areas and close to human habitation. As its name implies, this particular snake sports a distinctive "eye" mark on its hood, the only detail on an otherwise plain brown body. The other most widespread poisonous snake is the sixty-centimetre **Malayan pit viper**, whose dangerousness is compounded by its unnerving ability to change the tone of its pinky-brown and black-marked body according to its surroundings.

The ubiquitous shiny black or brown **common blind snake**, also known as the flowerpot snake, grows to only 17cm, and is as harmless as its worm-like appearance suggests. Also non-venomous but considerably mightier, with an average measurement of 7.5m (maximum 10m) and a top weight of 140kg, the **reticulated python** is Thailand's largest snake, and the second largest in the world after the anaconda. Tan-coloured, with "reticulated" black lines containing whitish oval spots, like eyes, the reticulated python is found near human habitation all over Thailand, especially in the suburbs of Greater Bangkok. It feeds on rats, rabbits, small deer, pigs, cats and dogs which it kills by constriction; if provoked, it can kill humans in the same way.

Other common Thai snakes include the **iridescent earth** or **sunbeam snake**, named after the sheen of its scales which glisten and change from black to a dark brown in the sunlight. Non-venomous and burrowing, this snake reaches a length of 1.2m and is found all over Thailand. South of Chumphon, the **mangrove snake** lives in the humid swamps that fringe the river banks, estuaries and coastal plains. Arboreal, nocturnal and mildly venomous, it can grow to about 2.5m and is black with thin yellow bands set at fairly wide intervals. Finally, the **golden tree snake** is the most common of Thailand's flying snakes, so called because they can glide from tree to ground. Frequently sighted in Greater Bangkok, this mildly venomous tree snake is not golden but green with a dense pattern of black flecks, and grows to about 1.5m.

Quite a few of Thailand's snakes can swim if they have to, but the country is also home to 25 species of **sea snakes**, whose tails are flattened to act as an efficient paddle in water. Most sea snakes are venomous though not aggressive. Of the poisonous ones, the commonest and most easily recognized is the **banded sea snake**, which is silvery grey with thirty to fifty black bands and a slightly yellow underside at its front end. It grows to 1.5m and inhabits shallow coastal waters, coming onto land to lay its eggs.

Marine species

The Indian Ocean (Andaman Sea) and the South China Sea (Gulf of Thailand) together play host to over 850 species of open-water fish, more than one hundred species of reef fish and some 250 species of hard coral.

Forty percent of Thailand's coral reef is protected within **national marine parks**, which are the most rewarding places to observe underwater life. The best of these are detailed in the guide and include Ko Similan, Ko Surin, Ko Tarutao and Ang Thong; Thailand's major diving bases have their headquarters on Phuket, Ko Phi Phi, Ko Lanta and Ko Tao, and in Ao Nang, Khao Lak and Pattaya. (See also p.73.)

Coral reefs are living organisms composed of a huge variety of marine life forms, but the foundation of every reef is its ostensibly inanimate **stony coral** – hard constructions such as boulder, mushroom, bushy staghorn and brain coral. Stony coral is composed of whole colonies of polyps – minuscule invertebrates which feed on plankton, depend on algae and direct sunlight for photosynthesis, and extract calcium carbonate (limestone) from sea water in order to reproduce. The polyps use this calcium carbonate to build new skeletons outside their bodies – an asexual reproductive process known as budding – and this is how a reef is formed. It's an extraordinarily slow process, with colony growth averaging somewhere between 5mm and 30mm a year.

The fleshy plant-like **soft coral**, such as dead man's fingers and elephant's ear, generally establishes itself on and around these banks of stony coral, swaying with the currents and using tentacles to trap all sorts of micro-organisms. Soft coral is also composed of polyps, but a variety with flaccid internal skeletons built from protein rather than calcium. **Horny coral**, like sea whips and intricate sea fans, looks like a cross between the stony and the soft varieties, while **sea anemones** have much the most obvious, and poisonous, tentacles of any member of the coral family, using them to trap fish and other large prey.

The algae and plankton that accumulate around coral colonies attract a whole catalogue of fish known collectively as **reef fish**. Most are small in stature, with vibrant colours which serve as camouflage against the coral, flattened bodies and broad tails for easy manoeuvring around the reef, and specially adapted features to help them poke about for food in the tiniest crannies.

Among the most typical and easily recognizable reef fish is the gorgeously coloured **emperor angel fish**, which boasts spectacular horizontal stripes in bright blue and orange, and an orange tail. The **moorish idol** is another fantastic sight, bizarrely shaped with a trailing streamer – or pennant fin – extending from its dorsal fin, a pronounced snout and dramatic black, yellow and white bands of colour. Similarly eye-catching, the ovoid **powder-blue surgeon fish** has a light blue body, a bright yellow dorsal fin and a white "chinstrap". The commonly spotted **long-nosed butterfly fish** is named for the butterfly-like movements of its yellow-banded silver body as it darts in and out of crevices looking for food. The bright orange **clown fish**, so called because the thick white stripes across its body resemble a clown's ruff, is more properly known as the anemone fish because of its mutually protective relationship with the sea anemone, near which it can usually be sighted. Equally predictable is the presence of **cleaner fish**, or cleaner wrasse, on the edges of every shoal of reef fish. Streamlined, with a long snout and jaws that act like tweezers, a cleaner fish spends its days picking parasites off the skins of other fish – a symbiotic relationship essential to both parties.

Some reef fish, among them the ubiquitous turquoise and purple **parrot fish**, eat coral. With the help of a bird-like beak, which is in fact several teeth fused together, the parrot fish scrapes away at the coral and then grinds the fragments down with another set of back teeth – a practice reputedly responsible for the erosion of a great deal of Thailand's reef. The magnificent mauve and burgundy **crown-of-thorns starfish** also feeds on coral, laying waste to as much as fifty square centimetres of stony coral in a 24-hour period. Its appearance is as formidable as its eating habits, with a body that measures up to 50cm in diameter protected by "arms" covered in highly venomous spines.

Larger, less frequent visitors to Thailand's offshore reefs include the **moray eel**, whose elongated jaws of viciously pointed teeth make it a deadly predator, and the similarly equipped **barracuda**, the world's fastest-swimming fish. **Sharks** are quite common off the Andaman coast reefs, where it's also sometimes possible to swim with a **manta ray**, whose extraordinary flatness, strange wing-like fins and massive size – up to 6m across and weighing some 1600kg – make it an astonishing presence. **Turtles** sometimes paddle around reef waters, too, but all four local species – leatherback, Olive Ridley, green and hawksbill – are fast becoming endangered in Thailand, so much so that the Royal Forestry Department has placed several of their egg-laying beaches under national park protection (see p.760), including those at Hat Mai Khao on Phuket, Thai Muang, Ko Surin Tai and Ko Tarutao.

Other commonly spotted creatures are the **sea urchin**, whose evil-looking spines grow up to 35cm in length, and the ugly but harmless **sea cucumber**, which looks like a large slug and lies half-buried on the sea bed. Deceptively slothful in appearance, sea cucumbers are constantly busy ingesting and excreting so much sand and mud that the combined force of those in a three-square-kilometre area can together redistribute one million kilogrammes of sea-bed material a year.

Environmental issues

Only in the 1970s did some sort of environmental awareness emerge in Thailand, when the politicization of the poor rural areas began to catch up with the power-brokers in Bangkok. For years farmers had been displaced from land on which they had long established a thriving ecological balance, to be resettled out of the way of the Bangkok-based logging interests. Discontent with this treatment finally led some of the farmers to join the student protests of 1973, and in the subsequent right-wing backlash many political ringleaders took temporary refuge in the north. Their experiences among the nation's dispossessed have ensured that the environment now plays a major role in the mainstream politics of Thailand.

National parks

One significant outcome of the new environmental awareness was the creation in the 1970s of a National Parks Division and a Wildlife Conservation Division within the Royal Forestry Department (RFD). In 1972 Thailand had just four **national parks**, but there are now 114 across the country, plus 24 national marine parks as well as various other protected zones. In all, they cover over thirteen percent of the country (a high proportion compared to other nations, such as Japan at 6.5 percent, and the US at 10.5 percent). However, as parks planner Dr Surachet Chettamart has warned, "Creating parks is not a numbers game, and when degraded areas are included, the whole parks system suffers. Some, such as Ko Phi Phi and Ko Samet, should be excised or reclassified since they have been transformed into holiday resorts."

The **touristification of national parks** such as Ko Phi Phi and Ko Samet is a hugely controversial issue, and was highlighted when the RFD allowed a film crew to "relandscape" part of Ko Phi Phi Leh in 1999 for the movie *The Beach* – to vociferous protest from environmental groups. There is no question that both Phi Phi and Samet have suffered huge environmental damage as a direct result of the number of overnight visitors they receive, and the contrast with national parks where the government has put its foot down – for example in Khao Yai, where all tourist businesses were unceremoniously kicked out in the early 1990s – is marked. More recently, the RFD began flexing its muscles in the

Ko Similan National Marine Park, closing three of the nine islands to divers, imposing tight bureaucratic controls on the number and type of boats allowed to bring snorkellers and divers to the archipelago and – most controversially – banning local fishermen from the area; the latter injunction caused intense outrage and resulted in two attempts on the life of the national park director involved. While most people understand that the role of the RFD is to conserve vulnerable and precious resources like the Similans, the dramatic hike in entrance fees payable by foreigners to national parks – from B20 up to B200 in 2000 – was greeted with cynicism and anger, not least because there is little sign of anything tangible being done with the money.

Deforestation

One of the biggest crises facing Thailand's environment is **deforestation**, the effects of which are felt all over the country. As well as providing shelter and sustenance for birds and animals (a single male tiger, for instance, needs about thirty square kilometres of forest to survive), forests act as an ecological sponge, binding soil and absorbing the impact of monsoon rains. When they are cut down, water and topsoil are both rapidly lost, causing devastating floods and mudslides – which happen with depressing regularity every rainy season. Though most commercial logging was formally banned in 1989, illegal activity has continued, and there is also the endemic problem of "influence": when a Bangkok big shot wants to clear a previously pristine area for a new property development, for example, it is virtually impossible for a lowly provincial civil servant to reject their plan, or money. An additional problem is the mass illegal harvesting of the **aloewood** tree within national parks such as Khao Yai. Aromatic aloewood oil is a prized ingredient of perfumes and incense and so the wood can fetch up to US$600 per kilogramme (it's said to be more valuable on the black market, gram for gram, than cocaine), which makes it a tempting prize for poachers.

Infrastructure projects and grassroots activism

Another major cause of deforestation is development of the country's **infrastructure**, and nothing has stirred as much controversy as Thailand's hydro-electric schemes, which might be a lot cleaner than the production and burning of lignite – the low-grade coal that's Thailand's major source of energy – but destroys vast areas and, of course, displaces countless people.

The construction of the **Pak Mun dam** in southern Isaan (see p.517) was typical. It was completed in July 1994 despite vociferous and at times violent protest from local people and environmental pressure groups. Over three thousand local farming families ended up losing their homes, and scores of fishermen had their annual incomes severely depleted, with inadequate compensation being offered by the Electricity Generating Authority of Thailand. To add insult to injury, a study by the independent World Commission on Dams, released in November 2000, showed that the dam is a financial as well as an environmental disaster. Affected families continue to lobby for reparation.

The one positive thing to come out of the Pak Mun debacle was the forming of the **Assembly of the Poor**. The women of the communities affected by the Pak Mun project started an anti-dam movement, and in 1995 joined forces with representatives from five other networks – consisting of people affected by other infrastructure projects, land and forest conflicts, slum issues and exploitation at work – to form the most powerful grassroots movement in Thailand. Uniting under the declaration that "the people must be the real beneficiaries of development, and the poor must participate in the decision-making on development projects that will affect them," the Assembly of the Poor has brought numerous development and poverty issues into the headlines, establishing protest villages at development sites and outside Government House in Bangkok. As a result of the Assembly's efforts, some new consultative and compensation measures have been introduced and certain controversial infrastructure projects have been shelved. The United Nations Development Programme now points to the Assembly as a model for grassroots struggles for sustainable development.

Mangroves and coral reefs

In the past, **mangrove swamps** were used by rice farmers to raise **prawns**, using the tides to wash the larvae into prepared pools. Some rice farmers even converted their paddies into prawn farms, but generally the scale of this aquaculture was small and sustainable. Unfortunately, big business has taken over in the last three decades, and today much of the prawn farming in Thailand is in the hands of a few companies. This has been bad for the local farmers, and disastrous for the ecology of the mangroves. Large-scale prawn farming uses vast amounts of sea water, which salinates the neighbouring land to the extent that rice farmers who used to produce two crops a year are now reduced to one small harvest. Furthermore, the chemicals used to feed the prawns and ward off disease suffocate the mangroves and contaminate the water used for irrigation, drinking and washing. This forces farmers to move their breeding pools along the coast, damaging yet more mangroves. With Thailand now the world's leading producer of black tiger prawns, some environmental action groups are calling for an international boycott until there's a proven supply of farmed tropical prawns.

Many of Thailand's **coral reefs** – some of which are thought to be around 450 million years old – are being destroyed by factors attributable to tourism. The main cause of tourism-related destruction is the pollution generated by the hotels and bungalows which have multiplied unchecked at many of the most beautiful sites on the coasts. The demand for coral souvenirs is exploited by unscrupulous divers and local traders, and some irresponsible dive leaders allow their customers to use harpoon guns, which cause terrible damage to reefs. Still, the destruction of coral by tourists is dwarfed by that wreaked by the practice of dynamite fishing and cyanide poisoning, which happen in areas away from the normal tourist haunts.

Endangered species and the wildlife trade

Though Thailand signed the Convention on the International Trade in Endangered Species – **CITES** – in 1983, and hosted the annual CITES conference in 2004, it continues to make money out of imported animals and animal products, and little seems to have changed since 1991, when the World Wide Fund for Nature accused Thailand of being the "wildlife supermarket of the world".

Most of the trade in endangered species is focused along the borders with Cambodia and Burma, where Thai middle-merchants can apparently easily acquire any number of creatures. Some will be sold as pets and to zoos, while others are destined for dining tables and medicine cabinets. The list of items netted in a raid on a trader's house in Nonthaburi in 2003 is not untypical: six live tigers, four live bears, two live orang-utans, nearly 1000 live snakes, four live pangolins, over eighty live turtles, four dead tigers, five dead bears, two dead leopards, a box of fresh tiger meat and bones. **Tiger** body-parts are especially lucrative and mostly end up on the black markets of China, Korea, Taiwan and Hong Kong, where bones, skin, teeth, whiskers and penis are prized for their "medicinal" properties; it's thought that much of Thailand's dwindling tiger population ends up this way. **Bear** paws and gall bladders are considered to have similar potency and are a star feature, along with other endangered species, at certain clandestine restaurants in Thailand catering to "gourmet" tourists from China and Korea; the traditional custom of slicing paws off a living bear and enhancing gall bladder flavour by taking it from an animal that is literally scared to death make this practice particularly vile. The Burmese border market at Thakhilek near Mae Sai (see p.409) is a notorious outlet for tiger and bear body-parts, while Chatuchak weekend market in Bangkok (see p.167) has long had a thriving trade in live animals – everything from hornbills to slow loris – though this may change following recent crackdowns.

Despite the CITES 1990 worldwide ban on all aspects of the **ivory** trade, Thailand has continued to be a major producer of worked ivory, importing so much raw ivory (a lot of it from Burma) that a 2002 report published by the monitoring agency Traffic cited Thailand as the "ivory trade giant" of South and Southeast Asia; in the previous year, the authors of the report had found over 88,000 ivory items on sale in shops in Bangkok and the provinces.

Under Thai law, traders in endangered species can face a four-year jail sentence and fines of B40,000 but, despite increasingly frequent and highly publicized raids on such dealers, to date no-one has been imprisoned and fines are clearly too small to act as a significant deterrent. On a more optimistic note, pressure groups such as the Bangkok offices of the World Wide Fund for Nature (Ⓦwww.wwfthai.org) and WildAid (Ⓦwww.wildaidasia.org) do seem to be having some effect on the national consciousness. In addition to running conservation projects, educational programmes and advertising campaigns, the two organizations have joined forces with the Ministry of Environment to set up a telephone hotline (Ⓣ1362) for tipoffs on suspected outlets and traders in endangered species, and calls have already resulted in successful raids.

Contributions by Mark Read and Gavin Lewis

Music

Music is an important part of Thai culture, whether related to Buddhist activities in the local temple (still a focal point for many communities), animist rituals, Brahmanic ceremonies or the wide range of popular song styles. The most interesting types of Thai music, *luk thung* and *mor lam*, are incredibly popular and distinctively Thai in character. But they – and Thai popular music in general – are largely ignored by visitors to the country. The little that tourists do tend to hear is classical or court ensembles at restaurants or the National Theatre, or the discordant pipes and drums that accompany Thai boxing (*muay Thai*).

The classical tradition

Thai classical dance and music can be traced back to stone engravings during the Sukhothai period (thirteenth–fifteenth centuries), which show ensembles of musicians playing traditional instruments, called **phipat**. The *phipat* ensembles include a large array of percussion instruments, rather like the Indonesian gamelan – gong circles, xylophones and drums – plus a raucous oboe called the *phinai*. The music was developed to accompany classical dance-drama (*khon* or *lakhon*) or shadow-puppet theatre (*nang*) – an ensemble playing for a shadow-puppet show is depicted in the magnificent *Ramayana* murals in Wat Phra Kaeo in Bangkok's Grand Palace complex.

Phipat music sounds strange to Western ears as the seven equal notes of the Thai scale fall between the cracks of the piano keyboard. But heard in the right environment – in a temple, at a dance performance or at a Thai boxing match – it can be entrancing. As there is no notation, everything is memorized. And, as in all Thai music, elements have been assimilated over the years from diverse sources, then synthesized into something new. Check out any of the international albums by the Prasit Thawon ensemble (Thawon was a National Artist).

Despite the country's rapid Westernization, Thai classical music has been undergoing something of a revival in the past few years, partly as a result of royal patronage. There have been recent experiments, too, that attempt to blend Thai classical and Western styles – often jazz or rock – led by adventurous groups like **Kangsadan** and **Fong Naam**. Recently **Boy Thai** have followed their lead, albeit with a more pop-oriented sound, and have had some mainstream success with two albums. The movie *Homrong*, about a famous *ranat* (xylophone) player in pre-World War II Siam, proved surprisingly popular in 2004.

There are regular dance and classical music performances in Bangkok at the National Theatre and the Thailand Cultural Centre (see p.185). Somewhat lacklustre **temple dancing** can usually be seen at the Erawan Shrine on Thanon Rama I and the *lak muang* shrine behind the Grand Palace; at these venues, people give thanks for their good fortune by paying for the temple musicians and dancers to go through a routine. A number of Bangkok restaurants also mount music and dance shows for tourists, including regular shows by Fong Naam, the resident band at the *Tawandang German Brewery* (see p.183), and **Duriyapraneet**, the latter being the country's longest-established classical band.

Folk music

Thailand's folk musics are often referred to as **pleng phua bahn**, which encompasses styles from the country's four distinct regions (central, north,

△ Thai drum

northeast and south), with more than eighty languages and dialects. Despite the rapid social change of the past two decades, numerous folk styles are still enthusiastically played, from the hill-tribe New Year dances in the far north to the all-night singing jousts of northeastern *mor lam glawn*, to the haunting Muslim vocals of *dikir* in the deep south.

Most Thais are familiar with the exciting central folk styles like *lam tad, pleng choi and pleng I-saw*, which often feature raunchy verbal jousting between male and female singers. Styles like these and the ever-popular *mor lam* from the northeast (see p.834) are incorporated into modern popular styles like *luk thung* (see p.833).

One notable folk style to have grown in popularity in recent years is the up-tempo and danceable northeastern instrumental style known as **bong lang** (the name comes from a wooden xylophone that is attached vertically to a tree). *Bong lang* is thought to predate Indian-Thai culture, and while it is clearly an ancient music, the style continues to be refined. As recently as the late 1970s, the *phin hai*, a jar with rubber stretched across the mouth, was introduced (though often only to put a cute young woman at the front of the band); its sound, made by plucking the rubber, is similar to that of a double bass.

The best place to see *bong lang* is upcountry, especially in Kalasin province in central Isaan between November and March. Folk music also features prominently at the major festivals held in the northeastern cities of Khon Kaen, Ubon Ratchathani and Udon Thani, particularly at Songkhran (April), the Bun Bang Fai rocket festival (May), and the Asanha Puja candle festival (July); check with TAT for specific dates and locations.

Popular styles

Despite the crippling problem of music piracy and a market dominated by a few major companies, the Thai **pop scene** remains vibrant and full of surprises. Thailand is the second biggest music market in Southeast Asia after Indonesia, and Bangkok is a major regional centre for pop music and popular culture.

Western orchestration for Thai melodies had been introduced in the 1930s and this led to the development of *dontree sakol*, or modern music, in the form of big band and swing, country and western, Hollywood film music, rock 'n' roll, and so on. In the early days, two distinctive Thai genres developed: *luk grung*, a schmaltzy romantic ballad form, popularized by Thailand's most beloved popular composer and bandleader Euah Sunthornsanan and his Suntharaporn band; and *luk thung* (Thai country). **Luk grung**, with its clearly enunciated singing style and romantic fantasies, was long associated with the rich strata of Bangkok society; it's the kind of music that is played by state organs like Radio Thailand. However, it was largely transformed during the 1960s by the popularity of Western stars like Cliff Richard; as musicians started to mimic the new Western music, a new term was coined, *wong shadow* (*wong* meaning group, *shadow* from the British group, The Shadows). This trend led to the development of *string*, westernized Thai pop, in the 1980s.

String

The term **string** came into use as Thai-language pop music rapidly developed in the economic boom times of the 1980s. S*tring* encompasses ballads, rock and alternative, disco, techno/house, heavy metal, reggae, ska and rap; whatever trend is popular in the US, UK and increasingly Japan (with a nod to Taiwan and Korea) gets picked up quickly and reassembled with Thai lyrics and a particular local flavour that often favours sweet melodies.

Megastars like veteran **Thongchai "Bird" Macintyre** generally record on either of the two major labels, Grammy and RS Promotion, though another

Discography

CDs are taking over from cassettes, even in the provinces (where the mix is 70 percent *luk thung*, 25 percent *string* and 5 percent international). In Bangkok, ask the vendors at the day and night markets, or the stores on Thanon Charoen Krung (New Road). Most major *luk thung* or *mor lam* artists release a CD/cassette every three months, which is often given an artist's series number. Old-style recordings of Suraphon Sombatjalern and the like can be found on the ground floor of the Mah Boon Krong Centre at the Bangkok Cassette store or at Pantip Plaza. All the releases listed here are CDs except where stated; the rest are Thai cassettes.

Classical

Fong Naam *The Hang Hong Suite* (Nimbus, UK). A good introduction to the vivacious and glittering sound of classical Thai music, from one of Thailand's best ensembles. The CD includes some upbeat funeral music and parodies of the musical languages of neighbouring cultures. *The Sleeping Angel* (Nimbus, UK) is also a splendid recording.
The Prasit Thawon Ensemble *Thai Classical Music* (Nimbus, UK). Brilliant playing (and outstanding recording quality) from some of Thailand's best performers, mainly of *piphat* style. Includes the overture *Homrong Sornthong* and, on *Cherd Chin*, some scintillating dialogues between different instruments.
Various *Thailande* (Auvidis/UNESCO, France). An atmospheric disc of three contrasting ensembles from Chiang Mai. Intricate textures that draw you in.

Modern music (Thai sakol)

Euah Suntaraporn *Chabab Derm* (*Old Songs*) *Vols 1–5, 6–10* (Bangkok Cassette). Modern Thai music was popularized by the late master Euah. Some of the most popular Thai songs ever were performed by the Suntaraporn band and a bevy of singers.

Hill-tribe music

Various *Thailand: Musiques et Chants des Peuples du Triangle d'Or* (Globe Music, France). Recordings of the traditional music of Thailand's main hill-tribe groups: Meo, Lisu, Shan, Lahu, Yao, Akha and Karen.

Chao ley (sea gypsy) music

Various *Sea Gypsies of the Andaman Sea* (Topic, UK). The traditional music of the nomadic fisherfolk in southern Thailand, mostly recorded in the Surin islands.

Folk music

David Fanshawe *Music From Thailand and Laos: Southeast Asia Recordings* (Arc Music, UK). Excellent range of folk music from different regions of both countries.

Luk thung

If you can't find any of the albums below, go for a compilation of past albums, usually under a title like *Luam Hits* (Mixed Hits).
Got Chakrapand Arbkornburi *Jareon, Jareon* (*New, New*) (GMM Grammy, Thailand). Big hit during 2003 and 2004, following his performance in a telenovella on a *likay* troupe. Also check out any of his Greatest Hits compilations.
Pompuang Duangjan In Thailand, the best of many cassettes to go for is *Pompuang Lai Por Sor* (*Pompuang's Many Eras*) (Topline, Thailand). Her early spine-tingling hits can be found on several CD compilations from Bangkok Cassette, some recorded when she was known as Nampung Petsupan (Honey Diamond from Supanburi).
Monsit Khamsoi *Khai Kwai Chuay Mae* (*Sell the Buffalo to Help Mum*) and *Sang Nang* (*While I'm Away*) (both on Sure, Thailand). He came from nowhere and was considered too ugly to make it, but with his humility and that fabulously soft emotive voice, he captured the hearts of the entire nation and proved to be the best male *luk thung* singer to emerge for years.

Sodsai Rungphothong *Rak Nong Porn* (*I Love Young Porn*) (Topline, Thailand). The killer comeback by veteran Sodsai – the title track sold two million. Classic old-style *luk thung* – jangling temple bells and brass blaring, and Sodsai wailing over it all.

Sayan Sanya *Luk Thung Talap Thong* (*Luk Thung from the Golden Tape*) (Onpa, Thailand). Heir to Sombatjalern's throne, sweet-voiced Sanya has never sounded better than on this greatest hits collection.

Suraphon Sombatjalern *Luam Pleng* (*Mixed Songs*) *Vols 1–4* (Bangkok Cassette, Thailand). Greatest hits by the king of *luk thung*. Great voice, great songs, great backing – Siamese soul.

Various *Mon Rak Luk Thung* (*Enchanting Countryside*) (RS Promotion, Thailand). Runaway bestseller from the TV series based on the 1969 movie (see p.842).

Various *Mon Rak Transistor* (*A Transistor Love Story*) (UFO, Thailand). From the hit movie about a young country boy who tries to make it in the big city as a *luk thung* singer (see p.845). Includes Surapon's wonderful theme song, *Mai Lerm* (*Don't Forget*).

Various *The Rough Guide to the Music of Thailand: Lukthung and Morlam: The Hidden Sounds of Asia* (World Music Network, UK). Good review of some current *mor lam* and *luk thung*, despite confusing liner notes.

Mor lam/northeastern music

Jintara Poonlarp *Luam Hit Baet Pi* (*Mixed Hits from Eight Years*) (Master Tape, Thailand). Poonlarp has conquered *mor lam* over the past decade with her powerful husky voice.

Banyen Rakgan *Luk Thung, Mor Lam Sood Hit* (*Luk Thung, Mor Lam Top Hits*) (Rota, Thailand). Sixteen scorchers from the first national *mor lam* star. Rakgan's voice is a standout. Good example of the big-band *mor lam* sound.

Isan Slété *Songs and Music from North East Thailand* (Globestyle, UK). Excellent selection of traditional *mor lam*. Vocal and instrumental numbers, played by a band of master musicians.

Pornsak Songsaeng *Gaud Mawn Nawn Pur* (*Holding the Pillow in my Delirium*) (Onpa, Thailand). *Mor lam*'s top male act, a fine singer with a deep, distinctive voice.

Various *Instrumental Music of Northeast Thailand* (King, Japan). Wonderful collection of *bong lang* and related instrumental northeastern styles. Lively and fun. Unmissable.

Various, featuring Chaweewan Damnoen *Mor lam Singing of Northeast Thailand* (King, Japan). The only female *mor lam* National Artist, Chaweewan Damnoen, headlines this fine collection of many *lam* (singing) styles. Most *mor lam glawn* narrative and dance styles, even spirit-possession rituals, are included.

String and Songs for Life

Carabou *Made in Thailand* and *Ameri-koi* (both Krabue, Thailand). Two classic albums from the Songs for Life giants. *Made in Thailand* was right in tune with the times and targeted social problems like consumerism, the sex trade and a failing education system. *Ameri-koi* (*Greedy America*) is even more nationalistic than the previous one, but it also hits out at Thai migrant workers exploited by labour brokers.

Modern Dog *Modern Dog* (Bakery Music, Thailand). This album of alternative rock marked an important change of direction for the Thai rock scene.

Kantrum

Darkie *Darkie, Rock II: Buk Jah* (Movie Music, Thailand). The first-ever *kantrum* crossover album achieved nationwide stardom for the King of Kantrum. Darkie's booming voice moves from rap-like delivery to moans and wails, shadowed closely by the fiddle and some funky riddims. Unmissable.

Darkie *Kantrum Rock Vols I & II* (available on separate cassettes). Benchmark recordings by *kantrum*'s only major star: Darkie's fine wailing voice is featured in rock-*kantrum*, *kantrum* and *kantrum luk thung*.

major star, **Tata Young**, is now signed to BEC-Tero and recently released her first international album in English. Grammy, which controls more than half the market, has an umbrella of labels that releases everything from best-selling soft rockers **LoSo** and **Mai Chareonpura** to the current top-selling *luk thung* act **Got Chakrapand**. Their most famous Thai rock act, though, is the talented brothers **Asanee & Wasan**, now producing a new generation of rockers on their own label.

Since the mid-1990s, Bakery Music, originally an independent label but now linked with BMG, has led the two major pop trends to develop. Bakery broke the **alternative** scene with **Modern Dog**, probably the country's best rock act of the last decade, and helped develop the rap scene with the top-selling Thai language rapper **Joey Boy**. They also picked up on the popularity of Japanese culture and music with Thai youth and started a label, Dohjo, which specializes in **J-pop** (Japanese-influenced pop), and produces a Thai *manga* comic.

The **live** scene in Bangkok has expanded dramatically since the late 1990s, as some students and young people, perhaps tired of formulaic pop, have formed their own "underground" bands – mainly punk, thrash, electro-clash and what Thais call "heavy" (heavy metal). DIY albums feature at gigs and there is an annual "Fat festival" that showcases many of the bands. Campuses like Ramkhamhaeng University are good places to get information on upcoming events. Bangkok is the best place to catch gigs – check the *Bangkok Metro* and *Farang* monthly listings magazines and the English-language newspapers, the *Nation* and *Bangkok Post* for dates.

Songs for life

Another big genre is **pleng phua chiwit**, or "songs for life", which started as a kind of progressive rock in the early 1970s, with bands like **Caravan** (no relation to the British songsters) blending *pleng phua bahn* (folk songs) with Western folk and rock. Caravan were at the forefront of the left-wing campaign for democracy with songs like *Khon Gap Kwai* (Human with Buffaloes):

Greed eats our labour and divides people into classes
The rice farmers fall to the bottom
Insulted as backward and ignorant brutes
With one important and sure thing: death.

Although an elected government survived from 1973 to 1976, the military returned soon after and Caravan, like many of the student activists, went into hiding in the jungle. There they performed to villagers and hill-tribes people and gave the occasional concert. When the government offered an amnesty in 1979, most of the students, and Caravan too, disillusioned with the Communist Party's support for the Khmer Rouge in Cambodia, returned to normal life.

In the 1980s a new group emerged to carry on Caravan's work, **Carabou**. The band split up but has had several reunions; their influence is still strong, with leader Ad Carabou still in the limelight but now more as a businessman selling his own brand of "tonic" drink, Carabou Daeng, via the band's gigs. However, despite the bloody street riots of 1992 (in protest at the then military-installed government) once again bringing "songs for life" artists out to support the pro-democracy protests, since the 1980s the strong social activism of Caravan's early years has generally been replaced by more individual and personal themes. The current top act is fresh-faced singer-songwriter **Pongsit Kamphee**, whose earnest approach and rise through the ranks (he was reportedly once a stagehand for Caravan) have garnered him a sizeable following.

Musically, the genre has changed little in 25 years, remaining strongly rooted in Western folk-rock styles. Songs for life fans should check out cassette stalls at Bangkok's Chatuchak Weekend Market (see p.166), several of which specialize in this genre.

Luk thung

Go to one of the huge **luk thung** shows held in a temple or local stadium on the outskirts of Bangkok, or to any temple fair in the countryside, and you'll hear one of the great undiscovered popular musics of Asia. The shows, amid the bright lights, foodstalls and fairground games, last several hours and involve dozens of dancers and costume changes. In contrast with *luk grung*, *luk thung* (literally, "child of the field") has always been associated with the rural and urban poor, and because of this has gained nationwide popularity over the past forty years.

According to *luk thung* DJ Jenpope Jobkrabunwan, the term was first coined by Jamnong Rangsitkuhn in 1962, but the first song in the style was *Oh Jow Sow Chao Rai* (Oh, the Vegetable Grower's Bride), recorded in 1937, and the genre's first big singer, **Kamrot Samboonanon**, emerged in the mid-1940s. Originally called *pleng talat* (market songs) or *pleng chiwit* (songs of life), the style blended together folk songs (*pleng phua bahn*), central Thai classical music and Thai folk dances (*ram wong*). Malay strings and fiddles were added in the 1950s, as were Latin brass and rhythms like the cha-cha-cha and mambo (Asian tours by Xavier Cugat influenced many Asian pop styles during the 1950s), as well as elements from Hollywood movie music and "yodelling" country and western vocal styles from the likes of Gene Autry and Hank Williams. In 1952, a new singer, **Suraphon Sombatjalern**, made his debut with a song entitled *Nam Da Sow Vienne* (Tears of the Vientiane Girl) and became the undisputed king of the style until his untimely murder (for serious womanizing, rumour has it) in 1967. Sombatjalern helped develop the music into a mature form, and was known as the "King" of the genre, along with his Queen, sweet-voiced Pongsri Woranut.

Today, *luk thung* is a mix of Thai folk music and traditional entertainment forms like *likay* (travelling popular theatre), as well as a range of Western styles. There are certainly some strong musical affinities with other regional pop styles like Indonesian *dangdut* and Japanese *enka*, but what is distinctly Thai – quite apart from the spectacular live shows – are the singing styles and the content of the lyrics. Vocal styles are full of glissando, wavering grace notes and wailing ornamentation. A singer must have a wide vocal range, as the late *luk thung* megastar **Pompuang Duangjan** explained: "Making the *luk thung* sound is difficult, you must handle well the high and low notes. And because the emotional content is stronger than in *luk grung*, you must also be able to create a strongly charged atmosphere."

Pompuang had the kind of voice that turns the spine to jelly. She rose to prominence during the late 1970s, joining **Sayan Sanya** as the biggest male and female names in the business. Like Sombatjalern, both came from the rural peasantry, making identification with themes and stories that related directly to the audience much easier. Songs narrate mini-novellas, based around typical characters like the lorry driver, peasant lad or girl, poor farmer, prostitute or maid; and the themes are those of going away to the big city, infidelity, grief, tragedy and sexual pleasure. Interestingly, it is not always the lyrics that carry the sexual charge of the song (and if lyrics are deemed too risqué by the authorities the song will be subject to strict censorship) but rather the vocal style and the stage presentation, which can be very bawdy indeed.

With the advent of TV and the rise in popularity of *string*, the number of large upcountry *luk thung* shows has declined. It's not easy, said Pompuang, to tour with over a hundred staff, including the dancers in the *hang kruang* (chorus). "We play for over four hours, but *string* bands, with only a few staff members, play a paltry two hours!" Her response to the advent of *string* and the increasing importance of promotional videos was to develop a dance-floor-oriented sound – **electronic luk thung**. Few *luk thung* singers are capable of this, but Pompuang had the vocal range to tackle both ballad forms and the up-tempo dance numbers. Her musical diversification increased her popularity enormously, and when she died in 1992, aged only 31, up to 200,000 people, ranging from royalty to the rural poor, made their way to her funeral in her home town of Suphanburi.

Since Pompuang's death, the top *luk thung* slot has been occupied by **"Got" Chakrapand Arbkornburi**, whose switch from pop to full-time *luk thung* has brought many younger listeners to the style, while the reigning female singer is **Suranee Ratchasima**. Bangkok's first 24-hour *luk thung* radio station, Luk Thung FM (90MHz), was launched in 1997, and it's even hip for the middle class to like *luk thung* these days. Listeners have been snapping up collections of *luk thung* classics, and several veteran singers have relaunched their careers, including **Sodsai Rungphothong**, who had a monster two-million seller with his *Rak Nong Porn* album. A new generation of singers has also emerged, with artists like **Monsit Kamsoi**, **Arpaporn Nakornsawan**, **Yingyong Yodbuangarm**, **Mike Piromporn**, **Tai Orathai** and **Fon Thanasunthorn**. There is some truth, however, in the criticism that some new *luk thung* stars are being artificially manufactured just like their pop and rock counterparts, and there's a tendency to rate a pretty face over vocal expertise.

For many years, *luk thung* was sung by performers from the Suphanburi area in the central plains, but more regional voices are being heard in the genre now, with northeasterners now outnumbering these singers. A slightly faster rhythm, *luk thung* Isaan, has developed, led initially by **Pimpa Pornsiri**, who called the style *luk thung prayuk*. The south, too, has its own *luk thung* star, in the enormously popular **Ekachai Srivichai**. But the most surprising development has been the emergence of not one but two blonde-haired, blue-eyed foreigners singing *luk thung* and *mor lam*. First up is Swede **Manat "Jonas" Andersson**, who rose to national prominence with his debut album, *Pom Cheu Jonas*; he's already a fixture on the *luk thung* circuits. Anglo-Dutch singer **Kristy Gibson** sings mainly *luk thung Isaan* and *mor lam*; her debut album, *Der Kha Der*, was also received raptuously by *luk thung* fans.

Mor lam

Mor lam is the folk style from the poor, dry northeastern region of Isaan, an area famed for droughts, hot spicy food, good boxers and great music. Over the last fifteen years, the modern pop form of this style has risen dramatically, at *luk thung*'s expense. Traditionally, a *mor lam* is a master of the *lam* singing style (sung in the Isaan dialect, which is actually Lao), and is accompanied by the *khaen* (bamboo mouth organ), the *phin* (two- to four-string guitar) and *ching* (small temple bells). Modern **mor lam** developed from *mor lam glawn*, a narrative form where all-night singing jousts are held between male and female singers, and from *mor lam soeng*, the group-dance form. Both still play an important part in many social events like weddings, births and deaths, festivals and temple fairs. A *mor lam* may sing intricate fixed-metre Lao epic poems or may relate current affairs in a spontaneous rap. In the large groups, Western instruments like guitar (replacing the *phin*) and synthesizer (for the *khaen*) are used.

The style came to national prominence more than twenty years ago, when a female *mor lam* singer, **Banyen Rakgan**, appeared on national TV. In the early 1980s the music was heard not only in Isaan but also in the growing slums of Bangkok, as rural migrants poured into the capital in search of work. By the end of the decade stars like **Jintara Poonlarp** (with her hit song "Isaan Woman Far From Home") and **Pornsak Songsaeng** could command the same sell-out concerts as their *luk thung* counterparts. The current bestseller is

Siriporn Ampaiporn, whose strong vocals burst upon the scene with the monster-selling *Bor Rak Si Dam* album.

The format of a *mor lam* performance is similar to that of *luk thung* shows – lots of dancers in wild costumes, comedy skits and a large backing orchestra – as is the subject matter. The music is definitely hot, especially if you see it live, when bands will often play through the night, never missing the groove for a minute, driven on by the relentless *phin* and *khaen* playing. To some people, the fast plucking style of the *phin* gives a West African or Celtic tinge; the *khaen* has a rich sound – over a bass drone players improvise around the melody, while at the same time vamping the basic rhythm. Male and female singers rotate or duet humorous love songs, which often start with one of the *mor khaen* setting up the beat. They sing about topical issues, bits of news, crack lewd jokes or make fun of the audience – all very tongue-in-cheek.

Musically, however, *mor lam* and *luk thung* are very different; *mor lam* has a much faster, relentless rhythm and the vocal delivery is rapid-fire, rather like a rap. You'll immediately recognize a *mor lam* song with its introductory wailing moan "*Oh la naw*", meaning "fortune". *Mor lam* artists, brought up bilingually, can easily switch from *luk thung* to *mor lam*, but *luk thung* artists, who only speak the national central Thai dialect (Siamese), cannot branch out so easily.

In the 1990s, *mor lam* musicians headed off the challenge of increasingly popular *string* bands by creating **mor lam sing**, a turbo-charged modern version of *mor lam glawn* played by small electric combos. The number of large touring *luk thung* or *mor lam* shows has declined in recent years, owing to high overheads, TV entertainment and the popularity of *string* bands, so *mor lam sing* satisfies the need for local music with a modern edge.

Mor lam sing was followed quickly by a more-rock-oriented *mor lam* sound (this is a little similar to Grand X in the 1980s, which played a mix of rock and *luk thung*), led by funky little combos like **Rocksadert**, actually much better live than on recordings.

Kantrum: Thai-Cambodian pop

"Isaan nua (north) has *mor lam*, Isaan dai (south) has *kantrum*," sings **Darkie**, the first – and so far only – star of **kantrum**, Thai-Cambodian pop, in his song, "Isaan Dai Sah Muk Kee" (Southern Isaan Unity). His music is a very specific offshoot, from the southern part of Isaan, where Thai-Cambodians mix with ethnic Lao and Thais. So far *kantrum* is only popular in Isaan, and that seems unlikely to change, as few people outside the region speak either Cambodian or the Thai-Cambodian dialect, Suay, in which the songs are sung.

Modern *kantrum* has developed from Cambodian folk and classical music, played in a small group consisting of fiddle, small hand drums and *krab* (pieces of hardwood bashed together rather like claves). This traditional style is now quite hard to find in Thailand; some ten or so years ago, musicians started to electrify the music, using both traditional and Western instruments. Shunning the synthesizer preferred by his competitors like Khong Khoi, Oh-Yot and Ai Num Muang Surin, Darkie puts the wailing fiddle centre-stage, cranks up the rhythms (*kantrum* has a harder beat than even *mor lam*) and sets off with his deep, distinctive voice. In 1997, he broke new ground with *Darkie Rock II: Buk Jah*, the first *kantrum* crossover album to have success in the mainstream pop market. Sadly, in 2001, at the young age of 35, Darkie passed away.

John Clewley
(Adapted from the *Rough Guide to World Music*)

The hill tribes

Originating in various parts of China and Southeast Asia, the hill tribes are sometimes termed Fourth World people, in that they are migrants who continue to migrate without regard for established national boundaries. Most arrived in Thailand during the last century, and many of the hill peoples are still found in other parts of Southeast Asia – in Vietnam, for example, where the French used the *montagnards* ("mountain dwellers") in their fight against communism. Since 1975, a large percentage of the one million refugees that Thailand has accepted from Burma, Laos and Cambodia has been hill-tribe people. Some, however, have been around for much longer, like the Lawa, who are thought to have been the first settlers in northern Thailand, though these days they have largely been assimilated into mainstream Thai culture.

Called **chao khao** (mountain people) by the Thais, the tribes are mostly pre-literate societies, whose sophisticated systems of customs, laws and beliefs have developed to harmonize relationships between individuals and their environment. In recent years their ancient culture has come under threat, faced with the effects of rapid population growth and the ensuing competition for land, discrimination and exploitation by lowland Thais, and tourism. However, the integrity of their way of life is as yet largely undamaged, and what follows is the briefest of introductions to an immensely complex subject. If you want to learn more, visit the Tribal Museum in Chiang Mai (see p.334), or the Hill Tribe Museum and Handicrafts Shop in Chiang Rai (see p.403) before setting out on a trek.

Agriculture

Although the hill tribes keep some livestock, such as pigs, poultry and elephants, the base of their economy is **swidden agriculture**, a crude form of shifting cultivation also practised by many Thai lowland farmers. At the beginning of the season an area of jungle is cleared and burned, producing ash to fertilize rice, corn, chillies and other vegetables, which are replanted in succeeding years until the soil's nutrients are exhausted. This system is sustainable with a low population density, which allows the jungle time to recover before it is used again. However, with the increase in population over recent decades, ever greater areas are being exhausted, and the decreasing forest cover is leading to erosion and micro-climatic change.

As a result, many villages took up the large-scale production of **opium** to supplement the traditional subsistence crops, though the Thai government has now largely eradicated opium production in the north. However, the cash crops which have been introduced in its place have often led to further environmental damage, as these low-profit crops require larger areas of cultivation, and thus greater deforestation. Furthermore, the water supplies have become polluted with chemical pesticides, and, although more environmentally sensitive agricultural techniques are being introduced, they have yet to achieve widespread acceptance.

Religion and festivals

Although some tribes have taken up Buddhism and others – especially among the Karen, Mien and Lahu – have been converted by Christian missionaries bringing the incentives of education and modern medicine, the hill tribes are predominantly **animists**. In this belief system, all natural objects are inhabited by spirits which, along with the tribe's ancestor spirits and the supreme divine spirit, must be propitiated to prevent harm to the family or village. Most villages have one or more religious leaders, which may include a priest who looks after the ritual life of the community, and at least one shaman who has the power to mediate with the spirits and prescribe what has to be done to keep them happy. If a member of the community is sick, for example, the shaman will be consulted to determine what action has insulted which spirit, and will then carry out the correct sacrifice.

The most important festival, celebrated by all the tribes, is at **New Year**, when whole communities take part in dancing, music and rituals particular to each tribe: Hmong boys and girls, for instance, take part in a courting ritual at this time, while playing catch with a ball. The New Year festivals are not held on fixed dates, but at various times during the cool-season slack period in the agricultural cycle from January to March.

Costumes and handicrafts

The most conspicuous characteristics of the hill tribes are their exquisitely crafted **costumes** and adornments, the styles and colours of which are particular to each group. Although many men and children now adopt Western clothes for everyday wear, with boys in particular more often running around in long shorts and T-shirts with logos, most women and girls still wear the traditional attire at all times. It's the women who make the clothes too – some still spin their own cotton, though many Hmong, Lisu and Mien women are prosperous enough to buy materials from itinerant traders. Other distinctive hill-tribe artefacts – tools, jewellery, weapons and musical instruments – are the domain of the men, and specialist **blacksmiths** and **silversmiths** have such high status that some attract business from villages many kilometres away. Jewellery, the chief outward proof of a family's wealth, is displayed most obviously by Lisu women at the New Year festivals, and is commonly made from silver melted down from Indian and Burmese coins, though brass, copper and aluminium are also used.

Clothing and **handicrafts** were not regarded as marketable products until the early 1980s, when co-operatives were set up to manufacture and market these goods, which are now big business in the shops of Thailand. The hill tribes' deep-dyed coarse cloth, embroidered with simple geometric patterns in bright colours, has become popular among middle-class Thais as well as farang visitors. Mien material, dyed indigo or black with bright snowflake embroidery, is on sale in many shops, as is the simple but very distinctive Akha work – coarse black cotton, with triangular patterns of stitching and small fabric patches in rainbow colours, usually made up into bags and hats. The Hmong's much more sophisticated **embroidery** and **appliqué**, added to jacket lapels and cuffs and skirt hems, is also widely seen – Blue Hmong skirts, made on a base of indigo-dyed cotton with a white geometric batik design and embroidered in loud primary colours, are particularly attractive.

Besides clothing, the hill tribes' other handicrafts, such as knives and wooden or bamboo musical pipes, have found a market amongst farangs, the most saleable product being the intricate engraving work of their silversmiths, especially in the form of chunky bracelets. For a sizeable minority of villages, handicrafts now provide the security of a steady income to supplement what they make from farming.

The main tribes

Within the small geographical area of northern Thailand there are at least ten different hill tribes, many of them divided into distinct subgroups – the following are the main seven, listed in order of population and under their own names, rather than the sometimes derogatory names used by Thais. (The Thai Yai – or Shan – the dominant group in most of the west of the region, are not a hill tribe, but a subgroup of Thais.) Beyond the broad similarities outlined above, this section sketches their differences in terms of history, economy and religion, and describes elements of dress by which they can be distinguished.

Karen

The **Karen** (called Kaliang or Yang in Thai) form by far the largest hill-tribe group in Thailand with a population of about 500,000, and are the second oldest after the Lawa, having begun to arrive here from Burma and China in the seventeenth century. The Thai Karen, many of them refugees from Burma (see box on p.296), mostly live in a broad tract of land west of Chiang Mai, which stretches along the border from Mae Hong Son province all the way down to Kanchanaburi, with scattered pockets in Chiang Mai, Chiang Rai and Phayao provinces.

The Karen traditionally practise a system of **rotating cultivation** – ecologically far more sensitive than slash-and-burn – in the valleys of this region and on low hills. Their houses, very similar to those of lowland Thais, are small (they do not live in extended family groups), built on stilts and made of bamboo or teak; they're often surrounded by fruit gardens and neat fences. As well as farming their own land, the Karen often hire out their labour to Thais and other hill tribes, and keep a variety of livestock including elephants, which used to be employed in the teak trade but are now often found giving rides to trekking parties.

Unmarried Karen women wear loose white or undyed V-necked shift dresses, often decorated with grass seeds at the seams. Some subgroups decorate them more elaborately, Sgaw girls with a woven red or pink band above the waist, and Pwo girls with woven red patterns in the lower half of the shift. Married women wear blouses and skirts in bold colours, predominantly red or blue. Men generally wear blue, baggy trousers with red or blue shirts, a simplified version of the women's blouse.

Hmong

Called the Meo by the Thais (a term meaning "barbarian"), the **Hmong** (free people) originated in central China or Mongolia and are now found widely in northern Thailand; they are still the most widespread minority group in south China. There are two subgroups: the **Blue Hmong**, who live around and to the west of Chiang Mai; and the **White Hmong**, who are found to the east. Their overall population in Thailand is about 110,000, making them the second-largest hill-tribe group.

Of all the hill tribes, the Hmong have been the quickest to move away from subsistence farming. In the past, Hmong people were more involved in opium production than most other tribes in Thailand, though now many have eagerly embraced the newer cash crops. Hmong clothing has become much in demand in Thailand, and Hmong women will often be seen at markets throughout the country selling their handicrafts. The women, in fact, are expected to do most of the work on the land and in the home.

Hmong **villages** are usually built at high altitudes, below the crest of a protecting hill. Although wealthier families sometimes build the more comfortable Thai-style houses, most stick to the traditional house, with its dirt floor and a roof descending almost to ground level. They live together in extended families, with two or more bedrooms and a large guest platform.

The Blue Hmong dress in especially striking **clothes**. The women wear intricately embroidered pleated skirts decorated with parallel horizontal bands of red, pink, blue and white; their jackets are of black satin, with wide orange and yellow embroidered cuffs and lapels. White Hmong women wear black baggy trousers and simple jackets with blue cuffs. Men of both groups generally wear baggy black pants with colourful sashes round the waist, and embroidered jackets closing over the chest with a button at the left shoulder. All the Hmong are famous for their chunky **silver jewellery**, which the women wear every day, the men only on special occasions: they believe silver binds a person's spirits together, and wear a heavy neck ring to keep the spirits weighed down in the body.

Lahu

The **Lahu**, who originated in the Tibetan highlands, migrated to southern China, Burma and Laos centuries ago; only since the end of the nineteenth century did they begin to come into Thailand from northern Burma. They're called Muser – from the Burmese word for "hunter" – by the Thais, because many of the first Lahu to reach northern Thailand were professional hunters. With a population of about 82,000, they are the third-largest hill-tribe group: most of their settlements are concentrated close to the Burmese border, in Chiang Rai, northern Chiang Mai and Mae Hong Son provinces, but families and villages change locations frequently. The Lahu language has become the *lingua franca* of the hill tribes, since the Lahu often hire out their labour. About one-third of Lahu have been converted to Christianity (through exposure in colonial Burma), and many have abandoned their traditional way of life as a result. The remaining animist Lahu believe in a village guardian spirit, who is often worshipped at a central temple that is surrounded by banners and streamers of white and yellow flags. Village houses are built on high stilts with walls of bamboo or wooden planks, thatched with grass. While subsistence farming is still common, sustainable agriculture – plantations of orchards, tea or coffee – is becoming more prevalent, and cash crops such as corn and cotton have taken the place of opium.

Some Lahu women wear a distinctive black cloak with diagonal white stripes, decorated in bold red and yellow at the top of the sleeve, but traditional costume has been supplanted by the Thai shirt and sarong amongst many Lahu groups. The tribe is famous for its richly embroidered **yaam** (shoulder bags), which are widely available in Chiang Mai.

Akha

The poorest of the hill tribes, the **Akha** (Kaw or Eekaw in Thai) migrated from Tibet over two thousand years ago to Yunnan in China, where at some stage they had an organized state and kept written chronicles of their history – these chronicles, like the Akha written language, are now lost. From the 1910s the tribe began to settle in Thailand and is found in four provinces – Chiang Rai, Chiang Mai, Lampang and Phrae – with a population of nearly 50,000 in about 250 villages. The greatest concentration of Akha villages is in Chiang Rai province followed by northern Chiang Mai, near the Burmese border – recently many Akha have fled persecution in politically unstable Burma. A large Akha population still lives in Yunnan and there are communities in neighbouring Laos as well as in Burma.

The Akha are less open to change than the other hill tribes, and have maintained their old agricultural methods of **shifting cultivation**. The Akha's form of animism – *Akhazang*, "the way of life of the Akha" – has also survived in uncompromised form. As well as spirits in the natural world, *Akhazang* encompasses the worship of ancestor spirits: some Akha can recite the names of over sixty generations of forebears.

Every Akha village is entered through ceremonial **gates** decorated with carvings depicting human activities and attributes – even cars and aeroplanes – to indicate to the spirit world that beyond here only humans should pass. To touch any of these carvings, or to show any lack of respect to them, is punishable by fines or sacrifices. The gates are rebuilt every year, so many villages have a series of gates, the older ones in a state of disintegration. Another characteristic of an Akha villages is its giant **swing** (also replaced each year), and used every August or early September in a swinging festival in which the whole population takes part.

Akha **houses** are recognizable by their low stilts and steeply pitched roofs, though some may use higher stilts to reflect higher status. Even more distinctive is the elaborate **headgear** which women wear all day; it frames the entire face and usually features white beads interspersed with silver coins, topped with plumes of red taffeta and framed by dangling hollow silver balls and other jewellery or strings of beads. The rest of their heavy costume is made up of decorated tube-shaped ankle-to-knee leggings, an above-the-knee black skirt with a white beaded centrepiece, and a loose-fitting black jacket with heavily embroidered cuffs and lapels.

Mien

The **Mien** (called Yao in Thai) consider themselves the aristocrats of the hill tribes. Originating in central China, they began migrating southward more than two thousand years ago to southern China, Vietnam, Laos and Thailand; in southern China they used to have such power that at one time a Mien princess was married to a Chinese emperor. In Thailand today the Mien are widely scattered throughout the north, with concentrations around Nan, Phayao and Chiang Rai, and a population of about 41,000. They are the only hill tribe to have a written language, and a codified religion based on medieval Chinese Taoism, although in recent years there have been many Mien converts to Christianity and Buddhism. In general, the Mien strike a balance between integration into Thai life and maintenance of their separate cultural base. Many earn extra cash by selling exquisite embroidery and religious scrolls, painted in bold Chinese style.

Mien villages are not especially distinctive: their houses are usually built of wooden planks on a dirt floor, with a guest platform of bamboo in the communal living area. The **clothes** of the women, however, are instantly recognizable: long black jackets with glamorous looking stole-like lapels of bright scarlet wool, heavily embroidered loose trousers in intricate designs which can take up to two years to complete, and a similarly embroidered black turban. The caps of babies are also very beautiful, richly embroidered with red or pink pom-poms. On special occasions, like weddings, women and children wear silver neck rings, with silver chains decorated with silver ornaments extending down the back, and even their turbans are crossed with lengths of silver. A Mien woman's wedding headdress is quite extraordinary, a carefully constructed platform with arched supports which are covered with red fabric and heirlooms of embroidered cloth. Two burgundy-coloured fringes create side curtains obscuring her face, and the only concession to modernity is the black insulating tape that holds the structure to her head.

Lisu

The **Lisu** (Lisaw in Thai), who originated in eastern Tibet, first arrived in Thailand in 1921 and are found mostly in the west, particularly between Chiang Mai and Mae Hong Son, but also in western Chiang Rai, Chiang Mai and Phayao provinces, with a population of around 30,000. Whereas the other hill tribes are led by the village headman or shaman, the Lisu are organized into patriarchal clans which have authority over many villages, and their strong sense of clan rivalry often results in public violence.

The Lisu live in extended families at moderate to high altitudes, in houses built on the ground, with dirt floors and bamboo walls. Both men and women dress colourfully; the women wear a blue or green parti-coloured knee-length tunic, split up the sides to the waist, with a wide black belt and blue or green pants. At New Year, the women don dazzling outfits, including waistcoats and belts of intricately fashioned silver and turbans with multi-coloured pom-poms and streamers; traditionally, the men wear green, pink or yellow baggy pants and a blue jacket.

Lawa

The history of the **Lawa** people (Lua in Thai) is poorly understood, but it seems very likely that they have inhabited Thailand since at least the eighth century; they were certainly here when the Thais arrived eight hundred years ago. The Lawa people are found only in Thailand; they believe that they migrated from Cambodia and linguistically they are certainly closely related to Mon-Khmer, but some archeologists think that their origins lie in Micronesia, which they left perhaps two thousand years back.

This lengthy cohabitation with the Thais has produced large-scale integration, so that most Lawa villages are indistinguishable from Thai settlements and most Lawa speak Thai as their first language. However, in an area of about 500 square kilometres between Hot, Mae Sariang and Mae Hong Son, the Lawa still live a largely traditional life, although even here the majority have adopted Buddhism and Thai-style houses. The basis of their economy is subsistence agriculture, with rice grown on terraces according to a sophisticated rotation system. Those identified as Lawa number just over ten thousand.

Unmarried Lawa women wear distinctive strings of orange and yellow beads, loose white blouses edged with pink, and tight skirts in parallel bands of blue, black, yellow and pink. After marriage, these brightly coloured clothes are replaced with a long fawn dress, but the beads are still worn. All the women wear their hair tied in a turban, and the men wear light-coloured baggy pants and tunics or, more commonly, Western clothes.

Film

Until recently, Thai cinema was almost impenetrable to the outside world. Thai films were shown exclusively in Thailand, in their original language, and considered to be of little interest to a foreign audience. But the West began to take notice of Thai cinema in 2000, when films such as *Iron Ladies*, *Tears of the Black Tiger* and later *The Legend of Suriyothai* showed that Thai directors had the style and wit to entertain non-Thai-speaking audiences. Many larger-budget Thai films are now released outside Thailand and with English subtitles.

A brief history

Thailand's first **cinema** was built in 1905 in Bangkok, behind Wat Tuk on Thanon Charoen Krung, and for a couple of decades screened only short, silent films from America, Europe and Japan. Though nothing remains of the earliest film-theatres, the recently renovated Art-Deco Sala Chalermkrung, which was built in 1933 in Bangkok's Chinatown, is still in use today as a venue for live theatre and the occasional screening (see p.185).

The **first home-grown film**, *Chok Sorng Chan* (*Double Luck*), made by the Wasuwat brothers of the Bangkok Film Company, didn't emerge until 1927, and it was another five years before *Long Thang* (*Going Astray*), the first Thai film with sound, followed.

During the 1920s, a few foreign film companies came to Thailand to film the local culture and wildlife. One early classic from this period is *Chang* (1927; available on video), which tells the simple story, in documentary style, of a family who live on the edge of the forest in Nan province. *Chang's* American directors Merian Cooper and Ernest B. Schoedsack later drew on their experiences in the Thai jungle for their 1933 classic, *King Kong*.

Though Thai film-making continued throughout the 1930s and 1940s, it was virtually suspended during World War II, before re-emerging with a flourish in the 1950s. The **1950s, 1960s and 1970s** were a golden period for the production of large numbers of hastily made but hugely popular low-budget escapist films, mainly action melodramas featuring stereotypical characters, gangsters and corny love interest. Many of these films starred **Mitr Chaibancha**, Thailand's greatest-ever film star. He played the handsome hero in 265 films, in many of them performing opposite former beauty queen **Petchara Chaowarat**. Of the 165 movies they made together, their most famous was *Mon Rak Luk Thung* (*Enchanting Countryside*, 1969), a folk-musical about life and love in the countryside that played continuously in Bangkok for six months and later spawned a best-selling soundtrack album (see p.831). Nearly every Thai adult can recall the days when Mitr co-starred with Petchara, and when Mitr fell to a dramatic death in 1970 – during a stunt involving a rope ladder suspended from a helicopter – it caused nationwide mourning. He was cremated at Wat Thepsirin in Bangkok (off Thanon Luang in Chinatown), where photos of the cremation ceremony and the crowds of fans who attended are still on display. Though non-Thai speakers are denied the pleasure of seeing Mitr and Petchara in action, you can get a good idea of the general tone of their films from the 2000 hit *Tears of the Black Tiger*, described on p.845, which affectionately parodies the films of this period.

For many years after Mitr's death, Thai cinema continued to be dominated by action melodramas, though a notable exception was *Khao Cheu Karn* (*His*

Name is Karn), the first Thai film to tackle corruption in the civil service – it was released in 1973, not long before mass student demonstrations led to the ousting of the military government, and was made by Chatri Chalerm Yukol, who went on to direct the 2001 epic *The Legend of Suriyothai*, described on p.845. The other stand-out of film of the 1970s is *Phlae Khao* (*The Old Scar*, 1977), in which director Cherd Songsri uses traditional rural Thailand as a potent setting for a tragic romance that ends with the heroine's death.

With competition from television and large numbers of imported Hollywood films, Thai film production dwindled during the 1980s, but in 1984 the **Thai National Film Archive** was set up in Bangkok, behind the National Gallery at 4 Thanon Chao Fa, where it continues to preserve not only Thai films but also many of the wonderful posters used to promote them (see box on p.844 for more on film-poster art). A rare stand-out film from the 1980s is Yuttana Mukdasanit's coming-of-age drama *Butterflies and Flowers* (*Pee Sua Lae Dok Mai*, 1986), which is set in a Muslim community in southern Thailand and looks at the pressures on a poor teenager who ends up smuggling rice across the nearby Malaysian border. The film won an award at the Hawaii International Film Festival.

By the 1990s, the Thai film industry was in a rather sorry state and the few films still produced were mainly trite melodramas aimed at an undiscerning teenage audience. But everything started to change for the better in 1997.

Modern Thai cinema

The Thai film industry is currently enjoying a remarkable re-birth and it all started in 1997 with the release of Pen-Ek Ratanaruang's *Fun Boy Karaoke* and Nonzee' Nimibutr's *Daeng Bireley's and the Young Gangsters*. Fuelled by a new wave of talented directors and writers, including Nonzee and Pen-Ek, this resurgence has seen Thai films benefiting from larger budgets and achieving international acclaim. The new breed of Thai film-makers has moved away

Outdoor film shows

Before TVs became a standard fixture of every village home, the only way anyone living outside a town could see a movie was when the **travelling cinema** pitched up. These outdoor film shows, or *nang klarng plaeng*, were hugely popular well into the 1980s, when an estimated 2000 travelling screens were regularly staging film shows all over the country. Their popularity has since declined but they are not yet extinct and, if you get the chance, the shows are well worth attending. These days, *nang klarng plaeng* are most common in the northeast, the poorest and least urbanized region of the country. If you spot a large cinema screen in a field, park or temple grounds, then there is probably going to be a film show that night. They're usually staged either as part of a fair, or in honour of a family occasion such as a birthday or funeral. Anyone is welcome to attend the film show and spectators may or may not be charged a small entrance fee. Chances are the movie will be wild kung fu, corny romance, gruesome horror or lurid action melodrama, but you're very unlikely to get English subtitles.

Even if you don't get to witness an outdoor film show first hand, you can see one in action in Pen-Ek's charming tragi-comedy *Mon Rak Transistor* (see p.845). In the film, the heroine attends a *nang klarng plaeng* showing of a Hollywood movie. A voice-over man sits at a microphone translating the dialogue for his audience of northeastern villagers – cheaper than getting the film dubbed into Thai – and manages to direct a few flirtatious lines of his own at the heroine as he does so.

from traditional action melodramas and soap operas to create films that are more imaginative, realistic and stylish. With a new emphasis on production values, they also look very good, yet it is the fresh, distinctly Thai style that most charms Western audiences, a style summed up by one Thai film commentator as "neo-unrealist", and by another as being influenced by the popular *likay* genre of bawdy, over-the-top Thai street-theatre (see p.66), where actors use song and dance as well as speech to tell their story.

Daeng Bireley's and the Young Gangsters (*Antaphan Krong Muang*) was the surprise hit of 1997; **Nonzee Nimibutr** showed in this story of 1950s gangsters that he is one of the few Thai film-makers able to appeal to the international festival circuit as well as local cinema-goers. He followed it up with the even more successful *Nang Nak* in 1999, giving the big-budget treatment to a traditional nineteenth-century Thai ghost story about a woman who dies while in labour, along with her unborn child. The film broke all box-office records and grossed US$150 million. In *Jan Dara* (2001), the 1930s story of a young man who despises his womanizing stepfather, yet eventually becomes just such a person, Nonzee pushed the envelope of what was acceptable in Thai cinema by including scenes of rape and lesbianism that would not have been permitted a decade earlier. *Okay Betong* (2004) follows a former monk forced to deal with the modern world when, after a bomb attack kills his sister in the politically turbulent deep south, he forsakes his insular northeastern monastery and journeys south to Betong to find his young niece.

In a wry tale of messages received from beyond the grave, **Pen-Ek Ratanaruang**'s first film *Fun Bar Karaoke* (1997) looked at how the lives of

Posters and billboards

Until the 1990s, domestic and foreign films were always promoted in Thailand with **original Thai artwork**, especially commissioned to hang as billboards and to be reproduced on posters. The artists who produced them really poured their hearts into these images, interpreting the film in their own style and always including an extraordinary amount of detail. Unlike the films themselves, Thai film posters were rarely subject to any censorship and as a result they were often far more eye-catchingly graphic and explicit than Western artwork for the same films. Posters for horror films (always very big in Thailand) depicted particularly gruesome, blood-drenched images, while ads for the (illegal) screenings of soft-porn movies often displayed a surprising amount of naked flesh.

The Thai poster for **Apocalypse Now**, painted by Tong Dee Panumas in about 1980, is a classic. Tong Dee used as his starting point the close-up image of Marlon Brando that graced most posters in America and Europe. He re-rendered this in his own style then added an eye-boggling montage of scenes from the film: soldiers standing among ruined Khmer temples, Robert Duvall looking out at the carnage of war, great clouds of napalm-fire, Dennis Hopper photographing it all, Martin Sheen in sweaty close-up, and more.

Locally produced posters are still used to advertise films in Thailand, but for over a decade now they have featured photographic images instead of original artwork. However, there's still a chance to admire the exuberant creativity of Thai cinema art because many provincial cinemas continue to employ local artists to produce their own **billboard** paintings every week. Look for these giant works of art above cinema doors, at key locations around town, and on the sides of the megaphone trucks that circulate around town screeching out the times and plot lines of the next show. In seven days' time they will have been dismantled, reduced to a pile of planks and painted over with the artwork for next week's film.

modern middle-class Thais are still affected by traditional superstitions. His next film *6ixtynin9* (*Ruang Talok 69,* 1999) was a fast-paced thriller set during the Asian financial crisis, with a down-on-her-luck woman stumbling upon a horde of money. Pen-Ek followed this with *Mon Rak Transistor: A Transistor Love Story* (2003), a bitter-sweet love story about a naïve boy from the country with ambitions to be a *luk thung* singer. It's full of charm and the popular soundtrack is available on CD (see p.831). Pen-Ek's *Last Life in the Universe* (2003) is a much darker, more melancholy affair, following two very different personalities – a suicidal Japanese man and a Thai girl – who are brought together in grief.

The scriptwriter on Nonzee's *Daeng Bireley's* and *Nang Nak* was Wisit Sasanatieng who, in 2000, directed **Tears of the Black Tiger** (*Fah Talai Jone*). This gentle send-up of the old Thai action films of the 1960s and 1970s uses exaggerated acting styles and irresistible comic-book colours to tell the story of handsome bandit Dum and his love for upper-class Rumpoey. Writer-director Wisit grew up watching the Spaghetti Westerns of Sergio Leone and includes more than a few passing references to those films.

Another notable name is director Bandit Rittakol, who enjoyed domestic success with a series of comic films in the 1980s and 1990s before tackling the highly sensitive issue of Thailand's radical pro-democracy movement in **The Moon-Hunter** (2001). Based on an autobiographical script by Seksan Prasetkul, one of the student leaders of the October 14 uprising in 1973, the film takes an intelligent look at what happened to the leftist groups after they toppled the corrupt military government.

There have been a number of other recent high-profile international successes. The warm and off-beat comedy **Iron Ladies** (*Satri Lek,* 2000) charts the often hilarious true-life adventures of a Lampang volleyball team made up of transsexuals and transvestites. **Bangkok Dangerous** (*Krung Thep Antharai,* 2000) is a riveting thriller directed by brothers Oxide and Danny Pang, effectively counterbalancing a brutal tale about a deaf and dumb hitman with the story of his love affair with a girl who knows nothing about his occupation. Heavily influenced by the fast-paced Hong Kong gangster films of John Woo, this contains a number of chase scenes shot in the streets and alleys of Bangkok. The sixteenth-century epic **The Legend of Suriyothai** (2001) broke the mould in a different way. A visually stunning historical blockbuster whose B400 million budget made it the most expensive Thai film ever made, it tells the true story of a queen of the Ayutthayan court who gave her life defending her husband during a Burmese invasion. Keen to give international appeal to this complex portrait of court intrigue and rather partisan take on Thai-Burmese relations, director Chatri Chalerm Yukol brought in Frances Ford Coppola to edit a shortened version for Western audiences. Tanit Jitnukul's **Bang Rajan: Legend of the Village Warriors** (2000) also tapped the patriotic vein in its bloody, big-budget dramatization of the legendary brave but futile attempt by Thai villagers to repel the Burmese invasion of 1767, which ended in the sacking of Thailand's then-capital, Ayutthaya.

Interest in these and other ground-breaking Thai films has been so significant over the last few years that since 1998 there has been a **Bangkok Film Festival** every January (see p.62 for details). Meanwhile, entire festivals of Thai films have also been held in London and Tokyo and Thai films have been enthusiastically received at many international film festivals, including Cannes.

Neil Pettigrew

Books

We have included publishers' details for books that may be hard to find outside Thailand; other titles should be available worldwide. Titles marked ★ are particularly recommended.

Travelogues

Steve Van Beek *Slithering South* (Wind and Water, Hong Kong). An expat writer tells how he single-handedly paddled his wooden boat down the entire 1100-kilometre course of the Chao Phraya River, and reveals a side of Thailand that's rarely written about in English.

Carl Bock *Temples and Elephants* (Orchid Press, Bangkok). Nineteenth-century account of a rough journey from Bangkok to the far north, dotted with vivid descriptions of rural life and court ceremonial.

Donna Carrière *Year of the Roasted Ear: Travels, Trials and Tribulations in Southeast Asia*. Amusing and sharply observant account of the Carrière family's disaster-ridden holiday in Thailand and Malaysia.

★ **Karen Connelly** *Touch the Dragon* (Silkworm Books, Chiang Mai). Evocative and humorous journal of an impressionable Canadian teenager, sent on an exchange programme to Den Chai in northern Thailand for a year.

Tristan Jones *To Venture Further*. Amazing tale of how the author, a veteran adventurer and an amputee, pioneered the crossing of the Kra Isthmus in a longtail boat staffed by a disabled crew.

Charles Nicholl *Borderlines*. Entertaining adventures and dangerous romance in the "Golden Triangle" form the core of this slightly hackneyed traveller's tale, interwoven with stimulating and well-informed cultural diversions.

★ **James O'Reilly and Larry Habegger** (eds) *Travelers' Tales: Thailand*. An absorbing anthology of contemporary writings about Thailand, by Thailand experts, social commentators, travel writers and first-time visitors.

Tom Vater *Beyond the Pancake Trench: Road tales from the Wild East* (Orchid Press, Bangkok). Filmically described snapshots of life in twenty-first century Thailand, from a self-confessed seeker after marginal experiences. Also covers exploits in Cambodia, Laos, Vietnam and India.

Culture and society

Michael Carrithers *The Buddha: A Very Short Introduction*. Accessible account of the life of the Buddha, and the development and significance of his thought.

Philip Cornwel-Smith and John Goss *Very Thai*. Why do Thais decant their soft drinks into plastic bags, and what lies behind their penchant for Neoclassical architecture? Answers and insights aplenty in this erudite, sumptuously photographed guide to contemporary Thai culture.

James Eckardt *Bangkok People* (Asia Books, Bangkok). The collected articles of a renowned expat journalist, whose interviews and encounters with a gallery of different Bangkokians – from construction-site workers and street vendors to boxers and political candidates – add texture and context to the city.

Sanitsuda Ekachai *Behind the Smile* (Thai Development Support Committee, Bangkok). Compilation of features by a *Bangkok Post* journalist highlighting the effect of Thailand's sudden economic growth on the country's rural poor.

Sandra Gregory with Michael Tierney *Forget You Had A Daughter: Doing Time in the "Bangkok Hilton" – Sandra Gregory's Story*. The frank and shocking account of a young British woman who was imprisoned in Bangkok's notorious Lard Yao prison after being caught trying to smuggle 89 grammes of heroin out of Thailand.

Roger Jones *Culture Smart! Thailand*. Handy little primer on Thailand's social and cultural mores, with plenty of refreshingly up-to-date insights.

★ **Elaine and Paul Lewis** *Peoples of the Golden Triangle* (River Books, Bangkok; Thames and Hudson, UK). Hefty, exhaustive work illustrated with excellent photographs, describing every aspect of hill-tribe life.

Father Joe Maier *The Slaughterhouse: Stories from Bangkok's Klong Toey Slum* (Post Books, Bangkok). Catholic priest Father Joe shares the stories of some of the Bangkok street kids and slum-dwellers that his charitable foundation has been supporting since 1972 (see Basics p.82).

Trilok Chandra Majupuria *Erawan Shrine and Brahma Worship in Thailand* (Tecpress, Bangkok). The most concise introduction to the complexities of Thai religion, with a much wider scope than the title implies.

★ **Cleo Odzer** *Patpong Sisters*. An American anthropologist's funny and touching account of her life with the prostitutes and bar girls of Bangkok's notorious red-light district.

★ **Phra Peter Pannapadipo** *Little Angels: The Real-Life Stories of Twelve Thai Novice Monks* (Post Books, Bangkok). A dozen young boys, many of them from desperate backgrounds, tell the often poignant stories of why they became novice monks. For some, funding from the Students Education Trust (described on p.83) has changed their lives.

Phra Peter Pannapadipo *Phra Farang: An English Monk in Thailand* (Post Books, Bangkok). Behind the scenes in a Thai monastery: the frank, funny and illuminating account of a UK-born former businessman's life as a Thai monk.

★ **Pasuk Phongpaichit and Sungsidh Piriyarangsan** *Corruption and Democracy in Thailand*. Fascinating academic study, revealing the nuts and bolts of corruption in Thailand and its links with all levels of political life, and suggesting a route to a stronger society. Their sequel, a study of Thailand's illegal economy, *Guns, Girls, Gambling, Ganja*, co-written with Nualnoi Treerat, makes equally eye-opening and depressing reading.

Denis Segaller *Thai Ways* and *More Thai Ways* (Post Books, Bangkok). Fascinating collections of short pieces on Thai customs and traditions written by a long-term English resident of Bangkok.

Pira Sudham *People of Esarn* (Shire Books, Bangkok). Wry and touching potted life stories of villagers who live in, leave and return to the poverty-stricken northeast, compiled by a northeastern lad turned author.

Richard Totman *The Third Sex: Kathoey – Thailand's Ladyboys* (Silkworm Books, Chiang Mai). As several *kathoey* share their life stories with him, social scientist Totman examines their place in modern Thai society and explores the theory, supported by Buddhist philosophy, that *kathoey* are members of a third sex whose transgendered make-up is pre-determined from birth.

S. Tsow *Thai Lite* (Asia Books, Bangkok). Humorous, occasionally insightful, collection of feature articles on a diverse range of subjects by a Bangkok-based journo.

William Warren *Living in Thailand.* Luscious coffee-table volume of traditional houses, with an emphasis on the homes of Thailand's rich and famous; seductively photographed by Luca Invernizzi Tettoni.

History

Anna Leonowens *The English Governess at the Siamese Court.* The mendacious memoirs of the nineteenth-century English governess that inspired the infamous Yul Brynner film *The King and I*; low on accuracy, high on inside-palace gossip.

Pasuk Phongpaichit and Chris Baker *Thailand's Crisis.* Illuminating examination, sometimes heavy going, of the 1997 economic crisis and its political, social and cultural causes and effects, co-authored by a professor of economics at Bangkok's Chulalongkorn University and a farang freelance writer.

Michael Smithies *Old Bangkok.* Brief, anecdotal history of the capital's early development, emphasizing what remains to be seen of bygone Bangkok.

★ **William Stevenson** *The Revolutionary King.* Fascinating biography of the normally secretive King Bhumibol, by a British journalist who was given unprecedented access to the monarch and his family. The overall approach is fairly uncritical, but lots of revealing insights emerge along the way.

John Stewart *To the River Kwai: Two Journeys – 1943, 1979* (Bloomsbury). A survivor of the horrific World War II POW camps along the River Kwai returns to the region, interlacing his wartime reminiscences with observations on how he feels 36 years later.

William Warren *Jim Thompson: the Legendary American of Thailand.* The engrossing biography of the ex-intelligence agent, art collector and Thai silk magnate whose disappearance in Malaysia in 1967 has never been satisfactorily resolved.

Joseph J. Wright Jr *The Balancing Act: A History of Modern Thailand* (Asia Books, Bangkok). Detailed analysis of the Thai political scene from the end of the absolute monarchy in 1932 until the February 1991 coup; plenty of anecdotes and wider cultural references make it a far from dry read.

★ **David K. Wyatt** *Thailand: A Short History.* An excellent treatment, scholarly but highly readable, with a good eye for witty, telling details. Good chapters on the story of the Thais before they reached what's now Thailand, and on recent developments. His *Siam in Mind* (Silkworm Books, Chiang Mai) is a wide-ranging and intriguing collection of sketches and short reflections that point towards an intellectual history of Thailand.

Art, architecture and film

★ **Steve Van Beek** *The Arts of Thailand* (Periplus, Singapore). Lavish and perfectly pitched introduction to the history of Thai architecture, sculpture and painting, with superb photographs by Luca Invernizzi Tettoni.

Jean Boisselier *The Heritage of Thai Sculpture.* Expensive but accessible seminal tome by influential French art historian.

★ **Susan Conway** *Thai Textiles*. A fascinating, richly illustrated work which draws on sculptures and temple murals to trace the evolution of Thai weaving techniques and costume styles, and to examine the functional and ceremonial uses of textiles.

★ **Sumet Jumsai** *Naga: Cultural Origins in Siam and the West Pacific*. Wide-ranging discussion of water symbols in Thailand and other parts of Asia – a stimulating mix of architecture, art, mythology and cosmology.

Steven Pettifor *Flavours: Thai Contemporary Art* (Thavibu Gallery, Bangkok). Takes up the baton from Poshyananda (see below) to look at the newly invigorated art scene in Thailand from 1992 to 2004, with profiles of 23 leading lights, including painters, multi-media and performance artists.

★ **Apinan Poshyananda** *Modern Art In Thailand*. Excellent introduction which extends up to the early 1990s, with very readable discussions on dozens of individual artists, and lots of colour plates.

Dome Sukwong and Sawasdi Suwannapak *A Century of Thai Cinema*. Full-colour tome tracing the history of the Thai film industry and all the promotional artwork (billboards, posters, magazines and cigarette cards) associated with it.

William Warren and Luca Invernizzi Tettoni *Arts and Crafts of Thailand*. Good-value large-format paperback, setting the wealth of Thai arts and crafts in cultural context, with plenty of attractive illustrations and colour photographs.

Natural history and ecology

Ashley J. Boyd and Collin Piprell *Diving in Thailand*. A thorough guide to 84 dive sites, detailing access, weather conditions, visibility, scenery and marine life for each, plus general introductory sections on Thailand's marine life, conservation and photography tips.

Boonsong Lekagul and Philip D. Round *Guide to the Birds of Thailand* (Saha Karn Bheat, Thailand). Worth scouring second-hand outlets for this hard-to-find but unparalleled illustrated guide to Thailand's birds.

★ **Craig Robson** *A Field Guide to the Birds of Thailand*. Expert and beautifully illustrated guide to Thailand's top 950 bird species, with locator maps.

★ **Eric Valli and Diane Summers** *The Shadow Hunters*. Beautifully photographed photo-essay on the birds'-nest collectors of southern Thailand, with whom the authors spent over a year, together scaling the phenomenal heights of the sheer limestone walls.

Literature

Alastair Dingwall (ed) *Traveller's Literary Companion: Southeast Asia*. A useful though rather dry reference, with a large section on Thailand, including a book list, well-chosen extracts, biographical details of authors and other literary notes.

M.L. Manich Jumsai *Thai Ramayana* (Chalermnit, Bangkok). Slightly stilted abridged prose translation of King Rama I's version of the epic Hindu narrative, full of gleeful descriptions of bizarre mythological characters and supernatural battles. Essential reading for a full appreciation of Thai painting, carving and classical dance.

Khammaan Khonkhai *The Teachers of Mad Dog Swamp* (Silkworm Books, Chiang Mai). The engaging story of a young teacher who encounters opposition to his progressive ideas when he is posted to a remote village school in the northeast. A typical example of the "novels for life" genre, which are known for their strong moral stance.

★ **Chart Korpjitti** *The Judgement* (Thai Modern Classics). Sobering modern-day tragedy about a good-hearted Thai villager who is ostracized by his hypocritical neighbours. Contains lots of interesting details on village life and traditions and thought-provoking passages on the stifling conservatism of rural communities. Winner of the S.E.A. Write award in 1982.

Nitaya Masavisut (ed) *The S.E.A. Write Anthology of Thai Short Stories and Poems* (Silkworm Books, Chiang Mai). Interesting medley of short stories and poems by Thai writers who have won Southeast Asian Writers' Awards, providing a good introduction to the contemporary literary scene.

Kukrit Pramoj *Si Phaendin: Four Reigns* (Silkworm Books, Chiang Mai). A kind of historical romance spanning the four reigns of Ramas V to VIII (1892–1946). Written by former prime minister Kukrit Pramoj, the story has become a modern classic in Thailand, made into films, plays and TV dramas, with heroine Ploi as the archetypal feminine role model.

J.C. Shaw *The Ramayana through Western Eyes* (DK Books, Bangkok). The bare bones of the epic tale are retold between tenuously comparable excerpts from Western poets, including Shakespeare, Shelley and Walt Whitman. Much more helpfully, the text is interspersed with key scenes from the murals at Bangkok's Wat Phra Kaeo.

S.P. Somtow *Jasmine Nights*. An engaging and humorous rites-of-passage tale, of an upper-class boy learning what it is to be Thai. *Dragon's Fin Soup and Other Modern Siamese Fables* is an imaginative and entertaining collection of often supernatural short stories, focusing on the collision of East and West.

★ **Khamsing Srinawk** *The Politician and Other Stories* (Silkworm Books, Chiang Mai). A collection of brilliantly satiric short stories, full of pithy moral observation and biting irony, which capture the vulnerability of peasant farmers in the north and northeast, as they try to come to grips with the modern world. Written by an insider from a peasant family, who was educated at Chulalongkorn University, became a hero of the left, and joined the communist insurgents after the 1976 clampdown.

Atsiri Thammachoat *Of Time and Tide* (Thai Modern Classics). Set in a fishing village near Hua Hin, this poetically written novella looks at how Thailand's fishing industry is changing, charting the effects on its fisherfolk and their communities.

Klaus Wenk *Thai Literature – An Introduction* (White Lotus, Bangkok). Dry, but useful, short overview of the last seven hundred years by a noted German scholar, with plenty of extracts.

Thailand in foreign literature

★ **Dean Barrett** *Kingdom of Make-Believe*. Despite the clichéd ingredients – the Patpong go-go bar scene, opium smuggling in the Golden Triangle, Vietnam veterans – this novel about a return to Thailand following a twenty-year absence turns out to be a rewardingly multi-dimensional take on the farang experience.

Botan *Letters from Thailand* (Silkworm Books, Chiang Mai).

Probably the best introduction to the Chinese community in Bangkok, presented in the form of letters written over a twenty-year period by a Chinese emigrant to his mother. Branded as both anti-Chinese and anti-Thai, this 1969 prizewinning book is now mandatory reading in school social studies' classes.

Pierre Boulle *The Bridge Over the River Kwai*. The World War II novel that inspired the David Lean movie and kicked off the Kanchanaburi tourist industry.

Alex Garland *The Beach*. Gripping cult thriller (made into a film in 1999) that uses a Thai setting to explore the way in which travellers' ceaseless quest for "undiscovered" utopias inevitably leads to them despoiling the idyll.

Spalding Gray *Swimming to Cambodia*. Entertaining and politically acute account of the late actor and monologist's time in Thailand on location for the filming of *The Killing Fields*.

Michel Houellebecq *Platform*. Sex tourism in Thailand provides the nucleus of this brilliantly provocative (some would say offensive) novel, in which Houellebecq presents a ferocious critique of Western decadence and cultural colonialism, and of radical Islam too.

Christopher G. Moore *God Of Darkness* (Asia Books, Bangkok). Thailand's bestselling expat novelist sets his most intriguing thriller during the economic crisis of 1997 and includes plenty of meat on endemic corruption and the desperate struggle for power within family and society.

Collin Piprell *Yawn: A Thriller* (Asia Books, Bangkok). Enjoyable page-turner that spins a good yarn from the apparently disparate worlds of scuba-diving and Buddhist retreats. Set mainly in Pattaya and a thinly disguised Ko Pha Ngan.

Darin Strauss *Chang & Eng*. An intriguing imagined autobiography of the famous nineteenth-century Siamese twins (see p.218), from their impoverished Thai childhood via the freak shows of New York and London to married life in smalltown North Carolina. Unfortunately marred by lazy research and a confused grasp of Thai geography and culture.

Food and cookery

Vatcharin Bhumichitr *The Taste of Thailand*. Another glossy introduction to this eminently photogenic country, this time through its food. The author runs a Thai restaurant in London and provides background colour as well as about 150 recipes adapted for Western kitchens.

Jacqueline M. Piper *Fruits of South-East Asia*. An exploration of the bounteous fruits of the region, tracing their role in cooking, medicine, handicrafts and rituals. Well illustrated with photos, watercolours and early botanical drawings.

Travel guides

Oliver Hargreave *Exploring Chiang Mai: City, Valley and Mountains* (Within Books, Chiang Mai). Thorough, updated guide to the city and out-of-town trips, with plenty of useful small-scale maps, written by a long-time resident.

Thom Henley *Krabi: Caught in the Spell – A Guide to Thailand's Enchanted Province* (Thai Nature Education, Phuket). Highly readable features and observations on the attractions and people of south Thailand's most beautiful region, written by an expat environmentalist.

William Warren *Bangkok*. An engaging portrait of the unwieldy capital, weaving together anecdotes and character sketches from Bangkok's past and present.

Language

Language

Language

Thai belongs to one of the oldest families of languages in the world, Austro-Thai, and is radically different from most of the other tongues of Southeast Asia. Being tonal, Thai is extremely difficult for Westerners to master, but by building up from a small core of set phrases, you should soon have enough to get by. Most Thais who deal with tourists speak some English, but once you stray off the beaten track you'll probably need at least a little Thai. Anywhere you go, you'll impress and get better treatment if you at least make an effort to speak a few words.

Distinct dialects are spoken in the north, the northeast and the south, which can increase the difficulty of comprehending what's said to you. **Thai script** is even more of a problem to Westerners, with 44 consonants to represent 21 consonant sounds and 32 vowels to deal with 48 different vowel sounds. However, street signs in touristed areas are nearly always written in Roman script as well as Thai, and in other circumstances you're better off asking than trying to unscramble the swirling mess of symbols, signs and accents. For more information on transliteration into Roman script, see the box in the Introduction.

Among **language books**, *Thai: A Rough Guide Phrasebook* covers the essential phrases and expressions in both Thai script and phonetic equivalents, as well as dipping into grammar and providing a menu reader and fuller vocabulary in dictionary format (English–Thai and Thai–English). Of the pocket dictionaries available in Thailand, G.H. Allison's *Mini English–Thai and Thai–English Dictionary* (Chalermnit) has the edge over *Robertson's Practical English–Thai Dictionary* (Asia Books), although it's more difficult to find.

The best **teach-yourself course** is the expensive *Linguaphone Thai*, which includes six cassettes; Routledge's *Colloquial Thai* covers some of the same ground less thoroughly. For a more traditional textbook, try Stuart Campbell and Chuan Shaweevongse's *The Fundamentals of the Thai Language*, which is comprehensive, though hard going. G.H. Allison's *Easy Thai* is best for those who feel the urge to learn the alphabet.

Pronunciation

Mastering **tones** is probably the most difficult part of learning Thai. Five different tones are used – low, middle, high, falling, and rising – by which the meaning of a single syllable can be altered in five different ways. Thus, using four of the five tones, you can make a sentence just from just one syllable: "mái mài mâi măi" meaning "New wood burns, doesn't it?" As well as the natural difficulty in becoming attuned to speaking and listening to these different tones, Western efforts are complicated by our tendency to denote the overall meaning of a sentence by modulating our tones – for example, turning a statement into a question through a shift of stress and tone. Listen to native Thai speakers and you'll soon begin to pick up the different approach to tone.

The pitch of each tone is gauged in relation to your vocal range when speaking, but they should all lie within a narrow band, separated by gaps just big enough to differentiate them. The **low tones** (syllables marked ̀), **middle tones** (unmarked syllables), and **high tones** (syllables marked ́) should each be pronounced evenly and with no inflection. The **falling tone** (syllables marked ^) is spoken with an obvious drop in pitch, as if you were sharply emphasizing a word in English. The **rising tone** (marked ˇ) is pronounced as if you were asking an exaggerated question in English.

As well as the unfamiliar tones, you'll find that, despite the best efforts of the transliterators, there is no precise English equivalent to many **vowel and consonant sounds** in the Thai language. The lists below give a rough idea of pronunciation.

Vowels

a	as in dad.
aa	has no precise equivalent, but is pronounced as it looks, with the vowel elongated.
ae	as in there.
ai	as in buy.
ao	as in now.
aw	as in awe.
e	as in pen.
eu	as in sir, but heavily nasalized.
i	as in tip.
ii	as in feet.
o	as in knock.
oe	as in hurt, but more closed.
oh	as in toe.
u	as in loot.
uay	"*u*" plus "*ay*" as in pay.
uu	as in pool.

Consonants

r	as in rip, but with the tongue flapped quickly against the palate – in everyday speech, it's often pronounced like "l".
kh	as in keep.
ph	as in put.
th	as in time.
k	is unaspirated and unvoiced, and closer to "g".
p	is also unaspirated and unvoiced, and closer to "b".
t	is also unaspirated and unvoiced, and closer to "d".

General words and phrases

Greetings and basic phrases

When you speak to a stranger in Thailand, you should generally end your sentence in *khráp* if you're a man, *khâ* if you're a woman – these untranslatable politening syllables will gain good will, and are nearly always used after *sawàt dii* (hello/goodbye) and *khàwp khun* (thank you). *Khráp* and *khâ* are also often used to answer "yes" to a question, though the most common way is to repeat the verb of the question (precede it with *mâi* for "no"). *Châi* (yes) and *mâi châi* (no) are less frequently used than their English equivalents.

Hello	sawàt dii
Where are you going?	pai năi? (not always meant literally, but used as a general greeting)
I'm out having fun/ I'm travelling	pai thîaw (answer to pai năi, almost indefinable pleasantry)

Goodbye	sawàt dii/la kàwn
Good luck/cheers	chôk dii
Excuse me	khăw thâwt
Thank you	khàwp khun
It's nothing/it doesn't matter	mâi pen rai
How are you?	sabai dii reŭ?
I'm fine	sabai dii
What's your name?	khun chêu arai?
My name is...	phŏm (men)/ diichăn (women) chêu...
I come from...	phŏm/diichăn maa jàak...
I don't understand	mâi khâo jai
Do you speak English?	khun phûut phasăa angkrìt dâi măi?
Do you have...?	mii...măi?
Is there...?	...mii măi?
Is...possible?	...dâi măi?
Can you help me?	chûay phŏm/ diichăn dâi măi?
(I) want...	ao...
(I) would like to...	yàak jà...
(I) like...	châwp...
What is this called in Thai?	níi phasăa thai rîak wâa arai?

Getting around

Where is the...?	...yùu thîi năi?
How far?	klai thâo rai?
I would like to go to...	yàak jà pai...
Where have you been?	pai năi maa?
Where is this bus going?	rót níi pai năi?
When will the bus leave?	rót jà àwk mêua rai?
What time does the bus arrive in...?	rót theŭng...kìi mohng?
Stop here	jàwt thîi nîi
here	thîi nîi
there/over there	thîi nâan/thîi nôhn
right	khwăa
left	sái
straight	trong
north	neŭa
south	tâi
east	tawan àwk
west	tawan tòk
near/far	klâi/klai
street	thanŏn
train station	sathàanii rót fai
bus station	sathàanii rót meh
airport	sanăam bin
ticket	tŭa
hotel	rohng raem
post office	praisanii
restaurant	raan ahăan
shop	raan
market	talàat
hospital	rohng pha-yaabaan
motorbike	rót mohtoesai
taxi	rót táksîi
boat	reua

Accommodation and shopping

How much is...?	...thâo rai/kìi bàat?
How much is a room here per night?	hâwng thîi nîi kheun lá thâo rai?
Do you have a cheaper room?	mii hâwng thùuk kwàa măi?
Can I/we look at the room?	duu hâwng dâi măi?
I/We'll stay two nights	jà yùu săwng kheun
Can you reduce the price?	lót raakhaa dâi măi?
Can I store my bag here?	fàak krapăo wái thîi nîi dâi măi?
cheap/expensive	thùuk/phaeng
air-con room	hăwng ae
ordinary room	hăwng thammadaa

| telephone | thohrásàp | blanket | phâa hòm |
| laundry | sák phâa | fan | phát lom |

General adjectives

alone	khon diaw	easy	ngâi
another	ìik…nèung	fun	sanùk
bad	mâi dii	hot (temperature)	ráwn
big	yài	hot (spicy)	pèt
clean	sa-àat	hungry	hiǔ khâo
closed	pìt	ill	mâi sabai
cold (object)	yen	open	pòet
cold (person or weather)	nǎo	pretty	sǔay
		small	lek
delicious	aròi	thirsty	hǐu nám
difficult	yâak	tired	nèu-ai
dirty	sokaprok	very	mâak

General nouns

Nouns have no plurals or genders, and don't require an article.

bathroom/toilet	hǎwng nám	foreigner	fàràng
boyfriend or girlfriend	faen	friend	phêuan
		money	ngoen
food	ahǎan	water/liquid	nám

General verbs

Thai verbs do not conjugate at all, and also often double up as nouns and adjectives, which means that foreigners' most unidiomatic attempts to construct sentences are often readily understood.

come	maa	sit	nâng
do	tham	sleep	nawn làp
eat	kin/thaan khâo	take	ao
give	hâi	walk	doen pai
go	pai		

Numbers

zero	sǔun	eleven	sìp èt
one	nèung	twelve, thirteen, etc	sìp sǎwng, sìp sǎam…
two	sǎwng		
three	sǎam	twenty	yîi sìp/yiip
four	sìi	twenty-one	yîi sìp èt
five	hâa	twenty-two, twenty-three, etc	yîi sìp sǎwng, yîi sìp sǎam…
six	hòk		
seven	jèt	thirty, forty, etc	sǎam sìp, sìi sìp…
eight	pàet	one hundred, two hundred, etc	nèung rói, sǎwng rói…
nine	kâo		
ten	sìp	one thousand	nèung phan
		ten thousand	nèung mèun

Time

The commonest system for telling the time, as outlined below, is actually a confusing mix of several different systems. The State Railway and government officials use the 24-hour clock (9am is *kâo naalikaa*, 10am *sìp naalikaa*, and so on), which is always worth trying if you get stuck.

1–5am	tii nèung–tii hâa
6–11am	hòk mohng cháo–sìp èt mohng cháo
noon	thîang
1pm	bài mohng
2–4pm	bài săwng mohng–bài sìi mohng
5–6pm	hâa mohng yen–hòk mohng yen
7–11pm	nèung thûm–hâa thûm
midnight	thîang kheun
What time is it?	kìi mohng láew?
How many hours?	kìi chûa mohng?
How long?	naan thâo rai?
minute	naathii
hour	chûa mohng
day	waan
week	aathít
month	deuan
year	pii
today	wan níi
tomorrow	phrûng níi
yesterday	mêua wan
now	diăw níi
next week	aathít nâa
last week	aathít kàwn
morning	cháo
afternoon	bài
evening	yen
night	kheun

Days

Sunday	wan aathít
Monday	wan jan
Tuesday	wan angkhaan
Wednesday	wan phút
Thursday	wan pháréuhàt
Friday	wan sùk
Saturday	wan săo

Food and drink

Note: Descriptions of Thai fruits are given on pp.50–51.

Basic ingredients

Kài	**Chicken**
Mŭu	**Pork**
Néua	**Beef, meat**
Pèt	**Duck**
Ahăan thaleh	**Seafood**
Plaa	**Fish**
Plaa dùk	**Catfish**
Plaa mèuk	**Squid**
Kûng	**Prawn, shrimp**
Hŏy	**Shellfish**
Hŏy nang rom	**Oyster**
Puu	**Crab**
Khài	**Egg**
Phàk	**Vegetables**

Vegetables

Makĕua	**Aubergine**
Makĕua thêt	**Tomato**
Nàw mái	**Bamboo shoots**
Tùa ngâwk	**Bean sprouts**
Phrík	**Chilli**
Man faràng	**Potato**

Man faràng thâwt	Chips	Hèt	Mushroom
Taeng kwaa	Cucumber	Tùa	Peas, beans or lentils
Phrík yùak	Green pepper	Tôn hŏrm	Spring onions
Krathiam	Garlic		

Noodles

Ba miì	Egg noodles	Kwáy tiăw/ ba miì rât nâ (mŭu)	Rice noodles/egg noodles fried in gravy-like sauce with vegetables (and pork slices)
Kwáy tiăw (sên yaì/ sên lék)	White rice noodles (wide/thin)	Phàt thai	Thin noodles fried with egg, bean sprouts and tofu, topped with ground peanuts
Ba miì kràwp	Crisp fried egg noodles	Pàt siyú	Wide or thin noodles fried with soy sauce, egg and meat
Kwáy tiăw/ ba miì haêng	Rice noodles/egg noodles fried with egg, small pieces of meat and a few vegetables		
Kwáy tiăw/ba miì nám (mŭu)	Rice noodle/egg noodle soup, made with chicken broth (and pork balls)		

Rice

Khâo	Rice	Khâo niăw	Sticky rice
Khâo man kài	Slices of chicken served over marinated rice	Khâo pàt	Fried rice
Khâo mŭu daeng	Red pork with rice	Khâo rât kaeng	Curry over rice
Khâo nâ kài/pèt	Chicken/duck served with sauce over rice	Khâo tôm	Rice soup (usually for breakfast)

Curries and soups

Kaeng phèt	Hot, red curry	Kaeng sôm	Fish and vegetable curry
Kaeng phánaeng	Thick, savoury curry	Tôm khàa kài	Chicken coconut soup
Kaeng khĭaw wan	Green curry	Tôm yam kûng	Hot and sour prawn soup
Kaeng mátsàman	Rich Muslim-style curry, usually with beef and potatoes	Kaeng jèut	Mild soup with vegetables and usually pork
Kaeng karìi	Mild, Indian-style curry		

Other dishes

Hâwy thâwt	Omelette stuffed with mussels	Kài pàt nàw mái	Chicken with bamboo shoots
Kài pàt bai kraprao	Chicken fried with basil leaves	Kài pàt mét mámûang	Chicken with cashew nuts

Kài pàt khǐng	Chicken with ginger
Kài yâang	Grilled chicken
Khài yát sài	Omelette with pork and vegetables
Khǎnom jiin nám yaa	Noodles topped with fish curry
Kûng chúp paêng thâwt	Prawns fried in batter
Lâap	Spicy ground meat
Mǔu prîaw wǎan	Sweet and sour pork
Néua phàt krathiam phrík thai	Beef fried with garlic and pepper
Néua phàt nám man hoy	Beef in oyster sauce
Pàt phàk bûng fai daeng	Morning glory fried in garlic and bean sauce
Pàt phàk lǎi yàng	Stir-fried vegetables
Pàw pía	Spring rolls
Plaa nêung páe sá	Whole fish steamed with vegetables and ginger
Plaa rât phrík	Whole fish cooked with chillies
Plaa thâwt	Fried whole fish
Sàté	Satay
Sôm tam	Spicy papaya salad
Thâwt man plaa	Fish cake
Yam néua	Grilled beef salad
Yam plaa mèuk	Squid salad
Yam thuù phuu	Wing-bean salad
Yam wun sen	Noodle and pork salad

Thai desserts (khanǒm)

Khanǒm beuang	Small crispy pancake folded over with coconut cream and strands of sweet egg inside
Khâo lǎam	Sticky rice, coconut cream and black beans cooked and served in bamboo tubes
Khâo niǎw daeng	Sticky red rice mixed with coconut cream
Khâo niǎw thúrian/ mámûang	Sticky rice mixed with coconut cream and durian/ mango
Klûay khàek	Fried banana
Lûk taan chêum	Sweet palm kernels served in syrup
Sǎngkhayaa	Coconut custard
Tàkôh	Squares of transparent jelly (jello) topped with coconut cream

Drinks (khreûang deùm)

Bia	Beer
Chaa ráwn	Hot tea
Chaa yen	Iced tea
Kaafae ráwn	Hot coffee
Kâew	Glass
Khúat	Bottle
Mâekhǒng (or anglicized "Mekong")	Thai brand-name rice whisky
Nám klûay	Banana shake
Nám mánao/sôm	Fresh, bottled or fizzy lemon/ orange juice
Nám plào	Drinking water (boiled or filtered)
Nám sǒdaa	Soda water
Nám tan	Sugar
Kleua	Salt
Nám yen	Cold water
Nom jeùd	Milk
Ohlíang	Iced coffee
Sohdaa	Soda water
Thûay	Cup

Ordering

I am vegetarian/ vegan	Phǒm (male)/ diichǎn (female) kin ahǎan mangsàwirát/ jeh
Can I see the menu?	Khǎw duù menu?
I would like…	Khǎw…
With/without…	Saì/mâi saì…
Can I have the bill please?	Khǎw check bin?

Glossary

Amphoe District.
Amphoe muang Provincial capital.
Ao Bay.
Apsara Female deity.
Avalokitesvara Bodhisattva representing compassion.
Avatar Earthly manifestation of a deity.
Ban Village or house.
Bang Village by a river or the sea.
Bencharong Polychromatic ceramics made in China for the Thai market.
Bhumisparsa mudra Most common gesture of Buddha images; symbolizes the Buddha's victory over temptation.
Bodhisattva In Mahayana Buddhism, an enlightened being who postpones his or her entry into Nirvana.
Bot Main sanctuary of a Buddhist temple.
Brahma One of the Hindu trinity – "The Creator". Usually depicted with four faces and four arms.
Celadon Porcelain with distinctive grey-green glaze.
Changwat Province.
Chao ley/chao nam "Sea gypsies" – nomadic fisherfolk of south Thailand.
Chedi Reliquary tower in Buddhist temple.
Chofa Finial on temple roof.
Deva Mythical deity.
Devaraja God-king.
Dharma The teachings or doctrine of the Buddha.
Dharmachakra Buddhist Wheel of Law (also known as Wheel of Doctrine or Wheel of Life).
Doi Mountain.
Erawan Mythical three-headed elephant; Indra's vehicle.
Farang Foreigner/foreign.
Ganesh Hindu elephant-headed deity, remover of obstacles and god of knowledge.
Garuda Mythical Hindu creature – half-man half-bird; Vishnu's vehicle.
Gopura Entrance pavilion to temple precinct (especially Khmer).
Hamsa Sacred mythical goose; Brahma's vehicle.
Hanuman Monkey god and chief of the monkey army in the *Ramayana*; ally of Rama.
Hat Beach.
Hin Stone.
Hinayana Pejorative term for Theravada school of Buddhism, literally "Lesser Vehicle".
Ho trai A scripture library.
Indra Hindu king of the gods and, in Buddhism, devotee of the Buddha; usually carries a thunderbolt.
Isaan Northeast Thailand.
Jataka Stories of the five hundred lives of the Buddha.
Khaen Reed and wood pipe; the characteristic musical instrument of Isaan.
Khao Hill, mountain.
Khlong Canal.
Khon Classical dance-drama.
Kinnari Mythical creature – half-woman, half-bird.
Kirtimukha Very powerful deity depicted as a lion-head.
Ko Island.
Ku The Lao word for *prang*; a tower in a temple complex.
Laem Headland or cape.
Lakhon Classical dance-drama.
Lak muang City pillar; revered home for the city's guardian spirit.
Lakshaman/Phra Lak Rama's younger brother.
Lakshana Auspicious signs or "marks of greatness" displayed by the Buddha.
Lanna Northern Thai kingdom that lasted from the thirteenth to the sixteenth century.
Likay Popular folk theatre.
Longyi Burmese sarong.
Maenam River.
Mahathat Chedi containing relics of the Buddha.
Mahayana School of Buddhism now practised mainly in China, Japan and Korea; literally "the Great Vehicle".
Mara The Evil One; tempter of the Buddha.
Mawn khwaan Traditional triangular or "axe-head" pillow.
Meru/Sineru Mythical mountain at the centre of Hindu and Buddhist cosmologies.
Mondop Small, square temple building to house minor images or religious texts.
Moo/muu Neighbourhood.
Muang City or town.

Muay Thai Thai boxing.
Mudra Symbolic gesture of the Buddha.
Mut Mee Tie-dyed cotton or silk.
Naga Mythical dragon-headed serpent in Buddhism and Hinduism.
Nakhon Honorific title for a city.
Nam Water.
Nam tok Waterfall.
Nang thalung Shadow-puppet entertainment, found in southern Thailand.
Nielloware Engraved metalwork.
Nirvana Final liberation from the cycle of rebirths; state of non-being to which Buddhists aspire.
Pak Tai Southern Thailand.
Pali Language of ancient India; the script of the original Buddhist scriptures.
Pha sin Woman's sarong.
Phi Animist spirit.
Phra Honorific term – literally "excellent".
Phu Mountain.
Prang Central tower in a Khmer temple.
Prasat Khmer temple complex or central shrine.
Rama/Phra Ram Human manifestation of Hindu deity Vishnu; hero of the *Ramayana*.
Ramakien Thai version of the *Ramayana*.
Ramayana Hindu epic of good versus evil: chief characters include Rama, Sita, Ravana, Hanuman.
Ravana/Totsagan Rama's adversary in the *Ramayana;* represents evil.
Reua hang yao Longtail boat.
Rishi Ascetic hermit.
Rot ae/rot tua Air-conditioned bus.
Rot thammadaa Ordinary bus.
Sala Meeting hall or open-sided pavilion.
Samlor Passenger tricycle; literally "three-wheeled".
Sanskrit Sacred language of Hinduism; also used in Buddhism.
Sanuk Fun.
Sema Boundary stone to mark consecrated ground within temple complex.
Shiva One of the Hindu trinity – "The Destroyer".
Shiva lingam Phallic representation of Shiva.
Soi Lane or side road.
Songkhran Thai New Year.
Songthaew Pick-up used as public transport; literally "two rows", after the vehicle's two facing benches.
Takraw Game played with a rattan ball.
Talat Market.
Talat nam Floating market.
Talat yen Night market.
Tambon Subdistrict.
Tavatimsa Buddhist heaven.
Tha Pier.
Thale Sea or lake.
Tham Cave.
Thanon Road.
That Chedi.
Thep A divinity.
Theravada Main school of Buddhist thought in Thailand; also known as Hinayana.
Totsagan Rama's evil rival in the *Ramayana*; also known as Ravana.
Tripitaka Buddhist scriptures.
Trok Alley.
Tuk-tuk Motorized three-wheeled taxi.
Uma Shiva's consort.
Ushnisha Cranial protuberance on Buddha images, signifying an enlightened being.
Viharn Temple assembly hall for the laity; usually contains the principal Buddha image.
Vipassana Buddhist meditation technique; literally "insight".
Vishnu One of the Hindu trinity – "The Preserver". Usually shown with four arms, holding a disc, a conch, a lotus and a club.
Wai Thai greeting expressed by a prayer-like gesture with the hands.
Wang Palace.
Wat Temple.
Wiang Fortified town.
Yaksha Mythical giant.
Yantra Magical combination of numbers and letters, used to ward off danger.

Rough Guides

advertiser

...music & reference

Trinidad & Tobago

Africa & Middle East
Cape Town
Egypt
The Gambia
Jordan
Kenya
Marrakesh DIRECTIONS
Morocco
South Africa, Lesotho & Swaziland
Syria
Tanzania
Tunisia
West Africa
Zanzibar
Zimbabwe

Travel Theme guides
First-Time Around the World
First-Time Asia
First-Time Europe
First-Time Latin America
Skiing & Snowboarding in North America
Travel Online
Travel Health
Walks in London & SE England
Women Travel

Restaurant guides
French Hotels & Restaurants
London
New York
San Francisco

Maps
Algarve
Amsterdam
Andalucia & Costa del Sol
Argentina
Athens
Australia
Baja California
Barcelona
Berlin
Boston
Brittany
Brussels
Chicago
Crete
Croatia
Cuba
Cyprus
Czech Republic
Dominican Republic
Dubai & UAE
Dublin
Egypt
Florence & Siena
Frankfurt
Greece
Guatemala & Belize
Iceland
Ireland
Kenya
Lisbon
London
Los Angeles
Madrid
Mexico
Miami & Key West
Morocco
New York City
New Zealand
Northern Spain
Paris
Peru
Portugal
Prague
Rome
San Francisco
Sicily
South Africa
South India
Sri Lanka
Tenerife
Thailand
Toronto
Trinidad & Tobago
Tuscany
Venice
Washington DC
Yucatán Peninsula

Dictionary Phrasebooks
Czech
Dutch
Egyptian Arabic
EuropeanLanguages (Czech, French, German, Greek, Italian, Portuguese, Spanish)
French
German
Greek
Hindi & Urdu
Hungarian
Indonesian
Italian
Japanese
Mandarin Chinese
Mexican Spanish
Polish
Portuguese
Russian
Spanish
Swahili
Thai
Turkish
Vietnamese

Music Guides
The Beatles
Bob Dylan
Cult Pop
Classical Music
Country Music
Elvis
Hip Hop
House
Irish Music
Jazz
Music USA
Opera
Reggae
Rock
Techno
World Music (2 vols)

History Guides
China
Egypt
England
France
India
Islam
Italy
Spain
USA

Reference Guides
Books for Teenagers
Children's Books, 0–5
Children's Books, 5–11
Cult Fiction
Cult Football
Cult Movies
Cult TV
Ethical Shopping
Formula 1
The iPod, iTunes & Music Online
The Internet
Internet Radio
James Bond
Kids' Movies
Lord of the Rings
Muhammed Ali
Man Utd
Personal Computers
Pregnancy & Birth
Shakespeare
Superheroes
Unexplained Phenomena
The Universe
Videogaming
Weather
Website Directory

Also! More than 120 Rough Guide music CDs are available from all good book and record stores. Listen in at www.worldmusic.net

Rough Guides maps

Rough Guide Maps, printed on waterproof and rip-proof Yupo™ paper, offer an unbeatable combination of practicality, clarity of design and amazing value.

CITY MAPS

Amsterdam · Barcelona · Berlin · Boston · Brussels · Dublin
Florence & Siena · Frankfurt · London · Los Angeles
Miami · New York · Paris · Prague · Rome
San Francisco · Venice · Washington DC and more...

COUNTRY & REGIONAL MAPS

Andalucía · Argentina · Australia · Baja California · Cuba
Cyprus · Dominican Republic · Egypt · Greece
Guatemala & Belize · Ireland · Mexico · Morocco
New Zealand · South Africa · Sri Lanka · Tenerife · Thailand
Trinidad & Tobago Yucatán Peninsula · and more...

US$9.99 Can$13.99 £5.99

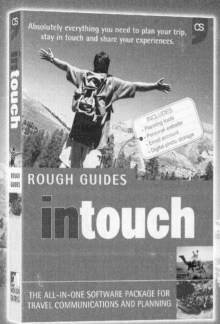

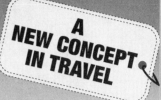

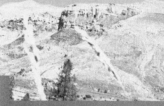

STA TRAVEL
450 BRANCHES WORLDWIDE
SPECIALISTS IN TRAVEL FOR STUDENTS & YOUNG PEOPLE
LOW COST FLIGHTS > OVERLAND & ADVENTURE TOURS
ACCOMMODATION > TRAVEL INSURANCE > CAR HIRE
CITY & CLUBBING BREAKS > ROUND THE WORLD > GAP YEAR
SKI & SNOWBOARD > TRAVEL HELP > WELL TRAVELLED STAFF
STA TRAVEL LTD
ABTA 99209
3206 ATOL PROTECTED
0870 160 6070
www.statravel.co.uk

Index

and small print

A Rough Guide to Rough Guides

In the summer of 1981, Mark Ellingham, a recent graduate from Bristol University, was travelling round Greece and couldn't find a guidebook that really met his needs. On the one hand there were the student guides, insistent on saving every last cent, and on the other the heavyweight cultural tomes whose authors seemed to have spent more time in a research library than lounging away the afternoon at a taverna or on the beach.

In a bid to avoid getting a job, Mark and a small group of writers set about creating their own guidebook. It was a guide to Greece that aimed to combine a journalistic approach to description with a thoroughly practical approach to travellers' needs – a guide that would incorporate culture, history and contemporary insights with a critical edge, together with up-to-date, value-for-money listings. Back in London, Mark and the team finished their Rough Guide, as they called it, and talked Routledge into publishing the book.

That first *Rough Guide to Greece*, published in 1982, was a student scheme that became a publishing phenomenon. The immediate success of the book – with numerous reprints and a Thomas Cook prize shortlisting – spawned a series that rapidly covered dozens of destinations. Rough Guides had a ready market among low-budget backpackers, but soon also acquired a much broader and older readership that relished Rough Guides' wit and inquisitiveness as much as their enthusiastic, critical approach. Everyone wants value for money, but not at any price.

Rough Guides soon began supplementing the "rougher" information about hostels and low-budget listings with the kind of detail on restaurants and quality hotels that independent-minded visitors on any budget might expect, whether on business in New York or trekking in Thailand.

These days the guides – distributed worldwide by the Penguin group – offer recommendations from shoestring to luxury and cover more than 200 destinations around the globe, including almost every country in the Americas and Europe, more than half of Africa and most of Asia and Australasia. Our ever-growing team of authors and photographers is spread all over the world, particularly in Europe, the USA and Australia.

In 1994, we published the *Rough Guide to World Music* and *Rough Guide to Classical Music*; and a year later the *Rough Guide to the Internet*. All three books have become benchmark titles in their fields – which encouraged us to expand into other areas of publishing, mainly around popular culture. Rough Guides now publish:

- Travel guides to more than 200 worldwide destinations
- Dictionary phrasebooks to 22 major languages
- History guides ranging from Ireland to Islam
- Maps printed on rip-proof and waterproof Polyart™ paper
- Music guides running the gamut from Opera to Elvis
- Restaurant guides to London, New York and San Francisco
- Reference books on topics as diverse as the Weather and Shakespeare
- Sports guides from Formula 1 to Man Utd
- Pop culture books from *Lord of the Rings* to Cult TV
- World Music CDs in association with World Music Network

Visit **www.roughguides.com** to see our latest publications.

Rough Guide Credits

Editorial and layout by Departure Lounge, www.departurelounge.biz
Text editor: Sarah Hudson
Layout: Lee Redmond, Debbie Woska
Cartography: Melissa Baker, Miles Irving, Katie Lloyd-Jones
Picture research: Jj Luck
Proofreader: Karen Parker

Editorial: London Martin Dunford, Kate Berens, Helena Smith, Claire Saunders, Geoff Howard, Ruth Blackmore, Gavin Thomas, Polly Thomas, Richard Lim, Lucy Ratcliffe, Clifton Wilkinson, Alison Murchie, Fran Sandham, Sally Schafer, Alexander Mark Rogers, Karoline Densley, Andy Turner, Ella O'Donnell, Keith Drew, Andrew Lockett, Joe Staines, Duncan Clark, Peter Buckley, Matthew Milton; **New York** Andrew Rosenberg, Richard Koss, Yuki Takagaki, Hunter Slaton, Chris Barsanti, Steven Horak
Design & Pictures: London Simon Bracken, Dan May, Diana Jarvis, Mark Thomas, Jj Luck, Harriet Mills; **Delhi** Madhulita Mohapatra, Umesh Aggarwal, Ajay Verma, Jessica Subramanian
Production: Julia Bovis, John McKay, Sophie Hewat
Cartography: London Maxine Repath, Ed Wright, Katie Lloyd-Jones, Miles Irving; **Delhi** Manish Chandra, Rajesh Chhibber, Jai Prakesh Mishra, Ashutosh Bharti, Rajesh Mishra, Animesh Pathak, Jasbir Sandhu, Karobi Gogoi
Cover art direction: Louise Boulton
Online: New York Jennifer Gold, Cree Lawson, Suzanne Welles, Benjamin Ross; **Delhi** Manik Chauhan, Narender Kumar, Shekhar Jha, Rakesh Kumar
Marketing & Publicity: London Richard Trillo, Niki Smith, David Wearn, Chloë Roberts, Demelza Dallow, Kristina Pentland; **New York** Geoff Colquitt, Megan Kennedy
Finance: Gary Singh
Manager India: Punita Singh
Series editor: Mark Ellingham
PA to Managing Director: Julie Sanderson
Managing Director: Kevin Fitzgerald

Publishing Information

This fifth edition published October 2004 by
Rough Guides Ltd,
80 Strand, London WC2R 0RL.
345 Hudson St, 4th Floor,
New York, NY 10014, USA.
Distributed by the Penguin Group
Penguin Books Ltd,
80 Strand, London WC2R 0RL
Penguin Putnam, Inc.
375 Hudson Street, NY 10014, USA
Penguin Books Australia Ltd,
487 Maroondah Highway, PO Box 257,
Ringwood, Victoria 3134, Australia
Penguin Books Canada Ltd,
10 Alcorn Avenue, Toronto, Ontario,
Canada M4V 1E4
Penguin Books (NZ) Ltd,
182–190 Wairau Road, Auckland 10,
New Zealand
Typeset in Bembo and Helvetica to an original design by Henry Iles.

Printed in Italy by LegoPrint S.p.A

896pp includes index
A catalogue record for this book is available from the British Library

ISBN 1-84353-273-5

1 3 5 7 9 8 6 4 2

Help us update

We've gone to a lot of effort to ensure that the fifth edition of **The Rough Guide to Thailand** is accurate and up-to-date. However, things change – places get "discovered", opening hours are notoriously fickle, restaurants and rooms raise prices or lower standards. If you feel we've got it wrong or left something out, we'd like to know, and if you can remember the address, the price, the time, the phone number, so much the better.

We'll credit all contributions, and send a copy of the next edition (or any other Rough Guide if you prefer) for the best letters. Everyone who writes to us and isn't already a subscriber will receive a copy of our full-colour thrice-yearly newsletter. Please mark letters: "**Rough Guide Thailand Update**" and send to: Rough Guides, 80 Strand, London WC2R 0RL, or Rough Guides, 4th Floor, 345 Hudson St, New York, NY 10014. Or send an email to **mail@roughguides.com**

Have your questions answered and tell others about your trip at **www.roughguides.atinfopop.com**

Acknowledgements

The **authors** jointly would like to thank: Abigail Batalla and Richard Hume at London TAT; Ron Emmons; Phil Cornwel-Smith; staff at TAT offices in Bangkok, Phitsanulok, Khorat, Hat Yai, Ko Samui, Narathiwat and Surat Thani; Fran Sandham for the feature on Bangkok tailors; Victor Borg for information on drugs penalties; Tom Vater for background on the *chao ley*; Richard Lim; Bangkok Airways.

From **Lucy**, thanks to: Apple and Noi; Slotthee; Pirom and Aree; Chai and Tham in Amphawa; Sam in Kanchanaburi; Khun Charin in Kamphaeng Phet; Nit and You; Jame, Mawn and Serge in Trat; Tan and Michel; Khun Sud, Khun Naa and Ronnie in Sukhothai; David on Ko Si Chang; Jonathan Buckley; Fred Gilardone.

Readers' letters

Thanks to all the readers who have taken the time and trouble to write in with comments and suggestions. Listed below are those who were especially helpful: apologies for any errors, omissions or misspellings.

Allen Ackerman, Esmé Allen & Stuart Foulkes, Martin Allen, Kiersten Aschauer, Ed Ashby, Karen Aslett, Tony Awerner, K. Babu, Robert Bachweizen, Jatinder Bahia, Lisa Barley, David Barnes, Julie Baxter, Jane Bell, Alison Berry, Graham Biles, Rubert Blum, Sharon Bolton, Julia Bonn, Alex Borione, Norbert Braun, H. van den Broek, Adrian R. Brown, Thomas Brown, Anna Burgess, Steve Burroughs, Hans Buyl, Fionnuala Callaghan, Denise Callahan, Leanna Cashen & Gareth Evans, Steve Chapman, Julia Charles, Vanessa Cheeseham & Gilbert Dedominicis, Chris, Chuanhui, James Clarke, Yoav Cohen, Gwyn Cole, Katie Collins, Karin Conroy, Frances Cornford, Paul Costa, Brian Cox, Holly Crofton & Jamie Dixon, Peter Cunningham, Justin Dane, Lorraine Davies, Debbie, Alex Diez, Matthew Dillon, Mark J. Dodds, Ron Doering, Barry Doherty, Don Dunlop, Sean Dwyer, Ursula Esser, D. Fletcher, Leanne Fogarty, John & Marilyn Francis, Tim Frier, Jelle de Gee, Bart van Geleuken & Sakia Ligthart, Maggy Goossens, Quinton & Irene Gradwell, Gary & Luke Hampson, Tony Harrould, Bettina Hartas, Linda Hartley, Kevin Harvey, Noel Hathorn, Christian Hawkins, John Heebink, Alex Herrmann & Isabelle Rzehulka, Alan Hickey, George van der Hilst, Gerard Holohan, Emma Hooijberg & Flo Herold, Anne and Kenneth Hoy, Atle Ingebrigtsen, William Ingram, Michelle Jarman, Dorothy Jekill, Miriam Jones, Mark Kater & Esther Wolfs, Jason Kennedy, Jim Kennedy & Julie Swettenham, Paul D. Kester, David Kitching, Kornelis Klevering, E. Knott, Ian Knowlson & Ragnhild P. Sandvik, Jesse Koche, Wenche Kristoffersen, Andrew Ktoris, Kajanga Kulatunga, S. Laurence, Ann Marie Lee, Paul J. Lee, Howell Lewis, Josephine Lindop, N. Lipp, Arjen van Loenen and Edith Beerdsen, Iris Lohrengel, Fatima Lopes & Vasco Silva, Hien Luong, Matt and Donna Maciejewski, Sarah Martinsson, Gavin Mason & Stephen Penning, Rod McCormick, Lyn McCoy, Chris McCullough, Larry McGuirk, Penny McKenzie, Donald Mcvean, Matt Mecke, Tony Messenger, Dafydd Meurig, Robin Miles, Ron Morris, Michael Mueller, Keith Mundy, Jane Murphy, K.P. Narayan, Sheila Nelson, Neil Noe & Sara Ladewig, Therese Nordenskar, Tessa Lyander Nordsten, Heidi Nunn & Darren Hern, Maureen O'Keefe, P. John O'Neill, Thomas Ormes, Peter Peirson, Alexandra Pitman, N Platt, Sara Platt, Jan Plihal, Rowena Poston, Elsie Rasmussen, Helen Read, Heather Rhodes, Andreas Rieck, Anna Ritchie & Sean Quigley, Bill Ryan, Jackie & Pete Sanders, Vivian Schatz, Steve Scott, Matt Sheriff, Debbie Slonowsky, Kate Smith, Maya Smith, Michael Smith, Jonny Söderström, Thomas Sourmail, Ruud Spek, Rachel Stevens, Hoe Yen Tam, Anna Taylor, Dawn & Neil Taylor, Stephen Taylor, Les Thompson, Tony, Laura Vella, Pete & Nikki Vesey, Clive Walker, Colin Waller, Jason Weetman & Daniela Nussbaum, Bjorn & Karen Weynants, Lennart Widell, Melanie Wielens, Maja Wildisen, Joe Willard & Ginette Morley, Helen Williams, Simon Williams, Timmy Williams, M.T. Willis, Brendt Wohlberg, Matthias Zehner.

Photo Credits

Cover credits
Main front: Ayutthaya © Powerstock
Front top: Elephant © Alamy
Front lower: Durian fruit © Robert Harding
Back top: Rice fields © Alamy
Back lower: © Robert Harding

Colour introduction
Koh Phi Phi © David Noton/Taxi/Getty Images
Rice fields © Lee Corbett/www.travel-ink.co.uk
Spools of silk © Joel W. Rogers/Corbis
Four eyes © Anthony Ellis
Monks at sunset, Chiang Mai © Thailand Tourist Board
Spirit house, Ko Samet © www.travel-ink.co.uk
Wat Arun and the Chao Phraya River, Bangkok © Chris Caldicott/Axiom
Gecko © Robert Harding
Thai boxing match, Bangkok © P. Treanor/Trip
Red Karen, northern Thailand © James Mann
Thanon Khao San, Bangkok © Neil Setchfield
Hua Hin train station sign © B. North/Trip
Prachuap Khiri Khan © Chris Scott

39 things not to miss
01 Wat Phumin, Nan © G. Corrigan/Robert Harding
02 Sea canoe, Krabi © Ellen Rooney/Robert Harding
03 Similan Islands © André Seale/Alamy
04 Loy Krathong, Sukhothai © Robert Harding
05 Great hornbill, Khao Yai National Park © Barbra Leigh/Corbis
06 Full moon party at Hat Rin, Ko Pha Ngan © Robert Harding
07 Phanom Rung © C. Rennie/Trip
08 Silkworms, Ban Prasat © Chris Scott
09 The National Museum, Bangkok © Martyn Evans/www.travel-ink.co.uk
10 Ko Mak, Ko Chang archipelago © Phil Cawley/Alamy
11 Ko Nang Yuan islets, Ko Tao © John S. Callahan/Alamy
12 Traditional massage © Robert Harding
13 Rafting down the Mae Khlong River, Umphang © Fred Gilardone
14 The Grand Palace, Bangkok © A. Tovy/Trip
15 Jim Thompson's House, Bangkok © Robert Harding
16 Ao Wong Duan, Ko Samet © Robert Francis/Robert Harding
17 Wat Yai Suwannaram, Phetchaburi © Robert Harding
18 Wat Phu Tok © Paul Gray
19 Hat Khlong Dao, Ko Lanta © Nicholas Pitt/Travelsnaps/Alamy
20 Amulet market, Bangkok © Alain Evrard/Robert Harding
21 Reclining Buddha, Wat Pho, Bangkok © Peter Charlesworth/Asiaworksphotos.com
22 Songkhla © Paul Gray
23 Death Railway, Kanchanaburi © Robert Harding
24 Doi Inthanon National Park, Mae Hong Son loop © Galen Rowell/Corbis
25 Vegetarian festival, Phuket © Robert Harding
26 Khao Sok National Park © David Noton/Alamy
27 Sticky-rice basket © Steve Gorton/Dorling Kindersley
28 Ko Tarutao National Marine Park © Paul Gray
29 Night market, Kanchanaburi © Robert Harding
30 Salad dishes, Chiang Mai © Robert Harding
31 Buddha in a bodhi tree, Wat Phra Mahathat, Ayutthaya © Paul Gray
32 Mekong River © Charcrit Boonsom/ Robert Harding
33 Wat Phra That Doi Suthep, Chiang Mai © Robert Harding
34 Tom yam kung © Simon Reddy/ www.travel-ink.co.uk
35 Laem Phra Nang © Robert Harding
36 Wind chimes, Chatuchak Weekend Market, Bangkok © Victor Borg
37 Wat Mahathat, Sukhothai © www.travel-ink.co.uk
38 Songkhran © Alain Evrard/Robert Harding
39 Axe pillows, Ban Sri Than © Lucy Ridout

Black and whites
Bangkok tuk-tuks © www.travel-ink.co.uk (p.40)
Wat Pho © Victor Borg (p.88)
Rama IX Bridge, southern Thonburi © Gerhard Jörén/Asiaworksphotos.com (p.148)
T-shirt stall, Thanon Khao San © Neil Setchfield (p.189)
Buddha in a bodhi tree, Wat Phra Mahathat, Ayutthaya © Paul Gray (p.208)
Early morning, Sangkhlaburi © Lucy Ridout (p.245)
Kamphaeng Phet © Charcrit Boonsom/www.travel-ink.co.uk (p.292)
Mae Sariang, Mae Hong Son © Peter Charlesworth/Asiaworksphotos.com (p.310)
Wat Phra Singh, Chiang Mai © Peter Charlesworth/Asiaworksphotos.com (p.329)
Elephant and mahout near Chiang Rai © D. Maybury/Trip (p.397)
Ko Chang © Ben Davies/Asiaworksphotos.com (p.420)

Phra Abhai Mani's mermaid, Ao Hin Kok © www.travel-ink.co.uk (p.443)
Mekong River © Charcrit Boonsom/www.travel-ink.co.uk (p.474)
Prasat Muang Tam © Ellen Rooney/Robert Harding (p.499)
Mekong sunset, Sang Khom © Jim Holmes/Axiom (p.539)
Ko Nang Yuan, Ko Tao © John S. Callahan/Alamy (p.558)
Hat Rin, Ko Pha Ngan © Rob Cousins/Robert Harding (p.613)
Laem Phra Nang © Robert Harding (p.638)
Ao Phang Nga © Robert Harding (p.696)
Ao Phra-Ae, Ko Lanta © Nicholas Pitt/Travelsnaps/Alamy (p.734)
Ko Tarutao National Marine Park © Paul Gray (p.742)
Songkhla National Museum © Paul Gray (p.770)
Wat Sri Sawai, Sukhothai © Tibor Bognar/Trip (p.806)
Thai drum © Luca Invernizzi Tettoni/Robert Harding (p.828)

Index

Map entries are in colour

A

B

INDEX

C

D

E

F

INDEX

L

M

N

O

P

R

S

T

U

V

W

Y

INDEX

MISS BUNCLE'S BOOK

Persephone Book Nº 81
Published by Persephone Books Ltd 2008
Reprinted 2009, 2010 and 2015

First published in 1934 by Herbert Jenkins Ltd.

Endpapers taken from 'Flower vase lit by rays from a table lamp', a screen-printed cotton and rayon designed by Vanessa Bell for Allan Walton Textiles in 1934

Typeset in ITC Baskerville by Keystroke, Wolverhampton

Printed and bound in Germany by GGP Media GmbH, Poessneck

978 1903155 714

Persephone Books Ltd
59 Lamb's Conduit Street
London WC1N 3NB
020 7242 9292

www.persephonebooks.co.uk

MISS BUNCLE'S BOOK

by

DE STEVENSON

with a new preface by

ALINE TEMPLETON

PERSEPHONE BOOKS
LONDON

CONTENTS

PREFACE

I first made my acquaintance with *Miss Buncle's Book* when I was, I suppose, about fourteen, with a reading habit which meant that if I had no book of my own immediately to hand, I trawled my parents' bookcases with the desperation of a chain-smoker who has smoked the last fag in the packet. *Miss Buncle's Book* wasn't immediately promising: it had a shabby, faded orange cover, poor quality paper and a motif inside which showed a lion sitting atop a book, whose pages proclaimed, 'Book Production War Economy Standard.' I must have been particularly desperate that afternoon, since I took it off the shelf.

It was, to my surprise, extremely funny – funny in a gently satirical, wholly engaging way. I devoured it, and as was my practice with favourite books, went back later and read it again. I still do, sometimes. I went on to the sequel, *Miss Buncle Married,* which, though it never had quite the impact of the first book, I also read and reread, despite the fact that – presumably in the interests of the aforementioned economy – Chapters Twelve to Fifteen had been omitted. It was only years later that I ran down another copy and discovered what had happened inbetween. A lot of things, previously rather mysterious, at last made sense.

Over the years, I would find DE Stevenson's books, as her granddaughter put it to me, 'a soothing balm' at times of stress and exhaustion. None, though, had quite the charm and originality of *Miss Buncle's Book*.

Its author, according to novelist Molly Clavering, was 'a quiet woman with curls of silvery hair, blue eyes and a low-pitched, unforgettable voice, wearing for choice good tweeds and well-cut plain shoes, [who] frequently astonishes people to whom she is pointed out as a famous author.' Dorothy Emily (DE) Stevenson, with more than forty hugely successful novels to her name and millions of fans all over the world, had little to do with the trappings of fame.

She was content with the life of an ordinary, well-to-do middle-class woman in a Scottish country town, with the gentle entertainments of tea parties with neighbours, drives in the beautiful Borders countryside, her crossword puzzles and her voracious reading – and her writing, of course. A tour of France and Italy when she was a young girl, and a visit to Mauritius in the Fifties to see her son, were among her rare trips abroad, and her media exposure was limited to a couple of interviews with Woman's Hour and In Town Tonight – then a popular equivalent of modern chat shows. Yet even today, there are fan sites in the United States, where dedicated 'DESsies' subject her novels to detailed analysis, swap notes about possible reprints and reminisce about the circumstances of their first encounter with her books. She is still much loved.

Dorothy made an early start to her writing career, beginning when she was eight. 'At first,' she wrote, 'members of the family were amused and interested but very soon they became bored beyond measure and decided I must stop, but I couldn't stop – my head was too full of stories. So I made a sort of nest in the box room, and wrote and wrote.'

It was not surprising that writing should come naturally to her. Born in Edinburgh in 1892, Dorothy was the daughter of one of the 'lighthouse' Stevensons, the famous engineering family, responsible for many of the great lights around the Scottish coast and abroad, and her father's first cousin was the even more famous Robert Louis. Sadly, she never knew him: he died in the South Seas when she was four years old, but she always felt particularly close to him, even writing, in later life, of a spiritual encounter with him on a Scottish moor.

She was educated at home in Edinburgh with governesses. August was spent at North Berwick, the east coast holiday resort which, like St Andrews a little further north, was famous for its bracing climate, its sandy beaches and its golf. Dorothy took her golf seriously and it was only the outbreak of war which cheated her of a place in the Scottish Ladies' golf team.

By then she was married to an army officer, Captain James Peploe. He too had distinguished connections. The artist Samuel Peploe was his father's half-brother and during the Second World War his widow brought a large number of paintings to the house in Moffat for safekeeping then afterwards, to the regret of the present family, took them all away again.

It was a hard time for a young army wife, in the middle of the First World War, and soon with the first of her four children – Patsy, who tragically was to die of of measles and a mastoid infection in 1928. Her husband came through his war service; Dorothy later put her experiences to good use in her first big success, *Mrs Tim of the Regiment*, in 1932.

At the outbreak of the Second World War, the Stevensons were living in Bearsden in Glasgow, where James was in the Territorial Army, but the Blitz drove them at last to look for a quieter place. They found it, fifty miles away, in 1 North Park, Moffat, a 'temporary' move which lasted until Dorothy died aged 81.

Moffat, in the central Borders of Scotland, is a picturesque small town, the first 'spa town' in Scotland, still retaining much of its Victorian charm. Huddled among the hills, it has wonderful walks – to Dorothy, one of its great attractions – and all around is stunning scenery, like the Grey Mare's Tail waterfall and the Devil's Beef Tub, where the Border Reivers would hide their stolen cattle. She wrote, 'I sometimes thought of Moffat as an island, surrounded not by water but by comfortable hills and moors,' and it became a favoured holiday destination for Robin, Rosemary and John, her children – indeed, it is still home to her granddaughter Wendy. Dorothy is buried in the cemetery above the town, with a simple headstone with her husband's and her own names, and underneath, 'Authoress DE Stevenson' and an epitaph, 'So long thy power hath led me/Sure it still will lead me on,' taken from the hymn, *Lead Kindly Light*.

Her last book, *Gerald and Elizabeth,* was published in 1969, only four years before her death. Despite the demands of family, house moves and the war, she had produced a book a year, more or less, and sometimes two – written in longhand on loose-leaf paper, leaning on a baize-covered sheet of plywood on her knees – from the time *Mrs Tim* came out. Even before that, she had *Meadow Flowers*, a book of French poems she had translated, privately printed, and in 1923 *Peter West*, the first of her novels, was published. In it you see the first hints of the author she would become. 'Adelaide laughed. She made a point of laughing at Edward's jokes,' with its sly humour, is typical of DE Stevenson's keen observation. But much of the book, produced as a serial for *Chambers Journal*, is heavy-handed and unconvincing and had no great success; her career only really started eleven years later.

With one startling exception – *An Empty World* (1936) was science fiction, set in 1973 after the massive destruction of life of earth by a giant comet – her books are commonly described as romantic fiction. The current genre 'relationship novels' might be a better category for them, though the relationships she depicts are of a very different type. Love, when it comes to the heroine – as it almost invariably does – is a delicate, insidious emotion grown in friendship and respect; any blatant display is shown as both vulgar and insincere.

Landscape has an important place in her books. She was a proud Scot, even dedicating her first book 'to all who love Scotland, her tears and smiles, her dark woods and sunlit moors, and the plain and homely folk in the lonely villages of the north,' but her stories set in tranquil English villages also have a magic of place. Some favourites, like 'Wandlebury', are the setting for several novels, giving a comforting sense of familiarity to a new cast of characters.

DE Stevenson divided her books into two categories: 'Some [are] light and amusing, some serious studies of character.' Yet even in those which, I think, she might have characterised as light and amusing, she created attractive people. She loved her characters, and her readers loved them too. She also had a habit, which endeared the novels further to her readers, of bringing popular figures back in walk-on parts in later books. It was if she were offering admission to a society which quietly carried on its own life, even when no one was watching, with the privilege of catching up, from time to time, with news of an old friend while discovering new ones. 'I write,' she said simply, 'about people everyone would like to meet.' There was a strong suspicion in the family that some of them did, in fact, have a basis in people Stevenson had met in Moffat, though this was always denied.

Miss Buncle's Book, her fourth novel, published in 1934,was an immediate success. It was in its fifteenth printing by the time my mother bought her utility edition, and the sequel, *Miss Buncle Married,* with its dedication, 'To those who liked Miss Buncle and asked for more' came out two years later. The third in the series, *The Two Mrs Abbotts,* appeared towards the end of the war.

Barbara Buncle, plain, unfashionable, patronised and ignored, is an unlikely heroine – but then so too was Jane Eyre. The only daughter of respectably middle-class parents, she has had a sheltered village life even after their death, living off the dividends which so reliably came through the letter-box at appropriate times and cared for by Dorcas, the maid who had been her own nurse when Miss Buncle was 'a small fat child in a basketwork pram.' It is the nineteen thirties, though: the chill winds of depression are blowing and the dividends dwindle and dwindle. The possibility of doing without domestic help occurs to neither mistress nor maid, Dorcas being as much family as any blood relation could be. Nor, it seems, does the idea of Miss Buncle finding a job, since this would be so unsuitable as not even to be discussed. Since Dorcas didn't fancy hens or paying guests, she suggests a book. And Miss Buncle, despite her claim, 'I have no imagination at all', writes it, with results she could never have foreseen.

Silverstream, the village where Miss Buncle lives, is so carefully realised that the reader could readily find the way from house to house to shops to church. It is idealised, of course, but it gives a glimpse into a vanished world: there are still butchers and bakers and greengrocers, with delivery boys to take out the orders; you pop up to London for a new hat, if female, or if male a fitting with your tailor; the whole village – apart from the servants cooking lunch, of course – meets at church on a Sunday morning. Gossip has the place of today's celeb mags, and its content is usually about as accurate – a useful plot device which DE Stevenson does not scruple to exploit.

The First World War changed many things, but between the wars the life of the provincial middle-class still remained much as before. Yet in this novel Stevenson shows the cracks beginning to appear. The Depression is never mentioned explicitly, but lack of money, and fear for the future, is a repeated theme. Even so, a lady is still expected either to have a private income or to get married and taking paid employment would be a shameful admission of poverty, excluding her from polite society. A household might have to make do with one maid instead of a staff, but there could be no question of the lady of the house doing domestic chores. A young girl taking a walk without a maid in attendance is definitely frowned upon. Miss Buncle's Silverstream is bound by conventions which would have been entirely familiar to the Victorians.

So perhaps the most surprising feature of the book is the warmly described lesbian relationship between gruff Miss King and pretty Miss Pretty. Only six years earlier, the hugely shocking *The Well of Loneliness* by Radclyffe Hall had been ruled obscene by a British court, and the *Sunday Express* had thundered, ' I would rather give a healthy boy or a healthy girl a phial of prussic acid than this book.' It seems unlikely that, given her audience, Stevenson would have set out to shock; it might even seem reasonable to wonder if, like Queen Victoria, she was unaware of the very existence of lesbians. And yet, Miss King says cryptically, 'There was a book, some years ago . . . It distressed us very much at the time, but it had nothing to do with us and I decided to ignore it,' which would suggest that her creator was well aware of these issues. In Silverstream society the ladies, if seen as eccentric, are simply accepted at face value.

The novel is, of course, all about Barbara Buncle's book and its consequences. Mr Abbott, her amiable publisher, was fascinated by 'a novel about a woman who wrote a novel about a woman who wrote a novel. It was like a perspective of mirrors such as tailors use, where the woman and her novel were reflected back and forth to infinity.' As the author, DE Stevenson adds yet another series of reflections, which perhaps does something to explain its sparkling quality.

Most of DE Stevenson's books are now out of print, but American websites eagerly circulate news of any new editions. A good second-hand copy of *Mrs Tim of the Regiment* can change hands for over £100. So what is the attraction of books that are so much of a time and place which certainly isn't the cruel modern world? Oscar Wilde's Miss Prism, asked about her lost three-volume novel, explained, 'The good ended happily and the bad unhappily. That is what fiction means,' and perhaps part of the attraction is that in Stevenson's novels these rules comfortingly still apply.

Dorothy was known to say, 'My books are my lighthouses': an interesting remark, given her pride in her engineering ancestors. Such a flimsy thing, a book, compared to the towering landmarks they created. Was there, perhaps, a trace of defensiveness there? But *The Pen is Mightier* – was the title of Barbara Buncle's second book, and it is a curious irony that just as the Stevenson books are creeping back into print, modern satellite systems are extinguishing one by one the lanterns of the Stevenson lighthouses.

DE Stevenson took a delight in writing, as she said, 'simply to please myself and amuse others,' and three quarters of a century later she is still amusing and her delight is contagious in the delicious entertainment which is *Miss Buncle's Book.*

Aline Templeton
Edinburgh, 2008

CHAPTER ONE

BREAKFAST ROLLS

One fine summer's morning the sun peeped over the hills and looked down upon the valley of Silverstream. It was so early that there was really very little for him to see except the cows belonging to Twelve-Trees Farm in the meadows by the river. They were going slowly up to the farm to be milked. Their shadows were still quite black, weird and ungainly like pictures of prehistoric monsters moving over the lush grass. The farm stirred and a slow spiral of smoke rose from the kitchen chimney.

In the village of Silverstream (which lay further down the valley) the bakery woke up first, for there were the breakfast rolls to be made and baked. Mrs Goldsmith saw to the details of the bakery herself and prided herself upon the punctuality of her deliveries. She bustled round, wakening her daughters with small ceremony, kneading the dough for the rolls, directing the stoking of the ovens, and listening with one ear for the arrival of Tommy Hobday who delivered the rolls to Silverstream before he went to school.

Tommy had been late once or twice lately; she had informed his mother that if he were late again she would have to find another boy. She did not think Tommy would be late again, but, if he were, she must try and find another boy, it was so important for the rolls to be out early. Colonel Weatherhead (retired) was one of her best customers and he was an early breakfaster. He lived in a grey stone house down near the bridge – The Bridge House – just opposite to Mrs Bold at Cosy Neuk. Mrs Bold was a widow. She had nothing to drag her out of bed in the morning, and, therefore, like a sensible woman, she breakfasted late. It was inconvenient from the point of view of breakfast rolls that two such near neighbours should want their rolls at different hours. Then, at the other end of the village, there was the Vicar. Quite new, he was, and addicted to early Services on the birthdays of Saints. Not only the usual Saints that everybody knew about, but all sorts of strange Saints that nobody in Silverstream had ever heard of before; so you never knew when the Vicarage would be early astir. In Mr Dunn's time it used to slumber peacefully until its rolls arrived, but now, instead of being the last house on Tommy's list, it had to be moved up quite near the top. Very awkward it was, because that end of the village, where the old grey sixteenth-century church rested so peacefully amongst the tombstones, had been all late breakfasters and therefore safe to be left until the end of Tommy's round. Miss Buncle, at Tanglewood Cottage, for instance, had breakfast at nine o'clock, and old Mrs Carter and the Bulmers were all late.

The hill was a problem too, for there were six houses on the hill and in them dwelt Mrs Featherstone Hogg (there was a Mr Featherstone Hogg too, of course, but he didn't count, nobody ever thought of him except as Mrs Featherstone Hogg's husband) and Mrs Greensleeves, and Mr Snowdon and his two daughters, and two officers from the camp, Captain Sandeman and Major Shearer, and Mrs Dick who took in gentlemen paying guests, all clamouring for their rolls early – except, of course, Mrs Greensleeves, who breakfasted in bed about ten o'clock, if what Milly Spikes said could be believed.

Mrs Goldsmith shoved her trays of neatly made rolls into the oven and turned down her sleeves thoughtfully. Now if only the Vicar lived on the hill, and Mrs Greensleeves in the Vicarage, how much easier it would be! The whole of the hill would be early, and Church End would be all late. No need then to buy a bicycle for Tommy. As it was, something must be done, either a bicycle or an extra boy – and boys were such a nuisance.

Miss King and Miss Pretty dwelt in the High Street next door to Dr Walker in an old house behind high stone walls. They had nine o'clock breakfast, of course, being ladies of leisure, but the rest of the High Street was early. Pursuing her previous thoughts, and slackening her activities a little, now that the rolls were safely in the oven, Mrs Goldsmith moved the ladies into the Colonel's house by the bridge, and the gallant Colonel, with all his goods and chattels, was dumped into Durward Lodge next door to Dr Walker.

These pleasant dreams were interrupted by the noisy entrance of Tommy and his baskets. No time for dreams now.

'Is this early enough for you?' he enquired. 'Not ready yet? Dear me! I've been up for hours, I 'ave.'

'Less of your cheek, Tommy Hobday,' replied Mrs Goldsmith firmly.

* * *

At this very moment an alarm clock started to vibrate furiously in Tanglewood Cottage. The clock was in the maid's bedroom, of course. Dorcas turned over sleepily and stretched out one hand to still its clamour. Drat the thing, she felt as if she had only just got into bed. How short the nights were! She sat up and swung her legs over the edge of the bed and rubbed her eyes. Her feet found a pair of ancient bedroom slippers – which had once belonged to Miss Buncle – and she was soon shuffling about the room and splashing her face in the small basin which stood in the corner in a three-corner-shaped washstand with a hole in the middle. Dorcas was so used to all this that she did it without properly waking up. In fact it was not until she had shuffled down to the kitchen, boiled the kettle over the gas ring, and made herself a pot of tea that she could be said to be properly awake. This was the best cup of the day and she lingered over it, feeling somewhat guilty at wasting the precious moments, but enjoying it all the more for that.

Dorcas had been at Tanglewood Cottage for more years than she cared to count; ever since Miss Buncle had been a small fat child in a basket-work pram. First of all she had been the small, fat child's nurse, and then her maid. Then Mrs Buncle's parlourmaid left and Dorcas had taken on the job; sometimes, in domestic upheavals, she had found herself in the role of cook. Time passed, and Mr and Mrs Buncle departed full of years to a better land and Dorcas – who was now practically one of the family – stayed on with Miss Buncle – no longer a fat child – as cook, maid, and parlourmaid combined. She was now a small, wizened old woman with bright beady eyes, but in spite of her advancing years she was strong and able for more work than many a young girl in her teens.

'Lawks!' she exclaimed suddenly, looking up at the clock. 'Look at the time, and the drawing-room to be done yet – I'm all behind, like a cow's tail.'

She whisked the tea things into the sink and bustled round the kitchen putting things to rights, then, seizing the broom and the dusters out of the housemaid's cupboards, she rushed into Miss Buncle's drawing-room like a small but extremely violent tornado.

Breakfast was all ready on the dining-room table when Miss Buncle came down at nine o'clock precisely. The rolls had come, and the postman was handing in the letters at the front door. Miss Buncle pounced upon the letters eagerly; most of them were circulars but there was one long thin envelope with a London postmark addressed to 'John Smith, Esq'. Miss Buncle had been expecting a communication for John Smith for several weeks, but now that it had come she was almost afraid to open it. She turned it over in her hands waiting until Dorcas had finished fussing round the breakfast table.

Dorcas was interested in the letter, but she realised that Miss Buncle was waiting for her to depart, so at last she departed reluctantly. Miss Buncle tore it open and spread it out. Her hands were shaking so that she could scarcely read it.

ABBOTT & SPICER
Publishers

Brummel Street,
London EC4
–th July.

Dear Mr Smith,

I have read *Chronicles of an English Village* and am interested in it. Could you call at my office on Wednesday morning at twelve o'clock? If this is not convenient to you I should be glad if you will suggest a suitable day.

Yours faithfully,
A Abbott

'Goodness!' exclaimed Miss Buncle aloud. 'They are going to take it.'

She rushed into the kitchen to tell Dorcas the amazing news.

CHAPTER TWO

DISTURBER OF THE PEACE

Mr Abbott looked at the clock several times as he went through his business on Wednesday morning. He was excited at the prospect of the interview with John Smith. Years of publishing had failed to dim his enthusiasms or to turn him into a soured and bitter pessimist. Every new and promising author found favour in his eyes. He had given up trying to predict the success or unsuccess of the novels he published, but he went on publishing them and hoping that each one published would prove itself a bestseller.

Last Friday morning his nephew, Sam Abbott, who had just been taken into the firm of Abbott & Spicer, suddenly appeared in Mr Abbott's sanctum with a deplorable lack of ceremony, and announced 'Uncle Arthur, the feller who wrote this book is either a genius or an imbecile.'

Something stirred in Mr Abbott's heart at these words, (a sort of sixth sense perhaps) and he had held out his hand for the untidy-looking manuscript with a feeling of excitement – was this the bestseller at last?

His sensible, publishing, business-man self had warned him that Sam was new to the job, and had reminded him of other lamentable occasions when authors who had promised to be swans had turned out disappointing geese, but the flame which burned within him leapt to the challenge.

The manuscript had gone home with him that night, and he was still reading it at 2 a.m. Still reading it, and still in doubt. Making allowances for the exaggeration due to his youth and inexperience Sam had been right about *Chronicles of an English Village*, and Mr Abbott could not but endorse his opinion. It was not written by a genius, of course, neither was it the babblings of an imbecile; but the author of it was either a very clever man writing with his tongue in his cheek, or else a very simple person writing in all good faith.

Whichever he was, Mr Abbott was in no two opinions about publishing him. The Autumn List was almost complete, but room should be made for *Chronicles of an English Village*.

As Mr Abbott turned out his light – about 3 a.m. – and snuggled down comfortably in bed, his mind was already busy on the blurb which should introduce this unusual book to the notice of the world. The author might have his own ideas about the blurb, of course, but Mr Abbott decided that it must be very carefully worded so as to give no clue – no clue whatever – as to whether the book was a delicate satire (comparable only with the first chapter of *Northanger Abbey*) or merely a chronicle of events seen through the innocent eyes of a simpleton.

It was really a satire, of course, thought Mr Abbott, closing his eyes – that love scene in the moonlit garden for instance, and the other one where the young bank clerk serenaded his cruel love with a mandolin, and the two sedate ladies buying riding breeches and setting off for the Far East – and yet there was simplicity about the whole thing, a freshness like the fragrance of new mown hay.

New mown hay, that was good, thought Mr Abbott. Should 'new mown hay' go into the blurb or should it be left to the reader to discover? What fools the public were! They were exactly like sheep . . . thought Mr Abbott sleepily . . . following each other's lead, neglecting one book and buying another just because other people were buying it, although, for the life of you, you couldn't see what the one lacked and the other possessed. But this book, said Mr Abbott to himself, this book must go – it should be made to go. Pleasant visions of bookstalls piled with neat copies of *Chronicles of an English Village* and the public clamouring for more editions passed dreamily through his mind.

The author must come and see him, thought Mr Abbott, coming back from the verge of sleep. He would know then, once he had seen the man, whether the book was a satire or a straight story, and he must know that (the mystery intrigued him) but nobody else should know. John Smith must be bidden to the office at the earliest possible moment for there was no time to waste if the book was to go into the Autumn List – John Smith, what a name! An assumed name, of course, and rather a good one considering the nature of the book.

Sleep hovered over Mr Abbott darkly, it descended upon him with outstretched wings.

On Saturday evening, after a day's golf, Mr Abbott read the book again. He took it into his hands with some trepidation – it was probably not so good as he had thought

– things looked different at 2 a.m. – he would be disappointed when he re-read the thing.

But Mr Abbott was not the least bit disappointed when he re-read the thing, it was just as good today as it had been last night – in fact it was better, for he knew the end and could now appreciate the finer points. It made him chuckle, it kept him glued to his chair till the small hours, it drifted along and he drifted along with it and time was not. It was the characterisation, Mr Abbott decided, that made the book. The people were all so real, every single character was convincing. Every single character breathed the breath of life. There was not a flat two-dimensional character in the book – rather unusual that! There were glaring faults of construction in the thing (in fact there was not much attempt at construction about it) – obviously a tyro, this John Smith! And yet, was he? And yet, was he? Weren't the very faults of construction part of the book's charm?

The first part of *Chronicles of an English Village* was a humdrum sort of affair – it was indeed a chronicle of life in an English Village. It might have been dull if the people had not been so well drawn, or if the writing had not been of that amazing simplicity which kept one wondering whether it were intended to be satirical or not. The second part was a sort of fantasy: a golden boy walked through the village playing on a reed pipe, and his music roused the villagers to strange doings. It was queer, it was unusual, it was provocative and, strangely enough, it was also extremely funny. Mr Abbott was aware, from personal experience, that you could not lay it down until the end.

The name of the book was poor, Mr Abbott thought. *Chronicles of an English Village* sounded dull; but another name could easily be found, a name that would focus light on the principal incident in the book, the incident upon which the whole story turned. What about 'The Golden Boy' or 'The Piper Passes'? Perhaps the latter was too sophisticated for such an artless (or was it an artful) story. It might be called 'Disturber of the Peace', thought Mr Abbott. Yes, that was rather good. It had the right ring about it; it was easy to remember; it cast the necessary light upon the boy. He would suggest the title to John Smith.

It will have been deduced from the foregoing that Mr Abbott was a bachelor – what wife would have allowed her husband to sit up till all hours for two nights running reading the manuscript of a novel? None.

Mr Abbott *was* a bachelor, he lived at Hampstead Heath in a very pleasant little house with a small garden. A man and his wife – Rast was their name – 'did' for Mr Abbott and made him extremely comfortable. Their matrimonial differences were frequent and violent, but these were confined to the kitchen premises and were not allowed to interfere with their master's comfort. A slate hung upon a hook on the kitchen dresser, and if the Rasts were not upon speaking terms they communicated with each other through the medium of a squeaky slate pencil. 'Wake him 7.30' Rast would write, and Mrs Rast would glance at the slate on her way to bed and appear at Mr Abbott's bedside at 7.30 precisely with a spotless tray of morning tea. Lucky Mr Abbott!

The letter summoning John Smith was despatched early

on Monday – it was the first thing Mr Abbott had seen to on his arrival at Brummel Street – and now here was Wednesday morning, and Mr Abbott was expecting John Smith. There was the usual box of cigars on Mr Abbott's table and two boxes of cigarettes – Turkish and Virginian – so that whatever sort of man John Smith might be, his taste could be catered for with the least possible trouble or delay. Mr Abbott was not quite his usual self this morning, he was excited, and the typist found him distrait. He was not giving his whole mind to the drawing up of a water-tight contract with Mr Shillingsworth, who was a best seller and quarrelled with every publisher in turn, and it was important, nay, it was imperative, that Mr Abbott's whole mind should be given to the matter.

'I think you had better come back later,' Mr Abbott was saying. 'I must think it over carefully.'

At this moment there was a knock at the door and the small page boy announced hoarsely, 'Miss Buncle to see you, sir. Shall I bring her up?'

'Buncle!' cried Mr Abbott. 'Buncle – who's Buncle?'

'Says she's got an appointment at twelve.'

Mr Abbott stared at the imp while he rearranged his thoughts. Miss Buncle – John Smith – why hadn't he thought that it might be a woman?

'Show her up,' he said sharply.

The typist gathered up her papers and departed with the swift silence of her tribe, and a few moments later Miss Buncle stood before the great man. She was trembling a little, partly from excitement and partly from fear.

'I got your letter,' she said in a soft voice, and showed it to him.

'So you are John Smith,' he announced with a humorous lift of his brows.

'It was the first name I thought of.'

'It is an easy name to think of,' he pointed out. 'I rather thought it was too bad to be true.'

'I don't mind changing it,' she told him hastily.

'I don't want it changed,' said Mr Abbott. 'There's nothing wrong with John Smith – but why not Buncle? A good name, Buncle.'

Her face blanched. 'But I live there!' she cried breathlessly.

Mr Abbott caught her meaning at once. (How quick he was, thought Miss Buncle. Lots of people would have said, 'Where do you live?' or, 'What has that got to do with Buncle?' but this man grasped the point in a moment.)

'In that case,' he said, and raised his hands a little, palm upwards – they both laughed.

Contact was now definitely established, Miss Buncle sat down and refused both kinds of cigarettes (he did not offer her the cigars, of course). Mr Abbott looked at her and wondered. How had she felt when she wrote *Chronicles*? Was it a straight story or a satire? He was still in doubt. She was obviously a simple sort of person – shabbily dressed in a coat and skirt of blue flannel. Her hat was dreadful, her face was pale and rather thin, with a pointed chin and a nondescript nose, but on the other hand her eyes were good – dark blue with long lashes – and they twinkled a little when she laughed. Her mouth was good too, and her teeth – if they were real – magnificent.

Meeting Miss Buncle in the street, Mr Abbott (who was rather a connoisseur of feminine charms) would not have looked twice at her. A thin, dowdy woman of forty – he would have said (erring on the unkind side in the matter of her age) and passed on to pastures new. But here, in his sanctum, with the knowledge that she had written an amusing novel, he looked at her with different eyes.

'Well,' he said, smiling at her in a friendly manner, 'I've read your novel and I like it.'

She clasped her hands together and her eyes shone.

This made him add – quite against his principles – 'I like it very much indeed.'

'Oh!' she exclaimed ecstatically. 'Oh!'

'Tell me all about it,' Mr Abbott said. This interview was proceeding on quite different lines from what he had imagined, arranged, and decided; quite differently, in fact, from any other interview between an author and a publisher in which Mr Abbott had ever participated.

'All about it!' echoed Miss Buncle helplessly.

'Why did you write it? How did you feel when you were writing it? Have you ever written anything before?' he explained.

'I wanted money,' said Miss Buncle simply.

Mr Abbott chuckled. This was a new kind of author. Of course they all wanted money, everybody did. Johnson's dictum that nobody but a donkey wrote for anything except money was as true today as it had ever been and always would be, but how few authors owned to the fact so simply! They either told you that something stronger than themselves compelled them to write, or else that they felt they had a message to give the world.

'Oh! I am quite serious,' said Miss Buncle, objecting to Mr Abbott's chuckle. 'You see my dividends are so wretched this year. Of course I ought to have known they would be, after all the papers said, but somehow I didn't. The dividends had always come in regularly and I thought – well, I never thought anything about it,' said Miss Buncle truthfully, 'and then when they didn't come in – or else came in only about half the usual amount – it gave me rather a shock.'

'Yes,' said Mr Abbott. He could visualise Miss Buncle sitting there in the midst of a crashing world waiting with perfect confidence for her dividends to come in, and the dividends failing to come in, and Miss Buncle worried about it and realising at last that *her* world was crashing as well as the outside world. He could visualise her lying awake at night with a cold sort of feeling in her heart and wondering what she had better do about it.

'So then you thought you would write a book,' suggested Mr Abbott sympathetically.

'Well, not just at first,' replied the author. 'I thought of lots of other things first – keeping hens for one thing. But I don't care for hens much. I don't like touching them, they are such fluttery things, aren't they? And Dorcas doesn't like them either. Dorcas is my maid.'

'Susan?' enquired Mr Abbott with a smile and a motion of

his hand towards the manuscript of *Chronicles of an English Village* which lay between them on the table.

Miss Buncle blushed, she neither confirmed nor denied that Dorcas was Susan (or Susan, Dorcas). Mr Abbott did not press the point.

'Well, so hens were definitely ruled out,' he prompted.

'Yes. Then I thought of paying guests, but there is already an establishment for paying guests in Silverstream.'

'You couldn't take the bread out of Mrs Turpin's mouth.'

'Mrs Dick,' corrected Miss Buncle quickly.

'Very ingenious,' commented Mr Abbott, 'and of course Susan – I mean Dorcas – wouldn't have liked PG's either.'

'She didn't like the idea at all,' Miss Buncle assured him.

'So then you thought of a book.'

'It was Dorcas really,' said Miss Buncle, giving honour where honour was due.

Mr Abbott felt like shaking her. Why couldn't she tell him about the book like a human being instead of having to have everything dragged out of her by main force? Most authors were only too ready to discuss the inception of their books – only too ready. He looked at Miss Buncle, feeling that he wanted to shake her, and suddenly found himself wondering what her name was. She was Elizabeth in the book of course – Elizabeth Wade – but what was her real name – Jane? Margaret? Ann?

'And how does Dorcas like the book?' enquired Mr Abbott.

'She hasn't read it yet,' replied Miss Buncle. 'She hasn't much time for reading and I wasn't very keen for her to read it. You see I don't think she will like it much, she likes something exciting. My book's not exciting is it? At least the first part isn't. But life in Silverstream is rather dull and I can only write about what I know. At least –' she added, twisting her hands in her effort to explain her limitations as an author and be perfectly truthful about it all – 'At least I can only write about *people* that I know. I can make them *do* things, of course.'

Somehow Mr Abbott was sure that she was thinking of those passionate love scenes on the terrace in the light of the Harvest Moon. He was almost persuaded now that *Chronicles of an English Village* was a straight story – no satire intended – it did not matter in the least, of course, because nearly everybody would think otherwise, but he did want to be sure.

'How did you feel when you wrote it?' he asked her suddenly.

'Well,' she replied after a moment's thought, 'it was difficult to start, and then it went on by itself like a snowball rolling down a hill. I began to look at people with different eyes, and they all seemed more interesting. Then, after a bit, I began to get quite frightened because it was all mixed up in my mind – Silverstream and Copperfield – and some days I didn't know which was which. And when I walked down to the village to do my shopping it was sometimes Copperfield and sometimes Silverstream, and when I met Colonel Weatherhead I couldn't remember whether he had really proposed to Dorothea Bold or not – and I thought I must be going mad or something.'

Mr Abbott had heard this kind of talk before and it had never impressed him very much. Miss Buncle did impress him because she wasn't trying to, she was simply answering his questions to the best of her ability and with the utmost truthfulness.

'Copperfield is actually Silverstream?' enquired Mr Abbott.

'Yes – you see I have no imagination at all,' said Miss Buncle sadly.

'But the second part – surely the second part is not all true?' gasped Mr Abbott.

Miss Buncle admitted that it was not. 'That was just an idea that came to me suddenly,' she said modestly. 'They all seemed so smug and settled, I thought it would be fun to wake them up.'

'It must have been fun,' he agreed.

From this point they went on to discuss the name, and Mr Abbott explained his ideas on the subject. The title was a trifle dull, not a good selling title. He suggested *Disturber of the Peace*. Miss Buncle was only too ready to bow to his superior knowledge of such things.

'And now for the contract,' said Mr Abbott cheerfully. He rang the bell, the contract was brought and with it came Mr Spicer and two clerks to witness the signatures. Mr Abbott could have cheated Miss Buncle quite easily if he had wanted to; fortunately for her he didn't want to, it was not his way. You make friends with the goose and treat it decently and it continues to lay golden eggs. In his opinion *Disturber of the Peace* was a golden egg but whether Miss Goose Buncle would lay any more was beyond the power of man to tell. She said herself that she could only write about what she knew – or rather (and wasn't this an important distinction) about *people* she knew. It was an admission made by no author that Mr Abbott had ever met before – a staggering admission. But to take it at its worst there was no reason to suppose that Miss Buncle had exhausted the whole essence of Copperfield in one book. Mr Abbott wanted other books from Miss Buncle, books about Copperfield or any other place provided that they had the same flavour.

This being so, Miss Buncle was asked to sign a very fair contract with Abbott & Spicer Ltd, in which she promised the first option of three more novels to the firm.

'Of course I may not write any more,' she protested, aghast at this mountain of work which had reared itself so suddenly in her path.

Mr Spicer looked somewhat alarmed at this admission of sterility, but Mr Abbott was all smiles.

'Of course you may not,' he comforted her. 'Sign your name just there – but somehow or other I think you will.'

So she signed her name – Barbara Buncle – very neatly, exactly where she was told, with Mr Abbott's very fat fountain pen, and the others put on their spectacles – at least Messrs Abbott & Spicer did, the clerks were too young to require any artificial aid – and signed too, in a very business-like way, and soon after this Barbara Buncle found herself in the street, slightly dazed and exceedingly hungry for it was long past her usual hour for lunch and she had breakfasted early.

Brummel Street was crowded and noisy, Miss Buncle was jostled by newsboys selling afternoon editions of various papers and by business men hurrying to unknown but obviously important appointments. Nobody took any notice of Miss Buncle except to say 'Sorry' or 'Pardon me' when they nearly bumped her into the road.

The open door of a small restaurant seemed a refuge; she found a table and ordered coffee and buns and chocolate éclairs for she had an unsophisticated palate and a good digestion. Then, laying her handbag with the copy of the contract on the table beside her plate she considered herself, and the strange sequence of events which had brought her to this pass.

'I'm an author,' she said to herself. 'How very odd!'

* * *

Colonel Weatherhead was in the Silverstream train – he had been in town paying a visit to his tailor – and waved his paper at Miss Buncle as she came along the platform.

'Come along, come along,' he said, quite unnecessarily, for Miss Buncle was coming along very well, and the train was not thinking of starting.

'I didn't know you were in town,' said Miss Buncle as the Colonel took her umbrella and placed it on the rack.

'And I didn't know you were,' he replied. 'You have had a successful day, I trust.'

Colonel Weatherhead had a gallant and slightly jocular manner with the fair sex which had come out very successfully in *Disturber of the Peace*. In spite of this he was really a very nice man, Miss Buncle thought. She had not been too unkind to him, she had merely drawn him as he was – and after all she had given him a very nice wife; Dorothea Bold was a dear.

Miss Buncle said she had had a very successful day.

'Hats or the dentist?' enquired the Colonel naming the two reasons which usually brought the inhabitants of Silverstream to town.

Miss Buncle said it was neither, and blushed. She was feeling a little guilty over her enormous secret.

'Aha – I see I must not enquire further,' said the Colonel archly. 'Some fellers have all the luck – by Jove they have!'

Miss Buncle looked down and smiled, she would not be drawn. If Colonel Weatherhead liked to think she had gone to London to meet a man he must just continue to think so. And of course I did, thought Miss Buncle to herself, but not in the way he thinks – or pretends to think, for of course he doesn't really think I went to meet a man, but he thinks that I would like him to think so.

It was rather muddled put like that, but Miss Buncle knew what she meant herself which was the main thing.

The train started without anyone else invading their solitude.

'Would you like the window up or down?' asked Colonel Weatherhead attentively. 'This one up and that one down? How pleasant to get a little fresh air. I can't think how anyone can live in London and breathe.'

Miss Buncle agreed, and added that it was the noise she disliked.

'Dreadful!' said the Colonel. 'Dreadful!'

Part of her hoped that Colonel Weatherhead would now settle down comfortably to the perusal of his papers and leave her in peace, but the other part hoped that he would continue to talk. He was such excellent copy, and, although *Disturber of the Peace* (such an excellent name suggested by that nice clever Mr Abbott) was finished and done with, she had got into the habit of watching people and listening to them. It had become second nature to her.

Colonel Weatherhead did not continue to produce copy for Miss Buncle; he took up a paper and scanned it but without seeing anything to interest him. The visit to his tailor had disturbed him, and he was still smarting under the disclosures of the tape. Two inches round the waist since January – quite horrible! An hour's digging in the garden before lunch might help, and perhaps an extra ten minutes' physical jerks before breakfast.

Miss Buncle was also immersed in secret thoughts, but hers were pleasant. The houses sped by, and were gradually replaced by orchards and fields.

CHAPTER THREE

MRS GREENSLEEVES

Mrs Greensleeves lay in bed enjoying her breakfast and looking at her correspondence. She was a pretty woman and she liked pretty things. The pink satin quilt, the frilled pillows with their pink silk bows, the breakfast tray with its white cloth and pink china were all carefully chosen. Mrs Greensleeves liked to think that they expressed her personality, and perhaps they did. Nobody saw her in bed except her maid – for Mr Greensleeves had departed from this cold and weary world some years ago – but the mirror was adjusted so that she could see herself and she enjoyed the picture.

On this particular summer's morning Mrs Greensleeves' correspondence consisted of two horrible bills – which she didn't see how she could possibly pay – and a chatty letter from her greatest friend, Iris Stratton.

'My dearest one,' Iris had written, 'Fancy that Ernest Hathaway appearing at Silverstream! Too intriguing! I've been making enquiries as you asked me – you know I'd do anything for my beloved Vivian – my dear, the man is rolling. He was at Oxford with Bob and Bob knows all about him. You can take it from your little Iris that he's full of ill-gotten gains. His father was in oil, or something, anyway he left thousands. His mother's dead too and Ernest was brought up by an old uncle, a clergyman in the North. Bob doesn't know why he has gone and buried himself at Silverstream unless he is writing a book – he's brainy, of course, and frightfully serious and goody-goody. – Not Bob's style at all and not yours either – what? Bob's still potty about you. I've trotted out some nice girls for him but he won't look at them. He's very jealous of you taking an interest in EH. I wish you would think seriously of Bob, you know I would like you as a sister-in-law. I believe you quite like Bob only he hasn't enough money for you – nasty little treasure-hunter that you are! – I bet you would be happier with Bob on two-pence-halfpenny than buried with EH in a country parish. I don't see *you* in a country parish taking round soup and blankets to the sick and the needy. Perhaps you think you could dig him out of it. Tell me what he's like when you write and whether you are *really* interested in the creature: Why don't you come up to town and have a binge, you must be getting positively mouldy at Silverstream. There's nothing much on just now, of course, but it would be fun. – IRIS.'

Vivian sighed and the letter fluttered on to the pink silk quilt – she had let her tea get cold while she read it. If only I could sell up the house and take a flat in town, she thought, but town's no fun without money. Nothing is any fun without money, I must have money somehow.

She lay back and considered ways and means. Iris was right, she was growing mouldy in Silverstream; it was dull as ditchwater, nothing ever happened. There was such a dearth of men in the place that she had actually made friends with one of Mrs Dick's paying guests. He was amusing and admiring – though common – and he had a car. He was better than nothing, that was all that could be said. Unfortunately he had begun to get a little troublesome just lately, Vivian would have to put him in his place and there would be no more joy-rides in Mr Fortnum's car. What a nuisance it all was! She sighed again and her eyes fell on the bills – something would have to be done about it. She took up the letter again and read the parts concerning Ernest Hathaway very carefully.

The next day was Sunday. Vivian Greensleeves rose from her pink bed much earlier than usual, she had mapped out her campaign and decided that there was no time to be lost. When she was dressed she surveyed herself in the glass. The effect was charming but rather too – well *too smart*. Perhaps the black hat would be better for the occasion. She changed her hat and rubbed some of the red off her lips.

On her way down she looked in at the kitchen door and said, 'I'm going to church, Milly. There may be a gentleman to lunch. Make a cheese soufflé in case.'

She was inconsiderate and overbearing, but Milly stayed with her because she was generous in a careless way. She let

Milly out a great deal, when it suited her, and gave Milly her frocks and hats when she was tired of them (which was long before they showed any signs of wear).

Milly was annoyed about the gentleman coming to lunch for it was her afternoon out, and it was doubtful, now, whether she would get out at all. At the best it would be late before she had cleared the lunch and washed up.

'I suppose you'll want coffee,' she said sullenly.

'Of course I shall want coffee,' replied Mrs Greensleeves.

She was perfectly aware that Milly was in a bad temper, but not in the least worried about it. She hummed a little song as she tripped off to church in her high-heeled shoes.

The Snowdons were coming out of their gate as she passed, they were all dressed up in their Sunday clothes. Mr Snowdon lifted his hat to Mrs Greensleeves and remarked in a cheerful voice that it was a fine day. The Misses Snowdon greeted Mrs Greensleeves with cries of delight. They were no longer young but they were full of skittishness. Miss Olivia was fat and red, she was the musical one. Miss Isabella was thin and pale, she was the poetical one. They admired each other with a great admiration, and Mr Snowdon admired them both, and they both admired him. They were an extremely happy family, but perhaps somewhat annoying to their friends; for they were all so full of each other's excellences that they had no admiration or interest for the excellences of outsiders.

On this particular Sunday morning Olivia was full of Isabella's latest poem; it was about a violet, and she had sent it to *Country Lore* and it had been accepted. Vivian Greensleeves was obliged to walk along with the Snowdons and listen to all this. Few of us have the necessary unselfishness to hear with gladness the talents of others extolled or to listen with patience to the successes of those whom we despise – Vivian hated it more than most people.

'I must speak to Barbara Buncle,' she said, and hurried on in the middle of the story. It was rude, of course, and the Snowdons were annoyed; they discussed the bad manners of Vivian Greensleeves all the way to church.

Meanwhile Vivian had hurried on and nearly overtaken Miss Buncle, but not quite. She did not really want to speak to Miss Buncle, nor to be seen walking with her – dull, frumpy creature! She was wearing a brown silk dress that had seen its best days long ago, and a light blue hat. It almost made your eyes water, Vivian decided. She slackened her pace a little, but not too much, for the Snowdons were behind.

The little Church of St Monica was cool and dim – very pleasant after the bright glare outside. Vivian took up a strategic position beneath the pulpit. He was nice-looking, she decided. She liked his thin, ascetic face, his sleek black hair and his dreamy grey eyes set wide apart. His forehead was high and his head beautifully shaped. The choir sang better than usual, and not so slowly; he seemed to have made a difference already in the church.

There was the usual gathering in the churchyard after the service. Vivian saw the Bulmers, with their two small children, talking to Mrs Bold. Miss Buncle was walking across the fields with old Mrs Carter – they lived next door to each other. The Snowdons were in animated conversation with Mrs Walker, the doctor's wife.

Vivian avoided them all and strolled about by herself looking at the grey tombstones with their worn inscriptions – some of them were so worn as to be illegible – and was glad that she was alive.

Colonel Weatherhead passed her, looking very smart in a new grey flannel suit. He waited for Mrs Bold at the lych gate and they walked away together – they lived opposite each other at the far end of the village near the bridge.

She'll never get him, thought Vivian, looking after the two figures with a malicious smile. He's far too much of a bachelor and too set in his ways – what a pair of fools!

The choir boys came tumbling out of the vestry, with their hob-nailed boots clattering on the steps. They threw on their caps and went tearing home over the fields. Would the man never come? Vivian wondered. What on earth could he be doing? Ah, there he was!

He walked quickly with his eyes on the ground, immersed in his own thoughts. Vivian had to touch him on the arm as he passed her.

'I'm Mrs Greensleeves,' she said, smiling sweetly.

Mr Hathaway took off his hat and shook hands with her. 'What a lovely day!' he said. She was sure he said that to everybody.

'I wondered if you would come and have lunch with me, Mr Hathaway,' she said in a friendly manner. 'It would give me so much pleasure.' She saw refusal in his face, and added quickly, 'I knew Mr Dunn so well. I should like to get to know you. It is such a *help* –'

She saw that she had said the right thing and left it at that – she was very cunning.

'I have got the Children's Service,' he told her doubtfully.

'Not till three,' she pleaded. 'And my house is not far.'

Mr Hathaway would rather have gone home; he was still new to his work and he found it took a lot out of him, but perhaps it was his duty – it *was* his duty to make friends with his parishioners, of course.

Vivian was thinking what a pity he's not tall! He looked taller in the pulpit, but he can't be more than five feet six. He looks strong and athletic though. Vivian sighed, she liked tall men.

'Well, it's very kind of you –' said Ernest Hathaway, with a smile.

They left a message at the Vicarage and walked up the hill together. Vivian began to talk about the sermon, and asked one or two fairly intelligent questions about it. Mr Hathaway answered them conscientiously. He was rather dull, she decided. For one thing he seemed quite unconscious that he was walking with a pretty woman. He's never once looked at me, she thought, I might have been Barbara Buncle for all the impression I have made on him.

Vivian's eyes were not so useless, she had noted the cloth of his black suit, it was fine and smooth; his shoes were handmade and beautifully shiny. Fancy him having all that money, she thought – what a waste!

In spite of her bad temper Milly produced a good lunch. The cheese soufflé was a trifle curdled and lumpy, but it was quite eatable. Mr Hathaway did not notice its deficiencies for he was talking about himself, and his ambitions. Like most people he enjoyed talking about himself to a sympathetic listener. It crossed his mind that Mrs Greensleeves was a nice woman.

'I'm afraid I've talked all the time,' he said as he went away to take the Children's Service.

'It has been *so* interesting,' said Mrs Greensleeves, hiding a yawn. 'Come and have supper with me on Wednesday night – just a little plain supper – then you can give me an innings,' she smiled at him.

Mr Hathaway reminded her, a little sternly, that Wednesday night was a Saints' Vigil and that there was a service at St Monica's at eight o'clock. She looked suitably chidden, and asked him to come on Thursday instead.

'I'm afraid I have been rather naughty about Saints' Days lately,' she told him, veiling her brown eyes with long black lashes.

There was no time now to point out the enormity of being lax, for the children would be waiting. Mr Hathaway decided as he strode off down the hill that here was a soul to be saved. He had already suspected that his predecessor had been a somewhat careless shepherd. Mrs Greensleeves was obviously a sweet, good little woman by nature – a trifle worldly perhaps, but fundamentally sound. She must be gathered into the fold. It was exactly what Mrs Greensleeves intended him to think.

On Thursday night Mr Hathaway appeared looking very smart in a well-cut dinner jacket. Vivian Greensleeves had taken a lot of trouble over the 'little supper' – it was just right. There were shaded candles on the table which shed a very pretty soft light on Vivian's beautiful arms. She leaned her elbows on the table and told her guest a great deal about herself. The greater part of the story came directly from a book which Vivian had just read, it was called *A Brand from the Burning*. Vivian softened it down a good deal, she did not want to appear too flaming a brand, or Mr Hathaway might be afraid of having his fingers burned. Vivian was, of course, more sinned against than sinning, but she was definitely a strayed sheep. They sat on the sofa together afterwards and Mr Hathaway did his duty by her. He showed her the error of her ways and besought her to repent. Mrs Greensleeves repented very prettily with tears. Mr Hathaway was forced to comfort her. He rather enjoyed the experience. It was impossible to complete the saving of Vivian's soul in one evening, and Ernest Hathaway was not one to grudge his time when the saving of a soul was in question. He promised to come again. He came again, quite often. It was soon rumoured in Silverstream that Mrs Greensleeves had become an enthusiastic church-goer, Milly Spikes may have had something to do with the spreading of the news. Milly did the shopping in the village for Mon Repos.

'It 'asn't done 'er any good so far,' Milly said, in answer to a piously expressed hope of her aunt, Mrs Goldsmith, at the bakery. 'More cantankerous than ever, that's wot she is. It's the Vicar she's after, if you ask me.'

‘Not really?’ Here was a piece of news worth having, and straight from the horse’s mouth, so to speak. Somebody came in at that moment for a cutting loaf – they would have to wait, that was all. Aunt and niece had their heads together over the counter. ‘And she said . . . and he said . . . and in comes Mr you know who . . . and she said . . . but don’t you say I told you, for Mercy’s sake.’ It was all very thrilling.

CHAPTER FOUR

MR HATHAWAY

It was not only Vivian Greensleeves who found in the new Vicar an acquisition to Silverstream, the Tennis Club also benefited from his presence, and benefited very considerably. Mr Hathaway played an excellent game of tennis, he was streets ahead of anybody else in the club; but a fairly even match could be made if the Vicar were given an absolute rabbit as a partner – and there were plenty of rabbits to choose from.

Barbara Buncle was one of the most frequent of the Vicar's partners, she was a keen player, but her game never seemed to improve. The more she tried the worse she seemed to get, it was really very discouraging.

One fine afternoon in September, towards the end of the tennis season, Barbara Buncle walked down to the club. There was a match in progress, and those who were not taking part in the struggle were watching it from the verandah of the small pavilion. Barbara changed her shoes and joined the audience. It was an exciting game to watch, Mrs Bulmer and the Vicar against Mr Fortnum and Olivia Snowdon. They should have been evenly matched, for Miss Snowdon was one of the best players in the club, and Mrs Bulmer one of the worst, and this should have counterbalanced the Vicar's superiority over Mr Fortnum; but this was mere theory, and did not allow for the psychology of the players at all. Barbara Buncle perceived that the Vicar and Mrs Bulmer were going to win. The Vicar was in great form and he had managed to inspire his partner with unusual confidence. She was playing several degrees above her usual form, whereas their opponents were getting on each other's nerves and in each other's way and becoming more and more annoyed with each other. Miss Snowdon – in spite of her obesity – was a most energetic performer on the tennis court, she swooped here and swooped there, poaching in Mr Fortnum's court and getting extremely red and hot. Mr Fortnum was annoyed at having his strokes interfered with, he withdrew to a corner and left Miss Snowdon to do as she liked – if she wanted to play a single, let her. He sulked and became careless. Miss Snowdon glared at him every time he missed the ball.

Barbara watched it all with interest, it was such fun to watch people and see how they reacted to one another's personality. Vivian Greensleeves was watching it too, she did not care for tennis, but she had begun to come down to the courts in the late afternoons, nobody quite knew why. She sat in a deck chair with a good deal of very neat leg clad in beige silk stocking exposed to view. She looked cool and graceful and very pretty. The women members did not take much notice of Vivian, if she liked to come down she could come, they didn't mind much either way, but some of the men were quite pleased to sit and talk to her between the sets. The women members felt that she was not really a Silverstreamite, not really one of themselves. Miss Snowdon declared that she was 'not good form', and Miss Isabella Snowdon added that her clothes were 'ootray'. Vivian was fully aware of their opinions; she, on her part, despised the whole lot of them. She thought them frumpy, and dull, and incredibly stupid. Her sole reason for appearing at the tennis club was to keep an eye on Ernest Hathaway. If he came, so must she; but she was bored stiff by the whole performance; she felt, and looked, as alien as a bird of paradise in a murmuration of starlings.

The game was almost finished – it *was* finished to all intents and purposes, for Mr Fortnum was beaten and not all the energy and vim of Miss Snowdon could pull him through.

'Olivia has such beautiful style,' announced Miss Isabella Snowdon to all who cared to hear. She merely wished to point out, in a thoroughly ladylike manner, that it was not dear Olivia's fault if her side was losing.

'It would have made a better game if they had had Dorothea Bold instead of Olivia,' said Miss King firmly.

'Oh, Miss King, how can you say such a thing?' cried Miss Isabella in horrified tones.

'Merely because it happens to be true. Dorothea is a more reliable player than Olivia,' replied Miss King firmly, and moved away.

'Horrid old thing!' said Miss Isabella to Barbara Buncle who happened to be sitting next to her. 'It's just jealousy, that's what it is. She may dress herself up like a man, and talk and smoke like a man, but she's nothing but a cat – that's what she is.'

'I rather like Miss King,' said Barbara placidly, and she looked at Miss King's tall commanding figure as it strode off across the court with some affection. Of course she *was* rather funny with her deep voice, and her short hair, and her strange habit of wearing tailored coats and skirts with collars and ties like a man, and very often she was to be seen with a cigarette in the corner of her mouth, and her hands in her pockets; but, after all, these little peculiarities did nobody any harm, and there was something rather nice about the woman. At any rate she would never say behind your back what she would not say to your face (like some people one could name). You always knew exactly where you were with her, she said what she thought without fear or favour.

Miss Isabella looked at Barbara with contempt – fancy standing up for Miss King! But of course nobody in Silverstream cared what Barbara Buncle thought, the woman was nothing but an idiot. She wondered idly what Barbara Buncle was thinking about now, sitting there with that silly vacant smile upon her face. She would have been surprised if she could have read the thoughts that prompted the silly smile.

The truth was that Barbara was feeling somewhat pleased with life today, and she had good reason to be pleased, for, only that morning, a parcel of books had arrived from Messrs Abbott & Spicer – six neat copies of *Disturber of the Peace* with the firm's compliments. She had spent the whole morning reading her book, and marvelling at the astounding fact that she had written every word of it, and here it was, actually in print, with a smart red cover, and a jacket with a beautiful picture of a Golden Boy playing on a reed pipe.

The jacket was just a *little* disappointing because the Golden Boy was quite different from Barbara's conception of him. For one thing he seemed to have goats' legs and his ears were pointed in a peculiar way – Barbara had imagined quite a human, ordinary sort of boy – but that was, after all, a mere detail and you could hardly expect a strange artist to depict a Golden Boy exactly as you had imagined him.

The set was over now, and the players were returning to the pavilion talking about the various strokes which had made or marred their fortunes in the game. Mr Hathaway was illustrating a back-hand drive to Mrs Bulmer. He was a kind man, always ready to help the rabbits to improve their status.

'What about a men's four?' suggested Dorothea Bold, 'Here's Dr Walker coming – it would be splendid to watch.'

'Awfully sorry, I must go now,' said the Vicar, struggling into his blazer. 'The truth is my uncle is coming for two nights –'

He said goodbye to everybody and strode off. He was late, for the set had lasted longer than he had expected, he wondered if it would matter much if he broke into a run. Would it do Silverstream any harm to see its Vicar doubling along the High Street like an ordinary young man? Perhaps it was better just to walk quickly. When you became a Vicar it seemed necessary to stifle so many natural impulses.

Uncle Mike wouldn't mind him being a bit late – there was no foolishness of that kind about Uncle Mike – but Ernest was longing to see Uncle Mike after all these weeks, and to add to his pleasure it was delightful to be going to entertain Uncle Mike in his very own house.

The Reverend Michael Whitney was Ernest Hathaway's uncle, guardian, tutor, his father in God, and general confessor. He had looked after Ernest ever since the latter had been left an orphan at eleven years old. Ernest had spent all his holidays at the big old-fashioned country rectory, a corner of which was amply sufficient for the bachelor Rector's needs. Uncle and nephew – an oddly assorted couple – had walked and talked together and fished various small streams in the neighbourhood with more or less success. Uncle Mike had devoted one entire summer holiday to the important task of teaching Ernest to hold a straight bat, to keep his eye on the ball and step out to it. There was a certain telling pull to leg which Uncle Mike had imparted to Ernest and which had brought that young man laurels on more than one occasion.

Ernest owed everything to Uncle Mike, and he knew it and was grateful. It was nice to be able to entertain Uncle Mike in return. He was only coming for two days, of course, but Ernest had managed to include most of Uncle Mike's favourite dishes in the two days' menu. He hoped Mrs Hobday would make a success of the dishes and not forget the orange salad, nor make the curry too hot.

As Ernest put his hand on the gate and vaulted lightly into his own garden he saw that Uncle Mike had arrived, and had established himself in a deck chair on the lawn beneath the chestnut tree. Ernest waved his hand, and shouted, 'Don't get up.'

'I can't,' said Uncle Mike (his figure was not of the type that rises easily from deck chairs), but his round fat face beamed with pleasure as Ernest came towards him across the lawn.

'Been teaching your parishioners to play tennis?' asked Uncle Mike chuckling.

'Trying to,' smiled Ernest.

'Not getting stuck-up, are you?'

'Trying not to,' smiled Ernest again.

'How often have I warned you against the Sin of Pride?' demanded Uncle Mike with mock severity.

'Hundreds of times,' Ernest agreed with mock humility.

They both laughed. It was very pleasant to joke with somebody who understood. Ernest was happy, the garden was full of the late-afternoon golden sunshine and the song of birds, it was quiet and peaceful after the chatter of the tennis club. He sat down on the grass beside Uncle Mike and took off his hat.

'You're very comfortable here,' Uncle Mike told him. 'I like the look of that woman you've got – Mrs Hobday, isn't it? Your bookcase fits into the library nicely, doesn't it?'

'I'm too comfortable,' Ernest replied tersely.

'You said so in your letter,' agreed Uncle Mike. 'I didn't know what you meant. How can a person be too comfortable? I suppose you have got one of your wild-cat ideas –'

'Yes, I have,' Ernest owned smiling a little, 'at least you will probably think it is a wild-cat idea.'

'I have no doubt of it. Let's hear the worst.'

‘It’s like this, Uncle Mike,’ Ernest said, clasping his hands round his knees and looking up at the other man with his frank gaze, ‘I’ve got too much money.’

The fat man began to laugh, he laughed and wheezed and laughed again.

‘You’ve got your asthma –’ said Ernest anxiously.

‘You’re enough to give anyone – asthma,’ gasped Uncle Mike. ‘Absolutely unique in this planet – don’t you know that the – whole world is on the verge of bankruptcy?’

‘I’m not talking about the whole world,’ replied Ernest. ‘I’m talking about myself. Here am I, a strong healthy man, living in luxury – it’s not right.’

‘You can help people, Ernest.’

‘There is nobody here that needs help,’ Ernest replied, ‘nobody really poor. Of course I can give money away to people, but it doesn’t do much good – in fact I’m beginning to see that it does harm. People here think that I’ve got plenty of money and they come to me with tales – not always strictly true – and expect me to help them.’

‘Human nature,’ suggested Uncle Mike who had seen a good deal of human nature in his time.

‘It’s doing harm,’ Ernest told him, ‘my money is doing harm in this parish. Instead of giving, they take. It’s not right. St Paul said people should give to the Church, and support their priests.’

‘You find them grasping?’ enquired Uncle Mike.

‘Only because I’m well off – I’m sure of that, or at least nearly sure –. They are only grasping because they think I can afford to give.’

'Well, you can.'

'Yes, but the system is all wrong. The whole thing is back to front – oh it's so difficult to explain –' Ernest cried, waving his arms. 'My mind is so full of it all that I simply can't put it into words. Look at the Apostles, look at St Francis! They stripped themselves of their worldly goods (perhaps it was to teach people to give) and they didn't starve, did they?'

'People fed them,' replied Uncle Mike. 'People don't feed saints nowadays, they ask them why they are not on the dole, and advise them to apply for parish relief.'

'Now don't be horrid, Uncle Mike,' said Ernest, as if he were, once more, only eleven years old. 'You can understand if you want to. It's really quite simple – here I am living in luxury and getting fat and lazy. It's frightfully bad for me, and it's bad for other people too. Mrs Hobday is wasteful and extravagant, and I don't care – why should I? – People come and ask me for money and I give it to them because it's less trouble to give it to them than to refuse – it's bad, bad, bad.'

'Well, supposing it is bad – what is the remedy?' enquired Uncle Mike uneasily.

'I ought to be able to live on my stipend.'

'You couldn't,' replied Uncle Mike, 'we went over all that before you came here. The living was offered to you because you had private means. It is such a poor living that no man who had not private means could take it –'

'That's another wrong thing,' said Ernest excitedly. 'A living shouldn't be offered to a man because he has private means – the labourer is worthy of his hire – it is debasing the church – no living should be so poor that a single man couldn't live on it.'

'The world is far from perfect,' Uncle Mike said (he had lived in the world a long time and had learnt to take the bad with the good, like a Gregory powder in jam). 'The world is far from perfect. There are lots of things wrong but you can't change the world.'

'I don't want to change the world – at least perhaps I do want to, but I'm not such a fool as to think I can – that isn't the point. The point is that there's something wrong *here*, something wrong in my life and I've got to change it. I'm going to try and live on my stipend, Uncle Mike. After all a man should be able to live on very little. Look at St Francis –'

'Well, go ahead then,' said Uncle Mike who was beginning to feel rather weary, and had no wish to hear any more about St Francis at the moment. 'Go ahead and try to live on it for a bit. I don't suppose it will do you any harm. Try to keep your expenses down to three pounds a week –'

'That wouldn't be any good,' interrupted Ernest, shaking his head, 'I wouldn't be able to do it.'

'Of course you wouldn't. Isn't that just what I've been telling you?' asked Uncle Mike in exasperation. And how could he? How could Ernest, who had always had as much money as he could spend, suddenly start living on three pounds a week? (Especially when there was no real necessity for it. If you had to do a thing you just had to, and there was the end of it.) It was not that the boy was extravagant, exactly, but he always liked the best of everything, and, since his father had left him well provided for, there seemed to be no reason why he should not have the best of everything. Mr Whitney had nothing to complain of about Ernest's spending. The boy spent wisely, and he had always been generous in a wise manner, but up to now, he had managed to go through his large yearly income without the slightest difficulty.

'I shan't be able to live on three pounds a week unless I have only three pounds a week to live on,' Ernest was saying. 'If I have only three pounds to spend, I can't spend more.'

'Can't you?' enquired Mr Whitney.

'Well, I shan't, anyhow,' returned Ernest, 'and what I want to do is this, I want to arrange for all my money to go to various charities, to go to them straight off just as it comes in, so that I shan't have it at all, even if I want it. You can get a deed of gift made out, or something like that, I suppose.'

Mr Whitney gasped.

'Here's a list of charities I've thought of,' Ernest continued, taking the list out of his pocket and handing it over. 'You can probably suggest others. Of course the capital is tied up in the trust or I could have got rid of it much more easily – it's a pity.'

'It is indeed,' replied Mr Whitney with deplorable sarcasm.

'I'm afraid it's going to be a bit of a nuisance for *you,*' continued Ernest. 'But I don't see how else I can arrange it, or who else I could get to do it for me –'

At this point Mr Whitney ceased to listen, he knew Ernest sufficiently well to know that when Ernest got an idea into his head nothing would remove it. The only thing to be done was to safeguard the rash youth from the consequence of his wild-cat scheme. If Uncle Mike took the management of the wild-cat scheme into his own hands he could keep part of the money in reserve for Ernest when he wanted it (as he most assuredly would want it). Yes, that would be the best way – he would fall in with Ernest's plan and agree to distribute the money, and of course he would distribute the greater part of the money as Ernest wished; but part of it – say five hundred pounds – he would bank safely in Ernest's name so that it would be there if required, and if not required it could be distributed at the end of the year. A year of poverty would do Ernest no harm – no harm at all. In fact it would be quite a valuable experience for Ernest. He had always had too much money, and too much money was bad – not that it seemed to have done Ernest any harm –. Mr Whitney had been worried about Ernest's affluence at one time, but when he saw that the boy was turning out all right in spite of the money, he had ceased to worry. It was strange how things worked out. Mr Whitney had wished that Ernest might have the experience of poverty, and now Ernest had chosen to have it, and Mr Whitney was worried. But there was really nothing to worry about, thought Mr Whitney, comforting himself – he hated having to worry about things – because everything would be quite all right, and it would do Ernest good to count the pennies for a year. As long as the boy did not starve himself it would be all right, he must keep an eye on Ernest and see that he did not do that, of course.

They discussed the whole matter again after dinner – the dinner had been very satisfactory – and it was decided that Ernest should sign a paper making over his year's income to

Uncle Mike. Uncle Mike would then distribute the money to various charities as he thought best. (Ernest didn't mind very much who got the money as long as he was rid of it – he had begun to look upon it as a burden – perhaps the burden that Christian had carried strapped to his back.) At the end of a year the matter would be reconsidered. Mr Whitney insisted on the year's probation – Ernest might want to marry, or he, himself, might die, anything might happen in a year –

'Good,' said Ernest at last, stretching his arms, 'I'm free.'

'You are bound,' thought Mr Whitney but he was too wise to say so.

* * *

The next morning was a Saint's Birthday. Ernest and Uncle Mike walked down through the garden to the little church. The dew glistened on the grass like millions of diamonds, a lark was singing blithely.

Ernest thought that he had never enjoyed anything more deeply and perfectly than that Early Celebration, his heart was full of peace and happiness. It was too wonderful to talk about. After it was over they walked back through the sunlit garden, very near together in spirit.

'Do you think I'm a fool, Uncle Mike?' asked Ernest suddenly.

'If you think it the right thing to do you are right to do it,' replied Uncle Mike quietly. 'I believe the experience will be valuable.'

CHAPTER FIVE

MRS WALKER

Mrs Walker – the doctor's wife – was the first person in Silverstream to read *Disturber of the Peace*.

It was a foggy evening in October, very raw and damp for the time of year. Incidentally it was the fifth anniversary of the Walkers' wedding day, and Sarah Walker had arranged a nice little dinner with all the doctor's favourite dishes to celebrate the occasion. But woman proposes and God disposes – Sarah knew when she heard the telephone bell that it was an urgent call.

It was quite absurd that she should know from the way the bell rang that it was an urgent call (it might just as well have been a telegram from her father remembering, belatedly, the occasion; or a message from Mrs Featherstone Hogg bidding her to tea; or half a dozen other things of no importance whatsoever) but Sarah always declared that she knew the moment the telephone bell rang whether or not it was the hand of God summoning John from her side, and the strange thing was that she was very often right.

So, tonight, when the bell rang, and John ran downstairs to answer it, and returned to say, 'It's the Sandeman baby arriving,' she had already got over her disappointment about the anniversary dinner and had decided to counter-order everything (seeing the feast would be but an empty farce without John, and besides, she did not really enjoy salmon and oxtail herself, but only liked to see John enjoying them) and have a poached egg and a cup of cocoa on a tray in the study.

'I'm frightfully sorry,' said Dr John, 'but it can't be helped. Don't wait up for me, Sally. Dear knows when I'll be home – have you seen my rubber gloves?'

'There's a new pair in the drawer in the Surgery,' Sarah said, 'the others split. Never mind, we'll pretend it's tomorrow. Be sure to make it a boy.'

This was a recognised joke, so the doctor chuckled dutifully.

'Take your muffler – the big grey one,' Sarah added, 'it's a horrible night.'

He kissed her and tore himself away.

The study was a cosy, rather shabby room with red curtains, shaded lights, and a few good prints on its plain, cream-coloured walls. Two deep leather armchairs stood on either side of the fire.

Sarah sighed, drew back the curtains and peered out at the night. She could not make out whether it was raining or not, the mist was heavy, and the street lamps were surrounded by an orange-coloured nimbus. She felt glad that she had made John take his muffler. She wondered how long Mrs Sandeman's baby would take to arrive. Her mind strayed back three years, it was on a night like this that the twins had made their unexpected appearance in the world – how horrible it had been! She had never appreciated John at his full value until that dreadful night, his kindness, his gentleness, his marvellous strength.

The parcel of books from the library was on the table. Sarah undid the string and turned them over with her long thin fingers. What had they sent this time? She rejected a fat biography, and dipped into a historical *réchauffé* – too dull. She was not in the mood for improving literature tonight, something light and amusing would pass the time better. What about this one – *Disturber of the Peace* by John Smith? She took it up and sank into the doctor's chair (it was the more comfortable of the two for John's weight had broken some of the springs, and flattened out the others, whereas Sarah's chair was still in its pristine state of bulgy hardness despite her five years' occupancy). Nell, the setter – who had never set at anything more exciting than a crow – lay down comfortably at Sarah's feet.

'I shall wait up for him however late it is,' Sarah told her. 'He can't be later than twelve, can he, Nell? I shall make him a cup of Benger's, and you shall have some too.'

Nell wagged her tail, it was a pity she couldn't talk, but she understood every word you said – at least the Walkers declared that she did.

Sarah turned on the reading lamp and opened the book; quiet fell in the room as she began to read. She read quickly, for, since the advent of the twins, she had not been very strong, and people who are not very strong usually read a great deal, and people who read a great deal read quickly – besides the book ran along so easily, it swept you along –

Sarah laughed softly, and Nell stirred in her sleep and raised her beautiful head.

'You know, Nell, you miss a lot by not being able to read,' Sarah told her. 'These people are real live people – they are quite delicious.'

Nell wagged her feathery tail, it was good when the goddess descended from the clouds and spoke to you, it gave you a cosy safe feeling in your inside.

Sarah read on. You couldn't help reading on. She read on till the fire died down and she had to rouse herself to mend it – dreadful if John returned cold and wet to find a half-dead fire! As she put on a piece of coal, her mind, freed from the witchery of the printed page, swept back over what she had read. It might be Silverstream, she thought. Copperfield – Silverstream – how queer! And Major Waterfoot is exactly like Colonel Weatherhead, and Mrs Mildmay might easily be Dorothea Bold –

She knit her brows and turned back the pages, growing more and more suspicious that this was no mere coincidence of names and personalities. She was looking for that bit about the doctor who had been sent for by Mr Gaymer. Here it was –

'Dr Rider was a tall, broad-shouldered Scotsman with a whimsical mouth and a pair of shaggy eyebrows; he brought a cheery atmosphere of health and vigour into the most hopeless of sickrooms. Children loved him and he could do what he liked with the most unmanageable mother's darling in Copperfield. But for those with imaginary ailments he had short shrift, and was apt to prescribe castor oil for malingerers, a peculiarity which did not endear him to their hearts.'

It was John to the life. Sarah lay back in her chair and laughed and laughed. Who on earth could have written this book? Somebody in Silverstream obviously; somebody who knew everybody in Silverstream; one of John's patients. She turned to the cover and saw that the author called himself John Smith – it did not help her much, anybody might be John Smith. Well, she thought, let's go over all the people in Silverstream who might have written it, and eliminate the impossibles, there aren't so very many people in Silverstream. Could it be Colonel Weatherhead? No, not his style at all, besides he could never have written such a true and penetrating description of himself. Could it be Mr Dunn? Too old and dull. The new Vicar? Hardly, he was too busy with his saints, and besides he had not had the time to get to know the people of Silverstream as this man knew them. Mr Fortnum? No, the book was too unkind to him. Mr Snowdon? No again, and for the same reason. That left the military people and Mr Featherstone Hogg. Sarah eliminated the military people, they were too taken up with themselves and their own affairs, they were birds of passage and scarcely knew Silverstream. Mr Featherstone Hogg was far too much in awe of his wife to draw her as she was drawn in this amazing book, for Mrs Horsley Downs was Mrs Featherstone Hogg to the life. Her languid elegance and her assumption of superiority were touched in with inimitable skill. There was even a description of one of her musical evenings when all Copperfield had been bidden to listen to Brahms, and to partake of lukewarm coffee made of coffee essence and anchovy paste sandwiches – Mr Featherstone Hogg would never have dared –

There was Stephen Bulmer of course, everyone in Silverstream knew that Mr Bulmer was engaged in writing a book about Henry the Fourth. But this book was not about Henry the Fourth, and Sarah was pretty sure that Stephen Bulmer had not written it. She visualised his long thin face and the unpleasant lines upon it – deep lines from the base of his nose to the corners of his cynical mouth, and deep vertical lines between his brows.

Horrid thing! – thought Sarah – horrid, selfish, bad-tempered thing! She felt very strongly about Stephen Bulmer because Margaret Bulmer was her friend, and Meg had been such a gay, pretty little creature before she married him, and now she was neither pretty nor gay. Meg was a loyal soul and said very little about Stephen – even to Sarah – but Sarah knew that she was unhappy. As for the children, they were like two little mice, unnaturally quiet and subdued. They came to tea with the twins, sometimes, and were alarmed by the noise these robust infants made. 'We're not allowed to play noisy games at home, it disturbs Daddy,' small Stephen had said. She had told John what he had said, and John had been quite violent about it – John adored children.

Sarah had now exhausted the masculine element in Silverstream. It might easily be a woman, she thought, perhaps if I read on I shall see –

She read on.

The book was doubly amusing now, she was always stopping to say, 'It's Miss King, of course – Miss King *exactly*. And this is Olivia Snowdon. Oh, *what will* she say when she reads it?' Stopping to laugh, or to clap her hands softly, or to re-read some especially spicy description of a well-known person.

It was midnight when she finished the first part of the book, a complete picture of the village; quiet and uneventful, very busy in its own estimation, the people full of gossip and curiosity about the affairs of their neighbours. So far not a thing had happened in Copperfield that could not have happened quite easily in Silverstream. The book was as uneventful as that, and yet it had not been dull. The first part occupied two-thirds of the book and ended with the words, 'And so the village of Copperfield slept beneath the stars.'

Sarah looked up at the clock, it was midnight and John had not returned. She hoped there was nothing wrong. It was a first baby, of course, and first babies were apt to keep people waiting. Mrs Sandeman was a nice little thing. Captain Sandeman was nice too. Quite young and very devoted to his wife – he would be having a wretched time, poor soul.

Sarah sighed, turned over the page and read on.

'Down the path from the hills came a boy playing on a reed pipe. He was a tall slim youth, barefooted with a tattered goat-skin round his body. The sun shone upon his golden hair, and on the fine golden down which clothed his arms and legs. He came into Copperfield over the bridge. The clear notes of his pipe, mingled with the song of the river, came to the ears of Major Waterfoot who was digging in his garden. He straightened his back and looked up. The clear notes stirred something in his heart, something deep and elemental that had been slumbering for years. Mrs Mildmay – on the other side of the road – heard the music also. It was music only in the sense that bird-song is music. It was – if such a thing can be imagined – the essence of bird-song. There was in it the love song of the male bird courting his mate, showing off his voice and boasting of brave deeds; and there was the call to adventure and the violence of battle; and lastly there was the satisfaction of mating, and the joy of the first egg. Mrs Mildmay felt that her life was very empty. She looked across the road at the chimneys of the Major's house which could be seen above the tree-tops, and she sighed.'

(Unlike Mrs Mildmay, Sarah chuckled. She wondered if John Smith had meant her to chuckle – or not.)

The golden boy piped on through the High Street and up the hill, and then down again past the vicarage and the old church which slumbered quietly by the river. Wherever he went he left behind him unrest and strange disturbance. People woke up, cast aside the fetters of conventional behaviour and followed the primitive impulses of their hidden natures. In some hearts the clear sweet music woke ambition, in some it woke memories of other days and prompted kind actions. Some of its hearers were driven to acts of violence, in others it kindled love.

At least John Smith said that the music kindled love, but Sarah Walker – who knew something about that commodity, something more, she suspected, than John Smith – would have said that the emotion which the boy's pipe kindled in the hearts of its hearers was not love at all, but passion.

After this things began to happen in Copperfield – incredible things – Major Waterfoot discovered that he had loved Mrs Mildmay for four years without ever having suspected it, so he rushed across the road and found Mrs Mildmay in her garden, and proposed to her with a fervour which almost made Sarah's eyebrows disappear into her hair. (It may be remarked in parenthesis that Sarah's eyebrows were a distinctive feature, darker than her hair and beautifully arched.) This was the love scene which had made such an impression upon Mr Abbott. It was a passionate scene, and had either been written by somebody who knew very little about such matters or somebody who knew a great deal. It was either very innocent – or else it wasn't.

Sarah read it twice and was still undecided about it, she left it and hastened on in the wake of the piping boy. Copperfield seethed with emotion. The very buns on Mrs Silver's spotless counter were charged with electricity. Mr Horsley Downs, who had never been capable of saying boo to a goose, developed a superiority complex, and, not content with bullying his wife in private, actually went the length of inserting a notice in the *Copperfield Times* to say that he would not be responsible for his wife's debts, and that she had been a chorus girl when he married her. Mrs Nevis rose from her grave where she had been reposing peacefully for three years and turned up at her old home in the middle of a dinner party to the consternation of her husband and daughters (the Snowdons of course). She had always been a thorn in their flesh on account of her plain homely Yorkshire accent and habits, which she had never been able to eradicate on her elevation to a higher sphere of life. Her appearance at the feast, all smiles and affection after her three years' absence, and the horror-stricken family and embarrassed guests, were drawn with the pen of a master. Then Edith Gaymer (Margaret Bulmer of course) eloped with old Mrs Farmer's son (Harry Carter of course), and Mr Mason (who was obviously Mr Fortnum) serenaded Mrs Myrtle Coates, playing all night long on a mandolin in her garden, and breathing his last beneath the firmly closed windows of his cruel charmer. In fact everyone did something queer, even Miss King and Miss Pretty (they were called Earle and Darling in the book but Sarah had got beyond troubling her head with such details) were seized with the spirit of adventure and decided to start upon an expedition to Samarkand. They each ordered a pair of riding breeches from Sharrods, and the book closed – very suitably – on that high note.

Sarah heard John's key in the front door as she raced through the last page.

* * *

'You don't mean to say you waited up!' Dr John exclaimed, filling the doorway of the study with his huge bulk. He was half annoyed with her for disobeying orders, and wholly pleased to find a smiling and wide-awake Sarah.

'Was he a tired, cold boy, then?' she enquired twining her arms round his neck and kissing the wrinkles at the corners of his eyes.

'He was, rather,' admitted John Walker laughing, but, strange to say, he felt – all at once – much less tired, and quite warm and comfortable.

He sat down by the fire, which, thanks to Sarah's care, was full of leaping, warming, cheering flames, and listened to her light footsteps going down the passage to warm his Benger's for him. What a blessed darling she was – thought Dr John – and how lucky he was, and how unworthy of her dear warm love! There had been a time, after the twins were born, when he thought he might lose her. She seemed to be going downhill – down, down, down – and nothing that he could do, or think of, seemed to stop that steady decline. Not prayer, nor cod-liver oil, nor iron injections had seemed of the slightest avail, and he knew only too well where that hill ended. And then, quite suddenly and for no reason that he could see, she had begun to climb up again, and here she was, still with him; still spoiling him; still making him love her more and more and more every day.

He stretched his arms and yawned luxuriously – 'Nice fire, Nell,' he said. Nell agreed fervently.

The steps were coming back now along the passage – not quite such light careless steps this time, for Sarah was carrying the tray, and there were three bowls of Benger's on the tray and a tin of Marie biscuits –

'You don't mean to say –' said Dr John.

'I promised her,' replied Sarah gravely. She gave Nell her Benger's and put down the tray in front of the fire on a small stool. The doctor took his and stirred it slowly.

'Have a biscuit,' Sarah said.

They sat in the two big chairs with their bowls of Benger's and the tin of Marie biscuits between them, and he began to tell her about his case. She was completely trustworthy and tremendously interested in all his cases, and Dr John had discovered long ago that it was not only a pleasure to talk to his wife about his work, but also that it was actually a help to him to put his difficulties and doubts before her. It helped to clear his mind and to make things plain to himself, and her intelligent questions often served to throw light upon puzzling problems. Sometimes Dr John teased his wife about her interest in his work, and told her that she had picked his brains for five years, and that she thought she was as good a doctor as he was; and then, just to teach her, he would break into technicalities of medical jargon and Sarah would toss her head and say, 'What's the good of all those silly Latin names? It doesn't help to cure people to call their diseases by names of five syllables. Of course you only do it to bamboozle the poor things and make them think that you are a great deal cleverer than you really are.'

Tonight he had a lot to tell Sarah, and Sarah listened with a little frown of concentration (she understood most of it, and wildly guessed at the rest, for she had read some of John's books on the sly, so that she might follow with a reasonable amount of intelligence when John talked to her). He told her what a ghastly time he had had, and how anxious he had been, and how they had telephoned to London for a specialist to come at once, but the baby decided to come first, and to come in a very unusual manner – a very eccentric troublesome sort of baby it had been. But everything was all right now, except that the Sandemans would have to pay the specialist for coming down from London in the middle of the night, and looking at Mrs Sandeman and saying, 'You all right? That's right,' and looking at the baby and saying, 'Nice little chap – he's all right,' and going home again in his car.

"They won't mind,' said Sarah wisely.

'Perhaps not, but I do,' replied the doctor.

'Why? Would you rather he had come and said they were all wrong?'

He laughed, it was no use arguing with Sarah, she always got the best of it. Her dancing brain could make circles round his big, sure, slow-moving mind –

'You were very naughty to wait up,' he told her, changing the subject. 'I might have been there all night.'

'It was that book,' Sarah said. 'I meant to sit up until twelve – and then I simply had to finish it. My dear, *you are in it*.'

'Me? Nonsense,' he said, smiling at her excitement.

'It's not. You are,' she told him eagerly. 'Everyone in Silverstream is in it. It's all about Silverstream –'

'Well then, you are in it too, I suppose,' he replied, humouring her, but not believing that it was actually true. 'I can't be in it without you, or there would only be half of me – less than half of me –' he laughed comfortably.

'I'm not in it,' she said, wrinkling those eyebrows of hers, for it had not struck her until this moment that she was about the only person in Silverstream who did not figure in *Disturber of the Peace*. 'But, of course, you are only mentioned once or twice – just as a doctor who goes about giving his malingering patients castor oil –'

He shouted with laughter at that, and she had to remind him that the twins were sleeping overhead.

'– But you must read it, and then you'll see for yourself,' she added, when he had moderated and apologised for his unbridled mirth, 'just you read it, Dr John.'

He took the book in his hands and looked at it idly.

'Not *now*, for mercy's sake,' she gasped, seizing it from him and hiding it behind her back. She had experienced the strange allure of *Disturber of the Peace*, and had no wish to see him start upon it at this hour of the morning.

'You silly kitten!' he exclaimed humorously, 'you don't really suppose I would sit up all night reading a novel? Tell me about it while I finish my Benger's.'

She complied, knowing that it was good for him to take his mind off his work before he slept. He was such a conscientious old darling, worrying himself to death about every case, heartbroken if one of his patients slipped through his fingers, taking all the blame if things went wrong, and giving all the credit to Nature or nursing if things went right.

'Well, you're Dr Rider,' she told him, clasping her lovely hands round one knee, and looking up at him with a whimsical smile. 'You've gone up in the world, you see. And Colonel Weatherhead is Major Waterfoot – so he's come down. And Barbara Buncle is Elizabeth Wade – I can't see the connection there, but she *is* –. And Dorcas is Susan – she's frightfully good. And Miss King and Miss Pretty are Miss Earle and Miss Darling, and Mrs Featherstone Hogg is Mrs Horsley Downs – she is screamingly funny –. And the Bulmers are the Gaymers, and Mrs Dick is Mrs Turpin and Mr Fortnum is Mr Mason and the Sandemans –'

'Stop, stop!' cried the doctor.

She stopped and sat there smiling at him and swinging her foot a little.

'Is this all *true*?' he asked. The question was quite a legitimate one, for Sally had a puckish sense of humour, and more than once she had spun him tales of amazing events full of the most circumstantial details, and he had followed her, blundering along credulously in his elephantine way, only to be told at the end that the whole thing had been fabricated in her own busy head. So, tonight, the suspicion arose in his mind that this was merely one of Sally's 'take ins,' and that in a moment or two she would burst out laughing and tell him that he was a darling old donkey and that she had made it all up.

'It's all true, honour bright,' Sally said, nodding at him gravely, too much taken up with the queerness of it all to resent the aspersions on her veracity.

'Well what do we *do*, then?' he asked, standing up and stretching himself. 'It can't be a very exciting book if it is all about Silverstream – Silverstream's worst enemy couldn't accuse it of being exciting. What *happens* in the book? What do we all *do*?'

'Oh, my dear!' she cried, 'that's just it – what you all *do*.'

'It seems to me there are breakers ahead,' said Dr John solemnly.

CHAPTER SIX

MRS CARTER'S TEA-PARTY

The first breaker broke a few days later at old Mrs Carter's tea-party, and the full force of the wave fell upon the head of Barbara Buncle. They were all sitting in the drawing-room round the Jacobean gate-legged table, and there was a bowl of chrysanthemums – the very last, Mrs Carter assured them – in the centre. Barbara knew when she saw the china that Mrs Featherstone Hogg was expected, and her spirits fell a degree for she did not like Mrs Featherstone Hogg. Barbara had met Dorothea Bold on the doorstep and they had gone in together, and Miss King and Miss Pretty were there already. But not for these would Mrs Carter have produced her best eggshell cups and saucers, that filmy drawn-thread-work tea-cloth, those lusciously bulging cream buns.

'Agatha said she would look in later,' said Mrs Carter in confidential tones. 'She's such a busy bee we must take her when we can get her.'

Mrs Featherstone Hogg was less like a busy bee than anybody Barbara could think of. She was tall and willowy and tired, so tired that you could not help feeling it was good of her to trouble to speak to you at all. She did not speak much to you, of course, if you were an unimportant person like Barbara Buncle. Barbara sometimes wondered what it was that gave Mrs Featherstone Hogg her social position in Silverstream. Why did everyone flock to her dull parties and consume the poor fare provided for them there? Why did everybody do what she told them to do? Why did old Mrs Carter produce her best china and linen for Agatha's delectation? Was it because of her rude manner? or was it because she bought her clothes from the most expensive place in London?

It was this tired and languid lady that Mrs Carter compared to a busy bee and something shook in Barbara's interior at the ineptness of the description; but it would never do to laugh, nobody in Silverstream laughed at Mrs Featherstone Hogg. Barbara turned quickly to her nearest neighbour, who happened to be Angela Pretty, and asked her if she had put in her bulbs yet. Of course it was just like Mrs Featherstone Hogg to say she would 'look in later' – she was not like an ordinary mortal who was expected to arrive at the time appointed for her arrival – Barbara made a mental note of the phrase and then remembered with a twinge of disappointment that *Disturber of the Peace* was finished, and that nothing more could be added to its teeming pages. Perhaps I *will* write another, she thought to herself in surprise.

Angela was twittering on about her bulbs – the exact amount of moisture they required and the exact number of days one should keep them in the dark to promote the growth of healthy roots – it was very dull. Barbara detached one ear from Angela to listen to what the others were talking about.

'She is coming to me tomorrow,' Mrs Carter was saying. 'Such a sudden decision, but, of course, I am delighted to have the dear child. I am putting her in the old nursery, it is the pleasantest room on that floor, and has a delightful view over the river. It gets all the morning sun, and sunshine is just what she requires after her operation – plenty of sunshine and fresh milk, the doctor said – so, of course, dear Harry thought of me at once.'

Barbara could not see why he had thought of old Mrs Carter in connection with the doctor's prescription. Sunlight and milk were no part of the good lady's *régime*. She hardly ever went out of doors even in the summer, unless to go to church or to tea with a friend, and Barbara had never beheld her neighbour imbibing milk except as an accompaniment to a cup of tea. But of course Harry was her son, so he must know her better even than Barbara did; or, perhaps, his thoughts went back to his childhood and milk puddings, and he connected his mother with these – it was rather far-fetched, but the subconscious mind was so marvellous nowadays –

'I don't think you heard that, Barbara, dear,' said Mrs Carter kindly, 'you were talking to Angela. Harry is going out to India with his regiment and dear little Sally is coming to me to be built up after her appendicitis. *Built up*,' repeated Mrs Carter, obviously delighted with the term, and nodding her beautifully waved grey head with solemn emphasis.

‘How nice for you – and for her of course,’ exclaimed Barbara. She had lived for so long amongst these people and had suffered so many afternoon teas that she was able to say the expected thing without thinking about it at all. You simply put a penny in the machine and the expected thing came out at once, all done up in a neat little packet, and suitably labelled. The machine worked without any effort on Barbara’s part, it even worked when the real Barbara was absent and only the shell, dressed in its shabby garments, remained sitting upright upon its chair. The real Barbara often flew away like that and took refuge from the dullness and boredom of Silverstream in the scintillating atmosphere of Copperfield.

‘It will be nice for us all in Silverstream – there are so few young people here,’ said Angela Pretty prettily.

At this moment – Barbara was just handing Mrs Carter her cup for some more tea – the door opened, and Mrs Featherstone Hogg burst in. She appeared to be carrying something in one hand, holding it away from her as if it were a poisonous reptile or a loathsome toad.

‘Filth!’ she cried. ‘Filth!’ and flung it on to the table all amongst the cakes and china and chrysanthemums. It lay there, half resting upon a dish of cream buns, and half propped up against the damson jam – it was a copy of Barbara Buncle’s book.

‘My dear Agatha!’ exclaimed Mrs Carter with pardonable surprise. The rest of the party was too aghast for speech, it was as if a bombshell had burst among them; even Barbara was amazed and pained at the transformation which her simple story had wrought upon the elegant, languid personality of Mrs Featherstone Hogg.

'You are in it too,' said 'dear Agatha', incoherently to her hostess. 'You haven't read it, I suppose, or you wouldn't be sitting there like a graven image. You wear a wig, you know, and false teeth, and you put pectin in your damson jam to make it set, and your son elopes with a married woman – Mrs Farmer is your name.'

'She's mad,' whispered Mrs Carter white to the lips.

Mrs Featherstone Hogg laughed shrilly. 'Oh no, I'm not mad,' she said. 'I'm quite sane, I assure you. I intend to have the man up for libel. Edwin has gone up to town to see our lawyer about it – I sent him straight up in the Daimler. The man will find he can't trifle with *me*. He'll be sorry he was born before I've done with him. You're in it too,' she added, pouncing upon Dorothea Bold so fiercely that the poor woman nearly choked on a piece of dry seed-cake. 'And you – and you – and you,' she continued, pointing with her heavily ringed fingers at the remaining three guests.

Miss King found her voice first. Perhaps it was the manliness of her attire that gave her confidence in her own capabilities, or perhaps it was her confident and capable nature which promoted the manliness of her attire. It does not really matter which, the important thing is that Miss King believed she was a capable sensible person and this belief was a great help to her in emergencies such as the present one.

'Do you mean that we are all described in that book?' demanded Miss King in her deep quiet voice, and she pointed to the somewhat battered copy of *Disturber of the Peace* which lay dejectedly upon the buns.

'I've told you so, haven't I?' shrieked Mrs Featherstone Hogg. 'Are you all deaf or imbecile that you can't understand plain English?'

Barbara Buncle never knew how she got away from that dreadful tea-party. She had a vague idea that she had made her exit in the wake of Miss King, and that Miss King had remarked upon the beauty of the night and added that Mrs Featherstone Hogg had rather given herself away, hadn't she? Some people's elegance was only skin-deep, scrape off a little bit of the veneer and you got the real wood – common deal in this case, Miss King suspected. Barbara made some non-committal reply, and staggered home – fortunately it was only next door – and she sat down in her comfortable chair beside her own cheerful fire and held her head.

Presently she rose and went to the telephone. She must speak to Mr Abbott. If anyone could help her he could, but she did not think anyone could help her. It was a sort of blind instinct that made her fly to Mr Abbott.

They told her at the office that he had gone home some time ago, and, after an agonising delay, and much consultation among themselves, they consented to give her the telephone number of his private residence. Barbara was almost in tears when she got on to him at last.

'It's going splendidly,' his cheerful voice proclaimed. 'Nothing to worry about. I've put a second impression in hand – we shall probably need a third –'

'But they *know*,' she squeaked. 'They know it's them – they are going to start libel actions –'

‘They won’t do anything of the sort,’ he assured her in his comforting deep voice. ‘No lawyer would look at it. Now don’t worry, and don’t say another word over the telephone. I’ll come over and see you tomorrow afternoon and you can tell me all about it.’

Barbara put down the receiver and stood there for a few minutes looking at it thoughtfully.

CHAPTER SEVEN

FIRST FRUITS

'There's absolutely nothing to worry about,' said Mr Abbott. He was standing in front of Miss Buncle's fire in Miss Buncle's comfortable, though rather shabby, and old-fashioned drawing-room and smiling at her cheerfully. 'Any respectable lawyer would turn down the case. He would look a fool appearing in court with a case like that, and his clients would be made to look worse fools. We have only got to say, "The portrait which you find so ugly was never intended to be a portrait of you. If you really think you are like that we are sorry for you and offer you our sincere sympathy."'

Barbara actually smiled. It had taken Mr Abbott half an hour's hard work to obtain that smile. Now that he had obtained it, he liked it immensely, and he liked her teeth – he had decided quite definitely that they were real.

'Of course they don't know it's me,' Barbara said hopefully.

(It was curious, Mr Abbott thought, that a woman who could write good English should be unable to speak it, he had noticed this little peculiarity of Miss Buncle's before, it amused and intrigued him.)

'No,' he agreed, 'and you are perfectly safe with *us*.'

'Oh, I hope so,' cried Barbara. 'I should have to leave here if they found out who it was.'

'Surely it is not as bad as all that!'

'Quite as bad,' Barbara told him nodding emphatically, 'of course they haven't all read it yet but Mrs Featherstone Hogg is furious, and Mrs Carter doesn't like the bit about her wig and the pectin in her jam. She is frightfully proud of her damson jam, you see, but I'm sure there is pectin in it, I'm sure it would never set like that without pectin – mine won't – besides I saw the packets in the grocer's basket.'

She was beginning to talk now. Mr Abbott urged her on with encouraging noises and nods. He had already noticed that Miss Buncle was either monosyllabic and completely inarticulate, or else overpowered by a stream of words which forced themselves between her lips like water from a bursting dam.

'I suppose I should never have written it,' continued Miss Buncle sadly. 'But you see I had to do *something* – I told you about the dividends, didn't I? – and the only thing I could do was to write a book, and the only kind of book I could write was about people I knew. And then another thing was that I never really thought or believed *in my bones* that the book would be published. I just finished it and sent it up –'

'And why to *me*?' enquired Mr Abbott with much interest. 'I mean why did you send the book to *me*? Perhaps you had heard from somebody that our firm –'

'Oh, no,' she exclaimed. 'I knew nothing at all about publishers. You were the first on the list – alphabetically – that was all.'

Mr Abbott was somewhat taken aback – on such trifles hang the fates of bestsellers!

'And then when you took it,' continued Miss Buncle, quite oblivious of his reaction to her naïve admission, 'when you actually said you would publish it, I was so excited that I forgot about the people being so like the people here. It seemed so funny to be a real author – so important somehow. When I thought about it at all (which wasn't often), I thought, perhaps they'll never see it or read it at all (heaps of books are published and you never hear about them) and even if they do read it they'll never think it could possibly be them – in a book I mean. But really and truly I scarcely even thought about it at all,' said Miss Buncle, trying hard to be absolutely exact, and to explain her extraordinary density in the matter.

'It was quite natural,' Mr Abbott told her.

'But of course I see now that I should never have written it at all.'

'That would have been a pity,' said Mr Abbott with his mind on the mounting sales of *Disturber of the Peace*. 'A pity for me, and a pity for you. The book is doing so well.' He took out his pocket-book and produced a large white note which he laid down beside her on the table. 'Just a little something on account,' he added, smiling at her surprise. 'I thought perhaps you might be glad to have it with Christmas coming on. I shall want a receipt of course.'

Barbara looked at it – she could not believe her eyes – and then she looked at Mr Abbott.

'But I couldn't –' she said tremulously.

'My dear girl, I am not a philanthropist. You've earned it,' said Mr Abbott. 'I didn't bring you a cheque, because if a cheque from us goes through your bank it might give the show away. Banks are supposed to be soundproof,' said Mr Abbott, talking on to give this extraordinary woman time to get over the shock of receiving a hundred pounds. 'But my experience is if you want to keep a thing dark the fewer people who know about it the better. So you can pay that in, and nobody will know where it has come from. . . . You can say it is a present from your uncle in Australia,' added Mr Abbott chuckling. 'Make him a sheep-farmer with a benevolent disposition, or a gold digger who has struck lucky if you like.'

It took him ten minutes to convince the extraordinary woman that this was her own money which she had earned by the sweat of her brow, and that there was more coming which she would receive in due course.

Mr Abbott had said that he was not a philanthropist, and he was not. He was merely a man who did business in his own way. He called himself a student of psychology. Authors – he was wont to say – were kittle cattle. He prided himself on his management of authors. Mr Abbott had produced the hundred pound note for several reasons. To begin with, *Disturber of the Peace* had earned it and was well on its way to earn more. Of course he need not have paid Miss Buncle anything on account, there was nothing about it in the contract. If he wanted to be strictly business-like he would have waited until February – when his books were made up – and sent her a cheque for what was due, but he did not want to be strictly business-like. It amused him to surprise and please people, and perhaps especially to surprise and please Miss Buncle. Then Miss Buncle was distressed about the stir caused by her book and Mr Abbott knew of nothing more soothing to worry or distress than a nice round fat cheque (or bank note). Lastly – and this was the most subtle reason of all – lastly he wanted another book from Miss Buncle, and he wanted it soon, before the *éclat* of *Disturber of the Peace* had died away and John Smith had faded out of the fickle memories of the great British Public, and he knew that – paradoxical as it might sound – a nice fat cheque (or bank note) was not only a soothing and comforting balm to troubled authors, but it was also a spur.

Miss Buncle signed the receipt for a hundred pounds on account of her novel with a trembling hand. It was not nearly such a neat signature as that which had appeared upon the contract. He didn't know – he couldn't possibly have known – that in spite of all her economies, in spite of stinting and scraping, of eschewing meat, and eating margarine instead of butter, and diluting the milk, and buying the very cheapest tea that floated like dust on the top of your cup, Miss Buncle's account at the bank was overdrawn by seven pounds fifteen shillings and would soon have been overdrawn by more; for the dividends, which had been steadily decreasing, had now practically ceased.

There were tears in Miss Buncle's eyes as she signed the receipt and folded up the amazing note. Fancy that tiny piece of paper representing so much! It really *was* rather astonishing (when you come to think of it) what that tiny piece of paper represented – far more than a hundred sovereigns (although in modern finance less). It represented food and drink to Barbara Buncle, and, perhaps, a new winter coat and hat; but, above all, freedom from that awful nightmare of worry, and sleep, and a quiet mind.

CHAPTER EIGHT

MISS KING AND MR ABBOTT

Mr Abbott was very busy when Miss King called to see him, but he agreed to 'give her ten minutes'. The truth was Mr Abbott could not resist the temptation of seeing Miss King, for she had written on her card 're *Disturber of the Peace*'.

Miss Buncle's book intrigued Mr Abbott, and Miss Buncle herself intrigued him. She was such a queer mixture of simplicity and subtlety (at least he thought she was). She spoke bad grammar and wrote good English. She was meticulously truthful in all she said (it was almost as if she were on oath to speak the truth, the whole truth and nothing but the truth all day long and every day of the week). She lived her solitary life amongst all those people, with her tremendous secret locked up in her breast; going about amongst them looking as if butter wouldn't melt in her mouth, but taking careful note of all they said and did, and then going quietly home and writing it all down. They were after her now like a pack of hounds, but they didn't know that the fox was in the very midst of them, under their very noses, disguised as one of themselves – it was a piquant situation and Mr Abbott fully appreciated it.

'But I must be very careful,' said Mr Abbott to himself, as the imp went away to fetch Miss King for the ten minutes' interview, 'I must be very careful.'

Miss King accepted the chair which Mr Abbott offered her with his pleasant old-fashioned bow, but declined a cigarette. You couldn't smoke a man's cigarettes and then threaten him with a libel action.

'I have only a very few minutes to spare, Miss – er' – he glanced at the card which lay on the table – 'Miss King,' said Mr Abbott blandly.

'A very few minutes will be sufficient for my purpose,' replied Miss King in her most capable manner. 'I have merely called to request you to withdraw *Disturber of the Peace* from circulation.'

'Dear me!' said Mr Abbott, blinking, 'that is surely very – er – drastic.'

'Desperate diseases demand desperate remedies,' said Miss King sententiously.

'And what is your objection to the novel?' enquired Mr Abbott gently. 'It seems to me a very harmless sort of novel. I would not compare it for a moment with a desperate disease. In fact I found it amusing – light reading, of course, but distinctly amusing –'

'It is a horrible book,' said Miss King, losing a little of her business-like calm. 'It is causing a great deal of misery and trouble to innocent people –'

'How can that be?' wondered Mr Abbott aloud.

'You will withdraw it immediately,' continued Miss King, taking no notice of his interruption. 'You will withdraw the book from circulation. I have been empowered by several people in Silverstream to come today and ask you to withdraw it.'

'And if I refuse?' enquired Mr Abbott softly.

'You will not refuse,' Miss King told him, trying to make her voice sound confident, 'you do not wish to – to be had up for libel, I suppose.'

'No,' said Mr Abbott simply.

'Well, you will,' declared Miss King. She knew that she was putting her case badly. She knew – although she had not admitted it to herself – that her case was already lost. She was nervous, and her flow of language – business-like language – had deserted her. Coming up in the train she had overwhelmed Mr Abbott with her eloquence and brought him to his knees. But Mr Abbott was so different from what she had imagined, so quiet and calm and sure of himself, so benign-looking. If he had been angry or rude she could have dealt with him much more easily. She had never imagined that a publisher was like this.

'I'm afraid you must be more explicit,' said Mr Abbott with unruffled calm.

'I thought I had been explicit.'

'Oh, no,' he said, shaking his head at her sorrowfully, 'you have told me what you want, but surely you can't expect me to comply with the request of a complete stranger without any adequate reason being offered. My business is run on strictly business lines, I do it to make money,' said Mr Abbott, lifting his brows apologetically.

'So I supposed,' said Miss King with some sarcasm. 'And

that is the reason I'm here. You will save money if you withdraw the book immediately. You ask me to be explicit and I will be explicit. My friends and I intend to put the matter into the hands of our lawyers and you will find yourself involved in a costly action for libel unless the book is withdrawn immediately – that is the position in a nutshell.'

'Have you consulted your lawyer, Miss King?' asked Mr Abbott, still with that peaceful smile.

'I fail to see how that affects the position.'

'It doesn't, really,' he admitted, 'I only wondered if you had. In any case your suggestion is impracticable. The novel is selling well and –'

'I don't care how it is selling – if it is selling well that is all the more reason to stop it,' cried Miss King incoherently. 'How would you like to be pilloried in a horrible book like that? Every small detail of your domestic life laid bare – your most sacred secrets dragged into the limelight and trampled upon – how would you like it, I ask you?'

'My dear lady!' exclaimed Mr Abbott, surprised and pained by her vehemence, 'my dear lady, people often imagine that their personalities have been drawn upon in a novel. I put it to you that you are mistaken, that the secrets exposed in *Disturber of the Peace* are not your secrets at all. Authors must be credited with a certain amount of imagination, you know. They seldom draw their portraits from life –'

'Portraits!' she cried, 'This is not a portrait, it's a photograph.'

Mr Abbott looked at her and decided that it was. She was Miss Earle of course. Miss Buncle had drawn her with a faithfulness which was almost staggering. He felt a little annoyed with Barbara for a moment – it was scarcely necessary, for instance, to have mentioned that small mole upon her chin and the three longish hairs which grew from it. The mole would have been omitted from a portrait of Miss King, or else idealised and made to look like a beauty spot, but in a photograph there was no such evasion of the truth –

He realised suddenly that Miss King had changed her tactics; she was appealing now to his better nature; she was throwing herself on his mercy; she had begun to tell him her life-story – or at least the part of it which she considered relevant to the occasion –

'So there we were,' she was saying, 'both orphans, without anybody dependent upon us, nor any near relations. I had a house, larger than I required. Miss Pretty was homeless. We both possessed small incomes, too small to enable us to live alone in comfort. I was about to sell my house (for I could not live in it alone) when the suggestion was made that we should pool our resources and live together – what more natural? By this means we were enabled to live comfortably in my house. The companionship was pleasant, the financial problem was solved. There was a book some years ago,' continued Miss King incoherently, 'it distressed us very much at the time, but it had nothing to do with us, and I decided to ignore it – this book is far worse – it's all about us – it's far far worse –'

'You have misread the novel entirely,' said Mr Abbott uncomfortably. 'I assure you that you have misread it. There is nothing in it to cause you the slightest distress. The author is a particularly simple-minded – er – person.'

'But Samarkand!' exclaimed Miss King, trying to keep the sound of tears out of her voice. 'Why Samarkand of all places?'

'I don't know anything about Samarkand,' said Mr Abbott truthfully, 'but to me it has an adventurous sound, and I feel convinced that that was what it was intended to convey –'

'A dreadful Eastern place – full of vice and – and horribleness,' cried Miss King.

'No, no. *Adventure*,' replied Mr Abbott, waving his hands wildly – 'Deserts and camels, you know, and Sheiks and Arabs riding about on milk-white steeds, and oases with palms – all that sort of thing. But at the same time,' he added retreating into safety again, 'at the same time I feel sure you are mistaken and the characters are surely imaginary – purely imaginary. It is merely an unfortunate coincidence that they seem to bear some resemblance –'

'Who is this John Smith?' demanded Miss King suddenly, interrupting Mr Abbott's flow of eloquence with a lamentable lack of ceremony, 'Tell me that. Who is the man? He must be somebody living in Silverstream of course, but who? That's the question. Bulmer is the only man I know of who writes books, and he would not make his wife elope with another man – it's simply unthinkable –'

'I'm afraid our time is up,' said Mr Abbott, looking at his watch regretfully. 'I have given you rather longer than I intended, but it has been a most interesting conversation –'

'I shall remain here until you tell me who John Smith is,'

said Miss King firmly – he could scarcely throw her out, she reflected.

Mr Abbott smiled and shook his head. 'Quite impossible, my dear lady,' he said. 'Besides, why should you suppose that you would know him?'

'Because he knows me,' replied Miss King with incontrovertible logic.

'I feel sure you are mistaken,' said Mr Abbott.

'I shall remain here until you tell me,' said Miss King.

It looked as though they had reached an impasse, but Mr Abbott was a man of resource – there were other rooms in his office. He rose quickly and reached the door before Miss King had perceived his intention. 'By all means remain here,' he invited her with his courtly little bow. 'You will excuse me if I leave you – I have an appointment' and was gone.

Miss King realised at once that she had been out-generalled. She sat still for a few moments, looking round the cosy little room and wondering whether the clue to the mystery might be found here by a determined woman. Surely it must lie at her hand, here in the sanctum of the senior partner of Abbott & Spicer's firm. The walls were papered with light brown, the carpet was thick and soft and brown, the curtains were of dark brown velvet. On a small oak table in the corner stood a book-trough containing two large dictionaries, a copy of *Who's Who*, and a London Post Office Directory. In the other corner was a small safe. A large glass-fronted bookcase took up the length of one wall. Above the mantelpiece there was an oak shelf containing Abbott & Spicer's latest publications. Miss King rose from her chair and took down *Disturber of the Peace*. She glanced through it with a shudder of distaste, but there was nothing to be learned from it – no clue to be gained as to who had perpetrated it – it was merely an ordinary copy of the book such as could be bought at any bookstall for the exorbitant sum of seven and sixpence.

Gaining confidence, Miss King now turned to the desk – it was a large oak desk and it stood in the middle of the room, carefully arranged so that the light from the window should fall over Mr Abbott's left shoulder. The drawers of the desk were all locked except one, in which was an assortment of paper and envelopes. On the desk stood a telephone of the usual pattern. There was also a manuscript entitled *The Flames of Hell*, by Hesa Feend. (Mr Abbott had been considering its merits and demerits when Miss King had interrupted his morning's work.) Miss King glanced at it with disgust. The large sheet of blotting paper on the desk was virgin, save for a signature which Miss King decided was that of Mr Abbott himself. The waste-paper basket contained two circulars, and a review of Mr Shillingsworth's latest novel just published by the firm. Nothing remained to be investigated but the safe. Miss King investigated the safe fruitlessly.

She glanced once more round the room – how tantalising it was to be here in this room with the clue so near and not to be able to find it! If I could only find out who it was, she thought, with a sigh. The room lay before her, perfectly open. Mr Abbott had given her the freedom of the room, but she had found nothing. Was it any use waiting in case Mr Abbott might return, or Mr Spicer might come in to get something? She thought not.

She went over to the door and put her hand on the knob. Had he locked her in? she wondered suddenly. Mr Abbott had done nothing so ungentlemanly, the handle turned, the door opened, Miss King was standing in the passage. With some little difficulty she found her way down various long corridors and iron steps, and in a few moments she had reached the street.

Miss King was in such a hurry to shake the dust of Abbott & Spicer's from her feet that she ran straight into the arms of a man – a tall thin man – who was about to enter the building.

'Mr Bulmer!' she exclaimed in amazement.

Mr Bulmer looked as startled as herself and somewhat sheepish into the bargain.

'If you have come to see that man it's no good,' she told him breathlessly. 'He's a perfect fool,' (she had forgotten for the moment that he had outwitted her), 'one of those solid smiling fools that nothing will move or excite.'

'I don't want to move or excite Mr Abbott,' replied Mr Bulmer sourly. 'I merely want to find out the name of the man who wrote that novel about Silverstream. Mrs Featherstone Hogg lent it to me yesterday and I sat up reading it half the night. Have *you* read it?' he asked, looking down at Miss King with sudden suspicion.

'Of course – that's why I'm here.'

'You don't like it – eh?' he asked, smiling in rather an unpleasant sort of way.

'No more than you do,' retorted Miss King, who was always at her best if people turned nasty. She wondered if she should press home her point – men did not care to be deserted by their wives. It was not true, of course. Margaret Bulmer had not really gone off with Harry Carter – at least if she had, Miss King had not heard of it – but the book said that she had. The book had exposed Mr Bulmer's selfishness and cruelty so frankly that you felt quite glad Margaret had escaped from him; you did not blame her for it. On the other hand Mr Bulmer was angry about the book, he might be a good ally in the fight against Abbott & Spicer and the mysterious John Smith. Miss King decided not to press the point home.

'The book must be withdrawn from circulation,' said Miss King firmly.

Mr Bulmer laughed bitterly. 'So that was your idea. Why don't you go to the zoo and ask the lion to give you his ration of meat? You would be more likely to succeed.'

'What do you mean?' she enquired.

'I mean, *Disturber of the Peace* is a best seller. A publisher doesn't get hold of a best seller every day of the week. Abbott won't withdraw it – he'd be a fool if he did.'

'What are *you* going to do?' she asked him. 'You're going to do something, I suppose – you've come here to see the man, haven't you?'

'My idea was merely to get hold of the author's name and strangle him slowly,' replied Mr Bulmer with a nasty smile. 'Quite a primitive idea compared with yours, isn't it? But more likely to succeed –'

'I asked him that too,' said Miss King.

'Well, keep on asking,' Mr Bulmer replied sarcastically. 'Perhaps in time he will get tired of saying no. Come up and see him constantly – publishers love to have their mornings wasted for them – put off your visit to Samarkand for a few weeks, and sit upon Mr Abbott's doorstep.'

'Samarkand,' cried Miss King, goaded to frenzy. 'I'm not going to Samarkand – why should I? What's it got to do with you where I go? I shall go to Samarkand if I like –'

She put up her umbrella and plunged away from him down the teeming street.

CHAPTER NINE

MRS BULMER

Margaret Bulmer knew quite well that something had upset Stephen but she did not know what it was. He had said nothing to her about the book which had been lent to him by Mrs Featherstone Hogg, nor had he offered it to her to read. On the contrary when Stephen Bulmer had finished the book he had looked about his study for some safe place to hide it, and, finding none really safe from the prying eyes of wives and housemaids, he had deliberately made up the fire, and, tearing the book to pieces in his thin claw-like hands, had fed it to the flames. Slowly and bit by bit *Disturber of the Peace* had been reduced to ashes in Mr Bulmer's grate. He felt a sort of queer satisfaction in the rite. The copy belonged to Mrs Featherstone Hogg, of course (she had paid seven and sixpence for it), but that didn't matter in the least. He was not afraid of Mrs Featherstone Hogg, if she asked for the book it would give Mr Bulmer the greatest pleasure to reply that he had burnt it – he hoped she would ask for it.

After he had finished burning *Disturber of the Peace* he went up to bed very quietly. Margaret had been in bed for hours. He took great care not to waken her, for somehow he did not want to face Margaret's clear gaze just now. He was not really like David Gaymer, of course, but perhaps he had been just a little inconsiderate now and then.

Margaret was not asleep, she was merely pretending to be asleep because it was easier, and she was so tired. She was surprised when Stephen came up to bed quietly instead of stamping about in his dressing-room as he usually did, and throwing his boots on the floor. She was even more surprised when he crawled into bed without putting on the light and telling her that his hot-water bottle was stone cold. She wondered vaguely if Stephen were ill, but decided that he couldn't be ill, or he would have wakened her up to find the aspirin tablets and to warm some milk for him – she drifted off to sleep.

In the morning Stephen was still 'queer'. He came down to breakfast shaved and dressed instead of having breakfast in bed as he usually did, and, instead of immersing himself in *The Times*, he was quite conversational. He even spoke kindly to the children (who were too astounded at this unusual behaviour to answer him at all) and asked Margaret what she was going to do with herself – *he* was going to London by the ten-thirty. Margaret replied that she was going to give the children their lessons. She caught him gazing at her in a queer way when he thought she was busy with the tea-cups. She was relieved when he departed to catch his train.

Margaret thought about it all as she ordered the dinner and gave the children their lessons. Of course it was quite a usual thing for Stephen to sit up half the night; he said he could write better when the house was quiet. (The house was quiet all day as it was possible for any house to be. Everyone was provided with carpet slippers and there was soundproof felt on the stairs. If Stephen were not writing, he was asleep, or thinking, and, whichever of these pursuits he was engaged upon, the house had to be quiet. At the slightest sound the door of the study would fly open and Stephen would emerge white with fury and stamp up and down the hall raging like a maniac, and demanding of his Maker why he could not get a little peace in his own house. Sometimes Margaret took the two children out into the woods for a picnic lunch, and urged them to run about and make a noise. She tried to make them play games such as she had played in her childhood, and to shout and sing, but it was no good. The children were like two little mice. She couldn't get a loud sound out of them. Margaret worried about the children quite a lot, it was not natural for children to be so quiet, but she could do nothing. They were terrified of Stephen, of course, that was the reason – terrified of his rages and his loud strident voice. They would creep past his door like ghosts, they would stop suddenly in the midst of their quiet games and listen with strange intent looks upon their little faces.)

Now that Stephen had departed for the train the house woke up a little. Margaret could hear the two maids talking in the kitchen, a saucepan fell on the floor with a clatter, and one of them laughed.

Margaret wondered what was the matter with Stephen today, and last night. Why had he gone to town? What was it that he had burnt last night in the study grate? She was sure that he was upset about something. Stephen was frequently upset, either in mind or stomach, but the strange thing was that he had never been known to show it in this fashion. Usually when Stephen was upset he was *more* irritable and morose, not *less*.

'No, Stevie dear, this is an adding sum,' said Margaret, 'it's not subtraction like we did yesterday. You remember how to add, don't you? Take your pencil out of your mouth, Dolly.'

It really was very queer about Stephen. The more she thought about it the more queer it seemed. She wondered whether she should give the children a holiday and run over to see Sarah Walker and tell her about it – Sarah was so wise. She would not say too much to Sarah – just that Stephen did not seem quite like himself. Of course Sarah could not advise her without knowing in what way Stephen was not like himself, but Margaret did not want advice, she wanted to be reassured, she wanted sympathy, she wanted a nice long talk with Sarah. It was strange that she should want sympathy and reassurance because her husband had been more considerate than usual – or less inconsiderate – but it really just meant that her world was shaking under her feet.

So Margaret gave the children a holiday, and told them to rush about and play hide-and-seek and make a lot of noise because Daddy had gone to London, and then she ran upstairs and pulled on a tammy, and caught up her last year's coat with the worn fur collar (because of course in these hard times she could not afford a new winter coat although she had noticed rather enviously that her maids had each afforded one) and sped along the streets to see Sarah, feeling guilty, and happy, and worried, all at the same time. Guilty because of the holiday, happy because she was going to see Sarah whom she loved, and worried because Stephen had been so queer.

The sky was blue and there was a lightness and brightness in the air due to a touch of frost. It really was a lovely morning. Margaret tripped along and her spirits rose because it was so lovely. Everything was bright and shining, the river was shining like polished silver, the trees were flaunting their autumn colours in the clear sunlight. She passed Tanglewood Cottage and waved her hand to Barbara Buncle who was making a bonfire in her garden.

'Lovely smell!' she shouted to Barbara in a friendly manner, and Barbara waved her rake in reply.

* * *

The maid said that Mrs Walker was in. That was one of the good things about Sarah, she always seemed to be there if you wanted her. And another good thing was that however busy she might be – and of course she must be busy sometimes – she never seemed to be busy when you wanted her, but could always sit down and chat in a comfortable leisurely manner whatever time of day it happened to be.

All this flashed across Margaret's mind as she was shown into the doctor's study, and Sarah rose from the desk where she had been adding up accounts and held out her hands.

'How lovely!' Sarah said. 'I was just longing for some excuse to escape from those horrible things.' They sat down beside the fire – Sarah poked it into a nice blaze – and talked about their children. Margaret complained that hers were too quiet, and Sarah declared that hers were too noisy, and they both laughed a little because they understood each other perfectly and were happy in being together.

'I can't think why we don't see each other more often,' Sarah said, and Margaret agreed that *she* couldn't either, except, of course, that they were both busy with husbands and children and things.

Sarah was looking at her friend with new eyes borrowed from *Disturber of the Peace*, and she saw that what the mysterious John Smith said was true. Margaret was worn down by her husband's bad temper just as a silver sixpence is worn down by constant rubbing against coarser coins. Margaret's prettiness was almost gone, and her vivacity was almost gone. (Today she was prettier than usual, and more vivacious, because she had come quickly through the brisk air to see her friend.) And Sarah thought – as all happy wives think – I would never have stood it all these years. I would have left the brute long ago. I ought to have thought about her more, and been kinder to her, for I am so blessed. And she thought of John (who had been called out in the middle of breakfast to succour Mrs Goldsmith's youngest grandchild in convulsions, and had not yet returned) and smiled very tenderly.

Margaret said, 'You know, Sarah, I really came because I was worried about Stephen.'

'Is he ill?' enquired the doctor's wife.

'No, in fact he seemed particularly well,' replied Margaret surprisingly. 'He sat up half the night, but he wasn't writing

– at least he wasn't writing his book – and then this morning he got up early and went to London.'

Sarah murmured commiseratingly – she was slightly fogged as to why she should commiserate, but commiseration was evidently required, so, like a good friend, she supplied it.

'I know it sounds silly put like that,' Margaret owned, 'but somehow Stephen was not like himself at all.'

Sarah thought that any deviation from Stephen's usual self must be an improvement, but she did not say so. She said – 'I know what you mean.'

'Yes. He spoke to the children at breakfast instead of reading the paper. He was quite talkative, and more – more considerate,' said Margaret. She had not meant to say that, because of course it implied that Stephen was not as a rule considerate; but somehow the words had popped out and there it was: Sarah knew now that Stephen had been considerate, and that it was such a very unusual thing for Stephen to be considerate that Margaret was worried about it.

Sarah wrinkled her brows and thought about the problem which had been presented to her. It would have puzzled Sherlock Holmes, she felt, for there were no clues at all to work on, and Margaret was not being frank with her. Margaret had only told her about half the story, and even that had come out by accident.

'Dear old Meg,' said Sarah suddenly, laying a friendly hand on Margaret's arm, 'if you are really worried, and really want my help, you'll have to tell me the whole thing.'

Margaret had seen that five minutes ago, and she was torn in twain. She hated to be disloyal to Stephen, she hated women who told tales about their husbands; but on the other hand she really was worried – supposing Stephen had gone up to town to meet a *woman* – and Sarah was completely trustworthy. So after a moment's thought she told Sarah the whole thing – all about his quietness in coming up to bed, and his endeavour not to waken her, and how the morning had found him full of kindness and amiability, and she told Sarah about the very queer way he kept looking at her when he thought she was not looking at him.

Sarah was appalled at the revelation – not of today's kindness of course, but of previous brutality. Margaret seemed to think it was quite natural that Stephen should be selfish and morose, she seemed to think that husbands had a right to make everybody round them miserable. Sarah would have liked to say, 'for goodness' sake leave the man before he has utterly destroyed you,' but of course she didn't say that; as a matter of fact she didn't say anything, she just gazed at Margaret with her large grey eyes open to their widest extent.

'Do you think it's a woman, Sarah?' Margaret asked with bated breath.

'Nonsense!' said Sarah.

'It was almost – almost as if he were trying to propitiate me,' Margaret pointed out.

Well, it did look like that, but there was another idea beginning to move in Sarah's brain. She marshalled the facts at her command: Stephen had sat up very late, but he was not writing about Henry the Fourth (so Margaret said). What was he doing then? He was reading (he must have been reading since he wasn't writing, that was obvious) and he must have been reading something that enthralled him, something that he could not lay down. Sarah had been similarly enthralled not long ago. Her agile mind leaped very easily over the gap in her deductions and fastened itself firmly upon the hypothesis that Stephen had been reading *Disturber of the Peace*, by John Smith.

Supposing Stephen had been reading *Disturber of the Peace* last night, what effect would it have had upon him?

'Sarah –'

'Wait,' she said quickly, 'I'm thinking.'

Margaret waited hopefully.

Sarah thought. Supposing Stephen recognised himself as David Gaymer, it would have given him a bit of a shock, wouldn't it? David Gaymer was not a lovable character, he was selfish and irritable, he bullied his wife and domineered over his children. Sarah had thought when she read about David Gaymer, this is a bit overdone. Stephen's horrid, but he's not quite so horrid as all that. But today's little talk with Margaret had shown her that David Gaymer was not a bit overdone, he was Stephen Bulmer down to the very last button on his waistcoat. David Gaymer wrote books, he was writing the *Life of Alva*. She remembered thinking at the time that Stephen should write a life of Alva in preference to *Henry the Fourth*. It seemed more suitable.

But let's follow this out, Sarah entreated herself. How would Stephen feel when he recognised himself? He would be very angry at first, 'I'm not like that,' he would say, and then he would think about it and remember things.

And then after a bit he would read on, and find his wife getting alienated from him – Edith Gaymer was drawn very sympathetically in the book – and finally going off with another man, a man who could give her the love and sympathy she had so sadly lacked. And he would be torn between disgust for David Gaymer and sympathy for Stephen Bulmer. 'Good Heavens!' he would exclaim, 'is Margaret really thinking of leaving me? What should I do without Margaret?' He would begin to think about Margaret and what kind of life she was having with him, and perhaps he would realise – for he was by no means a stupid man, only blinded by his selfishness and bad temper – that Margaret was having a pretty poor life of it with him, and that nobody could blame her very much if she *did* think of leaving him.

Stephen could not fail to see himself in David Gaymer, for there was no exaggeration about John Smith, nor did he beat about the bush. He simply described the characters and told his tale, and the characters were so real that they made the tale seem real too – even the fantastic part of the tale seemed probable. Of course Sarah was not in the book herself, but she was sure she would have recognised herself at once if she had been so honoured because John Smith had the knack of breathing the very essence of the people he described into the pages of his book.

John Smith had held up the mirror to poor Stephen and had said, 'Here you are, old chap! I hope you like yourself. Those nasty marks from your nose to the corners of your mouth, and those others between your brows are marks you put there yourself, you know. You can't blame God for those.'

And poor Stephen had replied, 'Good Heavens, is that me?' (or he would probably have said, 'Is that I?' for he was a pedantic and serious soul) and he would gaze at Margaret – just as she had described 'in a queer way' – wondering if it could possibly be true that she was thinking of leaving him, and he would make an effort to be less like David Gaymer. And lastly he would fly up to town to tackle the publisher and find out who this man was – this John Smith who seemed to know more about himself and his wife than he himself knew.

So that although Sarah had very little to go on it all fitted beautifully. And, besides, she was quite sure that she was right in her deductions, which was the main thing, because if Sarah were quite sure she was right about anything she always was – John said so too.

Margaret had waited patiently all this time, and now she was to be rewarded for her patience.

'Now listen,' Sarah said (quite needlessly, for of course Margaret was all ears. Hadn't she been sitting there waiting for about five minutes merely to hear the pearls of wisdom fall from Sarah's lips?). 'Now listen, Margaret. I've thought it all out and I'm quite sure I'm right. Stephen's not after a woman, and there is absolutely nothing for you to worry about.'

'D'you think he's lost a lot of money?' enquired Margaret. This reasonable but somewhat alarming idea had occurred to her while she was waiting for Sarah to speak.

'No I don't,' said Sarah firmly. 'If he had lost a lot of money he would have behaved quite differently about it. Stephen was sitting up last night reading a novel.'

'But he never reads novels,' interpolated Margaret.

'He was reading a novel last night,' Sarah told her. 'It's a novel called *Disturber of the Peace*, and it has just come out. It really is a most extraordinary book. I will give it to you to read.'

'I can get it from Stephen, he will give it to me to read,' suggested Margaret.

'He will do nothing of the sort,' replied Sarah. 'Stephen will keep it away from you. He will hide it; he will burn it rather than let you have one peep at it.'

Margaret's eyes bulged.

'No, there's nothing *like that* in it,' Sarah said. 'At least, I could see nothing wrong at all. Angela Pretty had hysterics over it, of course, and John had to tear round and administer sal volatile – but really it's quite harmless and very amusing.'

'It sounds like it,' said Margaret ironically.

'It is *really*,' Sarah assured her.

'Well, why hysterics?' enquired Margaret, not unreasonably.

'I don't quite know,' said Sarah, wrinkling her brows. 'I couldn't understand what John was driving at. He was furious about the book – said the man ought to be hanged and all that sort of thing – but he hasn't read it yet of course. He was just going by what *they* said. I'm going to make him read it himself.'

'Why on earth did Angela have hysterics?'

'Well, it was partly because she didn't want to go to Samarkand,' replied Sarah.

Margaret gazed at her in amazement.

'They go off to Samarkand in the book,' Sarah explained patiently (Meg was really rather dense about the whole thing).

'You mean Miss King and Angela Pretty go to Samarkand in a book?'

'Yes – at least they start off at the end.'

'Start off at the end,' echoed Margaret stupidly.

'Start off to Samarkand at the end of the book,' explained Sarah.

'And what do they do when they get there?'

'It doesn't say, it just says they are going, and they order riding breeches and things.'

'But what has all that got to do with Stephen?' enquired Margaret after a short silence in which she had tried to make some sense of these extraordinary disclosures, and lamentably failed in the attempt.

'Nothing at all,' replied Sarah promptly. 'It was you who asked me all about Angela's hysterics and Samarkand and put me off the track. The thing that has to do with Stephen is that you are in the book too.'

'Me!' cried Margaret in astonishment. 'And do I go to Samarkand too?'

'No, of course not. What would you do at Samarkand?'

'What does anybody do there?'

'Well, you don't go there, anyhow,' said Sarah, wishing that Margaret would be quiet and allow her to tell the story in her own way – and indeed they would have got on much quicker if she had.

'What do I do then?' said Margaret. She had never been in a book before, and she was rather thrilled about it all.

'You climb out of your bedroom window and elope with Harry Carter,' Sarah told her.

Margaret was so dumbfounded that Sarah got her wish, she was able to continue without further interruption. 'So now you see the whole thing. Stephen read the book last night and he's been thinking about it ever since and wondering if there is any truth in it, and now he's dashed off to London to find out who the author is, so that he can wring his neck or something.'

'But whatever shall I say to Stephen?' exclaimed Margaret.

'If I were you I should pretend I hadn't read the book at all,' said Sarah. 'I know you haven't read it yet, but you had better stay to lunch and read it this afternoon. You had better just go on as usual and pretend you haven't heard anything about it. It will do Stephen no harm to keep on looking at you and wondering,' said Sarah with fiendish satisfaction. 'And you can sort of keep him guessing,' she added.

'Keep him guessing?' asked Margaret.

'Yes, keep him guessing,' said Sarah, and she went on to point out to her bewildered friend various ingenious ways in which she could keep her husband on tenterhooks.

But it was not until Sarah had put the book into Margaret's hands, and settled her comfortably in the doctor's chair, and gone out with a basket full of flowers and oranges and calves'-foot jelly for the Hobday child – who was ill again poor lamb – that Margaret began to understand what all the fuss was about.

She began to read *Disturber of the Peace* because Sarah said she was to read it, but as she went on and recognised all the people she knew, drawn just as they were, without one jot omitted or one tittle added, she became engrossed. And then Stephen appeared upon the scene, and it was just Stephen exactly – so much so that she blushed for his nakedness. For herself she almost wept. John Smith showed her herself as she had not realised she was – a woman hungry for tenderness, snatching at happiness and love, her last chance before she grew too old.

Margaret lunched with Sarah and spent the afternoon finishing the book, and as she put it down she said, 'He knows everything about me, that man, except one thing, and that one thing is the strongest thing in my life. If it had not been for that one thing, I would have gone away and left Stephen long ago – just as Edith Gaymer did – but I couldn't leave the children – not for any man on earth – so I shall stay with him always, and grow old and ugly, without ever having known what it is to be loved.'

She felt Sarah's arms round her, and Sarah's voice in her ear telling her not to cry.

'The children love you frightfully,' Sarah whispered, 'and Stephen will improve – I know he will. Look at how different he was this morning. You've been too lenient with him – too doormatty, Meg darling – take a firm line. It will be better for Stephen and better for everyone if you make him behave. I don't suppose he's happy being horrid – nobody is,' said Sarah wisely.

CHAPTER TEN

'FEU DE JOIE'

Barbara Buncle waved her rake to Margaret Bulmer and continued to gather up the dead leaves and the prunings from her gooseberry bushes and apple trees and to pile them on to her bonfire. She had deposited the hundred pound note in her bank that morning, and it was necessary to celebrate the occasion in some way and to work off her excitement. What could be more fitting to celebrate the occasion than a bonfire? Great victories, Kings' Coronations and the birth of heirs have all been celebrated by bonfires, so why not the advent of peace and prosperity to Tanglewood Cottage?

The beauty of Barbara's bonfire lay in the fact that nobody knew it was a celebrating bonfire – nobody but herself. The gardener who worked occasionally in Tanglewood garden passed, and called out, 'I see you are burning up your leaves, Miss.' Burning up her leaves! What a way to speak of a bonfire.

Margaret Bulmer had shouted, 'Lovely smell!' It was rather nice, thought Barbara, sniffing, but it was the flames she liked, the little red flames that licked round the twigs and shot up suddenly – she threw on some more twigs just to see the flames shoot up.

What fun it had been that morning at the bank! Barbara had gone in soon after the bank had opened, and the young man with the fair hair and the supercilious expression (Mr Black his name was, and he was one of Mrs Dick's paying guests) had looked up from his desk and seen who it was and gone on writing for at least two minutes before he came to see what she wanted. No need to bother about that old frump, he had said to himself – or Barbara thought that he had. Barbara was sure that he knew her account was over-drawn, perhaps he had been told not to cash any more cheques for Miss Buncle. When he had quite finished what he was doing he lounged over to the counter and she produced the note.

'Ha, don't often see these chaps about!' he had remarked in his familiar way which Barbara detested.

'A little present from my uncle,' said Barbara, quite casually, as if it were quite a usual occurrence to receive hundred pound notes from your uncle.

'Must be a rich man, your uncle,' suggested Mr Black, filling up forms – his manner had altered towards her, at least so Barbara imagined, he was much more respectful and attentive. It was the rich uncle in the background she supposed .

'Oh, he is, and so generous. He lives in Birmingham,' said Barbara glibly. She was amazed at herself when she found what she had said – such dreadful lies, and they had tumbled out of her mouth without the slightest effort. It really was rather appalling. She had intended to domicile her rich uncle in Australia as Mr Abbott had humorously suggested, but it had suddenly struck her that perhaps the money in Australia was different from our money. It might have the name of an Australian bank inscribed upon it – or a kangaroo or something. Barbara did not know, and she had no idea how to find out; so, all things considered, it seemed easier for the rich uncle to reside in Birmingham. Barbara had never been to Birmingham, and, to her, it seemed almost as far away from Silverstream as Australia, and therefore almost as safe.

She was thinking about all this, and piling leaves on to her bonfire, and the smoke was swirling round her, blackening her face and making her eyes pour with water, when suddenly a voice announced:

'Ooh – a bonfire!'

Barbara looked all round to discover where the voice came from, and finally found herself gazing into a pair of very blue eyes which were peering over the fence dividing her garden from that of old Mrs Carter. The blue eyes, some fair curls, and a red tammy was all that was visible above the fence.

'I suppose – I suppose I couldn't come and help,' said the voice plaintively. 'I love bonfires.'

'Do come and help,' Barbara said. 'There's a gap in the fence lower down the garden –'

The eyes disappeared instantly, and, a few moments later, there was a rustle of dry leaves dispersed by flying feet and a young girl appeared – a somewhat breathless young girl in grey tweeds, a slim willowy creature with a rose-leaf complexion and a small pretty mouth, rather a firm wilful mouth for such a fairy-like creature, Barbara decided.

'I'm Sally,' said the girl, when she had recovered her breath.

Barbara remembered now. It was at that dreadful tea-party when Mrs Featherstone Hogg had burst in like a bombshell and had thrown *Disturber of the Peace* on to Mrs Carter's tea-table. They had been talking about Sally at the time. Sally was coming to live with Mrs Carter because she required sunshine and milk.

'But I thought Sally was a child,' said Barbara vaguely.

'You would,' replied Sally darkly. 'I mean if you heard Gran talking about me you would think I was about seven instead of seventeen. She treats me like an infant – tells me to change my stockings and wash my hands for lunch, and sends me up to bed at eight o'clock every night. *Me*, who has kept house for Daddy for two years – it's a bit steep, it really is.'

'Steep?' enquired Barbara.

'A bit thick,' Sally explained kindly, 'absolutely the pink limit.'

'Yes,' said Barbara, somewhat bewildered.

'I knew you would think so,' Sally told her. 'The moment I saw you I said to myself *there's* a sensible person.' She sat down on a convenient log and stirred the bonfire dreamily with an apple branch. 'I said to myself there's a sensible person, I must speak to her or I'll go mad. You don't know how beastly it is to be treated like an imbecile and followed about all day long and stuffed with milk. You see I was mistress in Daddy's house and I did what I liked. We had a lovely time together. We had little dinners, and twice a week we went out to restaurants and then on to a play. And of course all the subalterns called just as if I were grown-up. We were at Malta before that – it was too marvellous. Have you ever been to Malta?'

'Never,' replied Barbara sadly.

'You must, you simply must,' said Sally, turning her face up to Barbara and almost dazzling that staid person with the bewildering beauty of her smile. 'Everyone ought to go to Malta. There's the most heavenly bathing there, and dances every night, and darling little Snotties to dance with, and tennis parties – you *do* play tennis, I suppose.'

'A little,' replied Barbara, with truthful modesty.

'You'd love it,' Sally told her, 'you'd simply adore it. I'd like us to go together and then I could show you everything – don't you hate this dull hole?'

'Well –' said Barbara doubtfully.

'I knew it,' Sally said eagerly. 'I knew you were like me – pining to get away. Daddy's gone to India and left me here with Gran, and I simply can't bear it.'

'It must be dull for you,' Barbara admitted.

'It's simply foul,' replied the remarkable girl. 'I was yearning to go to India. I'd heard so much about it from everyone, and it seemed almost too good to be true when Daddy heard that he had been posted to Calcutta. It was all settled, and I was looking forward to it more than words can tell, and then my appendix went rotten.'

'Dreadful!' said Barbara sympathetically.

'Ghastly – simply ghastly,' Sally agreed. 'They yanked it out of me of course, and I thought everything would be all right, and then the doctor – who was an absolute fiend – went and told Daddy that India was out of the question for me, and

I must be fed up. I was fed up all right I can tell you. Fancy Daddy going off to India alone,' Sally said tremulously.

'Dreadful!' said Barbara again, she hoped the girl was not going to cry. (She need not have worried, Sally was made of sterner stuff.)

'Have you ever had appendicitis?' enquired Sally more cheerfully.

'Never,' replied Barbara.

'Well, don't,' Sally advised her. 'It's absolutely foul. It came on gradually with me, and I used to wake up at night and feel like David – "My reins chasten me in the night season," *you* know. It gave me a sort of friendly feeling for David. I wonder if he had a touch of appendicitis.'

Barbara was feeling more and more bewildered, she was not used to this kind of conversation. She tried to fix her mind upon David and the facts known to her about him, so as to determine whether it could have been appendicitis he suffered from; but before she could do so Sally had abandoned the subject.

'Lovely bonfire!' Sally said, poking it so that the flames shot up with a roaring, crackling sound. 'The French call it "feu de joie" – I think that's an awfully good name for it, don't you? Is this a "feu de joie" or is it just burning rubbish?'

'It's a "feu de joie",' Barbara replied incautiously.

'Oh! That makes it ten times nicer,' cried Sally. 'Let's pile on more sticks until it's as high as the house. What's it for?'

'Well, it's for *me*,' Barbara said lamely. 'I can't tell you exactly –'

'A secret?'

Barbara nodded.

'How too marvellous!' breathed Sally. 'Oh, I *do* think it was good of you to let me come and help you with it.'

They worked away happily, piling more sticks on to the 'feu de joie' so that the flames sank down for a minute and then leapt up higher than ever. It became so hot that they could not go near it. They poked at it with long sticks and laughed and the smoke poured into their lungs and made them cough; it was tremendous fun.

At last, worn out with their efforts, they retired to a short distance and sat down on a log to admire their handiwork.

'Gran would have a fit if she could see me sitting here,' announced Sally placidly. She took a somewhat sticky paper bag out of her pocket and offered Barbara a toffee-ball. Barbara took one, she liked toffee and she was not foolishly fastidious.

'Perhaps you had better not sit here, then,' Barbara pointed out, her utterance somewhat obstructed by the large ball of toffee.

"It's quite all right as long as she doesn't *see* me,' replied Sally, 'and she won't see me, because Mrs Featherstone Hogg came in to see her and talk about that book, and Gran didn't want me to hear what they said so she told me to take a sharp walk. I hate sharp walks, don't you?'

'What book?' enquired Barbara, knowing quite well, but hoping that she was mistaken.

'*Disturber of the Peace*, of course. They all talk about it night and day. Have you read it? I had to creep down after

Gran had gone to bed and pinch it out of the drawing-room. Gran said it was not suitable for young people.'

Barbara chuckled; she couldn't help it, for when Sally quoted from 'Gran' she put on the old lady's voice and manner so exactly that it almost seemed as if Mrs Carter were sitting beside her on the log. She chuckled, but at the same time she was beset with fears – they were talking about her book night and day, were they?

'Something tickled you?' enquired Sally cheekily.

Barbara didn't answer this, she tried to make her voice sound stern as she pointed out the wickedness of reading books banned by your grandmother.

'Of course you have to say that,' said Sally unrepentantly, 'but you don't really think it's wicked. I had to read the book when they were all talking about it all the time, hadn't I? Besides Gran's such an old stickler, she thinks I ought to read *Little Women* and *The Fairchild Family*.'

'You are under her care,' said Barbara virtuously.

'Worse luck!' Sally agreed with a sigh. 'But it's such rot, I've read whatever I liked for years. Daddy didn't mind what I read. I've read far worse things than *Disturber of the Peace*. There's nothing horrid about it at all. It's simply a *scream*. I had to stuff the bedclothes into my mouth when I came to the bits about Gran and Mrs Featherstone Hogg.'

'Did you think it was funny?' asked the author with interest.

'I should jolly well think it is,' replied Sally, 'but to me it's not just a funny book, it's something far better –'

'Is it?'

'It's a kind of – a kind of allegory,' continued Sally gravely. 'Here's this horrible little village, full of its own affairs and its own importance, all puffed up and smug and conventional and satisfied with itself, and then suddenly their eyes are opened and their shackles fall off and they act according to their real natures. They're not shams any more, they're real. It's simply marvellous,' Sally said, turning a shining face upon the astonished author.

Barbara's heart warmed at this unsolicited praise. She had heard the child of her brain maligned and anathematised, she had been obliged to sit dumbly and hear it called filth; but now, here, at last was somebody who appreciated its worth. Barbara looked at Sally with affection and respect.

'He's wakened them all up,' Sally was saying, 'wakened them all up and made them see themselves as others see them. Of course that's what he meant to do. Have you read it?'

'Y – es,' said Barbara.

'Perhaps you didn't read it as carefully as I did,' Sally said consolingly. 'I was so interested, you see, I seemed to get right inside the man's brain. I can see exactly what he meant when he wrote it – I know exactly what he felt – he's a marvellous man. I should like to marry John Smith,' said Sally, nursing one knee and gazing at the bonfire with shining eyes.

'You – you would like to – to *marry* him?' echoed Barbara in amazement.

'Yes,' replied Sally. 'He's the sort of man I admire – absolutely fearless. I'm sure he's tall and strong with shaggy sort of hair that keeps falling over his forehead until he tosses his head and shakes it back. He's not exactly good-looking of course, but he has a humorous mouth and nice eyes – piercing grey eyes that look straight through you. I can see him striding about the country with a drawn sword in his hand – *Disturber of the Peace* is a drawn sword – ready to attack all the dragons of modern life at a moment's notice, freeing poor little worms like Mr Featherstone Hogg from their shackles, and trampling on stupid conventions and shams. He doesn't care what people think of him, of course, he only cares to do good, to help the weak and expose the humbugs – I wonder if I shall ever meet him,' said Sally softly, almost reverently. 'I'm afraid I shan't ever meet him, it would be too good to be true. I expect he has left Silverstream now and gone to some other horrid smug little place to waken it up and give it beans.'

Barbara was absolutely dumb – she had no idea that she had written such a marvellous book, nor that its effects upon Silverstream were so far-reaching. She was much too honest to credit herself with all those noble motives. She had written *Disturber of the Peace* to make a little money for herself, because she needed money very badly, but it was pleasant to think that more had gone into it than she had intended. If all that Sally said were true she was a public benefactor, and not – as she had been led to believe – a criminal of the deepest dye. As for John Smith, it was most extraordinary but he seemed quite real to Barbara; she could see him – just as Sally had described – striding about the country, a modern Jack the Giant Killer, with his shaggy hair and piercing grey eyes.

'People like Gran and Mrs Featherstone Hogg have no right to criticise a splendid man like that,' Sally continued, 'he's as far above their mouldy little minds as the stars. They don't understand him of course, but other people will. All over the country people are reading his book and leading better and nobler lives because of it.'

Barbara felt she could go on listening to this sort of conversation for hours. What an extraordinary girl Sally was – a very clever girl indeed, with sense far beyond her tender years. Unfortunately time was flying and she felt bound to point out the fact to her companion. Mrs Carter had lunch at one o'clock and punctuality was something of a fetish at The Firs.

Sally sprang up. 'I wonder if Mrs Hogg will still be there,' she said, 'I called her Mrs Hogg this morning and she didn't like it a bit. I can't bear her, can you? I suppose you couldn't ask me to tea some day, could you?'

'I could,' replied Barbara. 'Would Mrs Carter let you come?'

'Why not? You are quite respectable, aren't you?' enquired Sally in her direct manner.

'Oh yes – at least. . . .' It crossed Barbara's mind that perhaps she wasn't quite respectable now, by Mrs Carter's standard. If Mrs Carter knew that she was John Smith – but Mrs Carter didn't know, so it was all right.

Sally had been watching her face, poised ready for flight.

'Aren't you?' she now demanded, with gleaming eyes. Quite obviously she was hoping that her new friend was *not* quite all that Gran could desire, and therefore much more exciting to know.

'Of course I am, don't be silly,' Barbara said, a tiny bit annoyed, though she couldn't have said why.

‘All right – don’t get ratty,’ Sally adjured her, ‘I suppose it was too much to hope for –’

And she fled.

* * *

This conversation with Sally Carter cheered Barbara on her way, and she needed cheering for it was a way strewn with boulders. Not only did the inhabitants of Silverstream discuss and vilify *Disturber of the Peace*, but people from all over the country wrote letters praising or blaming its author – curiously enough the praise was almost as disturbing as the blame, so entirely incomprehensible was it to the innocent and bewildered John Smith. Then there were the newspapers with their stupefying reviews. Mr Abbott had advised Miss Buncle to contribute to a press cutting agency (she was lamentably ignorant in these matters), and Barbara, who was acquiring a habit of doing what Mr Abbott told her, obediently contributed two guineas to one of these, hitherto unheard of, establishments.

A shower of criticism immediately descended. There was scarcely a single day when the postman failed to bring words of praise or blame to Tanglewood Cottage. Barbara read them all with care, and rejoiced or sorrowed according to the meed which was measured unto her. Sometimes she was completely puzzled by the critics’ views upon her book and once or twice she was visited by the unworthy suspicion that the critic could not have studied *Disturber of the Peace* with the meticulous care it deserved before writing his considered opinion of it.

'This book is uneven,' complained *The Morning Mail*, 'the plot is good but the characterisation is poor. There never were such people as those depicted in *Disturber of the Peace*. Major Waterfoot is a type of retired officer which never existed except in the vivid imagination of our younger novelists. We would recommend John Smith to study life at first hand before attempting to write about it.'

'We can thoroughly recommend *Disturber of the Peace*, by John Smith, to anyone who is feeling blue,' announced *The Evening Clarion*. 'It is the funniest thing we have read for a long time. We hail a new writer to the ranks of Britain's humorists.'

'Brilliant Satire,' exclaimed *The Daily Post*. 'Every page is a masterpiece of the most delicate ridicule. The characters are delineated with a sure hand. Mr Smith is to be congratulated upon his first novel.'

The Literary News was not so kind – '*Disturber of the Peace*, by John Smith (Abbott & Spicer 7*s* 6*d*),' it announced, 'is one of those futile novels that behoves us to ask ourselves – as we lay it down with a sigh of relief – why it has ever been written. It is dull and prosy, the sentiment mawkish, the characters unconvincing. A dull Major living in a country village falls in love with his next-door neighbour, who is a widow of independent means, but nothing happens until the god of love descends from Olympus to rouse him from his lethargy – why the god of love should take the trouble is a matter which the author fails to explain, and indeed it would be exceedingly difficult of explanation. There is a preposterous love scene in the lady's garden, the Major seduces her, and the book ends with the couple contemplating a honeymoon in Samarkand. There are some subsidiary characters and incidents dragged in to pad out the story, but this is the main theme and we do not feel that many of our readers will care to waste their time upon rubbish of this description.'

'A Romantic Story of Love in a Village,' said *The People's Illustrated* in capital letters. 'Those of us who are weary of the so-called brilliant novel of modern life will enjoy the old-world fragrance of Copperfield. There is nothing in *Disturber of the Peace* to bring a blush to the most modest cheek. The characters are drawn with a loving and discriminate hand. We seem to know them quite well ere we lay down the book – to know them and to love them as we know and love our friends. It is to be hoped that Mr Smith will give us more novels from his pen of this same elevating type.'

'Who is John Smith?' enquired Mr Snooks who wrote the literary column for *The Weekly Guide*. 'He seems to be a young man of singular discernment. There is no muddled thinking in his novel, every sentence is clear and concise and relevant to the purpose. Mr Smith is somewhat scornful of love, he writes of love with his tongue in his cheek – the result is exceedingly funny. I can heartily recommend the book to those with a sense of humour.'

'The last novel on our list is *Disturber of the Peace*, by John Smith (Abbott & Spicer 7*s* 6*d*),' said *The Morning Sun*. 'It is a type of novel we do not care to recommend to our readers, but no doubt it will gain large sales. It concerns itself chiefly with the description of characters under the influence of unbridled or perverted passions.'

* * *

The writers of these criticisms would doubtless have been pleased if they could have seen John Smith poring over their words. Barbara tried in vain to arrive at some definite conclusion as to the merits of her book. But no sooner had one review plunged her into the depths of despair by saying that *Disturber of the Peace* was as dull as ditchwater, or perverted and immoral, and not fit for a respectable human being to read, than another cutting arrived, by the next post, informing all who cared to know that it was a charming book, clever, brilliant, elevating or supremely funny. It was certainly very puzzling. Meantime the sales went up by leaps and bounds and Mr Abbott sent her congratulatory notes and urged her to start another book at once on the same lines.

CHAPTER ELEVEN

COLONEL WEATHERHEAD AND THE BISHOP

Colonel Weatherhead was pulling up Bishop's weed in his garden. He had a fearful tussle with the Bishop every autumn, for the Bishop was entrenched in a thorn hedge at the bottom of the garden near the river, and however much of him Colonel Weatherhead managed to eradicate there was always enough root left embedded in the thickest part of the hedge to start him off again next year.

Colonel Weatherhead had a kind of sneaking admiration for the Bishop – here was an enemy, worthy of his steel. The Colonel went for him tooth and nail, he dug and tore and burned the Bishop, and the sweat poured off him in rivulets. Sometimes he stood up, and straightened his back, and felt himself round the waist, and wondered if that horrible two inches had diminished at all.

He was in the thick of the fight, and his hair was standing on end, and his face and hands were scratched with thorns, and one of his brace buttons had flown off in the struggle – in fact he was as filthy and as completely happy as a little boy making mud pies – when he heard a car drive up to his front door. He peered through the bushes and saw that it was Mrs Featherstone Hogg's car, and there was Mrs Featherstone Hogg herself, getting out of the car and going into his house.

The Colonel swore a regrettable oath, he did not like Mrs Featherstone Hogg at the best of times, but even supposing he had liked her immensely she would have been unwelcome just now. Colonel Weatherhead was in no condition to appear before a lady. He would be in no condition to appear before a lady until he had soaked himself in an extremely hot bath and changed all his clothes.

The Colonel now perceived to his horror that Simmons was coming down the garden to find him – Simmons was the Colonel's soldier servant, an excellent creature in his way, and thoroughly conscientious, but somewhat lacking in initiative. Colonel Weatherhead made a rapid reconnaissance of his position and sprinted for the toolshed. It was a dark musty place (as toolsheds so often are) filled with worn-out tools, and a wheelbarrow and a lawnmower, and festooned with spiders' webs; but the Colonel was already as dirty as any man could be, so there was no need to be fastidious. He crawled underneath the wheelbarrow and pulled a piece of sacking over his legs. He was concerned to find that he was breathing heavily, it was partly the short sprint and partly the excitement, but it showed he was out of training. I must shorten the tobacco ration, he thought, regretfully.

Simmons looked all round the garden faithfully. He even glanced into the toolshed, although it was unlikely that Colonel Weatherhead would be there, then he returned to the house and informed Mrs Featherstone Hogg that the Colonel seemed to have gone out.

'What do you mean?' enquired that lady haughtily. 'You said Colonel Weatherhead was in the garden.'

'I thought he was, ma'am,' replied Simmons.

'Either the Colonel is out, or else he is in,' said Mrs Featherstone Hogg. 'What do you mean by saying he seems to have gone out?'

'Well, I can't find him, ma'am,' Simmons returned, scratching his ear in perplexity, 'and yet I'd take my affy davvy he's somewhere about, for he wasn't dressed to go out, so to speak.'

'It's most annoying,' Mrs Featherstone Hogg said. 'I suppose it is no use waiting for the Colonel – you don't know when he will be in?'

'No ma'am, I don't – and that's the truth. I don't know where he's gone, and I don't know when he'll be back.'

Mrs Featherstone Hogg looked at him with disapproval, then she produced a brown paper parcel and laid it on the table. 'You will give this parcel to Colonel Weatherhead directly he comes in,' she informed Simmons, 'and tell him that I came down here specially to see him – you understand?'

Simmons replied that he did.

'It is very *important*,' said Mrs Featherstone Hogg.

Colonel Weatherhead waited until he heard the car drive off before he emerged from his lair. He was even dirtier than he had been, there were spiders' webs in his hair, and his face was streaked with soil, and he had torn a jagged rent in his trousers with a nail. His language might have set fire to the toolshed if it had not been so damp –

Should he have another go at the Bishop, or should he return to the house and bathe? That was the question. He consulted his watch and found that there was half an hour before tea. He took up the fork and hesitated – bath or Bishop? A spider chose the moment to crawl over the Colonel's ear.

'Ugh, damn and blast!' he cried, rubbing his ear with a thoroughly grimy hand, and decided for a bath. The decision had been made for him by a spider (not for the first time had this intelligent insect helped a gallant soldier to make an important decision at a critical moment. It will be remembered that Robert the Bruce was similarly guided). Robert Weatherhead put the fork into the toolshed and went up to the house.

Simmons was waiting for him when he emerged from the bathroom clean and pink as a newly-washed baby.

'Mrs Featherstone 'Ogg was here, sir, and I was to say she came down special to see you, sir, and this parcel's very important,' he recited glibly.

The Colonel slapped on his braces and grunted.

'I looked everywhere for you, sir.'

The Colonel grunted again.

Simmons laid the parcel on the dressing-table with reverent care and departed to the kitchen. He had shifted the responsibility of the parcel, his conscience was clear.

'I wonder where the old codger *was*,' he said to his wife as he sat down to his tea, and spread his bread with a liberal helping of butter and stretched out his arm for the jam.

''Iding,' suggested Mrs Simmons promptly.

'But I looked all over the place – I looked in the toolshed even –'

'More fool you!' retorted his better half scornfully, 'if 'e *'ad* bin in the toolshed it would 'ave meant 'e didn't want to be found. What call 'ad you to be 'unting for the pore gentleman in the toolshed? None. If 'e didn't want to be found it was yore place not to find 'im – see?'

Simmons saw. 'You *are* a one!' he said in awed tones.

Colonel Weatherhead glanced at the mysterious parcel as he put on his collar and struggled with his stud – it looked like a book. He put out one hand and felt it – yes, it was a book, he could feel the hard edges of the cover through the brown paper. Why had Mrs Featherstone Hogg sent him a book? What kind of a book would it be? Colonel Weatherhead was pretty certain that Mrs Featherstone Hogg's taste in literature was different from his – it would be one of those high-brow books, deadly dull. He left it on the dressing-table and went downstairs to have his tea. There was a novel of Buchan's waiting for him to read, it had just come from the library – much more his style.

The Colonel drank his tea and read his Buchan, he was very comfortable after his exercise and his bath. He ate two crumpets, they were fattening, of course, but he felt entitled to them after his strenuous work.

At seven o'clock the telephone bell rang, and Simmons came to report that Mrs Featherstone Hogg was on the line and wished to speak to him. Colonel Weatherhead lifted the receiver and heard a voice say –

'Have you read it?'

'Read what?'

'The book I left for you, of course.'

'Oh, yes. No, I haven't read it yet. Been awfully busy, you know.'

'Read it,' said the voice that purported to be the voice of Mrs Featherstone Hogg but did not sound like hers. 'Read it immediately.'

'Yes, yes,' agreed the Colonel.

'I'm going to London on important business, but I shall be home on Saturday. I want to hear exactly what you think of it.'

'Yes, yes. All right, my dear lady,' soothed Colonel Weatherhead to the excited voice at the other end of the telephone, so unlike the usual languid, die-away tones of Mrs Featherstone Hogg.

Something must have stung the old girl properly, he thought, as he returned to John Buchan and his comfortable fire.

That was Wednesday, it was not until Friday morning that he undid the wrappings of the book sent to him by Mrs Featherstone Hogg, and looked at it curiously. He was sufficiently in awe of Mrs Featherstone Hogg to feel that it would be wise to have read the book before she returned from London (or at any rate glanced through the thing). She would probably ring him up and ask him if he had done so, it was too much to hope that she would have forgotten all about it. Most people in Silverstream did what Mrs Featherstone Hogg told them to do, it was easier in the long run, they found.

On first inspection the book seemed quite an ordinary sort of novel – not at all the high-brow stuff that he had expected. He started on it about eleven o'clock on Friday morning, for it was raining hard, and much too wet to go out and dig; besides he was somewhat stiff after a last struggle with the Bishop which had absorbed the major part of Thursday.

Disturber of the Peace amused him – 'Damned good,' he commented as he read the description of Major Waterfoot, 'not unlike that feller in the Dragoons.' At one o'clock he laid it on the table, open and face downwards to keep his place, and went in to his solitary lunch. At one-thirty he was back in his chair, reading.

The rain fell steadily all afternoon and the Colonel read on. He chuckled once or twice and decided that the people were very real, it might almost be Silverstream. Simmons brought in his tea, and he continued to read.

Colonel Weatherhead finished the book about seven o'clock and sat and thought about it for a bit. It was an amusing and interesting book – he liked it – but he couldn't see, for the life of him, why Mrs Featherstone Hogg had been so excited about it. He would never have supposed that it was her style at all. The people in the book appealed to him, they were real live people, just the sort of people you met every day. Copperfield was a typical English village, and the people were typical English people. They were quite contented with their lot, they went on day after day doing the same things and saying the same things – a bit futile, wasn't it? They never got anywhere, nothing ever happened to them except that they grew old. And then suddenly that Golden

Boy came along with his pipes and stirred them all up. Fancy if a Golden Boy came to Silverstream and stirred us all up! Colonel Weatherhead thought. He reviewed his own life, it was pretty futile, pretty empty and lonely. It would become even more so as time went on and he got older and couldn't do all the things he liked doing, such as walking, and digging, and fighting with the Bishop. Gradually all these things would desert him and he would be nothing but an old crusty crock. It was a horrible thought. He poked the fire fiercely, and went up to dress for his solitary dinner.

The evening stretched before him like a desert. Damn that book, he thought, it's upset me. It's upset me frightfully. Something queer about that book to upset me like this –

As he sipped his coffee he noticed that the rain was no longer beating against the windows. He pulled aside the blind and looked out, it was fine. The moon sailed like a silver crescent in a cloudless sky, the stars were brilliant.

'I shall go out, Simmons,' said the Colonel. 'Bring my galoshes, will you?'

Simmons brought his galoshes and he went out. The air was very sweet after the rain. The moon silvered the leaves of the evergreens, the bushes dripped heavily, the hedge was a mass of diamonds. The moon turned the flooded paths to silvery streams.

'Dashed pretty!' said Colonel Weatherhead, it made him feel quite poetical. But all the same it was a sad eerie sort of scene, not the sort of scene to cheer you up when you were feeling a bit blue, not the sort of scene to be out in all by yourself. The gorgeous moonlight reminded the Colonel of that love scene he had just been reading about, when Major Waterfoot had proposed in such a dashing manner to the pretty Mrs Mildmay. He had thought it 'dashed good' at the time, it had made him feel quite young and ardent – that's the way to propose to a woman, by Jove it is! – he had thought. That fellow knows what he is writing about. But, unfortunately, thinking of it now, made the Colonel feel even lonelier than before.

He splashed along the drive in his galoshes and went through the gates on to the road, it would be cleaner on the road. Mrs Bold's small house was just opposite, he could see the lighted windows of her dressing-room through the – now almost bare – branches of the trees. The pink curtains which were drawn across the windows gave it a particularly cosy appearance.

'I haven't seen her for days,' he said to himself, hesitating before the gate of Cosy Neuk. 'Hope she's not ill or anything. Nice sensible little woman – pretty too – perhaps it would be neighbourly to enquire.'

He pushed the gate open and went in.

Mrs Bold was sitting on a sofa by the fire making herself a 'nightie' of peach-coloured crêpe-de-chine. She huddled it into her work basket as the Colonel was announced and looked up, a trifle flustered.

'Just looked in to see how you were getting on,' he apologised.

'How nice of you! I was feeling so lonely,' said Mrs Bold smiling at him pathetically.

By Jove, *she* was lonely *too*, thought Colonel Weatherhead

– must be dashed lonely for a woman living by herself, and she was always so bright and cheery. Plucky little creature! Pretty little creature! He was emboldened to pat the hand which she held out to him – Mrs Bold made no objection.

'Well,' he said, 'it *is* lonely living alone – nobody to talk to or anything.' He sat down beside her on the sofa and told her all about how lonely he was, living in The Bridge House all by himself. Mrs Bold listened and sympathised.

It was very cosy and comfortable in Mrs Bold's drawing-room. The fire burned brightly, Colonel Weatherhead noticed that it was composed of coal and logs – an ideal fire. He said so to his hostess. They talked about fires and found that their tastes tallied exactly – it was astonishing.

Colonel Weatherhead began to think he had been a fool. He had known Mrs Bold for four years – she had lived opposite his gate for that period – and, although he had always liked and admired the little woman in a vague way, he had never, until this moment, realised how charming she was, how sensible and intelligent, how sympathetic.

He glanced at her sideways, her eyes were fixed upon the fire which irradiated her small round face with rosy light – how pretty she was! Her hair was pretty too, it was brown with reddish glints in it, and it curled prettily round her forehead and at the back of her neck. She was talking about the Coal People, and telling Colonel Weatherhead what trouble she had with them. She had ordered two tons that morning, and the men had insisted on bringing the heavy carts into the garden instead of carrying it in bag by bag as they usually did. The consequence was they had broken a drain pipe which had been put too near the surface of the drive. She had known this would happen – it had happened before when she moved into the house and the furniture van had driven in – but the coal-man wouldn't listen to her and now she would have to send for a plumber. Colonel Weatherhead had no idea – she told him – how dreadfully these sort of people imposed on a lone woman.

'Don't be one any more, Dorothea,' said Colonel Weatherhead earnestly.

This fell far short of the dashing manner in which Major Waterfoot had proposed to Mrs Mildmay, but it was quite as effective. Dorothea was in his arms and he was kissing her before he knew where he was – it was a delightful sensation.

The Colonel did not go home until it was quite late; the moon was still shining, but it did not make him feel sad, in fact it made him feel somewhat light-headed. Simmons and his wife had gone to bed long ago of course. The Colonel let himself into his silent house and went to bed also – he had all sorts of strange unusual feelings. Presently he went to sleep and dreamed about Dorothea.

CHAPTER TWELVE

MRS FEATHERSTONE HOGG

Mrs Featherstone Hogg did not enjoy her two days in London. She had not intended to go to London herself just now, it was not the right time of year for London. Christmas was coming on and the hotel was crowded, she could not get a room to suit her tastes. The streets were wet and draughty, the shops were stuffy and overheated, there was flu about – and Mrs Featherstone Hogg was terrified of flu – but in spite of all these horrors which she had known about before ever she started she was obliged to go to London because of Edwin's stupidity. Edwin's visit to the lawyer had been a complete failure, he had returned to Silverstream with the information that Mr Spark was of the opinion that they had no case for a libel action against Abbott & Spicer. It was always unsatisfactory to bring up a case of libel based upon a novel. It was so unsatisfactory that it was scarcely ever attempted. Nothing would be gained by it.

Edwin appeared to think that he had done all that was necessary in consulting Mr Spark. Mrs Featherstone Hogg did not share his views, and she told him so all the way up to London in the car.

'Do you mean to tell me that you will allow any low-down scribbler to say what he likes about me without moving a finger to have him punished?' she enquired.

'Well, I asked Spark,' Edwin pointed out.

'You asked Spark,' repeated Mrs Featherstone Hogg, scornfully.

'Yes, I asked Spark, and he said it was no use.'

'So you decided to do nothing about it,' declared the lady, her eyes flashing dangerously. 'It's nothing to you, I suppose, if I am insulted, ridiculed, held up to scorn? Have you no pride, Edwin? Can you sit at your ease and have it bruited abroad that I was in the chorus when you married me?'

'But you were, Agatha,' Mr Featherstone Hogg pointed out with amazing indiscretion.

'You liar!' screamed Agatha. 'I had a speaking part.'

'You said, "Girls, girls, what a wonderful time we are having!"' said Mr Featherstone Hogg reminiscently. 'And then you all danced. You were third from the end in the front row.'

'Well, and what of that? It's nothing against a girl if she has to earn her own living, is it?'

'Nothing,' replied Mr Featherstone Hogg promptly. 'Nothing in my opinion – it was you who –'

'Stop it now,' cried his better half holding her ears tightly.

'I was only going to say it was you who seemed ashamed of it,' said Mr Featherstone Hogg mildly. 'I'm not, and never was.'

The interview with Mr Spark took place that afternoon. It was a very unsatisfactory interview. Mr Spark merely reiterated the arguments which he had used to Mr Featherstone Hogg; he hadn't even read the book which Mrs Featherstone Hogg had sent him to read; he did not see any object in reading the book; he thought the matter was closed. Mrs Featherstone Hogg disabused his mind of this idea. She commanded him to read *Disturber of the Peace* and made an appointment with him for the following day.

Mr Spark read the book and enjoyed it – especially the bits about Mrs Featherstone Hogg – but he was even less anxious to take the case to court after he had read it. He visualised the scene in court – everyone giggling, the judge making witticisms – what barrister would take such a case? He imagined the roars of laughter as the passages objected to by his client were read aloud. (Mrs Featherstone Hogg had marked the offending passages in red ink so that there should be no mistake about it.)

When the Featherstone Hoggs appeared on the following day at the appointed hour Mr Spark had decided on his line –

'My dear Mrs Featherstone Hogg,' he said, rising and offering her a chair, 'I have been reading the novel (quite a second-rate affair and not worthy of your notice, I assure you), and the character which you object to is not you at all. You have been too sensitive altogether.'

'It is Mrs Horsley Downs.'

'I know, I know. You marked it for me. It bears – I admit – some small resemblance to you; but that is merely a coincidence. Fundamentally you are totally unlike Mrs Horsley Downs – totally unlike. Of course it is quite natural that anyone with your sensitive nature should be hurt by – by the mere suggestion that a character in a novel of this description should be based upon your unusual personality, but believe me you are labouring under a misconception, believe me the resemblances are mere chance resemblances, the differences are fundamental. I would even go so far as to say –'

'Nonsense,' said Mrs Featherstone Hogg, unmoved by this peroration. 'The thing is a libel. It's not only a libel upon me, it's a libel upon the whole of Silverstream. I've got the whole of Silverstream behind me – they'll all bring actions –'

'I *very* much doubt it,' said Mr Spark. 'The case would serve no good purpose and would bring a great deal of unpleasant ridicule upon the plaintiffs.'

At this stage in the proceedings, Mrs Featherstone Hogg completely lost her temper. (In her defence be it said that she had been having a very trying time for the last ten days. *Disturber of the Peace* had disturbed her peace most thoroughly. The foundations of her social position in Silverstream were shaking, and her social position in Silverstream was of supreme importance to Mrs Featherstone Hogg.) She raged and stormed at Mr Spark and Edwin, she pointed out that the book was a disgusting book, it had ridiculed her, she wanted an abject apology and large damages. She explained, somewhat incoherently, that the character of Mrs Horsley Downs was a horrible character and not in the least like her, but that it was obviously intended for her, because it was exactly like her, and that therefore it was a libel and as such ought to be punished to the utmost rigour of the law. She said the same thing a dozen times in different words, but always loudly, until Mr Spark thought his head would burst. Her language became more picturesque and less polite every moment. Mr Spark began to wonder whether she really had been in the chorus when Mr Featherstone Hogg had been so misled as to marry her and elevate her to a higher sphere of life.

When, at last, she paused for breath, Mr Spark merely shook his head and said that it was no use.

'You mean you refuse to help us?' asked Mrs Featherstone Hogg, incredulously.

'I do,' replied Mr Spark with spirit. The Featherstone Hoggs were wealthy clients, and he could ill afford to lose them, but there were limits to his endurance, and he had reached the limits now.

'We shall go elsewhere then,' announced Mrs Featherstone Hogg, rising, and gathering up her sables with the air of a tragedy queen.

Mr Featherstone Hogg had contributed absolutely nothing to the conversation – if conversation it could be called. He had remained in the background twiddling his thumbs and wishing from the bottom of his heart that he had stayed at home. But now that the interview was at an end and Agatha had said all that she wanted to say he leant forward a little and cleared his throat.

'Did you speak, Edwin?' enquired his wife, turning upon him with a quelling glance.

'No, but I'm going to,' replied the worm, turning at last. He too had read *Disturber of the Peace* and the seeds of rebellion had been planted in his heart by that amazing publication. The seeds had taken some time to germinate, for Edwin's heart was poor soil in which to grow rebellion, but they were beginning to grow now.

'I intend to take Mr Spark's advice,' said Mr Featherstone Hogg, blinking a little nervously.

'*You* intend to.'

'Yes, Agatha. I intend to take Mr Spark's advice. I have no money to throw away upon a hopeless lawsuit. I have no wish to look ridiculous –'

'You look ridiculous already,' snapped Agatha.

Mr Featherstone Hogg took no notice of this un-ladylike remark. He found his hat and gloves and shook hands with Mr Spark.

'I may be calling upon you in a few days to make some alterations in my Will,' said Mr Featherstone Hogg in very distinct and somewhat significant tones.

'Any time that suits you,' the lawyer replied effusively.

'I may come – or again I may not. It all depends upon circumstances,' said Mr Featherstone Hogg.

'Just as you please – my time is at your disposal,' said Mr Spark. 'You might like to have a look over your Will with me. Perhaps there are some minor points you would like to revise.'

'It is a major alteration I have in mind,' said Mr Featherstone Hogg firmly.

Mr Spark accompanied the couple to the door with admirable courtesy. He stood upon the step, bowing until the Daimler had borne them away. Then he went back to his sanctum, and shut the door carefully, and laughed and laughed and laughed.

CHAPTER THIRTEEN

COLONEL WEATHERHEAD AND MRS BOLD

The first thing that Mrs Featherstone Hogg did on her return to Silverstream was to ring up Colonel Weatherhead. Simmons answered the telephone and informed her that the Colonel was out.

'When will he be back?' enquired Mrs Featherstone Hogg.

'I don't know at all, ma'am.'

'Where has he gone? Has he gone to London?'

'Oh no, ma'am – I think he's over at Mrs Bold's.'

Mrs Featherstone Hogg rang off. It was most annoying, the man was never in when she wanted him. She supposed that Colonel Weatherhead had gone to talk it all over with Dorothea Bold. It seemed obvious, but, wasn't it a trifle – well – indelicate? In *Disturber of the Peace* Major Waterfoot had proposed to Mrs Mildmay – some people said he had seduced her – surely that put their prototypes in a very awkward position. Most people would have wanted to avoid each other, at any rate, until the first strangeness of the position wore off. Still, some people were queer, not everybody had such sensitive feelings about matters of this kind as *she* had, and anyhow it was their own affair, if they liked to talk it over with each other it did not affect Mrs Featherstone Hogg. She decided to go down to Dorothea's and meet the Colonel there, they could all talk it over together and decide what was to be done.

She ordered the car to come round directly after lunch. It had just brought her down from London and the chauffeur had started to clean it, but that did not disturb Mrs Featherstone Hogg in the least. Cars were there to be used; chauffeurs were there to drive you when and where you wanted to be driven. It had started to rain and Mrs Featherstone Hogg's chauffeur was not very pleased about it.

It will be seen that Mrs Featherstone Hogg had by no means abandoned her campaign against John Smith. The action for libel was definitely off, Edwin had been most unreasonable about the whole thing. He had told her – as they drove away from Mr Spark's door – that he did not wish to hear another word upon the subject, and she had bowed to his decision. She was obliged to bow to Edwin's decision because he had been so very queer about his Will. As it stood the Will suited Agatha exactly – it left her everything without any restriction whatever – why alter it then?

Agatha had no wish to lose Edwin, he was, as a rule, quite docile, and very little trouble, he never interfered with her, and he gave her a generous allowance; but we must all die sometime, and Edwin was twenty years older than Agatha, and suffered from a weak heart. It was only reasonable to suppose that he would pass on to a better land before she did. Agatha felt that she could bear the loss more courageously if she had all Edwin's money to comfort her in her bereavement – every penny of it without any stupid restrictions about re-marriage, or anything else –

Mrs Featherstone Hogg thought all this over very carefully and decided that she would say no more about the libel action, it was safer not to. Edwin was not *likely* to do anything very drastic, but he might – he had been quite unlike his usual self ever since the somewhat stormy interview with Mr Spark. The libel action must go, but that was no reason why John Smith should get off scot-free. Something else must be thought of, somehow or other the mystery of the book's authorship must be solved and the man punished.

Before going down in the car to see Dorothea Bold, she rang up Mr Bulmer on the telephone and they had a long conversation about *Disturber of the Peace*. Mr Bulmer told her that he was alone in the house, he had sent Margaret and the children to her people in Devonshire for a long visit. It seemed wiser, said Mr Bulmer. Mrs Featherstone Hogg praised his forethought. Neither of them mentioned why it was wiser to banish Margaret from Silverstream at the moment, but both knew that it was because Mr Bulmer did not want his wife to read *Disturber of the Peace*, nor to hear it discussed by the inhabitants of Silverstream. Mrs Featherstone Hogg wished that she could have banished Edwin before he had been contaminated by the book. She heaved a sigh.

'What are you doing about it?' enquired Mr Bulmer. 'Are you going to sue them for libel?'

Mrs Featherstone Hogg replied that it was all off – the laws of England were in such a decadent condition – they must take the law into their own hands. Did Mr Bulmer think it would be a good plan to hold a Meeting in Mrs Featherstone Hogg's drawing-room and invite all the people who were annoyed about *Disturber of the Peace*?

Mr Bulmer thought the plan sound.

Surely between them they would elucidate the mystery of John Smith – suggested Mrs Featherstone Hogg – a clue here and another clue there, put together they would discover John Smith.

Mr Bulmer thought they might.

Mrs Featherstone Hogg said she would let him know what day – she thought perhaps Thursday – it would give them time to collect everybody. Besides it was the half-day in Silverstream so Mrs Goldsmith could come too, she had heard that Mrs Goldsmith was annoyed about *Disturber of the Peace*.

By this time Mr Bulmer was tired of the conversation, he replied briefly that Thursday afternoon would suit him, and rang off.

Mrs Featherstone Hogg got into her car which had been waiting at the door for twenty minutes –

'Mrs Bold's house,' she said laconically.

She was pleased with the idea of the Meeting – it was an inspiration. It had come to her quite suddenly when she was speaking to Mr Bulmer (great inspirations often come quite suddenly and unexpectedly to their fortunate recipients). Surely the combined brains of Silverstream would discover the identity of John Smith. It had become an absolute obsession to Mrs Featherstone Hogg, the thing had got on her nerves, she felt she could not rest until she had found him. Once they knew who it was they could decide what was to be done, everything depended upon who the man was. Whether it was the sort of man who could be terrorised, ostracised, or horse-whipped. At the very least he could be made to apologise and hounded out of Silverstream. In this case the punishment must be made to fit the criminal. Mrs Featherstone Hogg decided that Colonel Weatherhead would be the best person to wield the horse-whip should the horse-whip be necessary. She was a little doubtful as to what horse-whipping really was, but Colonel Weatherhead would know.

Mrs Featherstone Hogg had now reached her destination. The Daimler could not drive into Cosy Neuk because the drive was up. There was a large hole right in the very middle of Dorothea's drive and several men in overalls were standing round, smoking clay pipes and talking about it. One man was in the hole, up to his armpits, he was the only one who was not smoking and talking; he was merely leaning against the edge of the hole listening to the others. Two pick-axes and several large shovels were lying about, or propped against the gate, it had started to rain again, and there was a very disgusting smell –

Mrs Featherstone Hogg took out her handkerchief and sniffed it delicately, it was scented with Rose d'Amour, and it put up a fairly effective barrage against the other and much less pleasant odour, which was coming from the hole in Dorothea's drive.

Mrs Featherstone Hogg looked out at the rain, and decided to send a message to Dorothea by her chauffeur. It was no use plodding through the rain and mud and ruining her shoes unless Dorothea was at home and could see her. She was explaining all this to the chauffeur when suddenly the men standing about the hole were galvanised into activity. They seized pick-axes and spades and tore fiercely at the drive. The man in the hole stopped listening – there was nothing to listen to now of course – and began to throw up spadefuls of mud from the depths of the hole.

Mrs Featherstone Hogg wondered what had happened to induce such sudden industry, and then she saw that Colonel Weatherhead had emerged from the house and was coming down the drive. He was wearing a very dirty Burberry and a tweed cap. He stopped and spoke to the foreman and peered into the hole. Mrs Featherstone Hogg could not hear what he was saying but it looked as if he were giving instructions as to what was to be done. What business was it of Colonel Weatherhead's? It was not his drive. The faulty drain (there was unfortunately no doubt that it was a faulty drain) was not his either – it was Dorothea's. Anyone would have thought that Dorothea might look after her own drains.

Colonel Weatherhead finished talking to the foreman and looked up and saw the car. Mrs Featherstone Hogg beckoned to him through the window. He was not at all pleased when he saw who it was, but there was no escape this time – no handy toolshed to hide in. The Colonel walked over to the car and greeted its occupant with a singular lack of enthusiasm.

'Have you read the book?' asked Mrs Featherstone Hogg eagerly. 'Come into the car for a minute or two – it's so cold with the door open.'

'I'm very wet,' objected the Colonel.

'Never mind that. Come in. I want to speak to you.'

Colonel Weatherhead got in reluctantly, and the door was shut.

'Well, have you read it?' demanded Mrs Featherstone Hogg. 'What do you think of it?'

'Charming,' replied the Colonel. 'Most amusing book I've read for a long time.'

'Charming? Amusing?'

'So true to life,' added the Colonel. 'That soldier feller – Rivers or something – was the dead spit of a feller I used to know in India – ha, ha – couldn't help laughing when I read it. Haven't laughed so much over a book for years.'

'But it's *you*,' cried Mrs Featherstone Hogg in amazement. 'Can't you see that it is yourself, libelled, held up to ridicule; it's a caricature of *you*.'

'Me?'

'Yes of course.' (Good Heavens, how dense the man was!)

'But why should it be me?' enquired Colonel Weatherhead. 'I mean I don't know the feller who wrote it –'

'You may not know who he is, but he knows you all right – can't you see that the book is all about Silverstream – the whole thing is a wicked caricature of Silverstream – an outrageous attack on innocent people.'

'Nonsense,' said the Colonel.

'Didn't you *see* it?' demanded the lady irately.

'No I didn't. Who *are* the people anyway? Who's that Mrs Thingumbob – the woman that the soldier feller gets engaged to?'

'Dorothea Bold, of course,' replied Mrs Featherstone Hogg, scornfully.

Colonel Weatherhead was silent.

'It's the frightful wickedness of it,' said Mrs Featherstone Hogg. 'It's the frightful wickedness of it, that – that makes me so angry. Here we are all living together like a – like a happy family' (this was a good comparison, she thought, she must make a note of it for her speech at the Meeting) – 'and then that horrible man comes along and spoils everything. Nothing will ever be the same again,' she added pathetically, with her mind on Edwin and his rebellion – Edwin who had always been so mild and reasonable but was now asserting himself and making strange and sinister threats about Wills.

Colonel Weatherhead was still silent, he was not a quick thinker, he was wondering whether it could possibly be true. If so it was very queer – very queer indeed. He had done exactly what the book said (or at any rate as near as made no odds). What would Dorothea say when she heard about it? How would it affect his new relationship with that charming and altogether delightful person? Dreadful if she thought that he had proposed to her because he had read it in a book. It would be difficult to explain that the book had nothing to do with it, because, in a way, the book had everything to do with it. Dorothea might be annoyed. It would make them look slightly ridiculous in Silverstream if their union had been foretold in a book. People would say they had lived opposite to each other for four years and couldn't make up their minds to marry each other until they read it in a novel. Not a nice thing for all Silverstream to be saying – not nice at all.

'The man must be found,' Mrs Featherstone Hogg was saying, she had said a lot more – all about herself and Edwin, and how the character of Mrs Horsley Downs was not in the least like her, and that she didn't see how a man she didn't know could possibly have found out all that about her private affairs, and that obviously he didn't know anything about her at all, or he could never have written such an outrageous libel – but Colonel Weatherhead had not been listening. He came to the surface again just in time to hear her saying that the man must be found.

'What man?' asked the Colonel.

'John Smith of course – only his name isn't John Smith.'

'Why?'

'Because he must be somebody in Silverstream, somebody who knows us all – otherwise he couldn't have written about us in his book.'

'Oh I see – well I expect it's that Bulmer man. He writes books, it must be him.'

'I ask you, would he be likely to make his wife run away with Harry Carter?' said Mrs Featherstone Hogg impatiently. 'Would any man be likely to do such a thing?'

'Run away with Harry Carter!' echoed the Colonel.

'Would he be likely to make her do that?' repeated Mrs Featherstone Hogg, getting more and more enraged at the Colonel's stupidity.

'I've often wondered why she didn't run away with somebody,' he said vaguely, 'nice little woman, far too nice for a cantankerous beast like Bulmer –'

'Well, what do you think ought to be done?' she asked trying to bring him back to the point, they would never get on at this rate, and John Smith *must* be found.

'Done?' asked the Colonel.

'Yes, do you think he ought to be horse-whipped?'

'Well, I don't really blame Carter, y'know. She must have been dashed unhappy with that sour-faced husband of hers. It's not like going off with the wife of a brother-officer – not quite so rotten – besides Carter's gone to India with the Fiftieth. I suppose he's taken her with him –'

'What *are* you talking about?' cried Mrs Featherstone Hogg. 'She hasn't run away with him yet –'

'Send Bulmer an anonymous letter, then,' suggested Colonel Weatherhead with sudden brilliant inspiration. 'That'll put a stopper on it.'

'She's not going to run away – at least so far as I know – Mr Bulmer's sent her to Devonshire to spend Christmas with her people –'

'She'll enjoy that.'

'She may or she may not – that's scarcely the point. We're not talking about the Bulmers at all.'

'Oh – I thought we were,' said the bewildered Colonel. 'I thought you said Mrs Bulmer had run away with Harry Carter.'

'It's only in the book – it's all in the book – didn't you read it?' asked Mrs Featherstone Hogg angrily. She felt she would like to shake the man, he was so hopelessly dense. She was not far off shaking him if the truth were told.

'Good Lord!' said Colonel Weatherhead. He tried to remember the book in detail, but Dorothea had swamped his mind and the book – read through rapidly – had faded into an indistinct blur. He could remember quite distinctly his own reaction to it, and the love scene in Mrs Mildmay's garden, but not much else.

'Don't you think John Smith ought to be horse-whipped?' said Mrs Featherstone Hogg, savagely.

'What's the feller done?'

'He wrote it – he's the author of it,' said Mrs Featherstone Hogg, trying very hard not to lose her temper completely. It was so important to keep on friendly terms with Colonel Weatherhead, because he was the only man who could possibly be visualised horse-whipping John Smith. And John Smith must be horse-whipped, she was convinced of that now. He had caused such a lot of trouble and worry. If it had not been for John Smith, Mrs Featherstone Hogg would have been sitting at home over a nice fire reading or sewing comfortably, instead of boxed up in a draughty car, with the rain pattering on the roof, trying to talk to an imbecile. John Smith must certainly be horse-whipped and the Colonel was the man to do it, therefore the Colonel must be won over; his stupidity must be tolerated with superhuman patience, he must be wheedled, flattered, cajoled, infuriated, and so roused to action.

'Listen to me,' said Mrs Featherstone Hogg, laying her hand upon the Colonel's arm, 'you had better read the book again, carefully, and then we can talk it all over quietly together, and decide what is to be done. I am having a Meeting at my house on Thursday at half-past three and tea afterwards. Tell Dorothea I shall expect her too. I will go round in the car and invite everybody in Silverstream – everybody must come.'

'All right,' said the Colonel. He realised that the interview was over and he was glad. He wanted to get away and arrange his thoughts. (He did not care a bit whether Mrs Featherstone Hogg found John Smith, or whether that gentleman received the punishment she so vehemently desired to mete out to him: he only cared for the possible effects which these extraordinary disclosures might have upon Dorothea and himself.) Besides it was bad for his rheumatism to sit in a cold car with wet shoes on, and the legs of his trousers all damp and clammy from the drips off his waterproof –

He said 'Goodbye' to Mrs Featherstone Hogg, stepped out of the car with alacrity, and went home to have a bath and change his clothes. Dorothea was coming to dinner with him.

* * *

So far nobody knew of their engagement. They had decided to keep it a secret, but they would not be able to keep it a secret for long. The servants would soon guess what was afoot, and, in a few days, the news would be all over Silverstream. And now the whole thing was complicated by that book, if what Mrs Featherstone Hogg said was true. Colonel Weatherhead thought about it in his bath and all the time he was dressing.

He came down to find that Dorothea had arrived and was standing on tiptoe in front of the drawing-room mantelpiece arranging her hair in the mirror. There was something very sweet and feminine about her as she patted her curls into shape. He crept in very quietly and kissed her on the tip of her ear – it was very neatly done, Major Waterfoot himself could not have done it better –

Dorothea screamed, and blushed, and told him he was a wicked man – positively wicked. 'Supposing Simmons had seen you,' she pointed out, 'what *would* he have thought?'

'Simmons never thinks,' replied Colonel Weatherhead. 'He leaves all the thinking to his wife. Jolly good idea too,' added the Colonel chuckling.

'Now, now!' threatened Dorothea.

They were very circumspect during dinner, and Simmons saw nothing that he shouldn't have seen. They discussed Dorothea's drains, and from thence wandered on by some strange bypath to chrysanthemums. Dorothea's were all frosted, but the Colonel still had a few which he had protected from the night-frosts with elaborately rigged sacking.

'Mrs Carter still has some,' Dorothea said. 'I was having tea with her the other day and such a queer thing happened. Mrs Featherstone Hogg burst in; she was in a frightful rage about a book – she practically threw it at us and said it was filth and that it was all about *us*.'

'Did you read it?' enquired the Colonel anxiously.

'No. She left it for Mrs Carter to read, but I must get hold of it. I shall ask for it at the library.'

'Don't,' said Colonel Weatherhead, taking her hand,

which lay conveniently near him on the table. 'Don't read it, Dorothea. Why should you waste your time and – and soil your beautiful mind reading filth?'

They gazed into each other's eyes adoringly, then with a sigh Dorothea withdrew her hand – Simmons was coming in with the pudding.

'I rather wondered what the book said about me,' said Dorothea, returning to the subject which intrigued her somewhat. 'You wouldn't think there was much material for a book in a place like Silverstream. Mrs Featherstone Hogg was really very queer about it, she told Mrs Carter that she wore a wig – that Mrs Carter wore a wig, I mean – I've always thought her hair looked too good to be true. Mrs Carter didn't like it.'

Colonel Weatherhead was trying to make up his mind whether to make a clean breast of the whole thing, or whether to pretend that he knew nothing about it. His inclinations veered to the latter course – it was much the easier – but he was rather afraid that Dorothea might hear Mrs Featherstone Hogg's account of it and realise that he had not been quite open with her. That would be disastrous. There was a third course open to him, the course of telling Dorothea a little, and making light of it. This course was fraught with difficulties, but, on the whole, it seemed best.

'Mrs Featherstone Hogg is absolutely crazy about that wretched book,' said Colonel Weatherhead, trying to laugh convincingly. 'She came down here this afternoon and made me sit in her car with her, and she talked at me until I didn't know whether I was standing on my head or my heels. What an awful woman she is!'

'Did you read the book?' enquired Dorothea.

'I glanced through it,' replied the Colonel casually. 'She sent it to me, and then kept on ringing me up and asking what I thought of it. I saw nothing very much in it – quite an ordinary novel, I thought.'

'*Am* I in it?'

'There was nobody the least like you in the book. Nobody half so pretty and charming, and sweet, and dainty,' said the Colonel gallantly (Simmons had brought their coffee and departed for good, so it was quite safe).

Dorothea laughed roguishly.

The Colonel leaned over and kissed her hand.

They smiled into each other's eyes.

'We've wasted years,' said Colonel Weatherhead, with a sigh. 'Years, and years, and years. One, two, three, four,' he added, telling them over on Dorothea's fingers.

Dorothea did not know the correct answer to this. Privately she thought that Robert was right, but it was his fault that the years had been wasted – not hers – so she said nothing.

The Colonel was not talking at random when he said they had wasted years, he had an idea at the back of his mind, but he didn't know how to broach it to his beloved. He could not see how to go on. Perhaps it would be better to approach the subject from a different angle.

'Those drains of yours have a horrible smell,' he said thoughtfully.

Dorothea withdrew her hand (it will be remembered that he had been counting her fingers), she was a little hurt at the aspersion on her drains, it was a frightful come-down from wasted years to drains.

'Everybody's drains smell when they're blocked,' said Dorothea shortly.

'I know, I know,' he said hastily. 'But what I mean is it's not healthy for you – it would be dreadful if you got ill or anything. I've been thinking it over carefully while we've been talking. Your drains are blocked; the weather is ghastly (it does nothing but rain); and I've finished with my Bishop, for this year – I hope I've finished the brute for good, but I can't be certain of that, of course, until next spring – there's nothing to keep us here as far as I can see, absolutely nothing.'

'Nothing to keep us here?' enquired Dorothea who was considerably puzzled by the connection between the weather and her drains and the Colonel's Bishop. Who was the Colonel's Bishop? Was he some troublesome relative who required consideration – an older brother perhaps, or possibly an uncle? She had never heard Robert say that he had a brother who was a Bishop.

'Dorothea,' said the Colonel, who had beaten about the bush to no purpose and was tired of the game, 'Dorothea, I want to marry you.'

Dorothea was surprised. She had already promised to marry Colonel Weatherhead (or Robert as she now called him). She had thought – with good reason – that the matter was decided.

'I know you do, Robert,' she said feebly.

'But I want to marry you now, at once,' he told her urgently. 'Don't you see how everything points to our getting married immediately? The weather, my Bishop, your drains, *everything*. We'll go up to town on Monday and get married quietly, without any fuss, and go off to Monte Carlo for Christmas. Say you will, Dorothea darling.'

'Robert!' she exclaimed in amazement.

'Why not?' he enquired in wheedling tones. 'There's nothing to stop us, and everything to – to – you know what I mean, I can't think of the word – it's absolutely the hand of Providence pointing. The weather is as foul as your drains, and my Bishop is done for –'

'Who is your Bishop?' interrupted Dorothea somewhat irritably for such a good-natured woman. '*Who on earth is your Bishop?* You've been talking about him for ages, and I don't see what he has got to do with our getting married –'

Colonel Weatherhead roared with laughter.

'Good Heavens! I thought everyone in Silverstream had heard about my Bishop – I can't be such a garrulous old bore after all – have I never told you about my struggles with the brute every autumn?'

'Never,' said Dorothea primly, 'and I really do not think you should speak of a Bishop in that way, Robert dear. He may be very trying at times – I am sure he is – but after all we must remember that he is consecrated – consecrated with oil,' said Dorothea vaguely, 'and therefore –'

'It's a weed,' gasped the Colonel between his spasms of laughter. 'Bishop's weed – it grows in my hedge – it has roots like an octopus –'

Dorothea did not join in his mirth. How was she to know that it was a weed he was talking about? She saw nothing very funny in the misunderstanding.

Colonel Weatherhead took out a large white silk handkerchief and mopped his eyes. When the film of moisture was removed he was horrified to find that his ladylove was offended. She was sitting up very straight in her chair gazing before her at the picture of the Colonel's grandfather, in oils, which hung upon the dining-room wall.

'Never mind the stupid old weed,' he said hastily. 'It's just one of my silly jokes – damn silly joke, I know. Somehow I always enjoy my fight with the Bishop's weed. It's the only fight I'm fit for now, and the old soldier enjoys a fight. Let's go into the drawing-room, shall we?'

Dorothea was immediately appeased. They went into the drawing-room arm in arm. Simmons had built up the fire to an alarming height – he had been brought up in the Army, of course, where coal is free – Dorothea thought it was rather extravagant but it was certainly very cosy on a cold night. They toasted their toes and talked about themselves and were very happy.

The Colonel walked home with his guest. It was still raining and everything was dripping wet – they nearly fell into the hole in Dorothea's drive which had escaped their memory for the time being.

'What about Monday?' whispered the Colonel.

'Not *Monday*,' she pleaded.

'Why not Monday? What's the matter with Monday?' he demanded boldly.

'Too soon. How can I get my clothes ready?'

'We'll stop in Paris and get clothes,' he told her with diabolical cunning. 'Listen, Dorothea. We don't want a lot of fuss and bother in Silverstream. Let's give them the slip. Just vanish quietly and tell them nothing about it until it's all over. We'll send them postcards from Paris or Monte, then they'll have time to talk themselves out before we get home. What do you say?'

Dorothea wanted fuss as little as he did. She could almost hear the gossips saying, 'Well, it's taken her four years. I wonder how she managed to hook him in the end. He must be in his dotage, I suppose.' That is what they would *all* say when they heard of her engagement, and she would know they were thinking it when they offered her their congratulations.

'Well,' she said, wavering.

'You will!' he jubilated. 'Hurrah!'

He really was quite like a boy, and it was much more exciting, being engaged to him, than she had expected. Fancy his planning all that about Monte Carlo for Christmas – you would never think him capable of such a dashing idea. It was rather a nice idea too, it would be lovely to get away from Silverstream for a bit and bask in the sun. Robert was really a dear, she loved him. She had wanted him for years and she had almost despaired. He had always been friendly and neighbourly, ready to help and advise her in any emergency that required male help and advice – when her tree fell, for instance, it was Colonel Weatherhead who arranged with the man to come and cut it up for her – but he had never shown the slightest signs of wanting to marry her until last night. What had suddenly wakened him up? Dorothea wondered, as she shut and bolted the front door and went slowly and thoughtfully up the stairs to bed.

She lighted the gas fire in her bedroom and thought about it all, sitting in a low chair and warming her knees the while. There was nobody to consult about her marriage, she was independent, her money was her own. She had two sisters, both married. One lived in London and the other in a country parsonage. They would be surprised, of course – perhaps even rather amused, for they were both younger than herself and both very much married matrons – but they would be quite nice about it, she knew. I can stay with Alice while Robert arranges about the wedding, she thought. Alice was always quite pleased to give her house-room for a few days when she wanted it.

Dorothea had decided to humour Robert's boyish whim, there was no reason against it. I wonder how old he is – she thought – perhaps nearly sixty, but he doesn't look it, and anyhow it doesn't matter. I'm not as young as I was, and Robert's a dear. The drawing-room at The Bridge House is rather dull – she thought – but I could brighten it up with some of my own things. Perhaps Robert would throw out a bow-window in the drawing-room, that would make a lot of difference.

After a little she got up and began to pull out drawers and burrow into tissue paper. I shan't take much – she thought – it will be fun getting things in Paris – pretty things. Fancy him suggesting that!

Dorothea paused for a moment with a silk scarf in her hands. It almost looked as if – as if he knew a good deal about women. He was so glib about it. Had he taken other women to Paris to choose clothes? Well, I can't help that – she told herself sharply – what does it matter anyhow? Get on with the job, Dorothea.

She got on with it.

CHAPTER FOURTEEN

SUNDAY AND MONDAY

The next day was Sunday. The newly-engaged couple had decided to go to church separately, to sit in their separate pews and to behave as if nothing had happened. It was rather fun to deceive Silverstream, and Silverstream would be all the more surprised when it received its postcards from Paris.

Dorothea tripped along sedately – it was a lovely morning, the clouds had all vanished and the sun was shining brightly through the bare trees – she did not know whether Robert was ahead of her, or behind. (Her clocks were all different, clocks are one of those mysterious things that never go so well in a woman's house, clocks need a man to keep them in proper subjection.) First she thought that Robert must be ahead of her, and hurried on, and then she was sure he was behind her, and dawdled.

Barbara Buncle was just coming out of her gate when Dorothea passed, they walked along together talking about the sunshine and how nice and warm it was for December. Dorothea liked Barbara, she felt sorry that Barbara's clothes were so appalling. Probably Barbara was very badly off, but even so she might have done better than that. The truth was she looked less peculiar in her everyday garments because they were tweeds and jerseys – you couldn't go far wrong with tweeds and jerseys. On Sundays poor Barbara looked a perfect sight, her hat was frightful.

'Why don't you get a new hat, Barbara?' she said suddenly.

'Well, I did think of it, but this one is still quite good,' replied Barbara.

'Give it to Dorcas and buy another,' suggested Dorothea, daringly.

'Perhaps I will,' said Barbara, and why shouldn't I? she thought – why shouldn't I have some nice clothes now that I can afford it? The only bother is I never seem to be able to get nice ones. I always feel an absolute guy in new clothes. How nice Dorothea looks!

'How nice you look, Dorothea!' she said.

'Do I?'

'Yes. You always look nice, of course, but today you look even nicer than usual.'

'You *lamb*!' said Dorothea.

Colonel Weatherhead passed them, and bowed gravely.

'A pleasant morning after the rain, Mrs Bold,' he remarked as he went by.

Dorothea laughed inwardly – he was a naughty boy! Barbara collected the phrase for her new novel. 'A pleasant morning after the rain,' was exactly what Major Waterfoot would have said. Not to Mrs Mildmay, of course, for they were married now and it was not a remark that a man was likely to make to his wife, but Major Waterfoot could say it to somebody else – it was too good to waste.

The new novel had started, and it was proving uphill work. Inspiration had not visited Barbara, she was toiling at it nobly, if somewhat hopelessly. It will never be as good as *Disturber of the Peace*, she thought.

The three people with their secret thoughts – so secret and so diverse – entered St Monica's together. Mrs Carter and Sally were close behind. Mrs Greensleeves was already in her pew. Miss King and Angela Pretty were hurrying across the field-path followed by Mrs Goldsmith and her family. The Bulmers were there, and the Snowdons, and the Featherstone Hoggs, even the two young men from Mrs Dick's had come to church this morning. The sunshine after the rain had lured them all out. Of all our Silverstream friends only the Walkers were absent. The doctor scarcely ever went to church, and Sarah had stayed at home because the twins had a feverish cold.

Mrs Carter sat in the same pew as Barbara Buncle. Usually they sat one at either end of the pew with four vacant seats between them, but today Sally was there to fill the vacancy. Barbara could not help noticing that Sally was a little restless during the service, she seemed doubtful when to stand up, and when to kneel down. She fluttered the leaves of her prayer-book in the vain endeavour to find her place. Sally doesn't go to church often – Barbara decided.

During the sermon a small piece of paper was pushed into Barbara's hand. 'I'm coming to tea with you today,' was written on it. Barbara looked at her, and nodded and smiled, she felt pleased and excited at the idea of Sally coming to tea – it was nice that Sally wanted to come. Perhaps

Sally would talk about *Disturber of the Peace*, she liked hearing Sally talk about it. Mrs Featherstone Hogg was having a meeting at her house on Thursday to talk about it, and she had asked Barbara to go. 'There will be tea afterwards,' Mrs Featherstone Hogg had said. Barbara did not want to go to the meeting and hear them discussing *Disturber of the Peace*. She knew exactly what they would say about it. The tea was no inducement to those who knew Mrs Featherstone Hogg's teas. Barbara had endured many teas at The Riggs, so she knew exactly what to expect – shallow cups with grey-looking lukewarm liquid and a sandwich containing banana paste or gentleman's relish, you didn't know which it was going to be until you bit into it. Still, it would look funny if I didn't go – Barbara thought.

She tried to fix her mind on the sermon. It was all about loving your neighbour, and how you must seek out the good in people and only see the good. Mr Hathaway said that was the way to make people good – by refusing to see the evil. Barbara wondered if this were true, and, if so, how deep it went. If you refused to see the evil in a murderer, did that cure him? Doubtful. Mr Hathaway had passed on to the subject of money. Money was the root of all evil. St Francis had no money, he had nothing, and he was superlatively good. People had too much money nowadays – Mr Hathaway said – our lives should be simplified, a man needed very little in this world, it was in the next world that a man should lay up treasure. 'Sell that thou hast, and give to the poor,' said Mr Hathaway. 'And now –'

Barbara stood up, wondering whether Mr Hathaway

had done that, it was said in the village that he had lots of money.

Vivian Greensleeves did not listen much to the sermon, she had other things to think of. She had made considerable progress with the Vicar since that first luncheon party and the supper that followed. He bored her frightfully but that could not be helped, the main thing was that he had money. Vivian needed money more and more. The shops in Silver-stream were beginning to get impatient. Her dressmaker in London had sent her a lawyer's letter demanding instant payment of her account. It was all so unjust – thought Vivian – if she had had money she would have paid her bills gladly, but she couldn't give the wretches money when she had none to give them. Ernest Hathaway was her only hope, she must just make the best of him, and once they were married she need not listen to his dull and stupid dissertations any more.

After the service Vivian waited for the Vicar in the church-yard and they walked up the hill together. Ernest Hathaway had drifted into the habit of lunching with Vivian on Sundays. It was now an understood thing that she should wait for him after Matins and that they should walk up the hill to Mon Repos together.

Today they talked about some books which Mr Hathaway had lent Mrs Greensleeves to read. They were incredibly dull books, but Vivian had actually read them – or partially read them – so as to have some intelligent questions all ready to ask him when they met. She had decided that her campaign must be speeded up – Mr Hathaway admired her, and liked her, she knew. It was almost time he proposed. Today she would ask him to call her Vivian. He would be quite pleased to call her Vivian, she thought, and she was right. Ernest was quite ready to call her Vivian – he asked her to call him Ernest, and discoursed for some minutes about the religious significance of Christian names. Vivian didn't care a jot for their religious significance, but she listened meekly. After all, whatever significance he attached to her Christian name, it was a step in the right direction to call her by it.

Ernest called her by it several times with a great deal of pleasure. He was very proud of this sheep which he had shepherded so energetically into the fold. He thought she was beautiful, and, now that she had repented of her sins and remedied her omissions, she was also good. What more could any man want than a good and beautiful wife?

* * *

Sally arrived at Tanglewood Cottage for tea as arranged. Barbara had nothing to give her for tea, she had not expected a guest, and, being Sunday, she could not rush out and buy buns from Mrs Goldsmith as she would most certainly have done had the day been an ordinary day. But there was a nice fire and they made hot-buttered toast and scorched their faces and were thoroughly happy.

'I've been thinking of getting a new hat,' said Barbara suddenly.

Sally pricked up her ears. 'How exciting!' she exclaimed, and, visualising the hat which had sat next to her in church that morning, she added fervently, 'Yes, you really should.'

‘I’m so bad at choosing hats,’ sighed Barbara. ‘That’s the worst of it. I never seem to get one that really suits me, and Miss Bonnar has such a poor selection.’

‘My dear – you would never buy a hat at Miss Bonnar’s!’ cried the horror-stricken Sally.

‘But I always go to Miss Bonnar –’

‘Nonsense, you must go to town of course. Go to Virginia’s.’

‘Where’s that?’ enquired Barbara with interest.

‘She’s a friend of mine,’ Sally confided. ‘She has a little shop for hats and frocks in Kensington High Street. I’ll write a note to her, if you like, and tell her not to rook you.’

‘Will you really?’

‘Rather. It will be doing her a good turn too. And really she’s a frightfully decent sort, and frightfully clever at knowing exactly what will suit you.’

‘I’ll go tomorrow,’ Barbara said dashingly. ‘And I’ll get some really nice clothes as well as a hat.’ Why shouldn’t she? The hundred pounds in the bank seemed every reason why she should.

‘Have your hair waved first,’ advised Sally as she went away regretfully, at seven o’clock. ‘But don’t let them cut it off whatever you do, it wouldn’t suit you at all, but they’re sure to want to do it.’ She came back from the gate to add, ‘Give my love to Virginia and tell her I’m miserable.’

Thus it fell out that Barbara and Dorothea Bold were both passengers in the 10.30 train to London on Monday morning. (Colonel Weatherhead had gone up by the 8.15 to transact some important business and to make enquiries about a Special Licence.)

Barbara hailed Dorothea cheerfully and they selected an empty third-class carriage and bestowed themselves therein.

'I'm going to stay with Alice for a day or two,' said Dorothea truthfully – it seemed better to forestall any questions with an appearance of absolute frankness.

'How nice!' said Barbara. 'I'm only going up for the day. I'm going to have my hair waved, I think.'

'Oh do,' cried Dorothea. 'Go to my woman – she's simply marvellous.'

Barbara noted the address and thought how nice people were. It was all being made so easy for her. First Sally and now Dorothea had flown to her rescue. They talked in a friendly desultory sort of fashion all the way to town and parted at the station – Dorothea to go off to her sister's, in a taxi, with her luggage, and Barbara to board a bus which her friend assured her would land her quite near the marvellous woman who would transform her lank locks into ravishing waves.

The ravishing waves took some time to materialise. It was an amazing experience, Barbara decided, and she was not quite sure that she liked the result. Her old hat certainly looked most peculiar perched on the top of her undulating coiffure. However, she paid her money without a murmur and marched out of the shop – she was nearly sure that the girl at the desk was giggling at her appearance.

She lunched frugally at a Corner Shop and then set out to look for Virginia. 'A little yellow shop,' Sally had said, 'with one small hat in the window and the name above the door in black letters.' It was difficult to find, because it was really so very small and unassuming, but Barbara found it at last wedged in between a huge drapery establishment and a flourishing flower shop. She pushed the door open and went in.

The little shop was empty save for a few fragile-looking gilt chairs and long mirrors which showed Barbara her own form at several distressing angles. No wonder that girl laughed, thought Barbara disconsolately, I look an absolute freak with my hair like this. I wonder if there's anything on earth that would straighten out a permanent wave. I don't suppose there *is* anything short of cutting it all off at the roots.

These desperate reflections were cut short by the appearance of a young woman gowned in black, with a supercilious expression who offered Barbara a gilt chair and enquired what she could do for 'Moddam'. Barbara was too terrified to speak, she merely handed over the letter from Sally and waited the result.

'Oh I see,' said the young woman in patronising tones. 'A letter for Moddam. Kindly wait for a few moments until I find out if she is disengaged.'

Barbara had not long to wait, she only just had time to seize her hat with both hands and pull it down on to her hair before Virginia herself appeared with Sally's letter in her hand. She was rather like Sally – Barbara thought – only taller, and dark instead of fair.

'How nice of Sally to send you to me,' she said in a friendly manner. 'Do come in here, won't you?'

Barbara was quite ready to go anywhere, she found herself being ushered into a large room at the back of the shop – a large square room hung with coats and hats and frocks of every shape and hue.

'Now we can talk,' said Virginia. 'Tell me all about Sally. She says she's miserable, is she?'

'She says she is,' said Barbara, blinking a little. 'But I really don't think she is *very*.'

'Because if she is, something will have to be done about it,' said Virginia firmly. 'We can't have Sally being miserable, you know. I wanted her to come in with me when Colonel Carter went to India without her, but the doctor said she would be better in the country.'

'Milk and sunshine,' suggested Barbara.

'Yes, that was the idea,' replied Virginia. 'But milk and sunshine are no good if you're miserable. You must let me know if you think she'd be better here. You live near her, don't you?'

'Next door,' Barbara said.

'Sally's a dear, isn't she?'

They discussed Sally for several minutes.

'And now,' said Virginia at last, 'you want some things, don't you? Sally says I'm to choose for you. Take off your hat.'

Barbara removed it thankfully, once more it had slid up and was perched on the top of her head.

Virginia stared at her with narrowed eyes. 'Bottle green with your nice complexion,' she decided, 'or that new shade of wine – let's see –' and she dived into various cupboards.

They spent three crowded hours together in the large square room. Virginia was most exacting, she flung dresses on to Barbara and tore them off again. 'It's not your style at all,' she told Barbara when the latter expressed a preference for a brown crêpe-de-chine with a straight bodice and flared skirt. 'Sally would kill me if I let you have it. Just wait a moment till I find what I am looking for,' and she burrowed into the cupboard again.

Barbara tried on coats and jumpers and frocks and hats until her newly-waved hair was like a wind-blown haystack.

'I'm so sorry about your hair,' Virginia said. 'It's awful of me to rumple you up like this, but we *must* get the right thing. You must wet it and set it in waves when you go to bed – I'll give you a net.'

When at last Barbara emerged from the shop she felt somewhat dizzy, and tremendously excited – she had never known until now that clothes could be exciting. There were a few alterations to be made, but Virginia had promised to send off the things on Thursday. She would get them on Friday morning. Barbara had spent nearly fifty pounds but she had got her money's worth and she knew it. There was a bottle-green coat with a fur collar and a hat to match, and a jumper suit to go with it; and there were two 'little frocks' and an evening gown – and there were slips and stockings and shoes to match.

CHAPTER FIFTEEN

MORE ABOUT MONDAY

Barbara little knew that, while she was enjoying herself in London and buying a complete set of new clothes under the expert advice of Virginia, *Disturber of the Peace* was having a busy day in Silverstream, but such indeed was the case. It was spreading rapidly like the desperate disease to which Miss King had compared it. Mrs Featherstone Hogg was its most valuable publicity agent, she went round in her car distributing invitations to her drawing-room meeting and copies of *Disturber of the Peace* to all those who had not read it. She did not realise that John Smith obtained royalties upon every copy of this book that was sold, or she would have confined her expenditure upon the book to narrower limits. It would have distressed her exceedingly to think that she was putting money into the pocket of the detestable John Smith.

Mrs Featherstone Hogg's drawing-room meeting was to be representative. It was not to be confined to any one class of person. She would throw open her drawing-room to everyone in Silverstream who was mentioned in *Disturber of the Peace* – it was a noble gesture.

She asked Mrs Goldsmith, and one of her daughters, and she asked Mrs Dick and two of her paying guests, and she asked the military people who were merely mentioned in passing. She even asked the old gravedigger from St Monica's who had been terrified (so said *Disturber of the Peace*) by the sight of Mrs Nevis (or Snowdon) arising from her grave to attend the dinner party given by her family. Unfortunately Mr Durnet was frightfully hard of hearing, and they could not make him understand what it was all about, but his daughter promised to have him all ready and send him up to The Riggs on Thursday at three-thirty.

The Snowdons had received their invitation on Sunday and had spent Sunday evening reading *Disturber of the Peace*. Nobody knows what they said about it in the privacy of their home – they said very little outside – but Miss Isabella, who was of a nervous temperament, awoke screaming in the middle of the night and declared – when her adoring relatives appeared in her bedroom in *déshabillé* – that her mother had come back from the dead.

'That's impossible, Isabella,' said Mr Snowdon with unwonted sternness.

'It may be impossible but it is true all the same,' said Isabella tearfully. 'She was standing there at the end of my bed, just where you are standing. And she called me "Izzy". You know how I hated it when she called me Izzy.'

The cook had now appeared upon the scene with her hair in curl-papers and her eyes starting out of her head.

'It's gallstones, that's what it is,' she announced, 'my married sister was taken just the same and she had four. They gave them to her at the hospital in a bag.'

It was some time before Miss Olivia could persuade her that Miss Isabella was in no pain, and induce her to return to bed. Meanwhile Mr Snowdon was endeavouring, without much success, to soothe his younger daughter, by assuring her that she had been the victim of a nightmare.

'But I saw her distinctly,' Isabella declared, 'I was awake at the time. I know I was.'

'You couldn't have been.'

'I was, I was,' cried Isabella hysterically.

Peace was ultimately restored by the administration of two aspirin tablets, and Mr Snowdon and Olivia covered the sufferer with her disarranged bedclothes and tiptoed softly from the room. They discussed the whole matter in whispers on the landing. Olivia thought that Dr Walker should be summoned, but her father disagreed. It was inadvisable to reveal family secrets to outsiders if it could be avoided. They must think of other means of laying the spectre which had disturbed dear Isabella's rest.

'What other means?' demanded Olivia, in an urgent whisper. 'You know how sensitive the poor darling is. Once she gets an idea like that into her head –'

Mr Snowdon shivered – not entirely because he was cold – he was remembering other occasions when ideas became fixed in dear Isabella's head and produced nightmares. He felt he was too old now to go through all that sort of thing again. When you grew older you required refreshing sleep during the night if you were to be any use at your office during the day.

'What about Chemical Food?' he suggested.

Olivia was afraid that Chemical Food would be inadequate.

Mr Snowdon sighed and agreed that Olivia might be right, they must think of something else.

They went back to bed.

* * *

Mrs Greensleeves was another to whom *Disturber of the Peace* brought unrest. She met Mrs Featherstone Hogg in the butcher's on Monday morning.

'I was just coming to see you,' said Mrs Featherstone Hogg, with unwonted friendliness – hitherto she had treated Vivian with contempt and had scarcely deigned to see her when they met – 'I want you to come to my drawing-room meeting on Thursday afternoon. You will come, won't you?'

'What's it about?' asked Vivian suspiciously. 'Is it Foreign Missions or something?'

'It's about *Disturber of the Peace*,' replied Mrs Featherstone Hogg.

'*Disturber of the Peace*,' echoed Vivian, 'what on earth is that?'

Mrs Featherstone Hogg was amazed. 'Do you mean to say you haven't read that dreadful book?' she demanded incredulously. 'I thought everyone knew about it. You must read it at once, it's the wickedest book that has ever been written.'

She had no time to say any more, for she was late for lunch already, but she had said quite enough to arouse Vivian's interest to boiling point. Vivian went into Miss Renton's there and then, and bought a copy of the book to take home with her. Miss Renton was doing a tremendous trade in John

Smith's novel, she had had to order a special consignment of copies from London and even these were nearly exhausted. Everybody in Silverstream wanted to read *Disturber of the Peace*, and everybody wanted to read it at once. The library copy was booked for weeks ahead by those who were poor or too thrifty to pay seven and sixpence for a copy of their own.

Vivian put the copy of *Disturber of the Peace* under her arm and walked home quickly. It had started to rain again – she put up her umbrella and nearly bumped into Dr Walker, who was hastening home also.

'Isn't this weather awful?' Vivian said crossly.

Dr Walker agreed with her. His car was being decarbonised and he had had a busy morning. The afternoon would probably be worse. People usually chose the moment when the doctor's car was out of action to hack their fingers to the bone, or scald their children with boiling tea, or fall downstairs. He had no time to stop and talk with Mrs Greensleeves.

Vivian thought the doctor was curt, she went home in the rain with her book, and started to read it with avidity. ('The wickedest book that has ever been written' was sufficient recommendation to whet the appetite of the most jaded novel-reader.) At first it seemed quite an innocent sort of book, but after a little she recognised its peculiarity, and when she was half way through she recognised the libellous portrait of herself. She was so enraged by the impudence of the thing that she hurled the book across the room. 'No wonder Mrs Featherstone Hogg said it was wicked,' she announced fiercely. And then of course she had to get up and fish it out from under the piano and finish it, and the end was a hundred times more wicked than the beginning.

Vivian flew into the most fearful rage, she stormed about all over the house like a lunatic – even Milly Spikes, who was no stranger to her mistress's temper, was alarmed by the violence of her rage and retired to the scullery in company with the cat until it should have spent itself somewhat –

The idea of this man (who was he? John Smith) writing about her private affairs in a horrible twopenny-halfpenny novel! And writing about her private affairs in such a way too! As if she – Vivian – would have anything to do with that horrible man who lodged with Mrs Dick as a paying guest. She had been kind to him, of course, at one time, when she was bored to tears by the dullness of Silverstream – you must have somebody to talk to, and Mr Fortnum was the best that Silverstream could provide. But she had soon found out that nothing was to be gained from Mr Fortnum's friendship – he had sold his car for one thing so he couldn't even take her for an occasional run – and she had choked him off fairly easily. So it was all the more maddening to have the whole affair raked up like this. Supposing Ernest read the book and recognised the portrait? He was coming along so nicely now, Vivian thought her financial troubles were practically settled.

Oh how maddening it all was! How utterly maddening! How dare that horrible man write such lies about her – such disgusting lies!

Vivian wept tears of sheer rage.

It was in the midst of this storm that Ernest Hathaway walked in, heralded by Milly. Vivian had quite forgotten that she had asked him to supper.

The sight of Ernest pulled Vivian together as nothing else could have done, she hid the book under a convenient cushion and looked up at him with dewy eyes.

'Oh, Ernest, I'm so miserable,' she sobbed, changing the tears of rage to tears of woe at a moment's notice.

Ernest was aghast to find his beautiful penitent in tears, he sat down on the sofa and tried to comfort her, soon she was weeping softly in his arms. She continued to weep for several minutes while she tried to find some plausible and pathetic story to account for her tears. Then she stopped weeping and told it to him.

She was lonely, she said, terribly lonely and somebody had been unkind to her because she had nobody to protect her. It was a much longer story than that of course and complicated by sobs, and assurances that she was not going to burden Ernest with her small troubles, but that was the gist of it. The person who had been unkind to her dwelt in London, she would not reveal his name under any persuasion whatever, it was her own fault for not seeing that he was a horrid sort of man from the very beginning –

Ernest listened and sympathised and eventually when Vivian had almost given up hope, he asked her to marry him.

* * *

We must now return to Dr Walker who had nearly collided with Vivian Greensleeves in the High Street. It will be remembered that he was hastening home to lunch after a busy morning. He was frightfully late for lunch, of course, and Sarah had had hers, and gone out, but she had left a message for Dr John on the telephone block. Sometimes these messages left by Sarah for her husband's perusal were slightly unofficial, but they were always perfectly clear. She did not allow her sense of humour to interfere with business; she only used it as a sauce to make the boiled fish more interesting – so to speak. Sarah loved a joke. Why not indulge herself since it did nobody any harm and did John good? John took life so awfully seriously, it was good for him to be shaken up a little now and then. Today she had written, 'Please go and look at Angela's Pretty chest.'

Dr John smiled as he tore off the leaf and put it carefully away in his notebook. He kept every letter and every scrap of paper that Sarah had ever written to him. He was – he knew it himself – quite foolishly sentimental about Sarah. When he had put the leaflet safely away his brow clouded over, and he slipped his stethoscope into his pocket and went in next door.

Angela's chest lay heavily upon the doctor's mind. There was nothing definite about it (it was one of those doubtful borderline cases which are really more anxiety to their medical man than a definite disease. Last year he had had a specialist down from town to look at Angela, and Angela had been ill for a week with sheer fright, and the specialist had said, 'There's nothing definite, nothing at all yet, but keep an eye on her.' So helpful after all the fuss; and every cold that Angela took, settled firmly on her chest).

Today Dr John was full of jokes with Angela. He pretended to upset the tumbler and caught it in the air, and he teased her about her new bed-jacket, and told her all about the latest mischief perpetrated by the twins. He was so cheerful that he left Angela feeling much better, and much happier about herself; feeling, indeed, that it had been quite an unnecessary expense to send for him at all.

But as he went downstairs, the clouds gathered once more upon the doctor's brow, and he went into the drawing-room, where Ellen King was writing, and shut the door behind him.

'Well John?' she said, rather breathlessly.

'I don't like these continual colds,' he said. 'I don't like them, Ellen.'

These two were old friends, they had always lived next door to each other (for Dr John's father had been Silverstream's doctor before Dr John was born). Ellen and John had played together as children, and together had climbed every climbable tree in the two adjoining gardens. Dr John had a great respect for Ellen King, and a great compassion, she was such a lonely sort of creature and ridden by a curious temperament. Her excellent brain had never been developed and turned to use. Ellen would have made a good doctor or lawyer (the stuff was there), but her father had abhorred clever women and had denied her the opportunity of a decent education.

'What do you mean, exactly?' she asked him anxiously.

'I don't mean anything very much,' Dr John told her. 'In fact I mean exactly what I say – I don't like these continual colds that Angela gets. Could you possibly go away?'

'Go away? You mean to Bournemouth or somewhere?'

'Bournemouth? No. I mean to Egypt. It is warm and dry there. Just for the rest of the winter, of course.'

'I suppose we could if it is necessary – I mean of course we could if it is necessary,' she amended in sudden alarm.

'I wouldn't like to say it is necessary, but it is advisable,' he replied, choosing his words carefully.

Miss King knew that he was wondering whether they could afford it, and she answered him as if he had put the question.

'We have got a little, put away for a rainy day,' she said, smiling a trifle wanly.

'It's raining all right,' he replied pointing to the window.

'But not very hard?' she asked him.

'No,' he said. 'Just a shower, Ellen, just a shower. But we want to get Angela off to some place where she will get sunshine and dry air to breathe. Wait and go after the New Year. I'll look in tomorrow when you've thought it over, and we can arrange the whole thing.'

'John!' she said suddenly. 'Shall I let Angela go alone? I could take up some sort of work – no, don't say anything yet – I believe I'm bad for Angela, John. I have begun to think she would be better without me. She depends upon me too much. Sometimes I think she is beginning to lose her identity altogether –'

'What on earth are you talking about?' said Dr John furiously, taking a few strides across the floor and back again to his usual station in front of the fire. 'What on earth are you talking about, Ellen? I thought you had more sense. Angela would depend upon anybody who happened to be there to depend upon. It's her nature to – to lean – Angela is weak in body, and soul, and mind.'

'I know,' said Ellen, 'I know all that, John, but I love her just the same. I love her too much. I fuss over her too much – I agonise over her –'

'Look here, we all agonise over people we love. But we mustn't fuss – that's the important thing. It's difficult not to fuss, but we mustn't do it, Ellen. I don't think you do fuss over Angela. I think you're very sensible with her.'

'I've begun to doubt it,' Ellen replied. 'You don't know how she depends upon me for everything. She can't even decide what to wear without asking me what I think. That's bad, isn't it, John?'

'It's the woman's nature,' he said impatiently. 'You've done such a lot for her, you've been wonderful to her, Ellen. Believe me it's not your fault that she's weak and vacillating – you're not bad for her, it's absurd and ridiculous to think so. As for her going to Egypt by herself, the thing's simply unthinkable, I couldn't countenance it for a moment. I'd rather she stayed here, infinitely rather. You must go and look after her, she needs you. For pity's sake don't go and get a lot of foolish ideas into your head.'

'John, have you read that book?'

'Have I read it? Did Sarah give me a moment's peace until I had read the wretched book? Have I had a moment's peace ever since with everybody talking about it, and having hysterics over it? – Don't talk to me about that book, Ellen,' said Dr John half in fun and half in earnest.

‘But what do you think of it, John?’ she demanded, disobeying his injunction promptly.

‘Well, I’ll tell you what I think about it if you like. I know I’m in the minority in my opinion, but that can’t be helped. I think it was written by a very simple-minded person – a woman. Yes, I’m almost certain John Smith is a woman. I wouldn’t mind betting you a fiver that it’s a woman, if you like to take me on. And I don’t think the book is meant to be unkind or libellous at all. I think John Smith sat down at her desk, and wrote that book in absolute good faith, merely describing people as she saw them, putting in every smallest detail about them just as she saw it.’

‘But the second part,’ objected Ellen.

Dr John laughed. ‘The second part ran away with her – that’s obvious. The book suddenly took the bit in its mouth and bolted with John Smith, and she just sat back and held on like grim death and let it run. I confess that it amused me, Ellen – I know this is heresy in Silverstream, but it amused me immensely. It didn’t strike me as a satire, nor could I find anything nasty in it. You can read it both ways, I know, especially some parts like the love scenes, but I’m pretty certain that John Smith intended nothing nasty. I’m pretty certain that it’s just a simple story, written by a very innocent person – a person totally ignorant of the world, and worldly matters – perhaps even rather a stupid person.’

‘And who is it?’ she asked him, thoughtfully.

‘There you have me,’ the doctor owned, stroking his chin. ‘There, I admit, you have me cold. I have not the remotest idea who can have written that book, although, obviously, I must know the author quite well.’

'She must be a local person,' Ellen agreed, she had quite accepted the doctor's diagnosis of the author's sex.

'Of course she must be. And somebody who knows us all intimately. Everybody will tell you that the book is full of discrepancies, of course. Mrs Carter says that it is quite wrong about her hair,' said Dr John with twinkling eyes, 'and Mrs Featherstone Hogg denies that she was ever in the chorus –'

'Was she?' enquired Ellen breathlessly.

'I'm sure I don't know, and if I did I wouldn't tell you,' was the whimsical reply. 'Bulmer says he's the soul of amiability, and Mrs Dick doesn't feed her paying guests on congealed bacon fat, and I assure you here and now that I never prescribe castor oil for lead swingers – as a matter of fact I know a trick worth two of that – but all the same I am convinced that John Smith knows us all pretty well, and that, therefore, we must know John Smith.'

'That's what I said to Mr Abbott,' Ellen agreed.

Dr John was edging towards the door, he hoped that Ellen would let him go and have his lunch – it was after two o'clock and he was feeling somewhat empty – but she hadn't finished with him yet.

'You're not really anxious about Angela, are you?' she asked, following him into the hall.

'Not if you go away,' he replied firmly. 'I shall be worried if you stay here. Lord! I wish I could get away from this abominable climate, and take Sarah – you're lucky.'

'You wouldn't let Sarah come with us?' suggested Ellen hopefully.

'Kind of you,' he said, struggling into his coat, and retrieving his hat from the stand, 'very kind indeed, and of course I'd let her. But I don't think she'd go. Persuade her if you can. I'd miss her abominably, of course, but I'm all for it, if you can get her to go. I tried to send her away when she was ill, but she was twice as ill at the mere idea –'

'You were anxious about her, I know,' said Ellen.

'Anxious? I was demented,' replied the doctor. 'I don't want anyone to go through that particular hell if I can help it. That's why I'm banishing you to Egypt.' He was on the doorstep now, poised for flight – if only the woman would stop talking and let him get home.

'Why don't you send us to Samarkand while you're about it?' she demanded, with a deep chuckle. 'I believe you're in league with your female John Smith.'

Dr John waved his hat at her 'Good! Splendid!' he cried. 'That's the spirit – that's more like the good old Ellen King I know so well. Tell them all that you and Angela are off to Samarkand – and, Ellen,' he added in lower and more confidential tones, 'don't forget to order those riding breeches, will you? You'd look fine in them –'

CHAPTER SIXTEEN

THE DRAWING-ROOM MEETING

Barbara Buncle was a little late for the drawing-room meeting on Thursday afternoon. She had been working at her new novel all the morning, and then, just as she was in the middle of dressing, Sally had appeared and had wanted to hear all about her adventures in town, and all about Virginia and the new clothes. Barbara tried to talk and dress at the same time but she was not used to it, having been an only child with no sisters to initiate her in the art.

'That stocking's inside out,' Sally told her, 'and there's a tiny hole in the heel. You had better give it to me to mend while you put on your hat.'

Barbara complied meekly, her new outfit had not arrived yet, so she had to wear her old hat – the one that looked so ridiculous upon her new hair.

'You can't go like that,' said Sally frankly. 'Haven't you got any other hats at all?'

'None that I could wear,' admitted Barbara sadly.

Sally put down the stocking which she had mended neatly, and rummaged in Barbara's wardrobe. She unearthed an old black felt which Barbara had intended to give to Dorcas, twisted it this way and that in her small capable hands, and finally crammed it on to Barbara's head, back to front, and told her to go.

'You'll be fearfully late if you don't hurry,' she said, just as if it were not her fault at all that Barbara was late, 'Gran started hours ago. And I want you to listen to everything that everybody says and remember it all to tell me. I'd give anything to be there.'

Barbara promised, and seized her umbrella, and fled, quite forgetting about the hat.

Mrs Featherstone Hogg had arranged all her chairs around the drawing-room walls, they were filled with people. She herself was seated in the middle with a card-table in front of her, covered with a red cloth, and laden with writing materials. Beside her sat Mr Bulmer wearing his gloomiest expression.

Mr Bulmer's gloom was due partly to domestic difficulties which had arisen in the absence of his wife, and partly to the feeling that he looked a fool sitting in the middle of Mrs Featherstone Hogg's drawing-room on a bedroom chair. He had tried to efface himself upon the sofa beside Mrs Goldsmith, but Mrs Featherstone Hogg had pounced upon him, and dragged him forth and seated him at her side; and there he was, for all the world like an exhibit in a show – a secondary exhibit, of course, for Mrs Featherstone Hogg was obviously the primary exhibit herself.

The Meeting had not yet started when Barbara arrived, so she was not late after all, or else the Meeting was late in starting. She slipped – as inconspicuously as possible – into a seat beside Sarah Walker and looked round the room.

Miss King was sitting near the window beside Mrs Carter, and beyond them was Mrs Dick flanked by two of her gentlemen paying guests – Mr Fortnum and Mr Black. (The latter was Barbara's supercilious young friend from the bank, of course.) Then came the three Snowdons, Mrs Greensleeves and Captain Sandeman, and Mr Featherstone Hogg. Mrs Goldsmith was alone upon the sofa but she filled more than half of it quite comfortably. She looked very solemn and important in a black silk cloak trimmed with astrakhan. Mr Durnet was near the door, he was all in his Sunday clothes and was obviously quite bewildered to find himself in The Riggs drawing-room. I'm glad I didn't let Dorcas come, thought Barbara. Dorcas had been invited, of course, but she had shown no signs of wanting to attend the meeting, and Barbara hadn't pressed her in any way. Barbara felt she could bear the ordeal better if Dorcas were safely at home.

Barbara Buncle looked round the room and saw all her puppets (with a few exceptions) assembled together for the purpose of reviling their creator. She wondered if any other author had ever beheld such a curious sight. It would be exciting to write a play, Barbara thought, to see your creations put on the garment of mortality, to hear your words issuing from their mouths. But a play must always be a little disappointing, no actor can completely satisfy an author, there must be some discrepancy between the author's conception of a character and the actor's expression. This was far better than any play, for the actors were themselves. They couldn't act out of character if they tried, for they *were* the characters – as large as life and twice as natural.

A strange mist hovered before Barbara's eyes. Was this Silverstream, or was it Copperfield? Was that Mrs Horsley Downs, or was it Mrs Featherstone Hogg?

Sarah Walker recalled her to reality – 'I really ought not to be here because I'm not *in* it,' she whispered, 'John's coming later if he can possibly get away. Isn't it *funny*?' Barbara agreed that it was, and enquired after the twins' cold.

'Oh it's much better thank you,' said their mother. 'They are out today for the first time. I do like your hat, Barbara.'

'Good gracious!' exclaimed Barbara, 'I'd forgotten about my hat – what on earth can it look like?'

'Silence!' cried Mrs Featherstone Hogg, and she tapped loudly on the card-table with a hammer.

'Ladies and gentlemen,' said Mrs Featherstone Hogg. 'It is now ten minutes to four, and two of our – of our number have not come yet. There are other absentees, of course, but they have been unavoidably – er – prevented from attending. I will read their apologies later. But these two people have sent no word, they said they would come and I was expecting them. They are very important to our – to our cause. I refer of course to Colonel Weatherhead and Mrs Bold. Does anyone know why they have not turned up?'

'Dorothea Bold has gone to London to stay with her sister,' said Barbara in a small voice.

'How very strange!' said Mrs Featherstone Hogg. 'She might have let me know. Colonel Weatherhead promised to tell her about the Meeting. Well there is just the Colonel to wait for, then, and the point is shall we wait a little longer for him, or carry on without him?'

A babble of talk immediately broke forth as everyone present began to explain to her neighbour or to her hostess why it was absolutely necessary to wait for the Colonel's arrival, or to carry on with the Meeting at once. Barbara was swept into Copperfield (the new novel was all about Copperfield too, of course), she contemplated the scene with delight, she was a sponge, soaking up ambrosia.

Mrs Featherstone Hogg consulted in undertones with Mr Bulmer and then rapped upon the table. The Meeting relapsed into silence.

'Mr Bulmer says I ought to have opened the Meeting by explaining that I am the chairman and he is the president,' she said loudly. 'But of course the Meeting has not been opened yet. I merely wished to ascertain whether everybody thinks we should start without Colonel Weatherhead or wait until he comes.'

'Very unconstitutional,' remarked Mr Bulmer loudly.

'But look here,' said Mr Black (from the bank). 'Look here, you don't need a chairman *and* a president, surely, I mean it's not usual. Either the chairman presides or the president takes the chair, I mean –'

Mrs Featherstone Hogg took no notice of the objections and interruptions. She considered Mr Black's objection foolish. It was her Meeting, and she would do as she liked about presidents and chairmen, she certainly was not going to take instruction from Mr Black.

'Colonel Weatherhead is very important to us,' said Mrs

Featherstone Hogg, keeping firmly to the point, 'and I consider we should wait until he comes.'

'Why not telephone to the feller?' suggested Captain Sandeman, sensibly. 'He's probably forgotten all about it.'

The chairman considered this, and decided that it was a good idea, so Mr Featherstone Hogg was sent to telephone to the Colonel and find out if he had started.

The Meeting waited patiently, all except Mr Bulmer, who showed signs of strain. He had no use at all for Colonel Weatherhead, and considered that the business in hand could have been transacted quite as efficiently without the Colonel's presence. As a matter of fact he had the same feeling about two-thirds of the people invited by Mrs Featherstone Hogg. She had made a fool of the whole thing by asking old Durnet and Mrs Goldsmith. The former was practically an imbecile in Mr Bulmer's opinion – a good many people were practically imbeciles in Mr Bulmer's opinion. He tapped irritably on the table with his fingers, and crossed and re-crossed his legs.

After some time Mr Featherstone Hogg returned to say that the exchange could get no reply from The Bridge House.

'You should have told them to ring again,' said Mrs Featherstone Hogg crossly.

'I did,' he replied.

There was nothing more to be done about the Colonel, so Mrs Featherstone Hogg was obliged to start the proceedings without him. She rose from her chair and rapped upon the table with her hammer.

'Ladies and gentlemen,' said Mrs Featherstone Hogg, referring to her notes, which she had compiled that morning with considerable care. 'Ladies and gentlemen, we have met together today to discuss this book – *Disturber of the Peace* – which has been flung into our peaceful village like a poison bomb. Before the publication of this book we were all living together like a big happy family, but now there are rifts in the lute and the music is discordant and harsh. We have all suffered from the effects of this book – some in one way and some in another. I have no time to go into each individual case today, it is sufficient to say that all have suffered – that is why we are here. Books like *Disturber of the Peace* are a deadly menace to society. They undermine the foundations of English life. An Englishman's house is his castle, it is into the sacred precincts of this castle that *Disturber of the Peace* has entered, destroying the fragrance of the home, and violating its privacy. We of Silverstream must lead the way, it is our duty and our privilege to show England that the home is still a sacred spot and cannot be violated with impunity.'

Mrs Featherstone Hogg had marked on her notes, 'Pause for applause.' She paused hopefully.

Mr Black was the only member of the Meeting who realised what was expected of him. He clapped feebly, but it is impossible to clap alone, so he left off almost immediately.

'There is only one thing to be done,' continued Mrs Featherstone Hogg, returning to her notes. 'The author of this sacrilege – John Smith he calls himself – must be found. He must be dragged out of his hole like a rat, and punished severely, as an example to the world. It is to do this that we have met today.' She sat down.

Mr Bulmer rose somewhat wearily and said, 'I was under the impression that I was president of this Meeting. The impression was evidently erroneous,' and sat down.

The Meeting applauded loudly, but whether the applause was intended to encourage Mr Bulmer or to confirm him in his impression it is difficult to say.

Mrs Featherstone Hogg bobbed up again. 'I am sorry that Mr Bulmer is not satisfied with the way the Meeting is being conducted,' she announced in defiant tones. 'I would like to remind him that we are here today to put our heads together and find John Smith. Small points of procedure are of secondary consideration compared with our main object. The Meeting is now open for discussion.'

There was dead silence.

Mrs Featherstone Hogg waited for a minute or two and then bobbed up again.

'Perhaps I haven't explained properly,' she said. 'The Meeting is now open, and anybody who has anything to say can say it now.'

'I'd like to put in a word,' said Mrs Goldsmith, suddenly. 'It's about my buns. It said in that book that my buns was full of electricity. I'd just like to say that's not true, and anybody who says it *is* true is telling lies. There's no electricity comes near my buns. I don't hold with these new electric ovens for baking, I don't. My oven's a brick oven, heated with an ordinary furnace, same as my father used. The dough's rolled by 'and. There's no electricity comes near my buns, and no seconds neither. I use nothing but first-grade flour in my bakery – there's people living not a hundred miles from here who couldn't say the same – and that's the truth,' added Mrs Goldsmith, leaning back and fanning her hot face with her handkerchief.

Mrs Featherstone Hogg rapped on the table – 'I'm sure it is very interesting to hear about Mrs Goldsmith's methods of baking,' she announced in patronising tones. 'But I don't see how that is going to help us in our search for John Smith. We could all point out the horrible lies that he's written about us if we liked, but what good would that do? I must ask the members of this Meeting to keep to the matter in hand or we shall be here all night.'

'Perhaps I shouldn't have spoke up like I did,' said Mrs Goldsmith apologetically. 'But it's hard to have people making wicked aspirations about my buns and lie down under it.'

'Quite right too,' said Mrs Dick, nodding her head so that the ostrich feather round her hat waved like a milk-white pennon in the breeze. 'Quite right too. Stand up for yourself, I say, for there's nobody else going to stand up *for* you. And while we're on the subject I'd just like to mention that if my guests are late for their breakfasts their breakfasts are kept hot – there's nobody in my establishment is asked to eat congealed bacon fat like it says in that book – Mr Fortnum and Mr Black will bear me out,' she added firmly, looking towards the paying guests who had accompanied her to the Meeting.

'That's right,' said Mr Fortnum hoarsely.

'– And there's another thing,' continued Mrs Dick. 'Just one more thing, and I'll have done, for I'm not going into the question of my mattresses in Mrs Featherstone Hogg's drawing-room. It's enough to say that they're all good horse-hair mattresses every one of them, and anyone who says they're stuffed with potatoes is a liar – what I really want to say is this: my guests are all respectable and well-behaved, and I've never had a gentleman of the name of Mason staying in my establishment, and if I did have, I'd have seen to it that he behaved as a gentleman ought. None of my gentlemen ever spent all night in a lady's garden playing on a mandolin. Mr Fortnum plays the ukelele and very nice it is of an evening in the drawing-room and the other gentlemen singing –'

Mrs Featherstone Hogg rapped on the table –

'Mr Bulmer will now read out the apologies from the absentees,' she said loudly.

'It ought to have been done at the beginning,' said Mr Bulmer crossly.

'I know, I forgot about it.'

'You had better do it yourself.'

'Very well,' said the chairman, 'if you don't want to do it, I will.' She took up a sheaf of papers and cleared her throat. 'Mrs Bulmer is away from home and therefore regrets that she cannot be present. Dr Walker is unavoidably detained, but hopes to come in later. Miss Pretty is in bed with a feverish cold, she much regrets that she is unable to be present at Mrs Featherstone Hogg's drawing-room meeting, but hopes it will be a great success. (I am sure we are all much obliged to Miss Pretty for her kind message.) Colonel Carter has sailed for India and regrets that he is unable to attend.

Major and Mrs Shearer regret that owing to a previous engagement they are unable to accept Mrs Featherstone Hogg's kind invitation to her drawing-room meeting. Miss Dorcas Pemberty regrets that she is unable to be present. Mrs Sandeman is unable to be present as she is still in bed, she much regrets that she cannot accept Mrs Featherstone Hogg's kind invitation. I think that is all, we can now proceed with the – er – proceedings,' said Mrs Featherstone Hogg, and she sat down.

'What are you going to do when you find John Smith?' enquired Miss King in her deep sensible voice. 'It appears to me that you can't do anything at all. No reputable lawyer will touch the case with a barge pole.'

'Leave that to me,' replied the chairman of the meeting in a voice that boded ill for John Smith.

'I move that the vote of the meeting shall be taken on the point,' said Miss King firmly.

Sarah Walker seconded the motion and Mrs Featherstone Hogg was forced to ask for a show of hands. Hands were shown on the point, and it was found that the majority lay with Miss King. In other words they all wanted to have some say in what punishment should be meted out to John Smith rather than leave the matter entirely in their chairman's hands.

'I think we should send him to Coventry,' said Isabella Snowdon, savagely.

'Poof – what would John Smith care for that,' snorted Mr Bulmer. 'A good ducking in the horse-pond is what he wants.'

'It all depends on what sort of a man he is,' Mr Snowdon pointed out. 'As Miss King so rightly says, no lawyer will touch the case – but there are other means of procedure.'

'What means?' demanded Mr Bulmer.

'Most men have a weak spot,' replied Mr Snowdon significantly.

'You mean we could find out something disgraceful about his past, and blackmail him?' enquired Sarah Walker, sweetly.

'I never mentioned blackmail,' retorted Mr Snowdon. 'I merely said that most men have a weak spot. In dealing with a person of John Smith's calibre one cannot be squeamish. The man obviously needs a lesson. Find his weak spot and you have him at your mercy.'

'What's it all about?' enquired Mr Durnet suddenly in a piping voice. 'What's it all about? Ella said we was going to 'ave tea. It's a long time coming.'

'After the Meeting,' shouted Mr Black who was sitting next to the old man. 'AFTER THE MEETING.'

'Yes, eating. That's what Ella said,' piped Mr Durnet disconsolately. 'But I don't see no signs of eating, nor drinking neither.'

Mrs Featherstone Hogg took no notice of the interruption. 'You're all quite wrong,' she said firmly. 'John Smith ought to be horse-whipped, that's the only thing for a man like him. And horse-whipped he will be, if I have any say in the matter.'

'You haven't,' said Mr Bulmer. 'You are the chairman – or at least you are supposed to be the chairman – and therefore you have no say in the matter beyond giving a casting vote.'

‘If I had known that I wouldn’t have been the chairman,’ replied Mrs Featherstone Hogg with some heat. ‘Do you mean to say that because I am the chairman I have to sit here like a dummy, and not give the meeting the benefit of my ideas?’

Mr Bulmer did not attempt to answer this question, perhaps his experience was insufficient to deal with such a fine point.

‘Who’s going to do the horse-whipping?’ he enquired, passing on to safer ground. ‘Who’s going to horse-whip the man and probably find himself in gaol over the affair? That’s what I want to know.’

‘Colonel Weatherhead, of course,’ said Mrs Featherstone Hogg calmly.

The entire meeting gasped with amazement.

‘I’d like to see the fun,’ announced Captain Sandeman.

‘So’d I,’ agreed Mr Black, ‘but the Colonel’s an oldish man for a job like that, and we don’t know what size of a chap this John Smith will be. I’d like to know the size of a chap before I said I’d tackle him – still I admire pluck.’

‘It’s a pity more people are not as brave as the Colonel,’ said Mrs Featherstone Hogg with asperity. She had pondered for so long over the horse-whipping business that she was now convinced in her own mind that the whole thing was settled with Colonel Weatherhead. It would have been almost impossible to disabuse her mind of the conviction that Colonel Weatherhead had agreed with alacrity to horse-whip John Smith. Fortunately, nobody present was in a position to try.

‘I wouldn’t mind taking him on if he was smaller than me,’ retorted Mr Black, who felt that the chairman’s remark was especially addressed to him, and resented the aspersion upon his personal courage. ‘But it wouldn’t be the least use me undertaking the job if I couldn’t be certain of getting the better of the chap.’

Captain Sandeman was heard to murmur something, and was asked by the chairman to repeat his remark. It was obvious that she hoped he was a volunteer, he was young, and strong, and had broad shoulders, and his profession was militant.

‘I just said – “First catch your hare”,’ said Captain Sandeman.

‘Very pertinent too,’ remarked Miss Olivia Snowdon.

‘Good Heavens! What’s impertinent about it?’ demanded Captain Sandeman indignantly, ‘I merely said – “first catch your hare”. It’s a proverb. It means you can’t punish the man till you’ve caught him. “First catch your hare, then cook him.” You can’t cook John Smith till you’ve bowled him over, can you? We aren’t within a hundred miles of finding out who the feller *is* yet.’

‘I know, I know,’ soothed the harassed chairman. ‘Nobody said impertinent.’

‘Miss Snowdon did.’

‘I said pertinent,’ Miss Snowdon remarked scornfully. ‘Perhaps you do not realise that pertinent means to the point, it means the reverse of impertinent. The word has now lost its original meaning, of course –’

‘Is it necessary to go into the etymological meaning of the word?’ enquired Mr Bulmer in a tired voice.

'I considered it necessary to explain my meaning to Captain Sandeman,' returned Miss Snowdon, with some heat.

Mrs Featherstone Hogg thought it was time to interfere. She rapped on the table with her hammer.

'We must really confine ourselves to the business in hand,' she said sternly. 'We keep on wandering away from the point –'

'It's the chairman's business to prevent that occurring,' retorted Mr Bulmer.

'I've been trying to,' Mrs Featherstone Hogg said, with pardonable irritation. 'I've been trying to keep people to the point ever since we started. If you think you could do it so much better you had better be chairman and conduct the meeting yourself.'

'God forbid!' exclaimed Mr Bulmer.

'I'm only trying to help you all,' continued the chairman in pathetic accents. 'I've had you all here today to try to get to the bottom of this – of this distressing affair.'

'And very kind of you it is, ma'am,' put in Mrs Goldsmith who had determined to ally herself with her best customer at all costs. 'Very kind of you to take all the trouble you have taken, and to have us all here today in your nice drawing-room – so it is. I propose a vote of thanks to Mrs Featherstone Hogg,' she added with sudden brilliant inspiration.

'Very unconstitutional!' exclaimed Mr Bulmer.

'Very kind of you, Mrs Goldsmith,' said Mrs Featherstone Hogg, with a defiant look in Mr Bulmer's direction. 'Very kind indeed of you, and I'm glad somebody appreciates my efforts, but the only thing is a vote of thanks comes at the end of the proceedings.'

'Does it?' enquired Mrs Goldsmith in an interested voice. 'Well, I never was at a drawing-room meeting before, so I didn't know. I've been to Quaker Meetings of course. My aunt who lives in Herefordshire is a Quaker, and we used to stay with her when we were young. And of course at Quaker Meetings you just speak as the spirit moves you, so I thought it was the same kind of idea –'

'Well, it's not,' said the perplexed chairman. 'If anyone has anything to say which will throw light upon the identity of John Smith we shall be only too pleased to listen to them, but if not I must request members to remain silent.'

'How would it do if we all remained silent for ten minutes?' suggested Miss Isabella Snowdon, timidly. 'Those who cared to pray for guidance could do so, of course, and the others could just concentrate upon the problem. The power of thought is so immense and so – so – er – powerful, I feel sure that we should gain something valuable in that way.'

'I didn't know this was going to turn into a séance, or I should have stayed at home,' announced Mr Bulmer, who was getting more and more irritable every moment.

'My sister never suggested a séance nor anything to do with spiritualism,' cried Miss Olivia, rushing into the fray. 'Concentrated thought is an entirely different matter –'

'The Meeting should have been opened with prayer,' suggested Mrs Dick, who had suddenly thought of this contribution to the debate.

'I think it would have been most unsuitable,' said Miss King, firmly.

'When you've all finished quarrelling I would like to tell you about my idea,' Vivian Greensleeves announced. There was something significant in her tone which quelled the rising storm. Everybody looked at her, of course, which was exactly what Vivian liked. She lay back with her legs crossed, smiling in a mysterious manner, and toying idly with the tassels on the arm of her chair. It was the first time that Vivian had opened her mouth since she had arrived, except to yawn once or twice in a ladylike manner behind her hand – she had been waiting, more or less patiently, until everybody present had made complete fools of themselves; she considered that she had now waited long enough, and was ready to contribute her quota.

'We shall be very glad to listen to your idea,' Mrs Featherstone Hogg announced graciously.

'Well,' said Vivian Greensleeves, slowly. 'I've been thinking it over ever since I read the book, and it seems to me there's only one person in Silverstream who is not caricatured in the book and held up to scorn, only one person who knows us all well enough to write about us and is not in the book herself. I think that John Smith is Mrs Walker.'

Everybody immediately turned and gazed at Sarah Walker. It would have taken a more brazen person than Sarah not to blush in the blaze of limelight suddenly thrown upon her.

'Oh!' she said.

'Oh no, it's not her,' cried Barbara Buncle.

Mrs Featherstone Hogg swallowed once or twice. There seemed to be a sort of lump sticking in her throat – possibly a form of excitement. Why had she not thought of Mrs Walker herself? Sarah had just the sort of perverted sense of humour which disfigured *Disturber of the Peace*. Sarah knew them all, she had opportunities of hearing things about her neighbours which are denied to the wives of stockbrokers. Sarah had ample time to write, for she was by way of being delicate and did not go about much. She made an excuse of her delicacy to abstain from such excitements as tea-parties and musical evenings at The Riggs. What more likely than that she stayed at home and ridiculed them all? Sarah went her own way, and lived her own life, she did not bow to the sovereignty of Mrs Featherstone Hogg. Mrs Featherstone Hogg did not like Sarah, she was pretty sure it was Sarah who had written the book.

Several other people seemed to be arriving at the same conclusion; Mrs Carter was arguing loudly with Miss King; Mrs Goldsmith was arguing loudly with Mrs Dick; the Snowdons were whispering amongst themselves; Mr Bulmer was glaring at Sarah like a gargoyle.

Mr Bulmer was convinced that Mrs Greensleeves had hit the bull's-eye with her first shot. He disliked Sarah intensely, and, moreover, he knew that Sarah disliked him (Sarah never made any concealment of her likes and dislikes). Sarah was Margaret's closest friend, of course Margaret had told her all about him, and she had travestied him in her hateful book. The thing was obvious.

Mr Bulmer plucked at Mrs Featherstone Hogg's sleeve and whispered in her ear.

The chairman rose, and rapped upon the table.

'Mrs Walker,' she said solemnly. 'It is my painful duty to ask you in the name of this Meeting whether or not you wrote the novel, *Disturber of the Peace*. Please do not let us have any prevarications, we desire the truth, the whole truth and nothing but the truth.'

Sarah leapt to her feet, she was furious. How dared Mrs Featherstone Hogg put the question in that way? As if she, Sarah Walker, told lies!

'I *will* tell you the whole truth,' she cried, nerved by wrath. 'I did not write *Disturber of the Peace*, but I wish I had. I wish I had the brains to do it. I think it is a very clever and amusing book, and I hope it will do you all good to see yourselves as others see you for once in a way. A set of smug hypocrites – that's what you are. It's a great pity there aren't more John Smiths about.'

Having said her say, Sarah made for the door, and Barbara, who had had quite enough of the drawing-room meeting, got up and followed her. The remainder of the company was too astounded to move.

Barbara seized the door out of Sarah's grasp and closed it gently but firmly behind her. She heaved a sigh of relief – they had escaped without being torn in pieces – and pursued the flying Sarah down the stairs. In the hall was a tall familiar figure struggling out of its great-coat. Sarah flung herself into its arms and began to laugh hysterically.

'John,' she cried, 'John, John, John!'

Barbara stood on the stairs and gazed at them, open-mouthed.

'Sally dear!' cried the amazed Dr John. 'Sally dear, what on earth's happened?'

'They all think John Smith is me,' cried Sarah, gasping for breath.

CHAPTER SEVENTEEN

INSPIRATION

Barbara Buncle rushed home and shut herself up in the small room which she had begun to call her study. She cast her hat and coat on to the nearest chair and seized her fountain pen. Words were hammering in her brain. They poured out on to the paper in an endless stream. The floor was gradually covered with sheets of closely written foolscap. It looked as if a snowstorm had been raging in the study when Dorcas came in to say that supper was ready.

'Go away, I'm busy,' said Miss Buncle without raising her head.

'Now, Miss Barbara, don't be contrary,' said Dorcas, firmly. 'I've poached you an egg, and you can't go wasting eggs at two and eleven a dozen.'

'Eat it yourself, then,' suggested the author.

'I'll do no such thing,' Dorcas replied. 'Come along now, Miss Barbara, do. You hadn't much dinner you know, and I'm quite sure you didn't get no tea worth talking about at that old skinflint's party.'

'I had none,' said Barbara, raising a flushed face from her writing table.

‘There,’ cried Dorcas triumphantly, ‘what did I tell you?’

‘If you bring the egg here I’ll eat it,’ said Barbara in despair. ‘Only for goodness’ sake go away and don’t talk to me –’

Dorcas went away, she was beginning to get used to living in the house with an author. It was not comfortable, she found, and it was distinctly trying to the temper. Dorcas often thought with regret of the good old days when the dividends had come in punctually, and Miss Barbara had been an ordinary human being; taking her meals at regular hours, going up to bed as the clock struck eleven, and coming down for breakfast in the morning as the clock struck nine.

I believe hens would have been less bother after all, Dorcas thought, as she prepared a tray with the poached egg, a cup of cocoa, and two pieces of brown toast set out upon it in appetising array – Authors! said Dorcas to herself with scornful emphasis – Authors indeed! – Well, I’ll never read a book again but what I’ll think of the people as has had to put up with the author, I know that. – Preparing meals, and beating the gong, and going back ’alf an hour later to find nobody’s ever been near them, and the mutton fat frozen solid in the dish, and the soup stone cold – and them ringing bells at all hours for coffee, ‘and make it strong Dorcas – make it strong!’ and them writing half the night, and lying in bed half the day with people toiling up to their bedrooms with trays. – Authors – poof! said Dorcas to herself – but I never could abide hens neither – and she took up the tray and marched across the hall and pushed open the door of the study with one foot, and crunched heedlessly over the foolscap-covered floor, and dumped the tray down on the foolscap-covered desk.

'Go away,' said Barbara impatiently. Her pen was still skimming over the paper like a bird.

'Well I'm not going, then,' Dorcas replied. 'Not till I see you eat that egg and drink that cocoa with my own eyes, I'm not. For as soon as ever my back's turned you'll forget all about it.'

Barbara knew she was cornered. She took up the knife and fork and made short work of the poached egg.

'I was hungry,' she admitted in a surprised voice.

'Well, and what did you expect?' enquired Dorcas. 'With no tea, and as much dinner as would fatten up a fly – anybody would be hungry, I should think. Drink up your cocoa, Miss Barbara, before it gets cold and nasty.'

The meal was soon disposed of, Dorcas picked up the tray and made for the door –

'Oh, and Dorcas –'

'Yes, Miss Barbara.'

'I'd like a cup of coffee about eleven – before you go up to bed – and make it strong, Dorcas.'

'Yes, Miss Barbara,' said Dorcas, she pulled a face at the author's bent back and shut the door firmly.

* * *

On Friday morning Barbara lay in bed just as Dorcas had expected. She was worn out with the spate of inspiration which had kept her chained to her desk until the early hours of the morning.

'Well, you do look a ghost and no mistake,' Dorcas said, as she contemplated the recumbent figure of her mistress, and noted with dismay the dark smudges beneath Miss Buncle's eyes.

'I know,' said Barbara, 'I was writing nearly all night, that's why.'

'You'd better take a few days off it,' Dorcas advised, 'or we'll be having Dr Walker here, wanting to know what's wore you out like that.'

'Oh, I can't do that,' replied Barbara. 'It's only just beginning to – to roll along smoothly, and Mr Abbott's in a hurry for it. I must stick into it for a bit. Perhaps later on I might take a few days –'

'I'd be willing to try hens, Miss Barbara, if you're agreeable.'

'Hens?' enquired Barbara, toying with her bacon distastefully.

'You give up writing and we'll try hens,' wheedled Dorcas. 'My nephew has a fine hen-farm in Surrey. He'd be willing to start us off with a few, and give us some hints –'

The author sat up in bed and gazed at her in amazement. 'Dorcas, I could never give up writing *now*,' she said, incredulously (nor could she, the vice had got her firmly in its grip, as well ask a morphinomaniac to give up drugs). 'You don't know how exciting it is, Dorcas. It just sweeps you along and you've no idea of the time –'

'I guessed that much,' interpolated Dorcas, grimly.

'And look at the money I've made,' continued the complacent author. 'A whole hundred pounds, and more coming soon, Mr Abbott says. How long would it take to make a hundred pounds out of hens?'

Dorcas knew a little about her nephew's profits, and she was forced to admit, regretfully, that it might take years to make a clear hundred pounds out of hens.

'Well, you *see*,' said Barbara triumphantly, 'it would take years of work and worry to make a hundred pounds out of hens, and I can make it quite easily in a few months just by enjoying myself.'

'I'm not enjoying myself.'

'I know it's trying for you, but I can't help it, I really can't. When I feel it all bubbling over in my head it just *has* to come out, or I'd burst or something – you can have all my clothes if you like.'

Dorcas looked at her in consternation – what new horror was this? Had the strain of writing all night deranged the poor lady's brain, or did she contemplate remaining in bed for the rest of her life, and having trays brought up to her?

'All your clothes, Miss Barbara?' echoed Dorcas.

'Yes, all of them,' replied Miss Buncle, waving a negligent hand towards the wardrobe. 'Take them all away, out of the cupboard and the drawers. You can give some of them to your niece if you like – or sell them. Do whatever you like with them, Dorcas, but don't bother me about it.'

'You'll feel better after you've had a nice sleep,' Dorcas suggested, anxiously.

Barbara yawned, 'Yes, I am sleepy,' she admitted, 'I feel all empty and peaceful. I should think people feel exactly like this after they've had a baby –'

'Really, Miss Barbara, I don't know what you'll say next,' complained the scandalised Dorcas.

Barbara giggled, and snuggled down in bed. 'I'll sleep till lunch time,' she announced.

Dorcas took up the breakfast tray and left the room – all was peace.

Barbara Buncle slept, and as she slept she dreamed that she was walking down the village street. There was a kind of misty radiance in the air, so she knew that this was Copperfield. She walked along with a springy step and her beautifully polished brown shoes hardly touched the ground. She was so happy – she was always happy in Copperfield. Everything always went right in Copperfield, people did as she wanted them to do, they were never rude about her book, they were never cross or patronising. In Copperfield she had everybody under her thumb – even Mrs Horsley Downs was obliged to obey her orders. Mrs Horsley Downs couldn't walk across the street unless Barbara allowed her to. In Copperfield Barbara herself was just as she wanted to be, she was younger, and prettier and more attractive. People looked at her as she passed, not because she was a 'sight', but because she was pleasant to behold. Her hair was beautifully dressed, her clothes were perfect, her petticoat never hung down below her skirt, her stocking never developed a hole in the heel – in fact she was not Barbara Buncle any more, she was Elizabeth Wade.

Elizabeth Wade it was, who tripped along the Copperfield streets that fine morning. Elizabeth Wade clad in a complete new outfit from Virginia's little shop. She was wearing the bottle-green coat with the grey fur collar and the little hat to match, and beneath the bottle-green coat was the jumper suit which went with it so beautifully.

Elizabeth Wade went into the bakery to buy buns.

'I can recommend these, Miss,' said Mrs Silver with a smile, 'these are full of electricity. Please let me send up a dozen for you to try, there will be no charge to *you*, of course, Miss.'

Miss Wade gave her gracious consent and left the shop. How pleasant it was to be so popular! The sun was streaming down and filling the High Street with its golden beams, Elizabeth was dazzled by the brightness of the light. She closed her eyes for a moment, and when she opened them again she saw the Golden Boy. He was dancing along in the middle of the street playing on his pipe – lifting it up towards the sky and bending down again, first to one side and then to the other; bending and swaying from side to side, up to the sky and down to the ground, and all the time the music flowed from his pipe, a thin clear trickle of notes.

Elizabeth was not in the least surprised, why should she be surprised? He was her own Golden Boy, not the hybrid creature that had appeared upon the cover of *Disturber of the Peace*. He was her own Golden Boy, she had created him herself. He passed quite close to Elizabeth Wade, as she stood in the doorway of the bakery, and disappeared up the hill.

The bright light faded. Elizabeth rubbed her eyes and opened them to find her faithful slave standing at her bedside with a large tray. The sun was shining in at her open window and the birds were twittering blithely amongst the leaves of the ivy which covered Tanglewood Cottage.

'I've had a lovely sleep, Susan,' said Elizabeth/Barbara stretching her arms.

'It's Dorcas,' said that worthy in a humouring voice. 'It's your own Dorcas, Miss Barbara. Here's your dinner, sit up now and take it while it's nice and hot. Look, I got a little pigeon for you – isn't that nice now? And Mr Abbott's just rung up on the telephone to say he's coming down this afternoon to see you, and here's a postcard from Paris – it's come by air.'

Barbara sat up the better to deal with this mass of information. Copperfield had vanished, and with it Elizabeth Wade. It was Barbara who held out her hand for the postcard, not Elizabeth Wade. The postcard was a highly-coloured photograph of the Eiffel Tower and written upon it in Dorothea Bold's large round hand was the following amazing message – 'Enjoying our honeymoon tremendously. Love from us both. Dorothea Weatherhead.'

'They're married, Dorcas,' exclaimed Barbara.

'That's what I thought, Miss Barbara,' Dorcas replied. (We must not blame Dorcas too severely. Postcards are fair game, and it was not every day that one arrived from Paris – by airmail too. It would have been scarcely human if Dorcas had not glanced at it as she took it from the postman – and Dorothea's hand was particularly round and clear.) 'That's just what I thought they were,' said Dorcas, 'and a very nice couple they'll make. I expect it's *Disturber* that's done it.'

'D'you really think it could be?' Barbara said, with her eyes like saucers. 'D'you really think so, Dorcas? I *would* be glad if I thought that. D'you think they read my book and went straight off and got married? How wonderful it is!'

She lay back and thought about the mighty power of the pen, quite oblivious of the fact that her nice pigeon was getting cold.

* * *

When she had thought about it enough, and finished her lunch, Barbara got up and had a hot bath. Her new garments had arrived – Virginia had kept her promise faithfully – and Barbara decided to wear one of her new frocks this afternoon. A bath seemed a fitting preliminary to the donning of the slinky, soft, wine-coloured creation which lay curled up in its neat brown box all padded out with rustling tissue paper.

When she had bathed, and dressed, and finished doing her hair, Barbara slipped the frock very carefully over her head and turned to look at herself in the long mirror which swung on a wooden frame beside her chest of drawers. She was quite startled at the change in her appearance – it was Elizabeth Wade who looked back at her from the quicksilver depths of the mirror (not Barbara Buncle at all). Elizabeth Wade with flushed cheeks and bright eyes enhanced by the deep red frock which swept in a pretty curve to her ankles, and added a couple of inches to her height.

The doorbell rang while she was still contemplating Elizabeth and she went downstairs to greet Mr Abbott.

'You don't mind my turning up like this,' Mr Abbott said. 'I had a slack afternoon and there were one or two things I wanted to talk to you about –'

He stopped suddenly and gazed at his hostess in surprise. He was a mere man, of course, and he had not the remotest idea what had caused the amazing difference in Miss Buncle's appearance. He only knew that she was much more attractive than he had thought, much prettier too, and years younger –

'I must have been blind,' he said aloud.

'Blind?' enquired Barbara.

'Oh, I mean – er – I had some difficulty in finding your house again,' explained Mr Abbott, 'couldn't have been looking where I was going or something –'

'Well, anyway, here you are,' said Barbara smiling at him. She was full of self-assurance today and happy in her mastery of the situation. She was Elizabeth of course, that was the reason for it. Elizabeth Wade always knew what to do and say on every occasion – how unlike Barbara Buncle!

'I've been working so hard,' she told him, sitting down beside the fire and motioning Mr Abbott to the sofa with a gracious wave of her hand. 'Do smoke Mr Abbott, won't you – Dorcas is quite worried about me, she thinks it would be better if we were to try keeping hens.'

'No, no!' laughed Mr Abbott, taking a cigarette out of his tortoise-shell case and tapping it gently on his thumb-nail. 'No, no, Miss Buncle. We're not going to let you off so easily. We're going to keep your nose to the grind-stone. There's no rest for the best-seller, you know.'

'Am I really a best-seller?'

'Pretty good. The reviews have been very helpful –'

'Helpful!' cried Barbara in amazement. 'Some of them said I was immoral and perverted.'

'I know. It was simply marvellous,' replied Mr Abbott, holding out his cigarette and watching the smoke curl upwards with appreciation and content. 'It really was simply marvellous. In my wildest and most optimistic moments I scarcely dared to hope that they would misread you to that extent.'

'Then – then it was a good thing?'

'Couldn't have had better reviews if I had written them myself. The sales leapt up –'

Barbara was astounded. How strange people were! What an incredible sort of world this business of writing had opened up before her eyes!

'And how's Copperfield?' enquired Mr Abbott. 'Anybody found John Smith yet?'

'No.'

'There are lots of people out for his blood.'

'I know,' said Barbara sadly.

'A Miss King called on me one day,' Mr Abbott continued with twinkling eyes. 'I gathered that she was rather peevish at being banished to Samarkand. And she was followed by a Mr Bulmer – a sour-faced individual, who wanted a little talk with Mr John Smith about his wife –'

'I know,' said Barbara again. 'It's simply dreadful the way they all go on. They had a Meeting here yesterday, and decided that I was to be horse-whipped, only it seemed rather difficult to get volunteers for the job.'

Mr Abbott laughed, 'First catch your hare –' he said.

'Captain Sandeman said that too.'

'Then Captain Sandeman is a sensible man. What about the new novel, Miss Buncle? How is it going?'

'Like mad,' replied Barbara. 'But of course it's all about Copperfield too. I don't know how to write about anything else –'

'Don't worry. You write what you feel you want to write, and never mind what Copperfield says. Copperfield ought to be flattered at being immortalised by your pen.'

'Now you are laughing at me,' said Barbara, provocatively. It was really Elizabeth who said it of course, Barbara would never have dared, but Mr Abbott wasn't to know that his hostess had suddenly changed into a totally different woman.

'I never laugh at charming ladies,' he told her.

They sparred in a friendly manner until Dorcas appeared with the tea. Dorcas approved of Mr Abbott, he was a real London gentleman. To show her appreciation she had made some little cakes, and put on her best muslin cap and apron.

'Smart. That's what he is,' Dorcas said to Milly Spikes who had got the afternoon off and was having a cup of tea with her in the kitchen.

'I like 'em smart,' agreed Milly.

Dorcas was not very proud of her friendship with Milly Spikes. In fact she would not have admitted its existence. 'She likes to come in now and then for a cup of tea,' Dorcas would have said if anyone had hinted that she liked Milly. But Dorcas did like Milly all the same, and, although she frequently told herself that Milly was 'low' and not her style at all, she was always very pleased to see Milly and to listen to her gossip. Milly knew everything that happened in Silverstream. She got all the village news from Mrs Goldsmith who was her aunt; and the news about the gentry filtered to her ears (which were preternaturally alert, and occasionally glued to keyholes) through the medium of Mrs Greensleeves. Mrs Greensleeves was not as reticent about her affairs, and the affairs of her neighbours, as she might have been if she had taken the trouble to understand the mentality of her maid. The remainder of the Silverstream news was garnered by the indefatigable Milly in the kitchens and servants' halls of Silverstream, where, owing to her good-nature and amusing tongue, she was *persona grata* with one and all.

Milly's tales lost nothing in the telling, and it was 'as good as a play' when she really got going, and imitated Mrs Greensleeves' somewhat affected tones or described her rages which broke forth periodically when the tradesmen sent in their bills. She heartily despised her employer and spoke of her with contempt – a thing quite definitely 'not done' in the opinion of Dorcas –

Dorcas was torn between her disapproval of Milly's stories and her enjoyment of their racy character.

'I s'pose you 'eard all about Mrs Featherstone 'ogg's drawing-room meeting,' said Milly, helping herself to Miss Buncle's jam with a liberal hand. 'Seems to 'ave been a sort of free fight from wot I 'ear. They all fixed on Mrs Walker as being John Smith –'

'Well, they fixed wrong,' interpolated Dorcas.

'I know that,' said Milly calmly.

'And how d'you know that so certain?'

'Easy as A B C. I took a walk up to the doctor's after supper larst night an' 'ad a little chat with Nannie – you know Nannie Walker, silly old fat 'ead, ain't she? Well, Nannie says Mrs Walker never does no sort of writing except the doctor's accounts an' suchlike. She reads, and knits the twins' jumper suits. That's proof enough for me. A person can read when they're knitting, but they can't write, can they? Not unless they've got a double set of 'ands, they can't.'

'A regular Sherlock 'Olmes, aren't you?' enquired Dorcas with a trace of irony in her tone.

'Well, I can put two and two together as well as most,' replied Milly amiably, 'and a good deal better than some. I found out more in 'arf an hour from the twins' old Nannie than all Silverstream sitting round The Riggs drawing-room the 'ole blessed afternoon. They 'ad old Mr Durnet there if you'll believe me – wot on earth they 'oped to find out from that pore dotty old man is more than I can see. And in the middle of the Meeting the pore old soul ups an' says, "When's my tea coming, that's wot I wants ter know." Aunt Clarer said 'e did, an' I don't blame 'im neither. It beats the band, don't it, Dorcas?'

Dorcas was forced to agree that it did. She was beginning to wish she had not been so scornful about Mrs Featherstone Hogg's drawing-room meeting. What a score it would have been if she could have said to Milly, 'Ah yes, of course, I was there myself.' How Milly's young eyes would have bulged at the news. But Dorcas hadn't been there, and she was beginning to get a little tired of Milly's second-hand account of the proceedings, so she changed the subject very successfully by remarking,

'That's a nice hat you've got on, Milly.'

'*She* give it me,' replied Milly with a wink. 'Had me eye on this 'at ever since she got it. She gave three guineas for it, if you please.'

'Lor'!' said Dorcas, looking at the hat with increased respect.

'It's too smart for 'er now she's after the Vicar,' continued Milly. 'That's 'ow I got it.'

'I thought she was after that Mr Fortnum.'

'You *are* be'ind'and,' said Milly mischievously. 'It's the Vicar now, and she's as good as got 'im too. Calls 'im Ernest to 'is face – an' 'e *is* earnest too. She thinks 'e's got plenty of money –'

'Well, he has, hasn't he?' enquired the thoroughly interested Dorcas.

'No 'e 'asn't,' said Milly, lowering her voice confidentially, 'everyone thought 'e 'ad money when 'e come, but Mrs 'Obday says it's not true. She says the poverty of the pore young gentleman is beyond words. 'E goes about with 'oles in 'is boots the size of five shilling bits, and she spends all 'er time trying to darn 'is socks because 'e 'asn't a penny to buy new ones. Mr 'Obday tol' me 'imself 'e 'as to put 'is foot down strong, or she'd be taking the scraps of meat out of their own mouths to feed the Vicar – fair gone on 'im Mrs 'Obday is.'

'Lor'!' exclaimed Dorcas in amazement.

Milly had finished with the Vicar now, she emptied out the dregs of her tea and studied the cup carefully.

'Do mine, Milly,' Dorcas said, handing over her cup to the amateur fortune-teller, 'what's that big square-looking thing, there?'

'Ooh, that's a wedding, that is! A wedding in the 'ouse. It 'ull be Miss Buncle – wot's the London gentleman like?'

'Biggish man,' said Dorcas thoughtfully, 'nice eyes, dark hair, greyish over the ears –'

'That's 'im. See, 'e's down there near the bottom of the cup – biggish man –'

'Where? Let's see,' entreated Dorcas.

'An' that's a flitting – see, down the other side? Means you're going to move, that's wot that means – and those dots all over the place is money coming in –'

CHAPTER EIGHTEEN

A HISTORY LESSON

It was decreed by the Powers That Be that Sally Carter was to have some instruction. Dr Walker had been consulted and had given his opinion that an hour's study every morning would do Sally no harm. The truth was Mrs Carter was finding difficulty in employing her grand-daughter. Sally was not domesticated, she disliked household toil, and the suggestion that she should help with the jam was met with a firm refusal. Sally had never made jam, she didn't know how to make jam, and she wasn't going to go into the kitchen and display her ignorance to the cook.

Mrs Carter's habit was to rise about eleven, and what was Sally to do with herself until then? What Sally did was to wander about the damp garden and catch a cold in her head. So Mrs Carter called in the doctor, and they put their heads together and decided that a little study – just an hour every morning – would do Sally less harm after her operation than mooning about and catching cold. 'And she's woefully ignorant,' Mrs Carter said, shaking her beautiful grey curls in dismay, 'I don't know what Harry has been thinking about, I really don't. He has kept the child with him all the time, roaming about the world – a year in this school, and six months somewhere else, and then a governess for a bit until Harry found her making eyes at him and sent her away – the poor child knows nothing, positively nothing. It is deplorable. Who can we find in Silverstream to teach the child? Who *can* we find, Doctor? You know *everybody*, of course, so perhaps you can help me.'

'I wonder if Hathaway would take it on,' said Dr Walker thoughtfully.

'You mean the new Vicar?' enquired Mrs Carter in a surprised voice.

'Well, I don't know, of course,' said Dr Walker, cautiously. 'He might not consider it for a moment – but then again, he might. I happen to know he's not very well off, and he might be glad to make a little extra in that way.'

'But my dear doctor, I thought he had plenty of money.'

'So we all thought, but he hasn't.'

'Are you quite certain?' asked Mrs Carter incredulously.

'Quite certain. My information is from a reliable source,' replied Dr Walker. 'Perhaps he has lost it all, like many unfortunate people in these troublous times, or perhaps he never had as much as rumour gave him. Anyway, there it is. Hathaway is a poor man, and a well-educated man and he must have a lot of time on his hands,' said the busy doctor, 'and I can't think of anybody else at all.'

The last argument clinched the matter as far as Mrs Carter was concerned. She was really desperate. She sat down the moment the doctor had gone and wrote a little note to Mr Hathaway (Mrs Carter always wrote little notes), putting her difficulties before him, and asking him in a most tactful manner whether he could possibly spare an hour in the morning to initiate her grand-daughter into the mysteries of Latin and History.

Ernest was somewhat startled when the little note reached him per Mrs Carter's gardener. He wouldn't have minded coaching a boy, but this was evidently a girl – grand-daughters usually were – and it seemed just a trifle *infra dig* to coach a girl. On the other hand there was the money question, and the money question was troubling Ernest very badly at the moment. Three pounds a week had seemed quite a lot when he had started so gaily on his new *régime*, but by the time Mrs Hobday's wages had come off it, and the weekly bills had been settled, there was nothing left over for such necessary items as the replacement of underwear, the soling of shoes, a pair of winter gloves, or seeds for the garden. – The Apostles and the Saints had lived in warmer climes, and under totally different conditions, of course –

After a few weeks, in which he vainly endeavoured to live below his income, Ernest began to wonder what would happen when his suits wore out, or if he had to call in the doctor, or see the dentist about his teeth. There was also his library subscription to think of – a mere nothing in the old days, but now a serious consideration. It must be met somehow of course, for it was absolutely necessary for a man in his position to have new books and keep abreast of modern thought. It was his duty to do so, and he would starve himself sooner than neglect his duty.

Ernest sat and thought about it for a long time, and then he rummaged about and found an old tobacco tin, and made a hole in the lid. Every week he tried to drop a few shillings into the box, and every week they had to come out again to meet some unexpected demand upon his purse.

He had told Mrs Hobday that he would have much less money in future, and had asked her to be as economical as she could. She had taken the news very calmly. Everybody was losing their money nowadays. It was a pity, but it couldn't be helped. Why, just the other day Mrs Hobday's own brother had lost all his savings in one fell swoop. It was rubber or something, Mrs Hobday thought. 'I tell you what we'll do, sir,' she said helpfully. 'We'll shut up the 'ouse, all except your bedroom and the study, and then we needn't have that girl, Karen, any more. A good-for-nothing slop of a girl she is! I'll manage the whole thing myself easy.'

It had not been any part of Ernest's scheme to throw a girl out of work, but he realised that something pretty drastic must be done, unless of course – but he wasn't going to contemplate that for a moment, he would last out the year supposing he starved, supposing his clothes fell into rags. It was unthinkable to go crawling back to Uncle Mike with the admission that he had failed.

It is interesting to note that he was already thinking about the year not as a term of probation, but as a definite task to be faced. Perhaps Vivian had something to do with this. He had begun to get interested in Vivian at this juncture – interested, but no more.

Some weeks after the dismissal of Karen he had to speak to Mrs Hobday again. He hated the job – hated it all the more because Mrs Hobday was so frightfully nice, and had been so kind to him and so decent about it before. He put it off from day to day, brooding over it, and making himself utterly wretched about it, but at last he pulled himself together and went off to look for her. He found her making his bed.

'We must keep the bills down, I'm afraid,' he said, feeling extremely shy and embarrassed. 'D'you think if I had just an egg or something for my supper it would make any difference?'

'That's all right, sir,' she replied, beating up his pillow with her capable work-stained hands. 'I've been getting the best of everything, seeing you were a gentleman as has been used to it – so to speak. I'll keep the bills down to what you say. Only of course you're bound to notice a bit of difference. Stooing steak isn't the same as best steak and no amount of cooking will make it the same. And while we're on the subject, sir, Hobday was asking if you'll mind if I went 'ome nights. I'd take a bit less if I could get 'ome about six and cook Hobday's supper. I could leave your supper all ready, and you could 'eat a cup of cocoa for yourself. I'd be 'ere early in the morning to see to the breakfast of course.'

Ernest consented, he was wax in Mrs Hobday's capable hands.

'I 'ardly liked to ask,' continued Mrs Hobday. 'But it would make a lot of difference if you really don't mind. You see my girl's been running up expenses – she's a good girl, Mary is, but she's young. She 'asn't the eye to pick out the best bit of meat at the butcher's. And then Rosy's ill again an' that makes more work. She gets the bronchitis every winter, that child does. As soon as ever the wind comes cold it strikes 'er in the chest. I don't know what we'd do without Dr Walker, he's such a kind gentleman, 'e was in seeing Rosy yest'day afternoon. I took a run down 'ome just to see what was 'appening, an' I run straight into Dr Walker, 'e's coming again tomorrow to see Rosy. Mrs Walker was in too with a basket full of oranges and jelly and a bunch of flowers. Mrs Walker would do you good just to look at 'er if you was ill, let alone what she brings.'

'I don't think I know Mrs Walker,' Ernest said.

'She goes to church pretty regular too,' replied Mrs Hobday. 'Except if the twins is ill, or anything – a tall slim lady she is, with brown 'air, and grey eyes, and 'er eyebrows go up and down a lot when she talks. You wouldn't forget Mrs Walker once you'd talked to 'er – and the doctor's a fine man – *kind* that's what they are.'

'You must go down to your home when you want,' Ernest said (he felt vaguely that he could be just as kind as the Walkers), 'especially when your child is ill. Don't mind about me. I'll manage quite all right. Your first duty is to your home, of course.'

'Thank you kindly, sir, but I'll manage to run both 'ouses – that's nothing to me. As long as you've got your 'ealth you can do anything you set your mind to. That's what I always say. I've said it to Hobday often when 'e's been a bit down in the mouth about 'is work. You see, sir, Hobday's a boilermaker by trade. 'E used to go to Bulverham every day, but the works is closed down now, and 'e's 'ad to take a job on the roads. Lucky to get it too. But Hobday gets a bit down in the mouth every now and then. "When am I going to get back to me own work?" he says to me. I'm sorry for 'im, too. It's 'ard when you can't get your own work, isn't it, sir? Just like as if *you* 'ad to go for a schoolmaster or something – I hope you don't mind me making the remark, my tongue do run away with me sometimes.'

'No, of course not – yes, it is exactly the same, and I do feel very sorry indeed for your husband,' said Ernest trying to answer all her questions at once and getting a trifle mixed up in the attempt.

That was only last week, and here was Ernest going for a schoolmaster just like Hobday. He felt even more sympathy for Hobday now that he knew exactly what it felt like to have to take up work which was not really your own line. Of course it was much worse for Hobday, because Ernest's was only a temporary thing. Now that he was definitely engaged to Vivian there was no question of carrying on with the experiment after the year was up. He must tell Vivian soon about his financial affairs, but there was no hurry about it. He had a lurking suspicion that Vivian would not understand the motives which had prompted his experiment in Poverty – she might even think him rather a fool.

Perhaps I *am* rather a fool, Ernest thought, wearing myself into a shadow quite unnecessarily. At any rate I don't seem to be much use at this job. His financial affairs had not benefited very much from the new arrangement with Mrs Hobday. The few shillings he had saved on her wages went into the tin, of course, but they came out again almost directly to buy a new spade for the garden – and only this morning the kitchen kettle had developed a small hole in its bottom – it was extraordinary how the money dribbled away.

'I *must* teach that little girl,' thought Ernest sitting down at his desk and taking up his pen to reply to Mrs Carter. 'There's nothing else for it – and I ought to be glad of the opportunity, ungrateful wretch that I am!'

But all the same he sighed, as he sealed up his letter, and gave it to the gardener who was waiting for a reply. It was rather a come-down, after all his noble aspirations, to start teaching Latin and History to a little girl.

So far, little has been said about Ernest's aspirations, and the reason why he had accepted the living at Silverstream which was really rather a backwater and had, hitherto, been held by ancient or unambitious men. Ernest was neither ancient nor unambitious, but he felt that he could chew the cud of his learning for a while, and read and meditate, and, eventually, when he had got his somewhat chaotic ideas into order, he could write a book.

It was certainly quiet enough at Silverstream, and now that he was alone at night in the big empty Vicarage it was really rather eerie. Sometimes Ernest thought he heard strange noises and went round the house with a thick stick, and an electric torch looking for burglars, but it had never been burglars yet. It was just the old house creaking in the wind, and talking to itself about all it had seen, and the big cheerful families which it had sheltered and sent forth into the world.

Ernest made up his mind, at last, that he would give up his nocturnal rambles. They wasted his time and made him feel lonely, and it was unlikely – when you thought about it seriously – that any sane burglar would choose the Vicarage for his nefarious purposes, considering that the Vicarage was almost empty and contained nothing of the slightest value for a burglar to take. It was much more likely, Ernest thought, that a sane burglar would choose The Riggs which was glittering with silver plate, or The Firs which boasted a valuable collection of eighteenth-century snuff-boxes. So he ceased to listen to the strange noises at night, and, after a little while, he ceased to hear them.

* * *

Sally was annoyed when she was informed of the arrangement with the Vicar. The idea of a grown-up woman like herself being sent back to the schoolroom like a troublesome child was galling in the extreme. But the whole thing was settled before she heard of it at all, and she was obliged to bow to the inevitable. Sally donned her most sophisticated garments, as a sort of mute protest against the indignity of it, and presented herself at the Vicarage punctually at ten-thirty. Her injured feelings were somewhat soothed by the Vicar's reception of her.

'Oh!' cried Ernest, leaping from his chair, 'are you – I mean I didn't know – are you – are you Miss Carter? – I thought it was going to be a child.' (His amazement and consternation were all that could be desired.)

'Gran treats me like one,' replied Sally, taking command of the situation at once. 'It really is most annoying – I suppose it's because Gran is so old herself.'

'I suppose it is,' agreed Ernest.

'Old people never seem to think that children grow up – they think you remain at the same age always. And of course Gran remembers Daddy being a little boy, and eating bread and milk for his supper, so I suppose it is difficult for her to realise me at all.'

'I suppose it is,' said Ernest again.

'People's brains work slowly when they get old. They don't pick up new impressions, you know. A doctor explained that to me once. It was very interesting indeed.'

'Yes, it must have been,' said Ernest helplessly, He was quite at a loss as to how he was going to begin the lesson. How on earth was he to start teaching Latin and History to this very self-possessed young lady? Lord's *Modern Europe* which he had found and decided upon as being the very thing for his purpose, now seemed entirely inadequate support. So too, the Latin Primer which he had unearthed last night from a box of old books and carried down to the study with triumph and satisfaction. The young lady was taking off her gloves, she evidently expected him to start at once. Ernest ran his hands through his hair in despair.

Sally had begun to enjoy herself, she was fully aware of Ernest's dilemma.

'I had this at school of course,' said Sally, taking up the well-worn primer. 'But I expect I've forgotten all about it by now. Do we start at the beginning?'

'Yes,' agreed Ernest. 'At least I don't know. Perhaps you would rather do some translations. The primer is rather dull. You see I didn't know you were – I thought you were – I mean I just got those books out because –'

'But I'm really very ignorant,' Sally told him, opening her blue eyes very wide, and gazing at him innocently. 'You'll be horrified when you find how little I know. I've forgotten everything I ever learnt.'

How blue her eyes were!

'Perhaps I might take off my hat,' suggested Sally.

'Oh yes,' he said, 'yes, of course, do take it off if it's more comfortable.'

Sally took it off, and gave her head a little shake so that her golden curls fluffed out round her head like a halo. Ernest had never seen anything so pretty in his life, he gazed at her with fascinated eyes.

'Well, I suppose we had better begin, hadn't we?' she enquired, sitting down at the table. 'Yes I suppose we had,' replied Ernest, trying to pull himself together.

'We mustn't waste our time,' Sally pointed out.

Ernest agreed. He took up the Latin Primer and laid it down again – it was awfully dull.

'What about history?' suggested Sally. 'I'm awfully ignorant about history, you know.'

'We had better start with history, then,' Ernest said.

'Everyone should know something about history, shouldn't they?' Sally demanded.

Ernest was sure that she was right. They opened Lord's *Modern Europe* and glanced through it together.

'I think this is too – too elementary for you,' Ernest said suddenly, closing the book and looking at his pupil – he found it difficult not to look at her. And when he looked at her he could think of nothing except how pretty she was. He looked away again, and tried to collect his scattered wits. 'Modern thought has progressed so enormously,' said Ernest. 'Dates are not considered so important nowadays, it's the background that really matters. It's understanding how the people lived, what kind of things they had to eat, and what they felt and thought.'

'Dates are dreadfully dull,' Sally agreed. 'I never could learn dates. What you say sounds so interesting.'

Ernest glowed, he said some more about it, elaborating his theory. They discussed the manner in which history should be taught. Meanwhile the time flew. It was half-past eleven before they had decided where to begin.

'I'm afraid we haven't done much work,' Ernest said guiltily as his pupil rose and pulled on her hat.

'We've cleared the ground,' Sally pointed out. 'It's most important to clear the ground. And you have found out how little I know –'

'Oh, but I haven't at all,' Ernest assured her. 'I mean you're so intelligent. So alive.'

Sally liked being called intelligent and alive, it was better to be intelligent than clever (who had said that?) Sally rather suspected that she was both, and perhaps she was right. She went home quite pleased with herself, and told Gran that the ground had been cleared. Gran had had a peaceful morning so she was easily convinced that the experiment was a success.

CHAPTER NINETEEN

MISS BUNCLE'S HOLIDAY

Mrs Carter was expecting Barbara Buncle to tea, she was somewhat surprised when Elizabeth Wade arrived instead.

'My dear Barbara!' she said, peering at her guest short-sightedly, 'My dear Barbara, what have you been doing to yourself? Not monkey glands, I hope.'

'Just a new coat and hat, that's all,' replied Barbara slightly dashed at her reception.

'And you've had your hair permanently waved,' Mrs Carter pointed out. 'I must say it's a great improvement to your appearance. It always is an improvement to anybody with straight hair. Mine is naturally wavy, of course,' she added defiantly – Mrs Carter was trying hard to live down the wicked aspersions cast upon her hair by John Smith –

'How nice for you!' said Barbara, sighing.

'Sally has started lessons with the Vicar,' said Mrs Carter, changing the subject rather abruptly. 'It is such a blessing for the dear child to have some definite employment in the morning when I am busy.'

'With the Vicar?'

‘Yes, he’s very badly off – so Dr Walker says. I don’t know how Dr Walker found out, except that he seems to know everything. Of course that’s how Sarah got all the information for her book – although a great deal of it is incorrect –’

Barbara followed this disjointed and not altogether logical sentence with some difficulty. She seized upon the main point – or at least what she considered to be the main point.

‘But Sarah didn’t write it,’ she said firmly.

‘How do you know? I’m perfectly certain she wrote it. Who else could have written it? Look at the opportunities she has. I’m certain the doctor tells her everything. I would never have Dr Walker again if it were not for the fact that he understands my rheumatism so well. But I shall cut Sarah when I see her,’ added Mrs Carter with satisfaction.

‘She didn’t write it,’ said Barbara again.

‘Well, I’d like to know who did, then. You didn’t stay until the end of the meeting, of course. We all decided that John Smith was Sarah Walker – it was unanimous, except for Ellen King, who always disagrees with everybody. Even old Mr Durnet held up his hand –’

‘I don’t suppose he had the slightest idea what he was holding up his hand for,’ interrupted Barbara.

‘Well, he held it up anyway – and wasn’t it a clear proof of guilt, getting in such a rage and dashing out of the room like a maniac without even saying goodbye to her hostess?’

‘I did the same,’ said Barbara bravely. She had not realised until this moment that she had been guilty of a breach of manners. Ought she to have said ‘goodbye’ to Mrs Featherstone Hogg, and ‘thank you very much for having me’?

I suppose I ought to have – thought Barbara – but if I had thought that at the time I wouldn't have come away at all, I simply couldn't have done it before everybody, so perhaps it's just as well I forgot my manners.

'Oh, *you*!' laughed Mrs Carter. 'Nobody even thought of you. You could never have written *Disturber of the Peace*. Sarah Walker has brains. I don't care for the woman at all – never did. She has no idea of how a lady ought to behave. The way she hob-nobs with the village people and doesn't pay proper respect where proper respect is due! I never could understand what *you* could see in Sarah Walker – but she certainly has brains of a kind –'

Barbara was hurt, and amused, intensely relieved, and very much annoyed all at the same time. There was a queer bubbly feeling in her inside at the mixture of emotions. She felt inclined to shout, 'Well, I did write it then, you silly old thing!' but she managed to stifle the inclination. She merely reiterated her conviction that Sarah had not written *Disturber of the Peace*.

'It's no use keeping on saying that, Barbara,' said Mrs Carter irritably. 'If Sarah didn't write it, who did? Agatha Featherstone Hogg and I made a list of everyone we knew in Silverstream and went through it one by one, most carefully. Everyone is either in the book themselves – or else absolutely incapable of writing it. But in any case it doesn't matter much now, we shall soon know for certain whether Sarah wrote it or not.'

'You will soon know for certain?'

'Agatha has a plan,' explained Mrs Carter. 'At least the

plan really originated with Mrs Greensleeves. Agatha has merely adopted it and they are working it out together.'

'And what is the plan?' Barbara asked breathlessly.

'Well, I can't tell you about it, because I promised Agatha I would tell nobody. Of course it wouldn't matter telling you, Barbara, but a promise is a promise. Personally I think the plan is a trifle risky, but Agatha will be careful.'

'Goodness!' said Barbara feebly. She was alarmed at the news. If the plan had been Mrs Featherstone Hogg's concoction she would not have worried so much – Mrs Featherstone Hogg was vindictive but not subtle – but Mrs Greensleeves was of a different calibre, she was cunning and sly as a vixen.

'Yes,' said Mrs Carter with satisfaction, 'yes, we shall soon know for certain whether or not it was Sarah Walker. Did you get a postcard from Paris, by any chance?'

Barbara admitted that she had.

'Disgraceful! Positively indecent!' said Mrs Carter, warming up again. 'I don't know what the world is coming to, nowadays.'

'I think it's nice that they got married,' Barbara said, trembling a little at her temerity in contradicting her hostess.

'Nice!' exclaimed old Mrs Carter. 'It's certainly not *nice*. The word is misused nowadays to a ridiculous extent. The word *nice* means fastidious, discreet – was it either fastidious or discreet for two people, whose names are being bandied about the world in a third rate novel, to rush off to Paris together? I suppose they *are* married,' added Mrs Carter, in a tone which implied that she had grave doubts on the subject.

'Dorcas was saying that they would make a very nice – er – I mean charming couple.'

'Dorcas!' snorted Mrs Carter, 'what does Dorcas know about it? It's a great mistake to talk things over with servants, you shouldn't pay any attention to what Dorcas says.'

'I don't, unless I agree with her,' said Barbara simply.

The conversation was getting more and more unpleasant. Barbara longed for Sally to come in and rescue her. She wondered where on earth Sally was, all this time. Once Sally appeared upon the scene Mrs Carter would cease talking about disgraceful marriages, for she was very careful what she said before her grand-daughter – quite unnecessarily careful considering Sally's knowledge of the world and its wicked ways.

'The amount of harm that book has done!' said Mrs Carter, raising her eyes to the ceiling. 'This dreadful hole-and-corner wedding, the Bulmers' home broken up and Isabella Snowdon's nightmares are all directly attributable to that book – not to speak of the discomfort and worry it has caused to people like Agatha and myself –'

Sally drifted in silently when tea was nearly over. She was all in brown today, russet brown like a November beech leaf. She sat down and sipped a large tumbler of milk with obvious distaste.

'Where have you been, Sally?' enquired her grandmother anxiously. 'I hope you haven't been wandering about outside, it's far too cold for you to be out at this time of night.'

'I was walking.'

'Where did you go, dear? All by yourself?'

'I met Mr Hathaway,' said Sally, carelessly. 'He came along.'

'That was good of him,' said Mrs Carter. 'Very kind indeed of him to take you for a walk. I hope you are not imposing too much on Mr Hathaway's good nature.'

Sally did not seem to think this required an answer, she sipped her milk, and crumbled a biscuit in her fingers.

'Don't make crumbs, dear,' said Mrs Carter. 'You can ring the bell for Lily to take the tea away, if you like.'

Sally ceased crumbling and rang the bell for Lily without speaking. When Sally had stayed at The Firs as a small child it had been a treat to ring the bell for tea to be cleared away, and Gran seemed to think it was a treat still. These small things annoyed Sally – she knew it was silly to be annoyed, but she was annoyed just the same.

Barbara felt sorry for her today, she looked sad, and withdrawn – the child was suffering within herself. Perhaps she was fretting for her father. It must be frightful for her – Barbara thought. Half an hour of old Mrs Carter's conversation had left Barbara somewhat worn – what must it be like to have nobody but Mrs Carter, and Mrs Carter all day long, and every day? Barbara remembered her promise to Virginia to keep an eye on Sally, and felt a trifle guilty. She had been so engrossed in her new book that she had not seen as much of Sally as she had intended.

'Sally must come and have tea with me again,' she said.

'I'm sure the child would enjoy that,' said Mrs Carter, graciously. 'Wouldn't you, Sally? Say thank you to Miss Buncle.'

'Yes, thank you, Miss Buncle. I would like to come,' said Sally with a wan smile.

She's ill – thought Barbara in dismay – she's pining away under our very eyes. I must try to cheer her up, poor little soul! Aloud she said –

'Well, what about tomorrow at four o'clock?'

* * *

The following morning was damp and unpleasant. Barbara glued her nose to the window and tried to determine whether it was actually raining or not. She decided that in any case it was not nice enough to go out for a walk. This was annoying because she was taking a little holiday and she was therefore free to enjoy herself. The new novel had absorbed all her thoughts and energies for days, and she felt exhausted, and a trifle stale – 'I shall take a holiday,' she had said, throwing down her pen and shutting her desk firmly, and she was making herself take it. Today was the second day of her holiday and she was already weary of it; Silverstream was a cold bleak place compared with Copperfield.

Barbara longed for the sunny atmosphere of her spiritual home where she could do as she liked, and say what she pleased, and nobody could contradict her unless she allowed them to do so; where there was no fear of anyone discovering who she was; and where nobody made secret and alarming plans to unmask John Smith – or, if they did, she knew beforehand exactly what they were and could foil them at will.

She wandered round the house getting in the way, and moving things about so that Dorcas couldn't find them when she wanted them.

'Why ever don't you go and write your story, Miss Barbara?' said Dorcas at last in exasperation.

'I'm taking a holiday,' said Barbara peevishly.

'You don't seem to be enjoying it much,' Dorcas said looking up from the kitchen table where she was rolling out the pastry for a pie. 'It's not my idea of a holiday mooning round the house with a long face –'

'I wish I was dead,' Barbara said. 'I wish I had somebody to talk to, I wish –'

'You better go out, Miss Barbara,' said Dorcas crossly. 'What's the good of wishing you was dead, and then wishing you had somebody to talk to? You couldn't talk if you was dead. If you was to go out for a nice walk you might meet somebody to talk to, and I'd get on with my work – I'm behind 'and as it is.'

'I'll go for a fastidious discreet walk,' Barbara said, 'that's what *nice* means. Did you know that, Dorcas? Well it does. I'll go out for a fastidious walk if you like – it would be more discreet to stay at home with all the talk that's going on in Silverstream. I know now exactly what a wanted man feels like.'

'A wanted man?'

'Yes, a man wanted by the police for murder or something. John Smith is wanted in Silverstream, you know, very badly wanted, and every time I walk down the High Street I expect to feel a heavy hand on my shoulder, and hear Sergeant Capper's voice saying, "I arrest you in the name of the law," or whatever it is that they say to a wanted man.'

'How you do rave on, Miss Barbara. Sergeant Capper would never arrest *you*.'

ꝏꝏꝏꝏꝏ

'It would really be John Smith he was arresting,' Barbara explained, sitting down on the edge of the kitchen table and watching Dorcas fit her neat oval of dough on to the top of the pie. 'John Smith is wanted for the murder of Mrs Featherstone Hogg's reputation – and Mrs Carter's too of course – Sergeant Capper would have to arrest John Smith even if he didn't want to –'

'Get your 'at like a dear, Miss Barbara,' Dorcas besought her. 'The rain's off now, and it's nice and bright. I declare I don't know what I'm doing with you standing over me talking all that nonsense. I'm not sure now as I haven't gone and put sugar in the potatoes by mistake.'

Barbara looked out of the window and saw that it had really cleared up, and the sun was struggling through the clouds. She went upstairs and put on her new coat and hat, and she took a new pair of grey gloves with fur gauntlets out of a drawer and put them on. She was wearing her new clothes every day now – it seemed rather extravagant, but she couldn't help it, she had taken a dislike to her old clothes for the new ones had opened her eyes to their frightfulness. They were scarcely worthy to be called clothes, Barbara thought, they were merely coverings for the body. She wondered how on earth she had ever worn them.

It was Elizabeth Wade – looking very Elizabeth Wade-ish – who issued forth into the fitful winter sunshine and went strolling down to the shops.

I might go in and see Sarah – she thought – as she passed the doctor's house. It would be rather nice – no, rather pleasant – to have a chat with Sarah. Sarah was about the only person in Silverstream except Sally who approved of *Disturber of the Peace*, she wasn't in it of course, but she was in the new novel. She was 'nice' in it, of course, because Sarah *was nice* – not in the least fastidious, or discreet, but just nice. It gave Barbara a warm feeling in her heart when she remembered how Sarah had stood up for the much maligned *Disturber of the Peace* before all those old cats. Yes, she must certainly go in and see Sarah.

There was another reason urging Barbara to go and see Sarah, and a much more important one. Sarah was not 'coming out' very well in the new novel. It was easier – Barbara found – to portray people who were a bit odd like Miss King, or catty and patronising like Mrs Featherstone Hogg. Sarah was none of these things, and her portrait was rather 'wishy-washy' in consequence. She would take a good look at Sarah this morning and try to absorb her personality so that when she sat down at her desk to write about her there would be something to write about.

Sarah was embroidering a brown teddy bear on a blue linen overall for one of the twins. She had a slight cold, and the doctor had forbidden her to go out, so she was feeling a little bored and was delighted to see Barbara. Barbara was rather a dear.

'Goodness, you're all new!' she exclaimed. 'How nice you look! How on earth did you manage to afford a new coat in these hard times?'

'I got a little money unexpectedly,' said Barbara with perfect truth. (She preferred to tell the truth if she could.)

'I wish I had,' said Sarah. 'My relations are all frightfully healthy at present. Sit down near the fire, Barbara dear. Wasn't that meeting ghastly!'

Barbara agreed that it was.

'Mrs Featherstone Hogg ought to be drowned,' continued Sarah. 'She really ought, and Stephen Bulmer, and the Greensleeves woman. Silverstream would be ever so much pleasanter to live in if they were all drowned. I still boil all over when I think of the way she stood up and asked me not to tell lies in front of everybody. I would have loved to tell them I had written the book just to see their faces. Ellen King is very nearly as bad, she got John all het up about *Disturber of the Peace* until I made him read it. Then, of course, he agreed with me that there was nothing disgusting about it. I can't understand Ellen King at all, she's usually such a sensible sort of person. I can't see anything in the book for her to make a song and dance about – can you?'

'No, I can't,' said Barbara. She had not intended to be hard on Miss King, she liked her. The fact was that Barbara had always been of the opinion that Miss King found Silverstream a trifle dull, there was little scope in Silverstream for Miss King's energies and capabilities, and it had been with friendly intent that she had arranged an adventurous holiday for her in Samarkand.

'You've read *Disturber of the Peace*, of course,' Sarah said. 'What a well-chosen name it is! We have had no peace in Silverstream since it was published, have we? Don't you think it's amusing, Barbara? I laughed and laughed when I read it. I couldn't leave it and go to bed.'

Barbara was intensely gratified, she preened herself inwardly.

'I suppose you think I wrote it?' asked Sarah with twinkling eyes.

'No, I don't,' replied Barbara, 'but the others do – I mean Mrs Carter and Mrs Featherstone Hogg and all of them. They've got some deep plan that's going to prove you wrote it. Mrs Carter wouldn't tell me what the plan was, she had promised not to tell anybody, but she was full of it. I thought I'd better warn you.'

'It was dear of you,' said Sarah, 'but I didn't write the book so they can't prove that I did.'

'I know, but I didn't like the way she spoke of the plan, she looked sort of mischievous. I can't explain what I mean but it made my blood run cold.'

'I don't give a damn for any plan made by Hogg and Carter,' said Sarah naughtily. 'It's bound to be futile and foolish –'

'But this is really Mrs Greensleeves' plan, the others have only adopted it.'

'That's different. Vivian Greensleeves hates me, for some reason. I know she hates me because she is always so frightfully sugary – and of course it was her suggestion that I was John Smith – and of course she doesn't like John Smith at all. John Smith was really very unkind to Vivian Greensleeves,' said Sarah, sniggering a little, 'that Romeo and Juliet scene with Mr Fortnum and Mason was just a *trifle* beneath our friend Vivian – not very much beneath her, I fancy, there was just enough truth in it to be intensely galling.'

'She's dangerous, Sarah.'

'She's a snaky sort of person,' Sarah said, wrinkling her brows, 'but I don't see what she could do to me, I don't really see what she could *do*.'

Barbara didn't see either but she felt that something nasty was brewing.

The twins were just coming in from their morning walk as Barbara went away.

'Aren't they lambs?' said their mother proudly – and they really were like two little lambs in their white fur coats and caps. Each lamb was hugging tightly beneath one arm a very shabby disreputable looking teddy bear, more precious in the sight of its owner than all the other toys in the nursery put together. The teddy bears went everywhere with the twins and shared their beds, and meals, and walks. They had been worn threadbare with love and kisses.

'Have they been good, Nannie?' Sarah asked.

'Very good,' said Nannie fondly. It was her invariable reply to Sarah's invariable question – no matter how wicked the twins had been she always assured their mother that they had behaved like angels. She punished them herself of course, but she never 'told on them'. Nannie adored them, she had had them 'from the month' and they were the joy and pride of her heart. Even their wickedness was of an endearing nature.

Barbara shook hands with the twins gravely, she was never at her best with children. She was under the impression that children didn't like her, they always stared at her so solemnly with their large innocent eyes. Her relations with Sarah's twins were further complicated by the fact that she never knew which was Jack and which was Jill – for Sarah dressed them both alike quite regardless of their sex. It was so awkward not to know whether you were addressing a male or a female.

'I can't think why John Smith didn't put them in his book, can you?' Sarah said, 'they're quite the loveliest, darlingest lambs in Silverstream. Goodbye, Barbara dear, and thank you for coming. I'll keep my wits about me and look out for squalls.'

* * *

Miss King was just going in at her own gate as Barbara passed, and Barbara, although she would fain have avoided the woman, was obliged to stop and speak to her.

'What horrid damp weather,' Barbara said, wondering what we would do without that safe topic of conversation. 'And so warm and unseasonable, isn't it? I do hope it will clear up and be nice and frosty for Christmas Day. I like Christmas Day to be frosty, don't you?'

'It never is,' Miss King pointed out.

'I expect we shall have a cold spell later,' continued Barbara. 'After all this mild wet weather we are practically bound to. Don't you think so?'

'Well, it won't affect me, anyway,' said Miss King blithely, 'Angela and I are off to Samarkand next week,' and passed in.

Barbara was left outside, staring at the gate as if there were something peculiar the matter with it.

CHAPTER TWENTY

CHIEFLY ABOUT SALLY

Christmas came and went, Silverstream went to church and gave each other small and somewhat useless presents just as it always did at this season of the year. Sally's history lessons progressed on unconventional lines. Mr Hathaway had ordered from his library some of the modern books about historical people and they were reading them together. It was scarcely history in the accepted sense of the word, but it was much more interesting than Lord's *Modern Europe*. They read aloud in turn and discussed what they read, exchanging ideas, and getting to know each other pretty well in the process. Ernest learnt quite as much as Sally at these history lessons – not much history, of course, but there are other things just as important as history. The conversation was apt to wander off into other fields, and linger there until Ernest suddenly remembered that he was giving Sally a history lesson and they returned hastily to their book.

They went for several walks together (not many, because Ernest's garden claimed such a large proportion of his time and energy), they explored the little byways of Silverstream and the woods, and they visited Twelve-Trees Farm once or twice because Ernest wanted to see one of the farmer's sons, who had sprained his leg and couldn't come to church. Dick Billing served well as an excuse for a walk up the valley and the Billings were delighted with the new Vicar's kindness and attention. Of course, there was no need to talk about history during these occasional rambles.

Ernest was so innocent and inexperienced in worldly matters that he was able to keep Sally and Vivian quite apart in his mind. Sally was a pretty child and a charming companion of whom he was growing very fond. Vivian was the woman he was going to marry.

Sally began to like Mr Hathaway very much. She had been rather scornful of him at first and had decided that he was 'soft', but she soon revised her opinion. Ernest wasn't 'soft', he was just 'different'. It took Sally a little time to understand him because she had never met anyone the least like him before. He was a new kind of being to Sally who was used to captains and subalterns and an occasional young man about town. Ernest had an entirely different point of view from these gay and self-possessed young creatures. His vocabulary was different, his character was different, his mind worked in a different way. But once she began to understand Ernest, she began to like him, and the more she understood him the better she liked him.

One morning – a few days after Christmas – Mrs Hobday knocked discreetly upon the door while the lesson was in progress, and asked for three shillings to pay the laundry. Ernest found his old tobacco tin and peered into it.

'I'm afraid there's only two and threepence here,' he said regretfully, 'I thought there was more, but, of course, I had to pay carriage on the books, hadn't I?'

‘They can wait till next week,’ said Mrs Hobday, who knew the secrets of the tobacco tin, and accepted this strange financial arrangement with the equanimity of her kind.

‘No,’ said Ernest firmly, ‘you had better give them the two and threepence while it’s here. Otherwise it will just fade away and the bill will be double next week. Tell them to add on the ninepence to their next account.’

Sally was amazed at this poverty. She knew what it was to be economical, of course, and to go without a new hat when you wanted it very badly, for soldiers are proverbially poor; but she had never realised that you could be so short of money as this. Fancy not having three shillings wherewith to pay your laundry bill – how ghastly!

‘It’s awkward being so poor,’ said Mr Hathaway to Sally quite frankly and somewhat apologetically, when he had replaced the empty tin in his drawer. ‘I try to save a little in that old tin, but there’s always something coming along that has to be paid. I was hoping to get my shoes mended next week.’

Sally gazed at him with wide eyes.

‘I don’t mind really,’ he said, laughing a little at her distress, ‘it’s rather fun pinching and scraping and trying to live on my stipend – it’s like a game –’

How brave he was!

‘Don’t worry,’ Ernest continued, ‘I shall be all right – you mustn’t look so sad about it, you know.’

‘You’ll have the money for my lessons, of course,’ Sally pointed out.

‘I oughtn’t to take it, really,’ replied Ernest, ‘I’m afraid you’re not learning much from me.’

‘Oh, I am!’ declared Sally, ‘I’m learning lots. Gran ought to pay you ever so much for my lessons, and she ought to pay you every week, I shall tell her about it.’

They discussed the question with the utmost frankness. Sally had been brought up with soldiers, a class which is completely frank as regards money. Having very little to come and go on, and knowing to a halfpenny what each other is drawing in the way of pay, the Army Officer has no false pride about his financial affairs. Ernest was perfectly frank, also, because he had never been poor, and he was not really poor now. This poverty of his, as he had told Sally, was merely a sort of game. Sometimes it was a troublesome, worrying sort of game, but there was nothing bitter, and real, and grinding about it. Poverty is easy to bear if it is only temporary, easier still if it is an entirely voluntary burden.

The next morning Sally appeared with an envelope containing two weeks’ salary from Mrs Carter for the instruction of her grand-daughter, which the said grand-daughter had extracted from Mrs Carter with firmness and tact.

Ernest was quite pleased to see the money – which Sally assured him he had ‘honestly earned’ – and not at all embarrassed at taking it from his pupil’s hands. Together they placed it in the tobacco tin, and Ernest promised to have his shoes mended at once. It was high time he did something about his shoes, for he did not possess a pair without large holes in the soles, and these large holes let in the water most uncomfortably when he walked about the muddy lanes of Silverstream.

They were just settling down comfortably to a perusal of

Elizabeth and Essex, by Lytton Strachey, when the doorbell rang and Mrs Greensleeves was shown in to the study. Mrs Greensleeves was beautifully dressed in navy blue, with black fox furs, and a quiet but obviously costly black felt hat set at a jaunty angle on her elaborately waved hair.

Sally had no use for Mrs Greensleeves, she had met her like before, and her sharp eyes had sized up that wily lady the moment they had beheld her sitting at her ease in Gran's drawing-room and laying down the law to Gran and Mrs Featherstone Hogg about *Disturber of the Peace*. And, besides her own infallible instinct, Sally had John Smith's word for it that Mrs Greensleeves was no good.

It was, however, quite obvious to Sally that Mr Hathaway did not share her views, and the views of John Smith, about his unexpected visitor. He seemed enchanted to see her and apologised profusely for being in the middle of a lesson. He was shy, and embarrassed, and meek, and propitiatory – almost as if he had been found out doing something wrong – and his excuses for Sally's presence were not altogether tactful. Sally was annoyed; she had every right to be here – far more right than Mrs Greensleeves if it came to that – and she did not like being apologised for. She had ceased to think of these hours with Mr Hathaway as lessons (except, of course, that Gran must pay for them), and it was humiliating to be shoved back into the schoolroom before Mrs Greensleeves whom she disliked and despised.

'It doesn't matter at all,' said Sally, seizing her hat and cramming it on to her golden curls.

'Oh, but you mustn't go,' said poor Ernest. 'We have only

just begun our lesson. Mrs Greensleeves won't mind waiting, or coming back later.'

Mrs Greensleeves said she wouldn't dream of disturbing a lesson, but, unfortunately, she could not come back later, she merely wanted to speak to Mr Hathaway privately for a few minutes. Perhaps Miss Carter could wait.

It appeared, however, that Miss Carter could not wait either, Gran would be expecting her and it was quite unthinkable to keep Gran waiting of course. She wasn't very sure whether she would be able to spare the time to continue her readings with Mr Hathaway, Gran was getting old, and required a lot of attention.

Ernest gazed from one to the other in dismay, he was quite helpless in this sudden and unexpected dilemma. He was being paid for Miss Carter's lessons, and therefore it was his duty to give them to her at the appointed time, but how could he let Vivian go away when she wanted to speak to him? Vivian would be annoyed if he sent her away – besides they were engaged, so, of course, he wanted to talk to her.

Sally read him like a book – he was fairly easy to read – and departed in high dudgeon and walked about Silverstream for an hour. She wasn't going home, and she wasn't going to tell Gran about it until she had made up her mind definitely whether she was going to continue her readings with Mr Hathaway or not (it sounded so much better to call them readings – and of course that was what they really were).

Sally walked quickly up the hill and into the woods. At one moment she was furious with Mr Hathaway for being such a fool, and the next moment she was sorry for him for being such an innocent. 'I wonder if they are engaged,' she said aloud, slashing at an unoffending bush with her umbrella. 'I bet they are engaged or he wouldn't have been so terrified of offending her. How could he be such an idiot as to fall in love with a horrible little cat like Vivian Greensleeves! She's years older than he is – five years older at least – and not a bit his style. She cares for nothing but clothes –'

A sudden thought struck her, and she stopped slashing and leaned against a convenient tree. Vivian Greensleeves would never marry a poor man. 'She can't know he's so poor,' said Sally to herself, 'or she wouldn't want him.' It was an amazing thought, amazing and comforting. It was a sort of loop-hole in the blank wall, it was a ray of sunshine in a dark place. Perhaps Vivian Greensleeves had heard – as all Silverstream had heard – that the new Vicar was a wealthy man, perhaps she didn't know that he had lost all his money.

Sally closed her eyes and thought about it deeply, she could think much better when her eyes were shut. She would save the poor young man from the clutches of Mrs Greensleeves, she would save him in spite of himself. The only thing to be settled was *how* she was going to save him.

Thinking all this over and over inside her head, Sally went home and was wonderfully docile and obedient to her grandmother, drinking up her milk without a murmur, and sitting reading very quietly in the corner of the sofa for the remainder of the morning.

'May I go out for a walk, Gran?' Sally asked, when they had finished lunch and were drinking their coffee in the drawing-room. 'It is so nice and sunny today, I feel a walk would do me a lot of good.'

Mrs Carter saw no reason why Sally should not go for a walk; she, herself, liked to sit down quietly with a book after lunch, and sometimes she closed her eyes and snoozed for a little in a ladylike manner; but children were different, of course, and the doctor had said most distinctly that Sally was to have sunshine.

'I think you might, dear,' said Gran, 'perhaps Lily had better put on her things and go with you –'

'Oh, Gran! It's Lily's afternoon out,' said Sally reproachfully.

This was an argument that could not be met, Gran would rather have gone for a walk with Sally herself than have filched an 'afternoon out' from her admirable and highly efficient parlourmaid.

'Well, I suppose you had better go alone then,' she said, with a little sigh. 'I don't like you walking about alone, but it can't be helped. Don't go too far, dear, and don't overtire yourself or get your feet wet.'

Sally promised to obey these dull injunctions with unusual docility and departed to call on Mrs Greensleeves.

* * *

Vivian Greensleeves was in when Sally called, she often took a little nap after lunch herself – there was nothing else to do in Silverstream except sleep. She had just composed herself comfortably upon her pink bed, and closed her eyes, when Milly came in to say that Miss Carter had called.

'Miss Carter!' exclaimed Vivian irritably.

'Mrs Carter's grand-daughter,' said Milly, 'the young lady from The Firs.'

'I know all that,' said Vivian. 'What does she want to see me for?'

Milly had no idea, Miss Carter hadn't said why she wanted to see Mrs Greensleeves, she had just called.

'Well, I suppose I had better see her,' said Vivian reluctantly. 'Some idiotic message from the old lady, I suppose – curse her!'

She arose reluctantly from her bed and powdered her nose. She did this quite instinctively and not because she wanted to appear at her best before Sally Carter.

Sally was waiting in the drawing-room, she rose when her hostess appeared and they shook hands gravely. It crossed Vivian's mind that the Carter child was much younger than she had thought, she couldn't possibly be more than fifteen. The impression was due to the fact that Sally had donned an entirely different set of garments from those she usually wore. With the old blue school hat which had been stowed away in the bottom of her hat box for the last three years, and the belted waterproof, and the coloured woollen scarf wound round her neck, Sally would have passed anywhere for a schoolgirl. Nor had she been content merely to lay aside her attractive and sophisticated clothes (Sally was nothing if not thorough), she had laid away her grown-up manner as well.

'I hope you don't mind me coming,' she said shyly.

Vivian replied conventionally that she was very pleased to

see her – she could not well do otherwise – and asked her to sit down.

'Silverstream is awfully dull, isn't it?' said Sally opening her eyes very wide. 'I expect you find it awfully dull too, don't you?'

'Yes, I do,' replied Vivian fervently. She wondered what on earth the child had come for. Why didn't she say what she had come for instead of sitting there gazing round the room with those intensely blue and innocent eyes?

'Have you a message for me?' she asked at last.

'Oh, no,' said Sally. 'No, I haven't. You see Gran didn't know I was coming. I expect you think it's rather queer me coming to see you like this – I just – I just wanted to see you –' said Sally, looking down and twisting one of the buttons of her waterproof in an embarrassed manner.

Vivian smiled – she thought she understood now why Sally had come. The child had evidently taken a fancy to her this morning, one of those schoolgirl passions which one reads about in psychological novels. And wasn't it quite a natural thing that Sally should take a fancy to somebody so entirely different from the dull and stodgy people with whom she was surrounded? Of course it was.

'It was nice of you to come,' said the pleasantly flattered Vivian – even a schoolgirl's admiration was worth having in a place as dull as Silverstream.

'Oh, no, it was nice of you to *see* me,' replied Sally humbly.

'I'm sorry you are feeling dull here – I expect you had a much gayer time with your father, hadn't you?'

'Yes. There were parties in the winter, and we used to

play tennis at school in the Summer Term. Daddy was always moving about, of course, so I went to lots of different schools.'

'Rather nice,' suggested Vivian to whom a constant change of scene seemed very desirable.

'In some ways,' Sally agreed, 'but I didn't learn very much, because I was just getting used to one kind of teaching when I moved on to something quite different. Gran says I'm very ignorant for my age, so that's why I'm having lessons with Mr Hathaway.

'I see,' said Vivian. She was interested. It had seemed such a queer arrangement when she had broken in upon them in the middle of the lesson that morning. She had even felt a trifle – just a trifle – jealous. Perfectly ridiculous of her to feel jealous of an infant like this! She had tried to find out from Ernest why on earth he had taken on the job of teaching Sally Carter but he had not given any satisfactory explanation of his reasons. Ernest could be very obstinate when he liked.

'It's very kind of Mr Hathaway to spare the time,' Vivian continued, when she had sorted things out in her own mind. 'I suppose he is doing it to please Mrs Carter.'

Sally nodded. 'Partly to please Gran, and partly, of course, because he needs the money so badly,' she told Vivian with childish frankness.

'Mr Hathaway has plenty of money,' said Vivian sharply. 'You needn't think the money is any object to him. I expect your grandmother asked him to do it and he didn't like to refuse.' It would be just like Ernest, she thought, to feel he was obliged to teach the child when Mrs Carter asked him.

Sally shook her head sadly, 'I know people think Mr

Hathaway is rich, but he's frightfully poor really. He's lost all his money you know. It's frightfully sad. I shouldn't think anyone has ever been so poor before.'

'Nonsense,' said Vivian, but all the same her heart missed a beat. Supposing the child was right? Supposing Ernest really *had* lost all his money and she had wasted all that time and taken all that trouble for nothing? 'What makes you think he has lost all his money?' she asked, trying to make her voice sound casual but not succeeding in deceiving Sally's sharp ears.

She's horrified – Sally thought, hugging herself with delight at the success of her plan – she's trying hard not to believe it, but she knows it's true all the same. Aloud she said sadly, 'Dr Walker told Gran, and I know it's true because he hadn't enough money to pay his laundry bill until he got the money from Gran for my lessons. Oh, I do think it's sad, don't you, Mrs Greensleeves?'

'It's more than sad – if it's true,' replied Vivian in a strange voice – and I'll find out whether it's true or not before I'm a day older – she added to herself fiercely.

Sally had now discovered the black cat. This sagacious animal usually remained in the kitchen with Milly and the food, both of which he infinitely preferred to his official mistress. Today for some reason, known only to himself, he was sitting on the black mat in front of the drawing-room fire, and, when Sally called to him invitingly, he stretched his back and walked slowly across the floor.

'Oh what a darling cat!' Sally exclaimed. 'Is he yours? Puss, puss, puss – what's his name, Mrs Greensleeves?'

She continued to praise and stroke the pussy's glossy back. He really was a dear, and she was intensely grateful to him for helping her to change the subject. She felt instinctively that she had said enough about Mr Hathaway's poverty, enough to upset Mrs Greensleeves and to place a thorny doubt in her mind. Mrs Greensleeves would never know a moment's peace until she had found out definitely whether the staggering news was true or not, and that was all that Sally wanted. So she stroked the cat's ears and slid her small hand along his ridgy back until he purred like a miniature Rolls-Royce.

'But his clothes are so – so *good*,' said Vivian, who was too closely interested to abandon the subject.

'I suppose he got them before he was poor,' said Sally naïvely.

CHAPTER TWENTY-ONE

MRS SNOWDON'S MEMORIAL

Ernest was delighted to see his pupil appear as usual the following morning, he had been afraid she would not come. She had been annoyed and offended, he knew, at the arbitrary way in which Vivian Greensleeves had cut short their lesson. Vivian shouldn't have done it, of course, and he shouldn't have allowed Vivian to do it, but he had been absolutely helpless at the time – a mere shuttlecock between the two. Looking back upon the scene Ernest decided that he had played a poor part, he should have been firm, he should have sent Vivian away and finished the lesson with Miss Carter; but he could not have done it all the same. It crossed his mind that Vivian had been a little inconsiderate, and somewhat domineering. Was he taking unto himself a domineering wife? St Paul said that a woman should be obedient to her husband. Of course he was not Vivian's husband, she would be different when they were married. Strangely enough the thought of being married to Vivian had ceased to thrill him. Ernest wondered why. A week ago, ten days ago, the mere thought of being married to Vivian had been sufficient to send delicious shivers up his spine. It's just that I'm getting used to the idea – Ernest thought.

When the mystic hour of ten-thirty drew near, Ernest found that he could not sit still. He went and looked out of the window several times – would she come, or was she really hurt and offended? How awful if she didn't come any more, if she discontinued her lessons! They had had such pleasant hours together, he liked to hear her reading, she had such a pretty voice, and he could look at her undisturbed – he liked looking at her.

If she doesn't come I shall go and call, Ernest thought, I was at fault about the whole thing and I must apologise. Perhaps if I apologise she will forgive me for being such a weak idiot. He left the window – impelled by a sudden idea – and went into the kitchen to find Mrs Hobday.

'Oh, Mrs Hobday,' said Ernest. 'If anybody calls while I am giving Miss Carter her lesson please say I am engaged. The lesson must not be interrupted.'

'Yessir,' said Mrs Hobday. 'I'm sorry about yesterday, I really am. But Mrs Greensleeves was so obstinate and you 'adn't said nothing definite about not being disturbed. I really didn't know wot to do.'

'I know, it was my fault, Mrs Hobday,' Ernest told her. 'Entirely my fault – but you'll know another time.'

'Oh, I will, sir,' replied Mrs Hobday. She won't get in again and worry the poor lambs – added Mrs Hobday to herself – not unless it's over my dead body, she won't. – Mrs Hobday was another who had no use for Vivian Greensleeves.

At this moment the doorbell rang, it rang so loudly that Ernest – whose nerves had been on edge all morning – nearly jumped out of his skin.

'That'll be Miss Carter now,' said Mrs Hobday taking off her apron.

'Don't bother, I'll answer it,' Ernest told her, and he ran to open the door. Sally was standing on the step, she smiled in a friendly manner when she saw Ernest.

'Am I late?' she enquired.

'No, not a bit,' replied the Vicar, 'but I was so awfully afraid you wouldn't come – I couldn't help it yesterday – I'm such an ass – you aren't angry, are you?'

'I was, at the time,' Sally admitted, following him into the study. 'But I'm not now, not a bit.' She stood and smiled at him.

What a darling! thought Ernest. He had a sudden feeling that he would like to kiss her – a most extraordinary feeling for a man who was engaged to somebody else – of course it would never do to kiss her, it would be a frightful thing to do. Sally held out her hand and they shook hands gravely.

'It won't happen again,' Ernest said, 'I've told Mrs Hobday to say I'm engaged if anyone calls.'

'No,' said Sally. 'No, I don't think it will happen again.' She took up *Elizabeth and Essex* which was lying all ready on the table with a book-marker in the place. 'Shall I read first, or will you?' she enquired.

'You read,' Ernest said, and he composed himself very happily and contentedly in his chair to watch her.

* * *

Several days later Ernest, taking a little stroll round the churchyard, was surprised and somewhat pained to see that a large pink marble sarcophagus had appeared as if by magic upon the Snowdons' family grave. He was the more distressed because the little churchyard had hitherto been happily free from monstrosities of this nature. It was such a pretty little churchyard, peaceful and beautiful, with several fine old trees lending dignity to the scene, and the river murmuring past as if it were singing an endless lullaby to the sleepers.

Ernest paused and hesitated – there appeared to be several men employed in giving the finishing touches to the regrettable erection. He decided to go and speak to them – perhaps even remonstrate in a tactful manner. At any rate he could find out the reason for its sudden appearance among the simpler and more tasteful monuments. As he drew near Ernest perceived that Mr Snowdon was there himself, speaking to the men and giving them some instructions about the lettering. 'PEACE BE ST' had already been inscribed in large gold letters upon one side of the stone – it was a curious text to have chosen, Ernest thought.

An older – and wiser – man than Ernest would have turned back on seeing the perpetrator of the outrage himself. Tombs and tombstones are delicate subjects for an outsider to intrude upon at the best of times, and Ernest was not as calm as he should have been to deal with a delicate subject – in fact he was extremely annoyed. What business had Mr Snowdon to destroy the amenities of Ernest's pretty churchyard with his execrable taste? The thing was a perfect eyesore.

He said, 'Good afternoon,' to Mr Snowdon, and asked, somewhat unnecessarily, what was being done.

'I am erecting a memorial to my dear wife,' said Mr Snowdon in throaty tones.

'But there was already a memorial to Mrs Snowdon here,' Ernest pointed out.

'Merely a temporary one,' replied the bereaved husband. 'Merely temporary.'

'It was a granite cross, wasn't it?' enquired Ernest, pursuing the subject unwisely.

'Yes,' replied Mr Snowdon briefly.

'A granite cross is usually considered a sufficiently permanent type of memorial. As a matter of fact I liked it better than this.'

'Did you?'

Mr Snowdon's tone proclaimed that he did not care whether the Vicar liked it or not. If Mr Snowdon thought fit to change the granite cross for a marble sarcophagus, it was no business of the Vicar's – interfering man, poking his nose into matters that did not concern him.

Ernest walked round to the other side of the enormous slab and saw that the inscription here was finished. Mr Snowdon had caused the words 'REST IN PEACE' to be cut upon this side of his dear wife's memorial. The Vicar did not care for the wording at all, it had a Roman Catholic ring about it, his annoyance was in no way appeased.

'I suppose you have obtained permission to erect it,' Ernest asked indiscreetly.

'I have,' replied Mr Snowdon.

Ernest sighed, there was nothing more to be done about the wretched thing. He was just turning away when the marble sarcophagus hit him once more in the eye – it literally got up and hit him. It was a ghastly thing. It was too appalling for words. It spoilt that whole corner of the churchyard.

'Do you think it is quite – er – suitable?' said Ernest, returning once more to the attack. 'I mean it is so – so different from all the other stones, so – so very – er – large, and – and heavy. The stone sarcophagus has quite gone out of fashion, you know.'

'You think so?' enquired Mr Snowdon, with dangerous meekness.

'It really has,' Ernest assured him, 'perhaps you don't know the origin of the custom of covering the entire grave with a large heavy stone. It was used to keep wolves and jackals from disturbing the grave –' Ernest was warming up to his subject now, he felt that if he explained the whole thing carefully to Mr Snowdon he might see the error of his ways and consent to have the pink marble atrocity removed and the granite cross restored. Vivian could have warned Mr Snowdon that he was in for a lecture on memorials and their historical and religious significance, but Vivian wasn't there, of course. 'They were at first confined to foreign lands,' continued Ernest, 'where wolves and jackals abounded, roaming about graveyards and digging up bones. One can easily understand how the idea of the large heavy stone covering the entire grave was evolved. The idea was brought home by the Crusaders who had seen it during their travels and the practice of covering the tomb with a stone memorial became fairly common in England. It died out, I am glad to say, and was only revived for a short period during the panic caused by the trial of Burke and Hare. You will, of course, remember that these men were found guilty of despoiling newly made graves in order to procure anatomical specimens to sell to students and hospitals. I feel convinced that the panic caused was out of all proportion to the facts of the case, but naturally bereaved relatives felt anxious to protect the graves of their dead from desecration. Those days are now past and modern taste leans towards a simpler form, it prefers to dispense with all that is superfluous and meaningless. The sarcophagus is both superfluous and meaningless – it is even more meaningless than usual in this case for I believe Mrs Snowdon has been dead for some years –'

'Thank you,' said Mr Snowdon with elaborate sarcasm. 'Thank you very much. I am sorry to interrupt your eloquence but *I* have other things to do. When I want to hear another sermon from you I shall come to church, but this one will last me for some time I fancy. Meanwhile perhaps you will be good enough to mind your own business and allow me to mind mine. If I choose to erect a certain type of memorial upon my family grave, I shall do so. *Good* afternoon, Mr Hathaway.'

Ernest retired, baffled and conscience-stricken. He realised too late that he had been treading on delicate ground with elephantine feet. He had offended Mr Snowdon without achieving his object. Ernest brooded over the matter as he went home. It seemed to him a very strange thing to take down a granite cross and put up a marble sarcophagus after a woman had been dead and buried for three years. What was the meaning of it? The lettering was different too, for the granite cross had borne the inscription, 'She is not dead, but sleepeth.' Ernest remembered it distinctly because he had liked it, he had thought when he read it that it was a beautiful idea to put our Lord's consolatory words to Jairus upon a memorial tombstone. They had a deep significance, they carried with them a promise – the promise of resurrection.

Ernest felt sorry these words were not upon Mrs Snowdon's grave any more (he had a strange feeling that Mrs Snowdon was sorry too), but this was by no means the worst part of the unfortunate affair, even the hideous erection itself was not the worst part of it; far worse than these was the knowledge that he had been tactless and indiscreet. Uncle Mike had warned him of the pitfalls of his calling – 'Tread warily,' Uncle Mike had said. 'You may think they're fools, but *you're* a fool if you let them see it, and don't offend the "little ones", whatever you do, or you will be much happier and more comfortable at the bottom of the sea with a millstone round your neck.' This much from Uncle Mike and, already, at the very beginning of his incumbency, he had offended one of his most important parishioners.

Ernest was so upset that he could think of nothing else, he mooned round the house for a bit, and finally decided to go and have tea with Vivian. He must talk it over with somebody and Vivian was obviously the person with whom to talk it over. He was going to marry Vivian, she was going to share all his troubles and worries; well, she could begin by sharing this one – thought Ernest. Besides, of course, he *wanted* to tell Vivian all about it, she was so sweet and womanly and sympathetic, and she knew a good deal about the world. She could advise him whether he should write to Mr Snowdon and apologise, and if so what he should say. Perhaps between them they should concoct a conciliatory letter to Mr Snowdon.

Ernest thought all this as he breasted the hill. He hadn't seen Vivian for several days, indeed he had not seen her since that dreadful morning when she had interrupted Miss Carter's history lesson. That was Wednesday, and today was Saturday – practically three days without a glimpse of Vivian! It was strange that he had not noticed this before. He wondered why she had not dropped in to see him as she usually did either in the morning, when he was working in the garden, or in the afternoon, when he was reading in his study. Perhaps she had been busy, or perhaps it was because the weather had been so dreadful – it had rained all yesterday and most of the day before, he remembered.

He found Vivian having tea in front of the drawing-room fire. It was a cosy scene. How nice that she was alone! Ernest went forward eagerly.

'Well, what do you want?' Vivian asked sharply. The mere sight of him caused her to boil with rage, for she had discovered that what Sally had told her was true. In fact once she began to make enquiries it appeared that everybody in the village was aware of Ernest's financial difficulties, everybody except herself. The village was full of the most astounding tales of the poverty at the Vicarage. She was told about the enormous holes in his shoes (which could be seen to great advantage during the Litany) and about the even more enormous holes in his socks, which Mrs Hobday was obliged to wrestle with because the poor gentleman could not afford new ones. She was even told that Ernest had invested in a pair of hair clippers and had endeavoured, with startling results, to cut his own hair so as to save a monthly ninepence at the Silverstream barber's gentlemen's saloon. Nearly all the shops had tales to tell of poor Ernest's amateur efforts in economy. He bought broken rolls at Mrs Goldsmith's and odd scraps of meat at Mr Hart's, and the outside leaves of cabbages at Miss Clement's fruit and vegetable emporium. Mrs Hobday had put him up to it of course, they told Mrs Greensleeves, the poor gentleman would never have thought of things like that himself.

Thus it was that when Ernest walked into her drawing-room looking pleased to see her, and expecting her to be equally pleased to see *him*, Vivian's blood simply boiled with rage, and instead of welcoming him with open arms as Ernest had expected, she looked at him as if he were some new and particularly loathsome species of slug and enquired what he wanted.

'You haven't been to see me for ages,' Ernest told her, slightly damped by this unusual reception.

'I've found you out, you see,' replied Vivian, trying to speak calmly and not succeeding very well.

'You've found me out?'

'Yes.'

'But I haven't done *anything*,' said poor Ernest.

'Oh no! you haven't done anything, have you?' demanded Vivian scornfully, 'you haven't lied and deceived me at all, have you?'

'No, I haven't,' replied Ernest with some spirit.

'You thought you had taken me in nicely, didn't you?' continued Vivian with rising heat. 'Coming here and pretending to everybody that you were rich and strutting about in fine clothes, and all the time you haven't a penny – not enough money to have your shoes mended –'

'Oh, is that all?' said Ernest, beginning to see daylight through the fog, 'I can explain that quite easily, you see –'

'Yes, that's all,' Vivian interrupted furiously. 'That's *all* and it's quite enough too –'

'But Vivian, if you would listen for a moment I can explain –'

'I don't want to listen to you any more, I've listened to you quite enough, I'm sick of listening to you –'

'But Vivian –'

'The idea of you coming here,' she cried, 'the very idea of you coming here and pretending to be so good and pious – a sort of saint on earth – and all the time you're nothing but an impostor.'

'I'm not an impostor.'

'You are an impostor, and a liar and a cheat. The very idea of you coming to propose marriage to me when you hadn't a single penny to bless yourself with. What do you think I want to marry you for? I suppose you think I would be happy and content to live all my life in a mouldy country vicarage, pinching and scraping, and counting every halfpenny? Well you're mistaken, then. I suppose you think you're so good and wonderful that any girl would be proud to marry you and darn your socks for the rest of her life? Well, you're mistaken there, too – thoroughly mistaken. You bore me to death,' said Vivian vindictively. 'Do you hear that – you bore me to death.'

Ernest heard it, he could not fail to hear it, for Vivian's voice was loud and somewhat shrill. He found that his knees were shaking for he was unused to scenes of this kind. He gazed at Vivian with horror – was this really Vivian, this woman with the hard eyes and the shrill shrewish voice? Was this the same Vivian who had listened to him so sympathetically, who had brought him her troubles and doubts to be smoothed away? Was this the lamb that he had brought back with such pride and joy to the fold?

You bore me to death, Vivian had said. He bored her. Why then had she listened to him and encouraged him to talk to her? Why had she sought him out, visited him at the vicarage, invited him to her house, and, above all, why had she promised to marry him? It seemed a most extraordinary thing to Ernest, he could not understand it at all, he was utterly bewildered. He gazed at Vivian and decided that she looked strange, she looked like an unknown woman, he felt as if he had never seen her before.

'Then it was – it was because – because you thought I had money,' he said slowly, his brain clearing as he spoke, 'you said you would marry me because you thought I had money?'

Vivian didn't like it put quite like that, it sounded all wrong, somehow, as if *she* were in the wrong and not Ernest at all.

'People must have money you fool!' she said with slightly less rancour, 'how do you suppose people can live without money?'

'They need a little, certainly.'

'I need lots,' Vivian said frankly. 'It's only idiots and imbeciles who say that money isn't important. Money is the most important thing in the world. I would be perfectly happy with lots and lots of money –'

'And a husband who bored you,' suggested Ernest, looking at her very gravely and waiting for her answer with some anxiety.

She laughed a trifle hysterically. 'With the Devil himself,' she cried.

CHAPTER TWENTY-TWO

THE CHILDREN'S PARTY AT THE RIGGS

The Featherstone Hoggs' children's party was fixed for the second week in January. They gave one every year, usually on Christmas Eve and a large and elaborately decorated Christmas Tree was the *pièce de résistance*; but this year, with all the excitement over *Disturber of the Peace*, and the drawing-room meeting, the children's party had slipped out of mind.

Mrs Featherstone Hogg disliked the children's party intensely, she only gave it because it was the 'right thing' for the most important lady in the neighbourhood to give a children's party, and because Lady Barnton from Bulverham Castle could always be induced to come to it and bring her small nieces when she could not be induced to come to any other of Mrs Featherstone Hogg's various parties or At Homes.

Christmas Eve had passed, and there was no mention of a children's party. Mr Featherstone Hogg had not forgotten about it, he liked the Children's Party (it was the only kind of party he did like), but he thought perhaps Agatha had had enough to bear this year so he said nothing about it. Perhaps they might have one at Easter instead; by Easter Agatha would have settled down a little. He decided to leave it at that. He was astonished when Agatha reminded him about it, the first mention of it usually lay with him. In spite of Lady Barnton, Agatha always approached the Children's Party with reluctance. It was such a bore, she always said, it was so noisy, the children made such a mess –

So, when a few days after the New Year Agatha suddenly enquired with an amiable smile whether they were going to have a Children's Party this year, Edwin looked up from his marmalade with surprise (they were at breakfast).

'I thought you were too upset, Agatha,' said Edwin with solicitude. 'I wasn't going to bother you about it this year.'

'One mustn't be selfish,' Agatha replied smiling wanly. 'One mustn't allow one's own feelings to interfere with the enjoyment of others.'

'No,' said Edwin, a little dazed by this altruism.

'I shouldn't like the children to be disappointed just because I happen to be miserable.'

'No,' said Edwin again.

'Of course the little Bulmers are away – banished from their home all because of that unspeakable book,' continued Agatha in languid tones. 'But we could have the Walker twins and the little Shearers, and Mrs Carter's grandchild (she's rather old, of course, and a pert, unmannerly sort of girl, but we shall have to ask her), and Lady Barnton and her nieces, and the Turners, and the Semples from Bulverham –'

Mr Featherstone Hogg was pleased, he did not analyse Agatha's motives. It was enough for him that they were to have the party, and have it, apparently, without the usual fuss. It was nice that they were going to have it after all, he always enjoyed it. Children were so jolly, he liked them, and they liked him. Children did not look through him, nor snub him because he was small and insignificant as so many grown-up people did. He was rather a 'dog' with children and he enjoyed being a 'dog'. Last year he had dressed up as Santa Claus and had been a tremendous success, in fact the success of the evening. It was too late to be Santa Claus this year, of course, but he would think of something else to amuse them, something entirely new. Mr Featherstone Hogg finished his breakfast hastily and went off to find the 'list' which he kept securely from year to year amongst his papers in his meticulously neat desk.

They fixed the date there and then and the invitations were issued immediately. Agatha pointed out that schools usually started towards the end of the month, and Lady Barnton's nieces – at least the two elder ones – would be going away soon.

Sarah Walker was not altogether surprised when she found that her name was omitted from the twins' invitation to the children's party at The Riggs. She could scarcely expect to be invited after her somewhat discourteous exit from the drawing-room meeting. The invitation card bore the information that Mrs Featherstone Hogg was having a children's party on the tenth of January and would be delighted to see Master and Miss Walker and Nurse. Well, anyhow Nannie would enjoy it – thought Sarah – even if the twins didn't. The twins were still rather young to enjoy parties and they had so few that they were apt to become over-excited and obstreperous. But Nannie would manage them (she managed them better than Sarah), and she would enjoy taking them and showing them off to the other Nannies. It was rather dull for Nannies in Silverstream, there were so few children. Now that the Bulmers had gone the little Shearers were the only other children in the place. Sarah had been glad when the Shearers came in and she found they had small children and a Nannie that *her* Nannie approved of. Fortunately Nannie had friends in Silverstream, she liked the Goldsmith girls, and Dorcas, and she was not above an occasional chat with Milly Spikes; but Nannies are a class apart and these people – though well enough in their way – were not really congenial to her. At the Featherstone Hoggs' party Nannie would meet several other Nannies, she would be in her element. It was therefore almost entirely for the sake of their guardian that Master and Miss Walker accepted the kind invitation of Mrs Featherstone Hogg.

Dr Walker had an urgent call to Bulverham on the afternoon of the party so he could not convey his offspring to The Riggs as had been arranged. Sarah was obliged to order a taxi for them; it was rather extravagant, of course, but fortunately parties did not happen very often in Silverstream.

The twins were ready some minutes before the taxi arrived, and came into the drawing-room to wait.

'How sweet they look, Nannie!' Sarah cried, hugging them both at the same time.

Nannie agreed that they did. They were dressed in blue silk tunics embroidered with white daisies round the collars and cuffs. Their fair hair was bobbed neatly round their white necks. They had white silk socks and white buckskin shoes with small silver buckles. Nannie was intensely proud of them, it was so unusual to see twins – a boy and a girl – exactly alike. Nannie enjoyed the distinction of having such charges, she was openly amused and secretly flattered when people – and other Nannies especially – could not tell them apart. 'They're not a bit alike really,' Nannie would say, laughing a little at the joke. 'I could tell which was which in the dark.'

'There's the taxi,' said Sarah suddenly. 'You had better not keep him waiting, Nannie. Tell him to come back for you at six, that will be late enough for them.'

Nannie promised to remember to tell him, she enveloped the twins in their white fur coats, and shepherded them into the taxi.

The party was just sitting down to tea when they arrived. Nannie counted about fifteen children, there were more grown-ups, of course. Mrs Featherstone Hogg welcomed the Walkers affably and found two seats so that the twins could sit together – they were never happy apart.

'What a dear little couple they are!' said Mr Featherstone Hogg.

Nannie smiled with a satisfied air, she had made a rapid survey of the table, and discovered that there wasn't a child in the room who could compare with her two, not one. She stood behind their chairs and buttered their buns for them and saw that they didn't eat anything unsuitable. Lady Barnton's youngest niece had a fat Nannie and *she* stood behind her child's chair. Nannie looked at the fat Nannie and decided that she was the right sort, she made a tentative remark and the two were soon chatting together happily. The Shearers' Nannie was at the other side of the table looking after the Shearer baby who was only eighteen months – just old enough to want all he saw in the way of cakes and too young to be allowed to have them. Nannie Shearer's hands were amply full, trying to keep him quiet and feeding him with sponge cake.

'I never seen twins as alike as yours, are they girls or boys?' said the fat Nannie admiringly.

'One of each.'

'Well, I never. I'm sure nobody could tell the difference if they were paid for it. I had twins once but they were both girls, and they weren't so like each other either.'

Mrs Greensleeves now appeared at Nannie's elbow, she had come to 'help with the children.' She spoke to Nannie in a friendly way and admired the twins.

'Did you make their little tunics?' she asked.

'Mrs Walker made them,' replied Nannie. 'Mrs Walker makes nearly all their clothes, she's a beautiful knitter too.'

'I wonder how she finds the time,' said Mrs Greensleeves inquisitively.

Nannie didn't answer, she thought it was a silly remark to make. What else had Mrs Walker to do but to make nice clothes for the twins? She had three maids and a nurse so there was no need for her to do a hand's turn in the house. Still, apart from her silly remark, Mrs Greensleeves seemed nice and she had a tall gentleman with her that Nannie rather liked the look of, and a tall lady. Nannie decided that they were a brother and sister for they had the same kind of nose, slightly hooky.

Mrs Greensleeves sat down beside the twins and talked to them. They were quite friendly with her, and Jack offered her a bite of his chocolate biscuit.

'Just pretend to bite it,' Nannie advised her.

Mrs Greensleeves pretended.

'Here,' said the tall gentleman. 'Is that a girl or a boy making up to you, Vivian? I don't mind so much if it's a girl –'

'I've no idea which it is,' replied Mrs Greensleeves, laughingly.

The children's tea was nearly over now, and the other Nannies were going downstairs to the housekeeper's room to have theirs. Mrs Greensleeves suggested to Nannie that she should go with them.

'I'll look after the twins,' she promised.

There seemed no reason why Nannie should not go. The twins were quite happy with Mrs Greensleeves, they were moving into the drawing-room now, for some games, so there was no chance of the twins over-eating themselves upon unsuitable food while she was gone.

'You're sure it will be all right, madam?' Nannie asked. 'You won't let them get too wild, will you? If they're not happy you could ring and send for me, couldn't you?'

'We'll look after them,' said the tall gentleman, 'off you go and have your tea, Nannie.'

Nannie went as far as the door and waited, they were quite

happy, they had not even noted her departure. Somebody had started to play the piano and dozens of coloured balloons had been let loose on the floor. The children were all laughing and scrambling after them. She went downstairs to the housekeeper's room and joined the other Nannies. It was a cheerful and pleasant party.

Nannie was away about half an hour. When she came back up the stairs she heard the sound of musical chairs in the drawing-room – a few bars of music and then silence, and then loud shrieks, and then another few bars of music. Musical chairs was rather beyond the twins. Nannie hoped they hadn't been allowed to play, it was a rough game for tiny children – she hastened her steps. The door of the drawing-room was open, she stood in the doorway and looked all round the room for the two little blue figures. She saw the Shearer children, and the Semples and the Turners, but where were Jack and Jill? In about a minute Nannie was certain that they were not in the room, Mrs Greensleeves and the tall gentleman had also vanished. She wondered what on earth had happened – there was the possibility that they had fallen down and hurt themselves and been taken upstairs to have a knee bandaged or something, but it didn't seem likely. Surely Mrs Greensleeves would have rung the bell for her if anything had gone wrong. She began to feel a little nervous and frightened, perhaps it was silly of her to have left them, they were so small, but what could have happened to them here?

Presently she edged round the room and touched Mrs Featherstone Hogg on the arm.

‘Please, madam, where are the twins? It’s about time I was getting on their things to go home. Mrs Walker does not want them to be late.’

Mrs Featherstone Hogg seemed excited, her face was very flushed and her eyes were glittering strangely – almost as if she had been drinking, Nannie thought –

‘Oh, they’ll be all right,’ she said.

‘But where are they?’ demanded Nannie.

‘Mrs Greensleeves is looking after them. I think she and Mr Stratton took them out for a run in Mr Stratton’s car.’

‘A run in his car,’ echoed the twins’ guardian in dismay.

‘They were too small to join in the games.’

‘But I should have gone too – Mrs Walker wouldn’t like it. Mrs Walker will be annoyed about it –’

‘They will be quite safe in Mr Stratton’s car. He and his sister are staying with Mrs Greensleeves for the weekend.’

‘Oh, why did I leave them?’ cried Nannie. ‘And it’s so frightfully cold and damp. When will they be back?’

‘Mr Stratton will probably take them straight home,’ said Mrs Featherstone Hogg. ‘You had better go home too, and then you will be there when they arrive.’

Nannie was aghast, how could she possibly go home without the twins? She couldn’t possibly. Mrs Walker would be furious, and with good cause. She began to explain all this to Mrs Featherstone Hogg. Meanwhile the musical chairs was continuing with its maddening pauses, the noise was increasing. Nannie had to shout louder and louder to make herself heard above the din.

‘I can’t help all that,’ said Mrs Featherstone Hogg, interrupting Nannie's explanations and lamentations crossly. 'If they're so precious you shouldn't have left them.'

She left Nannie there gaping, and swept across the room to speak to Lady Barnton.

The whole thing was utterly beyond Nannie's comprehension, such a thing had never happened to her before in all her years of Nannie-hood. She turned it over in her mind and decided to telephone to her mistress for orders. Mrs Walker would probably be angry about it but that couldn't be helped, it was too serious to be hidden or glossed over. She made her way out of the hot noisy drawing-room and hunted about the house until she found a telephone. It was in Mr Featherstone Hogg's study, but Mr Featherstone Hogg was playing with the children so he was not there. Nannie was so panic-stricken by now that she would not have cared for half a dozen Mr Featherstone Hoggs, she rushed to the telephone and gave the doctor's number in a trembling voice – 'If only the doctor is back,' she prayed. 'Oh God, please let the doctor answer it.'

Unfortunately the doctor was not back. Mrs Walker answered the phone, and Nannie was obliged to explain the whole thing to her mistress. She explained exactly what had occurred as clearly as her state of mind would allow her – 'I shouldn't have left them,' she wailed down the telephone. 'But really they seemed all right, and I never thought of anything like this. Never.'

'It's not your fault at all, Nannie,' said Mrs Walker in a peculiar voice. 'I was an absolute fool to let them go, I should have thought of it – oh Nannie, nobody would *harm* them, would they?'

‘Harm them!’ cried Nannie.

‘Never mind,’ said Mrs Walker. ‘I’ll come straight up and see Mrs Featherstone Hogg at once. You had better wait there till I come. Try to find out where they’ve gone.’

‘How?’ enquired Nannie. ‘Who shall I ask?’

‘I’ll come at once,’ Mrs Walker said. ‘Wait for me in the hall.’ And she rang off.

Sarah was shaking all over with fright – but she tried to pull herself together. No good to collapse now, she must get her babies back first. If only John had been here, he was so strong and dependable; but there was no knowing when John would be back, she must tackle the matter herself. She kept on assuring herself that they wouldn’t dare to harm the twins, they were just doing it to frighten her, of course, that was all. If only I had somebody to go with me – thought poor Sarah. Who could she get? Ellen King would have been the person, but Ellen King had gone, and Margaret had gone, and Dorothea was honeymooning at Monte Carlo. There was Barbara Buncle of course – Barbara was a nice kind creature and it was she who had warned Sarah that some deep scheme was being laid to her undoing. If only I had taken it more seriously – Sarah thought, as she lifted the receiver and gave Barbara’s number –

Barbara was writing when Dorcas came to say that Mrs Walker had rung up. She laid down her pen and went to speak to Sarah.

‘They’ve done it, Barbara,’ said Sarah’s voice in her ear.

‘Done what?’

‘They’ve stolen the twins. I thought I had better let you know. I’m going straight up to see Mrs Featherstone Hogg.’

‘Good gracious!’ said Barbara, trying to take in the situation, and make up her mind what was to be done.

‘Unless they return the twins immediately I shall get the police,’ Sarah continued in a queer hard voice. ‘But I don’t want to do that if I can get them back without. Nobody could do them any harm, could they, Barbara. It’s just to frighten me, isn’t it?’

‘It’s just bluff,’ Barbara assured her. ‘It’s just bluff. We’ll get them back at once. Don’t worry, Sarah – or at least don’t worry more than you can help. It will be quite all right when I’ve seen Mrs Featherstone Hogg. Wait for me and we’ll go up together and make her – no, you *must* wait for me,’ she added, as Sarah began to say she couldn’t wait a single moment. ‘It will be much better if you wait for me – I’ll run all the way – I can’t explain now but I can make everything all right.’

She rushed upstairs and dragged on her clothes anyhow. Dorcas was waiting for her in the hall.

‘Lor’, Miss Barbara, you’re never going out now?’

‘Yes,’ said Barbara breathlessly. ‘I’m going up to The Riggs. If I’m not back in two hours you can ring up your friend Sergeant Capper and tell him to search for my dead body in the cellars – where’s my umbrella, Dorcas? Where on earth’s my umbrella?’

‘In the stand, of course. But, oh, Miss Barbara, what *do* you mean? For goodness’ sake don’t go and do nothing rash, now –’

‘It’s all right,’ Barbara told her, fumbling with the safety chain on her front door. ‘It’s all right, Dorcas. I don’t suppose they can do anything to me, really. I was just joking – just joking, Dorcas. Don't worry. I'll be back in an hour or an hour and a half –'

She fled down the path. Poor Sarah, it was frightful. It must all come out now, of course. She must tell Mrs Featherstone Hogg that *she* was John Smith – not Sarah at all, and then they would give Sarah back her babies. She ought to have owned up before; but who would have thought the plan would have been such a fiendish plan as this? Of course it was all a gigantic piece of bluff, but still –

The road into the village had never seemed so long, Barbara ran, and walked, and ran again. She pictured Sarah's agony of mind, she wondered if it would have been better and quicker to ring up Mrs Featherstone Hogg and explain matters over the telephone – perhaps it would have been better. On the other hand it might not have been so efficacious. Better to do the thing thoroughly, as it had to be done. Better to face it out in person – more difficult of course, but braver, to walk into the august presence and say, 'I'm John Smith so please give Sarah back her babies at once –'

As she neared the doctor's house she expected to see Sarah waiting for her on the doorstep ready-dressed to fly to the rescue of her twins. But there was no sign of Sarah, the house was perfectly quiet, the door was shut. Barbara rang the bell and waited impatiently. It seemed hours before Fuller answered the door (Fuller was the doctor's parlourmaid, she had been with the Walkers for years. She knew Barbara well, of course).

'Oh, Fuller!' said Barbara breathlessly. 'Isn't Mrs Walker ready?'

'Mrs Walker's engaged,' said Fuller. 'She said I was to ask you to wait a few minutes in the drawing-room.'

Barbara was amazed at the information that Sarah was engaged. What could be so important as to engage her at this critical moment with night coming on and the twins lost?

'Who is it, Fuller?' she enquired as they passed the door of the study.

'It's a strange lady,' whispered Fuller. 'Not a Silverstream lady. I never saw her before – Miss Stratton her name was.'

'Fuller! D'you think it's all right?' asked Barbara anxiously. 'I mean she couldn't *do* anything to Mrs Walker, could she?'

'Lor'!' exclaimed Fuller, startled for once out of her propriety. 'Lor', Miss Buncle! You don't reely think anyone would 'arm the mistress, do you?'

They paused outside the study door and looked at each other with wide eyes. Miss Buncle's nerves had been completely upset by the kidnapping of the twins, and the distressing knowledge that it was her fault. It would be her fault too if the stranger did Sarah bodily harm. She visualised the stranger stabbing Sarah between the shoulder blades and escaping out of the study window; she visualised Sarah lying on the floor in a pool of blood, breathing her last. Miss Buncle frequently bemoaned the fact that she had no imagination, but one feels she must have had a little to visualise such a terrible scene in the placid atmosphere of the doctor's hall. The atmosphere was not so placid as usual tonight, of course, even Fuller seemed a little upset, and not quite her ordinary machine-like self. Barbara wondered if Fuller knew about the twins, she probably did.

'Couldn't you go in, and *see*?' suggested Barbara in trembling accents. 'Do go in, Fuller. You could pretend you were going in to draw the curtains or something –'

'The curtains have been drawn *hours*,' said Fuller. 'But perhaps I could go in and say you had come, Miss.'

'Yes, oh yes, *do*, Fuller,' entreated Barbara.

She remained outside the door while Fuller went in, and waited, trembling. She heard Fuller say, 'Miss Buncle is here, madam,' and Sarah reply, 'Please ask her to wait in the drawing-room, Fuller.' A strange, rather high-pitched voice added, 'We have nearly finished our business – may I use your telephone?' then Fuller came out again and the door was shut.

'It's quite all right, Miss,' Fuller said in a relieved tone. 'They're signing papers on the doctor's table.' She led Barbara to the drawing-room, made up the fire and left her to her own devices.

Barbara was bewildered. It was so queer for Sarah to be transacting business with a strange woman instead of dashing up to The Riggs to rescue her twins. What could be the meaning of it? Sarah had sounded absolutely frantic when she had spoken to Barbara on the telephone. 'I can't wait a moment,' she had said, and here she was calmly signing papers on the doctor's table, and making no attempt to do anything about the twins. I suppose I must just wait – thought Barbara helplessly – it wouldn't be any use me going up to The Riggs without Sarah. Besides, she said I was to wait.

She walked about the room, restlessly; counting the patterns on the carpet, and, when that was done, looking at the photographs. More than half the photographs depicted the twins at various stages of their short career – the twins in long clothes, the twins in short clothes, the twins in practically no clothes at all, the twins standing on a staircase in jumper suits, the twins playing in the garden in overalls. In no case could Barbara determine which was which.

'Goodness!' said Barbara aloud. 'Goodness, how I wish she would come! It's worse than waiting at the dentist.'

She decided to shut her eyes and try to remember all the furniture in the room, perhaps that would pass the time and keep her from going mad. There's the piano, thought Barbara, and the cabinet with the Dresden figures, and the two armchairs near the fire, and the chesterfield of course. And there's a nest of tables near the door, and a lacquer screen –

'Are you ill, Barbara?' said Sarah's voice suddenly. She had come in quietly and found Barbara sitting there with her eyes shut and murmuring to herself – no wonder she thought Barbara was ill.

'Oh Sarah!' cried Barbara, opening her eyes and jumping up out of her chair. 'Thank goodness you've come at last. I'm John Smith.'

'So am I,' smiled Sarah with remarkable calm.

'But I really am,' cried Barbara, seizing her arm and shaking it fiercely. 'I wrote the book, Sarah, do you hear? We've only got to go up to The Riggs and tell them that I'm John Smith, and not you at all, and they're bound to give us the twins immediately.'

'It's sweet of you, Barbara,' said Sarah affectionately. 'It really is perfectly sweet of you to think of it, but they'd never believe you, for a moment, you're such a rotten liar, you know. But you're an absolute lamb to think of doing it. I'm not John Smith either, of course, but they've got it firmly fixed in their heads that I am and nothing will convince them otherwise. So the only thing –'

'But, Sarah, if I go and tell them that I am John Smith – I am, really and truly.'

'It's all right. It's all settled,' said Sarah. 'They are sending the twins home at once.'

'Thank goodness!' exclaimed Barbara, sinking back in her chair with a sigh of relief.

'Yes, they only wanted me to sign a paper saying that I apologised for all the things I had said about them, and that they were all quite untrue –'

'And you signed it?' gasped Barbara.

'Of course I signed it,' said Sarah laughing. 'D'you think it mattered to me what I signed so long as I could get Jack and Jill home safe and sound? I just signed my name wherever the woman told me to sign it and she went away quite pleased. She's a friend of Vivian Greensleeves and Vivian had evidently roped her in to the plan without giving her much idea of what it was. She was quite decent really – I don't think she liked her part very much.'

'You signed a paper saying you were John Smith?' enquired Barbara again in bewildered tones.

'Yes, I told you, Barbara,' replied her friend. 'I signed everything she had with her. I signed a letter to the publisher as well. She telephoned to her brother from here and he said the twins were all right and he would bring them back in about twenty minutes.'

'But Sarah, you signed a letter to the publisher?'

'Yes, Barbara, I did. Mr Abbott will be surprised when he gets it, but I don't expect it will worry him much. I expect publishers often get letters from raving lunatics, don't you?'

'What did it say?'

'Oh, I don't know. I didn't read it very carefully. Just that I wanted my novel suppressed or something – *my* novel mark you!'

'It's really mine,' Barbara told her. 'I had better go and see Mrs Featherstone Hogg and explain it all.'

'My dear, it's not necessary. They're quite pleased now and the twins will soon be back. I'd really rather you didn't go and muddle it all up, if you don't mind. You see nobody would believe you and it would complicate matters.'

'It would clear matters up.'

'No, it wouldn't,' Sarah said firmly. 'It would complicate the whole thing, and I might not get the twins back or something. I wish I hadn't been such a fool as to let them go to that party. I should have smelt a rat when they didn't invite me –'

'Who could have thought –'

'Nobody except Vivian Greensleeves, it's exactly the sort of plan she would think of. I wonder if Mrs Featherstone Hogg is giving her something for doing it. You will notice that Mrs Featherstone Hogg is keeping well out of it all herself.'

'You could have them up for kidnapping,' suggested Barbara wildly.

'I don't think so,' replied Sarah, wrinkling her brows. 'They've been pretty wily about the whole thing, you know. Vivian and Mr Stratton took them for a run in his car – it's a new car, the sister told me, and he's very proud of it – we couldn't prove that he had any intention of not bringing them home. As a matter of fact I expect he would have brought them back safely whether I signed the beastly papers or not – but I wasn't going to risk anything. I wonder what I had better do about telling John. Shall I tell him or not? He would be frightfully angry, of course. What would you do about it if you were me?'

Barbara had no idea what she would do if she were Sarah, she was completely bamboozled by the whole affair.

'Perhaps I had better tell John about it,' continued Sarah thoughtfully. 'He might hear a garbled version of it from somebody else.'

'Yes,' said Barbara dazedly. 'Well, I think I'll just go home now, Sarah. Dorcas will be worried, and I can't do any good here –'

'You might wait until they come – until somebody comes,' said Sarah quickly, 'just in case of – of anything. I'm upset, I'd hate to wait here all alone with nobody to talk to. Nannie will be back in a minute or two – I telephoned to her that everything was all right, the poor soul was completely flummoxed –'

'No wonder,' exclaimed Barbara.

The twins arrived first. The bell rang, and Fuller discovered the two little figures on the doorstep. They ran into the house, quite happy and full of excitement at their unusual adventures. They had no idea, of course, that their mother had aged about ten years in their absence.

'Me an' Jack had a lovely d'ive,' cried Jill.

'I 'ike Bob,' said Jack. 'He gave me a chockit.'

Sarah swept them into her arms and hugged them ecstatically, they were both a little surprised at the fervour of her embrace.

'You're squashing my nose, Mummie,' said Jill reproachfully in a muffled voice.

'Well, I think I'll go home now,' Barbara said. 'You'll be all right now, won't you?'

'I haven't half thanked you,' said Sarah, raising a flushed face and tear-filled eyes. 'You're a real friend, Barbara dear. It was splendid of you to come so quickly and to think of that plan of yours. I'd have let you do it, if it would have got my babies back any quicker, but it was easier the other way. Perhaps some day we shall know who John Smith really is.'

'It's me,' said Barbara in a last despairing effort. 'It really is me, Sarah. Really and truly.'

'We wrote it together, didn't we?' Sarah said, smiling and nuzzling into her babies' necks like a mother-cow. 'And Jack and Jill helped too – didn't you my precious loves? You filled Mummy's pen for her so that she could write funny stories about Mrs Featherstone Hogg.'

'I got a paper yat out of a c'acker,' cried Jack, escaping from his mother's arms and jumping up and down in front of her, 'I got a paper yat out of a c'acker.'

'I got a fistle,' shouted Jill, 'Mummie I got a lickle fistle –'

Barbara went away and left them – there was nothing more she could do. Sarah didn't need her any more, Sarah was perfectly happy.

CHAPTER TWENTY-THREE

MISS BUNCLE'S DAY IN TOWN

Barbara Buncle had been bidden to lunch at The Berkeley with her publisher. It was the most exciting thing that had ever happened to her, she was excited for days beforehand.

Even Sally – who was deeply immersed in important affairs of her own – was aware that Barbara was unusually animated and gay.

When the great day arrived, Barbara decided to go up to town early and combine the outing with a shopping orgy; she therefore arrived at The Berkeley with weird-shaped brown paper parcels hanging painfully upon every finger – a solecism of which Elizabeth Wade would never have been guilty.

Mr Abbott had been waiting for ten minutes, and he was surprised to see her with so many parcels, but she was so flatteringly pleased to see him that he forgave her all her sins immediately. He led the way to a table, which he had reserved, near the window, and sufficiently far from the band to make conversation possible, and helped the waiter to disentangle Barbara's fingers. Then they sat down and the lunch began.

Barbara enjoyed it all tremendously. She was Elizabeth most of the time, of course, for this was an Elizabethan sort of party – having a *tête-à-tête* lunch at an expensive restaurant with a distinguished-looking man – but sometimes she was Barbara for a few minutes, and then she felt a little shy, and awkward, and humble.

Mr Abbott was very attentive. He had become increasingly attracted by Miss Buncle and today she was at her best. Her appearance was a credit to him, her conversation intrigued him. You never knew what Miss Buncle was going to say next. At one moment she seemed a sophisticated woman of the world, and the next she seemed as innocent and confiding as a child. Mr Abbott could not know that he was really entertaining two ladies to lunch at The Berkeley, that two ladies were laughing at his jokes and his light badinage – so appropriate to the occasion.

The conviction had been growing in Mr Abbott's mind that Miss Buncle was the woman he had been waiting for all his life. She was attractive to look at, she was good-tempered and full of fun and she was obviously extremely healthy. He found her amusing and provocative. She was clever enough, but not too clever (Mr Abbott did not like a woman to be better off in the way of brains than he was himself; Miss Buncle wasn't). Last, but not least, there was something very fresh and innocent about her which appealed to Mr Abbott immensely.

It sounds very matter-of-fact put like this, but Mr Abbott was a matter-of-fact businessman. It was his nature to weigh the pros and cons before he decided upon anything important. He was tremendously attracted by Miss Buncle but he was not exactly swept off his feet by her charms – perhaps he was rather old to fall in love in a headlong fashion, perhaps he was rather old to be swept off his feet –

Mr Abbott decided that he would wait until he had the manuscript of the new novel in his hand before offering the author his heart. Whether or not Miss Buncle accepted him – and he had no idea what her feelings were – the proposal was bound to unsettle her mind, to knock her off her balance, so to speak. Once the new novel was completed he did not mind whether there was another John Smith or not. If she wanted to write she should write, and if she did not want to write she need never write another word – he would be her dividends. But he did want just one more John Smith, and he wanted it soon, for the amazing sales of *Disturber of the Peace* were waning now and it was the right moment to publish another novel from the pen of John Smith – 'There is a tide in the affairs of men, which, taken at the flood, leads on to fortune.' Mr Abbott felt that it would be a thousand pities to lose the tide.

'And what is the new novel to be called?' enquired Mr Abbott with interest.

'Well, I thought of calling it *The Pen is Mightier –*,' Barbara said confidentially, 'but I don't mind if you can think of something better – at least not very much,' added Barbara, not altogether truthfully, for she would mind a good deal if the new novel had to be called something else. She was rather pleased with the name, it expressed her deepest convictions – had she not seen in the last few months what a mighty weapon the pen could be?

'I like the name,' replied Mr Abbott. 'Of course I haven't

read the novel yet, but I like the name. How soon can you let me have it?'

'It's nearly finished.'

'Good,' said Mr Abbott smiling.

'But I don't know how to finish it. I've come to a stop,' said Barbara, tasting her pêche Melba and deciding that it must have come straight from Paradise.

'Bad,' said Mr Abbott, frowning.

'I've thought and thought,' said Barbara with a sigh. 'Sometimes the whole thing seems the most awful rubbish, and I feel like throwing it in the fire.'

'No, no!' exclaimed Mr Abbott anxiously. 'No, no – that would never do. Don't do that on any account. It's just that you are stale.'

'I suppose I am,' said Barbara sadly.

'All authors get stale,' said Mr Abbott with a comforting smile, 'even the very best of best-sellers. I tell you what. Send it to me, if you like, and I'll read it over. I might be able to make a suggestion which would help you.'

'Would you really?' said Barbara, brightening up at once. 'Would you read it and see what you think? Wouldn't it be a fearful bother for you, Mr Abbott?'

'It would be a pleasure,' he replied gallantly.

After lunch Mr Abbott took his guest to see a film which was said to be 'THE MOST STUPENDOUS AND UTTERLY AMAZING PRODUCTION OF OUR TIME.' Mr Abbott was stupendously bored at the amazing production, and he was glad to note that Miss Buncle was also bored. He was glad, not because he liked to bore his guests with stupendous productions, but because it showed more unmistakably than anything that had gone before that Miss Buncle was the right woman. If *His Wonderful Pal* bored Barbara Buncle, she would do. Most of the women round them and a good many of the men were following the hair-raising adventures of *His Wonderful Pal*, with tense interest. In a way Mr Abbott admitted that it *was* amazing.

It was amazing that anybody could have contemplated the filming of such a thing and of course the sum spent upon the production was stupendous – he didn't need the programme to tell him that – but the story was so puerile that it would not have contented an average child of ten years old. It was simply an excuse for scenery and love scenes. – *He* cheated at cards – at least *they* said he had, and everybody thought he had except 'His Wonderful Pal'. *She* believed in him, of course, but *he* told her he couldn't possibly marry her until he had vindicated himself. To vindicate himself he had to visit the court of the Great Mogul (nobody knew why he had to do this, and most of the audience was too drugged by the really amazing scenery to have any critical faculty left).

'His Wonderful Pal' followed him at a discreet distance to watch over his safety, and passed through incredible adventures in the jungle, carrying them off with a sang-froid beside which the sang-froid of Elizabeth Wade paled into insignificance. 'His Wonderful Pal' arrived at the court of the Great Mogul just in time to save her lover from the machinations of a man in whose truth and loyalty *he* had never doubted – it was *her* woman's instinct that warned her he was

No Good. Most people with two eyes in their head would have seen from the very beginning that the man was No Good (what could you expect of a man with a wall-eye and a black gap in his front teeth?), but the lover trusted him implicitly in spite of these indications of a black heart and was very nearly in the soup.

The arrival of 'His Wonderful Pal' at the court of the Great Mogul was accompanied by earthquakes, and tropical thunder and lightning; and the Great Mogul's Palace fell down, column by column, and crushed everybody to death – except, of course, the lovers. These fortunate survivors were quite oblivious of the fate of the Great Mogul and his myrmidons, nor did they make any attempt to succour the wall-eyed traitor who was pinned by the leg under a fallen column and was expiring in agonies. They left him to his well-deserved fate and escaped together through alligator-infested swamps, and tiger infested jungles, and carried on intermittent but harrowing love scenes – on one occasion whilst being pursued by a rogue elephant.

Her sang-froid had disappeared by now, but not her permanent wave, and she wept huge oily tears and declared that if *he* didn't marry her she would throw herself over a cliff – which had most conveniently appeared in the middle of the jungle – and thus end her useless and miserable existence. 'Do people really behave like that?' Barbara whispered to Mr Abbott.

'God forbid!' replied that gentleman fervently. 'Shall we go?' Barbara nodded, she had forgotten that a nod cannot be seen by one's companion in the gloom of a picture house.

'Would you like to go out?' Mr Abbott repeated after a minute or two. During this time 'His Wonderful Pal' had almost thrown herself over the cliff but not quite, of course. *He* had just managed to catch her in time and the two were now locked in a frantic embrace. . . . A woman sitting just in front of Mr Abbott was sobbing openly into her handkerchief. . . .

'Yes, let's go,' whispered Barbara.

They went as quickly and silently as they could, stumbling over people's umbrellas and treading on innumerable toes. Everybody was furious with them for blocking out the scene at the most critical, or at any rate one of the most critical moments in the drama.

'Whew!' said Mr Abbott, as they emerged into the cool bright air of day. 'Whew, what an experience. I feel quite battered. What about a cup of tea?'

Barbara thought it would be nice, and they found a small tea-shop, requisitioned a small table, and gave their order.

'I could never think of anything like that,' Barbara said, as she drew off her gloves and put them on an empty chair – she was referring of course to the incredible adventures they had just witnessed.

'Thank God for that!' exclaimed Mr Abbott reverently.

'I have no imagination, you see,' Barbara continued sadly, 'I can only write about real things – things that really happen, I mean. How do people think of things like that? They must have quite different brains from ordinary people.'

'Yes,' said Mr Abbott vaguely. He was watching Miss Buncle demolishing crumpets and his admiration at the feat was intense – what a digestion she must have! His lunch was still lingering in the region of the second button of his waistcoat, yet he was sure he had eaten no more than she had –

'I've no idea how people think of things like that,' continued Mr Abbott, when his surprise had somewhat abated. 'I wish they didn't, don't you? Perhaps they dream them after a visit to the Zoo and a heavy supper of toasted cheese.'

Barbara laughed, and then sighed. 'It would be rather nice to be able to write things like that. People seem to enjoy them – (I suppose if they cry it does mean they're enjoying themselves?) – and there would be no chance of people recognising themselves and being cross about it. I don't know what I shall find to write about when I have finished *The Pen is Mightier* –'

'Copperfield played out?' enquired Mr Abbott sympathetically.

'Just about it, I'm afraid.'

'Don't worry, something will turn up. Take a little holiday after *The Pen is Mightier* –. You really deserve a little holiday, you know.'

CHAPTER TWENTY-FOUR

THE PEN IS MIGHTIER –

The Pen is Mightier – was waiting for Mr Abbott when he got home from the office next day. He tore it open eagerly, he was quite excited about it. Miss Buncle was an enigma to Mr Abbott, both as a woman and as an author. Sometimes he felt he understood her quite well, and sometimes he felt that he did not understand her at all. He hadn't the remotest idea what her new book would be like – it might be the most appalling rubbish, or it might be a bestseller. Mr Abbott was rather afraid that *Disturber of the Peace* was a sort of fluke and that Miss Buncle might never write another word worth reading, but he might be quite wrong of course, he hoped he was quite wrong. He settled down comfortably to read.

The Pen is Mightier – was still 'all about Copperfield', just as Miss Buncle had said. Mr Abbott recognised the same characters in it as had appeared in *Disturber of the Peace*, but there were new characters too: Mr Shakeshaft, the Vicar, Miss Claire Farmer, a grand-daughter of old Mrs Farmer (who had worn a wig and put pectin in her famous damson jam) and Mrs Rider, the doctor's wife.

Mr Shakeshaft was depicted as a serious, devout young priest, deeply in the toils of Mrs Myrtle Coates, who supposed him to have a great deal of money. Mrs Myrtle Coates had appeared in the pages of *Disturber of the Peace* (Mr Abbott remembered the character distinctly), she was, in modern parlance, a 'gold digger', and had been mixed up with an unpleasantly second-rate young man. This new imbroglio with the Vicar of Copperfield was no credit to Mrs Myrtle Coates, she led him on in a shameless manner, and then threw him over at the last minute, because he had lost all his money in a bank smash. So much for the Vicar and Mrs Myrtle Coates.

The main theme of the book was concerned with the fortunes and misfortunes of Elizabeth Wade – Miss Buncle's other self. Miss Wade wrote a book, and the story of Miss Wade's career as a novelist was the story of Miss Buncle's own extraordinary experiences. Miss Wade wrote a book and placed it with Messrs Nun and Nutmeg (the name made Mr Abbott roar with laughter). This spicy firm published Miss Wade's book and it immediately became a bestseller. The book was 'all about' Copperfield, and Copperfield was annoyed or pleased according to how it found itself in Miss Wade's book. Miss Wade's book, which was entitled *Storms in a Teacup*, by J Farrier, was discussed and criticised very harshly by the Copperfieldians – at least by those of them who had no discernment, the others saw genius, which, of course, was clearly proved by the absolutely unprecedented sales. The theme was unusual, and intriguing. Mr Abbott had never before read a novel about a woman who wrote a novel about a woman who wrote a novel – it was like a recurring decimal, he thought, or perhaps even more like a perspective of mirrors such as tailors use, in which the woman and her novel were reflected back and forth to infinity. It made your brain reel if you pursued the thought too far, but there was no need to do so, unless you wanted to, of course. So much for the main theme.

The character of Mrs Rider, the doctor's wife, was clearly and sympathetically drawn. Mr Abbott liked her immensely. She was really a charming creation. Mrs Rider was suspected of being the author of *Storms in a Teacup*, and had rather a thin time of it in consequence. She was the victim of an absurd and altogether incredible conspiracy, hatched by the Myrtle Coates and Horsley Downs lot, to prove her authorship of the book. Mr Abbott was rather doubtful about this incident, he wondered whether Miss Buncle would mind if he suggested its deletion. The kidnapping of the Rider baby was rather too improbable and unconvincing, even for a novel like *The Pen is Mightier –*, and most people would take it for farce. He decided to think it over carefully, and speak to Miss Buncle about the kidnapping business.

The Pen is Mightier – was a complicated sort of book, it had so many threads. There was the Myrtle Coates thread, and there was the conspiracy against Mrs Rider, and there was the main theme all about Elizabeth Wade and her book, and besides these there were several smaller threads all intertwined one with the other in a decidedly ingenious manner. Mr Abbott disentangled them in his own mind – Mr Horsley Downs had cast off his fetters and was having a much better time of it than he had in *Disturber of the Peace*. He amused himself very pleasantly and innocently by taking actresses to lunch at The Berkeley. (This must have been added last night for it bore the authentic stamp, and the ink was still blue.) The Gaymers, the Waterfoots and Miss Earle took subsidiary places in *The Pen is Mightier –*. They had been dealt with faithfully in Miss Buncle's previous book. The Gaymers' divorce was touched on lightly; the Waterfoots sent post-cards from Rome to say that they were exploring the Forum and found it intensely interesting; and Miss Earle and Miss Darling were 'seen off' to Samarkand accompanied by the good wishes of their friends.

All these stories merged into each other, but they were really distinct stories and Mr Abbott surmised that they were true – or very nearly true. He could vouch for the complete and almost terrifying veracity of the Elizabeth Wade story, and his own portrait, labelled Mr Nun, amused him immensely – Barbara was always kind to people she liked.

The book was very like *Disturber of the Peace*, but it was handled more firmly, it was better, funnier, more even in texture. Miss Buncle's writing had come on a lot, and yet it had not lost the extraordinary simplicity which some people had taken for satire. Mr Abbott was delighted with *The Pen is Mightier –*.

Towards the end Miss Buncle had gathered in her threads with a cunning hand, and they were all gathered in and finished off neatly except the main thread of all. Elizabeth Wade was left – as it were – hanging in the air. It was this that had stumped Miss Buncle – how was she to finish off

Elizabeth Wade, seeing that Barbara Buncle was by no means finished off?

Mr Abbott saw the difficulty. The book required something to round off the main theme and complete it, something definite. It was the more difficult, of course, because *The Pen is Mightier* – was all true, there was no fantastic element in this book like the Golden Boy in the latter half of *Disturber of the Peace*. It was all true, therefore the *dénouement* must be true also, otherwise the result would be inartistic.

Mr Abbott sat and thought about it for a long time, and then he smiled. He saw the end of the book quite clearly, and it was an end that satisfied him – he hoped sincerely that it would satisfy Miss Buncle. He found a sheet of foolscap and outlined his idea for the completion of *The Pen is Mightier* –, it did not take him long for it was only an outline, of course, and he made it as bare as possible because he did not want it to appear as if there had been a strange hand at work in the completion of Miss Buncle's book. The letter which he enclosed with the manuscript and the notes took him much longer to write, and he re-wrote it several times before he was satisfied with its wording. Then he packed up the whole thing and sent it back to Miss Buncle by registered post.

Mr Abbott reflected, as he procured his receipt at the Post Office, that this was – perhaps – a unique way of proposing to a lady. He hoped Miss Buncle would take it in the right spirit and appreciate its fine points; he hoped that she would do it justice in her book. It was all to go into the book, of course, that was the whole idea: – Elizabeth Wade's confession to her publisher of having got stuck with her new novel: Mr

Nun's offer to read it, and his suggestion for the end, coupled with a proposal of marriage to the fair author. *The Pen is Mightier* – would end with the wedding of Mr Nun and Miss Elizabeth Wade – no better ending could be possible. It finished off Elizabeth in great style and it was just the sort of finishing off that *The Pen is Mightier* – required.

* * *

Barbara Buncle was delighted with Mr Abbott's suggestion for ending her novel, she saw at once that it was exactly what she needed. Wedding bells would make an artistic *finale* – how clever Mr Abbott was to have thought of it!

It was not until she had digested the foolscap sheet, and laid some tentative plans for Elizabeth's wedding, that she turned to Mr Abbott's letter, and discovered that he had sent her a proposal of marriage. The letter was not long, it merely said that he hoped Mr Nun's suggestion would meet with Elizabeth's approval. He realised, he said, that everything in the book was true, and he hoped that the end would be no exception to the rule. Could she – he enquired, and the words were underlined lest she should fail to perceive their significance – could she possibly see her way to making his suggestion for the ending of her book come true? The letter concluded with the information that he would come over on Friday afternoon for her answer.

Barbara was amazed, she read the letter several times before she could convince herself that it really meant what she took it to mean. She was absolutely staggered at the idea of anybody wanting to marry her. Mr Nun had fallen in love with

Elizabeth Wade, of course – what more natural considering the charms of that fortunate woman? – but for Mr Abbott to confess to a like passion for Barbara Buncle was the most incredible thing on earth. She had long ago decided that Mr Abbott was quite the nicest man she had ever met, he was reliable, and kind and loyal, she had trusted him and leant on him when everybody had been so unkind about *Disturber of the Peace*, and he had not failed her. She had never before had a proposal of marriage in any form, but she realised – in spite of her inexperience in such matters – that Mr Abbott's proposal was unique. It was delicate, it was flattering, it was clever. Of course, Mr Abbott was a very clever man, she had realised that at their first interview when he had been a complete stranger to her. He was now her friend and she valued his friendship tremendously – but could she marry him? It was such a surprise that he should want her to marry him, she had never thought of such a thing for a moment. This is so sudden – Barbara thought – and smiled at the aptness of the hackneyed phrase.

I can't marry him, I can't possibly – Barbara thought. And yet she wouldn't like to lose him, to lose his friendship and his support. If she refused to marry him would he continue to be her friend? It would never be the same, of course, there would always be that feeling of embarrassment between them. The mere idea of losing Mr Abbott's friendship filled her with dismay. She began to wonder if she could possibly marry him, she began to think she might.

Dorcas brought in the supper and found her reading and re-reading Mr Abbott's letter.

'What do you think of marriage, Dorcas?' enquired Barbara, in a conversational tone.

'It's that Mr Abbott!' Dorcas exclaimed, dropping the toast-rack in her excitement. 'I knew it, Miss Barbara. I just knew it. It was in my cup – a wedding in the house and a biggish man looking towards it. That's Mr Abbott I said – I really did. Oh, Miss Barbara, I'm so glad!'

'But Dorcas, I haven't made up my mind –' cried poor Barbara in dismay.

'No, Miss Barbara, of course you haven't. But it *will* be lovely – fancy seeing you a bride, all in white with orange blossoms in your hair! Oh, and he's such a nice gentleman too. So free and easy. I will say this for Mr Abbott, he knows what's what, he does. Oh, Miss Barbara, how happy I am.'

'But I haven't decided anything – I probably won't marry him at all, Dorcas. I've got to think it all over – nothing is settled yet –'

'No, Miss Barbara, of course not. It would never do to jump at him, it wouldn't be proper at all. But I can't help thinking about the wedding. I *do* like weddings, don't you, Miss Barbara? We can turn out this room for the reception, and have a buffet across the corner. I shall get one of Mrs Goldsmith's girls to help: she wouldn't mind giving me a hand, an' it would be ever so much nicer than having a stranger, don't you think so, Miss Barbara? And the twins are just right for pages – the doctor's twins – all dressed up in white satin and carrying your train –'

It was hopeless to argue with Dorcas, Barbara gave it up in despair.

'Well, anyhow, you're not to say a word to anybody,' she said firmly. 'I haven't decided anything, and I won't be rushed like this. It's a dead secret, Dorcas. Every bit as dead as *Disturber of the Peace*.'

'I won't say nothing,' Dorcas promised. 'Mum's the word, Miss Barbara. But you won't mind me thinking about it, will you? I couldn't promise not to think about it, not for ten pounds, I couldn't.'

'Well, don't talk about it anyhow,' Barbara said.

Dorcas sighed, there was lots more she could have said about the wedding, but she supposed it was no use trying to say it. She had thought of several most important points to discuss with Miss Barbara, but if Miss Barbara would not discuss them she must just hold her tongue. She took up her tray with manifest reluctance and turned to leave the room.

'Oh, and Dorcas,' said Barbara. 'I shall be writing late, tonight, so don't forget my coffee.'

'You'd much better go to bed, Miss Barbara,' said Dorcas sensibly, 'there'll be no more need for you to write now that you've got a husband to keep you.'

In spite of the fact that she had got – or was possibly going to get – a husband, Barbara wrote all night. The end came out beautifully. There was a touching scene in the garden when Elizabeth accepted Mr Nun's heart and hand. It was summertime, and Mr Nun came for his answer dressed in tennis flannels, with a light-blue blazer enhancing his manly charms. Elizabeth was sitting in the arbour, and Mr Nun was so impatient to get to her, that he vaulted lightly over the hedge and came to her across the grass. Elizabeth was coy, she placed her finished manuscript in his hands and said: 'Reginald, dearest, there is my answer,' and left him in the arbour to digest it at leisure. Reginald read the end at top speed and found that it gave him his heart's desire – he rushed into the house to claim his bride.

All Copperfield was bidden to the wedding and all Copperfield came with alacrity – even Miss Earle and Miss Darling were summoned from Samarkand to attend. – Elizabeth was loved and admired and respected in Copperfield. Nobody had the slightest idea that she was J Farrier, that much discussed author of *Storms in a Teacup*, and there was no reason why anybody should ever know now. The wedding had done away with the need for the dramatic exposure which Barbara had been toying with reluctantly. The wedding was a far nicer ending than the dramatic exposure of J Farrier. Thus it was that all Copperfield came gladly to Elizabeth's wedding, bearing gifts, and the villagers erected a triumphal arch. The wedding was solemnised in the little church of St Agatha's by the sad-faced Mr Shakeshaft, who could not help comparing the good fortune of Mr Nun with his own blasted hopes. It was a brilliant wedding, the sun shone upon the bride, and the birds burst into song as she appeared at the church door after the ceremony, a radiant vision in spotless white.

All Copperfield now repaired to the bride's charming house for the Wedding Breakfast, and each and all of the assembled guests proffered congratulations and good wishes in characteristic phrases. It was a little like the last scene in a

Christmas Pantomime where all the characters appeared to make their bow.

Barbara finished *The Pen is Mightier* – just as the clatter of the milk-cans sounded in the road. She laid down her pen and went to the window. Dawn ought to have been breaking over the hills, but it was doing no such thing, and would not be doing any such thing for another two hours at least. The milk-cart was the only thing to be seen through the leafless trees. It was drawn up beneath the lamp-post so that the milk-man could see which can was the right one for Tanglewood Cottage – a poor substitute for the breaking of dawn which Barbara felt was her right.

She yawned and stretched herself for she was very stiff and cramped. The joy of achievement – and what an achievement – buoyed her up, so that she did not feel tired at all, but she was very hungry. Dorcas would be coming down soon, thought Barbara, she would get Dorcas to boil an egg for her – perhaps two eggs – and then she would go to bed and sleep till tea-time, for she must be fresh and rested when Mr Abbott arrived.

Writing all that about Elizabeth's wedding (her own wedding, really, for was she not Elizabeth?) had made the idea of marrying Mr Abbott seem quite familiar. It was not surprising and alarming any more. She had been rather foolish to be so perturbed at the idea. There was nothing to be surprised and alarmed at in a wedding, people got married every day, and they continued to be much the same as before. Marriage did not alter people much, as far as Barbara could see.

Elizabeth had gone forward bravely to meet her fate, the sun had shone upon her and the birds had sung with joy, she was actually married now – Elizabeth was actually married. – She wasn't Elizabeth Wade any more, she was Mrs Reginald Nun, and soon – or perhaps not exactly *soon*, but some day – Barbara would be Mrs Arthur Abbott.

CHAPTER TWENTY-FIVE

MISS BUNCLE AND MR ABBOTT

Barbara carried out the first part of her plan with the greatest ease. She ate her lightly boiled eggs and endured, with meekness, the scoldings of Dorcas. Then she went to bed and fell immediately into a deep and dreamless sleep. She awoke at two o'clock and found the sun shining. It was ridiculous to remain in bed any longer. She was refreshed by her sleep, thoroughly refreshed, but she found that she was somewhat restless and apprehensive. She must get up and move about. She must go out or something – anyhow it was quite impossible to remain in bed. The meeting with Mr Abbott which had seemed a mere detail when she was divided from it by the gulf of sleep had suddenly assumed a terrifying guise. He would be here in two hours – in less than two hours – and he would want an answer to his proposal. Would Mr Abbott propose again by word of mouth? Perhaps he would propose in the dashing manner of Major Waterfoot – how dreadful that would be! What on earth would she do if he fell on his knees before her, and declared in trembling accents that he could not live without her another moment. (Barbara could not quite *see* Mr Abbott doing it, but you never knew.) Elizabeth might have managed such a scene with success, she would have known exactly what to do, of course, but Elizabeth was married now – Elizabeth could not help her. Elizabeth had managed her own love affair with consummate ease, she had placed her novel in Mr Nun's hands, and had said, 'Reginald, dearest, there is my answer.' It was all very well for Elizabeth to do things like that, Barbara couldn't. To start with Barbara could not imagine herself addressing Mr Abbott as 'Arthur', she supposed she would have to if she were going to marry him, but it would take her some time to get used to it.

Barbara was dressed by now, and there was still an hour before Mr Abbott was expected. She decided to go for a walk – a good sharp walk would be the best cure for her unsettled nerves.

'You're never going out, Miss Barbara!' Dorcas exclaimed, when she appeared downstairs with her hat and coat on. 'What if the poor gentleman arrives before you get back?'

The words gave Barbara a sudden idea – it was such an excellent idea that she wondered why on earth she had not thought of it before.

'Give him this, Dorcas,' she said, dumping the fat untidy manuscript of *The Pen is Mightier* – on the kitchen table. 'If he comes before I get back just give him this from me, and tell him I left it for him to read.'

'But he'll be wanting to see *you*,' said Dorcas, reproachfully. 'He won't want to sit down and read all that rubbish the moment he arrives. Really, Miss Barbara, you might have a little consideration for the poor gentleman, I do think.'

‘Just give it to him,’ said Barbara, and she disappeared hastily out of the back door. There was no time to be lost. Mr Abbott might arrive earlier than he had said, and it would be dreadful if he arrived before she had made good her escape.

She ran down the garden and squeezed through the gap in the fence and made off across the fields towards the church.

It was five o’clock before Barbara could make up her mind to return to Tanglewood Cottage, and even then it took all her courage. She crept into the hall like a burglar, and peeped in at the half-open door of the drawing-room. Mr Abbott was sitting in front of the fire having tea, he looked very happy and quite at home in Barbara’s drawing-room. He was just pouring out a second cup when he looked up and saw his runaway hostess.

‘Don’t be frightened of me,’ he said, smiling at her in a friendly manner. ‘I’m warranted not to bite.’

Barbara laughed, it was so reassuring, so utterly different from what she had expected.

‘Let me offer you some of your own excellent tea,’ Mr Abbott continued, waving the teapot at her hospitably. ‘You must be cold and hungry. Dorcas informs me that you had no lunch. It is really very naughty of you to go out without your lunch and wander about in the cold, and get chilled to the bone. When we are married I shall not allow you to do such silly things – we *are* going to be married, aren’t we, Barbara, dear?’

‘Yes,’ she said, ‘I think so. At least if you really want to be. I’m quite happy like this.’

'Of course I want to be,' replied Mr Abbott, ignoring the latter half of her remark. 'I want to be married very much indeed. Do come and have some tea, Barbara.'

She sat down rather gingerly at the other side of the fire, and accepted the cup which he had poured out for her. So far all had been well, and she was nearly sure now that Mr Abbott was not going to kneel down and break into impassioned speech – what a mercy it was that he was such a sensible sort of man!

'This is cosy,' said Mr Abbott. 'I'm very happy. I hope you are happy too. We suit each other exactly, and I am very fond of you, Barbara. I will be very good to you, my dear – don't be frightened of me for goodness' sake,' he added quickly. 'Have some hot-buttered toast.'

Barbara was not really frightened, it was impossible to be frightened of Mr Abbott any more. He was so nice and friendly – just the same as he always was, only nicer and kinder. She ate quantities of hot-buttered toast, and felt much better. She began to feel quite safe and happy. She began to feel that some day – perhaps quite soon – she might manage to call him Arthur.

They discussed *The Pen is Mightier* – and Mr Abbott told her that he thought it was even better than *Disturber of the Peace*. The only thing he was at all doubtful about was the kidnapping of the Rider baby. People didn't kidnap babies in this country, Mr Abbott said, and it seemed a pity to introduce one improbable episode into an otherwise probable and even veracious chronicle of everyday affairs.

'But it did happen,' Barbara pointed out. 'It all happened exactly like that, except that it was really twins.'

Mr Abbott gazed at her in amazement.

'It's all true, every word,' Barbara continued. 'Mrs Greensleeves did it – Mrs Myrtle Coates, you know – just as I wrote it. I could never have imagined it because I've got no imagination at all.'

'Well I'm jiggered!' said Mr Abbott, heavily.

'Truth is stranger than fiction,' added Barbara with a satisfied smile. She was pleased at having thought of this exceedingly apt proverb, it was almost as good as *The Pen is Mightier than the Sword*, and would have done almost as well as a title for her book – almost as well, but not quite.

Of course Mr Abbott could say no more about the improbability of the episode. An episode that has actually happened in real life cannot be said to be too improbable for a novel. So Mr Abbott abandoned the subject, and, after suggesting one or two minor alterations, he asked if he might take the manuscript away with him tonight and put it in hand at once. He had brought the contract with him and Dorcas could be called in to witness Barbara's signature, if she approved of the idea. Barbara agreed and summoned Dorcas from the back premises.

The contract was a very different contract from the one which Barbara had signed for *Disturber of the Peace*. John Smith was a bestseller now – or at any rate as near to a best seller as made no odds. Miss Buncle was to get a large sum in advance, and excellent royalties as well. It was a good contract even for a best seller, but Miss Buncle never looked at it. She took up Mr Abbott's fat fountain pen and enquired where she was to write her name.

'But you haven't read it!' exclaimed Mr Abbott in surprise.

'I suppose it's just the same as before, isn't it?' asked Barbara. 'Why should I bother to read it over if you say it's all right?'

Mr Abbott was touched at her complete confidence in him, but somewhat startled at her ignorance of financial matters. She evidently quite failed to realise that her stock had gone up since *Disturber of the Peace* had been published, and that her market value had increased a hundredfold. It was a good thing – he thought – that she would have him to take care of her in future, and see that she was not swindled out of everything she possessed.

Dorcas signed her name upon the contract with a considerable amount of heavy breathing, and returned to the kitchen with all speed. She was busy roasting a duck for their suppers, and she was rather anxious about it. How awful if it 'caught' while she was signing their stupid papers – something to do with the wedding, Dorcas supposed. She, also, had not bothered to glance through the contract, but that was chiefly because of the duck.

There was only one thing which had to be decided immediately. Mr Abbott was a little anxious as to how Barbara would take it, he approached the subject with all the tact he could command.

'I like the way you've finished *The Pen is Mightier* –,' he told her, with an ingratiating smile.

'It was your idea entirely,' she told him.

'I mean I like the manner in which you have carried out my idea,' he explained. 'The wedding is excellent, and all Copperfield coming to the feast is a delightful touch – one of the best things you've done, Barbara – it is delicate farce (if such a thing can be).'

'Farce!' said Barbara somewhat perplexed at the word, 'But it's not funny at all. At least it's not meant to be funny, I didn't mean –'

'I know, I know,' he said. 'Never mind. It doesn't matter about that. Everybody will like it immensely and that's the main thing. What I want to put before you is this, the end of your book is going to be true in essentials, but we can't make it altogether true – I'm explaining it badly,' he cried, running his hand over his smooth hair, and looking at Barbara in a harassed manner. 'I mean we can't have our wedding here in Silverstream.'

'Why not?' Barbara enquired. She had already begun to look forward to the wedding. It was to be the same as Elizabeth's wedding – or as near that ideal ceremony as possible. Of course you could not arrange for sunshine and bird-song in Silverstream as you could in Copperfield. Barbara realised that, and bowed to the inevitable like the philosopher she was; but she did want her wedding to be at the same church, and to be attended by the same people as Elizabeth's wedding, and she did want to appear before the inhabitants of Silverstream as a pure white bride.

'Why not?' enquired Barbara again, for Mr Abbott hadn't answered her the first time. 'Why can't we have our wedding here in Silverstream, and everything just like Elizabeth and Mr Nun?'

'Well,' said Mr Abbott. 'Well, you see, Barbara, the moment we publish *The Pen is Mightier* – everyone in Silverstream will know that you are John Smith. They couldn't help knowing it, if they tried, because Elizabeth Wade is Barbara Buncle to the meanest intelligence, and Elizabeth Wade wrote *Storms in a Teacup*, and *Storms in a Teacup* is *Disturber of the Peace*.'

Barbara saw – 'Fancy me not noticing that!' she said, sadly.

'It's a pity but it can't be helped,' said Mr Abbott.

'I suppose you couldn't keep back *The Pen is Mightier* – till after the wedding, could you?'

'I could,' agreed Mr Abbott, 'and I would too, if that would be any use. We could quite easily be married before the book is published, but there's another thing to be thought of. Don't you see what will happen when you send out the invitations to the wedding with my name on them? Wedding invitations usually have the name of the bridegroom inscribed upon them, don't they?'

'Yes, what will happen?'

'Everybody will say, "Mr Abbott" – who on earth is Mr Abbott? Is he the publisher fellow? How is it that Miss Buncle knows Mr Abbott so well?'

'Of course they will,' said Barbara sadly. 'How clever you are! Far cleverer than me. I would never have thought of that until it had happened.'

'Not clever at all,' Mr Abbott said, preening himself a little – it really was very pleasant to be appreciated at one's true worth. 'Not clever at all, Barbara, dear. It is just my business brain. Your brain runs on other lines. Now, I could never have written *Disturber of the Peace*, and *The Pen is Mightier* –,' said Mr Abbott with perfect truth. 'People are made differently (and how fortunate that they are, what a dull world it would be if we were all alike!). One person can do one thing and another person can do something else. Together we shall be complete, invincible, perfect,' said Mr Abbott ardently and he leaned forward, and laid his hand on Barbara's knee.

It was a strong, comforting, safe sort of hand. Barbara rather liked the feeling of it lying there on her knee – she smiled at him.

'You see how it is,' he continued. 'I should have loved you to have a beautiful wedding like Elizabeth's, but it simply can't be done. Directly Silverstream realises that you are John Smith your life will be a burden to you. They can't do anything very desperate, of course, but they can make things extremely unpleasant –'

Barbara knew that he was right, she would have to leave Silverstream. She found that she did not mind very much. She had lived in Silverstream all her life but the last few months had been too great a strain upon her nerves, she was not happy in Silverstream. The reason for her unhappiness was not far to seek, she never had a moment's real peace. She never knew when somebody was going to pounce upon *Disturber of the Peace*, and tear it to bits; she never knew when somebody would stop her in the street and denounce her as John Smith; she felt positively sick every time the telephone bell rang in case somebody had found her out. Barbara felt that it would be a great relief to get away from Silverstream and leave all her fears, and all her troubles, behind.

She loved Copperfield, of course, but the books were finished now and Copperfield was fading from her mind. She could no longer enter Copperfield at will, the door was shut

– she had shut it herself, of course, but she could not open it again.

'Will you be very sorry to leave Silverstream?' Mr Abbott asked her, sympathetically.

'No,' said Barbara, 'I don't really think I shall mind very much.'

'Good,' he said, smiling and rubbing his hands.

CHAPTER TWENTY-SIX

COLONEL AND MRS WEATHERHEAD

The Weatherheads returned to Silverstream about the beginning of March. They had had a delightful time at Monte Carlo and had settled down into married harness with the greatest of ease. The Colonel was delighted with his pretty, agreeable wife, and had no idea that he was completely under her thumb.

Barbara was the first person in Silverstream to call upon the newly married couple. She had always liked Dorothea Bold, and she was anxious to see what Dorothea Weatherhead was like. What had marriage done to Dorothea? Besides, it was something to do, to walk down to the bridge and call. It would take the best part of an afternoon and would serve to kill time. Barbara was very restless these days, she couldn't settle to anything.

The Weatherheads had taken up their abode in Cosy Neuk while The Bridge House was being altered to suit their requirements. They were delighted to see Barbara Buncle and asked her to stay to tea. They told her all their news, first about their adventures at Monte Carlo and then about the alterations at The Bridge House. It was being painted and papered from attic to cellar – they told Barbara – and a bow-window was being thrown out on the south side of the drawing-room.

'I may tell you that's my idea entirely,' said Colonel Weatherhead with no little pride. 'The room was dull and cold. A south window will make all the difference.'

Barbara complimented him on his sagacity.

'It's convenient being so near at hand,' said Dorothea, chipping into the conversation. 'Robert can keep an eye on the workmen and see what they are doing. You've no idea how it keeps them up to the mark to have a man after them. They never pay any attention to a woman.'

'It was only because Dorothea wanted somebody to chivvy the plumbers who were doing her drains that she consented to marry *me*,' put in the Colonel chuckling.

'Yes, that was the reason,' agreed Dorothea, 'you really ought to get a husband, Barbara. They're quite useful if the drains go wrong, or if you want a bow window built out.'

'My drains never go wrong,' Barbara replied, smiling inwardly, 'and I couldn't possibly afford a bow-window. Besides nobody would want to marry *me*, would they?'

They both protested vehemently, but insincerely, at her modesty. Barbara was aware of the insincerity of their protestations – her writing had made her perspicacious of her fellow creatures – and she hugged herself with delight to think of their amazement when they heard –

'And how's Silverstream?' enquired Dorothea, as she sat down behind the tea-table, and arranged the cups with her pretty plump hands.

Barbara told her that Silverstream was just the same as ever.

'Not entirely,' said Colonel Weatherhead, chuckling and winking at his new wife. 'Been a bloodless revolution at The Riggs, hasn't there?'

'Now don't be naughty, Robert,' Dorothea entreated him. 'I'm sure Barbara wouldn't be interested in nasty gossip about poor little Mr Featherstone Hogg.'

'I'm dashed sure she would be,' returned the Colonel.

'Of course I would,' cried Barbara. 'It's too cruel to rouse my curiosity like that. I insist on hearing all about it.'

'You tell her then,' Dorothea said.

'Well, it's not very much really. It's only rather funny when you know the Featherstone Hoggs, and know how the poor little feller has always been kept in order, and squashed on every occasion. Dolly and I saw the little feller in town one night at that new smart restaurant in Mayfair – Silvio, or something. He was dining *tête-à-tête* with a young lady and enjoying himself tremendously. He was far too much taken up with his fair companion to see us.'

'She looked like a chorus girl,' Dorothea put in, 'frightfully made up, and the least possible amount of clothes. I don't know what "Agatha" would have said if she had seen "dear Edwin" and his companion that night.'

They were in the middle of tea when Sarah Walker arrived to pay her call. She kissed Dorothea and told her that she was a wicked woman –

'The idea of keeping us all in the dark like that!'

'It was all very sudden, you know,' replied Dorothea blushing prettily.

'You must blame me, if there's any blame going,' said the Colonel. 'The whole thing was entirely my fault and I'm not a bit sorry, either.'

'You dreadful soldier-men,' said Sarah, shaking her head in dismay. 'You're a wild, dangerous lot, and no mistake.'

'I'm going to have an At Home,' announced Dorothea, changing the subject abruptly, 'you and Barbara must both come, and help me with it. I don't want Silverstream to feel done out of its Wedding At Home.'

Sarah wrinkled her brows. 'It's sweet of you, Dorothea, but I don't think I will. You see Silverstream doesn't like me much at the moment. They all think I'm John Smith.'

'They think you are John Smith?' enquired Dorothea in a bewildered voice. 'Who on earth is John Smith?'

'That's just what everybody wants to know – or at least they did until they fixed on me.'

'But who is he? What has he done?'

'You don't mean to say you haven't read the book?' exclaimed Sarah in amazement. 'I thought everybody in the whole world had read it – *Disturber of the Peace*, by John Smith,' she added, on seeing that her hostess had no idea what she was talking about, 'you've read it, haven't you, Colonel?'

'Oh, I know now!' cried Dorothea. 'It's that book Mrs Featherstone Hogg was so furious about. Robert read it just before we went abroad. He said there wasn't much in it – didn't you, Robert?'

'Not very much,' said Robert, uncomfortably.

'I bought it in London to take abroad with me,' continued

Dorothea, 'but the queer thing was it disappeared – so I never read it after all.'

'Disappeared?' enquired Sarah with interest.

'Yes, vanished completely. I put it in the top of the lunch basket to read it in the train, and when I opened the basket it had gone – wasn't it odd?'

'Very odd indeed,' Sarah replied, 'but I really wouldn't bother about it any more, if I were you. As the Colonel so rightly says there is not much in it.'

Colonel Weatherhead looked at her gratefully – what an eminently sensible, charming, and agreeable woman Mrs Walker was! Just the very friend for dear Dolly – the friend he would have chosen for her himself.

Barbara left the tea-party early. She was expecting Arthur to supper, and she was pleasantly thrilled at the prospect of seeing him. She had not seen Arthur for nearly a week, he had been so busy trying to get all his business cleared up and put in order so that he could take a nice long holiday with a clear conscience. And, besides the pleasure of seeing Arthur again, there was another pleasure in store tonight, Barbara was looking forward to it immensely. Arthur had promised to bring with him an advance copy of *The Pen is Mightier –*. The book was going to be published quite soon now; in fact, as soon as certain important arrangements had been completed.

As she walked home, Barbara thought about the Weatherheads very contentedly. It was obvious that their marriage had been a success, they both seemed very happy. The Weatherhead marriage was her most successful achievement

– or perhaps it would be more correct to call it the most successful achievement of *Disturber of the Peace*. They had done exactly what they were told, and made no fuss about it whatever. She felt a proprietary interest in the Weatherheads.

Next to the Weatherheads in order of merit Barbara put Miss King and Miss Pretty. They had departed to Samarkand just after the New Year. At least they had said they were going to Samarkand. Barbara was in some doubt whether their flight south had really ended in Samarkand, for the postcards which had arrived in due course, and had been displayed on the mantelpieces of Silverstream, seemed to be views of the pyramids, varied by an occasional sphinx. Barbara had always been led to believe that these interesting and ancient monuments were exclusively Egyptian.

Margaret Bulmer was also one of the successes achieved by *Disturber of the Peace*, but in an entirely different manner. Margaret had returned from her long visit to her parents, looking ten years younger, to find a much more considerate and agreeable husband. The truth was that Stephen had missed her quite a lot, the house had not been nearly so comfortable without Margaret to oil the wheels of the domestic machinery. Stephen was determined to take no risks, and he laid himself out to be agreeable to his wife. Moreover an old shed at the bottom of the garden had been converted into a very comfortable writing room for Stephen, so he was able to carry out his researches into the character and attainments of Henry the Fourth without being disturbed by the noise of his offspring and dependants. The house was more comfortable for everybody now that there was no longer the need for complete and absolute silence. Mr Bulmer's writing room was all the more necessary because the children had been thoroughly spoilt by their grandparents during their long visit. They were now a pair of ordinary, healthy, noisy children and no longer little white mice. All this was directly attributable to the influence of *Disturber of the Peace*, so that although Margaret had not actually followed her prescribed destiny and eloped at midnight from her bedroom window with Harry Carter, Barbara felt quite justified in claiming Margaret as another success.

And lastly there was Mr Featherstone Hogg. Barbara was so glad to hear that he was really having a nice time. She liked Mr Featherstone Hogg, he had always been kind to her. Barbara liked to repay kindness with kindness so she had given him a nice time in *The Pen is Mightier* –. A chance remark of old Mrs Carter's anent Edwin's unfortunate penchant for the stage, coupled with her own experiences at the Berkeley, had shown Barbara in what way Edwin could be entertained (she might not have imagination but she was certainly ingenious), and it appeared that she had chosen well for him. She had entertained him exactly as he liked to entertain himself. Barbara was glad.

CHAPTER TWENTY-SEVEN

SALLY'S SECRET

The next morning was fine and sunny. Sally came dancing in to see Barbara with a copy of the *Daily Gazette* in her hand.

'Look,' she cried, 'look, Barbara! John Smith has written a new book. It's coming out next week. Oh, I am excited about it, aren't you, Barbara? I wonder what he's written about this time. It's called *The Pen is Mightier* – doesn't it sound thrilling? No pen could be mightier than John Smith's, could it?'

Barbara tried hard to register surprise, she decided that she was not a born actress. Fortunately Sally was too full of her great news to notice Barbara's attempts. She did not wait for answers to her various questions. Sally rarely expected answers to her questions, and Barbara knew her well enough now not to bother about finding any. By the time you had found an adequate answer Sally had flitted on to something quite different.

'Gran rang up Mrs Featherstone Hogg,' continued Sally delightedly. 'She shut the door of the library so that I shouldn't hear what she was saying, but she was so excited and talked so loud, that I heard quite clearly in the hall. They are both ordering copies of it to be sent to them the moment it comes out. They hope it will give them some clue to John Smith. – Are you ordering a copy, Barbara? You had better do it soon. The first edition will be sold out directly. Will you lend me your copy to read if Gran sits on hers? Oh, I do think John Smith is marvellous!'

'You're going to marry him, aren't you?' enquired Barbara wickedly.

'Oh, that was just my nonsense,' said Sally, actually blushing, 'you mustn't take all I say for gospel truth, Barbara dear. When I'm excited I just gas on, and say all sorts of rubbish. How could I possibly want to marry a man I've never even *seen*?'

'It does seem impossible. But of course you know exactly what he's like, and that makes a lot of difference. Big and strong – isn't he – with a humorous mouth and piercing eyes and long tousled hair –'

'You're teasing me now. What a horrid person you are! Do be good, Barbara, and I'll tell you a secret. It's a frightfully important secret too. I'm in love.'

'Not really? Not with John Smith?'

'Silly, it's true. I'm engaged,' Sally said, fishing down the front of her jumper and displaying a ring set with diamonds. '*Now* will you believe it's true?'

Barbara was forced to believe such indubitable evidence, she was suitably impressed.

'We're going to be married directly I hear from Daddy. I've written to tell Daddy all about it. Oh Barbara, he's a marvellous man!'

'I know. You always said he was.'

‘Not Daddy (although of course he’s marvellous too). I mean Ernest’s marvellous – Mr Hathaway, you know. Barbara, he’s too sweet for words. I adore him. Of course I’ve been in love before,’ continued Sally, looking very wise and experienced, ‘but never the least like this – this is the real thing. We’re just waiting now for Daddy’s letter and then we’ll get married and live happily ever after.’

Barbara looked at her in distress. ‘Sally dear,’ she said anxiously. ‘I don’t think your father will consent to your marrying Mr Hathaway. He’s very nice, of course, but he’s so frightfully poor – what would you live on?’

‘That’s just the amazing thing, my dear. He’s not poor at all. He’s written and told Daddy exactly how much he has, and it’s lots,’ said Sally, opening her blue eyes very wide. ‘He gave away all his money for a whole year just to see what it was like to be poor. He’s so *good*, you know, Barbara. His ideals are so wonderful. I shall never be able to live up to Ernest’s ideals.’

‘Of course you can if you try.’

‘Yes, perhaps,’ Sally agreed. ‘If I try very hard – but isn’t it wonderful, Barbara? Isn’t it just like a novel to fall in love with a poor man, and then find he’s rich beyond the dreams of avarice?’

Barbara agreed, she hugged Sally and told her how frightfully glad she was.

Sally was rather young of course, but she had seen more of the world than many older people and she was quite capable of managing her own life. Barbara had always thought Mr Hathaway a nice young man – rather serious perhaps, but

Sally would liven him up. It seemed very suitable, and she thought that Sally would be happy. She was in a condition of mind to believe that marriage was a desirable state.

'And you'll come to the wedding, won't you, Barbara?' Sally said, disengaging herself from Barbara's embrace.

'If Barbara Buncle still exists, Barbara Buncle will be there,' replied that lady. (And that's really rather clever of me – she thought – because I shan't *be* Barbara Buncle any more, I shall be Barbara Abbott. It's a pity I shan't be at the wedding of course, but I can't be, so it's no use thinking about it.)

Sally's news was really astounding, she could hardly believe it was true. She wished she had known about it before so that she could have put it all into *The Pen is Mightier –*. It would have added considerable interest to the story of Mr Shakeshaft if she had married him off to his pupil – just like Swift and Stella, Barbara thought regretfully. There might even have been a double wedding at St Agatha's. No, the wedding was Elizabeth's and Elizabeth's alone. It would never have done to filch any of the glory from Elizabeth; but the story about Mr Shakeshaft being a rich man after all – a sort of prince in disguise – was a distinct loss to *The Pen is Mightier –*. Why didn't I think of it? sighed Barbara. I have no imagination at all. It would have finished off Mr Shakeshaft so happily and made Mrs Myrtle Coates look even more of a fool. It is, of course, the obvious end, only I was too blind and stupid to see it.

'What *are* you thinking about, Barbara?' demanded Sally.

'I'm wishing I had a little imagination,' replied Barbara. She was always truthful when it was possible so to be.

'Never mind, old thing! We can't all be John Smiths,' said Sally, squeezing her arm affectionately.

CHAPTER TWENTY-EIGHT

JOHN SMITH

The Pen is Mightier – arrived in Silverstream. It seemed that practically everybody had ordered copies in advance. By twelve o'clock Mrs Featherstone Hogg was on the telephone summoning her forces.

'Of course it's Barbara Buncle,' she said to Mr Bulmer. 'Who would have thought that frumpy little object would have the audacity to write such wicked books? You've read the new one, I suppose, *it's worse*.'

'I've glanced through it – just glanced through it casually,' replied Mr Bulmer, who had had his nose glued to the pages of *The Pen is Mightier* – ever since it had arrived. 'The novel is not worth *reading*.'

'Of course not,' agreed Mrs Featherstone Hogg. 'I just glanced through it too, just to see whether I could find any clue to John Smith's identity, and it's perfectly plain now.'

Mr Bulmer agreed.

'I'll call for you in the Daimler in about ten minutes,' added Mrs Featherstone Hogg. 'We can't *do* anything to her, I suppose, but we can go down to Tanglewood Cottage and have it out with her.'

Mr, Bulmer agreed with alacrity.

Mrs Featherstone Hogg rang up Vivian Greensleeves and arranged to pick her up on the way; the Weatherheads were invited but refused; Mrs Carter agreed to meet the others at the gate, so too, the Snowdons.

Mrs Featherstone Hogg could not think of anyone else to ask, she did not want people like Mrs Dick and Mrs Goldsmith – they only complicated matters. She had made the mistake of asking too many people to her drawing-room meeting and she was determined not to repeat it. Of course it was a great pity that Ellen King was not here –

Mrs Carter was coming out of her gate as the Daimler drove up to Tanglewood Cottage and disgorged its occupants.

'Isn't it awful?' cried Mrs Carter, hastening towards the others. 'Isn't it perfectly awful to think I've been living next door to him – to her – to John Smith I mean – all this time? I never was so mistaken in anyone, it just shows how *deep* she is.'

'I always considered Barbara Buncle half idiotic,' agreed Mrs Featherstone Hogg.

'The books in no way disprove your opinion,' gasped Miss Snowdon, who had just arrived upon the scene, very breathless, with her father and sister in tow.

'That's what I think,' agreed Mr Bulmer. 'They're idiotic books.'

'Hullo!' exclaimed Vivian Greensleeves (who had been looking about her while the others talked), 'look at that. What does that mean?' She pointed to a large white board which was fixed securely in a tree near the gate. They all looked at it, and saw that it bore in new black lettering the announcement:

TANGLEWOOD COTTAGE

THIS DESIRABLE RESIDENCE FOR SALE

THREE BEDROOMS, TWO RECEPTION, BATHROOM,

H & C

(*Apply* MRS ABBOTT, c/o Abbott & Spicer,
Brummel Street, London, EC4)

'She's going away,' Mr Snowdon suggested.

'Can you wonder?' cried Mrs Carter. 'What sort of a life would she have in Silverstream after this?'

'I wonder who Mrs Abbott is,' said Vivian.

Mrs Featherstone Hogg was shaking the gate fiercely. 'It seems to be locked, she's frightened out of her wits, I suppose.'

'Quite likely,' agreed Miss Snowdon.

They all gazed up the drive. Vivian pointed out that there were the wheel marks of a large car in the soft ground. They were quite recent wheel marks.

'Who can have driven in?' Mrs Carter wondered.

'She's probably bought a car,' said Mr Bulmer.

'Barbara Buncle!' cried Mrs Carter incredulously, 'The woman is as poor as a church mouse.'

'Is she?' said Mr Bulmer sarcastically. 'Is she really? She must have made hundreds out of her first novel, and even more out of the new one.'

'Hundreds out of that rubbish?' cried Mrs Featherstone Hogg.

'Yes, hundreds. It's just those trashy novels that make money, nowadays,' said Mr Bulmer bitterly. (His bitterness was caused by the fact that *Henry the Fourth* was now completed, and was going the rounds of all the Publishing Houses in London, and returning every few weeks, to its author, with the sure instinct of a homing pigeon.)

'Well, it's no use standing here all day,' said Vivian Greensleeves, crossly.

They agreed that it was not. Mrs Featherstone Hogg shook the gate again, but with no result.

'We could go in through my garden,' suggested Mrs Carter. 'There's that gap in the fence – Sally uses it. I shall have it blocked up immediately, of course.'

It was an excellent idea, and the whole party turned to follow her.

At this moment another car drove up and was seen to be the doctor's Alvis. Sarah had also procured a copy of *The Pen is Mightier* –, and had spent the morning reading it, and discovering its authorship. She had given the doctor no peace until he had agreed to bring her down to Tanglewood Cottage in the car.

'They'll kill her,' she told him, with exaggerated concern.

Dr John didn't think that they would actually kill Miss Buncle, but he agreed that it might be as well to go down and see what was happening.

'Hullo!' said Sarah, stepping out of the car, 'everybody seems to be calling on John Smith this morning.'

'Did you ever know such a wicked deception?' cried Mrs Carter.

'Who would ever have thought it was Barbara Buncle?' cried Miss Isabella Snowdon.

'Barbara told me about it months ago,' replied Sarah nonchalantly.

'She told you she was John Smith?'

'Yes, months ago' (but of course I didn't believe her, added Sarah to herself).

The whole party stood and gazed at Sarah in amazement. They had so much to say that they couldn't find words to say anything at all.

'Well, never mind that now,' said Mrs Carter. 'Come along – this way – through my garden.'

They followed Mrs Carter through her gate, and down the somewhat muddy path that led to the gap in the fence. Dr Walker and Sarah came last, by themselves. They were not strictly of the party, they were merely here to see that nothing happened –

'What are you going to say, Agatha?' enquired Mrs Carter, rather breathlessly, of Mrs Featherstone Hogg.

'Words will be given me,' replied that lady, confidently, as she squeezed through the fence in the wake of the fat Miss Snowdon.

They approached the house through the shrubbery where Barbara had had her 'feu de joie'. The trees were budding now, and there were some early daffodils amongst the long grass; but the party had no eyes for the beauties of spring, they were one and all engaged in framing cutting sentences to hurl at John Smith. They couldn't *do* anything, of course, but they could say a good deal.

They approached the house in silence, and stood in a little group upon the lawn. They stared at the house, and the house stared back at them with closely shuttered windows. It wore the unmistakable, forlorn look of a deserted nest.

Barbara Buncle had gone.

Persephone Books publishes the following titles:

No. 1 *William – an Englishman* (1919) by Cicely Hamilton
No. 2 *Mariana* (1940) by Monica Dickens
No. 3 *Someone at a Distance* (1953) by Dorothy Whipple
No. 4 *Fidelity* (1915) by Susan Glaspell
No. 5 *An Interrupted Life: the Diaries and Letters of Etty Hillesum 1941–43*
No. 6 *The Victorian Chaise-longue* (1953) by Marghanita Laski
No. 7 *The Home-Maker* (1924) by Dorothy Canfield Fisher
No. 8 *Good Evening, Mrs. Craven: the Wartime Stories of Mollie Panter-Downes 1939–44*
No. 9 *Few Eggs and No Oranges: the Diaries of Vere Hodgson 1940–45*
No. 10 *Good Things in England* (1932) by Florence White
No. 11 *Julian Grenfell* (1976) by Nicholas Mosley
No. 12 *It's Hard to be Hip over Thirty and Other Tragedies of Married Life* (1968) by Judith Viorst
No. 13 *Consequences* (1919) by EM Delafield
No. 14 *Farewell Leicester Square* (1941) by Betty Miller
No. 15 *Tell It to a Stranger: Stories from the 1940s* by Elizabeth Berridge
No. 16 *Saplings* (1945) by Noel Streatfeild
No. 17 *Marjory Fleming* (1946) by Oriel Malet
No. 18 *Every Eye* (1956) by Isobel English
No. 19 *They Knew Mr. Knight* (1934) by Dorothy Whipple
No. 20 *A Woman's Place: 1910–1975* by Ruth Adam
No. 21 *Miss Pettigrew Lives for a Day* (1938) by Winifred Watson
No. 22 *Consider the Years 1938–1946* by Virginia Graham
No. 23 *Reuben Sachs* (1888) by Amy Levy
No. 24 *Family Roundabout* (1948) by Richmal Crompton
No. 25 *The Montana Stories* (1921) by Katherine Mansfield
No. 26 *Brook Evans* (1928) by Susan Glaspell

No. 27 *The Children Who Lived in a Barn* (1938) by Eleanor Graham
No. 28 *Little Boy Lost* (1949) by Marghanita Laski
No. 29 *The Making of a Marchioness* (1901) by Frances Hodgson Burnett
No. 30 *Kitchen Essays* (1922) by Agnes Jekyll
No. 31 *A House in the Country* (1944) by Jocelyn Playfair
No. 32 *The Carlyles at Home* (1965) by Thea Holme
No. 33 *The Far Cry* (1949) by Emma Smith
No. 34 *Minnie's Room: the Peacetime Stories of Mollie Panter-Downes 1947–65*
No. 35 *Greenery Street* (1925) by Denis Mackail
No. 36 *Lettice Delmer* (1958) by Susan Miles
No. 37 *The Runaway* (1872) by Elizabeth Anna Hart
No. 38 *Cheerful Weather for the Wedding* (1932) by Julia Strachey
No. 39 *Manja* (1939) by Anna Gmeyner
No. 40 *The Priory* (1939) by Dorothy Whipple
No. 41 *Hostages to Fortune* (1933) by Elizabeth Cambridge
No. 42 *The Blank Wall* (1947) by Elisabeth Sanxay Holding
No. 43 *The Wise Virgins* (1914) by Leonard Woolf
No. 44 *Tea with Mr Rochester* (1949) by Frances Towers
No. 45 *Good Food on the Aga* (1933) by Ambrose Heath
No. 46 *Miss Ranskill Comes Home* (1946) by Barbara Euphan Todd
No. 47 *The New House* (1936) by Lettice Cooper
No. 48 *The Casino* (1948) by Margaret Bonham
No. 49 *Bricks and Mortar* (1932) by Helen Ashton
No. 50 *The World that was Ours* (1967) by Hilda Bernstein
No. 51 *Operation Heartbreak* (1950) by Duff Cooper
No. 52 *The Village* (1952) by Marghanita Laski
No. 53 *Lady Rose and Mrs Memmary* (1937) by Ruby Ferguson
No. 54 *They Can't Ration These* (1940) by Vicomte de Mauduit
No. 55 *Flush* (1933) by Virginia Woolf

No. 56 *They Were Sisters* (1943) by Dorothy Whipple
No. 57 *The Hopkins Manuscript* (1939) by RC Sherriff
No. 58 *Hetty Dorval* (1947) by Ethel Wilson
No. 59 *There Were No Windows* (1944) by Norah Hoult
No. 60 *Doreen* (1946) by Barbara Noble
No. 61 *A London Child of the 1870s* (1934) by Molly Hughes
No. 62 *How to Run your Home without Help* (1949) by Kay Smallshaw
No. 63 *Princes in the Land* (1938) by Joanna Cannan
No. 64 *The Woman Novelist and Other Stories* (1946) by Diana Gardner
No. 65 *Alas, Poor Lady* (1937) by Rachel Ferguson
No. 66 *Gardener's Nightcap* (1938) by Muriel Stuart
No. 67 *The Fortnight in September* (1931) by RC Sherriff
No. 68 *The Expendable Man* (1963) by Dorothy B Hughes
No. 69 *Journal of Katherine Mansfield* (1927)
No. 70 *Plats du Jour* (1957) by Patience Gray and Primrose Boyd
No. 71 *The Shuttle* (1907) by Frances Hodgson Burnett
No. 72 *House-Bound* (1942) by Winifred Peck
No. 73 *The Young Pretenders* (1895) by Edith Henrietta Fowler
No. 74 *The Closed Door and Other Stories* by Dorothy Whipple
No. 75 *On the Other Side: Letters to my Children from Germany 1940–46* by Mathilde Wolff-Mönckeberg
No. 76 *The Crowded Street* (1924) by Winifred Holtby
No. 77 *Daddy's Gone A-Hunting* (1958) by Penelope Mortimer
No. 78 *A Very Great Profession: The Woman's Novel 1914–39* (1983) by Nicola Beauman
No. 79 *Round about a Pound a Week* (1913) by Maud Pember Reeves
No. 80 *The Country Housewife's Book* (1934) by Lucy H Yates
No. 81 *Miss Buncle's Book* (1934) by DE Stevenson
No. 82 *Amours de Voyage* (1849) by Arthur Hugh Clough
No. 83 *Making Conversation* (1931) by Christine Longford

No. 84 *A New System of Domestic Cookery* (1806) by Mrs Rundell
No. 85 *High Wages* (1930) by Dorothy Whipple
No. 86 *To Bed with Grand Music* (1946) by 'Sarah Russell' (Marghanita Laski)
No. 87 *Dimanche and Other Stories* (1934–41) by Irène Némirovsky
No. 88 *Still Missing* (1981) by Beth Gutcheon
No. 89 *The Mystery of Mrs Blencarrow* (1890) by Mrs Oliphant
No. 90 *The Winds of Heaven* (1955) by Monica Dickens
No. 91 *Miss Buncle Married* (1936) by DE Stevenson
No. 92 *Midsummer Night in the Workhouse* (1962) by Diana Athill
No. 93 *The Sack of Bath* (1973) by Adam Fergusson
No. 94 *No Surrender* (1911) by Constance Maud
No. 95 *Greenbanks* (1932) by Dorothy Whipple
No. 96 *Dinners for Beginners* (1934) by Rachel and Margaret Ryan
No. 97 *Harriet* (1934) by Elizabeth Jenkins,
No. 98 *A Writer's Diary* (1953) by Virginia Woolf,
No. 99 *Patience* (1953) by John Coates
No. 100 *The Persephone Book of Short Stories*
No. 101 *Heat Lightning* (1932) by Helen Hull
No. 102 *The Exiles Return* (1958) by Elisabeth de Waal
No. 103 *The Squire* (1938) by Enid Bagnold
No. 104 *The Two Mrs Abbotts* (1943) by DE Stevenson
No. 105 *Diary of a Provincial Lady* (1930) by EM Delafield
No. 106 *Into the Whirlwind* (1967) by Eugenia Ginzburg
No. 107 *Wilfred and Eileen* (1976) by Jonathan Smith
No. 108 *The Happy Tree* (1926) by Rosalind Murray
No. 109 *The Country Life Cookery Book* (1937) by Ambrose Heath
No. 110 *Because of the Lockwoods* (1949) by Dorothy Whipple
No. 111 *London War Notes* (1939–45) by Mollie Panter-Downes
No. 112 *Vain Shadow* (1963) by Jane Hervey